Understanding the Law

3rd Edition

3rd Edition

Understanding
the Law

DONALD L. CARPER   NORBERT J. MIETUS   BILL W. WEST

WEST WEST LEGAL STUDIES IN BUSINESS
Thomson Learning™

Australia • Canada • Denmark • Japan • Mexico • New Zealand • Philippines
Puerto Rico • Singapore • South Africa • Spain • United Kingdom • United States

Understanding the Law, 3rd Edition by Donald L. Carper, Norbert J. Mietus, and Bill W. West

Vice President/Team Director: Jack W. Calhoun
Acquisitions Editor: Scott D. Person
Senior Developmental Editor: Jan Lamar
Marketing Manager: Michael Worls
Production Editor: Peggy K. Buskey
Manufacturing Coordinator: Georgina Calderon
Internal Design: Jennifer Lambert
Cover Design: Matulionis Design
Cover Illustrator: Matulionis Design with images Copyright © 1999 PhotoDisc, Inc.
Production House: Cover to Cover Publishing, Inc.
Printer: R.R. Donnelley & Sons Company, Crawfordsville Manufacturing Division

Printed in the United States of America
1 2 3 4 5 02 01 00 99

For more information contact West Legal Studies in Business, South-Western College Publishing, 5101 Madison Road, Cincinnati, Ohio, 45227 or find us on the Internet at http://www.westbuslaw.com

For permission to use material from this text or product, contact us by
• **telephone: 1-800-730-2214**
• **fax: 1-800-730-2215**
• **web: http://www.thomsonrights.com**

Library of Contress Cataloging-in-Publication Data

Carper, Donald L.
    Understanding the law / Donald L. Carper, Norbert J. Mietus, Bill
W. West. -- 3rd ed.
        p. cm.
    Rev. ed. of: Understanding the law / Donald L. Carper . . . [et
al.].
    Includes index.
    ISBN 0-538-88549-1
    1. Law--United States. I. Mietus, Norbert J. II. West, Bill W.
III. Understanding the law. IV. Title.
KF386.C29 1999
349.73--dc21   99-26785

This book is printed on acid-free paper.

BRIEF CONTENTS

CONTENTS

UNIT I

The Legal System and Basic Principles of Law 1

CHAPTER 7

TORTS: PRIVATE WRONGS   301

PREFACE

This is our new millennium edition, a point worth noting if for no other reason than there won't be another. Joshing aside, we believe this is a particularly appropriate time to pioneer a little, within the traditional constraints of a textbook. Thus, in preparing for this new edition, we broaden our horizons, combining serious classroom and hallway listening with our more usual updating methodology. While listening, we often heard the notion that students seem to be changing a lot. To punctuate this point, we have heard college students referred to as the "sound bite" generation, a presumed reference to the impact of television, if not the Internet. We also have heard from students that we professors may be increasingly stubborn, insisting upon teaching the way it has been done before, the inelastic "tried and true" technique. Even as the role of computer technology in teaching and learning expands exponentially, we continue to hear these interesting, opposing, and not overly flattering views. Of course, neither view is completely accurate, but we think we have incorporated important insights from both in this, our third edition of *Understanding the Law*.

In our modern society, every well-educated person should understand the fundamentals of law and our legal system, which traditionally do not change as rapidly as the reported changes in our students. The beauty of our legal system is, of course, its adherence to principles even as it responds to the ever-changing long-term needs and demands of society. To emphasize the adaptability of our laws and legal system, we make comparisons between certain aspects of our society as they existed at the beginning of the twentieth century and today. What better time to make such comparisons than at the beginning of a new millennium? Thus compared, the invitation to extrapolate into the future is compelling.

In 1900, the United States was a racially and linguistically diverse society consisting of 76 million "foreigners" living without most of today's civil rights and amenities—and without most of today's legal problems. Our laws and legal system have successfully responded to an industrial revolution, two world wars as well as other wars, the civil rights movement, benefits from technology beyond one's wildest dreams, and a population increase of almost 200 million. Can this act be repeated in the coming century? In the near future, almost everyone sees a continuing service revolution, accelerating computer and communications technology, and unimaginable benefits from genetic engineering—all in a still rapidly expanding population. Wherever possible, we suggest issues that are likely to arise in the early years of the twenty-first century. Perhaps proposed changes in our judicial system that are designed to accommodate the future will themselves become the legal issues of the highest importance. These are mentioned for students to ponder.

We attempt to highlight selected issues in law by using an increasing number of what we call "gavels"—examples, cases, and hypotheticals, each identified in the textbook with a gavel icon. Often we submit these gavels on issues that are on the horizon, as yet unresolved, to prompt reasoned student discussion. Thus, we present many opportunities for students to begin mastering the separation of emotion from reason. Both the societal comparisons "then" and "now," and the liberal use of gavels, have been tested and greeted with astonishing success in our classes. Our technique has been to present stimulating issues with clarity and simplicity. Students appreciate our deliberate simplification of difficult concepts as well as our avoidance of arcane terminology, whenever possible, without loss of accuracy. We continue to provide clear definitions of technical terms when first used and have generously expanded the glossary for quick reference. We have added the addresses of useful Web sites, in some cases where much more than sound bites are presented. We do this with one reservation: Web sites still are not stable addresses. If you find an address that does not work, peeling back the address to its main page may enable you to find the information you seek. Your favorite search engine can duplicate or perhaps improve our efforts as well.

In preparing this edition, we accept the premise that computer and communications technology, genetic engineering, and the changing demographics of our society will combine to create the most significant new legal issues likely to arise within the first decade of the new millennium. We have sprinkled throughout the book the kinds of issues we expect these forces to generate. One such issue concerns congressional representation and state reapportionment following the 2000 census. Our first case example in Chapter 1 again concerns gerrymandering. In Chapter 2, a case example concerns the use of statistical sampling in taking the census. The struggles from the 1990 census are only now dwindling. With the census of 2000, we expect gerrymandering and reapportionment battles to be fought with intensity in many states, with resultant major shifts in political power. Shifts in political power obviously translate into shifts in rules of law.

On a different note, we have good reason to believe that our "changing students" share considerable interest in the most perplexing issues pertaining to the immediate future. We resist the temptation to shy away from the burgeoning legal (and ethical) issues presented by genetic science and its forthcoming impact upon the family. Demographic changes well underway exacerbate legal issues between generations, as the baby-boomers take their votes into their early retirement years, with demands expressed in what is now called elder law. Age discrimination, along with estate planning, driver restrictions, elder abuse, and environmental protection, are legal issues that come to mind. And so we attempt to captivate our "changing students" with concepts of law that respond to the same issues that are reflected in the "sound bites" they allegedly hear. Our primary mission remains the publication of a textbook that provides an introduction to law appropriate for all college-level students as part of their formal, general education for life.

Regardless of the nature of new issues, many ancient principles of law underlying our constitutional form of government remain supremely applicable today—and will tomorrow as well regardless of societal changes. With the conviction that a well-informed citizenry is crucial to the long-term survival and success of our society, we again discuss these principles in connection with thought-provoking, still-evolving *new* issues. For example, we point out the concern of neighbors who want to know about the nearby presence of a convicted sexual offender. But we also identify the conflicting notions that once a debt to society is paid, it is paid; of privacy; and of futility where one solution creates a greater problem elsewhere. By applying legal principles to conflicting and even contentious issues, we attempt to enliven the law for our students at the same time that we invite them to think. Besides which, it makes teaching more fun. Certainly more fun than the alleged pedagogy of the "tried and true."

Finally, we have expanded our presentation of laws governing our students' significant legal, economic, and family concerns. After all, most college students will marry (and sometimes divorce); have families (with interest in genetics); buy homes or rent living quarters; use credit; become employees (and sometimes employers); drive on crowded, often hazardous streets and highways; and ultimately confront the deaths of loved ones. These are the topics to which students relate the most. Same-sex marriage; designer babies; rules of homeowner associations; personal safety of renters; workplace harassment; inheritance; and the presence of slow elders in fast freeway lanes never fail to involve the participatory interests of our students.

SUPPLEMENTS

For the instructor

INSTRUCTOR'S MANUAL WITH TEST BANK

The *Instructor's Manual* continues to be written by the authors. Each chapter of the manual provides a chapter overview, along with teaching suggestions. The *Test Bank* has a minimum of 20 multiple-choice, 15 true-false, 10 fill in, and 3 essay questions.

THOMSON LEARNING TESTING TOOLS™

Computerized Testing Software contains all of the questions in the printed test bank. This program is an easy-to-use test creation software compatible with Microsoft Windows. Instructors can add or edit questions, instructions, and answers, and select questions by previewing them on the screen; selecting them randomly, or selecting them by number. Instructors can also create and administer quizzes online, whether over the Internet, a local area network (LAN), or a wide area network (WAN).

TEN COMPLIMENTARY HOURS OF WESTLAW

West's computerized legal research gives instructors and students access to U.S. Code, federal regulations, and numerous special libraries. With *WestLaw*, you also have access to Dow Jones News/retrieval, a comprehensive source of business and financial information.

COURT TV TRIAL STORIES

In courtrooms across America, dramatic stories of people in conflict unfold every day. Since 1991, Court TV has covered hundreds of cases, each one a balance of right and wrong, fact and fiction, truth and lies. Court TV's *Trial Story* series features highly relevant cases condensed into one-hour programs. Each *Trial Story* captures the whole story of a trial, including news footage, courtroom testimony, and interviews with defendants, plaintiffs, witnesses, lawyers, jurors, and judges. Each *Trial Story* video engages students while presenting important legal concepts.

CNN *LEGAL ISSUES* VIDEO UPDATE

You can update your coverage of legal issues, as well as spark lively classroom discussion and deeper understanding, by using the CNN, *Legal Issues* Video Update. This video update is produced by Turner Learning, using the resources of CNN, the world's first 24-hour, all-news network.

BUSINESS LAW AND LEGAL ENVIRONMENT VIDEO LIBRARY

The Video Library includes seven different types of professionally produced legal videos: *Drama of the Law* and *Drama of the Law II*, *The Making of a Case*, *Law and Literature*, *Ethics in America*, selected mock trial videos, *Equal Justice Series*, and *West's Business Profiles*.

SUPREME COURT AUDIOCASSETTE LIBRARY

These audiotapes feature 10 unedited arguments made before the Supreme Court.

For the Student

QUICKEN® BUSINESS LAW PARTNER® 3.0 CD-ROM

The *Quicken® Business Law Partner®* CD-ROM is included with the text as a special complementary supplement for the course. This valuable product contains numerous sample documents, including forms and letters that are useful for personal business as well as in the workplace.

YOU BE THE JUDGE SOFTWARE

This easy-to-use program presents students with new cases and directs them to resolve the relevant issues.

ACKNOWLEDGEMENTS

Donald L. Carper and Bill W. West accept full responsibility for this edition, relieving Norbert J. Mietus and the late T. E. Shoemaker. We are indebted to many persons who have assisted with this new edition. Don Carper would like to ac-knowledge assistance in finding valuable Web sites to his son, Scott D. Carper. Bill West would like to acknowledge the valuable critiquing of the manuscript by Stacy M. Baba.

Our reviewers for this edition again are an eclectic group, representing pro-grams in business, legal assistance, and political science. They are:

Norma C. Connolly, Montclair State University
John L. Frank, Chippewa Valley Technical College
Terry L. Hull, Southwest Texas State University
Linda M. Moran, Santa Rosa Junior College
Gene C. Wunder, Washburn University

We wholeheartedly accept the appropriateness of their occasional plaudits, and just as completely reject each and all of their thoughtless criticisms. In truth we truly appreciate the hard work of the reviewers who give us helpful feedback on our scholarship and approach. We responded to the many helpful suggestions ex-cept when they were at odds with each other.

DEDICATION

To Roy R. Van Cleve (1926–1997)

He served his country as a soldier; its young men and women as an educator; Wyn, Van, and Kathleen as a loving husband and father; and me as a role model and friend. He was a man of real excellence. I miss him.

Don L. Carper
January 2000

THE LEGAL SYSTEM AND BASIC PRINCIPLES OF LAW

UNIT 1

INTRODUCTION TO LAW

*L*et reverence for the laws be breathed by every American mother to the lisping babe that prattles on her lap; let it be taught in schools, in seminaries, and in colleges; let it be written in primers, spelling-books, and in almanacs; let it be preached from the pulpit, proclaimed in legislative halls, and enforced in courts of justice. And, in short, let it become the political religion of the nation; and let the old and the young, the rich and the poor, the grave and the gay of all sexes and tongues and colors and conditions, sacrifice unceasingly upon its altars.

Abraham Lincoln Address before the Young Men's Lyceum of Springfield, Illinois, January 1837.

Welcome to the study of law for your general education. As you leave college and begin your careers, and possibly marry and start families, the laws of our society will play an ever-increasing role in your lives. As educated members of society, your understanding of our legal system will be meaningful in voting and actively participating in community, state, and federal issues and affairs. From a more practical standpoint, your education about our law and legal system will help you guide your families toward happier and more financially successful lives. We do not assume that you are interested in becoming attorneys at law, although it is a noble calling and some of you may eventually decide to attend law school and become members of the bar, i.e., lawyers. Instead, most of you will select from a variety of careers and lifestyles, seeking to make your lives as meaningful as possible while living in a complex society that surrounds us with many opportunities and obstacles. *Understanding the Law* is designed to help you recognize opportunities and overcome obstacles in reaching your goals.

Each individual and family engages in business activities in the sense that money is earned to buy needed and desired goods and services. Family members must be prepared to deal with a myriad of businesses as consumers, employees, and active members of communities that are involved in issues of growth and congestion. Community leaders increasingly deal with such difficult problems as neighborhood crime, traffic, homelessness, and environmental protection. Understanding the laws that affect you will not become easier as the twenty-first century unfolds.

3

Already you have learned something about the law, simply by experiencing life. For example, you know that intentionally injuring another person, stealing, or damaging someone else's property is unlawful. You know that in an automobile collision, the careless driver is held responsible, and when both drivers have been careless, they share the blame. You know that divorce creates issues of alimony, division of family property, and financial support for children and changes in their parental custody. You know that employers must provide safe working conditions for their employees. You know that you must conform to rules in casting your vote in elections, in registering for admission to college, in driving on public highways, and in obtaining certain drugs.

You probably could write a reasonable definition of the law. Perhaps you would correctly conclude that laws are rules that must be obeyed to avoid the imposition of sanctions (legal penalties). More precisely, the dictionary declares: **law is** a body of rules of conduct prescribed by controlling authority, and having binding legal force.[1] But this traditional definition of law is static, a "snapshot" emphasizing law's nature as a set of written rules.

Consider law as dynamic, continuously changing and evolving, always responding to the needs of society for solutions to evolving new issues. There are many specific, written rules, such as speed limits. But there also are conflicts between rules and their application to changing situations. For example, there is no established rule relative to the responsibility of tobacco companies to reimburse states for money the states previously paid for the care of those made ill from cigarettes. That important law is evolving in many courts in the country. Consider the evolving Internet that is changing traditional laws of privacy, free speech, and crime, as well as many rules of commerce and consumerism.

It is perfectly logical for laws to change continuously in response to the evolving characteristics of and the issues within our society. That is, law changes as we change. Each new or modified law must conform to the immutable principles of our Constitution or ultimately be discarded. Thus, the laws of our society are both dynamic and predicated upon immutable principles.* The vast majority of changes in our laws do not violate the broad constitutional principles upon which our society is based. Does society change the law or does the law change society? This "Which comes first, the chicken or the egg?" variety of question is unanswerable. Consider that in some states recent changes in the law require that motorcycle riders wear helmets. Did these new laws change society? Or did society recognize a need (through its representative officials) and require a change in the law? The answer to both questions is "yes." What is important is that, either way, our legal system and laws are dynamic and respond to the legal issues that arise within our changing society. In a nutshell, the study of law is the study of a moving target. As you will study in Chapter 2, some changes are quite immediate, as when legislatures respond to popular demands. In contrast, courts are structured to accommodate change more slowly, at a more reflective pace.

As this is written (January 1999), the end of the twentieth century is rapidly approaching. A new millennium will have begun by the time you graduate from college. Sweeping changes already are on the horizon. Understanding the

---

*Ours is a democracy in which the "immutable principles" mentioned are derived by reference to our Constitution. Not all are expressed; many are implied. For example, the much-publicized right of privacy is an unspecified constitutional principle upon which both abortion and interracial marriage have been based. These interpretative principles or laws are declared by the U.S. Supreme Court, as will be discussed more fully in Chapter 2.

fundamentals of our law and its system will better prepare you to participate fully in these sweeping changes. As one century draws to a close, what better time to look backward to the turn of the twentieth century to examine (if not marvel at) and learn from 100 years of changes in our society and in our laws?

When William McKinley became president in 1897, a great industrial revolution was well underway in this country. Railroads were spreading from the east to the great cities in the west. Coal was fueling the furnaces used in making steel, which in turn was used to manufacture train rails. Following the invention of the gasoline engine, automobiles soon would become mass produced, changing the face of our nation forever. The Wright brothers had yet to give birth to the airplane industry, and space exploration was science fiction. As we approach the year 2000 and a new century, we are experiencing another magnificent technological revolution, which links not seaboards but the entire world. In this modern yet still embryonic revolution, the demands upon the legal system already are reaching new heights of complexity. For example:

- The Internet is causing a re-examination of principles of free speech, privacy, and the protection of minors from sexually explicit materials.

- Applications of computer technology rapidly are changing the federal laws governing intellectual property, especially copyright and patent laws.

- Boosted by computer technology, the science of biotechnology is about to present our society and its legal system with intensely serious social and legal issues involving genetic alteration of plant and animal life, human cloning, and even the possibility of allowing parents the opportunity to produce "designer" babies. Already it has been declared that the unique product of human intervention into natural processes of animal and plant life may be patented, thereby creating the incentive of global monopolization.

- Computer-assisted aeronautical design stands upon the threshold of The HyperSoar, a commercial passenger and/or military airplane that would fly at ten times the speed of sound, leaving the atmosphere after takeoff, then shutting down its power and skimming over the fringes of the earth's atmosphere like a flat rock skimming across the surface of a lake.[2] Flight time between any two places on earth could be achieved in no more than two hours; four round trips between San Francisco and London could be made each day. Such a shrinking of the globe portends changes in the laws of international commerce dealing with such matters as illegal replication and distribution of products, other unfair business practices, and nearly instantaneous financial management. The merging of global cultures through such proximity in time portends legal issues of presently unimaginable dimensions.

In addition to the technology revolution, natural forces are also exacerbating today's issues. Consider the following:

- There has been a population explosion with its myriad social issues, and the problem is growing exponentially. For example, demands for changes in education, reapportionment, health management, and immigration policy are intensifying. Political conflicts over these kinds of issues already are so intense that, in some situations, U.S. courts are performing legislative functions following a stalemate by state officials (e.g., in management of schools, reapportionment, and even public transportation). On the one hand, our population is aging, setting the stage for fierce competition between workers and retirees for the nation's wealth and benefits. On the other hand, according to the Census Bureau, the so-called "Millennium Generation" now has 70.2 million children, while at the peak of the "Baby Boomer Generation" there were only 69.9 million. "This is a revolution in waiting that will redefine society in the 21st century just as baby-boomers shaped social, political and economic changes in the last half of the 20th century."[3] Unlike the Baby Boom Generation, which came about after a surge of births following World War Two, the Millennium Generation arises as much from immigration as from the "baby boom echo" (offspring of baby boomers). Already, children ages, 6 to 12 are estimated to influence the spending of $500 billion each year—by influencing "mom." The influence ranges from food and restaurants to switching from the once "cool" minivans to the preferred sport utility vehicles.[4]

- Environmental issues abound from global warming to air and water pollution, presenting our society with problems it alone cannot resolve. Our legal system is already in high gear making laws to meet these forthcoming challenges.

Looking backward we see that although our legal system has resolved the issues presented by changing lifestyles, attitudes, and mores, we also see that some solutions are resting on tenuous footing, as reflected by 5–4 decisions of the U.S. Supreme Court. Although resolved by law, volatile and contentious issues such as abortion, flag burning, prayer in schools, and affirmative action are not fully resolved by society, a substantial portion of which patiently waits for a replacement Supreme Court Justice. Proponents of other issues that have been previously resolved await each new election to garner a few more votes in Congress or in a state legislature. In this sense, by looking backward, perhaps you can better appreciate the importance of your participation in the future resolution of these issues.

A historical perspective can sharpen our understanding of the outlook for our laws and for our legal system in the early years of the coming new millennium. Does the outlook portend major changes, such as reform of the court structure to accommodate a more complex society? Will a new specialized U.S. Supreme Court be required? Have the issues our legal system has dealt with over the past years strained it to the breaking point? "What now?" the reasoned person might ask, as we reach warp speed. Are there new issues that should be resolved by certain institutions in society other than courts? It is said that if we ignore history we are destined to repeat it. Here we are not studying history, but we must take it into consideration in contemplating the role of law and our legal system in the beginning of the new millennium.

LEGAL/SOCIETAL RELATIONSHIPS: 1900 vs. 2000

What do we take for granted today that was missing from our society on the eve of the twentieth century, when many of your great-grandparents were alive?

With the advantage of hindsight, we now know both the problems that were presented to our legal system in the twentieth century as well as their solutions. With some foresight, we hope to paint a picture for you of the kinds of problems facing our legal system today, on the threshold of the twenty-first century. Comparing the legal/societal relationships of 100 years ago with today's raises the question, "Is our legal system as constructed today capable of fulfilling adequately the demands our society will place upon it in the next century, or even in the next 25 years?" Consider the success of trial by jury over the preceding century—can you safely assume that it will be fully appropriate to our system of justice as we enter the new millennium? In most chapters of this textbook, you will find the kinds of issues that the future holds for our laws and legal system. But first we look backward to sharpen our views of how our society and its legal system can interact successfully in the near future.

COUNTING PEOPLE: TALLY OR STATISTICAL SAMPLE?

Just as once required in early Rome, the U.S. Constitution requires a head count, called a census, every decade. A census will occur in the year 2000. Why would a tally of our citizenry rise to the level of a constitutional mandate? This tally of the people (called an "enumeration" in our Constitution) is much more than informational. For example, and as you will read later in Chapter 2, our representational form of government allocates power (votes) based in part upon the number of persons resident within a certain state or geographical district. Thus, for example, Idaho, with its small population, is entitled to fewer U.S. Congressional seats (members entitled to vote) than, say, Illinois. Legislators from populous states such as Texas and New York can and do vote more benefits to their constituents (voters). The census is crucial for periodically changing the power structure of our representative form of government, thereby maintaining its fairness and logic.

At the turn of the twentieth century, taking a census was easier in the sense that the U.S. population was "only" 76 million. Today the U.S. is composed of more than 270 million people; thus, the census-taking process is very complicated and, according to many, quite flawed. For example, California, Texas, and Florida legislators contend that their people are undercounted because many residents are aliens who fear being counted and who, in essence, hide from the tally. Thus, certain incumbent politicians and minority groups are urging the 2000 census be made by statistical sampling methods rather than by head counting. Other states and groups object, undoubtedly fearing skewered results that would further weaken them. This is an excellent example of the complexity of issue the law faces today.* With congressional agreement impossible, the U.S. Supreme Court has accepted the responsibility of determining how the census shall be taken.

Often when there is an Internet source available to provide additional information on a topic that is discussed in the text, we will alert you to it in the margin. The Internet is changing the way we obtain information and is making it easier for you to have access to primary research and materials no matter where in the world they exist. You can learn whether or not statistical sampling will be permitted in the 2000 census by checking the case of *U.S. Department of Commerce v. U.S. House of Representatives*, docket number 98-0404. http://supct.law.cornell.edu/supct/index.html

---

*The census of 2000, like any census, is much more than a body count. The results of a census are studied by experts called demographers, who statistically analyze the results with reference to the distribution (location) and vital statistics (e.g., income, gender, and race) of the population. All of this information is used by politicians and activists to support their calls for changes in the laws on wide ranging issues, such as affirmative action, environmental protection, and social services.

OTHER LEGAL/SOCIETAL RELATIONSHIPS

What was our society like only one (extended) lifetime ago[5] on the eve of the twentieth century? With a flourishing economy fueled in part by the Klondike Gold Rush, William McKinley was re-elected president in 1900 on a platform that government should not control or discipline business. Riding the crest of victory over Spain in the Spanish-American War, Theodore (Teddy) Roosevelt became vice president. Unlike our present military capability for distance warfare, Roosevelt's "Rough Riders" fought eye-to-eye, although more U.S. soldiers died from contaminated meat than at the hands of the Spanish. On the brink of an industrial revolution and new status as a world power, changes were happening on the domestic front. Then, as now, people necessarily relied upon the ability of their laws to change responsively to their needs—and upon their legal system to oversee the process. Consider the following example of the U.S. Supreme Court in action:

> Minnesota law provided that "All labor on Sunday is prohibited, excepting the works of necessity or charity. . . ." Barber Petit was arrested, tried, and convicted of cutting hair and shaving beards in his barbershop on Sundays. He appealed all the way to the U.S. Supreme Court on the grounds that cutting hair and shaving beards was a work of necessity. What do you suppose was the result in 1899?[6]

The Court recognized the Sunday law of relaxation as "essential to the physical and moral well-being of society." The Court relied upon several precedents (prior court decisions) to the effect that shaving on Sunday was not a work of necessity. Even the House of Lords in England in earlier times had concluded that shaving customers was a worldly labor. Mr. Petit lost his appeal. Most cases before the U.S. Supreme Court were far more complex than Mr. Petit's case, involving commerce, taxation, admiralty, commercial transactions, water rights, and so on. The U.S. Supreme Court was composed of nine Justices, as it is today, and the structure of lower courts remains essentially unchanged. The point remains, however, that we live in an overwhelmingly more complex world.

Consider the role of women on the eve of the twentieth century. Their primary work was housework and child rearing. Perhaps 20 percent of women were in the paid labor force by 1900.[7] Of those employed outside the home, the vast majority were farmhands or domestics. Other than in the states of Utah and Colorado, women did not have the right to vote. The Klondike Gold Rush had fueled a "Gilded Age" as the twentieth century began, with affluence spreading throughout many American cities. Women in the upper classes became more athletic and "outdoorsy" than before. Although still corseted, the modern woman wore only one petticoat instead of the five previously worn. Bread was purchased in shops, freeing women from the chore of baking. Dining in fancy restaurants was a primary recreation, and their men enjoyed golfing and smoking Cuban cigars as a mark of attainment. At home, Jello was available for dessert. Only the homes of the upper classes had bathtubs, and fewer had showers, but this century began with the expectations of an ongoing Gilded Age with even more good (financial) times for our society. By the end of the century, trolleys (and to a very limited extent, cars) made travel easier, encouraging families from the wealthy class to move from urban areas to suburbs. The flight of people from cities to their suburbs had early beginnings. Upper-class families sent their children to the great Ivy League and other universities. And the national college entrance examination board was begun which created the SAT (scholastic achievement test) with which you are, no doubt, familiar. Nevertheless, women as a class were, for the most part, shortchanged in their protection by the law—from today's perspective. For example, upon marriage a woman's legal rights to property disappeared, property ownership being vested solely in her husband. But our law and legal system had been conceived by its founders as dynamic and, as it turned out, up to the task of coping with the dramatic changes in the extended lifetime of the twentieth century. The rights of women to vote and to own property independently were created under law, as were many other rights to the extent that few distinctions exist in the laws today that are based upon gender.

Consider some of the changes in our society brought about during the twentieth century, changes that placed extraordinary demands upon our legal system. Few people lived in the seven territories (Alaska, Arizona, District of Columbia, Hawaii, New Mexico, Oklahoma, and the Indian territories) in the 1890s, and most conveniences were found in or near the great cities. Although on the eve of an industrial revolution and as an emerging world power, in 1900 there were no airplanes, no manned spaceships, no satellites, no television sets or VCRs, no video cameras, no computers, no Internet, no color or sound movies, no suburban malls, no cellular or cordless telephones, no microwave ovens, no automatic dishwashers, no electric stoves, no trash compactors or disposals, no air conditioning, and no credit or debit cards. As for the implements of war, there were neither nuclear weapons nor submarines with inter-continental missiles to deliver them. On the other hand, Thomas Edison earlier had discovered and harnessed electricity, with the result that the phonograph (but not stereo) and household lighting were widely available in the cities. The first zeppelin had floated in the sky, but it wasn't over a Monday night football game. Individual transportation was by foot, horse or horse-drawn buggy, public transportation (rail and electric trolleys), and bicycle. There were only 13,824 motorcars in a country of 76 million people with a total of only 144 miles of paved roads in the entire United States. Mass production of automobiles was soon to follow the turn of the century, creating a love affair between the public and its cars that has left a most significant impact upon the entire century, including its laws. There were no McDonalds or Burger Kings or any other fast food places. The first hamburger wasn't served until the twentieth century began when, in early 1900, a man in Connecticut ground up some beef and served it between two pieces of toast without catsup or relish. Which came first, aspirin, or fast food? Aspirin had appeared a year earlier. It would be several years before vitamins were even discovered or refrigeration even invented. The towns and cities of the U.S. supported many small coffee bean roasting shops, much as Starbuck's and others dot our cities today. But the coffee roasters began a steady decline into oblivion when Hills Bros. of San Francisco first began packing pre-roasted beans into vacuum tins. For almost the entire century travelers to San Francisco would be greeted with the tantalizing aromas of coffee beans roasting at the Hills Bros.' plant. Technology already was creating its rewards and victims.[8]

Many interesting events at the beginning of the twentieth century have parallels to today's legal issues. Just before the turn of the century, Butch Cassidy and the Sundance Kid robbed a Union Pacific train in Wyoming and Gideons International began placing Bibles in hotel rooms; today, crime and religious

freedom share headlines and demand solutions through new laws or even constitutional amendment (school prayer). One hundred years ago, the last of the Indian
wars had been fought; today, Indian treaty rights to fish, gamble, and use natural
resources are in the news, with proposals for new enabling laws. A century ago the
first juvenile court was established in Illinois; today, juvenile and gang-
related crime prompts reactive laws. (For example, elementary school children in
Indianapolis must enter school through a metal detector to make sure no gun or
knife is being brought to class,[9] and convictions for gang-related crimes now are
being based on out-of-court [hearsay] testimony. A plethora of court decisions
have relaxed the rules to easier convict "gang" members.[10]) The United States government was already a leading employer at the turn of the century with a quarter
million employees, and only one-quarter of the U.S. commercial shipping fleet was
under sail power. Today, ocean pollution from petroleum-based products released
from steamships through disaster or otherwise continues to plague an environ-
mentally conscious world; new laws impose severe financial penalties and require
safety precautions, such as double hulls, "road maps" on the seas near coastlines,
and warrantless searches of vessels. A hurricane in Galveston, Texas, killed thousands of people in 1900, becoming the worst North American disaster in history;
today, natural disasters, fires, floods, hurricanes, and combinations of all occur annually, causing not only financial burdens but legal burdens of major proportions
(fraud in distribution of relief funds; liabilities for defective buildings, levees, etc.).
At the beginning of the twentieth century, grapefruit were made to grow sweeter
and gained public acceptance as a result; today, genetic engineering is modifying
food products to resist pests, to gain better size and marketing durability, and to
improve taste, while the legal implications of the genetic engineering of food products remains to be seen. A century ago the first drunk driving case involved a
horse-drawn taxicab driver; today, the Congress has under consideration a law to
compel states to adopt a tough national standard of .08 blood alcohol level figure
for drunk drivers (most states use a more lenient .10 standard).[11]

Obviously, most of today's necessities and conveniences were not available to
our society at the beginning of the twentieth century. But neither were there federal laws prohibiting discrimination on the basis of race, religion, or gender in the
workplace. Racial discrimination was alive and well at the beginning of the twentieth century. Because poll taxes and literacy tests were preconditions to voting in
many states, black Americans were segregated and powerless under the law to do
much about it. The constitutionality of the principle of "separate but equal" facilities based on race was well established.[12] More than one-half of the century
elapsed before that doctrine was overruled, when in 1954 the U.S. Supreme Court
declared that segregation was inherently unequal.[13] Although black Americans
could not legally be excluded from juries by the turn of the century, many states
relied upon racially selective jury selection practices. The infamous "Scottsboro
Boys" case probably marks the beginning of serious changes in the law to guarantee full participation by blacks on juries. The convictions and death penalties of
nine young blacks for the rape of two white women by an all-white jury was overruled because of discrimination in jury selection.[14]

But change in the law constantly was occurring. Our legal system was appropriate for the time and, as it turned out, supremely capable of coping with the
important issues that arose during the twentieth century. On the other hand,
some believe that our legal system already has begun to fail in its supremely challenging task of guiding our society.[15]

WHAT IS THE FORESEEABLE OUTLOOK FOR THE LEGAL SYSTEM IN THE COMING CENTURY?

With the knowledge of how the law and legal system has fulfilled its responsibility to meet radically changing times during the twentieth century, what can we foresee in the future for the law? What can be seen is complexity brought about by our expectation that the law, lawyers, and judges will continue to accept responsibility for solutions to an increasing number of precise issues within grand problems. Focusing on the arrival of the new millennium as a starting point for our outlook into the future is not unique. Academics across America are collecting information about the impact of the coming of the new millenium.[16] Here we suggest that the single most significant event likely will be an increasing role of the legal system in society, with a corresponding increase in the complexities of its procedures and the issues it resolves.

Our legal system shows no tendency to reject or limit the trend of accepting responsibilities (jurisdiction) over an increasing variety of issues. For example, relatively recently we have witnessed courts accepting the issues brought about by gerrymandering to right past wrongs (political action); by presidents abusing their trust and executive powers (court orders compelling testimony and submitting to civil litigation); by discrimination against persons on the basis of their health (e.g., AIDS, disability, mental health), sexual orientation (same-sex marriage), or religion (e.g., school prayer); by overruling laws created directly by people in the initiative process (propositions on ballots); and so on. These topics will become the focus of your studies later in this text, but here it is sufficient to identify significant problems being addressed more by courts and the legal system than by either the legislative or executive branches of government. We predict this trend will continue. Thus, your education about the law is more compelling than was your parents'.

There is a rationale that elected officials willingly choose to avoid the tough and controversial issues that always cost them votes, and leave these "no win" issues to the legal system where the judges are brave, if for no other reason, because the electorate participates less in their tenure. Abortion is one example where only the courts could resolve the issue, even though no constitutional provision could be identified to support the selected result. Even the U.S. Supreme Court could muster only a 5–4 decision, demonstrating that an issue so controversial could manage to be decided by only a single vote.[17] In short, it is increasingly important that well-informed citizens, like yourselves, be educated about our legal system, including the role of its judges and lawyers. Otherwise, citizens risk submission through ignorance and complacency to the latest sound bite or "spin" that seeks voter approval. Your understanding of the increasingly important legal system is critical over the long run, which is precisely why it is presented to you here.

We increasingly turn to the courts to solve our problems—both public *and* private. This produces a great strain upon our legal system, evident by the growth of alternative forums for dispute resolution (discussed fully in Chapter 3). The point here is that the future portends increasing legal costs of doing business and of protecting consumers. These costs are indirectly reflected in the prices of products as well as taxes used to support courts, judges, and governmental offices charged with providing public/legal services.

There is no reason to suspect that the demand for attorneys (e.g., legal solutions) will lessen or that their services will cost less as we proceed into the twenty-first century. Lawyers enjoy an oligarchy with the power (and willingness) to match their fees with the capabilities of their clients to pay. Increasing demand is producing more lawyers, who become safely ensconced within the parameters of existing firms, in turn, participating in an ever wider scope of increasingly specialized tasks. Unlike 1899, when lawyers wearing green visors drafted documents, examined titles, and appeared in court on what appears today to be simplistic matters, lawyers now are negotiators, contract and document preparers, transactional specialists, deal makers, catalysts of massive class actions by large groups of consumers, politicians and, of course, courtroom warriors armed with statutes authorizing, if not encouraging, litigation.

This is not to suggest that our dependence upon law, courts, and lawyers is either good or bad. It is merely a well understood phenomenon as we enter the twenty-first century. Educators often speak of the legal system as being composed of laws and courts. The logic is that laws are the rules of our society and courts ensure their enforcement. But what of attorneys? In reality, a person cannot pursue the solution of a substantial conflict or commercial transaction without an attorney's professional help. Although citizens are entitled under law to represent themselves, the reality is that such an attempt is ill advised for many obvious reasons. Thus, the attorney is the first person to become involved when legal issues and many business opportunities arise. Attorneys give advice, most of which is followed. They also perform other services as described in Chapter 4. The point is, attorneys must be acknowledged as an integral part of the legal system because laws and judges are powerless until attorneys bring matters into court.

We can foresee a growing population being served by expanding businesses and requiring greater governmental protection and services with expanding conflicts and issues, all requiring the services of lawyers. Do not misunderstand. Aside from the exasperation widely expressed by our society about lawyers, the law business is alive and well and adequately handling all the various clients it serves. With its ability to specialize and change to meet changing times, the prediction that the legal system (defined as to include lawyers) and the complexities it produces will continue to grow.

Throughout this book we will be explaining and simplifying what our law has become over the preceding 100 years. We liberally include observations about the beginning of the new millennium for your consideration. Following is a brief preview to the organization and content of this book. In Unit I, the first eight chapters, you will learn about our legal system and basic legal and business principles. In Unit II we include those specific areas of the law that we anticipate will most likely affect you personally and directly.

PREVIEW TO UNIT I: THE LEGAL SYSTEM AND BASIC PRINCIPLES OF LAW

OUR CONSTITUTION (CHAPTER 2)

Ours is a constitutional form of government; a society governed by laws enacted by representatives we choose, rather than by the ideas and whims of some supreme hereditary ruler or of an oligarchy. College graduates, especially, should be familiar with our Constitution and the protection it provides us from possible abuse by those who govern, while defining the structure and legitimate powers of the federal government. Why "college graduates"? Because it is you and others like you who will be primarily responsible for maintaining and managing our democracy in the years to come. Rising costs and other social reasons have moved college educations beyond the financial reach or goal of many otherwise qualified persons. This increases the obligations of leadership of those, like you, who do earn college and post-graduate degrees. On the one hand, knowing how our legal system works will help you take advantage of personal career and other opportunities. But in a larger sense, as an educated person you need to understand that ours is a constitutional democracy, and that our Constitution prohibits governments at all levels (city, county, state, and federal) from imposing arbitrary or otherwise improper rules and laws upon society. Consultive leadership depends upon education and wisdom, and that is the fundamental reason why your understanding of our Constitution is important.

In Chapter 2 you will learn or review that our Constitution both prescribes the organization of government and restrains federal, state, and local governments from arbitrary or oppressive regulation. To both organize and restrain, our Constitution separates government into three branches—the legislative, the judicial, and the executive. You will see how these branches of government can, and often do, overlap and even conflict.

As an example of how the law has been changing during this century, consider that in 1965 the U.S. Supreme Court, for the first time, declared that the U.S. Constitution guaranteed citizens a certain "right of privacy" that is implied from the phrase "due process." This is the same right of privacy that legalizes abortion, intermarriage, and the possession of pornography. Prior to 1965, these rights did not exist. There are, of course, countless other examples of how rights have been created or modified during the twentieth century.

Thus, Chapter 2 will provide you with much of the understanding you will need to evaluate proposed and actual changes in our laws and our legal system.

THE COURT SYSTEM (CHAPTER 3)

Most of you will be required to go to court sooner or later, and possibly more than once. Courts exist primarily to resolve disputes. Innumerable disputes (called cases, once in court) are handled by courts every business day. Disputes vary in content from simple traffic violations to complex, bitterly contested divorce proceedings. They range from arguments over price fixing between national corporations involving tens of millions of dollars, to accusations of murder and violent crime. Your appreciation of the breadth of court decisions will be enhanced by this course.

Your personal involvement in court will probably be as a juror or witness. Hopefully none of you will appear in criminal court as a defendant or victim, but this too could happen. You may have civil disputes with business associates, strangers, or even with friends or relatives whom you believe have violated your rights; you may end up in court to resolve serious differences over the conduct of family affairs.

From time to time, proposals to change our courts appear on election ballots. For example, delays in court proceeding are becoming legendary in heavily populated metropolitan areas. Generally, criminal trials take precedence over civil trials. The latter therefore may linger for years, especially in metropolitan areas, waiting for available courtrooms and judges. This impact of drug-related criminal cases is especially significant in the federal courts. Court administration, aided by computers and professional managers, is improving the efficiency in the handling of cases. Unfortunately, the trial dockets (calendars of pending cases) are overloaded in many of our metropolitan courts, with no end or solution in sight for the twenty-first century. We can expect proposals to achieve economies in time and money by reduction in the size of juries, and even by their elimination from certain types of cases. We also can expect changes in the administration of criminal cases that involve illegal drugs, because they take a large share of the time of courts, judges, public attorneys, and even space otherwise available for the incarceration of more violent offenders. Basic changes in the applicable laws and in court procedures should be carefully and thoughtfully made, with the participation of informed and concerned citizens such as yourselves.

Clearly it is important and useful to know where our courts are located, how they function, and the role they play in our society. The electronic media has capitalized on the public's interest in courts with TV shows, and the print media has responded by publishing novels based on lawyering and courtroom activities. Significant decisions of appellate courts, especially the U.S. Supreme Court, receive widespread media coverage when they are of popular interest and concern. In Chapter 3 you will obtain an accurate clarification to help you evaluate news reports of legal issues and to articulate your understanding to friends, associates, and others.

The Attorney–Client Relationship (Chapter 4)

Because of the complexities of modern life, it is very likely that you will, from time to time, require the services of an attorney. We describe attorneys as a part of our legal system because, realistically, there is almost no alternative to their services in resolving legal disputes. Attorney fees are a major component of the total cost of dispute resolution in courts, which makes attorney–client relations a serious concern of consumers who are directly affected. How do you locate and hire an attorney? What are customary attorneys' fees for typical types of services? Can you contest the payment of fees if the service you receive is unsatisfactory? If you are unhappy with the legal services you are receiving, can you fire your attorney? What if your attorney fails to keep you informed on the progress of your case? What is legal malpractice?

At a societal level, the questions are far more complex. When calamitous injuries occur to innocent victims, are contingent (percentage of recovery) attorney fees inherently unfair? We also consider the legal profession in its role in serving the needs of businesses, governments, labor unions, charities, religious groups, the military, and so on. In other words, the legal profession is the exclusive manager of the legal issues of all segments of our society, a responsibility that compels the fullest possible understanding of its operations.

In Chapter 4 you will receive a sufficient foundation for understanding the legal profession. It is unknown, however, whether or not the legal profession will change in response to highly publicized and widespread public dissatisfaction. Regardless, you will gain the understanding with which to assess the opposing sides of the ongoing debate about lawyers and the workings of their profession.

Joe Stropnicky made an appointment to hire attorney Judith Nathanson for legal assistance in obtaining a divorce. Judith rejected Joe as a client because he is male. She asserted her right to represent whom she pleases. Nathanson spent years building her practice specializing in representing women in family law. She felt no "personal commitment" toward men. Does Joe have any recourse against Judith?[18]

Businesses that hold themselves out to the public cannot refuse a customer on the basis of race, religion, gender, or other protected class of persons. Should lawyers be treated differently? Joe complained to the Massachusetts Commission Against Discrimination, which ruled in his favor. He was awarded $5,000 for his emotional distress in being rejected by Nathanson.

ADMINISTRATIVE LAW (CHAPTER 5)

You cannot qualify as a well-informed college graduate unless you are familiar with our form of government and its legal structure. Of course you're familiar with the three constitutionally derived branches of government: legislative, executive, and judicial. But how the functions of these branches interact in implementing and enforcing our written laws in the governance of our country is complex and significant. In addition to traditional state and federal lawmakers, hundreds of federal and state administrative agencies share responsibility to regulate the day-to-day business of our society. It is an established principle that regular lawmakers can delegate their constitutional lawmaking and enforcing functions to these specialized administrative agencies, which are assigned specific areas to govern.

In this chapter you will learn how administrative agencies, such as the Environmental Protection Agency (EPA), go about making rules and then enforcing their dictates. Sometimes new rules can be devastating to a business or others, as when, for example, the harvest of a commercial product such as the chinook salmon is restricted. In fact, as you will discover, most administrative rules have their detractors.

Viewed together, administrative agencies are sometimes described in less than loving terms as "the bureaucracy," causing delay upon costly delay and thriving in oceans of red tape. Nevertheless, the bureaucracy has important responsibilities, and it positively affects our lives and businesses every day. Individuals and businesses must use available administrative remedies before resorting to courts for redress of grievances; therefore, familiarity with fundamental appeal processes may be critical. These agencies form a major part of our legal system. In Chapter 5 we explore in detail how our administrative agencies function in the complex task of running the public business of the country. There you will find an organization chart that simplifies the structure of federal agencies in the overall scheme of our government.

CRIMES: PUBLIC WRONGS (CHAPTER 6)

Some conduct is so offensive it is deemed threatening and harmful to society in general, even though there may be but a single victim directly injured by the perpetrator. As the twentieth century winds down, crime is among the most worrisome problems in our society. As a result, society is demanding and receiving significant changes in laws governing crime and related punishment. Your informed participation in discussion of such changes during the years ahead may help to minimize obvious risks of enactment into law of politically inspired draconian measures. They may be an understandable response by legislators to demands of angry and worried citizens for action against what seem to be heinous crimes against innocent victims. But many, if not most, criminologists and penologists maintain that such overreaction is counterproductive. For example, the financial costs of life imprisonment for many more criminals can multiply without commensurate reduction in criminal activity. As you will study in Chapter 6, other popular legislative responses to public cries for protection include curfews, injunctions prohibiting specified conduct (loitering and associating) directed at an undesirable class of people (gangs) before a crime has been committed, expanded penalties for so-called "hate" crimes based on race or religion, and the enhancement of penalties for repeat offenders ("three strikes") who commit either violent (robbery) or nonviolent (illegal drug) crimes. One popular law enacted in response to public outcry requires notification of personal addresses to neighbors of sex offenders who already have fully served their sentences and paid for their crimes.

Congress and state legislatures have codified (prohibited by statute) various types of criminal conduct and have prescribed penalties for those convicted. Enforcement of the criminal law is almost exclusively the responsibility of various law enforcement bodies (e.g., the Federal Bureau of Investigation and state and local police departments). Private citizens normally do not enforce the criminal law, although some infrequently used laws authorize arrest by citizens under specified circumstances. In today's dangerous environment, citizen arrests are likely to become a rarity.

The topic of crime and punishment in our society carries with it issues involving race, and always has. A disproportionate percentage of African Americans are in the prisons and jails of the U.S., or otherwise under the jurisdiction of criminal authorities (probation and parole), than caucasians. Is this disparity linked more to race or to the government processes by which suspects are tried, convicted, and incarcerated? To what extent is the so-called war against drugs and the poverty surrounding some heavily populated inner cities reflected in these alarming statistics? Although there are no wholly satisfactory answers to these questions, as an informed citizen, you will be able to evaluate new proposals from differing perspectives, an academic and personal skill of great value.

TORTS: PRIVATE WRONGS (CHAPTER 7)

Some conduct may cause injury to another person although no crime is involved. For example, negligent (careless) operation of an automobile is often the cause of serious injury. But such negligent conduct does not threaten society in general, and therefore is not considered criminal in nature.* Nonetheless, the injured

---

*Some careless conduct is so reckless as to constitute a willful disregard for the safety of the public. Such gross negligence or recklessness is treated as a crime. Causing a vehicular accident while under the influence of alcohol or drugs is an example of such conduct, even when the offender had no specific criminal intent.

person is entitled to seek monetary compensation through legal action. The law of torts provides monetary damages for victims of wrongful and harmful or offensive conduct, whether intentional or negligent. It is a basic principle in law that for every wrong there is some remedy, and torts are private wrongs.

Employers are liable for the wrongful conduct of their employees done in the course of their jobs. Manufacturers, wholesalers, retailers, and sometimes repair businesses can be liable for injuries caused by defective products or services years after they were purchased. Some businesses are liable without any fault for injuries and damages to victims of dangerous activities, such as airplane crashes and chemical explosions or escape. And many victims of civil rights abuses, such as discrimination on the basis of age, gender, race, religion, or other protected categories, can recover damages for their treatment. When there are many victims of a civil wrong, they may be joined together in class actions to produce compensation without the necessity of separate lawsuits for each person. In other words, the tort law is the mechanism through which private wrongs are redressed. You will find that tort law is as controversial as it is interesting as you study Chapter 7.

CONTRACT LAW (CHAPTER 8)

Contracts are essential in getting the world's work done. Businesses and families alike rely on promises concerning the manufacture, distribution, and sale of goods and services. Contract law governs promises made for commercial purposes, including complex arrangements designed to keep the nation's economy operating. Contracts also govern the vast majority of activities that involve family finances, such as employment, investment, consumer purchases, home construction, and health care. The principles of contract law have not changed radically since the beginning of the twentieth century. Adoption of uniform laws of contracts among the states was an initial response to the increasing complexities of our society following World War Two. Called the Uniform Commercial Code, or UCC, these laws provided much needed uniformity of laws in commerce, such as who must suffer the risk of loss of goods that are in transit.

As the twenty-first century approaches, business is increasingly becoming a global effort. Furthermore, families will be conducting increasing amounts of business in cyberspace. These developments create important new issues and disputes relative to international contracts, many of which will be decided in court. We examine the laws of contracts in Chapter 8.

PREVIEW TO UNIT II: APPLICATIONS OF THE LAW TO THE INDIVIDUAL

FAMILY LAW (CHAPTER 9)

Unquestionably some aspects of family law will impact your life. The legal implications of living as a family can and do involve a great variety of laws. There are many examples with which to demonstrate the complexities existing between families and laws, beginning with the very definition of marriage.

Some clergy in the Methodist church perform "holy union" ceremonies for same-sex couples. Other pastors with a more conservative or fundamental view of the Bible vehemently object to this practice and threaten to withdraw from the church. Do these ceremonies create marriages?[19]

Legal marriage must be created in conformity with state laws, all of which, for example, require marital licenses and that members be of the opposite sex. However same-sex "marriages" or "unions" create families that are, in many states and in many ways, protected by law. For example, in those states, sexual orientation is not a valid basis for a landlord to refuse to rent living space. Today same-sex marriages continue to await legal authenticity.[20]

Family law is designed to protect family values. But differences of opinion as to those values can be significant. For example, in many states the family is thought to be protected by the criminalization of adultery. The federal government rewards families with certain tax benefits and provides financial and other assistance (e.g., withholding of income tax refunds) to states that have difficulty tracking down parents who are delinquent in child support payments. A variety of criminal and civil laws protect the family from abusive treatment. Clearly a well-informed citizenry must understand the essentials of family law.

Entering the twenty-first century, we find family law facing what promises to be the most controversial issue ever—the genetic alteration of humans, which offers prospective parents the choice of specific characteristics in their offspring (so-called designer babies). Already thorny issues of custody and the use of frozen and fertilized embryos following death or divorce have arisen in this blend of moral and legal issues.

In Chapter 9 you will learn about additional laws designed to protect family values as well as the potential involvement of it in your daily lives.

OWNING AND OPERATING MOTOR VEHICLES (CHAPTER 10)

Many legal issues arise from our nation's love affair with automobiles. To begin with, there is much information that drivers should know. Consider the following questions: What are the principles of law concerning ownership and leasing of automobiles? What are "lemon" laws? Who is responsible when accidents occur? What insurance must you have? What happens if you do not have insurance? What should you do if involved in an accident? If your passenger is injured, will your insurance company pay the medical expenses? Should all states adopt a no-fault plan for injury compensation? At the beginning of the twentieth century virtually all of these questions were irrelevant because only a few cars existed. As the twenty-first century begins, of course, our highways are glutted with motor vehicles; in fact, one of the most pressing problems will be determining how best to transport workers from suburbs to city employment centers. At the same time, there will be a much greater percentage of older drivers competing for space on the nation's highways. You will study the answers to these questions and more in Chapter 10. Related questions about the impact of motor vehicles of all kinds on our environment appear in other chapters, including laws encouraging the use of ethanol and electricity as replacements for petroleum-based fuels.

RENTERS AND LANDLORDS (CHAPTER 11)

Many of you are renting an apartment or sharing a rented home during your years at college. Most of you will probably rent housing for some time after college while saving for a down payment to buy a home. What are your rights as a tenant, and what duties do you owe your landlord? There are many questions that should be asked by prospective residents before signing a lease and committing to a rental unit. Can the landlord raise the rent? What if your landlord does not fix a leaking roof? If your belongings are stolen from your apartment, are you legally entitled to receive compensation from the landlord? Must your landlord provide safe living accommodations? Can your landlord secretly enter your apartment in your absence? Are you entitled to know what crimes have occurred in the rental premises before you sign a lease? What happens if you break your lease?

> Jamie moved into an apartment near the university she was attending. Jamie did not know, did not ask, and was not informed that the prior resident in her unit had been evicted for failure to pay rent following his arrest for the crime of forcible rape. She also did not know that the key to her apartment door had not been changed. Does the law require landlords to provide new keys on door locks when apartments are rented to new tenants?

No. But if Jamie had asked, the landlord would have been placed in the precarious position of either lying or telling the truth and re-keying the apartment. If the landlord opted to lie, and if Jamie became the victim of a crime following an entry into her apartment, the landlord would then be liable for substantial compensatory and punitive damages. The important laws pertaining to renters and landlords are outlined in Chapter 11.

HOME OWNERSHIP (CHAPTER 12)

A few years after college, almost all of you will be pursuing "the American Dream of owning your own home." How do you locate, finance, and purchase a home? Can two unrelated persons qualify for home financing? How large will your monthly payments be? Can your monthly payments increase? What happens if you miss a payment? Do you need the services of a real estate broker or sales agent when buying? When selling? Should you transfer credit card debt to a new home-equity loan?

> Joe, Stephanie, and their two young children purchased a lovely home in the suburbs for $325,000. They were unaware that a neighbor, Mr. Joshua Cox, previously had been convicted for a violent sexual assault upon a minor, had served five years in prison as a result, and had been released only two months before Joe's family arrived. Was the seller obligated to tell Joe and Stephanie about the neighbor?

The twentieth century principle of "let the buyer beware" has been changing to "let the seller beware," at least in regard to home purchases. Entering the twenty-first century, the new trend is that sellers must reveal all relevant known information that might bear upon the decision to purchase a home. The current address of felons who have been convicted of specified violent sexual assaults is public information—but must sellers tell prospective buyers? The answer is unknown, but with the trend as a guide, the most probable answer is that Joe and Stephanie should have been told by the seller. We consider the practices and laws affecting the "American Dream" in Chapter 12.

EMPLOYEE AND EMPLOYER RIGHTS AND DUTIES (CHAPTER 13)

Society increasingly demands that employers provide safe and humane workplaces, free of both physical dangers and of discriminatory practices based upon gender, race, ethnic origin, or other legally defined classifications. For example, permanent employees cannot be fired without good cause. The law may soon require health care for all employees, and employers may soon be held responsible for keeping workplaces safe from criminal attack. Already most employers must provide reasonable access for disabled employees and customers. Much is happening in the area of employer and employee relations.

> Joe had worked as a machinist for the Acme Lawnmower Company for 30 years, when at age 55 he was suddenly discharged for no apparent reason. Joe asked and was told that he was being replaced by a new, much younger machinist who was being hired at substantially less salary. Does Joe have a claim for discrimination on the basis of age?

Probably not. The prevailing rule is that the replacement of higher-paid employees with lower-paid employees is lawful even if the effect is to discharge older workers. Should Joe have had the opportunity to accept the lower, "market rate" of pay and retain his job? Employee rights and duties are discussed in Chapter 13.

WILLS, TRUSTS, AND PROBATE LAWS (CHAPTER 14)

Unfortunately, not all of the significant events in our lives are pleasant. Death must someday come to family members and others we love, including ourselves. But life goes on, and the law provides means of ensuring survivors that important financial matters of the deceased are properly handled. Are you prepared to share in these responsibilities? Who should have a will? How do you create a will? Do you need the services of an attorney to prepare a will? Should property be left equally, share and share alike, to heirs? When is a trust helpful in preparing for the financial aftermath of death? Is an attorney needed when a family member dies? Under what circumstances can a will be contested? How are family assets taxed when death occurs? What is a living will? A living trust? Can you leave instructions to prevent hookup to life support systems if you suffer a stroke or are in an automobile accident and become too incapacitated to make such a decision?

> Mary, age 87 and bedridden, had been lingering in a vegetative state for two years. Medical opinion was that she would never improve. She asked

her physician to help her commit suicide by lethal injection. She also asked her husband to take whatever means he could to end her life as mercifully as possible. Can Mary's physician or husband legally give her the relief she seeks?

No. Almost every state prohibits assisted suicide, and the U.S. Supreme Court has ruled that there is no constitutional right to die.[21] This situation is quite different from those in which the patient previously has signed a written directive that he or she desires that life support equipment be avoided, or even removed once hooked up. Many believe that laws should be expanded to include physician-assisted suicide. We present the challenging laws of estate planning and probate matters in Chapter 14.

Before proceeding to the specific legal topics found in Units I and II, some familiarity with the origins of our laws and our legal system will help you to appreciate their significance.

THE ENGLISH SOURCE OF OUR LAW

Before the eleventh century, England was an Anglo-Saxon society, a unified and relatively prosperous nation living mostly in villages. The economy was agricultural and the people were self-sufficient, growing grain, spinning wool, and even brewing beer for home consumption. Their kings headed powerful and wealthy aristocracies. Wealth was primarily tied to the landholding feudal system. Serfdom, in which people were born into vassalage and were required to work the aristocratic lords' hereditary lands, was widespread. Throughout the Saxon period, law was essentially a matter of local customs, and it changed very slowly. For the most part, laws were unwritten and reflected long-established customs and shared values; kings rarely issued laws binding the entire nation. Established legal systems provided monetary compensation for private wrongs and criminal prosecution for public wrongs. Generally, a person accused of a crime had either been caught in the act or had been found guilty in a strange proceeding during which witnesses and the accused engaged in "oath-swearing." This was a complicated procedure related more to the character of the accused than to evidence of a crime. There were no lawyers and no jury trials. Needless to say, this system was neither sophisticated nor flawless.

The Normans (Vikings who originally came from Scandinavia via northern France) were French in language,* viewpoint, and culture. Their system of law was based on the ancient Roman civil law, which was expressed mostly in detailed codes (systematic collections of rules) imposed by the ruler from above, in contrast to the Saxon practice of developing rules from below, based on customs of the people.

In 1066, William, Duke of Normandy led 5,000 men and 2,500 cavalry across the English Channel to defeat the Saxons in the Battle of Hastings. The Duke became known as William the Conqueror. The invasion was followed by decades of

*Norman French is very different from modern French.

regional uprisings and resistance characterized by extensive murder, oppression, famine, and fear, despite William's zeal for law, order, and justice.

The Normans retained the English common law of unwritten customs, except that church courts were introduced with authority limited mainly to spiritual matters and domestic (family) relations. England gradually underwent positive changes. A sense of national unity ensued, leading to a national system of law derived from both Anglo-Saxon and Norman influences. The Normans had already been influenced by the French, and the linking of England with the European continent, effected by the conquest, led to the introduction of elements of Roman civil law. Following numerous regional battles, William became King of England and ultimately obtained the allegiance of the people. Gradually, intermarriage between the native people and the invaders became common. As before, local justice continued to be the concern of local sheriffs, and the common law (law applied uniformly throughout the country) was characterized even then by equality before the law (the law applied the same to every person), respect for established rights, and impartial administration of justice.

The king's courts dealt with the common law (civil and criminal matters). The new Church Courts dealt with canon law (ecclesiastical law governing internal relations of the Roman Catholic church) and all aspects of marriage and succession. Disputes existed in some areas, such as legitimization of illegitimate children, which was not possible under canon law. Under common law, legitimization was accomplished by subsequent marriage of the parents. This was an important matter because it affected rights of succession to land.

By the twelfth century, sheriffs were being displaced by judges, who periodically visited places in the country to dispense justice. These "circuits" were precursors of the present U.S. circuit and district courts. The itinerant judges dealt with crimes such as murder, robbery, forgery, and arson. One judge, Glanvil, is credited with writing the *Treatise on the Laws and Customs of the Kingdom of England*, the first serious book on the evolving common law. In 1215, King John was forced to accept the *Magna Carta* (Latin: Great Charter), the basis of modern English constitutional liberty, commanding free elections and reform of the courts and barring imprisonment without a trial by a jury of peers. Trial by jury had evolved into permanency by way of the Magna Carta, and ultimately was incorporated into the U.S. Constitution. The Magna Carta essentially decreed supremacy of law over personal authority of the king and his aides. It was a precursor of our constitutional democracy.

For several hundred years the English system of courts evolved, influenced by conflicts and political interventions. High-ranking clergymen served as chancellors to the king; when the king's courts were unable or unwilling to provide a just solution to a legal problem, and the citizen appealed to the king, the matter would be referred to the chancellor—typically a high churchman in those days. As a man committed to justice and fairness, the chancellor was authorized to decide the cases without the assistance of a jury. These alternative courts became known as *courts of equity*. An example of a case in equity would be a dispute over the sale of a parcel of land in which the seller refused to transfer the title. The king's courts, by tradition, could do no more than award monetary damages. The chancellor (and, later, courts of equity) could and would order the seller to relinquish possession. Such decree of specific performance to this day remains an equitable remedy and is available in regular courts sitting without juries. Ultimately, jurisdictional conflicts refined the fundamental distinction between courts at law and courts in equity. This distinction endures in the U.S. today and determines important questions. However, unlike England, where courts in law and in equity were physically separated, each U.S. court today is empowered to render either equitable or legal relief. Equity is explained further in Chapter 3.

The eighteenth century brought England from medieval to modern times. The industrial revolution greatly affected the law as England changed from an agricultural society, where land was the principal form of wealth, to a society increasingly based on factories and industrial production. Machinery produced more goods at less cost with less labor; prices dropped, resulting in greater demand for goods. England prospered as trade expanded, and the law rapidly evolved, responding with many new principles of business law. But the transition was marred by many difficulties and abuses. By the end of the eighteenth century, the state of the law was described by an eminent historian, Sir Thomas Erskine May, in these pessimistic words:

> Heart-breaking delays and ruinous costs were the lot of suitors. Justice was dilatory, expensive, uncertain and remote. To the rich it was a costly lottery; to the poor a denial of right, or certain ruin. The class who profited most by its dark mysteries were the lawyers themselves. A suitor might be reduced to beggary or madness, but his advisers revelled in the chicane and artifice of a lifelong suit and grew rich.[22]

Over hundreds of years the common law of England had evolved into a framework of principles, found in both customs and statutes that were brought to the New World by the early colonial settlers. When the United States broke away from England after the Revolutionary War, we adopted the entire body of English common law as it existed in the eighteenth century—at least to the extent it does not conflict with U.S. federal and state laws. And that is the situation today; principles of the English common law are in effect throughout the country. Only Louisiana, purchased in 1803 from Napoleon, is different, retaining a variation of the Roman civil law that was then used in France.

> The Common Law of England so far as it is not repugnant to or inconsistent with the Constitution of the United States or the Constitution or laws of this state, is the rule of decision in all the courts of this state. California Civil Code, Sec. 22.2.

This California statute is representative of the reception of English legal doctrine and process in the courts of the United States. The Revolutionary War may have eliminated the power of the king over the colonies, but not the power of English legal thought over the United States.

English common law does not reflect any universal moral principles rooted in natural reason. Rather, its legitimacy arises from the tacit consent of the people as evident from custom and long usage. The technicality of the common law provides lawyers with their claim to expertise and serves by its very complexity to distinguish legal reasoning from the common sense reason of the populace.

MODERN COMMON LAW AND *STARE DECISIS*

Our form of government is a **federalism** (a union of states under a central federal government) that includes both federal and state courts, which function as either trial courts or appellate courts. As you will learn more fully in Chapter 3, trial

An excellent site about the history of English law is available. For example, read about the Laws of William the Conqueror. http://www.law.cam.ac.uk/

The Tarlton Law Library Guide to Legal History Resources on the Web at the University of Texas provides primary sources of law by private lawyer Thomas P. Vincent of Northhampton, Maine. http://www.commonlaw.com/

courts accept testimony and other evidence to determine guilt or innocence or to place financial responsibility. Appellate courts, on the other hand, review trial court procedures to ensure that correct laws were applied during trial. These appellate reviews, or written decisions, form the body of law called the common law, or case law.

Both federal and state appellate courts review cases based upon the constantly evolving principles of the common law that are expressed in the written decisions of courts. Who reads these written decisions? Members of the public, like yourselves, will learn about new, unfolding laws from television, the Internet, newspapers, and news magazines (but hopefully not from tabloids). Lawyers and scholars read and study court decisions as part of their professional responsibilities. Of course, judges read and study prior court decisions upon which they may decide the trials or cases before them.

Some principles of law derived through the common law apply to both state and federal court systems. For example, the doctrine of *stare decisis* (Latin: to stand by things that have been settled) mandates that once a rule of law is determined to be applicable to a particular set of facts involved in a case, it will be applied to all future cases that have similar facts. This doctrine binds courts of equal or junior rank to follow in its decisions the senior court that first applied the rule or principle. Essentially, lower state courts are bound to the principles established by higher appellate courts within the same state; lower federal courts are bound to the principles established by higher appellate courts within their respective jurisdictions. (The hierarchy of courts is outlined in Chapter 3.)

This important doctrine of *stare decisis* leads to stability and predictability in the law. For example, if a high court establishes the principle that a promise to marry is not enforceable in court nor is it compensable if broken, then routine legal research will alert all attorneys to the existence of that **precedent**. If a similar case arises, they will not waste time and money litigating the question; they know their court will be bound by the same earlier outcome under the doctrine of *stare decisis*. This doctrine is also commonly called the **doctrine of precedents**. Once a common law rule or principle is applied in a case it becomes a "precedent" and is binding on other courts in similar future cases. The appellate court's decision thus has become a part of the common law of that particular state.

Judges do not have the personal choice to disregard a precedent in the common law. Judges take oaths of office and are sworn "to comply with or be faithful to" the law.

J. Anthony Kline, a justice of a state appellate court, wrote a dissenting opinion in which, as a "matter of conscience," he refused to vote consistently with a state supreme court precedent. Does such a declaration violate the doctrine of *stare decisis*?[23]

Although the action of refusing to comply with a precedent flies in the face of the doctrine of *stare decisis*, it may be characterized as a narrow exception based upon the conscience of the justice that is "highly irregular and never to be lightly undertaken."

Stare decisis is not a straitjacket, however. If a principle has outlived its usefulness or has grown inapplicable because of changing social standards and circumstances, it may be overruled by a high court. Often a current case is not controlled by a principle previously applied in an earlier case simply because the two cases are distinguishable on their facts. The previous example of an unenforceable and uncompensable promise to marry would be distinguishable from a case where one of the prospective spouses had incurred considerable related expenses before the promise was broken. The earlier principle, therefore, would not apply to or bind the court's decision. Though the court, obviously, would not compel the parties to marry, it might establish a new principle in authorizing recovery of damages (an award of monetary compensation).

The common law of today is the body of rules derived from fundamental usages and customs of antiquity, particularly as they appeared in medieval England, and from modern judgments of appellate courts recognizing and applying those customs in specific cases. Since thousands of appellate cases are decided each year, the body of common law is enormous, even though most of these cases define no new principles. In preparing current cases, lawyers spend much time and effort searching earlier case records for principles of the common law that might be applicable. Thanks to computer technology, the task is less physically laborious today, but the information at the attorney's fingertips is nonetheless overwhelming in volume, let alone complexity. Before they can draft formal opinions or business documents or perform advocacy, lawyers must perform legal research of the applicable common, statutory, and regulatory (administrative agency) law. Lawyers, thus, are responsible to their clients more for researching than for knowing the law. For those of you who are interested in learning more about, or in practicing, legal research, we have included a summary of basic steps and included it in Appendix C.

Originally the common law of England was called unwritten law, because it evolved from the decisions of judges, based on customs and usages of the people, that had not been recorded, and obviously were not available in written form. Moreover, the decisions and opinions of the judges likewise were not recorded or printed in books; often judges exchanged their rulings orally. In contrast, codes and statutes (enacted by the king or a legislative body) were usually written (printed). Today, of course, most additions to the common law, made in appellate court decisions, are published chronologically in books, called **reporters**, and are referred to as **case law**. If case law were unwritten, both attorneys as well as the public would be unaware of decisions that had been made and of the appellate courts' rationale for those decisions.

MODERN SOURCES OF OUR LAW

Ours is a constitutional form of government, as explained in Chapter 2. In one sense, our Constitution is the ultimate source of our laws because it contains principles by which our nation is governed. Here we are concerned with those institutions of government that create the laws of our land.

Most educated adults are familiar with the basic structure of our federal government, divided by our Constitution into the legislative, executive, and judicial branches. Knowledge of this structure facilitates an understanding of how and where our laws are made and of how they are classified for clarity and comprehensibility. State and local governments also are structured into these three branches, and they operate in a manner similar to the federal system. We explore government and these branches in greater detail in Chapters 2 and 5. Here we briefly consider the sources of our laws.

LAWMAKING BY LEGISLATORS

Legislators, both state and federal, enact laws called statutes.* Local legislative bodies (e.g., for cities and counties) enact laws called **ordinances**. Collectively these statutes and ordinances are called the **written law**, as contrasted to **case law** (judicial decisions). Compilations of statutes by topic are called **codes**. For example, a state legislature may enact a statute lengthening the previous jail time for the crime of making an obscene telephone call. This statute will be compiled with, indexed to, and become a part of the state's "criminal" or "penal" code. There are numerous specialized codes in the states that group together statutes pertaining to particular subjects, such as the Vehicle Code, Health and Welfare Code, Corporations Code, and Business and Professions Code. These codes (often with slightly different titles) are generally available in any public law library, usually located in county courthouses.

The written law covers a staggering number of subjects, such as crimes, civil rights, housing, health, and indeed all matters that the legislative branch has the constitutional power to legislate upon. But it is important to understand that federal statutory law is limited to matters of federal **jurisdiction**.** State statutory law is limited to matters of statewide jurisdiction; a similar limitation is true for local ordinances.

Some difficult conflicts over jurisdiction have occurred. The language in which Article I, Section 8 of the U.S. Constitution enumerates the federal government's areas of jurisdiction is open to interpretation. Some believe that the courts have interpreted it too expansively, letting the federal government intrude on states' rights. Others argue that the federal reach should be extended even further, perhaps into such matters as shelter for the homeless. (We consider constitutional law in greater detail in Chapter 2.) When conflicts arise between federal and state jurisdictions, the U.S. Supreme Court makes the ultimate judicial decision through its interpretation and application of the Constitution.

Even when jurisdictions overlap—that is, when both the states and the federal government have jurisdiction—conflicts arise. The two may pass contradictory statutes. When that happens, the **doctrine of supremacy** applies, and the federal law prevails. For example, Amtrak, and all of its predecessor passenger trains, historically have dumped raw sewage on top of the railroad tracks and roadbeds. Permission for this practice dates back to early federal laws designed to encourage railroad construction. In 1989, Florida initiated a criminal nuisance charge against Amtrak, contending it dumped sewage on fishermen while they were sitting in a boat under a railroad trestle. In retaliation for the suit, Amtrak

*Often statutes are assigned titles, such as the Federal Racketeer Influence and Corrupt Organizations Act, called RICO.
**Jurisdiction refers to the subject matter for which Congress or state legislatures are empowered to enact laws. For example, Congress has jurisdiction to regulate the transportation of goods in interstate commerce; state legislatures do not. Court jurisdiction is explained fully in Chapter 3.

threatened to discontinue rail service to Florida. Faced with the doctrine of supremacy, the state yielded.*

Similar jurisdictional conflicts may exist between state and local governments. For example, local governments usually exercise exclusive jurisdiction over the zoning of real estate. Zoning laws restrict how land may be used. What if a state enacted a statute that authorized state officials to rezone real estate, regardless of local government rules? Does that differ from the common practice whereby state laws require suburban communities to accept construction of prisons and of treatment centers for drug addicts? Local ordinances may reflect NIMBY (not in my back yard) attitudes of neighborhoods, but just as state law bows to federal law, local law bows to state statutes.

Although proposed statutes are studied before their enactment, and although the end sought to be achieved is usually desirable and even necessary in the minds of proponents, the validity of a statute or ordinance still remains in doubt until it is challenged by some injured party and its validity is determined by an appropriate court. There is a presumption that a newly enacted statute or ordinance is constitutional, and few are held invalid by courts. Nonetheless, a person could be sentenced to jail for violation of a statute that later is determined to be unconstitutional and therefore void. At the end of this chapter, a sample U.S. Supreme Court decision is presented in which a state reapportionment statute was declared unconstitutional—after elections had occurred. The statute had created two new election districts to provide more congressional representation for African Americans living in North Carolina.

The question of the validity of a statute can be very complex. Is a statute or ordinance that prohibits sleeping overnight in a public place constitutional? What if its stated purpose is to maintain sanitary and safe public sidewalks and parks? But what if its true purpose is to drive homeless people out of the inner cities? Is the legal effect of the statute more or less important than its stated purpose? As you can readily see, the wise enactment of proper statutes by our legislators is no easy task.

Once the legislative branch enacts a law, uncertainty technically remains until the law is applied, then challenged in a trial, and finally judicially approved as constitutional. A statute or ordinance will not be ruled on by a court unless it is challenged by someone affected by its application, because courts do not render decisions based on hypothetical conflicts. There must be a case or controversy, properly presented to a court, before judicial action will be taken.

LAWMAKING BY THE EXECUTIVE BRANCH

The executive branch of government, at the federal, state, and local levels, collaborates with the legislative branch in the adoption of statutes. However, even if the president of the United States (or a state governor), as head of the executive branch, vetoes a proposed statute, the legislators have the power to override such action, usually with a two-thirds vote. This partnership in lawmaking is part of

---

*This incident prompted Congress to force Amtrak to modernize. Some Amtrak trains then converted human waste into a liquid that was sprayed onto the railroad tracks as a fine mist when the trains exceeded 35 miles per hour. Before the next century begins, Amtrak plans to have full waste-retention systems in place for all long-distance trains. Associated Press, Washington, 23 November 1991.

http://

You can find presidential executive orders in the Federal Register.
http://www.nara.gov/fedreg/

our system of checks and balances that encourages negotiation and compromise. The executive branch can also independently make certain laws. The president, state governors, and heads of local governments all have authority to issue certain directives that have the force and effect of law.*

Of much wider applicability and impact is the lawmaking power of thousands of federal, state, and local administrative agencies, which are specialized bodies created by Congress and by legislation at the state and local levels, to regulate specific activities. Administrative agencies investigate problems within their respective jurisdictions (an executive function); make laws called rules and regulations (a legislative function); and conduct hearings (similar to court trials) to determine if their rules have been violated and, if so, what penalties should be imposed (a judicial function). There are many important federal administrative agencies, numerous state agencies in each state, and a lesser number of agencies within each sizable local government.

You have probably read or heard about such prominent federal administrative agencies as the Central Intelligence Agency (CIA), Drug Enforcement Administration (DEA), Environmental Protection Agency (EPA), Farm Credit Administration (FCA), Food and Drug Administration (FDA), and the National Institute of Standards and Technology (NIST). Thousands of federal, state, and local administrative agencies continue to make and enforce innumerable laws each year on myriad subjects. You will learn more about lawmaking by administrative agencies in Chapter 5.

LAWMAKING BY COURTS

Federal and state judges preside over trials to settle controversies that are brought before them by parties to legal disputes. At the conclusion of each trial, the judge renders judgment in favor of one or the other of the litigants. Sometimes these judgments are based on a jury verdict. When there is no jury, the judgment is based on the trial court judge's evaluation of the evidence and his or her application of the law to the facts as found. Most of these judgments are never appealed. They resolve specific controversies and, to that extent, usually apply existing law. Occasionally, however, if the case is the first of its kind in that jurisdiction, the trial judge may formulate and apply a new rule of common law. Such a rule may then be reviewed by an appellate court. The appellate court's decision then would be followed by all other trial courts in that jurisdiction.

Usually when judgments are appealed to appellate courts, the essential question on appeal is whether or not the trial court judge made a prejudicial error. Error exists when a trial court judge misapplies the law in the conduct of the trial. For example, a trial judge may have erred by permitting the jury to consider irrelevant evidence. Not all errors of trial courts taint the outcome of the trial: only those that reasonably could have affected the outcome of the trial are prejudicial. Much irrelevant testimony is not prejudicial because it could not reasonably have affected the jury's verdict.

When error is claimed and an appeal is taken, the appellate court may affirm the lower court's decision, reverse it, send it back for a new trial (remand), or

---

*For example, in 1986 then-President Ronald Reagan ordered the random drug testing of certain employees working in interstate transportation. The issue of drug testing in other workplaces, and even in competitive sporting events, is an important ongoing issue today.

simply modify the trial court judgment in some manner. Whichever result is appropriate, the appellate court writes and usually publishes* a written opinion that typically (1) describes the nature of the controversy, (2) states what result was reached in the lower court, (3) reveals the basis upon which the appellant is appealing, and (4) declares and elaborates on its own decision, or "holding." In its decision, the court states the applicable rules of law as well as the rationale underlying its decision.

In making rulings, appellate courts interpret and apply relevant statutory law together with appropriate rules of common law derived from prior cases under the doctrine of *stare decisis*. If there is no controlling statute or principle of common law, which occasionally happens, the appellate court will create a new rule or extend an existing principle and apply it to the case. That new concept becomes a part of the continuous evolving common law to be followed by other courts in future cases. Thus, new law is created. For example, suppose that a state legislature enacted a law requiring a license and demonstrated ability for private persons to own and to use handguns, and when challenged, this law was declared by the U.S. Supreme Court to be constitutional. Thus, unlicensed persons could be punished by the state for owning or using a handgun. Is there any doubt this would be an important addition to our common law?

Judges who purposefully expand on the law in their decisions are often referred to as **judicial activists**. Judges who narrowly interpret the law by relying heavily on the doctrine of *stare decisis* are often referred to as **strict constructionists**. Either way, the interpretations of law set forth by judges constitute "judge-made" law, or common law. Sometimes court-made law is called **decisional law** or **case law**, since it is found in decisions of courts. Courts are reactive institutions; judges must wait for litigation to reach them before they can render a decision. Legislative bodies, on the other hand, can initiate new laws on any subject at any time they choose. Nonetheless, the judicial system has been responsible for many of the great social changes that have occurred in the United States.

Not all the language used by appellate courts in their written opinions becomes part of the common law. Much of it is explanatory, analyzing the facts of the case and elaborating on various legal principles that may or may not directly apply. Legal issues addressed in the opinion that are not logically necessary to support the ruling in the case are called *dicta* (Latin: for "remarks"). Being unnecessary language, *dicta* do not become part of the common law, although they may provide clues about how that judge's philosophy might be applied in future cases.

Sometimes it is quite clear which statutory language or principle of common law is applicable to a case. But the issue of how it should be applied to the specific facts may be quite complex. For example, in a murder trial there may be no disagreement about the applicability of a statute declaring that an unlawful killing with malice aforethought is murder. But the question of whether or not the particular defendant, who was severely impaired by illegal drugs at the time of the crime, can be legally capable of harboring "malice" (a state of mind prompting one to willfully kill the victim) may be open to argument. Following the trial (in which the trial court judge will have ruled one way or the other on

---

*Often an appellate court rules that its decision in a particular case on appeal is not of significance generally, and orders that it remain "unpublished." Such appellate court opinions are not valid precedents and are not printed in the books, called reporters, that contain published appellate court decisions.

the applicability of the issue), opposing appellate attorneys persuasively argue in favor of their contradictory positions when presenting their appeals to the court in written briefs and with oral arguments. Ultimately the legal controversy will be decided by an appellate court and a precedent may be set.

Through this decisional process, both federal and state appellate judges are making new law on a daily basis. With judges throughout the country "making law," can we expect decisions to be consistent?

> *. . . critical legal scholars—or simply 'crits'— . . . contend that decisions conflict with one another because they are based on different, and controversial, moral and political ideals. Lawyers cannot give a simple answer to a question, the crits say, because the legal system, like our society at large, cannot reconcile the contradictory instincts people feel when they confront social problems.*[24]

Does this mean the rule of law is flexible, depending on who is declaring it? If so, does that give added significance to the political appointment process underlying the selection of judges?

To assist you in understanding the way our appellate courts make and apply the law, excerpts from various important appellate cases are presented at the end of every chapter.

LAWMAKING BY THE PEOPLE

Many states have provisions in their constitutions that authorize citizens to place proposed new laws on ballots for direct vote by the people. These **initiatives** have resulted in laws approved by voters who had been disappointed by the inaction of their legislatures. To qualify proposed new initiatives for the ballot, proponents must obtain the signature of a specified number of qualified voters. One of the most widely publicized initiatives in recent times occurred in California. Proposition 209 dismantled affirmative action programs in public employment, education, and contracting. Like statutes, initiatives must pass the test of constitutionality as determined by courts. In 1996, California voters approved an initiative to legalize the possession and use of marijuana for medicinal purposes. A federal court promptly invalidated the law based upon the supremacy clause of the U.S. Constitution—federal laws that criminalize the use of marijuana control. You will learn more about the initiative process in Chapter 2.

TYPES AND CLASSIFICATIONS OF LAW

We have briefly considered the medieval sources of our contemporary law. We have also identified people and institutions that continually make and update our laws to help manage our highly complex modern society. We now turn to some definitions and classifications of U.S. law that will enhance your appreciation of its pervasiveness.

FEDERAL AND STATE LAW

We have already distinguished between common law and statutory law. Federal law consists of the U.S. Constitution, statutes enacted by Congress, treaties and Presidential orders, rules promulgated by federal agencies, and decisions of federal appellate courts. State law consists of state constitutions, statutes enacted by state legislatures, rules promulgated by state agencies, and the decisions of state courts.

> Every time you view a website, its contents already have been copied and stored in the random access memory (RAM) of your computer. Is this copying an infringement of the author's copyright protection?[25]

Copyright protection is granted to the authors of literary works by federal statutory law as it has been interpreted by federal courts. Thus, the question must be answered by reference to the federal law.

> Richard, a firefighter, demands financial compensation from a fertility clinic for impregnating his former wife by using frozen embryos that previously had been fertilized with his sperm. Can Richard recover damages for child support and emotional distress?[26]

Liability for wrongful birth, or negligence in handling fertilized embryos, is a subject governed by state statutory and case law. This question must be answered by reference to state law.

CIVIL AND CRIMINAL LAW

Civil law is the body of law, both federal and state, that pertains to civil or private rights enforced by civil actions. For example, the laws governing contracts are civil laws. Breach of a contract may result in a civil action for money damages to reimburse the person wronged for any financial loss suffered. **Criminal law**, as contrasted to civil law, is the body of statutory law, both federal and state, that declares what conduct is criminal and prescribes penalties for its commission. For example, a statute may define murder as an unlawful killing with malice aforethought. The precise definition of "malice aforethought" changes through interpretation by courts over the years, and thus courts have the continuing task of defining what conduct is criminal.

> David Cash, Jr., entered a rest room in a gambling casino in Las Vegas a few minutes after his friend Jeremy Strohmeyer. Cash looked over a stall and saw Strohmeyer with his hand over a small girl's mouth. After telling Strohmeyer to let her go, Cash left and did not report the incident. Strohmeyer later pled guilty to rape and murder of the child and was sentenced to life in prison. Was Cash guilty of any civil or criminal offense?[27]

Unlike some states, Nevada does not have a statute that criminalizes the failure to report a crime in progress. Thus, Cash was not guilty of any state crime. Crimes between private persons generally do not raise questions of federal law, and Cash is not guilty of any federal crime in this case. Under the common law there generally is no duty to protect strangers, and thus Cash probably is not liable for damages to the victim's parents for his conduct under the civil law of Nevada. Immoral acts are not always criminalized by the law.*

Many times the same act by a person can result in both criminal and civil penalties.

Orenthal Simpson was acquitted by jury of the crime of murdering both his former wife Nicole and Ron Goldman, a rescuer acting as a good samaritan. Thereafter, Simpson was sued in a civil court for the wrongful death of the victims. In the civil proceeding, the jury found Simpson responsible for the killings and liable for monetary damages. Do all criminal acts also result in civil liability for monetary damages?

No. For example, the crime of firing a handgun into the air within city limits may not injure any human, and there would be no victim to pursue a civil case. But most crimes do create victims who then are able to pursue civil remedies, as in the Simpson case.

The statutory law of individual states concerning crimes is collected in books often called Penal Codes. Civil laws, in general, are collected in books often called Civil Codes. You will learn about the very important differences between civil and criminal laws and trials in several future chapters.

PRIVATE AND PUBLIC LAW

Private law is the body of law regulating the rights and duties that exist between private persons ("persons" being a term that includes corporations). Contract law is an example of private law. **Public law**, on the other hand, includes constitutional, administrative, criminal, and international law, all of which are more directly concerned with public rights and obligations. Criminal law is of public concern because the next victim may be you or any other member of society. Administrative law, as will be seen in Chapter 5, protects consumers and the public from abuses by private businesses. It also protects the environment.

Many contend that jet skis are too noisy, leak oil and gas directly into the water, pose safety risks to bystanders, and damage natural resources. Some contend that all craft using outboard motors on America's waterways are equally offensive. Can the National Park Service (a federal administrative agency) adopt a rule with the force of law that bans the use of jet skis?[28]

Yes. Jet skis are banned at certain lakes and waterways that have been determined by the Park Service to be inappropriate for such use. Administrative agencies, such as the Park Service, continually assess the need for new regulations and create appropriate rules as required. These rules are examples of the public law of the land.

---

*Many members of the public were outraged at what they believed to be a serious moral offense by Cash. Protesters marched at UC–Berkeley where Cash is studying nuclear engineering and demanded his expulsion from the public university.

INTERNATIONAL AND DOMESTIC LAW

Law that concerns relations among sovereign nations is called **international law**. Reliance upon some form of international law dates to the Roman Empire or before and is typically based on custom. The precedents relied upon in international law are the acts of independent governments in their relations with one another, including treaties. When treaties or conventions exist (agreements between nations such as the Geneva Convention concerning human rights), they contain a procedural machinery to enforce their terms.

A United States EA-6B Marine jet, practicing low-level flying, hit and severed a ski gondola cable in the Italian Alps. Twenty people were killed. The U.S. claimed exclusive jurisdiction of the case under the North Atlantic Treaty Organization (NATO), an international mutual defense pact. Italy, spurred by the victims' families, claimed the jet had violated NATO's mandated flight patterns and it therefore did not apply. Trial and punishment therefore should take place in Italy. However, an Italian judge threw the Italian manslaughter case out of court, ruling that there was no domestic jurisdiction because of NATO. Thus the Marine pilot, Captain Richard J. Ashby, was returned to the U.S. for military trial (called court-martial) where he was acquitted of all charges by a jury of eight Marine officers on March 4, 1999.

Certain rules and principles are acknowledged in international relations. These understood rules pertain to such matters as territorial boundaries, use of the high seas, limitations on war, telecommunications, diplomatic and consular exchange, and the use of air space. The difficulty is that sovereign nations, by definition, exercise exclusive power or government within their boundaries and may or may not comply with these understood rules.

The United Nations (UN) is the primary mechanism that creates international law. It brings diplomacy, negotiation, and even propaganda to bear on world affairs. Through agreements, even military observers and peace keepers can be organized. In 1995 the UN established an International War Crimes Tribunal to prosecute persons accused of war crimes in the Bosnian war. All members of the UN comply with arrest warrants issued by the Tribunal. Many accused persons have been arrested; others are in hiding. Thus, criminal law also can be and is a matter of international law.

Our legal system may be expected to face global problems differently than in the past, when the disputes of nations were resolved through negotiations, the United Nations, or war. During World War Two, Japanese Americans were interred because of unfounded fears of espionage and loyalty, presenting domestic constitutional issues. Entering the twenty-first century, we are faced with the reality that the nature of war has changed. New electronically guided long-range missiles, so-called "Star Wars" weapons, are becoming increasingly threatening. Nuclear proliferation remains a serious challenge to international security. Moreover, weaponry now available in world markets can easily deliver genetically engineered toxins, diseases, and poisons over a wide area, resulting in the possible relaxation of domestic constitutional law, sacrificing the rights of individuals in the interest of general safety. Wars may be less likely to involve countries than to involve unidentified groups of people who, through acts of terrorism, fight for the political, financial, and religious issues they support. Thus, public security measures may involve restrictions on individual liberty by construction of fences or walls with temporary or permanent exclusion of citizens from public places. Electronic eavesdropping, by court authorization, already is being dramatically increased because it is an effective weapon against terrorists and criminals. Airport security already has modernized—and passengers are subject to warrantless searches. Many searches are based on stereotypes of personal appearances and behavior. Freedom of speech notwithstanding, jokingly mentioning a bomb while on or near an airplane is a criminal offense. Thus, international dangers affect both international and domestic law.

PROCEDURAL AND SUBSTANTIVE LAW

Procedural law consists of all the rules, or mechanisms, for processing civil and criminal cases through the federal and state judicial systems. Some cynics call it "lawyers' law" since its complexities and technicalities provide employment for attorneys.

Procedural law, in its pre-trial aspects, may dictate the dates and time limits within which papers must be filed, the size of paper to be used by attorneys, the size of print to be used, the fees that must be paid for the various documents upon filing them with the court, what information must be contained in legal papers, how witnesses and parties can be orally examined before trial, when and where the trial shall be held, what witnesses may be called, what issues may be presented to the trial court, and so on.

In its trial aspects, procedural law dictates how the jury may be selected, where the parties may sit in the courtroom and even if they may stand, what evidence may be offered to the jury, what questions may be asked of witnesses, and so on.

It is noteworthy that a separate body of procedural law governs the mechanics of processing appeals, and procedural law for civil cases differs from that for criminal cases. In short, the procedural law is as complex as it is vast, and cases that might have been won on their merits have been lost because of faulty lawyering with the applicable procedural law. A frequent type of attorney malpractice (professional negligence) involves procedural law mistakes, such as missing a critical deadline. If an attorney fails to comply with the civil procedural law, the court may, as a penalty, dismiss the case, with the result that the attorney's client loses. If a prosecutor fails to comply with the criminal procedural law, the court may dismiss the case and set the defendant free. Some of you may already have experienced this happy event when you went to court to challenge a citation for a traffic infraction. Because the citing officer was too busy with other duties and did not appear to testify, your case was dismissed.

Procedural law is so important that it receives basic constitutional protection in the Sixth Amendment to the U.S. Constitution (made applicable to the states by the Fourteenth Amendment, as explained in Chapter 2). The Sixth Amendment, as interpreted by the U.S. Supreme Court, requires that the government provide each citizen with procedural due process in criminal proceedings, including the right to have the advice of an attorney even if the accused is indigent, the right to confront accusers in a speedy and public trial by an impartial jury, and the right to be heard and to present a defense.

In 1985, Charles Ng was charged with torturing and murdering a dozen people in a California cabin where the victims had been kept as sex slaves. Ng fled to Canada, where he was arrested. But Canada refused to return Ng to California because California has a death penalty. After six years, the Canadian Supreme Court ruled that Ng must be extradited to the U.S. to stand trial. Meanwhile, the police had inadvertently destroyed some bullets and blood samples needed in the case. One key witness had died. Ng continues to use the procedural laws to challenge every attorney appointed for him and every judge assigned to preside over the trial. The files in the case are reported to weigh about six tons—which hopefully is an exaggeration. On Wednesday February 24, 1999 he was found guilty of 11 murders and sentenced to death marking commencement of the appeals process. By the time appeals are exhausted, the new millennium will be well underway. Has Mr. Ng been deprived of his right to a speedy trial?[29]

No. Charles Ng has waived his right to a speedy trial, believing, no doubt, that the passage of time is in his best interest. The public has no constitutional right to a speedy trial of criminal defendants. This case symbolizes a low point in the history of the procedural law.

Clearly the challenge of providing the mechanics for the processing of myriad cases of widely different nature has resulted in a complex body of procedural law. State and federal procedural laws are created by statute and by the courts themselves in publications called rules of court.

The **substantive law**, as contrasted to the procedural law, defines duties, establishes rights, and prohibits wrongs. Murder is prohibited by the substantive law; a license is required before entering the real estate sales business; there are speed limits and registration requirements for automobiles—all are duties imposed by substantive law. Earlier it was observed that Nevada did not have a law that criminalizes inaction, and therefore David Cash, Jr., was not guilty of a crime for failing to render assistance to the young girl murdered by Jeremy Strohmeyer. Such conduct is a crime in some states under their criminal substantive laws. The issue of which state's law should apply to Cash, and the time limits within which he must be prosecuted, are questions of the procedural law.

SUBJECT MATTER CLASSIFICATION

Law also is often classified on the basis of subject matter. Consider these representative distinct categories of law: corporation, admiralty, business, real estate, family, environmental, constitutional, labor, probate, corporate securities, and immigration. There are dozens of other legal specialties, and the list keeps growing. For example, a recent addition is elder law, pertaining to unique rights and duties of senior citizens.

Sam, 75 years of age and a resident of Sun City, Arizona, uses his golf cart for trips to the store and recreation center. Most residents of this retirement community also rely upon golf carts for transportation. But cars also use the roads and accidents happen. Should Sam be required by law to equip his golf cart with seat belts, turn signals, a windshield, and mirrors?[30]

By federal law, Sam is required to equip his golf cart as indicated. The National Highway Traffic Safety Administration (an administrative agency) has adopted rules to that effect, which some compare to similar state laws requiring motorcycle riders to wear helmets. Is it sufficient that a proposed law will, in all likelihood, protect family members from some perceived harm? Or should the potential good of a proposed law be balanced against its potential intrusiveness? But good, bad, or indifferent, golf carts are motor vehicles and, when on public streets, are subject to regulation like other vehicles.

Lawyers often refer to themselves in terms such as "trial lawyer," "corporate lawyer," "labor lawyer," or "lobbyist."* As noted in Chapter 4, when you need an attorney, you may need a specialist. Most specialists in the law have their own professional organizations, such as Trial Lawyers Associations and the National Academy of Elder Law Attorneys. A licensed attorney may practice in any field of law, but in many states the official state bar permits only those lawyers who have met certain standards of education and experience to become certified and to advertise themselves as certified specialists in the following fields: criminal law; family law; immigration and nationality law; taxation law; workers' compensation law; and probate, estate planning, and trust law. Other attorneys may practice law in those areas, but they cannot hold themselves out as certified specialists.

A SAMPLE U.S. SUPREME COURT DECISION

The following case illustrates some of the preceding introductory observations about our legal system. We selected the case because it is a split decision of the U.S. Supreme Court that illustrates the doctrine of precedents, judicial review of political enactments, protection of civil rights in a republic (with indirect representation), how courts make law, the distinction between public and private law, and an issue that is certain to be magnified in impact as the new millennium begins with a new census. The precise legal issue, racial gerrymandering,** is very complex. In this case, a new direction in the law is announced by the court in a very close split decision. The U.S. Supreme Court makes its decisions by majority vote, i.e., five or more Justices must agree. Any Justice who disagrees with the majority vote may, and often does, file (cause to be published) a dissenting opinion containing the basis for his or her disagreement. Four Justices dissented in the following case, *Shaw v. Reno.* Sometimes Justices who vote with the majority in a case nonetheless choose to express a different legal basis than the majority. Separate concurring opinions are filed in such instances.

---

*Not all lobbyists are lawyers but since legislators are constantly concerned with the passage of new laws and the amendment or repeal of old laws, lawyers are especially qualified for this endeavor. Oddly enough, if they are hired and paid as legal counsel, they generally need not register as professional lobbyists and are not subject to the rules that require lobbyists to disclose sources and amounts of income received.

**Gerrymandering is the intentional drawing of political districts by a political party (such as the Democratic party) that is in power so as to give itself a majority of voters in as many districts as possible while concentrating the voting strength of the other party (such as registered Republicans) into as few districts as possible. Using this technique, an incumbent party may control a legislature, although it generates only the same number of (or even fewer) votes as the other party in any election. The term "racial gerrymandering" describes the drawing of political district lines on the basis of race instead of on the basis of political party registrations. In an "at-large" election there are no districts and no possible gerrymandering. The candidates receiving the majority or plurality of votes win. The minority theoretically may have no representation. With "district" elections (such as for Congress and state legislatures), voters in the minority can be represented if they are a majority in any district. Racial gerrymandering sweeps a sufficient number of minority residents into the confines of a newly drawn district to create a new majority there.

The stark alternatives facing the Court in the *Shaw v. Reno* case have been simplified as follows: "Either states adopt bizarrely shaped districts to help minority members get elected, or states go back to the days when a state like North Carolina had a population that was 24 percent black and had no blacks in Congress."[31] Our courts exhibit no fear of facing the "tough" questions in our extremely diverse society. While adhering to the principle of *stare decisis*, our courts can and do maintain the dynamism of our laws, a conclusion supported by the case of *Shaw v. Reno*.

The following opinion, in *Shaw v. Reno*, has been edited for brevity. Frequently, in applying the doctrine of *stare decisis*, the Court, in its opinion, refers to earlier cases that support a relevant rule of law. Cases cited as precedent are identified by their citations, which are references to their names, volume, and page numbers where they may be found, and often by the year of their decision. For example, the case of *Shaw v. Reno*, which follows, may be found in volume 509 of the U.S. Reporter (which is a series of volumes containing only Supreme Court decisions) at page 630. It also may be found in volume 113 of the Supreme Court Reporter (a second set of volumes also containing all Supreme Court decisions) at page 2816. *Shaw v. Reno* was decided in 1993.

CONCLUSION

At the beginning of this chapter we welcomed you to the study of law for your general education. You now have been presented with an historical overview of the law and its relationship to our society during the twentieth century. You have seen the medieval sources of the common law contrasted with modern sources and how laws are classified and defined. Throughout the remainder of this text we suggest issues that are anticipated in the early years of the twenty-first century. Your understanding of the law and our legal system already is well underway.

CASE

SHAW V. RENO
509 US 630, 113 S.Ct. 2816 (1993)

Facts: Following the 1990 census, the North Carolina legislature enacted a reapportionment plan for the state's seats in the U.S. House of Representatives. A final version of the plan added two new congressional districts with irregularly drawn boundaries made for the purpose of surrounding an African-American majority of voters in each. The first district has been compared to a "Rorschach ink-blot test" and a "bug splattered on a windshield."[32] The second new African-American majority district is 160 miles long and, for much of its length, no wider than the Interstate 85 corridor. It winds in snakelike fashion through tobacco country, financial centers, and

manufacturing areas gobbling in enough enclaves to make an African-American majority. One state legislator has remarked that "if you drove down the interstate with both car doors open, you'd kill most of the people in the district."[33] Some voters brought suit contending the redistricting plan constituted an unconstitutional racial gerrymander because voters have a right under the equal-protection clause of the U.S. Constitution to participate in a color-blind electoral process.

Justice Sandra O'Connor delivered the opinion of the Court: Classifications of citizens solely on the basis of race "are by their very nature odious to a free people whose institutions are funded upon the doctrine of equality." (citations)* They threaten to stigmatize individuals by reason of their membership in a racial group and to incite racial hostility. (citations) Accordingly we have held that the Fourteenth Amendment requires state legislation that expressly distinguishes among citizens because of their race to be narrowly tailored to further a compelling governmental interest.

[W]e believe that reapportionment is one area in which appearances do matter. A reapportionment plan that includes in one district individuals who belong to the same race, but who are otherwise widely separated by geographical and political boundaries, and who may have little in common with one another but the color of their skin, bears an uncomfortable resemblance to political apartheid. It reinforces the perception that members of the same racial group—regardless of their age, education, economic status, or the community in which they live—think alike, share the same political interests, and will prefer the same candidates at the polls. We have rejected such perceptions elsewhere as impermissible racial stereotypes. . . . The message that such districting sends to elected representatives is equally pernicious. When a district obviously is created solely to effectuate the perceived

common interests of one racial group, elected officials are more likely to believe that their primary obligation is to represent only the members of that group, rather than their constituency as a whole. This is altogether antithetical to our system of representative democracy. . . . For these reasons, we conclude that a plaintiff challenging a reapportionment statute under the Equal Protection Clause may state a claim by alleging that the legislation, though race-neutral on its face, rationally cannot be understood as anything other than an effort to separate voters into different districts on the basis of race, and that the separation lacks sufficient justification.

Racial classifications of any sort pose the risk of lasting harm to our society. They reinforce the belief, held by too many for too much of our history, that individuals should be judged by the color of their skin. Racial classifications with respect to voting carry particular dangers. Racial gerrymandering, even for remedial purposes, may balkanize us into competing racial factions; it threatens to carry us further from the goal of a political system in which race no longer matters—a goal that the Fourteenth and Fifteenth Amendments embody, and to which the Nation continues to aspire. It is for these reasons that race-based districting by our state legislatures demands close judicial scrutiny. . . . .

Today we hold only that appellants have stated a claim under the Equal Protection Clause by alleging that the North Carolina General Assembly adopted a reapportionment scheme so irrational on its face that it can be understood only as an effort to segregate voters into separate voting districts because of their race, and that the separation lacks sufficient justification.

Justice White, with whom Justice Blackmun and Justice Stevens join, dissenting: . . . The State has made no mystery of its intent, which was to . . . (improve) the minority group's

---

*Following this quotation, the court referred to previous cases by their "citations," which means that the point is controlled by those cases upon the doctrine of *stare decisis*, a term explained earlier. Throughout this sample opinion, we will simply recite the term "citations" instead of repeating all of the citations recited in the opinion, to indicate the action by the Court.

prospects of electing a candidate of its choice. I doubt that this constitutes a discriminatory purpose as defined in the Court's equal protection cases—i.e., an intent to aggravate "the unequal distribution of electoral power." (citations) But even assuming that it does, there is no question that appellants have not alleged the requisite discriminatory effects. Whites constitute roughly 76 percent of the total population and 79 percent of the voting age population in North Carolina. Yet, under the State's plan, they still constitute a voting majority in 10 (or 83 percent) of the 12 congressional districts. Though they might be dissatisfied at the prospect of casting a vote for a losing candidate—a lot shared by many, including a disproportionate number of minority voters—surely they cannot complain of discriminatory treatment.

Justice Blackmun, dissenting: I join Justice White's dissenting opinion. . . . I . . . agree that the conscious use of race in redistricting does not violate the Equal Protection Clause unless the effect of the redistricting plan is to deny a particular group equal access to the political process or to minimize its voting strength.

Justice Stevens, dissenting: . . . The duty to govern impartially is abused when a group with power over the electoral process defines electoral boundaries solely to enhance its own political strength at the expense of any weaker group. That duty, however, is not violated when the majority acts to facilitate the election of a member of a group that lacks such power because it remains underrepresented in the state legislature—whether that group is defined by political affiliations, by common economic interests, or by religious, ethnic, or racial characteristics. . . . .

Justice Souter, dissenting: . . . In districting . . . the mere placement of an individual in one district instead of another denies no one a right or benefit provided to others. All citizens may register, vote, and be represented. In whatever district, the individual voter has a right to vote in each election, and the election will result in the voter's representation. As we

have held, no one's constitutional rights are violated merely because the candidate one supports loses the election or because a group (including a racial group) to which one belongs winds up with a representative from outside that group. . . . I would not respond to the seeming egregiousness of the redistricting now before us by untethering the concept of racial gerrymander in such a case from the concept of harm exemplified by dilution.

After *Shaw v. Reno*

Because of its population increase in the 1990 census, Georgia became entitled to an additional congressional seat. At that time, one district in Georgia was populated by an African American majority of voters. In 1991, the Georgia legislature adopted a "max-black" plan that had been drafted by the American Civil Liberties Union (ACLU) for the Congressional Black Caucus. This plan, approved by the U.S. Justice Department, created three majority black districts for Georgia in the 1992 elections; each elected black candidates.

After the case of *Shaw v. Reno* became law, some white voters sued alleging illegal racial gerrymandering, citing the stated policy of Georgia to maximize majority black districts. Ordered by a federal court to redraw districts, the Georgia legislature deadlocked and was unable to draw any reapportionment plan. In response to this failure, the U.S. District Court drafted its own plan containing one majority black district. This plan was used during the 1996 elections.

On appeal by several voters, the U.S. District Court plan was affirmed in another split decision by the U.S. Supreme Court in *Abrams v. Johnson*, ___U.S. ____, 117 S.Ct. 1925 (1997). Justice Kennedy wrote the majority opinion and was joined by Justices Rehnquist, O'Connor, Scalia, and Thomas.

Justices Breyer, Stevens, Souter, and Ginsburg dissented and, in their opinion, quoted from a precedent as follows:

> *. . . Just as a federal district court . . . should follow the policies and preferences of the state . . . in the reapportionment*

plans proposed by the state legislatures, whenever adherence to state policy does not detract from the requirements of the federal Constitution, a district court should similarly honor state policies in the context of congressional reapportionment.

. . . No one denies that, if one looks at the Georgia Legislature, one will find in them expressions of state "policies and preferences" for two majority-minority districts.

. . . The majority is legally wrong because this Court has said that a court should determine a State's redistricting preferences by looking to the "plans proposed by the state legislatures."

FOR CRITICAL ANALYSIS

A new census will occur in the year 2000 with some states gaining and other states losing congressional seats. Have the preceding U.S. Supreme Court cases resolved the problem of reapportionment by establishing sufficiently adequate guidelines for the states? Or do we enter the new millennium with the prospects of endless tinkering with reapportionment as special interest groups maneuver for gains in a population that rapidly is emerging without any racial majority?

CHAPTER QUESTIONS AND PROBLEMS

1. One view of equal protection is that the conscious use of race in drawing voting districts is permissible unless the plan is to minimize the voting strength of a minority group. The opposing view is that the conscious use of race in redistricting is unconstitutional regardless of the underlying motive. Which view, the first or the second, is a simplified version of the majority opinion in *Shaw v. Reno*?

2. Which of the following states would be most likely to favor taking the 2000 census by statistical sampling methods rather than by the traditional head count?
   a. Maine
   b. Illinois
   c. Florida
   d. Texas
   e. California

3. Assume there is a hypothetical fifty-first state called Columbia, which enacts the following statutes in its 2000 session:
   - Sec. 1. Makes it illegal for anyone under age 23 to possess a can of aerosol spray paint unless licensed by the state.

   - Sec. 2. Establishes an application form and sets a filing fee to obtain a spray-paint-possessor's license.
   - Sec. 3. Defines the tort of spray-paint trespass, and indicates the circumstances under which victims can sue and recover damages from spray-painting violators.
   - Sec. 4. Provides that owners whose properties are wrongfully spray-painted can sue in small claims court for damages not to exceed $25,000.
   - Sec. 5. Makes it a misdemeanor to sell or give a spray-paint can to any unlicensed person under age 23.

   With regard to each statute, determine whether it is a civil or criminal law, whether it is an example of public or private law, and whether it is procedural or substantive.

4. Which of the following crimes would not be characterized as a violation of the U.S. Constitution?
   a. The wrongful beating of prisoners by guards at a state prison.
   b. The robbery of a federally chartered bank.

c. The search of a student's car at a public university by a university parking ticket officer who was looking for contraband.

5. Attorneys do not have a monopoly upon the legal issues within our society because everyone, individual or corporation, has the constitutional right to represent themselves without an attorney. Is this an accurate generalization?

6. Identify which of the following acts are crimes and which are torts.
   a. Dirk, brandishing a gun, robs a convenience store.
   b. Dirk captures and rapes Monica in the parking lot of a mall.
   c. Dirk shoplifts clothes from his employer's store.
   d. Dirk seduces Monica, age 17.
   e. Dirk carelessly drives his car into a school bus, killing one child.
   f. Dirk crudely asks Monica to engage in a sex act with him.

7. Which of the following issues would most likely be decided by both state and federal appellate courts?
   a. Proper selection of jurors.
   b. Whether or not a witness lied during trial.
   c. Whether or not the jury came to the correct decision.
   d. Whether or not certain evidence should have been produced by attorneys during trial.
   e. Whether or not the trial court judge made erroneous rulings on objections to evidence.

8. There are nine U.S. Supreme Court Justices today, just as there were in 1900 when our population was 76 million. Today the U.S. population is 270 million.

Does this mean there should be:
a. more Justices to share the workload, or
b. that a new specialized court should be created to handle specified kinds of cases (say criminal appeals, only), or
c. that our Justices should be paid more, or
d. can you think of any other possible remedy?

9. Many principles that have evolved through interpretation by our Supreme Court are not expressed in the Constitution. Which of the following are examples of these unexpressed principles?
   a. The right of privacy upon which a woman's right to choose to have an abortion is predicated.
   b. The right to be free of unreasonable searches and seizures by government officials.
   c. The right not to be subjected to cruel and unusual punishment.
   d. The right to have an attorney in serious criminal cases.

10. Why are the thousands of often complex state and federal appellate decisions totaling tens of thousands of pages annually printed in expensive, hardcover books to collect dust in libraries? Why are they made fully available on the Internet? Who reads these long and, frankly, often boring recitals of the law, precedents, and legal theory? Surely all of these volumes cannot contain only significant and important cases. Why do we need volumes on the law in the 1800s, or in the 1920s? As an educated person, how would you answer these questions, if asked?

NOTES

1. *Black's Law Dictionary*, 6th ed. (West, St. Paul, MN, 1990).
2. The Hypersoar was designed by aerospace engineer Preston Carter of the Livermore National Laboratory, who announced that his design requires further analysis by the U.S. Air Force and university aeronautical engineers. David Perlman, *San Francisco Chronicle*, 11 September 1998.

3. Quotation from Gerald Celente, Director of the Trends Research Institute in Rhinebeck, New York. Dale Russakoff, *Washington Post*, 4 October 1998.

4. Quotation from Michael Kitei of Small Talk, a consulting firm that specializes in influencing children's spending. Dale Russakoff, *Washington Post*, 4 October 1998.

5. Although the life expectancy of a person born in the year 2000 is expected to be nearly 80 years, much medical opinion suggests that there is no inherent reason why life expectancy should not reach 100 years in the early part of the twenty-first century.

6. *Petit v. Minnesota*, 177 S.Ct. 164 (1899).

7. Alice Kessler-Harris, *Women Have Always Worked: A Historical Perspective* (New York: Feminist Press, 1981).

8. Much of the trivia about the turn of the twentieth century is from Traxel, *1898, The Birth of the American Century* (New York: Alfred A. Knopf, 1998).

9. Ashley H. Grant, Associated Press, 12 May 1998.

10. Associated Press, 25 August 1998.

11. Associated Press, Washington, 4 March 1998.

12. *Plessy v. Ferguson*, 163 U.S. 537 (1896).

13. *Brown v. Board of Education*, 347 U.S. 483 (1954).

14. *Powell v. Alabama*, 287 U.S. 45 (1932).

15. Max Boot, *Out of Order: Arrogance, Corruption, and Incompetence on the Bench* (New York: Basic Books, 1998).

16. Boston University has established a new Center for the Millennial Studies, a symbol of academic obsession with the year 2000. Yale University has sponsored a lecture series on millennial topics. The College of Notre Dame of Maryland has added courses on the millennium over the past year. The Andrew Mellon Foundation has begun funding millennial research, and The American Historical Review is requesting articles on millennialism. Boston Universities Center offers a full schedule of academic conferences through 2004 and publishes a newsletter, the *Millennial Stew*. According to the director of Boston Universities Center, "There's something about a round number, and the idea that we're at the dawn of a new age that is basic to human psychology and motivation." Joe Matthews, *Baltimore Sun*, 19 June 1998.

17. *Roe v. Wade*, 410 U.S. 113, 93 S.Ct. 705 (1973).

18. Paul Queary, Associated Press, 28 February 1997.

19. Don Lattin, *San Francisco Chronicle*, 23 May 1998.

20. Under the constitutional principle of Full Faith and Credit, (Art. 4, sec. 1), any one state conceivably would have to recognize as legal a same-sex marriage contracted in another state where such union was legal. To void this result, Congress enacted the Defense of Marriage Act of 1996, which defines marriage as a status involving members of the opposite sex. For analysis of same-sex marriage and equal protection, see the opinion of the Supreme Court of Hawaii in *Baehr v. Lewin*, 852 P.2d 44 (1993).

21. *Washington v. Glucksberg*, 117 S.Ct. 2258 (1997).

22. Theodore F.T. Plucknett, *A Concise History of the Common Law*, 5th ed. (Boston: Little, Brown, 1956), quoting Sir Thomas Erskine May, *Constitutional History*.

23. "Justice Kline Defends His Dissent," *California Lawyer*, September 1998, 25.

24. J. Frug, "Why Courts Are Always Making Law," *Fortune Magazine*, 25 September 1989, 245.

25. A hypothetical situation based on the U.S. Copyright Law of 1976.

26. Based on an event reported by Brian Macquarrie, *Boston Globe*, 18 September 1998.

27. Associated Press, Las Vegas, 9 September 1998.

28. *San Francisco Chronicle* Wire Reports, 17 September 1998.

29. Associated Press, Santa Ana, 15 September 1998.

30. Based on an article by Tim Malloy, Associated Press, 15 March 1998.

31. *San Francisco Chronicle*, 4 April 1994.

32. *Shaw v. Barr*, 808 F.Supp. 461, 476 (E.D. N.C. 1992) and *The Wall Street Journal*, 4 February 1992, A14.

33. *Shaw v. Barr*, supra, at 476–477 and *Washington Post*, 20 April 1993, A4.

2

OUR CONSTITUTION

The layman's Constitutional view is that what he likes is Constitutional and that which he doesn't like is unconstitutional. That about measures up the Constitutional acumen of the average person.

**Hugo Black, U.S. Supreme Court Justice,
New York Times,** *February 26, 1971.*

Already we have identified a number of weighty issues facing our society and its legal system in the early years of the new millennium, as contrasted with the issues faced a century ago. Then, an industrial revolution was beginning within a land that was sparsely populated but fabulously rich in resources. Now, an unimaginably wider range of issues extends from implications of advancing technology to predictable social conflicts in a land with fewer natural resources and a threatened environment. Yet there is a parallel today to the future our citizens faced in 1900. Then and now, the uncertainties of the future were offset by our confidence in our Constitution, the form of government it commands, and the civil liberties it guarantees. Then, as now, our Constitution is alive and well. What is this almost magical document?

Our Constitution is a voluntary agreement among our citizens that specifies national rules of governance and expresses our fundamental principles of justice. It also lists the inalienable rights of the people that bind them to cooperate for their general welfare. Written 11 years after the Declaration of Independence, the Constitution became operative in 1789. It is the world's oldest effectively functioning written constitution.

Our Constitution derives its legitimacy from the guaranteed right of the people to vote in the selection of their government representatives. This is also true of the written constitutions in all 50 states of the union. However, a democracy in which all of the qualified voters participate directly is obviously feasible only in very small political entities, such as some early New England towns. Our populous nation is a **republic**, meaning that its sovereign (supreme) power resides in the people but is exercised by representatives chosen through direct votes cast by qualified voters (i.e., qualified by age, citizenship, and registration) in free elections. The president and vice president are the only federal officials not elected directly; the electoral college, which is, however, elected by the people, chooses them.

43

WHAT IS CONSTITUTIONALISM?

Constitutionalism means "a fundamental law, or a fundamental set of principles and . . . [an] institutional arrangement, which would [actually] restrict arbitrary power and ensure 'limited government.'"[1] Thus, "the governing power is limited by enforceable rules of law, and concentration of power is prevented by various checks and balances so that the basic rights of individuals and groups are protected."[2]

Constitutionalism imposes limits on the exercise of government power. Many nations have constitutions, but that does not necessarily mean their citizens enjoy the fruits of constitutionalism. For example, a constitution that permits unlimited political power, whether in the hands of one, few, or many, does not provide constitutionalism. The Fascists' constitutions of Italy and Germany in the 1930s are an example. Neither included limitations on **arbitrary and capricious** uses of political power by the rulers. Arbitrary and capricious behavior has been aptly characterized as "willful and unreasonable action taken, without consideration of or in disregard of facts or without determining principle."[3] Even a constitution that provides limited political power, but establishes no mechanism to restrain the ruler's exercise of that power, fails to provide constitutionalism. For instance, a "freedom of the press" mandate in the Argentinean constitution did not prevent Juan Peron (president, 1945–1955) from destroying the world's largest Spanish-language newspaper, *La Prensa*, in Buenos Aires.

People enjoy constitutionalism only to the degree that their constitution limits power by specific provisions that effectively control the behavior of the ruling governors. One such control is having the judiciary serve as an enforcing watchdog on the exercise of powers by the executive and legislative branches, and even the lower levels of the judicial branch of government. The separation of powers concept is discussed more fully later in this chapter. A good example of its application occurred in 1952, when President Harry S. Truman ordered the secretary of commerce to seize and operate our country's privately owned steel mills after the United Steel Workers Union threatened to strike. Corporate managers retaliated by a "lockout" that kept the workers off their jobs. The president believed that a shutdown would impair the nation's ability to conduct the Korean War. Was the seizure order within the president's power? No. The Supreme Court held that "this seizure order cannot stand" for the following reasons:

1. The president's power, if any, to issue the order must stem either from an act of Congress or from the Constitution itself. The U.S. Supreme Court could find no congressional statute or constitutional provision that expressly authorized the president to take possession of private property as he did in the "steel mill" case.

2. Moreover, prior to this controversy, when the Taft-Hartley Act was under consideration in 1947, Congress had refused to adopt a law authorizing the seizure method of settling labor disputes that Truman used.

3. The order could not be sustained as an exercise of the president's military power as commander-in-chief of the armed forces. The commander-in-chief does not have the power to take possession of private property for the purpose of keeping labor–management disputes from stopping

production. The nation's lawmakers, not military authorities, should regulate labor disputes, declared the Court.[4]

The power of the U.S. Supreme Court to dictate to President Truman, and have him obey, demonstrates how constitutionalism helps to protect the people of the United States from abuses of executive power, however well meant such abuses may be.

Another example of separation and limitation of power took place in 1974, when the Supreme Court ordered President Richard M. Nixon to release subpoenaed tape recordings of discussions concerning a politically inspired burglary in the Watergate apartment house in Washington, D.C. Initially the president refused to release the tapes, claiming "executive privilege," e.g., the right to withhold recorded information he deemed important to the exercise of his presidential duties. The tapes showed that he had halted an FBI investigation, a serious obstruction of justice.

In 1997 Ms. Paula Jones filed a civil lawsuit for money damages against President William J. Clinton, alleging sexual harassment while he was governor of Arkansas. President Clinton asserted an "executive privilege" as justification for his request to suspend the litigation until after his presidency ended. Does the U.S. Constitution provide presidents with such an "executive privilege" to delay civil litigation?

No. The president contended that ongoing civil litigation would impair his ability to lead the nation—thus, it should be suspended by "executive privilege." The president was subpoenaed (ordered) to appear and testify in that litigation and he ultimately agreed to do so. Again, the judicial branch acted as an enforcing watchdog of the exercise of power by the executive branch of government.

WHAT IS CONSTITUTIONAL LAW?

Constitutional law in the United States has a variety of meanings. To the founders of our nation, it had to do with a concept known as **natural law*** and its corollary concept of **natural rights**. From the founders' perspective natural law was the higher law, in accordance with nature, applies to all men, and is unchangeable and eternal.** Natural rights are rights of human beings that exist regardless

---

*"But for natural law there would probably have been no American and no French revolution, nor would the great ideals of freedom and equality have found their way into the lawbooks after having found it into the hearts of men." See Alessandro Passerin D'Entreves, *Natural Law: An Introduction to Legal Philosophy* (London: Hutchinson and Co., 1951).

**See Marcus Tullius Cicero, *De re publica*, translated by George Sabine and Stanley Smith, Indianapolis, New York, Dobbs-Merrill (1960). A complete definition of natural law reads thus: "True law is right reason, harmonious with nature, diffused among all, constant, eternal; a law which calls to duty by its commands and restrains from evil by its prohibitions. . . . It is a sacred obligation not to attempt to legislate in contradiction to this law; nor may it be derogated from nor abrogated. Indeed, by neither the Senate nor the people can we be released from this law; nor does it require any but ourselves to be its expositor or interpreter. Nor is it one law at Rome and another at Athens; one now and another at a later time; but one eternal and unchangeable law binding all nations through all time." Marcus Tullius Cicero, *Lactantius, Div. Inst.* translated by Roberts and Donaldson (1871), vi, 8, 370.

of any other law. The founders believed they had incorporated natural-law principles into the Constitution in a manner consistent with the necessities of government or positive law.* **Positive law** is defined as any law enacted by the sovereign (supreme power) and deemed necessary to regulate an ordered society.** The natural-law doctrines found in the Constitution are reflected in the following fundamental beliefs, and they dictate the parameters within which legitimate governmental "positive law" must be exercised.[5]

1.   The *rights of man* are inalienable and indestructible.

2.   Paramount is the natural-law doctrine that the most fundamental rights of all human beings are life, liberty, and property.[6]

3.   Legitimate governments are obligated (by natural law) under their social contracts (constitutions) to protect and guarantee these rights to every person within their respective jurisdictions.

4.   The higher law acknowledges and promotes the principle of *private domain* into which governments should not intrude. Under this doctrine, the individual is free to do anything he chooses, unless specifically prohibited or circumscribed by reasonable positive law.*** This means that one may violate ethical standards, hallowed conventions, and Holy Writ, and yet not be answerable to the state unless the behavior involved has been prohibited or circumscribed by reasonable positive law. By contrast, many countries in today's turbulent world allow their citizens to do only that which is permitted by their man-made rules and decrees. All else that conflicts therewith is deemed prohibited.

5.   No person is allowed to be a judge in his or her own cause.[7] Thus, a Justice of the U.S. Supreme Court who has a personal interest in a controversy under appeal before the Court will refuse to participate in the case. A long-standing philosophical bias is not a disqualifying conflict of interest.

6.   No person is above the law—not legislators, not presidents, not judges.

In Chapter 1 we used the following case to describe the difference between civil and criminal law, and concluded that neither was applicable.

To view the political essays that are referred to as "The Federalist Papers visit: http://www.bus.miami.edu/ ~jmonroe/fedindex.htm

---

*"They are the principles of Aristotle and Plato, of Livy and Cicero, and Sidney, Harrington, and Locke: the principles of nature and eternal reason; the principles on which the whole government over us now stands." Quote attributed to John Adams. Clinton L. Rossiter, *The Political Thought of the American Revolution* (New York: Harcourt, Brace & World, 1953), 53.

**As is often true with philosophies, there is an inherent conflict between the pure precept of positive law and natural law. As proffered by Thomas Hobbes (1588–1679), positive law is essential to protect people from their primitive state, so when a law is enacted, people are duty-bound to obey it. Natural law presupposes a system of law grounded on its intrinsic truth rather than on any power of compulsion, and it is held to exist irrespective of and sometimes inconsistent with man-made laws. The tension between individual belief in and respect for natural law versus the positive laws of the state is not the subject of an abstract debate. One justification often given for civil disobedience is that the violator is actually complying with a higher law, namely natural law.

***This proscription on the law creates a conundrum. The natural right to an individual's private domain requires that the state enact a specific law before any person can be held accountable to the state for violating that law. On the other hand, because natural law exists without the necessity of any state declaration of its existence, such law could, of course, by its very nature be violated without its having been declared a part of the positive law. However, the violator of the natural law may suffer from sanctions, both temporal and, some ethicists would maintain, also eternal. If nothing else, a liar, thief, or murderer, for example, may suffer the agonies of ostracism from society, and often a troubled guilty conscience that can last a lifetime.

Late at night, David Thomas Cash, Jr., 19, observed his friend Jeremy Strohmeyer, 20, escort a very young girl into a restroom inside the Primadonna casino near Las Vegas. Shortly thereafter, Cash followed them inside, where he peered over the top of a stall. He saw Strohmeyer grappling with the girl, but said nothing and left. Later Strohmeyer rejoined Cash in the casino. After discussing the killing of the girl, Cash and Strohmeyer continued their evening of conviviality and gambling. Strohmeyer ultimately pled guilty to the rape and murder of the victim, and is serving life imprisonment without the possibility of parole (early release). Did Cash have a natural law right to choose to assist, or to ignore, the victim?

Yes. Recall from the paragraph 4 earlier: ". . . one may violate ethical standards, hallowed conventions, and Holy Writ, and yet not be answerable to the state unless the behavior involved has been prohibited by reasonable positive law." Under the natural law principle of private domain, Mr. Cash was free either to help the victim or to ignore her plight. Nevada has no statute (positive law) that criminalizes a refusal to prevent a crime from occurring. It is unclear whether or not a law requiring citizens to intervene in criminal conduct would be constitutional.

Important elements of the natural law and natural rights were included in the second paragraph of the Declaration of Independence:

> *We hold these truths to be self-evident, that all men are created equal, that they are Endowed by their Creator with certain unalienable Rights, that among these are Life, Liberty and the pursuit of Happiness. That to secure these rights, Governments are instituted among Men, deriving their just powers from the consent of the governed. That whenever any Form of Government becomes destructive of these ends, it is the Right of the people to alter or to abolish it, and to institute new Government, laying its foundation on such principles and organizing its powers in such form, as to them shall seem most likely to effect their Safety and Happiness.*

In January 1776, George Washington wrote of "the propriety of separation [from England on the basis of] . . . the sound doctrine and unanswerable reasoning contained in the pamphlet *Common Sense*." The author of *Common Sense*, Thomas Paine, summed up the spirit of the time in these lofty words:

> *But where, say some, is the King of America? I'll tell you, Friend. He reigns above, and does not make havoc of mankind like the royal brute of Britain. Yet, that we may not appear to be defective even in earthly honors, let a day be solemnly set apart for proclaiming the charter; let it be brought forth placed in the divine law, the word of God; let a crown be placed thereon, by which the world may know, that so far as we approve of monarchy, that in America the law is king. For as in absolute governments the king is law, so in free countries the law ought to be king; and there ought to be no other."[8] [Emphasis added]*

If the law is the "King of America," then who is the watchdog over the president of the United States?

The office of the U.S. special prosecutor (discussed later in this chapter) is the watchdog of the president or other high executive branch officials appointed by the president. The special prosecutor must refer evidence of violations of law by the president to the other branches of government (legislative or judicial) for appropriate action. Thus, no person is above the law—the "King of America," in Thomas Paine's memorable words.

When we speak of constitutional law today we mean the fundamental law or the supreme law of the land. Constitutional principles accorded special designation as constitutional laws are (1) judicial review, (2) separation of powers, (3) federalism, and (4) civil rights and liberties. These four special categories contain the most publicized and exciting principles of constitutional law.

WHAT IS JUDICIAL REVIEW?

Judicial review is the power and duty vested in the U.S. Supreme Court to declare null and void (i.e., of no validity or effect) any statute or act of the federal government or of any state government that violates the U.S. Constitution.* Although not specifically authorized in Article III (the Judicial Article of the Constitution), some form of judicial review was presumably envisioned by framers of the Constitution. According to Alexander Hamilton, the Supreme Court is the "least dangerous branch" because it controls neither sword nor purse.[9] He said the Supreme Court and not the Congress or the president should be the custodian of the Constitution. Further, he referred to "the medium of the courts of justice, whose duty it must be to declare all acts contrary to the manifest tenor of the constitution void. Without this, all the reservations of particular rights or privileges would amount to nothing."[10]

What *judicial review* meant, however, was not articulated until 1803, in the case of *Marbury v. Madison*.[11] This case did more than validate (i.e., give legal force to) judicial review of legislative and executive enactments and orders. Chief Justice Marshall enunciated a major power for the Supreme Court, recognizing it as the sole interpreter and custodian of the Constitution, to the exclusion of the president and Congress. With this declaration came the awesome duty of defining what the Constitution means and what it does not mean.

Although the exclusive judicial power of review has engendered heated controversy over the years, it also has been a stabilizing force for a growing and changing society. As national economic, social, and political conditions have changed, so too have attitudes and opinions of the people. This evolution is reflected in the leaders the people elect to office and in the Supreme Court Justices who are appointed. As a result, some long-standing Supreme Court decisions have been changed. What once was ruled constitutional thereafter is declared unconstitutional. For example, as the twentieth century began, racial segregation in schools was accepted and even endorsed by the "separate but equal" rule of *Plessy v. Ferguson*.[12] In 1954 however, the "separate but equal" rule was rejected

---

*Note that state supreme courts possess similar powers to nullify laws of their own legislatures that violate their respective state constitutions.

by *Brown v. The Board of Education of Topeka*.[13] As the new millennium begins, racial segregation in schools (and elsewhere) has been abolished.

Judicial review is not the exclusive process by which our Constitution can be changed. The people can and do make changes through the more difficult process of formal amendment. For example, women obtained the right to vote in 1920 by the Nineteenth Amendment to the Constitution.

WHAT IS SEPARATION OF POWERS?

Separation of powers is an indispensable element of our charter of government. The Constitution allocates powers of government according to function. The functional branches are legislative (law making), executive (law enforcing), and judicial (adjudicating).[14] Separation of powers provides an effective balance of power among the three branches of government. Different officials have unique and specific powers, and each branch operates under the direction of different persons. Each branch checks the other two to prevent them from garnering or exercising power illegally.[15] This institutional structure restrains a natural human tendency toward expansion of personal power. While preventing possible tyranny (i.e., despotic abuse of authority), the separation of powers permits officials to execute faithfully their constitutionally delegated powers.

The constitutional doctrine of separation of powers speaks of the relationships among the divisions of government. While there are indeed exclusive functions assigned to each (e.g., tax bills must begin in the House of Representatives), much of the work engaged in by the three branches of government is shared.

Congress may pass a bill; the president may sign or veto it. Congress may override the veto and enact the bill as law. The Supreme Court may strike down the statute as unconstitutional. If necessary, Congress may initiate a campaign to have the Constitution amended to accomplish the purpose of the statute, or more likely it may attempt to pass a new statute that is in conformity with the Constitution.[16] Note too that the president may be able to appoint new members to the Supreme Court (with the advice and consent of the Senate) who are sympathetic to his or her views.

To view important constitutional and governmental documents or to obtain references to many, visit http://www.lib.umich.edu/libhome/Documents.center/federal.html

Assume that President Clinton nominated Richard Westley to the U.S. Supreme Court. During confirmation proceedings conducted by the U.S. Senate, candidate Westley was asked, "Do you believe in the right of women to choose to have an abortion?" He answered simply, "No." The colloquy provoked widespread public concern, to which the Senate responded by killing the nomination.[17] Should Supreme Court candidates be required to reveal their deepest personal beliefs as a precondition to appointment?

Most members of the public probably would approve of a litmus test (single issue test that determines result) for nominees to the Supreme Court. However, over a lifetime a Justice will face an extraordinary number of important issues involving significant values, and most people, no doubt, also would prefer the appointment of highly qualified persons rather than persons sympathetic to one specific controversial issue—unless that issue was of supreme importance to the individual. The obvious conundrum typically is resolved by the refusal of candidates to respond specifically to such questions, reciting their loyalties to follow the rule of law.

It is reassuring to note that in the final analysis the power to decide an issue rests with the people, who may use their votes—"the power of the ballot box"— to elect representatives who are expected to comply with the expressed will of the people. However, the representatives are not legally obliged to do so. Even if they were, public opinion is usually divided and sometimes fragmented on controversial issues.

Pollsters who question randomly selected persons ascertain public opinion. The more persons who are polled, the greater the statistical accuracy of the result. Or is it? Are polls reliable or skewed by the phraseology and subject matter of the questions?

Elected officials do consider the results of polls in their decision making. However, many critics complain that poll results can be skewed by the way questions are asked, by the amount and quality of media interest in the issue, by respondents, who are indifferent to or uninformed about the issue at hand, or by respondents who color their answers based on their personal biases or suspicions. A straightforward question such as "How did you vote" is more likely to produce an accurate answer than a hypothetical question such as "How would you vote if the election were held today?" Even when the collective will of the people can be accurately determined, however, it may be ignored or countermanded if elected officials deem it unwise or ill-informed.

The presidential veto procedure is prescribed by Article I, Section 7 of the Constitution, which states, "Every Bill which shall have passed the House of Representatives and the Senate shall, before it becomes a Law, be presented to the President." Thereupon, "if he approves he shall sign it, but if not he shall return it, with his Objections to that House in which it shall have originated." If, after reconsideration it is approved by two-thirds of both houses, it shall become a law. Note that "if any Bill shall not be returned by the President within ten Days (Sundays excepted) after it shall have been presented to him, the same shall be a Law, in like manner as if he had signed it, unless the Congress by their adjournment prevent its Return, in which Case it shall not be a Law."

Each year Congress presents a budget to the president for signature into law. Typically, some of the proposed expenditures in the budget are intended primarily as political patronage. These so-called "pork barrel" budget items are included by the most powerful legislators in Congress, a tactic that assists them in their re-election campaigns.

Congress presented the fiscal year budget for the year 2000 to the president for signature or veto. Included was an item for ten million dollars for "parks and recreation" projects in Congresswoman Peavy's hometown. For years, Peavy had been a very vocal critic of the president. Can the president approve the budget yet, in retaliation, veto the proposed appropriation for Peavy?[18]

No. The power to make partial vetoes (called *line-item vetoes*) would have the practical effect of amending enactments by Congress. The president is not authorized by the Constitution to amend laws proposed by Congress.[19] Thus, the separation of the legislative and executive powers cannot be blurred by line-item vetoes.

HOW IS THE NATIONAL GOVERNMENT ORGANIZED?

LEGISLATIVE BRANCH (CONGRESS)

Article I of the Constitution delineates the organization and functions of the legislature. The legislative branch is *bicameral* (having two parts), with an upper house (the Senate) and a lower house (the House of Representatives). Members of the Senate originally were appointed by state legislatures, but in 1913 the Seventeenth Amendment changed the system to direct selection by popular vote. The Senate has 100 members, two from each state. Members of the House of Representatives are elected to 435 seats that are allocated to the states on the basis of population, as determined in the decennial national census.

For information about the organization and operation of government, visit http://www.yale.edu/lawweb/avalonavalon.htm

The basic function of the legislative branch is to enact laws. This is usually accomplished by a majority vote for or against enactment, amendment, or repeal. In both the House and the Senate, a quorum consists of a majority of the members who have been elected and sworn (i.e., taken an oath of office) to serve. Powers of the Congress are spelled out in Article I, Section 8 of the Constitution. They include the power to tax and borrow money, to regulate interstate commerce, to make laws regulating bankruptcies, to coin money, to establish post offices, to establish courts inferior to the Supreme Court, to declare war, and to govern the District of Columbia (the area of the nation's capital). However, Congress has great latitude in the detailed application of its enumerated powers by virtue of its blanket authority "to make all Laws which shall be necessary and proper for carrying into Execution" its stated powers.[20]

Information about Congress is available at http://www.house.gov/ and http://www.senate.gov/

Once the legislature enacts a law, its job is usually done. All persons subject to the newly enacted law are then required to comply. If necessary, lower-level government officials in the executive branch (e.g., police) enforce compliance. If and when the constitutionality of a statute is challenged, the dispute may ultimately be resolved by decision of the Supreme Court.

Sometimes newly enacted laws never become law.

Congress passed a law releasing alien Chinese students who were studying in the United States from the requirement of returning to China upon the expiration of their visas. (A visa is a document that grants a citizen of a foreign country legal permission to live, work, or study in the host country.) This was done because Congress believed that the Chinese government would punish most of these students for supporting the 1989 student uprising in Tiananmen Square and elsewhere in China. The proposed law was sent to the White House for signature by the president.

President George Bush vetoed the legislation on the grounds that Congress was interfering with foreign policy matters, a presidential responsibility. Moreover, the students were already protected against forced repatriation by his executive order, which directed the Immigration and Naturalization Service to extend the Chinese student visas indefinitely. When the bill was returned to the Congress, the House voted to override the veto, but the Senate did not; thus, the president's veto stood.

EXECUTIVE BRANCH (PRESIDENCY)

The president and vice president are each elected to a term of four years, with a limit of two consecutive full terms.* The constitutional process for choosing the chief executive and his or her running mate is cumbersome because the method is indirect, with state electors actually electing the president by casting electoral votes. The number of electors in each state is determined by the number of representatives the state has in the House, plus its two senators. Thus, currently each of seven states (Alaska, Delaware, Montana, North and South Dakota, Vermont, and Wyoming) and the District of Columbia has 3 votes, for a total of 24; populous California alone has 54; and New York has 33. These distributions of electoral votes will shift following the census in 2000.

In total, there are 538 electoral votes: 435 based on members of the House, 100 based on members in the Senate, and 3 from the District of Columbia. To win requires a majority of at least 270 electoral votes. Note that presidential elections and vacancies are further regulated by technical amendments to the Constitution.[21]

The unique electoral college has survived despite repeated efforts to alter or abolish it. This may be because it maintains the viability of political parties, which "in turn serve to identify issues and support candidates committed to advancing identified policies and programs. A new electoral college is created for every presidential election, that is, the people who serve as electors (casting votes) in the electoral college are different for each election.

Powers of the President

Section 2 of Article II of the Constitution specifies the following presidential powers. First and foremost, and of momentous importance during most of the twentieth century, is the power of the president as "Commander in Chief of the Armed Forces of the United States and of the militia of the several states, when called into actual service of the United States. . . ."[22]

While Congress retains to itself the power to declare war, the power "to make war" is granted solely to the president. It was during the Civil War that the commander in chief was declared to be the sole determiner of whether the hostilities were of ". . . such alarming proportions as will compel him to accord to them the character of belligerent"[23] and whether he would engage the armed forces of the United States in such hostilities. Advanced technology has changed the nature of modern warfare, thus further justifying the presidential power to respond quickly with military force to a military attack without congressional approval.

The president has the duty and power to make treaties, but they must be approved by a two-thirds vote of the Senate.[24] For example, three controversial yet

---

*"No person shall be elected to the office of the president more than twice, and no person who has held the office of president, or acted as president for more than two years of a term to which some other person was elected president, shall be elected to the office of the president more than once." (U.S. Constitution, Twenty-second Amendment)

vitally important treaties entered into by our country in the twentieth century were the Charter of the United Nations (1945); the North Atlantic Treaty Pact (1948), which created NATO (North Atlantic Treaty Organization), a defensive military alliance; and the North American Free Trade Agreement (NAFTA) among Canada, Mexico, and the United States. All three of these treaties were duly voted on and approved by the Senate. The president may also sign *executive agreements*, which do not require Senate ratification. For example, during the early months of World War Two, when German submarines were sinking many supply ships in an attempt to starve England into surrender, President Franklin D. Roosevelt signed an executive agreement giving the British 50 1914-type destroyers in exchange for 8 naval bases. This was entirely Constitutional, despite the fact that the United States had not yet declared war on Germany.

Recent treaties are all available on the Internet. For the full text of the North American Free Trade Agreement, visit http://www.itaiep.doc.gov/nafta/nafta2.htm

With the "advice and consent" of the Senate, the president appoints ambassadors, public ministers and consuls, Supreme Court Justices and presidential advisors.[25] Congress has empowered the president to choose other federal officers and commission heads. The Judiciary Act of 1789 gave presidents power to nominate appellate and district court judges for the federal courts. Congress must approve these appointments, a function that is another example of shared power between the branches of government.

You will find presidential executive orders in the federal register at http://www.nara.gov/fedreg/

The only constitutional method to remove a president from office is by a congressional proceeding called *impeachment*. This process is more appropriately discussed under the "judicial branch" in the next subsection.

Some scholars contend that the power to nominate Supreme Court Justices, who serve for life, is the single most important power of the president.

In the case of *Roe v. Wade*[26] the U.S. Supreme Court held for the first time that women have a constitutionally protected right to choose whether or not to have an abortion. Following this declaration, the states could no longer abolish abortion within their borders. Four Justices voted against the majority in *Roe v. Wade*. Could the replacement of one Justice potentially cause reversal of *Roe*, thereby altering or even eliminating the abortion law?

Yes. Many of the most controversial Supreme Court cases are decided by 5–4 votes. Nonetheless, presidential candidates historically have not announced the names of persons they would, if elected, nominate to the Supreme Court if the opportunity should arise. Nor do presidential candidates announce the names of possible appointees to their cabinets (department heads with the highest authority in an administration). Thus, voters make assumptions about their future based upon the campaign statements and track records of presidential candidates.

JUDICIAL BRANCH (COURTS)

Article III of the Constitution, the Judicial Article, declares, "The Judicial power of the United States shall be vested in one Supreme Court, and in such inferior courts as the Congress may from time to time ordain and establish."[27] Compared with detailed mandates given to the executive and legislative branches, Article III is sparse in providing guidance to the judiciary. Despite this lack of a closely defined role, the federal courts have become central to the doctrine of separation of

Many links to important aspects of our constitutional form of government are available at the White House home site http://www.whitehouse.gov/

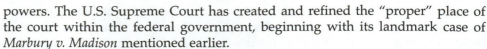

You will find both pending cases and current opinions of the U.S. Supreme Court at http://www.supct.law.cornell.edu/supct/

Resumes of Supreme Court Justices are available at http://www.supct.law.cornell.edu/supct/justices/fullcourt.hmtl

powers. The U.S. Supreme Court has created and refined the "proper" place of the court within the federal government, beginning with its landmark case of *Marbury v. Madison* mentioned earlier.

The power to determine the constitutionality of federal and state legislative enactments, as well as judicial review of actions taken by the executive branch, has given the U.S. Supreme Court major responsibility for maintaining the integrity of the Constitution. The Supreme Court is commonly thought to be the branch of government least likely to be swayed by political pressures and popular whims. One reason for this is because, like all federal judges Supreme Court Justices hold office for life, contingent only on good behavior. It is not uncommon for Supreme Court Justices to remain active on the bench well beyond the traditional retirement age of 65. For this reason, the Court was once referred to as "the nine old men." Currently, the Court is composed of the following Justices:

Stephen G. Breyer of Massachusetts (President Clinton, 1994)
Ruth Bader Ginsburg of New York (President Clinton, 1993)
Anthony M. Kennedy of California (President Reagan, 1988)
Sandra Day O'Connor of Arizona (President Reagan, 1981)
Chief Justice William H. Rehnquist of Arizona (President Reagan, 1986)
Antonin Scalia of Washington, D.C. (President Reagan, 1986)
David H. Souter of New Hampshire (President Bush, 1990)
John Paul Stevens of Illinois (President Ford, 1975)
Clarence Thomas of Georgia (President Bush, 1991)

All courts are empowered to issue orders to compel compliance with their rules and procedures. For example, courts authorize the issuance of subpoenas (orders to appear at a certain time and place) upon proper request by officials or lawyers (for their clients) who are engaged in litigation or investigation. Failure to comply with such a judicial order can prompt a court to hold the witness in "contempt of court." The court's penalty for contempt may range from a monetary fine to jail time.

In 1971 the U.S. Supreme Court approved the legality of a subpoena served upon President Richard Nixon (executive branch) to deliver to the Congress (legislative branch) certain tape recorded conversations that Nixon most certainly knew would end his term of office. He could have refused to obey the subpoena and destroyed the tapes. If Nixon had refused to comply with the subpoena and had destroyed the tapes, what would have happened?

Most likely the Congress would have impeached* President Nixon for failure to comply with a lawful subpoena approved by the U.S. Supreme Court. But it is not clear that disregard of a subpoena issued by Congress is a legal basis for

---

*Impeachment is a process for the removal from office of certain federal officers, including the president, that is provided for in the U.S. Constitution. To remove an official from office by impeachment requires a majority vote in the House of Representatives and a two-thirds majority vote in the Senate. In 1998 the U.S. House of Representatives voted to impeach President William Jefferson Clinton for obstruction of justice and perjury relating to his conduct following the infamous "Monica Lewinsky affair." The U.S. Senate, with Chief Justice William Rehnquist presiding, conducted an impeachment trial. On February 12, 1999, it voted 50 to 50 and 45 to 55 on the respective charges, thereby declining to remove the President from office.

impeachment. We never will know what would have happened then. But it is important to know how the three powers of government must interact, and that the gravity of the crisis then related to the president's willingness to comply with an order of the judicial branch of government. Unfortunately, uninformed citizens were destined never to understand the constitutional implications of "Watergate." Thus, they would not see the parallel in more current times.

In 1998 President Clinton was subpoenaed to testify before a federal grand jury, not as a witness, but concerning his personal conduct. Again, rather than create a constitutional confrontation about the obligation of a president to respond to a subpoena, President Clinton ultimately agreed to testify, and did. Could the president personally have appeared at the time and place to testify, but then refused to answer questions?

In Chapter 6 you will review the fundamental principle in our society that no person must testify against himself in a criminal proceeding. A person may volunteer to testify against himself, but he or she need not. President Clinton did not assert his privilege against self-incrimination, either because there was no criminal conduct about which he was concerned or because he simply waived his right. He became the first sitting president in history to testify before a federal grand jury (by closed-circuit television). But in either case, he ultimately chose the course of former President Nixon by complying with the dictates of the subpoena.

Federal judges can be removed from their courts only by death, voluntary retirement, or impeachment by the Congress of the United States.

The Honorable I. M. Deceptione, a federal district judge in Des Moines, Iowa, was tried and convicted of cheating on his income tax by filing a false return. He was sentenced to federal prison, where he remained for 18 months. After release, he promptly paid all fines, penalties, and taxes due, amounting to $52,000. Then, at his request, he was restored to his former position.[28] Can he be impeached?

Yes. Eight months after returning to his job as a judge, he was finally removed from the court by impeachment.

Congress is reluctant to use the impeachment procedure to remove public officials from office because it is costly, cumbersome, and time-consuming. But impeachment is the only way to remove federal judges from the public payroll even when they are proven guilty of criminal conduct. Fortunately, criminal acts by federal judges are rare.[29]

U.S. District Court Judge James Ware told a conference of federal judges and lawyers a riveting story of how his brother had been killed in 1963 by a racist's bullet in Alabama on the same day of the Ku Klux Klan's bombing of a Baptist church in which four black girls were killed. Later it was discovered and widely publicized that Judge Ware's story was a lie. What punishment, if any, do federal judges receive for conduct that goes to the heart of the credibility of the courts—honesty in public life?[30]

Previous to his misrepresentation, Judge Ware had been nominated for promotion to the U.S. Court of Appeals. After publication of his falsehood, Judge Ware withdrew his nomination. He also was publicly reprimanded by a panel of federal judges on the basis that his conduct "was prejudicial to the effective administration of the business of the courts." Judge Ware was not removed from office.

Under the Constitution, the Senate has the sole power to try all impeachments, and no person may be convicted without the concurrence of two-thirds of the members present. When political loyalty to the accused is involved, such a majority can be difficult to obtain unless the alleged offense is flagrant. Understandably, therefore, the practice is seldom used.

Congress sets the salaries for all federal employees, including judges. However, once the salaries for federal judges are set by Congress they can never be reduced for any reason during the tenure of judges then on the court.[31] This serves to forestall possible improper efforts to impose financial pressure on judges whose opinions are not favored. Of course, the salaries of new appointees may be lower than those of their predecessors, but this is unlikely to happen.

> Seymore Merit, a federal district court judge in Salt Lake City, Utah, was angry that Congress had not raised his pay for several years. He sued in the federal district court contending that he, and all other federal judges, had a constitutional right for pay raises. Does he?

Yes. The Supreme Court said that failure to raise the judge's salary by a percentage equal to the annual rate of inflation was unconstitutional, because the Constitution prohibits the reduction of the salary of federal judges.[32] Loss of purchasing power was considered the equivalent of a salary reduction. As a result, all federal judges had their salaries raised.

THE OFFICE OF SPECIAL PROSECUTOR

In 1978 Congress enacted the Ethics in Government Act which, among other things, provided for the appointment of an "independent counsel." This special prosecutor was empowered to investigate and, if appropriate, prosecute specified high-ranking government officials, including the president, for violations of federal laws. The special prosecutor is appointed by a federal court in response to a request from the U.S. attorney general (who is appointed by the president), following a preliminary investigation. The request is made when the attorney general believes there are "reasonable grounds to believe that further investigation or prosecution is warranted." The federal court then appoints an independent counsel and prescribes the prosecutorial jurisdiction and powers.

A special prosecutor cannot be removed from office by the president. The U.S. attorney general can remove a special prosecutor from office for good cause, for physical or mental incapacity, or for other factors that impair one's ability to perform. Congress does have the power to impeach the independent counsel.

> In 1998 Special Prosecutor Kenneth Starr submitted case files to Congress that were said to contain evidence of impeachable offenses that had been committed by President William J. Clinton. The evidence had been

obtained by compelling the sworn testimony of many witnesses, including the president. Does this power of a non-elected special prosecutor to issue subpoenas while investigating the president violate the separation of powers of the three branches of government?

No. The Constitution does not require the three branches to operate with absolute independence. Here there is no attempt by Congress to increase its own powers at the expense of the executive branch. Nor does the 1978 Act work any judicial branch usurpation of proper executive functions.[33] Because the special prosecutor cannot simply be fired and has the power to issue subpoenas compelling testimony of otherwise unwilling witnesses, such as the president, some argue that a new branch of government has been indirectly created. This branch, goes the argument, is not limited by the traditional "checks and balances" of the other branches. However, the judicial branch always has been empowered to issue subpoenas and retains the power to limit the jurisdiction and powers of any special prosecutor that it appoints. (The attorney general may nominate candidates, but the federal court selects them.) Congress can impeach a special prosecutor, or could simply refuse to take action upon any evidence produced by such a prosecutor.

WHAT IS FEDERALISM?

Federalism may be defined as a political arrangement in which two or more levels of government provide a variety of services for a given group of citizens in a specified geographic area. For example, Iowans are served by the national government and by their state government as well as by a variety of local governance structures.

For various definitions of federalism, see http://www.min.net/~kala/fed/define.htm

Scholars estimate more than 80,000 state and local governments* exist in the United States, each striving to meet the needs and wants of our complex, technologically driven society. This governmental profusion operates in a climate of political pressures, involving both competition and cooperation within and among various public officeholders. In effect, the U.S. Constitution prescribed some of this complexity when it reserved a large measure of sovereignty for each of the original 13 states, in accordance with Article IV and the Tenth Amendment.

In any event, we are a people served by, but also subject to, government rule that ranges from all-encompassing taxation mandated by our national Congress, to the narrowly defined rules for admission of toddlers to kindergarten as mandated by our local school boards.

The Constitution defines the lines of demarcation between the national government and the state governments. The national government has only those powers delegated to it, and such other powers that naturally flow therefrom.

---

*All governments within states were (are) created by the state legislatures under provisions in their respective state constitutions. The governments of cities, boroughs, and counties are most commonly recognized by citizens. Other varieties of local governments are school districts, flood-control districts, mosquito-abatement districts, and park districts. Under their charters of government (granted by state legislatures), they have budgets, collect taxes, and perform various other government functions.

Congress shall have the power "to make all laws which shall be necessary and proper for carrying into Execution the foregoing powers."[34] Some of these powers are exclusive as to the national government, such as "to coin Money" and "to make Treaties."[35] But other powers are shared, such as taxing and spending. As noted, all other powers "are reserved to the States respectively, or to the people."[36]

Our Constitution also limits the power of the national government; for example, it is prohibited from denying a request for a **writ of *habeas corpus*** (Latin: "you have the body"), a formal written order that an arrestee be brought before a court, usually to protect against abusive incarceration[37] without release on bail, pending a formal trial.

Under the Constitution, some powers are also denied to the states, such as the power to make a treaty. Finally, there are powers denied to both, such as the passage of **bills of attainder**, which are acts of the legislature punishing a named individual(s) or member(s) of a specific group without a judicial trial; and *ex post facto* **laws** (Latin: "after the fact"), which are retroactive laws that would punish alleged violators for acts lawful when committed, or that would increase the punishment applicable at the time the act was committed.

David Cash (mentioned earlier in this chapter) was not guilty of any crime by declining to rescue a young girl from his friend's murderous acts. In response to public outcry, assume that Nevada passed a statute that made failure to assist the victim of criminal behavior a felony (i.e., a serious crime). If the state of Nevada then arrested, prosecuted, convicted, and sent Cash to jail, what, if anything, could he do?

Under the preceding hypothetical example, Cash could sidestep the Nevada judicial system altogether and petition a federal court to protect him from this *ex post facto* law. The U.S. Constitution prohibits states from subjecting people to such laws regardless of the outcry or sentiment of most citizens. The federal court would order Nevada to release Cash.

WHAT CONSTITUTIONAL POWERS BELONG TO CITIZENS?

Although much power is delegated to the national government, and great power is reserved to states, it is the people who possess the ultimate power in our free society with its constitutional system. One of the great powers of the people is found in their right to vote.[38]

Every citizen wishing to govern personally must compete with political opponents and win this privilege by receiving a majority of the people's vote. "[T]hose who make public policy [laws] in this society are privileged to do so because they have won the struggle against others who seek the privilege of making policy."[39] It is by popular vote that lawmakers and governors are chosen.

Some state constitutions give qualified voters the right and power to bypass customary law-making procedures of state and local governments and to make laws directly. This is called the **initiative process**. It enables groups of voters, if sufficient in numbers, to originate and pass statutes, ordinances, and amendments to their respective constitutions without recourse to the legislature.

State legislatures may submit a **referendum** petition to voters for their approval or disapproval of an existing or proposed law. State constitutions as well as statutes can be created, amended, or disapproved through the referendum process. The **recall** petition enables voters to remove from office any elected state or local official before the expiration of his or her term. During most of the twentieth century, these three practices of direct democracy have given the people enhanced power of control over legislation and legislators.

These practices, especially the initiative process, are sometimes misused by well-financed special-interest groups, businesses, and professions to secure enactment of laws that favor their own purposes. Such groups may hire public relations firms to run a campaign for passage of certain desired legislation. With the use of direct-mail fund raising, and with payments offered to "vote hustlers" for each signature obtained, the public relations firms readily qualify their initiatives for the ballot. Later, absentee ballots may be mailed to persons who have signed the petitions to make it easy for them to vote on the particular proposal.

> Citizens have used the initiative process to establish a statewide lottery in California, to protect the moose in Maine, to encourage the death penalty in Massachusetts, to approve the sale of wine in local grocery stores in Colorado, to abolish daylight savings time in North Dakota, and to limit rights of gays in Colorado.[40]

Critics have condemned the initiative process as it is presently used. Controversial issues make their way onto the ballot and are often written in a manner so verbose and confusing that most people cannot reasonably evaluate the relevant pros and cons or fairly understand how they should vote. The confusion frequently is increased by slick media advertising. Despite the potential abuse inherent in the initiative process, however, it has the big advantage of increasing voter interest and participation.

> In 1996 California voters approved by majority vote a bitterly contested initiative. The effect of Proposition 209 was to prohibit affirmative action in public education, employment, and other state programs. Lawsuits were filed in federal court by minorities affected by the change in the law on the grounds that it would deny them equal protection under the law as guaranteed by the U.S. Constitution. What was the result?

In an *ex parte* (no opposition) hearing, a federal court judge initially suspended Proposition 209 pending a future trial.[41] Shortly thereafter, a higher federal court overruled the decision, and Proposition 209 then went into effect.[42] Thus, through the initiative process, a majority of the people were able to create a new law that the state legislative branch was unwilling to enact. Neither Proposition 209 nor similar bans on affirmative action have yet reached the U.S. Supreme Court.

THE POLICE POWER

Neither those who wrote the Constitution nor those who ratified it intended the national government to have authority over most details in the everyday lives of people. James Madison believed that limitation on the power of the national government was a major virtue of federalism,[43] whereby the **police power** is implicitly reserved to the states under the Tenth Amendment. The police power is the right to enact and enforce laws for the prevention of fraud and crime and to promote order, safety, health, morals, and the general welfare of the people. The police power is implemented by both state and local governments.

The city of Bellevue, Washington, passed an ordinance banning "obscenities" in all business establishments, including so-called "juice bars" where no alcoholic beverages are sold. The city ordinance defined "obscenity" to include totally nude dancing.[44] Is this ordinance a proper exercise of the police power?

No. Although the police power authorizes cities to enact laws that are deemed necessary to protect the welfare and morals of its residents, such laws must not violate some greater law, such as rights protected by the U.S. Constitution. The First Amendment to the Constitution guarantees citizens the right of free expression under most circumstances.

The presence of alcohol, however, is a special circumstance. An Indiana statute required dancers to wear "pasties" and "G-strings" in establishments where alcohol was sold. The U.S. Supreme Court upheld the law because there is a substantial governmental interest in maintaining order, which is a more important factor than any impairment the law may impose on free expression through nude dancing.[45] On these grounds, then, the city of Bellevue might possibly be able to regulate the location of "juice bars" if their proximity to institutions such as schools or churches violated some sense of community order.

The police power is thus an essential attribute of government but is subject to the limitations of the federal and state constitutions. Under the Constitution, the national government's power to regulate, control, and circumscribe human conduct is specifically tied to one or more of its delegated powers.[46] For example, the Federal Aviation Administration was established to provide for safety regulation in the manufacture of aircraft as a "necessary and proper" extension of Congress' power to "regulate Commerce . . . among the several States," as prescribed in the Constitution:

The Congress shall have Power. . . To regulate Commerce with foreign Nations, and among the several States. . . And To make all Laws which shall be necessary and proper for carrying into Execution the foregoing Powers, and all other Powers vested by this Constitution in the Government of the United States, or in any Department or Officer thereof.[47]

WHAT IS THE SUPREMACY CLAUSE?

According to the United States Constitution:

This Constitution and the Laws of the United States which shall be made in pursuance thereof; and all Treaties made, or which shall be made, under the Authority of the United States, shall be the supreme *Law of the Land; and the*

Judges in every State shall be bound thereby, any Thing in the Constitution or Laws of any State to the Contrary not withstanding.[48] *[Emphasis added]*

Thus, the Constitution and federal laws made under it, as well as decisions of the Supreme Court of the United States, together with related supporting opinions, are constituent parts of the "supreme law of the land." The significance of the **supremacy doctrine** is that it invalidates any conflicting state law by preemption, meaning that federal law takes precedence over state law in areas of control expressly delegated to the United States by the Constitution.[49]

An Arizona statute made it unlawful to operate a train of more than 14 passenger cars or 70 freight cars within the state. The law was a safety measure enacted under the state's police power. Was such state regulation of train lengths lawful?

No. Trains move into and out of Arizona, from and to other states. Interstate commerce is subject to federal regulation under Article I, Section 8. However, if the state regulation affects interstate commerce only slightly, or if national interests are served well by it, then states may regulate the particular interstate commerce.[50]

Today there is no argument about the supremacy of the national government. Most debate about proper state and federal roles has to do with "effectiveness": Should it be done nationally, or can it be done better locally? The availability of necessary funds and adequate resources are also important factors. States, counties, and cities that are "strapped for cash" eagerly seek federal funding for local projects such as public housing, mass transit construction, education, and indigent care. Also, major natural disasters require a national response. Federal resources are essential when local agencies are overwhelmed by major tasks of relief and reconstruction. Dramatic examples in recent years involved victims of hurricane winds along the Atlantic coast; flooding rivers in the great Mississippi Valley; and earthquakes, floods, and firestorms along the Pacific coast.

WHAT ABOUT TAXES?

In the famous case of *McCulloch v. Maryland*, Chief Justice John Marshall observed that "The power to tax involves the power to destroy."[51] Although primarily revenue-raising measures, taxes also are used to influence the behavior of people and the production and distribution of goods and services. Income taxes and estate and inheritance taxes (so-called *death taxes* on the privilege of giving and receiving part of a decedent's estate) tend to redistribute wealth. So-called *sin taxes* on liquor and tobacco products presumably tend to discourage harmful use of such products. Credits against the payment of taxes otherwise due by renters tends to ease the costs of housing. Tax benefits accorded parents of dependent children tend to ease family costs. And so on.

Taxes are never popular—but it has been said that they are the price of civilization. They are essential for the operation of government at all levels. The U.S. Constitution gives Congress "Power to lay [i.e., impose] and collect Taxes, Duties, Imposts [a generic term for taxes, usually referring to schedules of customs duties] and Excises [the term loosely applied to most taxes, including the sales tax, but excluding the income tax and the property tax]."[52]

For most employees, the personal income tax is collected from their employers, who are required to withhold proper amounts from wages or salaries earned. All wage earners are reminded of this each payday when they compare the difference between their "gross" and "net" earnings. The difference is a wide range of federal and state income taxes. Through the process of withholding income taxes, compliance and payment are comparatively simple and assured. Otherwise, at year's end taxpayers may find that they do not have enough money on hand to pay their taxes. But for persons with incomes from various investments, and for business firms, the income tax has evolved into a monstrous maze of confusing regulations. Professional certified public accountants and tax lawyers often disagree as to the proper interpretation of many clauses. Huge national CPA (certified public accountant) firms employ both accountants and tax lawyers to offer their customers full tax services. Less wealthy individuals obtain assistance in preparing their returns from tax-preparer businesses available in most cities in the United States. Computer programs also enable many people to prepare their own tax returns without professional assistance, and some may file (submit) them electronically.

The income tax on individuals and corporations has become the most important single source of revenue for the federal government. It is also imposed by most states and by some local governments. Economists justify it as the most equitable, or progressive, of taxes, especially when rates are graduated, because the levy is imposed in accordance with apparent ability to pay.

In contrast, the sales tax is regressive in that it imposes a disproportionately heavy burden on persons with *low* incomes. For example, the sales tax on an automobile is the same regardless of the purchaser's income. This sum may represent a substantial percentage of one person's disposable income yet hardly be noticed by another, more wealthy individual.

It also should be noted that the ability to pay taxes is not necessarily related to income. Wealth and annual income are not the same thing. For example, large land holdings—although subject to real-property taxes—may produce no taxable income for their land-rich owners. Likewise, persons of great wealth may own tax-exempt bonds issued by the federal or state governments or other public agencies. However, the interest rate on such bonds is generally lower than rates paid by private corporate borrowers. So the owner of tax-free bonds indirectly helps to support the government. Moreover corporations that reinvest all earnings and pay no dividends (which are taxable income) may, gradually, grow in value and increase the wealth of their shareholders, who pay no income taxes until their shares are sold, if ever, and then at reduced tax (capital gains) rates.

Obviously there is much to be considered in understanding income taxation. From a constitutional standpoint, there is no right to equality of wealth. That the more wealthy citizens may acquire more luxuries in life, or even better legal services, than less wealthy persons is of no constitutional significance. For example, criminal defendants are constitutionally entitled to *competent* legal services, not the best available legal services nor any particular lawyer of choice.

Harriet and Jannel, together for the preceding 15 years, are committed to a lifetime interpersonal relationship. They are both employed and own a

Our Constitution   Chapter 2   63

home together. Are Harriet and Jannel entitled to the same federal tax benefits as couples who are married under state laws?

No. Federal and state governments provide special tax benefits to married couples that are not available to unmarried persons regardless of their gender or personal relationship. Equal protection requires only that all persons who are similarly situated be treated comparably; for example, all married persons must be treated similarly under the tax laws. All unmarried couples, whether of the same sex or not, also are treated similarly under the tax laws.

WHAT IS THE COMMERCE CLAUSE?

In Article I, Section 8, the Constitution expressly grants the federal government the power to "regulate Commerce with foreign Nations, and among the several States, and with the Indian Tribes." This power to "regulate commerce" allows the federal government to regulate most business activities in the United States with uniform rules.

Commerce includes the buying, selling, and transporting of things of value from place to place. The Supreme Court has held that Congress has the power to regulate any activity, interstate or intrastate, that "affects" interstate commerce. **Interstate** means any activity that crosses state boundaries. **Intrastate** means any activity that occurs entirely within a state's boundaries. Thus, Congress can pass laws that regulate intrastate commerce if, but only if, interstate commerce is affected.

A farmer grows wheat she intends to be eaten only by her family. Can the federal government regulate this intrastate commercial activity?

Yes. The Supreme Court has held that wheat production is subject to federal regulation even if it will never be sold and will be eaten entirely by the farmer's family. The Court reasoned that home use reduces the demand for wheat, which is a sufficient economic effect on interstate commerce.[53]

Each state has an interest in regulating local activities. As part of their inherent sovereignty (power to govern), states possess police powers to regulate private activities to protect or promote the public health, safety, or general welfare of their citizens. For example, states have a clear interest in keeping their local roads and highways safe. However, when a state regulates the use of its roads and highways, those laws will also affect interstate commerce. A law setting a top speed on a highway affects all drivers, including interstate truckers.

If the state law affects interstate commerce, the courts may be asked to balance the state's interests with those of the federal government. The question is, does a state's exercise of its police power interfere with the federal government's right to regulate interstate commerce? Recall that the Constitution provides that when state and federal law conflict, federal law is supreme. The courts try to answer this question by balancing the interests of the state with those of the federal government. The courts will consider several factors, including the following:

1. What interest is the state furthering by its law?
2. Does the state law burden (make more difficult) interstate commerce?
3. Is there another way the state could accomplish its purpose without burdening interstate commerce?

Suppose Georgia passes a law requiring use of "contoured" rear-fender mudguards on trucks and trailers operating on its highways. All other mudguards are declared illegal. In 35 other states, such as the neighboring state of Florida, "straight" mudguards are either legal or required. There is evidence suggesting that contoured mudguards are safer than straight mudguards. Is the Georgia statute constitutional?

No. Truckers traveling through Georgia would have a problem. What is legal in Georgia is illegal in other states, including Florida, and vice versa. Clearly, the Georgia law would affect interstate commerce. Even though Georgia's purpose in passing the statute was to increase safety on the highways, a possible increase in safety would not justify requiring truckers to either avoid Georgia or change their mudguards before they pass through.

Kristina Shaman, a resident of Boca Raton, Florida, placed an order via the Internet with Leeward Winery in California for the delivery by mail of a case of chardonnay wine. A Florida statute provides that shipping alcoholic beverages into the state is a felony punishable by fine and jail. Can Florida constitutionally prohibit the U.S. Postal Service or a private carrier, such as United Parcel Service, from shipping alcohol interstate?

At first blush, it may seem odd that a state that many consider the gateway to drug trafficking would prohibit mail-order wine sales. However, Florida and many other states have recently adopted such prohibitory laws.[54] These state statutes tend to push up the prices and availability of rare wines and obscure brews, thereby affecting interstate commerce. However, these laws also protect the "dry" counties in many states where all alcoholic sales are prohibited, and also inhibit sales of alcohol to minors. The probability is that the laws, if tested, would be upheld as a permissible burden on interstate commerce. Note that the U.S. Postal Service would be immune from any state penalty under the doctrine of supremacy: only the shipper and possibly the purchaser could be held responsible.

WHAT IS THE BILL OF RIGHTS?

For reference information regarding the U.S. Constitution, and international law as well, see http://www.uni-wuerzburg.de/law

Bill of Rights is the all-inclusive title popularly given to the first ten amendments to the U.S. Constitution. The Bill of Rights mandates specific and general restraints on the national government to protect all persons from arbitrary and capricious acts by federal officials. Thus, the Bill of Rights originally applied only as a restraint on the national government. States were bound only by provisions on civil rights if and as specified in their own state constitutions.[55]

Following the Civil War, several amendments were added to the U.S. Constitution to protect and assist the newly freed slaves. In 1865 the Thirteenth Amendment formally outlawed slavery.[56] Previously, most African Americans had been denied liberty despite the contrary words of the Declaration of Independence* and despite the mandate of the Fifth Amendment that "no person shall be deprived of life, liberty, or property without due process of law."[57] Three years later, in 1868, the Fourteenth Amendment reiterated the right of all persons to liberty and extended the scope of its protection by binding all state and local governments with these words:

> *No state shall make or enforce any law which shall abridge the privileges or immunities of citizens of the United States; nor shall any state deprive any person of life, liberty, or property, without* due process *of law, nor deny to any person within its jurisdiction the* equal protection *of the laws."[58] [Emphasis added]*

The clauses guaranteeing due process of law and equal protection of the law were not defined at the time of the Fourteenth Amendment, leaving the work of definition and specific application to the judicial branch. The due process and equal protection clauses have been used by the Supreme Court to restrict the constitutionally reserved powers of the states.

Simply stated, the Supreme Court defines **due process** as the equivalent of fundamental fairness and **equal protection** as the prevention of invidious discrimination (i.e., differentiating offensively or unfairly). Thus, states cannot violate the due process or equal protection guaranteed to the people, regardless of what is contained in their respective constitutions. But the application of those terms to specific examples of state action was to evolve through Supreme Court decisions through an interpretive process referred to as *incorporation*.

INCORPORATION DOCTRINE

In its trailblazing decision in *Gitlow v. New York* in 1925, the U.S. Supreme Court announced, "[W]e may and do assume that freedom of speech and of press—First Amendment protections—are among the fundamental personal rights and 'liberties' protected by the due process clause of the Fourteenth Amendment from impairment by the States."[59]

With the *Gitlow* decision, the Supreme Court began a policy it has maintained ever since. As selected cases reach it, the Court has systematically imposed on the states most of the guarantees found in the Bill of Rights. Its ongoing impact is to bind both the national and state governments to the same standard of compliance regarding due process and equal protection.

THE FIRST AMENDMENT—AND FREE SPEECH

The First Amendment contains what is known historically as *primary rights*. It is no accident that this Amendment begins with the phrase, "Congress shall make

---

*"We hold these Truths to be self evident, that all Men are created equal, that they are endowed by their Creator with certain unalienable Rights, that among these are Life, Liberty, and the Pursuit of Happiness."

no law. . . ." Nor is it accidental that first among our primary rights is freedom of speech and press. They are "the matrix, the indispensable condition, of nearly every other form of freedom."[60] As Justice Hugo Black remarked, "Freedom to speak and write about public questions is as important to the life of our government as is the heart to the human body. . . . If that heart be weakened, the result is debilitation; if it be stilled, the result is death."[61] Accordingly, the Supreme Court has decided incrementally, one case after another, that the states must also guarantee to their citizens First Amendment rights of freedom of speech and press.[62]

The Court, however, has been unable to define free speech with precision. It has moved successively through certain legal expedients or "tests":

1. The "clear and present danger" test under which speech could be regulated by government was explained in *Schenck*.[63]

2. The "bad tendency" test was exemplified in *Abrams*. Here the Court accorded little importance to the guarantee of free speech, focusing almost solely on the impact of the challenged speech on the war (World War One) effort.[64]

3. The "preferred position" test was articulated in Justice Harlan Stone's famous footnote in the *Carolene Products* case. Stone presented the view that free speech enjoyed a preferred position in relation to other constitutional guarantees, calling for a more precise and searching scrutiny of legislation that might curtail "political processes."[65]

4. During the Cold War of the late 1940s and the 1950s, the Supreme Court upheld the conviction of 11 leaders of the American Communist Party by enforcing the Smith Act of 1940, which made it a crime to teach or advocate the overthrow of government by force. In doing so, the Court adopted the "probability" statement of the "clear and present danger" rule, as expressed by the highly respected Chief Judge Learned Hand, writing for the lower court majority: "In each case [courts] must ask whether the gravity of the 'evil,' discounted by its improbability, justifies such invasion of free speech as is necessary to avoid the danger."[66]

5. Political dissent during the late 1960s and early 1970s found the Court using the "ad hoc balancing" test. Using the "clear and present danger" test, the Court weighed the competing interests of free speech and law and order. Every ordinance attempting to serve the interests of the state must be drawn with "reasonable specificity toward the [speech] and conduct prohibited."[67]

Paladin Press published a book *Hit Man: A Technical Manual for Independent Contractors*, which provided instructions for would-be contract murderers. Lawrence Horn hired James Perry, a contract killer, to murder his ex-wife and their brain-damaged son, after which Horn expected to inherit a $2 million trust fund intended for the boy. Perry, using principles studied in the Paladin murder text, suffocated the boy and shot the ex-wife and an overnight nurse to their deaths. A sister of the ex-wife sued Paladin Press in a civil case for damages for aiding and abetting the murderer. Is the publication of an instructional book for murder protected by the First Amendment from a civil lawsuit?[68]

glossary

No. The Constitution does not shield from civil lawsuits bomb-making guides, assassination manuals, or similar works that exhort people to take the law into their own hands. Nor does the Constitution prevent the publication of libelous (untruthful) material and any subsequent civil lawsuits that may follow. The **prior restraint** of speech that is offensive for any reason is a judicial power that is exercised only in the most extraordinary circumstances.

The Court has been careful to protect expressive activity and symbolic speech,[69] and it has ruled that burning of the national flag of the United States, as political speech, can be restricted neither by the states nor by the Congress.[70]

IS COMMERCIAL SPEECH PROTECTED?

Commercial speech, which is defined as any communication that advertises a product or service for a business purpose to earn a profit, is also protected, but not as comprehensively as other speech.

Current issues of free speech are maintained at: http://www.freedomforum.org/speech/

San Diego enacted an ordinance that prohibited commercial outdoor advertising signs within the city limits. Sign owners sued the city for injunctive relief, claiming that the law violated their rights under the First Amendment. Does the ordinance violate the Constitution?

Yes. Speaking for the Court, Justice Byron B. White stated:

Prior to 1975, purely commercial advertisements of services or goods for sale was considered to be outside the protection of the First Amendment. . . . [But] in Virginia Pharmacy Board v. Virginia Citizens Consumer Council, *425 U.S. 748 (1976), we plainly held that speech proposing no more than commercial transaction enjoys a substantial degree of First Amendment protection. A State may not completely suppress the dissemination of truthful information about an entirely lawful activity merely because it is fearful of that information's effect upon its disseminators and its recipients. . . .*[71]

U.S. Beverage Co., produces Phat Boy, an inexpensive malt liquor that is sold in bigger bottles with a higher alcohol content than competing beers. It also sports a funky red, black, and yellow label and contains ginseng which some consider an aphrodisiac. ("Phat" is a 90s version of the word "cool.") A public interest group contends that Phat Boy is targeted to underage African Americans, much like cigarette ads featuring Joe Camel allegedly target teenagers. Does the Constitution protect focused commercial advertising?[72]

Yes, but to a lesser extent than other forms of speech. When alcohol is involved in any commercial activity, the states have an additional interest in protecting the public from harm. However, the North Carolina Alcoholic Beverage Commission received no complaints from the public, and the product was widely promoted and sold, not targeted in specific neighborhoods.

Is Symbolic Speech Protected? Even "Hate Speech"?

Although originally expressed as protection for spoken, written, or printed words, the First Amendment has been appropriately construed by the Court to embrace many forms of the communication of ideas.

Motion pictures, television programs, electronic tapes and disks, and fax transmissions have taken their place alongside the formerly dominant person-to-person speech and printed statements. In Des Moines, Iowa, the U.S. Supreme Court upheld the right of students to wear black armbands in school to show their opposition to the Vietnam War. The conduct was "a symbolic act that is within the Free Speech Clause . . . [and] was entirely divorced from actually or potentially disruptive conduct" that would interfere with appropriate discipline in the operation of the school.[73] As noted earlier, the symbolic act of burning an American flag is likewise protected under the First Amendment.

As indicated by these cases, the U.S. Supreme Court zealously erects ramparts around the cherished First Amendment freedoms to communicate.

Stanford University, a private institution, adopted a code stating that "one student cannot with purpose vilify another with fighting words that are ugly gutter epithets like 'nigger' and 'kike.'" The code also banned such hate-associated symbols as the swastika. Can a private university proscribe undesirable speech?

No. Stanford students challenged the code in state court where a judge promptly declared it unconstitutional.[74]

Again, in the recent past (1992), the U.S. Supreme Court unanimously condemned a St. Paul, Minnesota, ordinance that outlawed any hate-motivated expression (e.g., burning crosses, displaying swastikas) that "one knows or has reasonable grounds to know arouses anger, alarm, or resentment in others on the basis of race, color, creed, religion or gender."[75] In the **hate speech** case in question, a 17-year-old skinhead (i.e., an antisocial or delinquent youth who wears his hair closely cropped) was arrested after setting fire to a crude cross in the yard of a black family who had recently settled in a predominantly white neighborhood. Justice Antonin Scalia noted that such conduct "is reprehensible. . . . But St. Paul has sufficient means at its disposal to prevent such behavior without adding the First Amendment to the fire."[76] Note, however, that in the following year the Court unanimously upheld a Wisconsin statute that imposes harsher penalties on a criminal who "intentionally selects the person against whom the crime . . . is committed . . . because of the race, religion, color, disability, sexual orientation, national origin or ancestry of that person."[77] Most states now have similar "hate crime" penalty-enhancement laws.

In other cases, the Court has withheld the protective shield of the First Amendment from "fighting words," meaning words "which by their very utterance inflict injury or tend to incite an immediate breach of the peace" and conduct that is "directed to inciting or producing imminent lawless action and is likely to incite or produce such action."[78]

Reference in the Wisconsin statute to "sexual orientation" exemplifies increasing concern of legislative bodies and courts with the civil rights of homosexual persons, male and female. No doubt many homosexual persons have served with honor and distinction in military uniforms. In 1993 the Clinton administration took steps to permit them to openly disclose their sexual orientation. Opposition from top military commanders and others resulted in adoption of a compromise policy that is reflected in the advice, "Don't ask; don't tell; don't pursue."

Timothy McVeigh sent an e-mail with return address of "Boysrch," which prompted an investigation by the U.S. Navy. America Online revealed McVeigh's identity in violation of a federal privacy law. The Navy began proceedings to discharge McVeigh without benefits. Has the Navy violated the "Don't ask; don't tell; don't pursue" policy?

Yes. A federal judge ruled that the Navy's investigation into McVeigh's sexual orientation was a violation of the policy. McVeigh retired with full benefits and money damages from America Online.[79]

It is noteworthy that the members of the military are controlled by the Uniform Code of Military Justice, which closely prescribes conduct within the military services. Serious issues regarding the discharge of homosexual persons from the service, of women in combat roles, and of immoral sexual behavior continue to plague the military branches.*

Certain artists and their publishers have produced paintings, photographs, magazines, books, songs, videotapes, and compact discs that allegedly violate traditional and appropriate standards of morality and decency. Probably most people are not offended because they are not within the targeted markets for most of this bizarre art. However, programs on free television and cable television now enter most homes. Increasing numbers of viewers, both old and young, find excessive violence and perceived obscenity intolerable and are demanding government imposition of restraints or standards. But the practical difficulty of imposing effective controls is readily apparent from a reading of the 1973 case of *Miller v. California*, in which the U.S. Supreme Court decreed that to be legally condemned as obscene, the material must be such that

1. the average person,

2. applying contemporary community standards,

3. would find that the work taken as a whole appeals to the prurient (i.e., characterized by lustful thoughts) interest, and

4. the work depicts or describes in a patently offensive way sexual conduct proscribed by state law,

5. and whether—taken as a whole—it is lacking in serious artistic, political or scientific value.[80]

---

*The President is the "Commander in Chief of the United States. . . ." U.S. Constitution, Article II, Section 2. However, the President is not subject to the Uniform Code of Military Justice that applies to the military and prohibits, among other things, immoral sexual activity such as adultery.

The inherently subjective nature of the listed criteria, coupled with potentially thousands of different problems or cases, every one of which is unique in at least some respect, makes any comprehensive policing effort predestined to fail, except in the most egregious cases.

What is known is that nearly nude dancing by females (wearing "pasties" and "G-strings") is not inherently obscene and may be expressive conduct protected by the First and Fourteenth Amendments.[81] Essentially the determination of specifically what is obscene and, therefore, may be prohibited by state or local government is made by juries on a case-by-case basis.

Symbolic speech may also sometimes be deemed offensive because of historical implications related to race, religion, or other constitutionally protected classifications.

The mascot of Birmingham High School is an American Indian with a headdress that is based on Chief Pontiac, an Ottawa Indian who was an organizer of tribes against the invading English during the 1700s. The City of Pontiac, Michigan, is named after this Chief. The high school's team name is the "Braves." In response to demands of American Indian activists, the local board of education chose to change the mascots of four high schools, including the "Mohicans" and the "Warriors." Removing the "Braves" logo from the Birmingham High School gym floor and track and purchasing new gym clothes and uniforms will cost $240,000. The activists argued that portrayal of an American Indian with a headdress is sacrilegious.[82] Does the Constitution protect the use of insulting or sacrilegious speech?

Yes. However, there may be other reasons why a public school chooses to avoid offensive language or symbols. Even if offensive speech is protected from censorship by the Constitution, that does not mean it should be employed.

FREE SPEECH AND THE INTERNET

The Internet began in 1969 as an international network of computers among the military, defense contractors, and universities conducting defense-related research. Redundant connections were established to preserve communications even if some portions of the network were damaged in a war. Today, civilian networks link with one another, allowing tens of millions of people to communicate and access vast amounts of information from around the world. The Internet is a unique and wholly new medium of worldwide human communication the use of which will pose new challenges to our Constitution and legal system.

Solutions to new problems, especially involving government regulation of speech, will relate in part to the mechanics of the Internet. The number of "host" computers—those that store information and relay communications—increased from about 300 in 1981 to more than 10 million today. It is expected that at the beginning of the new millennium more than 200 million people will be using the Internet. These people can obtain access from many different sources. Most colleges and universities provide access for their students and faculty; many corporations provide their employees with access through an office network; many communities and local libraries provide free access; and computer coffee shops provide access for a small hourly fee.

Several major national "online services" such as America Online, CompuServe, the Microsoft Network, and Prodigy offer access to their own extensive proprietary networks as well as connections, called "links," to the much larger resources of the Internet. Anyone with access may send and receive electronic mail ("e-mail"), obtain automatic mailing list services ("mail exploders" or "listservs"), and participate in "newsgroups," "chat rooms," and the "World Wide Web." All of these communication and information retrieval methods can be used to transmit text; most can transmit sound, pictures, and moving video images. Taken together these tools are known as *Cyberspace*—located in no particular geographical location but available anywhere in the world to anyone with access to the Internet. The content on the Internet is as diverse as human thought.

The most significant category of communication over the Internet is the World Wide Web, which allows users to search for and retrieve information stored in remote computers, and sometimes to communicate back. The Web consists of a vast number of documents stored in computers all over the world. Some are files; others are more elaborate "Web pages" that contain "links" to other documents created by that site's author or to other related sites. To access a Web site, users simply type a known address into their computers or enter keywords into a commercial "search engine" in an effort to locate desired addresses. A particular Web page may contain the information sought by the "surfer" or, through its links, provide an avenue to other documents located anywhere in the world on the Internet. Access to most Web pages is free, although many allow access only to those who have purchased the right from a commercial provider. In this manner, any person can become a global publisher of information. No single organization controls membership in the Web, nor is there any centralized point from which individual Web sites or services can be blocked or regulated by government.

Sexually explicit material on the Internet includes text, pictures, and chat that range from the modestly titillating to the completely explicit. But users seldom encounter such content accidentally. Almost all sexually explicit images are preceded by warnings as to the content. And accessing a specific Web site requires affirmative steps more sophisticated than simply surfing a television set. Nonetheless, in 1996 Congress adopted the Telecommunications Act that attempted to prohibit the knowing transmission of obscene or indecent messages to any recipient under 18 years of age. The Supreme Court held that law to be an unconstitutional infringement of free speech guaranteed by the U.S. Constitution.[83] However, improper use of the Internet by individuals can result in civil or criminal penalties, such as by publication of libelous material (civil) or by conspiring to commit criminal offenses. Free speech does not equate to freedom from personal responsibility to comply with laws enacted under the police powers of the states.

THE FIRST AMENDMENT— AND FREEDOM OF RELIGION

Religious pluralism is a hallmark of American life, together with our commitment to religious freedom. In many parts of the world, governments maintain "official" religions and official religions maintain governments. In the United States, a wall has been erected between church and state; any significant breach of that wall by either government or church, no matter how compelling, is generally suspect. Yet attempts to promote or dissuade certain religions are made from time to time in spite of the Constitution's declaration that "Congress shall make no law respecting an establishment of religion, or prohibiting the free exercise thereof." What should be the government's position respecting religion? The Supreme Court has answered. The First Amendment (on religion) means this:

> *Neither a state nor the federal government can set up a church. Neither can pass laws, which aid one religion, aid all religions, or prefer one religion to another. Neither can force nor influence a person to go to or to remain away from church against his will or force him to profess a belief or disbelief in any religion. No person can be punished for entertaining or professing religious beliefs or disbeliefs, for church attendance or nonattendance. No tax in any amount, large or small, can be levied to support any religious activities or institutions, whatever they may be called, or whatever form they may adopt to teach or practice religion. Neither a state nor the federal government can, openly or secretly, participate in the affairs of any religious organizations or groups and vice versa . . . the [religious] clause was intended to erect "a wall of separation between church and state."[84]*

Accordingly, the Supreme Court has declared unconstitutional state attempts to promote "religious values" in public schools. In 1962, in a controversial decision (*Engel v. Vitale*),[85] the Court outlawed the recitation of a nonsectarian prayer in the public schools of New York State. The prayer was to be said aloud in class in the presence of a teacher at the beginning of every school day.* Speaking for the Court, Justice Hugo L. Black pointed out that the prayer violated the establishment clause of the First Amendment:

> *Its first and most immediate purpose [referring to the clause] rested on the belief that a union of government and religion tends to destroy government and to degrade religions . . . [G]overnmentally established religions and religious persecution go hand in hand. . . . It was in large part to get completely away from this sort of systematic religious persecution that the Founders brought into being our Nation, our Constitution and our Bill of Rights.[86]*

The Court has more recently said that even a one-minute period of silence for "meditation or voluntary prayer" is constitutionally impermissible.[87]

In 1984 Congress passed the Equal Access Act, making it unlawful for any public high school receiving federal assistance (funds) to prevent student groups from using school facilities for religious activities. If other student-initiated gatherings were permitted to meet at a high school, then there could be no denial of on-campus meetings for student-initiated religious activities. The Supreme Court had already declared constitutional student-initiated religious worship at state universities and colleges.[88]

Other activities involving religion are permissible in public schools. These include:

1. Silent prayer before tests so long as other students are not persuaded to participate.

---

*Prayer prescribed by New York Board of Regents; "Almighty God, we acknowledge our dependence upon Thee, and we beg Thy blessings upon us, our parents, our teachers and our country."

2. The teaching of the history of religion as distinguished from teaching religion.

3. The expression by students of their religious beliefs in the form of reports that are germane to their assignments.

4. Participation in religious clubs and the wearing of religious garb.[89]

COULD GUNS BE BANNED?

According to the Second Amendment:

A well regulated Militia, being necessary to the security of a free State, the right of the people to keep and bear Arms, shall not be infringed.[90]

When this amendment was penned, the common practice of states was to have large standing armies. There was a strong public sentiment that a large permanent army should not be part of the national government. Also, the amendment was designed to prevent Congress from disarming and abolishing state militias.

The Supreme Court has sustained this sentiment: "The Second Amendment guarantees *no right* to keep and bear a firearm that does not have some reasonable relationship to the preservation or efficiency of a well-regulated militia."[91]

States as well as the federal government may regulate some or all privately owned firearms if they so choose. According to the Court:

There is under our decisions no reason why stiff laws governing the purchase and possession of pistols may not be enacted. There is no reason why pistols may not be barred from anyone with a police record. There is no reason why a state may not require a purchaser of a pistol to pass a psychiatric test. There is no reason why all pistols should not be barred to everyone except the police.[92]

Different perspectives on the handgun control debate can be found at http://www.nra.org/ and http://www.cphv.org/

FREEDOM FROM UNREASONABLE SEARCHES

The Fourth Amendment recognizes "The right of the people to be secure in their persons, houses, papers, and effects against unreasonable searches and seizures."[93] But note that *reasonable* searches and seizures are permitted. Consequently, search warrants may be issued "upon probable cause, supported by Oath or affirmation, and particularly describing the place to be searched, and the persons or things to be seized."[94]

In two cases, *Wolf v. Colorado*[95] (1949) and *Mapp v. Ohio*[96] (1961), the Supreme Court imposed on the states the same standards of care in search and seizure procedures and the exclusion of evidence illegally obtained as that imposed by the Constitution on the national government. The Court said that citizens have a "right to privacy" and to be "free from unreasonable state intrusions. . . . We hold that all evidence obtained by search and seizures in violation of the Constitution is, by the same authority, inadmissible in a state Court."[97] This is known as the **exclusionary rule**, which is discussed more fully in Chapter 6.

SOBRIETY CHECKPOINT—A LEGAL GROUP SEARCH?

An interesting dichotomy exists between federal and state law in the matter of **sobriety checkpoints** established along highways, without prior notice, to intercept persons driving under the influence of alcohol or other drugs. In a Michigan case, the U.S. Supreme Court held that sobriety checkpoints do not violate the federal Constitution and **remanded** (i.e., sent back) the case for determination under the Michigan state constitution.[98] The Michigan Supreme Court held that the state constitution affords greater privacy than does the federal Constitution, and concluded that sobriety checkpoints *do* violate the Michigan constitution. In contrast, for example, California, with more vehicles on its highways than any other state, intermittently makes effective use of such checkpoints. Most other states authorize sobriety checkpoints on highways and prosecute offenders.

Amitai Etzioni sounds a sober warning about sobriety checkpoints. They might be labeled "group searches," he says, or "the search and seizure of the innocents" because most persons subjected to them are perfectly innocent. Screening gates at airports delay and inconvenience millions of passengers in order to deter and hopefully to prevent access to a minuscule minority of travelers. Similar group searches for weapons are routinely tolerated in the nation's capitol building, many courthouses, and numerous schools in "tough neighborhoods." Stricter, more time-consuming and even embarrassing tests of blood and urine for possible presence of illegal drugs are used for persons in such critical target groups as locomotive engineers and air traffic controllers. Etzioni comments that "as long as these measures are carefully circumscribed, they seem a necessary, albeit disconcerting, adaptation to the conditions of our time."* He concludes that "the real danger is that if we do not find effective ways to restore public order, constitutional order will be seriously challenged."[99]

At Madison High School in Milwaukee, Wisconsin, the principal ordered a random search of student lockers while he conducted investigative interviews of students. A gun and a quantity of cocaine were found in student Isiah's locker. Did the search violate Isiah's rights under the Fourth Amendment?

No. The Wisconsin Supreme Court ruled that, under the facts of the case, the students had no reasonable expectation of privacy and so, for Fourth Amendment purposes, no improper search had taken place.[100]

RIGHTS OF ACCUSED TO DUE PROCESS OF LAW

Guarantees under the Constitution to have the assistance of a lawyer during police questioning, after one is taken into custody or otherwise deprived of freedom

---

*As the twenty-first century begins, cities in at least one state are expanding their use of the "search of the innocents." In Buena Park and Ontario, suburbs of Los Angeles, California, police stop every fifth car and check the driver for a valid license. If the driver's license is not valid, the vehicle is impounded on the spot. Police reason that unlicensed drivers usually do not have liability insurance, an assertion that is said to justify the searches. The state highway patrol has declined to perform such blanket searches on the basis they may violate the U.S. Constitution. Associated Press, 16 January 1999.

in any significant way, and to be protected against compelled testimony and self-incrimination, are basic rights mandated by the U.S. Supreme Court for compliance by all states.[101]

A police undercover agent was planted in a cell with prisoner Perkins, who had been jailed for aggravated assault. Perkins was also under investigation for murder. The undercover agent asked Perkins if he had ever killed anybody. In answering the question, Perkins made statements implicating himself in the murder. Is this testimony that was given voluntarily but unknowingly by Perkins to a police officer admissible as evidence despite the way it was obtained?

Yes. The Supreme Court held that an undercover officer posing as an inmate has no obligation to warn an incarcerated suspect of any constitutional rights before asking questions, even though the response could be legally incriminating.[102]

Through a series of decisions based on Section 1 of the Fourteenth Amendment, the Supreme Court has imposed an obligation on the states to honor the human rights identified in the Fifth and Sixth Amendments. Included is the right to a speedy[103] and public trial[104] by an unbiased jury,[105] assuredly among the most vital of rights in a free society. To further guarantee a fair trial, the Court in other cases also incorporated the right to have **compulsory process*** for obtaining witnesses for the defense of the accused person,[106] and to the assistance of professional legal counsel in all cases[107] and at all stages[108] of criminal procedures to which the defendant is subjected. An exception is made as to counsel in appellate proceedings (although, in fact, appellants are generally assisted by counsel who are paid by the state).

You will find the first right of an accused to trial by jury in the Magna Carta, which also reveals much about life in medieval England. http://www.cet.com/~theoaks/historic/magnacarta.html

Chicago adopted an anti-loitering ordinance intended to curb the "expanding cancer" of urban gangs. Under the ordinance, people loitering (standing) in a public place could be ordered to move along if a police officer believed one or more was a gang member. Those who refused to move along could be arrested and sent to jail for up to six months, fined $500, and ordered to perform three weeks of public service—even without proof of criminal intent. Does the ordinance as applied deprive defendants of due process of law?[109]

Concern about criminal activity by members of urban gangs has prompted many local boards and councils to adopt ordinances designed to protect their residents. The Chicago ordinance is but one example. Ordinarily a person cannot be convicted of a crime by mere association and without criminal intent. The Supreme Court is expected to elaborate upon the constitutional requirements of such gang-related ordinances before the turn of the century. Similar attempts to enforce curfews have met with the constitutional objection that local government cannot restrict the freedom of young people to move about. The difficulty is that the benefits of a curfew may not outweigh the loss of freedom for children and their parents.

---

*Compulsory process means the Court, at the request of a defendant in a criminal prosecution, must use its legal powers to compel the appearance of witnesses in favor of the defendant (U.S. Constitution, Sixth Amendment).

The rights of persons accused of a crime are more fully described in Chapter 6.

EQUAL PROTECTION OF THE LAW IN EDUCATION

The equal right to education is arguably the first key to providing an opportunity for every student to realize her or his potential. The second, as shown in Exhibit 2–1, would be employment, and the third would be housing. The three are interdependent in a circular pattern:

1. Equal access to high-quality *education* provides the knowledge and skills essential for suitable *employment*.
2. Suitable *employment* provides the income required for desirable *housing*.
3. Desirable *housing* is likely to be found in neighborhoods with elementary and secondary schools that provide high-quality *education*.

And then the cycle is repeated.

Of course, the drama unfolds over a period of two or more decades. To give disadvantaged minorities benefits of education that others have routinely enjoyed, the U.S. Supreme Court acted decisively in the *Brown v. Board of Education of Topeka* cases discussed shortly. Implementation, however, has been difficult and time-consuming. At this writing, almost 40 years later, despite much progress, the education problem remains, exacerbated by "white flight" to the suburbs. When they married, many children of older residents in large cities found more desirable housing at affordable prices in new suburban subdivisions, readily accessible by private automobiles on new superhighways. This pattern accelerated the decline of the aging city neighborhoods, which now attracted lower-income

Exhibit 2–1:   Three Keys to Opportunity

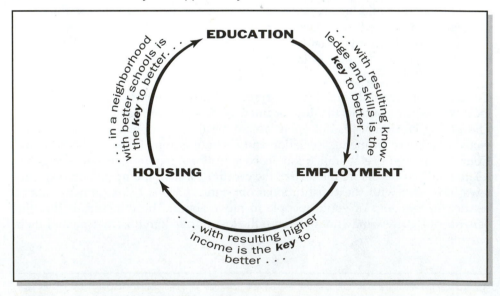

families, often minorities. Thus, the minority literally became the majority in the inner cities of a large number of metropolitan areas. Government attempts to integrate white and African American students in elementary and secondary schools were resented by many whites (and also by some African Americans), and in large measure were effectively frustrated by the migration to the suburbs.

The nationalization of equal opportunity continues to be a major priority of our legislatures and courts. Nowhere is this commitment by the federal government more evident than in the field of education at all levels. In 1954 a unanimous U.S. Supreme Court decreed that separation of the races in schools violated the right to *equal protection of the laws* guaranteed by the Fourteenth Amendment. Chief Justice Earl Warren declared that "segregation of children in public schools solely on the basis of race, even though the physical facilities and other 'tangible' factors may be equal, deprives the children of the minority group of equal educational opportunities. . . . To separate them from others of similar age and qualifications solely because of their race generates a feeling of inferiority as to their status in the community that may affect their hearts and minds in a way unlikely ever to be undone."[110] A year later, the Court ordered all public school districts to desegregate "with all deliberate speed."[111]

In 1976 the Court extended the principles of the *Brown* cases to private schools. It held that federal civil rights laws prohibited private nonsectarian schools from refusing to admit prospective students because they were black.[112]

Congress passed the Civil Rights Act of 1964, which is divided into subject matter sections called "titles." Title VI requires that all federal funds must be withdrawn from any school, college, or university that is guilty of discrimination on the "grounds of race, color, or national origin in any program or activity receiving federal financial assistance." (Gender, disability, age, Vietnam-veteran status, and disability of veterans were later added to the list.)

Christian National College (CNC), a private, coeducational liberal arts institution, declined all state or federal financial assistance in order to preserve its autonomy. However, many of its students received Basic Educational Opportunity Grants (BEOGs) from the U.S. Department of Education. The department required every participating institution to file a report certifying that no sex discrimination existed on its campus. Christian National refused to file the report and brought suit to prevent the department from cancelling all BEOGs.

What was the result?

CNC loses. The Court noted that failure to file a statement assuring an absence of gender-based discrimination is evidence of an intent to discriminate in violation of the law.[113] In similar cases involving tax-exempt organizations, such as religious schools, a failure to comply with legal orders to eliminate discrimination has resulted in action by the Internal Revenue Service (IRS) threatening to remove the tax-exempt status.[114]

Bob Jones University is a private learning institution whose founding principles include a specific religious belief. BJU receives no government assistance but the IRS denied its tax-exempt status because of its policy prohibiting interracial association and intermarriage. Can the IRS cause a private, religious university to pay income taxes (by denial of exempt status) while other religious organizations are exempt?

Yes. Even though all races can enroll, discrimination by racial affiliation (e.g., ban on intermarriage) is against public policy. The state has a compelling interest in banning racial discrimination in any form. The intent of the tax law is that entitlement to tax exemption depends on meeting "certain common-law standards of charity—namely that an institution seeking tax-exempt status must serve a public purpose and not be contrary to established public policy," which could not be satisfied by less restrictive means.[115] Loss of tax-exempt status could cause the closure of many otherwise worthwhile organizations.

Segregation in public schools that exists because of socioeconomic factors does not, in itself, violate the Constitution. For example, in one case the Court ordered removal of a court order that required busing of students to achieve integration goals in Oklahoma City—if as much had been accomplished as was practical.[116] But schools must adopt policies that remove the effects of past discrimination. Race neutral policies are not enough.[117] Otherwise the courts will intervene.

AFFIRMATIVE ACTION IN EDUCATION

African Americans in particular have been victims of discrimination in education, employment, and housing. **Affirmative action** is a process to eliminate continued discrimination (e.g., based on arbitrary classifications, such as race or sex) through the conscious adoption and implementation of policies favoring minorities in university admissions, public employment, and housing. Proponents argue that preferences are essential to erase the effects of prior and long-continued discrimination. Opponents argue that preferences themselves are an invidious form of discrimination—the claim is essentially that two wrongs do not make a right. There are other more sophisticated arguments concerning the possible indirect and psychological effects of preferential treatment.

Critics of racial preferences in education claim that what began as reasoned argument to overcome past discriminatory practices soon emerged as a series of numerical goals, quotas, and timetables created to bring African Americans, Asian Americans, Hispanic Americans, and Native Americans into the nation's colleges and universities. While there is much opposition to the way it is being done, there is no question that affirmative action is alive and well throughout the country.[118] But is it constitutional?

The Medical School of the University of California, Davis (UCD) set aside 16 class admissions for minority applicants. Allan Bakke, a white male and a top undergraduate student at the University of Minnesota and Stanford University, applied for admission to the UCD Medical School and was rejected twice. On both occasions, minority students with lower admission test scores, lower grade-point averages, and less impressive interviews were nonetheless admitted.

Bakke sued the university claiming he had been rejected because of his race, in violation of the Fourteenth Amendment and of Title VI of the Civil Rights Act of 1964. The trial court and the California Supreme Court found that UCD's admission plan did indeed violate the constitutional requirement of equal protection under the law. The U.S. Supreme Court accepted the case. How should it rule?

The U.S. Supreme Court found for Bakke* and declared the UCD admissions plan unconstitutional, thus affirming the decision of the California Supreme Court. The Court also held—with five votes and five different rationales—that ethnic diversity among medical students is an appropriate goal and therefore race can be one of the factors considered when students apply for admission.[119]

There have been no decisions by the Court to clarify this language. In fact, United States Supreme Court Justice Byron White said recently: "Agreement upon a means for applying the Equal Protection Clause to an affirmative action program has eluded this Court every time the issue has come before us."[120]

As noted earlier in this chapter, California eliminated all affirmative action policies through the initiative process (direct vote of the people). While the U.S. Supreme Court has authorized race-conscious admissions policies, California has chosen to achieve racial balance through other practices, such as improved outreach programs to fully qualified students. Other states have variations of processes in admissions and employment to achieve racial equality.

RIGHT TO PRIVACY

The right to privacy is the right to be left alone by other persons and by government. It is generally recognized as an essential component of personal dignity, peace of mind, and independence. Nevertheless, a right to privacy has not always been implicitly recognized and respected as a constitutionally protected right. There is no reference to privacy, as such, in the Constitution or the Bill of Rights. Indeed, it was not until 1965 that the U.S. Supreme Court recognized "the new constitutional right of privacy," in the words of Justice William O. Douglas. In the case of *Griswold v. Connecticut*, the Court held invalid a Connecticut statute that made it a criminal offense for married persons to use any drug or instrument to prevent conception. The Court held that the statute violated the First, Third, Fourth, Fifth, and Ninth Amendments, plus the equal-protection clause of the Fourteenth.[121]

The nation's highest court subsequently has used the declared and implicit right of privacy to affirm (1) the right of unmarried persons to have access to contraceptives, (2) the right of persons of different races to intermarry (also protected by the due-process and equal-protection clauses of the Fourteenth Amendment),

---

*Allan Bakke was finally admitted to UCD, received his medical degree, and continues the practice of his profession in Minnesota. In 1996 Senator Edward Kennedy declared to a Senate committee: "Dr. (Patrick) Chavis is a perfect example (of the positive results of affirmative action). He is the supposedly less qualified African-American student who allegedly displaced Allan Bakke . . . and triggered the landmark case. Today, Dr. Chavis is a successful ob-gyn in central Los Angeles, serving a disadvantaged community and making a difference in the lives of scores of poor families." Writing in *The Nation*, California State Senator Tom Hayden noted that while Allan Bakke became an anesthesiologist in Minnesota, Chavis was "providing primary care to poor women" in a mostly black community. "Bakke's scores were higher," Hayden admitted "but who made the most of his medical school education?" In 1996 Chavis' medical license was suspended by the California Medical Board for gross negligence and incompetence in the liposuction treatment of three women—one of whom died as a result. Jeff Jacoby, *Boston Globe*, "How Affirmative Action Can Be Fatal," (*New York Times* Service, 20 August 1997)

(3) the right of a woman to have an abortion under certain conditions, and (4) the right to possess obscene materials in one's home.[122]

Ohio passed a law making it a crime to possess obscene materials that depict minors having sex in any form or manner. Osborne was arrested for having photographs of children having sex. Does Osborne have a constitutional right of privacy to possess this particular matter in his home?

No. Osborne does have a right of privacy that shields him from accusations of possessing obscenity of all kinds except those involving children. The U.S. Supreme Court upheld the accused's conviction.[123]

The Court has held that the right of privacy does not extend to "places of public accommodation" and therefore adults do not have a constitutional right to acquire pornographic materials in bookstores or theaters.[124]

In *Eisenstadt v. Baird*, the Supreme Court tacitly recognized the right of heterosexual activity between consenting adults.* Does this apply to homosexual adult males? No. Georgia's statute prohibiting homosexual acts between adult males was found to be constitutional, on the grounds that the Constitution does not contain "a fundamental right to engage in homosexual sodomy,"[125] even in one's own home. Left undecided was whether a statute prohibiting sodomy between heterosexuals—husband and wife—is also constitutional.

Do "coerced" polygraph tests administered by private employers violate the right to privacy? Yes, at least in California. In the largest settlement of its kind (an out-of-court settlement), the Federated Groups agreed to pay $12.1 million to job applicants forced to take polygraph ("lie detector") tests as a condition of employment.[126]

It should be noted that the reliability of lie detectors is sufficiently uncertain that they are not accepted as evidence in court over a defendant's objection. This factor of unreliability differentiates lie detector tests from others, such as blood, urine, or breathalyzer tests.

Certain U.S. companies desire to sell encryption (secret code) software internationally. The software encodes e-mail and files to protect them from prying eyes. A supercomputer would need 10,000 years to break the code of a file with "128-bit" encryption. The U.S. Commerce Department requires that such companies provide them with a key with which to decipher the code. Does the Constitution's Right of Privacy guarantee citizens and companies the right to make private and secret encoded communications?[127]

The specific issue presented may never arise because encryption software is generally available on the international market. The right of government to ban encryption software unless a key is provided involves balancing national security interests against those of privacy and free speech.

---

*The state could not prevent the distribution of contraceptives to college students, many of them unmarried. Sexual acts between consenting unmarried adults are still illegal in some states.

Congress long ago banned the manufacture, sale, advertisement, and use of devices intended to secretly listen to and record telephone and oral communications.[128] Yet today sophisticated electronic spy equipment is accessible in "spy shops" and from mail-order companies. A stranger can monitor conversations inside a bedroom from a mile away, or spouses can track the movements of each other in the family car. Employers can listen to the conversations of every employee on the job. Although laws prohibiting the sale of spying equipment are on the books, lax enforcement, rapid changes in technology, and lack of public complaint have distorted (lowered) the public's expectation of privacy. Government cannot make wiretaps or otherwise perform searches without a prior search warrant, as will be discussed further in Chapter 6. But the Constitution does not guarantee a right of privacy to its citizens in the sense that they are protected from the intrusiveness of one another. The Constitution restrains only government from unreasonable intrusiveness.

The Privacy Rights Clearing House offers consumers information on how to protect their personal privacy. http://www.privacyrights.org/

NEW EXERCISES OF STATE POLICE POWER

The 1980s saw the emergence of a number of hotly contested issues pitting individual rights against the police power of the state to protect the public. State constitutions can require more stringent protective laws than are required by the U.S. Constitution. However, no state constitution or law can relax standards established by federal law, because of the doctrine of supremacy.

Among these problems, none are more difficult to resolve than the issues surrounding the disease called AIDS—acquired immune deficiency syndrome. For example, should individuals be subject to a mandatory AIDS testing program, especially those who work in certain high-risk areas or with high-risk persons? The general answer is no.*

Nebraska requires state healthcare workers with the mentally retarded to submit to blood tests for AIDS. Is such a requirement an unreasonable search of a person's body?

Yes. The Nebraska statute is unconstitutional. The Supreme Court, without comment, upheld a lower court's decision that blood tests for AIDS did violate the Fourth Amendment.[129] For now, the Supreme Court seems content to accept the doctrine that AIDS testing must meet the same constitutional requirements of reasonableness as other warrantless search and seizure practices.

Critics of universal blood testing charge that the Fourth Amendment "right of the people to be secure in their persons, houses, papers and effects, against unreasonable searches and seizure" is violated by indiscriminate blood testing (i.e., taking blood from one's body is a "search"). However, the Supreme Court said it was not unconstitutional to take blood from a person without his or her permission if that person is believed to be driving under the influence of alcohol. (In this case, the person in question was convicted of drunk driving on the basis of the amount of alcohol in his blood.)[130]

---

*Mandatory AIDS testing, like mandatory drug testing, involves an invasion of one's privacy that the Fourth Amendment seeks to protect.

Another area of constitutional conflict is mandatory drug testing. The legal status of drug testing in the private sector varies from state to state. While the Supreme Court has ruled that certain government drug-testing plans are constitutional, some authorities believe that the states will have to make their own decisions about drug testing. As long as drug testing meets a "reasonableness" test as to safeguards, such as providing sufficient notice and keeping the test results secret, the business community apparently will be permitted to continue testing employees and job applicants.[131]

EXPANDING SCOPE OF CIVIL RIGHTS LEGISLATION

President Lyndon B. Johnson left office under the cloudy skies of the unpopular Vietnam War. However, a legacy he took pride in was his "Great Society" program, the crown jewel of which was the Civil Rights Act of 1964. This statute forbids employers, employment agencies, and unions from discriminating in hiring, paying, training, promoting, or discharging employees on the basis of race, color, religion, national origin, or sex. Later law added the category of advanced age (over 40). However, courts subsequently have ruled that older workers can be replaced with younger workers if the purpose of the company is to save money by paying newer, younger workers less.

In 1990 Congress enacted the Americans with Disabilities Act (ADA), which was designed to prohibit discrimination against employees and prospective employees who happen to have disabilities. Going much further, "the ADA aims to prohibit public- and private-sector bias against 43 million disabled Americans in the work place and market place, in transportation and in telecommunications."[132] The law applies to public accommodations and entities that "affect commerce," thus affecting literally hundreds of thousands of places and enterprises in restaurants, theaters, motels, retail stores, and so forth. Excluded are private clubs and religious organizations. The ADA is explained more fully in Chapter 13.

The Constitution is a truly dynamic instrument, a bulwark of our freedom and independence. But it will always need to be reconsidered in light of technological change and social evolution. It embodies the fundamental principles that govern our society. The world never has seen a more perfect example of constitutionalism than is found in the United States of America. It endures because it embodies long-established customs, beliefs, political doctrines, and shared values of our society. It is a stabilizing force, yet it is dynamic, continually being interpreted by our legal system, always changing, and managing important questions that face us from day to day.

For a wide variety of census data, see http://www.census.gov/

In reference to the following case, every ten years the federal government takes a census (in Rome, the act of counting the people). The census of 2000 will be used for apportioning U.S. congressional representation among the states—the more people in a state, the more representatives it receives of the total 435 available. The census also forms the basis by which states apportion legislative districts, and provides a wealth of additional information about the population used by governments and businesses for a wide variety of purposes.

CASES

U.S. Department of Commerce v. U.S. House of Representatives

U.S. Supreme Court, Case 98–404 (1999)
(official citations not available at time of writing)

The Constitution's Census Clause authorizes Congress to direct an "actual Enumeration" of the American public every 10 years to provide a basis for apportioning congressional representation among the states. Pursuant to this mandate, Congress has enacted the Census Act (13 United States Code, Section 1 et. seq.) delegating the task to the Census Bureau under the Secretary of Commerce. The Census Bureau plans to use statistical sampling in 2000 to address a chronic "undercounting" of some identifiable groups, including certain minorities, children, and renters. For the last few decades the Census Bureau has sent census forms to every household, asking residents to complete and return them. The Bureau follows up by sending persons, called "enumerators" to personally visit all households that do not respond by mail. Despite this comprehensive effort to reach every household, the Bureau has always failed to reach—and has thus failed to count—a portion of the population. This shortfall is called the census "undercount."

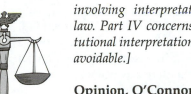

Under the statistical counting method, Indiana is expected to lose one representative to Congress. Furthermore, Indiana uses the federal census to draw districts for its legislative redistricting. Voters in some counties in Indiana will suffer "intra state dilution" vis-a-vis residents of counties with larger undercount rates, whose populations will surge through statistical sampling.

The Census Act, as amended in 1976, appears literally to authorize statistical sampling "except for the determination of population for purposes of [congressional] apportionment . . ." (Section 195).

[Parts I and II of the Court's opinion primarily concerned procedural law, i.e., the jurisdiction of the petitioners to bring the action. Part III concerned the substantive portion of the opinion involving interpretation of statutory law. Part IV concerns avoiding constitutional interpretation except when unavoidable.]

Opinion, O'Connor, J.:   An understanding of the historical background of the decennial census and the Act that governs it is essential to a proper interpretation of the Act's present text. From the very first census, the census of 1790, Congress has prohibited the use of statistical sampling in calculating the population for purposes of apportionment. . . . . The requirement that census enumerators visit each home in person appeared in statutes governing the next 14 censuses.

In 1976, the provisions of the Census Act at issue in this case took their present form. Congress revised Section 141(a) of the Census Act . . . . to authorize the Secretary to "take a decennial census of population as of the first day of April of such year, which date shall be known as the 'decennial census date' in such form and content as he may determine, including the use of sampling procedure and special surveys. 13 U.S.C. Section 141(a). . . . .

This broad grant of authority given in Section 141(a) is (modified) however, by the narrower and more specific Section 195, which is revealingly entitled, "Use of Sampling." The Section 141 authorization to use sampling techniques in the decennial census is not necessarily an authorization to use these techniques in collecting all of the information that is gathered during the decennial census. We look to the remainder of the law to determine what portions of the decennial census the authorization covers. When we do, we discover that . . . . Section 195 directly prohibits the use of sampling in the determination of population for purposes of apportionment. . . . .

As amended, the Section (195) now . . . . reads: "Except for the determination of population for purposes of apportionment of Representatives in Congress among the several States, the Secretary shall, if he considers it feasible, authorize the use of the statistical method known as 'sampling' in carrying out the provisions of this title." As amended, the section now requires the Secretary to use statistical sampling in assembling the myriad demographic data that are collected in connection with the decennial census. But the section maintains its prohibition on the use of statistical sampling in calculating population for purposes of apportionment. . . . .

In holding that the 1976 amendments (to Section 195) did not change the prohibition on the use of sampling in determining the population for apportionment purposes, we do not mean to suggest, as JUSTICE STEVENS claims in dissent, that the 1976 amendments had no purpose. . . . . Rather, the amendments served a very important purpose: They changed a provision that permitted the use of sampling for purposes other than apportionment into one that required that sampling be used for such purposes if "feasible." . . . .

JUSTICE BREYER'S interpretation of Section 195 is equally unpersuasive. JUSTICE BREYER agrees with the Court that the Census Act prohibits the use of sampling as a substitute for traditional enumeration methods. But he believes that this prohibition does not apply to the use of sampling as a "supplement" to traditional enumeration methods. This distinction is not borne out by the language of the statute.

O'Connor, J., delivered the majority opinion of the Court: With each part of the opinion attracting the vote of a different combination of justices.

With respect to:

- Parts I, III(A), and IV, Rehnquist, C.J., and Scalia, Kennedy, and Thomas joined.

- Part II, Rehnquist, C.J., and Scalia, Kennedy, Thomas, and Breyer joined,
- Part III(B) in which Rehnquist, C.J., and Kennedy joined.

There also was a concurring opinion: Scalia, J., filed an opinion concurring in part, in which Thomas joined, and in which Rehnquist, C.J., and Kennedy joined as to Part II.

JUSTICE STEVENS reasons from the purpose of the census clause: "The census is intended to serve the constitutional goal of equal representation. . . . That goal is best served by the use of a 'Manner' (of taking the census) that is most likely to be complete and accurate." . . . . That is true enough, and would prove the point if either (1) every estimate is more accurate than a headcount, or (2) Congress could be relied upon to permit only those estimates that are more accurate than headcounts. It is metaphysically certain that the first proposition is false, and morally certain that the second is (false). To give Congress the power, under the guise of regulating the "Manner" by which the census is taken, to select among various estimation techniques having credible (or even incredible) "expert" support, is to give the party controlling Congress the power to distort representation in its own favor. In other words, genuine enumeration may not be the most accurate way of determining population, but it may be the most accurate way of determining population with minimal possibility of partisan manipulation. The prospect of this Court's reviewing estimation techniques in the future, to determine which of them so obviously creates a distortion that it cannot be allowed, is not a happy one. (I foresee the new specialty of "Census Law.")

There also was a combination concurring and dissenting opinion: Breyer, J., filed an opinion concurring in part and dissenting in part. . . . .

The language of Section 195 permits a distinction between sampling used as a substitute and sampling used as a supplement. . . . . In answering the question whether this use of sampling remains a "supplement" because of its limited impact on the total headcount, I would give considerable weight to the views of the Secretary (Census Bureau).

There also were dissenting opinions: Ginsburg, J., filed a dissenting opinion in which Souter joined.

Stevens, J., filed a dissenting opinion, in which Souter and Ginsburg joined as to Parts I and II, and in which Breyer joined as to Parts II and III.

The Census Act . . . unambiguously authorizes the Secretary of Commerce to use sampling procedures when taking the decennial census. . . . . (It) contains two provisions that relate to sampling. The first (Section 141) is an unlimited authorization; the second (Section 195) is a limited mandate. . . . .

The limited mandate is contained in Section 195. That section commands the Secretary to use sampling, subject to two limitations: he need not do so when determining the population for apportionment purposes, and he need not do so unless he considers it feasible. The command reads as follows:

> *Except for the determination of population for purposes of apportionment of Representatives in Congress among the several States, the Secretary shall, if he considers it feasible, authorize the use of the statistical method known as 'sampling' in carrying out the provisions of this title.*

Although Section 195 does not command the Secretary to use sampling in the determination of population for apportionment purposes, neither does it prohibit such sampling. Not a word in Section 195 qualifies the unlimited grant of authority in Section 141.

FOR CRITICAL ANALYSIS

1. The census, taken by the "head count" and follow-up mailed questionnaire method, fails to produce totally accurate demographic data. Assuming *arguendo* that proposition is true, is the majority opinion putting form over substance? That is, which is more important, the substantive goal of equal representation or the procedure by which traditional representation is achieved?

2. You may have questions regarding the details of the statistical methods proposed by the Census Bureau. Although too lengthy to set forth here, they do appear in the full opinion of the Court which you may read at http://www.lib.umd.edu/ UMCP/GOV/supreme.html. Can you argue pro and con the issue whether or not Congress could be trusted to encourage statistical methods that would help it maintain its representative power structure?

3. The Court was presented with the choice of making its decision based upon the language of The Census Act, as amended, or by interpreting the Census Clause in the U.S. Constitution. Should the Supreme Court avoid interpreting the Constitution whenever possible? Or should it settle the matter once and for all by interpreting the Census Clause?

4. Is the potential for abuse in manipulating a statistical analysis an important, although unsaid, consideration in the majority view?

5. "Except for A, the Secretary shall perform B." Does this phrase mean the Secretary *may* perform A, but *shall* perform B? Or does it mean the Secretary *may not* perform A but *shall* perform B? As applied to the *Department of Commerce v. U.S. House*, can you articulate an argument supporting both interpretations? When interpreting the language of a statute, why shouldn't the Court ask the Congress to submit its interpretation of the statute at the time it was enacted?

6. Under this case, will the Census Bureau be permitted to use statistical

sampling to produce census figures that may be used for purposes such as allocations of federal funds to states, or by states for reapportionment of state legislative districts? What consequences can you foresee if one census result, by "head count" is used for federal congressional representation, and another census result, by statistical sampling, is used for all other purposes?

VERNONIA SCHOOL DISTRICT V. ACTON*
115 S.Ct. 2386, 132 L.Ed.2d 564 (1995)

The Vernonia School District in Oregon adopted a policy of randomly testing its interscholastic athletes for drugs by using urine tests. Three grade schools and one high school were affected in this small town where sports play a prominent role and athletes are admired. Both boys and girls are accompanied by an adult when samples are taken, but girls are afforded the privacy of a closed stall door. The adults listen for normal sounds of urination. After a samples is taken, it is given to the adult monitor, who checks it for temperature and tampering, and then transfers it to a vial. The samples are tested for amphetamines, cocaine, and marijuana, and are 99.94 percent accurate. Test results are kept in confidence by school officials and destroyed after one year. Athletes who test positive must participate in an assistance program or suffer suspension from athletics for the remainder of the season and the next athletic season.

The reason for adopting the drug-testing policy was to curb a sharp increase in drug use on campuses that apparently produced rudeness of students during class, outbursts of profane language, and other disciplinary referrals.

James Acton, a seventh-grader, signed up to play football but was denied participation because he and his parents refused to sign the drug-testing

consent forms. The Actons filed an action seeking an injunction (court order) preventing enforcement of drug testing. The Actons contended was that the drug testing amounted to a "suspicionless" search and therefore violated the Fourth and Fourteenth Amendments to the Constitution.

Justice SCALIA delivered the opinion of the Court: The Fourth Amendment to the United States Constitution provides that the Federal Government shall not violate "[t]he right of the people to be secure in their persons, houses, papers, and effects, against unreasonable searches and seizures. . . ." We have held that the Fourteenth Amendment extends this constitutional guarantee to searches and seizures by state officers, ... including public school officials, *New Jersey v. T.L.O.* 469 U.S. 325, 105 S.Ct. 733 (1985). . . . .

As the text of the Fourth Amendment indicates, the ultimate measure of the constitutionality of a governmental search is "reasonableness". . . .

Where a search is undertaken by law enforcement officials to discover evidence of criminal wrongdoing, this Court has said that reasonableness generally requires the

---

*Information on how to find decisions of the U.S. Supreme Court is available at http://www.lib.umd.edu

obtaining of a judicial warrant . . . . Warrants cannot be issued, of course, without the showing of probable cause required by the Warrant Clause. But a warrant is not required to establish the reasonableness of *all* government searches; and when a warrant is not required, ... probable cause is not invariably required either. A search unsupported by probable cause can be constitutional, we have said, "when special needs, beyond the normal need for law enforcement, make the warrant and probable-cause requirements impracticable." *Griffin v. Wisconsin*, 483 U.S. 868 (1987).

The first factor to be considered is the nature of the privacy interest upon which the search here at issue intrudes. . . . Legitimate privacy expectations are . . . less with regard to student athletes. School sports are not for the bashful. They require "suiting up" before each practice or event, and showering and changing afterwards. Public school locker rooms, the usual sites for these activities, are not notable for the privacy they afford. The locker rooms in Vernonia are typical: no individual dressing rooms are provided; shower heads are lined up along a wall, unseparated by any sort of partition or curtain; not even all the toilet stalls have doors. As the United States Court of Appeals for the Seventh Circuit has noted, there is "an element of communal undress inherent in athletic participation." *Schaill by Kross v. Tippecanoe County School Corp.*, 864 F.2d 1309 (1988). . . .

Having considered the scope of the legitimate expectation of privacy at issue here, we turn next to the character of the intrusion that is complained of. . . . [T]he degree of intrusion depends upon the manner in which production of the urine sample is monitored. Under the District's Policy, male students produce samples at a urinal along a wall. They remain fully clothed and are only observed from behind, if at all. Female students produce samples in an enclosed stall, with a female monitor standing outside listening only for sounds of tampering. These conditions are nearly identical to those typically encountered in public restrooms, which men, women, and especially school children use daily. Under such conditions, the privacy interests compromised by the process of obtaining the urine sample are in our view negligible. . . .

As to the efficacy of this means for addressing the problem: It seems to us self-evident that a drug problem largely fueled by the "role model" effect of athletes' drug use, and of particular danger to athletes, is effectively addressed by making sure that athletes do not use drugs. . . .

Taking into account all the factors we have considered above—the decreased expectation of privacy, the relative unobtrusiveness of the search, and the severity of the need met by the search—we conclude Vernonia's policy is reasonable and hence constitutional.

Justice O'Connor, with whom Justices Stevens and Justice Souter join, dissenting: The population of our Nation's public schools, grades 7 through 12, numbers around 18 million. By the reasoning of today's decision, the millions of these students who participate in interscholastic sports, an overwhelming majority of whom have given school officials no reason whatsoever to suspect they use drugs at school, are open to an intrusive bodily search. . . .

Blanket searches, because they can involve "thousands or millions" of searches, "pose a greater threat to liberty" than do suspicion-based ones, which "affect only one person at a time." *Illinois v. Krull*, 480 U.S. 340 (1987) (O'Connor, J., dissenting). Searches based on individualized suspicion also afford potential targets considerable control over whether they will, in fact, be searched because a person can avoid such a search by not acting in an objectively suspicious way. And given that the surest way to avoid acting suspiciously is to avoid the underlying wrongdoing, the costs of such a regime, one would think, are minimal. . . . .

For most of our constitutional history, mass, suspicionless searches have been generally considered per se unreasonable within the meaning of the Fourth Amendment. And we have allowed exceptions in recent years only where it has been clear that a suspicion-based regime would be ineffectual. Because that is not the case here, I dissent.

FOR CRITICAL ANALYSIS

1. Simply stated, is a search of all student athletes necessary, or would the search of only those students who exhibit some "suspicious" behavior be adequate? The degree of intrusion of a blanket search is minimal, but is even that degree reasonably necessary to achieve the goal sought? Under law, the answer is yes. Can you frame an opposing argument?

2. The random search for drivers under the influence of alcohol or drugs through the use of periodic "sobriety checkpoints" is constitutionally reasonable. By the same logic, the random drug testing of student athletes also should be adequate. Does this conclusion necessarily follow from the premise stated?

CHAPTER QUESTIONS AND PROBLEMS

1. The U.S. Supreme Court has experimented with but so far declined televising its proceedings.
    a. What are the pros and cons of televising oral arguments presented to the Court by opposing attorneys?
    b. Suppose Congress enacted a statute authorizing national television broadcasting companies the right to televise public proceedings of the Supreme Court. If the Supreme Court continued to deny such coverage, what constitutional issue would be presented?

2. Organizers of the annual Fiesta Bowl football game held in Arizona proposed establishing a race-specific scholarship fund for players of the competing teams. Are such scholarships unconstitutional because they are awarded only to members of one race? Would your answer be any different if the scholarships were awarded in schools where a history of intentional racial segregation existed?

3. Can government constitutionally regulate the content (i.e., censor) e-mail by banning "spam" (unwanted advertisements) and web sex or pornography (available on Web sites)?

4. Do state laws that criminalize sodomy between members of the same or opposite sex violate the constitutional right of privacy? Are such laws necessary in a free society?

5. America Online (AOL), an Internet service provider (ISP), paid online gossip columnist Matt Drudge for material. Part of the material AOL made available to the public stated that Sidney Blumenthal had a "spousal abuse" past. This information may be false and libelous. Is AOL's conduct protected by the First Amendment, or can Blumenthal win a case for damages for libel? Would your answer be the same if the libelous material was known by AOL to be untrue, but posted regardless?

6. Laws provide that employers must withhold the income taxes of employees from their paychecks and forward the taxes to the government. Which of the following ostensible justifications for such withholding laws is most important?
    a. The effect of the law is to improve the accuracy of each taxpayer's calculation of what total taxes were due for an entire taxable year.

b. Interest can be earned on the withheld money by government instead of by the taxpayers.

c. Employers are delegated the duty of collecting and remitting taxes to the government each month in order to save government administration costs.

d. Such a system makes tax collection more certain. There is no risk to the government that taxpayers will fail to set aside tax money to pay accrued taxes at year's end.

7. The City of Oakland passed an ordinance that prohibited the burning of all substances in residential yards within the city limits on days when a fire hazard warning was in effect. Violation was made a misdemeanor crime with a minimum fine of $500. Harry Haggerty, a political science major in college, invited student friends to his home in Oakland where, among other backyard activities, he intended to burn an American flag in protest to U.S. involvement in Iraq. If a fire warning were in effect, could Harry be convicted of the misdemeanor offense?

8. In an editorial comment, the highly respected British journal *The Economist* (27 March 1992, 15) opined, "Short of declaring war, nothing an American President can do has as much effect as appointing a justice to the Supreme Court." Do you agree? Why or why not?

9. Robert Lee, the principal of Nathan Bishop Middle School in Providence, Rhode Island, invited Rabbi Leslie Gutterman to deliver prayers at the public school graduation ceremony. When invited, the rabbi was asked to make the prayer at the ceremony nonsectarian, and he agreed to do so. Daniel Weisman, the father of a student, brought suit to prohibit school officials from including prayer in the ceremony. He was unsuccessful, and the ceremony took place with the Weismans in attendance. Weisman then sued in equity to permanently bar prayers at future ceremonies, including his daughter's high school graduation. The district court found that including prayer in public high school graduation exercises violated the establishment clause of the First Amendment. Does including a nonsectarian prayer in a public high school graduation ceremony constitute the establishment of a religion by government in violation of the First Amendment? [*Lee v. Weisman*, 505 U.S. 577, 112 S.Ct. 2649 (1992).]

10. Pursuant to its police power, a city adopted a noise ordinance under which noise of a specified amount of decibels in a residential area was a misdemeanor punishable by a $50 fine. At 1:30 a.m. a policeman pounded on the door of Sari Zayed and issued her a ticket in response to a neighbor's complaint of excessively loud snoring. Sari's defense was that she had tried to baffle the roar by rigging a mattress against the common wall. Thereafter, in response to public outcry, the City passed a resolution declaring that snoring was not a crime. This bizarre series of events occurred in Davis, California, in 1997.

a. Could the prosecutor continue with the case following the (*ex post facto*) repeal of the ordinance?

b. If the (*ex post facto*) repeal of a law permits a defendant's prior acts to be decriminalized, would this set the stage for government to excuse favored persons from otherwise criminal events?

NOTES

1. Giovanni Sartori, "Constitutionalism: A Preliminary Discussion," *The American Political Science Review*, December 1962.

2. *Webster's Third New International Dictionary* (Chicago: Encyclopedia Britannica, Inc., 1981).

3. *Elwood Investors Co. v. Behme*, 79 Misc.2d 910, 361 N.Y.S.2d 488 (New York, 1974).

4. *Youngstown Sheet and Tube Co. v. Sawyer*, 343 U.S. 579, 72 S.Ct. 863 (1952).

5. E. Corwin, *The "Higher Law" Background of American Constitutional Law* (Ithaca, N.Y.: Cornell University Press, 1967).

6. John Locke, *Two Treatises of Government* (London: Cambridge University Press, 1967).

7. *The Federalist*, No. 51.

8. Thomas Paine, *Political Writings*, (1837), 45–46.

9. *The Federalist*, No. 78.

10. *The Federalist*, No. 78.

11. *Marbury v. Madison*, 1 Cranch 137 (1803).

12. *Plessy v. Ferguson*, 163 U.S. 537, 16 S.Ct. 1138 (1896).

13. *Brown v. The Board of Education of Topeka*, 347 U.S. 483, 74 S.Ct. 686 (1954).

14. See U.S. Constitution, Art. I, Art. II, and Art. III.

15. *The Federalist*, No. 51.

16. *U.S. v. Eichman* and *U.S. v. Haggerty*, 496 U.S. 310, 110 S.Ct. 2404 (1990).

17. A hypothetical situation.

18. A hypothetical situation.

19. Based on *Clinton v. City of New York*, 118 S.Ct. 2091 (1998).

20. U.S. Constitution, Art. I, § 8.

21. U.S. Constitution, Twentieth Amendment, 1933; Twenty-second Amendment, 1951; Twenty-fifth Amendment, 1967.

22. U.S. Constitution, Art. II, § 2.

23. Prize cases, 67 U.S. 635 (1863).

24. U.S. Constitution, Art. II, § 2.

25. U.S. Constitution, Art. II, § 2.

26. *Roe v. Wade*, 410 U.S. 113, 93 S.Ct. 705 (1973).

27. U.S. Constitution, Art. III, § 1.

28. Impeachment of U.S. District Judge, *Facts on File* Yearbook Publication for 1986 (New York: Facts on File Inc., 1987).

29. J. Specter, "Impeachment: Another Look," *The National Law Journal*, 12 January 1989, 1.

30. Harriet Chiang, "Public Reprimand for Federal Judge," *San Francisco Chronicle*, 19 August 1998.

31. U.S. Constitution, Art. III § 1.

32. *U.S. v. Will*, 449 U.S. 200, 101 S.Ct. 471 (1980).

33. *Morrison v. Olson*, 487 U.S. 654, 108 S.Ct. 2597 (1988).

34. U.S. Constitution, Art. I, § 8.

35. U.S. Constitution, Art. II, § 2.

36. U.S. Constitution, Tenth Amendment, 1791.

37. U.S. Constitution, Art. I, § 9.

38. U.S. Constitution, Nineteenth Amendment, 1920; Twenty-third Amendment, 1961; Twenty-fourth Amendment, 1964; Twenty-fifth Amendment, 1967; and Twenty-sixth Amendment, 1971.

39. Fred Krinsky and Gerald Rigby, *Theory and Practice of American Democracy* (Belmont, CA: Dickenson Publishing Co., 1967) , 105.

40. James MacGregor Burns, J.W. Peltason, and Thomas E. Cronin, *Government by the People* (Englewood Cliffs, NJ: Prentice-Hall, 1989), 606.

41. Thelton Henderson, U.S. District Court Justice, 1996.

42. *Economic Equity v. Wilson*, 110 F.3d 1431 (1997). Application to the U.S. Supreme Court for a stay (suspension pending trial) was denied. 118 S.Ct. 17 (1998).

43. *The Federalist*, No. 51.

44. A hypothetical situation.

45. *Barnes v. Glen Theater*, 501 U.S. 560 (1991). *City of Rancho Cucamonga v. Wainer Consulting Services*, 213 Cal.App.3d 1338 (1989).

46. *The Federalist*, No. 51.

47. U.S. Constitution, Art. I, § 8.

48. U.S. Constitution, Art. VI.

49. *Martin v. Hunters Lessee*, I Wheaton 304 (1816) and *Cohens v. Virginia*, 6 Wheaton 264 (1821).

50. *Southern Pacific v. Arizona*, 325 U.S. 761, 65 S.Ct. 1515 (1945) and *Edwards v. California*, 314 U.S. 160, 62 S.Ct. 164 (1941).

51. *McCulloch v. Maryland*, 4 Wheaton 316 (1819). See also U.S. Constitution, Art. III, § 1.

52. U.S. Constitution, Art. I, § 8.

53. *Wickard v. Filbum*, 317 U.S. 111, 63 S.Ct. 82 (1942).

54. Eun-Kyung Kim, Associated Press, 21 August 1997.

55. *Barron v. Baltimore*, 7 Peters 243 (1833).

56. U.S. Constitution, Thirteenth Amendment, 1865.

57. U.S. Constitution, Thirteenth Amendment, 1865.

58. U.S. Constitution, Fourteenth Amendment, 1868.

59. *Gitlow v. New York*, 268 U.S. 652, 49 S.Ct. 625 (1925).

60. *Palko v. Conn.*, 302 U.S. 319, 58 S.Ct. 149 (1937).

61. *Milk Wagon Drivers Union v. Meadowmoor Dairies*, 312 U.S. 287, 60 S.Ct. 259 (1941).

62. *Near v. Minnesota*, 283 U.S. 697, 51 S.Ct. 625 (1931) and *Bridges v. California*, 314 U.S. 252, 62 S.Ct. 190 (1941). See also *DeJonge v. Oregon*, 299 U.S. 353, 57 S.Ct. 255 (1937) and *Cox v. Louisiana*, 379 U.S. 536, 85 S.Ct. 466 (1965).

63. *Schenk v. U.S.*, 249 U.S. 47, 39 S.Ct. 247 (1919).

64. *Abrams v. U.S.*, 250 U.S. 616, 40 S.Ct. 17 (1919).

65. *U.S. v. Carolene Products*, 304 U.S. 141, 58 S.Ct. 778 (1938).

66. *Dennis v. United States*, 341 U.S. 494, 71 S.Ct. 857 (1951).

67. *Coates v. Cincinnati*, 402 U.S. 611, 91 S.Ct. 1686 (1971).

68. "Judge Decries How-to Book for Murderers," *Los Angeles Times* (Richmond, VA), 8 May 1997. "Publisher Can Be Sued for Killings," Chronicle News Service, 11 November 1997. Hearing by U.S. Supreme Court denied, *Enterprises v. Rice*, 97-1325.

69. *Hazelwood School District v. Kuhlmeir*, 484 U.S. 260, 108 S.Ct. 562 (1988) and *Frisby v. Shultz*, 487 U.S. 474, 108 S.Ct. 2495 (1988).

70. *U.S. v. Haggerty* and *U.S. v. Eichman*, 496 U.S. 310, 110 S.Ct. 2404 (1990).

71. *Metromedia Inc. v. City of San Diego*, 453 U.S. 490, 101 S.Ct. 2882 (1981).

72. Based on a report by Wendy Hower, *Raleigh News & Observer*, 15 March 1998.

73. *Tinker v. Des Moines School District*, 393 U.S. 503, 89 S.Ct. 733 (1969).

74. Bill Workman, "Ban on Hate Speech Struck Down," *San Francisco Chronicle*, 2 March 1995.

75. *R.A.V. v. City of St. Paul*, 505 U.S. 377, 112 S.Ct. 2538 (1969).

76. *R.A.V. v. City of St. Paul*.

77. *Wisconsin v. Mitchell*, 508 U.S. 476, 113 S.Ct. 2194 (1993).

78. *Chaplinsky v. New Hampshire*, 315 U.S. 568, 62 S.Ct. 766 (1942).

79. *New York Times*, 13 June 1998.

80. *Miller v. California*, 413 U.S. 15, 93 S.Ct. 2607 (1973).

81. *Barnes v. Glen Theater, Inc.*, 501 U.S. 560, 111 S.Ct. 2456 (1991).

82. Associated Press, 20 September 1997.

83. *Reno v. A.C.L.U.*, 117 S.Ct. 2329 (1997).

84. *Everson v. Board of Education of the Town of Ewing*, 330 U.S. 1, 67 S.Ct. 504 (1947).

85. *Engel v. Vitale*, 370 U.S. 421, 82 S.Ct. 1261 (1962).

86. *Engel v. Vitale.*

87. *Wallace v. Jaffree*, 472 U.S. 38, 105 S.Ct. 2479 (1985).

88. *Board of Education of the Westside Community Schools v. Mergens*, 496 U.S. 226, 110 S.Ct. 2356 (1990).

89. Joan Lowy, Scripps Howard News Service, 1 March 1998.

90. U.S. Constitution, Second Amendment, 1791.

91. *Lewis v. U.S.*, 445 U.S. 55, 100 S.Ct. 915 (1980).

92. *Adams v. Williams*, 407 U.S. 143, 92 S.Ct. 1921 (1972).

93. U.S. Constitution, Fourth Amendment, 1791.

94. U.S. Constitution, Fourth Amendment, 1791.

95. *Wolf v. Colorado*, 338 U.S. 25, 69 S.Ct. 1359 (1949).

96. *Mapp v. Ohio*, 367 U.S. 643, 81 S.Ct. 1684 (1961).

97. *Mapp v. Ohio.*

98. *Michigan Department of State Police v. Sitz*, 496 U.S. 444, 110 S.Ct. 2481 (1993).

99. Amitri Etzioni, "Group Searches Are Here To Stay," *The National Law Journal*, 18 October 1993, 15.

100. In the Interest of Isiah B., Wisconsin Supreme Court, 176 Wis.2d 639, 500 N.W.2d 637 (1993).

101. *Malloy v. Hogan*, 378 U.S. 1, 84 S.Ct. 1489 (1964) and *Miranda v. Arizona*, 384 U.S. 436, 86 S.Ct. 1602 (1966). *Miranda* is discussed in Chapter 6.

102. *Illinois v. Perkins*, 496 U.S. 292, 110 S.Ct. 2394 (1990).

103. *Klopher v. North Carolina*, 386 U.S. 213, 87 S.Ct. 988 (1967).

104. In re *Oliver*, 333 U.S. 257, 69 S.Ct. 499 (1948).

105. *Parker v. Gladden*, 385 U.S. 363, 87 S.Ct. 468 (1966) and *Duncan v. Louisiana*, 391 U.S. 145, 88 S.Ct. 1444 (1968).

106. *Washington v. Texas*, 388 U.S. 14, 87 S.Ct. 1920 (1967).

107. *Argersinger v. Hamblin*, 407 U.S. 25, 92 S.Ct. 2006 (1972) and *Gideon v. Wainwright*, 372 U.S. 335, 83 S.Ct. 792 (1963).

108. *Argersinger v. Hamblin* and *Gideon v. Wainwright.*

109. *Chicago v. Morales*, 97-1121.

110. *Brown v. Board of Education of Topeka*, 347 U.S. 483, 74 S.Ct. 686 (1954).

111. *Brown v. Board of Education of Topeka*, 349 U.S. 294, 75 S.Ct. 753 (1955).

112. *Runyon v. McCrary*, 427 U.S. 160, 96 S.Ct. 848 (1950).

113. *Grove City College v. Bell*, 555 U.S. 535, 104 S.Ct. 1211 (1984).

114. *Grove City College v. Bell.*

115. Modified from and based on the case of *Bob Jones University v. U.S.*, 461 U.S. 574, 103 S.Ct. 2017 (1983).

116. *Board of Education of Oklahoma City v. Dowell*, 498 U.S. 237, 111 S.Ct. 630 (1991).

117. *U.S. v. Fordice*, 505 U.S. 717, 112 S.Ct. 2727(1992).

118. *Steelworkers v. Weber*, 443 U.S. 193, 99 S.Ct. 2721 (1979) and *Sheet Metal Workers v. Equal Employment Opportunity Commission*, 478 U.S. 501, 106 S.Ct. 3063 (1986).

119. *University of California Regents v. Bakke*, 438 U.S. 265, 95 S.Ct. 2733 (1978).

120. *Wygant v. Jackson Board of Education*, 476 U.S. 267, 106 S.Ct. 1842 (1986).

121. *Griswold v. Connecticut*, 381 U.S. 479, 85 S.Ct. 1678 (1965).

122. *Eisenstady v. Baird*, 405 U.S. 438, 92 S.Ct. 1029 (1972); *Loving v. Virginia*, 388 U.S. 87, S.Ct. 1817 (1967); *Roe v. Wade*, 410 U.S. 113, 93 S.Ct. 705 (1973); *Doc v. Bolton*, 410 U.S. 179, 93 S.Ct. 739 (1973); and *Stanley v. Georgia*, 394 U.S. 557, 87 S.Ct. 1243 (1969).

123. *Osborne v. Ohio*, 495 U.S. 103, 110 S.Ct. 1691 (1990).

124. *Paris Adult Theater I v. Slayton*, 413 U.S. 49, 93 S.Ct. 2628 (1973).

125. *Bowers v. Hardwick*, 478 U.S. 186, 106 S.Ct. 284 (1986).

126. *The Wall Street Journal*, 23 June 1989.

127. Carolyn Said, "Software Firm Skirts U.S. Law on Encryption," *San Francisco Chronicle*, 20 March 1998.

128. Title 18, U.S. Code.

129. *Washington Post*, 31 October 1989. Also see Lifson, "History of HIV Infection," *San Francisco Chronicle*, 27 December 1989.

130. *Schmerber v. California*, 384 U.S. 757, 86 S.Ct. 1826 (1966).

131. "Drug Testing Becomes a Corporate Mine Field," *The Wall Street Journal*, 21 December 1989.

132. R. Samborn, "More Lawsuits?" *The National Law Journal*, 25 March 1991, 1.

3

THE COURT SYSTEM

Sir Thomas More: The law, Roper, the law. I know what's legal and not what's right. And I'll stick to what's legal.

William Roper: Then you set man's law above God's.

Sir Thomas More: No, far below; but let me draw your attention to a fact—I'm not God. The currents and eddies of right and wrong, which you find such plain sailing, I can't navigate.

William Roper: So . . . you'd give the Devil benefit of the law!

Sir Thomas More: Yes. What would you do? Cut a great road through the law to get after the Devil?

William Roper: I'd cut down every law in England to do that!

Sir Thomas More: Oh? And when the last law was down and the Devil turned round on you where would you hide, Roper, the laws all being flat? Yes, I'd give the Devil benefit of law, for my own safety's sake.

Robert Bolt slightly and reverently edited from his play "A Man for All Seasons."

It is often stated and generally believed that persons residing in the United States of America are governed by law, not by people. "A government of laws, and not of men" are words written in 1774 by John Adams, first vice president and second president of the United States.[1] This means that decisions establishing and affecting rights and duties are not based on the personal values of certain individuals but rather are made by the courts according to existing rules while using fair and impartial processes. Sir Thomas More, quoted above, would no doubt approve of the United States' emphasis on established rules rather than individual discretion, but like all human creations "a government of law" is not perfect. The oft-heard condemnation of government "red tape" is sometimes a veiled criticism of the rule of law, and complaints about the law often concern the processes that are relied upon to ensure fair and impartial application of law.

Indeed, providing for the application of the rule of law in a fair, impartial, and consistent manner, while remaining efficient, is a difficult task, especially in the United States, which contains such a diversity of ethnic origins and cultural backgrounds. Yet it is that very diversity that makes the rule of law so vitally important for the resolution of disputes with "equal justice under law" for all.

92

The creation, recognition, and enforcement of our rights and duties are responsibilities shared by the legislative, executive, and judicial branches of government. However, the nature and manner in which laws are made and shaped differs dramatically depending on its source. Probably no other country is more reliant on its judges and its courts than the United States. One hundred and fifty years ago, French political scientist Alexis de Tocqueville noted the unique importance of courts in the American political system. "Restricted within its limits, the power granted to American courts to pronounce on the constitutionality of laws is yet one of the most powerful barriers ever erected against the tyranny of political assemblies."[2]

Although the power of courts can and does restrict arbitrary abuse of power, bias can creep into the court system. As an example, consider the following episode in traffic court.

> *The Traffic Court judge found himself facing two attorneys, both of whom he knew very well. Both were charged with speeding violations. "Gentlemen," he said, "I could not be truly objective in either of your cases, so I'm going to let you judge each other's case." Both lawyers agreed. Attorney Number One climbed to the bench. "You are charged with driving 40 in a 25 mile per hour zone. How do you plead?" he asked Attorney Number Two. "Guilty," was the response. "I fine you $50," said Number One. Then they exchanged places. "You are charged with driving 40 in a 25 mile zone," said Number Two. "What is your plea?" "Guilty," said Number One. "Then I fine you $200," said Number Two. "Hey! that's unfair," said the first. "I fined you only $50." "Yes," was the reply, "but there is too much speeding going on. This is the second case we've had like that today."*

Although the purpose of the story is to amuse, it illustrates the injustice of an inconsistent and unfair decision made by a biased judge. **Bias** is a preconceived belief about some person or fact that makes it difficult to be neutral, dispassionate, or fair in evaluating that person's rights and duties, guilt or innocence. A judge is biased when he or she has a personal interest in the outcome of a case or has reached a conclusion about a case before hearing the evidence and legal arguments.

The U.S. system of justice strives to provide both reasonable consistency and neutrality. This requires the elimination of judicial bias, including rejection of personal values that conflict with legal values. The independent neutral forum, where facts are determined and rules applied for resolving legal disputes, is the *court system*.

The role of lawyers is not to be overlooked in the operations of courts. Courts would not be effective without the service of attorneys who shape their clients' cases, present legal issues to courts, quickly object to improprieties offered by opposing counsel, and so forth. We discuss lawyers more fully in the following chapter, but here we note the dependence of our courts upon the legal profession. This always has been true. In the frontier days of the west following the discovery of gold in 1849, law and order of a sort was preserved by vigilantism. The goal of vigilantes was simple enough: to establish order and stability in mining camps, cattle towns, and the open range. The procedures of the vigilantes, unlike legal procedures today, featured simplicity and certain, severe punishment.

It was the frontier attorneys, not trained in law schools but rather by apprenticeships and experience, who encouraged and supported procedures to bring offenders into courtrooms, where fair and less arbitrary procedures could be applied. On the decline following the Civil War, vigilantism remains only as a reminder of the importance of due process brought about by court procedures that guarantee fair treatment for all. By the turn of the century, in 1900, lawyers had been educated in college and in law schools and were relied upon then, as today, to present their clients' disputes to the courts. The dependency of the courts upon the bar (the legal profession) was total then as now. Of course, there weren't as many lawyers then—according to the 1900 census, only 4,278 persons declared themselves to be practicing attorneys. Nor were there as many courts. Today, most of our courts are jammed with cases and more federal judges are said to be urgently needed. And with more courts handling more and increasingly complex issues, we can be assured of more attorneys.

WHAT IS A COURT?

Clearly it is important and useful to know where our courts are located, how they function, and the important role they play in our society. The media has capitalized on the public's interest in courts with movies and TV shows, and the publishing industry has reaped huge rewards from novels based on courtroom activities. Significant decisions of appellate courts, especially the U.S. Supreme Court, receive widespread media coverage and many citizens worry about the future consequences of important decisions. For example, how can veterans accept the burning of the American flag as protected speech? How can religious people accept denial of a moment's prayer in school? How can taxpayers, investors, and businesses accept refusal of line-item veto power to eliminate wasteful expenditures? The public has an acute interest in such decisions which become the topic of lively debate on the Internet, in coffee shops, on talk radio, and so on. Because the actions of courts receive such expansive notoriety, it is obvious that you, as educated citizens, must be familiar with the functions of courts.

Courts are public facilities, available to private persons, business organizations, and government agencies, where legal disputes are heard and decided. Courts offer their tax-supported services practically free to users. Under the U.S. Constitution, courts are essentially independent of the other branches of government.* This independence protects the courts from potential interference by the executive or legislative branches.

A court is both a place and a system. It is a place where you may go to peacefully resolve your legal disputes with others ("I'll see you in court!"). The word *court* is also used to describe all the court system participants, including judges, attorneys, clerks, witnesses, parties, and the public ("Court is in session"); and sometimes only the presiding judge or justice ("If the court please, may I be heard at this time?").

Courts are also part of a system, as there are different courts for different types of legal disputes, each with different specified procedures. Some courts

*The courts are not totally independent of the other two branches. For example, the executive branch of government makes judicial appointments, collects taxes, and distributes funds necessary to pay judges and otherwise operate the judicial system. The legislative branch sets salaries and benefits of judges and often confirms judicial appointments. But it would be unconstitutional for the legislative branch to influence courts through pay or benefit cuts or other intimidating laws.

determine the facts of individual disputes (trial courts); others review decisions of lower courts for correctness, consistency, and fairness (appellate courts). Appellate judges, both in the state and federal systems, have the power to make new law, and do. To understand the courts, it is useful to recognize some of their different functions, including those of trial and appellate courts.

WHAT IS A TRIAL COURT?

Trial courts conduct the initial proceedings in legal disputes. These proceedings have three distinct purposes: (1) to determine the facts of the dispute ("What happened between the competing parties?"), (2) to determine what rules of law should be applied to the facts, and (3) to apply those rules to the facts.

> Marya Martinez signed up for ski instruction at Heavenly Mountain in Idaho. Gary Graf, a certified ski instructor, fitted Marya with rental skis. He then taught her how to snowplow (i.e., a beginning maneuver for turning, reducing speed, or stopping). Later that afternoon, Marya was showing her new skills to Luther Thomas, whom she had just met during lunch. Her show was short. Marya fell and suffered a spiral fracture of her right leg, just above the ankle. Her bindings had failed to release her boot from the skis when she fell. She sued Gary in a civil action for damages, alleging that he had carelessly adjusted the bindings too tightly. Who will win?

No one knows who will win because the facts have not yet been judicially determined. Did Gary secure the bindings too tightly? Did Marya, or anyone else, tamper with the bindings after Gary set them? Did the bindings fail because they were too tight or because Marya had allowed ice to accumulate beneath her boot? Were the bindings manufactured in a defective manner? Was there a contract that disclaimed or limited Gary's liability? A civil trial will determine the answers to these and other relevant factual and legal contentions. In the trial, Marya is the **plaintiff** (person seeking relief in a civil trial) because she is seeking to recover **damages** (money) from Gary, the **defendant** (in a civil trial, the person whom a lawsuit is brought against). The entire process, designed to resolve (i.e., decide or settle) the legal controversy, is called a **lawsuit** or **litigation**.

Marya's attempt to collect damages from Gary is an example of a *civil dispute* (also called a *civil action* or *civil lawsuit*). **Civil disputes** are private controversies between persons.* A civil dispute is sometimes defined broadly by stating what it is not. It is not a matter involving criminal law. A **criminal dispute** (also called a *criminal action* or *criminal case*) is brought by government to determine whether an accused (also called a *defendant*) is guilty of an act committed against the public and in violation of a penal statute.

Civil matters and criminal matters are separate fields of law; in large cities, attorneys and judges often specialize in one or the other. The dependence of

---

*The term *persons* for most situations in law includes humans, as well as artificial persons, such as government bodies and different types of business entities, including corporations.

courts upon attorneys is such that it would be foolhardy for a civil case attorney to defend an accused murderer even before an impartial jury. There are similarities as well as differences between civil and criminal matters. Both involve formal proceedings before a court. Both are conducted to resolve disputed questions of fact and law that will, in turn, define applicable rights and duties of the parties involved. Different terminology, however, is often used. For example, a defendant found to be responsible in a civil trial is said to be *liable,* while in a criminal trial such a person is said to be *guilty.* The accused in both cases, though, is called a *defendant.*

In a criminal trial, a prosecutor (e.g., a public prosecutor or district attorney) from the local governing unit (county) represents the public on behalf of the state. If a federal crime is involved, an attorney from the Department of Justice represents the public. While government can be a party in either a civil or criminal matter, only the government can prosecute a criminal action, because *crimes—* although usually committed against private persons—are prosecuted as public offenses against all society. Procedures differ substantially in criminal actions from those used in civil actions. The focus of this chapter is on the civil court system, although we make some references to the criminal system. (See Chapter 6 for a more complete discussion of criminal procedure.)

Most court proceedings and court records are open to public scrutiny, thereby assuring us that no secret "kangaroo court" sessions take place. Court TV broadcasts trials of high interest to national, and sometimes worldwide, audiences. However, public attendance at trial can be restricted or barred for security reasons. Sometimes one or both parties request privacy, and the court will agree when there is an overriding reason why the public should be excluded from hearing the details of the dispute or seeing witnesses whose privacy ought to be protected. Even if the proceeding is closed to the public, a verbatim transcript of the trial is prepared so reviewing courts may be apprised of precisely what was said and by whom. Moreover, the press follows important and/or interesting cases and, in recent years, has adopted an investigative posture when dealing with all aspects of government, including courts.

The attorney general of Maryland filed a civil suit against Cottman Transmission Systems, Inc., relating to allegations of fraudulent activities. Cottman was accused of removing automobile transmissions for inspection and maintenance when this costly action was unnecessary. The attorney general distributed news releases elaborating the allegations against Cottman. When the attorney general made additional claims, Cottman asked the court to close the courtroom except for parties directly involved in the proceeding.[3] Did the court agree to do this?

Initially, yes. Cottman's counsel convinced the trial court judge that the press releases harmed their client's ability to obtain a fair trial, and so the public was barred. Before trial began, however, a higher court overruled this decision.

While restricting access to civil law proceedings is uncommon, restricting access to criminal law proceedings is even more rare. The possibility of secret trials resulting in loss of individual liberty through a jail sentence is an anathema to our democracy. Equally disturbing would be the secret exoneration of a favored celebrity. Criminal proceedings may be conducted in private only in extraordinary situations that are demonstrated to, and then justified by, the trial court judge.[4]

An exception to the openness in most court cases is the juvenile court proceeding, which is conducted privately in most states in order to protect youthful offenders. The media typically cooperates with the juvenile courts by not publicizing the names of juveniles accused of status offenses (e.g., truancy and running away) and even conduct considered criminal if committed by adults.

At the turn of the twentieth century, in 1900, there were no special laws for juveniles. But as the industrial revolution progressed and spread across the country, bringing increasing opportunities for mischief by juveniles in the cities, the states began adopting laws protecting minors (under 18) from the adult criminal system. As the twenty-first century, nearing 2000, begins, a considerable body of thought holds that people reach maturity at an age younger than 18, at least for purposes of the criminal law. The states increasingly are willing to treat children of 16, 14, and even younger as adults by sentencing them similarly to adult criminals.

WHAT IS AN APPELLATE COURT?

Within a specified time following the trial court's final determination (a *judgment*), the losing party can **appeal**, which is a formal request to a higher court to review the trial judge's ruling. These review courts are called **appellate courts**. Consisting of three or more judges, called justices, these courts review decisions of trial court judges for substantive and procedural correctness. In civil cases, there is no right to have the state's highest court consider an appeal. In criminal cases resulting in the death penalty, the right to an appellate review by the state's highest court is guaranteed. This is a safeguard against imposing an irreversible penalty without thorough review of all aspects of the conviction. Lawyers research the written opinions of appellate courts in earlier cases to determine what law should be applied to the problem facing their clients. This is one example of how trial courts depend upon attorneys.

The appellate court works from a verbatim record (court transcript) of what was said and what *evidence* was accepted in the lower court, such as photographs, models, charts, business records, contracts, and so forth. Appellate courts do not listen to witnesses, accept new evidence,* make new determinations of fact, or utilize a jury. Instead, the court receives written briefs prepared by lawyers that contain legal arguments as to how the law was incorrectly stated or applied to the facts as presented to the trial court. This is an example of how appellate courts rely on attorneys. The appellate court accepts as true the facts found by the trial court, which considered all the testimony of all witnesses along with all other evidence, and upon so doing decides whether rules of substantive and procedural law were properly applied by the trial judge. However, appellate judges may also "weigh," or evaluate, the factual evidence as presented in the trial court and

---

*Examples of evidence are testimony of witnesses, photographs, documents, handwriting samples, dented fenders, and so on. In weighing the believability of testimony evidence, the jury also considers the demeanor, eye contact, dress, and mannerisms of a witness.

then decide whether, as a matter of law, the facts were sufficient to justify the judgment.

If the appellate court concludes that the trial court erroneously applied or interpreted the law, it may modify or reverse the judgment or decision, and either enter a new judgment or *remand* (return) the case to the trial court for a new trial or other proceedings in compliance with the appellate court's instructions. In other words, the trial court is instructed to "do it right this time." Merely finding an error at the trial court level is not sufficient to overturn the trial court's judgment. If an error is minor, it is believed unlikely that it would affect the case outcome. The error found must be serious, requiring correction by the appellate court in order to avoid a miscarriage of justice. Therefore, it can be concluded that when a reversal occurs, the trial court judge is deemed to have made a serious error in one or more legal rulings.

In the previously discussed *Cottman* case, the trial court judge's decision to ban the press was appealed and reversed even before the trial took place. The Maryland appellate court stated:

> To close a court to public scrutiny of the proceedings is to shut off the light of the law. How else will the citizenry learn of the happenings in the courts—their government's third branch—except through access to the courts by the people themselves or through reports supplied by the media? A . . . corporate entity involved as a party to a civil case is entitled to a fair trial, not a private one.[5]

Relative to the number of cases heard in trial court, very few cases are appealed. The cost to appeal can be prohibitive in time, money, and peace of mind. Although the parties may not be pleased with the outcome of the trial, they nonetheless have had their "day in court."

Thus, to win a corrective action by an appellate court, the **appellant**, the party who appeals the case to a higher court, must show that an error by the court prejudiced the appellant's cause. The **appellee**, the party against whom the appeal is brought, will contend that no error was made, or that any error did not affect the outcome of the trial. Clearly the trial is the crucial, potent, and final source of justice for most persons involved in litigation.

WHAT IS JURISDICTION?

To understand the courts, we must understand **jurisdiction**. In Latin, *juris* means "law," and *diction* means "to speak." Thus, "the power to speak the law" is the precise meaning of the term *jurisdiction*. It refers to the geographic area within which a court has the right and power to operate (that is, "speak"). It also refers to the persons over whom and the subject matters about which a court has the right and power to make decisions that are legally binding. Obviously, the term is used many ways, but always in relation to the right and power of the courts to act. Jurisdiction is about (1) political boundaries (states, federal government, territories, foreign countries, etc.), (2) the type of dispute and dollar amount involved, and (3) persons and property. In other words, jurisdiction is about a plaintiff choosing the right place to sue, choosing the right court in that place, and

For an article about the use of cameras in the courtrooms see http://www.ajs.org/camera3.html

There is an excellent discussion about jurisdiction at the Nolo Press Web site http://www.nolo.com and http://www.nolo.com/ChunkCM/which_court.html

applying rules of fairness governing when a person must appear in court to defend his or her liberty or property.

POLITICAL BOUNDARIES OF STATE AND FEDERAL COURTS

Government power begins and ends at geographical boundaries. It is clear to most that the courts of one sovereign power ordinarily have no authority over someone present in another sovereign power absent extraordinary reason. The United States is, however, a country with shared political boundaries, and the states are not entirely sovereign. Federalism exists in the U.S. court system as well as in the executive and legislative branches of government. Simply put, we have both federal and state court systems. There are 52 court systems—one for each of the 50 states, the federal government,* and the District of Columbia. They have much in common and are interrelated, but still each is an independent system. Interestingly, a party seeking judicial resolution of a dispute often may have the choice of which court system he or she wishes to use.

When both a federal court and a state court have the power to hear a case, they have **concurrent jurisdiction**. Which court, federal or state or both, has power or authority over a given matter is a question of jurisdiction, as provided for in the constitutions and/or statutes of the federal government and of the respective states.

> While walking along a busy street in Tallahassee, Jorge Cepada, a citizen of Florida, was struck by a crate that flew off a move-yourself rental driven by Gretchen Smalter. Desiring compensation for his injuries, Jorge intended suing Gretchen in the convenient Florida courts. May he do so? Could he instead sue in a federal court?

When Gretchen allegedly injured Jorge in Florida, both the Florida state courts and the U.S. District Court had concurrent jurisdiction. An injured victim has the right to use the courts of the state where harm occurs. A plaintiff also has the right to bring suit in the courts of the state in which he or she is a resident (in this case, Jorge is a resident of Florida). The right to use a federal court includes situations in which the parties to a dispute are each citizens of different states. When such diversity of citizenship exists, a plaintiff may either file an action in federal court (assuming the claimed damages are in excess of $75,000) or in state court. The federal basis for jurisdiction is called *diversity of citizenship* (discussed further on page 105). In diversity of citizenship cases, the federal court applies the substantive law of the state in which it sits, such as the state's law of negligence. Significantly different procedural rules apply in federal civil courts than in state courts, and attorneys are quick to seize upon advantages sometimes available in this regard. Note that diversity jurisdiction allows persons to use the federal courts when their claims do not otherwise involve any federal law. Claims based on federal law may be filed in a federal court without the need for diversity jurisdiction.

---

*Federal courts include courts for the U.S. Territories, Puerto Rico, Virgin Islands, Canal Zone, Guam, and the Northern Mariana Islands.

JURISDICTION OVER SUBJECT MATTER

Subject matter jurisdiction determines which types of cases a court can hear. Probate courts—courts that handle only wills and estate matters—exemplify courts of **limited jurisdiction**, meaning courts authorized to hear specific limited types of cases. A court of **general jurisdiction** is a court that can hear and decide almost any type of case.

The subject matter jurisdiction of a court is usually defined in the constitutional or statutory law that creates the court. It may refer to the type of case, its seriousness as reflected by the amount of money requested by the person bringing the lawsuit, or the type of relief requested of the court. For example, a court may be able to hear only cases where the damages requested are $20,000 or less, or when the court is asked to order a person to do or not do something.

In criminal matters, the seriousness of a crime may determine which court hears a case. For example, a murder trial is held in the trial court of general jurisdiction rather than one of limited jurisdiction. Whether the proceeding is a trial or an appeal is perhaps the most obvious subject matter limitation on jurisdiction.

Venue

The proper place for trial within a state that otherwise has appropriate jurisdiction for either a civil or criminal case is called its venue (French: "to come"). Venue is the local place, within the geographical boundaries of a larger jurisdiction, where a case is most appropriately tried. Proper venue reflects a policy of closeness—that is, a court trying a suit should be close to where the incident leading to the suit occurred or close to where the defendant resides.

All things being equal, the following rules are typical:

1. In divorce cases, proper venue is the county of the family residence.

2. In automobile accident cases, proper venue is the county where the accident occurred or where the defendant resides.

3. In breach of contract cases, proper venue is where the contract was made, or where it was breached, or where the defendant lives.

4. In criminal cases, proper venue is the county in which the crime occurred or where the defendant was apprehended.

All things are not equal, however, when a significant event occurs that makes a different venue more likely to produce a just result. For example, excessive publicity in the county where a crime occurred may unreasonably prejudice an accused's right to a fair trial. Under such circumstances, courts will grant a **motion for change of venue** and order the case be tried in a more appropriate place.

In the spring of 1992, a jury in Simi Valley, California, found four white Los Angeles police officers not guilty of using excessive force in the arrest of a black man, Rodney King. The highly publicized case involved accusations that the officers used unlawful force during Mr. King's arrest. A bystander, who had videotaped the use of force against King, made the tape available to the television media. The tape was played on television over and over, and the resulting publicity caused the police officers to request a change of venue from Los Angeles, where they argued they could not get a fair trial. The request was granted, and the trial was transferred to Simi Valley. A not guilty verdict by the Simi Valley jurors was followed by several days of rioting in southwestern Los Angeles. Many commentators announced that, in their opinions, the defendants had escaped conviction only because the change of venue placed the trial in Simi Valley where only 2.2 percent of the residents are African American. In the Simi Valley trial, no blacks served on the jury.*

Venue also can be changed within a single county, from one judicial district to another.

O.J. Simpson resided in, and was accused of committing a murder in, Los Angeles County. Ostensibly to avoid the possibility of race-based riots, the district attorney of Los Angeles personally moved the place for the trial of O.J. Simpson from the largely "white" Santa Monica (where Simpson lived and where the murders occurred) to the largely "black" downtown. Both places are within Los Angeles County. Simpson was found not guilty of the murders by the predominately African American jury. Did the change of venue from Santa Monica to downtown Los Angeles affect the outcome of the case?

One can only speculate as to what the outcome might have been had the venue not been changed. Suffice it to say that the defense was delighted with the change in venue—the prosecuting attorneys were not consulted about the change even though their supervisor, the district attorney, made the decision.

JURISDICTION OVER PERSONS AND PROPERTY

In our previous example (page 99), if Gretchen can be served with a *summons*— an order informing her that a lawsuit has been filed against her—within the boundaries of Florida, the Florida state court has the power and right to hear the case. Under such circumstances, Jorge's Florida court would have **in personam jurisdiction** over Gretchen, meaning power over her. The most common means of obtaining *in personam* jurisdiction in a civil case is by personal service of a summons and complaint on the defendant who is within the boundaries of the state in which the suit is commenced.

Assume the address given to Jorge by Gretchen shows her new home is in Oklahoma and by the time the suit is filed Gretchen lives in Oklahoma. Can Jorge still sue Gretchen in Florida or must he now sue in Oklahoma?

---

*After the acquittal on state criminal charges, the federal government filed federal criminal charges in Los Angeles alleging that the four police officers had violated Rodney King's civil rights. The federal jury found two officers, Powell and Koon, guilty; the two other officers were found innocent. Motions by the defendants for a change of venue in this trial were denied. The federal government does not prosecute all defendants who are acquitted of state criminal charges involving civil rights violations. It can be argued legally that the government makes its selection upon political bases, in cases that generate significant publicity and public outrage. Would the U.S. have prosecuted the police in the Rodney King case if there had been no public release of the videotape of the event?

Clearly, if the process server (a person in the business of serving summons upon defendants) can find Gretchen within Florida, Jorge can sue in the Florida court. But, if Gretchen had returned to Oklahoma before Jorge engaged the services of a lawyer and begins litigation, the question is whether or not the Florida court could obtain jurisdiction over an Oklahoma citizen who never returns to Florida. The answer is yes, because Florida, like all states, has a **long-arm statute**. Long-arm statutes subject nonresident defendants to local jurisdiction for wrongful activities they engage in while physically within a state even if they have left the state by the time they are sued. Long-arm statutes also can obtain jurisdiction over some activities of a defendant that occurred outside the state but that caused harm within the state.[6] If a person drives a motor vehicle within a state, he is deemed to give his agreement to appear and answer for any harm he causes while driving in that state (called *implied consent*). Jorge won't even be required to hire a process server in Oklahoma, although that would be permissible; service of the summons by registered mail to Gretchen's home would typically be adequate. Defendants also give implied consent to jurisdiction of states in which they do business. Thus, consumers in Florida can use their local courts to sue out-of-state companies who do business in their state. When defendants are not subject to long-arm statutes, plaintiffs can always sue a defendant in the state of residence.

Although *in personam* jurisdiction is the most common way to get jurisdiction over a defendant, sometimes a dispute involves ownership or title to property. In these cases plaintiffs will seek *in rem* **jurisdiction** (Latin: "against a thing"). *In rem* jurisdiction empowers courts to declare rights against the world rather than just the named defendant(s). If the legal question involves ownership of real property located in Alaska, for example, the appropriate court to hear the case would be the trial court where the property is located in Alaska. Parties known to the plaintiff, who have an interest in the property, have a due-process right to receive fair notice of any proceeding based on *in rem* jurisdiction, as well as a right to participate in the case.

HOW ARE STATE COURT SYSTEMS ORGANIZED?

The typical state court system consists of both trial and appellate courts. Consider the typical state court system shown in Exhibit 3–1. It has three main levels: (1) trial courts of general or limited jurisdiction, (2) intermediate appellate courts, and (3) the highest court (usually named the supreme court). Although most state court systems provide two levels of appeal, some states have but one appellate court.* Also, unfortunately, titles of state courts are not uniform; names of courts in one state frequently apply to quite different courts in another state. Confusion can be avoided by focusing on the function a court performs: trial or appellate.

The typical state will have a trial court of general jurisdiction, often called the *superior court*. That court may hear money matters with unlimited dollar limits and serious criminal matters. All states have courts with limited subject matter jurisdiction, often called special *inferior trial courts* or *minor judiciary courts*. A

Two excellent Web sites for information about state court systems are
National Center for State Courts
http://www.ncsc.dni.us
and
National Law Journal State Court referral site
http://www.ljextra.com/courthouse/states.html

*States with only one appellate court are Delaware, Maine, Montana, Nevada, New Hampshire, North Dakota, Rhode Island, South Dakota, Vermont, West Virginia, and Wyoming.

Exhibit 3–1:   A Typical State Court System

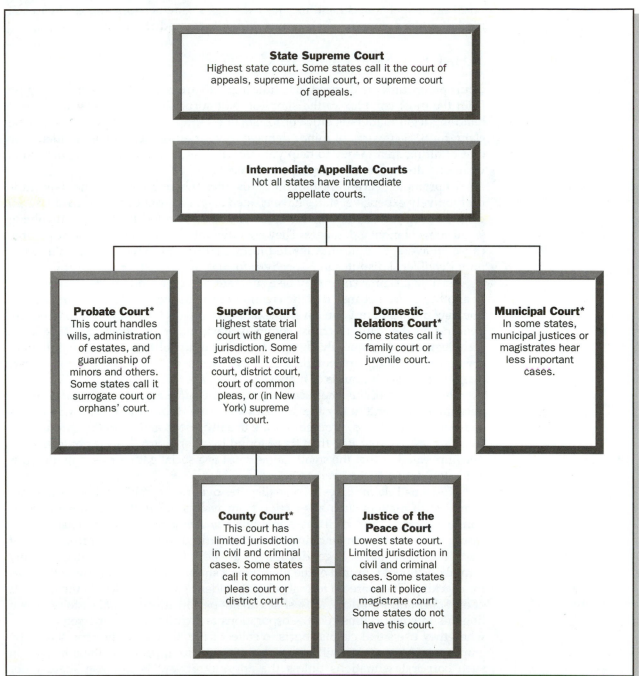

*Courts of limited jurisdiction, such as probate, domestic relations, municipal, or county courts, may be separate courts or may be part of a trial court of general jurisdiction.

small claims court, discussed shortly, is an example of an inferior trial court of limited jurisdiction. Small claims courts hear claims involving relatively small dollar amounts. A domestic relations court, which handles only divorce actions and child custody cases, is another example of a court of limited jurisdiction. Local municipal courts handling, for example, misdemeanors and civil cases of modest dollar amounts are also courts of limited jurisdiction.

WHAT ARE SMALL CLAIMS COURTS?

Court procedures are devised to handle a great variety of legal problems ranging from the most complex to the simplest. Not surprisingly, the usual manner of handling legal matters is efficient for small or simple cases. If you have a legal claim for $1,500 worth of minor damage to your automobile in an accident, the cost of hiring an attorney to help you recover that amount through court action would no doubt exceed your hoped-for recovery.

To promote peaceful resolution of disputes where a conventional lawsuit is prohibitively expensive, states have created a special trial court, called the **small claims court**. Jurisdiction of this court is usually limited to disputes involving small sums of money damages. They are often referred to as the *people's court*, because an average adult with limited formal education may obtain resolution of minor civil legal disputes in a speedy, informal, and user-friendly forum.

The small claims court may be a separate court, or a designated subdivision of another court. Because it is the creation of each state, particulars vary widely. The maximum amount of recoverable damages ranges from $1,000 to $17,500, depending on the state, the most common maximum range being $2,500–$5,000. State legislatures frequently change the dollar limits of these courts in inflationary times to continue to provide inexpensive access to the courts for civil matters involving modest amounts of money.

The purpose of the small claims court is the same as any other trial court: to determine facts and apply the law. However, the dynamics of the small claims court are more relaxed, proceedings are usually faster, and procedures to use the court are less complicated than those found in other courts. This is not to say it is uncomplicated or that the small claims court is a social gathering—only that it is less intimidating to the average litigant.

Most small claims cases involve disputes over money, although some are concerned with matters such as eviction from residential rentals. Divorce actions, criminal matters, and civil cases involving *in rem* jurisdiction are examples of cases not accepted in small claims court. The procedural rules differ from those of traditional trial courts. Legal documents are kept to a minimum; often the only formal document required of the plaintiff is a simple pre-printed form with boxes for checking. There are no formal rules of evidence and no juries. In the interests of economy and simplicity, most states do not permit attorneys at law to represent litigants in small claims court. Corporations are artificial, legal persons, and so when they use small claims courts to collect debts they must be represented by employees. Most states will not allow attorneys to appear for litigants even in such corporate situations unless the attorney at law is the sole shareholder and/or an officeholder of the corporation.

Each party explains the dispute, calling on witnesses for corroboration or for additional facts. Each party also presents any supporting documents or other physical evidence. The judge may ask questions and then, without any elaborate commentary or research, decide the case. Sometimes the judge will rule at the conclusion of the trial, but often the judge will inform the parties of his or her decision later by mail. In some states parties can appeal the case, but in many

http://

Look up the small claims court monetary limits for your state at http://www.nolo.com/ChunkCM/CM19.html

http://

If you want additional information about small claims courts, such as procedures or whether or not attorneys are allowed in court, check http://www.halt.org/SmallClaims/smallclaimsinfo.html

situations the small claims court plaintiff does not have that right—his or her use of a small claims court is deemed a waiver of the right to a jury and to appeal. The defendant, however, generally retains a right to a **trial *de novo*** (*de novo* means "new" and the term means a right to a completely new trial hearing*).

Small claims courts help "the little person" get his or her "day in court" without the delays and costs that accompany use of traditional courts. However, because business firms often have a substantial number of small claims, they appear most frequently as plaintiffs in small claims court actions.**

Various television programs such as *The People's Court* popularize small claims courts. Technically these proceedings are *arbitrations,* (a private third party is selected by the parties to hear and resolve the dispute) rather than trials, but they illustrate the types of disputes heard and resolved in small claims courts.

WHAT IS THE FEDERAL COURT SYSTEM?

Like the state court system, the federal court system consists of both trial and appellate courts. The two principal appellate courts are the U.S. Courts of Appeals and the U.S. Supreme Court.

FEDERAL TRIAL COURTS

The federal government has one trial court of general jurisdiction called the **U.S. District Court**. The country is divided into 93 districts. Each district consists of a number of judges doing business in a number of different courtrooms and even in different buildings. How many judges are "sitting" (i.e., conducting the court's business) is related to the population within each district. In populous areas, the districts are geographically small; in rural areas, they are large. There is at least one U.S. District Court in every state and territory in the United States, even though individual court boundaries may include more than one state. U.S. District Courts conduct trials concerning federal matters, such as federal crimes and enforcement of federal statutes. **Diversity of citizenship jurisdiction** exists when a plaintiff is a citizen of one state and the defendant is a citizen of another state, or when one party is a foreign country or a citizen of a foreign country and the other is a citizen of the United States. The amount of claimed damages in a diversity of citizenship case must be at least $75,000.[7] In settling such controversies, the particular U.S. District Court involved applies federal *procedural law* (which involves the manner in which rights and duties are to be enforced) and the *substantive law* (which involves the defining of rights and duties) of the appropriate

If you are interested in the origins of the National Judiciary, read the article by Philip B. Kurland at http://www.apsanet.org/CENnet/thisconstitution/kurland.html

You may look up information on federal courts at the federal court Web site http://www.uscourts.gov/

---

*The defendant, unlike the plaintiff, did not choose the small claims court forum and usually is not deemed to have waived the right to an appeal. In the normal appeal, the trial record is reviewed to determine if the trial judge made an error. If a party has a right to a trial *de novo*, the prior court record is not considered (note that small claims courts do not keep a record of transcripts), and the defendant is automatically given a new day in court. Although the new trial occurs at a higher level court, the trial usually remains informal and is decided by a judge without a jury. See M. Barrett, The Constitutional Right to Jury Trial: A Historical Exception for Small Monetary Claims, 39 Hastings L.J. 125 (1987). See also, *Crouchman v. Superior Court*, 45 Cal.3d 1167, 755 P. 2d 1075, 248 Cal. Rptr. 626 (1988) and *Iowa Nat. Mut. Ins. Co. v. Mitchell*, 305 N.W. 2d 724 (Iowa, 1981).

**In number apparently about one-half the plaintiffs are businesses, according to one report. See "The Role of the Small-Claims Court," *Consumer Reports*, November 1979, 666.

state, usually the state where the court is located.[8] When a federal court hears a case because of diversity jurisdiction, an example of *concurrent jurisdiction* exists because at least one state court would also have had the power to hear the case, if the plaintiff had chosen to file the case there.

> Jorge, a resident of Florida, wishes to sue Gretchen, an Oklahoma resident, to collect damages for injuries and losses arising from the motor vehicle accident that occurred in Florida (see page 99). If the amount of damages requested exceeds $75,000, Jorge can sue in a U.S. District Court sitting in either Florida or Oklahoma. Can he alternatively file the case in a state court?

Yes, as noted earlier, he can. Because the accident occurred in Florida, the most convenient state court would be Florida's. Using a long-arm statute, he could get jurisdiction over Gretchen through use of the mail. Jorge could also file the lawsuit in Oklahoma, Gretchen's resident state, and obtain jurisdiction there. This accident provides an example of a legal dispute in which concurrent jurisdiction exists.

When cases can be tried only in federal courts or only in state courts, **exclusive jurisdiction** exists. A person filing for a discharge in bankruptcy, which is a constitutional legal right that releases one from the duty to pay one's debts, can file the petition* only in a federal court. States also have exclusive jurisdiction in certain subject matter areas—for example, in divorces and adoptions. The concepts of concurrent and exclusive jurisdiction are illustrated in Exhibit 3–2.

FEDERAL APPELLATE COURTS

U.S. Courts of Appeals

The **U.S. Courts of Appeals** review the decisions of the U.S. District Courts located within their respective circuits. The country is divided into 12 circuits or geographical areas, each with a U.S. Court of Appeals. The number of judges, courtroom-building locations, and geographic size of the circuits vary greatly.** As with state appellate courts, the U.S. Courts of Appeals review cases brought to the court's attention by parties contending that the federal trial judge made an error of law. The federal system also has a U.S. Court of Appeals for the federal circuit, which has nationwide jurisdiction to hear appeals from all district courts in patent cases, as well as certain claims against the federal government. Also heard before this court are appeals from specialized courts (e.g., the U.S. Claims Court and the U.S. Court of International Trade) and claims arising from decisions of federal administrative agencies.

---

*A petition is the appropriate filing to institute a bankruptcy proceeding.
**The Washington, D.C. Circuit is the smallest circuit in geographical size and is responsible only for the nation's capital. The largest geographical circuit is the ninth (Alaska, Arizona, California, Guam, Hawaii, Idaho, Montana, Oregon, Nevada, the Northern Mariana Islands, and Washington). The number of judges per circuit ranges from six sitting circuit court judges in the first circuit (Maine, Massachusetts, New Hampshire, Puerto Rico, and Rhode Island) to twenty-eight authorized judges in the ninth circuit. At this writing, a proposal to split the ninth circuit was under consideration by Congress.

Exhibit 3–2: Exclusive and Concurrent Jurisdiction

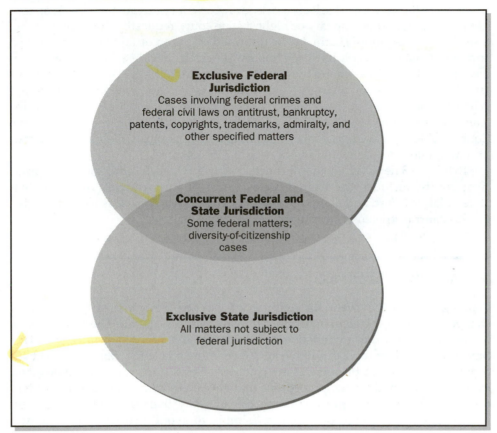

Exclusive Federal Jurisdiction
Cases involving federal crimes and federal civil laws on antitrust, bankruptcy, patents, copyrights, trademarks, admiralty, and other specified matters

Concurrent Federal and State Jurisdiction
Some federal matters; diversity-of-citizenship cases

Exclusive State Jurisdiction
All matters not subject to federal jurisdiction

U.S. Supreme Court

The highest level of the federal court system is the **United States Supreme Court**. Under the U.S. Constitution, there is but one such court. The court consists of nine Justices.* It has original, or trial, jurisdiction in rare instances—for example, in legal disputes in which a state is a party, cases between two states, and cases involving ambassadors. Most often it acts as the court of final appeal for federal Courts of Appeals and, in less frequent situations, the highest state appellate courts when they have decided cases on the basis of federal law.

Many cases compete for the attention of the U.S. Supreme Court, and in some cases the Court is required to take action (mandatory jurisdiction). An example of a mandatory case would be an appeal from either a federal or state court where the lower court has held that an act of Congress is unconstitutional. However, most appeals are discretionary (discretionary jurisdiction) and the Court is free to select which cases it will hear and decide. The selection process is accomplished

---

*The Constitution does not specify the number of Supreme Court Justices, and since its inception the number has varied. However, since 1869 the number has remained at nine. In 1937, an attempt was made by President Franklin D. Roosevelt to "pack the court" with six additional Justices who would presumably be sympathetic to his "New Deal" reform legislation. This maneuver was vigorously opposed and rejected by Congress.

by the *rule of four*, which means that the case is selected if four of the nine justices so choose. When the Court selects a case for review, it issues an order (**writ of certiorari**) to the Court of Appeals, or highest state court, requesting the record of the case. A writ of certiorari (Latin: "to be informed of") is an order by which the U.S. Supreme Court exercises its discretionary power to decide which lower court cases it will hear. To be among these cases, an important federal question must be raised, such as one involving a constitutional issue (e.g., freedom of speech). When the Supreme Court declines review of a case, the practical effect is affirmance of the lower court decision, which continues binding the parties. The Court is able to hear only a small percentage of the appeals filed annually, and formal opinions are delivered in only about 115–130 cases.[9]

Exhibit 3–3 depicts the federal court structure, which, in addition to the principal courts, includes the United States Court of International Trade, United States Claims Court, and United States Tax Court. Each of these is a special jurisdiction court restricted to hearing particular types of cases.

TRIAL PROCEEDINGS

This Web site has a lawsuit divided into five stages: investigation, notice, pleading, discovery, and trial. See the discussion of each by the law firm of Babbitt & Johnson in West Palm Beach, Florida. http://www.babbitt-johnson.com/suite.html

Looking back at the twentieth century, we can see that most of the dramatic changes in our legal system occurred following World War Two. The first 50 years of the century saw the law functioning in a slower, if not more leisurely, way. The procedures guiding cases through courts were more relaxed by far in the first half of the century. Today, procedures are complex. Meritorious cases can be lost because of errors made in the procedures that are necessary in maneuvering a civil case through the court process. Some litigants pay their opponents a sum of money, often called "nuisance money," simply to avoid incurring the expenses that complexity always seems to create.

HOW IS A CIVIL CASE STARTED?

Recall the example where Marya Martinez was injured in a skiing accident that she believes would not have occurred but for the carelessness of her ski instructor, Gary Graf (page 95). If Marya decides to sue Gary Graf, her attorney will begin the case by filing a document called a **complaint** with the county clerk. The complaint briefly states the facts she believes justify her claim, the basis for jurisdiction of the court, and the request for damages or other relief she seeks. Martinez is the plaintiff, and the complaint is almost always prepared by her attorney, who is satisfied that she has a **cause of action** (legally appropriate basis for suing).

County clerks maintain files, generally in alphabetical and numerical order, of every case filed in their respective counties. These records are open to the public. A filing fee (from $50 to $100 or more) is charged at the time of filing. When the complaint is filed, the clerk issues a **summons** (prepared by the plaintiff's attorney) by endorsing it on behalf of the court. The summons is a notice of a lawsuit; it informs the defendant that a lawsuit has been filed against him or her in the named court and that the defendant has a prescribed time (e.g., 30 days) to personally appear or respond to the complaint. You may recall the importance of the summons in obtaining jurisdiction of the defendant, as described earlier in the case involving Jorge Cepada and Gretchen Smalter. If the defendant fails to

Exhibit 3–3: The U.S. Court System

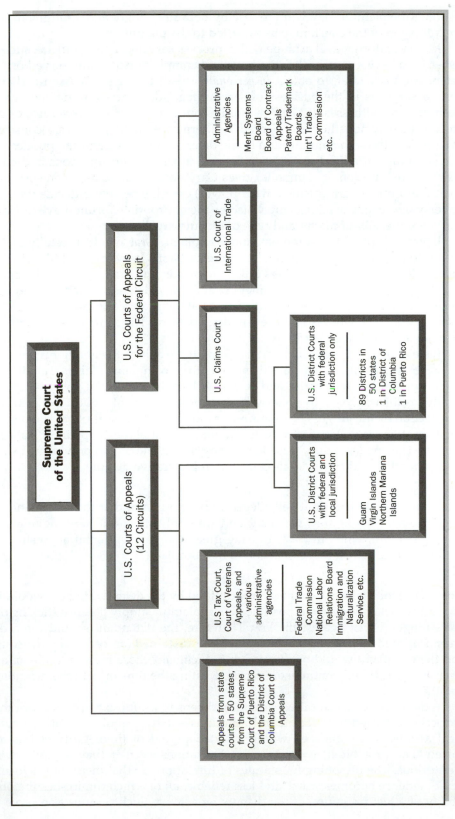

respond, the plaintiff may win the case by **default** (forfeit), and a judgment, the final decision of the court, may be awarded to the plaintiff.

Marya's attorney will arrange with a **process server** or a local official, such as a sheriff, to have a copy of the summons and complaint personally served on the defendant, Gary Graf, to obtain *in personam* jurisdiction. As discussed earlier, a process server is in the business of serving legal documents on defendants or plaintiffs and witnesses. If Gary cannot be found, or if he evades service of the process, he may nonetheless be served by alternative methods such as "constructive service" through a notification to the defendant by mail and the publication of a summons in a local newspaper. Serving a copy of the summons and complaint (or publication of summons) gives Gary notice that he has been sued and gives the proper court jurisdiction (or power) over his person to decide the controversy. The court, of course, must also be the appropriate forum (have jurisdiction) over the subject matter and type of dispute involved.

Upon receipt of the summons and complaint, Graf would typically hire a lawyer to represent him to uphold his interests. Graf's lawyer would file with the county clerk responsive pleadings called an **answer** and mail a copy to the plaintiff's lawyer. The answer is a document containing a defendant's denial and personal allegations of fact. In the answer, Graf may admit to any parts of the complaint that he believes are true and deny the rest. The complaint and answer together are called the **pleadings**.

Instead of an answer, Graf's attorney might be able to file another type of responsive document, asking for a dismissal of the complaint. This is called a **demurrer** or **motion to dismiss** and is used when the complaint, even if true, is legally insufficient to justify an answer. A **motion** is a formal request to a court for some action by the judge. The demurrer or motion to dismiss is often called a "so what" motion, as its legal effect is to say that even if all of the plaintiff's allegations are true, no legal duty was breached by the defendant. To provide an example of a motion to dismiss, let us consider an illustrative dispute.

Plaintiff Archibald Cantwell alleged in his complaint that the defendant professor "wrongfully, viciously, and wantonly stuck out her tongue at the plaintiff, while in class, causing great and severe mental anguish." Did Archie state a cause of action in his complaint?

No. Even if the plaintiff's claims were admitted by the defendant, there would be no legal recovery (judgment) possible for the plaintiff simply because sticking out one's tongue is not against the law. Therefore, the defendant should file a demurrer or motion to dismiss, which would be **sustained** (agreed to) by the court, and the complaint would be dismissed. If Archibald chose instead to file an answer, the case would continue on to trial, wasting the time of both the defendant and the court.

A demurrer can also raise procedural defenses, as, for example, a claim that the action is barred by a **statute of limitations**—statute requiring that particular legal actions be commenced within a stated period of time. Tardy claims are barred (i.e., prohibited) by statutes of limitations even if they are otherwise meritorious. The reasoning for statutes of limitation are that memories fade and other evidence becomes scarce and less reliable, all of which diminishes the possibility of a just resolution of the dispute by a court. Such statutes also serve to eliminate what could be an ongoing threat of suit that would otherwise interfere with the defendant's life.

Once Marya's complaint and Graf's answer are filed, the factual contentions of each party are stated on the record. Plaintiffs and defendants almost always disagree with each other's version of what had happened; these factual disagreements are much of what must be resolved at trial.

Following receipt of summons and complaint, Graf might voluntarily or unwittingly do nothing. Doing nothing is rarely a smart choice; here it would pave the way for Marya to obtain an uncontested judgment, called a **default judgment**. As explained earlier, a judgment is a final expression by the court telling who wins and who loses. Unlike a judgment following a trial, a default judgment may be issued by the judge following a trial in which the defendant is absent, and who, it is therefore assumed, does not contest the accuracy of the plaintiff's claims. The judge simply takes minimal evidence from the plaintiff to ensure that the claim is not frivolous or improper in some respect. Following such an *ex parte* (Latin: "with one party") **trial**, which often takes only minutes of the court's time, a judgment typically is awarded the plaintiff. So, doing nothing can be a costly mistake. Even if he is going to concede fault and liability, Graf would be wise to file answer to the complaint and then try to negotiate a compromise limiting the damages he must pay or providing a reasonable payment schedule.

How Is a Criminal Case Started?

In contrast to a civil case, a criminal case is formally begun by the issuance of an **accusation**, which formally charges a specified person with commission of a particular crime. An accusation is usually initiated by the district attorney (under which circumstance it is called an **information**) or by a body called the **grand jury***** (under which circumstance it is called an **indictment**). Misdemeanor cases typically are initiated by the filing of a complaint. These terms and criminal procedures are discussed in Chapter 6.

What Are Pretrial Procedures?

Once a civil lawsuit begins by the filing of pleadings, a year or more may elapse before the trial. In some crowded metropolitan areas, the volume of cases filed, together with shortages of judges and courtrooms, cause seriously congested calendars, which in turn necessitate undesirable delays in settling cases for trial. In rural and less populous jurisdictions, the trial may occur as soon as the opposing attorneys are prepared. In populous urban areas, delays of three to four years sometimes occur. Courtroom delay has become one of the most serious problems facing this country's legal system. In recent years, many states have begun experimenting with new administrative methods to expedite the process. Many states actively encourage alternatives to litigation, such as arbitration. The legal system is flexible enough to allow for alternatives to the courts in many

For an example of the different statutes of limitations in a state, look them up for the state of Indiana at http://www.state.in.us/hcc/html/scc/statute/html For the different times in each state for a negligence lawsuit, consult the following site, which contains excerpts from the book *Winning Your Personal Injury Claim* by Evan K. Aidman, Esq. http://www.legalaidman.com/8b-state.htm

*A body composed of a number of jurors that varies from state to state, sometimes 6, sometimes 12, and occasionally more than 12. The grand jury inquires into crimes committed in the city or other geographic region from which the members are drawn, makes determination of the probability of guilt, and then issues indictments (formal accusation of crime) against supposed offenders. (24 American Jurisprudence, Grand Jury § 2.)

situations. Alternatives to litigation are called **alternative dispute resolution (ADR)** and are discussed in Chapter 4.

Discovery

One of the most time-consuming, expensive, and intrusive aspects of going through civil trials today is a process called **discovery**. Discovery includes the use of a group of methods to learn facts about the dispute. Nonexistent early in the twentieth century, many believe that discovery has escalated into an arsenal of weapons that is often abused by attorneys. Should discovery be streamlined to keep pace with life and times in the twenty-first century? Many business contracts today contain arbitration agreements (discussed in Chapter 4) that avoid going to court if and when future disputes arise between the contracting persons. One major reason why many, perhaps most, financial businesses (e.g., banks, stock brokerages) and HMOs (health maintenance organizations) choose this judicial by-pass is to avoid the costs, intrusiveness, and delays associated with discovery procedures.

Although courtroom availability is the most common reason for a delay in a trial date, counsel for one or both of the parties may seek delay because more time is needed for discovery procedures. The stated goals of discovery are to (1) educate each party as to the facts surrounding the controversy, (2) promote voluntary settlement of the controversy by revealing strengths and weaknesses in the cases of each party, and (3) eliminate surprises that might otherwise arise during the trial, possibly leading to a miscarriage of justice.

Depositions and interrogatories are the most common types of discovery. A **deposition** is the questioning of a witness or adverse party by the opposing attorney, long before the trial, under oath, in the presence of a court reporter and the other party's attorney. **Interrogatories** are a form of discovery in which written questions are directed to a party, who must then reply under oath with written answers.

Marya Martinez hired Sally Sharpe as her attorney in the case against Gary Graf. Sharpe's complaint and summons issued by the court were personally served on Graf. He promptly hired a lawyer, Scott Dasse, who prepared and filed an answer. Graf contended that he adjusted Marya's bindings carefully and properly and was not negligent. Graf's answer also alleged that Marya was negligent in two respects: (1) being under the influence of alcohol at the time of her injury and (2) being careless in allowing ice to form beneath her boots. The pleadings were filed, joining the issues of fact. What is the status of the proceedings?

Attorney Sharpe is seeking a money judgment against Graf to compensate Marya for her injury on the theory that Graf was negligent. Attorney Dasse, on behalf of Graf, is contending that Graf was not negligent and that even, if he was, Marya was equally careless as to her own safety and so she should be denied a money judgment. Both attorneys will need more information in order to prepare for trial.

Depositions.   Sharpe wants to know the exact setting Graf had used in adjusting Marya's bindings, then she can seek expert advice as to what should have been the proper setting. Sharpe could mail a notice of taking deposition to Graf's attorney, requesting that Graf appear in Sharpe's office at a stated time to be questioned under oath with a court reporter present. The court reporters will use mechanical shorthand to record all testimony. In many states, electronic shorthand equipment and recording machines also are used. During this deposition, which Graf must attend, Sharpe could ask him, among other things, what setting he had used on Marya's bindings. Of course, Graf's attorney will respond by taking Marya's deposition.

> At Marya's deposition, Dasse asked the following question: "Miss Martinez, do you date frequently?" Attorney Sharpe immediately objected, shouting that she would not allow her client to be subjected to irrelevant questions by Dasse. Must Marya answer the question?

At the deposition, attorney Dasse cannot force Marya to answer a question if she refuses. He could, however, seek a court order requiring her to answer the question if the question is deemed appropriate by the judge. Courts have the power to compel the parties to comply with the discovery procedures. If the order is granted and Marya still refuses to answer, her entire case may be dismissed or another sanction (penalty) imposed. Attorney Dasse will need to explain to a judge why the question is appropriate because its relevance to the case is not obvious.

After the deposition, the court reporter prepares a hard (paper) copy of all questions and answers. This document is made available to the witness, who makes any necessary corrections before signing and returning it. If the witness is unavailable at the trial, or is present but changes the version of the story given at the deposition, the transcript itself may be introduced as evidence and used to impeach (i.e., discredit) the witness. In complex cases, depositions may require several days of testimony under oath. The cost of taking depositions is a major expense of litigation and one significant reason why alternatives to litigation are often sought.*

Written Interrogatories.   After the deposition, attorney Dasse thought of some additional questions that he would like to ask. He sent the following **written interrogatories** to Marya through her attorney:

1. Please state the address of Luther Thomas.
2. Please state each date you visited a doctor and your total medical bill expenses.
3. Please state whether or not your medical bills are being paid by an insurance company. If so, please state the company's name and the applicable policy number.

---

*As undeniably useful as discovery is, it is costly and can be subject to abuse. Litigants can request large quantities of documents based on possible relevance, and the expense of this production of documents is borne by the person producing them. The federal courts and many state court systems are experimenting with discovery rules in an attempt to preserve discovery's value while limiting its excesses. Examples of new rules include requiring a party to provide relevant discovery without it being requested by the other party and harsher penalties (sanctions) available to the courts for instances where abuse of discovery rules exist. Some authors have suggested eliminating discovery altogether. Lorn Kieve, "Discovery Reform," 11 ABA Journal 79 (December 1991).

If Marya fails to answer the written interrogatories, Graf's attorney may seek an order from the court compelling answers. Attorneys may serve hundreds of written interrogatories in preparation of a complex case. They are less expensive than depositions because no court reporter is needed, and since they are written they tend to be more concise than the ramblings that frequently accompany oral interrogations. Furthermore, parties responding to interrogatories must search their files and records for information they "cannot recall." A disadvantage is that they allow a witness to consult with counsel and draft an answer that, while true, discloses as little as possible and states even that as favorably as possible. The questioning attorney is not present to detect signs of uneasiness and possible evasion or concealment, nor is he or she able to immediately pursue promising leads suggested by oral responses during depositions.

Motion to Produce.   The **motion to produce** may result in an order made by a judge at the request of counsel. It compels the opposing party to provide specified evidence that he or she currently controls or possesses, and that is believed to be relevant in the case.

Dasse believed that Marya's diary might provide important information. He therefore filed a motion to produce with the court after his request to produce it had been refused. The motion requested an order compelling Marya to deliver her diary to Dasse for his inspection. Will the motion be granted?

Dasse's motion will not be granted unless he can demonstrate to the court specifically what may be contained in the diary that would be relevant to the issues in the case. That appears doubtful unless, for example, Dasse can offer proof that Marya has been deceitful and he has reason to believe that the diary would confirm the deceit.

At the time of trial, either attorney may ask the court for a **subpoena** (Latin: "under penalty"), a written order directing a person to appear in court and testify as a witness. If it is believed that the witness has books or documents needed for a full disclosure of the facts, the court may issue a **subpoena** *duces tecum* (Latin: "under penalty bring with you"), requiring that identified documents or physical evidence be brought to court.

Discovery in Criminal Matters

In a criminal case, discovery is limited because of the defendant's **privilege against self-incrimination**. (A **privilege** is a legal right.) This legal right, in brief, allows that a defendant cannot be compelled to testify against him- or herself in a criminal case. The privilege is derived from the Fifth Amendment to the U.S. Constitution, and it is often referred to in slang terms as "taking the Fifth."

The government prosecutor does not have this same right, as the prosecutors are not on trial. The Sixth Amendment to the U.S. Constitution gives the accused the right "in all criminal prosecutions . . . to be confronted with the witnesses against him. . . ." Therefore, the government prosecutor must allow examination of the evidence against the defendant, including names of witnesses against the defendant. However, physical evidence (such as weapons, clothing, and stolen

The law office of Myron Milch in New Jersey provides a sample order for discovery at http://www.milchlaw.com/form7.html

goods) may be impounded (seized and held) by the district attorney, pending trial. The defendant does, however, have the right to inspect all such evidence before trial. The apparent advantage of one-way discovery for the criminal defendant is more than counterbalanced by the state's greater resources to independently investigate and discover facts surrounding alleged criminal activity.

Motion for Summary Judgment

If there are no disputes over facts that need to be resolved, it is possible that the case can be decided without a trial. In a **motion for summary judgment** the moving party argues that there are no significant questions of fact and that the applicable law requires that the moving party be awarded judgment. This motion might be made to the court after discovery, when a party believes discovery has shown that there are no real disputes as to the facts. If the motion is granted, no trial takes place. The party against whom a motion for summary judgment is granted (or any other adverse order that terminates the case) would have the right to appeal.

The Pretrial Conference

Either party or the court can request a **pretrial hearing** or **conference**, which usually takes place after the discovery process is over. The conference consists of an informal discussion between the judge and the attorneys. Its purpose is to identify the matters that are in dispute and to plan the course of the trial. At the pretrial hearing, the judge may encourage the parties to settle without a trial (an out-of-court settlement). These "settlement conferences" are sometimes attended by the parties to the litigation, as well as by their attorneys. Possible "before trial" steps in a civil dispute are set forth in Exhibit 3–4.

WHAT IS A JURY?

A **jury** is a group of men and women selected according to pre-established procedures to ensure lack of bias, who are sworn under oath to inquire of certain matters of fact and declare the truth based on evidence presented to them. A jury is also referred to as a **trier of fact**. This broad definition of a jury includes many types of juries used in the Untied States including grand jury, petit jury, special jury, coroner's jury, and sheriff's jury. Our discussion focuses on those juries selected to hear and decide specific legal disputes rather than investigative juries, such as grand juries.

In the United States, litigating parties often request a jury trial. Whether the request is granted will depend on whether the requesting party has a legal right to a jury trial. Many U.S. citizens believe that they have a right to a jury trial in all legal matters, but they are wrong. Litigants do, however, have a right to a jury trial in many matters. Whether they have a right to jury trial may depend on whether the trial is criminal or civil, raises matters "in equity" or "law," or whether it takes place in state or federal courts.*

---

*Article III, Section 2 of the Constitution provides that, "the Trial of all Crimes . . . shall be by Jury. . . ." The Sixth and Seventh Amendments also provide for the right to a jury trial. The Sixth Amendment, referring to criminal cases, provides that "In all criminal prosecutions, the accused shall enjoy the right to a speedy and public trial. . . ." The Seventh Amendment states, "In Suits at common law, where the value in controversy shall exceed twenty dollars, the right of trial by jury shall be persevered. . . ."

Exhibit 3-4: Steps in a Civil Case—Before Trial

*In many states, nonbinding arbitration may be required in addition to or in lieu of the settlement conference.

Tort or breach of contract occurs.

Victim does nothing.

Victim consults attorney, who investigates and may negotiate with prospective defendant or his/her attorney.

No basis for action: matter is dropped.

Basis for action is established, but dispute is settled out of court, possibly by alternative dispute resolution (ADR).

Plaintiff's attorney prepares complaint and summons and files them with proper court.

Copies of complaint and summons are delivered to defendant (by process server).

No response is received: plaintiff gets judgment by default.

OR

Defendant's attorney files answer to complaint.

OR

Defendant's attorney files demurrer to complaint.

Denied by judge at hearing (proceed to trial).

Sustained by judge at hearing.

Plaintiff drops action.

Plaintiff revises complaint and starts over.

Plaintiff contests demurrer at appellate court.

Discovery by plaintiff and defendant. Includes depositions, interrogatories, and motions to produce.

Settlement conference with judge.*

Proceed to trial.

OR

Matter not settled. Case proceeds.

Matter settled. Case dismissed.

People's Bank, a Connecticut corporation, filed an action to foreclose on a home owned by William and Nadine Podd, husband and wife, alleging the Podds failed to pay their monthly mortgage payments. The Podds requested a trial by jury. People's Bank objected. Do the Podds have a right to jury trial in this lawsuit?[10]

Any party to a civil lawsuit in the federal court system has the constitutional right (under the Seventh Amendment) to trial by jury in cases at law, "where the value in controversy shall exceed twenty dollars." A right to a jury trial in a civil case in state courts is not guaranteed by the federal Constitution,[11] although state constitutions usually provide for this right. The case of *People's Bank v. Podd* was filed in a Connecticut state court raising issues of state civil law. The Connecticut constitution provides for a right to a jury trial, but the Connecticut supreme court has held that this right exists only in those cases where a right to jury trial existed at the time of the Constitution's adoption (1812). The court concluded the action brought against the Podds was an equity action and so the state needn't provide the Podds a jury trial. We discuss equity actions in more detail later in the chapter.

The right to a jury trial is more certain in matters of criminal law. The murder trial of O.J. Simpson made most Americans acutely aware of the role of juries. In addition to issues of selection, sequestration, crime scene visitation, and evidence tampering, the public was presented with the possible issue of nullification of law.* A trial by an "impartial jury" is a constitutional right (under the Sixth and Fourteenth Amendments) in any criminal matter, federal or state, where a serious penalty such as a jail sentence or imprisonment of more than six months may be the punishment.[12] Criminal defendants may waive their right to jury trials for various reasons (such as a **plea bargain**, where they admit guilt to a lesser offense than they were charged with, thereby sparing the state of conducting costly trials with uncertain outcomes). A judge alone then makes the necessary findings of fact and imposes a sentence.

In usual cases a jury concludes and decides the **questions of fact**—historical events that must be proved to win a lawsuit. For example, in a dispute about a fight between two students William and Norbert, there probably will be a disagreement as to who started the altercation. A question of fact is presented and is generally answered by the jury, with a verdict in favor of the defensive fighter. If there is no jury, the trial judge decides questions of fact.

Questions of law are the appropriate legal rules to be applied in the trial. The judge decides or answers the questions of law in the trial. For example, in the fight between William and Norbert, the judge determines the legal rules appropriate to decide the case (e.g., the definition of battery and self-defense would probably be among the legal rules applied). The judge also makes a ruling of law when allowing or disallowing certain evidence, ruling on motions, or instructing the jury which legal principles should be applied to the facts during their deliberations. A question of law, not fact, also arises whenever the constitutionality of a statute or executive action is an issue. As constitutionality is a question of law, not fact, a jury does not decide whether a statute is constitutional.

---

*The power of a jury to reject the law and evidence to acquit a defendant it believes is guilty. This concept is discussed in more detail later in the chapter.

The deference that a jury must give the judge's jury instructions differs in civil and criminal cases. In a civil case, if the jury ignores the law, the judge has the duty and the power to overturn the jury verdict. The judge's power is restricted in a criminal case, although the judge can declare a defendant not guilty even if the jury decided to convict the defendant. However, in a criminal case, a judge cannot overturn a jury verdict of not guilty because he or she believes the jury is wrong or has ignored the law. This residual power of the jury in a criminal case is called **jury nullification**. Thus, for example, in a criminal case, although a jury could not find a law unconstitutional, it could legally refuse to convict a defendant because they think the law is unconstitutional, or unfair, or for any other reason. A judge is not free to disregard the jury's verdict of not guilty unless the judge finds jury corruption or misconduct (e.g., one or more jurors had been bribed).

Defendant Douglas E. Datcher was indicted for attempted distribution of a controlled substance and related charges. A conviction on all charges could lead, under non-discretionary federal sentencing guidelines, to a minimum 25-year sentence. Datcher, believing that conviction of the offenses would mandate punishment that was too harsh, made a motion to the court to allow him to ask potential jurors during the *voir dire* process (see page 119) about their attitudes toward punishment and to argue the issue of punishment to the jury during closing argument. Should the court allow Datcher to discuss the severity of punishment when the jury's only role is to determine guilt or innocence on the charged crimes?[13]

The defendant's motion was partially granted. "[T]he defendant may argue possible punishment to the jury but may not *voir dire* the jury on this issue." This is so even though "that jury, upon learning of the draconian sentence hanging over his head, would deem penalty too great and thus let the defendant go free pursuant to the power of a jury nullification." This case considers the importance of a jury as a watchdog of government in a criminal case. Although the court acknowledges the inherent right of a jury in a criminal case to disregard the law, this court and others have held it improper to inform the jury that they have this power.

Prospective Jurors

The jury is a group of persons selected from a panel of randomly designated citizens of the local region to decide a particular civil or criminal case. A jury is considered the fairest instrument of justice on the theory that it tends to neutralize individual bias from the courtroom by drawing together a number of persons of diverse interests and backgrounds. No single person—not even a highly educated, coldly analytical, scrupulously honest, professional scientist—is totally objective, so it is hoped that the combination of differing perspectives will provide the balance needed for just decisions. Judges, lawyers, witnesses, scholars—and most important, litigants themselves—generally agree that the jury system works well most of the time.

Usually litigants in emotionally charged cases, both civil and criminal, prefer the consensus of a jury of their peers (equals) to the decision of one judge. On the other hand, many attorneys believe that, in complex business litigation, a jury can be overwhelmed and thoroughly confused by a flood of technical language. Thus, they think that in such cases their clients will fare better by waiving their right to a jury trial and relying on the expertise of the judge or an arbitrator.

It is important that the jury selection process be random. Otherwise, people would justifiably suspect its integrity. In criminal cases especially, the jury is sometimes the sole barrier between the individual and the awesome power of the prosecuting government. The selection begins with preparation of a list or panel of prospective jurors. Most states prepare such lists from voter registrations. Because minorities, the poor, and young adults do not register to vote at the same rate as the rest of the population, these groups are likely to be underrepresented on juries. For this reason, many states use other sources of names for prospective jurors, such as driver-registration records, telephone directories, hunting and fishing license lists, utility customer lists, or census rolls. Some accept volunteers for jury duty.

The Jury Selection and Service Act regulates jury selection in federal cases.[14] This act provides that names selected from voter registration lists should be supplemented with names from additional lists to help ensure selection of juries that better represent a diverse community.

Exemptions from Jury Service

A few classes of people are automatically exempt, or disqualified, from jury duty in many states. In federal courts, disqualified groups include noncitizens; minors; residents of less than one year; persons unable to read, write, and understand English; persons with mental or physical infirmities that would impair their capability as jurors; and convicted felons. States have adopted similar exemptions.[15] In addition, persons may be temporarily excused or indefinitely exempted when absence from a job or family would cause an unreasonable hardship.

It is illegal for an employer to penalize or discriminate against an employee for serving as a juror by docking vacation time.[16] Some employers continue to pay the salaries or wages of jurors, less the modest fees received from the court, but this is not compulsory. Jurors are presently paid $40 per day in the federal court system and usually less in state courts. Such small sums are inadequate pay for most jurors who are not receiving any income from their employers. Consequently, jury duty that may last for weeks or longer may mean a significant financial sacrifice. Yet jury service is a citizen's duty in a democracy. Persons refusing to serve without an acceptable excuse can be found in contempt of court, resulting in fines and/or imprisonment.*

Voir Dire

The French phrase *voir dire* (pronounced *v'wah deer* and meaning "to speak the truth") refers to the questioning of prospective jurors to find possible bias. Understandably, attorneys try to *seat* (select) jurors who they believe to be sympathetic to their clients' position. Thus, an accountant accustomed to arithmetic precision may not be welcomed as a juror by a defendant relying on an

*In December of 1998, a Los Angeles judge fined 41 people $1,500 each for failing to make themselves available as jurors or appear to explain their absence. *Sacramento Bee*, December 10, 1998, A4.

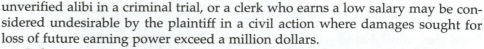

A Web site for a jury
consulting firm, The
Wilmington Institute in Dallas,
Texas is found at
http://www.wilmington-
institute.com/

unverified alibi in a criminal trial, or a clerk who earns a low salary may be considered undesirable by the plaintiff in a civil action where damages sought for loss of future earning power exceed a million dollars.

In large cities, private companies are available to research potential juror lists for cases when a sizable amount of money is at stake. Such research firms provide "jury books" containing past juror voting records and other personal information. These books are sold to attorneys to assist them in identifying favorable prospective jurors. In major trials, where the stakes are high, sociologists and psychologists have been hired by lawyers to analyze the physical appearance, education, social status, economic condition, personality, and general cultural background of each prospective juror. The idea is to predict attitude and probable voting conduct in the forthcoming trial. Such assistance in jury selection raises many questions about the accuracy of character evaluation and the ethical propriety of this practice, especially if only one side has access to such information.*

On behalf of Marya Martinez, attorney Sharpe demands a jury trial. On the day set for trial, Sharpe and attorney Dasse meet with Judge Miller in chambers. Sharpe requests permission to personally *voir dire* the prospective jurors. Dasse does not object. Will Judge Miller grant this request?

Possibly. Historically, judges have had the power to either conduct *voir dire* themselves or to allow the attorneys to do so. Most states follow the lead of the federal court system where *voir dire* is conducted by the judge, but only after considering specific questions offered by the attorneys. Using a judge usually expedites the questioning and serves to preclude the use of inappropriate questions. Some attorneys try to argue their case in *voir dire,* which is not a valid purpose of the jury selection process.

Judge Miller grants Sharpe's request and orders that the two attorneys conduct the *voir dire.* One of the questions Sharpe asks each prospective juror is whether he or she has ever been a ski instructor. One person answers "yes." Is this sufficient evidence of juror bias? If so, what recourse does Sharpe have against it?

Prior experience or knowledge of a situation may or may not show a person is biased. Everyone possesses inclinations and opinions consistent with his or her culture, education, family background, experience, and so forth, but not everyone allows these to prejudice his or her thinking. What matters is whether a certain experience or inclination tends to make a person unable to decide fairly a particular case. Some types of experience are more likely than others to do this. If bias is evident or likely, the judge may excuse the prospective juror **for cause** (bias or the appearance of bias is shown). In Marya's trial, a prospective juror who was once a ski instructor would probably not be as impartial as someone without this

---

*Legal consulting firms provide pretrial opinion polls, profiles of "ideal jurors," mock trials and shadow juries. They also coach lawyers and witnesses and prepare designs for courtroom graphics. When such assistance is utilized, critics suggest that the jury is not composed of one's peers.

experience. Thus, bias is likely. The judge might properly excuse that prospective juror for cause.

There is no limit on the number of challenges for cause, which can be granted, with a showing of bias. In jury selection for a trial concerning a highly publicized Brink's warehouse robbery in Boston, some 1,000 prospective jurors were excused for cause. Because of newspaper accounts over the years before the first arrest in the case, most of those excused had definite opinions as to the guilt of the defendants.[17]

Even if no bias is demonstrable, each attorney in either a civil or criminal action can challenge peremptorily (without cause) and thereby excuse from service a limited number of prospective jurors (six, for example, in civil actions, and generally more in criminal actions). The purpose of a **peremptory challenge** (dismissal of a juror for an undisclosed personal reason of the dismissing party) is to permit parties to eliminate some prospective jurors for any reason or for no reason. Some clients simply do not like the looks of a particular prospective juror. A well-known ditty goes:

> I do not like thee, Dr. Fell;
> the reason why I cannot tell.
> But this I know and know full well,
> I do not like thee, Dr. Fell.

Although no reason need be stated for a peremptory challenge, such challenges cannot be used to accomplish the illegal and impermissible purpose of excluding persons on the basis of their race or gender.* Once peremptory challenges are exhausted or waived (given up or unused), the designated number of jurors are sworn to fulfill their duty faithfully, and the trial begins. If the trial is expected to last very long, one, two, or more extra jurors (called *alternates*) are selected and remain in the courtroom throughout the trial. In the infamous criminal trial of O.J. Simpson, for the first time in U.S. history, more alternate jurors (15) were selected than jurors (12). Alternate jurors vote only if a regular juror dies or withdraws because of illness, family hardship, misconduct, or other conflict. If by the end of a trial there are not enough jurors remaining to render a verdict, a mistrial results unless both parties agree to accept the verdict of the smaller panel.

A preschool molestation case in Los Angeles took more than two-and-one-half years before the jury adjourned to consider their verdicts. By that time all six alternate jurors had replaced vacancies that occurred during trial. If the jury had lost another juror before the verdicts were rendered, a mistrial would have occurred in a trial that cost over $15 million. After three months of deliberations the jury reached verdicts on 65 counts (separate criminal charges) against two defendants. One defendant was found not guilty on all charged counts. The other defendant was found

---

*A number of recent far-ranging Supreme Court decisions have changed the nature of the peremptory challenge process. It is now impermissible to dismiss a juror on the basis of race in both criminal and civil cases by either party. See *Batson v. Kentucky*, 476 U.S. 79, 106 S.Ct. 1712 (1986); *Powers v. Ohio*, 499 U.S. 400, 111 S.Ct. 1364 (1991); *Edmonston v. Leesville Concrete Co.*, 500 U.S. 614, 111 S.Ct. 2077 (1991); *Georgia v. McCollum*, 505 U.S. 42, 112 S.Ct. 2348 (1992); *Holland v. Illinois*, 493 U.S. 474, 110 S.Ct. 803 (1990); *Hernandez v. New York*, 500 U.S. 352, 111 S.Ct. 1859 (1991). In 1994, the limitation on the use of peremptory challenges was extended to make exclusions based on gender also impermissible. See *J.E.B. v. Alabama* 511 U.S. 127, 114 S.Ct. 1419 (1994).

not guilty on all but 13 counts. As to these counts the jury was unable to reach a verdict. As the jury finished its deliberations without losing another juror, there was no mistrial.[18]

Jury Size and Vote

Since the middle of the fourteenth century, juries in England were composed of 12 persons. Probably for that reason, laypersons as well as scholars in the United States had long assumed that the Constitution, when referring to a jury, meant a jury of 12 persons. In federal criminal court trials, 12 jurors are the required number, although criminal verdicts have been upheld with 11 jurors.[19] In civil cases, the number of jurors required has been reduced to 6 in many district courts. According to the U.S. Supreme Court, this reduction to 6 jurors in a civil case satisfies the Seventh Amendment.[20]

The U.S. Supreme Court has held that the Fourteenth Amendment does not require that state court juries (as opposed to federal ones) be composed of 12 persons in either civil or criminal cases. As few as 6 members have been found constitutional in a state court,[21] although a jury of 5 in a criminal case has been disallowed.[22] For reasons of efficiency and economy, about one-fourth of the states have reduced the size of juries to 6–8 jurors in both civil and criminal matters. Currently no state provides for fewer than 12 jurors in cases where the death penalty could be imposed, although that may be constitutionally permissible.

Although the United States is indebted to England for its commitment to trial by jury, today's United Kingdom began significantly curtailing the right to juries in civil cases in 1933. This action was a response to the growing complexity of civil law and the time and expense consumed by the jury process. A civil jury is now the exception in the United Kingdom.[23]

The number of jurors required to agree on a verdict is an additional important question in American jurisprudence. Historically, to reach a verdict in criminal cases the jury vote had to be unanimous. Thus, in criminal actions one juror has been able to block the prosecutor's attempt to convict the accused. Such power is an affirmation of the importance of each juror. The requirement of the unanimous jury is the rule in federal and most state criminal prosecutions.[24] A few states allow for a guilty verdict without requiring a unanimous jury (for example, Oregon permits a conviction by 10 out of 12 jurors),[25] although a unanimous vote for a verdict in a state 6-person jury criminal case is required.[26] In most civil cases, however, a three-fourths majority (9 of 12 jurors) is sufficient. On the other hand, in the federal court system civil juries are required to render unanimous verdicts.*

Clearly, a reduction in jury size together with relaxed voting percentages for a verdict will do much to change the role of the jury in our society. In addition, some states are reducing the number of types of cases in which a jury is considered appropriate. For example, states with no-fault automobile insurance plans largely bypass the jury process in automobile-related personal injury cases. Many states have decriminalized such matters as minor traffic offenses and removed a

---

*Federal Rules of Civil Procedure §48 states, "The court shall seat a jury of not fewer than six and not more than twelve members. Unless the parties otherwise stipulate, (1) the verdict shall be unanimous and (2) no verdict shall be taken from a jury reduced in size to fewer than six members."

person's right to a jury trial in such cases. In the federal system, there is a presumption that offenses punishable by incarceration for six months or less are petty offenses for which jury trials are unavailable.[27] In addition, there is an important area of U.S. jurisprudence where the Constitution does not require jury trials and legal history has not provided them, namely all matters "in equity." Recall the gavel on page 117 where the Podds were unsuccessful in their request for a jury trial in the foreclosure action brought against them. Most laypersons are uninformed on the important subject of equity, which we address next.

WHAT IS AN ACTION OR CAUSE IN EQUITY?

The United States legal system, like that of the United Kingdom, distinguishes between what are called disputes *at law* and *in equity*. The distinction between law and equity is not based on logic but on history. As discussed in Chapter 1, in medieval times certain types of cases in England were decided by chancellors (government administrators) rather than in the king's court. The chancellors were often also religious aides to the king. In most disputes, an aggrieved person could seek and obtain monetary relief from a regular king's court. In the king's court, a judge would decide the case, sometimes with the assistance of a jury. Such were matters "at common law," and monetary damages usually were the only relief available from the king's courts.

A person unable to obtain relief from a regular court would appeal to the king, who would refer the citizen to the king's chancellor. As a general proposition, chancellors became involved only when there was no adequate remedy at law, when monetary damages were not sought or did not satisfy the need of the party seeking relief. These actions became known as actions "at equity." The chancellors decided matters brought before them based on their conscience, community norms of conduct, and principles of equity, or fairness.

Today, all but a few U.S. courts have combined powers of law and equity.[28] However, differences between the two methods of relief remain in the handling of certain types of disputes, available remedies, and the procedural rules applied to the actions. For example, matters involving the family were and are matters in equity, and an example of a type of dispute heard only as a matter in equity. Thus, if a dispute involves a divorce or dissolution or marriage, adoption, name change, or juvenile problem, a court sits in equity without a jury and usually applies different procedural rules.

Other civil cases in equity based on the claimant seeking a different remedy include the following:

1. An action requesting the court to order the defendant to comply with a contract by performing as promised (e.g., when the subject of the sales contract is unique, such as an original painting by van Gogh or a parcel of land), and the buyer wants performance, not monetary damages (**specific performance**).

2. An action requesting the court to rescind an agreement to sell one's home, because of the undue influence of a relative (**rescission**).

3. An action to bar a person from continuing to hunt unlawfully on someone else's property, or to end an unlawful strike by a union (**injunction**).

Note that in each example of equity, money damages are not sought. The monetary remedy at law was either inadequate or unavailable. However, today

See the discussion on the equitable remedy of INJUNCTION at the THE 'LECTRIC LAW LIBRARY(TM) http://www.LECTLAW.COM// DEF/i046 most courts, even in an equity action, strive to give full relief requested, including monetary damages if appropriate. Except in a few states, a modern court can grant both a remedy at law and at equity. For example, an aggrieved songwriter might be awarded an injunction barring the infringer (wrongful user) from using her copyrighted song without permission and also be given dollar damages for the prior illegal use. Examples of civil cases at law include actions to recover money for (1) injury caused by negligence of the defendant, (2) loss of earnings caused by defamation of character by the defendant, (3) money lost as the result of the defendant's fraud and deceit, and (4) profits lost due to breach of contract by the defendant. Exhibit 3–5 provides a contrast between matters at equity and at law.

However, criminal cases are not matters in equity.* There is no right to trial by jury in equity cases. The constitutional right to a jury was limited in the Seventh Amendment of the Constitution to civil matters, which are "suits at common law." The distinction between *common law* and *equity* was well known by the drafters of the Constitution. Jury trials in equity matters did not exist in England, as the chancellor relied on his own good conscience and sense of what was just. Since juries were available at law, a person who sought relief in equity waived the right to common-law procedures, including the jury. In some states, a judge in equity may use an advisory jury but is not obliged to take and/or apply its verdict.

A judge sitting in a matter in equity has awesome power. The judge is both the finder of fact and law and controls the powerful remedies available only in equity. Courts of equity not only provide different remedies but also often oper-

Exhibit 3–5:   Contrast Between a Matter in Equity and a Matter at Law

	Equity	**Law**

Subject Matter	Family law
	Probate
	Trusts
	When remedy at law
	  is inadequate
		Everything that is not
		  a matter in equity

Nature of Trial	No jury	Jury

Remedies	In contracts:
	  Reformation
	  Rescission
	  Specific Performance
	Injunctions
	Restitution
		Money damages

*If a juvenile commits an act that would be criminal if committed by an adult, the matter is generally considered a matter in equity. It is technically not considered a criminal matter, although a deprivation of liberty can and often does result if the minor is found responsible. Although an equitable matter, some due process protection still applies because of the potential for deprivation of liberty. However, there is no right to a jury trial. Many states provide for the criminal prosecution of minors as if they are adults in certain situations. If the minor is tried as an adult, the case is transferred from the court of equity to the criminal courts and all rights and jeopardies of criminal defendants apply.

ate using different procedures and guidelines, including what are called equitable maxims. A *maxim* is a proposition or statement which provides a guide to a judge's exercise of his or her discretion. A few examples of equitable maxims are provided and explained in Exhibit 3–6.

Defiance of a judge's order can place a person in ==contempt of court== and subject him or her to summary arrest and imprisonment. Contempt of court is ==willful disobedience of a judicial order or obstruction of the work of the court.== Some of the most controversial cases in the history of law have involved the exercise of a judge's equitable power.

> Dr. J. Elizabeth Morgan was a party to a legal action involving visitation rights concerning her minor female child, Hilary. She maintained that the child's father had sexually abused her daughter. Although the husband strenuously denied this allegation, Morgan refused to obey an unsupervised visitation order in favor of her husband and placed the girl in hiding. Judge Herbert Dixon held Dr. Morgan in contempt of court. How could the court enforce its order?

Dr. Morgan was taken to the District of Columbia jail, where she spent the next 759 days for refusing to disclose the whereabouts of her child. She was finally released after a special law requiring her immediate release was passed by Congress and signed by then-President George W. Bush. As the court matter was in equity, no jury had been involved. Dr. Morgan had been jailed for her continuing refusal to follow the court's order, even though she had committed no crime.[29] During the 1990s, Susan McDougal spent 18 months in jail for civil contempt for her refusal to answer questions posed by Special Prosecutor Kenneth Starr about President William J. Clinton's involvement in the Whitewater Development Corporation.[30]

An even more dramatic case demonstrating the awesome power of a court of equity involved prison inmates in Texas. The United States District Court for the Southern District of Texas held that the conditions of confinement in the state violated the U.S. Constitution. To implement and ensure compliance with the

An update on the Elizabeth Morgan case can be found at http://www.seattletimes.com/news/nation-world/html98/altmorg_050198.html

Exhibit 3–6: Equitable Maxims

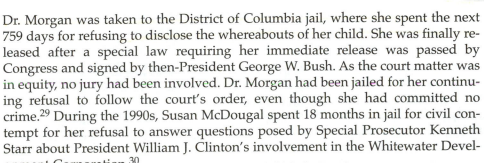

A maxim is a proposition or general statement. Some common maxims relating to actions in equity follow:

1. Whoever seeks equity must do equity. (Anyone who wishes to be treated fairly must treat others fairly.)
2. When there is equal equity, the law must prevail. (The applicable law will determine the outcome of a controversy in which the merits of both sides are equal.)
3. One seeking the aid of an equity court must come to the court with clean hands. (Plantiffs must have acted fairly and honestly.)
4. Equity will not suffer a right to exist without a remedy. (Equitable relief will be awarded when there is a right to relief and there is not adequate remedy at law.)
5. Equity regards substance rather than form. (Equity is more concerned with fairness and justice than with legal technicalities.)
6. Equity aids the vigilant, not those who rest on their rights. (Equity will not help those who neglect their rights for an unreasonably long period of time.)

court order, the entire prison system of Texas was put under the control of a Special Master of the court.[31]

Returning to Marya's case against Graf, we can see that since it is an action at law, either party may demand a jury trial. If neither party demands a jury, the right is waived and the trial will proceed with the judge alone determining the truth of all factual contentions.

HOW IS A TRIAL CONDUCTED?

After the jury is selected in a civil case, the plaintiff's attorney proceeds first because the plaintiff has the **burden of proof**. This is the duty to present evidence that supports the allegations in the complaint (the facts). In civil cases, the burden of proof is satisfied by presenting a **preponderance of evidence**. That is, according to the evidence, it is more likely than not that the allegations in the complaint are true. If the jury agrees that the plaintiff more likely than not is right, the burden is met, and they must return a verdict for the plaintiff. In a criminal case, however, the burden of proof is much greater. The state, represented by a prosecutor, has the burden of proving the guilt of the defendant **beyond a reasonable doubt**. This means the finder of fact must be firmly convinced of the defendant's guilt.* The proof of guilt must preclude any other reasonable interpretation of the facts and be inconsistent with any other rational conclusion.

While Marya Martinez was in the hospital, she told her father that Gary Graf took her wallet after she fell. This incensed Hernando Martinez, Marya's father, who demanded that Graf be prosecuted for theft. The criminal case came to trial months before the civil case, and the jury found Graf not guilty. Does this mean that Marya will lose her civil case?

No. Marya's civil case concerns the civil issue of negligence in adjusting her ski bindings. The criminal case dealt with subsequent independent, unrelated behavior. In some situations, however, a single act can result in civil liability and also a criminal penalty. For example, if Graf had deliberately struck Marya in the face without legal excuse or justification, he should be found civilly liable for damages and criminally guilty of battery. Theoretically, though, the defendant Graf could win the criminal case and lose the civil case. Such a result could happen because of the different burdens of proof involved. Moreover, the trials take place at different times with different juries and different procedural rules. The

---

*"The beyond a reasonable doubt standard is a requirement of due process, but the Constitution neither prohibits trial courts from defining reasonable doubt nor requires them to do so as a matter of course," *Hopt v. Utah*, 120 U.S. 430, 99 S.Ct. 2781 (1887). Supreme Court Justice Kennedy referred to the following "beyond a reasonable doubt" jury instruction as "clear, straightforward and accurate" in his concurring opinion in *Victor v. Nebraska*, 511 U.S. 1, 114 S.Ct. 1239, 1253 (1994); "The government has the burden of proving the defendant guilty beyond a reasonable doubt. Some of you may have served as juror in civil cases, where you were told that it is only necessary to prove that a fact is more likely true than not true. In criminal cases, the government's proof must be more powerful than that. It must be beyond a reasonable doubt. Proof beyond a reasonable doubt is proof that leaves you firmly convinced of the defendant's guilt. There are very few things in this world that we know with absolute certainty, and in criminal cases the law does not require proof that overcomes every possible doubt. If, based on your consideration of the evidence, you are firmly convinced that the defendant is guilty of the crime charged, you must find him guilty. If on the other hand, you think there is a real possibility that he is not guilty, you must give him the benefit of the doubt and find him not guilty."

law allows both victims (society at large and Marya in particular) their "days in court"—society (the state) is hurt by the alleged public crime, and Marya (a private party) is hurt civilly by the alleged private tort. Because one charge is civil and one is criminal, there is no **double jeopardy** (being tried twice for the same offense), which would be unconstitutional as violative of the Fifth Amendment.* A notorious example of this split possibility occurred after the not guilty verdict in the O.J. Simpson criminal trial. The parents of Nicole Brown Simpson and Ron Goldman sued for the wrongful death of their children. The jury in the civil case found Simpson liable (legally responsible) for the deaths.[32]

Procedures in a criminal trial are essentially the same as those for a civil case. However, under the U.S. Constitution (Fifth Amendment), a defendant in a criminal case cannot be compelled to testify. This is not true in a civil case, unless the testimony would tend to incriminate and possibly subject the defendant to prosecution for some crime.

Opening Statements

The plaintiff's attorney begins the trial by making an **opening statement**—a summary of what the plaintiff expects to prove in the trial. Then the defendant's attorney may, but need not, make an opening statement telling what the defendant expects to prove in the trial. Such statements are often used to inform the jury, in broad outline, of what they can expect to hear as the trial unfolds.

Evidence

After the opening statements, the plaintiff's attorney presents the plaintiff's **case-in-chief**. This involves calling and questioning witnesses and introducing into evidence documents, photographs, or other things that bear on the issues. **Evidence** is everything that the "finder of fact" (the jury, or judge when there is no jury) is entitled to consider in arriving at a determination of the facts. For example, the oral testimony of witnesses presented under oath is evidence; commentary of the attorney about that evidence is not. Attorneys are hired after the events in question have taken place and are thus not competent to testify as witnesses. Their role is to elicit evidence, comment on it, and argue about its significance. Of course, if the attorney's interpretation of the testimony of the witnesses is persuasive, the jury will be influenced by it.

Whether evidence should or should not be admitted is a question of law; therefore, the judge rules on all objections attorneys may make as to the admission of particular evidence. Evidence is admitted if the judge believes it will be useful in resolving issues in the case. Many rules concern what evidence is and is not admissible. For example, to be admitted evidence must be **relevant** (related to the fact in dispute). **Irrelevant evidence** (evidence not related to the fact in dispute) is not admissible.

Sharpe called Marya as her first witness. Marya recites her story. Sharpe sits down and attorney Dasse begins his cross-examination. "Isn't it a

---

*Separate criminal trials brought by different governmental entities even upon the same set of facts are generally not considered to be double jeopardy. For example, after the accused police officers in the Rodney King beating case were found not guilty of state criminal charges, the federal government was successful in bringing federal criminal charges against two of the officers for depriving Rodney King of his civil rights. See footnote on page 101.

fact, Ms. Martinez, that immediately before you fractured your leg you got drunk on wine with a gentleman, Luther Thomas, who you picked up in the bar?" Sharpe objects to the question. Will the judge sustain or overrule the objection?

The objection will be **sustained** (the judge will not allow the question to be answered). The question is compound; that is, it contains two or more questions, one concerning sobriety, the other concerning whether, and where and how, she met Luther Thomas. It also contains a conclusion which is inflammatory: "drunk." Attorney Dasse will probably be instructed to rephrase or drop the question. The question appears to be designed more to intimidate the witness than to extract information. The ruling by the judge is a ruling on a question of law.

A better form of questioning would be as follows:

Dasse: Isn't it a fact, Ms. Martinez, that immediately before you fractured your leg you were drinking wine?

Martinez: Yes, sir.

Dasse: With whom were you drinking wine?

Martinez: Luther Thomas.

Dasse: And did you know him previously?

Martinez: No.

After Sharpe has called all of the plaintiff's witnesses and introduced into evidence all relevant documents and other physical evidence (such as the ski boots), she *rests* (ends) the plaintiff's case. The defendant may now offer a *motion to dismiss* the case, claiming that the plaintiff has failed to establish a ***prima facie*** (Latin: "at first sight; on the face of it") case. A plaintiff is required to offer sufficient evidence of the defendant's wrongful conduct to justify an award of monetary damages or other relief. For example, if a preponderance of the evidence proved only that the defendant "thrust his middle finger in the air as an obscene gesture," the plaintiff could not win. There was no *prima facie* case and the judge would not permit the jury to return a verdict for the plaintiff. Under those circumstances, the defense need produce no evidence and can figuratively "stick its tongue out" at the plaintiff.

A plaintiff is required to offer facts that prove a *prima facie* case before a defendant is required to respond with a defense. The court will grant a motion to dismiss only if the plaintiff has failed to produce evidence about some significant aspect of the case. If this motion is denied by the judge, the defendant's attorney may make an opening statement (provided that it was not made at the beginning of the trial).

The defendant's case-in-chief also begins by calling witnesses. Of course, the plaintiff's attorney has the right to cross-examine the defendant's witnesses immediately after their direct examination, as the defendant's attorney did when the plaintiff's case was presented. After the defense rests, the plaintiff may offer additional evidence limited to rebutting the defense, but not opening new issues. And, of course, the defense has one final opportunity to rebut, limited to whatever was presented in the plaintiff's rebuttal.

Motion for a Directed Verdict

After the parties have rested their respective cases-in-chief, either may ask the judge to decide the matter by making a **motion for a directed verdict**. This motion is a request to a judge that he or she enter the requested verdict instead of allowing the jury to present its verdict. It is based on the alleged absence of sufficient facts to allow any other verdict than the requested one. The judge could, for example, properly direct a verdict in favor of the plaintiff if, despite the evidence presented by the defendant, no reasonable person could agree with the defendant. Granting such a motion is unusual; even if the evidence appears to be legally conclusive for one party, the judge normally allows the jury to provide its independent opinion.

Summation

After all the evidence has been offered, each attorney argues the case before the jury. In other words, each attorney tells the jury what he or she believes was proved in the trial and tries to persuade the jury to agree. The **summation** is not evidence or even a discussion; rather, it is a speech made by the attorney designed to persuade the jury. Persuasive speeches by political candidates pale in comparison to ruminations by attorneys. In our civil case example, the plaintiff's attorney would begin, followed by the defendant's attorney, and then the plaintiff's attorney concludes. Marya's attorney, Sharpe, might argue as follows:

> *Ladies and gentlemen of the jury, you have heard all the evidence. It is now your duty to determine the facts. I believe we have shown by a preponderance of the evidence that the injury was caused by Mr. Graf. I remind you that Marya's medical bills were $5,742.53. She missed one month of work, at her rate of pay of $3,195 a month. She had to wear a cast from her waist to her toes for six months. What is this worth in dollars? Put yourself in her shoes—excuse me, cast. Why all this expense and all this pain and anguish? Why? Because the defendant, this careless ski instructor, Gary Graf, fastened the bindings down on Ms. Martinez's foot with unprofessional disregard for her safety and well being. The evidence is clear: Gary Graf was not thinking about bindings. Gary Graf did not pay attention to his serious duty. Gary Graf was clearly negligent. And so it is now your duty to lessen the harm he caused. Simple justice requires you to return a verdict in favor of Marya.*

Attorney Dasse might argue to the jury:

> *Ladies and gentlemen, it is our duty to pierce the veil of emotion with which counsel is attempting to surround us. Let us look at the facts. Unfortunately, the plaintiff was injured. No one feels good about that, especially Gary Graf. However, the fact Ms. Martinez was injured is not a reason to hold Gary Graf responsible. Skiing is a sport with risks. Marya cannot transfer responsibility for her own safety to another person if the risk materializes. Marya decided to ski. She failed to exercise the appropriate care that would have prevented her accident. Feeling sorry for her is natural. We all feel sorry for her. But this does not justify a verdict against Mr. Graf. The simple facts are that Ms. Martinez was not thinking about skiing; she was more interested in impressing her date after spending a good part of the day drinking wine. She was injured not because of any negligence of Gary Graf. Bindings don't work if they are icy, and had she been sober she would have seen the ice when she put her skis back on. She was*

negligent. Now she is trying to obtain a bonanza at the expense of my client, a hard-working, sincere, very professional gentleman. Ladies and gentlemen of this jury, you know your duty: return a verdict for Gary Graf.

Instructions to the Jury

After the summation, the judge will instruct the jury on the law (**jury instructions**) that must be applied to the facts that the jury decides are true. Typically, each attorney will submit proposed instructions to the judge. The judge decides on the instructions to give to the jury. The instructions might include the following, but would be considerably more exhaustive:

You are instructed that statements of witnesses, sworn to tell the truth, constitute evidence that you may consider. Comments of the attorneys are not evidence. You are instructed that if the defendant failed to use reasonable care and secured the bindings too tightly, he was negligent. You are further instructed that if the accident was caused by ice between the boot and ski, and not by the adjustment to the bindings, the plaintiff was negligent.

Deliberation and Verdict

After the instructions, the jury will retire to a private room to **deliberate**, and by vote (usually a three-fourths majority is decisive in a civil case) return a **verdict**, the jury's decision.

If the jury returns with a verdict deemed to be wrong as a matter of law, the judge in a civil case has the power to render a contrary judgment, sometimes called a **judgement n.o.v.**, which is a **judgment *non obstante veredicto*** (Latin: "notwithstanding the verdict"). In effect, the judge is the thirteenth juror, with the power to veto the others' decision and to substitute a different one. (Recall that in a criminal case the judge cannot veto a verdict of "not guilty.")

After a verdict, the judge may grant a motion made by the losing party for a new trial. The judge will not grant a *motion for a new trial* unless some serious mistake of law (called *error*) has occurred. Sometimes the judge may think that the damages awarded by the jury are excessive or inadequate and may therefore grant a motion for a new trial unless the plaintiff or defendant, as the case may be, agrees to a modified award. To avoid the costs and uncertainties of another trial, the parties may compromise and agree to the modified award. The steps in a jury trial are identified in Exhibit 3–7.

HOW IS A CASE ENDED?

The concluding pronouncement of a court is its judgment. A judgment may declare a status (e.g., divorced), order one to do or not do something (e.g., pay money damages or transfer a title to land), impose a sentence (e.g., go to jail), or otherwise resolve a controversy.

In an auto accident case, the jury became convinced that the plaintiff should be compensated for harm to her left leg, which was crushed and had to be surgically removed. The accident was caused by the negligent operation of a truck by the defendant. The jury returned its verdict in the plaintiff's favor for $1,300,000. Is the verdict the voice of the court?

Exhibit 3-7: Steps in a Civil Case—Jury Trial

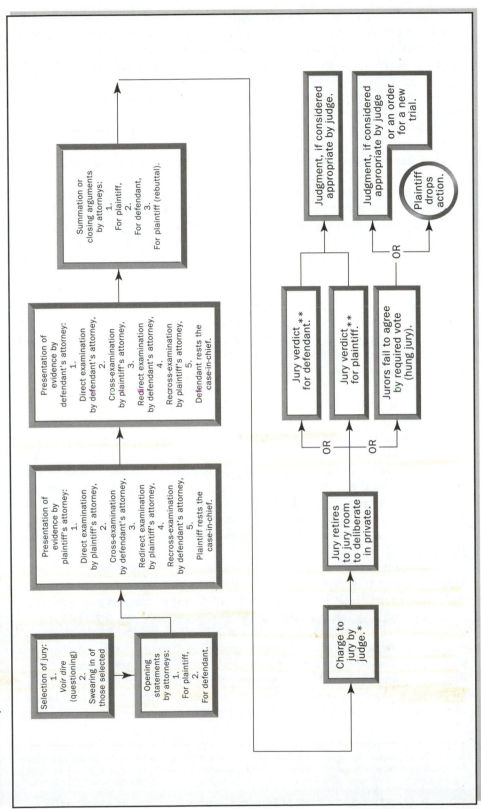

*A judge may direct a jury to return a certain verdict when, if all testimony on one side were believed, the other party nonetheless would be entitled to win.

**In rare cases, a judge may grant a judgment *non obstante veredicto* (Latin: "notwithstanding the verdict"), setting aside the jury's verdict because in the judge's opinion it is wrong as a matter of law.

No. The verdict is the expressed opinion of the jury. Based on the verdict, the court will usually issue a judgment for damages. As noted earlier, if the court concludes that the jury verdict is unreasonable in the light of the evidence, it can prevent a miscarriage of justice by reducing the amount of damages, ordering a new trial, or granting a judgment notwithstanding a verdict.

In divorce proceedings, the judgment of the court will be termination of the marriage. In a paternity case, the judgment of the court will be a declaration that the defendant is or is not the natural father. In a suit to end mass picketing and violence in a strike, the judgment of the court will be an injunction. In a suit to compel someone to do something that was promised by contract, the judgment of the court will be a decree of specific performance.

In criminal cases, the verdict will be guilty or not guilty.* If it is "not guilty," the judgment of the court must correspond to the verdict. However, if the verdict is "guilty," the judge may overrule the jury and acquit the defendant, or the judge may order a new trial to avoid a miscarriage of justice. In most cases, the judge has the power to impose a sentence, then suspend it, and place the defendant on probation.

Once a party has received a judgment, the judicial branch of government has completed its work, unless the matter is appealed. Sometimes a party to the action may return to court if the order of the court is not obeyed. In divorce, for example, after support payments have been ordered, either party may return and request an increase or decrease in payments because of changed circumstances, needs, or ability to pay.

Collecting a Judgment

If the defendant does not appeal and the time for appeal passes, a losing defendant is considered a **judgment debtor**, meaning one against whom a judgment has been entered but who has not paid the judgment. The judgment debtor may voluntarily pay the judgment, or pay the judgment after the plaintiff demands payment. However, if the judgment debtor fails to pay, the legal system provides a method of satisfying the debt provided the defendant has assets that can be identified and seized. State statutes generally call for payment of interest (usually at the annual rate between 6 and 10 percent) to accrue on the unpaid balance of the judgment until fully paid.

Assistance in collecting the dollar amount of the judgment is provided by the executive branch of government, usually through the office of the county sheriff or federal marshal. Officials will not do anything simply because you have won a lawsuit and have not been paid. A **judgment creditor**, one who has won a judgment but is as yet unpaid, must first provide a copy of the final judgment, identify assets owned by the judgment debtor, and give specific instructions to a sheriff or marshal before he or she will assist in collecting the judgment. The court order directing the sheriff to confiscate property of the defendant is called a **writ of execution**. Such a writ may be used to **garnish** (confiscate) part of any debt owed to the judgment debtor by others, usually unpaid wages due from the

A site with excerpts from *Collecting a Small Claims Court Judgment: You're on Your Own*, by Lisa Goldoftas and Stephen Elias, Nolo Press, is found at http://www.tenant.net/Court/nolo/nn247.html

---

*Of course, it is possible that a jury will be unable to reach a decision. In 1994, a pair of criminal cases captured national media attention. Erik and Kyle Menendez were accused of the first-degree murder of their parents. At the trial, the fact that the brothers had killed their parents was admitted, but both brothers defended their action on the basis of self-defense. Two juries, one for each brother, heard the case; neither jury was able to agree on a verdict. The two brothers were retried and found guilty and sentenced to life imprisonment without the possibility of parole.

debtor's employer(s). After being paid in full, the judgment creditor must provide the judgment debtor with a signed *satisfaction of judgment* document as evidence of that fact.

Judicial means exist for compelling cooperation of the judgment debtor in identifying his or her assets—namely, by means of an **order of examination**, which is a judicially authorized inquiry about the judgment debtor's assets. Usually, the judgment debtor is either summoned to court and asked questions about assets owned or required to respond to a questionnaire about such assets. It is, however, a fact of legal life in this country that if a plaintiff wins a case but the defendant does not have sufficient assets or insurance to pay the judgment, the plaintiff will probably recover little or nothing. The U.S. Constitution (Article I, Section 8) gives Congress the exclusive right "to establish uniform laws on the subject of Bankruptcies." Under federal statutes, almost all debts, including most judgments, can be discharged by the bankruptcy of the defendant debtor. In addition, federal bankruptcy laws and state consumer statutes provide that certain property is exempt from debt collection by judicial or other means. Thus, the bankrupt is not stripped of all possessions. So analysis of the possibility or impossibility of collection should be one of the first considerations before deciding to sue, even though collection is the last step in an ordinary civil lawsuit. Possible steps in a civil dispute resolved by court action are set forth in Exhibit 3–7 on page 131.

A criminal trial is procedurally very similar to a civil trial and is explored in Chapter 6. Trial procedures in the U.S. District Courts are governed by the Federal Rules of Civil and Criminal Procedure and closely resemble state procedures.

WHAT HAPPENS IF EITHER PARTY APPEALS?

As previously discussed, procedures before a federal or state appellate court differ greatly from trial court procedures. Appellate courts hear appeals from trial courts and do not conduct trials. The only question on appeal, as a general proposition, is whether or not the law was applied correctly by the judge during the trial proceedings. Appellate courts do not consider new evidence or hear witnesses. If the appellate court holds that the law was applied correctly, the judgment of the trial court is **affirmed** (upheld).

The jury found Jack Malum guilty of cocaine possession. During the trial, the judge instructed the jury, in part, as follows: "I instruct you that a crime is committed when one attends a party at which cocaine is being used, regardless of whether or not the defendant participated in such activity." Will an appeal by Mr. Malum be successful?

Yes. An appellate court would conclude that the court's instruction to the jury was an erroneous statement of the law. Mr. Malum did not receive a fair trial because mere attendance at a party is not in itself a crime, yet the jury was told that it was.

Appellate courts consist of three or more justices. Most of their work is done in private and consists of reading *transcripts* (official copies of the proceedings in the trial court) of cases on appeal. The appellate court assumes that all facts found by the trial court are true. In order to make the court's decision, they will study

Exhibit 3–8:   Steps in a Civil Case—After Trial

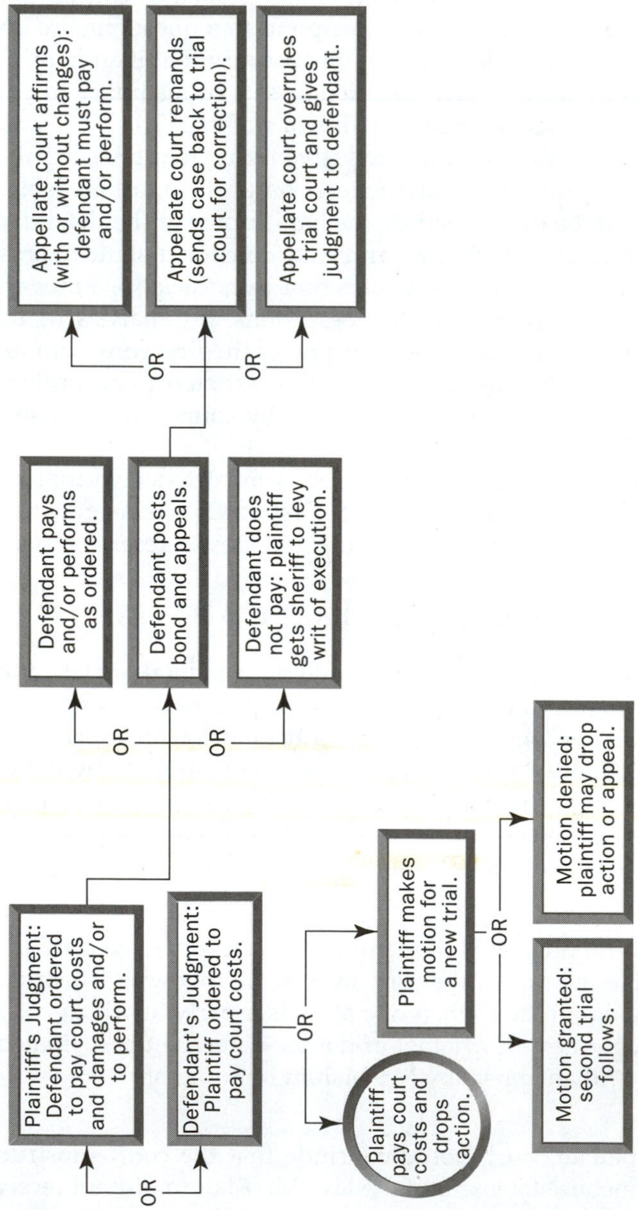

Plaintiff's Judgment: Defendant ordered to pay court costs and damages and/or to perform.

OR

Defendant's Judgment: Plaintiff ordered to pay court costs.

OR

Plaintiff pays court costs and drops action.

OR

Plaintiff makes motion for a new trial.

OR

Motion denied: plaintiff may drop action or appeal.

Motion granted: second trial follows.

Defendant pays and/or performs as ordered.

OR

Defendant posts bond and appeals.

OR

Defendant does not pay: plaintiff gets sheriff to levy writ of execution.

Appellate court affirms (with or without changes): defendant must pay and/or perform.

OR

Appellate court remands (sends case back to trial court for correction).

OR

Appellate court overrules trial court and gives judgment to defendant.

the applicable law and examine briefs filed by the attorneys for the appellant and the appellee and study the applicable law. A *brief* is a written legal argument addressed to the appellate court discussing or arguing why the judgment from below should be affirmed or reversed, modified, or perhaps *remanded* (sent back) to the trial court for further specified action. Before the appellate court makes its decision, the respective attorneys often make oral arguments to the appellate court, within limited allotted times. The concluding steps in a civil trial are provided in Exhibit 3–8.

A SAMPLE STATE APPELLATE COURT DECISION

The case presented here is a New Jersey state appellate case. Although we provide an edited case at the end of most chapters, this chapter presents a virtually complete appellate case in the words of the court. Limits of space and time preclude inclusion of the full text of other cases. This is an interesting case decided on procedural grounds that provides an opportunity for thorough analysis.

In *Trustees of Columbia University v. Jacobsen,* a college student cross-complains when the university seeks payment of owed tuition. The student claims that the university did not provide him with wisdom and truth. He pursues his claim even after his mother paid the tuition. Consider here the function of the trial court and appellate court in this case. Also note the importance of pretrial procedures on the disposition of the case. The first part of the case identifies the pleadings made and the rulings of the trial court. The second part presents the underlying facts of the dispute. The third part presents the analysis and conclusion of the court.

CASE

TRUSTEES OF COLUMBIA UNIVERSITY V. JACOBSEN

New Jersey Superior Court, Appellate Division,
53 N.J. Super. 574, 148 A.2d 63 (1959)

Columbia University brought suit against a student to recover money due on two promissory notes signed by the student in payment of the balance of his tuition owed. The student filed a counterclaim for deceit based on alleged false representations by the university as to what it would teach him.

Judge Goldman delivered the opinion of the court: Defendant appeals from a summary judgment of the Superior Court Law Division, dismissing his counterclaim with prejudice and denying his counter-motion for summary judgment. . . .

I

Columbia brought suit in the district court against defendant and his parents on two notes made by him and signed by them as co-makers, representing the balance of tuition he owed the University. The principal due amounted to $1,049.50, but plaintiff sued for only $1,000, waiving any demand for judgment in excess of the jurisdictional limit of the court. Defendant then sought to file an answer and counterclaim demanding, among other things, money damages in the sum of $7,016. The counterclaim was in 50 counts which severally alleged that plaintiff had represented that it would teach defendant wisdom, truth, character, enlightenment, understanding, justice, liberty, honesty, courage, beauty and similar virtues and qualities; that it would develop the whole man, maturity, well-roundness, objective thinking and the like; and that because it had failed to do so it was guilty of misrepresentation, to defendant's pecuniary damage.

The district court clerk having refused to accept the pleading because of the amount demanded, defendant moved to transfer the action to the Superior Court. Plaintiff consented, but before an order could be entered defendant's mother paid the amount due and plaintiff thereupon discontinued its action. After transfer to the Superior Court defendant filed a supplement to this answer and counterclaim in which he [further demanded] Columbia to return the sum paid by his mother.

Plaintiff then moved in the Superior Court for an order dismissing the counterclaim and for the entry of summary judgement . . . (Defendant) appeared pro se throughout the entire proceedings below as he does here.

Following oral argument the Law Division judge . . . concluded that the statements attributed by defendant to plaintiff did not constitute a false representation. The judgment under appeal was then entered.

II.

Following a successful freshman year at Dartmouth defendant entered Columbia University in the fall of 1951. He continued there until the end of his senior year in the spring of 1954, but was not graduated because of poor scholastic standing. Plaintiff admits the many quotations from college catalogues and brochures, inscriptions over University buildings and addresses by University officers cited in the schedules annexed to the counterclaim. The sole question

is whether these statements constitute actionable misrepresentation.

. . . Although the remedy of summary judgment is admittedly drastic and cautiously granted . . . the remedy should not be withheld where, as here, there is no genuine issue of material fact.

The attempt of the counterclaim, inartistically drawn as it is, was to state a cause of action in deceit. The necessary elements of the action are: a false representation, knowledge or belief on the part of the person making the representation that it is false, an intention that the other party act thereon, reasonable reliance by such party in so doing, and resultant damage to him.

We are in complete agreement with the trial court that the counterclaim fails to establish the very first element, false representation, basic to any action in deceit. Plaintiff stands by every quotation relied on by defendant. Only by reading into the imagined meanings he attributes to them can one conclude—and the conclusion would be a most tenuous insubstantial one—that Columbia University represented it could teach wisdom, truth, justice, beauty, spirituality and all the other qualities set out in the 50 counts of the counterclaim.

A sampling from the quotations cited by the defendant will suffice as illustration. Defendant quotes from a Columbia College brochure stating that

"*. . . Columbia College provides a liberal arts education . . . A liberal arts course . . . has extremely positive values of its own. Chief among these, perhaps, is something which has been a principal aim of Columbia College from the beginning: It develops the whole man. . . . [Columbia's] aim remains constant: to foster in its students a desire to learn, a habit of critical judgment, and a deep-rooted sense of personal and social responsibility. . . . [I]ts liberal arts course pursues this aim in five ways. (1) It brings you into firsthand contact with the major intellectual ideas that have helped to shape human thinking and the course of human events. (2) It* *gives you a broader acquaintance with the rest of the world. (3) It guides you toward an understanding of people and their motivations. (4) It leads you to a comprehending knowledge of the scientific world. (5) It helps you acquire facility in the art of communication . . ."*

He then cites the motto of Columbia College and Columbia University: "In lumine tuo videbimus lumen" ("In light we shall see Light") and the inscription over the college chapel: "Wisdom dwelleth in the heart of him that hath understanding." He also refers to an address of the president of Columbia University at its bicentennial convocation:

*"There can never have been a time in the history of the world when men had greater need of wisdom * * * I mean an understanding of man's relationship to his fellow men and to the universe * * * To this task of educational leadership in a troubled time and in an uncertain world, Columbia, like other great centers of learning in free societies, unhesitating dedicates itself. * * *"*

We have thoroughly combined all the statements upon which defendant relies in his counterclaim, as well as the exhibits he handed up to the trial judge, including one of 59 pages setting out his account of the circumstances leading to the present action. They add up to nothing more than a fairly complete exposition of Columbia's objectives, desires and hopes, together with factual statements as to the nature of some of the courses included in its curricula. As plaintiff correctly observes, what defendant is seeking to do is to assign to the quoted excerpts a construction and interpretation peculiarly subjective to him and completely unwarranted by the plain sense and meaning of the language used. . . .

At the heart of defendant's counterclaim is a single complaint. He concedes that

"I have really only one charge against Columbia: that it does not teach Wisdom as it claims to do. From this charge ensues an endless number of charges, of

which I have selected fifty at random. I am prepared to show that each of these fifty claims in turn is false, though the central issue is that of Columbia's pretense of teaching Wisdom."

We agree with the trial judge that wisdom is not a subject which can be taught and that no rational person would accept such a claim made by any man or institution. We find nothing in the record to establish that Columbia represented, expressly or even by way of impression, that it could or would teach wisdom or the several qualities which defendant insists are "synonyms for or aspects of the same Quality." The matter is perhaps best summed up in the supporting affidavit of the Dean of Columbia College, where he said that "All that any college can do through its teachers, libraries, laboratories and other facilities is to endeavor to teach the student the known facts, acquaint him with the nature of those matters which are unknown, and thereby assist him in developing mentally, morally and physically. Wisdom is a hoped-for end product of education, experience and ability which many seek and many fail to attain."

Defendant's extended argument lacks the element of fraudulent representation indispensable to any action of deceit. We note, in passing, that he has cited no legal authority whatsoever for his position. Instead, he has submitted a dictionary definition of "wisdom" and quotations from such works as the Bhagavad-Gita, the Mundaka Upanishad, the Analects of Confucius and the Koran; excerpts from Euripides, Plato and Menander; and references to the Bible. Interesting through these may be, they do not support defendant's indictment. If his pleadings, affidavit and exhibits demonstrate anything, it is indeed the validity of what Pope said in his Moral Essays:

"A little learning is a dangerous thing; Drink deep, or taste not the Pierian spring . . ."

The papers make clear that through the years defendant's interest has shifted from civil engineering to social work, then to physics, and finally to English and creative writing. In college he became increasing critical of his professors and his courses; in his last year he attended classes only when he chose and rejected the regimen of examinations and term papers. When his non-attendance at classes and his poor work in the senior year were called to his attention by the Columbia Dean of Students, he replied in a lengthy letter that "I want to learn, but I must do it my own way. I realize my behavior is nonconforming, but in these times when there are so many forces that demand conformity I hope I will find Columbia willing to grant some freedom to a student who wants to be a literary artist." In short, he chose to judge Columbia's educational system by the shifting standards of his own fancy, and now seeks to place his failure at Columbia's door on the theory that it had deliberately misrepresented that it taught wisdom.

III.

In light of our conclusion that defendant has failed to state a cause of action in deceit based on fraudulent representation, we need not deal with plaintiff's further contentions that (1) even assuming an unequivocal representa-

tion by Columbia that it would teach wisdom, this amounted to nothing more than a promise to do something in the future and therefore was not an actionable misrepresentation of fact; and (2) the counterclaim is defective for failure properly to plead the particulars of the alleged fraud.

* * *

The judgment is affirmed.

FOR CRITICAL ANALYSIS

1. Was there a trial in this case? Why or why not?

2. The court said the defendant appeared *pro se*. What does that mean, and what effect did it have on the case? Use the glossary and consult Chapter 4 for the answer.

3. What legal result was the plaintiff trying to accomplish by its lawsuit? The defendant?

4. Why did the plaintiff reduce its claim to $1,000?

5. Did either the plaintiff or defendant present evidence in the proceeding discussed in the case?

CHAPTER QUESTIONS AND PROBLEMS

1. In regard to small claims court:
   a. Why do many states not allow attorneys to represent litigants in small claims court? (Note that in all states parties can consult counsel before and after the trial.)
   b. What are the differences between television programs such as *The People's Court* and *Judge Judy* and a typical small claims court? The success of popular television programs such as these is not without controversy. What are the pros and cons of these types of programs?

   c. What should the appropriate maximum dollar amount be for small claims court (if any)? What should be the basis for determining the appropriate jurisdictional amount?

2. While driving her car in Colorado, Pearldean Norset, a resident of Alabama, negligently struck Carl Broadnorf, a resident of Arizona. As a result of the accident, Carl suffered more than $22,000 in property damage, $40,000 in medical expenses, and $15,000 in lost wages. Carl wants to know

whether he can obtain jurisdiction over Pearldean in the following courts:
a. Federal District Court in Colorado.
b. Alabama State Trial Court.
c. Colorado State Trial Court.
d. District of Columbia Trial Court.
e. Federal Circuit Court of Appeals for the Ninth Circuit (includes Arizona).

3. In regard to courts and trials:
a. Name each of the courts of your state and properly display them on an organization chart.
b. What are the pros and cons of permitting each side in a case to exercise one peremptory challenge of the judge assigned to the case? Would your arguments be different depending on whether the case is criminal or civil?
c. Do you believe a judge can influence a jury by such seemingly innocent conduct as smiling, eyebrow raising, grimacing, and so on during the testimony of witnesses? How can any such effect be combated?

4. Sylvester is on trial for the assault and battery of his roommate, Arnold. Sylvester hit Arnold after Arnold refused to stop playing grunge music on his guitar. Sylvester was trying to study for a test. Sylvester intends to argue self-defense, arguing a physical noise attack. One of the prospective jurors has spiked green hair and a nose ring. Suggest a strategy that would best serve Sylvester's interests in dismissing the juror. Use the correct legal terms.

5. About jury nullification:
a. What is it?
b. Are jurors instructed by the judge as to existence of the power of jury nullification? Why or why not?
c. Does the power of jury nullification exist in both civil and criminal trials?

6. About Trial and Appellate Courts:
a. Define each.
b. What is the purpose of each?
c. Do juries assist both? Explain.

d. Do both exist in state and federal systems?
e. Do witnesses testify before each? Explain.

7. Thomas, William, and Ella McCollum were white defendants facing criminal charges of assault and battery against two African Americans. Before the trial began, the prosecution requested that the court prohibit these defendants from exercising their peremptory challenges in a racially discriminatory manner. The prosecution claimed that the defendants' attorneys intended to eliminate African American jurors from the panel, and that it would be possible for them to do so given the number of peremptory challenges available to the defendants. The trial court held, and the Georgia Supreme Court affirmed, that "neither Georgia nor federal law prohibits criminal defendants from exercising peremptory strikes in a racially discriminatory manner." The defendants, of course, agreed, arguing that the prohibition against discriminatory use of peremptory challenges by the state is to provide due process for a criminal defendant and that any restriction on the use of peremptory challenges by the defense would deny defendants the right to a fair trial, The state argued that because it is prohibited from dismissals on racial grounds, the defense should be similarly restrained. In addition, the prosecution argued that discrimination in the selection of jurors is, in effect, discrimination against the excused jurors, which should not be allowed by the court whether engaged in by the prosecution or by the defense. How did the court decide? *Georgia v. McCollum*, 505 U.S. 42, 112 S.Ct. 2348 (1992).

8. Walter Martin brought an employment discrimination suit against the New York Department of Mental Hygiene and Dr. Stuart Keill, a regional director of the department. Although Dr. Keill knew of the lawsuit and the nature of the

claim, he was not served with a copy of the complaint and a summons. Could Martin pursue the case against Dr. Keill without such service? [*Martin v. N.Y. State Department of Mental Hygiene*, 588 F.2d 371 (1978).]

9. Martha obtained a contested divorce from her husband, Donald Anderson. The trial court judge entered judgment of divorce. Donald asked the trial court to "vacate" (rescind or erase) the judgment, but the court refused his request. On Donald's appeal, the appellate court agreed that the trial court judge was erroneous in his ruling. Does this mean that Donald and Martha are married again? [*Anderson v. Anderson*, 869 S.W.2d 289 (Mo. 1994).]

10. Joshua Southard was cited for speeding and failing to yield to an emergency vehicle. He requested a trial in the Cape Girardeu County Circuit Court. Mr. Southard was found guilty and fined. He appealed, claiming that the circuit court lacked subject-matter jurisdiction and that the proper court to hear the case was the municipal court. He was correct: the appropriate court was the municipal court. The county circuit court did, however, have the power to hold a trial *de novo* after an original trial in municipal court. (Recall that a trial *de novo* is a type of appeal wherein a party is allowed a second complete trial in a different court.) Mr. Southard, when requesting the hearing, incorrectly stated to the circuit court that the municipal court had previously heard his case and rendered a judgment. The prosecution argued that although the circuit court was not the appropriate court for an initial trial, that because Southard "stated that judgment had been rendered against him in the municipal court, he should not be allowed to take advantage of an error of his own making." Did Southard win his appeal arguing that the court lacked subject-matter jurisdiction? [*City of Jackson v. Southard*, 869 S.W.2d 280 (Missouri, 1994).]

NOTES

1. "Novanglus Papers," *Boston Gazette*, 1774, No. 7. "Novanglus" was a pseudonym used by John Adams, signer of the Declaration of Independence and, later, second President of the United States.
2. Alexis de Tocqueville, *Democracy in America*, ed. J.P. Mayer and Max Lerner (New York: Harper and Row, 1966), 93.
3. *Maryland v. Cottman Transmissions, Inc.*, 75 Md.App. 647, 542 A.2d 859 (Md., 1988).
4. *Richmond Newspapers v. Virginia*, 448 U.S. 555, 100 S.Ct. 2814 (1980).
5. *Maryland v. Cottman Transmissions, Inc.*
6. An example of such an activity is production of a product or material in a foreign state that is used or consumed by a person in the state where jurisdiction is sought. Florida's general long-arm statute is a representative long-arm statute and is found at West's F.S.A. § 48.193
7. 28 U.S.C. §§ 1331 & 1332.
8. *Erie Railroad v. Tompkins*, 304 U.S. 64, 58 S.Ct. 817 (1938).
9. "The Supreme Court," Supreme Court Historical Society, 1992, 11.
10. *People's Bank v. Podd*, 1993 WL 382514 (Conn.Super.).
11. *Minneapolis and St. Louis R.R. Co. v. Bombolis*, 241 U.S. 211, 36 S.Ct. 595 (1916).
12. *Duncan v. Louisiana*, 391 U.S. 145, 88 S.Ct. 1444 (1968) and *Baldwin v. New York*, 399 U.S. 66, 90 S.Ct. 1886 (1970).
13. *United States v. Datcher*, 830 F.Supp. 411 (M.D. Tennessee, 1993).
14. The Jury Selection and Service Act of 1968, 28 U.S.C. §§ 1861–1974.
15. As of 1992, twenty-six states have no exemptions for professionals. Robert Litan, "Verdict: Assessing the Civil Jury System" (Washington D.C., The Brookings Institution, 1993), 380.
16. Federal statute protects jurors from being discharged, intimidated, or coerced by their permanent employer based on federal jury service. 28 U.S.C. § 1875.
17. *Commonwealth of Mass. v. Geagan*, 339 Mass. 487, 159 N.E.2d 870 (1959).
18. After a second three-month trial, the second jury also deadlocked as to the guilt or innocence of the last remaining defendant, Raymond Buckey. The Los Angeles county district attorney decided to not retry the case. 76 *American Bar Association Journal* 28 (April 1990).
19. *U.S. v. Araujo*, 62 F.3d 930 (7th cir. 1995).
20. *Colgrove v. Battin*, 413 U.S. 149, 93 S.Ct. 2448 (1973).
21. *Williams v. Florida*, 399 U.S. 78, 90 S.Ct. 1893 (1970), a non-capital criminal case, and *Colgrove v. Battin*, a civil case.
22. *Ballew v. Georgia*, 435 U.S. 223, 98 S.Ct. 1029 (1978).
23. Woolf and Williams, *Juries, Justice for a Generation*, (Plenary Sessions American Bar Association, The Senate of the Inns

of Court and the Bar. The Law Society of England and Wales, 1985), 9.

24. *Apodaca v. Oregon*, 406 U.S. 404, 92 S.Ct. 1628 (1972).

25. *Apodaca v. Oregon*. Also see *Johnson v. Louisiana*, 406 U.S. 356, 92 S.Ct. 1620 (1972). The Oregon plan allows 10 to 12 verdicts (i.e., ten out of twelve votes) in all cases except capital ones (those cases calling for the death penalty), which require unanimity.

26. *Burch v. Louisiana*, 441 U.S. 130, 99 S.Ct. 1623 (1979).

27. *Blanton v. North Las Vegas*, 489 U.S. 538, 109 S.Ct. 1289 (1989).

28. Delaware's Court of Chancery still provides an example of the separation of courts of law and equity. The Delaware Courts of Chancery may not hear any case in which a sufficient remedy may be had by common law or statute. 10 Del. C. § 341 and Del. Const. Art. IV, § 7 and § 10.

29. West's Summary of American Law, Annual update (St. Paul MN: West Publishing 1990), 63.

30. David Rouella, "Is Criminal Contempt Overkill?" *National Law Journal*, 11 May 1998, A6.

31. *Ruiz v. Estelle*, 679 F.2d 115 (1982).

32. This verdict was rendered in a different venue (Santa Monica) than the criminal trial (Downtown Los Angeles) by a different and predominately Caucasian jury. A news report on the jury verdict can be found in *USA Today*, 5 February 1997.

4

THE ATTORNEY–
CLIENT RELATIONSHIP

A *law firm receptionist answered the phone the morning after the firm's senior partner had died unexpectedly.*

"Is Mr. Smith there?" asked the client on the phone.

"I'm very sorry, but Mr. Smith passed away last night," the receptionist answered.

"Is Mr. Smith there?" repeated the client.

The receptionist was perplexed. "Perhaps you didn't understand me. I'm afraid Mr. Smith died last night."

"Is Mr. Smith there?" asked the client again.

"Madam, do you understand what I'm saying?" said the exasperated receptionist. "Mr. Smith is dead."

"I understand perfectly," the client sighed. "I just can't hear it often enough."

Adapted from a statement made at a U.S. Senate confirmation hearing of a Supreme Court Justice.

An ideal legal system meets the somewhat inconsistent goals of stability and flexibility. It is also understandable and accessible to everyone. In previous chapters we have discussed constitutional law and the legal doctrine of *stare decisis*, both of which work toward balancing the goals of stability and flexibility. In this chapter we will consider the two additional goals of an ideal legal system, understandability and accessibility. Are the laws of the country known, comprehensible, and adequate—in other words, is knowledge about United States law available to the general population and do people have access to adequate legal redress (i.e., damages or other remedy) through the legal system? After a close look at lawyers and their role in the American legal system, we will discuss alternatives to the use of lawyers and, indeed, to the use of formal legal structures. Lastly, we have included in Appendix C a reference to legal research methods.

142

Lawyers have been targets of criticism in the guise of humor, and otherwise, throughout history, but the classic quotation is undoubtedly from Shakespeare's play, *Henry VI, Part II*: "The first thing we do, let's kill all the lawyers."* Why is so much animosity displayed toward lawyers? In an era of political correctness where jokes and comments about gender, ethnic origin, and even sexuality are considered bad form and even the basis of punishment (e.g., public apology or resignation from office), negative comments about lawyers are still common and socially acceptable. Who are lawyers, or attorneys at law, and what functions do they perform in our legal system? Is one required to use a lawyer to have access to the legal system? Before addressing these issues, the first question to ask and answer is: What is the special importance of advocacy (i.e., pleading the cause of another person) within American jurisprudence? Advocacy is so important partly because of the adversarial nature of the American legal system.

The practice of law at the beginning of the twentieth century was radically different from today. Consider a few of the most obvious contrasts:

- At the turn of the twentieth century, the prestige of and personal satisfaction from the practice of law was, in large part, its own primary reward—not money.

- One hundred years ago, the image and reputation necessary for attorneys to obtain clients was gleaned in a quiet and professional word-of-mouth way—not by glitzy ads, promotions, flyers mailed to strangers, billboards, online come-ons, crowds of attorneys at sites of catastrophes and nearby hospitals, etc.

- Today's adversary system (explained fully later in the chapter) empowers opposing attorneys as warriors, authorizing them ethically to put winning above considerations of truth and justice. At the turn of the twentieth century, attorneys exercised a professional self-restraint under which winning was not the only consideration.

- In years past, civility existed among the members of the bar, who took one another at their word. Urban lawyers today rarely if ever accept another attorney's word and require a written follow-up memorandum to preserve their oral understandings—a new bumptious and combative behavior between attorneys too often permeates the practice of law.

- Lawyers formerly became partners with one another, sharing their liabilities as well as profits. Today, lawyers are shareholders in their corporate law businesses, shielding their personal wealth from their businesses.

In a nutshell, lawyering is becoming a corporate business guided by business principles.[1]

---

*The use of this quote as pejorative is ironic because, within the context of the play, the words speak well, not ill, of lawyers. In the play, the Duke of York foments revolution through the use of Jack Cade. Cade fancies he will be king after a peasant revolution. As king he intends to be worshipped as a god, to require all in the kingdom to dress alike, to "be the parliament of England" through his mouth alone, and to require all women to surrender their virginity to him before any marriage. In the ramblings between Cade and one Dick the butcher, the environment for despotism is discussed. Dick opines that to advance Cade's evil goals, "The first thing we do, let's kill all the lawyers." Cade says, "Nay, that I mean to do."

WHAT IS THE ADVERSARY SYSTEM?

The backbone of the U.S. legal system is the adversary method of resolving disputes. In an **adversary system**, parties to legal actions are opponents. The judge is independent and neutral, unlike magistrates in so-called inquisitorial systems (discussed shortly). This fairly simple concept has enormous ramifications. Courts make decisions based on facts brought to their attention by the proponents and opponents in the legal conflict. Each party is responsible for producing evidence and rules of law that support the specified side of the dispute. The competitors are openly partial and biased for their side. Each party (contestant or participant) earnestly asserts every available supporting reason to merit victory. Every theory revealed and asserted is a theory considered and subjected to attack by the opponent. In effect, the judge acts much as a referee in a sporting contest, ensuring that the procedural rules created to maintain civility and fairness are properly followed.

Another major feature of the adversary system is the requirement of a moving party. Thus, courts depend on attorneys to organize and present their cases. In civil matters, for example, legal questions are not considered by a court unless a moving party brings a problem to the attention of the court by filing a lawsuit. Each party is then independently responsible for presenting its case. The moving party, or plaintiff in a civil lawsuit, must meet a required burden of proof before the defendant must respond. In a criminal case, the moving party (for example, a county district attorney) is from the executive branch of government, not the judicial branch.

> He spoke to the jurors as if he were alone with them, the way two people can be alone in a crowded public park. His notes were at the counsel table . . . but he never paused to look at them. He told the jury about the tragedies the Woburn families had endured, and then, the tone of his voice growing harsher, about W.R. Grace and Beatrice Foods.
>
> When Schlichtmann was done, the crowd in the gallery remained quiet for a long moment. Judge Skinner broke the spell by calling a brief recess. The crowd, elbow to elbow in their seats, seemed to let out a collective breath, and began talking among themselves as they shuffled out to the corridor.[2]

The adversary system is the essence of what many consider to be the most just legal system the world has ever known. But it also has shortcomings and critics. The adversary system places a premium on advocacy skills, on being able to articulate ideas clearly and to present information in both written and oral form, in order to convince decision makers of the merits of a cause. Yet the merits of a legal position are not necessarily related to one's ability to persuade others. Therefore, parties to a legal conflict generally hire advocates—lawyers—who possess the required talent.

Of course, access to the system is critically important—redress is not possible if access is denied. The means and methods used to seek legal redress are often complicated, specialized, and daunting to the casual user. Because the clerical personnel of courts do not assist parties to disputes except to provide the place and the preliminary paperwork for the dispute to be resolved, parties who decide to sue without using attorneys are doubly disadvantaged. In addition to their ignorance of the legal process, they also may find court personnel unhelpful and sometimes even hostile.*

The contrasting **inquisitorial system**, mentioned previously, exists in many other countries as diverse as Argentina, France, and China. Under the inquisitorial system, judges need not depend on the testimony of the parties once the matter is before the court. Judges can investigate the dispute, question witnesses, and independently seek out evidence before a trial. Although attorneys are still necessary in countries with such systems, their role and the role of a trial is often seen as less critical to the administration of justice.**

If you are [ ] law of a particular nation, satisfy that curiosity by using the Emory Law Library Electronic Reference Desk at http://www.law.emory.edu/LAW/refdesk/country/foreign/

ATTORNEYS AT LAW

An **attorney at law** (also called a **lawyer**) is a person authorized by law to represent clients in legal matters. Attorneys also draft documents involving legal rights and duties and give expert advice on legal questions. Countless businesses and public organizations routinely look to lawyers for such help. More than two-thirds of the adults in the United States have consulted attorneys for assistance with personal legal problems. Most of these problems involve the preparation of wills, the purchase or sale of real property, divorce or marriage dissolution, serious personal injuries caused by other persons, consumer problems (e.g., disputes with landlords or lenders), or difficulties with governmental agencies.[3] Every person during her or his lifetime should anticipate direct or indirect involvement with an attorney. Accordingly, one should be familiar with the legal profession and learn how to select, *retain* (hire), cooperate with, and evaluate an attorney's performance.

Lawyers are noted for having the ability to sort through complicated descriptions of human events to determine which facts are important and to analyze the relationship of those facts to legal rules and principles. Lawyers generally have the special ability to advocate positions through the use of oral and written argument. They are expected to be able to do this while remaining emotionally neutral, or at least in control of emotions that could disrupt their ability to analyze clearly. On the other hand, "lawyers are accused—rightfully so—of taking simple issues and making them more complicated and of finding every possible permutation, instead of looking for the relatively straightforward answer to the problem placed before them."[4]

WHO MAY PRACTICE LAW?

Generally, only licensed attorneys may perform legal services for others, their clients. Most state legislatures have created state bar associations to regulate

*A court clerk attempting to assist a party who is not represented by an attorney might be found to be practicing law without a license in violation of state criminal statutes.
**In the interest of accuracy, it should be noted that in most modern legal systems the distinctions between adversarial and inquisitorial methods are not as great in practice as in theory. For example, in the adversary system judges do, within limits, ask witnesses questions and make limited suggestions to counsel about what evidence should be provided to the court. In inquisitorial systems, counsel represents parties and the scope and degree of judicial inquiry are often limited.

If you are interested in law school, they are all linked at the Emory Law Library site at http://www.law.emory.edu/LAW/refdesk/education/schools.html

lawyers and the practice of law. The rules of such associations, together with applicable federal and state statutes, combine with the inherent powers of the court to regulate and govern the legal profession. Each state sets its own qualifications for admission to practice law within its borders. However, all states permit attorneys to hire non-attorneys, often called legal assistants, to perform legal services under their indirect supervision. Thus, non-attorneys actually perform a considerable amount of legal services.

An attorney must have a separate license from each state in which he or she wishes to practice law.* A candidate for a license to practice law must possess good moral character, complete certain minimum educational requirements,** pass an examination on the law (called a *bar examination*), and take an oath to support the law and conform to rules of professional conduct of that state. A person has no inherent right to be able to practice law or to represent others in court. The practice of law is considered a privilege granted to those who demonstrate fitness in intellectual attainment and moral character.[5]

Bonnie Cord and Jeffrey Blue, an unmarried couple, bought a home and resided together in a rural area of Warren County. Bonnie, an attorney licensed to practice law in Washington, D.C., applied for a license in Virginia. Duncan Gibb, judge of the Circuit Court of Warren County, denied her application because her living arrangement "would lower the public's opinion of the Bar as a whole." Bonnie appealed to a higher court. What should have been the result?

Bonnie won the case and her license because her conduct did not affect her fitness to practice law.[6] The same result has been reached where an applicant admitted a sexual preference for persons of the same sex.

With a few exceptions, no one is required to use a lawyer in a legal proceeding. A party to a case before a trial court may appear *in propria persona* (Latin: "in one's own person") or *in pro se* (Latin: "for him or herself"), that is, without the services of a lawyer. Generally, though, it is not advisable to go to court without a lawyer. A common saying even among lawyers is "one who serves as his own lawyer has a fool for a client!" Thus, lawyers when personally sued usually use another lawyer for themselves. All of us, even lawyers, are emotionally involved in our own cases; we need educated, experienced, and unemotional counsel to analyze issues dispassionately and argue them persuasively before judge and jury. It is important to have an independent advocate.

---

*Occasionally, an attorney will represent a client in the court of a state other than the one where he or she has a license. The attorney can do so after receiving permission from the court of that state. The granting of the right is referred to as *pro hac vice*, (Latin: "for this occasion"). It is customary for a court to require that the out-of-state attorney associate with a local attorney for the duration of the case. In recent years, attorneys, particularly those who work in-house for large companies, have questioned the propriety of state-by-state licensing of attorneys, arguing that it is in effect an illegal barrier to interstate commerce. In a 1998 California Supreme Court case, a New York lawyer was denied recovery of fees for representation of a client in a California arbitration. There was no associated California counsel. *Birbrower v. Superior Court of Santa Clara County*, 17 Cal. 4th 119, 949 P.2d 1 (Cal., 1998).

**The educational requirements vary depending on the state. Most states require that any person wishing to take the state bar examination must be a graduate of a law school accredited by the American Bar Association. Law school provides a graduate professional education and so virtually all law students possess a baccalaureate degree before entering law school.

A defendant in Superior Court decided to be his own lawyer, which some say was mistake number one. His second mistake was the first question he asked the victim: "Did you see my face clearly when I took your purse?" The sentence: Two to ten years.[7]

Each federal court (e.g., U.S. Supreme Court, U.S. Courts of Appeals, U.S. District Court) recognizes its own separate bar or group of attorneys permitted to practice before it. Although there are separate federal regulations, permission to practice law in the federal courts is granted to attorneys licensed in any state without requiring further legal education or passing an additional examination.

Government regulation of the legal profession exists because the attorney–client relationship requires technical expertise and is fiduciary in nature. A **fiduciary relationship** is one involving a person in a position of trust who undertakes to act for the benefit of another. The attorney as a fiduciary must exercise the utmost good faith, honesty, and fairness toward that client. Licensure is designed to protect the public by seeking to ensure that every attorney is competent, honorable, and worthy of that trust reposed by the client. Because the practice of law is a licensed profession, offering legal services without professional certification as an attorney violates a criminal statute.

An attorney's license can be suspended or revoked for failing to maintain professional standards, including obeying the law, or for providing services in an incompetent and unethical fashion. However, attorneys are not required to disclose to prospective clients whether or not they have ever been disciplined for unprofessional conduct, whether or not they are under treatment for any relevant mental or addictive health problem, or how many times they have been sued by former clients. Many states also require that each attorney complete a certain number of continuing-education law and practice courses within a prescribed time to retain their professional license.

SPECIALIZATION

As with a license to practice medicine, a license to practice law is a broad grant of power. It permits an attorney to undertake a wide variety of legal tasks. Common sense for both lawyer and client suggests that a general-practice attorney should undertake only routine matters for a client. A complex legal problem should be referred to a specialist, who will be familiar with the intricacies, procedures, and detailed rules in that particular area of law. All areas of law practice include unwritten norms, knowledge of which allow the specialist to bring a legal problem to a faster, more satisfactory conclusion than can an attorney not well versed in the particular area.

Attorneys may choose to specialize in any one or more areas, such as divorce or family law, probate and estates, criminal law, administrative law, real property law, personal injury law, small business law, and consumer law. These specialties usually correlate with the most common public needs. Other specialties include antitrust law, labor or employment law, tax law, bankruptcy law, intellectual property law, international law, workers' compensation law, water law, and elder law (a relatively new legal specialty serving America's aging baby boomers). Attorneys may also be classified as performing either office or litigation (court-related) services. For example, one real estate attorney may perform only office services while another performs only court cases. On the other hand, criminal lawyers are litigators. A client should learn the specialty of any attorney he or she consults.

Many states* allow specially educated and experienced attorneys to identify themselves as certified specialists if they have met the standards of education and experience set by the state bar. In Arizona, for example, certified specialties now include bankruptcy, criminal law, family law, estate and trust, injury and wrongful-death litigation, real estate law, tax law, and workers' compensation law.[8]

Geographical location plays a role in the type of law services available. For example, antitrust, patent, immigration, and securities specialists are found in populous urban areas, while general practitioners are usually found in suburbs and rural communities. Family, small business, criminal, and probate law attorneys are found in all communities of any significant size.

ASSOCIATIONS OF LAWYERS

You can find a listing of the largest 250 law firms in the United States at the National Law Journal Web site at http://www.ljx.com/firms/

A lawyer may choose to practice alone, combine with one or more other attorneys in a law partnership, or (in most states) conduct business as a professional corporation. Law partnerships and corporations currently range in size from 2 to more than 2,334 attorneys.** The nature of the practice of law has changed dramatically in the last 60 years. The following quotation from Erwin Griswold captures some of the changes occurring during his lifetime in the law.

> [G]ood openings for young lawyers were not easy to find. When I finished law school [Harvard] in 1928, I made the rounds of the New York law offices. I did receive a number of offers, but they were all at the fixed rate of $125 a month. Practically no member of my class at law school had a position at the time of our graduation. It was taken for granted that you would first take and pass the applicable state bar examination, and then knock on the doors of law offices in the city of choice and hope that some sort of an opening could be found. There was not a great deal of change until after the close of World War II.***

Most attorneys who associate with others do so in some form of partnership or a professional corporation. When professionals, including lawyers, form organizations, they do not necessarily gain all the advantages that exist for other businesses. For example, there are generally no restrictions on who may be a shareholder (part owner) in the usual corporation. But in a professional law corporation, non-legal professionals (e.g., legal secretaries, legal assistants, and investigators) are not allowed to be shareholders. In addition, although the corporate form usually protects a shareholder from all personal liability for the debts of the firm, it does not completely protect a shareholder in a professional corporation. To protect the public, such corporations may not shield attorney

---

*Including Alabama, Arizona, Arkansas, California, Connecticut, Florida, Georgia, Louisiana, Minnesota, New Jersey, New Mexico, South Carolina, Texas, and Utah.

**The largest law firm in the country is Baker & McKenzie. Like other large law firms, it has offices in several states and in several countries overseas. *The National Law Journal* publishes an annual survey of the nation's largest law firms each September. If current trends continue, some observers predict that law firms will continue to grow in size and a smaller number of firms will someday dominate much of the nation's legal work. Thomas Gibbons, "Law Practice in 2001," 76 *American Bar Association Journal* 69 (1990).

***Today it is most unlikely that a top Harvard graduate would need to go door to door to find employment, and the starting salary would be most attractive. Erwin Griswold, *The National Law Journal*, 30 December 1991, 17. Adapted from the book, *Ould Field, New Corne: The Personal Memoirs of a Twentieth Century Lawyer* (St. Paul, MN: West Publishing, 1991).

shareholders from liability for wrongful errors and omissions (malpractice) arising from the practice of law.*

Lawyers in all but the smallest "boutique" firms are often assisted by **legal assistants**** (persons qualified to perform a wide range of administrative and semilegal tasks), secretaries or personal assistants, investigators, and office managers. Medium to large size partnerships include attorneys offering a wide variety of specialized legal services. On the other hand, some law firms limit their entire practice to a single specialty. For example, some firms specialize in the defense of automobile injury cases. These firms are employed by automobile insurance companies to represent their customers who are involved in automobile accidents.

Prestige within the legal community is often related to the size of the firm. The larger the firm, the greater its prestige and, usually, the higher the fees it charges the client. This phenomenon is partly the result of large, well-established firms attracting top graduates from elite law schools. Members (owners, or "equity-partners") of these firms often earn high personal incomes, serve wealthy clients, and occupy luxurious offices. The solo practitioner, rightly or wrongly, is often found at the bottom of the image and income ladder.[9] The nature of the practice of law appears to be changing drastically. While the evolution of legal practice from solo practitioners to large firms has been going on for more than 60 years,*** the establishment of the megafirm with offices in different cities, states, and countries is a more recent innovation.

Types of law practice also offer different levels of prestige. An example of the strong sentiments about one type of practice is expressed in the following newspaper quote from a judge (with obviously strong, but not necessarily accurate, opinions) who was contemplating his return to practice.

> When he goes back into practice, Winner said he will accept any kind of case except divorce cases. "I'll represent whores, pimps, or newspaper reporters, but I'm not going to try divorce cases," he said. "There is no end to them, and no end to the calls at home. There's also no satisfactory solution to any of them. The cause of most divorces is that there isn't enough money, and if there isn't enough money to support one family, there sure isn't enough money to support two."[10]

Public attorneys (e.g., public defenders, district attorneys, U.S. attorneys, and county counsels) represent various local, state, and federal governments. Attorneys in public service are usually bound by the same rules of professional conduct as are attorneys in the private practice of law.****

Interested in becoming a paralegal? See The National Federation of Paralegal Associations Web site at http://www.paralegals.org/

---

*Various types of statutory schemes protect clients of professional corporations. One type will not allow shareholders to have limited liability. Another requires the professional corporation or limited liability partnership to purchase insurance against professional malpractice (errors and omissions insurance). The insurance may be a condition for an initial and a continuing certification to do business. A third scheme requires all shareholders to personally guarantee all corporate obligations for malpractice as a condition for certification.

**Persons, qualified through education, training, or work experience, who are employed or retained by a lawyer, law office, governmental agency, or other entity in a capacity or function which involves the performance, under the ultimate direction and supervision of an attorney, of specifically delegated substantive legal work, which work for the most part, requires sufficient knowledge of legal concepts that, absent such assistant, the attorney would perform the task. American Bar Association definition.

***In the years immediately after World War Two approximately 65 percent of lawyers in this country practiced alone. Albert Blaustein, *American Lawyer* (Westport, Conn.: Greenwood Publishing, 1972).

****One exception is when an adversary proffers an offer to compromise. Private attorneys are bound to disclose such vital information to their clients. A public district attorney, however, need not reveal all proffered offers for plea bargains to anyone.

Generally, free legal counsel for civil matters is not available to low-income people through government offices. However, many communities have established legal aid offices that provide limited legal advice in civil matters and assistance to people who cannot afford an attorney. In personal injury cases, legal services are available from private attorneys on a **contingency fee** basis. The fee (a percentage of the amount recovered) is contingent on the outcome of the case. In other words, no fee is paid unless money is won for the client. (Further discussion of attorney fees appears later in this chapter.)

If you wish to know more about the Legal Services Corporation go to their Web site at http://www.ltsi.net/lsc/index.html

The federal **Legal Services Corporation (LSC)** assists states in providing legal assistance to the underprivileged through grants to local legal service providers to the poor. Created in 1964, the LSC has encountered some controversy since advocacy for the poor often has unpopular political ramifications. Cases brought by the LSC often name other government agencies as defendants, creating political backlash and resentment. President Ronald W. Reagan attempted several times to eliminate the Legal Services Corporation but was thwarted by Congress, although funding to the agency was significantly cut. No matter who is president, federal budget difficulties have severely curtailed the effectiveness of the LSC.[11] The appropriation for the LSC in 1996 was less than that received in 1980, despite population growth and inflation. A 1994 study reported that there is "one LSC lawyer for every 6,000 to 7,000 poor people, compared with a national average of one lawyer for every 320 people."[12]

Many bar associations and legal commentators urge lawyers to allocate part of their time to civil *pro bono publico* (Latin: "for the public good") services free of charge. Many attorneys do contribute their time and effort to serving poor people who have legal problems, but the need is far from being met to the satisfaction of all concerned. Partly because of the lack of financial ability of poor persons to pursue their legal rights, Congress and state legislatures have added "fee shifting" provisions to some statutes they enact. Under these statutes, attorneys will represent poor persons with good cases because if they win, the government will pay all attorney fees. Many attorneys specialize in representing poor persons, usually in matters concerning their civil rights or treatment by government, because they collect generous fees for their service. And it is not difficult to solicit business from victims who do not have to pay attorney fees in advance. To some, fee shifting is the only way to protect poor people. To others, fee shifting statutes are like adding gasoline to the fires of litigation, which many believe already to be out of control.

Assistance to indigent persons accused of crimes is provided without charge through state and federal public defenders' offices. Courts will appoint private attorneys when public attorneys are not available. These private attorneys are paid standardized fees by state governments. Under the Sixth Amendment, legal assistance is a constitutional right for all persons accused of crimes punishable by imprisonment, even if they cannot afford to hire private legal counsel.

Some "store front lawyers" or "law clinics" operating out of strip malls and other such quarters provide routine legal services for lower fees. This type of law practice began in the 1970s with the relaxation of rules prohibiting advertising. These attorneys often represent clients in limited areas such as family law, criminal defense, and probate matters. To lower costs, they emphasize standardized legal forms and procedures for routine matters. In recent years, many of these clinics have added other legal specialties to their services.

Group and prepaid legal service plans are designed to make legal services available at reduced cost to members of unions or other organizations, such as financial institutions. These plans are usually limited in scope but do provide low-cost assistance for routine legal matters (e.g., simple wills, document review, and warranty enforcement).

A form of legal services that became popular in the late 1960s is the **public interest law firm**. These firms offer assistance in particular areas such as employment, minority rights, civil rights, political rights, family law, and environmental law. Public interest law firms are often funded by grants from private charitable organizations. Public interest firms represent opposite sides of controversial legal issues.

WHAT ARE PROFESSIONAL ETHICS?

A useful definition of **ethics** appeared in the book *Ethics in the Corporate Policy Process*:

> *Ethics is a process by which individuals, social groups, and societies evaluate their actions from the perspective of moral principles and values. This evaluation may be on the basis of traditional convictions, of ideals sought, of goals desired, of moral laws to be obeyed, of an improved quality of relations among humans and with the environment. When we speak of "ethics" and ethical reflection, we mean the activity of applying these various yardsticks to the actions of persons and groups.*[13]

Read about current issues in legal ethics at the Web site devoted to this topic. http://www.legalethics.com/

Ethical issues are about what is fair and just. They address the question: What is the right thing to do in a situation? Ethics and the law, although not identical, do go hand in hand.

Professional ethics are written rules of prohibited conduct that are adopted by and binding upon members of a professional group. A common assumption about groups claiming to be composed of professionals is that they commit themselves to public service and written rules of ethics.

Professional rules of conduct (rules and codes of ethics) for attorneys are established and enforced to protect the public and to preserve and improve the reputation of the bar. A breach of these rules may lead to an attorney's being disciplined for unethical conduct. Discipline may take the form of (1) disbarment, (2) suspension from practice for a stated period of time, (3) probation, or (4) *reproval* (formal private or public censure). In 1983 the American Bar Association drastically revised its Model Code of Professional Responsibility and incorporated it into the current Model Rules of Professional Conduct. As of the fall of 1998, 38 states and the District of Columbia had adopted all or significant portions of the Model Rules into state law or court rules. Most remaining states have adopted modified versions of a prior statement of the code. The ABA's Project 2000 is scheduled to make recommendations regarding new rules or revisions to the Model Rules sometime in the year 2000.

> *In the nature of law practice, however, conflicting responsibilities are encountered. Virtually all difficult ethical problems arise from conflict between a*

lawyer's responsibility to clients, to the legal system and to the lawyer's own in-terest in remaining an upright person while earning a satisfactory living. The Rules of Professional Conduct prescribe terms for resolving such conflicts. Within the framework of these Rules many difficult issues of professional discre-tion can arise. Such issues must be resolved through the exercise of sensitive pro-fessional and moral judgement guided by the basic principles underlying the Rules.[14]

Charging an unconscionable and exorbitant fee, stealing a client's funds, im-properly soliciting employment, neglecting a client's case, and misusing a client's funds are all examples of unethical conduct directly related to the attorney's pro-fession. Obviously, some unethical conduct involves criminal offenses. Other un-ethical conduct may expose the attorney to civil liability.

Attorneys may be disciplined for conduct involving *moral turpitude* (conduct contrary to justice, honesty, and good morals). Perjury, failure to pay income taxes, murder, larceny, participation in business fraud, child molestation, and sale of narcotics are all examples of crimes involving moral turpitude, and they sub-ject the offending attorney to professional discipline, in addition to separate crim-inal charges and individual civil lawsuits. Disciplinary hearings may take place even if questionable conduct does not directly relate to the attorney's ability to practice law. For example, former vice president and attorney Spiro T. Agnew was disbarred following his plea of *nolo contendere* (Latin: "I will not contest it"), a spe-cial form of guilty plea, to willful tax evasion.[15]

Grace Akinsanya retained [attorney] Pineda and paid him $1,500 as an advance fee to represent her in a real estate matter. After a few months, Akinsanya became dissatisfied with Pineda's inaction and she asked him to agree to a substitution-of-attorney. Pineda refused to sign a substitution-of-attorney form and would not return Akinsanya's files or refund any part of the advance fee. Only after the Superior Court sanc-tioned (punished) him for his actions did Pineda withdraw from the case and return Akinsanya's files.[16]

Based on these acts and six other similar acts of failure to perform services for clients, attorney Pineda was suspended from the practice of law for two years and placed on probation for five years.[17]

An important difference exists between the ethical obligations of private and public attorneys. A *private attorney* is ethically bound to zealously support and try to win the client's case. When an attorney represents a client in litigation, the at-torney is usually working with the record of historical events, which lawyers refer to as *facts*. The private attorney must resolve all doubts about facts and law so as to favor the client's interests. This is so because the private attorney in court is an advocate, not charged with the responsibility of passing judgment but only with advocating his or her client's position. The role of the attorney as advocate is one aspect of the adversary system of the United States.

A *public attorney*, such as a prosecutor or other government lawyer, has a pri-mary duty to see that justice is carried out, not simply to win a case. For example, a prosecutor must notify the defense of any evidence in a criminal case that obvi-ously tends to show the defendant's innocence. Although defense counsel is not obligated in the same way, he or she may not destroy, nor present as true, any evidence that is known as false, nor solicit or condone perjury in order to win a case.[18]

> Attorney Tak Sharpe represented the plaintiff in an automobile accident case that was nearing trial. To encourage a compromise, Sharpe telephoned the defendant, Sandra Broderik, instead of calling Ms. Broderik's attorney. Sharpe told Sandra that $17,500 would be a fair settlement. Sandra responded that she would prefer to discuss the matter with her attorney. Has Sharpe acted ethically?

No.[19] The Rules of Professional Conduct do not allow opposing counsel to communicate directly with another attorney's client concerning a pending case. Sharpe should have telephoned Broderik's lawyer. The purpose of this rule is to prevent an opponent's lawyer from intimidating the opposition or undermining the advice given by that client's counsel.

Questions of professional ethics are sometimes very complex and susceptible to misunderstanding. The attorney's job is to vigorously represent the client while honoring the law. For example, a criminal law attorney must attempt to persuade a judge and jury to free a client, even if he or she personally suspects or believes that the client is guilty of the offense. This is considered ethically correct because the lawyer's duty is to represent—not to judge—the client. Everyone is entitled to all available legal advantages. Even following conviction, the attorney will argue for probation rather than prison. A tax attorney will look vigilantly to find a *loophole* (an ambiguity by which the intent of tax law may be evaded) allowing a client to legitimately reduce or avoid tax payments. Ethically, this is proper as long as no evasion (violation of tax law) or fraudulent practice (such as forging documents) is involved. Congress often authorizes loopholes or tax shelters to encourage certain types of socially desirable investments. For example, Congress allows interest paid on home mortgages to be deducted from taxable income, reducing the income taxes paid by homeowners. (Of course, the taxpayer must request the deduction.)

> Tammy Forsberg was injured in a motorcycle accident. Her attorney, John Casey, obtained a settlement of which her portion was $23,233. Casey paid her $5,000 and refused to pay the rest. Forsberg hired a second lawyer, James Himmel, on a contingency fee basis to recover the remaining sum due from Casey. Himmel ultimately sued Casey and won a judgment of $100,000 for Forsberg but did not report the conduct of Casey to the state bar. What are the ethical implications of the conduct of Casey and Himmel?

The Illinois state bar disbarred Casey for his misconduct in failing to turn over the funds due Ms. Forsberg. Apparently, Casey had used the funds as if they were his own. Himmel was also found in violation of an ethical rule that makes it a duty of a lawyer to report to the proper authority knowledge of another lawyer's misconduct. The Illinois Supreme Court held that Himmel, in not reporting Casey's activities, had contributed to Casey taking additional funds from other clients in the interim, and he had done so because he put his desire for fees above the interests of the legal system. Although Himmel had practiced law without reproach for eleven years, he was suspended from the practice of law for one year.[20]*

ATTORNEY–CLIENT PRIVILEGE

The need to encourage full disclosure of facts by the client to the attorney has given rise to the **attorney–client privilege**, which ensures that all communications made by the client to the attorney will remain confidential. The attorney cannot waive the privilege or be compelled to reveal such communications, even in a court of law.[21] The privilege is designed to ensure fair and vigorous representation by encouraging open communications between the lawyer and the client. It applies in all states.

A criminal defense attorney learned from his client, Derrick Dagger, that in addition to the present crime with which Derrick was charged, he previously had murdered two young girls who recently had been reported as missing. The lawyer even learned the specific location of their bodies. Yet the attorney did not report this information to the authorities, to the parents of the girls, or to anyone else. Did the attorney behave ethically?

Yes, according to generally understood legal ethics. Others think not.[22] Although the attorney cannot waive the privilege, the client can do so. And an attorney cannot refuse to testify if the client waives the privilege. Rule 1.6 of the American Bar Association (ABA) Rules of Professional Conduct prohibits a lawyer from revealing "information relating to representation of a client unless the client consents after consultation." Cases involving difficult situations have brought these rules to public attention, if not understanding, over the years.

An anonymous client (referred to as J. Doe) contacted an attorney following Doe's involvement in a fatal hit-and-run accident. Doe instructed the attorney to offer a plea bargain with the prosecutor for minimal criminal charges while Doe remained anonymous. The prosecutor refused to bargain without revelation of Doe's identity. The victim's family sued the attorney to force disclosure of the client's name. Can the family get Doe's real name?

No. The Florida Circuit Court held that the information was privileged, and the attorney was not required to disclose the client's name.[23] Attorneys understand the natural public resentment that arises with such rulings. Nevertheless, "if the privilege is not maintained in 'hard' cases such as this, troubled individuals with legal problems will only dare to consult lawyers in 'easy' cases—where there is little to hide in any event."[24]

---

*The Supreme Court of Rhode Island found a similar failure to disclose to be appropriate conduct. The court noted that because of an instruction by the attorney's client not to disclose an embezzlement by a former attorney, the attorney was prohibited from disclosure under the attorney–client privilege. *In re Ethics Advisory Panel Opinion No. 92-1,* 627 A.2d 317 (1993).

In 1993 Deputy White House Counsel Vincent W. Foster, Jr., met with James Hamilton seeking personal legal representation. Hamilton took handwritten notes at the meeting. Nine days later, Foster committed suicide. Subsequently, a federal grand jury, at the request of Independent Counsel Kenneth Starr, issued subpoenas for the notes as part of the investigation of the president and his staff. Hamilton sought to quash the subpoena, arguing that the notes were protected by the attorney–client privilege. Starr's contention was that the attorney–client privilege should not prevent disclosure of confidential communications after the client has died, particularly if the information is relevant to a criminal proceeding. Did Starr get the notes?

No. In reversing the Court of Appeals for the District of Columbia Circuit, the U.S. Supreme Court stated, "[W]e think there are weighty reasons that counsel in favor of posthumous application [of the attorney–client privilege]. Knowing that communications will remain confidential even after death encourages the client to communicate fully and frankly with counsel. Clients may be concerned about reputation, civil liability, or possible harm to friends or family. Posthumous disclosure of such communications may be as feared as disclosure during the client's lifetime."[25]

The privilege has not, however, been held to cover all communications in all situations; for example, there is no privilege protecting communications made in the presence of others, or if the communication indicates an intent to commit a future crime, or if there is a statute requiring communications of a specific nature to be disclosed.

A federal law passed in 1988 requires attorneys to report to the Internal Revenue Service the identity of any client who makes a cash payment to them of $10,000 or more. Attorney Robert Leventhal filed the appropriate form with the IRS indicating receipt of a payment in excess of $10,000 but did not disclose the name of the client on the form. When ordered to complete the form, he declined, claiming such disclosures would violate the attorney–client privilege. Was Leventhal required to disclose the client name?

Yes. The federal appellate court held that the federal statute superseded both the state-created and the federal attorney–client privilege. The court also held that disclosure of the client's name was not the type of confidential communication protected by the privilege.[26]

CONFLICT OF INTEREST

Another major source of potential problems involving rules of ethics is the broad area of **conflict of interest**. In general, a conflict of interest is a situation in which an attorney and a client both have a real, perceived, or potential stake in a matter, for example, a financial matter. An obvious conflict is when an attorney, abusing her fiduciary capacity, convinces a client to name her as a beneficiary in a will or trust. A conflict less obvious to the general public has to do with representation of new clients by an attorney.* When accepting new clients an attorney must be vigilant in determining whether representing the new client conflicts with obligations owed to other clients (even previous ones). The magnitude of this problem has increased with the growth in law firm size. Conflicts of interest can also appear in appointments of counsel to represent indigent defendants accused of crimes.

> Judge Boles appointed Clayton Haley to represent Christopher, an indigent defendant charged with a crime. Haley asked to withdraw on the basis of a conflict of interest, stating his law partner was married to the county district attorney, Karen Price. Judge Boles held that no conflict of interest existed. Haley requested a judicial review on whether a conflict of interest existed. Did a conflict of interest exist?

The Texas appellate court agreed with Haley that the appearance of a conflict existed, which was sufficient to allow for Haley's dismissal as Christopher's counsel. The court held that in situations such as this the client is not free to accept or reject the attorney upon disclosure of the conflict because the client is not paying the bill for the attorney's services. In addition, the relationships in this defense could undermine public confidence in the criminal justice system.

SPECIOUS LAWSUITS

Despite a public perception to the contrary, it is unethical for a lawyer to file a meritless lawsuit. Concerns include protection of parties who would otherwise be the victims of baseless lawsuits and courts whose publicly supported time and facilities need to be protected from wasteful use. One example of rules designed to enforce this general concept is Rule 11 of the Federal Courts Rules of Civil Procedure.** This rule requires the court to punish lawyers and *pro se* plaintiffs who file meritless lawsuits. Punishments include requiring the plaintiffs to pay the defendant's court costs. The rule has been held by the U.S. Supreme Court to require all plaintiffs who sign legal papers, including plaintiffs represented by attorneys, to be subject to the rule.[27]

DEALING WITH AN ATTORNEY

IS AN ATTORNEY NECESSARY?

Lawyers are expected to assist with a seemingly endless stream of problems for private persons, businesses, government agencies, and other organizations.

---

*A lawyer shall not represent a client if the representation of that client may be materially limited by the lawyer's responsibilities to another client or to a third person, or by the lawyer's own interest, unless (1) the lawyer reasonably believes that representation will not be adversely affected and (2) the client consents after the consultation. ABA Model Rule of Professional Conduct 1.7 (b).

**The signature of an attorney or party constitutes a certificate by the signer that the signer has read the pleadings, motion, or other paper, that to the best of signer's knowledge, information and belief formed after reasonable inquiry is well founded in fact . . . and that it is not interposed for any improper purpose, such as to harass or to cause unnecessary delay or needless increase in the cost of litigation. . . . If pleading, motion, or other paper is signed in violation of this rule, the court shall . . . impose upon the person who signed it, a represented party, or both, an appropriate sanction.

Obviously, many clients consider attorneys an essential source of information, advice, and representation in a myriad of situations. Nonetheless, persons without the assistance of an attorney routinely resolve some legal problems. Among these are simple divorces, settlement of "fender-bender" car crash cases, simple handwritten wills, consumer purchase and sale contracts (such as "pink slip" certificates of vehicle ownership), and simple real estate purchase agreements. Numerous disputes involving small sums are within the jurisdiction of the small claims court (recall that law in such courts usually excludes attorneys, unless they are a parties in a case). Today there are excellent self-help books such as those published by Nolo Press* and legal software available such as *Business Law Partner* by Quicken. Unfortunately, too often persons in genuine need of legal advice or assistance fail to seek it, or delay in consulting an attorney. The result may be a permanent loss of a valuable legal right. A careful decision about self-help should be made.

Some general guidelines may help you decide whether to consult an attorney. Do consult an attorney if the matter can be characterized in any of the following ways:

1. The matter involves the risk of losing, or the possibility of obtaining, a sum of money that is significant to you.

2. The matter involves actual or possible physical or mental injury, suffered or threatened, that can be characterized as significant.

3. The matter seems very important for any other reason (e.g., a major impact on your life or that of a dependent, such as a child custody dispute).

4. The area of law is complex and/or you lack the time to carefully preserve or pursue your rights.

Not every dispute or problem ought to be taken to an attorney. Indeed, elementary economics militates against such petty litigiousness. The potential impact of events on one's life should be considered when considering the need for an attorney's services.

In recent years many critics have claimed that the United States has too many lawyers. The number of lawyers in our society allegedly has a negative effect on economic productivity and has engendered dissatisfaction among citizens. Indeed, lawyers have the dubious distinction of inspiring an anti-fan club called HALT (Help Abolish Legal Tyranny), which is at least partly the result of improper conduct by some lawyers. It is difficult to evaluate criticisms because reliable data for comparison with other nations generally does not exist. For example, comparative national counts of lawyers is misleading because legal professions in different countries perform different tasks. Thus, studies purporting to measure productivity as a function of the number of lawyers are often seriously flawed.[28]

Given that lawyer bashing is a socially acceptable form of class denigration, why do people wish to become lawyers, and why do lawyers remain in their profession? The following quotation from Harvey Rubenstein, President of the Delaware State Bar, offers one response.

The home page for HALT says it is the Organization of Americans for Legal Reform. As they have reservations about lawyers (a significant understatement), it is not surprising that they provide good self-help information. http://www.halt.org/index.html

West Publishing provides a legal dictionary on the Internet (Oran's *Dictionary of the Law*) for those who are self-help inclined. http://www.wld.com/general/sitemap.htm

---

*We frequently cite Nolo Press in this textbook. Nolo Press began publishing self-help legal resources in the late 1960s and, in our opinion, they have set the standard for accurate, easy-to-understand legal materials. As their publishing philosophy has been motivated by social goals, the materials they provide appear to be priced reasonably.

Why, then, do so many become and remain practicing lawyers? Maybe it is because lawyers really do take seriously their obligation to represent as best they can those who need help. Maybe it is because, once in a while, a lawyer is asked to plead a great cause that may affect the course of human events or make our society work a little better. Or maybe it is because, once in awhile, one lawyer may be the difference in one person's life. And to practicing lawyers, once in a while is enough.[29]

How Do You Find a "Good" Attorney?

Time, energy, and resourcefulness spent in finding an attorney will go a long way toward a satisfactory relationship and final result. Too often, the presence of a serious problem that prompts the search also prompts great haste in the selection process. An exhaustive search should not be necessary in order to avoid a "bad" attorney; to the contrary, in populous areas there are a number of qualified attorneys ready, willing, and able to perform the required service. But a cavalier approach to the selection process increases the chance of retaining an attorney who may not perform as well as others who are equally available.

Paid Advertisements

In the past, lawyers were prohibited by law and professional rules from advertising their services. The profession considered advertisement as not only unethical but also unbecoming conduct. Specifically, many members of the legal profession fear that advertising leads to extravagant and misleading claims and practices, creating rather than resolving conflict. Many attorneys also believe that advertising further tarnishes the general reputation of attorneys.*

Rules of conduct regarding publicity and advertising have been liberalized in recent years. In 1977, the U.S. Supreme Court ruled that the public had a right to information as to the availability and cost of routine legal services, and attorneys had a right to furnish that information.[30] States have formulated rules regarding advertising, although many issues are still debated. In recent years the Supreme Court has held that lawyers cannot be prohibited from sending direct mail solicitations[31] and communications to potential clients that they are certified to be specialists.[32] Claims about an individual attorney's competence or ability to achieve results are still considered unethical by the legal profession.

Initially, major firms with outstanding national reputations declined to advertise; recently, even they have begun to do it, though they generally avoid commercial television in favor of simple announcements, news releases, brochures, public television, newsletters, and advertisements in selected special audience magazines. A 1993 lawyer's poll found significant internal conflict among lawyers over advertising. Sixty-one percent of lawyers polled said their firms engage in some form of advertising. In the same poll, 87 percent of the lawyers believed that advertising has a negative effect on the image of the profession.[33] Most public libraries contain directories of attorneys with biographical information, including practice specialties and lists of representative clients.[34] Information

Some recommendations about what questions to ask a lawyer before you decide to engage her or his services can be found at the Organization of Americans for Legal Reform Web site at http://www.halt.org/ELS/elsB3.htm

---

*". . . [M]arketplace lawyer advertising, using all the sights, color, sounds, subliminal messages and not-so-hidden persuaders of commercial television, adversely affect not only the public's perception of those court officers, but also of the courts and the total judicial system." Justice Reynoldson, retired Chief Justice of the Iowa Supreme Court, "The Case Against Lawyer Advertising," 75 *ABA Journal* 60 (January 1989).

directories have been available for many years and have never been considered advertising. The Internet also provides various listings of law firms by bar associations, private organizations, and the law firms themselves.

Word-of-Mouth Advertising

Generally, the most reliable advertising is word of mouth. However, an attorney's reputation is more than simply "good" or "bad." Better questions concerning the reputation of a particular attorney include the following:

- What is the attorney's specialty?
- How long has the attorney been in practice?
- Does the attorney have a reputation for being a problem solver? Thorough? Expensive? Aggressive? Sincere? Or any other quality thought to be appropriate or inappropriate for the case?
- Do judges and attorneys generally think highly of the individual or firm?
- Is the attorney active in the community?
- Has the attorney been disciplined by the bar or been a defendant in malpractice cases?
- Is the attorney in good health?
- Does the attorney have a reputation for consuming alcohol to excess or taking harmful drugs?
- Is the attorney usually victorious in cases?
- Does the attorney make the fee arrangement clear?
- Does the attorney have a favorable reputation for keeping the client informed on case progress?
- Does the attorney work on the case or delegate the work to others?

The selection of an attorney should be accompanied by some introspection by the client. Clients should consider their own attitudes, goals, and objectives and, as dispassionately as possible, the nature of their claims. Some attorneys are problem solvers and others are "gladiators" (problem winners). A problem solver might complete the task in a short period of time, but the resolution may require considerable compromise on the part of the client. The gladiator might be victorious and provide more of what the client wanted, but may take considerably more time and require a different emotional commitment by the client. (Fewer than 5 percent of all civil cases actually go to trial, so even gladiators typically compromise; they just do it later in the process.) The problem solver may preserve a friendly, mutually profitable relationship for the client with the other party. This is seldom possible with a gladiator who may have embarrassed, angered, or even humiliated the opposing party.

A person in need of an attorney's services is advised to solicit help from several persons who might be in a position to obtain and relay information about the professional reputation of attorneys practicing in the community. Business managers, bankers, title company officers, city and county government officials, educators, merchants, stockbrokers, insurance executives, real estate personnel and, of course, lawyers are likely to have direct communication with and knowledge about members of the bar. They will often share their knowledge of the professional reputation of attorneys in the community. An employer is often a good source of information. Although most attorneys are listed in the Yellow Pages of the telephone directory, sometimes with large ads, such listings do not guarantee competence.

Meeting with the Attorney

Once a prospective client gets the name of one or two attorneys as possible selections, an office appointment may be made with each by telephone. An initial appointment of 30 minutes or so is often available without charge, or for a modest fee quoted in advance upon request. A prospective client has many questions concerning the rules of law thought to be applicable to the case. Unfortunately, there are usually a number of laws that may be applicable, and the attorney, pending further study, will necessarily be noncommittal. This is to be expected, because no attorney is capable of explaining all the law concerning a matter without careful research and preparation; nor is any attorney capable of predicting with certainty the outcome of any complex case.

No commitment to hire need be made at the first meeting; a simple "Thank you, I would like to consider the matter for a couple of days" permits a graceful departure. During the initial meeting, much can be learned from a few questions to the attorney:

* Do you frequently handle cases like mine?
* Is this your specialty? If not, how many cases of this type have you handled?
* Will you be doing all the work or will other persons be involved?
* Will you refer my case to another attorney in the firm or handle it yourself?
* Will this case conflict with any of your other obligations, court calendars, or appointments?
* Is it best to settle this matter now, even at a loss, rather than to be embroiled in a lengthy legal battle?
* May I have a copy of your standard retainer agreement?
* Will you please give me an estimate of my likely trial costs and fees for handling this matter to its conclusion?
* How will I be kept informed about the progress of the matter in your office?

Much can be learned about the prospective attorney by arriving for your meeting early and observing the law office in operation. Confusion and disorganization often suggest a lower quality of service. An office cluttered with files, papers, and books does not engender confidence. After you leave, will your file simply be part of the mess?

You should be aware that not all attorneys will appreciate being asked all of the questions just listed. Some will interpret your inquiries as an indication that you will be a "problem" or malcontent client. However, consumers of any service, including legal services, have the right to be informed and assured of the nature of the service they are to receive. If in the process of protecting your interests you are reasonable and courteous, a responsible attorney should not resent your questions. And if the two of you decide to do business together, you will be off to a good start, with mutual respect for each other.

Attorney Referral Services

Some communities offer bar association referral services, often listed in telephone white pages, Yellow Page Service Directories, and Web sites. These are associations of attorneys with various specialties. Often the participating attorneys will accept referrals only for specific types of cases. Or referrals may be made alphabetically. These attorneys are not selected on the basis of any particular qualifications. Frequently they are newer members of the bar seeking business and they may charge reduced rates for their services.

In addition to panels provided by bar associations, there are private business referral panels. These panels are similar to the bar panels. They often exist as a means of indirect advertising. The panel places advertisements seeking a particular kind of client, for example, a personal injury victim. Phone responses to the advertisement are then referred to panel members. Attorney members pay the referral business a fee for being allowed to participate.

Public Defenders

As noted earlier, a defendant accused of a serious crime (i.e., one for which the possible punishment is incarceration) has a constitutional right to be represented by a competent attorney at all stages of legal proceedings. If a defendant is indigent (unable to afford the services of a private attorney), the court will appoint an attorney, often called a **public defender**, to defend the accused free of charge. Contrary to some popularly held views, attorneys in public defender roles generally are very competent and zealous advocates for the defense. They are specialists. They handle a heavy caseload, develop vast experience in a short time, spend much time in court, and know the judges and court staff. Because they handle many criminal matters, they know the probable results of a plea negotiation or plea bargain. Records of numerous convictions reflect not incompetence on the part of the public defender but rather the fact that these lawyers are unable to choose their clients. Public defenders by inclination fight for the underdog, and they usually fight well. On the negative side, public defenders are often given too many cases to be able to devote the time and attention to any one case that a client accused of a crime might wish.

Solicitation

Most methods of solicitation, in which lawyers aggressively seek clients, are considered unethical. Public policy frowns on efforts to promote litigation, such as "ambulance chasing," where an accident victim is solicited to sign an employment agreement with an attorney. More sophisticated forms of solicitation, through a "capper" or "runner" who frequents likely places for generating legal business, are likewise unethical. Investigators, as well as nurses in emergency wards, have been used as cappers. They may receive an illegal referral fee from the attorney. Such payments frequently are made in cash in an attempt to avoid disclosure for the lawyer and to facilitate tax evasion for the capper. If solicited personally by an attorney or a capper, a prospective client should be aware that he or she is dealing with an unethical lawyer and should report the matter to the local or state bar association.*

Florida lawyer Shane Stafford arranged for Roy Blevins, a West Palm Beach police officer, to solicit personal injury cases for Stafford. In an 18-month period, Blevins referred ten or eleven cases to Stafford, including three automobile accident cases he investigated as a police officer. Stafford gave 15 percent of his legal fees to Blevins, who received approximately $11,000 total. Is such a referral arrangement legal and ethical?

This arrangement was neither legal nor ethical. The Florida Supreme Court held that "activities such as those pursued by Stafford are clearly prohibited. In recent years, perhaps no single aspect of the practice of law has received more public criticism than the unethical solicitation of clients." The Court found that Stafford had violated several disciplinary rules, including asking persons to recommend him for employment, dividing legal fees with a non-lawyer, and engaging in conduct that adversely reflects on fitness to practice law. The court suspended him "from the practice of law for a period of six months and upon reinstatement to the Bar, [he] shall be placed on probation for a period of two years." Three of seven judges dissented, believing the ruling correct but the punishment too lenient: "I think in order to restore the public's faith in our system of discipline it is necessary that we rid our ranks of this type of lawyer."[35]

HOW DO YOU HIRE AND FIRE AN ATTORNEY?

After a prospective client locates an appropriate attorney, the employment relationship is accomplished by contract. The attorney promises to represent the client in exchange for a promise of compensation. In some instances, an attorney will require a written agreement; in others, an oral agreement is considered adequate. Many states require that an attorney provide the client with a written contract shortly after undertaking the matter. Whether or not the law requires an agreement, the client should request a written agreement and ask that it be fully explained. An attorney has an ethical obligation to reject a frivolous case or a case raising issues where she or he lacks competence.**

The agreement will necessarily have limitations. It cannot guarantee any particular result or any particular completion date, and will usually not detail the

*Although individual attorneys in all states presently are restricted from solicitation, the U.S. Supreme Court has ruled that the American Civil Liberties Union (ACLU) and similar organizations of attorneys may solicit directly [*In re Primus*, 436 U.S. 412, 98 S.Ct. 1893 (1978)]; that the National Association for the Advancement of Colored People (NAACP) may solicit parents of school children in desegregation cases [*NAACP v. Button*, 371 U.S. 415, 83 S.Ct 328 (1963)]; and that a union may solicit its members to funnel their injury claims to a particular attorney [*United Mine Workers v. Illinois*, 389 U.S. 217, 88 S.Ct. 353 (1967)].

**Filing of frivolous and defamatory litigation justifies disciplinary action. The attorney is also vulnerable to a civil lawsuit for malicious prosecution, although such actions are seldom successful. See previous discussion concerning lawyer ethics.

step-by-step procedures the attorney will ultimately take. This lack of detail is not sinister, but instead realistic. Even the most common legal problem or case may entail many unpredictable complications. The client should carefully ask questions until all ramifications of the problem or case are at least generally understood.

Examples of questions a prospective client might ask include the following:

1. What is the computational basis of the fee to be charged? If hourly, is the "meter" running at the same rate while junior attorneys or paralegal personnel are working on the case? How much library or computer research is anticipated, and at what cost? Will the fee statement be itemized as to hours spent and tasks accomplished? How often will I be billed?

    a. If the fee is contingent (client and attorney share in any recovery), are costs to be deducted from the award before or after computation of the attorney's share? If the matter is settled quickly (and so the attorney's involvement is less than was anticipated) is the fee division reduced commensurately?

    b. What happens if the lawyer's work increases greatly—for example, when a new trial is granted or an appeal must be initiated?

    c. If a flat fee is charged, how will costs be paid? What does the fee include? What happens if there is an appeal? There should be a careful delineation of the work to be performed.

2. What specific important actions and events does the attorney predict will occur, and when are they most likely to happen?

3. What are the possible outcomes of the action, good and bad? Is there any point of no return; that is, a point beyond which the client cannot practically withdraw from the matter?

4. Will there be a need to refer all or any part of the case to another attorney? If so, how will the fee and work be affected and divided?

5. What will be the means (letter or telephone) and frequency of communications with the attorney or secretary? Will copies of all documents and correspondence routinely be sent to the client?

A client generally has the right to dismiss an attorney at any time for any reason. Difficulty may arise with respect to how much of the fee, if any, has been earned at the time of the discharge. The rule is easy to state but difficult to apply: the attorney is entitled to be paid the reasonable value of work done before discharge. In a contingent fee case, the attorney is entitled to be paid the reasonable value of the work done only when and if a recovery is obtained.

If the client discharging the attorney is unable to pay all fees the attorney has earned up to the time of discharge, a serious conflict may arise. The attorney demands payment while the client demands return of all documents (the file) connected with the case. The attorney may seek to pressure payment of accrued fees by refusing to release the file. In the absence of a statute giving the attorney the right to do so (called a *statutory* or *common-law retaining lien*), such conduct is illegal and probably unethical. However, many states do authorize such a lien.

A client may have difficulty hiring a new attorney for the case if one or more attorneys have been fired or have withdrawn. An attorney considering whether to accept such a case is usually suspicious of its merits and the client's emotional stability.* Care in selection of the best attorney at the beginning of the case is important for many reasons.

As a general rule, an attorney can terminate the employment relationship if there is a reasonable basis for the withdrawal. For example, the client's failure to pay the agreed fee is grounds for withdrawal. However, an attorney must (1) give reasonable notice to the client of intention to withdraw; (2) obtain court permission to withdraw if pleadings have been filed; (3) return the client's papers and money, where appropriate; and (4) refund any unearned fees. An attorney *must* withdraw from the employment when continued representation would require the attorney to violate a disciplinary rule. Other good reasons for withdrawal include failure of the attorney's health, materially affecting his or her ability to continue, or an awareness that a conflict of interest exists.

ATTORNEY FEE ARRANGEMENTS

Common methods for attorneys to be paid include payment on an hourly rate (e.g., $125 per hour), a flat fee for a service (e.g., $5,000 payable in two installments), a contingency fee (e.g., 35 percent of net recovery), or a combination of these methods. Tradition, business practice, and law tie certain types of fee arrangements to certain types of legal matters. For example, the contingency fee is common in personal injury actions but is considered an unethical method of billing in a family law matter.

> Elaine's husband Buck, a young doctor, was killed in the crash of a commercial "commuter" airplane. Buck was not in the airplane; he was in his medical office in San Luis Obispo, which was destroyed by the crash. Attorney Ian Page offered to represent her on a contingent fee basis for one-third of any net recovery. Page indicated no fees would be charged "unless and until" a recovery was made. Should Elaine hire Page?

No. As is the case in most calamitous events, there is no issue of "if." Recovery is assured because of the strict liability of defendants in such cases. Thus, it is only a matter of "when" fees will be paid. Obtaining a reasonable settlement will require negotiations, but one-third of, say, a $3 million settlement is unreasonable for the perhaps 100 hours necessary to represent Elaine. If Elaine asked attorneys to represent her for, say $250 per hour with payment deferred until settlement, she would receive offers from competent attorneys. Thus, it can be argued that contingent fees in calamitous personal injury or death cases where liability is certain (or even probable) are unethical because clients don't fully understand the arrangement or its alternatives. It is not uncommon for accident attorneys to refer to such cases as "jackpots" or "retirement" cases.

The flat fee is common for certain types of routine matters such as family law, criminal law matters, real estate title searches, trusts, and wills. In the last few years, more business clients have requested competitive bidding by two or more

---

*Shortly after beginning practice, new attorneys may be approached by a potential client who, with thick and tattered files, spins a tale of conspiracy, malevolence, and grievous harm. Believing they have found the case that will make their reputation, the young lawyers begin an investigation. Within a short time they find out every attorney in town is already very familiar with their client.

firms, as well as flat fees for matters that in the past were billed by the hour.[36] However, the hourly fee is still the dominant form of attorney billing and is used for all types of legal services.

The nature and, when feasible, the amount of the fee should be specified in a written attorney–client agreement. This freedom of contract is not, however, without limitation. In some instances, attorney fees are limited by statute or by the courts. Furthermore, when fee disputes arise, courts tend to give the benefit of any doubt to the client because of the usual bargaining superiority of the attorney.[37] In some states, the law presumes overreaching by the attorney if representation is begun before the fee is agreed on in a written contract.[38] In such instances, the attorney is hard pressed to justify and collect more than a minimal reasonable fee.

Although attorneys are free to charge their "going rate," the client's case must not be deliberately delayed for the purpose of coercing payment of a delinquent installment,[39] nor may an attorney charge an unconscionable or clearly excessive legal fee. The attorney is subject to discipline for making such an attempt.[40]

Actual fees charged for legal services are difficult to compare because of the many factors used in setting fees in specific cases. Hourly fees in large cities at the time of this writing range from $80 to $500 and more.* A flat fee for a simple divorce, with no significant property or child custody dispute, may range from $400 to $1,000; complex divorces for wealthy clients, on the other hand, may command fees in the tens of thousands of dollars. Contingency fees are rarely less than 25 percent of the net recovery or more than 50 percent. Astronomical fees in celebrated cases involving **class actions**,** national corporations, or prominent persons and politicians shed little light on fees charged for the routine legal problems of the ordinary consumer. It is, on the other hand, no doubt true that overhead costs prevent large firms from profitably handling legal matters in which small sums (less than $25,000–$50,000) are in dispute.

The following are important factors that normally are taken into consideration in setting an attorney's fee:

1. The time required.
2. The degree of legal skill needed and novelty of the legal question presented.
3. The customary fee charged in the locality for similar services.
4. The experience, reputation, and ability of the attorney.
5. The amount of money involved in the case.
6. The result obtained for the client.
7. Whether or not the case precluded the lawyer from accepting other legal work.
8. The nature and length of the attorney's relationship with the client.
9. Time constraints imposed by the client.
10. Whether the fee is certain or contingent.

*A 1994 Gallup survey found that the national average billing rate for law firm partners was $191 and $91 for associates. 80 *ABA Journal* 72–73 (March 1994).
**A class action is a lawsuit brought by a plaintiff for himself or herself and all others who are similarly situated. The plaintiff represents the interests of a group which is otherwise too large for each to be a separately named plaintiff.

The client should understand the possible conflicts created by various fee arrangements. For example, in a contingency fee arrangement, depending on how it is structured, either the attorney or the client "wants" a quick settlement while the other would be better off by proceeding through trial. In a flat-fee arrangement, the lawyer may have an incentive to dispose of the case as quickly as possible. An attorney paid by the hour might be tempted to overwork the case (i.e., with exhaustive research and discovery).

A variation on billing for services rendered is the **retainer fee**. A retainer fee is a sum of money paid an attorney solely in exchange for a promise to remain available for the client's consultation, if needed. Legal insurance plans often are a type of retainer fee. If the client calls the retained attorney, he or she will provide minor specific legal services without additional fees. If requested services are complicated or time-consuming (such as conduct of a trial), additional charges are billed as "earned" fees. The rate of additional fees might be according to the retainer agreement. Many attorneys also use the word "retainer" to describe the periodic receipt of earned fees from a regular client. At universities and colleges it is common for the student government association to enter a retainer contract with an attorney to be available for a certain number of hours a week to assist students with minor legal problems.

A growing number of states impose maximums on the percentage that may be charged in contingency fee contracts. In New Jersey, a maximum graduated scale is used in tort cases: from 50 percent on the first $1,000 of damages to 10 percent of any excess over $100,000.[41] In California, a special limitation exists for medical malpractice cases, from 40 percent of the first $50,000 of recovery to 10 percent of any excess over $200,000.[42] Similar statutory limitations exist in matters processed by administrative agencies rather than by courts (e.g., veterans' benefits, social security claims, and workers' compensation cases).

In addition, a fee charged by an attorney may be set by, or subject to the approval of, the court. An example of this would be fees of attorneys appointed to represent indigents or minors. When a fee limitation is applicable (by statute or court order), the client should ask whether the fee is prescribed or is a maximum allowed by law. In many cases, the statutory fee is a maximum and the client is free to negotiate payment of a lower fee (e.g., a probate fee).

Many countries, including Great Britain, provide that attorney fees (as well as court costs) are to be paid by the loser in a case.* In contrast, in the United States each party is usually responsible for his or her attorney fees, unless they agreed otherwise. (The loser always pays the court costs.)**

A person involved in a fee dispute with an attorney who cannot settle it through direct negotiation should contact the local bar association. Many local and state bar associations have established programs where disputed fees are

---

*Like most things, what appears simple at first blush is not quite so. Although the loser is responsible for reasonable attorneys fees (and costs) of the prevailing party in England, there are exceptions. Noting just one, many low-income persons in England are eligible for a government-funded legal aid program. Such persons are not subject to the cost-shifting rule.

**For example, a landlord suing a renter for past-due rent might benefit from a lease providing that the renter is to reimburse the landlord for any attorney fee expense incurred in collecting rent or enforcing the lease (this clause is commonly found in rental agreements). Many state statutes provide that if such a provision exists in the contract it will be construed to give the victor in the legal dispute, be it the landlord or the tenant, the right to reimbursement of legal fees. So, if a contract states only that it protects the landlord, the tenant will be awarded attorney fees if he or she wins the lawsuit.

reviewed in light of all applicable circumstances. Often a mutually satisfactory result is achieved without requiring further legal action. Some 47 states have programs providing for arbitration of attorney fee disputes to expedite settlement of client claims.*

> John Tyson, owner of a Burger King franchise, wanted to fire Jason, whom he suspected of repeatedly failing to comply with the posted policy requiring employees to wash their hands after using the bathroom. Tyson hired attorney Lisa Beck to advise him. Ms. Beck explained that the law must be researched and that a written opinion would be prepared. Completely convinced of Ms. Beck's self-proclaimed expertise, Tyson left her office. Unbeknownst to Tyson, Ms. Beck assigned the Tyson file to a summer law student intern. The intern did all the research and prepared an opinion based upon the firm's database of hundreds of letters to previous clients concerning when employees may be fired. Ms. Beck glanced at the report and asked her secretary to send it to Tyson under her signature with a bill showing 7 hours at $250 per hour for a total of $1,750. Beck's law firm paid its summer interns $20 per hour. Has malpractice (misfeasance) occurred?

Mr. Tyson would have no basis to suspect that anything was out of the ordinary. Oftentimes, the lawyer with whom a client meets does not perform all the legal services for the client. As far as the billing is concerned, attorneys are free to charge whatever they choose for their services and do not routinely disclose the names of persons to whom the work is delegated. The point is that you should enter into a legal service agreement like any other service agreement, understanding your rights and being vigilant in protecting your interests.

FINANCING ATTORNEY FEES

In some instances, a client may need to borrow money to pay attorney fees. A loan may be made by the creditor-attorney, a lending institution, or a third person (e.g., a relative). If the attorney finances the debt, a promissory note will be expected from the client. This arrangement may create a conflict of interest, because the attorney becomes both a creditor and agent of the client. An attorney may not use unreasonable collection methods; such conduct is unethical. Many attorneys are reluctant to sue a client to collect a fee (they believe it to be bad publicity) and simply demand cash in advance or refuse to extend credit to clients. Other attorneys are willing to sue clients for an unpaid fee because their fee agreements contain arbitration clauses—and publicity is suppressed.

FINANCING THE CLIENT'S CASE

As a legal case progresses costs often are incurred long before any recovery is possible. The following are costs in a typical personal injury case:

---

*States without programs are Arkansas, South Dakota, and West Virginia. Programs differ by state and sometimes even within a state. Some programs provide for mandatory binding arbitration and other programs encourage voluntary arbitration.

1. *Court cost.* The court charges fees (e.g., $100) to cover at least some of the administrative costs of processing the paperwork connected with litigation. Other court charges are made for such diverse items as daily fees paid to each juror in a jury trial (e.g., $20) and fees of expert witnesses.

2. *Investigation.* Most attorneys do not have the time, skill, or inclination to personally inspect the accident scene, photograph it, and talk to potential witnesses. These and similar tasks might be performed by a hired professional investigator for a fee.

3. *Discovery.* Sworn testimony is taken before a court reporter, usually in the office of the attorney who made the request. The session may be audiotaped or videotaped. Discovery is often very expensive, involving transcription costs as well as attorney fees.

4. *Medical examination.* The physical and sometimes mental condition of the victim is an issue in an injury case. Before trial, a physician will probably make one or more medical examinations. This procedure is distinguished from medical treatment. Some physicians specialize in examination of injury victims (and later provide testimony in court) rather than the treatment of patients, again for a fee.

5. *Expert witness fees.* Court testimony from experts is often necessary. Experts, as distinguished from lay witnesses, are entitled to give a formal opinion about a matter within their expertise. Lay witnesses are allowed to testify only as to what they saw, heard, or otherwise experienced. In an automobile accident case, for example, one or more physicians might testify as to the nature and extent of the victim's injury. An economist might testify as to the lost wages of the victim because of the injuries. A model maker may present a replica of the intersection involved, complete with model cars and signal lights. A computer expert may devise a computer simulation of many facets of an accident. All these experts are well paid for their time.

The sum total of these expenses can be many thousands of dollars. Most of these expenses are incurred whether or not—and certainly long before—any recovery is awarded and received.

Ethically, an attorney is permitted to "advance" litigation costs even though she or he is arguably creating an investment in the outcome of the client's case. The attorney might be tempted to suggest an early settlement not because it is in the client's best interest, but rather to recapture costs advanced as well as to participate in the recovery.[43] American Bar Association rules permit this practice if the client is ultimately responsible for reimbursing the attorney. The requirement of reimbursement is believed to militate against possible conflict of interest between the attorneys and the clients. Although the client is responsible for such costs, attorneys commonly absorb them when there is no recovery by not asking the client to pay. The attorney's duty to require reimbursement raises interesting ethical questions. Strictly speaking, payment of court costs for the client is **maintenance**, which is maintaining, supporting, or promoting the litigation of another. Maintenance is considered unethical and illegal because it encourages litigation.

Assuming the fee is contingent and the lawsuit is successful, litigation costs may be shared by the plaintiff and plaintiff's attorney. For example:

Gross recovery (in damages or settlement)	$100,000
Less net litigation costs incurred by plaintiff's lawyer, which equal:	
Total out-of-pocket litigation costs incurred (e.g., filing fees, investigation costs)	$ (17,250)
Portion of court costs recovered from unsuccessful litigant (e.g., jury fees reimbursed by defendant)	$ 2,750
Net recovery	$ 85,500
Less attorney's fee (35 percent of net recovery)	$ (29,925)
Client recovery after deduction of all expenses	$ 55,575

Litigation costs may be modest in some types of cases, such as a simple divorce, while litigation costs in antitrust cases may be hundreds of thousands or even millions of dollars in celebrated cases involving major corporations.

Charles Hall brought lawsuits against several defendants, alleging patent infringement regarding his waterbed innovations. To finance the lawsuit, he syndicated interests in the possible outcome of the suits. He raised $750,000.[44] May he finance his lawsuit in this fashion?

No. The doctrine of **champerty** forbids one from financially participating in the lawsuit of another. Champerty is defined as ". . . a bargain by [another] with a plaintiff or defendant for a portion of the matter involved in a suit in case of successful termination of the action, which the [other] undertakes to maintain or carry on at his own expense."[45] Society's concern is that investment in cases by outsiders encourages gambling and litigation.

WHAT IS LEGAL MALPRACTICE?

All states require a minimum standard of care from attorneys who perform legal services. One way this standard of care is monitored is through attorney discipline actions by the state bar or court. Clients can also sue attorneys who have injured them by careless or intentional wrongdoing. **Malpractice** is a tort occurring when an attorney fails to meet that standard of care, resulting in the client suffering a loss. This standard of care has been described in various ways, but generally an attorney is required to possess legal knowledge and skill and exercise due care and diligence. Attorney specialists are held to higher standards than those of other attorneys. Negligence by an attorney in handling a legal matter is malpractice. The tort of negligence is discussed in detail in Chapter 7.

To recover damages for attorney malpractice, the client needs to hire a second attorney to pursue the case against the lawyer accused of negligence. For the dissatisfied client, this is undoubtedly not a pleasant prospect. A malpractice case must be initiated within the time framework imposed by the applicable statute of limitations. This is usually within one to three years from the time of the negligent act(s).

In a malpractice trial, the purported victimized client must prove that, but for the attorney's negligence, the result in the earlier matter would have been more favorable to the client. The accused attorney may deny the charge or contend, "Yes, I may have been negligent, but the result was fair, adequate, and reasonable." The client winning a malpractice case still faces the problem of collecting the judgment. Attorneys who commit serious malpractice may also be the least able to pay a sizable judgment and the least likely to have purchased adequate malpractice insurance.

Mike Kline could not decide whether to consult an attorney about the neck injury he suffered when Dora Carson's car sideswiped him while he was skateboarding in a crosswalk. He had medical insurance and he expected his pain would soon stop. However, after nine months of continued distress and intermittent suffering, he consulted attorney Jules Doeshire about a suit for damages. Doeshire assured him he had a good case and prepared a contingency fee retainer agreement, which Mike signed. Several months later (13 months after the accident), attorney Doeshire contacted Mike and said that after further study he concluded that Mike really did not have a good case after all. "But not to worry; I won't charge you a cent," Doeshire told Mike. What should Mike do?

Mike should be very suspicious and either receive a full and completely satisfactory explanation of why Doeshire wishes to drop the matter or consult another attorney. It is possible that Doeshire committed malpractice by failing to file the complaint within the period of time permitted by the statute of limitations. Once an attorney accepts a case, it is his or her obligation to comply with procedural requirements. Failure to file documents within statutory time limits is one of the most common acts of malpractice.*

An attorney is not guilty of malpractice just because a case is lost. In every case with two or more adversaries, someone must lose and someone must win. A strategy decision that subsequently turns out to be disastrous is not usually malpractice. The attorneys representing Texaco in the *Pennzoil Co. v. Texaco, Inc.* case were considered to be among the most able attorneys in Texas, yet Texaco lost the case at trial and suffered damages of $10.53 billion[46] (see Chapter 11).

Attorney malpractice exists for a wide variety of negligent acts and omissions: failure to apply settled principles of law to the case, failure to protect the right to appeal, failure to draft pleadings (court-related documents) properly and promptly, failure to appear and defend, failure to assert all possible claims or defenses, failure to act in accordance with professional ethical standards, failure to present relevant evidence, lack of diligence in prosecuting a case once initiated, and misdrafting a will. An ounce of prevention in the careful selection of an attorney is worth a pound of cure in suing for malpractice.

In fairness, the following words from a former Chief Justice of the United States Supreme Court merit attention:

All of us have long known that there are problems in some areas of our profession which deserve and which receive criticism not only from the public but from the

---

*The American Bar Association claims that 11 percent of malpractice complaints involve failing to "calendar" or missing deadlines. W. Gates, "Charting the Shoals of Malpractice," 73 *ABA Journal* 62 (July 1987).

bar itself. The bar is the severest and most expert critic of the profession. At the same time, most citizens will acknowledge what history shows about the courageous lawyers who have been among the staunchest defenders of liberties. Virtually every advance in the cause of civil rights came at the hands of lawyers—often serving without compensation.[47]

UNAUTHORIZED PRACTICE OF LAW

Practicing law without a license is a crime, just as practicing medicine or dentistry without a license is a crime. A non-lawyer providing legal advice who bills a client for the service may not use the courts to collect the fee. Contracts for legal services by a non-attorney are illegal and void. Any payment made by the client is recoverable.

As discussed earlier in the chapter, all states provide for licensure as a prerequisite to practice. A person who does not have, or who fails to maintain, a license to practice law is forbidden to practice. It is sometimes difficult to decide whether a given act constitutes the offering of legal advice or simply the performing of standard business practice. Different states provide different answers. For example, in some states it is common for title companies to conduct title searches when real property is sold (albeit with the aid of in-house staff attorneys). In other states, independent attorneys perform this activity. Non-lawyers (such as real estate brokers) are generally permitted to complete blanks on forms that may affect legal rights. However, these must be standard forms, and legal advice may not be offered with the forms. Accountants prepare tax returns and suggest probable tax consequences but must be careful not to interpret tax statutes, rules, or cases or render tax planning legal advice.

There is currently popular support for relaxing the historical prohibition against the unauthorized practice of law to allow some routine legal matters to be handled by legal assistants, paralegals, or legal technicians. Legal assistants under the direction of lawyers already often perform such work. Lawyer supervision adds to the cost of such services, causing some consumers and non-lawyer providers to question whether the public is being protected or exploited. Routine matters usually include uncontested divorce pleadings, simple wills, eviction notices, simple bankruptcy filings, and probate of small estates. Exhibit 4–1 identifies the "practice of law" and other legally related work done by legal assistants under supervision of lawyers.

Some critics contend that the related services can be delivered to the consumer at lower cost, with higher pay for the legal service technician, by eliminating a superfluous middle person—the attorney. Opponents to the relaxation of unauthorized-practice laws are concerned that the dividing line between what is and what is not the practice of law will become even more confused and risky for consumers who do not appreciate or understand the difference in the educational preparation of legal assistants. Furthermore, it is difficult if not impossible to predetermine what is simple and routine.*

---

*Every attorney has been told by a client, "I just want a simple will," only to discover that either the client's circumstances or more detailed desires make that impossible.

Exhibit 4–1: Legal Work Permissible for Non-Lawyers under Supervision of Lawyers

<table>
<tr><th>Practice of Law</th><th>Work That May Be Done by Non-Lawyers*</th></tr>
<tr><td>

Accepting a case
Setting a fee
Evaluating the case and charting
  its course
Performing legal analysis
Giving legal advice
Participating in the formal
  judicial process (i.e.,
  depositions, hearings, trials,
  etc.)
Supervising legal assistants

</td><td>

Obtaining facts from client
Communicating information to
  client
Interviewing witnesses
Performing limited legal research to
  assist lawyer with legal analysis
Obtaining documents (i.e., police
  reports, medical records,
  employment records, deeds,
  plans, probate records, weather
  records, etc.)
Obtaining photographs
Preparing summaries
Preparing chronologies
Preparing itemization of claims
Preparing drafts of pleadings
Preparing drafts of interrogatories
  and production requests
Preparing drafts of responses to
  discovery requests
Preparing outlines for lawyer to use
  in deposing witnesses
Indexing deposition transcripts
  and preparing summaries of the
  evidence
Preparing exhibit lists

</td></tr>
</table>

*But performed under the supervision of a lawyer.

Source: Adapted from American Bar Association, Section of Law Practice Management, "Leveraging with Legal Assistants" (Chicago: ABA, 1993), 20.

Do-it-yourself probate kits (designed to assist the personal representative-executor or administrator in necessary procedures following death) and divorce kits are not considered to be the practice of law because the information is generalized and not tailored to the needs of a particular client.[48] In recent years, many self-help books and software in a variety of legal areas have been made available.

ALTERNATIVE DISPUTE RESOLUTION

According to George Herbert, an English poet who lived in the early 1600s, "Lawsuits consume time and money, and rest and friends." The words remain true in America as we begin the twenty-first century. They suggest that persons who are considering litigation should think twice and consider alternatives whenever possible. For example, when contracting, provisions for alternative dispute resolution may be included. Or, when a dispute arises, one party may suggest an alternative to the courts to which the other party may be only too happy to agree. When retaining an attorney for a civil law matter, a client should consider the use of alternatives to litigation such as negotiation, mediation, and arbitration. An attorney's willingness to consider these alternatives may be an important factor to use in deciding whom to employ to represent you.

As stated earlier, courts are available to resolve all disputes, be they complicated or simple. Our courts seek to protect the fundamental liberties of free speech, press, assembly, and religion, and they are available to decide such trivia as who gets to keep the "Blue Chip" stamp books in a dissolution of marriage.* For matters involving small sums of money, small claims courts are available to provide relief from complicated and costly legal procedures. Yet there are times when individuals and businesses may wish to avoid the complications and burdens of litigation for reasons other than the amount of money, time, goodwill, and peace of mind lost. These are times to consider **alternative dispute resolution (ADR),** a broad term used to describe methods of resolving disputes through means other than the traditional judicial process.

In Anglo-American jurisprudence, the most significant developments in ADR have occurred in recent years in response to the problems posed by lengthy delays in receiving a trial date. Efficiency-conscious business managers have been notably active in the search for more effective ADR methods for just this reason. Businesses can suffer financial losses from such delays.

Possible explanations for delays include population growth, too much crime, too many persons wanting to sue, too many laws and complex government regulations, and too many lawyers filing too many lawsuits. Whatever the explanation, the increased volume of filings has greatly extended the time necessary to resolve civil disputes, especially in major metropolitan areas. Delay is also caused by a shortage of judges and other court personnel, and especially by an even greater increase in criminal matters in the courts. Criminal matters take priority over civil matters and thus occupy the time of judges who otherwise would be available to hear civil cases. Delay imposes economic, social, and emotional costs.

Tanda Lee not only liked rap music, she liked it loud and late. Occupying her first house, she really appreciated freedom from repeated parental insistence that she "turn that thing down." Evan and Juanita Jenkins lived next door in the house they had purchased 40 years before. After one week of 3 A.M. concerts, Evan was unable to hide his anger. Dressed in his robe, he stormed over to Tanda's house and shouted, "Turn the blessed thing off!" Tanda was annoyed and shouted back, "I didn't move to get new parents. Anyway, it's a free country!" Then she turned the volume even higher. How do Evan and Juanita get some sleep?

Evan and Juanita have a number of legal options. They can phone the police, who will ask Tanda to show more consideration for her neighbors. Tanda probably is violating a public criminal statute against disturbing the peace, and Evan and Juanita could file a criminal complaint. They can also seek civil redress by suing

---

*The issue of who got custody of Blue Chip stamp books (stamps collected with the purchase of goods, which could later be exchanged for other merchandise) was a matter of major contention and anger between two divorcing parties in the first case handled by the author of this chapter. I went to law school for that?

Tanda, claiming that she has committed the tort of nuisance. In such an action, Evan and Juanita can claim money damages for past harm and request an injunction (equitable relief) prohibiting the loud music as a continuing nuisance.

The practical problem with all of these remedies is that they are costly in time, money, and tranquility. If Evan and Juanita use small claims court, where the cost of litigation will be minor, it still will be time-consuming and a drain on their peace of mind. Moreover, courtroom resolution ignores the fact that the parties will still live next door to each other after completion of the legal actions. The root of many problems referred to the courts is a defective human relationship, and such a relationship may continue and worsen after judicial intervention. The adversarial proceeding of a trial usually aggravates and exaggerates existing hard feelings. Neighboring parties thus often find new reasons to argue and land in court again.

Likewise, court resolution of business-related disputes may not be in the best interest of the contesting parties. Examples include consumer product disputes that affect company public relations and product reception, disputes over medical care in health maintenance organizations (HMOs), and environmental disputes that will affect community–government relations for years. With increasing frequency, business and government agencies are using ADR techniques in such cases instead of and in addition to the courts. Not only are such techniques usually easier and cheaper to use than the courts, they are more likely to lead to improved long-term understandings and harmony.

The most common types of ADR are:

- Negotiation.
- Mediation.
- Arbitration.
- Med-Arb.
- Private judging.
- Ombudsperson.
- Expert fact finding.
- Mini-trial.
- Summary jury trial.

Exhibit 4–2 compares the three most common types of ADR with a lawsuit.

NEGOTIATION

Negotiation is defined as communication for the purpose of persuasion. People tend to accept and live more graciously with a voluntary agreement than with a court-imposed solution, which will often rankle for years. There is an old saying in the law: "A bad agreement is better than a good lawsuit."

Although we all negotiate, most people can substantially improve their negotiation skills by observing a few rules. In recent years, several books (the most significant of which is perhaps Fisher, Ury, and Patton's *Getting to Yes*[49]) have stressed the importance and art of negotiation. Since the point of negotiation is to persuade, careful consideration of how best to present your views and seek acceptable results makes sense. Thus, good negotiation requires preparation. Moreover, negotiation, like most skills, can be improved. Indeed, it can be continuously improved. Skilled athletes do not stop trying to improve when they

Exhibit 4–2: Comparison of Alternative Dispute Resolution Methods with a Lawsuit

Characteristic	Negotiation	Mediation	Arbitration	Court Trial
Private or public process?	Private	Private	Private	Public
Who decides?	Parties	Parties	Arbitrator	Judge or jury
Adversary or cooperative?	Cooperative	Cooperative	Adversary	Adversary
Elapsed time to conclusion?	As long or short as it takes	As long or short as it takes	Usually 2 to 18 months	Usually 1 to 5 years (plus appeal, if any)
Costs of process?	Low	Low	Medium to high	High
Appeal?	Unnecessary	Unnecessary	Few grounds	Full right of appeal
Procedural rules?	Decided by parties	Decided by parties	Few and simple	Complex
Need attorney?	No	No	Yes	Yes
Discovery process?	No	No	Minimal allowed	Extensive allowed
Right to jury?	Unnecessary	Unnecessary	No	Yes, in most cases
Permanent record in files?	No	No	No	Yes

reach a certain level; in the same manner, one can always refine one's negotiating skills. There are many techniques of successful negotiation that can be taught, whether for legal disputes or everyday matters, including the use of supportable arguments, the avoidance of personalizing the dispute, giving as well as taking, and attempting to establish a relationship with the other party. Using even a few such techniques can improve the ability of most people to negotiate.

Perceiving negotiation as a form of ADR is useful because it legitimizes informal problem resolution by the client and even by the lawyer. Typically, by the time a dispute is referred to a lawyer, negotiation is thought to have failed. Although negotiation may well continue after a lawsuit is filed, it is then considered part of litigation strategy. Identifying negotiation as an ADR technique suggests a serious, professional approach to dispute resolution that may well enhance the possibilities of success. It may also encourage negotiation efforts by the lawyer earlier in the dispute, perhaps even prior to filing.

In contentious situations, parties often begin by demanding a recognition of rights and a remedy of grievances by the other side. The response is generally a counter for similar recognition. At this point, neither party is negotiating with the other. Neither is attempting to persuade; instead, they are talking at, not with, each other, though attempts at persuasion may follow.

In our hypothetical problem, Evan did not try to negotiate with Tanda when trying to get Tanda to reduce the volume of her music; he issued an order. Negotiation might have been more successful. If Evan tried negotiation and/or mediation and it did not work, he could still complain to the authorities (criminal action) and bring suit (civil action). Only if Evan arbitrated his claim (this would require Tanda's agreeing to arbitrate as well) would he be irrevocably substituting an ADR method for the traditional trial process. In other words, Tanda, like most persons with legal problems, has very little if anything to lose by attempting to negotiate a resolution to the dispute. The term *appropriate dispute resolution* recognizes that legal processes should not be used when more appropriate methods of dispute resolution are available.

MEDIATION

Mediation is the use of a neutral third party to assist contending parties to voluntarily resolve their dispute. A mediator, the person conducting the mediation, is chosen by the contending parties to facilitate communication between them in their effort to reach an agreement. Unlike an arbitrator, discussed next, the mediator has no power to impose a resolution to a dispute. He or she is not a judge and is not necessarily legally trained. Generally, the skills required to be a successful mediator include expertise in the specific problems underlying the dispute and exceptional communication skills. If the dispute is a family law problem, the mediator may be a social worker or family practice psychologist. If the dispute is about the breach of a construction contract, the mediator may be an architect, engineer, or construction law attorney. Besides possessing expertise in the given area, the mediator should be someone who listens well, is trustworthy, and can propose creative solutions.

Although mediation has been used in labor disputes for many years, its acceptance in commercial and other types of disputes has been significantly growing only since the 1980s. Because the mediation process does not lead to any findings or conclusions by the mediator, its form can vary substantially. However, appropriate behavior and techniques have been identified by organizations seeking to expand acceptance of the process. For example, a mediator may meet with each party separately—the meeting is called a *caucus*—to hear facts, opinions, and positions that someone might otherwise be reluctant to disclose with all parties present. The mediator may then act, with the approval of both parties, as a messenger to convey possible positions and resolutions between the parties so they can avoid face-to-face confrontation. To encourage the use of mediation, several states have provided that such communications by the parties are privileged and cannot be used in later court proceedings.

Mediators usually charge an hourly rate for their services, similar to what an attorney would charge. In these situations, parties normally split the cost of mediation. Sometimes mediators are available without charge, and low- or no-cost mediators are often available for family law, neighborhood, and consumer disputes.

One obstacle to mediation is that some attorneys think that tactics they intend to use in trial if mediation fails might be disclosed to their disadvantage during the mediation process. Another is that the mediation process requires some compromise by each party. A stubborn belief by either party that no compromise is possible will make mediation unproductive. Nevertheless, the most difficult part of most mediation is simply getting the parties to agree to the process.

The dispute between Evan and Tanda is the type that is usually best solved through mediation. **Neighborhood dispute centers**, common in major metropolitan areas, provide trained mediators to assist parties in resolving problems such as loud nighttime music. The mutual understanding that is required here for a long-term solution is not usually achieved through either the criminal or civil court process. The record of neighborhood mediation on such cases has been excellent—substantially more effective than court resolution.* As observed before, the most difficult task is getting both parties to engage in the mediation, which is strictly voluntary.

ARBITRATION

Arbitration is the most formal of the ADR processes. Here the *disputants*, parties in conflict, select a neutral third party, the *arbitrator*, to hear and decide their dispute. Unlike a mediator, an arbitrator becomes a private judge, and his or her decision is legally binding. Virtually any commercial matter can be submitted to arbitration. It is commonly used to resolve international commercial disputes.

Arbitrators must have contractual capacity (discussed in Chapter 8), must be impartial, and must be voluntarily selected by the parties. Usually they are experts in disputes similar to the one being arbitrated. Parties may agree on any number of arbitrators; it is common to have one arbitrator in a small dispute and three arbitrators when dollar damages are high. Although legal training is generally not required, many arbitrators are lawyers, and many retired judges serve as private arbitrators for a fee.

If you are curious about how to draft an arbitration clause, you can find advice and samples at http://www.hg.org/

---

*See "Talk, Don't Sue," *Changing Times*, August 1986, 49–52, an article that reports a settlement rate for mediation centers as high as 85 to 90 percent. Also see "Neighborhood Courts," *California Lawyer* (June 1982), p. 45 and "The Use of Mediation in the Resolution of Small Claims, Landlord/Tenant and Neighborhood Disputes," *St. Louis Bar Journal* (1986), 34. But also see "Mediating Neighborhood Conflict: Conceptual and Strategic Considerations," *Negotiation Journal* 3 (1987), 3. The authors point out that such centers often hear cases referred by the police or the courts. These agencies impose pressure to resolve the matter, but they must monitor recurring problems to really achieve success.

Arbitration may be selected to resolve a dispute through terms of a contract. Such contracts generally arise in two ways: after the dispute and, more often, before the dispute. Parties to a contract may agree that if a dispute arises about the contract, they will submit it to arbitration rather than use the courts. This agreement may be spelled out in an *arbitration clause* in the contract. Parties who do not have a contract providing for arbitration may agree to arbitrate any time after a dispute arises. (Note: In most tort actions, the parties do not have a prior contract relationship, and so arbitrations usually involve contract disputes.)

The parties in an arbitration can create their own procedural rules. State and federal statutes often provide for the procedures to be used when the parties have not done so. Furthermore, third-party associations such as the **American Arbitration Association (AAA)** provide procedural rules and administrative assistance for parties seeking arbitration. The parties can incorporate standard AAA procedural rules in contracts.

Procedural rules involving the arbitration hearing are more relaxed than rules in court (i.e., rules of evidence are basically dispensed with). An arbitrator acts as finder of both law and fact, as judge and as jury. Cases usually proceed as they would in a court, with the claimant first and the respondent second. The arbitrator provides a final resolution of the dispute, called an *award*, usually within 30 days after hearing the case.

A growing number of businesses use arbitration as a means of resolving disputes. Exhibit 4–3 shows sample clauses for contracts providing for arbitration.

Parties agree to arbitrate for several reasons:

1. Arbitration proceedings are private, while court actions are public. Sometimes parties want to handle their disputes in private.

2. Arbitration is usually speedier. Rather than wait for a courtroom, the parties can schedule an arbitration to take place within a short time.

3. Arbitrations are usually less expensive.

Exhibit 4–3:   Sample Arbitration Clauses

Pre-Dispute Clause
Any controversy or claim arising out of or relating to this contract, or the breach thereof, shall be settled by arbitration administered by the American Arbitration Association under its Commercial Arbitration Rules, and judgment on the award rendered by the arbitrator(s) may be entered in any court having jurisdiction thereof.

Post-Dispute Clause
We, the undersigned parties, hereby agree to submit to arbitration administered by the American Arbitration Association under its Commercial Arbitration Rules the following controversy: (cite briefly).

We further agree that the above controversy be submitted to (one) (three) arbitrator(s). We further agree that we will faithfully observe this agreement and the rules, that we will abide by and perform any award rendered by the arbitrator(s), and that a judgment of the court having jurisdiction may be entered on the award.

Reprinted by permission of the American Arbitration Association. http://www.adr.org/rules/commercial_rules. html1#StandardClause

http://

Review the checklist for drafting an arbitration clause on Hieros Gamos, the free legal research Web site, at http://www.hg.org/

The term *arbitration* usually means that a third party (or parties) will make a decision that is binding and final for the disputants, but variations of the process include non-binding arbitration (including court-annexed arbitration) and issue arbitration.* **Court-annexed arbitration** is usually a non-binding part of a process parties are required to participate in before they can go to trial. For example, the Hawaii court system has adopted a program of mandatory, non-binding arbitration for disputes involving less than $150,000. Colorado has a statute requiring all civil actions involving damages of less than $50,000 to be arbitrated, as part of a pilot project involving eight judicial districts in the state. In **issue arbitration**, part of a dispute is submitted to arbitration, and the arbitrator decides that part only—not the entire dispute.

In its purest form, however, arbitration provides a final resolution of the dispute, outside the public court system. It is sometimes referred to as an informal process, because procedural rules before and during the hearing are more relaxed (e.g., limitation of discovery). Although an arbitration may be informal when compared to the judicial process, it is the most formal of the ADR processes.

All the states and the federal government have statutes that allow the courts to enforce an arbitrator's award, if that becomes necessary. A losing party may appeal an arbitrator's decision to a court. However, except in cases of bias or obvious serious error, *courts seldom overturn arbitration awards*. Even an error of law made by an arbitrator is not grounds to overturn an arbitration award. Parties who have agreed to arbitrate disputes are not allowed to change their minds because they lose the case—not for any reason.

Greene agreed to construct a residence for homeowners Hundley and Butt. The construction contract provided that "[a]ny controversy relating to the construction of the residence or any other matter arising out of the terms of this contract shall be settled by binding arbitration . . . conducted pursuant to the Rules of the American Arbitration Association with regard to the Construction Industry Arbitration Rules." A construction dispute arose and was submitted for arbitration. After a two-day hearing, the arbitrator found for both parties and awarded $17,000 to the homeowners and $20,400 to Greene. The award lacked any explanation and the homeowners contested the award. Must the arbitrator provide support for his or her award?

No. Unless the agreement to arbitrate or arbitration rules require it, the arbitrator need not provide findings of fact or explanations in an award. "[T]he Arbitration Code does not require that an arbitrator enter written findings of fact in support of an award; nor does the Code require an arbitrator to explain the reasoning behind an award." The authority of an arbitrator gives her the "inherent power to

---

*Non-binding arbitration means the arbitrator's finding is not binding on the parties. Court-annexed arbitration is a common example of non-binding arbitration. Some states require parties to submit their lawsuits to non-binding arbitration as pre-condition to trial. An experienced volunteer attorney appointed to hear the case by the court hears the arbitration. Because a trial is generally a legal right of the litigants, the arbitration cannot be binding. To be binding, it must be voluntary. Although the findings of such an arbitration are not binding, there may be some risks (responsibility for court costs if the award is not improved at trial) in not accepting the finding.

fashion a remedy as long as the award draws its essence from the contract or statute."[50]

One variation of arbitration called **med-arb** combines mediation and arbitration. A neutral person is appointed to mediate the dispute. Failing that, the neutral person is authorized to resolve the dispute with a binding award. The methods used to conduct a med-arb often vary in format.

PRIVATE JUDGING

Private judging, also called *rent-a-judge*, allows litigants to bypass the formal court system and have their cases heard before retired judges as in a trial. Cases are tried before a referee selected and paid by the litigants and empowered by a state statute to enter decisions having the finality of trial court judgments. In California, and in the dozen or so other states with similar statutes, jurors can be selected from the public jury rolls to participate in such trials. Verdicts and judgments can be appealed to a state appellate court.

Private judging provides more flexibility and privacy than a normal trial. With private judging, parties can immediately schedule the trial and have access to usual trial procedures. However, unlike in arbitrations, parties using private judging have the traditional right to appeal adverse trial court rulings through the appellate courts. Private judging is nevertheless the most controversial ADR process. The costs are paid entirely by the disputants; therefore, private judging allows wealthy disputants to bypass the public trial calendar. In fact, the rent-a-judge system has been called "Cadillac justice." Parties who cannot afford it must wait their turn in the public courts.

Private courts are also criticized because it is feared they may lure away judges from the public courts through early retirement. Judges are paid more substantial fees by private clients than they earn as salaried public judges. Furthermore, hearings in private courts are not open to the public or the press. Wealthy corporations and other parties can shield their activities from the public eye. Finally, some observers believe that this private system of justice may delay needed reforms by taking some pressure off the public system.

OMBUDSPERSON

An **ombudsperson** or **ombud** is a third party usually selected by *one* of the disputing parties in an attempt to help resolve the dispute. The concept developed in the Scandinavian countries, where the ombudsman* is a public official appointed to hear and investigate citizen complaints against government. In the United States, the ombud can be either public or private and differs from a mediator in that he or she is actively involved in determining the facts and suggesting possible resolutions to the dispute. The ombud will investigate facts, propose and advocate solutions, and often make public his or her independent findings and recommendations. In some organizations, the ombud is a permanent employee who processes and regularly resolves disputes within the group. Like a mediator, an ombud has *no* authority to impose a solution. Unlike a mediator, the ombud, though starting as a neutral party, is not expected to remain neutral.

---

*In Swedish, the term *ombudsman* is not gender specific. In the United States, however, it is; hence the term *ombudsperson* or *ombud* is preferred.

Expert Fact Finding

Expert fact finding is a non-binding process in which an appointed expert investigates or hears facts on selected issues. At the conclusion, he or she makes findings of fact. These findings may assist in negotiations or may even be admissible in a more formal process. The recommendations often result in a negotiated settlement of the dispute. Fact finding may be part of a negotiation, a mediation, or an arbitration.

Mini-Trial

A **mini-trial** is a voluntary process through which parties, usually large business organizations, agree to an informal trial-like proceeding. The sides agree to the procedural rules, exchange information, and select a neutral advisor. The focal point of the process is to present facts of the case to a special private jury. The jury is composed of high-ranking officials of the disputant companies with authority to settle the dispute. As jurors, the officials learn about the dispute by hearing both sides. The now well-informed managers often can negotiate a settlement and avoid an actual court trial.

Summary Jury Trial

The **summary jury trial** is similar to the mini-trial: It is a process for cases already in litigation that have not yet settled. Before trial, parties present their cases to a private mock jury. The mock jury is composed of lay citizens chosen (and employed) to mirror what an actual jury would be expected to do. The presentations are brief and no witnesses are called. The jury is asked to return its verdict quickly. After the verdict, the attorneys question the jurors about their decision. The process is non-binding and is used to assist in a settlement. The lawyers gain insight about the probable results of an actual trial and the reaction of real jurors to their cases. If a settlement is not reached, both sides have the right to a full trial later.

Conclusions Regarding ADR

Litigation is risky, since the outcome is uncertain. It is time-consuming for attorneys and clients, and it is costly. Participants are also likely to suffer emotionally from drawn-out litigation. In the end, some 90–95 percent of all lawsuits are settled before trial, but often after years of waiting. Although litigation is often necessary, it is not always necessary. A decision to sue or to defend a suit through trial should be carefully thought out because of the direct and indirect costs involved.

Mr. Banks rejected a settlement offer of $22,500 in his breach of contract and tort action against eight former associates. He believed he was entitled to $500,000 in punitive damages. The case went to trial. The "good news" was that Mr. Banks won a jury verdict of $50,000. The "bad news" was that it took three years to resolve, during which time he was unemployed. His single-minded concern with the case alienated friends and relatives. The case cost him $105,000 in litigation expenses. During the prolonged dispute, he employed seven different lawyers, one at a time—six of them quit.

Mr. Banks won his case, so one could assume he was wronged. If, however, he had accepted the settlement offer he would have had a positive net recovery, rather than a negative victory with an out-of-pocket loss of at least $55,000 (litigation recovery of $50,000 minus litigation costs of $105,000). In the actual case this hypothetical example was based on, the plaintiff continued to be consumed by the case. He accused the judge, defendants, defense attorneys, and his own attorneys of a conspiracy against him.

Mr. Banks sought justice as he understood it, but he also sought vengeance. The court that heard the case was staffed by expensive professionals in an impressive but costly courthouse, to ensure a fair and impartial trial. Litigants generally overlook the expense of these services by the state. The plaintiff may or may not have felt vindicated even though he lost money, but did he violate a social responsibility to the public? Was his pursuit of "justice at any price" at too high a price to the public?

It is a simple truth that the shortest distance between two points is a straight line. A person aggrieved often expects that legal satisfaction is a simple matter of being given his or her deserved due. The "simple straight line" truth is not really that simple, and neither is the achievement of justice or legal satisfaction. A mountain or a canyon can make it practically impossible to travel in a straight line. A freeway, which bisects a straight line or path, will make it dangerous to proceed straight ahead without modifying your route around the freeway impedance. A similar problem exists in a quest for "equal justice under law."* The path to justice is seldom a straight line, even though we might wish it to be. The path is full of obstacles. They are, however, usually discoverable and surmountable for travelers assisted by knowledge, a sense of realism and common sense, and expert guides.

---

*Words inscribed in marble above the entrance to the U.S. Supreme Court building in Washington D.C.

CASE

NEW HAMPSHIRE V. GORDON
Supreme Court of New Hampshire, 141 N.H. 703, 692 A.2d 505 (1997)

In the fall of 1991, the victim, an administrator and teacher at New Hampshire Technical College in Nashua, began a consensual sexual relationship with the defendant, a student at the college. In July 1992, the victim informed the defendant that their relationship was over. In response, the defendant came to the victim's home and, after promising that he just wanted to talk to her, sexually assaulted her.

In September 1992, the defendant telephoned Judith Parys, a lawyer and his paralegal instructor at the college, and, crying, told her that he had had a relationship with the victim and "that things had gone wrong and that it was a mess." He told Parys that he was afraid the victim would have him removed from the college. Later the same day, the defendant called Parys again. He told her that "he had called [the victim] and, much to his surprise, that she had agreed to talk to him on the phone, . . . and that he didn't have to tie her up."

In October 1992, the defendant, who was shaking and looked like he had been crying, approached Parys after she finished teaching a class and told her that he had looked up the definition of rape in the New Hampshire statutes. He said that, based on the definition, "he was sure that he had raped [the victim] in the past."

The defendant was later charged with four counts of aggravated felonious sexual assault and one count of attempted aggravated felonious sexual assault. Before trial, he filed a motion in limine* to bar Parys from testifying against him, asserting that his communications with her were protected by the attorney–client privilege. The trial court denied the motion. The defendant was convicted on one count of aggravated felonious sexual assault.

BRODERICK, Justice delivered the opinion of the court: The defendant, Steven Gordon, was convicted of aggravated felonious sexual assault after a jury trial in Superior Court. In separate but consolidated appeals, the defendant argues that the trial court erred in admitting into evidence allegedly privileged statements he made to an attorney instructor. . . .We affirm.

The defendant argues that the trial court erred in denying his motion to exclude Parys' testimony based on the attorney–client privilege. It is generally recognized that "[a]n attorney–client relationship is created when (1) a person seeks advice or assistance from an attorney, (2) the advice or assistance sought pertains to matters within the attorney's professional competence, and (3) the attorney expressly or impliedly agrees to give or actually gives the desired advice or assistance." Here, the burden of proving the existence of an attorney–client relationship lies with the defendant. The defendant conceded at oral argument that he sought no legal advice in the September 1992 phone conversations. Consequently, we need look only at the October 1992 conversation at the college to determine whether an attorney–client relationship was established and, hence, whether the attorney–client privilege applies to that conversation.

At the hearing on the motion *in limine*, the trial court heard conflicting testimony on the question of whether the defendant's conversation with Parys at the college established an attorney–client relationship. The defendant maintained that Parys told him "to go look in the R.S.A.'s" and, when he returned, she advised him to "back off and give [the victim] her space." Additionally, he contended that Parys offered to "make some phone calls and get back to [him]."

---

*A motion *in limine* can be made (usually at the outset of a trial) to determine what evidence will or will not be allowed before the jury.

Parys' version of the conversation was quite different, however. She contended that the defendant informed her that "he had gone to the R.S.A.'s in the law library, had looked up the definition of 'rape,' and believed that he had raped [the victim]." Rather than offering legal advice, Parys testified that because of the defendant's "rambling," she "didn't have a chance to get a word in edgewise."

The credibility of witnesses is a factual determination within the sound discretion of the trial court. "[U]nless we find that no reasonable person could have come to the same conclusion," we defer to the trial court's credibility determination. *State v. Crotty*, 134 N.H. 706, 711, 597 A.2d 1078, 1082 (1991)

The trial court's determination that the defendant "did not . . . seek advice from Parys in her legal capacity" is adequately supported by the record. Parys testified that the defendant sought "absolutely no legal advice" and that she gave none. Additionally, she testified that she informed her classes—some of which the defendant attended—that she did not give legal advice and that she believed to do so could violate the Rules of Professional Conduct.

Even the defendant's own testimony does not support his argument that he sought legal advice from Parys in her capacity as an attorney. At the hearing on the motion *in limine*, the defendant read into the record his testimony from an earlier proceeding that when he spoke to Parys, he thought he was "talking to somebody in confidence. You tell somebody that you trust or that you're friendly with things that you wouldn't just openly stand out there and say. . . ." Speaking in confidence is not enough; "where one consults an attorney not as a lawyer but as a friend or as [an] . . . adviser . . ., the consultation is not professional nor the statement privileged." K. Broun et al., McCormick on Evidence § 88, at 322-24 (J. Strong ed., 4th ed. 1992).

Moreover, the defendant's conduct at two earlier proceedings, which the trial court considered in its ruling, does not support the existence of the privilege he now seeks to invoke. Prior to the defendant's trial, Parys twice testified—at a hearing on a domestic violence petition filed by the victim against the defendant and at a judicial review board hearing at the college—about the conversations she had with the defendant in September and October 1992. According to the defendant's testimony at the hearing on his motion *in limine*, at the domestic violence hearing, Parys indicated that she did not represent either party; the defendant apparently did not object. At the judicial review hearing, the defendant remarked about Parys: "I realize she's an attorney, but she's here as a witness. If she wants to play attorney, then she should represent somebody."

"A client has a privilege to refuse to disclose and to prevent any other person from disclosing confidential communications made for the purpose of facilitating the rendition of professional legal services to the client. . . ." N.H. R. Ev. 502(b). Because the defendant never established an attorney–client relationship with Parys, however, he cannot now assert the privilege as a shield against the admission of Parys' testimony.

Affirmed. All concurred.

For Critical Analysis

1. The authors of this book are attorneys. And though we are writing about the law, we do not intend to give specific legal advice to any students or other readers. Your class instructor is also likely to be an attorney. If you ask a question in class about a legal problem, or if you discuss a legal dilemma you are currently facing in a conversation with her or him, does the attorney–client privilege arise?

2. Who owns a privilege—the attorney or client or both? Why?

3. What additional facts might have led the court to believe a privilege existed?

CHAPTER QUESTIONS AND PROBLEMS

1. The legal profession is in the process of change. Following are some current issues involving changes that have impact on the public interest.

   a. Should attorneys who participate in formal courtroom trials be trained differently from other lawyers?

   b. Should charges concerning the unprofessional conduct of an attorney be heard and decided by attorneys, by non-lawyers, or by both?

   c. What limitations, if any, should be imposed on the right of attorneys to advertise for and to solicit legal business?

   d. Should there be limits to the fees charged by attorneys for legal services?

2. Contingent fee arrangements are said to make legal services available to persons who otherwise would be unable to pay; but contingent fee arrangements are also said to promote litigation unnecessarily, because potential plaintiffs (victims) have nothing to lose by suing. What do you think of these contentions?

3. Our founding fathers adopted (or, more correctly, retained) the English common law after the American Revolution. However, we have consistently refused to adopt the so-called English Plan for the payment of legal fees. The English Plan requires the losing party to pay both the plaintiff and the defendant attorney fees (as well as court costs). Presently, the loser in the U.S. always pays the court costs and his own attorney's fees (unless otherwise agreed by contract), but does not pay the attorney's fees of his or her opponent who has won the case. Some observers strongly recommend we adopt the English Plan. Do you agree?

4. Liability insurance is available to cover potential attorney malpractice. As with most liability insurance, the premiums charged have increased significantly in recent years. Malpractice insurance coverage for attorneys is usually not required either by law or by the Professional Rules of Conduct. As in many other liability situations, those who can most afford a major loss carry ample insurance, whereas those who have little financial ability are more likely to be without insurance. Should malpractice insurance or other proof of financial responsibility be required as a condition for the practice of law? Discuss.

5. The typical arbitration is a binding proceeding. That means that the arbitrator's decision cannot be appealed except for very limited reasons. What are the negative and positive aspects of arbitration because of this lack of appeal? Assume that during an arbitration the attorney representing one party became very angry, screamed obscenities at the arbitrator, and finally threw the exhibits onto the floor. Can the arbitrator hold the attorney in contempt?

6. In January 1991, Gail P. Carr-Williams, an attorney licensed to practice law in Michigan, applied to be admitted to the practice of law in Ohio without examination. After an initial recommendation that Carr-Williams' application be approved, the Board of Commissioners on Character and Fitness of the Supreme Court of Ohio appointed a panel to investigate Carr-Williams' application. The panel concluded that Carr-Williams had not satisfied her federal income tax obligations for several years and owed the Internal Revenue Service approximately $98,000 in taxes, interest, and penalties. She also owed state taxes of $14,000. What should the Board of Commissioners recommend as to her license to practice law in Ohio? [*In*

re Application of Carr-Williams, 63 Ohio St.3d 752, 591 N.E.2d 693 (Ohio, 1992).]

7. Attorney Edward M. Cooperman was retained to represent a client in a criminal matter. The client signed Cooperman's proffered fee agreement: "My minimum fee for appearing for you in this matter is Fifteen Thousand ($15,000) Dollars. This fee is not refundable for any reason whatsoever once I file a notice of appearance on your behalf." One month later, the client discharged Cooperman, but Cooperman refused to refund any portion of the fee. Cooperman had been warned by the local bar association grievance committee before this incident not to use nonrefundable fee agreements (meaning the fee is due independent of whether professional services are actually rendered). The attorneys' Code of Professional Conduct and Responsibility provides that an attorney "shall not enter into an agreement for, charge or collect an illegal or excessive fee" and upon withdrawal from employment "shall refund promptly any part of a fee paid in advance that has not been earned." Did Cooperman's fee arrangement violate the code? [Grievance Committee for the Tenth Judicial District v. Edward M. Cooperman, 83 N.Y.2d 465, 633 N.E.2d 1069, 611 N.Y.S. 2d 465 (N.Y., 1994).]

8. Mallard, an attorney admitted to practice before the U.S. District Court for the Southern District of Iowa, was selected by the U.S. magistrate to represent indigent inmates. The suit was filed against prison officials under a federal statute providing that federal courts may "request" an attorney to represent any person claiming poverty status. Claiming that he was not competent to handle a complex matter of that kind, Mallard filed a motion to withdraw. The magistrate denied his request and his appeal to the District Court and Court of Appeal was unsuccessful. Can the court compel attorney Mallard to represent an indigent civil litigant? [Mallard v. U.S. District Court for Southern Dist. of Iowa, 490 U.S. 296, 109 S.Ct. 1814 (1989).]

9. Richard Shapero, a Kentucky attorney, applied to the state Attorneys' Advertising Commission for approval of a letter that he proposed to send "to potential clients who have had a foreclosure suit filed against them." The letter advised the clients that federal law may prevent creditors from taking immediate action and that the recipients of the letters could call Shapero's office for free information on how to keep their homes. The commission did not find the letter false or misleading, but it would not approve it because an American Bar Association rule, which had been adopted by the Kentucky Supreme Court, prohibited direct-mail solicitation by lawyers if the mail was directed to specific recipients rather than to a general group of persons known to need the particular kind of legal services being offered. Since Shapero had targeted specific individuals for his advertising, the Kentucky Supreme Court affirmed the commission's finding. Shapero appealed to the United States Supreme Court, claiming that the rule violated attorneys' rights to free speech. Will Shapero succeed in his claim? [Shapero v. Kentucky Bar Association, 486 U.S. 466, 108 S.Ct. 1916 (1988).]

10. The Hembrees purchased a home. The purchase contract included the following clause: "Any controversy or claim arising out of or relating to this contract, or the breach thereof, shall be settled by arbitration in the city of contract origin, in accordance with the rules of the American Arbitration Association." The claim was arbitrated and the arbitrator found for the Hembrees on the theory of implied warranty. Such a warranty is a guarantee not stated in the contract. The seller and seller's realtor challenged the arbitrator's award in court, claiming the arbitrator exceeded his authority

because the theory of recovery was not part of the contract and the arbitrator's finding was a clear error of law. Is the arbitrator's authority strictly limited to the terms of the contract? If the arbitrator is clearly wrong as to the application of law, will the award be overturned by the court? [*Hembree v. Broadway Realty Trust Company, Inc.*, 151 Ariz. 418, 728 P.2d 288 (1986).]

NOTES

1. Richard Posner, *Overcoming Law* (Cambridge, Ma: Harvard University Press, 1997). Judge Posner reaches back to the guilds of medieval Europe as a platform for an economic evaluation of the legal profession today, which he concludes reflects an industrialization of service. The "transformation of the profession is the proximate consequence of a surge in demand for legal services" (p. 64).

2. Jonathan Harr, *A Civil Action* (New York, First Vintage Books Edition, 1996), 295.

3. B. Curran, "Survey of the Public's Legal Needs," 61 *ABA Journal* 848 (June 1978).

4. Ken Meyers, *National Law Journal*, 17 June 1991, 13.

5. *In re Keenan*, 314 Mass. 544, 50 N.E.2d 785 (Mass., 1943).

6. *Cord v. Gibb*, 314 Va. 1019, 254 S.E.2d 71 (Va., 1979).

7. *Sacramento Bee*, 9 February 1977.

8. See http://www.azbar.org/FindingLawyer/bls.asp.

9. Jerome Carlin, *Lawyer's Ethics* (New York: Russell Sage Foundation, 1966).

10. A copy of the published quotation is available (contact authors), although the source cannot be identified.

11. See generally, Ken Englade, "The LSC under Siege," 73 *ABA Journal* 66 (December 1987).

12. Claudia MacLachalan, "New Chief of Legal Services Presides Over Policy Changes," *The National Law Journal*, 4 July 1994, A11.

13. C. McCoy et al., *Ethics in the Corporate Policy Process: An Introduction* (Berkeley, CA: Center for Ethics and Social Policy, Graduate Theological Union, 1976), 2.

14. Excerpt from the Model Rules of Professional Conduct, American Bar Association, adopted August 1983.

15. *Maryland State Bar Assoc. v. Agnew*, 271 Md. 543, 318 A.2d 811 (Md., 1974).

16. *Pineda v. State Bar of Calif.*, 49 Cal.3d 753, 781 P.2d 1 (Cal., 1989).

17. *Pineda v. State Bar of Calif.*

18. E. Schnapper, "The Myth of Legal Ethics," 64 *ABA Journal* 202 (Feb. 1978).

19. *In the matter of Edward McIver Leppard*, 272 S.C. 414, 252 S.E.2d 143 (S.C., 1979).

20. *In re James H. Himmel*, 125 Ill.2d 531, 533 N.E.2d 790 (1989).

21. *State v. Alexander*, 108 Ariz. 556, 503 P.2d 777 (Ariz., 1972).

22. For both views, see Harry Subin, "The Criminal Lawyer's 'Different Mission': Reflections on the 'Right' to Present a False Case," 1 *Georgetown J. of Legal Ethics*, 125 (1987); and John Mitchell, "Reasonable Doubts Are Where You Find Them: A Response to Professor Subin's Position on the Criminal Lawyer's 'Different Mission,'" 1 *Georgetown J. of Legal Ethics*, 125 (1987).

23. *Baltes v. Doe*, 4 *Lawyers Manual of Professional Conduct* 356 (Fla. Cir. Ct., 1988).

24. Geoffrey Hazard and William Hodes, *The Law of Lawyering* (Englewood Cliffs, NJ: Prentice-Hall, 1989), § 90.2.

25. *Swidler & Berlin and James Hamilton v. United States*, US, 118 S.Ct. 2081 (1998).

26. *United States v. Leventhal*, 961 F.2d 936 (11th cir., 1992). See also, *U.S. v. Blackman*, C.A.9 (Or.) 1995, 72 F.3d 1418, certiorari denied 117 S.Ct. 275 (1996).

27. *Business Guides v. Chromatic Communications Enters*, 498 U.S. 533, 111 S.Ct. 922 (1991).

28. Ray August, "The Mythical Kingdom of Lawyers," 78 *ABA Journal* 72 (September 1992). An interesting rebuttal to lawyers as political fodder can be found in Charles Epp, "Let's Not Kill All the Lawyers," *The Wall Street Journal*, 9 July 1992.

29. Harvey Rubenstein, "On Being a Private Practitioner," 78 *ABA Journal* 140 (December 1992).

30. *Bates v. State Bar of Arizona*, 433 U.S. 350, 97 S.Ct. 2691 (1977).

31. *Shapero v. Kentucky Bar Association*, 486 U.S. 466, 108 S.Ct. 1916 (1988).

32. *Peel v. Attorney Registration and Disciplinary Commission of Illinois*, 496 U.S. 917, 110 S.Ct. 2281 (1990).

33. "Advertising Wars," 80 *ABA Journal* 72–73 (February 1994).

34. The most well-known directory is the *Martindale Hubbel Law Directory* (Summitt, NJ: Martindale-Hubbel).

35. *The Florida Bar v. Stafford*, 542 So.2d 1321 (Florida, 1989)

36. Darlene Ricker, "The Vanishing Hourly Fee," 90 *ABA Journal* 66 (March 1984).

37. *Baron v. Mare*, 47 Cal.App.3d 304, 120 Cal.Rptr. 675 (Ca., 1975).

38. 13 ALR3d 701 (1967).

39. *State of Kansas v. Mayes*, 216 Kan. 38, 531 P.2d 102 (Kan., 1975).

40. *Bushman v. State Bar*, 111 Cal.3d 558, 522 P.2d 312, 13 Cal.Rptr. 904 (1974) and *Florida Bar v. Winn*, 208 So.2d 809 (Fla., 1968).

41. *American Trial Lawyers Association v. New Jersey Supreme Court*, 66 N.J. 258, 330 A.2d 350 (N.J., 1974).

42. Calif. Bus. & Prof. Code § 6146.

43. American Bar Association, CPR 5, DR 5-103(b).

44. *The Wall Street Journal*, 22 November 1989.

45. 14 American Jurisprudence 2d § 3.

46. J. Shannon, *Texaco and the $10 Billion Jury* (Englewood Cliffs, NJ: Prentice-Hall, 1988).

47. Warren Burger, Chief Justice of the U.S. Supreme Court, in a speech to the American Law Institute, May 1978, as reported in the 64 *ABA Journal* 847 (1978).

48. *In re Thompson*, 574 S.W.2d 365 (Mo., 1978).

49. Roger Fisher, William Ury, and Bruce Patton, *Getting to Yes: Negotiating Agreement Without Giving In* (New York: Penguin Books, 1992).

50. *Greene et al. v. Hundley et al.*, 266 Ga. 592, 468 S.E.2d 350 (Georgia, 1996).

5

ADMINISTRATIVE LAW

*T*he rise of administrative bodies probably has
been the most significant legal trend of the last
century and perhaps more values are affected
by their decisions than by those of all the courts. . . .

Justice Robert H. Jackson,
U.S. Supreme Court Justice, 1941–1954.[1]

Justice Jackson's quotation expresses the belief of many legal scholars and political scientists regarding the importance of administrative agencies. This chapter
discusses the why, what, and how of the law of administrative agencies. First we
consider the why.

Ever bigger business, ruthless competition, unfettered consumption of natural resources, mismanagement of labor, and rapidly emerging new technologies
faced our society as it approached the beginning of the twentieth century.*[2] The
need for government regulation was expanding. Electricity, railroads, and the
telegraph and telephone led to national markets. Moguls rose to control steel, oil,
and the distribution of goods such as sugar, salt, and even matches. Competition
was combated with severe business practices, such as price cutting. Darwinian
battles by businesses featured the slashing of wages and the creation of ever more
efficiencies. For example, Bethlehem Steel Company studied the efficiencies of
different sizes of shovels and eventually began using 15 different types allowing
140 men to do the same work previously done by 600 using only one type. Time
and motion experts led the way. Even small independent bakeries became the targets of big business as technology made wide distribution of their goods possible.
The destruction of forests, grasslands, and rivers accelerated along with the industrial age—and with such destruction, the need for conservation. Already, the
Sierra Club had been founded to save Yosemite Valley. By the turn of the twentieth century, government regulation was lagging, although the disposal of oil in
waterways had been outlawed. Then, as now, Americans loved fast travel.
Bicycles featured tubular construction spoke wheels with ball bearings and air-
filled tires. The "wheels" were used for commuting as well as for traveling into
the countryside. The bicycle destroyed "the myth of the feminine fragility, and the
daringly split skirt that was required to ride it."[3] There were more than 4 million

---

*Some people would observe that some things never change.

bicycle riders by 1898. By 1898, the first gasoline-powered automobile had been sold and mass production was just around the corner. Big business was virtually unfettered in its growth.

Social problems also abounded at the turn of the twentieth century. Chastity before marriage was the accepted thought, but prostitution was rampant in the big cities. As noted in the *Ladies' Home Journal*, "the truth is the average man prefers mental repose rather than mental titillation in the companionship of women."[4] On the other hand, a few women did work as lawyers, dentists, barbers, and livery stable keepers. African Americans were flocking to the cities from the South, where there was no vote, no jobs, and no dignity; however, they were met with waves of European immigrants who were preferred by employers and who could blend into society more quickly. There were growing problems in admiralty, debtor's bankruptcy rights, property, commerce, in labor relations, and so on, all requiring sensible governmental regulation. In a nutshell, considering the wide range of obvious issues facing our society as it entered the twentieth century, how could a single Congress manage such a conglomeration of important issues? That it could not, already has been reflected by the creation of the Interstate Commerce Commission (discussed later in this chapter) to solve the many problems created by the railroads. But there were many more problems than those of the railroads—with nobody but Congress to solve them.

Laws cannot be passed without studying all possible ramifications, without the participation of affected parties, and without clear notions of the overall impact on society. How could the members of Congress resolve this clear dilemma? Could the law-making functions be delegated to specialized, expert organizations that could accumulate the expertise necessary to manage the businesses and affairs over which they would be given power? Indeed they could—and administrative agencies were born with this responsibility which has steadily grown into unfathomably huge proportions, as you will see in this chapter.

Today, 100 years later and on the brink of a new millennium, our society is perched upon the threshold of what promises to be an age of unprecedented technological advance together with the social implications of a rapidly expanding global population with commensurately declining natural resources and environmental degradation. The twentieth century of the industrial revolution, of world and other wars, of newly defined and protected civil rights, and of an unprecedented standard of living is drawing to a close.

Nobody suggests that life in our society during the early years of the twenty-first century will be anything but increasingly complex. Because of these anticipated complexities, the federal legislative branch of only 435 elected representatives and 100 senators could hardly be expected to provide the thousands of laws that will be necessary each year. The difference between the situation in 1900 and the situation today is the existence and ongoing effectiveness of administrative agencies at the federal, state, and even local levels of government. Many technical matters today require regulation beyond the understanding of most legislators, especially given the limited time they usually have to consider the multiplicity of pressing issues. For example, how can any one person be expected to cast votes with full comprehension during a legislative session when thousands of bills (proposed laws) are under consideration? Such bills include matters as diverse as fresh air circulation in commercial airlines, limitations on the chemical composition of fertilizers and insecticides and restrictions on use, salary requirements and job standards for civil service employees, control on the hunting of migrating birds, and proper safety equipment standards for two-wheel and three-wheel recreational vehicles.

Obviously, the legislative branch must delegate some of its powers in order to cope with the volume, and detailed specialized nature, of problems requiring legal and political solutions. Most delegations of congressional powers are made to administrative agencies. Federal agencies include, but are not limited to, the National Labor Relations Board, Federal Trade Commission, Small Business Administration, and the Internal Revenue Service. See Exhibit 5–1 for a listing of Executive departments and major independent federal administrative agencies.

Many of these agencies are empowered with a combination of legislative, executive, and judicial powers to accomplish the work of government with far greater efficiency than is possible if the tasks were performed by Congress. Although the exercise of these powers is subject to judicial review, the courts seldom overturn administrative agency rules and rulings. Administrators who govern agencies have been selected as experts in their specialized fields. The Congress has delegated to agencies the necessary powers to make rules (legislate), to administer and to enforce the rules (execute), and to investigate and prosecute violations of the rules (adjudicate).

In recent years there has been a backlash by business against extensive government bureaucracy, especially economic regulation. Some observers argue that agency rules create unreasonably and unnecessarily high compliance costs for business. They ask why bureaucrats should demand such voluminous reports, inspect our plants, condemn and confiscate our goods, tell us what to make and what to charge, and then investigate, prosecute, and punish us without jury trials—all at a high cost to business and to society (because these costs are usually passed along to customers in the form of higher prices). Some analysts complain that, furthermore, government agencies fail in their purpose to provide the regulation and protection private consumers need and deserve.

> There is more regulation with fewer benefits, and the whole process grows increasingly arbitrary and murky. The totality of federal regulations now comes to 202 volumes numbering 131,803 pages. This is 14 times greater than in 1950 and nearly four times greater than in 1965. There are 16 volumes of environmental regulations, 19 volumes of employment regulations.[5]

Not surprisingly, administrative agencies also have their enthusiastic supporters. Consumer advocates cheer them on. Many political scientists acclaim them as a logical evolutionary extension of our tripartite government, reflecting legitimate new needs for government control. Legislators, sensitive to public opinion, acknowledge that there appears to be no acceptable alternative.

> Public Citizen, a nationwide organization representing 120,000 consumers, and Patricia and Ben Christen, whose only son Cory died as a result of unregulated, misleading, commercially produced written patient drug information, hereby petition the Food and Drug Administration (FDA), to immediately recall, or seize if necessary, unregulated information that is being distributed with prescription drugs that is not consistent with or derived from a drug's FDA approved package insert. FDA's first priority should be to take action by recalling those PILs [Product Information Labels] whose inaccurate information is most likely to cause substantial harm if not corrected.[6]

Exhibit 5-1: The Government of the United States

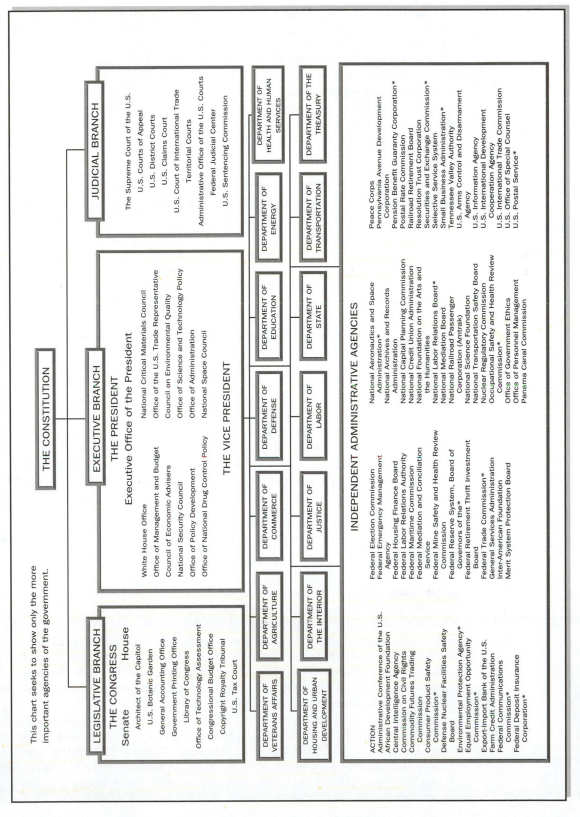

This chart seeks to show only the more important agencies of the government.

THE CONSTITUTION

LEGISLATIVE BRANCH

THE CONGRESS
Senate   House

Architect of the Capitol
U.S. Botanic Garden
General Accounting Office
Government Printing Office
Library of Congress
Office of Technology Assessment
Congressional Budget Office
Copyright Royalty Tribunal
U.S. Tax Court

EXECUTIVE BRANCH

THE PRESIDENT

Executive Office of the President

White House Office
Office of Management and Budget
Council of Economic Advisers
National Security Council
Office of Policy Development
Office of National Drug Control Policy

National Critical Materials Council
Office of the U.S. Trade Representative
Council on Environmental Quality
Office of Science and Technology Policy
Office of Administration
National Space Council

THE VICE PRESIDENT

JUDICIAL BRANCH

The Supreme Court of the U.S.
U.S. Courts of Appeal
U.S. District Courts
U.S. Claims Court
U.S. Court of International Trade
Territorial Courts
Administrative Office of the U.S. Courts
Federal Judicial Center
U.S. Sentencing Commission

DEPARTMENT OF VETERANS AFFAIRS

DEPARTMENT OF HOUSING AND URBAN DEVELOPMENT

DEPARTMENT OF AGRICULTURE

DEPARTMENT OF THE INTERIOR

DEPARTMENT OF COMMERCE

DEPARTMENT OF JUSTICE

DEPARTMENT OF DEFENSE

DEPARTMENT OF LABOR

DEPARTMENT OF EDUCATION

DEPARTMENT OF STATE

DEPARTMENT OF HEALTH AND HUMAN SERVICES

DEPARTMENT OF THE TREASURY

DEPARTMENT OF ENERGY

DEPARTMENT OF TRANSPORTATION

INDEPENDENT ADMINISTRATIVE AGENCIES

ACTION
Administrative Conference of the U.S.
African Development Foundation
Central Intelligence Agency
Commission on Civil Rights
Commodity Futures Trading Commission
Consumer Product Safety Commission*
Defense Nuclear Facilities Safety Board
Environmental Protection Agency*
Equal Employment Opportunity Commission*
Export-Import Bank of the U.S.
Farm Credit Administration
Federal Communications Commission*
Federal Deposit Insurance Corporation*

Federal Election Commission
Federal Emergency Management Agency
Federal Housing Finance Board
Federal Labor Relations Authority
Federal Maritime Commission
Federal Mediation and Conciliation Service
Federal Mine Safety and Health Review Commission
Federal Reserve System, Board of Governors of the*
Federal Retirement Thrift Investment Board
Federal Trade Commission*
General Services Administration
Inter-American Foundation
Merit System Protection Board

National Aeronautics and Space Administration*
National Archives and Records Administration
National Capital Planning Commission
National Credit Union Administration
National Foundation on the Arts and the Humanities
National Labor Relations Board*
National Mediation Board
National Railroad Passenger Corporation (Amtrak)
National Science Foundation
National Transportation Safety Board
Nuclear Regulatory Commission
Occupational Safety and Health Review Commission*
Office of Government Ethics
Office of Personnel Management
Panama Canal Commission

Peace Corps
Pennsylvania Avenue Development Corporation
Pension Benefit Guaranty Corporation*
Postal Rate Commission
Railroad Retirement Board
Resolution Trust Corporation
Securities and Exchange Commission*
Selective Service System
Small Business Administration*
Tennessee Valley Authority
U.S. Arms Control and Disarmament Agency
U.S. Information Agency
U.S. International Development Cooperation Agency
U.S. International Trade Commission
U.S. Office of Special Counsel
U.S. Postal Service*

*Major administrative agency.
Source: *U.S. Government Manual.*

This mixed reaction is understandable when one considers that administrative agencies are reaching into the workaday world to regulate the production of goods and services, which is essentially a private entrepreneurial effort in our capitalistic society. Not only do the rules imposed by administrative agencies often dictate how, when, and where things must be done, but they also significantly affect the profits realized by producers and the prices and quality of goods and services received by consumers. Although the emphasis in this chapter is on federal administrative law, most of the discussion applies equally to state and local administrative agencies as well.

WHAT ARE ADMINISTRATIVE AGENCIES?

Administrative agencies are collectively sub-branches of the executive branch of federal, state, and local governments. They are organizations of government officials created to achieve public goals and objectives. For example, Congress sets the rates at which a person's income is taxed, but the Internal Revenue Service (an administrative agency) has the duty to collect the tax. Typically, an **enabling statute** to accomplish government policy objectives defined in the statute creates an administrative agency. The nature of the agency, its powers, and its objectives are generally detailed in the enabling statute. To accomplish its given tasks, the agency may (and usually does) receive the power to make generally applicable rules and to determine in individual cases whether compliance with the law has occurred. Bureaucracies of administrative agencies have multiplied since the Great Depression of the 1930s, and so has administrative law. Today government—itself a product of law, and also a prolific creator of new law—extends its influence and control over a wide and expanding range of human activities (e.g., financial aid for farmers and landlords and food and shelter for the poor) and public facilities (e.g., schools and libraries, parks and prisons, airports and highways).

For a brief overview of administrative agencies and administrative law, go to the Cornell University Web site at http://www.law.cornell.edu/topics/administrative.html

glossary

WHAT IS ADMINISTRATIVE LAW?

Administrative law is defined in two very different ways. The first definition is that administrative law governs the creation, operation, and judicial review of administrative agencies. In other words, it defines the legal exercises and limits of administrative agency powers. The second definition is that administrative law is the composite body of substantive law created by the various administrative agencies in the performance of their assigned tasks. An example is all of the rules created by the Federal Trade Commission that have been adopted to prevent false advertising. This chapter focuses on the first definition.

Administrative law exists at the federal, state, and local levels of government. At the *federal* level, there are powerful administrative agencies such as the Federal Trade Commission (FTC) and the Federal Reserve Board (FRB). At the *state* level, agencies such as the Department of Motor Vehicles regulate vehicle and driver licensing. At the *local* level, agencies such as planning commissions regulate land use through zoning and building permits. At each level of government, the nature and limits of administrative power are important to everyone, along with the rules created by these agencies to complete their tasks.

BRIEF HISTORY OF U.S. ADMINISTRATIVE LAW

Some examples of administrative law can be traced to the earliest days of the republic. For example, in the aftermath of the Revolutionary War, veterans asked for financial benefits that had been authorized by Congress. To require Congress, or the courts, to review and make a decision on each application would have been exceedingly cumbersome and costly. Therefore, Congress delegated the problem to one bureaucracy. That special office has evolved over the years into today's giant Department of Veterans Affairs (VA), now a cabinet-level department.

The first major independent administrative agency was the Interstate Commerce Commission (ICC), created in 1887 to end certain abuses common in the railroad industry at the time: frenzied financing, arbitrary discrimination in rates among shippers and geographic areas, widely varying levels of service, cut-throat competition (below-cost pricing), and exploitive rate structures. The ICC brought order and commanded uniformity of service at reasonable rates and it did so for over 100 years. Contrary to popular opinion, government agencies do occasionally cease to exist, as did the ICC in 1996.[7]

A surge of interest in government regulation occurred under the New Deal of Franklin D. Roosevelt in the early 1930s. Legislation was introduced to control certain abuses of the free enterprise system that many believe led to the Great Depression. The Securities and Exchange Commission (SEC), the Federal Communications Commission (FCC), and the National Labor Relations Board (NLRB) came into existence at that time. Today these are huge agencies regulating the securities and stock markets, radio and television, and millions of workers.

An additional wave of new agencies was created in the 1960s, and again in the early 1970s, in response to demands for effective government action to end racial and sex discrimination in employment, to protect the consumer from commercial exploitation, to clean air and water pollution, and to provide workers with safe and healthful job environments. New agencies created in the 1960s and 1970s included the Equal Employment Opportunities Commission (EEOC), Consumer Product Safety Commission (CPSC), Environmental Protection Agency (EPA), and Occupational Safety and Health Administration (OSHA).

WHAT IS THE DIFFERENCE BETWEEN AN EXECUTIVE DEPARTMENT AND AN INDEPENDENT ADMINISTRATIVE AGENCY?

Administrative agencies are part of the executive branch of government, which is responsible for carrying out the functions of government. The first executive department agencies were the cabinet-level departments of War (later named Defense), State, and Treasury. These departments, created by the first Congress in 1789, have been joined by 11 more departments (see Exhibit 5–1). The heads of

Look at this Web site for a presentation of the various administrative agencies and commissions with links to each.
http://www2.whitehouse.gov/WH/Independent_Agencies/html/independent_links.html

these departments are called *secretaries*, and they are members of the president's cabinet. As such, they are directly answerable to the president. Thus, these departments are executive agencies, each headed by a single cabinet member who is under the direction and control of the president.

Most of the federal agencies referred to in this chapter, though, are not executive department agencies, but rather **independent administrative agencies,** meaning agencies within the executive branch whose operation and function is somewhat, although not totally, independent of all three branches of government, including the executive branch. So independent agencies are not directly controlled by Congress or the president.

A board or commission ranging in size from 5 to 11 members who, as noted, are not under the direct control of either the president or Congress heads each independent agency. The nature of the independence of these agencies is simple and effective. While most appointees to executive leadership positions serve at the pleasure of the president, appointments to independent agencies are for specific periods of time.

President Herbert Hoover appointed William Humphrey to the Federal Trade Commission for a seven-year term. Five years before the term expired, President Franklin D. Roosevelt, Hoover's successor as president, requested that Humphrey resign, stating, "I do not feel that your mind and my mind go along together on either the policies or the administering of the Federal Trade Commission. . . ." Humphrey declined, whereupon Roosevelt wrote Humphrey, "Effective as of this date you are hereby removed from the office of Commissioner of the Federal Trade Commission." Humphrey refused to vacate his office, claiming the Federal Trade Commission Act allowed removal of commissioners only for reasons of "inefficiency, neglect of duty, or malfeasance in office." Roosevelt maintained that as president of the United States he had the inherent power to remove members of the executive branch in whom he lacked confidence. Was Humphrey or the president correct?

The U.S. Supreme Court agreed with Humphrey. The court held that the president lacked the power to fire Humphrey, who could serve his appointed term unless found guilty of a failure to perform his job.

Much power comes and goes in subtle ways. Although the president is free to appoint to these positions, he or she is not free to fire any incumbent. Thus, the goal of policy independence is maintained. In addition, many appointments are for terms ranging from four to seven years. Thus, a newly elected president may have to wait until the end of the first term, or even into the second term, to replace such an appointed official.[8]

The language of the Supreme Court in identifying the nature and importance of this independence is noteworthy.

We think it plain under the Constitution that illimitable power of removal is not possessed by the President in respect of offices [such as FTC commissioners]. The authority of Congress, in creating quasi-legislative or quasi-judicial agencies to require them to act in discharge of their duties independently of executive control cannot well be doubted; and the authority includes as an appropriate incident, power to fix the period during which they shall continue in office, and to forbid their removal except for cause in the meantime. For it is quite evident that one who holds his office only during the pleasure of another, cannot be depended upon to maintain an attitude of independence against the latter's will.[9]

Agency names are not always helpful in determining whether they are independent or not. Administrative agencies go by names such as Commission, Board, Authority, Bureau, Office, Administration or Administrator, Corporation, and Division. In addition to administrative agencies that operate independent of the traditional government departments, there are the previously discussed departments that are dependent (i.e., the president retains the right to discharge without cause), such as the Department of State and the Department of Labor. These fit within the ordinary executive hierarchy, and the president appoints (with the advice and consent of the Senate), supervises, and fires the people heading these agencies at will. Sometimes these traditional departments also possess authority to create administrative rules, for example, the Internal Revenue Service (IRS) of the Treasury Department and the Social Security Administration of the Department of Health and Human Services.

Although no statistics are available, observers point out that the sheer volume of law generated by all types of administrative agencies exceeds the volume produced by both the legislatures and the courts combined. An example of a statutory language creating the composition of an independent administrative agency is provided in the 1964 statute that created the Equal Opportunity Employment Commission:

There is hereby created a Commission to be known as the Equal Employment Opportunity Commission, which shall be composed of five members, not more than three of whom shall be members of the same political party. Members of the Commission shall be appointed by the President by and with the advice and consent of the Senate for a term of five years.[10]

CREATION OF ADMINISTRATIVE AGENCIES

An administrative agency is legally created when an enabling bill (statute) is passed by Congress and signed by the president. These statutes specify the purpose(s) of the agency and the attributes of agency power, such as its composition (number of members, method of appointment, and length of terms). Of course, a newly created agency cannot perform any tasks until it is budgeted and staffed.

A reasonable question is whether there are limits on the ability of Congress to create administrative agencies and empower them to perform tasks of government previously assigned (to it) under the Constitution. This legal question involves the validity of delegating a constitutionally derived power from one branch of government to another branch of government. For example, the power of Congress to create law through statutes is delegated to an administrative agency that implements the delegation by creating regulations. Such delegations have been challenged in the court many times, but in only two cases has the

Supreme Court found that Congress exceeded constitutional limits by drafting too broad a delegation of power.[11]

In the midst of the 1930s depression, Congress enacted the National Industrial Recovery Act (NIRA). The NIRA authorized the president of the United States to approve codes of fair competition that had been prepared and submitted to him by trade and industry associations or had been created upon the president's own initiative. The act provided that violations of these codes could be punishable as crimes. The Schechter Poultry Corporation was held criminally liable for violation of the "Live Poultry Code." Schechter claimed that the code was the result of an unconstitutional delegation of power by Congress and thus unlawful and unenforceable. How did the Supreme Court rule?

A unanimous Supreme Court held that the delegation by Congress to the president in this statute was too broad, as it allowed the president to impose any regulation he (at the time, Franklin D. Roosevelt) chose on the poultry business. This "unfettered" power was "an unconstitutional delegation of legislative power."[12] However, subsequent challenges to broad congressional delegations have been uniformly upheld as valid.[13] In finding a delegation valid, the courts look for "[a] declared policy by Congress and its definition of the circumstances in which its command is to be effective. . . ."[14]

The following are among the guidelines considered by the Court to determine whether a delegation is valid:

- To whom is the delegation made? Is it made to an administrative agency, state government, president, private industry, or other?

- Is the delegation for a proper purpose? That is, is its purpose a legitimate exercise of government power?

- Have guidelines for delegated conduct been provided in the legislation? Are the guidelines broad or narrow in scope?

- Does the legislation provide for a fair process in creating regulations or administering tasks?

- Is the reason for the delegation an emergency?

- What is the nature of the delegation? For example, does it affect personal rights, such as denial of passports?

An example of a lawful delegation by Congress of defined power is the creation of the Federal Trade Commission (FTC). It was created by the Federal Trade Commission Act of 1914, which prohibits unfair and deceptive trade practices. The act describes the procedures the agency must follow to charge violators, provides for the judicial review of agency actions, and grants the power to investigate and to make rules and regulations. The FTC may force a company to stop an advertising campaign if it considers the advertisements to be "unfair or deceptive" to consumers. The FTC may even require a company to make announcements or advertisements that correct the false statements made in earlier advertisements.

OPERATION OF ADMINISTRATIVE AGENCIES

We can lick gravity, but sometimes the paperwork is overwhelming.

Wernher von Braun (1912–1977), German-born rocket scientist

Administrative activities have come to be called administrative process, in contrast to judicial process. **Administrative process** involves the administration of law by nonjudicial agencies, a modern development. **Judicial process** is the traditional administration of law by the courts. There are four basic functions of most administrative agencies: investigation, enforcement, rulemaking, and adjudication. Together, these functions are the administrative process. Combining them creates sufficient power and flexibility to allow the agency to accomplish its objectives. See Exhibit 5–2 for an illustration of how administrative law is created.

Generally, agency administrators are experts in the specialized fields to be regulated by the agency. Indeed, a primary justification for administrative

Current news on the topic of administrative law from the *National Law Journal* can be found at http://www.ljx.com/practice/administrative/index.html

http://

Exhibit 5–2: Administrative Law

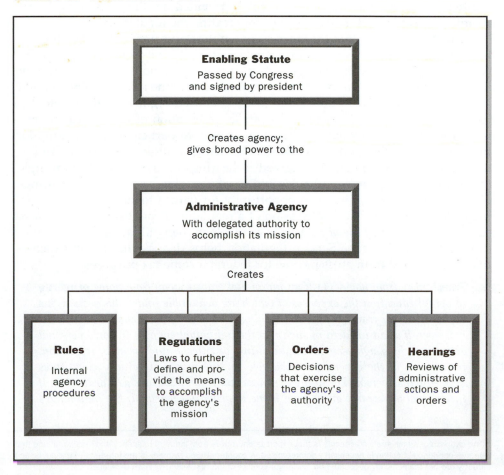

Enabling Statute
Passed by Congress and signed by president

Creates agency; gives broad power to the

Administrative Agency
With delegated authority to accomplish its mission

Creates

Rules
Internal agency procedures

Regulations
Laws to further define and provide the means to accomplish the agency's mission

Orders
Decisions that exercise the agency's authority

Hearings
Reviews of administrative actions and orders

agencies is that experts, free from direct political influence, can best create regulations and then adjudicate to accomplish important public policy objectives.*

Agency power is balanced by three external controls. First, the courts have the power to review agency actions. Judicial review is discussed later in the chapter. Second, the executive and legislative branches have political control over administrative agencies. Third, the **Administrative Procedure Act of 1946 (APA)** provides mandatory guidelines for federal administrative agencies carrying out their missions. The APA provides the basic requirements for agencies' rulemaking and adjudication of cases.

Our discussion of the operation of administrative agencies is directed to their most important administrative powers, including: the power to make rules and regulations (quasi-legislation), to investigate and enforce their orders (execution), and to review application of the rules to individuals (quasi-adjudication).

REGULATIONS AND RULEMAKING

On the basis of its own investigations, an agency establishes standards and detailed regulations and rules. Once adopted, regulations have the force of law, just as a statute passed by the legislature. To be valid, a regulation must be consistent with the U.S. Constitution (for example, it must meet due-process requirements), must not exceed the power conferred on the agency by Congress, and must be created consistent with procedural rules provided in the statute or in the Administrative Procedure Act (APA)[15] for creating the regulation.

The APA requires that the agency give notice of a proposed regulation, allowing interested parties an opportunity to participate in its formulation. In other words, people affected by the agency's proposed regulations must be permitted to participate or comment on the proposed rule before the rule is finally adopted. Notice usually involves publication of the proposed regulation, or of intent to regulate, in the *Federal Register*, the official publication of the federal government for all agency regulations. The opportunity to participate in the adoption process may involve polls, interviews, an open fact-finding hearing, and other means. Due process must be observed in hearings on new rules. For example, there must be reasonable advance notice of the time and place of hearings. Hearings might also provide an opportunity for parties to submit written comments to the agency. The final version of a regulation is published in the *Federal Register* as well. The *Federal Register* is available in many libraries. The following sample Internal Revenue Service regulation helps define what travel expenses may be deducted from gross income for federal income tax purposes.

> *Travel away from home. (1) If an individual travels away from home primarily to obtain education the expenses of which are deductible under this section, his expenditures for travel, meals, and lodging while away from home are deductible. However, if as an incident of such trip the individual engages in some personal activity such as sightseeing, social visiting, or entertaining, or other recreation, the portion of the expenses attributable to such personal activity constitutes nondeductible personal or living expenses and is not allowable as a deduction. If the individual's travel away from home is primarily personal, the individual's*

---

*One criticism of administrative agencies is that expert talent moves from industry to agency and vice-versa, and that true independence of action is necessarily compromised. A counter offered by many is the interests of the public and industry are not diametrically opposed, and few major conflict of interest scandals have developed.

expenditures for travel, meals and lodging (other than meals and lodging during the time spent in participating in deductible education pursuits) are not deductible. Whether a particular trip is primarily personal or primarily to obtain education the expenses of which are deductible under this section depends upon all the facts and circumstances of each case. An important factor to be taken into consideration in making the determination is the relative amount of time devoted to personal activity as compared with the time devoted to educational pursuits. 26 C.F.R. § 1.162-5 (e)

The Negotiated Rulemaking Act[16] provides a very different method of creating regulations. In the ordinary rulemaking process, just discussed, the agency staff studies the problem and reaches a tentative solution. That tentative solution is published in the *Federal Register* as a proposed rule, giving the public the opportunity to comment. After comment, the agency issues a final rule. In negotiated rulemaking, the agency invites representatives of all concerned parties, usually businesses, to meet to assist the agency in drafting the proposed rule. Thus, at the drafting stage, the agency takes into account these special interests along with the mandates of the enabling statute.

Administrative agencies also create internal procedural and interpretive *rules*. These rules are statements and opinions published by the agency, explaining how the agency interprets and intends to apply the laws it enforces. These internal rules also describe the agency's methods of operation and establish procedures for interacting with the agency. Interpretive rules do not have the force of law. They are not automatically binding on private individuals or organizations. Nor are they binding on the courts, as are statutes and regulations. Anyone who believes an agency rule is illegal or incorrect can challenge it in court. In practice, however, the courts give considerable weight to interpretive rules when deciding cases involving agency regulations. An example of a procedural rule is one listing factor the IRS uses in selecting which taxpayers to audit. An audit requires the taxpayer to produce the records (e.g., pay stubs and deducted-expense receipts) that were used to justify data contained in tax forms. The IRS "selection rule" to determine which taxpayers to audit would be, for example, a procedural rule to randomly audit one out of every 10,000 taxpayers.

INVESTIGATION

The work of an administrative agency is to execute its administrative tasks. That may involve the use of investigation, prosecution, negotiation, and any number of other administrative chores. Let us focus first on the agency's need to get information. For example, the Food and Drug Administration (FDA) is responsible for determining the safety and effectiveness of new drugs before approving them and allowing their sale in the United States. Accordingly, it requires studies from the company proposing the drug; the agency itself may also engage in studies. Sometimes manufacturers or interest groups voluntarily provide information needed by the agency, but sometimes they do not; in these cases, the agency must aggressively seek the information it needs. Obviously, to oversee an area or business, the agency must know about the activities and organizations involved.

A good source for information about government is the Interactive Citizens Handbook at the White House at http://www.whitehouse.gov/WH/html/handbook.html

A DC-10 jet crashed on takeoff at Chicago's O'Hare International Airport after its left engine and pylon dropped onto the runway. A total of 275

persons aboard the plane were killed, as well as 3 persons on the ground. The Federal Aviation Administration (FAA), aided by investigators from the National Transportation Safety Board, immediately began exhaustive studies of other DC-10s to determine, if possible, the cause of the disaster. Was the FAA able to order all 138 U.S.-registered DC-10s grounded while conducting its investigation?[17]

Yes, even though the loss in revenues for the affected U.S. airlines approximated $2.5 million a day. The grounding was ordered on June 6, 1979, and lasted 38 days. The grounding was lifted after the FAA determined that the disaster was caused by a crack in the aft bulkhead (rear wall) of the engine-support pylon, but only after the agency had issued orders (1) to the manufacturer to redesign the pylons, (2) to the airlines to end the maintenance procedure thought to have weakened the pylons and to begin more stringent maintenance inspections, and (3) to manufacturers and airlines to cooperate more closely with FAA engineers and inspectors in certifying the fitness of aircraft to fly.

Two of the most important investigative tools available to administrative agencies are the subpoena and the ability to search and seize. Both are helpful in determining policy and conducting an investigation. A **subpoena** is an order to produce a witness or a thing. Using a subpoena, the administrative agency can compel testimony. It can also compel production of documents, papers, records, and physical objects. Failure to comply with a subpoena can lead to a contempt citation punishable by fine or imprisonment.

Many agencies gather information through on-site inspections. Sometimes a search of a home, an office, or a factory is a way to get evidence to prove a regulatory violation. At other times, physical inspections are used instead of a formal hearing to correct or prevent an undesirable condition. Inspections and testing cover a wide range of activities. Inspections can be safety inspections of underground coal mines, safety tests of commercial equipment and automobiles, or environmental monitoring of factory emissions.

There may be a clash between the government's right to know information essential for public safety and well being and a private party's constitutional rights to due process and privacy, as well as freedom from self-incrimination. The Supreme Court has held that administrative agencies, such as the police, must comply with the **search-and-seizure** provisions of the Fourth Amendment.[18] The requirement for administrative warrants is less demanding than those for criminal warrants and there are some exceptions to the requirement that an agency get a warrant—for example, in the case of inspections of nuclear reactors at utility plants and certain other closely regulated industries. "While a search of a private residence generally must be conducted pursuant to a warrant in order to be reasonable, a warrantless administrative search of commercial property does not per se violate the Fourth Amendment."[19]

Craig and Marilyn Lesser of Union Grove, Wisconsin, were licensed dealers of long-eared, short-tailed lagomorphs—i.e., rabbits. Their rabbitry was subject to regulation and inspection under federal law by government agents. They were found to have unlawfully refused to allow inspections of their rabbitry on five occasions and were fined by the department secretary. The Lessers sought judicial review of the sanction, claiming that by inspecting and attempting to inspect their rabbitry without a warrant, their right to be free from unreasonable searches guaranteed by the Fourth Amendment was violated. Was a warrantless inspection of their rabbit farm lawful?

The inspections were held to be lawful and the court held that a three-part test for warrantless administrative searches was met.[20]

1. Is governmental regulation of the industry "pervasive"? "The Animal Welfare Act and the standards promulgated thereunder by the Secretary regulate many facets of the business. A license and the payment of a fee are required to engage in the sale of rabbits to a research institution. The operator of a rabbitry who sells rabbits for use in research cannot transport, purchase, sell, house, care for, or handle his rabbits without being subject to the Act or a standard. He must make and maintain records concerning the purchase, sale, transportation, identification, and previous ownership of his rabbits. And he is subject to loss of his license, civil penalties, and even criminal penalties, for failure to comply with the Act and the standards."

2. Are the warrantless inspections necessary to further the regulatory scheme? The court found the inspection scheme devised was necessary and reasonably related to the purposes of the law regulating the industry. "In rabbit farming many of the potential deficiencies that would violate the Act can be quickly concealed."

3. Did the inspection program advise the premises owner that the search was being conducted pursuant to the law, and was the discretion of the inspecting officers limited?

ENFORCEMENT

After concluding an investigation, the agency may start an administrative action. These actions may be brought against individuals or organizations. A complaint is the first step in an administrative action. Private citizens and organizations may sometimes also initiate complaints.* However, such claims always are prosecuted by the applicable agency. The agency acts as prosecutor, judge, and jury. Procedural safeguards against possible abuse of power by the agency protect persons subject to administrative investigations. When procedural safeguards are found inadequate, Congress may hold hearings and pass new laws constraining administrative powers. For example, in 1998, the Senate held hearings on IRS collection practices. These hearings led to new controls on IRS administrative discretion. Following is an excerpt from the reported testimony of Maureen O'Dwyer, an IRS employee.

> When first approached to give testimony before you, I was reluctant to do so, as I considered it to be a betrayal of my fellow employees. The IRS is an easy smear

The Federal Interagency Council on Statistical Policy maintains a site to provide access to the full range of statistics and information produced for 70 federal agencies. Check http://www.fedstats.gov/

---

*Some law schools give academic credit for law students persuading administrative agencies to pursue certain complaints. For an example see Ken Myers "Law Schools Suing for Extra Credit, Latest 'A' Got Rid of Clubs' Ladies Nights," *The National Law Journal*, 22 February 1993, 4.

and it has been reviled both justly and unjustly in the press. From the inside looking out, it is easy to distinguish between which accusations are true, and which are not. No one has risen to the defense of the service against the unjust accusations. I did not wish to add more fuel to the already raging fire, or to further demoralize my fellow employees by disclosing any other inequitable practices of the service. But our system of taxation is dependent on the taxpayer's belief that the tax laws they follow will apply to everyone and in the belief that they will be administered impartially.

The aging returns of small taxpayers are written up, unagreed and penalties are assessed. The taxpayer will receive a statutory notice; that is, it must respond within 90 days. If the taxpayer does not respond within this time frame, it will automatically lose its appeals rights and the right to petition tax court. Understanding these procedures is difficult for the unknowledgeable, small taxpayer. Without representation, the small taxpayer is vulnerable. The results can be costly.[21]

PROBLEM RESOLUTION

A majority of actions brought by administrative agencies are resolved without a formal adjudication. Regulated businesses generally wish to avoid the appearance of being uncooperative. Settlements preserve the resources of both the agency and the business. Agencies also work hard to prevent violations, and they usually negotiate with violators to avoid formal actions.

Between 1982 and 1992, more than 2,500 savings and loan associations and banks in the United States failed. These failures occurred in part because of questionable business practices of many of these financial institutions. In the wake of the failures, legal actions were brought by government agencies against individuals and business firms accused of negligent practices. In December 1992, three federal agencies announced a settlement of charges of wrongdoing with the certified public accounting firm of Ernst and Young. The firm agreed to pay $400 million; in exchange, the government dropped its legal action for damages. Ernst and Young did not admit or deny the charges brought, but explained that the settlement was necessary to stop an endless stream of lawsuits that were expensive to defend against.

In 1991, the APA was amended to authorize and encourage alternative dispute resolution (ADR) processes, including arbitration and mediation. This allows, but does not require, agencies and those they regulate to resolve conflicts regarding regulation enforcement without resorting to administrative hearings or court actions.[22]

HEARINGS OR ADMINISTRATIVE ADJUDICATION

Most agencies provide hearings as an alternative to court actions, when the agency threatens to deny a person some license, right, entitlement, or privilege. The agencies not only create rules consistent with their task but also enforce their rules through trial-like proceedings before **administrative law judges (ALJ)**. An

ALJ is a government employee appointed to hear administrative cases.* Sometimes the appointed heads of the agency hear the cases instead of, or on appeal from an earlier decision by, the ALJ. Sometimes adjudications are appeals of denials by agency staff of claims by citizens for government benefits. Examples of denied benefits might be the termination of social security benefits or of a government license. At the state level, similar quasi-judges are often called *hearing officers* as well as ALJs.

Some administrative agencies make policy by hearing and resolving individual disputes rather than by going through the regulation process. The National Labor Relations Board is one such agency. The Labor Management Relations Act is a detailed statute; rather than add additional regulations, the board and appointed hearing officers hear disputes under that act. The records of these proceedings are kept much in the manner of records of court proceedings. They form the basis of future rulings by the board and its hearing officers, as does the doctrine of *stare decisis* in the courts of law.

Process of Adjudication

After investigating a suspected rule violation, an agency may decide to file an administrative complaint against a party. An agency action may be prompted by complaints from private individuals or interest groups. For example, consumers who believe they were cheated often base FTC actions on alleged false advertising on a series of complaints.

Administrative Hearing

An administrative adjudication is somewhat similar to a trial. A lawyer may represent the charged party. Agency witnesses may be cross-examined, and evidence to counter that of the agency may be offered. There are, however, significant differences between an administrative hearing and a trial; for example, because there is no jury, the hearing officer decides both questions of law and of fact.

After the case is concluded, the ALJ gives an initial order, which may be appealed by either side. The appeal is made to the board or commission that governs the agency. Some boards consider all aspects of the case anew, as though no ALJ decision existed. Alternatively, the appeal may be taken to a federal court. The period in which one decides whether to appeal is usually very short.

If no appeal is taken, or if it is unsuccessful, the ALJ's initial order becomes the final order of the agency. If it is successfully appealed, the final order may come from the agency or from the decision of a reviewing court.

A final order may compel a party to pay monetary damages. In the alternative, a **cease-and-desist** order may forbid some specified activity. Such an order is similar to a court injunction. An ALJ may also order an agency to reinstate benefits previously denied by the agency.

Over a period of several months, three deaths occurred in a steel mill owned by USX Corp. The employees died by being burned, crushed, and

The ABA Administrative Procedure Database was developed and is maintained with the cooperation and support of the American Bar Association's Section of Administrative Law and Regulatory Practice and the Florida State University College of Law.
http://www.law.fsu.edu/library/admin/

http://

---

*Administrative law judges are usually attorneys. Sometimes they are employees of the very agency prosecuting the case. Certain safeguards exist to promote fairness in the proceedings. The ALJ is separated in the agency's organization from the investigative and prosecutorial staff. Private communication between the ALJ and anyone who is a party to an agency proceeding while the matter is pending is forbidden.

suffocated. The Occupational Safety and Health Administration (OSHA)—an administrative arm of the U.S. Department of Labor—was asked to investigate. After a finding of safety violations, OSHA recommended fines of $7.3 million. Does OSHA have the power to assess and collect these fines without USX having an opportunity to contest OSHA's findings?[23]

No. Although the agency has power to impose a fine, it cannot deny USX the opportunity to have a fact-finding hearing before an ALJ. However, at this particular hearing, USX pleaded guilty to the violations and promised to rectify the problem and follow OSHA's recommendations. The negotiated plea resulted in a much-reduced fine. Critics of such plea-bargaining* are answered by OSHA's declaration that it does not necessarily want violators punished; rather, it wants the safety problems corrected. OSHA's job is to make the workplace safer, not to raise money.

Due Process in Administrative Hearings

When do parties have a right to an administrative hearing? What government actions can be questioned in an administrative hearing? If you have a right to a hearing, what form does it take? Just as due process must be observed in hearings on new rules, it must also be observed in hearings on individual cases. In such cases, the ALJ or hearing examiner or officer has the powers of a regular judge in the conduct of a trial, and counsel may represent both the agency and the defendant. There is no jury, and the rules of evidence are usually relaxed in an administrative hearing. For example, hearsay evidence is usually admissible.

The ALJ's decision includes written findings of fact and of law, conclusions, and exceptions taken by the opposition. The agency has persuasive powers and may impose civil sanctions, suspension, cancellation or denial of licenses, confiscation of contraband, and other penalties. Any jail or prison sentence requires a conventional court trial.

Kelly was a New York City resident receiving welfare benefits under the federal program Aid to Families with Dependent Children (AFDC). The New York City Social Service agency, which was responsible for administering the program, terminated her benefits. The agency told Kelly that she could request an informal review meeting and a formal hearing. She sued, claiming she had a right to a hearing before her AFDC benefits were terminated. Does Kelly have a right to a hearing *before* the AFDC benefits are terminated?

Yes. The U.S. Supreme Court held that where benefits are a matter of statutory entitlement, the importance to the recipient must be weighed against the state's interest in efficient and expedient processes. As welfare benefits provide food, clothing, and shelter, Kelly had a right to a hearing before termination. Under the

*To plea-bargain is to agree to plead guilty to a crime on the promise of leniency in sentencing, or to agree to plead guilty to a lesser crime to avoid paying the penalty of a more severe crime. The plea-bargain removes the need for expensive and prolonged trials.

Fourteenth Amendment to the U.S. Constitution, the state may not "deprive any person of life, liberty or property without due process of law. . . ."[24] Here the court held that a termination of benefits without a prior termination hearing denied Kelly due process.

Since the *Kelly* case, the courts have attempted to balance the individual's interest and that of government. The question to be answered in every case is similar: If a government action adversely affects someone, does the person have a right to have the action independently reviewed? Accordingly, agencies normally offer to hold a preliminary hearing when the agency's contemplated action would deny a person some license, right, or privilege.

Closely related to the question of whether a person can demand a hearing is the inquiry as to what type of hearing it must be. Government agencies engage in literally millions of activities every day. How are citizens to be protected from arbitrary treatment without paralyzing the government's ability to make decisions and act effectively and efficiently? As stated by one commentator, "The fundamental policy problem of the administrative process is how to design a system of checks which will minimize the risks of bureaucratic arbitrariness and overreaching, while preserving for the agencies the flexibility they need to act effectively."[25]

At both the federal and state levels, statutes provide for hearings and often define their nature, while allowing procedures that provide greater rights to the aggrieved than those constitutionally required. At the federal level, the APA lists minimum requirements, including provisos (1) that a party must be given timely notice of the time, place, and nature of any hearing; (2) that the legal authority and jurisdiction under which the hearing is held must be stated; and (3) that the matters of fact and law claimed by the agency must be true.[26]

Judge Henry Friendly,[27] in an influential article published several years ago, identified 11 attributes of a fair hearing. While not all of these attributes are constitutionally required, many of them are what an American citizen expects as fair treatment not only from government but also from any large organization. With some editorial license, Judge Friendly's list is reproduced with a brief discussion and comparison of how each attribute affects an administrative hearing and contrasts with court processes:

1. *An unbiased tribunal.* In a court proceeding, a tribunal is a neutral court with a judge and/or jury deciding a case. In the usual administrative hearing, an agency employee who was not a party to the original decision is considered sufficiently unbiased. Should a trained neutral person independent of the agency be required? Generally the hearing officer or ALJ is required to be neutral, but he or she can work for and be paid by the agency.

2. *Notice of the proposed action and the grounds for the action.* In a judicial process, a complaint and summons are used to notify the party sued of the nature of the adverse claim. In an administrative action, some statement is expected about what government action is proposed, along with the legal reasons for the action.

3. *An opportunity to present reasons why the proposed action should not be taken.* Fundamental to all fair processes is an opportunity to tell, and justify with evidence, your view of the facts to the person reviewing the decision.

4.   *The right to call witnesses.* In a court trial, you have the right to subpoena witnesses. This means you can force a witness to attend your trial. While a party to an administrative hearing can call witnesses, the ability to compel their attendance is not always a legally enforceable right.

5.   *To know the evidence against you.* A person subject to a government action should be aware of all evidence used by the ALJ to make the decision. A hearing officer or ALJ should not receive evidence or opinions without sharing that information with the affected party. In administrative hearings, there are some situations where parties are not allowed to know all evidence against them. For example, a hearing to discipline a prisoner is an administrative hearing, but if testimony used to discipline the prisoner were provided to the prisoner, the adverse witness could face reprisals.

6.   *To have a decision based on evidence presented at the hearing.* If the decision is based on information presented at the hearing, then one has the opportunity to rebut it. If the ALJ makes a decision on facts learned outside the hearing, the claimant is denied a fair opportunity to contest the information. This right is almost always required.

7.   *Counsel.* Most administrative hearings will allow counsel but will not pay for it. Also, unlike in court proceedings, counsel is not required to have legal training.

8.   *Making of a record.* If a written record is not available, how can an unfair hearing be contested?

Darren R., father of Krista R. (a handicapped child), sought an administrative hearing to resolve a complaint he had made about the education provided for his daughter. Dissatisfied with the outcome of the hearing, he decided to sue the State Board of Education in federal court. In preparation, he requested that a written transcript of the administrative hearing be provided to him at government expense. His request was refused. Does he have a right to a free transcription of the recorded hearing?[28]

Trial courts provide verbatim records of trial, and so do some (but not all) administrative agencies. But what form does this record need to take—should it be summarized in writing, stenotyped (machine shorthand), or videotaped? The physical record in administrative hearings varies; all types of records are used by the different agencies. Audiocassette records are the most common. In the case upon which this gavel was based, the plaintiff was provided a verbatim taped recording of the administrative hearing. Dissatisfied, the plaintiff asserted that he was indigent and could not afford to pay the $3,000 fee to transcribe the tape. The statute authorizing this type of hearing allowed for an electronic record to be provided. The court rejected the plaintiff's contention that due process demanded a transcription for indigents. "The decision by Congress to give the states the option of maintaining a record by either electronic recording or written means is rational. It accomplishes the fundamental purpose of preserving a record, which might otherwise not be done, but spares the states the additional expense of transcribing the record. Congress could have felt this was as far as it wanted to go."[29]

9. *Statement of reasons for the decision.* If reasons for a decision are given, faulty reasoning can be challenged and appealed. If reasons are not given, how can a decision be appealed? A statement of reasons, even though brief, is usually expected as part of the administrative hearing process.

10. *Public attendance.* Open attendance in court trials is based on the general belief that the activities of government officials should be open to the public to protect individuals from possible abuse of government power. In administrative hearings, open attendance may be allowed, but often it is not.

11. *Judicial review.* As with court decisions, results of administrative hearings can also be appealed. Experience has shown, however, that courts seldom overturn administrative rulings or actions. Usually, the best chance for a successful appeal is within the agency. When appeals are taken outside the agency, courts involved are more likely to grant relief if the agency had violated due process in some way. Courts seldom challenge agency interpretation and application of the facts, because the agency is presumed to have expertise in the application of the facts presented.

Can an Administrative Agency Use ADR Processes?

In 1996, Congress made permanent a statutory scheme that began as an experiment in 1990. The Administrative Dispute Resolution Act and the Negotiated Rulemaking Act allow government agencies to use arbitration to decide disputes otherwise headed for administrative hearing or the courts. Use of mediation and other dispute resolution processes is provided for and encouraged. The law also approved the use of a negotiated rulemaking process discussed earlier in the chapter as an alternative to the usual regulatory rulemaking process.[30]

> Information on alternative dispute resolution in the administrative process can be found at http://www.adr.org/adminlaw.html

CONTROL OF ADMINISTRATIVE AGENCIES

Agency authority is held in check in several ways, some of which already have been discussed. The U.S. Constitution provides limits on agency authority, and so does the APA, which significantly affects the formal administrative process. The source of agency authority, the enabling statute, is also a limitation. Political control over agency power resides in both the executive and legislative branches of government. Judicial control is exercised by the independent review of agency action by the courts.

An example of political control over an administrative agency is the ability of Congress to amend the statute that defines agency power. Congress can specifically take away a power. Political control is also exercised through the budget process. The amount of money provided an agency in the yearly budget has as much influence over the agency as any formal control. Thus, the president, with the annual budget request, and Congress, in the appropriation legislation, dramatically affect an agency's ability to perform any task.

JUDICIAL REVIEW

The courts, with ultimate power to declare the law, provide a direct avenue for the review of agency action. However, not all agency action is held by the courts to be subject to judicial review. Nor does every individual have a right to challenge an agency's actions.

Scope of Judicial Review

The APA allows judicial review of most agency actions. This means that a court may prevent or undo any unauthorized action by an agency. Likewise, courts may compel agency action that has been unlawfully withheld. In reviewing administrative actions, courts are reluctant to review questions of fact—a deference based partly on the judicial attitude that those who hear and see the evidence firsthand are best able to evaluate it. Also, the agency is considered an expert in the topic it hears and, as such, usually is more knowledgeable about the topic contested than a reviewing judge would be. Finally, courts generally believe that wholesale review of agency actions would destroy the value of the more efficient agency process and worsen the problem of already crowded court calendars.

A *de novo* **review** (new proceeding) will, however, be granted if (1) a review is required by statute, (2) the agency's fact-finding proceeding was inadequate, or (3) new facts not heard in the original proceeding are to be raised.

Party Defenses to Agency Enforcement

The following are the broad bases for a defense to an agency action:

1. The agency exceeded the authority conferred on it by the agency's enabling legislation.
2. The agency improperly interpreted laws applicable to the agency action under review.
3. The agency violated a constitutional provision.
4. The agency acted in violation of the procedural requirements.
5. The agency acted in a manner that was arbitrary, capricious, or constituted an abuse of discretion.
6. The conclusion drawn by the agency was not supported by substantial evidence.

Parties seeking to have an agency action reviewed must satisfy several preliminary requirements, some of which are discussed here.

Environmentalists persuaded a court to require the Nuclear Regulatory Commission to reconsider its decision to grant an operating license to the Vermont Yankee Nuclear Power Corporation. The court held that the NRC was not adequately considering the dangers of nuclear fuel reprocessing and nuclear waste management. The NRC appealed to the U.S.

Supreme Court, claiming that the lower court had no power to interfere in the administrative process. Could the lower court legally interfere?

No. The courts do not have power to prescribe procedures that regulatory agencies must follow; at most, they may analyze whether the agency followed its own procedures and gathered sufficient evidence to support its actions. "Congress has made a choice to at least try nuclear energy, establishing a reasonable review process in which the courts are to play only a limited role," said the Supreme Court. A change, if any, must come from Congress. The courts should not attempt "to impose upon the agency [their] own notion of which procedures are best or most likely to further some vague, undefined public good."[31]

Reviewability

Arbitrary or capricious actions by agencies, or conflicts with basic law, will evoke responses from the courts. The challenger, or plaintiff, must show that the action is reviewable. The APA provides that the action of each agency of the government of the United States is subject to judicial review, except where there is a clear statutory prohibition of review. An enabling statute may restrict the scope of review as well as prohibit it.

The duties of the Port Authority of New York and New Jersey include the operation of the John F. Kennedy International Airport in New York City. When British and French airlines sought landing rights at the airport for their supersonic Concorde jet transports, residents in the vicinity of the airport protested because of an anticipated increase of noise. The Port Authority delayed in developing noise standards, but meanwhile banned the planes. British Airways sued, claiming the Port Authority's ban exceeded its powers and was unfair under the circumstances. The Port Authority was ordered by the court to permit Concorde flights immediately. The Port Authority appealed to the U.S. Supreme Court for a stay of the order, stopping or holding it in abeyance. Did the Supreme Court uphold the administrative agency in its ban on Concorde landings?

No. The application for stay was denied, and Concorde flights began. Administrative agencies must act reasonably or the courts can override their decisions, as here.[32] Prescribed procedures for review of an agency action are normally available within the agency itself. Despite the decision in the Port Authority case, recall that courts normally do not overrule agency decisions because, as discussed previously, agencies are recognized as experts in their fields.

Standing

The challenging party must have "standing to sue." **Standing** requires that a challenger have a direct stake in the outcome of the judicial proceeding. This direct interest can be shown if the challenger has been substantially affected by the agency's action. An injury to an economic interest, or even in some cases to an emotional, environmental, or aesthetic interest, is sufficient to show standing to sue. One reason for the requirement of standing to sue is to discourage petty lawsuits. The courts will require that a plaintiff show an actual injury by, or because of, an agency action. Protest lawsuits or lawsuits from taxpayers who are simply angry about some government action are dismissed because of lack of standing to sue.

The Trustees of the Loudoun County Library instituted a policy to block access to sexually explicit material through the library's publicly provided Internet access sites. An association of library patrons, Mainstream Loudoun, challenged the blocking policy and sued the Library Trustees. The Library Trustees defended on several bases, among them that "neither the individual plaintiffs nor Mainstream Loudoun have suffered an actual injury as a result of the Policy. Specifically . . . no member of Mainstream Loudoun has attempted to access blocked Internet materials in Loudoun County libraries, or petitioned a library to unblock a blocked site." Does Mainstream Loudoun have standing to sue the Library Trustees?

The court said Mainstream Loudoun had standing to sue. The complaint contradicted the Library Trustees claim, stating that several members *had* attempted to access blocked sites. For an association to have standing to sue on behalf of its members, "(1) its own members would have standing to sue in their own right; (2) the interests the organization seeks to protect are germane to the organization's purpose; and (3) neither the claim nor the relief sought requires the participation of the individual members in the lawsuit." All three criteria were found to exist.[33]

Exhaustion of Available Remedies

Courts are reluctant to interfere with the regulatory process, hoping the agency will correct its own mistakes. Until recently courts had been unwilling to review an action until the challenging party had exhausted all possible alternative means of resolving the controversy within the agency. In other words, a person seeking administrative relief or challenging an administrative ruling was expected to "exhaust available administrative remedies" before resorting to the courts. This stance, however, has come under challenge.

Darby was a South Carolina real estate developer specializing in the development and management of multifamily rental projects. In the 1980s, working with a mortgage banker's plan, Darby was able to obtain mortgage insurance from the Department of Housing and Urban Development (HUD). The plan was later determined to be inconsistent with a Department "Rule of Seven." The assistant secretary proposed to debar (suspend) Darby from further participation in HUD programs. Darby contested the suspension but, following an administrative hearing, an ALJ upheld an 18-month debarment from all federal programs. Darby failed to request a review from the HUD secretary within 15 days of receipt of the ALJ's determination. He later sought a judicial review of the ALJ's action. Did Darby's failure to avail himself of a HUD secretary review forestall his right to judicial review?

No. In a decision that surprised many administrative law scholars, the Supreme Court held that under the APA a plaintiff need not exhaust available administrative remedies unless a statute or specific agency rule requires it, and in this case none did. "It perhaps is surprising that it has taken over 45 years since the passage of the APA for this Court definitively to address this question. But where the APA applies, an appeal to 'superior agency authority' is a prerequisite to judicial review only when expressly required by statute or when an agency rule requires appeal before review and the administrative action is made inoperative pending that review."[34]

Knowledge of the requirement is still important because the law often requires that administrative options be exhausted before seeking judicial relief at both the federal and state level.

PUBLIC ACCOUNTABILITY

Several federal laws make agencies accessible and accountable to the public. The most significant of these public scrutiny laws are the Freedom of Information Act, the Government-in-the-Sunshine Act, and the Regulatory Flexibility Act.

Freedom of Information Act (FOIA)

The **Freedom of Information Act (FOIA)** requires that the federal government disclose most "records" to "any person" on request. Under the act government agencies are expected to publish most statements of policy and staff manuals that affect the public and are not already published in the *Federal Register*. Agencies are also required to indicate from whom and how much unpublished information may be obtained. The person requesting the information need not disclose why it is wanted. Certain records, such as information related to security risks or ongoing criminal investigations, are not retrievable. The news media and business firms make the most frequent requests under the FOIA. A refusal by a government agency to comply with a request or to provide requested information could be challenged in court.

Government-in-the-Sunshine Act

The **Government-in-the-Sunshine Act** prohibits secret agency meetings. It is an open-meeting law. Not only must most meetings of federal agencies be open for public observation, but advance notice must also be given of the meetings, along with the expected topics of discussion. Administrative hearings are not covered by the Sunshine Act, so they are conducted in private.

Regulatory Flexibility Act — glossary

The **Regulatory Flexibility Act** requires that whenever a new regulation will have a "significant impact upon a substantial number of small businesses," the agency must conduct a "flexibility analysis." This means that the agency must estimate and disclose the cost of the rule on small businesses. It must also consider any less burdensome alternatives. The act requires notice to small businesses about the proposed regulations.

SOME LEADING AREAS OF ADMINISTRATIVE AGENCY LAWMAKING

There are several broad areas where the administrative process of lawmaking and enforcement is especially important. Every regulatory agency was created in response to a specific need. Although critics abound, hardly anyone proposes abolition of all government regulation and control. The net result is a rejection of *laissez-faire* (French: "allow to act") capitalism and the substitution of a mixed economy in which government and private, profit-seeking businesses are closely interrelated.

BUSINESS FINANCE

Some areas of business greatly affect the economy and hence the general welfare; yet, if left alone, they are subject to abuse by unscrupulous and greedy manipulators. The government's response to this problem was the creation of three federal agencies: the Securities and Exchange Commission (SEC), The Commodity Futures Trading Commission (CFTC), and the Federal Reserve Board.

The SEC (1934)[35] regulates organized securities markets and the securities traded there. Securities law and regulations were established to provide purchasers of stock with enough information to make informed judgments about those purchases. Since its inception the SEC has required corporations to provide ample information to prospective investors. If information is not provided, or if the information provided is misleading or incorrect, the corporation—its directors and officers or its promoters—may be legally responsible to the buyers for losses suffered as a result. The SEC also regulates investment advisors. In 1997, the SEC responded and provided assistance to 48,169 complaints and inquiries from the public about the relations with security investment advisors.[36]

The CFTC (1974)[37] is similar to the SEC; it attempts to prevent manipulation, abusive trade practices, and fraud on commodity futures and option markets. Like the SEC, the CFTC regulates the futures professionals who trade in these markets.

The Federal Reserve Board (1913)[38] supervises and regulates most of the nation's banks and helps to set important national policies on extension of credit and supply of money in an effort to provide stability to the U.S. financial system and markets. The Federal Reserve Board provides various financial services to the U.S. government, financial institutions, and official foreign financial institutions.

The following press release provides a graphic example of the power of the FDIC to regulate and control financial markets. (The merger mentioned in the press release also required approval of the Department of Justice and resulted in the creation—at the time—of the largest U.S. bank.)

FDIC Press Release

Release Date: August 17, 1998

The Federal Reserve Board today announced its approval of the proposal of NationsBank Corporation, Charlotte, North Carolina, to merge with Bank-America Corporation, San Francisco, California, and thereby acquire all of Bank-America's bank, nonbank, and foreign subsidiaries.[39]

http://

Information on the Commodities Future Trading Commission can be found at http://www.cftc.gov/

COMMUNICATIONS

It is hard to imagine a more dynamic challenge to appropriate federal regulation than the topic of communications. When the last edition of this textbook was prepared, the Internet was mentioned twice in the entire textbook. The growth in just this one area of communications is utterly astounding. Add the growth of cellular phones and changes in the telephone market and you can quickly see the challenges existing in communications.

The Federal Communications Commission (FCC), established in 1934,[40] regulates communications across state and international borders in the attempt to maintain order where otherwise there would be chaos. The FCC oversees interstate and international communications by radio, television, wire, satellite, and cable. The following quote from the FCC chairperson captures some of the challenges facing this agency:

> When debate on the Telecommunications Act of 1996 took place, the Internet was only just beginning to emerge as a phenomenon in telecommunications. Most anyone who connected to a commercial online service did so at a mere 9600 bits per second. Building Web pages for a living seemed a risky proposition. If you wanted to buy a book from Barnes and Noble, you had to drive there. Today you can surf there. And even better, on the Net you've got a choice between Barnes and Noble or Amazon.com without leaving your home. Even as I speak, there are thousands of Americans who already are banking electronically from home, or acting as their own stock brokers, or buying their own airline tickets and choosing their own seats—all online. This year revenues from e-commerce are expected to be around $20 billion. That number is expected to grow to $350 billion in four years. In simple terms, this means more jobs and billions of dollars of growth added to the nation's economic output.[41]

Proposals to regulate the Internet are being considered as you read this text. Among issues under consideration are those involving pornography, copyright, spamming, credit, and gambling, to name but a few. To the extent anyone regulates the Internet, the FCC does.

The Cable Television Consumer Protection and Competition Act of 1992[42] authorizes the FCC and local city and county governments to regulate certain activities of the cable television industry. The law allows for the regulation of pricing (ensuring that cable rates are reasonable), the retransmission of local broadcasts, the requirement that certain technical standards are met, and for competition with microwave and satellite services and equipment.

The FCC regulates wire and radio communications common carriers, such as telephone and telegraph. The FCC also licenses radio and telephone circuits and assigns frequencies for their operation. The agency is responsible for all domestic wireless telecommunications programs, except those involving satellite communications including cellular services, personal communications services (PCS), paging, specialized mobile radio services, air-to-ground services, and basic exchange telecommunications radio services.

EMPLOYMENT PRACTICES

The complexities of fair employment practices led to the establishment of the National Labor Relations Board (NLRB) in 1935[43] to supervise union representation elections and to police relations between unions and management in order to prevent unfair practices by either. The Equal Employment Opportunity Commission (EEOC) was established in 1964[44] to investigate and resolve complaints of discrimination filed by employees, generally based on color, race, or sex, but also on religion, national origin, advanced age, and disabilities. The Pension and Welfare Programs Office of the Labor Department was established to enforce the Employee Retirement Income Security Act (ERISA), established in 1974,[45] which governs the integrity and fairness of private pension plans that supplement social security.

ENERGY

The organization chart for the Federal Energy Regulatory Commission (FERC) can be found at http://www.ferc.fed.us/intro/org2.htm

The United States is one of many highly energy-dependent nations. The major burden of meeting the country's energy needs has fallen on the Federal Energy Regulatory Commission (FERC) [1973][46] of the Department of Energy. Established in 1973, FERC is responsible for the following energy industries: electric utilities, hydropower facilities, and natural gas and oil pipelines. In recent years, FERC has implemented the Energy Policy Act of 1992, the purpose of which has been to reduce barriers to competition in the electric power industry.

Nuclear energy is regulated by the Nuclear Regulatory Commission (NRC), which was created by the Energy Reorganization Act of 1974[47] to ensure adequate protection of the public health and safety, the common defense and security, and the environment in the use of nuclear materials in the United States. The NRC licenses and supervises nuclear power plant reactors; research, test, and training reactors; and medical, academic, and industrial uses of nuclear materials. A major issue not dealt with in the late twentieth century has been the transport, storage, and disposal of nuclear materials and waste, a task also under the jurisdiction of the NRC.

The Nuclear Regulatory Commission itself was subject to investigation by at least six separate federal, state, and private groups after a frightening accident in March 1979 that caused an emergency shutdown of the Three Mile Island, Pennsylvania, nuclear power plant. A comprehensive study was made by a special 12-member presidential commission that made 44 recommendations, including one to abolish the 5-member NRC and replace it with an independent agency headed by a chief administrator with power to act quickly.

The NRC responded to the report by proposing that future nuclear power plants not be built near major population centers and that operating licenses be issued only after the states concerned have adopted emergency evacuation plans approved by the Federal Emergency Management Agency.[48] Obviously, the NRC has not been replaced, as recommended by the report.

ENVIRONMENT

Cattle feedlots and large poultry and pig farms produce polluted water that runs off into lakes and streams. Some pollutants may leach into ground waters as well. For years the federal Environment Protection

Agency (EPA) has regulated the discharge from factories, sewage treatment plants, and other nonagricultural sources into the nation's waterways. Can existing regulations be expanded to include agricultural pollution?[49]

Yes. In the twentieth century, the world has become heavily populated, urbanized, and industrialized. Consequently, the earth's capacity to handle the pollution being discharged into the air and water has become a major concern. In fact, the waste produced by industrial society has threatened and continues to threaten the existence of human life. There is a constant tension between the business goals of increasing profits and productivity and the social need to maintain and, where necessary, restore clean air and water. In the past 30 years, statutory and administrative laws that try to balance business goals with the need to protect the environment have become known as **environmental law**, an important and expanding type of government regulation.

In 1970, the Environmental Protection Agency (EPA) was created to coordinate federal regulation of environmental issues. This is the organization that administers most federal environmental policies and statutes. Federal laws provide the basis for issuing regulations to control pollution coming primarily from factories and motor vehicles. Stationary sources include electric utilities and industrial plants. The EPA sets air quality standards for major pollutants to protect vegetation, visibility, and certain economic conditions, as well as the breathability of the air. Regulations governing exhaust gases from automobiles are also included. Exhibit 5–3 is the formal statement of purpose of the Environmental Protection Agency.

The National Environmental Policy Act (NEPA) of 1969 requires that all federal agencies consider the environment when making important decisions. For every major federal action that significantly affects the quality of the environment, an **environmental impact statement (EIS)** must be prepared, analyzing the impact on the environment of the federal action and indicating alternatives

The EPA's twenty-fifth anniversary report can be found at http://www.epa.gov/oppe/25year/

Exhibit 5–3: EPA Statement of Purpose

The EPA's purpose is to ensure that:

- All Americans are protected from significant risks to human health and the environment where they live, learn, and work.
- National efforts to reduce environmental risk are based on the best available scientific information.
- Federal laws protecting human health and the environment are enforced fairly and effectively.
- Environmental protection is an integral consideration in U.S. policies concerning natural resources, human health, economic growth, energy, transportation, agriculture, industry, and international trade, and these factors are similarly considered in establishing environmental policy.
- All parts of society—communities, individuals, business, state and local governments, tribal governments—have access to accurate information sufficient to effectively participate in managing human health and environmental risks.
- Environmental protection contributes to making our communities and ecosystems diverse, sustainable, and economically productive.
- The United States plays a leadership role in working with other nations to protect the global environment.[50]

that might be taken. For example, building a new nuclear reactor involves federal action because a federal license is required. An EIS must analyze the project's impact on the environment. It must detail any anticipated adverse effects and alternative actions that might be taken. Environmental impact statements have become instruments by which private citizens, consumer interest groups, businesses, and others can challenge federal agency action that may harm the environment.

The Clean Water Act of 1972 established these goals and standards: (1) make waters safe for swimming, (2) protect fish and wildlife, and (3) eliminate the discharge of pollutants into the water. Federal regulations require a permit for dumping refuse into navigable waterways. The parties who need to dump refuse are directed to use the best available technology to minimize the possible harmful effects.

The Federal Insecticide, Fungicide, and Rodenticide Act (FIFRA) of 1947 as amended requires that pesticides and herbicides be (1) registered before they can be sold, (2) certified and used only for approved applications, and (3) used in limited quantities when applied to food crops. If a substance is identified as harmful, the EPA can cancel its registration after a hearing. If the harm is immediate, the EPA can suspend registration pending the hearing. The EPA may also inspect factories in which these chemicals are manufactured.

The Resource Conservation and Recovery Act (RCRA) of 1976 as amended provides the EPA with the authority to monitor and control hazardous waste disposal. Regulations require all producers of hazardous waste materials to label and package properly any hazardous waste to be transported.

The Comprehensive Environmental Response, Compensation, and Liability Act of 1980 (CERCLA), commonly known as *Superfund*, regulates the cleanup of leaking hazardous waste disposal sites. The act created a special federal fund for this purpose. The EPA can recover the cost of the cleanup from (1) the person who generated the wastes disposed of at the site, (2) the person who transported the wastes to the site, (3) the person who owned or operated the site at the time of the disposal, or (4) the current owner or operator.

FREE ENTERPRISE

The Federal Trade Commission (FTC), established in 1914,[51] shares watchdog duties with the Antitrust Division of the Justice Department in enforcing the federal laws against price fixing, monopolistic mergers, and various unfair trade practices. Maintenance of an open market with true freedom of enterprise remains an ongoing challenge. For many decades, the temptation to collaborate with competitors to allocate markets and fix prices has been irresistible for corporations in many fields.

The Superior Court Trial Lawyers Association of Washington, D.C. (SCTLA) went on a one-month strike for higher wages (higher hourly rates). SCTLA members are counselors in the criminal area (i.e., criminal lawyers) in private practice. They are registered with courts, indicating their availability to represent indigent defendants in cases assigned by the court.

After an investigation and hearing, the FTC ruled that the SCTLA boycott was illegal and barred any future, similar action. SCTLA appealed. A federal appeals court ordered the FTC to reconsider its decision and determine if the SCTLA had sufficient control of the market to make its boycott anticompetitive. The FTC appealed to the Supreme Court of the United States. Should the FTC be compelled to reconsider its ruling?

No. The Supreme Court said, "The social justification[s] proffered for [this] restraint of trade . . . do not make it any less unlawful." The Court here applies the toughest antitrust rule, the *per se* (in itself) rule. This means that the Court recognizes that some business activities, such as price fixing, are so anticompetitive that they are automatically (*per se*) prohibited. Thus these activities do not require proof that conspirators (in this case, SCTLA members) had a motive, or power, to control the market. The Supreme Court upheld the FTC ruling overturning the appeals court order and held that the SCTLA strike was inherently illegal. Therefore, evidence of SCTLA power to control the market was not required.[52]

TRANSPORTATION

According to economists, a transportation network is second only to education as a prerequisite for a productive society. Yet the technical complexities involved in such a system are beyond the range of skill and knowledge possessed by legislators or judges; regulators must have specialized technical education and typically make lifetime careers in the field.

The Department of Transportation (DOT) regulates the levels of service and rates of interstate railroads, common carrier truckers, and some waterway carriers. DOT also regulates airlines, although in recent years air carriers have had considerable freedom in route selection, level of service, and rate making. The Federal Maritime Commission (1936)[53] regulates ocean-going U.S. ships.

The Federal Aviation Administration (FAA), established in 1958,[54] regulates the manufacture of airplanes by certifying airworthiness, and also licenses pilots. Indirectly but vitally involved in transportation regulation is the National Highway Traffic Safety Administration (NHTSA).[55] Established in 1970, the NHTSA regulates quality and design in the manufacture of motor vehicles and tires in the interest of safety for drivers and passengers. The agency also sets and then enforces safety performance standards for motor vehicles and items of motor vehicle equipment. Information gathered by the NHTSA through its investigations and receipts of consumer complaints leads to several automobile safety recalls every year. Exhibit 5–4 is a recall notice made in 1998 of one of the most popular automobile models in America.

The automobile manufacturer is expected to notify customers of the safety defect and to make arrangements for appropriate repairs or modifications of the vehicle.

Other Areas

The foregoing discussion identifies many of the leading independent federal administrative agencies, but it is far from complete. Excluded, for example, are numerous federal offices or departments with administrative powers, as well as even more numerous state and local agencies and offices that make and apply administrative law. For example, administrative bodies at the state level usually supervise licensed trade and professional occupations, hospitals, nursing homes,

Exhibit 5–4:   Recall Notice from NHTSA

Toyota   **Years:**
Camry   **1994**
Number Involved: 104,928
Dates of Manufacture: April 1993–August 1994
NHTSA Recall No.: 98V155
Vehicle Description:
Description of Defect: The steering wheel set nut may not have been suffi-
ciently tightened, causing steering vibration and looseness. The nut can eventually
come off, allowing the steering wheel to separate from the steering shaft, loss of
vehicle control, and increasing the risk of a vehicle crash.
Remedy: Dealers will re-tighten the steering set nut.
Owner Notification: Owner notification was expected to begin during August
1998. Owners who do not receive the free remedy within a reasonable time should
contact Toyota at 1-800-331-4331.

and retirement facilities. When state legislatures made employers absolutely liable for injuries to workers suffered on the job under workers' compensation,
they created special administrative commissions to conduct necessary hearings
and make the required determination of injuries and of benefits payable.

At the local level, zoning decisions, variances from established standards,
and environmental impact statements are all under the surveillance and control
of agencies with powers to make administrative law.

Bradley Yance is a visionary investor in land. He often quotes the late Will
Rogers: "Invest in land; they ain't making any more of it." Bradley predicts that the city will expand mostly to the flat farmlands to the east.
Accordingly, over a period of 30 years he acquired a block of 2,000 acres,
which was eventually intersected by two superhighways. Bradley plans
to build a major shopping center on one side of the main road, with an
"edge" of three-story apartments and condominiums, and then a large
area of single family dwellings. On the other side of the main road, he
plans to build an industrial park for light industry, to be served by truck,
train, and helicopter. The time seems ripe for development. Will he be
able to go ahead with his ambitious project?

Not necessarily. Most large cities and counties have administrative bodies, such
as zoning commissions and planning boards that draft master plans for real estate development. Exercising the police power of government, they may unilaterally decide that certain areas shall remain agricultural and others shall become
residential, commercial, or industrial. Their decisions must be arrived at reasonably and after public hearings; but, in the final analysis, their judgment as experts
prevails, even though it may disappoint many and enriches a few. Haphazard development is economically wasteful and socially objectionable. Bradley Yance
will have to yield to the opinion of the administrators as to appropriate land use.

CASE

If your university is a public institution, then the due-process rules applicable to administrative agencies and discussed in the chapter apply to your school. If you are accused of cheating or otherwise run afoul of university administrators or, dare we say it, professors, you can expect certain minimum protection from expulsion or other treatment detrimental to your continued beneficial enrollment. The following case discusses due-process protections available in such a hearing. Consider the case in reference to the discussion of Judge Friendly's article on pages 205–207. If your university is a private school, you will probably find that it has provided rules very similar to those available at public institutions. Due-process protections are minimum requirements, and both public and private universities are free to provide more expansive protections—and they often do.

Nash v. Auburn University
812 F.2d 655 (11th Cir. 1987)

Two students, David Nash and Donna Perry, were accused of cheating on their anatomy examinations at Auburn University's School of Veterinary Medicine. At a university hearing to determine the merits of the charge, faculty members and student witnesses testified that they observed Nash and Perry examining specimens together in laboratory examinations and moving together from question to question at those exams. At the exams, Nash and Perry were seen suspiciously to signal each other and to exchange glances; on written exams, they were seen to look on each other's papers. Appellants frequently sat together at written exams in seats not assigned to them at the rear of the exam rooms. The students were suspended from the university at the conclusion of the hearing. Nash and Perry filed suit, arguing that Auburn University suspended them based on constitutionally inadequate procedures that violated their rights under the due-process clause of the Fourteenth Amendment. The U.S. District Court for the Middle District of Alabama entered judgment in favor of the university, and the students appealed. The Court of Appeals agreed with the District Court, holding that the students were provided with a fair hearing—notwithstanding the lack of advance notice of statements from accusing witnesses and the lack of opportunity to directly cross-examine witnesses. The court also

ruled that the students had been given adequate time to prepare for the disciplinary hearing.

Senior District Judge James E. Doyle delivered the opinion of the Court: Appellants were advised in writing on June 6, 1985, that they were charged with a violation of the Student Code of Professional Ethics (the code) of the Auburn University School of Veterinary Medicine. They were given "at least 72 hours to prepare a defense for the charge of academic dishonesty, in that while taking examinations during the 1984–1985 school year, information was allegedly obtained in an unethical manner." Appellants appeared with counsel at the hearing [and] objected that the notice was inadequate and too general to advise them of the charge[s]. [Counsel] requested a more specific notice and one additional day to prepare their defense. The following day each appellant received a written memorandum, dated June 11, 1985, advising them that they were charged with a violation of the code in "giving or receiving assistance or communication between students during the anatomy examination given on or about May 16, 1985." Included in the memorandum was a list of students and anatomy faculty witnesses who were expected to testify at the hearing in support of the charge against appellants.

A disciplinary hearing . . . was held on June 12, 1985. Both Nash and Perry attended, in the company of their attorney. The hearing was conducted by the non-voting student chancellor of the board, in the presence of appellants, witnesses, and student justices. There was no attorney for the board present. The chancellor allowed appellants' counsel to advise his clients during the hearing, but he was not permitted to participate in the proceedings. Appellants were to be allowed to question the adverse witnesses by directing their questions to the chancellor, who would then pose their questions to the witnesses.

After all of the testimony was presented supporting the charge, appellants were granted a short recess and then given an opportunity to present their defense. Appellants were allowed to present statements responding to the charge against them and rebutting the testimony of the student and faculty witnesses. They brought witnesses in their behalf who also made statements to the board and answered questions of the justices. After all of the presentations, the board again questioned appellants and the witnesses. After the board completed its questioning, appellants were given the opportunity to question the opposing witnesses by submitting questions to the chancellor, who would then direct the questions to the witnesses. Appellants instead asked the board several questions. Appellants asked for a recess, which was denied by the chancellor, and the hearing was concluded. After deliberating in private, the board decided unanimously that appellants were guilty of the charge of academic dishonesty. The justices recommended that appellants be suspended from school, with the opportunity to apply for admission again in one year. Appellants were notified of the board's decision and recommendation.

Appellants . . . appealed to the dean on June 13, 1985. Pursuant to the code, the dean referred the case to the school's faculty Committee on Admissions and Standards for its review and recommendation. On June 19, 1985, the committee held a day-long meeting to consider the appeal. The committee reviewed a copy of the materials presented to the board at its June 12 hearing and listened to an audio recording of the June 12 hearing. Appellants presented oral and written statements in their defense and answered questions from the committee. After deliberating, the committee voted unanimously to recommend that the dean uphold the board's findings and recommendation. The dean accepted the committee's recommendation and upheld the action of the board. Appellants later appealed to the president of Auburn University, who reviewed the written file in the case and concurred in their suspension.

Under the Fourteenth Amendment to the United States Constitution, no state may "deprive any person of life, liberty or property, without due process of law. . . ." It is alleged and not disputed that Auburn University is a creature of the state of Alabama. Further, it is assumed by the parties and by the district court that appellants have property and liberty interests in their continued enrollment at Auburn University and that their interests enjoy the protections of due process.

A. The Procedural Due Process Claims: "The Fundamental requirement of due process is the opportunity to be heard at a meaningful time and in a meaningful manner." *Goss v. Lopez.* What process is due is measured by a flexible standard that depends on the practical requirements of the circumstances. That flexible standard was translated by the *Goss* court to mean that high school students facing the deprivation of a property right by suspension from school must, at a minimum, "be given some kind of notice—and afforded some kind of hearing." [W]e broadly defined the notice and hearing required in cases of student expulsion from college: "[A]n opportunity to hear both sides in considerable detail is best suited to protect the rights of all involved. This is not to imply that a full-dress judicial hearing, with the right to cross-examine witnesses, is required."

The adequacy of the notice and the nature of the hearing vary according to an "appropriate accommodation of the competing interests involved." [T]hree factors are important when considering the constitutional adequacy of the procedures afforded in a given situation: First, the private interest that will be affected by the official action; second, the risk of an erroneous deprivation of such interest through the procedures used, and the probable value, if any, of additional or substitute procedural safeguards; and finally, the government's interest, including the function involved and the fiscal and administrative burdens that the additional or substitute procedural requirement would entail. The due process clause is not a "shield . . . from suspensions properly imposed," nor does it ensure that the academic disciplinary process is a "totally accurate, unerring process"; it merely guards against the risk of unfair suspension "if that may be done without prohibitive cost or interference with the educational process."

Nash and Perry argue that [Auburn] engaged in procedures, which deprived them of constitutionally protectible rights in their continued enrollment as veterinary students. They argue that inadequate notice failed to provide them the opportunity for a meaningful response to the charge of academic dishonesty. Specifically, they claim that the interval of time between the notice and the hearing was too short, and the notice did not apprise them of the substance of the evidence against them. They argue also that the hearing was inadequate to protect their interests from erroneous deprivation in that they were denied the opportunity to cross-examine witnesses. Further, they argue that the tribunal was unfairly prejudiced by the existence and the participation of a justice with knowledge of the charge. Appellants argue also that they were denied a meaningful appeal and that the cumulative effect of these individual abridgments of their rights denied them due process of law.

1. The Notice

a. Timing: There are no hard and fast rules by which to measure meaningful notice. "An elementary and fundamental requirement of due process . . . is notice reasonably calculated, under all the circumstances, to apprise interested parties of the pendency of the action and afford them an opportunity to present their objections."

Appellants urge . . . that a coercive atmosphere pervaded the June 10 hearing, providing appellants and their counsel no choice but to agree to the board's proposed timing of the restated notice and the rescheduled hearing. However, in the record of the June 10 hearing we find no evidence of coercion to give us concern that appellants' waiver might not have been knowingly given. In sum, appellants were given four days by the June 6 notice and an additional one day by the June 11 notice, for a total of about six days from the June 6 notice to prepare their defense at the June 12 hearing. Despite the severity of the charge of academic dishonesty and the severe sanction it carries, the time allowed appellants was reasonable. It enabled them to retain counsel who successfully argued in their behalf at the June 10 hearing for a more specific notice of the charge as well as for a delayed hearing. Further, appellants had sufficient time to appear at the June 12 hearing with witnesses in their behalf, bringing documentation to support their defense.

b. Content: Appellants argue that the notice in this case was deficient because it did not advise them of the nature of the testimony to be presented against them or of the facts underlying the charge of academic dishonesty. Appellants urge that the analysis by Professor Buxton of their May 16 examination answers was persuasive, complex testimony and came as a surprise. They argue that they were entitled to a summary of the testimony expected from Buxton and the other accusing witnesses at the June 12 hearing, because only such notice would have provided safeguards against their surprise at the testimony and would have ensured them a fair opportunity to respond. Had they known of Buxton's analysis before he testified, appellants suggest they would have presented expert, statistical testimony to rebut the inference that they cheated on the May 16 neuroanatomy exam.

There is no constitutional requirement that, to provide them an opportunity to respond, appellants must have received any more in the way of notice than a statement of the charge against them. Although the June 6 notice in their case was rudimentary, the June 11 notice specified that appellants were accused of academic dishonesty on the May 16 neuroanatomy exam and it included a list of accusing witnesses. On that notice, appellants obtained the assistance of counsel and brought to the June 12 hearing students and a faculty witness who testified as to their own interpretations of appellants' conduct throughout the school year and at the May 16 exam. Appellants were present at the entire June 12 hearing to hear the evidence against them, made a cogent defense, and undertook to discredit the adverse testimony, including Professor Huxton's analysis of their exam answers.

Despite the serious charge against appellants, who were hard-working students on the threshold of their careers, and the severity of the sanction imposed on them, we find that appellants were afforded constitutionally adequate notice and were adequately prepared by the notice to defend the charge against them.

2. The Hearing

a. Right to cross-examination: "The fundamental requisite of due process of law is the opportunity to be heard." However, the nature of the hearing "will depend on appropriate accommodation of the competing interests involved." Appellants rely on *Goldberg v. Kelly* (1970) to challenge the constitutional adequacy of their hearing on the ground they were not allowed to cross-examine the accusing witnesses. *Goldberg* taught us that "[i]n almost every setting where important decisions turn on questions of fact, due process requires an opportunity to confront and cross examine adverse witnesses." However, we have not expanded the *Goldberg* procedural requirements for quasi-judicial termination of welfare benefits in student disciplinary hearings. Where basic fairness is preserved, we have not required the cross-examination of witnesses and a full adversary proceeding. Due process requires that appellants have the right to respond, but their rights in the academic

disciplinary process are not coextensive with the rights of litigants in a civil trial or with those of defendants in a criminal trial.

Although appellants were not allowed to ask questions directly of the adverse witnesses at the June 12 hearing, it is clear that they heard all of the testimony against them. Appellants were told they could pose questions of the accusing witnesses by directing their questions to the presiding board chancellor, who would then direct appellants' questions to the witnesses.

We do not suggest that the opportunity to question witnesses would not have been valuable in this case. Although an important notion in our concept of justice is the cross examination of witnesses, there was no denial of appellants' constitutional rights to due process by their inability to question the adverse witnesses in the usual, adversarial manner. . . .

3. Fairness of the Tribunal

An impartial decision-maker is an essential guarantee of due process. "[B]asic fairness and integrity of the fact-finding process are the guiding stars." Appellants argue that the board was unfairly prejudiced at the June 12 hearing by the failure of a student justice to recuse himself. Appellants argue that the active presence of one student justice unfairly prejudiced the June 12 hearing and the deliberations of the board in this case, because that justice had prior knowledge of the charge of academic misconduct against appellants. They argue that a fair hearing and an unbiased decision were not possible in their case because the justice had not recused himself.

There is no evidence in the record, however, which suggests bias on the part of the student justice in question, such that he should disqualify himself from performing his duties on the board. He was familiar with appellants' conduct and with the general comments made about them by their classmates. In his contact with some potential student witnesses prior to the June 12 hearing, he explained the method of bringing information about violations of the code before the board chancellor. We agree with the district court that just "any prior knowledge of the incident" does not disqualify a decision-maker; neither this student justice's knowledge of the suspicions about appellants nor his contact with potential witnesses appear to have rendered him a biased decision-maker or to have denied appellants a tribunal free of bias.

4. The Appeal

[A]ppellants argue that their case was given only "perfunctory, fleeting review" by the dean of the school and the president of the university, both accepting the recommendations of the board and the committee, in violation of appellants' constitutional right to a meaningful appeal. We do not agree. The possibility that an erroneous decision may have been made by the board was diminished by the extensive review by the faculty committee. To impose two additional layers of *de novo* review, as appellants seem to request, would not have changed the nature of their opportunity to respond to the charge against them.

5. The Combination of Violations

The Student Code of Professional Ethics at Auburn University School of Veterinary Medicine provides rudimentary protections for students facing suspension on a charge of academic dishonesty. As we have explained, where appellants have challenged the adequacy of the notice and hearing provided them, Auburn's procedures met the constitutional minimum, but no more. They were given notice of the specific violation with which they were charged and were allowed an opportunity to respond at a hearing before an impartial tribunal, held within a reasonable time following the notice. Appellants were allowed to speak in their own behalf, to bring witnesses to support their defense, to confront their accusers, and to appeal their adverse decision to a committee of faculty members and then to officials of the school and the university. The judgment of the district court is affirmed.

FOR CRITICAL ANALYSIS

Considering this case and the text discussion, answer the following questions about the hypothetical university, Mid-State.

1. The policies of Mid-State University provide that students who disrupt class activities are subject to expulsion. Before expulsion can occur, however, the student is entitled to a conference with the dean of students. Jim is a student who has been accused of obstructing the administration of the school by engaging in a sit-in demonstration. He asserts that he is entitled to more procedural protection than afforded by the conference with the dean of students.

   a. Mid-State says that Jim enrolled at the university and therefore has waived any further protections than those granted him in the rules and regulations. Is this position well taken?

   b. Jim asserts that he is entitled to have his lawyer present during any procedures designed to expel him. Is this position reasonable?

   c. Jim states that he has the right to cross-examine the witnesses against him. Is he correct?

   d. Jim maintains that the dean of students is biased against him because of statements the dean has made to the effect that Jim is a menace and should be removed from the university. Is Jim's objection allowable?

   e. Would it make any difference to Jim if the university in question were a private rather than a public university? Restrict your answer to the right to a hearing and the general nature of such a hearing.

CHAPTER QUESTIONS AND PROBLEMS

1. What is the distinguishing characteristic of an independent administrative agency? What are the checks and balances on an administrative agency by the executive, legislative, and judicial branches of government?

2. Legal scholars have pointed out that "the sheer volume of law generated by all types of administrative agencies exceeds the volume produced by both the legislatures and the courts combined." Yet comparatively few cases involving the work of administrative agencies appear in the docket of the U.S. Supreme Court or in the dockets of the lower courts. Can you suggest a reason for this phenomenon?

3. Officials of the Internal Revenue Service (IRS) have repeatedly requested additional funds from Congress to enable them to audit more income tax returns, and to pursue individuals who don't even bother to file tax returns. The IRS confidently predicts that additional spending would result in hundreds of millions of dollars of additional income tax revenue. Why do you suppose Congress has resisted and generally rejected such IRS requests?

4. What recourse does a citizen have when an administrative agency, such as the Environmental Protection Agency (EPA), in its enthusiasm and dedication, imposes what one might consider to be unreasonable standards (e.g., for clean air, where the cost of eliminating perhaps the last 5 percent of pollution may be as high as the cost of eliminating the first 95 percent)?

5. Three deaths occurred in a chemical plant owned by Rivercity Chemical Corporation over a period of several months in 1999. The people died by being burned, crushed, and suffocated.

The Occupational Safety and Health Administration (OSHA)—an administrative arm of the U.S. Department of Labor—was asked to investigate. After a finding of safety violations, OSHA recommended fines of $8.3 million. Does an administrative agency such as OSHA have the power to assess and collect fines?

6. Martin Mazurie, a non-Indian, operated a bar on land he owned on an Indian reservation. A federal statute authorized Indian tribes to control the distribution of alcoholic beverages on their reservations. Mazurie, after denial of a tribal liquor license, was convicted of introducing spirituous beverages into Indian country. Mazurie appealed, claiming as a non-Indian landowner he was not subject to Indian authority and that the federal statute authorizing Indian tribe regulation of alcoholic beverages was an unconstitutional delegation of authority by Congress to a private body. The U.S. Court of Appeals agreed with Mazurie holding: "Congress cannot delegate its authority to a private, voluntary organization, which is obviously not a governmental agency, to regulate a business on privately owned lands, no matter where located." The Indian tribe appealed. Can Congress delegate power to an Indian tribe to regulate non-Indians on the reservation? [*U.S. v. Mazurie*, 419 U.S. 544, 95 S.Ct. 710 (1975).]

7. The plaintiffs, the Federal Defenders of San Diego (an organization of criminal-defense lawyers), brought suit to challenge the constitutionality of sentencing guidelines issued by the U.S. Sentencing Commission. The defendant commission challenged the plaintiffs' standing to bring the lawsuit. The plaintiffs argued that their members appear as counsel in 60 percent of Federal

Criminal cases that continue after an initial appearance. Do the Federal Defenders have standing to bring the lawsuit? [*Federal Defenders of San Diego, Inc., et al., v. U.S. Sentencing Commission*, 680 F.Supp. 26 (D.C., 1988).]

8. Ulmer G. Wilson, a New Orleans realtor, was unhappy when he discovered a "boot" on his car (immobilizing it). A note on the car's window gave a number to call to retrieve the car. After calling, he became even more unhappy. He was expected to pay $630 for previous parking violations and a $30 boot removal fee. Wilson refused to pay and the car was stored. The decision to "boot" Wilson's car had been made by Datacom, a private business under contract with the city to collect unpaid parking violations, receiving commission on all it collected. The decision to boot was made by Datacom based on a city ordinance allowing for immobilization of vehicles with three or more unpaid parking violations. Wilson had at least twenty parking tickets, nevertheless he contested the "booting," claiming it was a taking of his property without due process of law. He contented that the "booting" took place without proper notice and that the determination to "boot" was made by Datacom, a partial decision-maker who did not offer Wilson a hearing before booting the car. Was Wilson denied that right to a fair hearing with an impartial decision-maker? [*Ulmer G. Wilson v. The City of New Orleans*, 479 So.2d 891 (1985).]

9. As a general rule, administrative searches of businesses require a search warrant. The Department of Alcohol, Tobacco, and Firearms officials without a warrant inspected a liquor storeowner. The liquor storeowner claimed that the officers conducted a search in violation of his Fourth Amendment rights. The Department of Alcohol, Tobacco, and Firearms claimed that the liquor store is part of a "pervasively regulated industry" and as such there is a substantial government interest in warrantless searches. Can the department conduct a warrantless search? [*Donovan v. Dewey*, 452 U.S. 594, 101 S.Ct. 2534 (1981).]

10. Save The Dolphins is a nonprofit corporation whose primary purpose is to stop the incidental killing of dolphins in tuna fishing. The National Marine Fisheries Service (NMFS) made a film on an experimental tuna-fishing cruise. Save The Dolphins requested a copy of the film under the Freedom of Information Act. The NMFS declined to release the film because at the time the film was made the government had assured tuna boat captain Medina that "the film would not be shown to anyone but those involved in the research, since the scenes therein would depict fishing trade secrets and commercial information used by Medina's crew." Will NMFS be required to make the film available to Save The Dolphins? [*Save The Dolphins v. U.S. Department of Commerce*, 404 F.Supp. 407 (N.D.Ca., 1975).]

NOTES

1. *Federal Trade Commission v. Rubberoid Co.*, 343 U.S. 470, 72 S.Ct. 800 (1952).

2. For a detailed summary of society just before the turn of the twentieth century, see Davis Traxel, 1898. (New York: Alfred A. Knope, 1998).

3. Traxel, 72.

4. Traxel, 72.

5. From the "The Regulatory Juggernaut," *Newsweek*, 7 November 1994, 43.

6. Statement by Sidney M. Wolfe, M.D., Director, Public Citizen's Health Research Group Concerning Petition to Require FDA to Start Regulating the Content of Patient Information Leaflets for Prescription Drugs, 9 June 1998.

7. The Interstate Commerce Commission no longer exists. In 1996 its functions were transferred to the Department of Transportation. See the ICC Termination Act of 1995.

8. *Humphrey's Executor v. United States*, 295 U.S. 602, 55 S.Ct. 869 (1935).

9. *Humphrey's Executor v. United States.*

10. 42 U.S.C. § 2000e-4(a).

11. *Panama Refining Co. v. Ryan*, 293 U.S. 388, 55 S.Ct. 241 (1935) and *Schechter Poultry Corp. v. United States*, 295 U.S. 495, 55 S.Ct. 837 (1935).

12. *Panama Refining Co. v. Ryan* and *Schechter Poultry Corp. v. United States.*

13. *Loving v. United States*, 517 U.S. 748, 771, 116 S.Ct. 1737, 1750 (1996).

14. *Opp Cotton Mills, Inc. v. Administrator*, 312 U.S. 126, 144, 61 S.Ct. 524 (1941).

15. P.L. 404, 60 Stat. 237 (1946). The act has been amended several times. Major provisions can be found in 5 U.S.C. §§ 551-593 and 707-706.

16. P.L. 101-648, as amended P.L. 102-354 and P.L. 104-320, 5 U.S.C.A., §§ 561-579.

17. Facts on File, Transportation, p. 420 (1979).

18. See *Camara v. Municipal Court*, 387 U.S. 523, 87 S.Ct. 1727 (1967) and *Marshall v. Barlow's Inc.*, 436 U.S. 307, 98 S.Ct. 1816 (1978).

19. *Payton v. New York*, 445 U.S. 573, 100 S.Ct. 1371 (1980).

20. *Lesser v. Epsy*, 34 F.3d 1301 (7th cir., 1994).

21. CNN Live Event Special 09:39 a.m. ET April 30, 1998; Thursday 9:39 a.m. Eastern Time Transcript # 98043001V54. Content and programming copyright 1998 Cable News Network. Transcribed under license by Federal Document Clearing House, Inc.

22. 5 U.S.C. §§ 581-593.

23. "When Fines Collapse," *National Law Journal*, 4 December 1989, 74.

24. *Goldberg v. Kelly*, 397 U.S. 254, 90 S.Ct. 1011 (1970).

25. Ernest Gellhorn and C. Byse, *Administrative Law* (Mineola N.Y.: Foundation Press, 1987).

26. 5 U.S.C. § 554 (b).

27. Henry Friendly, Some Kind of Hearing, 123 *University of Pennsylvania Law Review* 1289 (1975).

28. Based on the case of *Edward B. v. Paul*, 814 F.2d 52 (1987).

29. *Edward B. v. Paul.*

30. P.L. 104-320.

31. *Vermont Yankee Nuclear Power Corporation v. Natural Resources Defense Council, Inc.*, 435 U.S. 519, 98 S.Ct. 1197 (1978).

32. *Port Authority of New York and New Jersey et al. v. British Airways et al.*, 434 U.S. 899, 98 S.Ct. 291, (1977) memorandum decision.

33. *Loudoun v. Trustees of the Loudoun County Library*, 2 F.Supp.2d 783 (E.D., Virginia, 1998).

34. *Darby v. Cisneros*, 509 U.S. 137, 113 S.Ct. 2539 (1993).

35. 15 U.S.C. §§ 77 et seq.

36. SEC 1997 Annual Report.

37. 7 USC § 2 et seq.

38. 12 U.S.C. § 221 et seq.

39. The press release can be found at http://www.bog.frb.fed.us/boarddocs/press/BHC/1998/19980817/

40. 15 USC § 21 et seq.

41. Speech by William E. Kennard, Chairman Federal Communications Commission to the National Association of Regulatory Utility Commissioners, Seattle, Washington, July 27, 1998.

42. P.L. 102-385, 106 Stat. 1460, 47 U.S.C. § 325 et seq.

43. 29 U.S.C. § 151 et seq.

44. 42 U.S.C. § 2000 et seq.

45. 29 U.S.C. § 1001 et seq.

46. 42 U.S.C. § 761 et seq.

47. 42 U.S.C. § 2011 et seq.

48. "Report of the President's Commission on the Accident of Three Mile Island" (Washington, D.C.: Government Printing Office, 1979).

49. Based on a press release, Bill Hord, "Farmer in Limbo over EPA Runoff Plan," *World-Herald Bureau*, 23 March 1998.

50. See http://www.epa.gov/epahome/epa.html.

51. 15 U.S.C. § 41 et seq.

52. *FTC v. Superior Court Trial Lawyers Association*, 493 U.S. 411, 110 S.Ct. 768 (1990).

53. 46 U.S.C. § 1301 et seq.

54. 14 U.S.C. § 81 et seq.; 49 U.S.C. § 1711 et seq.

55. 23 U.S.C. § 404 et seq.

6

CRIMES: PUBLIC WRONGS

*I*f there were no bad people there would be no good
lawyers.

Charles Dickens, The Old Curiosity Shop, 1841.

No area of law provokes more intense public reaction than criminal law. And the media capitalizes on the public's interest in crime, which borders on morbid fascination. Publicized cases frequently focus on issues that are controversial, perplexing, and provocative. Unfortunately, as a result, important but controversial issues are frequently obscured by emotions.

In the years around 1900, criminal behavior reflected the times: Train and bank robbery, mugging, prostitution, embezzlement, and fraud. Tammany Hall, a New York political machine noted for graft and corruption, marked the beginnings of organized crime. Every city contract and political nomination was controlled; no bridge or sewer could be repaired or brick laid without the purchased permission of Tammany Hall. But there were no juvenile laws shielding minors from criminal court and from adult penalties, no widespread fear of gang crimes, carjackings, homicides in schoolyards or in courtrooms, drug crimes, terrorist bombings, or serial killers and rapists. This is not to imply that our society at the beginning of the twenty-first century is plagued with crime. Actually, as the twentieth century ends, crime is reportedly decreasing. But the character of criminal behavior has been modernized, reflecting the crushing growth of high density populations within our cities, technology, the automobile, the popularization of drug use, and, according to some, the impact of television, movies, and the availability of idle time.

The impact of crime and law enforcement on our society is markedly different today than at the beginning of the twentieth century. Punishment is the direct consequence of apprehension for crime, but there also are indirect consequences of law enforcement upon society. For example, marijuana and its cousin, hemp, are illegal contraband in the United States. Thus, hemp cannot legally be grown in this country. But like soybeans, hemp can be used to produce an oil that in turn can be used in a wide variety of beneficial products, including cooking oil, cosmetics, and plastics. Hemp fiber can be used to make paper, cloth, and even structural panels stronger than plywood. Hemp seed can be ground for flour and even livestock feed. When grown in rotation with other crops, such as cotton, hemp increases their yields and reduces the need for pesticides. In short, hemp is a

You may obtain current statistics on crime from the Federal Bureau of Investigation at http://www.FBI.gov or the Justice Department at http://www.jrsainfo.org/

http://

potentially beneficial and valuable crop that is grown successfully in other countries, such as Canada, France, Germany, and England. One professor concludes that hemp, together with wheat, rice, straw, and kenaf, could fill the growing global shortage for fiber that is anticipated to be acute in the early years of the twenty-first century.[1] On the other hand, hemp contains a small amount of the same chemical found in marijuana. Existence of the chemical may not be significant, but hemp looks like marijuana and would make law enforcement more difficult. Thus, some officials contend that efforts to legalize hemp are a smoke screen to legalize marijuana.[2] The controversy surrounding legalization of hemp is both an example of how crime and its enforcement affect our society and an example of how the complexities of our legal system are compounding as we enter the new millennium.

Another indirect societal consequence of modern law enforcement is the privatization of prisons. States receive competing bids from private corporations to build and manage jails or prisons. The winning bidder builds and thereafter manages a prison in exchange for a daily fee for each inmate confined. Local businesses profit substantially from the nearby private prison. New jobs, increased retail sales, and new housing demand are some of the benefits. As private businesses, these jails can pay low wages to their labor force (inmates), perhaps less than one dollar per hour, to produce such products as computer circuit boards. With 1.8 million inmates in the United States, the private prison business is booming as we begin the new millennium. The prison industry lobbies government to maintain stiff sentencing laws because more prisoners means more profits.

Opponents to the privatization of prisons argue that inmates are not treated with the minimal standards required by law and produce products in competition with unions and other private businesses. Critics make an analogy between the conditions faced by today's incarcerated labor force and the working conditions at the beginning of the twentieth century that existed for children in the nation's coal mines and for women in the textile industry. Charges exist that prisoners are mistreated to extend their sentences to the maximum permitted by law. There also have been instances of sexual and physical abuse of inmates, although most states require that private prisons be accredited by the American Correctional Association. Despite such concerns, private prisons appear to be an expanding business for the new century.*

Looking toward the twenty-first century, society seems increasingly willing to treat minors as adults relative to the punishments they receive for criminal behavior. In most states, the move toward harsher treatment of juveniles is politically popular. But there is concern that juveniles in adult prisons "may be sexually and physically abused, permanently labeled as criminals, and denied access to rehabilitative services."[3]

The following questions illustrate many of the issues attracting intense public scrutiny as the twentieth century draws to a close:

- Is society morally responsible for criminal conduct through disregard of its less fortunate?

For a variety of arguments surrounding the hemp controversy, check
http://www.hemp.net/
and
http://www.crrh.org/hemptv/index2.html
and
http://www.geocities.com/CapitolHill/7247/

For information about the privatization of prisons visit http://www.ucc.uconn.edu/~Logan/

---

*For a history of private management of prisons, and the differing legal immunities that are applicable to public versus private guards, see *Richardson v. McKnight*, 117 S.Ct. 2100 (1997).

- Is the public victimized by repeat offenders who often are not apprehended or are punished too leniently if caught?
- Is blue-collar, back-street crime condemned while white-collar, "Wall Street" crime implicitly condoned?
- Are there different standards of justice for the rich and for the poor?
- Is capital punishment barbaric, or justified, or both?
- Should so-called victimless crimes (e.g., prostitution and gambling) be prosecuted?
- Why can insanity, even temporary insanity, excuse even the most heinous criminal conduct?
- Is the root cause of violent crime the creation of unwanted children in the homes of dysfunctional families? Or are the root causes moral and spiritual, or physiological and genetic, rather than social and economic?
- Are "abuse excuses" by perpetrators trivializing serious crime and producing too light sentences?
- Are too many nonviolent offenders being sentenced to prison?
- Does the uncertainty of punishment contribute to antisocial behavior?
- Is an average of 13 years on death row between original sentence and final appeal too long?
- Is the death penalty dehumanizing to society?
- Is criminal law being applied unfairly, producing a prison population disproportionately composed of young African American males?
- Is lawlessness encouraged by the apathy of too many citizens who, more or less unwittingly, buy goods that obviously are stolen, fail to report suspicious activities in their neighborhoods, and refuse to "become involved" as informants or as witnesses in criminal trials?

These are not easy questions and easy answers will not be forthcoming. To the contrary, people like you will be required to answer these questions either by choice or by default.

This chapter will familiarize you with the pervasiveness and complexity of these dilemmas through a survey of selected concepts of criminal law. There are no perfect solutions or antidotes for antisocial criminal behavior, but after studying the chapter you will better understand the dynamics involved and sharpen your thinking about what might be the best ways of dealing with the problem. Crime and punishment—or what happens when prevention fails—are the subjects addressed here.

WHAT IS A CRIME?

Certain human behavior is deemed to be so offensive and objectionable that it threatens the safety or common good of society. Such objectionable and antisocial conduct is therefore prohibited by statute. A **crime** has occurred when a prohibitory statute has been violated.* In summary, crime is a wrong against society, as defined by statute, and punishable by society. Criminals face a wide range of possible penalties, including monetary fines and forfeitures, incarceration, and even death, if arrested and convicted, though they sometimes are given the choice of performing some act that is beneficial to society, such as community service.

It is important to note the dual consequences of most wrongful behavior. That is, most crimes are also civil wrongs: a person who burglarizes a home is committing burglary, and also the civil wrong called *trespass*, and probably the civil wrong called *conversion* (theft) of another's property. In such a situation, the victim has the right to seek money compensation in the civil law even when society, through criminal law, punishes the wrongdoer. This principle has been vividly dramatized by the globally publicized case involving the infamous Orenthal J. Simpson.

In a criminal proceeding, Simpson was found not guilty of the double murder of his former wife Nicole and her friend Ronald Goldman. However, in a subsequent civil proceeding Simpson was found liable, or legally responsible, for those wrongful deaths and was ordered to pay $35 million in monetary damages to the families of the victims. Thus, the criminal law and the civil law acted independent of each other concerning a single wrong. There was no issue of "double jeopardy" in this case because double jeopardy is a safeguard that applies only to successive criminal trials for the same offense.

Under the U.S. Constitution, criminal statutes must describe the forbidden conduct clearly and precisely, so that all persons may know, after reasonable investigation or reflection, what is prohibited. For example, a law prohibiting "loitering," but without specifically defining the prohibited conduct, is unconstitutionally vague. The underlying principle of justice is that no one shall be held criminally liable for conduct that could not reasonably be recognized as forbidden. In general, we are entitled to a "fair warning" of the existence of a criminal law—thus, we can avoid the behavior it proscribes. The fair warning precondition requires the following:

1. The statute must be clear and specific. Defendants cannot be convicted of violating a "vague" statute.

2. Statutes will be "strictly" construed (interpreted) by courts to limit their scope as specifically as possible. Defendants cannot be convicted of behavior that is generalized in the prohibitory statute.

3. Courts cannot adopt a novel or creative interpretation of a statute to sweep certain behavior into its literal terms. Defendants cannot be convicted of behavior that would not be generally understood to fall within the scope of the statute.

---

*Some criminal statutes are mandatory—for example, those that command: "You must file a tax return and pay your income taxes without evasion" or "you must serve your country if drafted in time of war." Even these can be expressed as prohibitions of antisocial conduct.

Tennessee judge David Lanier was convicted of violating the constitutional rights of five women by assaulting them sexually. The federal statute the judge allegedly violated provided that it is a crime to "deprive a person of rights protected by the Constitution." Under the federal statute, if the deprivation of protected rights includes bodily injury, the prison sentence is enhanced to ten years. The jury found that two oral rapes by Judge Lanier caused the victims "bodily injury" and he received a 20-year sentence as a result of that finding. But Judge Lanier appealed, contending that he was ignorant that the words in the statute covered sexual assault. What was the result on appeal?

Judge Lanier won on appeal because he could not "reasonably anticipate" that his sexual assaults would violate the statute. The U.S. Supreme Court held that the "unlawfulness must be apparent."[4] In other words, Judge Lanier may have known that his behavior was improper, but he did not know that his sexual assaults deprived the victims of their Constitutional rights. At first blush, this may appear to violate the principle that "ignorance of the law is no excuse." However, the Court ruled only that "ignorance of a *nonspecific and vague law* is an excuse."

Most crimes are state crimes because they violate state statutes. In terms of volume, most federal crimes involve drug offenses. Congress has adopted statutes criminalizing drug transactions because they involve interstate commerce. But the violation of *any* federal statute (and there are many) is a federal crime that will be prosecuted in a federal court and, if conviction follows, will result in confinement in a federal prison. The case involving Judge Lanier exemplifies a federal crime.

The difficulties inherent in specifying the prohibited conduct in a statute is dramatized by the imprecision of the term "loitering." The definition of loitering has frustrated legislators trying to draft statutes that will constitutionally prohibit certain undesirable conduct associated both with so-called "homeless" people (e.g., aggressively begging, urinating in public, sleeping on sidewalks) as well as gang members (e.g., hanging out, dealing drugs, provoking other gangs). How can such conduct be defined and then prohibited when our freedom of association, i.e., to "hang out," is protected by our Constitution? Can police logically separate harmless loitering from activity that leads to drug dealing, drive-by shootings, and other violence the ordinance is intended to prevent? The status of these "anti-loitering" statutes is pending before the U.S. Supreme Court at the time of this writing. On the Web you can find the Court's solution and the new constitutional requirements of laws restricting loitering.

Crimes require criminal intent, with the exception of certain types of regulatory offenses, often called infractions, (e.g., failing to keep a restaurant kitchen adequately clean) and criminally negligent conduct, (e.g., bicycling or driving a vehicle while under the influence of alcohol). There is no universally accepted definition of the term; however, generally it means evil or wrongful purpose or design. Sometimes criminal statutes require specific criminal intent, as, for example, the intent to commit a robbery. Intent does not mean motive, which is a need, desire, or purpose that impels a person to act. A prosecutor need not prove the existence of an evil motive; a good motive never justifies a criminal act. Thus, a "mercy killing" is a crime regardless of its underlying noble motive.

The Illinois Supreme Court struck down a modern anti-loitering ordinance.[5] On appeal, that case is now (1999) pending before the U.S. Supreme Court.[6] It promises to be the leading case on the constitutionality of anti-loitering ordinances. You may find this case at http://supct.law.cornell.edu/supct/

Marilyn Harrell, a real estate broker in Maryland, publicly admitted unauthorized diversion of $5.7 million in proceeds from sales of federally insured properties that had been foreclosed. But she insisted that the bulk of the stolen money was used to provide housing for needy families as well as food for the poor. She had been entrusted with the money by the U.S. Department of Housing and Urban Development (HUD). Are her commendable purposes a legal defense to the crime of theft (which, under these circumstances, is also called *embezzlement*)?

No. Robin Hood's classic motive to help the poor was no defense for Marilyn, who has been dubbed "Robin HUD." She was convicted and sentenced to a prison term of 46 months, which she served.[7]

Criminal negligence is conduct that is without criminal intent and yet is sufficiently careless or reckless to be punished as a crime. Driving a vehicle while under the influence of drugs or alcohol is an example of criminal negligence. Leaving a handgun in one's home that is easily accessible to a child or leaving a child for a long period in a parked car are other examples.

Violation of state food quality regulations by a restaurant is an example of a **regulatory offense**, in which criminal intent is irrelevant (that is, not applicable) and therefore need not be proved. Failure to obtain a required business or professional license are other examples.

Derick Dagger thought about murdering his wife, Glynda, so he could inherit her money. Over a period of time, he developed and refined an elaborate scheme to commit the murder. He even wrote a step-by-step plan that he kept in his filing cabinet. Is he guilty of any crime?

No. Criminal intent, in the absence of any supportive overt act (i.e., an open, outward, manifested act), is not a crime. This is true even if one confesses to such an intent. The written plan could be hypothetical and is an insufficient overt act upon which to base a conviction. The desire to inherit money was Derick's motive, but a motive is not a crime.

In furtherance of his plan, Derick asked his lifelong friend, Patrick O'Leary, to assist him in murdering Glynda. Patrick declined to assist, but loaned his revolver to Derick for use in accomplishing the murder. Have any crimes occurred?

Yes. Derick has committed the crime of **solicitation**. Criminal solicitation is to strongly urge, entice, lure, or proposition another to engage in the commission of a crime. Patrick is guilty of **criminal facilitation** because he knowingly and substantially increased the probability that the crime would be committed; that is, he made it easier for Derick to effectuate his plan. Unlike a gun dealer in a normal retail sale, Patrick knew of Derick's intended crime and voluntarily assisted in its commission.

Suppose Patrick O'Leary had responded that he would be "happy to assist in the plan." Has another crime occurred? No. An agreement to commit a crime, standing alone, is not a crime. There is a constitutional limitation in criminalizing mere thought when there is no conduct in furtherance of the conspiracy. There must be some manifestation of the conspiratorial intent by what is called an *overt act*. But suppose that Patrick then demonstrated how to load and fire his gun, and Derick and Patrick agreed to divide the inheritance. Has another crime occurred? Yes. Under these circumstances, Derick and Patrick would be guilty of the crime of **conspiracy**. An agreement to commit a crime becomes a criminal conspiracy once a substantial act of preparation is performed by one or more of the conspirators in furtherance of their plan. Teaching how to load and use the gun is such an overt act.

Early that evening, while Glynda was preparing supper, Derick aimed the loaded gun at her through the kitchen window, but she kept moving, providing a poor target. Derick did not fire. Have any more crimes occurred?

Yes. Derick committed the crime of **attempt** to commit murder because he committed an act of perpetration—that is, he took a substantial step toward the commission of the crime. Because conspirators share each other's guilt, Patrick is also guilty of attempted murder.

If Derick and Patrick actually did all of the assumed acts, they would not necessarily be chargeable with, nor punishable for, each separate act. Some crimes are said to be included within, and merge into, the ultimate crime. For example, the crime of solicitation would merge into, and become a part of, the ultimate crime of attempted murder, for which both Patrick and Derick would be punishable.

Duress may negate the intent that must be present for a crime to have been committed. Duress is the forced participation in what otherwise would be a crime. It implies that a person's free will was overpowered, that he or she was coerced.

Following a Halloween party, Russell Pena and his girlfriend, Sara, age 20, were asleep at 4 A.M. in his car parked on private property. Patrolman Webb approached the car, smelled alcohol, and ordered Russell and Sara to get out. Sara was wearing only a fur coat over a sheer nightgown; Webb, searching for weapons, "closely" examined Sara's body with his flashlight. Webb ordered Sara to enter his vehicle so he could take her home for "protection," and departed, leaving Russell alone in the parked car. Fearing for Sara's safety, Russell followed and was subsequently arrested by Webb for driving while under the influence. His blood-alcohol level turned out to be .15 percent, which is presumptive evidence of intoxication. Russell contends he drove under duress because he feared for Sara's safety. Therefore, he argues, he did not voluntarily commit the crime. Is this a valid defense to the crime of driving under the influence of alcohol?

Yes. It is no crime to commit an act under duress arising from threats of harm to oneself or to another.[8] This case also illustrates the problem that frequently confronts juries in ascertaining the truth when presented with bizarre facts. Note, however, that killing another person is never excused or justified because it was committed under duress.

FEDERAL CRIMES

As previously noted, a crime is conduct that is proscribed by a statute enacted by the legislative branch of government. If the conduct violates a state statute, it is a state crime punishable by the state. If the conduct violates a federal statute, it is a federal crime punishable by the United States government. Examples of federal crimes are transportation of contraband (illegal property, such as certain harmful drugs) across state lines; bank robbery; forgery of a federal check; violation of certain civil rights protected by federal laws; wrongful interference with, or theft of, mail; evasion of federal income taxes; theft of U.S. government property; violation of securities laws; and physical violence on government property. In recent years, Congress has stiffened penalties for drug-related and various violent federal crimes.

In a highly publicized case, police officers Stacey Koon and Laurence Powell were charged with violating a state statute forbidding excessive force while arresting suspects. A bystander videotaped the events surrounding the arrest of Rodney King, who had been fleeing the police at high speeds on a freeway. Despite the provocative video, a state jury found the police officers not guilty of violating the state statute; however, a subsequent federal court jury found Koon and Powell guilty of violating the federal Civil Rights Act of 1964 for the same offensive conduct. Thus, one act can be both a state and a federal crime.[9] Double jeopardy does not apply because the federal and state governments are separate and distinct entities under the Constitution.

WHO ARE PARTIES TO A CRIME?

To define the degree of culpability (blameworthiness) of a participant in a crime, criminals historically have been classified as either a **principal** or as an **accessory**. A principal is a person directly involved in committing a crime. An accessory is a person who helps or assists a criminal activity without being present during commission of the crime. Principals receive more severe sentences than accessories. Under such classifications, a person who actually commits the crime, such as robbing a liquor store, is a principal in the first degree. Another person not as directly involved, the driver of the getaway car, for example, is classified as a principal of the second degree. A person who participated in the planning but who was not personally present at the scene of the crime is an **accessory before the fact**. One who assists the principals in evading capture is called an **accessory after the fact**.

A recent trend in many states, as in the federal system and in California and Illinois, is to classify all participants in a crime—the planner, the actual perpetrator, and the **aider** and **abettor**—as principals. A "lookout" is aiding and abetting in a crime and would be considered a principal.[10] Anyone who knowingly hides a fugitive, under this modern view, is called an accessory.

In a notorious case in California in 1971, Charles Manson was charged with the murders of the pregnant movie star Sharon Tate and others. Although not present at the scene of the crime, Manson, possessing hypnotic-like powers over members of his cult, commanded certain followers to commit the atrocity. Is Manson a principal or an accessory?

Although Manson never appeared at the scene of the crime, he was convicted as a principal to the crime of murder and sentenced to death.*

The particular manner in which one's own state classifies participation in criminal activity is not as important to know as the fact that, in all states, even slight participation in the commission of a crime may subject one to grave criminal penalties.

WHAT IS THE *CORPUS DELICITI*?

The *corpus delicti* (Latin: "body of a crime") is not the body of the deceased. The term refers to two essential elements of every crime: (1) the material being, or substance upon which a crime has been committed (as, in homicide, a dead person; in arson, a burned building) and (2) evidence of some person's criminal conduct (as, in homicide, a bullet hole in the corpse; in arson, glass fragments from a Molotov cocktail found at the scene). Evidence that a person is missing does not satisfy the requirement of a *corpus delicti*.

Margaret Lesher, widow and heiress of a $100 million estate, married professional buffalo rider T.C. Thorstenson following a whirlwind courtship. T.C. concealed from Margaret his previous marriage and allegations of domestic violence. Six months after their wedding, Margaret and T.C. were camping one evening by a desolate lake, sleeping in separate bags. In the morning, Margaret was missing. T.C. looked "everywhere" to no avail and then called the police. Margaret was found dead, floating in the lake near the campsite. An autopsy revealed only that Margaret had drowned. T.C. claimed his inheritance under Margaret's recently drafted will. Can T.C. be prosecuted for murder?

No. The general law is that no person may be tried for any crime unless, and until, the prosecutor has established a *corpus delicti*. In the T.C. Thorstenson case, there is no clear evidence that a crime has occurred and the *corpus delicti* cannot, therefore, be established. The drowning could have been accidental.[11] However, if the corpse had a head injury apparently inflicted by a weapon, T.C. might be

---

*Manson's death penalty was reduced to life imprisonment after the U.S. Supreme Court declared the death penalty, as then prescribed, to be unconstitutional. *Furman v. Georgia*, 408 U.S. 238, 92 S.Ct. 2726 (1972). When the death penalty was later restored by corrective legislation, its impact was prospective and did not affect the life sentence of Manson, who remains in prison to the day of this writing (1999).

investigated and, if corroborating evidence were presented, he could be charged with and tried for **homicide** (an unlawful taking of a human life).

Goldie Millar's $340,000 ranch home was discovered burned to the ground. Her body was never found. Her grandson, Michael Pyle, lived in the vicinity and was known to believe he was the sole beneficiary of her will. The sole evidence of wrongdoing was a telephone call by Michael to his wife reporting the fire and death of his grandmother two hours before these events actually took place. Can Michael be convicted of homicide even though no trace of Goldie's body was ever found?

Yes, because production of neither the body of the missing person nor the evidence of the means used to produce death is essential to establish the *corpus delicti* or to sustain a murder conviction. Michael's premature display of knowledge of the fire, the fire itself, and his grandmother's absence were critical factors supporting the first degree murder conviction.[12] Whenever a victim's body is missing, the *corpus delicti* must be established by other evidence that a crime occurred (for example, the testimony of an eyewitness). In any crime, the *corpus delicti* must be established before a criminal prosecution can take place against anyone.

As noted, the "body of the crime" must be proven before the defendant can be prosecuted. But what if the only evidence of the "body of the crime" comes from a confession by the accused?

Dennis Creutz admitted that he "might have touched" a 3-year-old girl in the vaginal area but "never thought he was doing anything wrong." The only other evidence of a crime were statements from the 3-year-old girl to the effect that she had been inappropriately touched with the hands and mouth of the defendant. Can the case proceed to trial?

No. In most types of criminal cases, prosecution cannot occur unless the *corpus delicti* is established by evidence other than a confession by the accused. This prevents convictions of, among others, "crackpots" who would readily confess to anything to obtain attention and even food and shelter in a prison.

However, in crimes against minors who are too young and therefore incapable of testifying in court, confessions of the accused can be used to establish the *corpus delicti*, following which a trial can proceed. In other words, the out-of-court corroboration by a witness who is too young to testify is sufficient to justify use of a confession for a *corpus delicti*. In the preceding example, however, the mere incriminating statements of Creutz do not constitute a confession. A confession is a complete acknowledgement of guilt and must encompass all the elements of the crime. A mere admission, such as Creutz made, is not a confession and therefore cannot be used to establish a *corpus delicti*. Thus there can be no trial.[13]

FELONY, MISDEMEANOR, OR INFRACTION?

States generally classify crimes on the basis of blameworthiness as either felonies or misdemeanors. The determinant is usually the gravity of the criminal act, which in turn determines the severity of the penalty imposed. Generally, a **felony** is a crime that is punishable by death or by imprisonment in a state prison for a year or longer. Sometimes felonies are divided into **capital crimes** (punishable by death or imprisonment) and **noncapital crimes** (punishable by imprisonment only). Statutes may declare that a certain crime, such as robbery, is a felony. If the statute is silent as to the gravity of the crime, but incarceration in a state prison is the prescribed punishment, the crime is a felony. Some statutes prescribe punishment as imprisonment in either a state prison or a county jail. These "wobblers" are public offenses that may be either a felony or a misdemeanor depending upon the actual punishment ordered by the judge.[14]

Some states have refined their system of crime classification. For example, in Illinois, murder is one separate category of felony. The penalty can be death or incarceration up to one's natural life. Various classes of less culpable crimes are as follows:

Class X felonies: Examples are solicitation of murder, aggravated sexual assault, and kidnapping for ransom. Minimum sentence is 6 years, maximum is 30 years.

Class 1 felonies: Examples are nonaggravated sexual assault and second degree murder. Minimum sentence is 4 years, maximum is 15 years.

Class 2 felonies: An example is armed escape from prison. Minimum sentence is 3 years, maximum is 7 years.

Class 3 felonies: Examples are involuntary manslaughter, incest, and aggravated battery. Minimum sentence is 2 years, maximum is 5 years.

Class 4 felonies: An example is bigamy. Minimum sentence is 1 year, maximum is 3 years.

Actual sentences imposed in Illinois are determined by the circumstances surrounding the crime, such as whether the victim was seriously injured, or whether the criminal was a repeat offender.[15]

A **misdemeanor** typically is punishable either by fine or incarceration in a jail for less than a year, or both. Some states have an additional classification for petty offenses, called **infractions** or **violations**. These carry no moral stigma and are punishable only by fine. Common infractions are illegal gaming, disturbing the peace, possession of alcohol by a minor, and presenting false evidence of age.[16] Illinois refines misdemeanors into three categories: Class A (e.g., prostitution, up to 1 year in jail), Class B (e.g., obstructing service of process, up to 6 months in jail), and Class C (e.g., glue inhaling, up to 30 days in jail).[17] These refinements in classification are examples of attempts to distinguish criminal acts on the basis of culpability (degree of wrongfulness), leading to appropriate differences in penalties imposed.

The U.S. Sentencing Reform Act of 1984 abolished the federal system of **indeterminate sentencing**. Indeterminate sentence statutes provide for a range of years of imprisonment (e.g., one to five years) rather than a specific period set by the judge. The indeterminate sentencing system had given federal judges broad discretion in setting the type and extent of punishment imposed. This resulted in great disparities in time actually served as well as sentences imposed because parole boards (officials with authority to set release dates) made actual release decisions tailored to the supposed amenability of each prisoner to rehabilitation. Many prisoners resented the uncertainties surrounding the subjective nature of decisions as to their actual release dates.

Historically, rehabilitation had been a primary goal of indeterminate sentencing. The federal Sentencing Reform Act of 1984 rejected imprisonment as a means of rehabilitation. Rather, it stated that punishment should serve the goals of retribution (to punish), education (to help prepare for legitimate employment), deterrence (to discourage repetition through fear), and incapacitation (to prevent repetition through confinement). The 1984 law abolished **parole** (suspension of part of a jail sentence) and made all sentences determinate, with sentence reduction allowed only for credits earned by good behavior while in custody. Binding sentencing guidelines now are established by the new U.S. Sentencing Commission, an administrative agency within the judicial branch of government. Felony and misdemeanor distinctions are unimportant because all criminal behavior is ranked in 43 different classes of severity, with corresponding sentences that vary depending on the defendant's record of prior convictions. This federal sentencing system has been severely criticized, primarily because it provides long sentences for relatively minor drug offenses. Judges object to it because it prevents them from exercising their discretion as to sentencing. Federal and state sentences are discussed later in this chapter, under the heading, "What Is the Punishment of Convicted Persons?"

The states vary widely in the severity of punishment that may be imposed by the sentencing judge for a particular crime. Some statutes prescribe determinate sentences, with a range of minimums and maximums. In all jurisdictions, a felony is substantially more blameworthy and more severely punished than a misdemeanor. At this writing, most states are re-examining their sentencing laws in response to widespread demand for harsher penalties for crimes.

WHAT ARE CRIMES AGAINST THE PERSON?

To be free of physical attack is of paramount value to all members of society. The right to life and physical security is the matrix of all the other inalienable rights of a person. Crimes of violence against persons therefore warrant the severest penalties. Yet, violence often grows out of emotions that are difficult to control. As a result, there are distinctions in moral culpability, and they are often subtle and difficult to apply. A discussion of the general rules that have evolved follows.

MURDER

Murder is the unlawful killing of a human being with **malice** (sometimes called **malice aforethought**), which denotes the highest degree of moral culpability or blameworthiness—an evil, cold-blooded state of mind. Both a paid killer and the person who did the hiring exemplify such a state of mind.

State laws classify murder into at least two categories—typically, murder of the **first degree** (or capital murder) and murder of the **second degree** (noncapital murder). Murder in the first degree may be punishable by death or by imprisonment for life with or without the possibility of parole. Murder in the second degree may be punishable by imprisonment for less than life.

Generally, any murder perpetrated by means of poison or torture, by ambush, during the commission of a dangerous felony (e.g., during rape or robbery), or by any other kind of willful, deliberate, or premeditated killing is murder of the highest degree. All other kinds of murder, as when some provocation exists, are deemed murder of a lesser degree. Premeditation is an important factor in determining the highest degree of murder and does not necessarily require any certain period of time to occur. A cold, calculated decision to kill may be arrived at in a short period of time. On the other hand, a sudden rash impulse, even though it includes an intent to kill, is not sufficient deliberation and premeditation to render an unlawful killing as "murder one." To be guilty of a deliberate and premeditated killing with malice aforethought, the slayer

1. must have weighed and considered the question of killing, and the reasons for and against such a choice, and

2. having in mind the consequences, have decided to commit, and

3. then actually have committed the unlawful act causing death.

These components are not easy to apply, as demonstrated by the following case.

> Ernest Martinez found his live-in girlfriend, Julie Ann, in his apartment in a compromising position with a man. Ernest climbed in the bathroom window, chasing Julie Ann and her friend out the front door into the streets. Martinez managed to hit the man on the head several times with a shower curtain rod, and then cornered Julie Ann in the rear alley. He beat her savagely in the alley until a neighbor asked what was going on. Martinez replied that he had "caught her in the act." He then dragged her back into his apartment, turned up the stereo, and beat her to death. Martinez was very jealous and often had warned Julie Ann about infidelity. Martinez contends he is guilty only of voluntary manslaughter because of the passion and rage he felt under the circumstances. How should the jury decide?

Martinez was found guilty of murder in the first degree on two separate theories: (1) there was evidence of premeditation and (2) his acts were murder by torture.[18] The intervention of the neighbor coupled with the act of turning up the stereo deprived the defendant of that intensity of passion that alone could have sufficed to reduce murder to voluntary manslaughter. There had been a "cooling-off period," supporting the finding of malice.

There are three general situations in which a defendant can be convicted of murder without personally killing anyone. The major shortcoming of these rules is that a relatively blameless defendant may receive the same severe punishment as a hardened killer.

Vicarious Murder Rule

Assume that A, B, and C all have conspired to kill the victim, but only A pulls the trigger. B and C are vicariously guilty of murder in the first degree. They are aiders and abettors and, as such, are principals. Massachusetts has adopted a "joint venture" theory of criminality in which individuals present at the scene of a crime, with knowledge that a codefendant intends to commit the crime, and who by agreement are willing and available to help that codefendant if necessary, are equally guilty.[19]

Felony-Murder Rule

Assume that A, B, and C have conspired to commit some inherently dangerous felony (such as armed robbery) but do not intend to kill anyone. Nonetheless, A pulls the trigger, killing the salesperson. B and C are also guilty of murder in the first degree even though they never intended that anyone be killed.* Even an aider and abettor (who, therefore, is also a principal) acting as "lookout" in the getaway car may be guilty of "murder one."[20]

Provocative-Act Rule

Assume that A, B, and C, although committing some dangerous crime, do not intend to kill anyone, and none of them pulls the trigger. Instead, A waves his gun, provoking some third party to fire the fatal bullet that kills C. A and B are guilty of murder in the first degree according to the provocative-act rule. This situation typically occurs with criminals fleeing the crime scene while being pursued by police. One defendant commits some act, such as firing a gun, that provokes the police to kill one of the criminals. The surviving perpetrators are guilty of murder.[21] The provocative-act rule has been rejected in many states including Pennsylvania, Colorado, New York, and New Mexico.[22]

The preceding rules involving vicarious responsibility are intended to deter criminal activity in which there is a high likelihood of an unintentional (i.e., careless or negligent) or accidental death.

Note that an aider and abettor to a felony that results in a homicide, such as a lookout or driver of a getaway car, who personally does not kill, who is not present at the killing, and who does not intend or anticipate the use of lethal force, cannot be sentenced to death. Such punishment would violate the Eighth Amendment, prohibiting cruel and unusual punishment.[23] Cruel and unusual punishment is discussed in detail later in this chapter. On the other hand, a getaway driver who has no intent to kill, and who does not personally commit a homicide, but who has a reckless indifference to life (such as evidenced by watching others perform a murder), can be sentenced to death.[24]

Juveniles Fernando and his two friends left their hideaway and drove into a rival gang's neighborhood intending to shoot "Cypress Park" members. On the first drive-by, shots were exchanged among shooters in Fernando's car, a rival gang member's car, and a nearby house. On a second drive-by, Caesar Sala, Fernando's shooter who was riding in the passenger seat, was fatally hit. Of what crime is Fernando guilty?

Fernando was found guilty of murder in the first degree under the provocative-act rule.[25] In many states, Fernando would be guilty of some felony other than murder.

---

*This felony-murder rule is disfavored by courts, although most states have some variation of felony-murder statutes. See *Suniga v. Bunnell*, 988 F.2d 664 (9th cir., 1992). Some states have reduced its classification to second-degree (Louisiana, New Hampshire, New York, and Pennsylvania) or third-degree (Maine and Wisconsin) murder. Among others, Hawaii, Kentucky, and Michigan have abolished it altogether.

Lawrence Hernandez entered Mr. and Mrs. Wolfe's coin shop in the afternoon, brandished a gun, and robbed them of coins and currency. Hernandez did not touch either of the Wolfes, but Mr. Wolfe died of a heart attack during the robbery. Of what crimes is Hernandez guilty?

Hernandez is, of course, guilty of armed robbery. In some states, he also is guilty of murder in the first degree under the felony-murder rule, which, as noted, is designed to deter negligent or accidental deaths as well as intentional homicides.[26] If an accomplice had been waiting in the car, acting as a lookout, he would be a principal and thus guilty with Hernandez of first-degree murder.

THE MALICE REQUIREMENT

The presence of malice aforethought may be implied from the conduct of the accused. Recall that when there is no malice, there can be no murder. Under such circumstances, the homicide is manslaughter.

Robert Rosenkrantz, age 18, was a "closet" homosexual, primarily because he feared reprisal from his father and family. His brother, Joey, discovered the truth and, along with his friend Steven, substantiated and revealed the truth to the family. Robert, under great mental strain, purchased an Uzi semiautomatic carbine, tracked down Steven, and killed him with a fusillade of bullets. Psychiatrists agreed that Robert was suffering from acute emotional disturbance. Robert appealed a second-degree murder conviction, arguing he was guilty only of voluntary manslaughter because there was no evidence of malice. What should be the result?

The second-degree murder conviction was affirmed on appeal.[27] Malice may be implied when, as here, the jury determines that no considerable provocation existed. Robert also unsuccessfully appealed that his sentence of 15 years to life plus 2 years for an 18-year-old using a firearm was cruel and unusual punishment in violation of the Eighth Amendment.

The Personhood Requirement

Malice is not the only statutory requirement of murder. The unlawful killing must be of a "human being." What constitutes a human being or "person" is among the more controversial issues in law.

For purposes of the Fourteenth Amendment to the U.S. Constitution, a fetus is not yet a person. Therefore, the respective states are free to define, as a matter of state law, when life begins, for the purpose of defining the crime of murder. The vast majority of states do not consider a fetus to be a person in a criminal law context; that is, there can be no murder of a fetus. California and a minority of other states (e.g., Illinois) amended their traditional murder statutes to include a fetus as a human being.[28] The emerging rule is that the unlawful killing of a fetus that has developed important human structures, usually seven to eight weeks after conception, can be murder.[29]

The U.S. Supreme Court has declared abortion legal throughout the country, and has also declared that the states can regulate abortions in the interest of protecting the "potentiality" of life.[30] Any distinction between a "human being" and a "potentiality of life" does not render unconstitutional the respective state's definitions of murder. The issue of abortion is discussed in Chapter 9.

MANSLAUGHTER

There are two general categories of **manslaughter**, both involving an unlawful killing of a person under some variety of emotional circumstances. **Voluntary manslaughter** is the most blameworthy because it is an intentional killing of a person. **Involuntary manslaughter** is an accidental killing. There is one further category in many states, **vehicular manslaughter**, specifically relating to deaths caused by the reckless driving of motor vehicles.

Voluntary manslaughter is an intentional killing—though without malice—in the heat of passion, as a result of severe provocation. As made clear by the Rosenkrantz case, discussed earlier, there must be a considerable heat of passion at the time of the killing from some substantial provocation. Otherwise, the homicide is murder. Robert Rosenkrantz was simply not in the heat of passion at the time of the killing. For example, he had purchased the Uzi many days before the killing, allowing plenty of time to "cool off."

Darwin Britcher agreed to drive two friends home from a teenagers' beer party. Britcher later testified that he had consumed only 9 beers and that it usually took 18 beers to impair his driving. His blood-alcohol level was determined to be .14 percent. He was speeding when his car left the road, hitting an embankment, a tree, and finally a telephone pole. Britcher and one passenger were seriously hurt; the other passenger died. Britcher was 19 years old. Can he be found guilty of, and be sentenced for, all three of the following crimes: (1) homicide by vehicle while driving under the influence of alcohol, (2) homicide by vehicle (for reckless driving), and (3) involuntary manslaughter?

Yes. There is no double jeopardy (twice being convicted for the same crime) in this case because the different crimes all contain different elements of proof, even though only a single accident was involved. For example, Britcher was recklessly speeding and he also was driving while intoxicated.[31] However, in most states Britcher's sentences on the various crimes would run concurrently (each year served in prison would count as a year served on each sentence) rather than consecutively. And in some states, he could be sentenced on only one conviction because they are all transactionally related. The *Britcher* case also exemplifies the complexities permeating criminal theory.

Note that in the *Britcher* case, one instance of drunken driving resulted in several felonies. In some states, if the manner in which a vehicle is driven is grossly reckless and careless of human life, malice may be implied and the charge then becomes murder in the second degree.

Robert Watson, having been out drinking, ran a red light at high speed and narrowly missed hitting another car by skidding to a stop. He took off, again at high speed, and collided with a Toyota at another intersection, skidding 292 feet before coming to a stop. The driver of the Toyota and his 6-year-old daughter were killed. Watson's blood-alcohol was .23 percent. Watson was charged with murder but contended he could be tried only for manslaughter because there was no proof of malice. Was Watson correct?

No. Malice may be implied from any conduct that has a high probability of resulting in a death and when it is done in wanton disregard for human life. Watson was speeding through city streets while intoxicated, an act presenting a great risk of death. He narrowly avoided one accident, only to cause another. These factors support a finding of implied malice. The jury verdict, guilty of murder in the second degree, was affirmed.[32]

> Carrie was born a "cocaine baby." As a result, she was undersized and ill. Cocaine was found in the bloodstream of her young mother, Melanie, as well as in the baby's urine. Melanie was charged with child abuse and with supplying drugs to a minor. Is Melanie guilty of the crime of being a bad and abusive mother? Or does the right of privacy protect Melanie's right to live her life as she sees fit?

Prosecutors estimate that several hundred thousand newborns are exposed to illegal drugs every year; these children are likely to be born prematurely and often die shortly after birth. If they survive the immediate postnatal period, they tend to be abnormally small and face increased risk of deformities and crib death. Should cocaine-using mothers be prosecuted for crimes upon their fetuses? Opponents of this idea argue that a "prenatal police force" would face the prospect of arresting not only users of cocaine, but also users of alcohol (also known to damage fetuses), smokers, and perhaps even women who must stand on their feet all day at their places of employment, a practice that is believed to cause damage to the fetus.

Several courts have refused to find mothers guilty of child abuse statutes on the grounds either that the "fetus" is not understood to be a "child" within the meaning of the statutes, or that the mothers did not have fair notice that they could face criminal charges for such behavior.[33] However, the South Carolina Supreme Court held that the statutory language "child" in its plain meaning included a "viable" (in the third trimester) fetus. The mother's conviction was affirmed.[34]

The final question is, if a pregnant woman has legal obligations to protect her fetus, how could she, at the same time, have the right to compel an abortion?[35]

In Chapter 9, we consider the related issue of civil remedies to protect fetuses from the behavior of their mothers.

RAPE

Sexual intercourse without the consent of the adult victim is the definition of the crime of **rape**. Rape statutes ordinarily apply to persons of opposite gender, while special statutes govern unlawful sexual conduct between same-sex adults. If the victim is a consenting minor, the crime is often called **statutory rape**. The purpose of statutes prohibiting sexual intercourse between adults and minors is to protect children. Presumably children cannot, because of their minority, give informed consent.

Mary Kay LeTourneau, age 35, a popular teacher in Seattle and the mother of four children, pleaded guilty to having sex with a 13-year-old boy who had been a student in her sixth-grade class. The two had originally met in her second-grade class. According to the victim, they had exchanged rings and planned the pregnancy that produced their daughter. Was Mary guilty of rape?

Yes. Mary was sentenced to seven years in prison, but the sentence was suspended after six months and probation granted.[36] Promptly following her release from jail in early 1998, Mary violated probation by again having sex with her underage victim. Her probation violated, Mary went back to jail to finish serving her seven-year sentence, although she was pregnant. Her daughter Georgia was born in October 1998—the same month a book co-authored by Mary and her underage victim was published in Europe. This bizarre case exemplifies how seriously the law recognizes the distinction between apparent and informed consent.

Although rape statutes are designed to protect minors, the offense can be committed by a defendant who is under age 18. Traditionally, children under age 14 are presumed incapable of committing rape because of their tender years. In one state the traditional immunity was overruled on the basis that there is "no sound legal or medical basis" for its application to rape. The conviction of a 13-year-old boy for the rape of an 11-year-old girl was approved.[37]

The crime of rape has received much public attention in recent years. Generally, attention has focused on the involvement of the victim in the administration of justice; that is, how the victim is treated immediately after the crime and to what extent the victim must endure humiliating trial tactics, often dealing with prior sexual experience(s). An isolated example exemplifying attitudes that sometimes surround rape prosecutions occurred when a grand jury in Austin, Texas, declined to indict (i.e., charge with crime) an accused knife-wielding rapist because the female victim had asked that he use a condom as some protection against AIDS or other sexually transmitted diseases (STDs).[38] The use of a condom can destroy the opportunity for scientific matching (almost comparable to fingerprint matching) of a semen specimen to a suspect.

Raymond Mitchell III telephoned a young woman, pretending vocally to be her boyfriend. She agreed to play a game by unlocking her door, wearing a blindfold, and then acting out any sexual fantasy she wanted. Raymond, fulfilling his part of the telephone agreement, then entered the blindfolded woman's home, engaged in sex with her, and silently left. They repeated this event twice a week for two months, during which the young woman erroneously believed her unseen suitor was her boyfriend. When charged with rape, Mitchell defended that the sex was consensual. What was the result?

Almost all states have some variety of "rape by fraud" laws that apply to situations in which a person's (usually a woman's) consent to sex is based on any sort of deceit. In the case of Mitchell, if he told the young woman that he was a specific person, that probably would be a sufficient lie to constitute a crime. But if he said, "I'm whoever you think I am," and the woman assumed it was her boyfriend, he probably could not be convicted. Mitchell, known as the "fantasy man," pleaded guilty in one other similar case through a plea bargain under which he received probation.[39]

Penalties for rape sometimes seem inadequate, as many felons have repeated sex-related offenses. Furthermore, when prosecuted, juries tend to be skeptical that the act was indeed without consent unless the victim risks death or severe bodily injury in an attempt to resist. Saying "no" is not as convincing to some juries as when the victim literally fights for her life.

There has been much reform; more is anticipated. For example, the Supreme Court of New Jersey has relaxed its state's definition of rape by declaring that sexual penetration alone meets the requirement of "physical force." No physical resistance by the victim is required. All other states (except Wisconsin) require proof of coercion or force in addition to penetration. Some believe the New Jersey court went too far, effectively requiring innocent men to prove that the women with whom they have sex consented to the act.*

Most states, responding to the need for reform, have enacted **rape shield statutes** protecting victims from courtroom questioning about prior sexual experience(s) with persons other than the defendant.

Ignacio Perea kidnapped an 11-year-old boy in Dade County, Florida, took him to a deserted warehouse, and raped him. Perea had a clinic receipt in his pocket indicating that he had tested HIV positive for the deadly AIDS virus. Of what crimes is Perea guilty?

A jury found Perea guilty of kidnapping (a felony discussed later in this chapter), rape, and attempted murder. This is the first time a jury had considered the AIDS virus to be a deadly weapon.[40] Other states have created new, specific crimes for those who engage in sexual contact while knowingly infected with the AIDS virus.

During trial for forcible "date" rape, there was evidence that the victim, Ms. M, initially consented to sexual intercourse with defendant David Vela, but changed her mind during the act. She told him to "stop." David nonetheless forcibly continued against her will. Is David guilty of any crime?

David is not guilty of forcible rape because Ms. M consented when penetration first occurred. The essence of the crime of rape is the outrage felt by the victim at being violated. If she retracts her consent during intercourse, but the male continues, she may certainly feel outrage, but of less magnitude than from nonconsensual intercourse. The male who persists once consent is withdrawn, however, may be guilty of another crime, such as assault and battery.[41]

---

*The New Jersey case involved a 17-year-old girl who consented to "kissing and heavy petting" in her home with a 15-year-old male houseguest, but who said "no" before penetration. She did not resist. *In the Interest of M.T.S.*, 129 N.J. 422, 609 A.2d 1266 (1992); *The National Law Journal*, 21 September 1992, 5.

EXTORTION AND KIDNAPPING

Autumn Jackson demanded $40 million from Bill Cosby to keep secret his alleged parenthood, and then signed a $24 million payoff agreement that was negotiated in an FBI sting. Although Jackson's mother had a sexual liaison with Cosby approximately nine months before Autumn's birth, Cosby's paternity is denied and unproven. Is it extortion to demand money to keep quiet a fact you believe to be true?[42]

Yes. What Autumn believed is not relevant (nor is Cosby's alleged parentage) to her wrongful demand for hush money in exchange for withholding a civil paternity prosecution. Note that the FBI was involved because the threat was forwarded across state lines, thereby invoking federal jurisdiction. Ms. Jackson was sentenced to 26 months in prison, but could be released in as few as 6 months if she completes a rehabilitation program. Notice that this example involved an attempt to extort money out of fear of publicity, not out of fear of physical harm to anyone.

Richard Alday telephoned the father of a 7-year-old boy to say that he had kidnapped his son. Alday demanded $15,000, threatening that the child would be "hurt bad" unless the money was paid. Before the payment of any ransom, it was discovered that the boy had not been kidnapped but had become lost when he wandered away from the family summer cabin. Alday was arrested. During prosecution for extortion, his attorney argued that no crime had been committed because no kidnapping had occurred. Did a crime occur?

Yes. **Extortion** is the crime of obtaining of money by the wrongful use of force or fear. Alday committed extortion when he tried to obtain money by threatening injury to the son.[43] This example of threatening physical injury is unlike the Cosby example of threatening publicity. Although there was no actual kidnapping in this case, it would have been a separate crime if it had occurred.

Extortion is recognized as an inherently vicious crime. Some states confine the meaning of extortion to the unlawful taking by an official under color of his office (e.g., "pay me now or I'll have you arrested"), while **blackmail** refers to an unlawful taking of money by a private person under some threat.[44] The threat may be to accuse the victim of a crime, or to expose some deformity, previous crime, or important secret of the victim. And, of course, as in the *Alday* case, any threat to injure a person is also extortion. It is no defense to extortion that the "facts" upon which the threats were based are later revealed to be untrue. It is the threat to reveal them, if the wrongdoer is not paid, that is a criminal act.

Kidnapping involves the use of force (or threat of force) in taking a person from one place to another against his or her will. Aggravated kidnapping occurs when an additional crime is involved, such as kidnapping to commit robbery, or to collect a ransom or reward, or to commit extortion. A typical sentence for aggravated kidnapping, without serious injury, is life imprisonment with the possibility of parole. Any homicide occurring during a kidnapping will trigger the felony-murder rule, enhancing the crime to murder in the first degree.

ROBBERY

Robbery is the taking of money or other personal property of another from his or her person or immediate presence by means of force or fear. A specific intent to steal is a necessary element of the crime. Robbery commands a greater penalty than theft (stealing without confrontation, discussed later) because there is a greater possibility of violence when the victim and offender are face-to-face. **Armed robbery** (use of a dangerous weapon) typically results in an enhanced penalty.

Carjacking is the wrongful taking of control of an occupied vehicle. It is a specialized version of robbery that typically results in an enhanced penalty due to the obvious likelihood of violence and danger to society.

Recall that even an accidental killing that occurs during the commission of a dangerous felony, such as armed robbery, elevates the homicide to murder of the first degree under the felony-murder rule, and that all participants, even the get-away driver, are equally guilty.

MAYHEM

A person is guilty of **mayhem** if he or she wrongfully dismembers, disfigures, or maims another person (e.g., cuts the tongue, severs a finger, puts out an eye, slits the nose, etc.).

Mrs. Lorena Bobbitt sliced off the penis of her sleeping husband, John Wayne Bobbitt, then fled from their home and ultimately tossed his member from her car into the street. Found by a passerby, Mr. Bobbitt's member was surgically re-attached. Is the crime reduced to battery because the dismemberment was not permanent?

No. Once the crime of mayhem occurs, the crime is not reduced by the success of a subsequent surgical or other repair. The permanency and nature of a dismemberment may affect the penalty imposed by the sentencing judge, however.

Bernie Lopez threw a beer bottle into a car, hitting Raul Morales and rendering him legally blind in the left eye. Bernie did not intend to damage Raul seriously, let alone render him partially blind. Is he guilty of battery or mayhem?

Bernie is guilty of mayhem. Specific intent to maim is not an element of the crime. All that is necessary is a general wrongful or criminal intent, such as Bernie had when he threw the beer bottle.[45]

ASSAULT AND BATTERY

Criminal assault is an unlawful attempt, coupled with a present ability, to commit a violent injury upon the person of another. If the assault is successful and injury results, a **criminal battery** has occurred. There can be no battery in criminal law without an assault because battery is a completed assault. For assault, there must be a present ability to injure. A menacing gesture with an unloaded gun is not an assault in the criminal law, although the result is different in the civil law (see Chapter 7). An unloaded gun cannot injure the victim unless it is used to pistol-whip or to club. Otherwise, there is no present ability to cause physical injury. On the other hand, one who fires at a service station attendant who is protected by bulletproof glass is guilty of assault. The shooter has the ability to strike out, and by shooting does in fact strike, even though the bullets cannot reach the intended victim.[46] Waving an unloaded gun toward another person may be a lesser crime than assault, such as brandishing a firearm.

HATE CRIMES AND TERRORISM

Violence directed at victims because of their race, religion, political affiliation, or other personal beliefs (e.g., supporting abortion rights) is loosely referred to as **hate crime**. Some states have included within their penalty enhancement laws those crimes that are based on hatred of the victim's sexual orientation. International terrorism or any antigovernment crime directed at randomly selected victims also may be classified within this category.

It is believed that the number of hate groups (often identified, for example, as Ku Klux Klan, skinheads, neo-Nazis, white Supremacists, and black separatists) as well the number of individuals harboring racial and government hatred is growing.[47] For this reason, legislation against hate crimes has also been on the rise. Most states and the federal government require penalty enhancements for hate crimes. Opponents of hate crime legislation, on the other hand, argue that the reason why crimes are committed does not affect the victim nor reflect the egregiousness of the act and should therefore be ignored.

STALKING

Stalking involves repeatedly being around or even secretly watching a person, making uninvited written or verbal communications, or making implied threats. It often involves telephone harassment or waiting for someone to appear. Victims typically are women between 19 and 39 years old and they are stalked repeatedly, some for years. Stalkers often are former husbands, boyfriends, or people the victims had lived with. A new crime whose notoriousness was assured by the film *Fatal Attraction*, stalking is prohibited in all 50 states. Court restraining orders are available to potential victims before any physical harm is inflicted. Although known to be widespread (about 1 in every 12 women report having been stalked), most stalking is not reported by the victims.[48]

Jonathan Norman, age 31, was arrested for attempting to enter filmmaker Steven Spielberg's home while carrying a "rape kit" containing handcuffs and duct tape among other paraphernalia. Norman's former lover, Charles Markovich, testified that it was Norman's secret intention to bind and rape Spielberg in the presence of his wife, Kate Capshaw. In defense, Norman's public defender contended that it is not a crime to have "weird thoughts" about someone famous, that Norman never entered Spielberg's property, that when told to leave, he does. Is Norman guilty of stalking?

Yes.[49] Although conduct may fall short of an attempted crime, it nonetheless may constitute stalking under state statutes.

WHAT ARE CRIMES AGAINST PROPERTY?

ARSON

Arson is the wrongful burning of real or personal property, either intentionally or recklessly—simple negligence is not enough. It is the classic crime against property. Punishment for arson typically varies with the type of property burned. For example, arson of an inhabited structure is more serious than arson of a vacant storage building. It is not arson to burn one's own property unless there is some fraudulent purpose (e.g., obtaining casualty insurance proceeds) or damage to the property of others.

BURGLARY

Burglary is the unlawful entry into premises, structures, and vehicles with the intent to commit larceny (theft) or any other felony. Some states have modified the common-law definitions of crimes against property that now vary among the states. Therefore, crime statistics may be skewed because, for example, identical terms may not indicate identical criminal acts. For example, one specialized crime triggering enhanced sentences is **home invasion burglary**, where gang members burst into the victim's home and quickly overpower all occupants. Unfortunately a variety of other crimes usually ensue, such as murder, rape, or robbery. In some states, burglary includes breaking into a vehicle for the purpose of committing larceny or theft—crimes we will examine next.

THEFT

Theft is the modern catchall term that embraces the unlawful taking of another's personal property. It includes the common-law crime of **larceny**, which is the wrongful taking of another's property without the use of force or fear. **Embezzlement** is a common-law form of larceny where an employee steals money from his or her employer. In embezzlement access to the money is lawful, as by a bookkeeper or government officer, but is wrongfully and secretly diverted to the personal use of the embezzler. **Larceny by trick** is the common-law crime of wrongfully obtaining property through some dishonest scam or fraudulent scheme. In all of these definitions, the modern term is simply *theft* and its definition includes the conduct previously called *larceny* under the common law.

Marsha Jones used her computer to obtain Mari Frank's name, social security and driver's license numbers. With her newly acquired identity Marsha was able to purchase a red Mustang convertible on credit. Unfortunately, while Mari Frank continues to defend herself from the collection agency that is attempting to collect the Mustang's price, Marsha continues to possess and drive the flashy car. Is it a crime to steal another person's identity?

Yes.[50] Nine states prosecute identity theft as a felony. In other states there is no crime for stealing identification, although other crimes may apply if the stolen identification is used to defraud a merchant, such as a Ford sales agency. Identity theft is a rapidly growing crime. If the offense involves interstate commerce, it also is a federal crime punishable by up to 15 years in prison.

Theft also can be defined by degree. The purpose in classifying criminal acts is to make the penalty fit the crime. **Grand theft** is a felony involving the taking of something of substantial value, as defined by statute (e.g., $400 or more in some states), or the taking of a certain kind of property, such as motor vehicles, firearms, or farm animals. Theft of personal property worth less than the statutory definition of substantial value, such as $400, is a misdemeanor and is called **petty theft**. Thus, for example, shoplifting may be either a felony or a misdemeanor depending upon the value of the stolen merchandise. Obviously, grand theft results in a harsher penalty than petty theft.

RECEIVING STOLEN PROPERTY

Knowingly buying stolen property is a crime. To be responsible for the offense, the accused must have known, or should have known, the property was stolen. Proof of knowledge may be inferred from the circumstances, such as adequacy of the price paid, the character of the vendor, the time and place of delivery, and so on. Ownership of the stolen property does not change; an innocent purchaser of stolen property must return it to the real owner and may seek reimbursement only from the person (generally the thief) who sold it to him or her.

> Sam purchased a car radio and CD player from Jaspar at the Greater Tuna Flea Market. The price was attractive, but not unusually low. Sam installed the unit and proudly showed it off to some of his friends at school. Donna noticed how similar the unit looked to one that had been stolen from her mother's car. She wrote down the serial number and took it home for comparison with her mother's warranty registration documents. The numbers were the same. Is Sam guilty of a crime? Who gets to keep the radio and CD player?

Sam is innocent of any wrongdoing. He did not know, and had no reason to suspect, that the radio had been stolen. Donna's mother still owns the radio and is entitled to its return. Sam theoretically could sue Jaspar for return of his money. More likely than not, Jaspar will be gone. Jaspar may or may not be guilty of a crime, depending on how he obtained the radio.

Misuse of a credit card, issuing a check knowing there are insufficient funds at the bank, and malicious mischief (vandalism) are examples of other crimes against property. "Keying" a car (scratching its painted surfaces with a key) is an example of malicious mischief that is remarkably costly to repair. Spray-painting graffiti is another example of costly vandalism that has provoked widespread concern and public outrage.* When crimes such as these involve small amounts of money or damage, they are misdemeanors. When victims suffer significant

---

*Spray-painting graffiti in public places is a very serious crime in Singapore. In early 1994, the conviction of Ohioan Michael Fay for the offense of malicious mischief was front-page news and a matter of national television coverage. The 18-year-old Fay was sentenced to four months in prison and six lashes (later reduced to four) across his buttocks with a 4-foot long, ½-inch thick, rattan cane. *San Francisco Chronicle*, 2 May 1994.

For information about the crime of shoplifting see http://www.employeetheft.com

financial loss as a result of the crime, courts usually impose a penalty and order the convicted defendant to make full restitution.

WHAT ARE CRIMES AGAINST PUBLIC HEALTH, SAFETY, AND WELFARE?

All states have adopted either the Uniform Controlled Substances Act or the Uniform Narcotic Drug Act. These laws classify drugs in schedules depending upon their harmfulness. For example, Schedule I drugs have a high potential for abuse and no generally accepted medical use. They include heroin, LSD, marijuana, mescaline, peyote, PCP, and cocaine base, as well as crack. There is an organized movement to legalize a restricted availability of marijuana on the grounds that it is a better or more effective painkiller for certain patients, such as cancer and AIDS sufferers. State laws created by the initiative process to legalize marijuana for such purpose have begun the appellate process, heading toward possible review by the U.S. Supreme Court.

Advocates of the legalization of marijuana distinguish between it as a "soft" drug and the "hard" drugs of cocaine and heroin. Current research, however, indicates that chronic use of marijuana causes chemical changes in the brain that are similar to those caused by withdrawal from cocaine, heroin, or alcohol. Thus, the susceptibility to using a "hard" drug, or alcohol, to relieve unpleasant symptoms of withdrawal from marijuana is increased.[51]

Schedule II drugs, such as opium, codeine, morphine, and amphetamine, have some accepted medical use. Further down the scale, Schedule V drugs have a low potential for abuse but may lead to some psychological or physical dependence.

Penalties are related to the activity (such as selling or manufacturing versus merely using) and the class of drug involved in the crime, and range from misdemeanors to felonies. For example, in California, using or being under the influence of cocaine, heroin, or marijuana is a misdemeanor with a maximum sentence of one year in county jail plus five years probation. On the other hand, possession for sale of these drugs is a felony punishable by up to four years in state prison.[52] In Florida, it is no crime to use or to be under the influence of a controlled substance. However, selling, buying, or manufacturing cocaine or heroin (Schedule I drugs) is a felony in the second degree with a penalty of up to 15 years plus a $10,000 fine.[53]

Much controversy surrounds the implications of imposing long prison sentences for drug offenses involving the less expensive yet very potent "crack" cocaine. Because poor, inner-city youths are more likely to be involved with "crack" than more affluent adults, the overwhelming majority of those imprisoned for its use are young African American males. Are there disparate penalties for users of inexpensive drugs compared to users of expensive narcotics? Perhaps.

Actor Robert Downey, Jr., was arrested in 1996 when police stopped his speeding pickup truck and found cocaine, crack, heroin, and a pistol. He pleaded guilty and was sentenced to three years probation. In 1998, Downey's probation was revoked for use of drugs and alcohol in violation of the court's previous order. He then was sentenced to six months in jail. However, he received four all-day furloughs from jail to complete the movie *In Dreams*. Deputy sheriffs had been asking for and receiving autographs from Downey, posing for pictures with him, and even letting the actor buy them lunch at the movie studio. Downey also was permitted to visit a plastic surgeon after a jailhouse fight. Are these "celebrity perks" legal?

No. Judges do have discretion to tailor sentences and to modify state incarceration procedures. It is not clear whether or not a "furlough" to participate in a movie is a proper exercise of that discretion. The judge in the Downey case was directed by a higher court to stop further "furloughs" pending further review, but Downey's sentence ended before a more definitive result could be made.[54] You might consider whether an inner-city African American youth, or any non-celebrity, would have received similar perks from the judge.

Some conduct that endangers the public health or safety is a misdemeanor.

Marcy Allen walked up to a metal detector in a public building. The bell sounded and her purse was searched. Marcy was carrying a key ring that was designed also as a can opener, windshield scraper, and hair lifter. It consisted of a cat head with two holes for eyes and sharp triangles for ears. By placing one's fingers through the "eyes," the key ring doubled as a sort of "brass knuckles" with sharp points (the ears of the cat). Marcy was charged with carrying an illegal weapon. What was the result?

States prohibit the buying or possession of certain kinds of implements that primarily can be used as weapons. So-called "brass knuckles" and switchblade knives are examples. But what of a key ring that happens to be shaped like a cat's head and, therefore, has pointy ears? The jury sided with the state and convicted Marcy of a misdemeanor. She was placed on six months probation.[55]

Other examples of misdemeanors are (1) going to the scene of an emergency for viewing when it results in impeding official personnel, (2) discarding a refrigerator with its door intact, (3) exhibiting the deformities of another person in exchange for money, (4) killing a farm animal while hunting, (5) operating machinery too close to high voltage wires, (6) attaching a burning candle to a balloon and releasing it, (7) donating blood or body organs while knowingly suffering from AIDS, (8) violating laws regulating food, liquor, drugs, and cosmetics, (9) violating fish and game laws, (10) allowing animals with known vicious propensities to be loose, (11) adulterating candy with laxatives or other chemicals, (12) cutting public shrubs, (13) selling alcoholic beverages after hours, and (14) firing a pistol up into the sky within city limits. In some states, one or more of these crimes may be felonies depending upon the circumstances involved.

WHAT ARE CRIMES AGAINST PUBLIC DECENCY AND MORALS?

One of the most controversial classifications of criminal behavior involves crimes against public decency and morals. Examples in this category are unlawful sexual intercourse, sodomy, and oral copulation. California is one state that does not restrict sexual activities between consenting adults in private places, but some states prohibit all "unnatural and lascivious" acts whether in private or not.[56]

> Responding to a telephone complaint that a burglary was taking place, police burst into a home discovering, instead of a burglar, the residents John Lawrence and Tyrone Garner engaging in sodomy. They were arrested, booked, and jailed overnight for violation of the Texas misdemeanor sodomy law. Lawrence and Garner pleaded "no contest," were fined $125 each, and then filed an appeal on the grounds that the law was unconstitutional. What will be the result on appeal?[57]

Lawrence and Garner argue that the sodomy law makes it illegal for homosexuals to engage in the identical sexual activity that is legal for heterosexuals—and is therefore unconstitutional. Many expect this and other similar cases to slowly work their way toward review of the entire subject by the U.S. Supreme Court. Until then, sodomy is a crime in some, but not all, states.

Other examples of behavior that is criminal in some, or all, states include incest (intercourse between specified classes of related persons), lewd conduct with children, adultery (intercourse between a cohabiting married and unmarried person), obscenity and indecency, prostitution and pimping (arranging for the prostitution of another), seduction, abortion (except pursuant to law or as allowed by the Therapeutic Abortion Act), child stealing by a parent, child neglect, failure to support a dependent, and gambling (except as specifically authorized by statute).

Sex perversion is a catchall crime that includes sodomy between consenting adults as well as lewd or lascivious acts with a child. In some states conviction of sex perversion or any other crime involving lascivious activity (such as rape, pimping, or prostitution) has for many years resulted in a continuing duty, after release from jail, to register with the local police as a sex offender. Such registration is intended to provide law enforcement with a list of "usual suspects" to be checked when sex crimes occur, but it has been difficult to enforce, is often ignored by law enforcement agencies, and has not proved to be an effective deterrent. However, in 1996, following the notorious murder of 7-year-old Megan Kanka, Congress passed a law encouraging states to adopt procedures disclosing the identity and residences of sex offenders. In response, the states have adopted statutes referred to as "Megan's Law." These statutes authorize law enforcement to publicize the identification and residential address of convicted sex offenders who are on parole or have served their sentences. The purpose is to protect families through disclosure. Names and addresses of convicted sex offenders are made available by CD-ROM held at local police stations, distributed by hand to households in the neighborhood, or made available on the Internet; sometimes photographs are also distributed to make identification by neighbors easy. Delaware requires that sex offender status be identified on drivers' licenses. This may cause prospective employers to hire someone else, but how it can help families avoid sex predators is unclear.

Critics of Megan's Law focus upon the fairness of subjecting persons who have served their time and paid their debt to society to a lifetime of harassment. Disclosure of sex offenders may result in an inability to retain employment or to enjoy the life available to others living in the suburbs without public shame.

To see the impact of Megan's Law, see
http://www.vsp.state.va.us

http://

There are also fears of vigilantism, although there are no examples of such at the date of this writing (1999). Some question the potential results when sex offenders are repeatedly "pushed" from one neighborhood to another, perhaps until finally locating in the inner-cities in high-density apartments and public housing. With the increased anonymity found in densely populated cities, the risk to poor children may be increased as more affluent children in the suburbs become more protected. Regardless, the public strongly favors implementation of Megan's Law,[58] and courts have upheld application of Megan's Law, ruling that it does not constitute additional punishment.[59]

Jonathan Hawes, age 29, planned to live with his mother in the small town of Dilley, about 25 miles from Portland, Oregon, upon his release from prison where he had served five years for sexually abusing two 10-year-old girls. Upon notification under Megan's Law, community members had a meeting with Hawes' mother. Tempers flared, there was talk of guard dogs, burning down the home, even killing Hawes. One resident shouted in the face of Hawes' mother, "When can I kill him?" The home where Hawes planned to live sits isolated from children in the middle of 27 acres of pasture. Ultimately members of the community offered to purchase the home, to get rid of Hawes, and then to sell the home later to a more acceptable person. Is Hawes legally obligated to sell and move?

No. But as his mother said, "If everyone in the community hates you, wants to sue you, wants to do you bodily harm, do you really have options?" An agreement of sale was reached and Hawes moved on.[60]

Some critics contend that undue and unjustified amounts of public law enforcement, money, and police attention are devoted to what they call "crimes without victims": deviant sexual behavior; fornication; homosexuality between consenting adults; cohabitation; prostitution; criminal abortion; illegal gambling; drunkenness in public; and the use of illegal drugs, including marijuana, heroin, and cocaine. These critics argue that our society is being regulated by "lifestyle police." Other people vigorously support what appears to be a hopeless, losing battle against each of these offenses. Among this latter group of people are those who believe that deviant sexual behavior and homosexuality are unnatural and unhealthful. Others contend that prostitution exploits and debases women, contributes to widespread venereal disease, and leads to other crimes, such as drug abuse. Those who oppose abortion point out that it sometimes threatens the mother's life while invariably destroying fetal life, and they believe that it represents a devaluing of human life that is harmful to society and morally wrong. Many contend that both illegal and legal gambling not only exploit gullible poor people but also divert funds from food and other necessities and commonly involve evasion of income taxes. And those who support laws against public drunkenness and the use of illegal drugs say that such laws are necessary to protect society from the actions of users as well as to discourage people from becoming users and suffering the ruinous effects of drug abuse and alcoholism —and then expecting taxpayers to finance their care and rehabilitation.

John V., age 16, screamed obscenities at his neighbor, Nancy W., who was driving past his house. Complaint was made and John was charged with violating a statute that prohibits "offensive words in a public place which are inherently likely to provoke an immediate violent reaction." Nancy had become angry, and then furious. She was incoherent, enraged, and humiliated, although she admitted she had "flipped off" John on prior occasions. John was convicted and placed on probation. He contends the law is unconstitutionally overbroad and vague, and has appealed. What should be the result?

John lost.[61] The right of free speech is not absolute. Not protected are the lewd and obscene, the profane, the libelous and insulting, or "fighting" words. For fighting words to be a crime, they must be uttered, as here, in a provocative manner, so there is a clear and present danger that an immediate breach of the peace will erupt. Such words are not protected because they are of such slight social value as a step to truth that any benefit is clearly outweighed by the social interest in order and morality.[62] Obviously, these are distinctions that are difficult to make, especially on a consistent basis, if only because the circumstances vary so widely.

WHAT ARE SOME EXAMPLES OF OTHER CRIMES?

WHITE-COLLAR CRIMES

The term **white-collar crime** is applied to nonviolent illegal acts committed by individuals or corporations in a business setting. Typical examples include theft, fraud, bribery, illegal kickbacks, embezzlement of money or trade secrets, prohibited "insider" information exchanges among securities dealers and corporate managers, and bid-rigging of construction contracts. There is a widespread perception that state and local prosecutors are swamped with traditional "street" crimes and display little interest in active pursuit of business crimes committed by white-collar professionals. There is another widespread perception that even those convicted of such crimes receive light sentences, and that their time is served in relatively comfortable "country-club," low-security prisons.

Although business crimes can be very complicated and difficult to prove beyond a reasonable doubt, there is reason to believe that both perceptions may change in the future as prosecutors increase their attention to white-collar crimes and ask for tougher sentencing.*

At age 16, Barry Minkow began a carpet-cleaning business in the family garage. Minkow became a youthful symbol of free enterprise by his early twenties as his company, ZZZZ Best, skyrocketed onto Wall Street and into homes across the United States through television advertising. On

*High-profile defendants convicted of multimillion dollar white-collar crimes involving securities include David Bloom (mail and securities fraud, 8 years); Paul Bilzerian (securities and tax fraud, 4 years plus $1.5 million fine); Stephen Wang, Jr., (insider trading, 3 years); and John Galanis (federal tax-shelter fraud, 27 years and state securities fraud, 7 to 21 years concurrently). *The Wall Street Journal*, 26 October 1988 and 28 September 1989. The champion of all white-collar criminals, Michael Milken, is discussed later in this chapter.

the way to this pinnacle of success, he swindled banks and investors out of $26 million with a pyramid of lies about company earnings and financial success. He essentially "cooked the books" of ZZZZ Best to obtain bank and investor monies. A jury convicted him of 57 counts of fraud, carrying a maximum of 403 years in prison and $50 million in fines. Eleven other defendants were convicted with Minkow. Can Minkow's victims recover their losses?

The victims did initiate costly and long-lasting civil actions to recover their losses, but the Minkows financial resources are not likely to allow payment. The judge ordered full restitution of $26 million.[63] Victims probably can deduct their losses on their tax returns and thereby reduce the income taxes they otherwise would be obligated to pay. Thus, indirectly, all other taxpayers share the loss because they have to pay more to offset the ultimate effect of those deductions. Barry Minkow did not serve 403 years in jail—he was sentenced to 25 years and served 7. While in prison Minkow became a "born-again" Christian earning a Master's degree in Christian Ministries. At last report, he is beginning a new life as a motivational speaker.

Giant corporations, as well as high-profile individuals, are more often charged with violating laws and regulations than smaller businesses and less well-known individuals. In February 1994, General Electric and the De Beers Centenary of Switzerland were indicted for conspiracy to fix prices of industrial diamonds in world markets. These companies are the largest world users of industrial diamonds, which are used in tools, not jewelry. De Beers group does business in just about every country in the world except the United States. In December 1994, a federal judge in Columbus, Ohio, dismissed the case, ruling there was insufficient evidence to warrant submission to a jury. The charges, although unproven, exemplify the government's enthusiasm in pursuing white-collar crime. The investigation took two-and-one-half years of intensive efforts.[64]

White-collar crime can occur in securities markets where stock markets can be used by insiders (owners and managers of businesses) to raise huge sums of money from investors seeking profits.

In 1988 a corporation, Bre-X, was formed by John Walsh. It was not successful until 1993, when it announced the discovery of a huge gold mine in Indonesia. The price of Bre-X stock began immediately to rise, attaining a level of $100 per share by 1996—yet no gold had been produced. Bre-X then announced that there were 40 million ounces of gold in its claim. The stock promptly soared to $281 per share. Later in 1996, Mr. Walsh and his wife Jeannette, the company secretary, began selling their stock, taking in some $20 million. In March 1997, a Bre-X geologist fell to his death from a helicopter in Indonesia—a death that was labeled a suicide. The stock crashed and became valueless by year's end. Independent tests revealed that there was no marketable gold in the mines. Mutual funds were the big losers in this white-collar fiasco.[65] What laws were broken?

Until accountants, securities fraud investigators, lawyers, financial market officials, and prosecutors sort through the records and documents surrounding this huge fraud, just what crimes are involved is unknown. The point is that white-collar crime, whether it involves fraud, embezzlement, securities violations, bribery, or other crimes, can be devastating to its victims and to the public. The suspicion often lingers that all of the missing money will somehow remain unaccounted for.

Tax evasion probably is the most familiar white-collar crime. Simply stated, it involves knowingly cheating on your income taxes, and it can be a serious crime—a felony. It is widely remembered that the infamous Al Capone, whose evil ways during Prohibition could not be successfully proven in court, ultimately was convicted for income tax evasion. The government pursued a less famous individual, Reuben Sturman, for some 29 years, trying to convict him on obscenity charges. Sturman masterminded a pornography empire that gave him a net worth estimated by authorities at $100 million, much of which had been laundered (i.e., funneled through other organizations—in this case, through Swiss and Caribbean banks—to create the appearances of business profits). The government's first break came in 1989 when, like Al Capone, Sturman was convicted of income tax fraud and sentenced to ten years in prison. He escaped from prison in 1992, only to be caught within two months. The Internal Revenue Service took 12 years to untangle Sturman's web of dummy corporations and foreign bank accounts; but that first tax evasion conviction led to other convictions for extortion and conspiracy. Sturman, now an old man, may spend the rest of his days in prison as another illustration of the tenacity of the government in pursuing white-collar tax evaders.[66]

In 1970, Congress passed the **Racketeer Influenced and Corrupt Organizations Act (RICO)** for use against organized crime and corruption in labor unions. Under RICO, organized crime members who are involved in an "enterprise" (the family) that engages, at least twice within ten years, in any of numerous specified criminal acts is chargeable with "racketeering."* RICO penalties include heavy prison sentences (up to 20 years) and forfeiture of any ill-gotten monetary gains.

Seizing an opportunity, federal prosecutors have utilized RICO on a widespread basis against white-collar criminals, whether part of organized crime or not. RICO has been used with considerable success against violators of securities laws. For example, Michael Milken was convicted under RICO of charges of scheming to manipulate stock prices, of trading on inside information, and of defrauding customers. His employer, the investment banking firm of Drexel Burnham Lambert, facing a RICO indictment, pleaded guilty to lesser charges and was fined $650 million. To qualify for a RICO prosecution, the accused must have been involved in a "pattern of racketeering activity." Abortion protesters who block access to abortion clinics can be sued by abortion-rights advocates for engaging in such a "pattern of racketeering activity."[67] Although the decision does not prohibit *peaceful* protests outside abortion clinics, nor stop protesters who trespass on clinic property without threatening clinic employees. Financial advisers who misrepresent money matters to their professional athlete clients also have been held to be engaging in a "pattern of racketeering activity."[68]

---

*The list of 40 criminal acts that underlie RICO includes murder, robbery, securities fraud, and use of the mail or telephone for illegal purposes. Lying twice on the telephone concerning a business contract theoretically could trigger a RICO indictment or lawsuit.

Obviously, federal courts are expanding the applicability of RICO to just about any collective wrongful activity, whether for economic gain or not. RICO's deterrent effect is real. For example, actual damages can be trebled in civil cases. In criminal cases, assets of an accused can be temporarily seized before a trial begins. The use of RICO continues to expand and promises to become an even more significant threat to white-collar criminals.

MISCELLANEOUS CRIMES

Legislatures have seen fit to proscribe a myriad of activities by written laws. These miscellaneous crimes include (1) abusing animals, (2) conducting cockfights, (3) altering telegrams, (4) "beating" vending machines or pay telephones, (5) removing articles from a corpse, (6) loitering around public schools, (7) offering a "dead or alive" reward, (8) tattooing a minor, (9) harassing another by telephone, (10) carrying a switchblade knife, (11) committing perjury (i.e., lying while sworn to tell the truth) or subornation of perjury (i.e., getting someone else to commit perjury), (12) killing protected species of birds, (13) bribing (i.e., paying money to a public official in return for some special consideration), and (14) defacing public property.

The foregoing examples are all state crimes. When criminal conduct involves interstate commerce or violates a U.S. statute, a federal crime has occurred. For example, perjury in a federal court is a federal crime. Killing certain species of birds or animals that are protected by federal laws are federal crimes.

The foregoing list shows the diversity in criminal laws deemed necessary to maintain peace and order in our politically organized, civilized society. There are thousands of miscellaneous crimes "on the books," including many outdated ones that are never enforced. Regardless of the "statutory blizzard" of crimes on the books, ignorance of the law is never a defense. If it were, no doubt most persons accused of a crime would plead such ignorance. Generally, the rules are reasonable and conform to standards of good conduct. The human conscience, or one's innate sense of what is sometimes called "natural law," normally provides a workable guide to what is, in the eyes of society, right and lawful and what is seriously wrong, hence punishable as a crime.

WHAT ARE SOME DEFENSES TO CRIMES?

SELF-DEFENSE

Violent conduct, which would otherwise be criminal behavior, is justified when used in defense of oneself or of certain other persons. All states recognize some form of the privilege of self-defense.

Harry Holland and his girlfriend, Cinnamon Clark, were listening to CDs in her apartment. A noisy party was underway next door. Suddenly there was a banging on Cinnamon's unlocked door, and it was flung open. There stood Butch Meen, butcher knife in one hand and beer bottle in the other. Harry's first thought was to run out the back door, but Cinnamon grabbed her pistol from the table drawer, aimed it at Butch's heart, and stared him right in the eyes. When Butch lunged toward her, Cinnamon, fearful of imminent and serious personal harm, killed him with a single well-aimed shot. Was the killing lawful?

Yes. The privilege of self-defense arises when one is confronted with a threat that causes a genuine and reasonable fear of imminent danger of great bodily injury. "Deadly resistance" is justified when the imminent peril is great. Since Butch held a butcher knife and bottle, Cinnamon's fear of great and imminent harm, including possible death, was reasonable and her defense was reasonable. If Butch had retreated, stepping backward, the killing would not have been justified, and Cinnamon would have been guilty of homicide, probably manslaughter. If Butch had lunged toward Harry alone, the killing would still be justified because she was entitled to defend Harry as well as herself.

Generally, the right to self-defense extends to members of one's immediate family or household and to others whom one is under a legal or socially recognized duty to protect. The fact that the acts occurred in Cinnamon's apartment increases the scope of the privilege of self-defense. Defense of habitation is rooted in the ancient principle that one's home is one's castle. It does not mean that a killing is justified merely because it takes place in the home of the accused; however, when at home, one is not obliged to retreat. On the other hand, when one is outside one's house (or apartment), one might be expected to retreat if possible to do so without added risk of harm. Thus, there is a general duty to retreat rather than to kill in self-defense. Even in the home, the killing must be in defense of life or to prevent probable grievous bodily injury, such as rape.

John Booth was released from prison and promptly, the same day, got drunk and decided to burglarize a house. Michael Lanier, a college student, and his fiancée were upstairs when they heard glass shattering downstairs. Lanier grabbed a bat, went downstairs, and confronted Booth, who was entering through the window. Immediately upon being struck by the bat, Booth began running away. Lanier chased him and continued to beat him into submission with the bat. Booth suffered a brain hemorrhage and fractured skull; his legs had been battered as well. Lanier was arrested for assault with a deadly weapon. Will the argument of self-defense work for Lanier?

The prosecutor dropped all charges against Lanier, citing (1) the outpouring of public support for Lanier, (2) the uncertainty of whether a jury from that community would convict, and (3) the fact that Lanier believed Booth to be a significant threat of death or serious physical injury.[69] As a general proposition, lethal force cannot be used to chase down an intruder who no longer poses any threat of imminent harm. But prosecutors often, as in the *Lanier* case, make the decision as to whether or not self-defense under all of the circumstances was justified. If Lanier had been a former convict who had served time for assault and battery on a police officer while resisting arrest for drunken driving, would the district attorney have prosecuted him for assault? If so, would that tend to suggest a dual standard of justice through selective prosecution?

Deadly force may not be used in defense against nondeadly force, such as slapping. Nor may it be used in defense of property when life is not threatened.

Thus, one may not set a deadly spring gun to fire if a door or window is broken into when one is not at home. If an intruder is hurt or killed, the person who set the gun is guilty of either murder or manslaughter and is also liable in a civil action for injury or wrongful death. Whether the crime was murder or manslaughter would be determined by the presence or absence of malice in the mind of the defendant who set the spring gun.

The right of self-defense is never a "license to kill." If less than deadly force is all that is reasonably required under the particular circumstances, then a killing in self-defense becomes unlawful and punishable as a crime. Once the danger is over, there is no justification for further retaliation.

Is Lack of Mental Capacity a Defense?

An insane person is not legally responsible for criminal conduct. The rationale is that our society's collective conscience does not allow punishment where it cannot impose moral blame. Nonetheless, an insane person may be committed for an indefinite period to a hospital for the insane, an approach that satisfies society's need for protection and its duty to assist those who are ill.

The historical difficulty with the defense of insanity results from the lack of a satisfactory definition of the term, coupled with clear and reliable criteria to enable juries to evaluate the mental condition and conduct of the accused. The defense of "not guilty by reason of insanity" has been eliminated by statute in Montana, Idaho, and Utah, and the U.S. Supreme Court has declined to review those laws.[70] In California, an **insanity defense** is available if the jury, in a separate trial for that purpose, determines that the defendant, by a preponderance of the evidence, was incapable (1) of knowing or understanding the nature and quality of the act or (2) of distinguishing right from wrong at the time the act was committed. In New York, a defendant is not criminally responsible if he or she lacked substantial capacity to know or appreciate (1) the nature and consequences of his or her act or (2) that such conduct was wrong.

Juries are accustomed to determining facts (e.g., did the gun belong to the defendant or not?). But when it comes to determining the sanity of the defendant, the jury must determine the correctness of an opinion. Insanity is an opinion expressed by psychiatrists until the jury says it is a fact. It is extremely difficult to determine that a certain state of mind is a fact, and its importance is questionable if the basic goal of society is to incarcerate defendants until they no longer are a threat to society. Some argue that all perpetrators of heinous crimes are "insane."

Defendant Jeffrey Dahmer was convicted of serial killing, of drilling holes in his living victims' heads and then pouring in chemicals to "zombify" them, of having sex with the corpses' viscera, and of keeping some body parts in his refrigerator, occasionally eating them. Should Dahmer have been punished as a criminal or treated as a desperately sick human being?

"Crazy" is different than legally insane. The Wisconsin jury trying the Dahmer case concluded that Dahmer was not insane.[71] But if Dahmer was not insane when he committed such grotesque and inhuman acts, one might ask, who is insane? As a matter of official policy, Wisconsin follows the Model Penal Code definition of mental responsibility: "A person is not responsible for criminal conduct if at the time of such conduct as a result of mental disease or defect he lacked substantial capacity either to appreciate the wrongfulness of his conduct or to conform his conduct to the requirements of law." Thus, Dahmer was judged able to appreciate the wrongfulness of what he did and able to refrain from doing it. The fact that he wanted to commit such "crazy" acts does not constitute legal insanity. Jeffrey Dahmer subsequently was murdered in prison.

Insanity need not be permanent, because some mental diseases or defects may be cured. Thus, in some states, the defense of **temporary insanity** is possible, whereby the accused is innocent of the crime because of insanity, and yet, being sane after the act, need not be confined in a mental hospital.

Insanity is to be distinguished from **diminished capacity**, which involves a different mental state. Some crimes are defined to require a specific intent on the part of the defendant. For example, capital murder requires the specific intent to kill. If by reason of delusion, narcotics, or alcohol, for example, the defendant's mental capacity is diminished to the extent that there can be no specific intent to kill, there can be no capital murder. The crime may be reduced to manslaughter because of the defendant's diminished capacity.[72] This defense has been eliminated by constitutional amendment in some states.

It is possible that an accused, sane at the time of the alleged crime, subsequently becomes insane. Insanity at the time of trial is not a defense to a crime committed during a prior time of sanity. However, a trial cannot proceed until the defendant is sane because a "fair" trial as guaranteed by our Constitution contemplates a rational defendant who can understand the charges against him or her and assist in a proper defense. Nor can a prison sentence be served by, nor an execution be administered to, an insane convict. In general terms, insanity suspends judicial proceedings as long as it continues. However, the defendant may be committed to a state institution for the insane until sanity is regained, at which time the criminal proceedings may resume.

Terrence Shulman was caught shoplifting a bottle of champagne from a supermarket. The champagne was to be a consolation gift to his girlfriend with whom he had just broken up because of his "addictive compulsive" shoplifting problem. Is kleptomania, or an "impulse control" disorder, or "addictive compulsive" behavior a defense to the crime of shoplifting?

No. There are understood to be about 23 million shoplifters in the United States, who steal about $25 million of merchandise each day. Few are believed to steal out of absolute financial need. Perhaps one-third steal for resale or to finance drug habits. But the vast majority of shoplifters (usually teenagers) steal as a response to personal or social pressures or in response to a compulsive impulse, such as kleptomania. The excitement created by getting away with the theft is said by many to be the one true reward of shoplifting. Because of the addictive and compulsive aspects of the crime of shoplifting, help from educational and counseling organizations, such as Shoplifters Alternative, is probably more effective than courts in reducing this crime.[73]

Criminal conduct is voluntary conduct. The defense of duress, discussed previously, is one example where participation in criminal conduct is not voluntary. Are criminal acts while asleep another example?

For unofficial statistics on who shoplifts and why, see the data compiled by a national security firm at http://www.unisen.com/articles.html#why For information on shoplifting in the military services, visit http://www.eglin.af.mil/public affairs/mar06/blotter.htm

http://

Early one morning, Kenneth Parks drove 14 miles to attack his wife's parents while they were asleep. He killed his mother-in-law with a butcher knife, severely injured his father-in-law, and then turned himself in to police. Kenneth had a sleep disorder and contended that, although perfectly sane, he simply had been sleepwalking while committing the homicide and attack. Is this defense sound?

Yes, at least in Canada. The Parks' case occurred in Ottawa, where a judge ruled that the acts were involuntary. His acquittal was upheld on appeal.[74] As difficult as it might be to persuade a jury, presumably an involuntary stupor or trance, caused by some innocent involvement, such as sleeping, would negate the required voluntariness. Note that a stupor or trance caused by drugs is not involuntary nor innocent because use of the drugs is a matter of personal choice.

WHAT IS ENTRAPMENT?

A defendant cannot be convicted of committing a crime if the government, acting through its law enforcement personnel, induced the criminal act. The defense of **entrapment** is an affirmative defense that must be proven by the defendant by a preponderance of the evidence, as in civil litigation; it does not have to be proven beyond a reasonable doubt. However, this defense is very narrow, limited in scope, and usually unsuccessful. It applies only when the conduct of the law enforcement agent was likely to induce a normally law-abiding person to commit the offense, when such a person would not otherwise be disposed to do so. That is, the question is not whether the particular defendant was induced to commit the crime, but whether any reasonable, law-abiding person would have been so induced.[75] There is no entrapment when undercover agents are merely negotiating the price of, and buying, illegal drugs from the defendant.[76]

Joe Shapiro, operating on Whidbey Island, Washington, negotiated with Richard Russell and others for the purchase of homemade methamphetamine, or "speed." Russell needed the very scarce, but legal, chemical phenyl-2-propanone to prepare the drug, and this was supplied by Shapiro. A month after the batch was prepared and delivered, Russell was advised that Shapiro was an employee of the Federal Bureau of Narcotics. Arrest and trial followed in due course. Had Russell been constitutionally entrapped?

No. Entrapment occurs only if the government agent implants the criminal design or idea in the mind of the defendant. The U.S. Supreme Court held that Russell had a predisposition to commit the crime and that the mere affording of opportunity by Shapiro was not entrapment.[77]

Even if the defendant is predisposed to criminal activity, the government may not engage in "outrageous" investigatory conduct, or evidence collected will be suppressed and the defendant set free.

Ralph "Sonny" Barger, the recognized leader of the Hell's Angels, was convicted of conspiracy to violate federal explosives laws based upon the testimony of Anthony Tait, an FBI informant who participated in a "sting" operation (investigative activity in which a suspected criminal organization is infiltrated by a government witness). The government investigation followed the murder of a Hell's Angel by members of the Outlaws Motorcycle Club. Barger contended that the government was guilty of outrageous investigative conduct: by hiring Tait on a contingent-fee basis; by having Tait travel from city to city throughout the country, spending $150,000 of government expense money recruiting Hell's Angels to retaliate against the Outlaws by blowing up their clubhouse in Chicago; and by inciting Barger, personally, to retaliate. Should the conviction be reversed?

No. The federal court acknowledged that the due-process clause of the Fifth Amendment requires fundamental fairness, and that some police conduct may be so egregious as to violate that command. But in this case the government merely responded to the real threat of gang retaliation, which could have caused great personal harm and property damage between two rival gangs with a history of violence.[78] Barger also contended that he had been entrapped, arguing that he had no predisposition to engage in criminal activity. His predisposition was, the court held, refuted by his personal involvement in the retaliatory scheme both before and after Anthony Tait's proposed plan of action was revealed.

WHAT IS THE STATUTE OF LIMITATIONS FOR CRIME?

A **statute of limitations** is a legislative determination that legal proceedings in connection with various types of civil and criminal acts may not be commenced beyond specified periods of time. Accordingly, such a statute may be a valid defense for the defendant. The criminal courts in metropolitan areas are already overcrowded with current cases. Such statutes are not intended to shield defendants from the law; rather, they prevent stale prosecutions in which witnesses' memories may have faded, making a "fair" trial exceedingly difficult, if not impossible, to obtain. Moreover, witnesses and principals may move, or die, and evidence may be obscured or lost. Furthermore, society is better served if wrongdoers resume normal, productive, law-abiding lives, without the psychological burden of possible arrest endlessly hanging over their heads.

The period of time specified in a statute of limitations commences upon commission or discovery of the offense. An accusatory pleading (indictment, information, or complaint) must be filed within the period prescribed. The statute is suspended, or tolled, by the absence of the defendant from the state; this eliminates flight as a possible method of avoiding prosecution. Although the limitation periods vary, for misdemeanors they usually are one year; for most felonies, they usually are three years. If the crime is either a misdemeanor or a felony, depending upon the sentence ultimately to be imposed, the limitation period is typically three years. There is no statute of limitations for certain serious crimes, such as murder.*

VICTIM'S RIGHTS

The last 20 years of the twentieth century have witnessed a gradual but pervasive trend to elevate the rights of crime victims, even if that requires lessening the rights of the perpetrators.

> *For too long, the victims of crime have been the forgotten persons of our criminal justice system. Rarely do we give victims the help they need or the attention they deserve. Yet the protection of our citizens—to guard them from becoming victims—is the primary purpose of our penal laws. Thus each new victim personally represents an instance in which our system has failed to prevent crime. Lack of concern for victims compounds that failure.[79]*

In response to the growing concern for victims' rights, Congress enacted the Omnibus Victim and Protection Act of 1982, providing, among other things, for victim-impact statements at sentencing, protection from intimidation, restitution from offenders (e.g., return of stolen property), and a general tightening of bail procedures.

The states have not remained on the sidelines. Since 1985, there has been an explosion of new legislation and constitutional amendments supportive of victims' rights in the criminal system. Most states now require that notice be provided to all victims, or to members of deceased victims' families, prior to sentencing proceedings. During these proceedings, victims or their families may express verbally (or in writing or by videotape, if they prefer) their views about the crime, about the convicted felon, and the need for restitution. Such victim-impact statements are often provided for the judge's use in sentencing. They typically contain information about the victim's economic loss, physical and psychological injuries, and how the crime caused changes in the victim's employment.

Lawrence Singleton had been convicted by a Florida jury of murdering a hitchhiking woman he had picked up and taken to his home. Singleton claimed that the victim, Roxanne Hayes, attacked him with a knife and that he was trying to grab the weapon when the blade plunged seven times into her body. In the penalty phase of the trial, when the jury must recommend either life imprisonment or death, the assistant state attorney reached back 20 years, to 1978, to call a previous victim of Singleton as a

---

*For example, in 1983 Mary Jane Dudley Maxwell Pugh Hall (Smith) was charged with, and convicted of, the shooting murder of her husband, Donald Pugh, back in 1970. *Hall (Smith) v. Commonwealth*, 8 Va.App. 526, 383 S.E.2d 18 (Virginia, 1989). Perhaps the record for justice delayed is the case of *Mississippi v. Sam Bowers*, the 73-year-old former Ku Klux Klan Imperial Wizard who was first accused in 1966 of ordering, but not participating in, the firebombing murder of activist Vernon Dahmer. Bowers was tried four consecutive times; in each trial an all-white jury deadlocked. Thirty-two years later after the murder of Dahmer, however, the prosecution, with the help of a surprise "confidential informant" as witness, obtained a guilty verdict. *New York Times*, 29 May 1998; Announcement of Anti-Defamation League, 21 August 1998.

witness in support of the death penalty. Do former victims have the right to testify in current proceedings to help persuade the jury to render the death penalty?

Yes. Mary Vincent traveled from California to Florida to testify, and told the jury, "I was raped, and I had my hands cut off" in 1978 when only 15 years old. Singleton used a hatchet and left Mary to die in a ditch invisible to the road. Somehow, without hands, Mary crawled up to the road, obtained help, and survived. Because Mary survived, Singleton was hunted down and convicted. Paroled from a California prison after serving just ten years, Singleton moved to Florida because many California towns resisted his residency. The Florida jury, after listening to Mary Vincent, recommended the death penalty.

Some state statutes restrict **plea-bargaining** in cases involving violence or serious felonies. (A plea bargain is an agreement under which an accused person agrees to plead guilty to a specified offense in exchange for a court-approved sentence.) These restrictive states will not agree in advance to any particular sentence in specified types of crimes, usually involving violence, such as rape.

Some states provide victims with information about possible civil remedies against the defendant, as well as the procedures to recover compensation from the innocent-victim restitution fund. Monies are collected for these innocent-victim funds from penalty assessments and restitution fines levied against convicted persons. Victims, otherwise without financial means, can apply for financial assistance for medical treatment, mental health counseling, loss of income, loss of support, funeral/burial costs, and rehabilitation.

For information about victim's rights see http://dir.yahoo.com/Society_and_Culture/

So-called "Son of Sam" laws impound the proceeds of sales by notorious criminals of their "story" to the media, such as movie and book rights.* Funds are escrowed until victims have had ample opportunity to sue in civil proceedings and obtain a judgment that then may be satisfied from the impounded funds. Any excess is returned to the felon. New York also created a Crime Victim's Board to administer all state programs dealing with crime victims. This was in response to some legislators expressing concern about expanding victims' rights despite the increased costs of imposing a myriad of new procedural duties upon the criminal justice system already overburdened by paperwork.

One problem with amending a constitution to provide victims' rights is that criminals' rights may be thereby abridged. As on a teeter-totter, the rights of one group may go up at the expense of the rights of the other. For example, articulate or powerful families of victims, who make unsworn and emotionally charged statements regarding the effects of a crime by one defendant, may produce a sentence that is more severe than that given to another defendant who does not face such pressures. Or plea bargains may be denied for those defendants whose victims have sufficient means to successfully urge full-blown prosecutions. Or probation may be denied when an especially articulate and persistent spokesperson makes demands upon the sentencing judge.

Some victims are found in jail. Those are victims of a judicial system that erroneously found them guilty.

---

*During 1977, New York was terrorized by multiple random shootings of young women and their companions committed by a killer dubbed the "Son of Sam" by the press. The killer, David Berkowitz, sold book rights to his story. This prompted the state to enact the first "Son of Sam" escrow law. New York Exec. Law, Sec. 632-a(l), McKinney 1982.

Freddie Pitts and Wilbert Lee, black men, were sentenced to death by an all-white jury for the murder of two white gas station attendants. After more than 30 years in jail, 9 of which were on death row, Freddie, 54, and Wilbert, 62, were found to be innocent. A white man, Curtis "Boo" Adams, was the guilty person.[80] As victims, can Freddie and Wilbert sue for compensation?

Persons who are convicted of a crime cannot necessarily recover compensation. As long as prosecutors acted reasonably and witnesses were truthful, there is no wrongdoer to sue. Florida, however, is an example of a state that does provide for compensation in such situations. Freddie and Wilbert each received $500,000 as compensation for their 30 years in jail.

Some victims of crime are witnesses to its commission.

Gloria Lyons and Denise Jones witnessed a homicide by Charles Lafayette, a member of the "Bloods gang." The slaying occurred during an argument over a $5 rock of cocaine. Gloria and Denise were reluctant to tell what they saw, for fear of "wearing snitch jackets," which they consider to be targets on their backs. What can the prosecutor do to safeguard these witnesses from retaliation?

You may compare victims' rights laws in Washington and Kentucky by visiting http://www.metrokc.gov/proatty/v_rights.htm and http://www.law.state.ky.us/victims/rights1.htm

Some states have witness relocation laws that provide some financial help for relocating endangered witnesses to new neighborhoods. Unfortunately, many such witnesses become lonely for and return to their old neighborhoods. The problem of witness protection in gang member prosecutions is an unresolved problem. In the preceding case, Gloria was executed in an alley within three days of testifying; Denise returned to her former neighborhood and was promptly murdered on the street. No arrests were made; however, Lafayette is in prison serving 25 years to life.[81] The tally: One murderer in jail and two witnesses dead with their murderer(s) still on the street.

The focus on victims' rights has become so intense in the waning years of the twentieth century that a field of study called "victimology" has emerged. Victimology is the study of the effects of crime on victims and the evaluation of victim-oriented policies and programs, such as victim-impact statements and innocent-victim funds. In addition to so-called "street crimes" (e.g., assault, robbery, drug dealing), those considered include domestic violence, white-collar, and hate crimes. In short, there is an increasing concern for the rights of victims of crime.[82]

WHEN ARE POLICE PERMITTED TO SEARCH AND SEIZE?

The Fourth Amendment to the U.S. Constitution prohibits unreasonable searches and seizures by government officials. It is aimed at protecting the privacy of people from unreasonable government intrusions, but it does not provide for any penalty against government officials when they violate its shield. However, decisions of the U.S. Supreme Court have established the so-called **exclusionary rule**, which acts as a deterrent to unreasonable police searches by prohibiting prosecutors from using improperly obtained evidence in a trial.[83]

Few rules have generated more public outcry over the years than the exclusionary rule. Often the public hears or reads in the news that a clearly guilty person has been released simply because the incriminating evidence was produced through an illegal search. To a very limited extent and subject to certain immunities, the victim of an unreasonable search may even bring a civil suit against the officer involved. Interestingly, no such rule is found in England, where relevancy remains the essential test of admissibility.

A search for, and seizure of, evidence may be authorized in advance by issuance of a search warrant. A proper judge or magistrate issues the warrant based upon "probable cause" (i.e., a reasonable ground) that incriminating evidence will be found. This may include authorization to perform electronic or telephonic eavesdropping. Warrants are granted only upon preparation of a sworn (under penalty of perjury) affidavit, which must contain the basis (such as the statement of a reliable informant) upon which the requesting law enforcement agency believes there is probable cause that criminal conduct is taking place.

A search and seizure may also be justified and legal in the absence of a search warrant when circumstances necessitate prompt, decisive action. The various states have developed many different rules with fine distinctions as to when a warrantless search is permitted. The states are free to adopt more stringent rules restricting searches than are required under federal law, but no state can permit searches that are prohibited by the Fourth Amendment. Situations in which a warrantless search may be permitted are as follows:

1. *Consent.* A person may freely consent to a search. Another occupant of one's apartment may also consent to a search of shared areas within the dwelling. Police also may search if they receive consent from someone who does not have the authority to give consent (such as a former roommate) if they reasonably believe the consent was legitimate.

2. *Incident to a lawful arrest.* During a lawful arrest, a defendant is taken into custody. The arresting officer then may make a search, generally limited to an "arm's length" area in which the defendant could reach for a weapon or destructible evidence. Once at the police station, during booking procedures, the warrantless search may take the form of a strip search for weapons or contraband. In many states, a person arrested for minor, misdemeanor offenses (such as unpaid parking violations) could be strip searched at the police station. Because of the unlikelihood that such arrestees might possess weapons or contraband, however, such practices are very rare.

3. *Motor-vehicle search based on probable cause.* A vehicle may be searched if there is probable cause to believe it contains contraband. Mobility of the vehicle underlies this exception to the rule requiring a search warrant in advance. Note that a traffic offense, such as speeding, may not be used as a pretext to justify a search for evidence of a different crime, but the observation of something "in plain view" is not an unreasonable search. Indeed, it is not considered a search at all and, thus, is not subject to the confines of the Fourth Amendment. For example, a handgun lying on

the floor behind the front seat, if seen by the officer, would justify a search of a vehicle that had been stopped for a routine traffic offense. The only restriction on the "plain view" doctrine is that the officer had a right to be in that place when the observation was made. **Sobriety checkpoints** set up by the highway patrol to detect drunk drivers do not violate the Fourth Amendment despite the absence of any individualized suspicion that a particular driver is under the influence. Neither the magnitude of the drunk-driving problem nor the state's interest in eradicating it can be disputed. The intrusion on the privacy of motorists stopped briefly at sobriety checkpoints is slight.[84] In the state of Georgia, police make prior public announcements and then identify with large signs the sites of forthcoming sobriety checkpoints. Contraband in plain view during a sobriety checkpoint stop clearly will be admissible in evidence against the accused.

In California, several cities have begun a new variation on the typical sobriety checkpoint. Buena Park and Ontario have instigated license checkpoints where every fifth car is stopped and the driver is asked to produce a valid driver's license. Drivers with no valid license have their vehicle impounded for up to 30 days. The avowed justification for random license checks is that drivers who don't have a valid driver's license usually don't have insurance either, and the program thus will deter accidents involving uninsured motorists.[85] The intrusion reflected by random license checks may be too great constitutionally to justify the goal of removing uninsured motorists from the highways. The California highway patrol has declined to participate in such stops on the grounds they may be unconstitutional. Meanwhile the license checkpoints are fully operational.

Officer Studnicka observed a van sitting on the shoulder of a state highway in the early evening. Thinking the van's driver might be having mechanical trouble, Studnicka made a U turn, turned on his flashing red lights, and came to a stop at the rear of the van. When asking driver Steven Hanson for his driver's license, Officer Studnicka observed an open can of Michelob beer near the dashboard. He then asked Hanson to get out, smelled alcohol, administered an "Alcohol Sensor" test, and arrested him for a DUI (driving while under the influence of alcohol or drugs). The van was impounded, during which procedure 8.7 grams of marijuana was found. Hanson moved the court for an order suppressing all evidence on the grounds that an illegal seizure had occurred, in violation of his Fourth Amendment rights. What was the result?

There was an improper seizure because the flashing red lights were a clear direction to Hanson, sitting in the van, not to drive away. In effect, Hanson was detained by the flashing lights. Officer Studnicka admitted that he had no suspicion of criminal activity when he turned on the red lights. Therefore, Studnicka had improperly restrained Hanson. All evidence was ordered suppressed and the charges against Hanson were dropped.[86] If Studnicka had not turned on the flashing red lights, the subsequent visual search would have been proper.

4. *Stop and frisk based on reasonable suspicion.* If an officer has a reasonable suspicion of criminal activity, or if a dangerous misdemeanor is occurring, the object of that suspicion may be detained, questioned, and "frisked" or "patted down" for a weapon.

5. *Hot pursuit.* A fleeing suspect may be pursued into a private building without a search (or arrest) warrant.

6. *Emergency.* Under emergency conditions, it may not be possible to obtain a search warrant before acting. An example would be a break-in to rescue the victim of a crime, seen through the window, who is in need of immediate assistance. Other evidence of a crime in progress (such as wet blood or sounds of agony) also justify immediate action by police.

7. *Open field.* An officer may search an open field suspected to contain contraband as long as there is no reasonable expectation of privacy therein. Police, trespassing in a neighbor's backyard and standing on their tiptoes, can visually search a defendant's backyard. The reasonable expectation of privacy, or zone of privacy, for the defendant is extended only to persons who happen to be less than 6 feet tall, or the height of the fence.[87] Observations from airplanes or helicopters (e.g., of fields suspected of being used to grow marijuana) generally do not require a search warrant. However, use of a thermal imaging device (i.e., one that registers heat from electric sun lamps) cannot be used without a warrant to detect an underground marijuana farm at a targeted property.[88] On the other hand, use of an infrared forward-looking device, aimed above a suspect's residence, to detect heat discharged by exhaust from lamps that might be used to grow marijuana inside the building does not violate the Fourth Amendment.[89] The difference between these two examples is that there could be no reasonable expectation of privacy regarding heat discharged from the residence through a vent.

8. *Abandoned property.* An officer may search an abandoned automobile or dwelling or personal property discarded by a suspect.

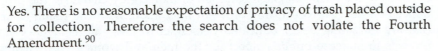

Jenny Stracner, a police investigator, examined the trash in a bag that Billy Greenwood and Dyanne Van Houten placed on the sidewalk near their home and discovered evidence of narcotics use. She used this evidence to obtain a search warrant of the house where quantities of narcotics were found. Was the warrantless search of the garbage constitutional?

Yes. There is no reasonable expectation of privacy of trash placed outside for collection. Therefore the search does not violate the Fourth Amendment.[90]

9. *Customs and immigration.* Customs and immigration officers do not need a search warrant in certain situations. For example, searches near the border, or places of entry to the United States, are exempt from the general requirements of probable cause. That is, those officers can detain and search persons if they have a "mere suspicion." Body ("skin") searches must be based upon "real, or reasonable, suspicion," and even a body cavity search (i.e., an intrusion beyond the body's surface) requires only a "clear indication," which is much less than probable

cause.[91] Conforming to a drug carrier's profile, behaving nervously, and wearing bulky clothing are typical bases for conducting a strip search.

10. *Mail to and from prisons.* Although domestic first-class mail cannot be searched without probable cause, there is an exception made for U.S. mail to and from prisons, all of which is subject to search. Some states prohibit the search of prison mail that is addressed to judges or lawyers from prison inmates.

11. *Searches by private citizens.* The Fourth Amendment is a restraint upon government, not upon individuals. Accordingly, evidence obtained from a search by a private citizen is admissible in evidence.

12. *Administrative inspections.* Certain pervasively regulated businesses (e.g., food establishments) are subject to warrantless inspections by administrative personnel as part of public necessity and licensing rules, and evidence discovered during such a search is accordingly admissible, even if unrelated to the inspection.

13. *Banks.* Banks and financial institutions supply information to government agencies pursuant to the Bank Secrecy Act without the necessity of a search warrant.

14. *Probation and parole.* As a usual condition to the granting of probation or parole, convicted felons waive their rights to a search warrant, and searches can take place at any time and any place.

As discussed earlier, the states are free to establish more stringent restraints upon the police than are required by the U.S. Constitution. Many states originally did further restrict their warrantless search requirements. Through adoption of victims' rights laws, as previously discussed, many states have relaxed their warrantless search rules to federal standards. In some states, federal officers continue to possess somewhat more latitude in performing warrantless searches than state officials, but this is not the modern trend. Determining the validity of a search is one of the most perplexing legal problems. It involves weighing the interests of the state in preventing crime against the interests of each person in maintaining privacy and freedom from unwarranted intrusion.

It is widely believed, and probably true, that some public officers, under the strain of daily action with dangerous and disagreeable suspects, are not always scrupulously considerate of the constitutional rights of the persons they search and arrest. Courts are reluctant to believe the stories of arrested persons when those stories are flatly denied by officers. Moreover, comparatively few defendants have the means or the inclination to thoroughly challenge the propriety of police conduct. However, this problem may abate with the rising salary scales that are attracting better educated personnel to law enforcement. Community projects to increase public respect for the men and women who engage in this necessary, but difficult, work may also help.

WHAT PROCEDURES LEAD TO A CRIMINAL TRIAL?

Criminal court procedures affect the quality of justice dispensed by our legal system and so are very important. But procedural safeguards can be frightening and mysterious to non-lawyers. The professional assistance of a qualified attorney for the accused person is thus advisable as early as possible in the criminal prosecution process. As soon as an investigation has included an individual, he or she should consult an attorney. The U.S. Supreme Court has declared that every accused person who cannot afford to hire a lawyer has a constitutional right to the services of professional counsel (usually a public defender) at public expense. Persons accused of minor crimes and infractions are excluded from this constitutional protection.

A discussion follows of the procedures that face those accused of serious crimes. All citizens should be generally familiar with these procedures. Exhibit 6–1 presents the typical steps in a criminal prosecution.

ACCUSATORY PLEADING

A person suspected of committing a state or federal crime becomes an accused following the issuance of an accusatory pleading. The most common types of accusatory pleadings are **complaint**, **information** (or affidavit), and **indictment**. Although the federal and state systems use documents with similar names, their procedures are somewhat different.

State Crimes

In some felony cases, the district attorney will prepare a complaint and file it with a judicial officer (usually called a *magistrate*), who is authorized to issue arrest warrants. If there is probable cause for the charges made against the accused, an arrest warrant will be issued. Following the arrest, a **preliminary hearing** will be conducted by a judge or magistrate to determine if an information should be issued binding the defendant for subsequent trial in the designated trial court. During this period of time, the defendant may be free on bail, which is discussed later in this chapter.

In other felony cases, the district attorney will request that the local grand jury convene. This is a group of selected citizens, not the type of jury sitting in jury trials. Following a secret session, the grand jury may issue an indictment charging the suspect with commission of a crime. The indictment is issued only if the grand jury is persuaded that there is probable cause that a crime has been committed by the defendant. Although the grand jury will hear evidence before issuing an indictment, the process has been widely criticized as being a mere "rubber stamp" procedure because the evidence in defense, if any, may be deemphasized or even withheld by the prosecutor. In 1994, a grand jury in Los Angeles was convened to determine whether or not to formally accuse O.J. Simpson of the murder of Nicole Brown Simpson and her friend Ronald Goldman. Before it issued its indictment, the California Superior Court in Los Angeles County suspended the powers of its grand jury on the basis that it had been prejudiced against O.J. Simpson by the massive publicity surrounding the murders. The district attorney then filed an accusation that led to a preliminary hearing. The municipal court determined that there was probable cause that the crime had been committed by O.J. Simpson, and the matter was set for jury trial. Sometimes the suspect is not even aware that the grand jury proceeding is taking place. After an indictment is issued, a warrant for the arrest of the accused will follow. Trial will follow apprehension and arraignment of the defendant.

Sometimes a grand jury will identify (but decline to indict) a person as a coconspirator with the defendant. Such an unindicted co-conspirator is neither arrested nor prosecuted, usually because of a lack of sufficient evidence to convict.

Exhibit 6–1: Typical Steps in a Criminal Prosecution

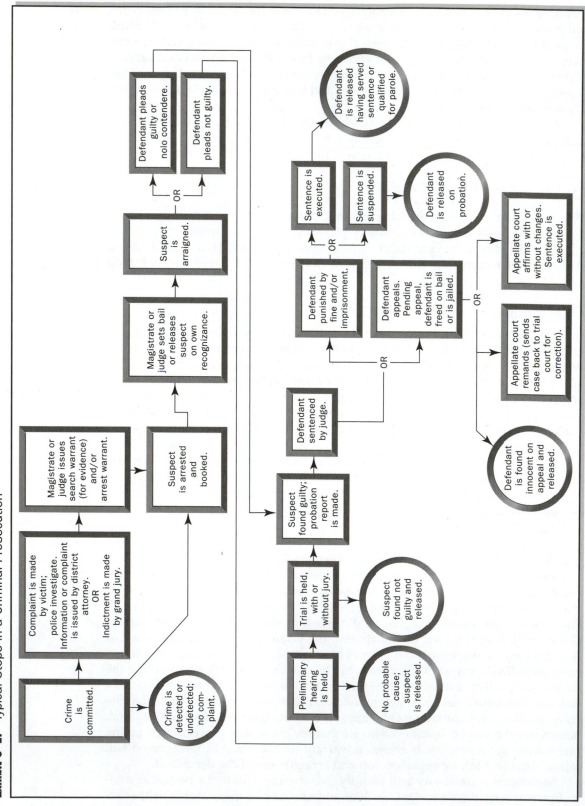

The decision to proceed against a suspect by complaint–preliminary hearing–information–trial, or more directly by indictment–trial, is left to the discretion of the prosecuting attorney. Frequently, if the suspect is a prominent person or political figure, the elected district attorney may prefer the indictment procedure, thereby delegating the decision to prosecute to a body of private citizens. In either process of accusation, it is important to recognize that there must be some kind of hearing to evaluate the prosecutor's case before the defendant is held for trial. This prevents an overzealous prosecutor from arbitrarily subjecting an accused to a criminal trial.

Regardless of the name of the accusatory documents utilized in a given state, they all provide the defendant with a clear understanding of the offenses charged so he or she may prepare a defense.

There are no indictments by grand jury of persons suspected of committing misdemeanors. Rather, misdemeanor suspects are accused by documents usually called *complaints*.

Federal Crimes

A complaint may be prepared by a federal official (such as a U.S. marshall or U.S. attorney) and submitted to a U.S. magistrate (i.e., a judicial officer, appointed by judges of federal district courts, having some of the powers of a judge) charging that there is probable cause to arrest a suspect. A private person cannot file such a complaint but may enlist the assistance of a U.S. attorney to instigate criminal proceedings. The magistrate then may issue a warrant for the arrest of the accused. Of course, for a crime committed in their presence, law enforcement persons can make an arrest without a warrant.

After arrest, the accused must be formally charged by federal information or indictment. A federal information is prepared by the U.S. attorney to formally charge persons accused of crimes for which the penalty is one year or less in a penitentiary. More serious crimes are prosecuted by federal indictment, which is a formal charge made by a federal grand jury composed of between 16 and 23 citizens who decide whether a crime has been committed and whether to institute criminal proceedings against a specific person. The federal grand jury listens to testimony and considers evidence presented by the U.S. attorney before making its decision. Many defendants waive their right to an indictment and choose to proceed by information for reasons of expediency.

Defendants accused of federal crimes are tried in the U.S. District Court before a federal judge (and jury, if a jury has been demanded and if the offense is serious enough to justify a jury). Incarceration for a federal offense is in a federal, rather than a state, penitentiary.

ARREST

After formal accusation by indictment or complaint, a warrant for the arrest of the accused is issued. To **arrest** is to take into custody for the purpose of bringing the person before a court. It is made by physical restraint or by the defendant's voluntary submission to custody.

Arrest may also occur in certain specified situations, before any accusatory pleading has been issued. This procedure differs slightly among the states. Generally, law officers may make a warrantless arrest (1) for a felony or a breach of the peace (perhaps a misdemeanor, such as simple assault) committed in their presence, (2) upon the accusation by a private person accusing another of a felony, or (3) upon probable cause or official information that the person arrested has committed a felony at some earlier time.

A private person can never obtain a warrant for the arrest of another. However, all states have either retained the common-law rules, or have enacted some variation thereof, whereby a private citizen may make a warrantless arrest, known as a "citizen's arrest." Generally, such an arrest may be made for a felony committed in the person's presence or for a misdemeanor that constitutes a breach of the peace then in progress. Whenever possible, arrests should be left to trained law enforcement officers. A citizen attempting an arrest faces the problem of restraining the arrestee, the possibility of violence, and the hazard of mistake, which could lead to a civil suit and damages for the tort of false imprisonment (arrest).

An officer or citizen making an arrest may search the arrestee if reasonably necessary to prevent destruction of evidence or to detect and confiscate any weapon or article useful to the arrestee in making an escape. The search must be reasonable. Indeed, an officer is privileged to stop and frisk, by pat-down, any person being lawfully questioned as a criminal suspect. The pat-down is reasonable if it is reasonably necessary for the officer's own protection. Such a suspect, however, should not be locked in jail for questioning or investigation unless there is an adequate basis (as previously described) to make a valid arrest. There is no adequate basis for an arrest for simple failure to identify oneself or to explain one's presence satisfactorily. The circumstances determine whether there is adequate basis for arrest. For example, refusal to explain one's presence at 3:00 A.M. in a warehouse district where recent burglaries have taken place would justify **detention** pending investigation, and possibly subsequent arrest. A detention is a temporary restraint of one's liberty to permit the police to determine if there is sufficient evidence to make an arrest. For example, a person may be detained long enough to perform a computer check on vehicle registration papers, or to obtain a drug-sniffing dog, or to obtain a possible eyewitness.

An officer making an arrest may use all force reasonably necessary to accomplish the restraint. The modern view is to discourage the use of deadly force in making an arrest. A private citizen may not use deadly force in making an arrest except in the case of one guilty of a violent felony (e.g., murder, arson, rape, or robbery). On the other side of the coin, it is the legal duty of everyone, innocent or guilty, to submit to a lawful arrest, and improper resistance is a separate crime.

Arrests are unnecessary in large numbers of situations involving illegal acts that occur in the presence of an officer, specifically misdemeanors, petty offenses, and infractions. The best example of an alternative to arrest is the ordinary traffic ticket, which is similar to the summons used in civil proceedings. The traffic violator is not a criminal and usually will abide by a written promise to respond to the citation, the traffic ticket. In a growing number of misdemeanors, including shoplifting and some narcotics violations, the summons is being used instead of arrest to facilitate and streamline the procedures for handling large numbers of cases.

BOOKING

After an arrest the accused may be **booked**, which involves searching, fingerprinting, photographing, testing for alcohol or drugs, and reasonably related activities. With respect to crimes involving the operation of motor vehicles while under the influence of alcohol or drugs, states have statutes establishing prohibited levels of blood-alcohol concentration (BAC). State maximum levels range from a low of .08 percent to .10 percent.* Still lower levels, such as .04 percent, have been adopted for application to commercial drivers and ship captains in some states, and .01 percent for drivers under age 21. Chapter 10 includes a guide to how many drinks result in various levels of blood-alcohol concentration.

Under criticism is the general practice of strip searching arrestees for the purpose of confiscating any weapon, contraband (i.e., any property that is unlawful to produce or possess), or other evidence. This practice obviously is demeaning and humiliating. It also is of dubious value when the soon-to-be-released arrestee is charged with an offense not involving drugs, contraband, a weapon, violence, or any other factor that would indicate a strong possibility of the presence of a concealed weapon. Some states prohibit strip searching in nonviolent misdemeanor cases.

The accused has certain rights after arrest, including the right to be promptly taken before a judge or magistrate, the right to be allowed bail (except in certain cases), the right to remain silent and, in serious criminal cases, the right to have an attorney present (a telephone call, without charge, must be permitted for this purpose). The right of an accused to be promptly taken before a judge or magistrate limits the possibility of unreasonable police interrogation ("the third degree") and affords an opportunity for the accused to have bail set (if it has not already been set and stated in the arrest warrant), to have constitutional rights explained, and to have an attorney appointed if he or she cannot afford private legal services.

BAIL

An accused who is arrested is physically taken to jail. But the state has no right to punish the arrestee, because the Fifth Amendment provides for a presumption of innocence. The purpose of **bail** is merely to help assure the defendant's presence for trial. Bail refers to the security given the court by the accused to assure later appearance for trial, in exchange for immediate release from custody. The amount of bail must be specified in the arrest warrant or, if arrest is without warrant, the magistrate will set bail after the arrest and booking. All crimes are "bailable," with certain exceptions. For example, the court may deny bail where there is a great likelihood the defendant will flee, as when a capital offense has been charged and the evidence of guilt is overwhelming.[92] But bail cannot be denied or set unreasonably high simply because a judge considers a defendant to be dangerous. The Massachusetts Supreme Judicial Council declared unconstitutional a statute that permitted a judge to deny bail simply because the judge believed the defendant to be dangerous. The court held that standards, such as found in the Federal Bail Reform Act of 1984, must be applied.[93]

Bail will be denied a person accused of certain extremely serious federal crimes if the government demonstrates by clear and convincing evidence, after an

---

*The trend is toward reduced permissible levels. California, Utah, Oregon, and Maine are among the dozen states that already use the lower .08 level. The U.S. Congress has considered, but not yet adopted, a federal minimum standard that would bind all states.

adversary hearing,* that no release conditions will reasonably assure the safety of the community. Bail for defendants accused of less serious federal offenses may be denied when, for example, there is a high degree of risk that the defendant will flee if released pending trial. When bail is denied, federal detainees are housed separately from convicted defendants, and other procedural safeguards apply.[94] In all cases, the policy is to be liberal in setting bail before any conviction takes place. Freedom while appealing a conviction is easily distinguishable from the situation before trial because there is no longer a presumption of innocence.

A **bail bond** is a document signed by both the accused and a bail bondsman binding them to pay to the state a specified sum if the accused fails to appear in court as directed. Bail bondsmen charge substantial fees in exchange for making such a promise, typically 10 percent of the sum specified as bail (e.g., $1,000 fee when the bail is $10,000). They rarely lose money because they secure their risk with collateral (such as stocks, bonds, mortgages, jewelry, or other valuables) and later go to great lengths to recover from the clients who "jump bail" (i.e., fail to appear in court as promised).

Every person accused of a crime is presumed innocent until proven guilty beyond a reasonable doubt and to a moral certainty, and therefore is entitled to release on bail with only limited exceptions, as previously noted. Under the Eighth Amendment, a judge or magistrate may not demand "excessive bail," but any amount may be too much for a poor person. Accordingly, at the federal level and in a number of progressive states, reforms have been enacted to permit release of the poor on their own **recognizance**, whereby the accused person simply promises in writing to appear for the trial. The court can attach other conditions to the prisoner's release, such as a promise not to contact the victim of the crime. Failure to fulfill conditions of release may lead to rearrest and may involve an obligation to pay a specified sum of money to the court.

ARRAIGNMENT

After being formally charged with a crime by the filing of an accusatory pleading (complaint, information, or indictment), the accused must be **arraigned**, meaning called into court, informed of the charge, and given an opportunity to make a response or plea. A public defender will be appointed to defend an accused who is unable to afford private counsel. In general, the defendant's plea may be either guilty, not guilty, *nolo contendere* (Latin: "I will not contest it"), or not guilty by reason of insanity. A plea of *nolo contendere* in criminal law is comparable to a plea of guilty. The only real distinction justifying its use is that a guilty plea can be used against the defendant as an admission against interest in subsequent civil litigation, whereas a plea of *nolo contendere* generally cannot. A guilty plea standing alone presumes that the defendant was sane at the time the crime was committed. Hence, the question of insanity must be raised by special plea, namely "not guilty by reason of insanity." In felony cases, a preliminary hearing (unless waived by the defendant) and trial will follow the defendant's plea. There is no

*An adversary hearing is a mini-trial, the purpose of which is to determine the potential danger to the community if the accused defendant is released on bail pending trial. The accused may have counsel, cross-examine witnesses, offer evidence, and so forth. There is no jury in these proceedings.

preliminary hearing in misdemeanor cases. If the plea is guilty, in either a felony or misdemeanor case, sentencing will then follow.

PLEA BARGAIN

Often, following arraignment, the district attorney or county prosecutor will decide that it is in the best interests of justice to offer a **plea bargain** to a defendant. Typically, the defendant agrees to plead guilty to some crime of lesser severity than the crime specified at the arraignment. In return, a judge agrees to a specified punishment and accepts the guilty plea on that basis. Once a judge has accepted a guilty plea, the judge cannot refuse to carry through the bargain that induced the plea.[95] The interests of justice are better served when the time, expense, and uncertainty of a trial can be avoided. For example, it may be uncertain whether a conviction for murder in the second degree or voluntary manslaughter can be obtained. It may be preferable to accept a guilty plea to the lesser charge than to incur the expense and difficulty of trial. There is an unending stream of cases to be disposed of, and plea-bargaining can be of benefit to the defendants—who are in jeopardy of a more severe sentence—as well as to the people represented by the prosecutor's office.

PRELIMINARY HEARING

A **preliminary hearing** is an evidentiary proceeding after a felony accusation, done before a magistrate or judge, to determine whether there is probable cause that the specified felony has been committed by the accused. The district attorney will call witnesses and present evidence in support of the charges. The accused need not, and usually does not, present any evidence because he or she is presumed innocent. However, most defendants' attorneys take advantage of the opportunity and cross-examine prosecution witnesses at length in order to learn as much as possible about the case. This defense strategy was viewed by millions of people who watched the preliminary hearing of O.J. Simpson on television. If the district attorney fails to prove a *corpus delicti*, the judge or magistrate will dismiss the charges immediately. As noted earlier, today's victims' rights legislation frequently has targeted the preliminary hearing as too inefficient and time-consuming. As a result, expedited preliminary hearings (i.e., featuring time allotments, fewer prosecution witnesses, and nearly automatic transfer for trial) move cases toward trial with a minimum of delay. Some critics contend that expedited preliminary hearings push cases to trial that should have been dismissed. The result, they maintain, is too many acquittals following costly, time-consuming jury trials.

In some states, a preliminary hearing is not conducted after an indictment, on the theory that there already has been an evidentiary hearing. This rule is subject to serious constitutional question because the grand jury is a one-sided proceeding with no judge or magistrate present.

After the preliminary hearing, assuming the prosecution has presented enough evidence to justify a trial, the matter will be set for jury or nonjury trial, to determine the guilt or innocence of the defendant. Preliminary hearings are not conducted in misdemeanor cases.

WHAT ARE THE CONSTITUTIONAL RIGHTS OF AN ACCUSED?

The legislative branch of government decides what activities are criminal and therefore prohibited. Commission of a proscribed act is a crime. Of course, the legislative branch of government has no power to prohibit that which the Constitution protects, such as the expression of opinion critical of government.

The executive branch of government, in turn, has the responsibility of arresting persons reasonably thought to have committed criminal acts.

The judicial branch has the responsibility for conducting trials of the accused. In the process, it is conceivable that the executive branch or the judicial branch could treat those accused of crimes in an unfair manner, thereby increasing the possibility that innocent persons may be convicted.

To minimize this possibility, certain fundamental rights are guaranteed by the U.S. Constitution, as well as by state constitutions, to every person suspected of involvement in criminal activity. For example, there is a right to be free from unreasonable searches and seizures, as described in a prior section of this chapter.

State constitutions are free to be more demanding than the U.S. Constitution in guaranteeing such rights. Thus, in some states, persons who are accused of a crime may enjoy expanded rights of protection from unreasonable prosecutorial activities.*

According to federal law, the police cannot arrest anyone without probable cause. Moreover, that person must be informed (1) of the right to remain silent, (2) that anything said can and will be used against him or her in a court of law, (3) that he or she is entitled to the presence and aid of a lawyer during questioning, and (4) that if he or she cannot afford to hire counsel, one will be provided free of charge.[96] These **Miranda warnings** technically are not constitutional rights; rather they are "procedural safeguards" imposed by the courts to preserve the integrity of the judicial system. Therefore, if the arresting officer fails to inform the arrestee of these rights, the court subsequently may reject as evidence anything said by the defendant that is of an incriminating nature, such as a confession. Rejection of such evidence by the court may result in dismissal of the case if there is no other evidence sufficient to convict.

Miranda warnings are required prior to custodial (while in custody) interrogation, but not before general investigatory questioning (e.g., Where do you live? What are you doing here? How did you get here?). The warnings relate to all offenses, regardless of their gravity (e.g., for driving under the influence of alcohol or drugs). Police can detain persons, during an investigation, for a reasonable time for some reasonable purpose, without making any arrest.** This "right to detain" can be based upon a reasonable suspicion of criminal activity involving

---

*Persons accused of a crime in California long have enjoyed broader state constitutional and statutory protections than are available to defendants accused of federal offenses. However, in June 1990, voters adopted Proposition 115, the Crime Victims' Justice Reform initiative, which literally equalized state and federal law. Affected were many criminal procedure laws, such as those instigating criminal charges, selecting jurors, conducting pretrial hearings, and even using federal law definitions of such diverse matters as "cruel and unusual punishment" and the right to privacy.

**For example, detention for an hour to obtain a drug-sniffing dog is a reasonable time. *U.S. v. Campbell*, 627 F.Supp. 320 (Alaska, 1985) aff'd 810 F.2d 206 (1987).

the detainee. The Miranda warnings need not be given until an arrest is contemplated. In petty misdemeanor cases or infractions (e.g., traffic violations), no arrest is contemplated, so Miranda warnings are inapplicable.

The accused is entitled to "due process" in all procedures following arrest. Bail, for example, is designed to prevent the punishment of one who is presumed innocent pending trial. There is a right to a speedy trial unless the defendant waives time and permits a later trial date. States typically provide that the defendant is entitled to commencement of trial within approximately 60 days of arraignment. But most defendants "waive time" to better prepare their defenses, or even simply to stall as long as possible. There is a right to be arraigned—that is, informed of the specific charges pending.

During trial, the defendant is entitled to an impartial jury and judge and is presumed innocent until found guilty. The state, representing the people, always has the burden of proof to convict "beyond a reasonable doubt." The defendant is entitled to be present in court in ordinary clothing* and is entitled to confront and cross-examine adverse witnesses, including informants.** A defendant has a right to conduct his or her own defense but must be able and willing to abide by rules of procedure and courtroom protocol. The Fifth Amendment provides that "no person shall . . . be compelled in any criminal case to be a witness against himself. . . ." This right is known as the **privilege against self-incrimination**. Accordingly, a defendant need not take the witness stand and testify in the proceeding. The prosecution must prove its case beyond a reasonable doubt without the use of the defendant's testimony.

Michael Vega was charged with vehicular manslaughter. Antoinette Marie Joseph was the sole witness able to incriminate him. Just before his jury trial was scheduled to begin, Michael married Antoinette, setting the stage for his wife not to testify against him. On motion of the defense attorney, Judge Constance Sweeney dismissed all charges, noting that the timing of the marriage was a "terrible violation of ordinary moral decency." Why did the judge dismiss the case?

As a variation of the privilege against self-incrimination, there is a privilege against incrimination by one's spouse. Thus Antoinette cannot testify against Michael without his permission—an unlikely circumstance.[97]

In trying to meet its burden of proof, the prosecution cannot suppress evidence favorable to an accused.[98] Thus, defendants may make a pretrial request for access to possibly favorable evidence. Furthermore, an involuntary confession made out of court is not admissible as evidence against the defendant, and a confession is involuntary if obtained by any form of compulsion, including false promises. Interestingly, the Fifth Amendment does not prevent police from

---

*A defendant cannot be compelled to be tried in jail attire because it may insinuate that the defendant has been arrested not only on the charge being tried but also on other charges for which he or she is being incarcerated. The presumption of innocence requires the civilian garb of innocence.

**A defendant is entitled to confront informants who are witnesses to the crime charged, not mere tipsters. *Bradford v. State*, 184 G.A.App. 459, 361 S.E.2d 838 (Georgia, 1987). Also, a defendant charged with child abuse does not always have the right to confront the victim in open court. *Maryland v. Craig*, 497 U.S. 836, 110 S.Ct. 3157 (1990).

requiring a defendant to participate in a lineup, repeat certain words that were uttered by a guilty person, submit to executing samples of handwriting, be fingerprinted, or be photographed. Both President William Clinton and defendant O.J. Simpson were required to give a sample of hair to the prosecution for DNA testing (explained in the next section). A defendant is entitled to subpoena defense witnesses and to have a "fair" trial, generally in a place where publicity about the case has not unreasonably tainted the proceedings, which must be open to the public.* Defendants may waive many of these rights if desired.

An accused cannot be placed twice in jeopardy for the same offense, but one wrongful act (such as rape) may be grounds for both criminal proceedings and a civil lawsuit for battery. A single criminal activity can involve violation of several statutory provisions and consequently result in several different crimes and punishments. Recall the preceding Darwin Britcher case (page 242) where three crimes were committed in one accident Britcher had while driving under the influence of alcohol. The constitutional safeguard against double jeopardy protects against a second prosecution following acquittal or conviction for a single crime, and against multiple punishments by the state for that offense.[99]

A defendant cannot be convicted for violation of an *ex post facto* law—one that punishes conduct that was not a crime when committed and was only later prohibited by statute.

Finally, a convicted defendant may not receive a sentence that is so disproportionate to the offense involved as to be fairly characterized as "cruel and unusual." This constitutional protection is discussed later in this chapter.

CAN INNOCENT PERSONS BE CONVICTED?

The basic purpose of the many constitutional safeguards we have considered is to minimize the risk of convicting innocent persons of crimes. In other words, the purpose is to ensure that justice is done to the extent humanly possible. To err by releasing a guilty defendant is thought to be preferable to incarcerating one who is innocent. Nevertheless, grievous mistakes are sometimes made.

Kirk Bloodsworth was tried and convicted of the brutal rape and murder of a 9-year-old girl. Bloodsworth was in prison and on death row for more than eight years when serious doubt of his guilt arose from the results of recent DNA testing** of semen specimens, which excluded him. Should Bloodsworth be released because of these test results?

Bloodsworth, his innocence confirmed, was promptly released from prison.[100] Like fingerprint comparison, DNA matching is admissible in evidence, although

---

*Global television coverage of the Orenthal J. Simpson murder trial prompted its label as the "Trial of the Century." Even before television was permitted in courtrooms, pretrial publicity has been a significant problem. For example, Giovanni Vigliotto, dubbed the "Sicilian Seducer" for his conviction of marrying and defrauding between 82 and 105 women, received national publicity (talk shows, made-for-TV movies, and even the *Guinness Book of World Records*) prior to his 1983 conviction in Arizona and sentence to 34 years in prison without possibility of parole. Defense attorneys contended it was the worst case of pretrial publicity ever, a comedy of errors, but Vigliotto lost his appeal and died while in prison. *Vigliotto v. Terry*, 873 F.2d 1201 (9th cir., 1989).
**DNA is the abbreviation for Deoxyribonucleic Acid, which is the substance that transfers genetic characteristics in all life forms.

unlike fingerprint analysis, it is not always absolutely conclusive. However, the overwhelming statistical probability of unique identification will be taken as conclusive in the minds of reasonable people. In a pioneering case,[101] the court ruled that any evidence that was generally accepted in the applicable scientific community was admissible (acceptable) in court. Thus, DNA evidence has become widely acceptable. As noted earlier, Orenthal J. Simpson was acquitted of the murder of two people despite DNA evidence that placed him at the scene of the crime. As a result of this acquittal, which many contend is a vivid example of jury nullification, an ongoing public resentment follows O.J. wherever he goes.

The ongoing saga of O.J. Simpson is continually updated at http://www.cs.indiana.edu/hyplan/dmiguse/other.html

WHAT IS THE PUNISHMENT OF CONVICTED PERSONS?

After conviction, judges impose sentences. State judges generally have more discretion in sentencing than do federal judges, who must comply with specific guidelines. State statutes prescribe the ranges of punishments that may be imposed. To help juries determine the degree of guilt (i.e., first- or second-degree murder) and make sentencing decisions, courts authorize the introduction of "expert opinion" testimony on a wide range of topics, such as the psychological profile of the defendant. The personal characteristics of defendants may bear upon their personal responsibility or upon the sentence that ought to be imposed. An **expert witness** is anyone qualified by knowledge, skill, experience, training, or education to offer a useful opinion.[102] Social scientists can and do offer an array of causes for crime: low verbal I.Q. (intelligence quotient) score, low levels of certain body chemicals and elevated levels of others, the presence of the XYY chromosome pattern in men, fetal alcohol and drug syndrome, a lack of religious involvement, extreme poverty, being raised in a single-parent family, the battered woman syndrome, and more. Many believe that, as we enter the new millennium, our legal system has become excessively tolerant of "abuse excuses" in which social causes and mental conditions are used to explain and ultimately excuse criminal behavior. According to this view, if our society continues to expand upon the traditional excuses of duress and insanity, our goal of encouraging and demanding personal responsibility will fail.[103]

Imprisonment and imposition of a fine are two basic forms of punishment. Either or both may be ordered, depending on what the statutory law requires and what a judge (and, in some cases, a jury) decides. Misdemeanants are confined in county jail, and felons are incarcerated in state prisons. Offenders guilty of federal crimes are incarcerated in federal penitentiaries.

The highly controversial death penalty is unique among all sentences in its irrevocability and rejection of rehabilitation as a possible outcome. It is discussed in greater detail later in this chapter.

PUNISHMENT FOR MISDEMEANORS

Ripley Offenbach tried to shoplift a pair of jeans from a department store. He was caught, entered a plea of guilty in the municipal court, and was sentenced to 60 days in jail. While confined, can Ripley simply loaf, eat nourishing food, and—in some jails—watch television?

Not necessarily. A prisoner is entitled to be fed, to receive medical care, and to be kept free from physical abuse* by prisoners or guards. However, there is scant management of prison guards and little to no solid information on abuses within prison walls.

County jail prisoners can be made to work on public roads and trails or on other jobs for the benefit of the public. Some counties have road camps for such purposes. However, commitment to such a camp, called the "farm," is selective and Ripley Offenbach, in the preceding example, may or may not be selected by jail officials. In some states, under **work furlough** programs, a prisoner in a county jail may work at regular outside employment during working hours and remain in confinement at other times. Under such programs, the sheriff collects the misdemeanant's earnings, withholding the cost of board, personal expenses, and administration and, if so ordered by the court, paying the surplus, if any, to appropriate dependents. Or, confinement may be served on weekends only. Assignments to the "farm" for work are made by the sheriff or other designated agency, whereas work furlough may be ordered by the sentencing judge.

In Illinois, misdemeanors are divided into classes A, B, and C, for which maximum sentences are 1 year, 6 months, and 30 days, respectively.[104] Most other states simply have a maximum of 1 year in jail; the judge specifies the exact time in accordance with circumstances surrounding the case.

Punishments can be tailored for a specific defendant and the circumstances surrounding his or her crime by offering probation, with conditions, in lieu of time in jail. The imposition of conditions in order to receive probation is loosely known as "creative sentencing." Conditions may involve community work, for example, but this can be rejected by the defendant who prefers to go to jail.

As punishment, four crab poachers in Florida agreed to parade around town for four Saturdays wearing signs that said, "It is a felony punishable by five years in prison and/or a $5,000 fine to molest crab pots. I know because I molested one." Is this a constitutional punishment?

Yes. This unique punishment was agreed to by the defendants, who preferred it to a more traditional punishment. However, there may be a limit as to how far judges can go with their creative sentencing. Judges have assigned very unusual conditions that many find offensive, for example, that prostitutes permanently move out of the county or that the names of "johns" (men who have been convicted of soliciting prostitution) be printed in the local newspaper.

Commonly, a county jail sentence imposed by the court may be shortened for good conduct—for example, ten days off for each month of such behavior. Additional time off may be granted for satisfactory completion of work assignments and for blood donations made to a blood bank.

PUNISHMENT FOR FELONIES

Traditionally, the legislative branch of government establishes either specified periods of confinement or minimum–maximum ranges for specified offenses. For

---

*Unfortunately, there is reason to believe that being raped, stabbed, or beaten has become part of the penalty paid by many prisoners. With the risk of contracting AIDS, prison rape can be a death sentence. *San Francisco Chronicle*, 14 June 1994.

example, in Illinois, second-degree murder warrants a sentence between 4 and 20 years.[105] Egregious circumstances surrounding offenses usually suggest which end of the scale will be applied by the sentencing judge.

> Richard Rowold fired his shotgun at a dog, missed, and accidentally shot his neighbor, Janet, who was in her backyard. Rowold was convicted of criminal recklessness for causing Janet's shoulder injury and was sentenced to three years in prison. However, the sentence was enhanced to eight years because he was a "habitual offender" guilty of two previous felonies; i.e., the federal crimes of mail fraud in 1980 and fraudulent use of an access device (cable TV decoder) in 1986.[106]

Statutory penalties for crimes can and do vary widely among the states. Capital crimes (punishable by death) may be punished by life imprisonment with or without the possibility of parole, or death. Capital punishment, called the death penalty by many, is discussed later in this chapter under the heading "When Is Punishment Cruel and Unusual?" because of the controversy surrounding that issue. Under traditional statutes for noncapital felonies, a specified minimum sentence is automatically increased when certain aggravating circumstances are present. Statutes specify increased or enhanced penalties for crimes if, for example:

1. The defendant has a prior conviction.
2. A weapon was used during the commission of the crime.
3. Great bodily harm was inflicted.
4. A particular class of victim is involved (e.g., a police officer).
5. The criminal motive was hatred of a protected class of persons (e.g., racial minorities).

Traditionally, three- or four-time felons face the impact of recidivist (repeat offender) statutes (as detailed in the discussion of cruel and unusual punishment). Some states have been echoing the former federal system by prescribing indeterminate sentences that authorize judges and parole boards to tailor the actual time served to the individual criminal. But changes in traditional sentencing formulas inevitably vary in response to ever-changing public demands. "Three strikes and you're out" is a response to public outcry that has been adopted in many states. The notion is that three felony convictions should result in incarceration for nothing less than 25 years to the maximum of life without possibility of parole.

> Andre Wilks, age 19, was arrested for breaking a car window and stealing a cellular telephone. He had a juvenile record of two purse-snatching convictions, crimes committed during one spree when he was 16. The district attorney offered him a plea bargain of 7 years in prison; if convicted by jury, he faced a three-strikes enhancement of 25 years to life in prison, even though it would be based on his juvenile record. Andre, against the advice of his lawyer, his mother, his uncle, the prosecutor, and even the judge, refused to accept the offer and chose trial by jury. During

trial, he perjured himself by denying everything. To his surprise and chagrin, the 12-year-old accomplice in the car burglary testified against him. Andre was convicted by the jury. Must the sentencing judge send Andre to prison for 25 years to life for stealing the cell phone?

The judge could "expunge" one of the prior juvenile convictions and thereby avoid the "three strikes and you're out" law. But, because Andre showed no remorse before conviction, and because he perjured himself, he was sentenced to 25 years to life in prison, where he will remain until long into the twenty-first century.[107]

Many states adopted "three strikes and you're out" laws in the 1990s, following the public fury over the case of Polly Klaas, a 12 year old from Petaluma, California, who was kidnapped from her bedroom and murdered in 1993 by a man with a long criminal record. However, most of them have put six or fewer defendants behind bars under those statutes. These states did not have many repeat offenders who were treated lightly under existing law, and had little need for the enhanced sentences provided by their three-strikes laws. California is a major exception where as many as one-quarter of the prison population is there under three-strikes sentencing, many of whom are serving 25 years to life.[108]

The publicized sentences imposed upon convicted defendants often are different than time actually served in prison. Many contend that criminals are not serving enough time and that there is too much of a gap between sentences set by judges and the amount of time actually served. Early releases can occur from a variety of reasons, such as early parole (discussed later in this chapter), credits for time served for "good time" (prison time without disciplinary action) and even court ordered release to relieve prison overcrowding. In reaction to public concern, 27 states (and the District of Columbia) now require violent offenders to serve at least 85 percent of their prison sentences. To encourage states to toughen their laws, the federal government grants funds to those that adopt the 85 percent minimum. An additional 13 states have lesser restrictions upon the early release of violent offenders. Overall, violent offenders (homicide, rape, robbery, or aggravated assault) who were released in 1997 had spent a little over four years in prison equal to 54 percent of their original sentence. About 18 percent of prisoners released in 1997 had served their full sentence.[109]

Ronnie Hawkins was convicted of petty theft, but it was his "third strike" and hence considered a felony. During his jury trial, although instructed by the judge to be quiet, Hawkins blurted out that he was HIV positive and was facing 25 years to life for petty theft—an apparent appeal to sympathy. He was considered disruptive. After his conviction, and during a sentencing hearing, Hawkins kept talking and interrupting the judge. Outraged, Judge Joan Comparet-Cassani ordered the bailiff to trigger a remote control device that caused 50,000 volts of electricity to surge into Hawkins. The jolt struck just above Hawkins' left kidney and continued for eight seconds, during which he "grimaced and sat stiff as a board." Hawkins was zapped with an electronic security belt intended to control violent defendants—and apparently to quiet them as well. Can defendants be physically punished while in the courtroom even though they have not been held in contempt, are not behaving violently, or are otherwise not threatening to harm anyone?

Judges are in control of their courtrooms and can and do take precautionary steps to protect themselves and others from violence. Electronic security belts are not uncommon to restrain violent defendants. The *Hawkins* case was unusual because his disruption took the form of talking too much.[110] Restraining or subduing a defendant in court is not considered "punishment" in the same way that "punishment" follows conviction. Rather, it is physical restraint or action that serves a nonpunishment purpose, i.e., order in the court. Nonetheless, upon petition by Hawkins, a U.S. District Court Judge issued a preliminary injunction prohibiting the use of stun belts in Los Angeles courts, stating: "a pain infliction device that has the potential to compromise an individual's ability to participate in his or her own defense does not belong in a court of law."[111]

Many contend that enhancing prison sentences under three-strikes laws for nonviolent crimes is unfair and accomplishes little more than filling up the nation's prisons. Others rebut by pointing to the recent downturn in crime rates, which they suggest is the direct result of harsher sentencing policies.

Does punishment end upon release from prison? Recall the discussion earlier concerning disclosure of the identity and residential address of convicted sex offenders under state statutes known as Megan's Law. Does the public's fear that sex offenders are habitual also apply to other felons?

Glenn Barker, age 40, served his sentence for murder, was released from prison, and obtained a job coaching youth basketball at the YMCA. But he was fired when police revealed his criminal record. He moved to another town, and according to his lawyer, "he's been employed, he's never had a parking ticket and he's never been in trouble or charged. He doesn't smoke, drink or dance the hoochie-coochie." The police then used Megan's Law as a basis to visit almost 1,000 homes distributing flyers of Barker's address and record. When does a criminal's sentence end?[112]

This is the first instance when Megan's Law has been selectively applied by police to an ex-con who was not a sex offender. Questions arise as to just which ex-cons police will choose to repeatedly expose. What are ex-cons supposed to do if they are excluded from employment and from neighborhoods? If one ex-con is exposed, should law enforcement be required to disclose all former convicts who committed similar crimes? Can police use Megan's Law as an excuse to harass selected ex-convicts?

For federal crimes, the U.S. Sentencing Commission has prepared a Sentencing Table. The vertical axis is divided into 43 units, each corresponding to a level of offense seriousness. The horizontal axis is divided into 6 units, each corresponding to a more extensive criminal history record. Judges base their sentence on where the unit representing the defendant's present crime intersects with that representing his or her past record. Opponents to this mechanical procedure refer to it as "sentencing by numbers" and decry the lack of judgment it allows. This opposition, especially by some federal judges, has been vocal and abundant.[113] Under the federal sentencing guidelines, all those convicted of a felony serve some time in prison, including white-collar criminal defendants. Although mired in constitutional law litigation since its inception, all parts of the Sentencing Reform Act of 1984 have been ruled constitutional by the U.S. Supreme Court. Therefore, the act is currently applied throughout the federal court system.[114] Federal judges can and do make "upward departures" from the sentencing guidelines when warranted by the egregiousness of the defendants' offenses.[115]

Much of the objection to sentencing by numbers was highlighted in a Department of Justice study released in 1994. Some 16,300 federal prisoners, or one in five, are "low-level" drug offenders—people with minimal or no prior criminal histories whose offenses involved neither violence nor sophisticated criminal activity. Their average sentence of seven years is reduced by good behavior to five years and nine months actually served.* These prisoners are the least likely to commit new crimes following release.[116]

In addition to fines and imprisonment, some professional persons convicted of crimes involving moral turpitude may suffer additional penalties, such as loss of professional license or employment. Teachers may lose their positions if convicted of criminal sexual misconduct on the basis of unfitness to teach or for lack of moral principles. Likewise, a license to practice law may be suspended or revoked for conviction of a crime involving moral turpitude, such as income tax invasion. In Chapter 4, you already learned about how lawyers are disciplined. Loss of professional license or position is not a substitute for a fine or imprisonment. It is an additional penalty that a professional person may suffer as the result of committing a crime.

WHAT ARE PAROLE, PROBATION, AND CLEMENCY?

Parole, probation, and clemency are three means by which punishment is ameliorated or rescinded. **Parole** suspends a sentence after incarceration has begun, as distinct from **probation**, which suspends the sentence before incarceration. Either a felon in a state prison or a misdemeanant in a county jail may be paroled. The decision is made by officials designated under legislative authority. The liberty of a parolee is conditional and may be suspended or revoked unilaterally for violation of conditions specified, such as avoiding certain company (e.g., former gang members) or activity (e.g., carrying a gun). Thus, parole consists of two parts. Parole *boards* are state administrative bodies that have the authority to decide when to release prisoners. If an indeterminate sentence exists (e.g., 25 years to life imprisonment), the board decides the exact time for release based on such matters as "good-time" credits (reductions in sentence for time spent in prison without discipline), other prison records, recommendations from prison officials, prosecutors, victims, and the prisoner's family and friends. Even if an indeterminate sentence does not exist, such boards often set the actual date of release and provide conditions for early release from prison, set the conditions of parole (i.e., refrain from consuming alcohol and from associating with known felons), and monitor the parolee's activities while on parole. Parole officers supervise convicts after their release. To prevent the early release of prisoners, many states have abolished parole boards, yet have retained parole officers. One result of

---

*Even under the federal sentencing system, a prisoner can often get credit for "good time." This means that if a prisoner serves time without breaking prison rules, a certain amount of the prison sentence is deducted. The amount of deduction for good time is approximately 50 days per year.

eliminating early release is to swell the prison populations. Traditionally parole officers were social workers who helped offenders find jobs. Entering the twenty-first century, parole officers are more like law enforcement officers concerned with surveillance, warrantless searches, and drug tests. Thus even more parolees are returned to prison for various offenses.*

The purpose of probation is to aid in rehabilitation. There is no absolute right to probation; it is a matter of discretionary decision for the judge. After conviction and before sentencing, a probation officer will, at the court's discretion, thoroughly examine the defendant's background and circumstances. A recommendation to grant or deny probation will then be made to the court. There are two types of probation, formal and informal. Once formal probation has been granted, a probation officer will continually supervise the defendant. If informal probation is granted, the defendant will be "on his or her honor" to comply with the conditions of release. Probation may depend on many events, such as compliance with all laws, search for gainful employment, restitution or return of stolen property or its value, abstention from using intoxicants, and submission to periodic tests for drug addiction.

In many states, the privilege of probation is limited by statutes. Thus, probation cannot be granted to a defendant in California who was armed with a deadly weapon during a prison escape; or who was guilty of kidnapping, murder, forcible rape, or train-wrecking; or who has two prior felonies. Traditional practices concerning probation will be severely limited if and when "three strikes and you're out" legislation is adopted throughout the country, as appears to be a possibility at the time of this writing.

When probation is granted, either the sentence is suspended pending successful completion of probation, or there is no imposition of any sentence at all during the period of probation. In either case, probation will be revoked if the defendant violates its terms or conditions. The original sentence may then become operative. However, revocation of probation may occur only after a hearing has been conducted to establish the fact of the violation. If probation is successfully completed, the defendant's conviction is legally erased.

A defendant has the right to refuse probation and accept the sentence in its place, but this seldom happens.

In addition, there are three kinds of **executive clemency**, meaning a formal act of mercy: **reprieve** (delay in execution of judgment), **commutation** (reduction of punishment), and **pardon** (release from punishment with restoration of all rights and privileges—e.g., voting rights). Governors of states possess the power of clemency over state criminals; the president of the United States possesses the power over persons guilty of federal crimes.

Joseph Yandle was convicted of first-degree murder for driving the getaway car for his accomplice, who entered the Mystic Liquor store in Medford, Massachusetts, and shot the store manager to death. Yandle

---

*Parole boards have been abolished in Arizona, California, Delaware, Illinois, Indiana, Kansas, Maine, Minnesota, Mississippi, Ohio, Oregon, New Mexico, North Carolina, Virginia, and Washington. As noted earlier, the U.S. Sentencing Commission has eliminated parole in certain federal offenses. There is no statistical evidence that abolishing parole boards has lowered crime rates in any state—but keeping serious criminals in prison longer undoubtedly prevents some crimes. Fox Butterfield, "Parole Board Cuts Aren't a Cure," *New York Times*, 10 January 1999.

was sentenced to life imprisonment without possibility of parole. After 23 years in prison, Yandle appeared on the *60 Minutes* TV program and said his crime was prompted by heroin, which he used to "numb" his memories of fighting in the Vietnam War. In patriotic response, the Board of Pardons recommended commutation of sentence; the governor agreed and Yandle was set free. Five years later it was learned that Yandle had been only a clerk in Okinawa, Japan, and had never fought in Vietnam. Yandle had lied because he "just wanted to go home." Can Yandle's commutation of sentence be revoked?

Yes. Yandle surrendered to officials and returned to custody while his commutation was in the process of revocation.[117]

In December 1990 Taro, a 5-year-old 110-pound Akita dog, injured Brie Halfond, a 10-year-old girl. Taro was ordered "forfeited" and killed under the New Jersey vicious-dog law. Lonnie and Sandy Lehrer, Taro's owners, began legal proceedings ultimately costing some $30,000 in fees while the state incurred twice that amount in costs plus $18,000 to house and feed Taro. Taro's fate ultimately involved the courts, the state legislature, and gubernatorial candidates and gained an international following. The legal issue was whether or not Brie had provoked Taro into the attack. The case finally reached the New Jersey Supreme Court, which let stand a lower court's order to put Taro to death. Can the governor grant executive clemency to Taro?

Yes. Governor Christie Whitman, fulfilling a campaign promise, used an executive order to remove a "forfeiture order" on the dog in lieu of a "pardon," which is a remedy reserved for human beings. Taro's life was spared.[118]

WHEN IS PUNISHMENT CRUEL AND UNUSUAL?

The Eighth Amendment to the U.S. Constitution prohibits government from inflicting **cruel and unusual punishment** upon persons convicted of crimes. Punishment can be cruel and unusual in any one of four ways:

1. The sentence can be totally disproportionate to the offense.
2. The prisoner may be subjected to inherently cruel abuse.
3. The method of punishment may be unacceptable to society.
4. The punishment may be inflicted arbitrarily.

Defendant Rummel was sentenced to life imprisonment under the Texas recidivist statute.* He was guilty of committing three felonies over a

---

*Almost all states have recidivist statutes that enhance statutory penalties to life imprisonment in the case of repeat offenders (recidivists). The purpose is to deter repeat offenders and to segregate persons who repeat crimes from the rest of society for long periods.

period of some 15 years, as follows: (1) fraudulently using a credit card to obtain $80 worth of goods, for which a sentence of 3 years was imposed; (2) passing a forged check for $28.36 for which a sentence of 4 years was imposed; and (3) obtaining $120.75 by false pretenses, the third felony, for which a sentence of life imprisonment was required under the recidivist statute.

Under Texas law, a defendant may be paroled within 12 years if he or she earns maximum good-time credit and if the parole board and the governor approve. Defendant Rummel contended that his penalty was so disproportionate to the crimes as to violate the Eighth Amendment prohibition against cruel and unusual punishment. He appealed to the U.S. Supreme Court. What was the result?

The Court upheld Rummel's sentence by a 5–4 split decision.[119] The court noted that although the crimes did not involve much money, the crime of obtaining $120.75 by false pretenses standing alone is a felony in 35 states. Further, his crime of passing a forged check of $28.36 would be theoretically punishable by some amount of imprisonment in 49 states. Thus, the Texas recidivist statute was allowed to apply.

The sentence of life imprisonment without possibility of parole for a defendant convicted of possessing a large amount of drugs (650 grams of cocaine) is not cruel and unusual punishment, according to the U.S. Supreme Court speaking in another 5–4 split decision.[120]

Davis was convicted by a Virginia jury of possessing 9 ounces of marijuana, with a street value of $200, for distribution. He was sentenced to prison for 40 years and fined $20,000. He appealed on the basis that the sentence was so disproportionate to the crime that it constituted cruel and unusual punishment. What was the result?

The U.S. Supreme Court, in a 6–3 decision, repeated its earlier declaration that federal courts should be reluctant to review legislatively mandated terms of imprisonment, and that successful court challenges to the proportionality of particular sentences should be exceedingly rare. The sentence was permitted to stand.[121]

Prison officials may properly use force (e.g., tear-gassing, clubbing, or even shooting) in defense of themselves or other persons. On the other hand, corporal punishment (physical injury as punishment) is constitutionally prohibited. Generally, however, the remedy for an aggrieved prisoner remains inadequate. An abused prisoner presumably can obtain a writ of *habeas corpus* (Latin: "you have the body"), a procedure prompting a court hearing, or the prisoner may sue under the Civil Rights Act of 1964 or in a common-law tort action.

William McKinney, a Nevada state prisoner, filed suit against prison officials claiming that his involuntary exposure to environmental tobacco smoke (ETS) from the cigarettes of his cellmate and of other inmates posed an unreasonable risk to his health, thus subjecting him to cruel and unusual punishment. There was no claim that injury already had occurred. What was the result?

Justice Byron White, writing for the majority of the U.S. Supreme Court, held that McKinney was entitled to a trial on the issue of whether or not he was being exposed to unreasonably high levels of ETS that posed an unreasonable risk of serious damage to his future health. Justice Clarence Thomas, with Justice Antonin Scalia joining, dissented, stating "I would draw the line at actual, serious injuries and reject the claim that exposure to the risk of injury can violate the Eighth Amendment."[122]

Prisoner Richard Black, while hanging out in the prison yard, heard someone, whom he believed to be a guard, yell "Stop that man!" Black thereupon chased a fellow inmate who had just struck another inmate with a pipe. Black was placed in punitive segregation for 18 months for "running in the yard." Is that punishment "cruel and unusual"?

Yes. Prison guards admitted that someone yelled "Stop that man" and that Black could have believed it to be a guard, even though it was not yelled by a prison official. Such punishment, without a prior hearing of any kind, violates the Eighth Amendment.[123]

In 1998 Theodore John Kaczynski, the so-called "Unabomber," pled guilty to using homemade explosives in murdering 3 people and injuring 23 others. Kaczynski will spend the rest of his life in prison, probably at "Supermax," a federal prison near Pueblo, Colorado, designed to house the "worst of the worst." Some argue that life in such a prison is inhumane. Kaczynski is confined to his cell for all but two hours per day for exercise, and is strip searched and shackled when leaving. Inmates may receive only five visitors each month, but no handshakes, hugs, or physical contact is allowed—speaking is by telephone and physical separation is by thick plexiglas. Accommodations are spartan and lonely. There is only one window and it faces the sky—the Rocky Mountains are not visible to Kaczynski. Others believe life in even a maximum-security prison is too easy. Kaczynski's cell is slightly larger than the cabin in the woods where he planned his bombings. It is equipped with a shower, a commode, an electric lamp, a concrete desk and stool, a cigarette lighter, and a 13-inch television. Kaczynski can order books of all kinds from his cell. Breakfast, lunch, and dinner are served in his cell and he has some choices of dishes. Three times a week he receives clean bedding and clothing and can write to his heart's content.[124]

Critics of **capital punishment** (death by execution) insist that it is not a deterrent to crime, is "cruel and unusual," and that it "degrades and dehumanizes" all who participate in its administration. They claim that it discriminates against the poor and minorities, citing statistics showing that most persons sentenced to die, in recent years, have been poor, male, and members of minority groups. This latter argument was especially persuasive in the decision by the U.S. Supreme Court limiting capital punishment. It held that a state may not leave the decision whether to impose capital punishment, upon a particular defendant, to the unguided discretion of a jury.[125]

If a state wants to authorize the death penalty, it has a constitutional responsibility to tailor it and apply its law in a manner that avoids any arbitrary and capricious infliction of the death penalty. The implicit assumption is that prosecutors, juries, and judges, if left to their own discretion, would discriminate against defendants on the basis of race. In other words, if a statutory procedure specifies the factors to be weighed and the procedures to be followed in deciding when to impose capital punishment, or specifies a mandatory death penalty for specified crimes, then capital punishment is constitutional.[126]

To sentence to death, when the crime is "outrageously or wantonly vile, horrible and inhumane," is too vague because virtually all homicides fit this description.[127] Also inadequate are the words "especially heinous, atrocious, or cruel."[128] However, when "cruel" is defined to mean the defendant intentionally inflicted extreme pain or torture upon the victim, above and beyond the pain necessarily accompanying the victim's death, there is sufficient clarity of standard to justify imposition of the death penalty.[129]

Illinois authorizes the death penalty when a defendant, 18 years or older, murders a peace officer or fireman on duty, a prison guard, or multiple victims; or if he or she commits murder during the hijacking of an airplane or public vehicle; or pursuant to a contract for hire; or to prevent testimony in any criminal case.[130]

An adult defendant with an IQ between 50 and 63, with a "mental age"—the ability to learn—of a 6-year-old child and with the social maturity—the ability to function in the world—of a 9- or 10-year-old, was convicted of murder and sentenced to death by a Texas jury. Does this sentence violate the prohibition against "cruel and unusual" punishment?

No. The U.S. Supreme Court held that the defendant's ability was not so disproportionate to the degree of personal culpability as to violate the Eighth Amendment's prohibition against "cruel and unusual" punishment, or even the ban on punishment of "idiots" or "lunatics."[131]

A 17-year-old male robbed a gas station in Kentucky, raped and sodomized a station attendant, and finally shot her to death so she could not identify him. In another unrelated case, in Missouri, a 16-year-old male robbed a convenience store and repeatedly stabbed the store's owner, leaving her to die. State courts in both cases imposed the death penalty. Is it "cruel and unusual" punishment to sentence a minor to death?

No. Evolving standards of decency are best reflected by the statutes adopted by state legislatures, which presumably mirror the will of the people. The Court noted that of the 37 states with laws that permit capital punishment, 15 declined to impose it upon 16-year-old offenders while 12 declined to impose it upon 17-year-old offenders. This does not establish the degree of national consensus sufficient to declare the death penalty cruel and unusual punishment when applied to minors.[132]

After convicting Russell Coleman of rape and capital murder, the jury was required to recommend death or life imprisonment without possibility of parole. The judge instructed the jury that the governor could commute (reduce) a sentence of life without possibility of parole, whereupon the jury recommended death. In truth, the governor does not have that sole authority and must first obtain the written consent of four state supreme court justices before reducing such a sentence. Was Russell Coleman denied a fair sentencing because of the incorrect information?

No. Arguably the jury opted for the death penalty out of fear that Coleman might someday be released from prison by a future governor. However, the U.S. Supreme Court held that even if the instruction was erroneous, there was no showing that it had a "substantial and injurious" effect on the jury. Under this 5–4 split decision it is increasingly difficult for federal courts to reverse state death penalties.[133]

Convicts may linger on death row for a dozen or more years pending the final outcome of appeals that determine the propriety of the procedures and laws applied in the original trial. Can living under the threat of a future death by execution for years itself constitute the prohibited cruel and unusual punishment? In one dissenting opinion, Justice Breyer suggested that delay of 23 years between sentencing and execution may be cruel and unusual punishment.[134]

Is it cruel and unusual punishment to execute a female for a capital crime? Although executions of women are infrequent, there is no constitutional distinction between execution of a man and a woman.*

The death penalty is unique among all forms of criminal punishment in (1) its rejection of rehabilitation as a fundamental purpose of our criminal justice system, (2) its total irrevocability, and (3) its conflict with our society's commitment to humane treatment of fellow human beings. Some who support it, however, ask whether there are reasonable alternatives for those few cases where death is adjudged a proper penalty. Is life imprisonment without possibility of parole, and perhaps without possibility of pardon, actually more cruel than death?

U.S. Supreme Court Justice Harry A. Blackmun voted for capital punishment throughout his legal career until 1994, when he reversed course in a case involving a man shot to death in a tavern. Blackmun, at this point, rejected capital punishment as inherently unconstitutional.** Justice Scalia, writing separately, noted that Blackmun did not select for his argument against capital punishment any of several more brutal murders pending before the Court as examples—such as the case of an 11-year-old girl raped by four men and then killed by stuffing her panties down her throat.[135] "How enviable a quiet death by lethal injection compared with that!" Sincerely held, yet divisive conflicts of opinion engendered by capital punishment clearly are here to stay.

For information about women on death row, see Victor L. Streib, *Death Penalty for Female Offenders, Jan 1, 1973 to Present*, Ohio Northern University, available at http://www.law.onu.edu/faculty/streib/femdeath.pdf

For updates on the death penalty debate and laws, use the index available at http://www.law.indiana.edu/law/v-lib/lawindex.html or obtain a variety of resources at The Death Penalty Page, http://law.fsu.edu/lawtech/deathpen/deathpen.html or http://www.essential.org/dpic/

CAN A DEFENDANT'S RECORD BE CLEARED?

State legislatures provide for the sealing (erasing) of certain criminal records as an aid to rehabilitation of defendants who have "learned their lesson." Usually, where the sentence is probation, and the defendant has successfully completed all

*In recent years, only three women have been executed: Velma Barfield in North Carolina, 2 November 1984; Karla Faye Tucker in Texas, 3 February 1998; and Judy Buenoano in Florida, 30 March 1998.
**Critics of Blackmun find contradiction between his recent rejection of capital punishment on the one hand, and his expressed pride in authorship of the majority opinion in *Roe v. Wade*, 410 U.S. 113, 93 S.Ct. 705 (1973), which legalized abortion, on the other hand.

the requirements of probation, the court will, upon motion, vacate the guilty plea or the finding of guilt, and dismiss the accusation or information. Thus, most legal disabilities that arise in connection with the conviction are legally erased. Such convictions ordinarily cannot be used thereafter to enhance the penalty for a subsequent conviction, although this traditional rule may be modified by variations of proposed "three strikes and you're out" legislation.

A defendant who was under 21 at the time of conviction for a misdemeanor may, upon completion of the sentence or probation, obtain an order of the court sealing all records pertaining to the conviction. Although the records are officially sealed in this manner, some applications for professional licensure inquire whether or not records exist and have been sealed, and, if so, what circumstance surrounded the crime. Otherwise, the defendant can answer questions as if the crime never occurred. Some types of misdemeanor records or infractions typically cannot be sealed, such as those pertaining to vehicle code violations, those involving registration as a sex offender, and those involving specified drug offenses.

WHAT SHOULD YOU DO IF ARRESTED?

A person placed under arrest, whether innocent or guilty, would be well advised to comply with the following suggestions (in the absence of more specific legal advice):

1. Do not strike an officer or resist arrest. If the officer is abusive, get the badge number and (if possible) the name. Be attentive and try to remember the specifics of the abuse involved.

2. Do not resist the officer searching you (e.g., patting down your body) and your car.

3. Do cooperate with fingerprinting and booking procedures. Even if these procedures are personally offensive, such as a strip search, no good can come from physical resistance. If given the choice between certain sobriety tests, be sure you understand your state's penalty for refusing all such tests before making that decision.

4. Do request (if not offered) the right to make a telephone call and use it to contact someone (parent, relative, friend) who can get a lawyer or assistance in posting bail and taking you home. If you cannot afford a lawyer, tell the magistrate or judge before whom you will be required to appear. You can request release on your own recognizance and the magistrate or judge will promptly make the decision on whether to grant your request.

5. Do not respond to detailed questions—beyond such harmless basics as name, address, and telephone number—until and unless you are advised to answer by your attorney. You cannot be penalized for remaining silent. As some attorneys advise, "put a zipper on your mouth."

6. When applicable, do immediately mention to the arresting officer any physical condition requiring medication, such as multiple sclerosis, epilepsy, or diabetes.

7. Be frank and honest in explaining in confidence to your attorney exactly what happened. Counsel is bound by law to respect this confidence, and will be better able to represent you if in possession of all the facts surrounding the incident. Your attorney cannot be compelled to reveal your conversation, even if it involves a confession of guilt.

CASES

PEOPLE V. FLAX
255 Ill.App 103, 627 N.E.2d 359 (1993)

Facts: Angelo Katselis and his wife Kiriaki owned and operated Harrison Cleaners in Chicago. At 6 P.M., October 22, 1987, Keefus Flax entered the store wearing a stocking as a mask. Flax demanded money. Mr. Katselis handed him $500 from the cash register. Then Mr. Katselis said, "I recognize you." In response, Flax took a gun from his pocket and shot and killed Mr. Katselis.

Flax was caught and convicted by jury of murder and armed robbery. He was sentenced to life in prison without parole, and for an additional 30 years for armed robbery. One ground for Flax's subsequent appeal was that the prosecutor's remarks during trial prejudiced his right to a fair trial.

Justice Gordon delivered the opinion of the Court: Defendant contends he was denied a fair trial by the following remarks made by the prosecutor in the opening statement:

> The evidence will also show that in October of 1987, the defendant, Keefus Flax, was also in business. He was in the business of murder and armed robbery.

The purpose of the prosecutor's opening (statement) is to inform the jury about what the prosecution intends in good faith to prove through the evidence to be presented. It is improper to mention matters which the prosecution knows will not be proved during the trial. The state contends that the prosecutor's

opening statement was not improper because it merely refers to the professional, businesslike manner in which the crime was committed, and such a conclusion was supported by the evidence. While this interpretation is arguably plausible, the remark should nevertheless have been avoided because it could also connote that defendant had been involved in other criminal activities.

Defendant also contends that the prosecutor's closing argument references to the defendant as a "bad man" and to the victim, his wife, and some witnesses as "good" people was improper. Statements arousing sympathy for, or commending the victim or the victim's family, while generally improper, can constitute harmless error where defendant is not substantially prejudiced. . . .

. . . The prosecutor's characterization of defendant as a "bad man" is a relatively mild pejorative in light of the seriousness of the crime committed. See e.g., *People v. Spreitzer*, 123 Ill.2d I, (annec.) 584 N.E.2d 477 [statement that to call defendant an animal "would be an insult to the animals" was held harmless error].

In view of the overwhelming evidence of defendant's guilt, there is no basis for concluding that the jury might have reached a verdict of not guilty had the State's Attorney not made the improper remarks.

The conviction is affirmed.

FOR CRITICAL ANALYSIS

1. The appellate court held that the prosecutor committed error twice, once in the opening statement by referring to the criminal "business" of Flax, and again in the final arguments by referring to Flax as a "bad" person and the victim as "good." If the prosecutor committed error, why wasn't the conviction overturned and the case remanded for a new trial?

2. If you were the district attorney prosecuting a particularly heinous case, would you be deterred by the *Flax* case from referring to the defendant in your case as a "bad person"? Or that he was in the "business of crime"? If your answer is "no," then how do you reconcile the doctrine of *stare decisis*? If you answer "yes," then what penalty is it that would deter you?

3. Can you describe the test the appellate court uses to determine under what circumstances an error by a prosecutor will result in a reversal of the conviction?

4. Suppose the defense lawyer in a criminal trial refers to the prosecutor as a "liar," a "crooked politician," and the recipient of a "bribe by the victim's family." Further assume that the jury returned a verdict of "not guilty." Will the prosecutor win a reversal on appeal?

PEOPLE V. CHEVALIER
136 Ill.2d 66, 136 Ill.Dec. 167, 544 N.E.2d 942 (1989)

This case was consolidated on appeal with a similar case (People v. Flores, *119 Ill.Dec. 214, 168 Ill.App.3d) because the issues on appeal are comparable. In each case, the defendant admittedly shot and killed his wife and was convicted of murder. Both contend that the evidence was sufficient to justify giving the juries permission (by appropriate instruction from the judge) to consider manslaughter as an alternative choice to murder.*

Justice Stamos delivered the opinion of the Court: The issue common to both appeals is whether the provocation on the part of the victim was legally adequate to reduce the homicide from murder to voluntary manslaughter. . . .

In each (case) defendant suspected his wife of marital infidelity. Just prior to the killing, the defendant and the victim had an argument, during which the victim admitted committing adultery and either disparaged the defendant's sexual abilities (*People v. Chevalier*) or flaunted the fact that she slept with her lover in the marital bed (*People v. Flores*). The victims were shot during these arguments.

In Illinois, adultery with a spouse as provocation generally has been limited to those instances where the parties are discovered in the act of adultery or immediately before or after such an act, and the killing follows such discovery. For these reasons, we hold that in each of the cases before us, the provocation claimed was, as a matter-of-law, insufficient to constitute the serious provocation necessary to reduce the homicide from murder to manslaughter.

FOR CRITICAL ANALYSIS

1. Note that during trial, the judge instructed the jury to find the defendants either guilty of murder, or not guilty. The

jurors were not given the alternative of finding the defendants guilty of manslaughter. Why did the trial judge refuse to give the jury that option?

2. There are precedents in Illinois under which husbands have been found guilty of manslaughter, but not murder, for killing their wives after a confrontation about adultery. By reference to the Court's opinion, can you distinguish those precedents from the Chevalier case?

3. Is the practical effect of the Chevalier case that husbands who promptly kill unfaithful wives receive substantially more lenient sentences than those who wait a few days? Do you think the same rationale ought to apply to wives who murder their husbands following physical spousal abuse? Can you distinguish between the two kinds of situations?

CHAPTER QUESTIONS AND PROBLEMS

1. Theodore Kaczynski, known as the Unabomber, pleaded guilty to killing 3 people and wounding 23 others using handmade bombs—a 17-year crime spree. Sentenced to life without possibility of parole, Kaczynski is in "Supermax," the Colorado federal prison designed to house "the worst of the worst." In a cell larger than his former cabin in the mountains, Kaczynski enjoys a shower, a commode, an electric lamp, a concrete desk and stool, a cigarette lighter, and a 13-inch television. He can order books, including novels. Breakfast, lunch, and dinner are delivered to his cell, and he makes limited selections from a menu. Freshly laundered clothing and bedding arrives three times a week. Although he can write to his heart's content, and receive five visitors per month, Kaczynski is isolated from other prisoners. [Cynthia Hubert, *Sacramento Bee*, 27 June 1998.]

   a. Do you think Ted Kaczynski was wise to plea-bargain for a life sentence rather than to face the risk of a death penalty from the jury?

   b. Do you think the attorney general was equally wise to offer the bargain?

   c. What changes, if any, would you recommend be made to the prison lifestyle?

2. Prison officials may deprive prisoners of any right that is reasonably related to legitimate penological interests. Thus, many states forbid beards, long hair and pony tails, earrings, and long sideburns as well as letters, numbers, and designs shaved onto the heads of inmates. Can you identify how each of the following rules may relate to a legitimate interest? Or are these simply mean-spirited attempts to make the lives of prisoners miserable?

   a. no beards
   b. no long hair or pony tails
   c. no earrings or other pierced jewelry
   d. no numbers and designs shaved onto heads
   e. no body-building machines
   f. no television

   Should exceptions be made on the basis of religion? Some Sikhs view unshorn hair as a supplication to God—cutting their hair makes them a renegade. Some Native Americans believe that long hair is a link to their ancestors. Some

Muslims hold that the Koran teaches that beards are a sign of manhood. What are the implications of such exceptions?

3. George, Milton, and Fernando, all 18, decided to rob a bicyclist on a trail in the early morning in Pacific Heights. They grabbed a bicyclist who, to their dismay, promptly produced a .25 caliber handgun and shot Fernando through the heart. George and Milton jumped in their car to speed away, but promptly crashed. The bicyclist never has been found. Of what crimes are George and Milton guilty?

4. Visit the Federal Bureau of Justice Web site at http://www.ojp.usdoj.gov/bjs/welcome.html and prepare to orally describe to class the crime statistics you find most interesting, and why.

5. Assume a violent rape occurred in a small, rural community and that DNA evidence was collected at the scene of the crime. The victim could describe her assailant only as a young Caucasian man between 18 and 30 years of age. Assume the police then ran a local newspaper advertisement requesting that all men in the suspected category come by the station to supply saliva samples for DNA matching. Approximately 15,000 males within the suspected category were believed to reside in the nearby communities. The police intended to test all DNA samples received and to question all males in the suspected category who declined to submit samples. What issues can you identify relative to this procedure of "blanket" testing of DNA as a police procedure?

6. What percentage of prospective jurors from across the nation do you assume would be "fair and impartial" if:
   a. one of the parties in the case was a homosexual or lesbian?
   b. one of the parties was an African American?
   c. one of the parties was a Hispanic?
   d. one of the parties was an Asian?
   e. one of the parties was a tobacco company?
   f. one of the parties was a politician?

What percentage of prospective jurors from across the nation do you assume would act on their own beliefs of right and wrong regardless of legal instructions from a judge?

Do you believe that responses of prospective jurors about such matters would be different once they were seated and participating in the solemnity of an actual trial?

7. In this chapter you read how one act, such as the assault and battery by police upon the suspect Rodney King, could be both a state and a federal crime without violating the prohibition against double jeopardy. You may recall that officers Koon and Powell, although acquitted of a state crime, were subsequently convicted of a federal crime—for the same offensive act. Under what circumstances do you think that federal prosecutors proceed against defendants who have been acquitted in state proceedings? Should federal prosecutors proceed against everyone suspected of committing a federal crime even though they previously were acquitted by jury in a state trial? In forming your rationale, consider that every time a state police officer violates the constitutional rights of any accused, by false arrest, for example, a federal offense also has occurred (violation of constitutional rights).

8. Earlier in this chapter you read that officers in a police vehicle cannot turn on its emergency lights if they stop to assist a motorist parked at roadside. In the case example you read, officer Studnicka turned on his flashing red lights when stopping to give possible assistance to Steven Hanson, who was parked in his van on the shoulder of the road. A beer was seen "in plain sight" of Studnicka, who then arrested Hanson for driving under the influence. A subsequent

search of the van revealed marijuana. Recall that the penalty ordered by the court for the illegal detention by Studnicka was suppression of the marijuana and alcohol evidence. Thus, Hanson was set free. Do you think Hanson was allowed to take his marijuana with him from court? Do you think the ruling of the judge would have been the same if, instead of marijuana, the police found the dead body of Hanson's wife in the van with a knife sticking from her chest? Explain the rationale of your answer.

9. Generally speaking, statutes—and the prosecutors, juries, and judges that enforce them—treat crimes against the person more harshly than crimes against property. The rationale is that human life is much more important than property of any description. Is there validity to the proposition that by downplaying crimes against property, society implicitly invites more serious crimes against persons? Present arguments both pro and con regarding this proposition.

10. Are you in favor of Megan's Law, which authorizes police to inform residents that a former sex offender is living in their midst? Should maps showing the specific location of residences be handed out at public expense? Should photographs be distributed for ease in identifying such persons, for example, in the local supermarket? To what other kinds of former felons should the practice be extended, if any? What constitutional issues can you identify relative to these practices?

11. On most Saturdays, Steve Mean played handball at a nearby park. He usually traveled by rollerblade via sidewalks then across a pedestrian overpass above the nearby freeway. Noticing a hole in the cagelike fencing along the overpass, Mean decided to drop a handball onto the freeway below to "see what would happen." Kristina Rey was driving to the mall when the ball struck and broke the windshield on her new Volkswagen. Startled, she jerked the wheel, sending her car directly into oncoming traffic. Kristina was killed instantly when an 18-wheel truck smashed into her Volkswagen head on. Of what kind of homicide is Steve Mean guilty?

NOTES

1. Mel Byrd, Director of Applied Research, North Carolina State University.
2. White House Office of National Drug Control Policy, as reported by Jeff Barnard, Associated Press, 27 July 1998.
3. William Glaberson, *New York Times*, 24 May 1998.
4. *U.S. v. Lanier*, 117 S.Ct. 1219 (1997).
5. *Chicago v. Morales*, 687 N.E.2d 53 (Ill., 1997).
6. *Chicago v. Morales* (97-1121).
7. *San Francisco Chronicle*, 23 June 1990.
8. *People v. Pena*, 149 Cal.App.3d Supp. 14, 197 Cal.Rptr. 264, (1983). See also *Commonwealth v. Martin*, 341 N.E.2d 1121 (Illinois, 1980).
9. *U.S. v. Koon*, 833 F.Supp. 769 (1993).
10. *People v. Jones*, 86 Ill.App.3d 278, 407 N.E.2d 1121 (Illinois, 1980).
11. C. Goodyear, *San Francisco Chronicle*, 20 October 1998.
12. *State v. Pyle*, 216 Kan. 423, 532 P.2d 1309 (Kansas, 1975).
13. *Creutz v. People*, 49 Cal.App.4th 822, 56 Cal.Rptr. 2d 870 (1996).
14. *People v. Municipal Court*, 88 Cal.App.3d 206, 151 Cal.Rptr. 861 (1979).
15. Illinois Code of Corrections, § 1005-8-1.
16. 17 Cal.Jur.III § 71.
17. Illinois Code of Corrections, § 1005-5-3.2.
18. *People v. Martinez*, 193 Cal.App.3d 364, 238 Cal.Rptr. 265 (1987).
19. *Commonwealth v. Noble*, 417 Mass. 341, 629 N.E.2d 1328 (Mass., 1994).
20. *State v. Tesack*, 181 W.Va. 422, 383 S.E.2d 54 (West Virginia, 1989).

21. *People v. Caldwell*, 36 C.3d 210, 681 P.2d 274, 203 Cal.Rptr. 433 (1984); *People v. Aurelio R.*, 167 Cal.App.3d 52, 212 Cal.Rptr. 868 (1985).

22. See, for example, *Commonwealth ex.rel. Smith v. Myers*, 438 Pa. 218, 261 A.2d 550 (Pennsylvania, 1970); *Alvarez v. Dist. Ct. for Denver*, 186 Colo. 37, 525 P.2d 1131 (Colorado, 1974); *People v. Wood*, 8 N.Y.2d 48, 167 N.E.2d 736 (New York, 1960); *State v. Harrison*, 90 N.M. 437, 564 P.2d 1321 (New Mexico, 1977).

23. *Enmund v. Florida*, 458 U.S. 782, 102 S.Ct. 3368 (1982).

24. *Tison v. Arizona*, 481 U.S. 137, 107 S.Ct. 1676 (1987).

25. *People v. Aurelio R.*, 167 Cal.App.3d 52, 212 Cal.Rptr. 868 (1985).

26. *People v. Hernandez*, 169 Cal.App.3d 282, 215 Cal.Rptr. 166 (1985).

27. *People v. Rosenkrantz*, 198 Cal.App.3d 1187, 244 Cal.Rptr. 403 (1988).

28. See, for example, California Penal Code, § 187.

29. In *The People v. Davis*, 30 Cal.Rptr. 2d 50, 872 P.2d 591 (1994), the California Supreme Court held that the fetus need only have progressed beyond the embryonic stage of seven to eight weeks for the murder statute to apply.

30. *Roe v. Wade*, 410 U.S. 113, 93 S.Ct. 705 (1973); *Webster v. Reproductive Health Services*, 492 U.S. 490, 109 S.Ct. 3040 (1989).

31. *Commonwealth v. Britcher*, 386 P.Super. 515, 563 A.2d 502 (Pennsylvania, 1989).

32. *People v. Watson*, 30 Cal.3d 290, 637 P.2d 279, 179 Cal.Rptr. 43 (1981).

33. *Reinesto v. Arizona*, 182 Ariz. 192, 894 P.2d 733 (1994); *Collins v. Texas*, 890 S.W.2d 893 (1994); *Nevada v. Encoe*, 110 Nev. 1317, 885 P.2d 596 (1994).

34. *Whitner v. State of South Carolina*, 492 S.E.2d 777 (So. Carolina, 1997); Certiorari to *U.S. Supreme Court* denied 26 May 1998.

35. *Time*, 22 May 1989, 104.

36. Associated Press, 15 November 1997.

37. *Commonwealth v. Walter R.*, 414 Mass. 714, 610 N.E.2d 323 (1993).

38. *National Law Journal*, 26 October 1992, 3.

39. Karin Miller, Associated Press, 3 February 1995.

40. *San Francisco Chronicle*, 2 March 1994, A7.

41. *People v. Vela*, 172 Cal.App.3d 237, 218 Cal.Rptr. 161 (1985); *Battle v. State*, 287 Md. 675, 414 A.2d 1266 (Maryland, 1980); *State v. Way*, 297 N.C. 293, 254 S.E.2d 760 (North Carolina, 1979).

42. Chronicle News Service, New York, 13 December 1997.

43. *People v. Alday*, 10 Cal. 3d 392, 315 P.2d 1169, 110 Cal.Rptr. 617 (California, 1973).

44. See 31 Am.Jur.2d, Extortion, Blackmail, and Threats, § 1.

45. *People v. Lopez*, 176 Cal.App.3d 545, 222 Cal.Rptr. 101 (1986). California Penal Code, §§ 203 and 204.

46. *People v. Valdez*, 175 Cal.App.3d 103, 220 Cal.Rptr. 538 (1985).

47. Richard A. Serrano, "Hate Groups on the Rise Across America," *Los Angeles Times*, 4 March 1998.

48. Associated Press, Washington, October 1997.

49. Associated Press, Santa Monica, 5 March 1998.

50. A hypothetical situation based on an actual case reported by the Los Angeles Daily News Service, 1 January 1999. In that reported case, Mari Frank had spent more than 500 hours and $10,000 attempting to clear her name.

51. Friedbert Weiss, Scripps Research Institute, La Jolla, CA, as reported by the Associated Press, Washington, 27 June 1997.

52. California Health & Safety Code, §§ 11,550 and 11,351.

53. Florida Crimes Code, § 893.13.

54. Associated Press, Los Angeles, 6 March 1998.

55. Associated Press, 16 April 1998.

56. Florida Crimes Code, § 800.02.

57. Reuters, Houston, 21 November 1998.

58. According to a New York State Attorney General's survey in March 1998, of those responding 92 percent favored Megan's Law. However, fewer (79 percent) favored putting the information on the Internet, a tactic that has been done in five states; Florida, Indiana, Kansas, Alaska, and Georgia. In 1999 Virginia became the first state to post the names, ages, addresses and photographs of sex offenders on the Internet. In California, the identity and address of some 68,000 sex offenders has been made available to the public, in some communities by maps and photographs delivered door-to-door by police.

59. Federal courts have upheld Megan's Law in Washington State, New York, and New Jersey. These federal courts have jurisdiction over a number of additional states. *Seattle Times*, 5 September 1997; Reuters, 22 August 1997.

60. Hans Greimel, "Neighbors Keep Molester Away by Buying His Home," Associated Press, *San Francisco Chronicle*, 13 August 1998.

61. *People v. John V.*, 167 Cal.App.3d 761, 213 Cal.Rptr. 503 (1985).

62. *Chaplinski v. State of New Hampshire*, 315 U.S. 568, 62 S.Ct. 766 (1942).

63. *San Francisco Chronicle*, 28 March 1989.

64. *The Wall Street Journal*, 18 February 1994.

65. *New York Times*, 6 May 1997.

66. *National Law Journal*, 13 September 1993, 8.

67. *National Organization for Women, Inc., v. Scheidler*, 510 U.S. 249, 114 S.Ct. 798 (1994).

68. *Terrell v. Childers*, 836 F.Supp. 468 (N.D. Illinois, 1993).

69. *San Francisco Chronicle*, 15 May 1997.

70. *San Francisco Chronicle*, 29 March 1994.

71. *National Law Journal*, 9 March 1992, 13.

72. *People v. Segal*, 54 N.Y.2d 58, 429 N.E.2d 107 (New York, 1981).

73. Judith Schoolman, New York, reported in *San Francisco Chronicle*, 16 March 1998.

74. Reuters, Ottawa, 8 August 1992.

75. *People v. Barraza*, 23 Cal.3d 675, 591 P.2d 947, 153 Cal.Rptr. 459 (1979).

76. *People v. Slatton*, 173 Cal.App.3d 487, 219 Cal.Rptr. 70 (1985); *People v. Kelley*, 158 Cal.App.3d 1085, 205 Cal.Rptr. 283 (1984).

77. *United States v. Russell*, 411 U.S. 423, 93 S.Ct. 1637 (1973).

78. *United States v. Barger*, 931 F.2d 359 (1991).

79. Proclamation signed by then-President Ronald Reagan when declaring the first annual Crime Victims' Week, April 1981.

80. Associated Press, 14 July 1998.

81. Associated Press, Los Angeles, 25 August 1998.

82. See McShane and Williams, "Radical Victimology: A Critique of the Concept of Victim in Traditional Victimology," *Crime and Delinquency* 38 (1992); Norris, Fran, and Krzysztof, "Psychological Distress Following Criminal Victimization in the General Population," *Journal of Consulting and Clinical Psychology* 62 (1994).

83. *United States v. Leon*, 468 U.S. 897, 104 S.Ct. 3405 (1984); *United States v. Peltier*, 422 U.S. 531, 95 S.Ct. 2313 (1975).

84. *Michigan Dept. of State Police v. Sitz*, 496 U.S. 444, 110 S.Ct. 2481 (1990).

85. Associated Press, 16 January 1999.

86. *State v. Hanson*, 501 N.W.2d 677 (Minn. App, 1993).
87. *National Law Journal*, 7 February 1994, 42.
88. *National Law Journal*, 7 February 1994, 6.
89. *U.S. v. Penny-Feeney*, 773 F.Supp. 220 (D.Hawaii, 1991).
90. *California v. Greenwood & Van Houten*, 486 U.S. 35, 108 S.Ct. 1625 (1988).
91. *United States v. Rodriquez*, 592 F.2d 553 (1979); *United States v. Ramsey*, 431 U.S. 606, 97 S.Ct. 1972 (1977); *United States v. Olcott*, 568 F.2d 1173 (1978).
92. New York Criminal Procedure Law, § 510.30 et. seq.
93. *National Law Journal*, 19 April 1993, 6, discussing the case of *Alme v. Commonwealth*, 414 Mass.667, 611 N.E.2d 2941 (1993).
94. The Bail Reform Act of 1984, 18 U.S.C. 3142(d). But see also *United States v. Salerno*, 481 U.S. 739, 107 S.Ct. 2095 (1987) for standards.
95. *United States v. Blackwell*, 694 F.2d 1325 (1982).
96. *Miranda v. Arizona*, 384 U.S. 436, 86 S.Ct. 1602 (1966).
97. Associated Press, Springfield, Massachusetts, 30 January 1999.
98. *Brady v. Maryland*, 373 U.S. 83, 83 S.Ct. 1194 (1963).
99. *N. Carolina v. Pearce*, 395 U.S. 711, 89 S.Ct. 2072 (1969).
100. *San Francisco Chronicle*, 29 June 1993.
101. *Frye v. United States*, 293 F.2d 1013 (D.C., 1923).
102. *Daubert v. Merrell Dow Pharmaceuticals, Inc.*, 509 U.S. 579 (1993).
103. James Q. Wilson, *Moral Judgment: Does the Abuse Excuse Threaten Our Legal System?* (New York: Basic Books, 1997).
104. Illinois Code of Corrections, § 1005-5-3.2.
105. Illinois Code of Corrections, § 1005-8-1.
106. *State of Indiana v. Rowold*, 629 N.E.2d 1285 (Indiana, 1994).
107. *Los Angeles Daily News*, 10 July 1998.
108. Associated Press, 10 December 1998.
109. Kalpana Srinivasan, "Criminals Seeing More Jail Time," Associated Press, 11 January 1999.
110. *Los Angeles Times*, 10 July 1998.
111. Associated Press, 28 January 1999.
112. Associated Press, Jackson, New Jersey, 26 November 1998.
113. *National Law Journal*, 27 July 1992, 17.
114. *United States v. Mistretta*, 488 U.S. 361, 109 S.Ct. 647 (1989).
115. *United States v. Bradley*, 917 F.2d 601 (1990); *United States v. Seluk*, 873 F.2d 15 (1989).
116. *National Law Journal*, 21 February 1994, 38.
117. Associated Press, Boston, 27 August 1998.
118. Jerry Gray, *New York Times*, 29 January 1994.
119. *Rummel v. Estelle*, 445 U.S. 263, 100 S.Ct. 1133 (1980).
120. *Harmelin v. Michigan*, 501 U.S. 957, 111 S.Ct. 2680 (1991).
121. *Hutto v. Davis*, 454 U.S. 370, 102 S.Ct. 703 (1982).
122. *Helling v. McKinney*, 509 U.S. 25, 113 S.Ct. 2475 (1993).
123. *Black v. Brown*, 524 F.Supp. 856 (1981).
124. Cynthia Hubert, *Sacramento Bee*, 27 June 1998.
125. *Furman v. Georgia*, 408 U.S. 238, 92 S.Ct. 1133 (1980).
126. *Gregg v. Georgia*, 428 U.S. 153, 96 S.Ct. 2909 (1976).
127. *Godfrey v. Georgia*, 446 U.S. 420, 100 S.Ct. 1759 (1980).
128. *Maynard v. Cartwright*, 486 U.S. 356, 108 S.Ct. 1853 (1988).
129. *State v. Breton*, 212 Conn. 258, 562 A.2d 1060 (Connecticut, 1989).
130. Illinois Criminal Code, § 9-1.
131. *Penry v. Lynaugh*, 492 U.S. 302, 109 S.Ct. 2934 (1989).
132. *Stanford v. Kentucky* and *Wilkins v. Missouri*, 492 U.S. 361, 109 S.Ct. 2969 (1989).
133. *Calderon v. Coleman*, No. 98-437, December 1998.
134. *Elledge v. Florida*, No. 98-54210, 13 October 1998.
135. *Callins v. Collins*, 510 U.S. 1141, 114 S.Ct. 1127 (1994).

TORTS: PRIVATE WRONGS

*T*he change that . . . overshadows and even controls all others is the industrial one, the application of science resulting in the great
inventions that have utilized the forces of nature on a
vast . . . scale: the growth of a world-wide market as
the object of production, of vast manufacturing cen-
tres to supply this market, of cheap and rapid means
of communication and distribution between all its
parts. . . . Through it the face of the earth is making over, even as to its
physical forms; political boundaries are wiped out and moved about, as if
they were indeed only lines on a paper map; population is hurriedly gathered into cities from the ends of the earth; habits of living are altered with
startling abruptness and thoroughness; the search for the truths of nature
is infinitely stimulated and facilitated, and their application to life made
not only practicable, but commercially necessary. Even our moral and religious ideas and interests . . . are profoundly affected.

John Dewey, The School and Society, *1899*.

The twentieth century began in a gilded age of prosperity for our people. For the
first time in history, our nation had achieved global economic and military significance. The booming economy was fueled by the expansion of the United
States in seizing the Spanish colonies of Cuba, Puerto Rico, and the Philippines
and in annexing Guam, Hawaii, and an island in the Samoas. Trade with the giant
markets in China, Korea, and Japan flooded western seaports such as Seattle,
Tacoma, and San Francisco with raw cotton from the South; fabric from New
England; and flour, iron, and steel from Chicago, Pittsburgh, and Kansas City.
Technology was exploiting electricity, while the automobile and airplane industries were in their infancy. There was a price to be paid for the booming economy,
however—an ever-increasing disparity between rich and poor, rampant racism
and sexism, and substandard housing and working conditions. The civil law system was facing the challenge of resolving a plethora of new and conflicting demands. The common law of England was in general effect throughout the United
States, including all of the common-law torts that, together with newly created
torts, form the basis of this chapter. Our civil law tort system, today referred to by
some as the "litigation explosion," was minute in scope and relatively simple in

301

1900. Horse-drawn buggy crashes did not provoke personal injury litigation as we know it today.

Our society enters the new century with similar expectations of the "good life" and a "long boom" of continuing prosperity. Only the nature of the economic revolutions has changed. The industrial revolution, fueled by the great Klondike gold rush of the 1890s, has evolved into today's scientific revolution in communications, electronics, and biotechnology.* Through two world wars, a Korean "police action," and the Vietnam and the Gulf Wars, our nation remains a global economic and military power. But both the role of civil tort law** and the legal system that shapes our daily lives have changed greatly over the past 100 years. As we shall see in this chapter, tort law "tomorrow" faces—and must resolve— some very unique problems.

Today, everyone is familiar with the highly publicized awards of money to victims of a wide variety of acts that society, through its legal system, deems to be wrong or simply unacceptable. These plaintiffs (victims who bring civil actions) recover damages (money) from defendants (those held responsible) in amounts typically set by juries. Most of these monies paid to victims come from insurance companies, who expect to take in enough money from premiums to pay all claims and then, of course, to retain a profit. Sometimes, though, it is not obvious that insurance companies are involved, nor is it clearly understood who is paying their premiums.

Thus, the civil law of torts shapes our society by shifting the risk of injury from victims to others who can better afford the costs (the "deep pockets"). Certain businesses (and sometimes persons) also are punished financially for actions deemed especially wrongful. These are punitive damage cases that discourage future wrongful conduct and, as well, enrich those victims whose lawyers can successfully pursue those kinds of claims. Thus, tort law is the vehicle through which both claims for compensation by victims and demands for punitive damages are administered.

Most injuries, and hence torts, arise from the role of individuals as consumers, as commuters, and as employees. Thus, buying and using products, commuting to and from work, and being safe and humanely treated during employment are three major responsibilities of the civil tort law.

At the beginning of the twentieth century, the notion of saving money and pinching pennies began to give way to the idea of consuming for "the good life." Much consumption begins in department stores, some of the world's largest and finest of which already were in the great cities by the turn of the century. New York, with 3 million immigrants of diverse nationalities, was the second largest city in the world and, perhaps, the largest in terms of retail sales. Plate glass was being imported from Europe for window displays, which involved movement, colors, toy ferris wheels, and mannequins wearing machine-made garments, making shopping irresistible. Yet many thought that advertising and window displays were a form of huckstering—the older generation regarded gawking at windows as vulgar. To overcome that view, stores hired "window gazers" as

---

*Biotechnology combines the use of engineering sciences and computer technology in the study of living organisms. The legal implications of genetic engineering are considered in Chapter 9.
**The modern law of torts (Latin: "to twist") concerns compensating victims for wrongful or unacceptable conduct and sometimes for public policy reasons.

shills to stand gaping at window displays.[1] With prosperity, fashion began replacing necessities. What was thought to be conspicuous consumption,* the idea to "shop till you drop," thus existed at both ends of the twentieth century. Today, remarkable displays of consumer products are visible in the recreational centers called malls, with their clusters of department stores, retail outlets, and services. Perhaps the most significant distinction between the consumer goods at the beginning and ending of the twentieth century is not in their variety, but in the laws that surround their manufacture, distribution, display, purchase, and use. That is the law of torts, while the business of buying, selling, manufacturing, and distributing is ruled by the law of contracts (covered in the following chapter).

We are consumers of products that may be defective, that may injure buyers and bystanders, that we may never even see (breast implants) or that may disappear (food products). Other products, such as legal, medical, and personal services, may not be as tangible as an automobile or a coffee maker, but can still cause considerable injuries and/or financial losses. We buy and equip homes with a myriad of products and store recreational "toys" in our garages, all of which can and do cause injuries. In using and enjoying the products we acquire, we can and do injure one another, as in automobile and boating accidents. We are also employees in businesses, where we make and distribute our goods and may violate one another's rights, such as the right to be treated equally and fairly regardless of gender, race, religion, sexual orientation, or physical condition. In other words, tort law affects our everyday conduct, making "the good life" a possible dream. It has grown and served our society commensurately with the consumer revolution of the twentieth century.

But the tort system is less than perfect. Manufacturers, retailers, insurers, and even doctors, being frequent defendants, contend that Americans are excessively litigious, file frivolous claims, and persuade juries to award excessive damages based on sympathy and emotions rather than on hard evidence. Perhaps the most notorious example of this contention is the widely remembered (and often misunderstood) case of the lady who sued McDonald's for injuries suffered when hot coffee spilled on her lap.

Stella Liebeck, age 79, having just purchased a cup of coffee from a McDonald's "drivethru," tried to remove its lid to add creme. The coffee spilled, burning Stella. Stella sued and recovered damages of $200,000 plus punitive damages of $2.7 million. What can we learn from this example of the tort law in action?

We can learn that the media, responding to considerable public interest, focuses upon the sensational aspects of tort cases, even at the expense of "the rest of

---

*The term "conspicuous consumption" was coined by the famous economist, Thorstein Veblen, in his work, *The Theory of the Leisure Class*. Veblen wrote: Much of the charm that invests the patent-leather shoe, the stainless linen, the lustrous cylindrical hat, and the walking stick . . . comes of their pointedly suggesting that the wearer cannot when so attired bear a hand in any employment that is directly and immediately of any human use. Elegant dress serves its purpose of elegance not only that it is expensive, but also because it is the insignia of leisure." Judy Crichton, *America 1900*, (New York, Henry Holt & Co., 1998) p. 113.

the story." McDonald's had some 700 claims for burns in the preceding ten years; knew that its coffee at 180–190 degrees was "scalding" hot and could cause third-degree burns, as it did on Stella; and knew that competitors sold coffee at the household range of 135–140 degrees. Stella suffered third-degree burns on her buttocks, inner thighs, and genitals and required skin grafts and eight days hospitalization. McDonald's rejected Stella's original offer to settle for $20,000. After the large verdict, the trial judge reduced the verdict to $160,000 general and $480,000 punitive damages. There are additional important facts surrounding the matter, but the lesson is that we, as educated persons, should not leap to conclusions from media versions of tort laws in action.

As noted earlier, the tort laws are less than perfect. The McDonald's example is useful for yet another example. Most civil lawsuits settle after the case is initiated (and thus, after it has been reported in the media). That is, the people involved decide to resolve their dispute privately. No judge or trial is involved. Almost everyone agrees that private settlement is the preferable alternative. However, private settlements are not made public, and thus the public remains forever ignorant of how the important cases are resolved. The public seldom learns about such settlements because, as a condition of the agreement, one or both parties demand a confidentiality promise. For example, the McDonald's "coffee" case ultimately was settled out of court, and whether McDonald's eventually paid more or less to Stella Liebeck than the sums noted above is and shall forever remain unknown to the public.

Many aspects of the tort system can and do create outcomes that may be less than perfect. Extraordinarily complex litigation remains within the province of the lay jury. Groups of strangers scattered across the country can and do join together in "classes" of victims to right a thousand, or a million, wrongs in a single trial. The refrain "everyone is suing everyone, and most are getting big money" is common. According to this argument, the massive, mushrooming litigation explosion is said to be making attorneys rich (they generally receive one-third of recoveries) at the expense of business.

A 6-year-old child was killed in an automobile crash because the rear latch on a Dodge Caravan was defective. A jury returned a verdict for the parents of $262.5 million.[2]

What is the reason for the growth of tort law since World War Two? For one, courts have been expanding the scope of tort liability, for example, by determining that manufacturers and sellers of defective products could be sued for injuries without proof of negligence or fault. We will learn more about such "product liability" later in this chapter. New statutes passed by Congress and by state legislatures that are intended to relieve suffering and injustice are another reason for the growth of tort law.* For example, the Civil Rights Act of 1964 has been interpreted to create tort liabilities for a wide range of violations of civil rights. These civil rights cases occur when the wrongdoer is a government employee, such as a police officer.

---

*Some refer to remedial legislation as "do-gooder" laws and argue that "laws that subordinate life, liberty or property to vague notions of 'the common good' inevitably lead to injustice." *Forbes*, 5 May 1997.

In response to a noise complaint, about 100 deputy sheriffs responded to a bridal shower of a Samoan American family. A melee followed during which deputies hit partygoers with flashlights and clubs. These "torts" by police violated the civil rights of the victims. A jury returned a verdict for 36 plaintiffs of $16 million that, through interest while on appeal, grew to the $25 million actually paid by the County of Los Angeles.[3]

Further expansion of tort law occurred with enactment of the federal Americans with Disabilities Act. The ADA has been interpreted expansively (including the condition of obesity and the affliction of AIDS within its protected classes), producing myriad lawsuits for violations of its terms. Many laws essentially benefit one group in society at the expense of another group, the latter group being better able to afford the solution. For example, businesses can afford to provide special accommodations to disabled customers who otherwise could not enjoy the same pleasures nor fulfill the same obligations of modern society. Thus, the tort law can and does shape social policy—indeed, some say it micromanages our lives.

In this chapter you will become acquainted with many of the rules governing the relationship between victims and the defendants who are at fault or are held liable regardless of fault. Even your understanding of the word "fault" must be slightly revised. The "fault" upon which most of our tort system functions puts blame upon persons who fail to live up to the standards that most of us regularly fail to achieve.

The multiple and diverse private controversies or lawsuits in tort law range in importance from the trivial to the profound. Most are overlooked or are settled amicably through direct negotiation or with the assistance of others. But whatever the seriousness of the disputes, they may be resolved by legal action in accordance with the law of torts.

WHAT ARE TORTS AND HOW ARE THEY CLASSIFIED?

A **tort** is a private wrong (other than a breach of contract) committed by one person (the **tortfeasor**) that injures another's (the victim's) person and/or property, for which the law allows the legal remedy of monetary damages.

Sometimes two or more persons, called *joint tortfeasors*, are liable for the particular injury to one or more victims, but any one of the joint tortfeasors may be required to pay all damages suffered by the victim(s). For example, assume an automobile accident happened because a curve on a state highway was not banked and because Tom Jones was driving with tires worn smooth—he failed to make the turn. Both Jones and the state are joint tortfeasors and fully responsible, but any award of money damages to an injured victim could be collected entirely from either. If Tom Jones were indigent, the victim most likely would recover all of the damages from the state with its "deep pockets."

Torts may be classified as intentional, negligent, or strict liability (including product liability).

An **intentional tort** occurs when a person purposely commits some act that injures the victim. As you might expect, most crimes are also torts because criminal acts almost always are intended and also injure the victim. Thus, the state may prosecute the wrongdoer in a criminal action for the public wrong to society, while the individual victim may sue in a civil action for the private wrong. Earlier you read about this dual role in the example where O.J. Simpson was found not guilty of murder, but civilly responsible for damages for committing the tort of battery resulting in wrongful death. But there is a significant difference between crimes and torts. In crime, the intent is evil. In torts, the intent may or may not be evil—all that is required is that some act be intended that causes injury. For example, a practical joke may be intended with no underlying evil motive, but if injury to a victim results, an intentional tort has occurred. Or consider a person who excitedly fires a pistol into the air as part of a Fourth of July celebration, only to learn that the bullet on its inevitable descent killed a child. An intentional tort has occurred because the handgun was fired intentionally, even though no evil intent existed. On the other hand, O.J. Simpson acted with evil intent when he committed the intentional tort of battery upon his victims. Thus, as noted, the intent behind the wrongful act necessary for tort liability may or may not be evil.

Understandably, many intentional torts are not crimes because many people do not act with a *guilty mind* (i.e., with intent to commit a crime against the person or property of another).

A second kind of tort is negligence. **Negligence** means carelessness. By failing to act as a reasonable, careful person would act under the same or similar circumstances, the tortfeasor inadvertently causes an injury that was foreseeable (one that a reasonable person could and should anticipate as being a possible consequence).

The third basic type of tort, **strict liability** (including product liability), arises under circumstances where the victim need not prove that the defendant acted negligently or was guilty of an intentional tort. Indeed, it is often referred to as "liability without fault." Thus, in some circumstances, the law establishes a social policy by which the risk of loss is shifted from specified victims to others in society, such as businesses, who can better afford the losses. All the victim must prove is the fact of the injury, the damages suffered, and that the injury was caused by a product or act to which strict liability attaches, such as an airplane crash or a defective consumer product.

TORTS BY INTENTIONAL CONDUCT

It has been said that the wiles of humans are infinite. In many situations, men, women, and children are motivated by greed, anger, revenge, lust, a perverted sense of humor, a distorted sense of justice, a craving for costly drugs, or a desperate quest for a quick "solution" to poverty or unemployment. So impelled, they purposely engage in antisocial conduct when they know or should know it may harm others. Deliberate conduct that is regarded by law as wrong and that causes injury to the person or property of another is an *intentional tort*. It clearly differs from negligence, which is careless, wrongful conduct. Because most persons do not deliberately commit acts that have a high probability of injury to others, intentional torts are encountered much less frequently than negligent torts. Eight of the most significant types of intentional torts are described below.

ASSAULT AND BATTERY

Assault is an intentional threat or attempt that places the **victim** (i.e., the person who is the object of a tort or crime) in fear or *apprehension* of an immediate harmful or offensive touching.

see glossary

> Lon Shark was arguing loudly with "Spike" Flack over a debt. Finally, Spike said, "Listen, dork, I've paid you off. Get lost!" He turned and began walking toward his pickup. Without uttering a word, Lon grabbed a baseball bat from the ground and swung violently at Spike's head, but missed. Oblivious of the act, Spike got into his pickup and drove away. Was Lon guilty of the tort of assault?

No. Because Spike was not aware of the deadly attempt, he suffered no fear of immediate injury. Putting another person in apprehension or fear of immediate injury is the wrongful act in assault. (Note that Lon could be found guilty of the *crime* of assault, and possibly of attempted murder, neither of which requires proof of the victim's mental apprehension, as explained in Chapter 6.)

A **battery** is the harmful or offensive touching of another person without justification, consent, or excuse. A successful right hook to the jaw of someone you don't like, as well as a slap in the face, are classic examples of a battery. A left hook that misses because the victim saw it coming and dodged in time is an assault. An assault usually precedes, but is not an essential element of, a battery. Criminal sexual attacks, including rape, are also civil law assaults and batteries.

> In Angola, Indiana, defendant Muir pleaded guilty to two felony counts of sexual battery, for which he was sentenced to six years in prison and fined $5,000. After the prison sentence was suspended, the victim brought a civil action for the intentional tort of battery and was awarded $17.5 million in damages.[4] Is the large judgment likely to be collectible?

Unfortunately, collection of such sizable judgments from irresponsible defendants is unlikely. Because many criminals do not have financial resources, they are not commonly sued by their victims for practical rather than legal reasons. The possibility of such large judgments no doubt discourages only the more financially responsible persons in society from committing intentional torts.

> As part of a medical experiment, employees of the University of Chicago (in cooperation with drug manufacturer Eli Lilly & Co.) caused the drug diethylstilbestrol (DES) to be administered at its Lying-In Hospital to some pregnant patients without their knowledge. The drug was designed to prevent miscarriages. Subsequently, more than 1,000 of the women alleged that their female children had suffered an increased propensity for cancer as a side effect of the drug. Were the women victims of actionable batteries?

Yes. Batteries occurred because the women did not consent to the experiment.[5] In medical practice, before administering experimental drugs, performing a surgical operation, or providing other treatment, doctors must obtain the **informed consent** of their patients. The patient must be told what risks are involved and what available alternatives exist. The consent need not be in writing and may be implied from conduct. However, doctors and hospitals are increasingly concerned about lawsuits and usually do insist on written consent for any surgery. In cases of true emergency, when consent cannot be obtained, it is not required.

In the Eli Lilly & Co. case, the hospital's action was a tort, even though certainly the hospital personnel intended no harm (quite the contrary). But the act of administering the drug was intentional. Note that even if the drug had no harmful effects—indeed, even if it had beneficial effects—there would have been batteries. Such touching without prior permission would be offensive because, in the words of the *Restatement of the Law of Torts*,* "it offends a reasonable sense of personal dignity."

Raviv Laor was going to the bathroom during a trans-Atlantic flight on Air France when a smoke alarm malfunctioned. Flight attendants, thinking someone in the lavatory was smoking, burst in, grabbed Raviv, and pulled him out onto the floor with his trousers around his ankles, exposing him to other passengers. Laor neither smokes nor drinks and opted for a non-smoking flight. He filed suit and publicly contended that the flight purser declared that "Americans were always screaming about their rights."[6] Suppose the jury believes that Raviv really was sneaking a smoke in the lavatory, does that mean his action for battery would fail?

International laws apply to international flights and issues may arise in Laor's lawsuit about which state's laws should be applied by the federal court. But this interesting event is an example of when otherwise lawful conduct may devolve into a battery. Assuming that flight attendants lawfully can break into a bathroom under certain circumstances (such as when smelling smoke) during a flight, can they also pull a passenger off the commode and unceremoniously down onto the floor? Without some justifiable necessity for such conduct, a battery must then have occurred. A good motive is no defense to an intentional tort.

One is required to tolerate the close proximity of other persons in crowded public places. Thus, for example, bodily contact with strangers—which may be unpleasant and offensive to some sensitive individuals—is quite legal when necessary or inadvertent, as in buses and trains during rush hours, even though similar touching might theoretically be actionable battery at other times of the day.

CONVERSION (CIVIL THEFT)

Any unauthorized taking of the personal property of another and wrongfully exercising rights of ownership is the tort of **conversion**. It can involve wrongfully

---

*The *Restatement of the Law* (of Torts, Contracts, etc.) consists of a series of authoritative volumes written by legal scholars of the American Law Institute. In clear language, they state the principal rules of existing law in the designated area, with numerous practical examples of their application. The *Restatements* identify trends in the law and present suggestions for desirable changes. Judges often cite the Restatements in their opinions. In this case, the *Restatement of the Law of Torts*, 2d edition, (St. Paul, MN: American Law Institute Publishers, 1934), 19 applied.

taking such things as (1) a house trailer, (2) stock certificates sold by a broker without authorization, (3) architectural plans for a residence, even though the building is in public view, and (4) the re-recording and sale of recorded musical performances owned by a record manufacturer.[7]

> Alexis finds a valuable single reflex camera in a leather case under a bench at Disney World in Orlando, Florida. A business card inside has the name, address, and phone number of Daniel Daze, with the words "Reward for Return." Alexis recalls the ditty "Finders Keepers, Losers Weepers" from her childhood and decides to keep the camera. Has she committed a crime or a tort?

Both. Alexis has committed the crime of larceny. She also is liable in damages to Daniel Daze for commission of the tort of conversion. Unfortunately for Daze, the crime and tort will probably go undetected and unpunished. Alexis, the finder, is known in law as a constructive bailee of the goods. A *bailee* is a person to whom goods are entrusted for use, storage, or other purposes. The bailee has temporary possession, coupled with a duty to return or dispose of the goods in accordance with the trust. A restaurant with coat checking, a parking garage, and a laundry are examples of bailees. As a bailee, Alexis should make a reasonable effort to find the owner, usually with the assistance of the local police. If no one claims the item within a reasonable time, the finder may keep the property.

A brief, temporary, and unauthorized interference with the personal property rights of another is termed a **trespass to chattel**. The owner is entitled to damages for the limited loss of possession and any actual harm to the property. But the wrongdoer is not compelled to pay the full market value. An example is the deliberate "keying" (scratching with a key) of a parked automobile (which is a tort and also the crime of malicious mischief). Repainting is costly and time-consuming, but such tortfeasors are usually juvenile "hit-and-run" types who are not likely to be caught.

FALSE IMPRISONMENT AND FALSE ARREST

The wrongful restraint of the physical liberty of another is called **false imprisonment.** It involves detention of the victim and restraint of his or her freedom of movement. There must be confinement within a given area, large or small, by means of physical barriers and/or physical force or threatened force. **False arrest** by an officer with legal authority (or even by one who pretends to have such authority) is a variety of false imprisonment. False arrest by a police officer also may be a violation of the civil rights of the victim, a federal offense.

Because of the prevalence of self-service in stores where merchandise is openly displayed, the crime of shoplifting reportedly costs merchants (and ultimately consumers) billions of dollars annually. The exact figure is unknown largely because some inventory shortages are also caused by employee pilferage. Attempts to reduce these losses through closer surveillance and the employment of plainclothes private security personnel have brought about many arrests—and along with them, charges of false imprisonment. Legislatures and police, however, are generally sympathetic to the plight of the storeowners. To help protect affected business firms, legislatures in many states have enacted laws that

For current but unofficial statistics on who shoplifts and why, see the data compiled by a national security firm at http://www.unisen.com/articles.html#why

establish the shopkeeper's privilege. These statutes permit a retail merchant or authorized employee to detain a person if there are reasonable grounds to believe that the suspect has shoplifted and if reasonable means of detection are used. To reduce the number of lawsuits and charges of abuse of privilege, prudent store security people use minimum restraint and promptly summon official police to conduct the search and make an arrest, if justified. As a further precaution, security people usually wait until the suspect has left the store and therefore cannot claim, "I'm still shopping," when detained.

The crime of rape constitutes two intentional torts, battery and false imprisonment. The locking of a child in a closet for an extended period may become the crime of parental abuse and the intentional tort of false imprisonment. Or, as a final example, discouraging a patron from leaving a bar by threatening to beat him up outside is a variety of false imprisonment.

INTENTIONAL INFLICTION OF MENTAL DISTRESS

Intentional infliction of mental distress, or as some states name it, **outrageous conduct,** occurs when one intentionally acts in a manner that reasonably may be expected to cause severe mental distress to another, the victim. To be actionable, the wrongful conduct must be describable as atrocious, utterly intolerable in today's society, and exceeding the bounds of all decency. This kind of conduct is so extreme and outrageous that it causes severe emotional distress, even though there is no physical touching of the plaintiff (as in a battery) or apprehension of an immediate harmful or offensive touching (as in assault). Because of the absence of physical harm, or its immediate threat, such claims have formerly been rejected. Claims of mental distress that are not evidenced by some tangible injury are easy to make, yet difficult to disprove. Nevertheless, most courts now hold that in a proper case such injury is real and compensable.

Mark Goldfarb, a student at Tennessee State University, was attending Professor Baker's class when an unidentified assailant surreptitiously entered the room and threw a pie that hit Baker. The professor immediately, but erroneously, accused Mark of the offense. The next day, Professor Baker barred Mark from the classroom and had him ejected from the building, still believing he was the culprit. Mark suffered emotional distress, especially because he was an ex-prisoner attempting personal rehabilitation; the accusation of lawlessness was particularly offensive to him. Mark sued the professor for the tort of outrageous conduct. Will he prevail?

No. The conduct was not actionable because the professor acted under provocation, and his conduct, although wrong, was the product of the sudden, unjustified, and humiliating attack.[8] This type of reflexive encounter is simply one of life's frictions and irritations for which there is no legal remedy.

Brendan Mcvey, 16, angry because his high school girlfriend Sara Phong, 15, broke up with him, mailed a nude photograph of Sara to Chris, the editor of the school newspaper. Before it was confiscated, the photograph was shown around campus, causing Sara humiliation and distress until the school year ended. Can Sara recover damages from Brendan and/or Chris?

A jury certainly would agree that the conduct of Brendan was intentional and outrageous. Although Brendan may be without funds to pay any court award, judgments may last from 10 to 20 years, and sometimes more. Thus, if Sara obtained a judgment, she would be a creditor of Brendan until he was as old as 36 and could, among other remedies, take part of his earnings through a procedure known as *garnishment*. Sara also may be able to convince a jury that Chris committed outrageous conduct by permitting the photograph to be seen by others— although that is a much closer question. If Brendan were 18 or older, he would also be guilty of a misdemeanor crime because Sara is a minor.

The tort of outrageous conduct sometimes arises when creditors, often with the assistance of collection agencies, pursue debtors in an especially aggressive manner. The problem became so acute that in 1977 Congress enacted the **Fair Debt Collection Practice Act**, which prohibits abusive tactics such as threats of violence or use of obscene language, harassing telephone calls, and publication of "shame" lists. In communicating with third parties to learn the location of a debtor, one may not even state that he or she owes a debt. Abused debtors may seek damages of up to $1,000 plus court costs and reasonable attorney fees. The act does not apply to creditors who do their own collecting, but in a proper case they may instead be subject to claims for outrageous conduct.

Torts committed by police often are characterized as violations of the victim's civil rights—but are common-law torts nonetheless.

Elbert Poppell, a former Mormon missionary, opened a "swingers' club" near San Diego. Guests donated $50 to attend weekend parties where they engaged in sex on mattresses throughout the house. Some guests were married couples, others were not, still others were complete strangers. Poppell previously was denied a business license for his purple "love bus" that was outfitted with beds and a hot tub. But no California laws were broken by Poppell because no money was exchanged between sex partners. His business was something like renting out one motel room to a large group of "members." But the police opposed the sex club and would park outside with lights flashing, ticketing guests for infractions such as broken tail lights and for parking illegally. Finally Poppell sued the City of San Diego in federal court claiming outrageous harassment. What should be the result?

A unanimous jury awarded him $200,000 in punitive and compensatory damages.[9] Although the police ostensibly violated no laws, their conduct was believed outrageous by the jury. Would it be similar if police stopped and administered a sobriety test to every patron leaving a "gay bar" after midnight, but stopped none of the patrons leaving a "sports bar"? There undoubtedly is a strong temptation on the part of some police to carry out, through selective enforcement or other improper tactics, the honestly believed will of the community. But the police, as well as other well-meaning persons, must focus their political beliefs upon changing local laws, not through individual actions that may result in personal liability.

Poppell was no pioneer in the neighborhood "swingers' club" activity. Another host, Bill Goodwin in Costa Mesa, California, invited guests on weekends to his "Panther Palace" featuring a 40-person hot tub, pool, and disco floor. As many as 100 guests of all professions and age groups attended these partner-swapping parties. There were no city ordinances against orgies, no violation of building codes, no broken zoning rules, and no requirement for a business license because no admission charge was made. The police did not harass Goodwin.[10] No tort occurred because there were no victims of this conduct thought by most people to be outrageous.

Serious actions taken to deprecate people because of their race, religion, physical characteristics, sexual orientation, etc., such as painting symbols on residences or etching epithets on plate glass windows, usually will constitute the intentional infliction of mental distress upon the victim. As a practical matter, most victims of this tort do not engage the services of an attorney and file a lawsuit because the wrongdoers are as insolvent as they are irresponsible.

DEFAMATION

glossary

The law imposes a general duty on all persons to refrain from wrongfully hurting another person's good reputation through false and harmful, unprivileged statements made to others. The breach of this duty is **defamation**. Breaching, or violating, this duty orally is the common law tort of **slander**; violating it in writing is the tort of **libel**. Defamation reduces the goodwill and respect a person has previously enjoyed and may subject her or him to ridicule, contempt, or possibly hatred by others. The critical element is the effect on third parties, people in the community. Thus, there can be no civil defamation without *publication*, which means communication to at least one third party. If one person lies about another to his or her face in private, or sends him or her a defamatory letter that only the victim reads, there is no civil defamation. If the letter is dictated to a secretary, there has been publication.

Thompson writes Andrew a private letter accusing him of embezzling funds. Peters calls Gordon dishonest and incompetent when no one else is around. All statements are false. Do these false communications result in civil liability for defamation?

No. The letter is not libel and the conversation is not slander. Neither Thompson nor Peters communicated their messages to a third party. If either Andrew or Gordon later publishes the false statements, they voluntarily damage their own reputations and therefore cannot recover. If a third party, by chance, overhears defamatory statements, the courts usually hold that this is a publication. Anyone who republishes or repeats defamatory statements is liable even if that person reveals the source of the statements. Most radio stations delay the broadcast of live programs, such as talk shows, for several seconds to avoid this kind of liability. Note, however, that newspapers and other media—without liability—publish reports containing defamatory statements that were absolutely privileged when made during legislative or judicial proceedings.

Special state laws protect specified businesses involving perishable crops from defamatory publications. The theory is that irreparable damage is done when the crop perishes, which may be long before a trial can be obtained.

> On her television program, Oprah Winfrey falsely warned the American people that "mad cow" disease could spread to people and, according to her guest, "make AIDS look like the common cold." Oprah added that she was "stopped cold from eating another burger." Within days of the show, cattle prices had plummeted to 10 year lows in what was dubbed the "Oprah crash." Cattle ranchers sued in federal court for violation of the Texas "veggie" laws that protect perishable products from false statements. Are cattle a perishable product?[11]

Perishable crops are extraordinarily vulnerable because their useful life as food is very short. Strawberries are an example of such a crop. However, the federal judge ruled that beef is not a perishable commodity, and that there was no liability for merely negligent misstatements. Thus, the cattle ranchers were required to prove, under ordinary business defamation rules, that Oprah's remarks were deliberate or at least reckless. Oprah won the case although the "mad cow" brain disease never has been found in cattle in the United States.

Slander

A false spoken or transitory gesture about the victim is *slander*. To succeed in proving slander, the plaintiff must prove actual monetary loss, technically called *special damages* (discussed later in this chapter). However, certain types of slander are so obviously harmful to reputation that special damages are presumed to exist and need not be proved. Such cases of **slander** *per se*, defamatory as a matter of law, exist whenever the defendant falsely publishes that the plaintiff (1) has committed a crime punishable by imprisonment; (2) has an existing venereal disease; (3) is unfit for his or her lawful business, trade, profession, or office (public or private); or (4) is guilty of sexual misconduct.[12]

Not every false statement about another person is actionable, even though it may contain vituperative, derogatory, or disparaging terms.

> In the presence of other persons, Marjorie Taylor, a high school teacher, told Monty Standby, her principal, that he was "plain stupid . . . not qualified . . . a disgrace to the profession" and "just like Lee Harvey Oswald . . . and Jack Ruby." Principal Standby sued. Who won?

Principal Standby won a jury verdict of $75,775 at the trial level. But judgment was reversed on appeal because Taylor's language was held to be not sufficiently defamatory, as a matter of law, to be slanderous.[13] Perhaps the judge found the comparison to Oswald and Ruby to be so preposterous that it made the outburst laughable, made in a fit of pique, and not likely to damage the reputation of the principal.

> Tawana Brawley, 15, claimed through her advisers, one of whom was the Rev. Al Sharpton, that she had been raped by a gang of white men that

included state prosecutor Steven Pagones. The publicity surrounding this accusation was considerable. A grand jury later found Tawana's story to be false. Steven Pagones sued Tawana and her advisers for slander. A jury awarded Pagones $345,000 damages against the advisers. Tawana defaulted (declined to defend), whereupon a judge awarded Pagones $5,000 in compensatory damages and $180,000 in punitive damages against her.[14] Can Tawana be protected from this judgment by the juvenile court laws that protect minors in criminal cases?

No. The judgment against Tawana will survive for up to 20 years, and will accrue interest at 10 percent. Thus, a portion of her wages as well as other assets may be taken in the future when she is an adult. Minors can seriously impact their financial futures through their civil misconduct. Recall that the theory underlying the tort of defamation is protection of the individual's reputation. A charge of rape, oftentimes difficult to defend, can cause untold grief to an innocent victim.

Libel

A false written or printed communication is *libel*. As such, it historically has been considered a more durable form of defamation than slander, with a stronger, longer-lasting impact. Accordingly, the cause of action may be successful even without proof of actual, out-of-pocket special damages, such as lost wages.

Britishers Helen Steel, a part-time bartender, and Dave Morris, an ex-postal worker, helped distribute a pamphlet claiming that McDonald's was cruel to animals, exploited children in its advertising, and that its low wages in Britain tended to depress salaries in the entire fast-food industry. The pamphlet contained other charges about the treatment of chickens used in McNuggets and the fat and salt content of Big Macs. Many other statements were contained in the pamphlet that ultimately were found to be false. McDonald's then sued Helen and Dave in what became known as the McLibel trial between David and Goliath. Without legal counsel, Helen and Dave called as expert witnesses vegetarians, environmentalists, libertarians, and animal rights activists from around the world. The English court took testimony from 180 witnesses over 313 court days sprinkled over 2½ years involving some 60,000 pages of documents. Lawyers for McDonald's were attired in wig and gown, as is traditional in English courts, while Helen and Dave wore jeans and sweatshirts. The McLibel trial became the longest in the history of England. At its end, the judge found that Helen and Dave had committed libel, and entered judgment for McDonald's for $96,000.[15] If McDonald's can collect none of the judgment, nor any of its huge legal fees from Helen and Dave, was the case an exercise in futility?

Sometimes considerations other than money control the decision to pursue litigation. Although unknown specifically, it might be deemed sensible for a company such as McDonald's to defend its reputation and thereby to dissuade others from publicizing untrue disparaging statements. On the other hand, many believe McDonald's suffered a public relations disaster through its litigation.

Privilege to Defame Others

Truth is an *absolute* defense against a defamation lawsuit. In other words, if a statement is true, then even though it damages someone's character, it is not defamatory. Such a statement, however, may violate the person's right to privacy, which is another intentional tort discussed later in the chapter. A **privilege** may also be a defense, since it is a legal right to do something. A privilege may be absolute or conditional. An **absolute privilege** gives the holder a right to act under all circumstances. A **conditional privilege** gives the holder a right to act under certain circumstances.

Public policy requires that certain persons be permitted and encouraged to express their ideas without restraint or fear of lawsuits for defamation. In our republic or representative democracy, legislative, executive, and judicial officers are encouraged to speak out for the common good. Legislators during legislative proceedings; judges, lawyers, jurors, and witnesses during judicial proceedings; top officials of the executive branch (notably the president and vice president, Cabinet members, and major department heads); as well as high-level officials of administrative agencies, acting in the official performance of their duties, have an absolute privilege to say anything, even if it is false, malicious, or self-serving. As noted earlier, the media (newspapers, magazines, and radio and television stations) have an absolute privilege in quoting the identified officials verbatim. Understandably, there is an absolute privilege between husband and wife for communications concerning third persons and for parents telling their children derogatory opinions about friends of the children.

A qualified privilege, or conditional privilege, exists for creditors who may, in good faith, exchange otherwise defamatory information about debtors whose creditworthiness is a mutual concern. A similar conditional privilege exists between employers with reference to qualifications of past and prospective employees. The privilege is qualified, or conditional, in the sense that the employer must act in good faith and without negligence. But note that the statements must be well-founded. Nevertheless, many employers refuse to express any opinion about the quality of performance of former employees, because of a fear of lawsuits claiming defamation. Even when one is vindicated, legal defense is costly.

The furor caused by defamation is better understood when one realizes that a person's reputation or good name is usually a delicate mental image in the minds of other persons in the community. It is a priceless possession available to both poor and rich, taking years to develop. Yet it is very fragile and can be shattered in seconds by one false statement. Defamation has been likened to cutting open a down-filled pillow in a violent windstorm. Fully restoring the good reputation, through denial by the victim and retraction by the liar, is like gathering up all of the thousands of tiny feathers that have scattered far and wide in the storm—impossible.

Special Status of Newspapers

A very important expansion of the right of newspapers to print libelous materials was made by the U.S. Supreme Court in 1964, in a famous case involving The *New York Times*. The Court held that the common law of libel is superseded in part by the First and Fourteenth Amendments to the U.S. Constitution, with reference to articles about public officials or public figures.[16] In effect, it gives the media a right of freedom of expression that approaches, but does not equal, the absolute privilege enjoyed by government officials as previously noted. The *New York Times* rule bars public officials or public figures from recovering for defamatory falsehoods unless they can prove the statement was made with actual malice. *Actual malice,* here, means that it was made with prior knowledge that it was false, or with reckless disregard as to whether it was true or false. Moreover, the defamation must be proved by clear and convincing evidence, which is more than the preponderance-of-evidence standard usually required in civil cases. Significantly, a number of state courts have applied the rule and extended it to nonmedia defendants as well.

Some 22 years later, in a 1986 case involving the *Philadelphia Inquirer,* the U.S. Supreme Court reinforced free speech–free press protection of the media. It held that under the U.S. Constitution, when a newspaper publishes a speech of public concern about a *private figure,* the plaintiff bears "the burden of showing falsity as well as fault (wrongfulness) before recovering damages." Generally, if a newspaper defames someone who is a private, rather than public, figure prompt retraction and apology are mitigating circumstances that may affect the award of punitive damages. The U.S. Supreme Court, to encourage freedom of expression, has ruled that punitive damages may not be awarded to private defamation plaintiffs in actions against media defendants (e.g., newspapers and radio and TV stations) without proof of actual malice. The media defendant remains liable only for actual monetary special damages, and these are likely to be modest.

In 1990, the Supreme Court imposed a new restraint on the press. It held that statements of opinion, as well as statements of fact, can be libelous. In the words of the court, saying "In my opinion Jones is a liar" is the same thing as saying "Jones is a liar."[17]

INVASION OF PRIVACY

Most states recognize the right of **privacy** by means of common-law case decisions, by statutes, and by state constitutions. *The Restatement of Torts* recognizes four broad categories of privacy invasion that may justify the award of damages:

1. Unreasonable intrusion on the seclusion of another.
2. Appropriation of the other's name or likeness.
3. Unreasonable publicity given to the other's private life.
4. Publicity that unreasonably places the other in a false light before the public.[18]

In one famous case, consumer advocate Ralph Nader's privacy was violated by General Motors Corporation after he had criticized their automobiles. GMC employed persons who threatened Nader, tapped his telephone, and attempted to entice him with women—all in a futile effort to silence him.[19] In another notable case, television talk-show host Johnny Carson blocked the use of the phrase "Here's Johnny" by a corporation engaged in renting and selling portable toilets.[20] But generally, public personages, such as sports and entertainment stars, cannot claim a right of privacy in their public image, performance, or duties. Such figures usually need, want, and solicit publicity to advance their careers—thus, in effect, waiving customary rights of privacy. Some advocates suggest that celebrities ought to be protected by statute from such apparent invasions of privacy as photographs in secluded but public places through high-powered telescopic lenses, or any obnoxious behavior in crowded public places such as restaurants or sports events.

All states, as well as the federal government, have enacted laws that supplement the tort of invasion of privacy. These include legislation concerning the wrongful opening of mail, electronic eavesdropping and telephone wiretapping, and disclosure of income taxes paid and welfare payments received. The notorious recording by Linda Tripp of private conversations she had with Monica Lewinsky in the scandal leading ultimately to the impeachment of President William J. Clinton raised the consciousness of the nation to the problem of telephonic privacy. Most states make the secretive recording of a telephone conversation a misdemeanor—although use of a cordless telephone typically results in loss of the right of privacy. The same result may follow from use of a cellular telephone because of the use of public airways for the transmission.

The tort law of privacy is not limited to celebrities. Everyone is entitled to protection from unreasonable invasions of privacy.

Ms. Nistle noticed but thought nothing of small scratches in the bathroom mirror of her apartment. Unbeknownst to her, construction workers, who were engaged in repairing the neighboring apartment, made the scratches to serve as peepholes. Ms. Nistle suffered humiliation and severe distress after learning that strangers routinely had been violating her privacy. Can she sue the landlord for the intentional tort of invasion of privacy?

No. The next-door construction workers were not agents or employees of the landlord, who personally did not scratch the peepholes or use them. Ms. Nistle could sue the individual construction workers for the intentional tort of invasion of privacy, but they probably were without substantial wealth.[21]

FRAUD

Fraud is a tort most frequently committed in sales of goods or services. It is also called **deceit** and sometimes **misrepresentation**. For fraud, the following elements must be present:

1. A false representation (i.e., a lie);
2. of a factual matter (not personal opinion, unless the opinion is that of an expert on the subject);
3. that is material (i.e., important enough to affect the decision of the intended victim);
4. known by the wrongdoer to be false, or made with reckless indifference as to its truth;
5. made with intent to induce action by the victim, who is unaware of its falsity;
6. and acting reasonably, the victim does justifiably rely on the lie in his or her decision; and
7. is injured as a result.

In a simple, often-repeated type of case, a seller of a used car may misrepresent the mileage,* the times and frequency of servicing and of overhaul, the number and identity of previous owners, or the number and nature of accidents, if any, in which the vehicle has been involved. A knowledgeable car buff might not be misled, but many amateurs would buy in trusting reliance and, if victimized, could therefore sue for damages.

Fraud may also occur under a wide variety of unusual circumstances, as the following cases indicate.

Peter Roberts, an 18-year-old Sears sales clerk, invented a quick-release socket wrench in his spare time. He applied for and received a patent in 1965. Thereafter, Sears negotiated to buy Peter's patent rights. He was told that (1) the invention was "not new," (2) the production cost would be 40 to 50 cents per wrench (Sears knew it would be only 20 cents), and (3) it would sell only to the extent promoted and, hence, was worth only $10,000. Peter agreed to accept a 2 cents royalty up to a maximum of $10,000. Within days, Sears was manufacturing 44,000 of Peter's wrenches per week. A half-million wrenches were sold in nine months. By 1975, more than 19 million wrenches had been sold for a net profit of more than $44 million, according to court records. Was Sears guilty of the tort of fraud?

Yes. A jury awarded Peter $1 million in damages. The U.S. Court of Appeals affirmed and also authorized Peter to rescind (set aside) his contract and sue Sears for breach of his patent. In 1982, a federal jury awarded Peter $5 million, and the judge increased this to $8.2 million on the grounds that the infringement was willful. In 1983, this decision was overturned by the Court of Appeals, which ordered a new trial. In September 1989, 25 years after receiving his patent, Peter and his attorney finally confronted Sears again in court. This time the trial was in its fifth day when the litigants reached a settlement agreement. At the time, a Sears spokesperson said that a term of the settlement was that neither side could comment on it.[22]

Dining at Yesterday's Restaurant in Mobile, Patrick Lamey ordered the "De La Mer" omelet. Afterwards, Patrick suffered nausea, vomiting, high fever, stomach cramps, and diarrhea. He was admitted to the hospital, where his condition was diagnosed as acute gastroenteritis. He was released in a few days. Patrick had no evidence that Yesterday's had been negligent or that the food was contaminated. But the menu stated that the "De La Mer" omelet contained crabmeat and trout when in fact it contained only codfish. Can Patrick simplify the proof needed by suing for misrepresentation?

---

*In a gross example of this offense, Chrysler Corporation was fined $7.6 million by a Federal District Court judge for selling 30 previously damaged vehicles as new cars and for odometer violations. Chrysler had previously entered a plea of no contest to the criminal charges. The fine supplemented an earlier settlement of more than $16 million in a civil suit. Records showed that between 1949 and 1986, Chrysler personnel had disconnected the odometers on about 60,000 new cars that were driven for periods of one day to five weeks by Chrysler executives before being placed on sale as brand new. In the 30 specially noted cases, the cars had been damaged while being driven by the executives, and repaired before sale as new. Reported in the *San Francisco Chronicle*, 11 August 1990.

Yes. Patrick easily could and did prove that the menu was a false misrepresentation of a material fact, that he relied upon it, and was damaged as a result. He recovered $27,500 damages.[23]

Tort law protects even the naive, the trusting, and the ignorant.

Soldier Steven Malandris, a truck driver in Korea, met and married Jung Ja, who was illiterate. Returning to the United States, their marriage was dominated by a quest for financial security. Steven worked as a baggage handler for United Airlines in Colorado; Jung Ja managed their money. They lived meagerly in order to save some $60,000, which they invested in United's stock. Steven met John Barron, an account executive for Merrill Lynch, Pierce Fenner & Smith, Inc. (a major securities firm), who prompted Steven to forge his wife's name to get access to the family money held as stock and to invest it in commodity options. Barron told Steven that there would be an "assured gain" and "no possibility" of any loss. However, soon $30,000 was gone. Jung Ja sustained permanent emotional injury, which allegedly "destroyed her ability to function as a human being." She rejected this world and lives only in anticipation of life after death. May Jung Ja recover damages for fraud?

Yes. A six-person jury in federal court awarded compensatory damages of $1,030,000, plus punitive damages of $3,000,000. When denying a motion for new trial, the judge commented, "This is not a case of a lost investment; it is the tragedy of a lost life."[24]

The children of Margaret Lesher, believing that her recent husband, buffalo rider T.C. Thorstenson, had murdered their mother to obtain part of her $100 million estate, sued him for fraud. They contended that Thorstenson had intentionally concealed one of his two previous marriages, the one in which he had been accused of spousal abuse. Margaret never would have married Thorstenson, her children contended, if she had known the truth. For their part, Thorstenson's attorneys argued that Margaret told their client a lie, that she was only 55 years old.[25] Are lies told between spouses the proper basis for a lawsuit for fraud?

Lies concerning the affection one does or does not feel about the other, made just before marriage or without regard to marriage, ordinarily are not justiciable. Thus, if one person relies upon the statement "I love you" and therefore takes some action that ultimately turns out to be regrettable, there is no basis for court action. However, lies of material facts may form the basis of an action for misrepresentation or fraud, even if the consequent action was to become married. In the Thorstenson case above, the outcome is not public because the case settled out of court.

Not all misrepresentations are tortious. A person commits no tort when he or she innocently does not know the information is false, but mistakenly tells you that a dog being sold to you is two years old when in fact it is five. Generally, if you are the victim of an innocent or a negligent misrepresentation, you have the option of rescinding the contract (by returning the dog and getting your money back) or renegotiating the sale price. Of course, a professional veterinarian seller who knows, or should know, the true age of the dog could be guilty of fraud under these circumstances.

Opinions of quality in advertisements and sales talks ("the finest car on the road," "enjoy the pleasure of the best in international travel," "the best in cordless telephones just got better") are actual examples of customary commercial "puffing" and are not actionable. A dissatisfied purchaser of automobile insurance claimed that the seller violated the New Jersey Consumer Fraud Act because its service did not live up to its slogan. The state supreme court disagreed, explaining that the slogan "You're in Good Hands with Allstate" is "nothing more than puffery";[26] there was no fraud. Social fibs likewise are not actionable (e.g., "I'll be there at 5 P.M." and the person doesn't arrive until 6 P.M., or not at all).

BAD FAITH

glossary

Persons pay premiums to insurance companies, who promise in exchange to pay money when some uncertain future calamity, such as an automobile accident, death, fire, or disability, occurs. If the insured persons fail to make timely payment of premiums, the insurance coverage may be cancelled. And if the insurance company fails to make a promised payment when some calamity occurs, the insured may sue for breach of the insurance contract. In the next chapter (about contracts), you will learn that punitive damages are not available for breach of contract. But courts have imposed a duty of "good faith and fair dealing" upon insurance companies, the violation of which may subject them to punitive damages. Violation of this duty is said to be the intentional tort of "bad faith."

The tort of bad faith in actions against insurance companies generally involves either of two scenarios.

In the first scenario, Joe Citizen pays premiums for automobile insurance with maximum liability coverage of, say, $100,000. Suppose Joe is involved in a car crash that seriously injures a victim in another car. The victim sues Joe for $150,000 but, learning of the insurance amount, agrees to settle out of court for the $100,000. However, Joe's insurance company rejects the offer, choosing instead to go to trial on a "roll of the dice" to see if a jury might return a verdict of less than $100,000. Instead, the jury verdict is $150,000. The insurance company pays the $100,000 policy maximum, thinking, "Well, at least we had a chance of saving some money." But Joe now must pay the $50,000 personally. Joe has been victimized by his insurance company, who violated its duty of "good faith and fair dealing" because it could have and should have paid its policy maximum to protect Joe. Courts in most states would permit Joe to sue his insurance company for "bad faith" and to recover the $50,000 above coverage limits plus punitive damages.

In the second possible scenario, the carrier delays payment of a legitimate claim. The reason may be an intent to earn interest on delayed payments, a desire to gamble on a less costly award by a jury, or an attempt to induce a needy claimant to settle for less because he or she can't afford to wait or litigate. Unreasonable delay in payment of a claim violates the duty of "good faith and fair dealing" and renders the insurance company liable for general and punitive damages.[27]

In theory, courts could impose a duty of good faith and fair dealing on any contract and permit a tort recovery of damages whenever a contract is breached under egregious circumstances. So far, courts are reluctant to extend tort recovery.

When calamities occur, insurance companies have a tremendous negotiating power over their dependent customers, which justifies the creation of a duty of good faith and fair dealing. Most other contractual relationships are not characterized by such unequal bargaining power and dependency.

TORTS BY NEGLIGENT BEHAVIOR

THE ELEMENTS OF NEGLIGENCE

Everyone has a *duty* (i.e., a mandatory obligation) imposed by law to behave with due care as a reasonable, prudent (i.e., cautious and careful) person would behave under the same or similar circumstances. If one fails to do so, and thus injures another's person or property, the victim may sue and recover damages from the wrongdoer for *negligence*.

To decide if a particular act constitutes compensable negligence, we can ask these questions:

1. Did the defendant owe a duty of care to the injured victim?
2. Did the defendant breach that duty through unreasonable conduct?
3. Did the plaintiff suffer an injury as a result of the defendant's breach of the duty of care?
4. Did the defendant's breach of duty cause the victim's injury?
5. Is there any social policy under which the defendant's liability ought to be cut off? For example, was the injury so remote from the defendant's act that it would be unforeseeable by a reasonable person?

The duty of care that every person owes to all others is judged by the flexible and variable standard of care of a hypothetical *reasonable person*. That is, we all are duty bound to act as carefully or prudently as a so-called reasonable person would act under all of the circumstances existing at the time. Otherwise, we may be liable to any victim we injure—if we owe that victim a duty of care and if there is no social policy cutting off our responsibility. Whether or not a defendant acted reasonably is a question for the jury (or judge when there is no jury).

Determinants of duty include the foreseeability of harm to the victim, the proximity or closeness between the unreasonable act and the injury, and the moral blameworthiness of the defendant. Also relevant are the public policy of preventing future harm; the financial burden on the defendant and the community in imposing the liability; and the availability, cost, and prevalence of insurance for the risk involved.[28] These above considerations have evolved under common law. Special rules, discussed later, have been added by state statutes.

The standard of care required is usually called ordinary care: What would a reasonable person have done under the same or similar circumstances? The law does not demand perfection. But any judgmental errors must have been understandable and excusable under the circumstances. Thus, for example, a "perfect" person driving on a busy highway and caught in a sudden and unusually heavy cloudburst, or dense duststorm, would carefully drive off the highway and onto the shoulder, and wait there for the passing storm to subside. However, practically, a reasonable person—seeing other vehicles still moving in both directions—

might assume that it was safe to drive on because the storm was only momentary and would shortly end. But the storm continues. Within seconds, our driver becomes one link in a chain reaction of rear-end crashes. Was the driver negligent? A jury would probably say, "No; it was an accident."

An accident is a sudden, unexpected, unintended happening that causes injury or death and/or loss of property. It may occur under circumstances where nobody is at fault, as in an earthquake or natural landslide. However, in most "accidents," one (or more) of the parties involved is at fault because of what someone did or failed to do. Automobile "accidents" are common examples of events that are usually caused by negligence. One example of an excusable accident is when a driver unavoidably loses control of the vehicle because of the sudden attack and painful sting of a bee.

One expert on torts, Edward J. Kionka, explains that the "reasonable person . . . is not the average or typical person, but an idealized image of such a person—a composite of the community's judgment as to how the typical community member ought to behave in each of the infinite variety of circumstances and activities in which there is a potential or actual risk of harm to the actor or others."[29] Community members sit on the juries that determine how the defendant ought to have behaved—some suspect that jurors themselves might behave less carefully than the standards they impose on others.

Failure to be reasonable may be seen in an act (e.g., setting fire to a building by flicking a cigarette butt) or an omission (e.g., neglecting to put out a small fire). It may be an intentional act (pushing the "pedal to the metal"), a careless act (reading a paper while driving), or a carefully performed but dangerous act (downhill skiing) that results in injury. Courts consider the nature of the act (whether it is outrageous or commonplace), how the act is performed (cautiously or carelessly), the relationship of the parties (landowner duty to trespasser), and the nature of the injury (serious or slight) to determine whether a duty of care has been breached.

The law of negligence has evolved by court decisions that arise in response to the injuries that occur as increasingly complex activities characterize our society.

Injo Kalen left a burning cigarette butt teetering on the edge of his girlfriend Amy's ashtray, which was sitting on the arm of the couch in her apartment. While Injo and Amy were dining in the other room, the butt became unbalanced as it burned and fell onto the cushions, which slowly began to burn. By the time the fire was noticed and extinguished, the couch and Amy's cashmere sweater were destroyed, and there were large burns in the carpet and smoke damage in the apartment. What are the legal consequences of this event?

Injo owed a duty of reasonable care to Amy and her landlord. That duty was breached when Injo failed to behave as a reasonable person by leaving the burning cigarette butt on the edge of the ashtray. Fire from a burning cigarette is a foreseeable consequence, and the damages were the proximate result of that negligence. Therefore, Injo is liable to both Amy and her landlord. Amy can agree to accept a specified sum from Injo for the value of her sweater (called *damages*). Amy's landlord, who owns the apartment and furniture, also could settle with Injo. But if the parties cannot settle the problem, Amy and/or her landlord could begin civil tort proceedings against Injo to recover damages. If Amy had renter's insurance, she also would be compensated by her insurance company for her sweater unless its value was less than the deductible portion of coverage. Most landlords carry fire insurance and would receive compensation from their casualty insurance company for damage to the building and couch as well. As a practical matter, both Amy and her landlord would probably accept payments by their insurance companies and take no further action.*

CAUSATION: ACTUAL AND PROXIMATE

Common sense and elementary justice tell us that one should not be liable for conduct that injures others unless there is a logical cause—effect relationship between the defendant's negligent act (or failure to act) and the plaintiff's injury. In simple fact situations, this principle is easy to apply. But when a sequence of events and persons is involved—as is often the case—the determination of cause and effect is difficult.

What if two independent forces combine to cause the injury? For example, suppose A builds an unreasonably large and roaring campfire near C's mountain cabin. B leaves an open container of gas on the ground at an adjoining campsite. Sparks from A's blazing campfire ignite B's gas can, causing a large enough fire to engulf and destroy C's cabin. Even if neither careless act alone could have produced that result, both A and B would be liable under the *substantial-factor test*, since both contributed substantially to the destruction of the cabin. The same would be true if *either* careless act alone would have been sufficient to destroy the cabin.

If a person fails in a duty of care and someone suffers injury, the wrongful activity must have caused the harm in order for a tort to have been committed. In deciding whether there is causation, the court will address two questions:

1. Is there **actual cause**? That is, did the injury happen because of the defendant's act, or would the injury have occurred anyway? If an injury would not have occurred without the defendant's act, then there is actual causation. Such causation can usually be determined by the descriptive *but-for* test. "But for" the wrongful act, the injury would not have happened.

2. Was the act the **proximate cause** of the injury? As a matter of social policy, how far should a defendant's liability extend or reach? The act not only was an important factor, it actually caused all the remote damages. But injuries can be so remote that, as a matter of public policy considerations of fairness, liability of the wrongdoer is simply cut off.

To be "proximate" as the term is used here, the cause need not necessarily be close or near to the resulting injury, in time or in space. But it must appear to be just and fair, and indeed feasible, to hold the defendant liable for the injury that did result.

---

*In theory, either Amy's or the landlord's insurance company that paid a claim would have the right to sue Injo for reimbursement of the money paid. This right of an insurance company to seek reimbursement from a wrongdoer for a claim paid to their customer is called *subrogation* (substitution of creditors). As a practical matter, insurance companies most often do not seek subrogation because the wrongdoer is without substantial financial resources.

So the wrong doer gets away with carelessness

Theoretically—and facetiously—we might trace all events of human history in an unbroken chain of events to Adam and Eve. Practically and justly, the result (the injury to the plaintiff) must not be unreasonably remote from the cause (the negligent act of the defendant). The proximate cause is the true cause "which, in a natural and continuous sequence, unbroken by any efficient intervening cause, produces injury, and without which the result would not have occurred."[30] The attempt to thoroughly define proximate cause is next to futile, but examples can simplify much analysis.

Brent Starr was testing the power of his new sports car on a clear two-lane highway in good weather. When he reached 90 mph, he lost control and the car crashed through a fence and into a high-voltage electricity pole. This caused a short circuit and power failure throughout the city of Barclay, 100 miles away. Among the many persons affected were the staff and doctors in General Hospital. Just as the power went out, surgeon Ramona Ramirez was making a critical incision near patient Albert Johnson's heart during open-heart surgery. As a result of the darkness and loss of power to essential equipment, she had to stop abruptly. The machines supplying vital oxygen and pumping blood went silent. Within minutes, Albert Johnson was dead. Is Brent Starr liable for Albert's death?

No. Brent's wrongful conduct was the actual cause of Albert's death. Under one test mentioned previously, it can be said that "but for" Brent's folly, Albert would not have died when he did. But Brent's act was not the proximate, legal cause because it was too indirect and remote from the death, which was not reasonably foreseeable by Brent.

Note that Brent would be liable for the damage to the fence and to the high-voltage electricity pole. It is also possible that General Hospital could be found guilty of negligence, and therefore liable, for failing to have a standby emergency electric power source available. (This is indeed standard practice in well-run hospitals, because power failures are not uncommon. But that would be another case.)

Brent Starr's car, after ramming the pole, caromed into the brush nearby, striking and killing Tom Sneed, who was hunting quail. Brent did not know that Tom was hunting there. Is Brent liable for Tom's death?

Yes. Here Brent's wrongful conduct was the actual and also the proximate or legal cause of the death. The negligent act was direct and close; there was no efficient intervening cause. With his eyes glued to the road, Brent probably did not even see Tom. Under the circumstances, however, the threat of injury or death from the speeding car to any person who happened to be in any of many potentially fatal locations on or along the highway was reasonably foreseeable in the law. What people really do and do not foresee is not decisive; what is foreseeable is a matter of law.

Thus, causation, both actual and proximate, must be proved to hold a defendant liable for negligence. There is proximate causation if there is "the ability to see or know in advance . . . that harm or injury is a likely result of acts or omissions.[31] If, and only if, a reasonably prudent person, under similar circumstances, could and would have foreseen the likelihood of injury from the defendant's conduct to any person in the situation of the victim, does the defendant have the duty to exercise reasonable care to refrain from such conduct. This point is discussed in practically every law school in the nation by reference to the following famous case.

> Standing at one end of a railroad station platform, a woman waits for her train to arrive. Suddenly there is a loud explosion at the distant other end of the platform. Vibrations resulting from the explosion cause some scales to fall on the woman, injuring her. Evidently, a railroad guard inside one car of a slowly moving train had reached out to grab a man who was running to get aboard. Another railroad guard—who was standing on the platform—gave the man a helping push from behind. The man happened to be carrying an unlabeled parcel, containing fireworks. When the parcel fell onto the railroad tracks, it exploded, whereupon Palsgraf, the woman at the other end of the platform, suffered injuries. She sued the railroad for damages. The jury found the guards to be negligent toward Palsgraf, and the trial court awarded her damages against the railroad, as the responsible employer. The railroad company appealed. Should the appellate court affirm the judgment?[32]

No. Palsgraf's complaint was properly dismissed. The injuries she suffered were not reasonably foreseeable—and were certainly not intentionally inflicted—by the railroad guards. Therefore, there was no duty to her that was breached by the guards or by their employer.* To prove negligence and to collect damages, Palsgraf would have had to show that the actions of the railroad guards as to her "had possibilities of danger so many and apparent as to entitle" her to be protected against those very actions. This she could not prove.

Without foreseeability, there is no duty to act or refrain from action. Without duty, there can be no negligence. Without negligence, there can be no fault. Without fault, there can be no liability, regardless of the extent of the injury. William Prosser and Page Keeton, leading authorities on torts, unequivocally state, "The question of foreseeability is not an element of causation and does not arise until the issue of causation has been determined."[33] Another legal scholar, Leon Green, properly points out that "Causation is a neutral issue, blind to right and wrong . . . but in absence of causal relation plaintiff has no case, and all other inquiries become moot."[34] After all, the linkage of cause and effect in any series of events may be coldly analyzed and *objectively* determined. Thereafter, one may inquire into whether any involved person (e.g., the defendant) *subjectively* could have and should have foreseen any of the described events or injurious effects.

Returning to Brent Starr's predicament in the earlier example, he could and should have foreseen that a person, such as Tom Sneed, might be in the bushes near the highway, perhaps hiking, hunting, resting, or bird-watching. But he

---

*The legal doctrine of *respondeat superior* (Latin: "let the master answer") holds the employer responsible to third parties for the acts of employees done in the course of, and within the scope of, their employment. It is discussed in Chapters 10 and 13.

could not reasonably have foreseen the tragic sequence of events in the hospital, nor could he have foreseen countless other resulting events at great distances from the scene of the crash, in areas served with electricity by the power line.

Recapitulating, to prevail in a negligence action the plaintiff must present a preponderance of evidence proving

1. existence of a legal duty to the plaintiff, and

2. breach of that duty by the defendant's action or failure to act, with

3. resulting legal causation, actual and proximate, of an alleged injury, which

4. justifies the award of damages in court.

Note that the weight of required evidence in civil negligence cases is not as demanding as in criminal cases, where the trier of facts must be convinced of their truth beyond a reasonable doubt. In civil cases, "preponderance" means that evidence in favor of the plaintiff is simply more convincing than evidence presented by the defendant in opposition. The weight of the plaintiff's evidence must be such that what is alleged is more believable, more convincing, more probable than not.[35]

Deborah Gaines arrived at the Preterm Health Services clinic to obtain her scheduled abortion. While sitting in the waiting room, John Salvi III opened fire and killed two receptionists. Deborah fled unharmed, but was "emotionally messed up" and could never return to any clinic for an abortion. The two guards on duty at Preterm also were emotionally traumatized. Deborah later gave birth to Vivian, who is learning disabled and hyperactive. Deborah has sued Preterm and the owner of the building for negligence that wrongfully caused the birth of Vivian. Deborah seeks damages with which to properly raise Vivian. The security guards also have sued Preterm for negligence. Was the claimed negligence (failure to provide safe premises) the proximate cause of the birth of Vivian?[36]

There was sufficient time following the Salvi shooting for Deborah to obtain an abortion at a different clinic. But, according to her lawsuit, she was "too emotionally upset" to do so. Unsafe premises may cause the foreseeable result of injury to the customer. But it is quite different to argue that unsafe premises may foreseeably result in the birth of a loving child.

Chicago police were pursuing a car over a traffic violation. The speeding car crashed, killing Jamil Khouri, severely injuring his son Omar, and slightly injuring his daughter Ahlam. The Khouri estate and family sued the City of Chicago as employer of the police who, it was claimed, negligently pursued the traffic violator whose car was in the fatal crash. Is the act of pursuing a fleeing criminal the proximate cause of injury to an innocent bystander?[37]

The City of Chicago settled the case paying a total of more than $4.5 million to the Khouri family. After that case, the United States Supreme Court ruled that the police were not responsible for the death of the passenger on a fleeing motorcycle who was killed when it crashed. The Court established a new rule that police essentially are not negligent nor is their conduct the proximate cause of resulting injuries during pursuits of suspects unless the actions of the police are so egregious that they "shock our conscience."[38] The U.S. Supreme Court had jurisdiction because the action was pursued as a violation of the federal civil rights of the deceased.

> Mukesh Rai, a devout Hindu, after ordering a bean burrito from Taco Bell, discovered to his dismay that he had begun eating a beef burrito in violation of a fundamental religious principle. Mukesh contends that Taco Bell was negligent and must pay for psychiatry costs, for a trip to England for a purification ceremony with Hindu masters, for a trip to India for the ultimate purification of bathing in the waters of the Ganges River, and for emotional distress, pain, and suffering.[39] Assuming that Taco Bell was negligent, were the damages claimed foreseeable?

On the one hand, there was a breach of contract when Mukesh did not receive the product he ordered. But damages from breach of contract are restricted to foreseeable and quantifiable monetary damages. The measure of damages in torts, as will be discussed later in this chapter, is more liberal in that nonquantifiable losses, such as pain and suffering, are compensable. Yet they also must be foreseeable. In today's multicultural society, is it unreasonable to require national retail organizations to be cognizant and protective of the differing religious and other beliefs, customs, and activities of customers?

> Darrell Parsons was riding his horse Poco along a bridle path when a garbage collection truck in a nearby restaurant parking lot picked up and emptied its trash-filled bin. The clanging noise spooked Poco, who began spinning, bucking, and finally bolting. Parsons was injured when he landed on the ground. Parsons sued the Crown Disposal Company for his injuries. What was the result?[40]

The case was thrown out of court summarily and never reached the jury trial Parsons sought. Appeals continued until the case reached the California Supreme Court some six years after the incident. The defense attorney asked rhetorically, "Why should we be liable if a horse operates like a horse and a trash truck operates like a trash truck?" If you believe the answer to this case was easy, you may be surprised to learn that two dissenting justices on the five member court believed that the victim was entitled to a trial by jury.

> Tired from an afternoon of drinking beer with friends while watching the Buffalo Bills on TV, Bill Brown was driving home. While passing down a street where homes were scattered among small warehouses, he didn't notice a fairly large, dilapidated cardboard carton near the gutter in the road ahead. Weaving slightly, Bill's car hit the cardboard box. To his dismay and horror, he saw in his rear view mirror that the carton had

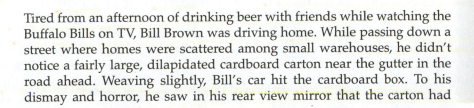

concealed a child. Kathy Wellington, age 3, had been walking on the curb, holding the carton over her head. She had evidently stumbled into the street, and the carton covered her completely. Her death was mercifully sudden. Kathy's parents now seek to hold Brown liable. Will they prevail?

No. Although Bill's clearly negligent conduct was the actual cause of Kathy's death, he is not liable. While it is foreseeable that a pedestrian might be in the vicinity, it is not foreseeable that a tiny person would be inside an old cardboard carton in the street.

INTERVENING CAUSES AND SHARED RESPONSIBILITY

An **intervening cause** is an independent force (either an act or a failure to act) that comes or happens after the defendant's negligent conduct has commenced. The natural sequence of events that could have caused an injury does not in fact take place. Instead, as an end result, an injury results that could not have been reasonably foreseen. Therefore, the original wrongdoer is not liable in damages.

Dimmwith foolishly keeps a can of gasoline in the trunk of his car, thereby creating risk of a foreseeable injury from explosion or fire. Now lightning strikes the car, exploding the car's built-in gas tank as well as the portable can. Nearby pedestrians are injured. Is Dimmwith liable to the victims?

No. The lightning, an unforeseeable natural phenomenon at that time and place, intervened, and the actual cause of the injuries from the explosion was the lightning.

Sometimes intervention of a human actor expands the scope of a negligent wrongdoer's liability. Consider the following hypothetical situation.

York and Waller are among a group of teenagers who walk to the end of a pier along the Atlantic coast in Florida. Waller objects when York engages in horseplay, but York persists, and with a quick push accidentally sends Waller into the deep water. Waller can't swim. He flounders, but is finally rescued by Himaet and is revived by prompt resuscitation. Himaet is also injured when a high wave tosses him against the piling of the pier. Is York liable for the injury to Waller? For the injury to Himaet?

York is liable for injuries to Waller for negligently pushing him off the pier. He also is liable to Himaet under the doctrine that "danger invites rescue." Thus, the intervention of the "Good Samaritan" Himaet expanded York's liability.

Most states have enacted **Good Samaritan laws** that effectively shield doctors and others from liability to an injured person when they stop along the way and render emergency aid. Of course, such volunteers are expected to use reasonable care under the circumstances, and they may not carelessly worsen the condition of anyone in distress. If intervening "Good Samaritans" are careless under the circumstances, they become liable for their own negligence. This can happen, as it did when the U.S. Coast Guard temporarily abandoned a search for a fisherman who subsequently died on a life raft five days after his boat had sunk. The death resulted because the USCG had negligently fouled up its own rescue-message transmission.[41]

On the other hand, some persons are totally insulated against the possibility of being held responsible for negligence. *The Restatement of Torts* states,

> *A child of tender years is not required to conform to the standard of behaviour which is reasonable to expect of an adult; but his (her) conduct is to be judged by the standard of behaviour to be expected from a child of like age, intelligence and experience. . . . It is impossible to fix the definite age at which children are capable of negligence.*[42]

However, some courts, as in Michigan, hold that a child under the age of 7 simply is incapable of negligence.[43]

VIOLATION OF STATUTES AS PROOF OF NEGLIGENCE

Legislation—at the federal, state, and local levels—often describes standards of conduct designed to prevent injuries. Violation of such statutes may be tortious. When a court determines that the particular statute applies to the facts of a case, in most jurisdictions the violation is *prima facie* (Latin: "on first appearance") negligence. An example would be a well-posted speed limit on a winding mountain road. Unless the defendant produces evidence that excuses the violation, negligence is conclusive. A possible excuse would be a sudden emergency, such as unexpected brake failure caused by defective design or manufacture.

PROFESSIONAL MALPRACTICE

Few areas of legal conflict have engendered as much heated debate as malpractice. Malpractice is negligence committed by a professional person. Malpractice is the failure to use that degree of care, learning, and skill ordinarily possessed and applied by the average prudent member of the profession in the same locality. Thus, a general practitioner of law or medicine in a small town is not expected to have the skills or facilities of a group of specialists in a large city.

Physicians and surgeons have been the prime targets of plaintiffs, but dentists, lawyers, accountants, architects, and engineers have comparable professional duties to those they serve and are increasingly being sued. Lawsuits have also been brought against other similar public-service types, such as pharmacists, chiropractors, insurance and real estate agents, and investment advisers. To help protect themselves against possible lawsuits, some contend that many doctors routinely order costly laboratory tests and X-rays as "security blankets" even when they are not essential for proper patient care.

Harvard University researchers examined some 31,000 medical records in a four-year-long study of malpractice (conducted in 51 hospitals in New York state), with results disclosed in 1990. They found 1,133 "adverse events" ranging from patients falling down to patients being infected during surgery. Twenty-five percent of the adverse events could be traced to negligence, yet only one lawsuit was filed for every 9.6 cases of detected negligence. If these figures are extrapolated to the entire total of 2.7 million patients who were hospitalized in New York state during 1984, about 100,000 patients were injured by improper medical treatment, and as many as 7,000 died.[44]

Thus, it could be that medical malpractice suits have touched only the tip of an iceberg of potential malpractice litigation.

PREMISES LIABILITY

The common-law duty of care that is owed to all persons generally is modified relative to the owners or occupiers of property. Owners and occupiers of real property (land and buildings) owe special care to certain classes of potential victims. We review the duties owed by landowners to trespassers, by homeowners to guests, and by business premises to their customers.

Trespassers on Land

Adult trespassers to real property are uninvited, generally unexpected, and unwanted. To them, minimal duty is owed—the owner (or occupier) must not set traps or spring guns to thwart or hurt trespassers or burglars, nor otherwise intentionally harm them. A landowner need not warn trespassers of dangerous natural conditions, but if trespassers are known to be on the premises there is a duty to warn of man-made risks they are not likely to discover (e.g., an attack guard dog).

It was the first day of the summer holiday. Jimmy Parker and Tom Rouble, both 10 years old, rode their bicycles into the country. They spotted an unattended tractor near the road, on the farm of Jensen Dairy, Inc. Tom said, "Let's see if we can start it!" Within minutes they were over the fence and fiddling with the controls of the machine. The engine started and in a sudden forward lurch, Jimmy was thrown off and broke his arm. Is Jensen Dairy liable?

abandoned refrigerator

Young children are an exception to the rules regarding trespassers. When children trespass because of natural curiosity about an **attractive nuisance** and are injured, the owner is liable. The tractor could be considered such an attraction. One of the most common attractive nuisances is a swimming pool. Many cities now have ordinances that specify the type of fencing that must safeguard pools from trespassing children. Attractive nuisances that are highly dangerous to children have included a fall by a 7-year-old girl from the second floor of a house under construction; an abandoned, burned-out semitrailer with melted remnants of red tail lights that fell on an 8-year-old boy; and an open sewer drain where a 19-month-old child was found drowned.[45]

In deciding whether the attractive-nuisance doctrine applies, courts consider (1) whether the defendant knew, or should have known, of the likelihood of trespassing children, and of the unreasonable risk of death or serious injury to them from an artificial (i.e., man-made) condition; (2) whether the children, because of their youth, do not realize the risk involved; and (3) whether the benefit of maintaining the condition, coupled with the burden or cost of eliminating the hazard, are slight compared to the risk to the children.

Sometimes enterprising attorneys try to characterize events most favorably to obtain the recovery of damages.

Pacific Bell installed two public telephone booths on the sidewalk within 20 feet of the parking attendant's booth for the adjacent parking lot. The telephone booths attracted young drug dealers who loitered nearby often harassing passers-by. Pacific Bell refused to relocate the booths after Alfonso Martinez, parking attendant, complained. After Alfonso was robbed and shot in the hand and back, he sued Pacific Bell on the theory that the telephone booths were an attractive nuisance.[46] Does Pacific Bell, under any theory, have a duty to protect a nearby parking attendant from harm by third parties?

Even if telephone booths were an attractive nuisance, they would not create liability for Pacific Bell for criminals who were attracted to the area. These criminals were not children and did not injure themselves.

Guests of Homeowners

Anyone who is upon or inside the homeowner's property with implied or express permission is a **licensee**. Social guests, U.S. Postal Service employees, public utility employees (e.g., meter readers), and building and health inspectors are licensees. Generally, the occupier of land owes the licensee a duty of reasonable care, but has no duty to inspect premises for dangerous conditions that are not obvious. However, once dangers are known, they must be repaired or the licensee must be warned.

Even policemen and firemen are licensees under the *firemans rule*. Probably the vast majority of fires are caused by negligence; yet once started, they also threaten the property of neighbors. Thus, public policy generally bars suits by firefighters for injuries suffered in performing their work in an *emergency* situation. But the owner is duty bound to warn the firefighters of any hidden hazards he or she is aware of, if there is an opportunity to do so. Failing this duty, the owner would be liable for injuries to the firefighter.

Many homeowners erroneously believe they can be held liable for any injury that occurs on their property. But if the homeowner is unaware of any danger, there is no liability or duty to warn of such condition. If a social guest stumbles on the concrete stairs leading to the front door, there is no liability. On the other hand, if a social guest slips on a throw rug that carelessly was placed on a newly waxed hardwood floor, there may be liability for failure to warn of the rather obvious danger.

Customers in Business Premises

Shoppers and customers in retail stores and patrons of restaurants, hotels, theaters, and amusement parks are called **invitees** in the law. They are there for business purposes and the owner or occupier of the premises is seeking to earn a profit from their presence. To them, the owner owes a high duty of care for their safety. He or she must routinely inspect for dangerous conditions and either correct them or clearly warn the invitees.

If a homeowner invites guests to a "lingerie party" hoping to make sales, the guests likewise have become business invitees to whom a high duty of care is owed.

Viola Velour was walking in the aisle of a supermarket, wearing her new high-heel pumps for the first time. Suddenly, her left ankle twisted, and she tumbled to the floor. As she fell, she grasped at an empty shopping cart nearby, and it came down on her head. The impact broke her dentures and caused a painful, unsightly gash in her face. She sued the owner of the supermarket for damages. Is there liability?

No. Viola was an invitee, but the market is not an insurer of her safety. The accident resulted from her inability to use high-heel shoes safely. To recover damages, she would have to prove that (1) the premises were in a dangerously defective condition; and (2) this condition was the result of the market owner's conduct, or that it existed long enough for the owner to be alerted and to correct it; and (3) the usual rules of causation were satisfied.

Sometimes produce in markets ends up on the floors, causing slippery spots. Customers who fall and are injured often bring "slip and fall" suits, which are fairly common. The question always arises as to the frequency with which the market inspects the floors for such spots and cleans them. A market is not reasonably required to inspect the floors every five minutes, and thus a "slip and fall" can occur under circumstances when the market simply is not negligent.

THE INJURY REQUIREMENT AND DAMAGES

There is no negligence if no one has been injured. To recover damages (receive compensation), a person must have suffered some loss, harm, wrong, or invasion of a protected interest. Essentially, the purpose of tort law is to compensate people for legally recognized injuries that result from unreasonable behavior. If no harm or injury results from a given action, there is no tort. Thus, the drunk driver of a speeding vehicle may be negligent, but until injury occurs there is no tort.

Patricia Burns, victimized by multiple sclerosis, claims that her doctor, Thomas Hanson, negligently failed to detect her pregnancy in time for her to obtain an abortion. She thus gave birth to Molly, whom she loves very much. But Patricia requires substantial funds (she asks for $1.6 million) to assist her with hiring in-house childcare and other workers to help her raise the healthy Molly.[47] Is having a healthy child a "wrongful birth" for which damages should be allowed?

In this case, the jury returned a verdict for the doctor. However, the trial judge refused to permit Patricia to testify to the jury that she would have had an abortion if she had known promptly of her pregnancy. The difficulty is, of course, in defining a new life as a measure of damages suffered by the parent. On the other hand, if a doctor commits negligence that proves to be disruptive and costly to the victim, shouldn't there be compensation? And if so, by what standard should the amount of damages be measured?

WHAT IS A *RES IPSA LOQUITOR* CASE?

Generally, in lawsuits involving negligence, the injured victim is the plaintiff and is required to prove that the defendant has breached a duty. In certain situations, however, courts infer that the duty was breached. In this type of case, the defendant must prove that he or she was not negligent. The inference of the defendant's breach of duty is known as the doctrine of *res ipsa loquitor* (Latin: "the thing speaks for itself"). This doctrine applies only when the event that creates the injury is under the exclusive control of the defendant, and it ordinarily does not occur without negligence.

> Mike Hubell is walking on the sidewalk alongside a building with a penthouse apartment on the tenth floor. The penthouse has an open terrace with a railing 3 feet high and 6 inches deep, decorated by a line of potted plants on the railing. Mike is knocked unconscious when he is hit on the head by a potted plant. It is later proven that the pot that hit him is similar to others on the penthouse railing, where one pot is missing. Mike is unable to prove how the pot happened to fall on him. Is this a *res ipsa loquitor* case?

This is a classic situation for application of the doctrine that "the thing speaks for itself." The pot evidently came from that penthouse terrace, which was under the exclusive control of the occupants of the apartment. It would not ordinarily have fallen unless someone was either careless or, possibly, intended to be "fiendishly funny."

The doctrine has been applied by unconscious patients undergoing surgery in hospitals. If such a patient suffers an injury that ordinarily does not occur in the absence of someone's negligence (as when a sponge is not removed from the surgical area), the doctrine can be invoked to shift the burden to the defense. Thus, the surgeon, surgical nurses, staff, and others will have to sort out the events among themselves.

WHAT ARE DEFENSES TO NEGLIGENCE?

Under certain circumstances, a defendant who might otherwise be liable because of his or her negligence can avoid payment of all or some of the damages by proving that the injured victim did one of the following:

1. Assumed the risk.
2. Also was negligent and, in most states, is entitled only to reduced damages, if any, under the doctrine of *comparative negligence*.
3. Also was negligent and, in a few states, is entitled to no damages under the doctrine of *contributory negligence*.

These three defenses are discussed in order.

Assumption of Risk

A person who voluntarily puts himself or herself in a risky situation, knowing the risk involved, and is then injured is not allowed to recover damages. This is the defense of **assumption of risk**. A plaintiff who knows and appreciates a given risk may assume it, thereby absolving the defendant of liability if injury results. In sports, especially, the hazards may be serious for both spectators and participants, and both may assume the risks of customary hazards of such games as baseball, basketball, football, and hockey.

In contact sports, participants assume the risk of injuries that are common and expected, even when an opponent is violating a rule of the game (e.g., when a jockey carelessly changes lanes during a horse race—a violation of a "foul riding" rule). But this does not give the contestants a *carte blanche* (French: "blank check") waiver of all violations of the rules. Conduct that is substantially outside the ordinary play of the game, especially if it is intentional, may give rise to tort liability.

Comparative and Contributory Negligence

Almost all states have adopted the rule of **comparative negligence**, under which a victim who is negligent may nevertheless recover damages from a defendant who is more negligent. Damages allowed are simply reduced in proportion to the amount of negligence attributable to the plaintiff. In other words, liability for damages is allocated to the parties in proportion to the fault each contributed to causing the injury, as determined by the jury (or judge when there is no jury).

T. Ray Vitesse was returning home in his heavy-duty pickup truck at dusk on a residential street, about an hour after sunset. He had several beers that afternoon. He later claimed he was not drunk, although he had forgotten to turn on his headlights. It was raining heavily at the time, and he felt mellow and refreshed as the raindrops splashed on his face through an open window. "Just cruising along" at only 10 mph over the posted speed limit (of 25 mph), his reverie suddenly ended as he crashed into the left side of Art Aritroso's sedan. Art was backing out of his driveway, but had failed to look both ways and hadn't turned his lights on until he was in the street. T. Ray suffered no injuries and his truck required no repairs, but Art's sedan was extensively damaged and he was badly injured. Art sued and the jury decided that his negligence constituted 25 percent of the total. Art's damages total $100,000. How much is he entitled to under the comparative-negligence rule?

The total damages recognized are reduced by the amount of the plaintiff's negligence, as long as it is not as great as the defendant's. Under this process, Art would get $75,000 (100 percent − 25 percent = 75 percent). He would have received $51,000 if his negligence had been 49 percent (100 percent − 49 percent = 51 percent), but nothing if it had been 50 percent or higher. (This is the case in Wisconsin, one of the first states to adopt comparative negligence.) Finally, in a number of states, under the "pure" comparative-negligence rule, contributory negligence never bars recovery. Damages are reduced in proportion to the amount of the plaintiff's negligence. Even if his negligence had been 99 percent, Art would nevertheless have received $1,000 (100 percent − 99 percent = 1 percent).

Previously, the rule of **contributory negligence** generally determined whether damages could be awarded at all for negligence. If two persons were involved in an accident and both were negligent, neither could recover any damages. Contributory negligence was held to be a complete bar to a negligence lawsuit. This was the rule even if one party "contributed" almost all of the negligence. Determination of contributory negligence is a question for the trier of fact. Not infrequently, a jury will temper strict application of the rule with compassion and common sense, and simply overlook minimal amounts of negligence by an otherwise deserving plaintiff. Moreover, the contributory negligence of a plaintiff is no defense for a defendant found guilty of willful and wanton misconduct (i.e., acting with reckless disregard for the plaintiff's safety, as by drunk driving).

This harsh rule of contributory negligence originated in England and was commonly applied in the United States during the 1800s, when railroads were first introduced. "Establishment-oriented" courts were interested in helping the new industry, and they applied the doctrine as a matter of law to collisions at grade crossings. The doctrine survived into the twentieth century and frequently blocked recovery of damages in automobile accident cases (where it is not unusual to find at least some negligence on the part of both drivers).*

Is the failure to use an automobile seat belt or shoulder harness (or airbag that inflates upon impact) evidence of contributory negligence? This issue is somewhat confusing. Belts generally reduce the severity of injury, but in some cases can cause internal injury. However, there is no documented proof that any person has died in a fiery accident because he or she could not unbuckle the seat belt. Indeed, the crash victim, if belted, is more likely to be conscious and better able to escape. If in the driver's seat, he or she is more likely to minimize further damage by maintaining better control of the car. Most states have mandated by statute the installation of seat belts, but not all require their use. Moreover, there is really no logical connection between a collision and the failure to use a seat belt. Consequently, most jurisdictions, including those of such populous states as Florida, New York, and Texas, have ruled that failure to use a seat belt does not constitute sufficient negligence to bar the plaintiff's lawsuit.[48] In some states such failure is negligence that may reduce damages if expert testimony proves how much less the injuries would have been had the belt been used.[49] The question should gradually become moot because federal law now requires that new models be equipped with either airbags or automatic seat belts/shoulder straps. A further discussion of negligence pertaining to automobile accidents is included in Chapter 10.

STRICT LIABILITY TORTS

As a matter of public policy, certain businesses must compensate persons who are injured by their products, services, or activities. In specified situations, the victimized plaintiff need not prove intent or negligence—the defendant is liable even if not at fault. This is true, for example, in the comparatively rare cases where the defendant keeps a wild animal, with dangerous propensities, that injures someone. Circus and carnival elephants, lions, and tigers may have been trained or tamed, but they remain wild. In contrast, some wild animals—such as deer, oxen, and monkeys—are excluded if they have been domesticated to live peaceably in the service of humans. Nevertheless, the owner of domestic animals, including dogs, is strictly liable for injuries inflicted by the animal if the owner knows of their dangerous propensities. Thus, a guard dog known to be vicious is not entitled to a first "free bite."

---

*A few states apply the doctrine of "last clear chance" to deny recovery if, despite the negligence of the defendant, the injured victim had the last clear chance to avoid the injury, but failed to do so. Thus, a driver who foresaw an approaching car straddling the white line, and who reasonably could pull over to the right, but who continued ahead with a resultant crash, would have had the last clear chance to avoid the injury and thus could not recover damages.

Of course, the owner of an ordinary dog or cat, not believed to be abnormally dangerous, would be liable if he or she directed the animal to harm another or negligently failed to prevent the harm. Animal behavior is often unpredictable and uncontrollable, and it is difficult to prove prior knowledge of viciousness. Therefore, some 30 states have enacted statutes that impose strict liability on owners of dogs that injure others, or specify that negligence need not be proved (e.g., as in roving dog cases and when leash laws are violated).

Certain activities are generally deemed to be so hazardous as to justify imposition of strict liability on the responsible actor. Examples of such ultrahazardous activities are fumigating buildings with poisonous gases and blasting with explosives in populated areas. Operating a nuclear reactor is an ultrahazardous activity. To date, there has been no Chernobyl-type disaster with loss of life in the United States. Nevertheless, Congress has responded to the potential threat with the Price-Anderson Act of 1957, which placed a liability limit on the nuclear power industry of $710 million in damages, with any additional claims to be paid by the federal government. The limit was raised in 1988 to $7.1 billion, and extended to cover university research reactors, nuclear weapons plants, and nuclear waste repositories.

WORKERS' COMPENSATION

A much more important category of strict liability is that imposed on employers when a worker is injured or killed on the job. In all states workers' compensation insurance laws now cover most employees, although farm or agriculture workers and domestic servants in homes are still excluded in some states. Under **workers' compensation**, workers receive (1) all medical treatment necessary to cure or provide relief from effects of employment-caused injuries or illness, (2) temporary or permanent disability payments, (3) vocational rehabilitation and retraining benefits when unable to return to the former job, and (4) legal assistance without charge. The benefit payments are not lavish, but they are reasonably certain, and the injured worker is not required (nor, indeed, permitted) to sue in order to obtain prescribed benefits. Claims are, of course, subject to review and approval in routine administrative hearings in which the worker is entitled to the assistance of legal counsel without charge. Note, too, that if a third party is responsible for the injury, the worker may sue and recover damages without limit in a conventional negligence action. A typical example would be when the injury is caused by defectively designed or built equipment that was used on the job. The injured worker can sue the third-party equipment manufacturer—but not his employer. Also, coworkers may be liable for injuries caused by intentional attacks or by willful or wanton negligence. Limited circumstances under which workers' compensation benefits would be denied are when the injury was the result of voluntary intoxication on the job, was intentionally self-inflicted, or when the injured worker was the aggressor in a fight.

Generally, workers' compensation is the exclusive remedy available against the employer in covered businesses.* This is a major improvement over the old

---

*An uncommon exception would be when the employer fraudulently conceals a hazardous working condition, such as the presence of asbestos particles. In such a case, substantial damages may be claimed by the injured worker in a separate action. See *Johns-Manville Products Corp. v. Contra Costa Superior Court*, 27 Cal.3d 465, 612 P.2d 948 (1980).

common-law rules, which permitted the worker to sue his or her employer—a costly and seldom prudent thing to do. For starters, the worker could be fired, if still alive. Thereafter, in court, the employer could avoid liability by proving that (1) the worker knew the hazards involved and assumed the risk (perhaps in exchange for a higher wage), or (2) the worker was guilty of contributory negligence, or (3) a coworker's negligence caused the accident.

> It was a glorious spring day as Willie Jon Fisher climbed to his workstation 125 feet above the bay. As a steelworker, he was paid premium wages for assuming the risk of his hazardous job on the new Silver Gate Bridge. In a burst of youthful exuberance, he removed his hard hat, waved to his pal Don Jones 20 feet above, and danced a quick jig on the beam where he stood. Jones shouted, "Simmer down and get to work!" But Willie fell, hitting a cross beam before the safety net caught his unconscious body. His injuries were permanent and he never returned to the job. Does his carelessness preclude his recovery of benefits?

No. Any covered employee injured on the job is entitled to benefits under the state's workers' compensation law.

At the beginning of the twentieth century, workers did not enjoy much protection under law. There was no workers' compensation, no safety laws governing workplaces, and no state fair employment agencies to assist workers. There weren't even any child labor laws, and thousands of children worked for almost no wages in the coal mines of Pennsylvania. Nor was there any minimum wage.

Pressures to speed up production have accounted for more accidents on the job in recent years. Increasing numbers of workers have filed successful claims for mental stress and for strain injuries caused by repetitive hand motions. Many workers complain about aching wrists, carpal-tunnel syndrome (from the Greek *karpes* for "wrist"), and sore fingers incurred in garment factories, meatpacking plants, post offices with letter-sorting machines, newspaper offices with video display terminals, supermarkets with bar-code scanners at checkout counters and offices with the ubiquitous keyboards. Employers complain because healthcare and workers' compensation premiums have risen, and workers complain that benefit payments are too low. Fortunately for employers, insurance premiums are a deductible business expense, and they can pass the cost along to their customers. On the receiving end, no federal income tax is assessed on workers' compensation insurance benefits (although social security disability payments may be subject to income tax).

DEFECTIVE PRODUCTS THAT CAUSE INJURY

Every year, millions of consumers are injured and thousands are killed by familiar products used in daily life. Usually, there is nothing wrong with the product, but the user has been careless or has failed to follow instructions for proper use and maintenance. Examples include trucks and automobiles; power boats; skis, bats, hardballs, and other sports equipment; guns and firecrackers; knives; and patent and prescription medicines. The most innocent-appearing and useful product, however, may in fact be lethal. For example, a child's pajamas may be made of highly flammable chemical fabric; a sleek sedan may have a steering mechanism prone to failure; and a wonder drug that prevents miscarriages may cause cancer in any female child born to the patient.

Under common-law rules, a person injured by a defective product may recover damages by proving that the product was negligently made. The negligence may be in the design, a lack of safety features, faulty materials or manufacture, or a failure to explain proper use and maintenance. Proving negligence in such cases is usually extremely difficult and costly, and often near impossible. The suspect product may be made with thousands of interrelated component parts; these may have been assembled many years before, in a factory located thousands of miles away, possibly in a foreign land.

An injured plaintiff might also allege a breach of a contractual warranty (see Chapter 8). However, there might be no warranties, or they may have expired, or recovery may be barred by failure to give proper prompt notice of the breach. Moreover, limited warranties often provide for no more than repair or replacement of the product if defective, or at best for a refund of the purchase price.

In 1962, the California Supreme Court provided a solution to the deficiencies of negligence and warranty theories by defining the new tort of strict liability for the manufacturer when a defective product is sold that injures a user. In this case, the product involved was an ingenious multipurpose power tool that could be used as a saw, a drill, and a wood lathe. It was purchased by the plaintiff's wife in 1955. In 1957, the plaintiff bought the attachments necessary to use the tool as a lathe to trim a large piece of wood. He had worked on a piece of wood several times without difficulty when it suddenly flew out of the machine and hit his forehead, causing a serious injury. Experts testified that an inadequate set of screws had been used by the manufacturer to hold parts of the machine together, and the machine's normal vibration caused the screws to be loosened, which brought about the accident. The court held, "A manufacturer is strictly liable in tort when an article he places on the market, knowing that it is to be used without inspection for defects, proves to have a defect that causes injury to a human being."[50]

In adopting the rule, the *Restatement of Torts* expanded the concept to include "injuries to any user or consumer or to his property," but qualified it by providing that the seller must be "engaged in the business of selling such a product . . . in a defective condition unreasonably dangerous to the user or consumer" and that it "is expected to and does reach the user or consumer without substantial change in the condition in which it is sold."[51] Many other jurisdictions, including such populous states as Illinois, Pennsylvania, and Texas, have adopted the rule. Contributory negligence of the plaintiff does not defeat his or her case. However, some states, using comparative negligence, allow a reduction in damages. In some jurisdictions, if the product was produced in accordance with the then-existing state of the art, the injury-causing design is not considered a defect.

The rule of strict liability for defective products shifts the burden of resulting injuries from the user to the manufacturer. Intermediaries such as wholesalers and retailers are also held responsible as they are better equipped to pursue the manufacturer. The manufacturer may purchase added insurance, which becomes a routine cost of production. But in any case, producers of products can pass along added costs to all customers in the form of slightly higher prices. Manufacturers are encouraged, moreover, to be more careful in product design, pre-sale testing, inspection, quality control in production, post-sale follow-up of performance, and prompt recall and repair when defects are disclosed. In recent years, many automobile models have been recalled for appropriate modifications to forestall costly strict liability litigation.

The following is a selection from a list of products for which liability has been imposed.

- Accutane (an anti-acne drug linked to birth defects).
- All-terrain vehicles.
- Bendectin and other teratogens (chemicals linked to birth defects).
- Chymopapain (a drug used to treat herniated disks).
- Dalkon shield (contraceptive device associated with inflammatory disease and spontaneous abortion in users; removed from the market in 1974).
- DES (a drug used to prevent miscarriages but discontinued because of increased risk of cancer in women who had fetal exposure).
- Halcion (a drug used as a sleep-inducing medicine).
- IUDs (a contraceptive device).
- Silicone gel breast implants.
- Tobacco products.
- Vehicle transmissions.

The largest and most notorious cases of strict liability as the twentieth century ends involve silicone gel breast implants and cigarettes.

Dow Corning corporation helped develop and sold tens of thousands of silicone gel breast implant devices. Thousands of women sued in a class action contending that their breast implants were defective, leaking silicone into their bodies and impairing their immune systems. Dow Corning, disputing the injuries, filed for bankruptcy due to the crush of claims. Later, under federal bankruptcy court rules, Dow Corning settled the cases, agreeing to pay $3.2 billion to those women who were injured by its product.[52]

The scientific report on breast implants is available on the Internet at http://www.fjc.gov/BREIMLIT/mdl926.htm

Class actions are procedural devices whereby groups of injured persons who are similarly situated can obtain redress in a single lawsuit, rather than filing hundreds or even thousands of separate cases. The silicone gel breast implant case is an excellent example of how large groups of victims are handled by the civil law tort system. Shortly after the Dow Corning settlement, a court-appointed panel of neutral scientists concluded after two years of study of more than 2,000 cases that there is no credible evidence that breast implants cause disease.[53] More than 1 million women have had silicone gel implants since the 1960s when they were introduced. The implants have been banned by the U.S. Food and Drug Administration since 1992, pending further analysis. The newly released report may affect any plans for further class actions.

Smoking presents many dilemmas to society. There no longer is any question that smoking is addictive (as are many other substances) and that it carries a high probability of contributing to lung diseases, especially cancer. Individuals cannot sue cigarette companies effectively because of the difficulties in engaging enough experts to prove causation. While it is one thing to show statistically that smoking contributes to lung cancer in the population, it is quite another thing to show that smoking (and not something else) caused an individual's lung cancer. Meanwhile, taxpayer (Medicaid) funded hospitals incur substantial costs in treating persons afflicted with diseases that likely were caused or exacerbated by cigarette smoking. Given these premises, almost all states joined together in filing litigation against the nation's four largest cigarette manufacturers.

> The tobacco industry settled lawsuits filed by most states by agreeing to pay about $206 billion as reimbursement for the Medicaid payments that had been incurred caring for patients of smoking-related diseases, and for future such costs through 2025. The states will receive portions of the $206 billion each year.[54] Is this "largest ever" settlement a back-breaker for the cigarette manufacturers, or the establishment of a social policy to shift more of the costs of smoking to smokers?

Tobacco manufacturing companies have agreed to pay the states a portion of their proceeds from cigarette sales. These payments will be tax deductible. The states will use the money to pay some hospital and other expenses of those who are afflicted with tobacco-related diseases and who are unable to care for themselves. For example, California is slated to receive $23.9 billion each year, although estimated health costs of smoking-related diseases is $42.5 billion each year. Furthermore, there is no requirement that the money actually be spent on smoking-related deaths. Thus, the settlement, spread out over more than 25 years, is a social policy akin to a "user tax" whereby cigarette users provide the funds with which to care for the illnesses created by cigarettes. Other provisions in the settlement restrict the kinds of advertising that will be permissible (no Joe Camel ads, but the Marlboro Man is okay). Immediately following the settlement, and to nobody's surprise, tobacco manufacturers announced a substantial price increase in cigarettes to offset the costs of the settlement. Since the price increase, Internet cigarette sales, some advertising no sales tax, discount prices, and free shipping, have been booming, as have sales of "black market" cigarettes bought in "low" tax states. Professional smuggling of "tax-free" export cigarettes is expected to increase.[55]

As the twentieth century winds down, smoking is prohibited or restricted in many public buildings, airplanes, buses, restaurants, workplaces, etc. Education about the inherent health risks of smoking has been widespread. What has been the effect on our society from this notoriety and what does the future portend? Price increases in cigarettes historically have induced many smokers to quit the habit. But a recent study by the Harvard School of Public Health presents a grim picture for the beginning of the new millennium—more college students than ever are smoking cigarettes. This result probably means that the 30-year decline in adult smoking has reversed. More than 25 percent of college students in the U.S. are smokers, according to the study. However, some 34 percent of noncollege adults of the same age smoke.[56] Cigarettes are distributed in a huge global market. The world's largest study of smoking deaths reveals that China makes up 20 percent of the world's population but smokes 30 percent of the world's cigarettes. Two-thirds of Chinese men under age 25 smoke. Globally, a record 4 million people will die of smoking-related illnesses in the year 2000, the first year of the new millennium.[57] If cigarettes were made of a controlled substance, similar to marijuana, with appropriate criminal penalties, would they be stamped out, saving all of these lives?

Everyone knows that guns can cause injury. Under what circumstances, however, may a gun manufacturer be held responsible for a defective gun?

> Michael Soe, age 14, took his father's Beretta 92 Compact L handgun from a camera bag and replaced its loaded ammunition magazine with an empty one. Unbeknownst to Michael, a cartridge remained in the gun's chamber. Michael then, while playing with the gun, shot his best friend Kenzo Dix in the heart, killing him instantly. Kenzo's parents sued Beretta Corp. for $7.5 million on the theory that the red dot on the gun's barrel that is raised one millimeter when a cartridge is in the chamber was too subtle and inadequate a warning. Berreta blamed the parent, for keeping the gun readily available and loaded. Berreta argued that a defense verdict would mean "personal responsibility is still a healthy concept in this society." Was the gun defective?[58]

This was the first jury trial involving the question of whether or not a handgun is defective in its design or warnings. Many other similar suits are pending in the United States. In the Kenzo Dix case, the jury returned a verdict for the defense.

The City of Chicago recently filed a lawsuit against gun manufacturers to recoup the cost of urban gun violence. The contention is that guns are defective products, unreasonably dangerous to the public health, much like cigarettes. Chicago also alleges that gun makers and dealers design, market, and sell easily concealable guns that are tailor-made for street warfare and not for sport. Such guns are sold in stores just outside Chicago, where they will be used within the city's limits. Other cities are filing similar lawsuits based more or less on the cigarette litigation.

Statutes of Repose — *glossary*

A **statute of repose** is a special statute of limitations that applies to specified defective products. Statutes of limitation set time limits within which lawsuits must be commenced—they are discussed fully later in this chapter. Because knowledge that a product is defective may not arise for many years, there is a public policy to extend the time within which victims may instigate their lawsuits for injuries they may sustain. However, it would be unfair to businesses to allow an unlimited number of years to pass before claims are asserted. Statutes of repose are a compromise of the interests of consumers on the one hand and manufacturers and sellers on the other. A statute of repose cuts off liability for a defective product following a specified number of years following its manufacture or sale, regardless of when the victim's injury occurs or is discovered. Statutes of limitation, on the other hand, do not begin to run until an injury has been discovered or should have been discovered by a victim using reasonable care. Statutes of limitation cover lawsuits generally and are discussed separately later in this chapter. There is no federal statute of repose. State statutes vary, but all cut off the time allowed for specified lawsuits usually pertaining to consumer products.

In addition to consumer products, statutes of repose may apply to medical and legal malpractice, to workers who are injured in the workplace, or even to renters who are injured by a defective product that is installed in their apartment. In malpractice cases, when they are applicable, statutes of repose typically cut off liability of the physician regardless of when the defect or harm is discovered by the victim. Thus, the "clock starts running" for possible liability for malpractice from the date the injury was inflicted. For example, one state's statute of repose cuts off medical malpractice lawsuits if they have not been commenced within five years of the physician's negligence, regardless of when the harm was discovered.[59] The "clock starts running" for construction or architectural design defect cases from the date of completion of the project, regardless of when the victim is injured.

Tom worked for the Acme Excavating Company performing maintenance duties on heavy equipment. In September 1999, a steel roller on a hydraulic conveyor that was transporting rock broke free, causing a large rock to severely break Tom's right leg. The conveyor was manufactured in 1972 by Zeland Equipment Co. and sold to Acme in 1980. Tom was covered by workers' compensation insurance and received medical and other financial assistance. His attorney advised him to sue Zeland under a defective product "strict liability" theory. Can Tom recover damages from Zeland?

The statute of limitations often is one year from the date of the injury—Tom has until September 2000 to commence litigation. But 27 years have elapsed since the conveyor was built by Zeland Equipment Co. and 19 years since it was sold to Acme. If there were a 25-year statute of repose, Tom's case would be barred. If the allowable period was 15 years, then Tom could sue Acme for product liability.[60]

Most statutes of repose are applied to lawsuits brought upon the theory of a defective consumer product. For example, Oregon cuts off a manufacturer's liability for a defective vehicle after eight years with only limited exception.[61] Victims generally have been unsuccessful in claiming that statutes of repose deny them equal protection of the law if their claim is barred at any time within the useful life of the product.[62]

WHAT ARE DAMAGES?

COMPENSATORY DAMAGES

Compensatory damages are also called *actual damages* because they consist of money awarded to the plaintiff for real (i.e., actual) loss or injury. Compensatory damages may consist of *special damages* and *general damages*. The word *damage* is often used to mean the loss caused by an injury. Perhaps just as often it is used to mean the *injury* itself (to a person, his or her property, or his or her rights). In the law, however, the plural version of the word *damages* means the *money awarded* by a court to a plaintiff in a civil action for loss and/or injury caused by a defendant's wrongful conduct. Damages may be awarded for a breach of contract, to put the plaintiff in the position he or she would have been in had the contract been performed as promised (see Chapter 8). They may also be awarded to a plaintiff because of a tort, for example, an injury suffered in an accident caused by the defendant's negligence. The money received reimburses the plaintiff for medical bills (of doctors and hospital), property loss (a "totaled" car), lost wages, and/or future "lost" income that cannot be earned because of the plaintiff's injuries. Damages also are designed to compensate for physical impairment (e.g., spinal injury or broken arm), mental anguish, and/or pain and suffering (both present and prospective, because they are expected to continue into the indefinite future).

> Jennifer, a 21-year-old college student majoring in music, was killed when she braked her Honda Civic as traffic slowed and was rear-ended by Carlos, who had been tailgating her for several miles. In a jury trial the attorney for Jennifer's family produced an expert witness who was prepared to testify that Jennifer had a 55-year life expectancy; that each day of her life she would have enjoyed her music, that she would have married and had the joy of a family as well as close friends and relationships, and many other benefits of living. All of these benefits are worth x dollars a day; therefore, the attorney for Jennifer's family claimed that the jury verdict should include, in addition to loss of future income and damages, an additional large sum of money representing Jennifer's daily loss of pleasure. Should the judge permit the jury to consider such testimony of "hedonic" damages?

The concept that an injured or deceased victim ought to be compensated for loss of future pleasure, in addition to the more traditional losses of consortium (shared companionship and support of marriage), pain and suffering, and earnings, is new. Called "hedonic" damages, it has met with disfavor by courts.[63]

Fines imposed against criminals as punishment go to the state. Damages awarded against tortfeasors in civil actions go to the plaintiff. If two or more tortfeasors are responsible for a given injury, each is fully liable to pay the entire judgment, but of course the plaintiff is entitled to only one full recovery. In most states, a tortfeasor who pays all or more than his or her share of the damages is entitled to contribution or partial reimbursement from the other wrongdoers.

If you can't collect

Special Damages

Special damages are often called *out-of-pocket costs* because they can be specified and precisely measured in terms of money. Common examples are the cost of a hospital stay, income lost because of absence from work, and the cost of repairing a car that was rear-ended. In awarding special damages for anticipated *future* losses, a jury may award the present value of such future sums, using an appropriate discount interest rate. The plaintiff gets a sum of money that, if invested at the selected interest (discount) rate, will grow over the years to precisely the amount that had been determined to be the total future monetary loss. Since World War Two, inflation has caused a continuing decline in the purchasing power of the dollar. This fact of life may also be taken into consideration in calculating future expenses resulting from the injury. Special damages are the actual result of the particular loss or injury; they flow from it naturally and proximately because of the unique combination of circumstances in any given case.

General Damages   *glossary*

General damages, the second kind of compensatory damages, are also the actual and proximate result of the particular loss or injury. They compensate victims for other than out-of-pocket monetary losses suffered. Prime examples include compensation for pain and suffering and compensation for mental distress caused by physical injuries.

> Annette Blenker, 37, was shopping at Berry's Market when a six-pack of long-necked beer bottles fell on her foot—she was wearing socks and sandals. Two months later she contacted Berry's and complained of her injury. She then sued for $2.5 million. According to her claim, Annette suffers from a rare nerve disorder that leaves her in constant pain. She walks on crutches, takes painkillers, and has trouble sleeping. Her doctors report that she is likely to suffer from RSD (reflexive sympathetic dystrophy) for the rest of her life. She consulted 11 different doctors, ranging from podiatrists to neurologists, anesthesiologists, an orthopedic surgeon, and a psychiatrist. What is the proper amount of damages?[64]

The jury returned a verdict to Annette of $388,000 for past and future economic damages and $87,000 for her pain and suffering. Jurors found no negligence in stacking the beer; instead, they found that the store employees failed to preserve an in-house videotape of the incident and that the store neglected to have a written policy on how to handle injured customers. The owner of Berry's Market was "shocked" at the verdict and cites it as an example of "lawsuit abuse" and the need for "tort reform." His expert witness testified that Annette's pain may be psychosomatic (bodily symptoms caused by mental or emotional disturbance).

In certain cases, a plaintiff may recover special and general damages for personal loss suffered as the result of harm done by the defendant to a third party, such as a spouse or child. For example, a spouse may recover for loss of **consortium** with the injured or deceased mate. *Consortium* includes companionship, affection, and sexual relations. Damages for consortium are not recoverable by unmarried persons, regardless of the intimacy or duration of the relationship. This is another example of unequal protection of the law and a reason why advocates contend same-sex marriages should be legitimized.

In early common law, if a victim died because of someone's tortious conduct, the death terminated all claims for damages. Today, however, **wrongful-death statutes** compensate immediate dependent relatives for loss of companionship and financial support resulting from the death. The award may be as high as millions of dollars, such as when the victim is a highly paid executive who leaves a surviving dependent spouse and children. On the other hand, the death of a single person with no children or other dependents could result in no cause of action. However, some states have **survivor statutes** that provide that a decedent's cause of action survives the death. It is owned by the decedent's estate, rather than by the surviving dependents (if any). Damages recovered by the estate are then distributed in accordance with the decedent's last will or by intestate distribution (see Chapter 14).

Punitive or Exemplary Damages

In certain cases, the civil law resembles the criminal law in sanctions imposed. It punishes especially blameworthy wrongdoers who intentionally hurt other persons. It does this by awarding **punitive** or **exemplary damages** to the victim, in addition to compensatory damages. The purpose is not to enrich the plaintiff, who has already been fully compensated for his loss or injury; rather, the purpose is to punish and make an example of the wrongdoer in order to deter him or her and others from a repetition of the offense.

Punitive damages are never awarded in breach-of-contract cases, unless they involve an intentional tort by the defendant, such as fraud or bad faith. They are awarded "where the wrong done . . . was aggravated by circumstances of violence, oppression, malice, fraud, or wanton and wicked conduct . . . and are intended to solace the plaintiff for mental anguish, laceration of his feelings, shame, degradation, or other aggravations of the original wrong, or else to punish the defendant for his evil behavior, or to make an example of him."[65]

Generally, punitive damages are available in cases of intentional tort, such as assault and battery, defamation, and fraud. They may also be awarded (1) in product-liability cases, but only where the defendant acted despicably with willful and conscious disregard of the rights and safety of others; (2) in premises-liability cases, where a tenant of an apartment building is the victim of criminal attack when the landlord knew of the danger of such attacks yet failed to take corrective action (e.g., by excluding unauthorized persons or preventing their access); and (3) where the defendant consumes alcohol to the point of intoxication when he or she plans to later operate a motor vehicle, and thereby harms another.[66]

Punitive damages have been likened to fines imposed on convicted criminals. But critics point out that fines are always paid to the state, and thus benefit all of society. By the same logic, they say, punitive damages should be paid to the state, for the benefit of all. At the time of this writing, a number of states seize part of punitive damages awarded in civil cases.* The U.S. Supreme Court recently let stand a Florida Supreme Court decision that allowed the state to take a substantial part of punitive-damage awards won in personal injury lawsuits.[67] Most states do not divert any portion of punitive damages into the public coffers, a position coming under increasing disapproval. In a case involving a fraudulent gold scam in Texas, the trial court judge approved an award of $75 million in compensatory damages and $100 million in punitive damages to the three victims. While affirming the result on appeal, one justice of the Texas Supreme Court made the following observation:

> I write separately to recommend that the Legislature enact a law apportioning one-half of punitive damage awards to the State. Presently, plaintiffs receive the entire award of punitive damages in Texas. For example, in this case three plaintiffs will share $100 million in punitive damages even though they were fully compensated for their injuries when the trial court awarded them more than $31 million in actual damages and $43 million in attorneys fees. Yet, the primary purposes for awarding punitive damages are to punish a defendant for reprehensible behavior and to deter similar conduct in the future. (citations) Also, punitive damages are generally awarded in situations in which the defendant's conduct has damaged society as a whole as well as the individual plaintiff. (citations) Thus the goal in awarding punitive damages is not to compensate the victim. Actual damages perform that function. Nevertheless, our law creates a

*For example, Florida, Georgia, Illinois, Iowa, Missouri, New York, Oregon, and Utah take a portion of punitive damage awards.

windfall for plaintiffs by allowing them to recover the entire award of punitive damages. I question whether this is a wise public policy.[68]

Municipalities can raise capital to build public improvements by issuing (selling) bonds to investors. These bonds create debts—investors are creditors. Monthly interest is paid to the investors as their bonds (loans) gradually are repaid. Banks, acting as trustees, offer the administrative service of receiving monthly bond payments and then distributing them to the rightful bond owners. Over many years some payments on bonds are unclaimed by bond owners. Patrick Stull, manager of the corporate trust department for Bank of America, noticed that unclaimed bond payments were being taken by the bank instead of being returned to the municipalities. In 1995, after being discharged, Stull filed a "whistleblower" lawsuit alleging that his discharge was retaliatory. "Whistleblower" laws protect employees who "blow the whistle" on fraudulent or illegal activities. Stull and defrauded bond issuers filed suit. The key issue in the case was whether or not Bank of America deliberately siphoned off the cash or simply could not keep its bookkeeping straight. Facing this issue, the Bank of America, denying any wrongdoing other than poor bookkeeping practices, settled the case by payment of $187 million. What role did punitive damages play in this settlement?

If a jury believed that Bank of America, with its sophisticated computer systems and accounting staff, could not possibly make such an obvious and huge error, and that therefore the bank was deliberately stealing money, it may have awarded punitive damages in an astronomical amount. The threat of punitive damages often influences the decision to settle. While attorneys against the bank will receive about $20 million, Patrick Stull will receive about $15 million for "blowing the whistle" on his employer.[69]

Generally, punitive damages may not be awarded in the absence of compensatory damages. However, a victim who has suffered no actual loss or injury may recover **nominal general damages** (usually 6 cents or $1), so that punitive damages may then be assessed against the wrongdoer. An example would be a "Peeping Tom" whose prurient gaze caused no monetary loss to the plaintiff. The victim recovers nominal damages to support an added award of punitive damages.

Judges or juries determine the proper amount of punitive damages by considering the nature and gravity of the offense as well as the defendant's ability to pay and the amount of compensatory damages awarded. Damage awards that are grossly inflated as a result of prejudice against large corporations, or passion, are typically substantially reduced or even rejected on appeal.

In a widely publicized case in 1989, a Los Angeles jury awarded the male lover of actor Rock Hudson $14.5 million in compensatory damages and $7.25 million in punitive damages, in an action against the estate of the deceased star. The jury found that Hudson, who died of AIDS, was guilty of conspiring with his personal secretary to keep the fatal affliction secret so that the plaintiff would continue his sexual relationship with the movie star. Is an award of damages justified?

Yes. However, the trial judge reduced the compensatory damages to $5 million and the punitive damages to $500,000, saying he would order a new trial on damages if the plaintiff refused to accept the reductions.[70]

WHAT BARRIERS CAN PREVENT COLLECTION OF DAMAGES?

A person with a perfectly good cause of action may never recover any money if (1) he or she fails to commence litigation promptly, and thus is barred from suing by an applicable statute of limitations or (2) he or she obtains a judgment but is unable to collect from a judgment-proof defendant.

STATUTES OF LIMITATION

Statutes of limitation "wipe the slate clean" for a wrongdoer after specified periods of time have elapsed without the filing of a lawsuit by the victim. They are legislative enactments that specify the limited periods of time during which the victim must formally initiate his or her action for legal relief, or, in the case of a crime, during which the government must prosecute the accused. (Chapter 6 more fully considers the length of statutes of limitations for crimes.)

It is psychologically counterproductive and ethically questionable to keep a potential civil lawsuit or criminal indictment hovering over a wrongdoer indefinitely. It discourages personal reform and tends to limit the individual's peace of mind as well as his or her social and economic productivity.

Statutes of limitation are designed to prescribe reasonable periods of time during which civil claims for damages may be filed (e.g., three or four years are common periods for breach of contract; one year is usual for the tort of negligence). Normally, persons become aware of the breach or injury within the specified time and are expected to sue for damages within that time. With the passage of time, evidence is lost, memories fade, witnesses move away or die, and it becomes very difficult, if not impossible, for a court to determine "the whole truth." However, in certain types of cases, the doctrine of strict liability supersedes traditional statutes of limitation. Thus, the doctrine permits a suit for damages *any* number of years after the allegedly defective product has been sold. This is permitted even if the product, when sold, had been manufactured conscientiously and was of acceptable quality as measured by the state of the art at the time. Because lawsuits are now being filed under principles of strict liability well beyond the statutory periods of limitation, substantial damages awarded to plaintiffs have been affecting the price and availability of domestic products. There is a considerable political movement favoring "tort reform" that focuses upon elimination of stale cases, punitive damage limitations, and other issues.

Statutes of limitation declare the time limits for most civil cases within which a victim must commence litigation against a wrongdoer. However, some civil cases request court relief other than money. For example, assume a homeowner contracts to sell but, at the last minute, changes his mind. Assume also that the buyer does not want to collect damages and instead asks the court to compel completion of the purchase. This remedy is known as *specific performance* (of a promise) and is equitable in nature because money is not sought. Cases for

The United States Chamber of Commerce spearheads the push by industry for tort reform. Their position may be reviewed at http://www.uschamber.org

http://

equitable remedies are governed by the **doctrine of laches**, which is based on the maxim that "equity aids the vigilant and not those who sleep on their rights." Hence, the court may refuse to give relief, in this case to the buyer, if the defendant (homeowner) has been misled or prejudiced by the plaintiff's unconscionable, unexplained, or unreasonable delay in asserting a right. Thus, if the buyer in our hypothetical did nothing for six months when the seller conveyed ownership to another, subsequent buyer, the court would deny specific performance. But since the statute of limitations for breach of contract is four years, the buyer could still sue the wrongful seller for money damages.

In most jurisdictions, an action to recover damages for tortious injury must be commenced within one year from the date of commission of the negligent tort. The period is generally the same for intentional torts, except for fraud. The defrauded victim may not even be aware of the injury until much later, and so the time limit is usually three years from time of discovery of the fraud. Generally, in medical and legal malpractice actions the statutory time does not begin to run until the plaintiff becomes aware of the injury suffered, while statutes of repose begin to run when the negligence occurs. Statutes of limitation are tolled and "the clock stops" while the defendant is out of the jurisdiction and during a plaintiff's minority. It is noteworthy that the statutory time limit for breach of contract (see Chapter 8) is typically two years for oral contracts and four years for written contracts and credit accounts. With crimes (see Chapter 6), the statutory periods of limitation reflect the gravity of the offenses. For felonies, three years from the date of commission is typical; for misdemeanors, one year. For murder, there is no time limit.

JUDGMENT-PROOF DEFENDANTS

Another barrier to collection of damages is that, even if found liable, the defendant may be **judgment-proof**, i.e., without sufficient liability insurance (if any) or other resources to pay. However, under state laws a judgment survives for years, perhaps ten on average, and may be renewed or extended a like period. Meanwhile, the judgment continues to grow from the effect of accruing interest, typically at 10 percent. Earnings made and other assets acquired by the debtor (e.g., through gifts or by inheritance) during the life of the judgment may be levied on by the unsatisfied judgment creditor. A *levy* is a process whereby a court official confiscates assets of a judgment debtor to satisfy the judgment. The creditor must first locate the debtor and identify the property to be confiscated—an easier task now that computer-assisted asset-search services are readily available. Nonetheless, socially irresponsible debtors often "skip," sometimes leaving the city, state, and/or country and providing no forwarding address. The difficulty the FBI has in tracking down "most wanted" criminals suggests the cost and practical impossibility of locating and collecting money from a determined "skip." Thus, winning a money judgment is no assurance of its collection.

CASES

RANDI W. V. MUROC JOINT UNIFIED SCHOOL DISTRICT
14 Cal.4th 1071, 60 Cal.Rptr.2d 263 (1997)

Robert Gadams desired to seek employment through the placement office at Fresno Pacific College, where he had received his teaching credential. Former employers were asked to provide references.

One former employer, Mendota School District, provided a letter of recommendation prepared by an official, Gilbert Rosette. Rosette's recommendation to Fresno Pacific College's placement office noted Gadams's "genuine concern" for students and his "outstanding rapport" with everyone, and concluded "I wouldn't hesitate to recommend Mr. Gadams for any position." Rosette allegedly knew, but did not mention, Gadams's history of improper contacts with female students. The contacts included hugging some female junior high school students, giving them back massages, making "sexual remarks" to them, and being involved in "sexual situations" with them.

Another former employer, Tranquility High School District, provided a letter of recommendation prepared by an official there, Richard Cole. Cole's recommendation to Fresno Pacific College's placement office was positive, but he did not mention information he allegedly possessed about Gadams while he was employed at Golden Plains Unified School District. Specifically, Cole knew that Gadams had been the subject of various parents' complaints, including charges that he "led a panty raid, made sexual overtures to students, sexual remarks to students. . . ." Nonetheless, Cole recommended Gadams for "almost any administrative position that he wishes to pursue."

Yet another former employer, Muroc Unified School District, provided a letter of recommendation prepared by an official there, David Malcolm. Malcolm's recommendation to Fresno Pacific College's placement office was positive. Malcolm described Gadams as an "upbeat, enthusiastic administrator who relates well to the students" and recommended him for "an assistant principalship

. . . without reservation." Malcolm allegedly knew that during Gadams's employment, disciplinary actions were taken against him for "sexual touching" of female students that caused him to resign.

Robert Gadams then was hired by Livingston Union School District as vice principal. Randi W., 13, a student at Livingston Middle School, was in Gadams's office when he offensively "touched, molested, and engaged in sexual touching" of her.

Randi W. brought suit against the school districts that recommended Gadams for employment on the theory, among others, that they were negligent for failing to disclose negative background information in their letters of recommendation to the placement office that provided them to her school's district.

The trial court dismissed the negligence aspect of Randi's action on the basis that the recommending school districts did not owe any duty to protect Randi because their recommendations were made only to a placement office.

CHIN, Associate Justice: . . . no California case has yet held that one who intentionally or negligently provides false information to another owes a duty of care *to a third person* who did not receive the information and who has no special relationship with the provider . . . .

Although the chain of causation leading from defendants' statements and omissions to Gadams's alleged assault on plaintiff is somewhat attenuated, we think the assault was reasonably foreseeable. . . . defendants could foresee that Livingston's officers would read and rely on defendants' letters in deciding to hire Gadams. Likewise, defendants could foresee that, had they not unqualifiedly recommended Gadams, Livingston would not have hired him. And finally, defendants could foresee that Gadams, after being hired by Livingston, might molest or injure a Livingston student such as (Randi W.). . . .

As for public policy, the law certainly recognizes a *policy of preventing future harm* of the kind alleged here. One of society's highest priorities is to protect children from sexual or physical abuse. (citations) Defendants urge that *competing social or economic policies* may disfavor the imposition of liability for misrepresentation or nondisclosure in employment references. They observe that a rule imposing liability in these situations could greatly inhibit the preparation and distribution of reference letters, to the general detriment of employers and employees alike. We have recently stated that "when deciding whether to expand a tort duty of care, courts must consider the potential social and economic consequences." (citations) Defendants argue that a rule imposing tort liability on writers of recommendation letters could have one very predictable consequence: employers would seldom write such letters, even in praise of exceptionally qualified employees. In defendants' view, . . . an employer would be better advised . . . merely to confirm the former employee's position, salary, and dates of employment.

In response, plaintiff asserts it is unlikely that employers will decline to write reference letters for fear of tort liability, at least in situations involving no foreseeable risks of physical injury to someone.

. . . we hold . . . that that the writer of a letter of recommendation owes to third persons a duty not to misrepresent the facts in describing the qualifications and character of a former employee, if making these misrepresentations would present a substantial, foreseeable risk of physical injury to the third persons.

Note: The case was returned to the Superior Court for trial by jury. The decision of the justices was split 4–3 on other issues in the case, but all agreed upon the portion quoted above in which new tort law was created.

FOR CRITICAL ANALYSIS

1. Suppose the former employer knew that Albert had an arrest record of assault and battery that grew from a bar fight. Must the employer reveal that information every time a prospective employer asks for references? Or must only sexual offenses be reported? Would the complete withholding of such information violate the duty "not to misrepresent the facts"? Isn't failure to reveal some fact as damaging as misrepresenting it?

2. Would the former employers in the Randi W. case have escaped liability if they had reported only the dates of Robert Gadams' employment? Or, to escape liability, must they reveal whatever sordid details they possess to future employers? What if the information they possessed about Gadams by his former employers was only rumor and unsubstantiated reports—could Gadams sue them for libel?

3. If the former employers reported the unsubstantiated information they possessed to all future prospective employers of Gadams, whether schools or any other businesses, would anybody employ him? Is it fair to warn only prospective employers who ask for references, and not others who accept prospective employees at their word? If your answer is "no," would you recommend publishing the names of such persons in some database available to all future employers?

DEBRA AGIS ET AL. V. HOWARD JOHNSON CO. ET AL.
371 Mass. 140, 355 N.E.2d 315 (1975)

Debra Agis, a waitress, sought to recover damages for mental anguish and emotional distress from her employer and the manager of the Ground Round (a Howard Johnson Restaurant). On May 23, 1975, Ms. Agis's manager had called the waitresses of the restaurant together and informed them that "there was some stealing going on," but that the identity of the person or persons responsible was not known, and that until the person or persons responsible were discovered, he would begin firing all the present waitresses in alphabetical order, starting with the letter "A." He then fired Debra Agis.

Ms. Agis filed a complaint stating that as a result of the manager's action she suffered emotional distress, mental anguish, and loss of wages and earnings. Her husband, James Agis, also brought suit for loss of the services, love, affection, and companionship of his wife.

The defendants moved to dismiss the complaint, alleging that even if everything the plaintiffs alleged were true, no action can be brought for emotional distress unless actual physical injury occurs. The Superior Court agreed with the defendants and dismissed the complaint. The plaintiffs appealed.

Justice Quirico delivered the opinion of the court: This case raises the issue whether a cause of action exists in this Commonwealth for the intentional or reckless infliction of severe emotional distress without resulting bodily injury. Counts 1 and 2 of this action were brought by the plaintiff Debra Agis against the Howard Johnson Company and Roger Dionne, manager of the restaurant in which she was employed, to recover damages for mental anguish and emotional distress allegedly caused by her summary dismissal from such employment. Counts 3 and 4 were brought by her husband, James Agis, against both defendants for loss of the services, love, affection, and companionship of his wife. This case is before us on the plaintiffs' appeal from the dismissal of their complaint.

The complaint alleges that, as a result of this incident, Mrs. Agis became greatly upset, began to cry, sustained emotional distress, mental anguish, and loss of wages and earnings. It further alleges that the actions of the defendants were reckless, extreme, outrageous, and intended to cause emotional distress and anguish. In addition, the complaint states that the defendants knew or should have known that their actions would cause such distress.

The defendants moved to dismiss the complaint on the ground that, even if true, the plaintiff's allegations fail to state a claim upon which relief can be granted because damages for emotional distress are not compensable absent resulting physical injury. The judge allowed the motion, and the plaintiffs appealed.

Our discussion of whether a cause of action exists for the intentional or reckless infliction of severe emotional distress without resulting bodily injury starts with our decision in *George v. Jordan Marsh Co.* (1971). While in that case we found it unnecessary to address the precise question raised here, we did summarize the history of actions for emotional distress and concluded that the law of the Commonwealth should be, and is, "that one who, without a privilege to do so, by extreme and outrageous conduct intentionally causes severe emotional distress to another, with bodily harm resulting from such distress, is subject to liability. . . ." The question whether such liability should be extended to cases in which there is no resulting bodily injury was "left until it arises," ibid., and that question has arisen here.

In the *George* case, we discussed in depth the policy considerations underlying the recognition of a cause of action for intentional infliction of severe emotional distress with resulting physical injury, and we concluded that the difficulties presented in allowing such an action were outweighed by the unfair and illogical consequences of the denial of recognition of such an independent tort. In so doing, we examined the persuasive authority then recognizing such a cause of action, and we placed considerable reliance on the Restatement (Second) of Torts § 46 (1965). Our examination of the policies underlying the extension of that cause of action to cases where there has been no bodily injury, and our review of the judicial precedent and the Restatement in this regard, lead us to conclude that such extension is both warranted and desirable.

The most often cited argument for refusing to extend the cause of action for intentional or reckless infliction of emotional distress to cases where there has been no physical injury is the difficulty of proof and the danger of fraudulent or frivolous claims. There has been a concern that "mental anguish, standing alone, is too subtle and speculative to be measured by any known legal standard," that "mental anguish and its consequences are so intangible and peculiar and vary so much with the individual that they cannot reasonably be anticipated," that a wide door might "be opened not only to fictitious claims but to litigation over trivialities and mere bad manners as well," and that there can be no objective measurement of the extent or the existence of emotional distress. There is a fear that "[i]t is easy to assert a claim of mental anguish and very hard to disprove it."

While we are not unconcerned with these problems, we believe that "the problems presented are not . . . insuperable" and that "administrative difficulties do not justify the denial of relief for serious invasions of mental and emotional tranquility. . . . That some claims may be spurious should not compel those who administer justice to shut their eyes to serious wrongs and let them go without being brought to account. It is the function of courts and juries to determine whether claims are valid or false. This responsibility should not he shunned merely because the task may be difficult to perform."

Furthermore, the distinction between the difficulty which juries may encounter in determining liability and assessing damages where no physical injury occurs and their performance of that same task where there has been resulting physical harm may be greatly overstated. "The jury is ordinarily in a better position . . . to determine whether outrageous conduct results in mental distress than whether that distress in turn results in physical injury. From their own experience jurors are aware of the extent and character of the disagreeable emotions that may result from the defendant's conduct, but a difficult medical question is presented when it must be determined if emotional distress resulted in physical injury. Greater proof that mental suffering occurred is found in the defendant's conduct designed to bring it about than in physical injury that may or may not have resulted therefrom." We are thus unwilling to deny the existence of this cause of action merely because there may be difficulties of proof. Instead, we believe "the door to recovery should be opened but narrowly and with due caution."

In light of what we have said, we hold that one who, by extreme and outrageous conduct and without privilege, causes severe emotional distress to another is subject to liability for such emotional distress even though no bodily harm may result. However, in order for a plaintiff to prevail in a case for liability under this tort, four elements must be established. It must be shown (1) that the actor intended to inflict emotional distress or that he knew or should have known that emotional distress was the likely result of his conduct; (2) that the conduct was "extreme and outrageous," was "beyond all possible bounds of decency" and was "utterly intolerable in a civilized community;" (3) that the actions of the defendant were the cause of the plaintiff's distress; and (4) that the emotional distress sustained by the plaintiff was "severe" and of a nature "that no reasonable man could be expected to endure it." These requirements are "aimed at limiting frivolous suits and avoiding litigation in situations where only bad manners and mere hurt feelings are involved," and we believe they are a "realistic safeguard against false claims. . . ."

Testing the plaintiff Debra Agis's complaint by the rules stated above, we hold that she makes out a cause of action and that her complaint is therefore legally sufficient. While many of her allegations are not particularly well stated, we believe that the "[p]laintiff has alleged facts and circumstances which reasonably could lead the trier of fact to conclude that defendant's conduct was extreme and outrageous, having a severe and traumatic effect upon plaintiff's emotional tranquility." Because reasonable men could differ on these issues, we believe that "it is for the jury, subject to the control of the court," to determine whether there should be liability in this case. While the judge was not in error in dismissing the complaint under the then state of the law, we believe that, in light of what we have said, the judgment must be reversed and the plaintiff Debra Agis must be given an opportunity to prove the allegations which she has made.

Counts 3 and 4 of the complaint are brought by James Agis seeking relief for loss of consortium as a result of the mental distress and anguish suffered by his wife Debra. There is no question that an action for loss of consortium by either spouse may be maintained in this Commonwealth where such loss is shown to arise from personal injury to one spouse caused by the negligence of a third person. The question before us is whether an action for loss of consortium may be maintained where the acts complained of are intentional, and where the injuries to the spouse are emotional rather than physical.

Traditionally, where the right to sue for loss of consortium has been recognized, intentional invasions of the marriage relationship such as alienation of affections or adultery have been held to give rise to this cause of action. We see no reason not to apply the same rule to the tort of intentional or reckless infliction of severe emotional distress. Similarly, the fact that there is no physical injury should not bar the plaintiff's claim. In [a previous] case, we hinted that "psychological

injury" could provide the basis for a consortium action. In addition, the underlying purpose of such an action is to compensate for the loss of the companionship, affection, and sexual enjoyment of one's spouse, and it is clear that these can be lost as a result of psychological or emotional injury as well as from actual physical harm.

Accordingly, we hold that, where a person has a cause of action for intentional or reckless infliction of severe emotional distress, his or her spouse also has a cause of action for loss of consortium arising out of that distress.

The judgment entered in the Superior Court dismissing the plaintiffs' complaint is reversed.

FOR CRITICAL ANALYSIS

1. Debra Agis was fired because her last name began with an "a," first in the alphabet. She was not accused of being a thief. This event was held to be sufficiently outrageous conduct to justify an action for damages, punitive damages (as an intentional tort), and for loss of consortium by her husband. Would a racial epithet be as outrageous? What about a disparaging remark about one's weight? Or skin complexion?

2. Under the *Agis* case, are all chain restaurants liable for damages each time their managers, who are distant from company headquarters, say or do something that upsets an employee? What limitations upon this liability can you identify in the *Agis* case? What limitations would you impose as judge? Employers are liable for the wrongful acts of their employees that are done in the course and scope of their employment. Are franchise restaurants "employees" of the franchising company, or are they "independent contractors" for whom no liability is incurred?

CHAPTER QUESTIONS AND PROBLEMS

1. Gramling, an expert in the use of explosives, obtained a city permit to level a ten-story building in the center of town by implosion. The explosives were carefully placed throughout the structure so that it would collapse inwardly and leave a heap of rubble on the site. Unfortunately, for unknown reasons, one charge on the third floor caused fragments of brick, concrete, and glass to fly outward. As a result, extensive and costly damage was done to plate glass in nearby buildings and to parked automobiles in the vicinity. There were also personal injuries. Is Gramling liable, even though he acted with a city permit and there was no evidence or claim of negligence?

2. Assume a jury rules that John was driving negligently and caused an automobile crash that injured the plaintiff.
   a. Does moral fault attach to John?
   b. Would your answer above be different if John were uninsured and unable to pay the judgment? If your answer is yes, what is the fault, driving negligently or being uninsured?
   c. Assuming John had adequate insurance, what consequences does he personally suffer as a result of his negligence? Does the accident go into his permanent employment records? Into a national database of negligent drivers? Or can he conceal it in all of his future personal transactions?
   d. Can society reasonably expect John to become a more careful and accident-free driver following his first accident?
   e. Is the law of negligence more about social policy or more about providing for compensation to injured persons?

3. Nick Dekker went into the Black Oak Restaurant for dinner. When leaving, he mistakenly took George Walton's hat from the coatrack and walked out the door. Walton observed the incident, ran outside, and yelled "Stop thief!" just as Dekker was driving out of the parking lot. Walton jumped into his own car and gave pursuit. He overtook a car driven by a man who looked like Dekker, although it was really Ferdinand Sinzant. Walton pulled alongside and forced Sinzant onto the shoulder of the road by easing his car along the front left side of Sinzant's car. When the cars stopped, Walton leaped out and smashed Sinzant in the mouth, knocking him unconscious. He put Sinzant into his car and drove back to the restaurant, where he phoned the police. When the squad car arrived, Sinzant regained consciousness, and Walton said, "Arrest this man, he's a thief!" The police refused to make the arrest because they had not observed any crime. However, they advised Walton that if he made a citizen's arrest, they would book Sinzant. Walton thereupon placed Sinzant under arrest. Meanwhile, Harry Hightower was injured when his car ran into, and badly damaged, the left rear of Sinzant's car, which was protruding slightly into the street with its lights out. At the time of the accident, Hightower was under the influence of marijuana. What torts have occurred?

4. During a wild party on the Fourth of July, Harry Hammer went outside and fired his 9mm pistol several times into the dark Los Angeles sky. Unfortunately, unlike the fabled arrow shot into the sky, Harry's bullet descended, hitting and penetrating Penalope's head and causing her modest but permanent injuries. Following the incident, Penelope lacked enthusiasm, complained of headaches,

and was easily frightened by loud noises. Harry had homeowner's liability insurance that would cover his negligent acts, and a good, permanent job paying him $6,000 a month. Would Harry's insurance policy pay for Penalope's injuries? Could Penalope obtain punitive damages from Harry?

5. Vera Babbitt, a mischievous prankster, called and told her friend Michelle that her fiance Gary was in a booth at the Hardball Sports Bar making out with a floozy. Before Vera could explain her message was a joke, Michelle slammed down the telephone, jumped into her Cherokee, and sped off to catch Gary in the act. Unfortunately, Vera cut off another driver and caused an accident, seriously injuring Billie Bellweather. What tort liabilities have arisen?

6. Harriet made a batch of brownies and donated them to the Girl Scouts to be sold as part of a fund raiser. Unfortunately, several purchasers of the brownies became deathly ill. Does the product-liability rule establish that Harriet is strictly liable for all injuries caused by the brownies?

7. Assume that a state enacted the following statute: "There shall be no recovery of damages based upon the commission of ordinary negligence." What ramifications can you think of that might flow from this unprecedented concept?

8. Johnson entered the defendant's store carrying her small child in an infant seat. When she tried to leave the store, she was stopped in a public place by a security officer who said that another employee had reported seeing her steal the infant seat. To show ownership, Johnson pointed to cat hair, food crumbs, and stains on the seat. After a 20-minute delay, the security officer apologized to the defendant and permitted her to leave. The trial court dismissed her action for false imprisonment, and Johnson appealed. Did the defendant have probable cause to detain Johnson, and was the 20-minute detention of Johnson reasonable in these circumstances? [*Johnson v. K-Mart Enterprises, Inc.*, 98 Wis.2d 533, 297 N.W.2d 74 (Wisconsin, 1980).]

9. Peter Wallis, a real estate broker, contends that before having sex, his girlfriend Kellie represented that she would use birth-control pills. But Kellie purposefully got pregnant, according to Wallis. He is suing Kellie for fraud and for conversion (civil theft) for wrongfully acquiring and misusing his sperm. Kellie contends that she was using birth-control pills and that his sperm given during sexual intercourse was not stolen or misused and should be considered a "gift" in the law. Kellie refused to obtain an abortion, moved out of their apartment, and gave birth to their daughter Taylor. Has Kellie converted Peter's sperm? Assuming that Mr. Wallis is correct in his contentions, what legal damages has he sustained?

10. Identify the tort that corresponds to each of the following crimes:
    a. Date rape.
    b. Robbery.
    c. Murder.
    d. Manslaughter by vehicle.
    e. Physical child abuse by a parent.
    f. Burglary.
    g. Shoplifting a dress.
    h. Crawling over a backyard fence and peeping through a bedroom window.
    i. Posting a naked picture of a former lover on the Internet.
    j. Practicing medicine without a license.

NOTES

1. David Traxel, *1898 The Birth of the American Century* (New York: Knopf, 1998).
2. Associated Press, 9 October 1997. Because verdicts are subject to appeal and often settled "out of court," the final amount paid may differ widely from the jury's award.
3. *The National Law Journal*, 2 November 1998.
4. *The National Law Journal*, 7 February 1994, 6.
5. *Mink v. University of Chicago and Eli Lily & Co.*, 460 F.Supp. 713 (M.D. Illinois, 1978).
6. Associated Press, New York, 3 July 1997.
7. *Matthew v. Page*, 354 So.2d 458 (Florida, 1978); *North Carolina National Bank v. McCarley & Co., Inc.*, 34 N.C.App. 689, 239 S.E.2d 583 (North Carolina, 1977); *Masterson v. McCroskie*, 194 Co. 460, 573 P.2d 547 (Colorado, 1978); and *A.M. Records, Inc. v. Heilman*, 75 Cal.App3d 554, 142 Cal.Rptr. 390 (1977).
8. *Goldfarb v. Baker*, 547 S.W. 2d 567 (Tennessee, 1977).
9. Associated Press, San Diego, 25 December 1996.
10. Associated Press, Costa Mesa, 2 May 1995.
11. Associated Press, Amarillo, 27 February 1998.
12. *Restatement of the Law of Torts*, 2d edition, (St. Paul, MN: American Law Institute Publishers, 1934), § 570–575.
13. *Stanley v. Taylor*, 4 Ill.App.3d, 98, 278 N.E.2d 824 (Illinois, 1972).
14. Associated Press, Poughkeepsie, N.Y., 10 October 1998.
15. Sarah Lyall, *New York Times*, 20 June 1997.
16. *New York Times v. Sullivan*, 376 U.S. 254, 84 S.Ct. 710 (1964); and *Philadelphia Newspapers, Inc. v. Hepps*, 475 U.S. 767, 106 S.Ct. 1558 (1986).
17. *Gertz v. Robert Welch, Inc.*, 418 U.S. 323, 94 S.Ct. 2997 (1974); and *Milkovich v. Lorain Journal Co.*, 497 U.S. 1, 110 S.Ct. 2695 (1990).
18. *Restatement of Torts*, § 652–A–E.
19. *Nader v. General Motors Corporation*, 298 N.Y.S.2d. 137, 31 A.D.2d 392 (New York, 1969).
20. *Carson v. Here's Johnny Portable Toilets*, 698 F.2d 831 (6th cir., 1983).
21. Based on *New Summit Associates Limited Partnership v. Nistle*, 73 Md.App.351, 533 A.2d 1350 (1987).
22. *Roberts v. Sears, Roebuck & Co.*, 673 F.2d 976 (7th cir., 1978); *San Francisco Chronicle*, 18 September 1989.
23. *Lamey v. Yesterday's Inc.*, 492 So.2d 988 (1986).
24. *Malandris v. Merrill Lynch, Pierce, Fenner, & Smith, Inc.*, 447 F.Supp. 543 (Colorado, 1977). On appeal, the award of compensatory damages was upheld, but the punitive damage award was reduced to $1,000,000. 703 F.2d 1152 (10th cir., 1983).
25. Charlie Goodyear, *San Francisco Chronicle*, 13 December 1997.
26. *Rodio v. Allstate Insurance Co.*, 123 N.J. 345, 587 A.2d 621 (New Jersey, 1991).
27. *Ledingham v. Blue Cross Plan for Hospital Care*, 29 Ill. App. 3d 339, 330 N.E.2d 540 (Illinois, 1975); *Grand Sheet Metal Products Co. v. Protection Mutual Insurance Co.*, 34 Conn.Supp. 46, 375 A.2d 428 (Connecticut, 1977); *McEvoy v. Group Health Cooperative of Eau Claire*, 570 N.W.2d 397 (1997).
28. *Thompson v. County of Alameda*, 614 P.2d 728, 167 Cal.Rptr. 70 (California, 1980).
29. Edward J. Kionka, *Torts in a Nutshell* (St. Paul, MN: West Publishing Co., 1992), 50.
30. *Wisniewski v. Great Atlantic & Pacific Tea Co.*, 226 Pa.Super. 574, 323 A.2d 744 (Pennsylvania, 1974).
31. Henry Campbell Black et al., *Black's Law Dictionary*, 5th ed. (St. Paul, MN: West Publishing Co., 1979).
32. *Palsgraf v. Long Island R.R. Co.*, 248 N.Y. 339, 162 N.E. 99 (New York, 1928).
33. William Prosser and Page Keeton, *Prosser and Keeton on Torts*, 5th ed. (St. Paul, MN: West Publishing Co., 1979), 43.
34. Leon Green, "The Casual Relation Issue in Negligence Law," *Michigan Law Review* 60 (1962), 543. See also *Weirum v. RKO General Inc.*, 15 Cal.3d 40, 539 P.2d 36 (California, 1975).
35. *Restatement of Torts*, § 328A.
36. Stephen Kiehl, *Boston Globe*, 3 September 1998.
37. *Khouri v. City of Chicago*, 92 L 15219 (Circuit Court, Cook Co., Ill); *National Law Journal*, 2 November 1998.
38. *County of Sacramento v. Lewis*, 96–1337; John Schwartz, *Washington Post*, 27 May 1998.
39. Hilary MacGregor, *Los Angeles Times*, 25 January 1998.
40. *Parsons v. Crown Disposal Company*, 63 Cal.Rptr. 2d 291 (California 1997).
41. *U.S. v. DeVane*, 306 F.2d, 182 (5th cir., 1962).
42. *Restatement of Torts*, § 283.
43. *Baker v. Alt*, 374 Mich. 492, 132 N.W.2d 614 (Michigan, 1965).
44. *The Wall Street Journal*, 1 March, 1990.
45. *Chase v. Luce*, 239 MN 364, 58 N.W.2d 565 (Minnesota, 1953); *Selby v. Tolbert*, 56 N.M. 718, 249 P.2d 498 (New Mexico, 1952); and *Hooks v. City of Detroit*, 31 Mich.App. 662, 187 N.W.2d 901 (Michigan, 1971).
46. George Markell, *San Francisco Chronicle*, 18 May 1998; *Martinez v. Pacific Bell* 275 Cal.Rptr.2d 878, 1990.
47. *Reuters*, Hartford, Conn., 5 November 1998.
48. *Brown v. Kendrick*, 192 So.2d 49 (Florida, 1966); *Abrams v. Woods*, 316 N.Y.S.2d 750, 64 Misc.2d 1093 (New York, 1970); and *Mercer v. Band*, 484 S.W.2d 117 (Texas, 1972).
49. See e.g., *Franklin v. Gibson*, 138 Cal.App.3d 340, 188 Cal.Rptr. 23 (California, 1982); *Yocco v. Barris*, 16 Ill.3d 113, 305 N.E.2d 584 (Illinois, 1973).
50. *Greenman v. Yuba Power Products, Inc.*, 59 Cal.2d 57, 377 P.2d 897, 27 Cal.Rptr. 697 (California, 1962).
51. *Restatement of Torts*, § 402A.
52. Associated Press, 10 November 1998.
53. *Los Angeles Times*, 2 December 1998.
54. Chronicle News Service, Los Angeles, 11 November 1998 and 21 November 1998.
55. Kenneth Howe, *San Francisco Chronicle*, 27 November 1998.
56. *Los Angeles Times*, 18 November 1998.
57. Study of 1.25 million Chinese jointly by Oxford and Cornell Universities and the Chinese Academies of Preventive Medicine, Emma Ross, Associated Press, 20 November 1998.
58. Henry K. Lee, *San Francisco Chronicle*, 10 November 1998.
59. *Hanflik v. Ratchford*, 848 F.Supp. 1539 (1989); *Craven v. Lowndes County Hospital Authority*, 263 Ga. 656, 437 S.E.2d 308 (Georgia, 1993).
60. This example based on the case of *Dinh v. Rust International Corporation*, 974 F.2d 500 (4th cir., 1992).
61. *Sealey v. Hicks*, 309 Or. 387, 788 P.2d 435 (1990).
62. *Olsen v. Freeman*, 117 Idaho 706, 791 P.2d 1285. (1990).
63. See e.g., *Ramos v. Kuzas*, 65 Ohio St. 3d 42, 600 N.E.2d 241 (1992); *McDougald v. Garber*, 73 N.Y.2d 246, 538 N.Y.S.2d 937 (1989); *Garcia v. Superior Court*, 49 Cal.Rptr.2d 580 (1996); and *Loth v. Truck-A-Say Corp.*, 70 Cal.Rptr. 2d 571 (1998).
64. Jim Doyle, *San Francisco Chronicle*, 27 June 1997.
65. *Black's Law Dictionary*.

66. *Grimshaw v. Ford Motor Co.*, 119 Cal.App.3d 757, 174 Cal.Rptr. 348 (California, 1981); *Penner v. Falk*, 153 Cal.App.3d 858, 200 Cal.Rptr. 661 (California, 1964); and *Taylor v. Superior Court*, 24 Cal.3d 890, 598 P.2d 854, 157 Cal.Rptr. 693 (California, 1979).

67. *Gordon v. Florida*, 585 So.2d 1033, 608 So.2d 800, 113 S.Ct. 1647 (Florida, 1993).

68. *General Resources v. Deadman*, 932 S.W.2d 485 (1996).

67. Sam Zuckerman, *San Francisco Chronicle*, 13 November 1998. There are both state and federal "whistleblower" statutes. See e.g., 31 U.S.C.A. 5328.

70. *San Francisco Chronicle*, 8 April 1989 and 22 April 1989.

8

CONTRACTS: ENFORCEABLE AGREEMENTS

*E*veryone lives by selling something.

Robert Louis Stevenson,
Scottish novelist, 1850–1894.

The law of contracts reflects our social values (commitment), interests (consumerism), and expectations (keeping promises) every day. How do people in our society make promises or commitments that are legally binding? What excuse is acceptable to justify breaking a legal commitment? Are there promises that are contrary to public policy and, therefore, void or invalid? If a promise violates the interests of society at large, will courts enforce it? If a child or an incompetent person makes a promise, will it be enforced? Answering these and other related questions is what contract law is about.

Through contracts, parties can create a greater degree of certainty as to the possible occurrence of future acts. The parties can create rights and duties upon which each might rely. Parties to contracts can also agree upon what are acceptable standards of conduct and how each party might be expected to behave relative to situations that may or may not occur.

Joseph needs 3,000 pumpkins for his urban pumpkin patch by late September to celebrate the Halloween season. He is acquainted with Paula, a local farmer, who is interested in selling the pumpkins. How can Joseph increase the probability of getting the pumpkins he needs when he needs them at a price he can afford?

A contract entered into with Paula in July for a September delivery of those pumpkins will increase the likelihood that Joseph will have the pumpkins when and where he needs them and at a price he can afford. Paula, on the other hand, no longer must worry about selling "ripe" pumpkins. If Paula fails to make delivery, Joseph will have rights against Paula to make good any loss because of Paula's failure to perform. The parties can arrange by the contract who is responsible for delivery, the expected grade and condition of the pumpkins upon arrival, whether the sale is for credit or cash, and on and on.

Contract law allows parties to make enforceable promises. If you think about it, you will realize that many promises people make do not create legal obligations. Sometimes the promises create *moral* rather than *legal* obligations. A moral obligation defines what you should do. Failure to perform a moral obligation, such as an agreement to give a friend a ride, does not usually create a legal liability. Sometimes promises create both a moral and a legal obligation (as when a friend promises to pay you for gas expenses to drive her to a neighboring city).

Rosalie invited an acquaintance, Jonathan, to a fund-raising dinner dance featuring the governor at the Pilothouse Restaurant on the Delta King in olde towne Sacramento. Jonathan accepted the offer and, eager to please Rosalie, spent $750 lavishly preparing for the evening. He got a haircut and purchased a new jacket, new shoes, and flowers. On the evening of the dance, Jonathan arrived at Rosalie's house and found out that she had already left for the evening. Jonathan is considering suing Rosalie for breach of contract to recover his expenses. Does he have a lawsuit?

Agreements to go on dates are not contracts; they are social arrangements. Although Rosalie may have breached a moral obligation, she is not required to pay Jonathan's expenses even though she did not keep the date.

One short, snappy definition of a **contract** is "an agreement that can be enforced in a court." The definition is accurate and easy to remember but not especially helpful. The authoritative *Restatement of Contracts** expands the definition of a contract to say it is "a promise, or a set of promises for the breach of which the law gives a remedy, or the performance of which the law in some way recognizes as a duty."[1] Contracts are the intelligent response to a felt human need to get things done with the cooperation of other human beings. They reflect the fact that in our technologically advanced civilization, marked by specialization and division of labor, with individuals highly dependent on each other, "No man is an island, entire of itself."[2] The U.S. Constitution expressly provides that "no State shall . . . pass any . . . Law impairing the Obligation of Contracts."**

Ordinarily, a contract is made when two (and sometimes more than two) parties exchange binding promises. In a promise, each party declares that she or he will (or will not) take a specified action in the future. If the contractual *promise* is not performed, the *contract* has been breached, and the party who failed to keep the promise must compensate the party to whom the promise was made. The non-performing party is usually required to pay money damages for failure to perform. In some situations, money damages cannot make the victim of the failure to perform "whole," and so a court of equity may require actual performance of the promised act.

---

*A *Restatement* is a treatise on law written and periodically reviewed by legal scholars. See Appendix C for further explanation.

**U.S. Constitution, Art. I, § 10. In the famous *Dartmouth College* case, the first Chief Justice of the U.S. Supreme Court, John Marshall, held that a charter of incorporation granted by King George III to Dartmouth College in 1769, which gave its trustees the right to govern the college forever, was indeed a contract. As such, it could not be rescinded, as was attempted by the New Hampshire state legislature, which had voted to transfer control of the College to a new board of overseers. *Dartmouth College v. Woodward*, 4 Wheaton 518 (1819).

In either case, the law seeks to give the party the benefit of the promise that was made. Understandably, punitive damages are not awarded; there is no crime and no tort, and generally no moral stigma attaches to the breach of contract. When a contractual promise is breached in the vast majority of cases, the parties agree to some acceptable alternative without litigation and the payment of damages.

Most people keep promises because of a sense of duty. Furthermore, keeping their promises is usually in the self-interest of both parties. Often the **promisor** (the person making the promise) and the **promisee** (the person to whom the promise is made) are not aware of the rules of contract law. They may rely on the good faith—the honesty and fairness—of the other persons who are involved. In business situations, however, parties should follow the rules of contract law carefully to avoid potential misunderstandings and disputes.

An Overview of the Promises We Live By

It is true that government statutes and court decisions prescribe the rules for creation, performance, and enforcement of contracts. But contracts are generally entered into privately, between private parties. Government agencies—local and federal—are not directly involved unless the government is itself a party to the contract. Of course, this happens often in our time of big government. Collectively, government is the nation's biggest employer, always under contract. It is the biggest buyer of goods and services, all under contract.

The Ubiquitous Contract

Contracts are legally binding links between producers and consumers throughout the world. They are the promises that are exchanged (and generally faithfully kept) to do the many things that get the world's work done. Literally billions of contracts are made and performed every day, often facilitated by the use of a common medium of exchange (money or credit).

Consider some ramifications of contracts in operation. Many millions of workers are employed under oral or written contracts. They work under contracts at every stage of production and distribution of goods and services. Each person contributes to the total effort that provides all of us with food, clothing, shelter, transportation, utilities, and entertainment. The seemingly limitless range of human needs and wants are thereby met through the fulfillment of contracts. The vast and incredibly complex public infrastructure of roads, highways, airports, harbors, schools, museums, fire and police departments, and sewage and refuse treatment and disposal systems has been constructed and is maintained by means of contracts. With relatively few exceptions, these binding agreements are performed without litigation. Were any substantial fraction of all contracts disputed, the country's court system would be overwhelmed and rendered inoperative. This is a tribute to the fundamental integrity and intelligence of most people. The widespread use of standardized contracts, common trade practices, and the uniformity and repetitiveness of most business dealings, of course, also explain it. People generally act with enlightened self-interest, serving the needs of others while gaining benefits of the contracts for themselves.

Examine the book you are reading—the paper, the ink, and the printing. Identify, if you can, the contracts involved in cutting trees, grinding them into pulp, and transforming the pulp—with the aid of water, chemicals, and heavy machinery—into rolls or sheets of paper. Don't overlook all the workers involved at each step, and the contracts they perform each day. Recognize the various transportation and communication facilities utilized from start to finish. Take any one of the above contract leads and pursue it to its sources; for example, the mining of minerals to produce the steel for the saws, trucks, ships, and other machinery. It is literally impossible to identify all the contracts that were involved, directly and indirectly, in placing this book at your disposal. One can convincingly argue that an incredibly complex yet effective network of contracts has implemented all human activity in our civilized, interdependent society.

What Is the Uniform Commercial Code (UCC)?

Elements of contract law vary from state to state and among major types of business enterprise. Many contracts are based on the common law, notably personal service agreements. Specialized statutes affect contract rights and obligations *in* security markets (for stocks and bonds), corporate financial transactions, and real estate dealings. But, overall, most contracts involve the sale/purchase of **goods** (i.e., all movable personal property that consists of things—other than money and securities), and these contracts are governed by the **Uniform Commercial Code (UCC)**.*

The full text of the Uniform Commercial Code can be found at http://www.law.cornell.edu/ucc/ucc.table.html

In the twentieth century, there has been an ongoing movement to create various "uniform" acts or codes to make state laws more consistent throughout the 50 states. The most pervasive and thus most significant uniform code is the UCC, which has been adopted, at least in part, by all 50 states as part of their statutory law. Because the UCC does not attempt to answer every contract question, generally accepted common-law rules still provide answers to most contract questions.

An important thing to know about any investigation of commercial law is whether the UCC governs a contract. Article 2 (Sales) is the most important part of the UCC for our discussion of contracts. Article 2 defines the rights and duties of contracting parties if the subject matter of the contract is a sale of goods. A **sale** is a transfer of ownership of goods in exchange for a price.

Also important to note is the emergence of expanded world markets and the law related to international sale transactions. The *United Nations Convention on Contracts for the Sale of Goods* became part of the law of the United States in 1988.** The convention applies to sales entered into by citizens of any two of the signatories, and it deviates from the UCC in some details. For example, unlike the

---

*The UCC, as amended, replaced seven other "uniform" acts and a variety of other legislative acts governing commercial activities. Currently, the following articles constitute the bulk of the official text:

1. General Provisions 2. Sales 2.A. Leases 3. Commercial Paper 4. Bank Deposits and Collections 5. Letters of Credit 6. Bulk Transfers 7. Warehouse Receipts, Bills of Lading and Other Documents 8. Investment Securities 9. Secured Transactions: Sales of Accounts and Chattel Paper.

**Among the other countries that have adopted this convention are Australia, Canada, France, Germany, Italy, Mexico, Sweden, and Switzerland.

UCC, the convention provides that any sales contract may be oral, whereas under the UCC, contracts for the sale of goods in excess of $500 must be evidenced by a written document. However, the contracting parties may expressly opt out of all or any part of this United Nations law.

HOW ARE CONTRACTS CLASSIFIED?

Generally, just two parties are involved in a given contract, but there may be multiple parties when appropriate. One person (and a "person" could be a corporation or partnership) called the **offeror** makes an offer to a second person, termed the **offeree**. The offeree may then respond to the offer with an acceptance. In effect, each party promises to do (or in some cases, promises *not* to do) something the other party wants to have done (or *not* have done). Generally, no special words need be used. Often there is preliminary negotiation or "bargaining." With a few exceptions (discussed later in this chapter), the contract may be oral, written, or implied from conduct and/or from some custom or usage of the particular trade; the agreement may also result from a combination of these methods of expression. Contracts may be classified as to method of expression, parties bound, legal effect, and extent of performance. A summary of these classifications is represented in Exhibit 8–1.

METHOD OF EXPRESSION

Any person capable of reading this sentence has probably been a party to countless contracts. The agreements may have been **express**, when made in words

Exhibit 8–1: How Are Contracts Classified?

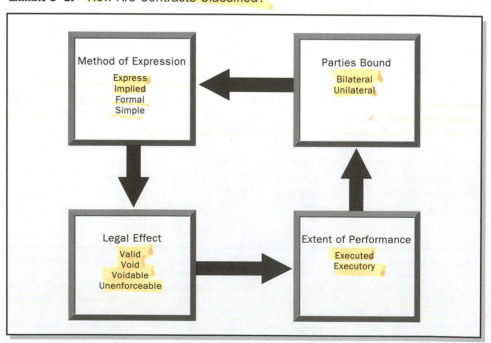

spoken or written, or they may have been **implied in fact**, when manifested in conduct or body language (e.g., an arm waved at a vendor in a stadium during a football game followed by the toss of money and a return toss of a bag of roasted peanuts). Contracts often are neither simply express or implied but combine express and implied terms.

Sometimes the law will imply and enforce an obligation even when there is no true agreement either express or implied between the parties. Such an obligation is called a *quasi-contract*. The law creates a quasi-contract when, under the circumstances, there would be unjust enrichment of one person unless he or she was required to pay value for a benefit received from someone else. The law provides that recovery in court is the reasonable value of the benefit received. Thus, a person may be required to perform as though a contract exists, even though no promise was made and no intent to be bound was manifested. A fairly common example of how a quasi-contract may come into being follows.

A surgeon stops her car at the scene of an automobile collision. She gives needed emergency aid to an unconscious victim at the accident. There was no agreement, yet the doctor has a legitimate claim in quasi-contract for the reasonable value of her services. In contrast, a passer-by with some knowledge of first aid who performed similar services is not entitled to any payment. Such an act would be that of a helpful volunteer, not of a professional who is customarily paid for such services.

Generally, the parties to an express contract or an implied in fact contract can use any language they please. In some cases, however, statutes prescribe the terms and exact language. Examples are negotiable instruments such as bank checks and promissory notes. These special types of contracts are called **formal contracts**; other types of contracts are called **simple contracts**, whether they are oral or written.

PARTIES BOUND

In most contracts, both parties exchange legally binding promises. Such an agreement is a **bilateral contract**; that is, a promise made in exchange for another promise. For example, Dawn agrees to try to find Angie's dog during a 24-hour period in exchange for Angie's promise to pay $50. If Dawn looks for the dog as promised, she is entitled to collect the $50 whether or not she succeeds in her search. Note that at the time the contract is created neither party has performed the promise they made to the other. In contrast, an offer for a **unilateral contract** is actually a potential agreement. One party makes a promise or offer to induce some completed *act* by another party. For example, Tore promises to pay $50 to anyone who will find and return his dog, dead or alive. No one is legally obliged to join in the search, nor is Tore obliged to pay unless the requested act is done and the dog is returned.

In May 1927, Charles A. ("Lucky") Lindbergh became the first person to fly across the Atlantic Ocean solo and nonstop from New York to Paris, using a single-engine monoplane, "The Spirit of St. Louis." Lindbergh was responding to a unilateral contract offer made by a St. Louis businessman to pay $25,000 to the first person(s) to perform the feat. After he was aloft and on his way (a substantial effort to perform), the offer could not be revoked or cancelled. Once the offeree has clearly started to perform, the law requires that the offeree have a reasonable time to complete the act, even though the offeree is not legally obliged to finish.

LEGAL EFFECT

If a contract complies with all essential elements (described in the next section), it is a **valid contract.** Sometimes the attempt to create a contract may be totally ineffective, and so there is no contract; in such a case, there is a **void agreement**. An example is an agreement to commit a crime or a tort. Sometimes an essential element of a valid contract is missing, and a party to the contract has the power to perform or withdraw without liability. Such contract is said to be **voidable**. For example, a minor (under age 18) may generally invalidate or void a contract even if freely and intentionally made. A parent or guardian may also take such action on the minor's behalf.

Finally, some contracts are valid yet **unenforceable**. A proper contract claim for money or performance may have become stale and unenforceable because enforcement was not sought before the time provided under the statute of limitations had passed. For example, a creditor may have a right to be paid the balance due on a retail store credit account. The typical statute of limitations requires that such creditors sue within four years of the due date, otherwise collection is barred.

EXTENT OF PERFORMANCE

If a contract has been fully performed by both parties, it is an **executed** contract. Sometimes parties to a contract say that they have "executed the agreement" when they have simply signed the written contract. But the parties must perform the promises contained in their contract before it is truly an executed contract.

If something remains to be done by either or both parties, it is an **executory contract**. Often sales contracts for goods, such as automobiles, are coupled with warranties as to performance for specified periods of time or extent of use (e.g., warranty for three years or 30,000 miles, whichever comes first). Although the basic contract may be executed, obligations created by the warranty remain for the specified time. Also, as noted in Chapter 7, if the user is injured by some defect in the product, the manufacturer may be strictly liable in tort for damages whether or not the warranty period has expired.

WHAT ARE THE REQUISITES OF A VALID CONTRACT?

There are six requisites for a valid contract: *competent parties* who make a *mutual agreement* with *genuine assent* supported by *reciprocal consideration* and which is legal in *formation and execution* and in the *form prescribed by law*. Let us examine each requisite.

COMPETENT PARTIES

The first essential for validity is **competent parties**, meaning that the parties who contract must have *legal capacity* to do so. The law generally expects that human beings will act as rational beings with freedom of will or of choice among alternative courses of action. Thus, the apparent agreement of a party may be negated by (1) infancy or minority (under age 18 in most states), (2) incapacitating mental condition that prevents the person from knowing the nature and consequences of a contract, or (3) incapacitating intoxication. Although most persons have full capacity (i.e., legal qualification or power) to contract, a large number do not. The law denies them the rights that flow from contracting, primarily to protect them from the burdensome duties of performance in foolish or improvident agreements. The restrictive denial also serves to protect them from possible exploitation by unscrupulous persons who might take unfair advantage of their ignorance, naivete, or incapacity.* In all three basic types of incapacity, the contract made is usually *voidable*, but only at the option of the incompetent person (or parent or guardian in control). The agreement is sometimes but seldom absolutely *void*. It is occasionally valid. Exhibit 8-2 illustrates the parallel status of minors, the mentally incompetent, and intoxicated persons.

Exception for Necessaries

An agreement to purchase goods or services that are **necessaries** is enforceable as a quasi-contract. In such a case, no valid contract exists, but a contractual remedy of reasonable compensatory damages is allowed to prevent unjust enrichment of the person who received the necessaries. Only the fair price would have to be paid, which might be different from the bargained-for price. Necessaries include such things as food, clothing, shelter, and medical care appropriate for a person's station in life. They must be truly needed, yet not be available from or provided by the parent or guardian of the incompetent.

Many business firms aggressively promote sales of cars, audiovisual and electronic equipment, and other items to minors, especially teenagers. They do this knowing that most of the purchases will not be returned even when the legal right to do so exists. To many teenagers, nothing is more precious than the freedom and independence provided by their very own car. Such persons are not likely to return cars, or indeed any other deeply coveted products, and demand refunds. Moreover, such items are usually acquired with parental knowledge and often with parental financial assistance. For big-ticket items, prudent retailers often require parental acknowledgement or approval and financial responsibility (e.g., by cosigning a promissory note or security agreement).

California Family Code § 6750 et seq. allows minors to engage in various entertainment industry venues. Read about filing petitions to approve minors' talent agency contracts and contracts in art, entertainment, and professional sports at http://home.earthlink.net/ ~barbdg/

MUTUAL AGREEMENT

The second essential of a valid contract is self-evident: The parties must come to a *mutual agreement*. There must be an *offer* by one and an *acceptance* by the other. There must be an agreement of the parties to the same thing (in Latin, a *consensus ad idem*). Thus, speaking quaintly, many laypersons and even some courts say

---

*In a few instances, the restriction is a form of punishment (as where prisoners are barred from most contract activity) or national defense (as where enemies in times of war are barred from contracting with American citizens).

Exhibit 8–2: General Patterns of Effects of Incapacity on Agreements (caveat: in some states variations exist in definitions and effects)

Contracting Party	Valid Contract	Voidable Contract	Void Agreements
Minor	■ *All* contracts, if married. ■ *All* contracts, if emancipated.* ■ *All* court-approved contracts. ■ Contract to enlist in armed service (at age 17) ■ In some states, contracts for loans incurred to pay for necessaries, including education and medical care.**	■ *Most* contracts. ■ To avoid liability, any goods received must be returned if still available. ■ *Some* states do not require a full refund even if goods cannot be returned, and even if minor lied about age; in most states the minor may disaffirm the contract, but is liable for any depreciation and wear and tear or use. ■ The contract may be ratified or avoided within a reasonable time after person reaches majority age.	■ *Some* attempts to contract; e.g., an apparent contract to name an agent or to dispose of real property.
Mentally incompetent person	■ *All* contracts, if person is merely neurotic. ■ *All* contracts made during a lucid interval of full sanity.	■ *All* attempts to contract made when person is entirely without understanding. ■ Any goods received must be returned, unless they are no longer available and other party acted in bad faith.	■ *All* attempts to contract, if person has been judicially declared insane and a guardian has been appointed.
Intoxicated person	■ *All* contracts, if the person is sober enough to understand the nature of the contract (even if he or she would not have made the contract if sober).	■ *All* attempts to contract made when person is too intoxicated to understand the nature of the contract. ■ Avoidance, to be effective, must be prompt after regaining sobriety and learning of the agreement.	■ *All* attempts to contract, if person has been judicially declared a victim of habitual intoxication and a guardian has been appointed.

*Living separate from consenting parents and managing own financial affairs.
**In most states this will be a quasi-contract rather than a "valid" contract.

there must be a "meeting of the minds." This subjective concept, however, is not strictly true. The law requires external or objective manifestation, in words or actions, of willingness to deal. Intent is decided by the objective theory of contracts. A party's intent to enter into a contract is judged by outward objective facts; persons are bound by what they express, either by their words or by their conduct. Internal, subjective thoughts remain secret. Before, during, and after an agreement of any complexity is entered, the parties seldom disclose the full content of their mental thinking about the terms of the contract.

The Offer

Three elements are necessary for an offer to be effective:

1. The offer must manifest an intention to be legally bound.
2. The terms of the offer must be reasonably definite and certain so a court can fashion a remedy.
3. The offer must be communicated to the offeree.

Adam and three other students ride to college each day in June's new-to-her automobile. Her car is worth $8,000. One cold morning just after everyone got into her car, it would not start. June yelled in anger, "I'll sell this car to anyone for $20!" Adam immediately dropped the $20 in her lap. Does Adam, the offeree, have a contract with June and a right to the car? Did June, the offeror, intend to create a contract?

For a valid offer, the person making the offer (called the *offeror*) must manifest an intent to be bound, to make a business agreement, a contract. The offer must not be made in obvious jest or in panicky fear. June's expression is obviously made in anger, excitement, or as a joke and it does not meet the objective-intent test. Since the offer is not effective, Adam's attempt to accept does not create an agreement. Likewise, an invitation to a social engagement or date is not a legal offer. If accepted, either party without legal liability may cancel it.

Most advertisements are also not legal offers to sell; instead, they are considered to be invitations to the world to come in and make offers to buy, to negotiate. Thus, under contract law an advertiser generally cannot be compelled to sell goods on the terms stated in an ad. Of course, if the ad is deliberately false or misleading, the advertiser may be liable for a tortuous or criminal act. Catalogs, price lists, circulars, and other pricing vehicles used by companies are treated in the same fashion as advertisements.

You put an ad in the classified section of the local newspaper offering to sell your favorite guitar for $75. Seven people call and "accept" your "offer" before you could remove the ad from the newspaper. If the ad is truly an offer, you would be bound by seven contracts to sell your guitar. But since *initial* advertisements are treated as *invitations* to make offers rather than as offers, you would have seven offers to choose from. You could accept the best one without assuming any liability for the six you reject.

The offer must be reasonably definite and certain. In case of a dispute, a court must be able to determine what the parties agreed to do.

Among the terms the court expects to find in a valid offer are:

1. Parties—who and how many.
2. Subject matter—what and how many.
3. Time of performance—when, delivery terms, warranties.
4. Price—how much and when to be paid.

Many common contracts are considered sufficiently definite and certain even though important terms are left unsettled. An example is a contract where one is hired to work and the duration of the employment is not stated; such a contract is considered an employment at will. Also, contracts for the professional services of a doctor, dentist, lawyer, or accountant are often made without clear knowledge of the full scope of the time and effort that will be needed, and so no fixed fee is given. In these situations, when the price is finally set it must be reasonable in light of all the circumstances. When such uncertainty is troubling or unacceptable, one can insist on a specific figure or an hourly rate, stated in advance. To cover contingencies, error is likely to be on the side of charging too much rather than too little.

Finally, the offer must be communicated to the person to whom is it made (called the *offeree*). Only the offeree or an authorized agent of the offeree may accept. In daily life, the parties to contracts usually identify themselves more precisely than as offeror–offeree. They may be known as student–university, seller–buyer, doctor–patient, employer–employee, lawyer–client, landlord–tenant, bailor–bailee, and so forth.

The Acceptance

To create a contract, the offeree must accept the offer by making a positive response to the offeror. General rules of contract law require that **acceptance** be a mirror-image response to the offer. It must be a timely, responsive, and unequivocal affirmation of a desire to enter into the contract on the terms of the offer. It also must be communicated to the offeror or to the offeror's authorized agent. The rules of acceptance for contracts involving the sale of goods (i.e., essentially movable and tangible things, other than money and securities) under the Uniform Commercial Code are more flexible as to what constitutes an acceptance. For all types of transactions, the courts will look for a timely response showing that the offeree wishes to be contractually bound.

Under the UCC, an offer to make a contract for the sale of goods is "construed as inviting acceptance in any manner and by any medium reasonable in the circumstances."[3] Generally, unless otherwise specified, the offeree may accept by the same or faster means than were used by the offeror. Today many communications of offers and acceptances are made by telephone, fax machines, e-mail, or overnight express delivery services. When an offer is made by U.S. Postal Service mail, the offeror impliedly authorizes the offeree to respond by mail, unless otherwise specified.[4] The acceptance is effective, and a contract arises, when the acceptance is properly posted (i.e., placed in the custody of the U.S. Postal Service with the correct address and proper postage), even if the letter of acceptance is lost in transit. The rule is often called the *deposit acceptance rule*.* Similarly, if Western Union telegram service or private overnight express delivery services are used, the acceptance is effective when the offeree gives the document to the delivery service.

How Long Does an Offer Last?

An offer, once made, does not last forever. It is ended by the *lapse of time*, if specified (e.g., "Let me know before Friday the 27th"). If no time is stated, then it ends after a reasonable time—an elastic concept that varies with the circumstances (e.g., a broker's offer to sell fresh strawberries may be good for a few hours; an offer made in June to sell loads of firewood may be good for several months).

Restatement (Second) of Contracts, § 30, provides that an offer invites acceptance "by any medium reasonable in the circumstances," unless the offer is specific about the means of acceptance. Under § 65, a medium is reasonable if it is one used by the offeror or one customary in similar transactions, unless the offeree knows of circumstances that would argue against the reasonableness of a particular medium (the need for speed because of rapid price changes, for example).

An offer is also ended by the destruction of the subject matter.[5] For example, Annabel offers to sell her pickup truck to Waukem. Before Waukem accepts the offer, the truck is damaged beyond reasonably practicable repair. Death or mental incompetence of either party also precludes acceptance and ends the offer.[6]

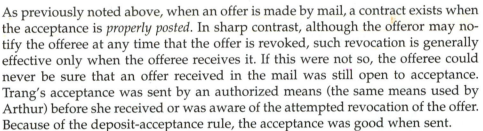

Saturday, Arthur mailed Trang an offer to sell his car for $1,000. On Monday, Arthur changed his mind and, not having heard from Trang, sent her a letter revoking his offer. On Wednesday, before she had received Arthur's letter of revocation, Trang mailed a letter of acceptance to Arthur. Trang demands that Arthur sell his car as promised, but Arthur claims that no contract exists because the offer was revoked prior to Trang's acceptance. Is Arthur correct?

As previously noted above, when an offer is made by mail, a contract exists when the acceptance is *properly posted*. In sharp contrast, although the offeror may notify the offeree at any time that the offer is revoked, such revocation is generally effective only when the offeree receives it. If this were not so, the offeree could never be sure that an offer received in the mail was still open to acceptance. Trang's acceptance was sent by an authorized means (the same means used by Arthur) before she received or was aware of the attempted revocation of the offer. Because of the deposit-acceptance rule, the acceptance was good when sent.

If a week was originally specified "to let you think it over," the offeror can nevertheless generally revoke the offer, without liability, before acceptance. Remember promises are enforceable only when a contract is formed, so a promise to keep an offer open can usually be broken without recourse. To avoid such possibility, the offeree may pay the offeror to keep the offer open for an agreed length of time by entering into an **option contract**.* An enforceable option is part of two separate, related contracts. One contract is an agreement that gives the offeree a fixed time to accept the offer in the second contract. During this period, the offeror does not have the legal right to revoke. The offeree pays the offeror something of value to create the option contract. An option contract is often used in the negotiation of real estate sales. The separateness of these aspects of option contract is reflected in the federal income tax laws, whereby option money is not taxed if it were purchase money.

Subsequent incompetence, or even death, does not terminate an offer made in an option contract (unless the offeror's personal performance is essential).[7] In such cases, generally a personal representative may perform, as by delivering goods or paying the price.

Now the offeree-option holder knows that he or she has the agreed-on option time to reflect, look at alternatives, or use the time to arrange financing. If the offeree-option holder decides to accept the original offer, any money paid for the option might be applied to the purchase price, if the parties had so agreed. If he or she rejects the offer, the offeror simply keeps that money as compensation for keeping the offer open.

Option contracts are the subject matter of major trading bodies such as the Chicago Board of Trade. http://www.cbot.com/

http://

---

*A merchant, unlike a casual seller of goods, may make a binding *firm offer* to keep the offer open for a stated time up to three months. It is not essential that the offeree pay for such a right, but the agreement must be in writing and signed by the merchant offer UCC § 2-205.

The parties may haggle over the terms of the contract. In doing so, an un-equivocal *rejection* of the offer by the offeree would end it. The rejection may take effect immediately, if made during oral negotiations; if mailed, it is effective only when received. Similarly, a *counteroffer* would end it.* Noncommittal words such as, "Your price sounds too rich for my diet, but let me sleep on that offer," would have no effect. Understandably, death or insanity of either party, or destruction of the subject matter, ends the offer.

RECIPROCAL CONSIDERATION

When a man keeps hollering, "It's the principle of the thing," he's talking about the money.

Frank Hubbard, *American humorist, 1868–1930*

The third requisite of a valid contract is the presence of *reciprocal consideration*. Consideration, in this context, simply means the value given in exchange for a promise or an act. The parties "bargain for," that is, freely negotiate, an exchange of promises and/or acts whereby each party ultimately enjoys some legal benefit and each suffers some legal detriment. Each party gives; each party receives. What is given and received must have legal value; generally it need not be equal or adequate by any other person's standards of valuation. Thus a promise of a gift is not legally enforceable because the donor is promised nothing of legal value in return. To say "Gee, thanks!" or "I love you!" is not consideration.

Recalling that in a bilateral contract each party is both promisor and promisee, study the following explanation of consideration provided by the *Restatement of Contracts*. Consideration may be (1) a return promise (e.g., to pay money or to give some service or property), (2) an act other than a promise (as in unilateral contracts), (3) a forbearance (where one party refrains from doing what he or she has a legal right to do), or (4) the creation, modification, or destruction of a legal relationship (where, e.g., the parties agree to become associated as business partners).

Jerry says to Max, "If you paint the garage green, I will pay you $100." Max paints the garage green. Can Max legally require Jerry to pay the $100? Is consideration present?

The answer to both questions is yes. The act of painting the garage is the consideration requested and in this case given in return for Jerry's promise to pay.

Suppose instead that Jerry says to Max, "In consideration of your not being as wealthy as my other friends, I will pay you $500 next Tuesday." Can Max legally require Jerry to pay him the $500? Does consideration exist?

---

*It is interesting to note that between merchants, an acceptance may be valid and binding on both parties "even though it states terms additional to or different from those offered or agreed upon. . . ." However, this provision of the UCC, § 2–207, is subject to a number of conditions that effectively maintain the offeror's control and ability to re-quire that acceptance comply with his or her terms if there is to be a contract.

No. Jerry's promise is not enforceable, because consideration is absent. Max did not pay anything (give consideration) for the $500 promised. Jerry simply stated his motive for an intended *gift* to Max. Note that use of the word *consideration* does not, alone, mean that consideration was given. Consideration is the sweetener that induces both parties to perform as promised. It conforms to the natural and customary human tendency to expect to receive something in exchange for something given, unless a gift is intended. Thus, in so-called illusory agreements there is no reciprocal consideration and therefore no contract. Examples would be where the parties "agree to agree," or when a supplier agrees to sell all goods of a given type that the buyer "may want," which may actually be none at all. This is distinguishable from a deal where the seller agrees to sell and the buyer agrees to buy all of the specified type of goods that the buyer may actually and measurably need or require during a stated period of time.

Similarly, there is no consideration when the promisor is already bound to do the act (e.g., when a police officer, for a promised fee, agrees to try to apprehend a burglar) or when some past consideration is involved (e.g., when A rescues B from drowning and *subsequently* B promises to pay A $5,000).

Under some special circumstances, consideration is not required as a matter of public policy. An illustration is a pledge or charitable subscription to a church or nonprofit hospital or school. The pledge states that it is for the purpose of erecting a library building, and it is made, in part, to induce others to contribute. Such a promise is legally binding in most states, even if the donor gets no valuable consideration in return. Of course, the charity must act in reliance on the pledge, for example, by contracting for construction of the new facility. Likewise, no consideration need be given by a creditor for a new promise by a debtor to pay a debt that has been barred from enforcement by bankruptcy (discussed later in this chapter) or by the statute of limitations.

Debra borrows $500 from Carter. She gives Carter a promissory note in which she promises to pay to the order of Carter the $500 with yearly interest of 7 percent one year from the date. A year passes, and no payment is made. Four more years (the statutory period of limitations for written contracts) pass, and still no payment is made. Carter has thereby lost the legal right to compel payment through court action. A year later, Debra has pangs of conscience and, apologizing and promising to pay the note in full, sends Carter a letter. Is this promise enforceable?

Yes, this promise revives the debt, even though Carter gave no new consideration. But if Debra verbally agreed to pay the debt, it would not be revived. An oral promise lacks the evidentiary value of the written note. A partial payment, identified as such by the debtor, would also revive the debt. Carter now has four more years in which to seek payment by court action.

GENUINE ASSENT

The fourth essential of a valid contract is that the agreement be made with the genuine assent, or real consent, of both parties. Assent is negated when either party acts under duress or because of undue influence. Assent, although given, is also fatally flawed if it resulted from fraud or certain types of mistakes.

Duress

http://

See definition of duress in Rupp's Insurance Glossary and Buyers Resource http://www.nils.com/rupps/ and http://homes.inresco.com/ Glossary/DURESS.html

An unusual occurrence in contract law, **duress**, happens when one party is prevented from exercising judgment and free will by some wrongful act or threat of the other party. It could result from threat of imprisonment (e.g., "I'll keep you locked up until you sign this contract!") or of physical injury to the other party or to a close relative or friend (e.g., "Sign here or I'll bash you so hard you'll never ever sign anything again!"). In addition, blackmail to induce consent to a contract is duress. The victim of the duress can generally choose to carry out the contract or to avoid the entire transaction, although duress involving a serious threat of violence leads to no contract at all, a void agreement. A threat of criminal prosecution would be duress; not so the comparatively common threat of civil suit to collect a debt. Why the difference? The first is a form of extortion or menace; the second is the voicing of a legal right to sue for money owed.

Economic need is generally not a basis for a finding of duress, even when one party charges a very high price for an item the other party needs. If the party charging the price also creates the need, however, economic duress may be found.

The Internal Revenue Service assessed a large tax and penalty against Sam Thompson. Thompson retained Earl Eyman to represent him to reduce the tax and penalty. The last day before the deadline for filing a reply with the IRS, Eyman refused to represent Thompson. He said he would reconsider if Thompson signed an agreement to pay a much higher fee than previously agreed. Is the agreement enforceable?

No. Although Eyman threatened only to withdraw his services, something he could legitimately do if done in proper time, he delayed his withdrawal until the last day. It would have been practically impossible at that late date for Thompson to get adequate representation elsewhere. Because Thompson was forced into signing the contract or losing his right to challenge the IRS assessment, the contract is voidable by him.

Undue Influence

Although peaceful and more subtle than duress, **undue influence** has the same effect: depriving a party of freedom of will in choosing a course of action. Wrongful persuasion and persistent pressure accomplish it. Typically, the wrongdoer asserts his or her position or authority or exploits the victim's misplaced confidence in the wrongdoer's apparent good faith and wisdom and, for example, obtains property from the victim at a price well below fair market value.

When Mabel Taylor reached her eightieth birthday, she was no longer able to drive her car. Her nephew, Ray, convinced Mabel that she should sell him the car for $50. Ray told Mabel that if she did not agree then he would no longer visit her. The actual value of the car was $7,000. This agreement is not enforceable because Ray is taking advantage of his special relationship with Mabel.

A suspicion of undue influence exists when parties are in a confidential or fiduciary relationship. Examples include that of parent and child, husband and wife, client and lawyer, guardian and ward, conservator and elderly conservatee, and principal and agent. Because one party relies so heavily on the other, the law requires the utmost good faith, scrupulous honesty, and full disclosure by the dominant party in dealings between the parties. To overcome a presumption of undue influence, the dominant party should make a full disclosure of all relevant facts; insist that the other party get the advice of qualified, independent counsel; and make honest, fair contracts.

Fraud

The essential elements of **fraud** are (1) false representation, a lie, (2) of a material (important) (3) fact (generally not a personal opinion, unless an expert is expressing it) (4) known to be false (or made with reckless indifference as to its truth or made with blameworthy ignorance of its falsity), (5) made with intent to deceive the victim and induce the victim to contract as a result of which (6) the victim is deceived and contracts in reliance on the lie, and (7) the victim is thereby injured.

A good site for information about fraud in consumer contracts can be found at the National Fraud Information Center of the National Consumers League at http://www.fraud.org/

Peter Pride, proprietor of "Cars You're Proud To Own," sold a used car to Lilly Le, a first-car buyer. Peter, who knew otherwise, said the car had one previous owner (actually, there had been two); had never been in an accident (actually, a rear fender, trunk and a bumper had been replaced after a collision); and had the original paint (the car had been repainted). The odometer showed 52,000 miles, and Peter said the engine had been overhauled (in fact, the odometer had been turned back from 66,000 miles, and the engine had been given only a tune-up). Peter had also claimed the car had new tires (they looked new to a neophyte but were actually retreads). Peter claimed the car was worth $10,000 but since he was trying to reduce his inventory, he'd let Lily "steal it" for only $7,500. Gullible Lily believed him, and relying on Peter's sales pitch bought the car for the asking price. She soon learned that in its actual condition, it was worth no more than $2,500. Is Peter Pride guilty of fraud? If so, what can Lily do?

Yes, Peter is guilty of fraud. He made a series of misrepresentations of fact, known to be false, intending to deceive Lily and to induce her to buy. Lily was deceived, and acting in reliance on the lies bought the car to her injury. Lily has several options.

She could *rescind* (cancel or undo) the contract, return the car, and demand a full refund of her $7,500.[8] In addition, she could sue for compensatory and punitive (or exemplary) damages (see Chapter 7). In a minority of states, Lily's compensatory damages would be the *out-of-pocket loss* suffered (i.e., the difference in value between what she gave—$7,500—and the value of what she got—$2,500—or a net $5,000). In most states, her compensatory damages under the **benefits-of-the-bargain rule** would be the difference between the value of what she received ($2,500) and the value of performance as misrepresented by the defendant Peter

($10,000), or a net $7,500. In either case, in most states Lily could also sue for punitive damages in addition to the compensatory damages because of Peter's intentional tort of fraud. Here the jury might award as much as $50,000 or more.*

Cullen contracts to purchase a hearing assistance dog from Estacio. The dog is blind in one eye but when Estacio shows the dog, he skillfully conceals this fact by turning the dog's head so Cullen cannot see the defect. All of the dog's senses are important in fulfilling the hearing assistance tasks. Is this concealment fraud?

Yes, this knowing concealment constitutes fraud. Another example of misrepresentation by conduct is the false denial of knowledge or information concerning facts that are material to the contract when such knowledge or information is requested. It is important that a purchaser ask many questions.

Mutual Mistake

When both parties have an erroneous idea or understanding about some fact that is an important element of the contract, there is a **mutual** or **bilateral mistake** that generally renders their agreement void, or voidable by either party. When both parties are mistaken about a material (i.e., important) fact, either party may rescind (i.e., cancel or annul the contract without liability). If the error were not obvious, the same court would not excuse the mistaken party.

Defendant Wichelhaus contracted to buy 125 bales of cotton from plaintiff Raffles. They agreed that the cotton would come from Bombay, India, to Liverpool on the ship *Peerless*. Buyer Wichelhaus reasonably thought the goods would arrive on a ship named *Peerless* that was scheduled to sail in October. Seller Raffles reasonably thought of another ship, which also happened to be named *Peerless*, but which was scheduled to sail from Bombay in December. When the cotton finally arrived, much later than expected by Wichelhaus, he refused to accept or pay for it. Was Wichelhaus legally bound by the alleged contract?[9]

No, according to this landmark old English case. Acting in good faith, the parties referred to different ships, sailing at significantly different times. The mutual mistake of fact rendered the agreement voidable. Note that different opinions as to *value* (e.g., of a parcel of land, a jewel, or a share of stock) or *expectations* of future value do not affect the validity of the contract. Likewise, a **unilateral mistake** (by one party) about value, expectations, or the applicability of a statute, such as a zoning law, generally does not affect the contract. However, suppose one party is mistaken or errs in submitting a bid on a construction job. The other party recognizes the obvious error but says nothing, and quickly signs the contract. A court of equity would permit the mistaken party to withdraw without liability.

---

*Peter has also violated a federal criminal statute, 49 U.S.C.A. § 32701 et seq., and undoubtedly state criminal statutes, as well (e.g. West's Ann.Cal.Vehicle Code § 11713) that regulate the sale of vehicles.

Jane Collins contracts to purchase one of two antique washing machines owned by Mike Heimer. Jane thinks she has purchased a white one, a premier model. Mike thinks Jane has purchased the beige one, his less valuable washing machine. Does a contract exist?

No. Jane and Mike have made a genuine mutual mistake of fact. Jane believes the contract subject matter is the white washing machine, while Mike believes it is the beige one. Nothing is more material than the subject matter of the contract. Since both parties are mistaken about the subject matter, no contract exists.

Suppose instead Jane contracts to buy the white washing machine, believing it to be worth $1,000 when it really is worth only $250. Can Jane escape the contract because of her mistake?

No. Jane's mistake is one of *value* or *quality*, not fact. A mistake of this nature does not normally affect the enforceability of the contract.

LEGALITY IN FORMATION AND EXECUTION

As the fifth, and in many cases, the final requisite for validity, the contract must be legal in its formation and in its proposed execution. Generally, an agreement may fail to qualify either because it is (1) contrary to some statute or (2) contrary to public policy (i.e., prevailing community standards as to what is contrary to the public good, or commonweal).

Violations of Statutes

The gangland expression, "There's a contract out on him," refers to an agreement to kill a designated victim. Such agreement is obviously illegal and void. The same summary condemnation would apply to any agreement to commit a tort. Not so clear is the legal status of agreements (1) to gamble or conduct lotteries, (2) to practice a trade or profession without a license, (3) to engage in profit-seeking business on Sundays, and (4) to charge interest rates that might be usurious. Consider the confusing status of these practices.

Gambling. Traditionally, gambling agreements, lotteries, and games of chance have been illegal when they involved three elements: (1) some payments by the gambler (2) for a chance (3) to win some prize. However, many states now have certain legal forms of gambling. Pressure to raise public revenues in recent years has led to this legalization (according to some observers, a highly regressive form of taxation). Critics object to such activity as economically wasteful (unless one regards the dubious entertainment effect to be a valuable product). They say that the gullible and the ignorant thereby squander money that would be better spent for necessaries, and that gambling promoters cynically pander to greed and unfounded hope by suggesting that "you, too, can get rich quick," despite astronomical odds against such a result.

Sometimes it is difficult to distinguish a gambling contract from the risk-sharing inherent in most contracts.

Jaime takes out a life insurance policy on an acquaintance, Botello. Jaime names himself as the beneficiary (the person to be paid) under the policy. Is this a legal contract or a gambling agreement?

The life insurance policy contract appears legal; however, Jaime is simply gambling on how long Botello will live. To prevent this type of contract, only someone with an **insurable interest** is allowed to recover on an insurance contract. An insurable interest exists when a person has a real economic risk related to the property or person insured. If your watch is stolen or damaged, for example, you suffer a real loss. If someone else's watch is stolen or broken, you may feel bad, but you suffer no direct economic loss. Thus, you have an insurable interest in your watch, but not in the other person's. Jaime cannot collect on an insurance policy on Botello's life (home or auto) because Jaime does not have an insurable interest in Botello or his property. If Jaime were a part owner in Botello's automobile, however, he could legally collect on an insurance policy on the auto because he has a property interest.

If an insurance company is aware a person applying for insurance lacks an insurable interest, the company should refuse to sell the policy. An insurer that sells a policy unaware that the holder lacks an insurable interest will claim lack of insurable interest as a defense to a claim for payment upon learning the truth. An innocent claimant will get a return of the premiums paid but not a payment on the policy.

See one state's (Missouri) grounds for refusal, revocation, or suspension of licenses required for enforceable contracts at http://www.moga.state.mo.us /statutes/C300-399/ 3370630.htm

Licensing. Many professions and trades require a license to practice (engage in business). Traditionally, the legitimate objective of such licensing laws has been to protect the public against unqualified practitioners. Too often, though, the dominant objective has been to limit entry in order to reduce competition in service and price. Nevertheless, contracts made by unlicensed persons are generally unenforceable; they cannot collect for services rendered. However, when the true objective of the licensing is to raise government revenues, failure to obtain a license does *not* render the contracts of the parties unenforceable or void. This would be true of a license required of all profit-making business firms in a city.

Paris was a real estate broker licensed in the state of Georgia. Paris contacted Cooper, a Florida resident who was interested in purchasing some Gulf County, Florida, acreage. Paris visited the property in Florida, helped prepare Cooper's written offer of purchase, worked with Cooper's attorney on the sales contract, and attended the closing of the sale in Panama City, Florida. As a result of this sale, Paris received a $315,070 commission. Can Cooper recover the commission on the basis that the contract is unenforceable because Paris was not licensed to conduct real estate transactions in Florida?

Yes. An agent must have a real estate license to represent a client in a real estate transaction and expect to collect a fee. Such licenses are granted by each state to protect the citizens of that state. A license in Georgia does not authorize the agent to practice in Florida. The agent could not collect the commission, and if the commission had been paid, the client could sue for its return.[10]

Blue Laws. In some states, strong support continues for traditional observance of the Sabbath as a day of rest and worship as mandated by the Mosaic Code.[11] Accordingly, **blue laws*** restrict the right to make or perform various contracts on Sundays. When such laws have been challenged as a violation of the First Amendment respecting establishment of religion, the U.S. Supreme Court has refused to interfere. Such observance is justified for needed rest and relaxation, the Court's reasoning goes; any day of the week could be designated for the purpose.

Usury. Most states regulate the maximum rates of interest that may be charged for certain loans of money. *Usury* is the practice of charging excessively high rates on loans. Today most states maintain some control over how much interest may be charged, but, for example, they allow rates as high as 40 percent a year or more on loans of no more than a few hundred dollars made by pawnbrokers and small loan companies. The extra interest charge is justified by the higher unit cost of processing such loans and by a higher risk of defaults by borrowers. The availability of such loans also helps to keep the borrowers out of the clutches of loan sharks, who may charge interest rates of 100 percent a year or more. Civil sanctions for usury vary among the states. In some states, the usurer is barred from collecting either principal or interest; in others, only the principal is payable; and additional variations exist. But observers suggest that many violations are unreported, often because of ignorance or fear of violent retaliation.

The purchase of goods on credit, subject to a carrying charge (some states call it **interest**) on the unpaid balance, has not been considered usury because there is no direct loan of money. However, as this practice has become very widespread, legal limits are now often imposed on the percentage rate that may be imposed. The typical carrying charge (or "interest rate") approaches 20 percent a year. This is a heavy levy, in light of the fact that the ordinary saver seldom earns as much as 5 percent in a bank savings account. Note that the federal **Consumer Credit Protection Act of 1968** (often referred to as the **Truth-in-Lending Law**) requires a full disclosure of the terms of contracts for sales on credit or for loans.[12] But it does not set any ceiling at the federal level on the rate of interest that may be charged, nor does it limit the price that may be charged for the goods or services sold.

Read about the historical development of the concept of usury, "The Usury Debate in the Seventeenth Century," at http://www.moga.state.mo/us/statutes/C300-399/3370630.htm

The charging of interest is an important moral issue in some religions. Read about interest and the Koran at http://www.humanities.ccny.cuny.edu/history/reader/islamtrade.htm

Violations of Public Policy

Some agreements are obviously contrary to public policy and therefore illegal and void. The list includes attempts to obstruct justice in court by bribing jurors, paying a witness to lie under oath (this is the crime of **subornation of perjury**), or paying a witness more than the modest legal fee prescribed by statute. (Note that counsel may engage experts for both the plaintiff and the defendant, to study and render their opinions about facts of the case. They are often called on to testify during the trial. Such expert witnesses may legitimately receive fees for their services far in excess of payments made to other witnesses.) Also included in attempts to obstruct justice is paying bribes to influence legislators, administrators, and judges. Banned also, by the Foreign Corrupt Practices Act, are bribes to obtain contracts with foreign governments.[13]

*Blue laws originally referred to strict rules in colonial New England that outlawed such practices as working, dancing, and drinking intoxicating liquors on Sundays. The term now refers to statutes that regulate commercial activities and amusements on Sundays. In contrast, "blue sky laws" regulate the sale of stocks and bonds and are designed to prevent fraudulent sale of securities worth no more than patches of blue sky.

Lobbying, properly practiced, is vital to the democratic process of legislation. Lobbyists outnumber legislators in Congress and in most statehouses. They are usually employed under contracts with special-interest groups to persuade legislators to vote in a certain way on legislation. To many persons, "lobbyist" is a term of infamy, no doubt because the practice of lobbying has too often in the past been corrupted by bribery or veiled purchases of favors. Nevertheless, lobbyists serve a useful purpose in providing important information on the pros and cons of present and proposed legislation. Any person may lobby on his or her own behalf; however, federal and state statutes generally require that persons who lobby for other individuals or groups must register, identify their clients, and disclose the source and amounts of payments received and dispensed.

Agreements that restrict trade and competition are generally illegal. Such contracts, called **covenants not to compete**, often violate one or more federal or state statutes and are often construed as common-law torts as well. These restraints of trade are against the public interest, which favors free competition. There are two major potential exceptions to this rule of illegality:

1. When the restraint of free trade is part of an otherwise enforceable contract for the sale of a business.

2. When a new employee agrees, as part of the employment contract, not to accept another employment position with any other employer who is a competitor of the present employer.

To be legal, such agreements must involve a legitimate business need and can be no more extensive in time, scope, and distance than reasonably necessary to protect the future related interests of the protected parties (i.e., the buyer of the business and the first employer). Courts also consider the effect of enforcement of such agreements on the public good—the restriction on the freedom to purchase goods and services cannot be excessive and is balanced against the contracting party's legitimate business need.

A promise by a person selling a store not to open a new store close to the old store is an example of a covenant not to compete. A shoe retailer selling her business might appropriately agree not to open a competing business anywhere in a sparsely populated county for perhaps two years; a seller of a company manufacturing heavy-duty earth-moving machines headed by a brilliant inventor whose unique products are sold worldwide, might properly agree not to open a competing business anywhere for three or more years. Thus, the buyer properly gets the benefit of the price paid for the *goodwill** value of the going concern.

In employment contracts, it is common for middle-level and upper-level managers to agree not to work for competitors or start new competing business firms for a specified time after leaving the current employment relationship. The restriction on competition must be reasonable; it should not be any greater than necessary to protect a legitimate business interest.

In 1982, Thomas Rector and four other employees of Paramount Termite Control Company agreed not to compete with their employer if they quit.

An agreement not to compete is an important part of many employment contracts, particularly in industries with unique business information. This article addresses the business context of such clauses.
http://www.njlegalink.com/library/labor/empcont.htm

Goodwill is the valuable intangible asset of a business that is developed over a prolonged period of time through successful contractual relations with satisfied customers and suppliers. Thus, an established business with goodwill normally enjoys higher profits than a new business of the same size but lacking such goodwill.

For two years after leaving Paramount's employment, they agreed not to "solicit business from any customer of Paramount where the purpose thereof is to provide the services of pest control with which customer the employee established contact while in the employ of Paramount at any time during the two years next preceding the termination of the Employment Agreement." The agreement covered the geographic areas the employees serviced as Paramount employees. Later, the employees resigned from Paramount and began working for a Paramount competitor that solicited business in the counties prohibited by the non-competition agreement. Paramount sought to enforce the promise. Did Paramount succeed?[14]

Yes. The Supreme Court of Virginia declared the restriction on competition was reasonable in time (two-year period) and in the geographic area covered. The court applied three criteria: (1) From the standpoint of the employer, was the restraint reasonable—no greater than necessary to protect a legitimate business interest of the employer? (2) From the standpoint of the employee, was the restraint reasonable—not unduly harsh and oppressive in limiting the employee's ability to earn a living? (3) Was the restraint reasonable as sound public policy? The court concluded that the restraint was no greater than reasonably necessary to protect Paramount's legitimate business interest. The five employees "had frequent contacts with Paramount's customers" and "were familiar with Paramount's methods of estimating the cost of its work, its specifications for doing the work, and its techniques of pest control." The court also found the geographic restriction reasonable, as it applied only to those counties in which the employees had previously worked and not in all counties within the state. Finally, because there was sufficient competition in the area, the court held the restrictions did not unreasonably restrain trade or violate public policy.

Read the California case of *Kolani v. Gluska* about an over-broad covenant not to compete at http://lalabor.com/cases/tradesecrets/broad_covenant_not_to_compete.html#top

What Is the Effect of Illegality?

An illegal agreement is void, and courts will normally not aid either party to the transaction. Exceptions are made and damages in tort or other relief may be awarded (1) when the violated law is intended to protect one of the parties (this is true, for example, when one party is the victim of usury), (2) when the parties are not equally blameworthy (e.g., when one party is the victim of fraud in illegal securities dealing, or when one party acts under duress or undue influence), and (3) when one of the parties repents and withdraws before the time set for performance (as in illegal bets over the outcome of a football game).

FORM PRESCRIBED BY LAW

The last requisite of a contract requires the contracts be in the **form prescribed by law** to be enforceable. This requirement exists only for those contracts for which statutes have created this as an additional requirement. Such contracts may be deficient in form, yet otherwise be valid. Thus, if the party who is entitled to raise the issue of form does not object, the contract may be routinely performed (executed) by both parties. After the contract is performed, the question of proper form is usually moot (no longer open to argument).

What Is the Statute of Frauds and Perjuries?

See this article about the Statute of Frauds by Attorney Ron Kilgard. http://www.dgsk.com/DOC/THESTA~1.htm

By statute, certain specialized contracts must contain prescribed language. This is true of fire and homeowner insurance policies. It is also true of contracts for loans and for sales of goods on credit under the Truth-in-Lending Act. But the most important legislation governing form in contracts was originated in 1677 in the English **Statute of Frauds and Perjuries**.[15] In essence, this statute provided that certain designated important contracts, to be enforceable in court, must (1) be in writing and (2) be signed by the party against whom enforcement is sought, or by his or her agent. Note that no problem as to form arises if the party *seeking* to enforce the contract has not signed. Such party could simply and promptly sign the document if the other party points out the lack of a signature.

The English statute is the original model for many versions adopted in most American states, all designed to prevent parties from subsequently fraudulently misrepresenting the actual terms of their agreements.

Writing important agreements encourages more careful draftsmanship and thus reduces potential misunderstandings and costly litigation. The requirement of a signature permits free and open negotiation and exchange of unsigned tentative drafts of the contract without fear of unintended or premature commitment. Including a sentence requiring the losing party, in case of litigation, to pay all court costs and reasonable attorney fees of the winner can discourage breaches of contracts and spiteful lawsuits. Better still, the written contract can provide for arbitration or some other specified alternative method of dispute resolution (see Chapter 4). Although the Statute of Frauds should encourage careful draftsmanship, any writing satisfies the requirement if it sufficiently expresses the agreement. Of course, the party against whom enforcement is sought must sign it. The writing could consist of a memorandum or letter(s), for example.

The following rules are better understood if certain technical words are first defined. The word **property** has a double meaning. It usually means the thing that is owned; in a strict legal sense, however, *property* means the rights of the owner to possess, use, and dispose of that thing. Property is broadly classified as real or personal. **Real property** is the land and things "permanently attached" to the land, such as buildings. It includes rights to airspace above the land, to water on the surface, and to the materials below the surface (e.g., oil, gas, and minerals). **Personal property** includes all movable property other than land. Both real and personal property appear in tangible and intangible forms. **Tangible property** has physical existence—it can be touched or seen. In contrast, **intangible property** has conceptual existence; an example is your reputation. Examples of *tangible real property* are the ground or land and buildings erected on the land. An example of *intangible real property* is an easement. An *easement* is the right to use another person's real property within prescribed limits and without removing anything from the property. An example would be an easement to go across another's land to get to the shore of a lake or river. Examples of *tangible personal property* include this book, your watch, and a Big Mac at McDonald's. Examples of *intangible personal property* are the copyright on this book, the design patent on your watch, and the goodwill enjoyed by owners of McDonald's fast-food restaurants. Under the UCC, a **sale** "consists in the passing of title from the seller to the buyer for a price."[16] The person who has *title* owns the property.

What Contracts Must Comply with the Statute of Frauds?

The Statute of Frauds applies to the following kinds of contracts:

1. *A contract for the sale of land or an interest therein*. Some states also require a lease for more than one year to be in writing. Thus, a month-to-month lease, or a lease of as long as one year, is valid even if oral. Under what is called the *equal-dignities rule*, the real estate broker's employment agreement (sometimes called a *listing*) to search for a purchaser of real property must also be in writing and properly signed.

2. *A contract for the sale of tangible goods for the price of $500 or more*. Under the UCC, *goods* "means all things . . . which are movable . . . other than the money in which the price is to be paid, investment securities . . . and things in action" (which are rights to recover personal property or money by means of a trial or other judicial proceeding) "also . . . the un-born young of animals and growing crops and other identified things attached to realty."[17]

    Certain important exceptions are made to this rule by the UCC. An oral contract for goods priced at $500 or more is nevertheless enforceable "if the goods are to be specially manufactured for the buyer and are not suitable for sale to others in the ordinary course of the seller's business." An example would be a unique and elaborate cabinet made with costly imported woods to hold a variety of audiovisual equipment, complete with a wet bar and built-in refrigerator. Before notice of repudiation of the contract is received, the seller must have "made either a substantial beginning of their manufacture, or commitments for their procurement." Furthermore, the buyer is bound "with respect to goods for which payment has been made and accepted or which have been received and accepted." Finally, the buyer is bound who "admits in his [her] pleading, testimony, or otherwise in court that a contract for sale was made."[18] The contract in such case would be enforceable, but only for the quantity of goods admitted.

    The UCC provides a special rule for merchants. Assume that between merchants a writing in confirmation of the sales contract and sufficient *against the sender* (who has signed) is received within a reasonable time, and the recipient has reason to know its contents. This will satisfy the requirement of a signed writing against *the recipient (even though he or she has not signed)*, unless the recipient gives written notice of objection to its contents to the sender within ten days after it has been received.[19]

3. *A contract that is not to be performed, and cannot possibly be performed within one year from the date of the agreement*. In calculating the time, the law ignores fractions of days, including any fraction of the date of the agreement. Thus, an oral contract for one year, to begin tomorrow, is enforceable. If it is to begin two or more days hence, it must be in writing and signed.

    Jamal is set to graduate from college. An employer orally contracts with Jamal to employ him for two years at $2,000 per month. Is this contract required to be in writing?

Yes. Because the terms of the contract exceed one year, this contract must be proved by written evidence to be enforceable. The oral agreement is insufficient proof of the existence of the contract. The one-year period begins to run the day after the contract is made, even if performance is not expected to begin until later.

4. A secondary, or underlying contract under which one person promises to pay or answer for the debt or duty of another, if such person fails to perform, or one in which an executor or administrator of an estate promises to pay a debt of the estate with his or her own money.

5. A promise made in consideration of marriage (e.g., "If you marry me, I will support your parents until they die"). Note that a contract to marry, and the actual contract of marriage, may be, and usually are, expressed orally: "Will you marry me?" "Yes." "I now pronounce you husband and wife."

6. The UCC requirement of a signed, written contract also applies to contracts for the sale of kinds of personal property not otherwise covered, in an amount or value beyond $5,000.[20] This provision does not apply to contracts for the sale of goods, securities, or security agreements, all of which are covered separately.[21]

Sufficiency of the Writing

The Statute of Frauds does not require a complete written contract signed by both parties. The statute can also be satisfied with a far less extensive writing—a memorandum. The memorandum can consist of any confirmation, invoice, sales slip, check, or telegram. Such items, singly or in combination, may be writings sufficient to satisfy the Statute of Frauds. Requirements of the statute for the memorandum are as follows:

1. It must be signed by the party against whom enforcement is sought.
2. It must contain at least the essential terms of the contract.

It is not required that both parties sign the memorandum. The essential signature is the signature of the person against whom enforcement is sought (person being sued).

Shelly agreed to lease Eric's house for three years for $600 a month rent. Shelly found an old standard-form lease, filled out the terms, signed it, and gave it to Eric saying, "Please sign this lease, Eric." Eric responded that he had changed his mind and now would like $750 a month rent. Can Shelly enforce Eric's oral promise to lease the property for three years at $600 a month? Does the lease she signed satisfy the Statute of Frauds?

Shelly cannot enforce Eric's promise as a lease for a three-year term must be in writing to be enforceable. Although Shelly prepared the lease, Eric did not sign it, and Eric is the party against whom enforcement is sought. In other words, for a party to enforce a contract, the writing must be signed by the other party. Thus, it is possible for a contract to be enforceable by one party, but not by the other.

The signature can be placed anywhere on the writing. It need not be at the end. And a signature can be initials or even a mark rather than a full name. The law does not require a witness, although without a witness it is hard to prove who created a mark and whether the mark was intended as a signature. Shelly could have made a deposit by check (noting purpose of the payment on the check) and then Eric's signature as an endorsement would undoubtedly have satisfied the Statute of Frauds.

DIRECT INVOLVEMENT OF THIRD PARTIES IN CONTRACTS

THIRD-PARTY DONEE AND CREDITOR BENEFICIARIES

If a contract is valid and legally enforceable, attention turns to the rights and duties of the parties. A relationship is created between parties to a contract called **privity of contract**. Parties in privity of contract have rights and duties because of the contract. Usually, third parties not in privity have no rights under the contract.

Most bilateral and unilateral contracts directly involve only the two original contracting parties. However, from the very inception of their agreement, one party may name and provide for a **third-party beneficiary**. For example, a parent in a contract for ordinary life insurance may name a child as a beneficiary of the policy. Since the main purpose is to confer a gift upon a third party, the child who has paid nothing therefore qualifies as a *donee beneficiary*.[22] As such, the child may enforce the contract and collect the proceeds of the policy upon the death of the parent. If the main purpose of the promisee buying the policy is to pay a debt or extinguish an obligation owed to a third party, then the third party is a *creditor beneficiary*.[23]

When Nikkel sold his gift and novelty shop to Oddeon, there were accounts payable (money owed to creditors) on the books with a total of $12,000 owed to five suppliers. Oddeon agreed to pay the balance due as part of the purchase price of the shop. Thus, the five suppliers were third-party creditor beneficiaries in the sales contract, and they have legal claims under the contract against Oddeon.

Beneficiaries of contracts (whether donee or creditor) can sue to enforce a contract that was made purposely for their benefit. Not all persons who benefit from contracts are given the right to enforce beneficial promises, however. The courts distinguish between intended beneficiaries (who can sue to enforce the contract) and incidental beneficiaries (who cannot).

An incidental beneficiary is a person who benefits from a contract but is not named and has no legally enforceable rights or duties under the contract. An example would be the benefit that people enjoy when the government builds a road under contract, or when private developers build a shopping center. Probably everyone has been an incidental beneficiary in many contracts.

ASSIGNMENT OF CONTRACT
RIGHTS AND DELEGATION OF DUTIES

After a contract has been made, the original parties generally may assign their contractual rights and/or delegate their contractual duties to others. Unless properly released from their duties, the parties remain liable for full performance following assignment of their rights. In special situations, as where they involve uniquely personal services, the duties may not be delegated. Thus without consent of the other party, a surgeon may not transfer an accepted duty of performing an operation. Likewise, unless otherwise agreed, one may not transfer rights to personal services. A transfer of rights may not be made if it could materially increase the burden of performance on the other party to the contract. Thus you cannot transfer your fire insurance policy to someone who buys your house, nor your automobile insurance to someone who buys your car. Indeed, such contracts specifically prohibit assignment to another party.

Nevertheless, valid transfers of contractual rights and duties occur with many variations. A common example that often involves multiple transfers is a contract for the construction of a private residence.

On June 1, 2000, Able Construction Company, a general contractor, agrees to build and sell a particular house to Baker on land it owns, for a contract price of $250,000. Promised delivery date is on or before November 1, that year. Able and a small crew of his employees prepare the site and lay the foundation. In separate contracts, on and after June 8, 2000, Able delegates all other construction work to independent contractors who are trade specialists in their fields (carpentry, plumbing, electrical work, painting, and so forth) for various prices. Able remains liable to Baker for the completed job as promised. On July 1, 2000, Baker learns that she is to be promoted and transferred by her employer to another city. Therefore, she sells the house to a friend, Newcomer, on August 10, 2000. She does this by assigning her rights and delegating her duties in the project to Newcomer. These contracts are graphically portrayed in Exhibit 8–3.

Note that Able might have assigned the right to part or all of the $250,000 price to a bank for a construction loan. Also, both Baker and Newcomer could have negotiated separate loan contracts with the house as security, to finance the purchase (see Chapter 12). Note, too, that Baker might have asked Newcomer to pay more or less than $250,000, but the parties agreed to the transfer at the original price.

HOW ARE CONTRACTS DISCHARGED?

The customary and usual way of discharging contracts is by **performance**. The reciprocal rights and duties of the parties are legally terminated when the parties have done what they have promised to do. Sometimes the performance is not precisely as promised, but the minor deviation may be a good-faith oversight or failure. In the house-construction example, assume the paint used was the proper quality and color but the wrong brand, or the garage door may have been

Exhibit 8–3: Example of Contract with Subsequent Delegation of Duties and Assignment of Rights

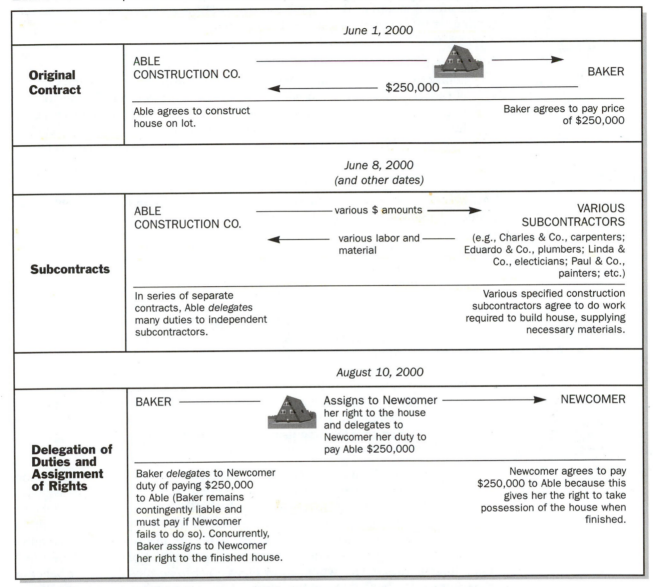

a half-foot wider than specified. The buyer must still "perform" by paying for such **substantial performance** by the general contractor, but may deduct an appropriate amount because of any deficiency in the builder's performance. The buyer need not pay extra for any improvements "volunteered" by the builder. Often businesspersons as well as ultimate consumers will accept an alternative or a variation of a promised performance simply because the deviation is not significant or does not reduce the value of consideration received. To insist on absolute compliance may end a mutually beneficial relationship.

Rather than engage in costly and acrimonious arguments and litigation, a party may **waive** (give up) or renounce legal contract rights. For example, an employer may do so when an employee under a year's contract quits without just cause after a month or two. Occasionally, a party will agree to accept some substitute for the original promised consideration.

Defft, a dentist, never refused to treat a patient, regardless of his or her ability to pay promptly for the service. When the charges for dental care of Gartner, an unemployed gardener, and his wife reached $600, they offered to redo Defft's lawn and trim all the trees and bushes on his lot in full payment or satisfaction of the debt. Defft agreed. This was an executory *accord*. When the work was completed, the debt was discharged by *accord and satisfaction*.

An **accord** is an agreement to perform an act to satisfy an existing contractual duty. A **satisfaction** is the performance of the accord agreement. For a contract to be discharged by accord and satisfaction, the parties must agree to accept a performance different from the performance originally promised. An accord and its satisfaction, or performance, discharge the original contractual obligation. Until satisfaction, the parties do not give up the rights they had before the accord.

Benton gets a judgment against Lorie for $6,000. Later, both parties agree that the judgment can be satisfied (paid) by Lorie's transferring her motor home to Benton. This agreement to accept the motor home instead of $6,000 in cash is the accord. If Lorie transfers her motor home to Benton, the accord agreement is fully satisfied, and the $6,000 debt is discharged. If Lorie refuses to transfer her motor home, the accord is breached. Since an original obligation is merely suspended in an accord, Benton can bring a lawsuit to enforce the judgment for $6,000 in cash.

In the hypothetical house construction, buyer Baker's contractual obligation might have been discharged if Able, the general contractor, had agreed with Baker and Newcomer to a **novation** (i.e., substitution of a new contract, debt, or obligation for an existing one between the same or different parties). Typically, a new contract is created with the same terms as the original one, but the novation substitutes a new party and discharges one of the original parties by agreement of all three parties.[24] This would allow Newcomer to be substituted for Baker in the contract. The bank that lent the construction money to Baker undoubtedly required her to sign a promissory note agreeing to pay. Had the bank deliberately marked the note "Cancelled" or destroyed it—a very unlikely possibility—the debt would have been discharged by *cancellation*. Similarly, any deliberate important change in a promissory note or other written contract by a party to the contract is a **material alteration**, and discharges the contractual obligation of the other party.

When there is a *material* (important) **breach**, or failure or refusal to perform a contract, the victim may *cancel* the contract with no liability and sue for damages. The right to sue, if utilized successfully, may be superseded by a judgment of the court. This, too, serves to discharge the contract, but by operation of law. Other means of discharging a contract by operation of law include (1) subsequent illegality—as when the Eighteenth Amendment prohibited "manufacture, sale, or transportation of intoxicating liquors;" (2) bankruptcy (the debts are not extinguished, but they cannot be enforced unless reaffirmed by the debtor with approval by the court);[25] (3) running of the statute of limitations (again, the debts are not extinguished, but they cannot be enforced unless reaffirmed by the debtor); (4) literal impossibility (as where a contract requires personal service and the individual dies); and (5) commercial impracticability, where "performance as agreed has been made impracticable by the occurrence of a contingency the non-occurrence of which was a basic assumption on which the contract was made."[26] Outbreak of war, surprise discovery of solid granite throughout much of the anticipated site of an underground garage, and a major earthquake are examples of circumstances in which performance might be excused because it has become commercially impracticable.

Circumstances can be such that both parties "want out." In such a case, a voluntary **rescission** is mutually agreed on. Anything already received is returned, and the *status quo ante* (previous situation) is restored.

WHAT REMEDIES ARE AVAILABLE FOR BREACH OF CONTRACT?

Vigorous contract activity is essential to a healthy economy. Through its laws, society seeks to encourage people to enter contracts and to perform as promised. Failure to do so is not conducive to goodwill and continued relations. But a breach of contract is not a crime and, except in unusual circumstances it is not a tort (e.g., when there is a breach of covenant of good faith and fair dealing). In a sense, contracting parties can usually regard a breach as a possible alternative to performance; it is surely not morally reprehensible if the victim of the breach is promptly "made whole" by being provided with money or some alternative performance that offsets any loss suffered.

If litigation becomes necessary, the defaulting party is generally obliged by a court to pay *compensatory damages,* sufficient to place the victim in essentially the same economic position or condition that would have resulted from performance of the contract. Only if the agreement were corrupted by a related tort, such as fraud, would punitive damages be awarded.

See these examples of liquidated damage clauses http://www.buildingteam.com/risk/contract/liquid.shtml

Armond agreed to sell his used Harley-Davidson motorcycle to Bushnell for $6,500. When Armond changed his mind and refused to complete the deal, Bushnell promptly bought a comparable model for $7,500 from Caldwell. Armond is liable to Bushnell for $1,000 in compensatory damages. If Bushnell was lucky enough to find a similar model priced at $6,000, she could still sue for *token or nominal damages* (typically 6 cents or $1). Armond would also be liable for court costs, but not for Bushnell's attorney's fees, unless that was provided for in the original sales contract.

Sometimes, the parties to a contract specify in advance what the damages shall lie in case of breach. Such **liquidated damage clauses** are often used in contracts for the construction of public buildings or commercial structures where damages are difficult to determine and prove. Courts will enforce such terms as long as the damages are not in fact penalties. They must be reasonable in the light of the anticipated or actual injury or harm caused by the breach.

When Metropolitan College contracted for its new classroom buildings (price $6 million), the general contractor promised to have it ready for occupancy two years thereafter, when the fall semester would begin on August 28. A liquidated damage clause called for the payment of $600 per school day (Monday through Saturday) of delay in completion beyond the promised date of August 28. Losses incurred would include rental costs for temporary portable buildings and the monetary value of burdens imposed on students, faculty, and staff from overcrowding and required reassignments. Therefore, this clause would be enforceable.

In some cases where money damages are inadequate, courts provide an *equitable, non-monetary remedy*. For example, since every parcel of land is unique, a buyer of land can compel delivery of possession by the owner who promised to sell. So, too, with unique works of art. For example, in 1989, an unidentified Japanese bidder at an auction agreed to pay $45.9 million for *Pierrot's Wedding*, a masterpiece from Pablo Picasso's famed "blue period."[27] Under U.S. law, a seller who refuses to deliver such a painting could be compelled to do so by a buyer who obtains a *specific performance decree* from a court of equity. Of course, if the painting has already been sold to another person who, unaware of the prior contract, bought in good faith and received good title, the victimized buyer would have to be satisfied with a money judgment. When appropriate, courts of equity may also issue *injunctions* (sometimes called *restraining orders*), which may prohibit a defendant from doing a specified act or command the defendant to do some positive act.

The talented and temperamental opera star Matilda Nocallara contracted—a full year in advance—to perform at a gala concert in New York City, promoted by Joy Jordane. A month before the scheduled date, Nocallara told Jordane that she was "indisposed" and planned instead to make "a less strenuous television appearance" that week in Los Angeles. What did Jordane do?

Jordane obtained an injunction from a court of equity, forbidding Matilda to perform in Los Angeles on the day of the scheduled concert. The court would not directly compel her appearance in New York because that would smack of involuntary servitude and would be difficult to enforce. In addition, the court would award Jordane dollar damages if Nocallara failed to keep her New York commitment.

WHAT SPECIAL PROTECTION IS PROVIDED FOR INDIVIDUAL CONSUMER CONTRACTS?

All persons are consumers. The most common consumer contracts are sales (purchase) agreements. Purchases are often made on credit, involving separate contracts to permit payment over extended periods of time. Sellers (i.e., manufacturers, wholesalers, and retailers) are generally more knowledgeable about their products and services than are most consumers. Moreover, sellers are more likely to have the assistance of attorneys in drafting contracts.

When one party has vastly superior bargaining power, a contract between that party and another may also be deemed unconscionable. Such situations usually involve an **adhesion contract**, defined as a contract drafted by a dominant party and then presented to the other party—the adhering party—on a "take it or leave it" basis. Unconscionable clauses, those that "shock the conscience" of a court, are more likely to be found in adhesion contracts than contracts where the parties truly bargained over terms.

> A welfare recipient with a fourth-grade education agrees to purchase a refrigerator for $2,000. He signs a two-year installment contract with a high but legal interest rate. The same type of refrigerator usually sells for $400 on the market. Is it possible that this contract is unconscionable?

Some courts have held this type of contract to be unconscionable, even though courts generally do not inquire into the adequacy of the consideration. To tell the consumer, "*Caveat emptor*—let the buyer beware," is no help when the buyer lacks the knowledge needed to evaluate the goods (be they simple clothing or complex electronic gear).

Over the years (dating back at least to 1906, when the federal Pure Food and Drug Act was enacted), government at all levels has been involved in protecting consumers against unfair practices of a comparatively small group of unethical businesspersons and firms that are always present somewhere in the marketplace. In the 1960s and 1970s, several important federal consumer protection bills were added. Although abuses continue, three broad categories of legislation (before-sale laws, during-sale laws, and after-sale laws) have given meaningful "teeth"—such as fines and prison terms—to the admonition, "*Caveat venditor*—let the seller beware."

BEFORE-SALE LAWS

Before-sale laws regulate the design, composition, and production of products for sale. They embrace such elements as quality, safety, purity, description, and packaging. For example, before-sale laws require emission devices to be installed in automobiles to reduce air pollution and tamper-proof packaging for over-the-counter drugs.

Since 1972, the **Consumer Product Safety Commission** has been charged with overseeing the safety of all consumer products other than autos, trucks, airplanes, boats, food, drugs, and cosmetics (which are the concern of other federal agencies).

The Consumer Product Safety Commission Web site is at http://www.cpsc.gov/

> *The U.S. Consumer Product Safety Commission (CPSC) announced today that John D'Angelo, owner and president of Utility Free Inc., a Colorado-based distributor of alternative energy products, was sentenced to nearly two years in jail for violating two laws enforced by CPSC. Mr. D'Angelo pled guilty to 15 counts of improperly shipping hazardous substances, including a highly corrosive, clear electrolyte solution. In December 1993, 15-year-old Justin Pulliam mistook the solution for water because Mr. D'Angelo had shipped it in a reused plastic*

one-gallon milk container that lacked appropriate warnings. The teenager drank it and died two weeks later from severe internal injuries.[28]

Probably the most important task of the CPSC is recall or corrective action orders on products produced and/or sold in the United States.

The Pure Food and Drug Act of 1906 is a legislative landmark in the area of consumer before-sale health protection. It marked the beginning of federal regulation of food and drugs in the United States. What caused the congressional action was the public outrage generated by a novel. The novel, published in 1905, was Upton Sinclair's *The Jungle*. It was an exposé of the Chicago meatpacking industry. The story was so revolting that no one who read it could remain unaffected. President Theodore Roosevelt demanded an immediate investigation of the Chicago meatpacking houses, supposedly after reading the following paragraph:

> *There was never the least attention paid to what was cut up for sausages; there would come all the way back from Europe old sausage that had been rejected, and that was mouldy and white—it would be dosed with borax and glycerine, and dumped into the hoppers, and made over again for home consumption. There would be meat that had tumbled out on the floor, in the dirt and sawdust, where the workers had tramped and spit uncounted billions of consumption germs. . . . It was too dark in these storage places to see well, but a man could run his hand over these piles of meat and sweep off handfuls of the dried dung of rats. These rats were nuisances, and the packers would put poisoned bread out for them; they would die, and then rats, bread and meat would go into the hoppers together. This is no fairy story and no joke; . . . there were things that went into the sausage in comparison with which a poisoned rat was a tidbit.*[29]

President Roosevelt ordered an investigation and the labor commissioner confirmed Sinclair's observations. Both the long-stalled Pure Food and Drug Act and the Meat Inspection Act were passed immediately.

Under the authority of the federal Nutrition Labeling and Education Act of 1990, the Food and Drug Administration now requires that nutritional information (per serving) be provided on labels on canned and packaged foods. Carefully examine the label on a can of your favorite soup, for example, and note the detailed listing of facts about the quantities therein of calcium, various types of fat, cholesterol, sodium, vitamins, and minerals. For many consumers, such information can literally be a lifesaver.

DURING-SALE LAWS

During-sale laws regulate truth in advertising, extension of credit, and contract terms and language. The Federal Trade Commission, created under the Federal Trade Commission Act of 1914, was originally primarily concerned with enforcement of the federal antitrust laws (i.e., the Sherman Anti-trust Act of 1890 and the Clayton Act of 1914). The FTC sought to prevent among business corporations unfair methods of competition that could lead to monopolies. More recently, the FTC has also been active as the principal federal agency regulating advertising.

The Federal Trade Commission provides a very helpful Web site at http://www.ftc.gov/

On September 21, 1998, Judge Wilkie D. Ferguson, Jr., in U.S. District Court, Florida, granted the FTC's request for a stipulated final order and permanent injunction against National Scholarship Foundation (NSF) to forbid advertising of student scholarship services. The FTC complaint stated NSF sent hundreds of thousands of postcards to potential college students and their families to solicit NSF's scholarship search services. When a consumer called the listed 800-number, a company representative told the caller that NSF could guarantee $1,000 worth of free grants and scholarships for a student if the caller paid a fee. In addition, the $189 fee would be refunded if anyone did not receive $1,000 or more in scholarship money through NSF within one year. In fact, the FTC charged that NSF did not fulfill its promise to find sources for its customers that lead them to $1,000 minimum scholarship(s) and that the service provided was generally worthless. In addition, according to the FTC, NSF rarely honored its refund guarantee.[30]

The most important section of the **Consumer Credit Protection Act of 1968** is known as the *Truth-in-Lending Act*, which requires a full disclosure of the comparative costs of buying goods for cash or on credit. On credit sales and loans of money, the creditor must disclose, in writing and in advance of signing, the total dollar finance charge and the effective annual percentage rate (APR) of the interest or finance charge. Sellers may not mislead gullible customers, for example, by quoting a credit cost of "only 1.5 percent a month." They must disclose that the equivalent interest cost per year is 18 percent. The act also provides for a three-day "cooling-off" period when a consumer agrees to borrow on the security of a second mortgage on a home. Under the law, the borrower may rescind and get back any money delivered to the creditor as long as he or she does it within the three days. The act places no limit on the rate or amount of interest or carrying charge, although some consumer advocates think it should.

The cooling-off rule of the Truth-in-Lending Act does not apply to first mortgages (or first deeds) on homes, because such credit has not generally been the basis for exploitation of unsophisticated homeowners in need of funds, and the interest rates have been reasonable. The three-day cooling-off period is a narrow exception that allows a party to escape a contract acceptance. Unfortunately, many consumers have heard of a "three-day rule" and think it applies to all consumer contracts. It does not.

Traditionally, garnishment (attachment of the salary or wages of a defaulting debtor) has been a principal remedy for unpaid creditors. To use this remedy, the creditor gets a court order (called a *writ of execution*) directing the debtor's employer to pay a certain portion of the employee's wages directly to the creditor until the judgment is paid in full. Sometimes employers fired workers who got into such financial trouble. Under the federal Consumer Credit Protection Act, normally the amount garnished may not exceed 25 percent of the worker's weekly take-home pay, or $60, or the amount by which the take-home pay exceeds 30 times the federal minimum wage, whichever is less. An employer may not discharge an employee simply because wages have been garnished for any one indebtedness.

The federal **Credit Card Act of 1970** controls certain practices of credit card companies. A consumer must apply for a credit card; it may not be thrust on the consumer without such request and consent. Moreover, the cardholder's liability for unauthorized use of the card by a thief or dishonest finder is limited to

Read all about debit cards at the National Consumers League Web site at http://www.nclnet.org/debitbro.htm and find out what to do if you lose your ATM or debit card at http://www.ftc.gov/bcp/conline/pubs/credit/atmcard.htm

a maximum of $50 per card. And even this limited liability for up to a maximum of $50 can be imposed only if

1. The cardholder requested and received the credit card, or signed or used it, or authorized another person to do so.

2. The card issuer provided a self-addressed, pre-stamped notification to be mailed by the cardholder in the event of loss or theft of the card.

3. The card issuer gave adequate notice of the $50 liability.

4. The card issuer provided positive means of identification (for example, signature or photo of the cardholder on the card).

5. The unauthorized use took place before the cardholder notified the issuer that such use might take place.

The **Fair Credit Reporting Act of 1970** gives consumers the right to check for accuracy of credit information about themselves that may be on file with credit reporting services, such as the Retailers Credit Association (RCA). The opportunity is provided to correct or explain inaccurate information.

The **Equal Credit Opportunity Act of 1974** forbids discrimination in extension of credit because of sex, marital status, race, or color, as well as religion, national origin, or advanced age; because the applicants get all or part of their income from a public assistance welfare program; or because the applicant has in good faith exercised a right under the Consumer Credit Protection Act.

In the past few years, the use of debit cards has increased significantly. ATM cards are a type of debit card. The National Consumers League estimates that two-thirds of American households will have a debit card by the year 2000. Although they often look like credit cards, they are very different. **Debit cards** draw against an account the user has with a financial institution or a prior payment of money the user has made to the card issuer. They do not involve an extension of credit. Instead of "pay later," they represent "pay now." Few of the consumer protections available when disputes arise are available with debit card use. The transactions are essentially cash transactions. If the debit card is stolen, federal law limits the holder's maximum liability to $50 if the loss is reported within two days of discovery. After two days liability increases to $500; if the loss is not reported within 60 days, the loss can be unlimited. However, debit card providers are free to provide more favorable terms to their customers, and they often do. Shop around.

AFTER-SALE LAWS

After-sale laws regulate credit billings, methods of debt collection, and warranties. The **Fair Credit Billing Act of 1974** is a response to problems that result when clerks with computers electronically provide invoices that may be erroneous. Consumers who believe (1) an accounting error has been made by the issuer of a credit card; (2) goods or services have not been delivered or accepted; (3) credit extensions have not been made or have been made incorrectly; or (4) payments or credits have been recorded incorrectly, may notify the creditor in writing within 60 days after the issuer mailed them the first bill with the error. The creditor (or issuer of the card) must investigate and respond promptly, normally within 30 days of receipt. Within 90 days, the creditor must either eliminate the error or explain why it believes the bill was correct. After notification, the creditor is temporarily barred from pressing for payment or reporting to a credit bureau, although statements may continue to be sent. Consumers are legally obligated to pay any part of the bill not in dispute. If the creditor admits an error, there can be no finance charges on the disputed amount. The creditor must submit a correct written notice of what is owed, and consumers must be given the usual time to pay before any finance charges or late-payment charges may be assessed. If it turns out that there was no error, consumers must pay finance charges on the disputed amount and make up any payments missed. The debtor who is not satisfied with the creditor's explanation is allowed a minimum of 10 days after receiving the explanation in which to protest. Thereafter, whether or not such protest was made, the creditor may sue or use other collection procedures. If there was a second protest, however, the creditor who notified credit bureaus and other creditors must mention the dispute and inform the debtor of the identity of the addressees.

Failure to comply with the stated rules makes the finance charges and first $30 of the disputed amount uncollectible, even if later events prove there was no error.

The **Fair Debt Collection Practices Act of 1977** outlaws a variety of unreasonably harsh tactics used in the past by overly aggressive debt collectors. Banned are late night and early morning telephone calls, the use of obscene and abusive language, threats to notify employers, false representation as police or official government agents, harassment with repeated phone calls, and similar unsavory behavior. Nothing in the law prevents creditors from using legitimate methods and conventional legal remedies to collect overdue debts.

WHAT WARRANTY PROTECTION DO YOU HAVE AS A CONSUMER?

A **warranty** is an assurance given by the seller of goods concerning the quality or performance of a product. Some warranties are implied by law and exist even if nothing is said about them; other warranties are expressed and may be oral, but are usually stated in the written contract. An **express warranty** can exist even if the seller did not intend to make one. The UCC does not require that the seller "use formal words such as 'warrant' or 'guarantee' or that he has a specific intention to make a warranty." It is necessary only that a reasonable buyer would believe that a particular representation (such as those just described) was part of the bargain. An **implied warranty** is one that the law implies from the nature or circumstances of the transaction.

Although warranties can arise in any sales transaction, it is important to distinguish between merchants and casual sellers. A **merchant** is a professional seller who deals in goods of the kind, or otherwise by occupation holds him- or herself out as having knowledge or skill peculiar to the practice or goods involved in the transaction.[31] Casual sellers are ordinary laypersons disposing of things they own.

Either a merchant or a casual seller may explicitly make the following express warranties:

1. *Warranty of conformity to description, sample, or model*—All goods supplied must conform to the sample or model shown at the time of the sale, or to the specifications provided.

A Businessperson's Guide to Federal Warranty Law can be found at http://www.freeadvice.com/gov_material/ftc-business-guide-to-fed-warranty-law-toc-5-87.htm

2.   *Warranty of conformity to seller's statement or promise*—The seller who openly states or writes a factual assertion about the goods is bound by that assertion.

In addition to express warranties, sales by either a merchant or casual seller create each of these implied warranties:

1.   *Warranty of title*—The seller has the title to the goods as claimed and the right to transfer or sell them.

2.   *Warranty against encumbrances*—The goods delivered will be free of liens or encumbrances—creditors' claims—of which the buyer is not aware at the time of contracting.

3.   *Warranty of fitness for a particular purpose*—If the buyer indicates the purpose for which the goods are needed and then relies on the seller's selection, the goods will be reasonably fit for the intended stated purpose.

When Peggy Butler visited Mac's Sport Shack, she told the salesperson that she was planning a backpack trip into the Great Smoky Mountains. Butler insisted on being outfitted with "Pathfinder" brand moccasin boots and a "Kozy" brand sleeping bag. After several days in the wilderness using this gear, she realized that neither product fit her needs. Her ankles were swollen, and she caught pneumonia. Is Mac's Sport Shack liable on a breach of warranty of fitness for a particular purpose?

No. A warranty is not given when the buyer insists on a particular brand, as here. Possibly Butler could hold the manufacturers liable if they had made express warranties as to the goods and these warranties were breached.

Merchant sellers alone make the following two additional implied warranties:

1.   *Warranty against infringement*—The goods sold are delivered free of any rightful claim of a third party under patent, copyright, or other legal protection.

2.   *Warranty of merchantability*—This is an extremely important warranty, promising that the goods are fit for the ordinary purposes for which such goods are used. Thus, a rocking chair (or stereo or toaster or umbrella) should function as such and last a reasonable length of time (which might be many years) under ordinary use.

Nonmerchantable goods include light bulbs that explode when switched on, pajamas that burst into flames at slight contact with a stove burner, high-heel shoes that break off under normal use, and shotgun shells that explode prematurely.

Official comments to the UCC state that contracts for sale by merchants of used or secondhand goods involve only such obligation as is appropriate to such goods. This obligation includes the customary implied warranty of merchantability, but the price, age, and condition of the goods at the time of the sale are considered in determining the scope of the warranty. Obviously, such a warranty may be of little value to the buyer, especially if the goods are worn out or in poor condition.

> You need a gallon of paint to match the color of your bedroom walls, a light shade somewhere between coral and peach. You take a wall chip sample to your local hardware store and request a gallon of paint of that color. Instead, you are given a gallon of bright blue paint. The salesperson has not breached any warranty of implied merchantability—the bright blue paint may be of high quality and suitable for interior walls. The clerk has, however, breached an implied warranty of fitness for a particular purpose.

MAY A SELLER DISCLAIM ALL WARRANTIES THAT OTHERWISE PROTECT THE CONSUMER?

A seller may generally **disclaim** (limit or negate) all warranties. Fortunately, because of competitive pressure, this seldom happens. To exclude the implied warranty of merchantability, the seller must conspicuously mention *merchantability* in the disclaimer or notice of exclusion. A statement that the goods are sold "as is" or "with all faults" also serves to exclude all implied warranties. However, the UCC provides that consequential damages may *not* be limited or excluded if the exclusion is **unconscionable** (i.e., against public policy). Limitation of such damages "for injury to the person in the case of consumer goods is prima facie unconscionable. . . ."[32] Also, if the goods are defective, the seller may be liable for damages under the tort doctrine of strict liability (see Chapter 7).

Formerly, sellers were often shielded from liability by legal requirements of *privity*, meaning that the plaintiff buyer seeking to enforce a warranty must be the party who contracted with the defendant seller. Thus, a consumer might sue a retailer who sold the defective product to him or her, but not the much wealthier manufacturer who made it. Most states have modified or rejected this archaic doctrine and hold all merchants or manufacturers in the chain of distribution liable for any breach. The UCC has extended the warranty protection beyond the buyer to include all members of the buyer's family or household and any of the buyer's guests, where they might reasonably be expected to use such goods and where the defective goods cause physical injury.[33] But in most states, innocent bystanders and others who are injured by a defective product must seek recovery on some other basis, such as strict product liability of manufacturers and intermediaries in a tort action, as noted previously.

> While trying to persuade Marjorie Ayers to buy an expensive personal computer system, Leon Cannon said that all parts were guaranteed and would be replaced without any charge if found defective within five years. The written purchase contract that Ayers later signed spoke of only a one-year warranty against defects in materials and workmanship. Moreover, it said that the customer would have to pay for half of

the usual labor charge. Which warranty terms actually apply to the purchase?

The one-year warranty terms apply—unless the buyer can satisfy a judge of the lie, or that she was the victim of mistake or fraud, or that the written contract was incomplete. This is the result of the **parol-evidence rule**, which presumes that the contracting parties have included all previous desired oral or written understandings in their final, integrated written agreement.[34] Thus, it is not enough for a consumer to get all-important contracts in writing; one should also make sure that the writing includes all desired terms and any oral assurances and that they are stated correctly and completely, including a clear statement of any warranty protection.

The federal **Magnuson-Moss Warranty Act of 1975,** designed to help protect ultimate consumers of personal, family, or household goods costing $10 or more, has added the concepts of *full* and *limited* warranties.[35] Under the act, no one is required to give a written warranty, but the seller who elects to do so must label it as either full or limited. If it is a *full warranty*, the seller agrees to fix the product within a reasonable time and without charge if it proves to be defective. If it cannot be fixed or if a reasonable number of attempts to fix it prove unsuccessful, the buyer has the choice of a full cash refund or a free replacement. (Some states have added *lemon laws*, which clarify and strengthen this rule.) No time limit may be placed on a full warranty, but if an otherwise full warranty has a time limit, it may be described, for example, as a "full five-year warranty." The seller must label any warranty that does not provide full protection a *limited warranty*. A warranty would be limited if, for example, the buyer had to pay any fee or transportation charge in order to utilize it. Implied warranties (e.g., of title or of merchantability) may not be disclaimed if any written warranty is given, but they may be defined and limited.

Typical language in an express warranty given by a representative manufacturer of consumer goods states that the product is warranted "against any defects due to faulty materials or workmanship for a one-year period after the original date of consumer purchase." In fairness to manufacturers, it should be noted that a warranty extended beyond the stated short period can be very costly to service. Buyers who neglect their possessions and fail to follow recommended maintenance schedules take unfair advantage of warranties. Yet all buyers pay for the added protection that most do not need, because the added cost is distributed over the price in all sales. A better alternative for some may be the purchase of "extended warranty protection" for an additional period of time for an additional charge.

The Federal Trade Commission (FTC) has independently imposed further regulations in cases where the consumer good costs more than $15. The seller is required to disclose the name of the warrantors, the nature and limitations (if any) of the warranty, and the fact that the buyer has legal rights to specified procedures for the enforcement of the warranty.

CASES

HAMER V. SIDWAY
124 N.Y. 538, 27 N.E. 256 (1891)

At a family celebration, in the presence of witnesses, William E. Story, Sr., promised to pay his nephew William E. Story, 2d, $5,000 if he would refrain from drinking, using tobacco, swearing, and playing cards or billiards (all legal activities for the nephew at that time) until he turned 21. The nephew assented and fully performed the conditions of the promise. When he reached 21, not quite 6 years later, he wrote a letter to his uncle, explaining that he had performed his part of their agreement and was thereby entitled to the $5,000. The uncle wrote a letter in response, reaffirming his promise. Unfortunately for the nephew, his uncle died some 12 years later without having paid him any money. The nephew assigned his claim to Hamer (the plaintiff in this case), but Sidway, the executor of the uncle's estate and the defendant in this action, rejected the claim. The executor's refusal was based on his belief that there was no consideration for the uncle's promise to pay because the uncle received no benefit from the nephew's performance. The following opinion of the New York Court of Appeals is a landmark statement on the rules of consideration, made in an interesting factual context. Keep in mind that $5,000 was worth much more in 1891 than it is today.

J. Parker wrote the following: The uncle received the letter, and a few days later he wrote and mailed to his nephew the following letter:

"Dear Nephew: Your letter of the 31st ult. came to hand all right, saying that you had lived up to the promise made to me several years ago. I have no doubt but you have, for which you shall have five thousand dollars, as I promised you. I had the money in the bank the day you was twenty-one years old that I intend for you, and you shall have the money certain.

Now, Willie, I do not intend to interfere with this money in any way till I think you are capable of taking care of it, and the sooner that time comes the better it will please me. I would hate very much to have you start out in some adventure that you thought all right and lose this money in one year. The first five thousand dollars that I got together cost me a heap of hard work. You would hardly believe me when I tell you that to obtain this I shoved a jack-plane many a day, butchered three or four years, then came to this city, and, after three months' perseverance, I obtained a situation in a grocery store. I opened this store early, closed late, slept in the fourth story of the building in a room 30 by 40 feet, and not a human being in the building but myself. All this I done to live as cheap as I could to save something. I don't want you to take up with this kind of fare. I was here in the cholera season of '49 and '52, and the deaths averaged 80 to 125. . . .

"Mr. Fisk, the gentleman I was working for, told me, if I left them, after it got healthy he probably would not want me. I stayed. All the money I have saved I know just how I got it. It did not come to me in any mysterious way, and the reason I speak of this is that money got in this way stops longer with a fellow that gets it with hard knocks than it does when he finds it. Willie, you are twenty-one, and you have many a timing to learn yet. This money you have earned much easier than I did, besides acquiring good habits at the same time, and you are quite welcome to the money. Hope you will make good use of it. I was ten long years getting this together after I was your age. Now, hoping this will be satisfactory, I stop. One thing more. Twenty-one years ago I bought you 15 sheep. These sheep were put out to double every four years. I kept track of them the first eight years. I have not heard much about them since. Your father and grandfather promised me that they would look after them till you were of age. Have they done so? I hope they have. By this time you have between five and six hundred sheep, worth a nice little income this spring. Willie, I have said much more than I expected to. Hope you can make out what I have written. Today is the seventeenth day that I have not been out of my room, and have had the doctor as many days. Am a little better today. Think I will get out next week. You need not mention [this] to father, as he always worries about small matters.

Truly yours, W. E. STORY. P.S. You can consider this money on interest."

The nephew received the letter, and thereafter consented that the money should remain with his uncle in accordance with the terms and conditions of the letter. The uncle died on the 29th day of January, 1887, without having paid over to his nephew any portion of the said $5,000 and interest. . . .

The question which provoked the most discussion by counsel on this appeal, and which lies at the foundation of plaintiff's asserted right of recovery, is whether by virtue of a contract, defendant's testator, William E. Story, became indebted to his nephew, William E. Story, 2d, on his twenty-first birthday in the sum of $5,000. The defendant contends that the contract was without consideration to support it, and therefore invalid. He asserts that the promisee, by refraining

from the use of liquor and tobacco, was not harmed, but benefited; that that which he did was best for him to do, independently of his uncle's promise—and insists that it follows that, unless the promisor was benefited, the contract was without consideration—a contention which, if well founded, would seem to leave open for controversy in many cases whether that which the promisee did or omitted to do was in fact of such benefit to him as to leave no consideration to support the enforcement of the promisor's agreement. Such a rule could not be tolerated, and is without foundation in the law. The exchequer chamber in 1875 defined "consideration" as follows: "A valuable consideration, in the sense of the law, may consist either in some right, interest, profit, or benefit accruing to the one party, or some forbearance, detriment, loss, or responsibility given, suffered, or undertaken by the other." Courts "will not ask whether the thing which forms the consideration does in fact benefit the promisee or a third party, or is of any substantial value to any one. It is enough that something is promised, done, forborne, or suffered by the party to whom the promise is made as consideration for the promise made to him." Anson, Cont, 63. "In general a waiver of any legal right at the request of another party is a sufficient consideration for a promise." Pars. Cont. "Any damage, or suspension, or forbearance of a right will be sufficient to sustain a promise." 2 Kent, Comm. (12th Ed.)

Pollock, in his work on Contracts (page 166), after citing the definition given by the exchequer chamber, already quoted, says: "The second branch of this judicial description is really the most important one. 'Consideration' means not so much that one party is profiting as that the other abandons some legal right in the present, or limits his legal freedom of action in the future, as an inducement for the promise of the first." Now, applying this rule to the facts before us, the promisee used tobacco, occasionally drank liquor, and he had a legal right to do so. That right he abandoned for a period of years upon the strength of the promise of the testator that for such forbearance he would give him $5,000.

We need not speculate on the effort which may have been required to give up the use of those stimulants. It is sufficient that he restricted his lawful freedom of action within certain prescribed limits upon the faith of his uncle's agreement, and now, having fully performed the conditions imposed, it is of no moment whether such performance actually proved a benefit to the promisor, and the court will not inquire into it; but, were it a proper subject of inquiry, we see nothing in this record that would permit a determination that the uncle was not benefited in a legal sense. . . .

The order appealed from should be reversed, and the judgment of the special term affirmed, with costs payable out of the estate.

All concur. [Hamer, the nephew's assignee, was found entitled to the $5,000 plus interest.]

FOR CRITICAL ANALYSIS

1. If *"drinking, using tobacco, swearing and playing cards or billiards"* were illegal for minors in New York at the time of William Story, Sr.'s offer, would consideration have been present?

2. Why do you suppose the nephew didn't demand payment from his uncle at the time he received his uncle's letter?

3. Could Sidway (the executor) argue the statute of frauds applies in this case? How would Hamer counter that claim?

LUCY V. ZEHMER
196 Va. 493, 84 S.E.2d 516 (1954)

This is a suit to compel specific performance of a land purchase contract claimed by defendant sellers to have been entered into as a joke. The circuit court entered a decree dismissing the suit, and purchasers appealed. The Supreme Court of Appeals held evidence showed that the contract represented a serious business transaction and good-faith sale and purchase of the farm, that no unusual circumstances existed in its making, and that purchasers were entitled to specific performance. This is another landmark contract case. In it, the court discusses the contract rules governing the manifestation of intent to contract and the contractual capacity of parties negotiating a contract while sipping distilled spirits.

J. Buchanan delivered the opinion of the court: This suit was instituted by W. O. Lucy and J. C. Lucy, complainants, against A. H. Zehmer and Ida S. Zehmer, his wife, defendants, to have specific performance of a contract by which it was alleged the Zehmers had sold to W. O. Lucy a tract of land owned by A. H. Zehmer in Dinwiddie county containing 471.6 acres, more or less, known as the Ferguson farm, for $50,000. J. C. Lucy, the other complainant, is a brother of W. O. Lucy, to whom W. O. Lucy transferred a half interest in his alleged purchase.

The instrument sought to be enforced was written by A. H. Zehmer on December 20, 1952, in these words: "We hereby agree to sell to W. O. Lucy the Ferguson Farm complete for $50,000, title satisfactory to buyer," and signed by the defendants, A. H. Zehmer and Ida S. Zehmer.

The answer of A. H. Zehmer admitted that at the time mentioned W. O. Lucy offered him $50,000 cash for the farm, but that he, Zehmer, considered that the offer was made in jest; that so thinking, and both he and Lucy having had several drinks, he wrote out "the memorandum" quoted above and induced his wife to sign it; that he did not deliver the memorandum to Lucy, but that Lucy picked it up, read it, put it in his pocket, attempted to offer Zehmer $5 to bind the bargain, which Zehmer refused to accept, and realizing for the first time that Lucy was serious, Zehmer assured him that he had no intention of selling the farm and that the whole matter was a joke. Lucy left the premises insisting that he had purchased the farm.

W. O. Lucy, a lumberman and farmer, thus testified in substance: He had known Zehmer for fifteen or twenty years and had been familiar with the Ferguson farm for ten years. Seven or eight years ago he had offered Zehmer $20,000 for the farm, which Zehmer had accepted, but the agreement was verbal and Zehmer backed out. On the night of December 20, 1952, around eight o'clock, he took an employee to McKenney, where Zehmer lived and operated a restaurant, filling station and motor court. While there he decided to see Zehmer and again try to buy the Ferguson farm. He entered the restaurant and talked to Mrs. Zehmer until Zehmer came in. He asked Zehmer if he had sold the Ferguson farm. Zehmer replied that he had not. Lucy said, "I bet you wouldn't take $50,000 for that place." Zehmer replied, "Yes, I would too; you wouldn't give fifty." Lucy said he would and told Zehmer to write up an agreement to that effect. Zehmer took a restaurant check and wrote on the back of it, "I do hereby agree to sell to W. O. Lucy the Ferguson Farm for $50,000 complete." Lucy told him he had better change it to "We" because Mrs. Zehmer would have to sign it too. Zehmer then tore up what he had written, wrote the agreement quoted above and asked Mrs. Zehmer, who was at the other end of the counter ten or twelve feet away, to sign it. Mrs. Zehmer said she would for $50,000 and signed it. Zehmer brought it back and gave it to Lucy, who offered him $5 which Zehmer refused, saying, "You don't need to give me any money, you got the agreement there signed by both of us."

The discussion leading to the signing of the agreement, said Lucy, lasted thirty or forty minutes, during which Zehmer seemed to doubt that Lucy could raise $50,000. Lucy suggested the provision for having the title examined and Zehmer made the suggestion that he would sell it "complete, everything there," and stated that all he had on the farm was three heifers.

Lucy took a partly filled bottle of whiskey into the restaurant with him for the purpose of giving Zehmer a drink if he wanted it. Zehmer did, and he and Lucy had one or two drinks together. Lucy said that while he felt the drinks he took he was not intoxicated, and from the way Zehmer handled the transaction he did not think he was either.

December 20 was on Saturday. Next day Lucy telephoned to J. C. Lucy and arranged with the latter to take a half interest in the purchase and pay half of the consideration. On Monday he engaged an attorney to examine the title. The attorney reported favorably on December 31, and on January 2 Lucy wrote Zehmer stating that the title was satisfactory, that he was ready to pay the purchase price in cash and asking when Zehmer would be ready to close the deal. Zehmer replied by letter, mailed on January 13, asserting that he had never agreed or intended to sell. Mr. and Mrs. Zehmer were called by the complainants as adverse witnesses. Zehmer testified in substance as follows: He bought this farm more than ten years ago for $11,000. He had had twenty-five offers, more or less, to buy it, including several from Lucy, who had never offered any specific sum of money. He had given them all the same answer, that he was not interested in selling it. On this Saturday night before Christmas it looked like everybody and his brother came by there to have a drink. He took a good many drinks during the afternoon and had a pint of his own. When he entered the restaurant around eight-thirty Lucy was there and he could see that he was "pretty high." He said to Lucy. "Boy, you got some good liquor, drinking, ain't you?" Lucy then offered him a drink. "I was already high as a Georgia pine, and didn't have any more better sense than to pour another great big slug out and gulp it down, and he took one too."

After they had talked a while Lucy asked whether he still had the Ferguson farm. He replied that he had not sold it and Lucy said, "I bet you wouldn't take $50,000 for it." Zehmer asked him if he would give $50,000 and Lucy said yes. Zehmer replied, "You haven't got $50,000 in cash." Lucy said he did and Zehmer replied that he did not believe it. They argued "pro and con for a long time," mainly about "whether he had $50,000 in cash that he could put up right then and buy that farm."

Finally, said Zehmer, Lucy told him if he didn't believe he had $50,000, "you sign that piece of paper here and say you will take $50,000 for the farm." He, Zehmer, "just grabbed the back off of a guest check there" and wrote on the back of it. At that point in his testimony Zehmer asked to see what he had written to "see if I recognize my own handwriting." He examined the paper and exclaimed, "Great balls of fire. I got 'Firgerson' for Ferguson. I have got satisfactory spelled wrong. I don't recognize that writing if I would see it, wouldn't know it was mine."

After Zehmer had, as he described it, "scribbled this thing off," Lucy said, "Get your wife to sign it." Zehmer walked over to where she was and she at first refused to sign but did so after he told her that he "was just needling him [Lucy], and didn't mean a thing in the world, that I was not selling the farm." Zehmer then "took it back over there . . . and I was still looking at the dern thing. I had the drink right there by my hand, and I reached over to get a drink, and he said, 'Let me see it.' He reached and picked it up, and when I looked back again he had it in his pocket and he dropped a five dollar bill over there, and he said, 'Here is five dollars payment on it. . . .' I said, 'Hell no, that is beer and liquor talking. I am not going to sell you the farm. I have told you that too many times before.'"

The defendants insist that the evidence was ample to support their contention that the writing sought to be enforced was prepared as a bluff or dare to force Lucy to admit that he did not have $50,000; that the whole matter was a joke; that the writing was not delivered to Lucy and no binding contract was ever made between the parties.

It is an unusual, if not bizarre, defense. When made to the writing admittedly prepared by one of the defendants and signed by both, clear evidence is required to sustain it.

In his testimony Zehmer claimed that he "was high as a Georgia pine," and that the transaction "was just a bunch of two dog-goned drunks bluffing to see who could talk the biggest and say the most." That claim is inconsistent with his attempt to testify in great detail as to what was said and what was done. It is contradicted by other evidence as to the condition of both parties, and rendered of no weight by the testimony of his wife that when Lucy left the restaurant she suggested that Zehmer drive him home. The record is convincing that Zehmer was not intoxicated to the extent of being unable to comprehend the nature and consequences of the instrument he executed, and hence that instrument is not to be invalidated on that ground. . . . It was in fact conceded by defendants' counsel in oral argument that under the evidence Zehmer was not too drunk to make a valid contract.

The evidence is convincing also that Zehmer wrote two agreements, the first one beginning "I hereby agree to sell." Zehmer first said he could not remember about that, then that "I don't think I wrote but one out." Mrs. Zehmer said that what he wrote was "I hereby agree," but that the "I" was changed to "We" after that night. The agreement that was written and signed is in the record and indicates no such change. Neither are the mistakes in spelling that Zehmer sought to point out readily apparent.

The appearance of the contract, the fact that it was under discussion for forty minutes or more before it was signed; Lucy's objection to the first draft because it was written in the singular, and he wanted Mrs. Zehmer to sign it also; the rewriting to meet that objection and the signing by Mrs. Zehmer; the discussion of what was to be included in the sale, the provision for the examination of the title, the completeness of the instrument that was executed, the taking possession of it by Lucy with no request or suggestion by either of the defendants that he give it back, are facts which furnish persuasive evidence that the execution of the contract was a serious business transaction rather than a casual, jesting matter as defendants now contend.

If it be assumed, contrary to what we think the evidence shows, that Zehmer was jesting about selling his farm to Lucy and that the transaction was intended by him to be a joke, nevertheless the evidence shows that Lucy did not so understand it but considered it to be a serious business transaction and the contract to be binding on the Zehmers as well as on himself. The very next day he arranged with his brother to put up half the money and take a half interest in the land. The day after that he employed an attorney to examine the title. The next night, Tuesday, he was back at Zehmer's place and there Zehmer told him for the first time, Lucy said, that he wasn't going to sell and he told Zehmer, "You know you sold that place fair and square." After receiving the report from his attorney that the title was good he wrote to Zehmer that he was ready to close the deal.

Not only did Lucy actually believe, but the evidence shows he was warranted in believing, that the contract represented a serious business transaction and a good faith sale and purchase of the farm.

In the field of contracts, as generally elsewhere, "We must look to the outward expression of a person as manifesting his intention rather than to his secret and unexpressed intention. The law imputes to a person an intention corresponding to the reasonable meaning of his words and acts. . . ."

At no time prior to the execution of the contract had Zehmer indicated to Lucy by word or act that he was not in earnest about selling the land. They had argued about it and discussed its terms, as Zehmer admitted, for a long time. Lucy testified that if there was any jesting it was about paying $50,000 that night. The contract and the evidence show that he was not expected to pay the money that night. Zehmer said that after the writing was signed he laid it down on the counter in front of Lucy. Lucy said Zehmer handed it to him. In any event there had been what appeared to be a good faith offer and a good faith acceptance, followed by the execution and apparent delivery of a written contract. Both said that Lucy put the writing in his pocket and then offered Zehmer $5 to seal the bargain. Not until then, even under the defendants' evidence, was anything said or done to indicate that the matter was a joke. Both of the Zehmer's testified that when Zehmer asked his wife to sign he whispered that it was a joke so Lucy wouldn't hear and that it was not intended that he should hear.

The mental assent of the parties is not requisite for the formation of a contract. If the words or other acts of one of the parties have but one reasonable meaning, his undisclosed intention is immaterial except when an unreasonable meaning which he attaches to his manifestations is known to the other party. . . .

The law, therefore, judges of an agreement between two persons exclusively from those expressions of their intentions which are communicated between them. . . .

An agreement or mutual assent is of course essential to a valid contract but the law imputes to a person an intention corresponding to the reasonable meaning of his words and acts. If his words and acts, judged by a reasonable standard, manifest an intention to agree, it is immaterial what may be the real but unexpressed state of his mind. . . .

So a person cannot set up that he was merely jesting when his conduct and words would warrant a reasonable person in believing that he intended a real agreement. . . .

Whether the writing signed by the defendants and now sought to be enforced by the complainants was the result of a serious offer by Lucy and a serious acceptance by the defendants, or was a serious offer by Lucy and an acceptance in secret jest by the defendants, in either event it constituted a binding contract of sale between the parties.

Defendants contend further, however, that even though a contract was made, equity should decline to enforce it under the circumstances. These circumstances have been set forth in detail above. They disclose some drinking by the two parties but not to an extent that they were unable to understand fully what they were doing. There was no fraud, no misrepresentation, no sharp practice and no dealing between unequal parties. The farm had been bought for $11,000 and was assessed for taxation at $6,300. The purchase price was $50,000. Zehmer admitted that it was a good price. There is in fact present in this case none of the grounds usually urged against specific performance.

Specific performance, it is true, is not a matter of absolute or arbitrary right, but is addressed to the reasonable and sound discretion of the court. . . . But it is likewise true that the discretion which may be exercised is not an arbitrary or capricious one, but one which is controlled by the established doctrines and settled principles of equity; and, generally, where a contract is in its nature and circumstances unobjectionable, it is as much a matter of course for courts of equity to decree a specific performance of it as it is for a court of law to give damages for a breach of it. . . .

The complainants are entitled to have specific performance of the contracts sued on. The decree appealed from is therefore reversed and the cause is remanded for the entry of a proper decree requiring the defendants to perform the contract in accordance with the prayer of the bill. Reversed and remanded.

FOR CRITICAL ANALYSIS

1. Why does the court require objective intention to contract? The contrasting term to objective is subjective meaning "peculiar to a particular individual." Why isn't subjective intent preferable; after all if you want to know what someone means can't you ask them?

2. Can you identify three separate contentions Zehmer makes to defend against Lucy's action? Why were they unsuccessful? Do you agree with the court's ruling?

3. Lucy testified that there had been an oral agreement to buy the farm for $20,000 "seven or eight years before." Why do you suppose Lucy had not sued to enforce that agreement?

CHAPTER QUESTIONS AND PROBLEMS

1. Regarding the elements of a valid contract:
   a. What are the five, and sometimes six, elements that are said to be essential for a valid contract?
   b. In which of the six elements does the law permit performance or execution at the option of one of the parties who might have legally withdrawn without liability? Explain.

2. Regarding breach of contract:
   a. Is breaching a contract comparable in moral culpability and legal effect to committing a tort or committing a crime? If not, how do these actions differ?
   b. Under what circumstances can a party who breaches a contract also be guilty of committing a tort?

3. Identify three contracts you have experienced or observed. Select one that is expressed in writing, one expressed orally, and one implied in fact from conduct. Classify each as to parties bound, legal effect, and extent of performance.

4. Clearly distinguish between a valid contract, a voidable contract, and a void agreement. Provide an example of each type of agreement and demonstrate how the court would treat each of your situations if they were litigated.

5. When is an acceptance to an offer sent by mail effective to form a contract if the acceptance was returned by mail?
   a. When it arrives at the offeror(s)?
   b. When you decide you intend to accept?
   c. When the acceptance is given to the secretary to mail?
   d. When your check clears the bank?
   e. When your letter of acceptance is mailed?
   f. What are the legal consequences, if any, if a timely sent, properly addressed and stamped letter is lost by the postal service?

6. Marcie and Bruce entered into a binding bilateral contract. The terms of the contract included that Marcie was to build a hang glider for Bruce, and that Bruce was to pay Marcie $18,000 upon its completion. After formation of the contract, Bruce decided he did not want the hang glider; because the contract was advantageous, however, he assigned all of his rights thereunder and delegated his duty of payment to his friend Shadoe. Shadoe paid Bruce $1,400 for the transferred right and immediately informed Marcie of the assignment. After Shadoe took delivery of the glider, he fled without paying Marcie. He was last seen by reliable sources gliding into Canada singing, "I did it my way." Characterize the contractual relationships of the parties and explain their respective rights.

7. Millie, a university psychology professor, says to her students, "All of you have worked hard, and if you continue to perform at a high level, I will pay for a pizza party for the class at the end of the year—if I think it is warranted." The students insist that they continued to "work hard," and they claim that the class grades "are high," but Millie gives no party. Can the students enforce Millie's promise?

8. Plaintiff, a minor, alleged that Schultz had made an oral contract with the plaintiff through his mother. In this alleged contract, Schultz agreed to give the plaintiff certain real estate if the plaintiff's mother would name the plaintiff (who was his grandson) after him. He also agreed to reserve (i.e., give) the plaintiff's parents a life estate (one that is good for their lifetimes only) in that real estate. The plaintiff's parents accepted the proposal, since they had already named their son after Schultz. However, Schultz never arranged for the title of the property to pass to the plaintiff. He did deliver possession of the real estate to the plaintiff's parents. The plaintiff requested that the court determine that he is the absolute owner of the real estate. The trial court agreed and awarded the property to the plaintiff, based on the alleged oral contract. The heirs of Schultz and the administrator of his estate appealed. Was the alleged contract between Schultz and the plaintiff's mother supported by consideration and therefore enforceable? [*Lanifer v. Lanifer*, 227 Iowa 258, 288 NW 104 (Iowa, 1939).]

9. When Tom Trousseau loaned Bob Barrow $100, he asked for an IOU. Barrow took a business card from his wallet and scribbled these words on its back: "IOU, old pal Tom, one hundred bucks," signed and dated it, and gave it to Trousseau. Is the card an enforcable written contract?

10. Defendant Robert Martin gave his American Express credit card to E. L. McBride, a business associate, for use in a joint business venture. Martin claimed he orally authorized McBride to charge up to $500 on the card. He also testified that he had previously sent a letter to plaintiff American Express asking them not to allow total charges on his account to exceed $1,000. McBride had returned the card to Martin and then disappeared. But McBride had actually charged approximately $5,300 to Martin's card. Under the Truth-in-Lending Act, is Martin liable for $50 or $5,300? [*Martin v.*

American Express, Inc., 361 So.2d 597 (Alabama, 1978).]

11. Quicken's Business Law Partner

   a. Access the document portion of Quicken's Business Law Partner. Complete the sales contract with a fictitious product and seller and buyer. Do you understand the various contract terms?

   b. Listen to Harvard Professor Arthur Miller's short lecture on whether or not loan documents should be in writing in the Ask the Expert financial category.

NOTES

1. *Restatement of the Law of Contracts*, 2nd edition, (St. Paul, MN: American Law Institute Publishers, 1981), § I.
2. John Donne, *Devotions upon Emergent Occasions*, Number 17, 1624.
3. Uniform Commercial Code (UCC) (St. Paul, MN: American Law Institute Publishers, 1987), § 2-206(1)(a). See also *Restatement of Contracts*, 2 § 30.
4. *Adams v. Lindsell*, 106 Eng. Rep. 250 (K.B., 1818).
5. *Restatement of Contracts*, § 3b.
6. *Restatement of Contracts*, § 48.
7. *Restatement of Contracts*, § 37.
8. *Restatement of Contracts*, §§ 163, 164.
9. *Raffles v. Wichelhaus*, 159 Eng. Rep. 375 (1864).
10. *Cooper v. Paris*, 413 So.2d 772 (Fla.App., 1st Dist., 1982).
11. The Ten Commandments, or Decalogue, and the other precepts spoken by God to Israel, delivered to Moses on Mount Sinai. *The Bible*, Exodus 20; Deuteronomy 5.
12. Consumer Credit Protection Act of 1968, 15 U.S.C. § 1601 et seq.
13. Foreign Corrupt Practices Act of 1977, 2 U.S.C. § 241 et seq.
14. *Paramount Termite Control Co. v. Rector*, 238 Va. 171, 380 S.E.2d 922 (Virginia, 1989).
15. Statute of Frauds and Perjuries, 29 Car. II, c. 3.
16. UCC, § 2-106(1).
17. UCC, § 2-105(1).
18. UCC, § 2-201(3).
19. UCC, § 2-201(2).
20. UCC, § 1-206(1).
21. UCC, §§ 2-201, 8-319, 9-203.
22. *Restatements of Contracts* 2d, § 302(l)(b).
23. *Restatements of Contracts* 2d, § 302(1)(a).
24. *Restatements of Contracts* 2d, §§ 423, 430.
25. U.S. Constitution, Eighteenth Amendment, ratified January 16, 1919, repealed by Twenty-First Amendment.
26. UCC § 2-615.
27. *San Francisco Chronicle*, 1 December 1989.
28. Press Release from the Consumer Product Safety Commission, January 1998.
29. Upton Sinclair, *The Jungle* (New York: Penguin Edition, 1985), 163.
30. Copies of the complaint and stipulated final order, as well as consumer education material associated with "Project $cholar$cam," are available from the FTC's Web site at http://www.ftc.gov and also from the FTC's Consumer Response Center, Room 130, 6th Street and Pennsylvania Avenue, N.W., Washington, D.C. 20580; 202-FTC-HELP (202-382-4357); TDD for the hearing impaired 202-326-2502.
31. UCC § 2-104(1).
32. UCC § 2-719(3) and § 2-302.
33. UCC § 2-318.
34. *Restatement of Contracts* 2d, § 213.
35. Magnuson-Moss Consumer Product Warranty and Guaranty Act, 15 U.S.C. § 2301 et seq.

APPLICATIONS OF THE LAW TO THE INDIVIDUAL

UNIT II

FAMILY LAW

*L*ove, the quest; marriage, the conquest; divorce, the inquest.

Helen Rolland, **Reflections
of a Bachelor Girl,** *1903*

Family law governs the legal relations of the basic social unit, the family. In general, family law has very little to do with happy families. Rather, family law is about protecting the family unit, especially children. Family law begins with rules expressed in state statutes designed by legislatures to protect the family institution. There are rules defining marriage, the mechanics of divorce, the basis for division of family assets upon divorce—all are set forth in state statutes. Wide variations exist in family law from state to state because legislative viewpoints reflect substantially different cultural and societal values. Understandably, these viewpoints often clash on the very sensitive and important principles applicable to the family. Religious beliefs, for example, probably conflict more frequently with family law than with any other categories of law.

As in other areas of law, when disputes arise between family members, we rely upon lawyers for assistance in presenting our family issues to judges and courts for resolution. These "divorce" lawyers present family law issues to judges (without juries, as family law is "in equity") for resolution. These judges, who typically specialize in domestic matters, rely heavily upon the recommendations of social service experts for such sensitive issues as child custody following the breakup of the marriage.

Lawyers often joke amongst themselves about their availability for our legal problems "from the cradle to the grave." In this book the distressing legal issues related to "the grave" are appropriately covered in our final chapter (pun intended). In this chapter you will discover that our need for family law begins long before "the cradle." Yes, facing the new millennium, our law increasingly is focusing upon protection of the fetus during pregnancy. The primary issue in society involving the unborn fetus has been the right of females to choose abortion. By the turn of the twentieth century, virtually every state had a law prohibiting or restricting abortion. It is noteworthy that women also did not have the right to vote. It was not until 1973 that the choice to abort a nonviable fetus became guaranteed under the U.S. Constitution.* But the issue of protection of the fetus is changing. Abortion no longer is the single issue.

In the early years of the new millennium there will be new laws designed to protect the unborn fetus from abusive behavior by its mother throughout pregnancy. The problem is so acute that confinement of the mother during pregnancy is, as you will learn, a distinct possibility, even though the U.S. Constitution guarantees the liberty of all.

Again we note the mushrooming complexities within our huge and diverse society. Looking forward, as we enter the new millennium there is scientific opportunity to "modify" or "adjust" a fetus before or after conception. Harnassing of the human gene creates opportunities and challenges in family law that make the issue of abortion pale in comparison. We have added a new section in this book to acquaint you with these issues facing society in the first few years of the twenty-first century.

There are emerging constitutional issues in family law, such as those presented by the demand for same-sex marriage, which would allow equality in taxation and financial benefits that traditional couples currently enjoy.

Already the law authorizes a variety of surrogacy arrangements under which persons otherwise incapable of having their own progeny can be rewarded. But legal issues defining the rights of the "natural parents" who are different from the "birth" mother continue.

At the beginning of the twentieth century, many children were called upon to work long hours for little pay and with little regard for their workplace safety or health. Facing the new millennium, we find that children are protected from abusive employment, but too many remain in need of protection from abuses by their parents, from other adults, and even from themselves. Child abuse is a violation of both criminal and family law, and is found in both of those chapters in this textbook. The scope of protective laws and issues cover a vast range of problems, from censorship of the Internet to the exclusionary zoning of "adult" bookstores; from sex, gore, and alcohol on TV to metal detectors in grade schools. This area of family law is rich with controversy, with prospects for new legal solutions undoubtedly eluding us well into the twenty-first century.

Most rules of family law are found in the civil law. But some are also found in the criminal law because certain conduct involving family members is so reprehensible that society, through legislation, expresses its disapproval by imposing criminal penalties. Child abuse and spouse-beating are examples of such conduct. Both criminal and civil statutes have been enacted principally to protect and enhance marriage and the family. Examples of criminal laws designed to protect the family include those proscribing adultery, bigamy, seduction accomplished by false promise of marriage, and incest (i.e., sexual intercourse between individuals who are so closely related to each other that marriage is forbidden by law). Examples of civil laws relating to the family declare that upon termination of the marriage, courts may distribute the family property equitably (in accordance with applicable state law) and define and order the continuing support rights and duties of family members.

---

*A fetus is viable when it theoretically could survive independent of its mother. In 1973, the law described viability as beginning after the first trimester (three months).

There is hardly an area of law more relevant to each of us than family law. Even if it does not touch one's life directly, its societal effects are felt by all.

A promise to "love, honor and cherish as long as we both shall live" is in fact easily and frequently revocable today. It is lamentable that many decide to live together without benefit of such vows and many who take them soon forget them. However, we are concerned here with legal, not moral obligations.[1]

For access to various state family law statutes, uniform laws, and other information visit http://fatty.law.cornell.edu/topics/divorce.html

http://

IS THE FEDERAL GOVERNMENT INVOLVED IN FAMILY LAW?

Although there is no national (federal) marriage or divorce law, a family member may become involved in a matter involving federal jurisdiction. For example, if American citizen Bruce Brown, husband and father, was caught at Nogales, Arizona, entering the United States with contraband, such as marijuana, he would be involved in a federal crime. But if Brown is jailed, the question of how his family would then be supported would be determined by principles of family law in the state of his residence. In addition, some federal laws are designed to protect the family when issues involving more than one state are raised. For example, the Child Abuse Prevention and Treatment Act of 1984 encourages states to adopt remedial statutes; the Omnibus Budget Reconciliation Act of 1981 provides for interception of income tax refunds payable to parents who are delinquent in their support obligations; the Parental Kidnapping Act of 1984 provides special penalties for "child-snatching" parents; and more recently the Uniform Interstate Family Support Act of 1992 streamlines the forced collection of support and establishes a commission to further study the problem. Further, the U.S. Supreme Court has held that former spouses who reside in different states may sue each other in federal court for damages (but not for divorce, alimony, or child custody) in federal court.[2] There is an emerging trend of federal courts accepting jurisdiction in family law matters that extend across state lines.[3] In the following case, a federal court applied the Illinois law regarding a breach of promise to marry.

Sharon Wildey, an attorney, sued her fiancé Richard Springs, III, for damages for ending their seven-week engagement, which had followed a whirlwind romance. She sued in federal court on the basis of diversity of citizenship. Sharon claimed she suffered depression and lost income by giving up her main client. Richard told Sharon that she could keep the $19,000 engagement ring and offered her $10,000 cash to help her "get through these times." She was thrice divorced and had four children; Richard was once divorced and had fathered three children. At the close of trial, Sharon's attorney asked the jury for damages of $365,000. What result do you predict?

The federal court jury awarded Sharon $93,000 for pain and suffering, $60,000 for lost income, and $25,000 for counseling.[4] This case was exceptional because few states permit legal actions seeking damages for breach of promise to marry on the general grounds that "pillow talk" cases ought not be resolved in court.

Congress is considering a greater federal involvement in family law. Consider the implications of the following proposed laws on family life.

- Removing the marriage penalty in the income tax.*

- Further curbing drunk driving by creating a low national standard for driving under the influence.

- Banning online gambling and curbing access by minors to pornography on the Internet.

- Making personal bankruptcy more difficult with greater repayment obligations when family credit card debts become overwhelming.

No one doubts the sincerity of the intentions to protect families that underlie new federal laws. But many such national laws fail to live up to their expectations when adopted. For example, federal law now bars the sale of cigarettes to persons under 18 years, yet minors are still able to purchase them in 4 out of every 10 attempts.[5] Are the new taxes on cigarettes likely to reduce their consumption by minors or more likely simply to raise funds? Alcohol has similarly been banned, yet there is a perceived need for federal laws to reduce driving under the influence and to protect the fetuses of minors from the alcohol syndrome.

WHAT IS MARRIAGE?

Marriage is a status, the legal union of husband and wife, entered into by means of a contract that is enforceable by courts. The legal relationship of marriage is based on state rather than federal law. When the status is created, the law grants enforceable rights to the parties and also imposes various mutual duties or obligations. Such official governance of the relationship is justified because marriage is recognized as essential for healthy, viable families and therefore the foundation of a healthy, viable society.

Alexis McVey and Martin Neiderhasen were exchanging wedding vows when Martin collapsed. He died of cardiac arrest in the ambulance. During their courtship, neither prepared a last will. Does Alexis have any legal rights to inherit from Martin?

Alexis has no rights of inheritance unless their vows were completed and their marriage proclaimed. The law treats Alexis and Martin just as it does any other unmarried persons. Martin's parents would inherit from him. If the marriage existed for only a moment, Alexis would have significant rights to his property in all states. This seemingly absurd hypothetical is based on an actual dispute between an alleged spouse and her bridegroom's parents.

*The marriage penalty is a term used to describe tax laws that create higher total income taxes on joint returns by married couples than would exist on individual returns filed by unmarried persons.

Statutes regulate the lawful creation of marriage. All jurisdictions currently prohibit the marriage of persons of the same sex. In 1989 Denmark became the first country to legalize same-sex marriages, called registered partnerships. Norway and Sweden soon followed suit. Registered partnerships, like marriages, can be "dissolved"; however, they do not allow for the adoption of children.[6]

In most states, a license between adults is prescribed for marriage. Parental consent is required for a minor (person under 18 years) to obtain a marriage license, but in special situations (e.g., pregnancy out of wedlock), some state courts are authorized to approve the marriage of underage persons. In Maryland, only parental consent is required for marriage of an underage pregnant girl.

> With her parents' blessings, Tina Akers and her boyfriend, Wayne, went to the courthouse, obtained a license, and were married. Wayne is 29 years old while Tina, eight months pregnant, is 13. Is this a new legal family or an example of parental child abuse or predatory and even pedophiliac sexual abuse and statutory rape?[7]

In Maryland, Tina and Wayne Compton and their newly born son, Austin, are a legal family. In other states, Wayne would have been charged with a crime and the marriage would not have been valid. Tina's father had married his wife Nancy when she was 16. They had eight children before their divorce. Although the marriage of very young teenagers was commonplace at the turn of the century, that practice gradually ended and largely disappeared following World War Two.*

All states prohibit marriage between members of the immediate family (ascendants–descendants, i.e., parent and child) and siblings (brother and sister) on moral and genetic grounds. Most also prohibit uncle–niece or aunt–nephew marriages, and some extend the prohibition to first cousins. A few continue to proscribe matrimony for certain relationships of affinity (e.g., stepfather–stepdaughter). Statutes typically require that a person entering marriage be of sound mind—not be insane, an idiot, an imbecile, or a lunatic—although doctors have difficulty diagnosing mental illness, and there is confusion as to what such terms mean in law. Most states used to require a health examination showing freedom from certain venereal diseases as a precondition for issuance of a marriage license. But that requirement has been eliminated in the vast majority of states. Solemnization is generally required by either a civil (justice of the peace or judge) or religious (minister, priest, rabbi, or the like) authority.

> Pauline Hall, while planning her marriage to George Bradshaw, became curious about whether she will be legally required to take and use George's surname. Is a wife legally required to take her husband's surname?

No. Wives customarily have taken the surname of their husbands. But such is not required by law. Many women choose to use both family surnames in combination. Thus, Pauline could choose to be known as "Pauline Hall-Bradshaw."

---

*For example, country music star Loretta Lynn married at 13 and was a grandmother by 29. *Washington Post*, 15 October 1998.

COMMON-LAW MARRIAGE

In 14 states,* a common-law marriage may arise when a man and a woman continue to live together as husband and wife but without legal formalities (health examination, marriage license, and proper solemnization). For a common-law marriage to exist, the parties must be legally qualified to marry, must cohabit and create the public impression that a marriage exists, and must intend that it exist.[8]

Sandra Jennings and actor William Hurt had a three-year sexual relationship while living in Manhattan. New York state does not recognize common-law marriages. But Sandra and William spent five weeks in South Carolina during Hurt's filming of *The Big Chill*. After they ended the relationship, Sandra sued Hurt in a New York court claiming that a common-law marriage, by mutual agreement, had existed under South Carolina's law. But Hurt often expressed his desire not to marry, and evidence of any agreement contrary to that desire was lacking. Sandra lost her case and appealed, contending, among other things, that the trial court wrongfully excluded Hurt's diaries from evidence. She also lost the appeal, prompting her attorney, Richard Golub, to publicly declare that the trial court judge, a woman, was so in love with Hurt that Jennings never had a chance.[9]

The law clearly requires considerable evidence in support of any determination that a common-law marriage exists. But once the common-law marriage is created, it is treated by the laws the same as all other conventional marriages. The vast majority of states do not permit cohabiting as a legal method of establishing a (common-law) marriage. In other words, most states do not provide for common-law marriage.

However, Article IV, Section 1 of the U.S. Constitution provides: "Full faith and credit shall be given in each state to the public acts, records, and judicial proceedings of every other state." Accordingly, states that do not themselves permit common-law marriages must recognize as valid a common-law marriage that previously was legally created elsewhere.

State laws traditionally restrict marriage to a man and a woman. Proponents of same-sex marriages argue that the heart of the public contract is an emotional, financial, and psychological bond between two people. That the two people cannot bear children is not relevant because no civil marriage license is granted on the condition that the couple bear children.

Nina Baehr and Genora Dancel applied for but were denied a marriage license in Hawaii. In court, they argued that they had a fundamental right to marry that was protected by the same constitutional right of privacy that legitimized abortion. Are Nina and Genora correct?

---

*Alabama, Colorado, Georgia, Idaho, Iowa, Kansas, Montana, Ohio, Oklahoma, Pennsylvania, Rhode Island, South Carolina, Texas, Utah, and the District of Columbia.

No. However, the state supreme court did rule that by restricting marriage to opposite-sex couples only, a sex-based discrimination occurred that violated the Hawaii Constitution unless the state could demonstrate a "compelling interest" to do so. More than a dozen states immediately enacted definitions of marriage excluding same-sex couples as "against public policy." The fear was that if same-sex marriages became legal in Hawaii, then under the full faith and credit clause of the U.S. Constitution, all other states would be required to recognize such marriages, just as they must recognize common-law marriages. Congress acted promptly by adoption of the Defense of Marriage Act of 1996, which sought to relieve states of any obligation to recognize same-sex marriages from other states. A number of states already have acted to prohibit same-sex marriages. And, in 1998 the people of Hawaii voted to change their state's constitution to ban same-sex marriages.[10]

> Certain "liberal" clergy in the Methodist Church perform "holy union" ceremonies for same-sex couples. Other pastors with a more "fundamental" view of the Bible vehemently object, to the degree of threatening to withdraw from the church.[11] Do these ceremonies create marriages?

No. Legal marriage must conform to state laws. As you will see in the following paragraphs, however, some legal benefits may attach to such relationships.

DOMESTIC PARTNERSHIPS

Married couples receive many financial benefits that are not available to unmarried couples who may have financial interdependence, shared living arrangements, and a commitment to mutual caring and love. Are such couples entitled to equal protection under law through equal access to financial benefits? Several cities in the U.S. have, by ordinance, created "domestic partnerships" under which registrants qualify for benefits that had previously been reserved for heterosexual married couples. The benefits include health insurance, bereavement leave, insurance, annuity and pension rights, and housing rights (as in rent-controlled apartments). Proponents intend to expand these benefits to include adoption and inheritance rights, federal income tax equality, and even veteran's benefits.

Opponents claim that a sexual relationship is not a precondition to receiving such benefits nor are any of the typical characteristics of a loving marriage. Theoretically, they argue, an elderly woman and her live-in nurse could qualify, or even a pair of fraternity brothers living as roommates. Marriage, on the other hand, is an anchor, a mechanism for economic and emotional stability that is not present when persons register as domestic partners.

THE "MARVIN MARRIAGE"

> Michelle Triola met noted actor Lee Marvin during the filming of *Ship of Fools*. The couple soon moved into the same household. Thereafter, Lee divorced his estranged wife, Betty, but in 1970 left Michelle to marry his childhood sweetheart, Pamela. Michelle sued for a share of Lee's

considerable earnings as well as compensation for the earnings she allegedly sacrificed for Lee's sake in giving up her career as a singer. Under Michelle's theory, she would have shared one-half of Marvin's earnings from *Ship of Fools* while his estranged wife would receive the other one-half as community property. What was the result?

Michelle ultimately lost her case. But the celebrated trial between Michelle Triola and Lee Marvin highlighted a trend, in some segments of our society, toward living together without the formality of a traditional marriage. The historical attitude of the courts had been to give no protection to either party of a so-called meretricious (based on pretense) relationship. Thus, upon separation, neither "pseudo-spouse" could obtain a share of the other party's earnings or accumulated wealth, or receive payments of alimony for continued support. Any contract that purported to create property or support rights in another in exchange for participation in a meretricious relationship was declared void as against public policy.

Departing from tradition, the California Supreme Court held that adults who live together and engage in sexual relations are, nonetheless, competent to contract to pool (i.e., combine) earnings, or to keep earnings and other property separate. The court stated that such an agreement might be express, implied (inferred from conduct), or based upon "some other tacit understanding." However, the contract could not be based on the exchange of sexual favors.[12] The California Supreme Court remanded the case to the trial court to determine if such an agreement existed between Triola and Marvin. The trial court rejected Michelle's contention that a contract existed, but awarded her $104,000 for rehabilitative compensation, called "palimony" by the media. That award subsequently was reversed on a second appeal because there was no evidence of a contract, and Michelle ultimately received nothing.[13]

A rash of similar lawsuits followed in California, setting a trend for courts in other states to grant relief to "discarded" companions when existence of a contract could be proved. But legislatures have remained reluctant to enact protective laws for cohabiting persons, usually citing public policy as a reason for discouraging cohabitation without marriage. In effect, some courts have discarded public-policy objections and recognized the economic value of the pseudo-spouse as a homemaker. Thus courts in many states now protect cohabitants by awarding division of property or payment of support through enforcement of an express (written or oral) or implied (inferred) agreement.[14] Furthermore, partners of homosexual unions receive Marvin-type relief in some jurisdictions.[15] On the other hand, some states continue to deny all relief to cohabitants on the grounds of public policy.[16]

WHAT ARE THE LEGAL CONSEQUENCES OF MARRIAGE?

OBLIGATION OF SUPPORT

The marital relationship implies a continuing and mutual obligation of support. Support includes food, shelter, clothing, medicine, and usually a wide range of consumer goods, all appropriate to the family's wealth and established standard of living. Management of the family budget is left to the wise or unwise (and sometimes spiteful) management of the spouses. It is a crime for parents to willfully fail to support their children. Moreover, some states have enacted statutes requiring adult children who have the financial means to support their indigent parents who receive government assistance. But courts seldom become involved in support disputes unless the marriage in question is in the process of dissolution or divorce. You will see, later in this chapter, that the family's budget (standard of living) before divorce is relevant to the issue of how much support (called *alimony*) should be imposed by law for the period following divorce.

> Robert Hamilton became disabled and could not work. His wife, Sally, a trained legal secretary, had been serving as housewife and homemaker. Sally declared that she would not seek gainful employment to support her husband and would henceforth terminate the marriage. Is Sally required to go to work to support Robert if the marriage remains intact? If it is terminated?

Yes, Sally will be required to apply her earning skills in support of her husband whether or not the marriage remains intact. Also, in this hypothetical case, she could be required to use property owned in her name for his support. However, Sally would not necessarily be indentured for life; courts will terminate lifetime support in many circumstances. At some point, the balance of equities would weigh in favor of public support of the disabled Hamilton, and Sally would be released from that obligation.

The specific criteria often used by courts in setting the amount of required support following termination of the marriage, and the length of time support must be paid, are reviewed later in this chapter.

PROPERTY RIGHTS

The legal rights of the spouses to their **marital property** (assets of the family, as defined by statute) upon divorce are somewhat different depending upon the applicable state law.

Uniform Marital Law Jurisdictions (Most States)

Under original common-law theory, title to all property owned by a woman was automatically vested in her husband upon marriage. During marriage, the wife owned no property. Marriage created one entity: the husband. A creditor who successfully sued the wife received a judgment against the husband, and thereby reached all of the family's nonexempt assets.

Rejecting the original common-law theory, 42 states have adopted some variation of the Uniform Marriage and Divorce Act, (UMDA), which, among other matters, creates a distinction between separate and marital property. This distinction is recognized by all states. **Separate property** is all property acquired before marriage or during marriage by gift or inheritance. The husband and wife are "partners" in their marital property earned during their marriage.

How marital property is handled upon divorce under the UMDA is explained later in this chapter. But during marriage, there is uncertainty in the law as to the extent to which creditors of one spouse can reach the family's marital property. Under the Uniform Marital Property Act (UMPA), all marital property can be reached by the creditors of either spouse. Courts in Maine have ruled, in the absence of any statute, that all marital property can be reached by creditors of either spouse during the marriage. This rule reflects the trend.[17] But courts in many states continue to rule that creditors of one spouse can reach only marital property that is held in that spouse's name. These states hold that property rights generally are based upon who holds title to the property. Creditors can reach only property held in the title of the debtor. However, even in these states property owners cannot change the title to property simply to avoid the claims of creditors. Such transfers can be set aside as fraudulent.

Community Property Jurisdictions*

All property acquired by the husband or the wife during marriage, other than by gift or inheritance, is **community property**. Unless agreed otherwise, the respective earnings of husband and wife during marriage are owned equally when received. Upon dissolution, accumulated earnings, as with all other community properties, are divided equally between the spouses because the ownership of community property is equal.

As stated earlier, separate property is property either brought into the marriage or acquired during marriage by gift or inheritance. Separate property retains its separate character as long as independent records are kept. For example, cash kept in a separate savings account will retain its separate property classification. **Commingling** of separate property and community property occurs when the two are so combined that they cannot reasonably be traced back to their original status. In such cases, the separate property has been transmuted into community property and has lost its former status. An example is cash brought into the marriage and subsequently combined in the family checking account with monthly community earnings. The status of property as separate or community can also be altered by an agreement between the spouses.

Gifts of Marital Property

Because both spouses own an undivided one-half interest in the community property, neither spouse can defeat the other's ownership rights by giving it away without consent.

In Bellevue, Washington, George was enamoured of his secretary, Vickie, and gave her a Jaguar XJS purchased with earnings from his accounting business. When his wife, Betty, learned of the gift, she insisted that the car be taken from Vickie. Can this be done legally?

Yes. Whenever either spouse gives away community property without the other's consent, the injured spouse can ask the court to set aside the transfer of property and order the property returned to the community. However, if the automobile was "given" to the secretary in exchange for services legitimately rendered, then

---

*Community property states are Arizona, California, Idaho, Louisiana, Nevada, New Mexico, Texas, and Washington.

the "gift" would be in the nature of a bonus, or wage, and would not be set aside. Realistically, in the preceding hypothetical example, the marriage probably would have deteriorated to the extent that Betty would pursue a dissolution (divorce) rather than continue the marriage while pursuing a lawsuit to return an improper gift from the community. In any divorce decree the court, in dividing the community property equally, would give Betty "credit" for her one-half value of the XJS.

Creditors of the Family

Unpaid creditors who obtain a judgment against either the husband or wife can reach all nonexempt community property to satisfy their claims. Property declared "exempt" by statute cannot be taken from anyone by any creditor (sufficient monies to obtain the necessaries of life are an example of exempt property). Accordingly, if a husband wrongfully punches a letter carrier, for example, severely injuring that person's eyesight, the victim can receive payment of the court judgment from the accumulated earnings of the defendant's wife, or from any other nonexempt community property. Of course, the husband's separate property would be liable for his torts committed during marriage and his personal debts incurred before his marriage; his wife's separate property would not. Reciprocally, the wife's separate property would be liable for her torts or other premarriage debts; her husband's separate property would not. However, either spouse's earnings during marriage may be diverted from the marriage and taken to satisfy premarital debts. To this extent, one does "marry" the preexisting debts of the spouse.

One spouse is not responsible for the crimes or torts of the other, and separate property is immune from fines or civil judgments against the other. Indirectly, of course, the innocent spouse is hurt if a fine is paid from community property or if, as a result of confinement, community property is not earned. Marriage does not shield one's separate property from his or her own creditors.

CIVIL LAWSUITS BETWEEN FAMILY MEMBERS

One traditional concept embodied in the common law has been that marriage melded a man and woman into a single legal entity. It logically followed that one spouse could not sue the other spouse, other than to dissolve the entity (as through divorce). This common-law rule, called the **doctrine of spousal immunity,** prohibits actions between spouses for torts, such as negligence and assault and battery. A justification for this immunity is to protect domestic tranquility. This doctrine does not prevent a victimized spouse from obtaining a divorce on grounds of adultery or extreme mental cruelty, but it does insulate many types of wrongful and abusive conduct by a family member. Consequently, the doctrine of spousal immunity currently is yielding to modern concepts and modifications by the courts (and legislatures) to permit lawsuits between spouses in various situations.

Wives have successfully sued husbands for both compensatory and punitive damages for wife-beating (recovery, $360,000); for intentional infliction of mental distress where a husband tried to hire a hit man (i.e., professional killer) to kill his wife (settled for a six-figure sum); for fraudulently undervaluing and selling marital property worth $800,000 for a price of $45,000 (recovery, $240,000); and for emotional distress when a husband had temper tantrums, doled out stingy amounts of cash, made his wife wear cheap clothes, and belittled her in front of their daughter (recovery, $362,000, forcing husband into bankruptcy).[18]

Shortly after her whirlwind courtship and wedding to Samuel B. McNeill III, Jo McNeill falsely told her husband that she was an attorney, had a master's degree in accounting, was suffering from cancer, and had an outstanding premarital judgment against her that could affect their assets. In reliance on these false statements, Samuel deeded title of his separate property, an exclusive waterfront home in Huntington Beach, California, into their joint names. Later, Jo falsely told Sam that she had only 90 days to live, encouraged him to put "their" assets into trust, and then gave him documents to sign that, in reality, transferred all of his assets to her. Soon thereafter the marriage deteriorated and Sam moved into a small rental cottage in Los Angeles near his work. Upon discovery of the truth, Sam sued his wife for fraud, and also sought recovery of his property. What was the result?

Misstatements of affection or feelings generally are not actionable. Noting that none of the false statements made by Jo McNeill concerned one party's feelings about the other, the trial court ruled in favor of Sam. On appeal, the judgement was upheld.[19] Children also may sue their parents in many states. For example, a daughter was permitted to sue her father for assault and rape;[20] a child sued her mother for negligently failing to buckle her seatbelt;[21] and a child injured *in utero* successfully sued her mother for negligence in jaywalking;[22] But the state of Florida, applying the doctrine of parental immunity, rejected a child's civil lawsuit for sexual abuse.[23] Maryland continues to apply parent-child tort immunity doctrine to actions based on negligence.[24] These actions between spouses, as well as lawsuits between children and their parents, are called *domestic torts*.*

Some argue that permitting lawsuits for injuries from domestic torts simply places another weapon in the hands of embittered and vengeful spouses. It drags soap operas into public courtrooms, implicitly forces the government (through its courts and legislatures) to prescribe what constitutes "normal" or "acceptable" interpersonal conduct, and exacerbates the litigation explosion. Others respond that spousal immunity should not be a shield against penalties for abusive conduct that would be civilly compensable if the parties were strangers. The question of what conduct ought to be compensable is not easy to answer. In the following example, we present actions based upon the intentional infliction of mental distress by one family member on another.

---

*There are significant financial advantages for attorneys who, in addition to accepting divorce cases (which are not usually lucrative), also take a related domestic tort case in which substantial contingent fees may be earned. Seizing the opportunity while the law evolves, lawyers are filing tort suits across the country, for intentional and negligent infliction of emotional distress; assault and battery; the transmission of or fear of transmission of sexual diseases; child-snatching; false imprisonment; defamation (libel or slander); fraudulent concealment of personal attitudes, beliefs or physical condition; and hiding assets during divorce proceedings. *The National Law Journal*, 23 September 1991, Attorneys may be expected to pursue only those defendants who have the means to pay judgments. Homeowners insurance policies will probably soon exclude domestic tort liability from coverage. Consequently, victims in wealthy families may benefit more from the recognition of domestic torts than victims in poor families. Stated bluntly, wealthy wrongdoers may be punished by monetary judgments, while judgment-proof poor wrongdoers escape unscathed.

A family court judge found that Mr. Hakkila's behavior in demeaning his wife, screaming at her, locking her out of the house and refusing to have sex with her was "... beyond the bounds of decency ... atrocious ... utterly intolerable" and constituted compensable negligent and intentional infliction of emotional distress. Should Mr. Hakkila be ordered to pay damages to his wife?

The case against Mr. Hakkila was thrown out on appeal.[25] In New Mexico, family members can sue one another but only if the wrongful conduct is sufficiently outrageous. ... "the threshold of outrageousness should be set high enough ... that the social good from recognizing the tort will not be outweighed by unseemly and invasive litigation."*

Why must intentional conduct between spouses be outrageous to justify civil liability? Presumably the law should not require a degree of civility between spouses that is beyond their capacity. People need to vent to some extent. About half of the states where the question has arisen have honored emotional-distress cases between spouses.[26] The other half of the states require extraordinarily outrageous behavior or the lawsuit is rejected.[27]

There also is a new potential for lawsuits by children against abusive parents, even when many years have elapsed since the alleged wrongful conduct. Many states hold that actions by children are not barred by the statute of limitations because it does not begin to "run" until adult survivors of child abuse overcome their memory blocks and discover (usually in psychiatric or psychological therapy) the acts that took place when they were young children. Even grossly negligent conduct by mothers during pregnancy (e.g., drug, alcohol, or nicotine abuse or rejection of prenatal care) may also give rise to civil judgments for damages in favor of the injured children.

Sexual abuse and severe physical abuse of a child are serious crimes discussed later in this chapter. Child abuse also is a domestic tort that, like other civil cases, may be proven by a "preponderance of the evidence." This burden of proof is much easier to meet than the proof "beyond a reasonable doubt" that is required for conviction in criminal cases. Perhaps the most perplexing dilemma clouding this particular domestic tort is how to identify and reject unjustified claims for damages sought many years following commission of the alleged acts. Such claims are based upon "recovered memory" that is recovered, perhaps after many years, during psychiatric therapy. The issue of the reliability of such recollections, the possibility that they were suggested rather than recollected, as well as the possibility of false claims are among the most difficult issues in such cases.

Claims of child abuse, made during contested custody proceedings (as distinguished from claims made during civil litigation) are discussed later in this chapter.

Not all abuse within families is by parents, nor are all civil lawsuits between family members designed to obtain money.

---

*That the husband insulted his wife in front of her friends by calling her an obsenity, mistreated her physically, locked her out of the house after she ripped the buttons off his shirt, called her "stupid" and "insane" and blamed their poor sexual relationship on her was held insufficiently outrageous to justify liability. *Haikila v. Hakkila*, 812 P.2d 132 (N. Mexico 1991).

Merle Haggard, 60, famous for singing "Okie From Muskogee" and "Workin' Man Blues," received a "continuous barrage of threats against his safety" from his son Marty, 39. Marty believed that Merle "owed him and his mother a lot of money." What civil remedy is available to protect the senior Haggard?

Haggard obtained a restraining order from court barring Marty from harassing or even coming near his father. Violation of such an injunction would be a contempt of court for which jail is the usual sanction.

WHAT LAWS GOVERN PARENTHOOD?

PRENATAL LAWS

For basic information about parenting, adoption, and family law in general, visit the informative Web site of NOLO Press at http://www.nolo.com

Perhaps the most controversial issue in family law is the question of abortion. In 1973, an overwhelming majority of states prohibited abortion unless necessary to preserve the life or health of the mother. In that year the leading and much-publicized case of *Roe v. Wade*[28] was handed down by the U.S. Supreme Court. It held that a pregnant female, married or single, in consultation with her physician, has an unqualified, absolute right to have an abortion during the first trimester (three months) of her pregnancy. This right cannot be vetoed by the natural father, by a parent, or by a husband. During the second trimester the right continues, but the abortion procedures may be regulated by the state, if it chooses, in ways that are related to maternal health (e.g., hospitalization). During the final trimester and when the fetus has become viable (capable of continuing its existence outside the womb naturally or by use of artificial life-support systems), the state may, if it chooses, prohibit abortion unless it is necessary for the health or preservation of the life of the mother. In the more recent *Webster* case, the U.S. Supreme Court held that a state may withhold the use of public employees and facilities to perform or assist abortions that are not necessary to save the mother's life.[29] Also, while *Roe* held that there is a compelling state interest in protecting a fetus (through regulation) once it has become viable, in *Webster*, the Court held that a state may regulate abortion before the fetus is viable by requiring medical tests to determine if the point of viability has occurred.

In 1990, the U.S. Supreme Court upheld (1) an Ohio law requiring an unmarried minor to notify at least one parent of her intended abortion and (2) a Minnesota law requiring an unmarried minor to notify both parents. The Court ruled that both laws were constitutional.[30] In both states, a procedure to bypass parental notification is provided if the female chooses to obtain a judge's order. In 1992, the U.S. Supreme Court declared that although a state cannot prohibit an abortion before a fetus is viable, it nonetheless can require that candidates for abortion first consider information about available and legal alternatives. Although states can thus regulate abortions before viability, the Court stated that they cannot do so in a way that "places a substantial obstacle in the path of a woman's choice."[31]

The mechanical trimester analysis of *Roe* has been shifted to the moment of viability, which today may occur earlier, at perhaps 23 to 24 weeks, or even slightly earlier. Whenever it occurs, the attainment of viability is the critical fact.

All of the U.S. Supreme Court decisions authorizing abortion have been 5–4 votes. In theory, the appointment of a single justice could shift the majority vote the other way.

Information on both sides of the abortion debate is available on the Internet at http://www/naral.org/ and http://www.prolife.org/ultimate/

LEGITIMACY

A legitimate child enjoys rights, and sometimes duties* of support; possesses rights of inheritance; and typically carries the father's surname. Such a child is the issue of his or her natural, married parents. Historically, an illegitimate child was a child born of an unmarried mother or born of an adulterous, incestuous, or bigamous relationship. Statutes today are inclusive and tend to resolve any doubt in favor of legitimacy through application of a legal presumption of legitimacy. For example, children conceived within a specified time of marriage or born within a specified time after divorce (or death) are presumed to be legitimate. Likewise, children born of a married woman are presumed to be legitimate; that is, fathered by the husband.

The presumption of legitimacy is difficult to overcome and usually will depend on the husband's showing of impotency or on a blood-typing analysis, which all but conclusively proves that the husband could not be the child's father. With modern blood-typing techniques and analyses, experts can establish statistical probabilities as to whether or not a suspect could be the natural father. Such tests also can show a high probability that a specific man is the father. Every state (except South Dakota) now has statutes providing for the admissibility of specified genetic tests in paternity cases.[32] Blood tests are not absolutely conclusive. In one case, the defendant contended that he had never even met the mother of the child he was accused of fathering even though blood tests revealed he had a 99.99 percent probability of paternity. The court believed the persuasive man.[33] DNA testing is even more conclusive.

Four poor children born out of wedlock to different mothers had their paternity established by DNA "sibling" testing of one another. Their deceased father was Larry Hillbloom, who crashed at sea leaving no DNA readily available. Hillbloom had sex with the teenage mothers of the half-brothers and sisters while he was on various other trips to the South Pacific. Hillbloom's will left everything to the University of California at Berkeley—nothing was said about any children. Can the illegimate children inherit?

Yes. Both legitimate and illegitimate children (once paternity is established) inherit unless specifically disinherited in the will. Not mentioning is not disinheriting. Thus, the four South Pacific children each received $90 million in their paternity suit.[34]

---

*As previously noted, in some states adult children are required to support their indigent parents who are receiving public assistance. There is no common-law duty of a child to support a parent.

The basic handicaps of an illegitimate child are financial. Until paternity is established by a court, the child does not inherit as an heir and has no right to paternal support.

There is a trend to equalize the rights of illegitimate (whose paternity is established) and legitimate children. Adopted children under the law are treated equally to natural children. This trend reflects the facts that increasing numbers of children are born out of wedlock and that such children are innocent of any wrongdoing. Thus, the U.S. Supreme Court has held that states may not discriminate against illegitimate children and that states must require that natural fathers support both their legitimate and illegitimate children.[35] Nor may a state create a right of action in favor of legitimate children for the wrongful death of a parent and exclude illegitimate children from the benefit of such a right.[36] And illegitimate children may not be excluded from sharing equally with other children in the recovery of workers' compensation benefits for the death of their parent.[37]

Custody of a child conceived out of wedlock remains with the mother as long as she is a suitable person. Otherwise, custody may be awarded to another suitable person, including the natural father.

Some states have adopted statutes that permit the illegitimate child with ascertained paternity to inherit from his or her father. In the absence of such a statute, the illegitimate child will inherit only from his or her mother.

In some states, an illegitimate child automatically becomes legitimated (or legitimized) upon the subsequent marriage of the child's parents. Other states require the father's acknowledgement (sometimes in writing) of the child's status to give him or her inheritance rights as an heir. And some states have equalized the rights of children in all respects, including inheritance.

Legal rights for nonmarital offspring have little meaning unless the natural father becomes identified. The fact of birth identifies the mother. The mother or child may bring a civil paternity action to establish the child's natural parentage. A male who is accused in a paternity action has a right to trial by jury. Usually the mother's testimony is admitted to show the requisite act of intercourse. Proof that an unmarried mother had sexual intercourse with other men during the period of possible conception is admissible; however, testimony concerning the mother's sexual activities before or after the time of possible conception cannot be considered by the jury.

If the mother prevails and paternity is established, the court's judgment will include an order of periodic support and reimbursement of medical costs, expenses of pregnancy, and her attorney fees. Once paternity is established, all states authorize their courts to order the payment of support because of state interest (welfare authorities may have the burden of support if the natural father is not held responsible). A few states also confer inheritance rights upon a child legitimated by a paternity proceeding. But even then, any child may be completely disinherited by the will of his or her parent. (See Chapter 14 for a more complete discussion of inheritance and disinheritance.)

SURROGATE MOTHER CONTRACTS

To obtain a biologically related child, a husband and wife may desire to artificially inseminate a contracting **surrogate mother**, who agrees to carry the fetus until birth and then relinquish her parental rights to the biological father. The natural father's wife then adopts the child. There are two basic kinds of surrogacy arrangements. In gestational surrogacy, the surrogate mother is not genetically related to the child. A fertilized egg is transferred into the surrogate mother's uterus to gestate until birth. The fertilized egg may or may not be genetically related to both the husband and wife who may have used the sperm or egg of a donor.

In 1985, William Stern and Mary Beth Whitehead entered into a surrogacy contract. It stated that Stern's wife, Elizabeth, was infertile, that they wanted a child, and that Mrs. Whitehead was willing to serve as the mother with Mr. Stern as the father. The contract provided that Mrs. Whitehead would become pregnant (through artificial insemination, using Mr. Stern's sperm), carry the child to term, bear it, deliver it to the Sterns, and thereafter do whatever was necessary to terminate her maternal rights so that Mrs. Stern could thereafter adopt the child. Mr. Stern agreed to pay $10,000 to Ms. Whitehead.

On March 27, 1986, Baby M was born; on March 30 she was delivered to the Sterns. Later that day, Mrs. Whitehead underwent an emotional crisis; she was deeply disturbed, disconsolate, and stricken with unbearable sadness. She had to have her child. Fearing that she may commit suicide, the Sterns returned Baby M in exchange for Ms. Whitehead's promise to return her child in one week. The struggle over custody then began in the courts and Melissa (Baby M) was returned to the Sterns pending final outcome of the litigation. Ms. Whitehead was permitted limited visitation.

The trial court ruled in favor of the Sterns. Ms. Whitehead appealed. What was the result?

The Supreme Court of New Jersey held that the surrogacy contract conflicted with the state's adoption laws, especially in calling for the payment of money and by providing for the irrevocable agreement of the natural mother to terminate her parental rights to facilitate the adoption. Also, the contract's basic premise, that the natural parents can decide in advance of birth which one is to have custody of the child, conflicts with the law that the child's best interests shall determine custody. Therefore, the court reasoned, the contract was void and unenforceable. The court then decided that custody with the Sterns was in the best interests of Melissa regardless of the invalidity of the contract. Ms. Whitehead lost custody but was awarded visitation rights.[38]

For reference materials about surrogacy arrangements and sample contract forms visit http://www.opts.com/ and http://www.surromomsonline.com/

Since *In re Baby M*, legislatures in a number of states have barred or severely limited the enforceability of surrogate contracts.* Nonetheless, surrogacy contracts continue to be utilized. A single firm specializing in surrogate parenting has successfully arranged 300 surrogate births, and thousands have occurred in the U.S.[39]

Crispina and Mark Calvert entered into a contract with Anna Johnson, who agreed to have their embryo (created by the sperm and egg of the Calverts) implanted into her uterus and to bear the child. The Calverts

*Arizona, Indiana, Kentucky, Louisiana, Michigan, New York, and Utah. See 29 *Idaho Law Review* 383 (1992–3).

agreed to pay Anna $10,000 and to purchase a life insurance policy on Anna's life for this service. Several months into the pregnancy, Anna claimed that she had "bonded" with the fetus and filed suit to be declared the legal mother. What was the result?

The California Supreme Court held that the law recognizes both genetic consanguinity (of the same blood) and giving birth as two means of establishing a mother and child relationship. However, when the two means do not coincide in one woman, the one who intended to bring about the birth of a child that she intended to raise as her own (Crispina Calvert in this case) is the natural mother.[40] Anna Johnson's attorney argued that the birth mother has the better case because the donor of the fertilized egg had never been pregnant and had never given birth.

In vitro fertilization (IVF) takes place in a petri dish (a glass dish with an overlapping cover for the culture of microorganisms), following which the fertilized egg is placed into the mother's uterus. It also is possible to freeze the fertilized embryo and implant it into a mother's uterus in the distant future.

Maureen Kass, 39, could not have children naturally because while in her mother's womb, she was exposed to the drug DES. Maureen and her husband, Steven, caused five of her eggs to be artificially fertilized by his sperm, and then frozen. They signed a contract stating that, upon divorce, the eggs would be donated to research and ultimately destroyed. But following their divorce, Maureen changed her mind; Steven objected, saying he did not want to have a child by his former wife. Maureen contended that the law should protect her maternal rights to her fertilized egg. Who wins?

The New York Court of Appeals upheld the contract.[41] The issue would not be so clear if there had been no contract to uphold. A male has no legal right to object to an abortion of the embryo; should he have a right to object to its gestation and birth before it has been implanted into a womb?

Cryopreservation of sperm makes artificial insemination possible without having to match ovulation cycles with sperm donations. The storage of large numbers of sperm samples permits infertile couples to select donor characteristics to assure a closer match to the sterile husband's own makeup. Selection can be based on race, height, body type, eye color, intelligence, religious background, and even national origin.[42] Fertilized embryos also can be frozen, for perhaps 100 years. Thus, women do not need to be subjected to surgery each time they need to get an egg—a dozen or more can be retrieved at one time.

At the beginning of the twenty-first century, an estimated 9,000 embryos are stockpiled in the country's freezers. Some of these fertilized eggs are forgotten or abandoned. Legal issues arise when storage bills are not paid. What if one or more of the donors dies? Can abandoned embryos be foreclosed upon and be given or sold in the open market? One set of "test tube orphans" (fertilized embryos) are residing in a deep freeze in Australia; its donors died in a plane crash leaving a multimillion dollar estate to their children, if they are ever born.[43]

Today a thriving surrogacy industry exists in this country, and thousands of IVF children have been born. Typically, these surrogacy arrangements involve fertilization of the woman's own egg with a male client's sperm. However, many arrangements, like the Crispina and Mark Calvert case, involve the renting of a womb for nine months to produce another couple's baby.

Legal issues presented in such cases concern validity of the underlying contracts, forfeiture of parental rights by surrogate mothers, assurance of adoption by wives of the natural fathers, the best interests of the children, inheritance rights following the intestate death of either of the biological parents, and commercialization of the whole process.

In addition to the legal issues, surrogacy raises many fundamental social, medical, and moral questions: Is surrogacy an acceptable positive solution to the problem of female infertility? Or is it an unnatural arrangement, and in effect a "forced baby sale" exploitive of poor women, even if they are paid for their cooperation? Should similar questions be asked about the use of fertility drugs, which have resulted in multiple births, even the birth of octuplets (eight siblings)? Later in this chapter we will consider whether or not the legal problems created by the use of human surrogates can be sidestepped by the use of artificial wombs.

PARENTING BY SAME-SEX COUPLES

Although same-sex marriages are not allowed in any U.S. state, some same-sex couples are treated as a family sufficiently to allow them to adopt a child. Whereas most adoption disputes involve attempted revocation of an adoption by a birth parent, in a lesbian relationship, the biological mother wants to add (not substitute) her partner as an additional "legal" parent. Some courts, reasoning that such an adoption is like a stepparent adoption, have permitted these adoptions.[44]

Partly because science provides new opportunities to "transplant" fetilized eggs, the law faces new challenges. One such challenge is the desire of lesbians to have and raise their "birth" children. For example, lesbian couples could select frozen sperm of preferred hereditary background from a bank, fertilize one of their eggs *in vitro*, and then transplant it into the womb of the other. One becomes the gestational mother, one is the hereditary mother. Later in this chapter, we review the state of science relative to family planning.

Related legal issues surrounding homosexuals as parents include legalization of same-sex marriage and the traditional difficulties of child custody and support, not to mention resolution of the many financial problems encountered when family relationships dissolve. Many argue that families require both sexes and that family law should become more restrictive relative to same-sex adoption. These issues are expected to fuel the demand for new family laws that protect the interests of children.

When adoption occurs, the law applies the same parenting rules that apply to all natural parents.

PARENTAL RIGHTS AND LIABILITIES

Freedom from governmental involvement in family affairs is a fundamental value in our society. While not explicitly stated therein, the U.S. Constitution implies a right to marry, to establish a home and bring up children, to educate one's children as one chooses, and a right to privacy—that is, to be let alone by the government in the private realm of family life. Parents thus have a constitutional right to autonomy in rearing their children, and the state cannot interfere except under "clear and convincing" proof of severe child abuse or abandonment.[45] Parents also must exercise reasonable care, supervision, protection, and control over their minor children. Willful failure to do so may be a crime, a variation of the misdemeanor called contributing to the delinquency of a minor.[46] The *Restatement of Torts* describes "a duty to exercise reasonable care so to control his minor child as to prevent it from intentionally harming others. . . ."[47] Parents are not criminally responsible for negligent parenting if they make reasonable efforts to control their children, but are unable to do so. There is no crime (or civil liability) visited upon parents for their children's general incorrigibility and bad disposition.

In general, parents have the right to custody of their minor children and are free to raise them as they see fit. Does the following case fly in the face of this rule?

Gregory Kingsley, age 12, was living happily with his foster parents, George and Lizabeth Russ, who had eight children of their own. George Russ had noticed Gregory while visiting the Lake County Boy's ranch, and soon applied to be his foster parent. (A foster family usually provides a temporary haven for a child until the child can be reunited with his or her family.) Before long, the Russes applied to formally adopt Gregory, but his natural mother, Rachel, objected. Gregory then contacted and hired his own attorney, Jerri Blair, to "sue his parents for divorce" so he could be legally adopted by George and Lizabeth. What was the outcome?

The State Circuit Court in Orlando, Florida, allowed Gregory Kingsley to "divorce" his natural parents, freeing him for adoption by George and Lizabeth.[48] However, this case does not contradict the broad rights of parents to raise their children as they see fit. The reality of the Gregory Kingsley case is that his parents, for various reasons, were not raising him at all. Gregory Kingsley was 12 at the time of his lawsuit—should a minimum age for such actions be established?

GENETIC ENGINEERING AND FAMILY PLANNING: LEGAL ISSUES

Education is a lifetime experience. There are nearly 15 million of you in college, and most of you will graduate from college in the twenty-first century, in the embryo of the new millennium. You most certainly will be affected by and participate in society's response to what many refer to as the "Biotech Century."* The accelerated pace of scientific discovery in biotechnology is the direct result of the marriage of the genetic and computer revolutions. The computer is being used "to decipher, manage and organize the vast resource of the biotech economy."[49] It is estimated that biological knowledge is currently doubling every five years; in genetics, the quantity of information is doubling every twenty-four months.

---

*Biotechnology is the use of the data and techniques of engineering and computer technology for the study of living organisms.

The U.S. Department of Energy is funding what is called the "Human Genome Project," with two hundred researchers working around the clock hoping to sequence the entire 3 billion base pairs of DNA that make up the total of 100,000 human genes by the end of 2003. Private companies also are racing to sequence the most important genes.[50] Although Congress has prohibited any government funding of research using human preembryos (fertilized eggs), private companies around the world are proceeding rapidly.

Private biotech corporations are interested in the potential profits from new medicines and vaccines that can be produced once the genetic code of disease is identified.* Driven by the rush to create and to monopolize the profits flowing from new discoveries, private business will provide new medicines and vaccines promising longer and healthier lives for families. Agricultural products that are improved (e.g., disease resistant) through genetic engineering also hold the promise for huge profits, and indirectly impact families through healthier children. Already there are thousands of genetically altered food products in the markets of the world. But here we are concerned with the laws and issues that are more directly surrounding the family. This rapidly developing science will begin impacting the family and family law in the earliest years of the coming century.

CURING CHILDREN THROUGH DRUGS AND TRANSPLANTS

Already, human genes have successfully been spliced into animal embryos, reducing the future risk of human rejection of transplanted organs from fully grown animals. It has become possible to produce cows that provide human milk (milk containing the human-like serum albumin) and pigs that grow human-like organs for transplant when needed.[51] Mice, rabbits, sheep, and cows have been genetically engineered to carry human genes, useful for producing various medicines. Private corporations hold patents to these human–animal combinations called chimeras. The next step already has occurred. A human cell's nucleus has been implanted into a cow's egg—its natural nucleus was sliced off. A hybrid cell, part human and part cow, was thus created and grew, quickly becoming more human-like as the human nucleus took control. Even though the hybrid is in the form of cells, the concept of half-human creatures stirs deeply felt beliefs.[52] Recently, patents have been requested on the process of mixing human cells with the cells of chimpanzees and pigs. A true chimera, one that is perhaps 30 percent human, is the goal. But at what point do constitutional rights kick in? The patent office has publicly announced that it will not grant patents on any "monsters." Patent law scholars have publicly responded there may be no choice under existing law. Many patents already have been granted on animals engineered to contain some human genes, cells, and tissues.[53]

For family members, what are the potential consequences of creating chimeras? A staggering number of pharmaceutical products are in the pipeline, ranging from anticancer to anticlotting drugs. One transgenic goat alone, "Grace," is valued at $1 million, the most valuable goat in history, for the anticancer drug it produces. Immediately after the cloned sheep "Dolly" was born, a second cloned sheep with a human gene, "Polly," was born. Animal clones could

For background as well as timely information on the Human Genome Project, visit its Web site at http://www.ornl.gov/TechResources/Human_Genome/home.html

---

*For example, the full genetic sequence of the bacteria chlamydia, best known as the cause of a sexually transmitted infection in women, has been identified and published. A solution to this disease is within sight.

be used to harvest organs for human transplantation; carrying human genes, these organs will be less likely to be rejected by their recipients. These animals would serve as "factories" for needed drugs and body parts. (More than 100,000 Americans die annually when no suitable organ is available.) Thus, there will be new cures and repairs for babies and children unless new family laws intervene. Should new family laws be adopted to restrict the dimensions of such human/animal combinations, or would this be futile in a global research environment?

"DESIGNER" BABIES IN THE FUTURE?

Ethical and legal issues arise when a human egg is fertilized in a petri dish and then is permitted to divide and grow in the dish before implantation into a surrogate's womb. What legal issues will arise when potential parents engage the services of geneticists to obtain "designer babies"?

With *in vitro* fertilization already an established process, genetic changes could be made in embryos outside the womb to correct deadly diseases, enhance mood, modify behavior, or change intelligence and physical traits. The "enhanced" embryo then would be planted in its mother's womb. The mapping of the entire human genome will allow the characteristics associated with specific genes to be studied and modified in the laboratory. The result: "designer babies." Even though environmental factors bear strongly on behavior, so also do genetics, as demonstrated by twins who have been raised in radically different environments.[54]

The mapping of the human genome, reproductive technologies, and genetic manipulation are by their nature the tools of *eugenics* (the movement to improve the human species through hereditary measures in mating). Eugenics was a popular movement at the beginning of the twentieth century, until it later was twisted by the insanities of Adolf Hitler. It was popularly believed that heredity was more influential than economic, cultural, or social factors in determining human behavior.

> *I wish very much that the wrong people could be prevented entirely from breeding; and when the evil nature of these people is sufficiently flagrant, this should be done. Criminals should be sterilized and feeble-minded persons forbidden to leave offspring behind them . . . the emphasis should be laid on getting desirable people to breed.*[55]

Indeed, many states enacted laws mandating sterilization under specified circumstances of family members who were criminals or "idiots." Today, "[g]enetic engineering is a technology designed to enhance the genetic inheritance of living things by manipulating their genetic code."[56] Like it or not, you are on the threshold of a new eugenics society. In germ-line therapy, genetic changes are made in the sperm, the egg, or in embryonic cells after fertilization and are carried on to future generations. Whatever is excised by genetic surgery is gone forever from the heredity of that future family. Genetic therapy that prevents the inheritance of some negative characteristic by future generations will likely be the first to be developed.

In 2010, Jean Luc and his bride Kristie consider and then decide not to obtain a genetic review of their *in vitro* embryo before it is implanted. They choose to let "nature run its course." Their son Injo is subsequently born with a lifelong defect that easily could have been deleted from the fertilized egg by simple gene surgery. Are Jean Luc and Kristie civilly liable to Injo for negligently failing to obain genetic screening?

In considering your answer to his hypothetical, do not assume the family members are angry with each other. Sometimes family suits are designed to obtain payment from an insurance company, as when a minor/passenger sues the parent/driver who is covered by insurance. Clearly, family law will be faced with difficult issues.

Parents in Massachusetts sued their doctor for his inability to extract fluid from the wife's uterus that would have revealed the presence of Down's syndrome. Had they known, they would have aborted the fetus.[57] Would prospective parents abort a fetus that was predisposed to obesity? More than one-half of all adults and more than 25 percent of all children are overweight or obese.[58] If lifelong illnesses are to be prevented by gene surgery, what about less serious characteristics? Would prospective parents choose to genetically eliminate myopia, dyslexia, left-handeness, or shortness? Already, sex screening is well established and opportunities sometimes are taken through abortion to achieve gender balance in the family. Would these families choose gene therapy to improve the physical characteristics of their babies, to produce "designer babies"? Such "designer babies" may be available only to the wealthy, who may also opt for gestation in an artificial womb to avoid the unpleasantries of pregnancy.*

Should children have the legal right to be told of changes made to their genetic sources? For many years, many children have had genetic roots different from their parents, because of adoption or sperm donation. Today, egg donation also is in widespread use; some 6,000 or more women have overcome their infertility in this fashion.** Do their children know? Most egg-transplant babies are currently too young to have been told about their origins. But soon into the next century, the issue will become acute. An overwhelming majority of parents of children conceived through sperm donation have not told their children, and many of those who have reportedly regret it.[59] So far, children do not have a legal right to know the truth. In some states, such as New York, the identities of sperm and egg donors are not disclosed to recipients—but records are maintained.

---

*Scientists theorize that early in the coming century a fetus will be grown in a totally artificial womb, from conception to birth, permitting a more predictable and safe environment and making genetic corrections easier. This process would add a new dimension to surrogacy contracts that could involve many presently unimaginable legal issues. Theoretically, a couple would contract to have either her or another woman's egg fertilized by either his or another male's sperm and gestated until birth in a rented glass womb. Thus, a true "test tube baby" is on the horizon.

By suppressing development of parts of such an embryo in an artificial glass womb, it may be scientifically possible to gestate body parts for future medical reasons, such as transplanting to humans. Because such organs would not have a head or nervous system, the applicability of law and the constitution may be avoided. And even if new laws prohibit such research in the United States, the likelihood of such global research is substantial.

Rather than suppress parts of such an embryo in an artificial glass womb, what if the contributor of the egg chose to "abort" or terminate the "test tube baby"? Such a woman then would have no claim to the right of privacy to deal with her own body—rather she would be in the constitutional shoes of the male who merely contributes sperm outside his body. Thus, such a gestating embryo may have constitutional protection in its own right.

**In vitro fertilization raises myriad legal issues when fertilized eggs stored in banks are abandoned by their owners, or when disagreements arise between their owners relative to their ultimate disposition. As the twentieth century winds down, these issues already are in our courtrooms. In one bizarre example, a fertility doctor, Lillian Nash, erroneously transplanted the embryo of an African-American couple into Donna Fusano's uterus along with an embryo created by Donna and her husband, who are caucasians. Twin boys were born, one black, whose custody has been volunteered to his genetic parents. Litigation is pending. Michael Grunwald. *Embryo Mix-Up is Double Trouble*, Washington Post, 31 March 1999.

CLONING BABIES

For an overview, including the history and last minute developments of human cloning, and exhaustive resources, visit http://library.advanced.org/24355/
For a more simplified version of human cloning, as well as questions of ethics, visit http://vetc.vsc.edu/vuhs/apbio/clone/

For centuries, science has been domesticating, breeding, and hybridizing animals and plants. But nature always has imposed limits on combinations of species. Today, microscopic bits of DNA from two species that could not mate in nature can be spliced together to create new life forms, to modify existing life forms, or to produce biological chemicals, such as insulin. In 1997, a scientist replaced the DNA in a normal sheep egg with the DNA from the mammary gland of an adult sheep. The splice worked—the egg grew and was then transplanted into the womb of a surrogate sheep, who bore Dolly, the famous cloned sheep. Thus, the DNA of an existing adult sheep was recreated in a newly born sheep that was gestated by a surrogate. Simply substitue the word "human" for "sheep" in the preceding sentence and you describe one of the most perplexing legal problems facing the family in the foreseeable future—human cloning.

Researchers have cloned a small group of genetically identical calves in a major step toward building herds of "designer cattle" with especially useful characteristics. Given the opportunity, would family members be willing to pay to clone themselves? To produce genetically identical children? If a fetus is not protected by the Constitution, then presumably it has no legal standing to object to its alteration. Or does it? What if, following legal separation, one parent chooses to genetically alter the embryo and have it transplanted in a surrogate mother? These unanswered questions are only meant to typify the many and esoteric kinds of family law issues that will be surfacing in the beginning years of the new millennium.

STATE PROTECTION OF MINORS

My mother loved children—she would have given anything if I had been one.

Groucho Marx, 1895–1977

Involvement of the state in family affairs is a modern trend. The purpose is protection of those family members who are least able to protect themselves. Out-of-wedlock births have contributed to a growing number of single-parent families, often requiring tax-supported public assistance. The state now also steps in when special needs arise, for example, to protect family members from serious harm caused by drug addiction or venereal disease, or in complications from difficult pregnancies. Finally, the state now engages in "co-parenting" through official acceptance of teenagers' decisions with regard to abortion and contraception.

Still another area of government protection of minors involves parental misconduct. Historically, parental immunity was considered necessary to preserve family harmony. For example, children could not sue their parents for personal injuries caused by parental negligence. In modern times, though, insurance covers damages caused by the negligent driving of the parent—at no apparent risk to family harmony. Thus, as indicated earlier in this chapter, parents are liable to their children for serious misconduct, parental immunity being a rapidly fading concept.

As a general common-law rule, parents are not liable for torts of their children causing injury to third persons. However, nearly half of the states have statutes creating parental liability up to certain specified limited amounts, often up to $10,000 or thereabouts, for their children's torts. Thus, in California, for example, parents would be responsible up to $10,000 for windows broken, cars keyed, or graffiti done by their minor children.[60] Some states require a showing of willful conduct by the minor before their parents are responsible, up to a statutory maximum amount of money. Many states also create parental liability for malicious mischief when their children damage school or other public property.

Antoinette Walker is a police officer in Oakland with responsibility to recruit new officers. She left her loaded handgun on her bedroom dresser where it was found by her 10-year-old son, who shot and wounded his 12-year-old brother. No adult was at home. What family law issues have arisen?

Antoinette could be charged with a crime—either misdemeanor or felony negligence in leaving a firearm readily available to minors. Handguns can be disabled by parents using trigger locks or simply by keeping them under lock and key. No crime was charged, however, raising the issue of selective enforcement—would an ordinary citizen have been prosecuted?[61] The separated father, Antoinette's husband, could sue in civil court for money damages or even to contest the existing custody arrangement. The wounded son may be entitled to recover damages from his mother for negligence. None of these events, however, took place in this family tragedy, as often they don't. Family law has implications for much injurious behavior amongst family members, but only when victims make complaints and attorneys bring their cases to court. Unfortunately, many abuses exist within families that are known only to the victims and perpetrators.

Some children need protection from each other. Metal dectectors are widely used in junior and senior high schools in major metropolitan areas. Recently, a grade school in Indianapolis began screening its elementary students for weapons. The policy is believed needed to protect students, teachers, and staff.[62] When minor students commit serious crimes against other students, especially involving guns or knives, they are prosecuted in juvenile court, the same as with off-campus crime. But lesser antisocial behavior among students, such as physical bullying, is ignored by the law. Such bullying, if occuring between strangers at a downtown mall, for example, would be a criminal assault and battery. Persistent schoolyard abuse (e.g., pushing and slapping or teasing about physical or mental characteristics) can be more damaging to its victims than isolated incidents off-campus. Yet such incidents largely are ignored by police and left for administrative discipline by school officials.

State statutes impose the obligation on parents to support their children until majority, or until earlier emancipation when the minor child becomes self-supporting. However, some states provide for postminority (over age 18) support by order of the divorce court or by statute.* Even when postminority support is

---

*California, Colorado, Illinois, Indiana, Iowa, Mississippi, Missouri, New Hampshire, New Jersey, New York, Oregon, Pennsylvania, South Carolina, and Washington.

not required, states will enforce marital agreements that call for such support. The general purpose of postminority child support is to pay for college education. In most states, child support is a joint obligation, although it may be apportioned between the parents according to their respective financial circumstances. It is a crime to willfully fail to support a child, and almost all states have computerized methods for tracking down deadbeat parents. But finding deadbeat parents is not the only problem. Often there simply isn't enough money to go around.

> Keith Jackson was elected school board president in San Francisco, overseeing 64,000 students and a $530 million budget. He receives $500 per month for his services. He had previously been hired by the district attorney to "track down deadbeat dads," but that job, for some unknown reason, lasted only three days. Keith is divorced and has two sons, 6 and 12, for whom the court has orderd $643 monthly child support. Keith is in arrearage of more than $5,000 and is falling further behind each month. Should a father run for an elected office that pays less than a court order for support, or should he obtain employment that pays enough for child support?

A court could order Jackson to search for a job that pays adequately for child support, and jail him if he refused. Public service as an elected official is important, but perhaps it is not as indispensable as being a supportive father.[63] The issue of child support is covered more fully later in this chapter.

Most parents choose to provide for their children, "the natural objects of their bounty," by will. However, a parent may intentionally disinherit his or her child (or children) completely, even if the child is a dependent minor of tender years. This rule of absolute testamentary freedom originated in the common law. Nevertheless, state statutes commonly provide that the child gets a share of the parental estate unless it is absolutely clear that the disinheritance was planned. In other words, disinheritance of a child cannot occur through oversight by a parent. If a disinherited child is mentioned in the will (for example, when a child is left a nominal amount), it is clear that the disinheritance was intentional and it will be upheld.

EMANCIPATED MINORS

The term *emancipation* means setting free. Therefore, an **emancipated minor** is "set free" from his or her parents. This means that the parents no longer have responsibility for or control over their emancipated child. Thus, parents also are set free, so to speak. Following emancipation, parents no longer have a legal duty to support or care for that child. Emancipated minors take on all of the rights and responsibilities of adults except for certain ones, such as being able to legally purchase alcoholic beverages. Nor is such a minor necessarily deprived of the benefits of juvenile court, discussed in the following section.

A number of states recognize the status of emancipation based on lawful marriage of the minor, or service in the military, or simply for becoming self-supporting. Some states provide a judicial procedure for declaration of the emancipated status.

In the fall of 1998, 17-year-old Dominique Moceanu, a member of the 1996 gold medal U.S. Olympic gymnastics team, filed suit in Texas requesting, among other things, future independence from her parents, saying they squandered her fortune and oppressed her for years. "I want whatever I have earned to be under my control so I know how my earnings are being used, and I want to be able to train and compete in the sport I love for the right reason—because I love it—not because my father tells me I have to make more money." Has Dominique stated sufficient grounds to become emancipated?

Yes. Before trial, Dominique and her parents settled the lawsuit and her parents agreed to the emancipation. The settlement was approved by court.[64]

JUVENILE COURT PROTECTION

I've been struck by the upside-down priorities of the juvenile-justice system. We are willing to spend the least amount of money to keep a kid at home, more to put him in a foster home, and the most to institutionalize him.

Marian Wright Edelman, **American lawyer**

Unfortunately, children sometimes are forced to live without adequate, or any, parental supervision; consequently, many become delinquent or even incorrigible. Legislatures have created juvenile court systems to protect minor children as well as the public in such situations. Unknown at the turn of the twentieth century, juvenile law and courts have burgeoned, especially following World War Two. Today there is much sentiment that juvenile laws and courts are too lenient and that more minors who engage in vicious crimes ought to be treated as adults.

Children are not under the jurisdiction of juvenile courts simply because they are minors (under age 18); rather, juvenile courts become involved only when necessary. For example, minor children who need proper parental care or who are destitute (with no home and without the necessaries of life) are within the jurisdiction of the juvenile court system. They can be declared "dependents" of the court, which then is free to make a wide variety of possible orders for their care, supervision, custody, and support. A dependent child may be taken from the custody of its parents and, for example, be placed in a foster home (as in the Gregory Kingsley case, discussed on page 428) or the home of a relative, or be subject to any other arrangement deemed by the court to be in the child's best interest.

Also subject to the jurisdiction of juvenile courts are minor children who commit acts that would be crimes if done by adults. Because juveniles may be confined against their will, they are entitled to many constitutional protections. For example, a minor in juvenile court has the right to representation by an attorney (without charge, if the minor is indigent) and cannot be compelled to be a witness against him- or herself. The burden of proof is the same as in criminal cases—generally, that is, "beyond a reasonable doubt." However, no right to trial by jury exists in juvenile court, nor is there a right to bail (although prehearing release is common).

Ordinarily, juvenile court hearings are not open to the public. If the accused person is found to have committed the charged offense, the court will declare the minor a ward of the court. Juvenile courts can make various orders, such as probation, fines, or commitments to juvenile homes, ranches, camps, or special jails for youthful offenders.

Parents can and do take control of unruly, out-of-control children who are truants from school and otherwise incorrigible by hiring "professional escorts" (moonlighting police and probation officers) to take their children to "behavior modification" camps in other locations, sometimes as far away as Jamaica. These children can be taken against their will because parents have the right and responsibility to determine what is best for their children.

Under specified conditions (usually the passage of a specified number of years), juvenile courts will officially seal all records pertaining to a minor's case. The minor then officially has no criminal record and will not be handicapped in the future when seeking employment.

Not all juvenile offenders are processed by juvenile courts. The nature of some youthful offenders, and the severity of their alleged misconduct (such as homicide, armed robbery, or rape), may lead the juvenile court to reject jurisdiction, thereby compelling the minor to stand trial as an adult and face harsher criminal procedures and possible penalties.

SEXUAL ABUSE OF CHILDREN

Sexual abuse of a child is a serious felony that is difficult to detect, usually occurring in complete privacy. The victimized child may be the only witness and may be reluctant or unable to testify adequately. Forced testimony by a child in open court may result in the child's suffering serious emotional distress that may adversely affect both the child and the usefulness of the information obtained. The scope of the problem in the United States is subject to considerable debate. One expert describes the public response as "sex-abuse hysteria," whose manifestations are overreacting, seeing danger when it does not exist, dramatizing, and so on.[65]

Nearly all of the states have adopted statutes designed to protect child witnesses from further harm caused by the humiliation and stress of testifying in open court. To balance the goal of protecting the child and the constitutional rights of the accused, various techniques are evolving to obtain testimony from involved children outside the presence of the person allegedly guilty of abusive conduct. For example, out-of-court statements (hearsay evidence) made privately by children to mental health or child protection professionals, who often use anatomically correct dolls, sometimes can be used in court.* This procedure assists many children who are unable to recall, report, or evaluate events accurately. Critics, however, point out that some experts, with the best of intentions, may come to faulty conclusions based on interpretations of the manner in which children manipulate dolls. Additional protective procedures include closed-circuit testimony from a private room, videotaping of such out-of-court testimony, and

---

*Admission into the record of such hearsay evidence is proper only when the "totality of circumstances" surrounding the testimony render the witness particularly worthy of belief. Out-of-court hearsay was ruled not admissible where the doctor conducted an interview without a videotape, asked leading questions, and had a preconceived idea of what the child should be disclosing. *Idaho v. Wright*, 497 U.S 805, 110 S.Ct. 3139 (1990).

allowing admission of hearsay evidence that otherwise would be excluded from the trial. But some of these protective laws may clash with the Sixth Amendment to the U.S. Constitution.

The Sixth Amendment grants an accused the right to confront all witnesses. Thus, the U.S. Supreme Court has denied the use of a screen in court to shield a child from visual contact while testifying.[66] But one exception to the right to eye-to-eye confrontation between the accused and the child while testifying in court has been approved by the U.S. Supreme Court. A 5–4 majority of Justices held that the Sixth Amendment does not invariably require face-to-face confrontation between a defendant and an adverse witness. It concluded that public policy, including the interest in protecting child witnesses from trauma, can justify an exception to the normal "preference" for face-to-face confrontation. The Court upheld a Maryland statutory scheme permitting a child to testify from outside the courtroom via closed-circuit television.[67]

Note that protection of the child from confrontation with the accused is a different problem than closing the trial to the public and press. Court proceedings almost always are open to the public; however, under appropriate circumstances, a judge can close the courtroom to protect a child from serious emotional injury.

Recall from Chapter 6 that proof of guilt in criminal cases must be "beyond a reasonable doubt." Moral certainty has been removed. Such a high standard of proof is not easily met with testimony that is incomplete, inconsistent, or even contradictory. The age and maturity of a child can make prosecution especially difficult in sexual abuse cases. The best example of the difficulties in determining the guilt or innocence of the accused is the notorious *McMartin* case (perhaps the longest and most costly criminal trial in U.S. history), in which one defendant was found not guilty of molesting numerous children while responsible for their care in a preschool. The jury in the three-year trial deadlocked on certain charges against the other defendant, and a retrial limited to those charges again resulted in a hung jury. Clearly emotions were very high, perhaps bordering on hysteria, in the local community, and the consequences were very serious with regard to everyone involved in such difficult, complex, and bewildering litigation.

In civil law divorce and child custody proceedings, more relaxed procedures and reduced standards of proof are applicable. For example, there is no right to trial by jury in divorce or custody matters.* Civil remedies also are quite different than criminal penalties for sexual abuse of a child. Whereas jail is the probable result of a criminal conviction for child abuse, a court order that all child visitation be supervised is one possible result of a civil proceeding. Monetary damages are another possible result of a civil remedy, as previously discussed.

The social and legal aspects of child abuse are rapidly evolving and few conclusions can accurately be drawn at the time of this writing.

MATERNAL ABUSE DURING PREGNANCY

The U.S. Constitution has been interpreted to guarantee women the right to choose to abort their fetuses under most circumstances at any time before viability (the first moment following which the unborn child could survive without its mother). The right of privacy also guarantees women the right to live their lives

---

*Only Texas permits trial by jury in divorce cases.

during pregnancy any way they please—with certain reservations. There is no constitutional right for women to live their lives during pregnancy in such a way that their future children predictably will be harmed.

Government fliers distributed at her high school warned Shirley that drinking alcohol during pregnancy was likely to cause serious health defects to babies. Several years later, Shirley began drinking whiskey heavily during pregnancy. Has Shirley committed a crime?

If Shirley were a resident of South Dakota, she could be made to attend a hearing (without a jury) and then be ordered by a judge to a detox center for days or to a treatment center for months. Fetal alcohol syndrome can leave its victims mentally and physically disabled for their entire lives, and the law in South Dakota has intervened to protect these unborn family members. Fetal alcohol syndrome affects about 1 in 500 children across the U.S., but it is about twenty times more prevalent in South Dakota (and some other states).[68]

The most pervasive abusive behavior by pregnant women consists of drug and alcohol use. Perhaps 11 percent of fetuses in the United States are exposed to illegal drugs.[69] This complex issue involves weighing the interest of society in healthy fetal life versus the mother's right to freedom of movement during part or all of her pregnancy. Earlier in Chapter 6, we mentioned the conflicting efforts of states to criminalize such behavior. The difficulties of such a family law are described in the *Johnson* case found at the end of this chapter.

Here the issue arises in the context of civil proceedings to confine abusive mothers in treatment centers, hospitals, or even the homes of relatives. Proposed laws are pending in a dozen or more states that would legalize the involuntary commitment to some kind of treatment facility for most or all of the gestational period of drug or alcohol abusers. But what about pregnant women who make other choices that adversely affect their fetuses, such as poor food and medicine choices, poor or no prenatal care, and even smoking? Is a civil proceeding to incarcerate a person a veiled device to avoid the constitutional rights enjoyed by those accused of crime? Some states proposing incarceration of future mothers put the matter under jursidiction of the juvenile court, where many rules are different and where trial by jury is not available. However, most constitutional rights are not suspended simply because the juvenile court has jurisdiction. How can society prevent the birth of "cocaine babies"? Can the unborn fetus be confined in a place where it is safe from abuse by its mother, such as a health institution, a foster home, or even the home of a responsible friend?

Darlene was pregnant with a viable fetus and critically needed a blood transfusion, which she refused on religious grounds. Darlene's refusal threatened the life of her unborn baby. Can the court order Darlene to submit to a blood transfusion to save her viable fetus?

No.[70] At the turn of the twentieth century, fetuses were protected by the laws making abortion illegal. As the twenty-first century approaches, the right of women to an abortion has been established. How that right will be reconciled with the rights of fetuses to be born free of harm from drug use or other abusive conduct by their mothers is evolving.

How May Marriage Be Terminated?

Dissolution (Divorce)

As there is a need for marriage, so is there a need for **divorce** (also called **dissolution of marriage**). Divorce ends the marriage but it does not necessarily terminate spousal responsibilities that arose from the marriage, such as the duties of child support and alimony. Divorce requires court proceedings, in which a judgment (or decree) in dissolution is rendered. Legislatures have traditionally permitted divorce for an "innocent" spouse from a "guilty" spouse; and this "fault" basis of divorce, in some form or other, is still in effect in some states. However, all states also provide for some variety of **no-fault grounds for divorce**.[71]

In response to widespread disenchantment with fault systems of divorce, many states have adopted some variety of no-fault divorce exclusively. The prevailing no-fault system requires proof of two elements: a breakdown of the marriage and the objective fact of physical separation of the spouses for some specified period of time, such as six months. This separation period offers the added benefit of preventing overly hasty divorces. Some states also retain the fault basis of divorce in order to provide immediate relief in severe cases or to allow judges to award unequal distributions of marital property. (Distributions of property and rights to spousal support upon divorce are covered separately later in this chapter.) A breakdown is established by testimony that the marriage is irretrievably broken because of the attitude of one or both spouses or because of a long-continued physical separation without a resumption of cohabitation. Following appropriate evidence of a breakdown, divorce is then available.

A primary advantage of no-fault divorce is that spouses are not required to "air their dirty laundry" in a courtroom, detailing each other's alleged misdeeds. Furthermore, private detectives are unnecessary to track spouses thought to be unfaithful. In fault systems, on the other hand, the stakes can be much higher because the more innocent spouse can benefit through uneven distribution of marital property and perhaps through award of a larger amount of support.

Under no-fault systems, an "innocent" spouse cannot prevent a divorce from occurring. People cannot be locked into marriage. But people facing divorce can use the law in retaliation.

The divorce proceedings by Donna Carroll, of Janesville, Wisconsin, prompted her husband to file criminal charges of adultery. This did little to save the marriage, but did cause Donna to perform 40 hours of community service. Facing a criminal trial, up to two years in jail, and as much as a $10,000 fine, Donna entered a plea bargain. Can the threat of criminal adultery charges be used by spouses to obtain larger divorce settlements?

Yes. Adultery is still a crime in about one-half of the states, including New York, Massachusettes, Connecticut, and Michigan. Enforcement of such statutes seldom occurs until a spouse brings charges during no-fault divorce proceedings.[72] However, there is a fine line between using legal proceedings as a club and the crime of extortion. (You may recall from Chapter 6 that the coercion of money under threat of harm is a felony called extortion.)

Some states permit civil remedies for alienation of affection. A third party can be sued by one spouse for "alienating" the affections of the other spouse—usually through sexual intercourse. While the "alienated" spouse may also be guilty of the crime of adultery, the third-party interloper may be civilly liable in damages. This kind of "heart-balm" lawsuit may be more of a vindication than a realistic legal remedy. For example, in North Carolina, Dorothy Hutelmyer sued secretary Lynne Cox for wrecking her marriage by sleeping with her husband Joseph. Dorothy was awarded a jury verdict of $1 million as damages, even though Lynne testified that Joseph's marriage already was wrecked as evidenced by a lack of sexual relations for the preceding seven years. The jury apparently rejected that contention in making the award. Adultress Lynne was broke, and even though she subsquently married Joseph, he is not liable for her debts.[73]

Recall our discussion of the modern trend to permit suits for damages in domestic torts. Critics of this development argue that they are "putting the fault back into no-fault divorces." Indeed, the family "dirty laundry" (e.g., wife-beating) can be aired in court as the basis for tort litigation, even if it is shielded from the court by no-fault divorce laws. Of course, this criticism applies only to a limited number of divorce cases where the alleged spousal misconduct is egregious enough to justify the filing of a separate domestic-tort lawsuit.

Although no-fault divorce is generally available throughout the states, new schemes to strengthen the marital vows are being proposed. The current "quickie divorce" system, according to proponents of these plans, promotes irresponsibility because spouses can "walk away" from their marriages very easily. Nearly one in two marriages can be expected to end in divorce. Children of broken homes are more likely to do poorly in school, suffer relationship problems, have babies out of wedlock, and get in trouble with the law. Not all sociologists agree with these conclusions, but there is a national movement afoot to make divorce more difficult. For instance legislation to create a two-tier system under which no-fault divorce would not be available if minor children were involved has failed to become law in any state—but is pending in some state legislatures. Other states are considering longer predivorce waiting periods and mandatory counseling. Louisiana now has an option type of marriage, called "covenant marriage," under which couples engage in premarital counseling and a mandatory two-year waiting period before divorce. Opponents refer to this as cheapening the institution of marriage by offering the choice of a "lite" or full-blown version. Another proposal is "divorce by persuasion," under which both parties would have to agree to the divorce. If one spouse disagreed, the other would have to purchase a ticket out through financial incentives or failing that, revert back to a "fault" basis for divorce.[74] The seeds of change are in the wind and may well affect your marriages and future families.

Although a couple may obtain a divorce without the services of an attorney, it is usuallly desirable to hire one where there are substantial family assets or liabilities that must be distributed, or if child custody or visitation rights are contested. Many persons with limited assets and no children obtain uncontested divorces by filling out appropriate forms without the assistance of any attorney. But there are many "divorce attorneys" in the world today, responding to a felt need. Unfortunately, this area of law is rife with opportunities for unethical behavior by attorneys. The very nature of divorce renders the clients extraordinarily vulnerable, emotionally as well as financially. The topic of legal ethics has been discussed in Chapter 4, but it is appropriate to note here that at least one state—New York—has by court rule adopted special ethical standards for divorce lawyers. One rule prohibits charging "up-front" nonrefundable fees. Such fees, collected before representation is undertaken, necessarily tends to dissuade the client from discharging the lawyer even if he or she is doing a poor job. Another clause prohibits so-called "couch fees," i.e., sexual favors from the client during representation. Yet another important clause requires written, instead of verbal, fee agreements. Contingent fees in divorce cases have long been prohibited, but are permitted in domestic tort cases.

ANNULMENT

Annulment is a declaration by a court that a purported marriage does not exist and never existed because of some defect present at the time of the marriage ceremony. Examples of such serious defects that could exist at the inception of the apparent marriage are incest, bigamy, mental incapacity, physical incapacity to consummate the marriage, insanity, and consent to marry resulting from fraud, dare, or intoxication.

When a defective marriage exists, only the innocent victim has the option to annul and must do so promptly upon discovery of the defect. False statements (e.g., that one is pregnant or that one will attempt to have a child) justify an annulment; less significant false statements (e.g., that one is rich or that one is a virgin) do not.

Even though a marriage is annulled, in the eyes of the law a child conceived prior to the annulment is deemed to be a legitimate child of the marriage that legally never existed.

On the second day of Mardi Gras in New Orleans, Carl, 21, met Maria, 17, at a Dixieland jazz concert. Within a week they were madly in love and decided to marry and begin a family of six children. They promptly applied for a marriage license and discovered that Louisiana enforced a three-day waiting period between the license and marriage dates. Impetuous, they drove to Texas and got married, although Maria had to lie about her age on their license. Within weeks, as their passions were cooling, Carl revealed that he "hated" children and that the divorce from his former wife was not yet final. What would Maria's attorney advise her?

Maria's lawyer would observe that Carl's lie about children was material and sufficient basis to annul the marriage. Further, a declaration that the marriage was void also was possible because Carl's divorce was not final. Although without significance in most states, Carl was guilty of bigamy. Maria also committed a crime when she lied about her age, but the court would not refuse to grant an annulment for that reason. Most likely, Maria would not be prosecuted for that misdemeanor. Carl also committed the intentional tort of fraud and could be sued civilly by Maria. If she could persuade a jury that she suffered substantial mental distress, such as humiliation and loss of sexual naivete because of Carl's wanton and malicious lies, Maria may recover substantial compensatory and punitive damages.

"BED AND BOARD" SEPARATION, SEPARATE MAINTENANCE, OR LEGAL SEPARATION

Many states provide for a partial termination of marriage. Separation a *mensa et thoro* (Latin: "from bed and board") allows the spouses to live apart without fixing desertion upon one or the other. Support obligations are established and property is divided by the court. However, the couple is not divorced and neither can remarry. This remedy of separation from bed and board derives from early English law when divorce was not available. The remedy is appropriate where the spouses (1) do not intend to remarry, (2) desire a complete settlement of their economic affairs, (3) want to preserve entitlements under certain public laws (e.g., social security), and (4) are opposed to divorce on religious grounds. Separate maintenance and legal separation are very similar to "bed and board" separation and provide the same benefits to the couple, except that property division normally is not adjudicated.

WHAT ARE A SPOUSE'S RIGHTS AND DUTIES UPON TERMINATION OF MARRIAGE?

MAINTENANCE (ALIMONY)

For information and opinion about gender bias in general and family law in particular, see http://www.attorneyetal.com/Previews/Ethics3.html

Upon termination of the marriage by divorce, *maintenance* (often called *alimony* or *support*) may be ordered by the court in both dollars per month and in duration of payments. Rehabilitative, or limited-term, alimony terminates at the end of a specified time period, during which the recipient seeks education, training, or experience to become self-supporting.[75] Permanent alimony or maintenance is indefinite in duration. Many couples who divorce arrive at a mutual agreement as to maintenance and thereby avoid the time, expense, and uncertainty of a court's decision. (Note that such marital agreements are subject to approval by the court.) But if the former spouses cannot agree, the judge, sitting as a court of equity and hence without a jury, considers all relevant factors and makes the award.

In 1979 the Supreme Court "de-sexed" alimony and held that gender-based alimony statutes were unconstitutional.[76] Alimony is required from either spouse if the other is in genuine need. One is in need, for example, if she (or sometimes he) cannot be self-supporting or if there is a child whose situation precludes employment by the parent with custody. Generally, marital fault is not a factor in determining whether or not alimony should be awarded, although some states specifically consider fault.*

The amount of alimony is related to the needs of the spouse receivng it and the ability of the other to pay. The following factors are considered by courts in setting and terminating alimony:

---

*Alabama, Connecticut, Florida, Georgia, Idaho, Louisiana, Michigan, Missouri, New Hampshire, North Carolina, North Dakota, Pennsylvania, Rhode Island, South Carolina, South Dakota, Tennessee, and West Virginia either take "fault" into consideration in setting the amount of alimony, or accept it as a bar altogether. See e.g., *Mathews v. Mathews*, 614 So.2d 1287 (Louisiana Ct. Ap., 1993) and *Cantwell v. Cantwell*, 334 N.C. 162, 432 S.E.2d 357 (North Carolina, 1993).

- Financial condition of the spouse seeking support as well as the ability of the other to pay.
- Length of the marriage.
- Age, health, education, and station in life of the parties.
- Occupations, vocational skills, and employability of the parties.
- Needs and opportunities for future income of the parties.
- Contributions of each in acquiring or maintaining marital property (including noneconomic contributions).
- Need of a custodial parent to occupy the marital home.
- Tax consequences involved.

Thomas Wilson had been married about four years when his wife Elma was injured in a fall. Her injuries resulted in a permanent neurologic deficit. She lacked "social judgment, common sense, and social intelligence." Two years later, the Wilsons agreed to divorce. Elma received $500 per month for two years, plus medical insurance for the same time. After those two years, Elma asked the court to extend alimony, anticipating further brain surgery and continued unemployment. The court extended alimony for one year, following which Elma asked for another extension, claiming no improvement in her condition or employment potential. What should the court order?

The trial court terminated the alimony, noting the shortness of the marriage and weighing society's obligation to assist Mrs. Wilson against Mr. Wilson's continuing obligation. In affirming the judgment, the appellate court observed that Mrs. Wilson was not a "displaced homemaker" but a "middle-aged bartender" with adult children. It further said, "While no one will dispute Elma's tragic disability, the clear trend is for trial courts to consider the totality of circumstances (in terminating support). . . ."[77]

The obligation of permanent alimony ends with the death of either spouse. Remarriage of the spouse receiving alimony also automatically terminates the duty to pay.

In the 1970s, the push for equality between the sexes resulted in a shift of state laws from permanent to rehabilitative alimony. But regardless of notions of equality, the reality often is that some women, especially those in their forties and fifties, could not go back to school and become doctors or lawyers and compete with their former husbands' earning capacity. As a result, such displaced homemakers often suffer a severe drop in their standard of living following divorce. Many such women lack saleable job skills or even knowledge about the changing workplace. Moreover, they often face illegal gender and age discrimination. For these reasons, courts in Ohio, Maryland, Louisiana, New York, Pennsylvania, and Florida have begun to require permanent, rather than limited-time, alimony awards. Contrary opinions continue to insist, however, that alimony should not be a "perpetual pension." Some believe that permanent alimony ought to be awarded to older women in marriages of long duration, but not to younger women who are capable of becoming self-supporting.

When circumstances change, alimony may be modified (even terminated) by petition to the court, which retains continuing jurisdiction until alimony is finally terminated. As previously noted, all relevant factors are considered by the court when hearing a petition to modify.[78] Often the changing factors relate to changes in the relative financial conditions of the former spouses. For example, a former husband can be reluctant to support his ex-wife while she is living with another man. Generally, cohabitation with another person in itself is not a sufficient basis for terminating alimony.[79] However, some states do provide for modification or termination of alimony under such circumstances.[80] These laws are equally operative if a former wife is paying support to her ex-husband.

Dentist Hall agreed to a divorce settlement in which his wife received the home, furnishings, and vehicle totaling more than $100,000 in value, plus annual alimony of $15,000. Three years later, he petitioned the court to terminate alimony due to changed circumstances. Robert Jones, who was sharing Hall's former home with his former wife, contributed nothing toward rent or maintenance, and engaged in sexual intercourse with her. The trial court terminated the alimony on the grounds that Hall should not be compelled to "support his divorced wife and her paramour in idleness and fornication." What was the result on appeal?

The judgment was reversed. Alimony may not be utilized as a club to regulate the ex-wife's sex life. On the other hand, the court did remand the case to the trial court for a reduction in alimony.[81]

PROPERTY DIVISION IN EQUITABLE DISTRIBUTION STATES

Other than community property jurisdictions, state laws authorize courts to distribute marital property "equitably" upon divorce, either in the form of property division or maintenance. The doctrine of equitable distribution awards a marital interest in all assets that were acquired with a material economic contribution by both spouses regardless of which spouse holds legal title. Savings or acquisitions from salaries or interest income and investment proceeds are obvious examples of marital property. Military pensions are less obvious.

The U.S. Supreme Court has held that military pensions cannot be awarded to divorcing spouses; otherwise important "military personnel objectives" would be threatened. For one example of such objectives, retirement (pension) payments are similar to a retainer, because retired military personnel may be required to return to duty at any time.[82] As a result of this decision, Congress enacted FUSFSPA* which gave states the choice of whether or not to treat military pensions as marital property, up to 50 percent of the pension going to the non-military spouse if the marriage has lasted ten years or more. Most states do consider military pensions as marital property. However, some married veterans are entitled to either pension or disability payments, and since the former are taxable income and the latter are not, these veterans often elect disability pay. To the chagrin of many, disability pay cannot be considered marital property.

---

*Federal Uniformed Services Former Spouses' Protection Act, commonly referred to by its acronym FUSFSPA, 10 U.S.C. 1409.

It is also not clear whether one spouse should be awarded a property interest in the professional license or degree of the other. How should an advanced degree, such as a Master's in Business Administration (MBA), or a professional license, such as a license to practice medicine, be treated upon divorce? Can they be assigned a dollar value and equitably distributed or divided? Suppose one spouse sacrifices his education to "put his wife through medical school." Upon a divorce immediately following the wife's graduation, should the husband be awarded half of the dollar value of the degree or license? If so, how should it be valued? In New York, it has been held that a husband's medical license was marital property under the state's equitable distribution law.[83] Following that decision, New York's highest court held that an academic degree obtained during marriage is also marital property subject to equitable distribution.[84] In the states that equitably distribute marital property, division of property is based upon such factors as length of the marriage, the parties' abilities to support themselves, and the property and income that was obtained during the marriage. Thus, a spouse has claim to an expected future stream of earnings resulting from an investment, or perhaps from an advanced degree. In North Carolina, professional degrees and licenses are separate property, but their value is taken into consideration in dividing marital property.[85] In Kentucky, a professional degree or license is considered in determining the standard of living to be maintained in setting alimony.[86] But it also has been widely held that college degrees and professional licenses are property rights that are not capable of being owned by a community (in marriage) and are not subject to distribution upon divorce.[87] In Utah, the goodwill of a solo practice dentist is not marital property,[88] nor is the goodwill of a CPA (certified public accountant) in Texas.[89] However, in most states "professional" goodwill, which may be defined loosely as enhanced earning power based upon special talents, reputation, business referral base, or uniqueness of services offered, is marital property that can be and is divided upon divorce.

"Celebrity" and "executive" goodwill are different than "professional" goodwill. The former terms refer to the fame and public idolatry of persons on the one hand and the professional and business reputations of individuals on the other. The goodwill from a business is distinguishable from the goodwill of a person. Goodwill in any form relates to the future earnings of money. Should the variety described as "celebrity" goodwill be appraised and divided upon divorce? States may be expected to apply the same rules to both varieties of goodwill, even though one is more easily connected with future earnings than the other.

In some states, restitutional alimony instead of property division may be awarded to reimburse one spouse for contributions made to the other in earning a professional degree.[90]

In many states, the nonmonetary contributions of a homemaker are considered to be the equivalent of the wage earner's monetary contributions. The starting point in making an equitable distribution is a presumption that equality is equity: an equal division is the most just.

For 32 years, Lorna Jorgenson Wendt ran the household and raised the Wendt's two daughters. Her husband Gary, 55, Chairman of GE Capital Services, testified that Lorna had no interest in business or his problems. Connecticut is an "equitable distribution" state and the divorce judge must decide on the worth of a stay-at-home wife. Lorna said, "I worked hard and I was very loyal." Gary said, "I worked hard. She didn't." The Wendt estate was valued as high as $100 million. What should the judge award to Lorna?

Lorna was awarded a multimillion dollar home in Stamford and a vacation home in Key Largo; $252,000 a year payable in monthly installments; and half of all stocks, bonds, and cash, all totaling about $20 million. In a community property state, Lorna would have received precisely one-half the total value of the family assets.

Sam's premarital house appreciated in value during his marriage with Sally. On the advice of her attorney, Sally agreed to quitclaim deed all her right, title, and interest, if any, in the house to Sam for a payment of $10. Did Sally lose her marital interest in the house?

No. The court ruled that all increase in value of a premarital house is a marital asset if the nonowner spouse takes an active role in its upkeep and management. The court will not uphold an unconscionable agreement.

The trend is to minimize relative fault of the spouses as a factor in property division.[91] However, many states consider economic fault (e.g., dissipation of marital assets pending divorce) in making an equitable division.[92] The criteria used in most states in making an equitable distribution of marital property between the spouses are comparable to the factors (previously listed) that are relied upon in setting alimony awards. Payments received in food stamps, in aid to families with dependent children (AFDC), and child support payments are not considered income to the recipient parent and therefore are not included as factors in dividing marital property.[93]

PROPERTY DIVISION IN COMMUNITY PROPERTY STATES

As stated earlier, community property is all property acquired by the husband or the wife during marriage other than by gift or inheritance. Community property must be distributed equally because each spouse is the "owner" of an undivided one-half interest. This is the most important distinguishing characteristic between community property and equitable distribution states.

Upon divorce, the court allocates the net value of each one-half interest to each spouse.* If the community property cannot be physically distributed equally, it may be sold and the cash proceeds divided, or a promissory note may be made from one spouse to the other to equalize the values received from an unequal physical distribution. (A physical distribution of assets is called a *distribution in kind*.) As discussed earlier, professional licenses or degrees may be marital property (in both equitable distribution and community property states) and are good examples of property that cannot be distributed in kind.[94]

---

*Wisconsin modified its community property laws in 1986 by adoption of the Uniform Marital Property Act. What was "community property" is now called "marital" property, but like community property, each spouse owns an undivided one-half interest. What was "separate" property is now called "individual" property. But the treatment upon dissolution or divorce is much the same as the other community property states.

Other assets, such as a promissory note requiring payment of money to the spouses, must be distributed to comply with the court's ordered distribution. One asset that may be distributed in kind is a cryogenically preserved (frozen) preembryo.

> When Junior L. and and Mary Sue Davis divorced, they owned seven cryogenically preserved preembryos. Ms. Davis desired to carry the preembryos to term; Mr. Davis objected and did not want to become a father against his will. The trial court ruled that the preembryos were human beings and awarded custody to Ms. Davis. During lengthy appeals, Ms. Davis remarried and changed her mind, desiring to donate the preembryos to another couple. Who should receive the preembryos, and why?

In a case of first impression, the Tennessee Supreme Court ruled against Ms. Davis, saying that preembryos do not enjoy protection as "persons" under federal law. "(There are) two rights of equal significance—the right to procreate and the right to avoid procreation. The equivalence of and inherent tension between these two interests are nowhere more evident than in the context of *in vitro* fertilization. None of the concerns about a woman's bodily integrity that have previously precluded men from controlling abortion decisions is applicable here. If the state's interests do not become sufficiently compelling in the abortion context until the end of the first trimester, after very significant developmental stages have passed, there is no state interest in these preembryos. Ordinarily, the party wishing to avoid procreation should prevail, assuming that the other party has a reasonable possibility of achieving parenthood by means other than use of the preembryos in question. If no reasonable alternatives exist, then the argument in favor of using the preembryos to achieve pregnancy should be considered. However, if the party seeking control of the preembryos intends merely to donate them to another couple, the objecting party obviously has the greater interest and should prevail."[95]

In some community property states (e.g., Washington and Texas), the court may divide the marital property in any manner it deems "just and equitable," not necessarily equally.[96] An unequal distribution of community property may act as a substitute for alimony.

All property either brought into the marriage or acquired by gift or inheritance is separate property, as mentioned earlier. Separate property is not typically subject to distribution by the court upon divorce and neither are its passive earnings (such as interest) if they are maintained separately with proper records. In a few states, however, all marital property is subject to distribution by the divorce court.

CHILD CUSTODY

Court awards of child custody and visitation rights are always based on the best interests of the child. Generally, parents are sensitive to their child's needs, and so they amicably agree on custody and visitation. In such instances, courts normally comply with the parents' joint request. However, when both parents demand custody or argue about visitation rights, the court must determine the best interests of the child and make appropriate orders. Forty-four states have adopted some form of the Uniform Marriage and Divorce Act, which specifies criteria for determining custody arrangements in the best interests of the child: (1) the wishes of the parents and the child; (2) the child's adjustment to his or her home, school, and community; and (3) the mental and physical health of all individuals involved. Although courts consider the wishes of the child, they weigh their importance by the child's age and maturity. It is not appropriate to ask a child in open court which parent he or she chooses to live with because it is not reckoned to be in the child's best interest to have custody turn on the transitory desires of a child.[97] Custody cannot be changed on the grounds that the custodial parent remarried across racial lines and is raising the child in a different cultural way, nor may race be considered in making initial custody awards, even if social stigma is proven.[98] However, the potential exposure of a child to secondhand smoke may prompt a trial court to condition the custody award on the absence of smoking by the custodial parent, or anyone else in the vicinity of the child. Children are especially vulnerable because their respiratory systems are less developed than adults—they inhale more frequently, and they are more likely to develop middle-ear infections. Children's exposure to secondhand smoke has even been characterized as child abuse.[99]

Children may be the parties most affected by divorce; they are undoubtedly the least able to protect their own rights, especially since the court receives most of its information about finances and emotional trauma from the parents. For this reason, one theory holds that children ought to be independently represented by their own attorney. Advocates of this theory applaud the case of Gregory Kingsley, previously discussed, who successfully "divorced" his parents by using his own attorney. On the other hand, a contrary theory holds that the illusion of power created by one's own attorney might be inimical to children's emotional well-being. Courts have the power to appoint a special guardian *ad litem* (Latin: "for the purpose of the suit") to protect the interests of the child. In Alaska and Wisconsin, courts have directed such guardians to vigorously advocate for the children in custody disputes.[100]

The granting of meaningful visitation opportunities may be expected to temper the impact of a change in custody unless visitation is used by a vindictive spouse as a weapon to prolong the agonies of divorce for all concerned. In such situations, the court may prohibit visitation or strictly limit its terms.

When divorced parents reside in different communities, split custody—where one parent has custody during summer, the other during the school year—may be an effective alternative.

Joint custody, in which the parents share responsibility for the child, became the most widespread choice of courts in the 1980s. In keeping with the trend, most state legislatures have expressed a preference for joint custody in their statutory guidelines. The theory is that, ideally, children need two actively involved parents in their lives.

Matthew and Martie have court-ordered joint custody of their only child, Roger. Living within the same city, both parents share all important issues, such as those created by religion, school, and sports activities. Roger lives with Mom on Monday–Thursday and with Dad on Friday–Saturday. Sundays are alternated. Matthew earns more than Martie and pays monthly child support. This arrangement is working smoothly and both parents remain flexible. What happens when Martie wants to move away to live with her new boyfriend, and to take Roger with her?

This hypothetical example shows both the benefits and the possible disadvantages of joint custody. When parents cooperate and circumstances permit, joint custody is very effective in providing the parental guidance needed by children. When parents are emotionally antagonistic, judges sometimes are asked to establish the specific custody changes on each vacation or holiday and to otherwise resolve normal parenting issues. The hiring of lawyers to formally dispute child custody issues further depletes the family funds available for the children. When one parent moves far away, the children necessarily lose the stability of a two-parent family. The emotional costs to the children and parents, as well as the financial costs, can be ruinous. Judges cannot be expected to solve all parenting issues by court orders. The toll upon children from marriages gone wrong cannot be measured nor cured by the application of family law. Simply stated, children are not best served when joint custody is awarded to parents who continue their bitterness and disagreements after the divorce. In keeping with this experience, many states now have neither a preference nor a presumption for joint custody awards.[101] The key to effective joint custody is joint cooperation between the parents.

Virtually everyone agrees that a mutually acceptable custody and visitation arrangement is the best method of minimizing the traumatic experience of divorce upon children. Through mediation, in which a professional and neutral third party attempts to reconcile the opposing views of the divorcing parents, agreements can be reached that otherwise would be impossible. Studies indicate that children of mediated divorces appear to adjust better and their parents appear to retain less hostility.[102] Indeed, California has adopted mandatory mediation proceedings that are applicable whenever child custody is disputed.[103] Critics of mediation contend that publicly funded mediators tend to push for agreements because they may measure their professional success and personal esteem by the number of "successful" outcomes they bring about. Private mediators charge as much as $300 per hour. If a full-blown social evaluation is ordered by the divorce court judge, such as when there are allegations of mental illness, drug or alcohol abuse, or child neglect, the costs may average in excess of $5,000 at a time when there already are insufficient family funds. Further, husband and wife may not have equal bargaining power, and one may give away some of his or her rights in reaching an agreement. This inequality may be especially significant where full disclosure of financial matters is not enforced as rigorously as it is in court proceedings, where formal discovery procedures are available.

All rational attempts to base custody fairly in the best interests of the child are made difficult, if not impossible, when false charges of child abuse are made by one parent, and/or the child, against the other parent (usually the father). The false charging of child abuse is referred to as the Parental Alienation Syndrome (or PAS).* In PAS, the "mother and children become so intent upon driving away

---

*One leading exponent of PAS at this time is forensic psychiatrist Richard Gardner, clinical professor of child psychiatry at Columbia University School of Physicians and Surgeons. Dr. Gardner acknowledges that no research confirms the existence of PAS, its causes if it exists, or the claim that a majority of child abuse accusations are false. *The National Law Journal*, 16 August 1993, 1.

the father that they launch a campaign of disparagement that can include falsely accusing him of sexually abusing his offspring."[104]

CHILD SUPPORT

In addition to custody orders, the court granting a divorce must make orders providing for the future support of the minor children. Statutory guidelines for setting the appropriate amount of child support presently exist in most states as a result of adoption by Congress of the Family Support Act.[105] State statutes typically consider the following factors:

- Child's necessities.
- Parent's standard of living and circumstances.
- Financial status of the parents.
- Earning capacity of each parent.
- Future educational plans of the child.
- Child's age.
- Earning ability and fiscal resources of the child.
- Duty of each parent to support other people.
- Value of care given by the custodial parent.

States also frequently take into consideration the need for and cost of day care. Most of the criteria listed relate to finances—but the legal obligation of support cannot exceed the financial capacity of the parent to pay it. One criterion listed credits the custodial parent with the monetary value of the care he or she gives. Would the value of that care be greater if the custodial parent—if a woman— were a "homemaker" mom or a "career" mom? What is the monetary value of daily love and affection? These examples of questions, and others that may occur to you, help explain the variable degree of subjectivity underlying support awards.

Original support orders can be modified by petition to the court when circumstances change. A frequent argument is that remarriage constitutes a significant change in circumstance. Allocation of the earnings of an ex-spouse between a former family and a second-marriage family can be a very sensitive issue. Traditionally, the common-law position has been that children should not be made to suffer from the existence of a new family in their father's (or mother's) life. The modern view is contrary: Remarriage may constitute a changed circumstance sufficient to justify a reduction in child support payments. And as remarriage can affect an ex-spouse's ability to pay child support, so may a change in career. Sometimes a new career will offer lower wages (necessitating a reduction in child support) in exchange for higher potential earnings in the future.

Collection of child support payments is far more difficult than ordering them. When the parent who is delinquent in making child support payments (the obligor) resides in the same state as the child, the custodial parent has several options: Legal procedures (often called the *levy of a writ of execution*) are provided for taking the delinquent parent's assets, including bank accounts and real property. However, certain portions of the debtor's assets are exempt from execution and cannot be taken. Legal procedures necessary to obtain relief by writ of execution can become so complex as to be ineffective, especially when the debtor does not have substantial assets. If the delinquent parent is employed, a wage assignment is an alternative. Under this legal mechanism, a portion of the parent's wages are withheld from weekly or monthly earnings and are forwarded to the custodial parent.

A judgment ordering the payment of child support also can be enforced by contempt proceedings when the failure to support is willful. Theoretically, an obligor who has the ability to pay the ordered child support but purposefully fails to do so can be jailed for contempt, that is, for violating the court's order. However, courts are reluctant to jail an employable parent. Jail precludes employment and contributes to an already crowded correction system. On the other hand, the threat of jail, or a short sentence for contempt of court, may act as a catalyst in encouraging a delinquent obligor to make the required child support payments.

When the parent who is delinquent in making child support payments resides out of state, another difficult problem exists. How can the custodial parent enforce the payment of child support by a former spouse who resides in another state? To alleviate this problem, most states have adopted the Uniform Reciprocal Enforcement of Support Act of 1968, called URESA, which recently has been streamlined by the Uniform Interstate Family Support Act of 1992 (UIFSA), which was immediately adopted by eight states: Arizona, Arkansas, Colorado, Montana, Nebraska, Oregon, Texas, and Washington. Most other states are in the process of adopting UIFSA, which essentially streamlines procedures and closes loopholes that had evolved under URESA. Under this special law, the prosecutor in the local state (residence of the custodial parent) initiates a formal legal proceeding in the foreign state (residence of the delinquent obligor), which will be prosecuted in the foreign state by its local prosecutor. The court in the foreign state enters a support order there and enforces it under local laws (including the issuance of a writ of execution or contempt of court proceedings, if appropriate). Monies collected in the foreign state are forwarded to the custodial parent.

If the failure to make support payments is a crime,* the foreign court can extradite (return) the delinquent obligor to the local state for criminal prosecution. The Child Support Recovery Act of 1992[106] made the willful failure to pay child support for more than one year a federal crime. This remedial legislation also created the National Commission on Child and Family Welfare, which has many enumerated duties relating to child custody, visitation, and domestic violence.

When court-ordered child support payments become delinquent, they do not disappear; rather, they accumulate and may be collected at any time in the future, in the same manner that other money judgments are collected, such as by levy of writ of execution to take assets or portions of the debtor's wages. Nor are accumulated child support liabilities discharged (eliminated) if the delinquent father successfully petitions for bankruptcy.

Even with existing legal remedies that are available to enforce child support (and alimony) payments, collection remains a serious problem in most states. It is widely acknowledged that custodial parents generally receive inadequate child support regardless of court orders. Congress recognizes interstate child support payment as a problem justifying federal support to states through contributions to improved computerized collection systems.

---

*The willful (deliberate) failure to supply necessaries of life to a child, without any excuse, is a crime. Failure to make such provision when the parent is financially unable to do so is not a crime.

How May Family Law Be Modified by Contract?

Premarital Agreements

A marital contract made before marriage is called an **antenuptial**, **premarital**, or **prenuptial agreement**. This type of agreement should be in writing to facilitate enforcement, and some states require that it be witnessed by a third person or notary public. They are increasingly popular as more and more persons prudently seek to establish and fix, before their nuptials, property division and/or support payments in the event that the marriage ends in divorce. Especially when either spouse has a disproportionately large estate of separate property, the premarital agreement can help to resolve future potential misunderstandings without costly litigation.

In response to this need, all states recognize premarital agreements. Many states have adopted some version of the 1983 Uniform Premarital Agreement Act.* Theoretically, premarital agreements can deal with (1) property and support rights during and after marriage, (2) the personal rights and obligations of the spouses during marriage, or (3) the education, care, and rearing of children. But the most common subjects of marital agreements are property divisions and support rights upon death or divorce. Furthermore, any contractual provision regarding the treatment of minor children is subject to modification by the court.

In most states, upon death of a spouse, the surviving spouse has an elective right to choose between inheriting under the decedent's will or rejecting the inheritance and taking instead a portion of the decedent's estate as provided for by statute. Premarital agreements may alter this option. On the other hand, this "elective" choice is not available in community property states because the surviving spouse is protected through ownership of one-half of the community property. But this community property ownership interest can also be altered by premarital agreement. Even states that do not permit contracts that alter the incidents of divorce do permit contracts that alter property distributions upon death of one spouse. (Inheritance is fully discussed in Chapter 14.)

Upon divorce, premarital agreements can alter court determinations concerning both property division and continuing support (alimony or maintenance). However, prenuptial agreements are void, as a matter of law, to the extent that they adversely affect the rights of minor children. Agreements affecting custody, care, or education of minor children can be valid but are subject to approval by the court. The court will void agreements if they adversely affect the children's best interests. Although about one-half of the states authorize premarital agreements that alter the legal incidents of divorce, some will not enforce agreements affecting support (alimony, maintenance, or child support).

Couples may include an arbitration clause in their prenuptial agreement concerning issues of spousal or child support. The best interests of a child and the interests of a spouse can be protected as well by the arbitration process as by a trial court.[107] However, this ADR (alternative dispute resolution) practice is not yet widespread.

---

*Arkansas, California, Colorado, Hawaii, Kansas, Maine, Montana, New Jersey, North Carolina, North Dakota, Oregon, Rhode Island, South Dakota, Virginia, and Texas. Many other states have either enacted their own legislation or are considering a version of the Uniform Act.

Arlene, a talented and promising young actress, had received her first multimillion dollar contract to perform the lead in a major movie production. She also was contemplating marriage to Bud, her off-again, on-again childhood sweetheart, who was a professional boxer with a low earning potential. Arlene decided to confer with an attorney concerning preparation of a premarital agreement. What might such a contract accomplish?

If Arlene and Bud lived in a community property state and did not have a premarital agreement, Bud would become the "owner" of one-half of Arlene's earnings after the marriage and would be entitled to his one-half of all community property acquired with her earnings upon any future divorce. This result could not be altered by the divorce court. A contract, on the other hand, could provide that all of Arlene's earnings would remain her separate property, and that upon divorce Bud would be entitled to a cash payment of, say, $100,000. In an "equitable distribution" state, the court would allocate Arlene's earnings based on the factors discussed earlier in this chapter. But Arlene and Bud also could agree in equitable distribution states that $100,000 would be distributed to Bud upon any future divorce—and that would resolve the issue. In some states, Arlene and Bud could agree that, upon any divorce, Arlene would pay alimony to Bud in some specified amount for some specified time. Courts, however, would not enforce such a promise that attempted to set support payments unless it was fair under all the circumstances. An agreement would not be necessary relative to distribution of assets upon Arlene's unexpected death. That matter should be covered by her last will, a topic we consider in our final chapter.

Prenuptial agreements theoretically can be updated during the marriage to reflect the desires of the spouses as their circumstances change from time to time.

As distinguished from prenuptial agreements, contracts made during marriage are called simply *marital contracts*, or *separation agreements* if they are entered while contemplating a forthcoming divorce. Marital contracts are intended to resolve the same sorts of future problems as antenuptial agreements, and receive comparable enforcement by the courts.

Courts will not enforce marital contracts of any kind that are unconscionable (unjust, unfair, or excessive). Preceding marriage, there often is unequal bargaining power between the prospective spouses, and the opportunity for overreaching (taking unfair advantage) may be available. Contracts signed immediately before the marriage ceremony are suspect and may be voided by the court. Similarly, a contract that is prepared by the attorney of only one of the parties is suspect; it should at least be reviewed and approved by counsel of the other party before signing. The courts' reluctance to automatically enforce all premarital agreements reflects a judicial tradition of protection of women from exploitation.

It is prudent for each spouse to receive independent legal advice before signing a premarital agreement. Legal representation minimizes the possibility of unfair overreaching and a possible subsequent declaration of invalidity by a court. This procedure also increases the likelihood that all assets will be disclosed and taken into consideration before the contract is signed. Because there is a public policy against divorce, courts will not enforce premarital agreements that are unconscionable or that promote divorce. A premarital agreement drafted so as to absolve a breadwinner from all obligations after divorce would, no doubt, be declared unconscionable and therefore would be unenforceable.

As a general rule, courts are more likely to enforce premarital agreements that affect property rights than those that affect support rights.

SEPARATION AGREEMENTS

As noted previously, a marital contract made during marriage, but when a divorce or dissolution is contemplated or is occurring, is called a *separation agreement*. These agreements are enforceable if each spouse fully discloses to the other all financial information and if its provisions are not unconscionable. Public policy favors private settlement of disputes, and courts will usually approve separation agreements as a part of the divorce proceedings. Parties to separation agreements should obtain legal counsel before signing because ramifications of such contracts are not readily apparent to, or understood by, a lay person. For example, will payments from one spouse be taxable income to the other? Will agreed upon support payments be subject to future modification by the court in case of changed circumstances (e.g., an unanticipated disability)? What would be the effect of a bankruptcy on the contractual obligations? Will the support provisions be enforceable by contempt powers of the court? What effect will a subsequent marriage of either spouse have upon the earlier separation agreement? The answers to these questions, as well as many others, may differ based on the needs and desires of the separating spouses and the law of the particular state. Accordingly, couples usually require the services of a qualified attorney to achieve results that are fair to both parties.

COHABITATION AGREEMENTS

Unmarried persons who live together as husband and wife may desire to protect their respective financial interests by entering into a *cohabitation agreement*. The first obstacle facing such a couple is the long-standing refusal of courts to enforce any contract purporting to exchange property for sexual favors.*

Mary orally agreed to "quit her job and be available to travel" in exchange for a man's promise to "take care of her for the rest of her life." Is the agreement enforceable?

Yes. The contract services do not necessarily include sexual favors.[108] In a few states, such as New York, an agreement for a lifetime of support requires a writing. In still other states, the contract could be interpreted as including sexual favors and therefore be violative of public policy.

Michele, 20, orally promised to "account to" Charles, 80, "all of her waking moments; to be at his beck and call as he should desire," for which

*There are exceptions, however, where states have rejected the illegal-consideration (sexual favors) doctrine. See, e.g., *Latham v. Latham*, 547 P.2d 144 (Oregon, 1976) and *Cook v. Cook*, 142 Ariz. 573, 691 P.2d 664 (Arizona, 1984).

services he would pay her $1,000 a month for the rest of her life. Is this contract enforceable?

This contract would not be enforceable in most states because it implies compensation in exchange for sexual favors, in violation of public policy. Public policy will not condone a contract that impliedly calls for the exchange of sexual favors.[109]

The preceding examples demonstrate the difficulties in establishing consistent laws for the enforcement of cohabitation agreements. Cohabitation agreements that do not contemplate the exchange of property for sexual favors are enforceable in most states, whether express (written or oral) or implied. You may recall the case involving Michelle Triola and Lee Marvin from earlier in this chapter (page 415). There, the court was willing to enforce even an oral agreement concerning financial support. But Michelle was unable to produce any evidence of such an agreement.

To increase the probability of enforcement of such an agreement, the parties would be well advised to obtain legal counsel for each person, fully disclose their respective financial resources, provide for a reasonable distribution of their properties upon any future parting of their ways, and express it all in writing.

CASES

JOHNSON V. STATE OF FLORIDA
602 So.2d 1288 (1992)

Jennifer Johnson gave birth to a boy whose urine contained benzoylecgonine, a breakdown product of cocaine. Fifteen months later Jennifer gave birth to a girl who also tested positive for a cocaine derivative in her urine. Florida has a statute that states: ". . . .it is unlawful for any person 18 years of age or older to deliver any controlled substance to a person under the age of 18 years. . . . Any person who violates this provision . . . is guilty of a felony in the first degree." Jennifer was convicted on two counts of delivering a controlled substance to her children. The theory of the prosecution was that Jennifer Johnson "delivered" cocaine to her two children via blood flowing through the childrens' umbilical cords in the 60- to 90-second period after they were expelled from her birth canal but before their umbilical cords were severed. Jennifer could not be prosecuted for giving birth to a drug-dependent child because that is not a crime in

Florida. Nor does Florida have a criminal statute prohibiting in utero transfers of controlled substances. Jennifer's convictions were appealed to the Florida Supreme Court.

Opinion of the Court: Justice Harding delivered the opinion of the Court. . . .There can be no doubt that drug abuse is one of the most serious problems confronting our society today. . . .Of particular concern is the alarming rise in the number of babies born with cocaine in their systems as a result of cocaine use by pregnant women. Some experts estimate that as many as eleven percent of pregnant women have used an illegal drug during pregnancy, and of those women, seventy-five percent have used cocaine. Report of the American Medical Association Board of Trustees, Legal Interventions During Pregnancy, 264 Journal of the American Medical Association 2663 (Nov. 28, 1990). Others estimate that 375,000 newborns per year are born to women who are users of illicit drugs. American Public Health Association 1990 Policy Statement. It is well-established that the effects of cocaine use by a pregnant woman on her fetus and later on her newborn can be severe. On average, cocaine-exposed babies have lower birth weights, shorter body lengths at birth, and smaller head circumferences than normal infants. 264 Journal of the American Medical Association 2666 (Nov. 28, 1990). Cocaine use may also result in sudden infant death syndrome, neural-behavioral deficiencies as well as other medical problems and long-term developmental abnormalities. American Public Health Association 1990 Policy Statement. The basic problem of damaging the fetus by drug use during pregnancy should not be addressed piecemeal, however, by prosecuting users who deliver their babies close in time to use of drugs and ignoring those who simply use drugs during their pregnancy. Florida could possibly have elected to make in utero transfers criminal. But it chose to deal with this problem in other ways. One way is to allow evidence of drug use by women as a ground for removal of the child to the custody of protective services, as was done in this case. . . .

At Johnson's trial, Dr. Tompkins testified that a mother's blood passes nutrients, oxygen and chemicals to an unborn child by a diffusion exchange at the capillary level from the womb to the placenta. The umbilical cord then circulates the baby's blood (including the exchange from its mother) between the placenta and the child. Metabolized cocaine derivatives in the mother's blood thus diffuse from the womb to the placenta, and then reach the baby through its umbilical cord. Although the blood flow is somewhat restricted during the birthing process, a measurable amount of blood is transferred from the placenta to the baby through the umbilical cord during delivery and after birth. . . .Dr. Stephen Kandall, a neonatologist, testified for the defense . . . that it is theoretically possible that cocaine or other substances can pass between a mother and her baby during the thirty-to-sixty second period after the child is born and before the umbilical cord is cut, but that the amount would be tiny.

. . . . in my view, the primary question in this case is whether (the statute) was intended by the Legislature to apply to the birthing process. Before Johnson can be prosecuted under this statute, it must be clear that the Legislature intended for it to apply to the delivery of cocaine derivatives to a newborn during a sixty-to-ninety second interval, before severance of the umbilical cord. I can find no case where "delivery" of a drug was based on an involuntary act such as diffusion and blood flow. . . . My review. . . leads me to conclude in this case that the Legislature expressly chose to treat the problem as a public health problem and that it considered but rejected imposing criminal sanctions. . . .

. . . . The California Medical Association has noted: While unhealthy behavior cannot be condoned, to bring criminal charges against a pregnant woman for activities which may be harmful to her fetus is inappropriate. Such prosecution is counterproductive to the public interest as it may discourage a woman from seeking prenatal care or dissuade her from providing accurate information to health care providers out of fear of self-incrimination.

The conviction of Jennifer Johnson was reversed.

Comment. Not all state courts agree with the Florida Supreme Court. In 1992, Cornelia Whitner was sentenced to eight years in jail after her baby was born with traces of cocaine in its system. The South Carolina courts relied on a statute prohibiting child "endangerment." Other states rely upon drug laws, charging that women were delivering drugs through the umbilical cords, as in the *Johnson* case. The South Carolina Supreme Court ruled that a viable fetus is a person under the meaning of the child abuse law—thus a child had been endangered. See also the cases cited in endnote 46 supra. [*New York Times*, 31 October 1997.]

FOR CRITICAL ANALYSIS

1. What are the pros and cons of the position that a woman has either or both, a natural law right or a right of privacy, under the U.S. Constitution, to control her body as she pleases both before and during her pregnancy?

2. If a theory of criminality in a proposed law is to be based on a child abuse statute, how would you define the term "criminal abuse"? For example, would you include smoking, abusive smoking, or prolonged exposure to secondhand smoke during pregnancy? Of accepting employment that meant standing at an assembly line for eight hours each work day? Of neglecting to obtain prenatal care? Of getting drunk?

3. If a theory of criminality in a proposed statute is to be based on a statute prohibiting the supplying of illegal drugs, how would you describe the extent of drug use that constitutes the crime? Would you include the occasional use of marijuana? Of cocaine? Of a misused prescription drug? Or would you reserve the determination until the newborn baby's blood could be tested? If so, would that be gambling with the health of the child?

IN THE MATTER OF ALISON D. V. VIRGINIA M.
77 N.Y.2d 651, 572 N.E.2d 27 (1991)

Alison and Virginia were living together in a home they owned. Intending a permanent relationship, they decided to become parents. Virginia was artificially inseminated and gave birth to a boy, ADM, in 1981. It was explicitly planned that the child would be theirs to raise together, and both were known to the boy as "mommy." After two years, Alison and Virginia separated and terminated their relationship. For several years, Alison contributed child support and enjoyed visitation with ADM while he was living with Virginia, his biological mother. Ultimately, Virginia severed all ties between ADM and Alison, prompting Alison's request for court-ordered visitation on the grounds that she was a parent entitled to visitation within the meaning of the term "parent" as used in Section 70 of the New York Domestic Relations Statute.

PER CURIAM

. . . . (Alison) claims to have acted as a "de facto" parent or that she should be viewed as a parent "by estoppel." Therefore, she claims she has standing to seek visitation rights. These claims, however, are insufficient under section 70. . . ."It has long been recognized that, as between a parent and a third person, parental custody of a child may not be displaced absent grievous cause or necessity." (citations to precedents). To allow the courts to award visitation—a limited form of custody—to a third person would necessarily impair the parents' right to custody and control. (Alison) concedes that (Virginia) is a fit parent. Therefore she has no right to petition the court to displace the choice made by this fit parent in deciding what is in the child's best interests. Accordingly, the order of the Appellate Division should be affirmed, with costs.

KAYE, J. (dissenting): The Court's decision, fixing biology as the key to visitation rights, has impact far beyond this particular controversy, one that may affect a wide spectrum of relationships—including those of long-time heterosexual stepparents, "common law" and non-heterosexual partners such as involved here, and even participants in scientific reproduction procedures. Estimates that more than 15.5 million children do not live with two biological parents, and that as many as eight to ten million children are born into families with a gay or lesbian parent, suggest just how widespread the impact may be. (citations).

But the impact of today's decision falls hardest on the children of those relationships, limiting their opportunity to maintain bonds that may be crucial to their development. The majority's retreat from the courts' proper role—its tightening of rules that should in visitation petititions, above all, retain the capacity to take the children's interests into account—compels this dissent. . . .

Most significantly, Virginia M. agrees that, after long cohabitation with Alison D. and before ADM's conception, it was "explicitly planned that the child would be theirs to raise together." It is also uncontested that the two shared "financial and emotional preparations" for the birth, and that for several years Alison D. actually filled the role of co-parent to ADM, both tangibly and intangibly. In all, a parent-child relationship—encouraged or at least condoned by Virginia M.—apparently existed between ADM and Alison D. during the first six years of the child's life.

While acknowledging that relationship, the (majority) nonetheless proclaims power-lessness to consider the child's best interest at all, because the word "parent" in the statute imposes an absolute barrier to Alison D.'s petition for visitation . . . . I cannot agree that such a result is mandated by Section 70, or any other law. . . .

FOR CRITICAL ANALYSIS

1. The court considered visitation as a "limited form of (parental) custody" to which Alison was not entitled under the statute. Under this theory, does a mother give a limited form of parental custody each day to a day care provider? Or is visitation something less than an intrusion into parental custody? Can you make an argument that visitation is only a change in physical, but not necessarily parental, custody?

2. Which view, the majority or dissenting, is more progressive given what you have learned about the future impact of surrogacy and genetic engineering upon the family? Does the majority, in effect, treat any person who is not a biological parent of a child as a "third person"? Can you formulate an argument in support of the dissent, that considerations other than biological relationship may serve the best interests of a child?

CHAPTER QUESTIONS AND PROBLEMS

1. Family law is in a state of change because of rapidly evolving social patterns. For example, there is an emergence of "informal marriage" (cohabitation with express or implied contract) alongside formal marriage (ceremonial or statutory). The "domestic partnerships" of homosexual persons also are a variety of "informal marriage." Both varieties of relationships, formal and informal marriage, often are terminated by choice, creating special legal consequences. Although you probably have not studied all the implications that can flow from marriage, from your generalized knowledge try to compare the implications of both types of relationships (formal marriage and cohabitation) on the following criteria:

   a. Federal and state income taxes.

b. Selection and use of surname.
c. Child support obligations.
d. Credit extension.
e. Expense of creating or ending the relationship.
f. Mutual support obligations.
g. Vicarious tort liability.
h. Recovery for lost consortium, or wrongful death.
i. Privilege not to testify against one another.
j. Immunities for sex crimes between spouses.
k. Division of assets upon death or termination of relationship.
l. Inheritance rights, absent a will.
m. Costs and coverage of health insurance.
n. Social security benefits.
o. Privacy in business matters upon termination of marriage.
p. Workers' compensation benefits.

2. It has been said that divorce is "the great American tragedy." Among measures suggested to reduce the divorce rate are higher age requirements for marriage, computerized analysis of personalities and backgrounds of prospective spouses, longer mandatory waiting periods after a marriage license is obtained, mandatory "marriage license training" (including instruction in the financial, social, psychological, and sexual aspects of marriage), trial marriage for a probationary period, and government day care centers for infants and preschool children to free mothers from the burdens of child care. What do you think should be done, if anything?

3. Which of the following promises are enforceable if contained in an antenuptial agreement?
a. Wife waives any claim for support upon any future divorce.
b. Husband agrees to raise children in a specified religion.
c. Both agree to a specified variety of sexual activities with a specified frequency.

d. Husband agrees to transfer certain valuable property to wife immediately upon marriage.
e. Wife agrees that husband may have custody of the children, if any, upon any future divorce.

4. What legal rights accrue in your state to an unmarried woman who lives with a man for 13 years "as husband and wife" who then is abandoned? Does it make any difference if she had received an oral promise of future support? What if they had a child? You may either refer to a legal encyclopedia located in your library or surf the Web. In either case, search under the subject index of "cohabitation," "same-sex marriage," and "domestic partnerships."

5. Bruce Vernoff, age 30, died suddenly of an allergic reaction. His wife, Gaby caused the extraction of Bruce's sperm from his body more than a day after his death. The sperm was kept frozen for more than a year before Gaby used it to become pregnant. On March 17 Gaby gave birth to a girl. Is it ethical (and legal) to harvest sperm (or eggs) from a corpse? Should consent of the deceased to the procedure be presumed? Who owns parts of a human body that remain "alive" after death? What if divorce proceedings were pending at the time of death? Should parents of an unmarried male who dies be able to harvest his sperm for future implantation in a surrogate mother to produce a grandchild? Should the disposition of sperm held in a sperm bank at the death of a donor be treated differently from sperm held in the decedent's body? Associated Press, *Dead Man's Sperm Used to Produce Baby*, 27 March 1999.

6. Does someone have a legal right to know whether or not she is genetically related to her father because her mother's egg was fertilized *in vitro* at a sperm bank? Should someone have a legal right to know the name of his genetic parent? Do

you apply the same rationale to donors who someday want desperately to find their genetic children, perhaps to leave them millions of dollars?

7. What legal problems can you think of that might arise if a surrogate mother changed her mind immediately following birth, and therefore refused to release her child to the natural father, as she had contracted to do? For example, what if she moved to another state and assumed a new identity and life—would she be guilty of child-snatching (kidnapping by a relative) or only responsible for breach of contract? Would your answer change if the surrogate mother were genetically related to the child (via her egg with *in vitro* fertilization)? Do any legal problems come to mind if a surrogate mother aborts the contracting parties' fetus?

8. Sharon Bottoms and April Wade were living together in a lesbian relationship. Sharon's mother, Kay, sought court ordered custody of Sharon's 2-year-old son Tyler on the grounds that Sharon's relationship with April made her an unfit mother. What should be the result? Are children raised in a homosexual family thereby disadvantaged in some way?

9. Suppose that John and Mary arrange to have their fertilized egg, or preembryo, frozen for future use. Suppose John is killed in an airplane crash. Should Mary have the legal right to bring the preembryo to birth? To hire a surrogate mother

for that purpose? To have genetic surgery performed upon it to change its future behavioral characteristics? To donate it to gene research? To donate it to another couple? What should be the rights of the genetic donors to custody of a preembryo?

10. If one spouse puts the other spouse through medical school by working and by delaying his or her own formal education, and if divorce occurs soon after the doctor completes residency, how might a court's judgment take these factors into consideration? What difference would it make if divorce occurs *before* the medical license is obtained?

11. Should divorcing spouses be permitted to bring tort actions against each other for precisely the same conduct that would entitle strangers to sue each other? Can you think of any conduct between spouses that arguably should not justify a domestic tort? Should the same rules of liability between spouses be interpreted to include liability between parents and their children?

12. Quicken's Business Law Partner—Pat, Sean's spouse, charges several purchases that remain unpaid. Creditors seek payment from Sean's separate property. Is Sean liable? Does it make any difference if the charges are for necessities? Consult Arthur Miller's commentaries.

NOTES

1. Associate Justice Haden, California Court of Appeal, speaking for the court in the case of *In re Marriage of Wilson*, 201 Cal.App.3d 913, 247 Cal.Rptr. 522 (1988).
2. *Ankenbrandt v. Richards*, 112 S.Ct. 2206 (1992).
3. *Rubin v. Smith*, 817 F.Supp. 987 (New Hampshire, 1993); *Lannan v. Maul*, 979 F.2d 627 (8th Circuit, 1992).
4. *Wildey v. Springs*, 840 F.Supp. 1259 (North Dakota, 1994), also reported in the *The National Law Journal*, 22 November 1993, 6.
5. Rayner Pike, Associated Press, 28 February 1998.
6. *The Wall Street Journal*, 8 June 1994.
7. Amy Argetsinger, *Washington Post*, 15 October 1998.

8. Texas Family Code Annotated, § 1.91.
9. *Jennings v. Hurt*, 160 App. Div.2d 576, 554 N.Y.S.2d 220 (1990).
10. Elaine Hersher, *San Francisco Chronicle*, 5 November 1998.
11. Don Lattin, *San Francisco Chronicle*, 23 May 1998.
12. *Marvin v. Marvin*, 134 Cal.Rptr. 815, 18 Cal.3d 660, 557 P.2d 106 (1976).
13. *Marvin v. Marvin*, 122 Cal.App.3d 871, 176 Cal.Rptr. 555 (1981).
14. *Levar v. Elkins*, 604 P.2d 602 (Alaska, 1980); *Carroll v. Lee*, 148 Ariz. 101, 712 P.2d 923 (Arizona, 1986); *Boland v. Catalano*, 202 Conn. 333, 521 A.2d 142 (Connecticut, 1987); *Donovan V.*

Scuderi, 51 Md. App. 217, 443 A.2d 121 (Maryland 1981); *Eaton v. Johnson*, 235 Kan. 323, 681 P.2d 606 (Kansas, 1984); *Hierholzer v. Sardy*, 128 Mich. App. 259, 340 N.W.2d 91 (Michigan, 1983); *Hay v. Hay*, 100 Nev. 196, 678 P.2d 672 (Nevada, 1984); *Morone v. Morone*, 50 N.Y. 2d 481, 413 N.E.2d 1154 (New York, 1980); and *Watts v. Watts*, 137 Wis.2d 506, 405 N.W.2d 303 (Wisconsin, 1987).

15. See *Whorton v. Dilingham*, 202 Cal.App.3d 447, 248 Cal.Rptr. 405 (1988); and *Small v. Harper*, 638 S.W.2d 24 (Texas, 1982).

16. *Hewitt v. Hewitt*, 77 Ill.2d 49, 394 N.E.2d 1204 (Illinois, 1979).

17. Checkoway, "Marital Property and Creditor's Rights," 4 *Maine Bar Journal* 254 (1989).

18. *The Wall Street Journal*, 2 February 1994.

19. *In re Marriage of McNeill*, 160 Cal.App.3d 548, 206 Cal.Rptr. 641 (1984).

20. *Barnes v. Barnes*, 603 N.E.2d 1337 (1992).

21. *Dellapenta v. Dellapenta*, 838 P.2d 1153 (Wyoming, 1992).

22. *Bonte v. Bonte*, 136 N.H.286, 616 A.2d 464 (New Hampshire, 1992).

23. *Richard v. Richard*, 599 So.2d 135 (Florida, 1992).

24. *Renko v. McLean*, 697 A.2d 468 (MD. 1997).

25. *Hakkila v. Hakkila*, 112 N.M. 77, 812 P.2d 132 (New Mexico, 1991) (cert. den. June 4, 1991).

26. *Simmons v. Simmons*, 773 P.2d 602 (Colorado, 1988); *Van Meter v. Van Meter*, 328 N.W. 2d 497 (Iowa, 1983); *Vance v. Vance*, 41 Md. App. 130, 396 A.2d 296 (Maryland 1979); *Davis v. Bostick*, 282 Or. 667, 580 P.2d 544 (Oregon 1978); *Noble v. Noble*, 761 P.2d 1369 (Utah, 1988); and *Stuart v. Stuart*, 143 Wis.2d 347, 421 N.W.2d 505 (Wisconsin, 1988).

27. *Harris v. McDavid*, 553 So.2d 567 (Alabama 1989); *Richard P. v. Superior Court*, 202 Cal.App.3d 1089, 249 Cal.Rptr. 246, (California, 1988); *Whittington v. Whittington*, 766 S.W.2d 73 (Kentucky, 1989); *Wiener v. Wiener*, 84 A.D.2d 814, 444 N.Y.S.2d 130 (New York, 1981); *Pickering v. Pickering*, 434 N.W.2d 758 (South Dakota, 1989).

28. *Roe v. Wade*, 410 U.S. 113, 93 S.Ct. 705 (1973).

29. *Webster v. Reproductive Health Services*, 492 U.S. 490, 109 S.Ct. 3040 (1989).

30. *Ohio v. Akron Center for Reproductive Health*, 493 U.S. 802, 110 S.Ct. 39 (1990) and *Hodgson v. Minnesota*, 497 U.S. 417, 1110 S.Ct. 2926 (1990).

31. *Planned Parenthood v. Casey*, 505 U.S. 833, 112 S.Ct. 2791 (1992).

32. Kaye and Kanwischer, "Admissibility of Genetic Testing in Paternity Litigation: A Survey of State Statutes," 22 *Family Law Quarterly* 109 (1988). For representative cases dealing with rebuttal of the presumption of legitimacy, see *Scheland v. Chilldres*, 852 S.W.2d 791 (Arkansas, 1993); *In re M.C.*, 844 P.2d 1313 (Colorado App., 1992); *Miller v. Kirshner*, 225 Conn 185, 621 A.2d 1326 (Connecticut, 1993); *In re Cooper*, 608 N.E.2d 1386 (Indiana Ct., app. 1993); *Jensen v. Runft*, 252 Kan. 76, 843 P.2d 191 (Kansas, 1992); *Johnson v. Van Blaricom*, 480 N.W.2d 138 (Minn. Ct. App., 1992); and *In re Tamara B.*, 585 N.Y.S.2d 757, (New York App. Div., 1992).

33. *State v. Hogan*, 613 So.2d 681 (Louisiana, 1993).

34. Lance Williams, *San Francisco Examiner*, 11 January 1998.

35. *Gomez v. Perez*, 409 U.S. 535, 93 S.Ct. 872 (1990).

36. *Levy v. Louisiana*, 391 U.S. 69, 88 S.Ct. 1509 (1968).

37. *Weber v. Aetna Casualty*, 406 U.S. 164, 92 S.Ct. L400 (1972).

38. *In re Baby M*, 217 N.J. Super. 313, 525 A.2d 1128, reversed at 109 N.J. 396, 537 A.2d 1227 (1988).

39. *The Wall Street Journal*, 21 May 1993; *The Business of Surrogate Parenting* (Albany NY: New York State Department of Health, Apr. 1992), 139.

40. *Johnson v. Calvert*, 5 Cal.4th 84, 851 P.2d 776, 19 Cal.Rptr.2d 494 (1993).

41. Associated Press, Albany N.Y., 8 May 1998.

42. Gina Kolata, "Clinics Selling Embryos Made for Adoption," *New York Times*, 23 November 1997.

43. Lisa M. Krieger, "Life on Ice: Frozen Embryos Proliferate," *San Francisco Examiner*, 9 May 1997.

44. *In re Evan*, 583 N.Y.S.2d 997 (New York, 1992); *Adoption of B.L.V.B.*, 628 A.2d 1271 (Virginia, 1993); *Adoption of Tammy*, 619 N.E.2d 315 (Massachusettes, 1993).

45. *Wisconsin v. Yoder*, 406 U.S. 205, 92 S.Ct. 1526 (1972); *Santosky v. Kramer*, 455 U.S. 745, 102 S.Ct. 1388 (1982).

46. See e.g., California Penal Code, § 272; *Williams v. Garcetti*, 5 Cal.4th 363, 853 P.2d 507, 20 Cal.Rptr.2d 341 (California, 1993); New York Penal Law, § 260.10(2); *People v. Scully*, 134 Misc.2d 906, 513 N.Y.S.2d 625 (1987); Kentucky Revised Statutes Ann. § 530.060(1).

47. *Restatement of the Law of Torts*, 2d edition (St. Paul, MN: American Law Institute Publishers, 1934), § 316.

48. *The Wall Street Journal*, 28 September 1992.

49. In the following paragraphs there are a sprinkling of quotations, all of which, unless otherwise indicated, are from Jeremy Rifkin, *The Biotech Century* (New York: Tarcher/ Putnam, 1998).

50. David Perlman and Carl T. Hall, *San Francisco Chronicle*, 24 October 1998.

51. Associated Press, Washington, 22 May 1998.

52. Nicholas Wade, "Biotech Firm Touts Potential of Cow-Human Hybrid Cells," *New York Times*, 13 November 1998.

53. Rick Weiss, *Washington Post*, 19 May 1998.

54. William Wright, *Born That Way: Genes, Behavior, Personality* (New York: Knoph, 1998).

55. Theordore Roosevelt to Charles B. Davenport, January 1913, *Charles B. Davenport Papers*, Department of Genetics, Cold Spring Harbor, NY.

56. Rifkin, *The Biotech Century*, 128.

57. Brian Macquarrie, *Boston Globe*, 18 September 1998.

58. James O. Hill, Director of the Colorado Clinical Nutrition Research Unit at the University of Colorado, quoted by Associated Press, 15 June 1998.

59. *New York Times*, 18 January 1998.

60. California Civil Code § 1714.1 & 3; and California Education Code §§ 10,606 and 28,801.

61. *San Francisco Chronicle*, 18 June 1998.

62. Associated Press, 12 May 1998.

63. *San Francisco Chronicle*, 12 May 1997.

64. *National Law Journal*, 2 November 1998 and 9 November 1998.

65. *The National Law Journal*, 6 September 1993, 1A.

66. *Coy v. Iowa*, 487 U.S. 1012, 108 S.Ct. 2798 (1988).

67. *Maryland v. Craig*, 497 U.S. 836, 110 S.Ct. 3157 (1990).

68. Gregg Aamot, Associated Press, 24 May 1998.

69. Judy Pasternak, *Los Angeles Times*, 4 May 1998.

70. *In re fetus Brown v. Darlene Brown*, 228 Ill.Dec. 525, 294 Ill.App.3d 159, 689 N.E.2d 397 (1997).

71. 20 *Family Law Quarterly* 444 (1987).

72. *Time*, 1 October 1990.

73. *Time*, 18 August 1997.

74. *Los Angeles Times*, 8 May 1998.

75. *Hanson v. Hanson*, 404 N.W.2d 460 (North Dakota, 1987); *Renfro v. Renfro*, 848 P.2d 830 (Alaska, 1993).

76. *Orr v. Orr*, 440 U.S. 268, 99 S.Ct. 1102 (1979).

77. *In re the Marriage of Wilson*, 201 Cal.App.3d 913, 247 Cal.Rptr. 522 (1988).

78. *Murphy v. Murphy*, 470 S.2d 1297 (Alabama, 1985); *In re the Marriage of Wilson*.

79. *Bliss v. Bliss*, 66 N.Y.2d 344, 497 N.Y.S.2d 344, 488 N.E.2d 90 (New York, 1985).

80. Alabama, California, Georgia, Illinois, Louisiana, Maryland, New York, Ohio, Pennsylvania, Tennessee, and

Utah permit modification in such cases. See *The Family Law Quarterly* 23 (1990), 546.

81. *Hall v. Hall*, 25 Ill.App.3d 524, 323 N.E.2d 541 (Illinois, 1975). In 1983, Illinois adopted Section 510(b) of its Marriage and Dissolution Act, which terminates alimony if the former spouse cohabits with another person.

82. *McCarty v. McCarty*, 453 U.S. 210, 101 S.Ct. 2728, (1981).

83. *O'Brien v. O'Brien*, 66 N.Y.2d 576, 498 N.Y.S.2d 743, 489 N.E.2d 712 (New York, 1985).

84. *McGowan v. McGowan*, 142 A.D.2d 355, 535 N.Y.S.2d 990 (1988).

85. *Dorton v. Dorton*, 77 N.C.App. 667, 336 S.E.2d 415 (North Carolina, 1986).

86. *Lovett v. Lovett*, 688 S.W.2d 329 (Kentucky, 1985).

87. See e.g., *In re Marriage of Aufmuth*, 89 Cal.App.3d 446, 152 Cal.Rptr. 668 (1979); *In re Marriage of Washburn*, 101 Wash.2d 168, 677 P.2d 152 (Washington, 1984); and *Lowery v. Lowery*, 262 Ga. 20, 413 S.E.2d 73 (Georgia, 1992).

88. *Sorensen v. Sorensen*, 839 P.2d 774 (Utah, 1992).

89. *Guzman v. Guzman*, 827 S.W.2d 445, (Texas, 1992).

90. *In re Francis*, 442 N.W.2d 59 (Iowa, 1989); *Wilson v. Wilson*, 434 N.W.2d 742 (S. Dakota, 1989).

91. *Aster v. Gross*, 7 Va.App. 1, 371 S.E.2d 833 (Virginia, 1988); but see *Pommerenke v. Pommerenke*, 7 Va.App. 241, 372 S.E.2d 630 (Virginia, 1988), where the court approved giving less than 10 percent of the assets to an adulterous wife.

92. See e.g., *Smith v. Smith*, 331 S.E.2d 682 (North Carolina, 1985).

93. *Bradley v. Bradley*, 336 S.E.2d 658 (North Carolina, 1985).

94. *In re marriage of Sullivan*, 37 Cal.3d 762 (1984).

95. *Davis v. Davis*, Sup.Ct. # WL 341632, 842 S.W.2d 588 (Tennessee, 1992). In Chapter 1 it was noted that some opinions are ordered "not published" and therefore cannot be used as legal precedent. This case was so ordered. Nonetheless, the case binds the parties and their preembryos. Also reported in *The National Law Journal*, 15 June 1992, A3.

96. Texas Family Code Annotated, § 3.63.

97. *Newberry v. Newberry*, 745 S.W.2d 796 (Missouri, 1988).

98. *Palmore v. Sidoti*, 466 U.S. 429, 104 S.Ct. 1879 (1984).

99. *The Wall Street Journal*, 17 August 1992.

100. *Veazey v. Veazey*, 560 P.2d 382 (Alaska, 1977); *DeMontigny v. DeMontigny*, 70 Wis. 2d 131, 233 N.W.2d 463 (Wisconsin, 1975).

101. 27 *Family Law Quarterly* (Winter 1994), 503.

102. Paquin, "Protecting the Interests of Children in Divorce Proceedings," 26 *The Journal of Family Law* 303 (1987-88).

103. California Civil Code, § 4607.

104. *The National Law Journal*, 16 August 1993, 1.

105. Public Law No. 100-485, 102 Statutes 2343 (1988).

106. Public Law No. 102-521, 106 Stat. 3403, 18 U.S.C. 228 (1992).

107. *Kelm v. Kelm*, an unpublished opinion of the Ohio Supreme Court, 1994 WL 85323 (Ohio App. 10). See also *The National Law Journal*, 4 February 1994, 39.

108. *Mullen v. Suchko*, 279 Pa.Super. 499, 421 A.2d 310 (Pennsylvania, 1980).

109. See *Roth v. Patino*, 298 N.Y. 543, 80 N.E. 2d 673 (New York, 1984) and *Rubenstein v. Kleven*, 261 F.2d 921 (1st Cir., 1958).

10

OWNING AND OPERATING MOTOR VEHICLES

*E*verything in life is somewhere else, and you get there in a car.

E.B. White, Author of Charlotte's Web

How people transport themselves and their products from one location to another is a major concern in all societies. Public policy issues arising from transportation questions will compete with other major issues in the twenty-first century. Where shall we live relative to where we work? How are goods best distributed in a worldwide market? What are the costs of different transportation systems? How much environmental harm is caused by pollution and how can it be minimized? Are large and efficient mass transportation systems economically feasible?

Automobiles are the most valuable item of personal property owned by most Americans. No other widely owned, mass-produced and distributed products are more costly than automobiles, trucks, and mobile motorized variations. No other item of personal property is as subsidized through public expenditures such as highways and fuels and through tolerance for air and surface pollution.

In one sense, the twentieth century began just as it is ending—with competition between automobiles powered by electricity and by other fuels (then, by gasoline, coal, or oil-fired steam; now by ethanol, natural gas, or one-half electricity and one-half gasoline). Although there were few gasoline-powered vehicles, most people in the major cities had seen them maneuvering through horse-clogged streets. A new independence and freedom was promised. "Trains kept their own schedules and never took you quite where you wanted to go, and horses got hungry, cold and tired. The auto was nothing but a dumb machine, but that was part of the joy."[1] One of the earliest proposed settlements from a crash was proposed by financier William K. Vanderbilt, who was "taking his father for a spin down the main street in New York, [when] he almost killed them both" in a collision with a "fishwagon." Vanderbilt promptly offered to compromise the case: "I'll settle for everything, my good fellow." What Vanderbilt meant was to pay for disposal of one horse and the purchase of another.[2] Even in 1900, with perhaps 8,000 *handmade* cars in the entire nation, there were fatal accidents with pedestrians and public outcries for "mancatchers" on the front of cars. The *New York Times* was calling for driver education, while the age of motor vehicle crashes and litigation was begun.

Electric cars were the simplest and the most pleasant to drive. "One owner wrote, 'There is no fire in it, no smell about it, nothing to break or get out of order; no gauges to watch, no tangle of oily, grimy parts.' Ready to start at a moment's notice, the electric vehicle was considered ideal for city use. . . . But batteries needed to be recharged every twenty to forty miles, and outside of the largest cities, recharging stations did not exist."[3] For most, the electric vehicle would be too expensive and too impracticable. Steam-driven vehicles made little impact— perhaps sitting on top of a boiler was unattractive. Gas-driven vehicles were taking over, although they were bumpy, noisy, rattling, and reeked of fuel. One gallon of gas, for ten cents, could transport two people for 25 miles.

The competition between gasoline and other fuels for vehicles is intensifying as the twenty-first century begins. Several global manufacturers already are offering limited selections of electric vehicles, part gasoline and part electric cars, and natural gas alternatives to the public.* Most can travel less than 100 miles before recharging, but engineers expect to extend that range substantially early in the new millennium. For about $25,000 you can purchase a three-wheeled two-seater made in Switzerland (called the S-Lem Active) that will travel about 50 miles on electricity or by foot pedal when the batteries go flat.

We conclude that the gasoline powered automobile with its considerable impact on the environment will fade away in the twenty-first century as we return, in a sense, to where we were with electric carriages silently meandering around our largest cities.

There may be substantial impacts upon the vehicle laws brought about by changing from gasoline to other less offensive fuels. For example, cars can have useful life expectancies of twenty and more years. Can government enact laws that keep older cars, sometimes called gross polluters, off the highways? Or must these owners be compensated for their losses as the changeover to electricity or other fuel becomes mandated?

Few human-made objects have had as extensive and intensive an impact on the law as the automobile. The registration of vehicles, collection of tens of millions of dollars in fees, and licensing of drivers are monumental, recurring tasks mandated by state statutes. Comprehensive vehicle codes govern rules of the road. Administrative agencies regulate vehicle manufacturers with particular emphasis on safety and fuel consumption. Other administrative agencies evaluate the environmental impact of new building construction to anticipate the effect on traffic flow and volume. Executive and legislative branches of the government, especially at the federal level, continue to struggle with the problem of maintaining a fuel supply for a nation on wheels. Collectively, millions of workers manufacture the vehicles, fuel them, service them, use them as tools, and ultimately dispose of them as scrap—a sizable problem in itself. International disputes often revolve around trade issues related to import and export of automobiles.

---

*Electric cars are now available from General Motors, Toyota, Chrysler, Ford, and others. On the outside they look exactly like ordinary pickup trucks, sedans, vans, or sports utility vehicles, and can reach speeds up to 80 miles per hour. Ford, for example, offers a Ranger on a three-year lease, $450 per month, which includes maintenance, insurance, and a battery charger. Erin McCormick, *San Francisco Examiner*, 25 October 1998. Honda and Toyota have announced production of automobiles powered by combined gasoline and electric motors. The vehicles use electric motors at low speeds and gasoline powered motors at higher speeds. While the gasoline motor is engaged it charges the electric engine battery, eliminating the need to plug in the car to recharge. Fuel economy is in the 60 mile per gallon range. Bob Mozley, National Motorist, Winter 1999, p. 12.

There is no body of law called motor vehicle law. However, previously discussed areas of law such as contracts, torts, and crimes have application to motor vehicles. We will also introduce personal property law as it relates to motor vehicles. The application of all these different areas of law to one type of personal property highlights both the rules and the importance of this type of property.

OWNING A MOTOR VEHICLE

An automobile is a form of **personal property**. **Property** is an aggregate of rights to a thing which are protected and guaranteed by government, including and especially ownership. Property is classified in many ways, most importantly as either real or personal. Property is either real or immovable, or personal or movable.[4] Real property is land and almost everything permanently attached to it, such as buildings, fences, trees, and roads. (See Chapters 11 and 12 for an in-depth discussion of real property.) Personal property* is not permanently attached to land, such as vehicles, merchandise in stores, food products, skis, boats, and backpacks. The general idea is that if property is not land or that which is permanently affixed to land, it is personalty (personal property), which is often referred to as property that can be easily moved. That mental image usually works until one tries to move a filled waterbed.

Ownership of personal property occurs many ways. Personal property can be created as you would create a painting or a clay pot. It can be transferred to another by gift. It can be bought, traded for, and found. In the case of motor vehicles, ownership usually results from a purchase.

IS A SPECIAL CONTRACT REQUIRED TO PURCHASE A MOTOR VEHICLE?

The sale of a motor vehicle is an ordinary contractual transaction subject to the law of contracts relating to personal property. The contract involves a sale of goods (tangible personal property) and is subject to the Uniform Commercial Code (See Chapter 8). The UCC relaxes some of the otherwise formal rules of common-law contract formation and performance and motor vehicles sales law is mostly uniform throughout the states.

Motor vehicles, of course, usually cost more than $500, and so the **statute of frauds** applies to such purchases. Accordingly, as evidence of an executory contract there must be some writing signed by the party to be obligated. This requirement is usually met with a standard form contract prepared by commercial sellers. Standardized (pre-printed) form agreements, including automobile sales contracts, are **adhesion contracts**, meaning they are drafted by a dominant party and then presented to the other party—the adhering party—on a "take it or leave it" basis. Unconscionable clauses, those that "shock the conscience" of a court, are more likely to be found in adhesion contracts than contracts where the parties

---

*During the first one-half of the twentieth century, items of personal property, such as lawn mowers, were called *chattels*. Thus, when you borrowed money to purchase furniture for your home, for example, you would sign a document called a *chattel mortgage* giving the creditor rights to repossess (or foreclose upon) the furnishings. This terminology has generally been abandoned in the United States.

truly bargain over terms. If language in an adhesion contract is ambiguous, courts will often interpret the language to favor the buyer, the party who did not draft the contract. Nevertheless, the buyer should be aware that the contract is written primarily to protect the interests of the seller, and is unlikely to have ambiguous terms or clauses.

The trunk of the car seemed too small to Bill Clark as he viewed the car he was thinking about buying. The salesperson, Frank, assured him there was adequate room in the trunk for luggage for a family of four. Frank also said: "If there isn't enough room, bring the car back and we will install a luggage rack." Bill signed a standard form automobile purchase contract that did not include any reference to the luggage rack. A few months later, Bill, unable to load four suitcases in the trunk, returned to the dealership expecting a new luggage rack free of additional charge. Does Bill have an enforceable right to a luggage rack?

Bill's claim would be thwarted by the **parol evidence rule**. This rule holds that when persons have signed a contract as their final and complete expression of intention (integrated contracts), then neither party may introduce in court any evidence of prior or contemporaneous oral or written material that adds to or modifies that written contract. The rule does not apply to less formal contracts—those not portending to be the final and complete expression of the agreement. However, standard form automobile purchase contracts do purport to be final and complete agreements. The lesson is clear and crucial: If important promises are made to you (e.g. warranties, credit terms, additional equipment), be sure they are included as part of the written contract.

In motor vehicle sales transactions, there are standard sales customs and techniques, and some states regulate contracts written by commercial sellers. A complete discussion of the mini-culture of "list price," "5 percent over invoice," and "clearance sales" are beyond the scope of this text. However, buyers are well advised to consult reliable sources for help in selecting the appropriate vehicle, (especially if previously owned), and for information on negotiating the best deal.*

The statute of frauds and parol evidence rule also apply to purchases from private owners. If there are warranties, any other promises, or an extension of credit, a written contract should be prepared containing these terms and the signatures of both the seller and the buyer to satisfy these requirements.

WARRANTIES FOR MOTOR VEHICLES

The seller of a new motor vehicle transfers title with any express warranties made and with several implied warranties. Recall from Chapter 8 that express

---

*Every April, the magazine *Consumer Reports* publishes an issue devoted to selecting and buying new and used cars. Several helpful books are available to assist the buyer of automobiles. A few examples include James Bragg, *Car Buyer's and Leaser's Negotiating Bible* (Random House, 1996); Mark Eskeldson, *What Car Dealers Don't Want You to Know* (Tech News Corp, 1977); Jack Gillis, Clarence Ditlow, Amy Curran, *The Car Book 1999: The Definitive Buyer's Guide to Car Safety, Fuel Economy, Maintenance, and Much More* (HarperCollins 1999); Ralph Nader and C. Ditlow, *Lemon Book: Auto Rights* 4th ed., (Moyer-Bell LTD. 1998); Jack Nerad, *The Complete Idiot's Guide to Buying or Leasing a Car* (Macmillan, 1996); Darrell Parrish, *The Car Buyer's Art: How to Beat the Salesman at His Own Game* (Bellflour, Ca.: Book Express, 1998); Remar Sutton, *Don't Get Taken Every Time: The Insider's Guide to Buying or Leasing Your Next Car or Truck*, 4th rev. edition (Penguin Books, 1997).

warranties are created by statements of fact made by the seller about quality, condition, description, and performance potential.

> Praneel X. Singh expressed his interest in the new model SRV. Walter, the number one salesperson at Autoworld, claimed, "This is the best new vehicle to be introduced in forty years." Is Walter's statement an express warranty?

Walter's *opinion* that the vehicle is "the best new vehicle to be introduced in forty years" creates no warranty; it is **puffing**, the word used to describe normal sellers' exaggerations about goods for sale. Similarly, statements such as, "It's worth a fortune" or "Anywhere else you'd pay more for it," do not usually create warranties. Whether the buyer's reliance on the seller's statement is reasonable is often the controlling factor. For example, a salesperson's statement that a car "will never breakdown" and "will last a lifetime" is so improbable that no reasonable buyer should rely on it. The how and where of the statement is also important in determining the reasonableness of the buyer's reliance. For example, it is generally more reasonable for a buyer to rely on a statement made in a written advertisement than on a salesperson's oral statement.

Also recall from Chapter 8 that *implied warranties* are warranties that arise in a sales transaction unless specifically disclaimed. The most important implied warranties in automobile sales transactions are usually the warranty of title and the warranty of merchantability. The **warranty of title** promises to the buyer that the seller possesses good title to the motor vehicle and can rightfully transfer title to the buyer. The **warranty of merchantability** refers to quality and is a promise that a vehicle is of usual and customary quality and as such is fit for its ordinary and intended use. Implied warranties of merchantability are made only by merchants. (Of course, an auto dealer is a merchant.) Given the value of a motor vehicle and its intended use, the implied warranty of merchantability is very extensive, unless limited by the seller. As you will see and should note, implied warranties of quality are almost always limited in some fashion by the seller.

> When Betty Orra bought her new automobile, she expected 100,000 or more miles of carefree motoring. She carefully maintained and serviced her vehicle. The car was sold with a written warranty from the dealer that included this language: "This warranty is in lieu of and excludes all other warranties, express or implied, including the warranty of merchantability." The warranty covered defects in materials or workmanship "for one year or 12,000 miles, whichever occurs first." Did Betty lose anything when she received this warranty?

Yes and no. The dealer statement is an attempted **disclaimer** sufficient to deny an implied warranty of merchantability in most contracts except those involving consumer goods, such as an automobile for personal use. A disclaimer is a specific statement indicating a particular warranty does not exist or limiting the warranty as to nature or duration. In a transaction for consumer goods, you can make a total disclaimer of the implied warranty of merchantability, but not a partial disclaimer. Total exclusion of an implied warranty of merchantability requires

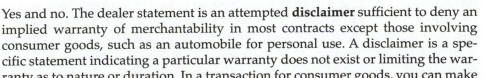

specific, legally acceptable language of disclaimer. The most common methods of a total disclaimer for an implied warranty of merchantability are (1) use of the terms "as is" or "with all faults" or (2) a statement that no other warranty, including that of merchantability, exists. The dealer did not use the "as is" form of disclaimer but relied on the alternative method. Although in a nonconsumer transaction this disclaimer would be effective, a federal law preempts the UCC in consumer transactions involving warranties. The federal Magnuson-Moss Warranty Act[5] (see Chapter 8) allows sellers of consumer goods to limit, but not eliminate, warranties of merchantability if any express warranty is given. Thus, the dealer cannot disclaim the warranty in the manner attempted. A merchant cannot give an express warranty and include an "as is" clause to eliminate the implied warranty of merchantability. Under Magnuson-Moss, a seller making an express warranty in a sales contract is not allowed to disclaim or modify either the implied warranty of merchantability or the implied warranty of fitness for a particular purpose. However, sellers can impose a time limit on the duration of an implied warranty. The time limit must be no less than the duration of the express warranty. Any limitation must also be reasonable, conscionable, and stated in clear and conspicuous language on the face of the warranty. All motor vehicle manufacturers provide express warranties, and the implied warranty of merchantability is often limited in time as part of the express warranty provision in the sales contract.* An acceptable limitation might read, "Any implied warranty of merchantability or fitness for a particular purpose applicable to this vehicle is limited to the duration of this written warranty."

Thus, Betty Orra did not lose her implied warranty of merchantability, but its limitation to 12 months was effective. The extent of the express warranty, both as to scope of coverage and length of coverage, is a very important issue when determining which motor vehicle to buy and how much to pay.

While negotiating to purchase a new Lincoln Navigator, Marvin Slick offered to waive his right to the "limited warranty" that was offered by the dealership. His persuasive argument to the sales manager was, "I believe in the car and don't need any limited warranty. So, I'll waive and give up the limited warranty if you will throw in my choice of 50 CDs." Would this be a good deal for the car dealer to make?

No. If the "limited" warranty is cancelled and nothing else is said, then the "full" warranty will control and the dealer's future responsibilities will be expanded.

Motor vehicle dealers often offer (at an additional cost) extended warranties to vehicle buyers. These warranties typically extend the time and expand the coverage provided by manufacturer warranties. These policies can be purchased from companies other than the original dealership and often at more favorable prices. Before deciding whether to purchase an extended warranty, one should become an informed consumer by studying the need for the product and the available extended warranties and prices. There are substantial differences in

---

*Some states have statutes that further restrict the ability of a seller to disclaim or limit implied warranties in consumer transactions. These state laws are upheld as long as they add to those rights provided by Magnuson-Moss.

price, scope, and length of coverage, and possible restrictions on who may service the vehicle.

A manufacturer providing a written warranty is also required to comply with Magnuson-Moss and applicable state laws. Magnuson-Moss does not require that the manufacturer or seller provide a warranty, but it does govern the wording of and extent of warranties when express warranties are given. If a seller makes an express written warranty involving consumer goods costing more than $10, the act controls how the warranty is to be given. Any warranty under the act must be labeled as "full" or "limited." In addition, if the cost of the goods is more than $15, the warrantor (the person making the warranty) must make certain disclosures in language that is easy to understand. The disclosures must state the names and addresses of the warrantor and must identify the product warranted, the procedures for enforcement of the warranty, and any limitations on warranty remedies.

A *full warranty* may not cover every problem arising from use of a consumer product, but it must give the buyer rights to free repair or replacement of any defective part. If the product cannot be repaired within a reasonable time, the consumer can choose a refund or a replacement without charge. The warranty does not cover damage that is caused by the consumer. A written consumer warranty that does not meet all the requirements of a full warranty is a *limited warranty*. The seller must state clearly that only a limited warranty is given. The Federal Trade Commission has the power to enforce many provisions of Magnuson-Moss and may sue businesses that fail to honor their written warranties.

Used cars purchased from dealers also carry implied warranties of merchantability because the dealers are still merchants even though the goods are used. Used cars purchased from private parties do not carry any warranty of quality unless made expressly by the nonmerchant seller (get these assurances in writing). Remember that all warranties of quality can be disclaimed by the words "as is." This is true even under Magnuson-Moss as long as no express warranty of quality is given.

WHAT ARE LEMON LAWS?

Margo O'Smalley was very excited when she bought her new convertible Aardvark Seven from Autoworld. She drove it off the lot and headed toward Slim's Health Club to show it to her friends. Two blocks from the dealership, the engine died. The car needed to be towed back to Autoworld. A very angry O'Smalley was not mollified when the sales representative said, "We'll be happy to repair or replace that cracked engine block." O'Smalley snapped back, "I expect to get a new and different Aardvark Seven. I am a consumer who won't be satisfied with a lemon." Will O'Smalley get a new car or must she allow the repair or replacement of the engine block?

The legal question is, did the dealership perform its contractual obligations when it delivered the vehicle? If the delivery is legally sufficient, Autoworld need only honor the warranty—either repair or replace the defective part. If, however, the delivery is insufficient under key UCC provisions, Autoworld must replace the defective car with a new one.

O'Smalley had a right to inspect her purchase before accepting it and becoming obligated to pay its purchase price. What is considered an appropriate inspection depends on the circumstances and the nature of the goods. In this situation, although O'Smalley received and took possession of the vehicle, a normal inspection would not have shown that the engine had a cracked block. Since she discovered that the vehicle was nonconforming almost immediately after receipt, she can return it and argue reasonably that she never really accepted it. O'Smalley really did indeed get a lemon[6] (sour deal), and she has a legal right to a full refund or a new vehicle under the UCC.[7]

There are additional rights under the UCC that may also be claimed to assist a buyer when there is a major and initial contract breach by the seller. Perhaps even if O'Smalley accepted the vehicle after a careful inspection, she could revoke her acceptance and enjoy the same rights (of replacement or full refund) as if she had rejected it initially. It is necessary that she revoke within a reasonable time after she discovers (or should have discovered) a sufficient reason for revocation, and before there is any substantial change in the condition of the goods (not caused by the defect).[8]

Access the site to the various state lemon laws from the Car Talk Web site of Tom and Ray Magliozzi (aka "Click and Clack, The Tappet Brothers"), renowned hosts of a radio program on auto care, at http://208.221.9.99/Tools/lemon-states.pl

Most problems with new cars are not as dramatic or immediate as O'Smalley's. All states have passed so-called **lemon laws** to provide protection for angry consumers who are dissatisfied with extensive warranty work and instead demand a new car or their money back. A lemon law provides that if a car is a lemon, the dealer must refund to the customer the purchase price of the car, plus sales tax, registration, and license fees, minus a reasonable allowance for use.[9] The problem, of course, is to define a "lemon" with sufficient precision and to enforce consumers' rights in a fair and prompt manner. If there is a major problem not permanently fixed in four attempts, or if a car is out of service for repairs for a cumulative total of 30 calendar days during a 12-month period, the car usually qualifies as a lemon. The covered period in different states ranges from the written warranty period, or 12 months to 2 years; sometimes coverage is based on miles driven (for example, 18,000 miles). Many lemon laws allow for the use of ADR methods, such as non-binding arbitration, to assist in the resolution of the dispute (see Chapter 4).

Mr. Hughes's new 1990 Dodge Caravan was a lemon. His first year of ownership was rewarded with seven separate trips to the dealer to repair transmission defects. Attempts to get Chrysler to replace the car within the time provided by the lemon law were unsuccessful. Hughes filed a lawsuit. The court entered judgment for Hughes in the amount of $74,371, including double the amount he paid for the vehicle and attorney fees. Do lemon laws always provide for a recovery that exceeds the price of the vehicle?

Wisconsin does but most states do not.[10] The Wisconsin statute specifically allows a court to award twice the customer damages plus attorney fees. The court opinion recites the transactional dilemma well: "We realize that car manufacturers do not deliberately set out to manufacture a lemon. Quite the opposite. In fact, it is in their own best interest not to do so. However, an unfortunate fact of life, seemingly as inevitable as night following day, is that occasionally a 'lemon' will slip through the line. And when that happens, another unfortunate fact of modern-day life is that the cost to the unlucky consumer who purchases that 'lemon' is far more than the cost of the car: interrupted, delayed, or even cancelled schedules; the time and the trouble, as well as the anxiety and stress that accompany those changes; the apprehensions that result every time the consumer gets back into that automobile wondering 'what next?' Dependability is a prime objective of every new car buyer. When that is taken away, the loss is far greater than the cost of the car. It is this fact that the legislature recognized when they enacted the lemon law. Its principle motivation is not to punish the manufacturer who, after all, would far prefer that no 'lemons' escape their line. Rather, it seeks to provide an incentive to that manufacturer to promptly return those unfortunate consumers back to where they thought they were when they first purchased that new automobile."[11]

WHAT ARE AUTOMOBILE LEASES?

In recent years, leasing has become a popular alternative to purchasing a vehicle. Technically, a "lease" is a common-law **bailment** for use. A bailment is created when personal property is temporarily delivered into the care of another without transfer of title. Thus, a bailment is created when you lend your car to a friend.

Virtually every study and analysis concludes that buying an automobile is less expensive than leasing over the full term of ownership.[12] However, monthly costs of leasing are reasonably low and the lease deposit is small, leaving the impression of a lower cost. Many consumers are also happy that at the end of the lease the car is simply returned to the dealer, or lessor. Although stings are attached to the car's return, most people view them as a very distant and unimportant problem. A person contemplating a lease should consider:

1. What is the term of the lease and what are the front-end, monthly, and back-end charges?* What additional charges, such as responsibility for repair, are occasioned by what events?

2. What limitations are imposed on total miles driven during the lease? What extra costs are incurred if the mileage limit is exceeded?

3. What warranty is offered with the leased automobile?

4. How and at what cost can the lease be terminated before it expires?

Anyone who leases an automobile should realize that the usual and normal costs of automobile ownership still exist in a lease. For example, costs such as license registration, liability and property insurance, emission certificates, gasoline, and maintenance remain costs of the buyer or lessee and are not changed by the normal lease. Also, bailment law and lease contracts require that personal property be returned in good condition. Thus, while an owner may neglect an automobile, a lessee does so with peril. There will undoubtedly be additional costs at lease return for excess mileage or wear and tear. Some leases contain important options at the end of the lease. If the car is worth more or less than a specified amount at the end of the lease, the consumer will receive a credit (unlikely) or pay a differential (likely) to guarantee the leasing company from any unpredicted depreciation or loss in value.

The Better Business Bureau administers a program to help automobile manufacturers and individual customers resolve disputes concerning alleged manufacturing defects.
http://www.bbb.org/complaints/BBBautoline.html

Keys to Vehicle Leasing: A Consumer Guide to Automobile Leasing is prepared by the Federal Reserve Board and is available at the Federal Consumer Information Center. http://www.pueblo.gsa.gov/cic_text/cars/key2leas/default.htm

*A "back-end" charge refers to costs the consumer pays at the end of the lease.

Some consumers who use their automobiles in their businesses, such as traveling salespersons and real estate agents, assume that they obtain tax benefits by deducting from their taxes the full amount of lease payments, plus all other related expenses. However, the tax laws do not play favorites with leased automobiles. Owners can also deduct their business travel expenses, including interest payments, and can depreciate (deduct) the cost of their vehicles gradually and proportionally over the years.

Many states levy a "use" tax against buyers in lieu of the sales tax they would otherwise pay if they had purchased the vehicle. Leases are covered by Article 2A of the Uniform Commercial Code. Bailments are discussed again later in the chapter.

Potente leased a new 1989 Peugeot through Peugeot Motors of America, Inc (PMA). A few months later, after experiencing problems with the vehicle, he sought relief under Ohio's "lemon law." PMA moved for summary judgment on the Lemon Law claim, arguing that Potente, as lessee, had no standing to bring an action under Ohio's lemon law. What was the result?

The court held that any consumer entitled to enforce contract warranties against the manufacturer had the right to enforce the state lemon laws. "A lease agreement which extends the manufacturer's warranty and the ability to enforce the warranty to the lessee falls within the protective ambit of Ohio's Lemon Law."[13] Most state lemon laws do extend to automobile leases, but not all.[14]

WHAT ARE AUTOMOBILE RECALLS?

Compare what you know about automobile safety in the U.S. with automobile safety information in Japan. http://www.osa.go.jp/ 980012e.html

Even after motor vehicles are sold, manufacturers have a continuing obligation to ensure their safety in normal use. Under federal law, manufacturers are required to notify consumers and the National Highway Traffic Safety Administration (NHTSA) of discovered safety defects and how they propose to eliminate or "cure" them. Recalls can be voluntary or mandated by the NHTSA. The manufacturer generally has the option of repairing the defect, replacing the vehicle, or refunding the price paid. Obviously, repairing the defect is the usual means of correction chosen by the manufacturers.

In early 1993, the National Highway Traffic Safety Administration requested that General Motors recall 4.7 million pickup trucks equipped with side-saddle gasoline tanks. "Since the side-saddle trucks were introduced in 1973, their gas tanks have sometimes ripped open and exploded in side-impact collisions. The GM trucks are 2.4 times as likely as pickups made by Ford Motor Co. to be involved in deadly crashes with fires, NHTSA says. This translates into about five deaths a year out of more than 40,000 on the nation's highways." GM was the defendant and loser in two cases with multimillion dollar product liability verdicts based on accusations of defective side-saddle gasoline tanks. In GM's defense, the NHTSA admitted that the vehicles passed all NHTSA safety tests in existence at the time the vehicles were manufactured. On December 2, 1994, four days before a public hearing to consider making the recall mandatory, the government dropped its recall effort. In exchange, GM agreed to spend $51 million on a variety of vehicle safety programs.[15]

PRODUCT LIABILITY

As made clear in the preceding GM truck example, manufacturers and sellers of goods, including automobiles, can be held liable to consumers, users, and bystanders for physical harm or property damage caused by the goods. This liability is called **product liability**. Legal theories of product liability include the contract theory of warranty and dual tort theories of negligence and strict liability (Chapter 7).

Product Liability Based on Warranty

An important part of product liability law is the breach of warranty theory. A person suffering physical injury or injury to other property because of substandard goods can seek recovery based on breach of warranty. The general rule is that consumers, purchasers, and even users of goods can recover from any seller for losses resulting from breach of implied and express warranties. In other words, most parties who are injured by goods can sue any seller of the goods, including the manufacturer on warranty theory.

This extensive right to recover is an exception to the usual requirement that a party be in *privity* of contract (direct contract relationship) with another to sue on a contract theory. The UCC has addressed the problem of privity by eliminating the requirement of privity for certain types of injuries and for certain beneficiaries.

Product Liability Based on Negligence

In Chapter 7, we discussed *negligence* as a failure to use the degree of care that a reasonable, prudent person would have used under the circumstances. If a seller does not exercise reasonable care and injury results, he or she is liable for negligence. A manufacturer must exercise due care to make a product safe. This due care must be exercised in all aspects of manufacturing the product. It includes product design and selection of the materials to make the product. It includes appropriate production, assembly, and testing of the product. It includes placing adequate warnings on the label to inform the user of potential dangers of which he or she might not be aware. And it extends to the inspection and testing of any purchased products used in the final product sold by the manufacturer. The failure to exercise due care is negligence. A manufacturer is liable to any person who is injured by a negligently made (defective) product. The manufacturer is liable for harm regardless of whether a sale or a contract to sell was involved.

Product Liability Based on Strict Liability

Under strict liability (introduced in Chapter 7), persons are responsible for their products regardless of the intentions or the exercise of reasonable care. The doctrine of strict liability applies to manufacturers, wholesalers, and retailers (also processors, assemblers, packagers, bottlers, and distributors) of personal property. A product may be defective because of production errors, design deficiencies, improper packaging, or failure to warn of dangers or to provide safety devices or instructions. A seller of any product in a defective condition that is unreasonably dangerous is subject to liability for physical harm caused to the ultimate user or to his property if (1) the seller is in the business of selling such a product and (2) the product is expected to and does reach the user without substantial change from the condition in which it was sold. See Exhibit 10–1 for the requirements to prove strict product liability.

Thus, under this theory, in any action against a manufacturer or seller, the plaintiff need not show how the product became defective. The plaintiff must, however, show that at the time of the injury, the condition of the product was essentially the same as it was when it left the hands of the defendant manufacturer or seller. All courts extend the strict liability of manufacturers and other sellers to injured bystanders.

> The motor of a car exploded, producing a cloud of steam. The steam caused a series of multiple collisions, since it prevented other drivers from seeing well. Is the automobile manufacturer liable for injuries caused by the explosion of the car's motor?

Yes, since the car motor was determined to be defective and the cause of the harm to the innocent third parties. Strict liability has also been expanded to include suppliers of parts and lessors of movable goods. Liability for personal injuries caused by defective goods extends also to those who lease such goods. Some courts hold that a leasing agreement creates an *implied warranty* that the leased goods will be fit for the duration of the lease. Under this view, if Rivercity Rent-a-Car leases an improperly maintained automobile, a passenger who is injured in an accident can sue Rivercity. (Liability here is based on the contract theory of warranty, not tort, because the lease is an ongoing contract.)

Frequently, a product injures a person because he or she did not use it carefully. Misconduct or misuse by a claimant can be a defense to reduce the claimant's recovery or to deny it altogether.

REGISTRATION OF MOTOR VEHICLES

The government requires that ownership of most types of motor vehicles be registered and that formal documents of ownership be properly executed. Similar requirements do not exist for most other types of personal property, such as stereos

Exhibit 10–1: Requirements of Strict Product Liability

The basic requirements of strict product liability are as follows:

- The product is sold in a defective condition.
- The defendant is in the business of selling that product.
- The product is unreasonably dangerous to the user or consumer because of its defective condition.
- The plaintiff (who need not be the purchaser) must suffer physical harm to self or property by use or consumption of the product.
- The defective condition must be the proximate cause of the injury or damage.
- The goods were not substantially changed from the time sold to the time of the injury.

and backpacks (nor for guns, although that has been proposed by gun-control advocates).

Advantages of Registration

Registration provides a method by which a state government can ensure vehicle owner compliance with safety and environmental requirements. To be registered initially, the vehicle must comply with minimal safety and pollution standards governing brakes, lights, and exhaust emissions. Registration of ownership also ensures orderly transfer of title. By requiring presentation and release of the certificate of ownership signed by the seller, the buyer has a better assurance of receiving good title and becoming the true owner. If the vehicle is stolen, the certificate of ownership and registration facilitates identification and restitution to the rightful owner. If a vehicle is involved in an accident in which property is damaged and/or a person is injured or killed, vehicle license numbers help trace the party responsible and facilitate follow-up measures. The issuance and renewal of the certificate of registration also serves as a convenient means of raising tax revenues for a variety of purposes, including highway construction and maintenance. Moreover, annual motor vehicle registration lists also aid selection of jury panels and the collection of unpaid traffic fines.

Licensing and Registration Procedures

Generally, a state will issue two certificates to the owners of motor vehicles: a certificate of ownership, or title, showing who owns the vehicle; and a certificate of registration, permitting operation of the vehicle on the highways of the state. License plates, or annual renewal tags, are also issued in conjunction with the certificate of registration.

With a few exceptions, such as U.S. government vehicles, a motor vehicle is licensed in the state where it is usually driven. When you move to another state, your vehicle registration generally remains valid for a limited period of time (30 to 90 days) before a local vehicle registration and license is required. At the time of yearly license registration, states commonly provide for emissions control device inspections and sometimes vehicle safety inspections. Some states require that the primary driver of the vehicle offer proof of financial responsibility (e.g., through ownership of an automobile liability insurance policy) before vehicle license plates are renewed.

Special laws also govern the vehicle and driver when traveling in foreign countries; information about these laws should be obtained from the country where you intend to travel and reviewed with a knowledgeable travel agent before departure.

Many counties and cities require the registration and periodic licensing of bicycles. The money generated from bicycle licensure is commonly used to maintain records that facilitate the recovery and return of stolen bikes.

Kitty Horrigan was carefully riding her new imported English motorcycle along a city street when Dick Guarno negligently lost control of his automobile and crashed into her. Guarno now claims Horrigan was also guilty of negligence because she failed to register her motorcycle as required by law. Is it considered negligence to drive an unlicensed motor vehicle on a public road?

No. Horrigan's failure to register her motorcycle had nothing to do with Guarno's negligence and will not prevent her from recovering damages for her injuries.[16] Horrigan is guilty of the infraction of driving an unregistered vehicle on a public street. Failure to sign title over to a new owner when delivering possession of a motor vehicle may leave the original owner liable to strangers who are injured by the motor vehicle in a later accident. Some states provide that the registered owner is liable (usually limited to some specified amount) for damage caused by the negligence of any authorized user of the vehicle.*

Usually, a certificate of ownership of a newly purchased vehicle lists two owners: a **registered owner** and a **legal owner**. Most automobiles are purchased on credit, and the lender retains a security interest in the vehicle. The purchaser-borrower is the registered owner (also called the **equitable owner**), with an ownership interest in the vehicle to the extent that the loan has been paid. Persons who refer to their equity in a vehicle mean the difference between the automobile's market value and the amount still owed to the lender. The lender (or creditor), having advanced the purchase money or sold the car on credit, retains a security interest in the vehicle and remains the legal (technical) owner until the loan is paid in full. A legal owner is generally not responsible for the manner in which the equitable owner uses or misuses the vehicle. The legal owner is primarily concerned with timely monthly payments. The lender's singular interest is in protecting the value of the collateral, increasing the probability that the loan will be repaid in full. For protection in the event that the car is damaged or stolen, the lender (legal owner) requires the equitable owner to carry adequate collision and comprehensive automobile insurance. The former covers damages to the vehicle caused by collision, the latter covers theft of the vehicle or damages caused by vandals. Careful and socially responsible owners also carry liability insurance to protect themselves from liability for possible injuries to others.

Because a registered owner has potential tort liability, it is very important to change registration simultaneously with the transfer of the vehicle. Requirements for a valid transfer of registration vary from state to state. It is common to require both a signed transfer of a certificate of ownership ("pink slip") and a notification to the department of motor vehicles requesting a change in the registered owner of the vehicle. The seller should file the notice of change of ownership, transferring potential liability to the buyer along with the ownership.

WHEN AND HOW MAY AN AUTOMOBILE BE REPOSSESSED?

It is unusual for people to have sufficient cash to buy an automobile outright. Yet, sellers still wish to sell automobiles and buyers still wish to buy them. Article 9 of the UCC provides a way for sellers to grant credit and maintain a low risk. Payment is guaranteed, or *secured*, by the car being purchased by the debtor. This is a type of **secured transaction**, meaning any transaction regardless of its form that is intended to create a security interest in personal property.

The importance to the creditor of being a secured creditor cannot be overemphasized. State laws that protect debtors generally do not hamper secured

The Florida Attorney General's Office provides advice on "How to Protect Yourself: Automobile Repossession" at http://legal.firn.edu/consumer/tips/tipautor.html

*The owner doesn't need to be present in the car for ownership liability to attach in California, District of Columbia, Florida, Idaho, Iowa, Massachusetts, Michigan, Minnesota, New York, Puerto Rico, and Rhode Island. The owner must be present in the car for liability to attach in Maryland, Mississippi, and Tennessee.

creditors. They have a preferred position if the debtor becomes bankrupt. Business as we know it would not exist without secured transaction law.

If the debt is paid, full legal ownership is returned or transferred to the purchaser. If, however, the debt is not paid, the creditor may exercise a right to seize or repossess the vehicle. Failure to pay a credit debt is called **default**. After default, a secured creditor can sue to collect the balance due on the debt, or enforce a security interest in the car by any available judicial process. The most common remedy is to take back the collateral. The debtor may simply return the collateral at the request of the secured party or the creditor may surreptitiously confiscate the car. When the secured party seizes the collateral, care must be taken to assure that no *breach of the peace* (as determined by state law) occurs. In other words, the creditor or the creditor's agent cannot forcibly enter a debtor's home, garage, or place of business without the permission of the debtor.

Max borrowed money from Acme Finance Company to purchase a car. Max gave Acme a security interest in the car to protect Acme from the possibility that Max would fail to pay his debt. After Max stopped making payments on the car, Acme sent Ben to seize it. Ben sneaked onto Max's property in the dead of night and made his way up the driveway where the car was parked. Ben jimmied a window of the car, hot-wired it, and drove it off. Is this a lawful repossession?

It appears to be a lawful repossession, as there was no confrontation with Max and no breach of the peace. And although Ben did go onto Max's property, he did not forcibly enter any building. However, to avoid possible confrontations with defaulting debtors, most car repossessions occur when the car is parked on a street or in a parking lot.

The secured party can sometimes keep the goods in satisfaction of the debt by following strict notice requirements under the UCC. Alternatively, the secured party can resell the goods and apply the proceeds (money received from the sale) toward the debt. Proceeds from a sale of retaken collateral must be applied in the following order:

1. Reasonable expenses stemming from the retaking, holding, or preparing for sale are covered first. When authorized by law and if provided for in the agreement, these can include reasonable attorneys' fees and legal expenses.

2. Satisfaction of the balance of the debt owed to the secured party.

3. Payment to owners of other security interests who have made a written demand received by the secured party before the proceeds have been distributed.

4. Return of any surplus amount received from the sale to the debtor.

Often, after proper disposition of the collateral, the secured party has not collected all that is owed by the debtor. Unless otherwise agreed, the debtor may be sued for any deficiency.

The debtor may be able to exercise the right of *redemption* of the collateral. The right of redemption is the right to have the collateral returned to the debtor. A redemption obviously must occur before the secured party disposes of the collateral. The debtor can exercise the right of redemption by paying the under-lying debt. All expenses related to the enforcement of the security interest by the secured party also must be paid.

DRIVING A MOTOR VEHICLE

WHY MUST DRIVERS BE LICENSED?

Kathy Jaren's license to drive had been revoked for proper cause. (She had been convicted of speeding on three occasions within 18 months.) She resented this interference with her freedom of movement and de-cided to drive anyway—but with extra care to avoid any trouble. As luck would have it, while driving safely and in compliance with the rules of the road, another motorist negligently ran a red light and rammed into her car. Will her lack of a driver's license have any effect on civil and criminal court proceedings?

No and yes. Unless there is some cause–effect relationship between the lack of the driver's license and the accident, the lack of license is immaterial. Kathy's rights in a civil action for damages resulting from the accident are not affected by her lack of a driver's license. However, she would be guilty of the offense of driving without a license, and for this she could be fined and/or jailed.

Driving is a privilege, not a constitutionally protected right[17], and is regu-lated by state or local government as an exercise of government police power.* Prospective drivers must demonstrate an ability to drive in traffic and must un-derstand the rules of the road. A license to drive may be suspended or revoked for violating the rules of the road, or even for an inability to demonstrate finan-cial responsibility after an accident. Demerit points are assigned for each infrac-tion, and a person's license can be suspended or revoked if too many points have been accumulated in a specific time period. Point systems vary from state to state. Exhibit 10–2 shows an example of the Alabama Driver's License Point System.

Auto insurance companies check government records for information about the driving records of people who apply for insurance or have policies with the company. The insurance companies routinely charge higher premiums or cancel coverage after one or more "moving" violations (an infraction based upon the car's motion). The individual must then purchase a minimum coverage policy at a premium price under what is called an *assigned-risk program*. Most states have an assigned-risk program under which insurance companies are required to sell insurance to high-risk drivers on a rotating basis. They are allowed to charge higher premiums to cover their risk.

---

*In recent years, several states have begun to use driver's license statutes as a means of regulating behavior not di-rectly related to driving a vehicle. For example, Wisconsin allows any municipal court to suspend a driver's license for nonpayment of any fines. In Kentucky, students who quit high school or have an academic deficiency lose their right to drive unless this would cause a family hardship. S. Garfield, "What License for DMV," *Sacramento Bee*, 27 March 1994.

Exhibit 10–2: The Alabama Driver's License Point System*

Points are assessed for violations as follows:
- Any driving conviction involving the ingestion of alcoholic beverages not otherwise requiring mandatory revocation of the driver's license—6 points
- Reckless driving—6 points
- Speeding (85 mph or above)—5 points
- Failure to yield right-of-way—5 points
- Passing stopped school bus—5 points
- Wrong side of road—4 points
- Illegal passing—4 points
- Following too closely—3 points
- Disregarding traffic control device (stop sign, traffic light, etc.)—3 points
- Speeding in excess of posted limits—2 points
- All other moving violations—2 points

The following points determine the suspension period length:
- 12–14 points in a 2-year period—60 days
- 15–17 points in a 2-year period—90 days
- 18–20 points in a 2-year period—120 days
- 21–23 points in a 2-year period—180 days
- 24 and above points in a 2-year period—365 days

After a traffic conviction is 2 years old, it loses its point count for suspension purposes but remains on a driver's record.

---

*http://www.wsnet.com/~aldps/psystem.html

Computer tracking has assisted some states in collecting payments for unpaid parking tickets. The department of government that renews vehicle registrations is kept informed by computer and simply withholds new license plates or tags until all fines are paid.

Generally, any competent adult may qualify for a driver's license upon passing a written test, a driving test, and a vision test. A minor of proper age (typically 16) may also qualify, but often must, in addition to the requirements for an adult, complete a driver education and/or driver training course. Several states have recently changed their laws on initial youth licensing to provide for a graduated licensing procedure, and other states are considering similar changes consistent with a model law specified by the National Committee on Uniform Traffic Laws and Ordinances. The significant requirement of the model law is a mandatory learner permit for at least six months, followed by at least six months in an intermediate licensing phase restricting night driving.

Some states require that parents sign and verify a minor's application and consent to be responsible for harm caused by their child while driving on a highway. Fortunately for most parents, this liability is usually limited. The amount of liability is often tied to the state's financial responsibility laws (e.g., $15,000 for injury or death, payable to any one person, and $30,000 payable to any number of persons, plus $5,000 for property damage as the result of any one accident for which their minor child is found to be legally responsible).[18] The requirement that an owner purchase insurance may be mandated by statute; if not, prudence and concern for others who may be injured by a child's negligence would dictate that a parent purchase at least the minimum coverage.

Parental liability for a child's damages caused with motor vehicles deviates from the general rule that parents are not vicariously responsible for their child's

For a list of states that follow the model law, as well as a state-by-state rundown of Youth Driver Laws, see the Institute for Highway Safety site at http://www.highwaysafety.org

http://

torts. Of course, parents are liable if the wrongful conduct of the child was committed at the parent's command, or in the course of the parent's business. In recent years, some states have extended the motor vehicle exception to include limited liability of parents for the willful misconduct of minor children.[19] Even in states where statutes create this parental liability, the minor tortfeasor is likewise liable. Realistically, however, the minor usually lacks the financial resources to pay the injured victim. Moreover, in cases of negligence the minor could escape a heavy judgment by bankruptcy, unless drunken driving caused the accident.

WHAT STANDARD OF CARE DOES THE LAW PRESCRIBE FOR DRIVERS?

The standard of care necessary when operating a motor vehicle is one example of the rules of negligence discussed in Chapter 7. The duty to act as a reasonable person requires that you, whether on or off the highway, refrain from carelessly injuring others. The question always is, were you as careful as a hypothetical reasonable person would have been under all circumstances surrounding the event? This broad duty may be violated willfully or negligently. Comparatively few people injure others willfully, with deliberate intent to harm. Such conduct could be criminal, and could result in a civil action for punitive damages as well as compensatory damages. In one case, the court said:

> *Here there is testimony from which the jury could find that defendant saw plaintiff 196 feet away in the paved portion of the roadway, and neither slowed nor sounded his horn. There is also the testimony that defendant's car swerved toward plaintiff immediately before the impact. Thus the evidence could support a jury finding that defendant was guilty of willful or wanton misconduct.*[20]

From time to time, most of us are careless. We fail to exercise reasonable care. We do not behave as an ordinary, prudent man, woman, or child of comparable age should behave under the same or similar circumstances. If someone is injured as a result of our negligence, we are generally liable for monetary damages. In the preceding case, there is some evidence of the intentional tort of battery.

Sometimes, of course, we may injure someone while we are acting without negligence or willful intent to harm. Then there is no liability. Such an injury could happen in a pure accident, a casualty that is sudden, unexpected, unforeseeable, and unplanned—perhaps the result of an unknown cause or the unpredictable result of a known cause. There is no liability, for example, when an injury results from a natural calamity (a violent storm) or from the victim's own carelessness (when a person, walking along while reading a paper, steps off a curb into a stream of traffic and is suddenly injured or even killed).

Robby Drexhage was driving on a freeway with his girlfriend, Karen, at his side, bragging to her about his car and about himself as a "hot driver." Suddenly, without notice to her or signal to other drivers, he accelerated within seconds to 95 mph. Visible ahead, moving at different speeds in three lanes, were about a dozen other vehicles. Robby rapidly passed them all, weaving skillfully from outside to inside lanes and back again. There were no highway patrol officers in sight, he was not arrested, and he did not cause an accident. Has he breached any legal duty?

Yes. He breached his general duty to drive as an ordinary prudent person exercising reasonable care for the safety of the lives and property of others. He did not respect the rights of his date Karen and all others on the highway. He breached specific duties to drive within the speed limits, to refrain from weaving in and out of traffic lanes, and to signal before changing lanes. Most criminal breaches of duty while driving go unpunished; fortunately, most such breaches do not cause injury to others. Robby committed no torts because there were no injured victims.*

MUST DRIVERS STOP AT ACCIDENT SCENES?

Gus Shikel, an expert in first-aid, was driving along a lonely country road when he came upon the scene of a one-car accident. The wrecked vehicle had collided with a utility pole. Inside were two adults and a child, all unconscious or in shock. One was bleeding profusely. Not wanting to get involved, Shikel drove on. Was he legally obliged to stop and render aid?

Not in most states. Generally, the law does not require one to be a good neighbor. The victims were strangers to whom Shikel legally owed no duty. The same result would apply if Shikel were a medical doctor. Shikel's retreat is likely an ethical violation, but it wasn't a legal one. However, if Shikel had in any way caused or contributed to the accident (as by drifting across the center line and forcing the oncoming driver into defensive maneuvers that resulted in the crash), he would be obligated to stop and would be criminally and civilly responsible if he failed to do so.

In any event, if he does stop—and one hopes that he would—and renders first-aid, under the common law he must do so with reasonable care under emergency situations. Conceivably, if one stops and renders aid, injured persons could sue the person providing assistance if that person failed to exercise reasonable care and thus aggravated the injuries. Such lawsuits are rare and recovery rarer still.

As discussed in Chapter 7, most states have specially enacted **Good Samaritan statutes** to shield volunteers from actions for ordinary negligence. North Carolina has a typical statute, stating that no person shall be liable for damages for injuries or death claimed to result from the rendering of first-aid or emergency healthcare treatment when the circumstances require prompt decisions and actions, and when the necessity is ". . . so reasonably apparent that any delay . . . would seriously worsen the physical condition or endanger the life . . . " of the patient.[21] Immunity is not available when the act is gross negligence, wanton conduct, or intentional wrongdoing. Nor does the statute relieve persons of liability for damages ". . . while rendering healthcare services in the normal and ordinary course of a business or profession."[22]

---

* Although not stated in the example, the conduct of Robby's high-speed maneuvering probably caused serious apprehension of serious physical injury in the minds of other drivers and of Karen as well. These victims could sue Robby for the intentional tort of assault and, although there were no physical injuries, could recover damages for mental distress and possibly punitive damages as well.

DOES A TRAFFIC CITATION PROVE CIVIL LIABILITY FOR AN ACCIDENT?

Kevin Harper was driving on the wrong side of a two-lane highway when he was involved in a head-on collision with Lisa Bowden. Lisa was proceeding legally in the opposite direction. Kevin was cited by the state patrol for violation of the vehicle code. Is he guilty of negligence *per se* (Latin: "of itself") because he was apparently violating a statute at the time?

Probably. **Negligence *per se*** means that proof of the act establishes the duty. Violation of a statute raises a ***prima facie*** (Latin: "at first sight") presumption or inference of negligence. If the plaintiff proves that the statute was violated and caused the accident, and the defendant introduces no contrary evidence, then the defendant is negligent. Violation of the statute must bear some relationship to the accident and be the cause in fact and proximate cause of the accident. For instance, violation of a statute requiring the driver to be licensed would not bear any relationship to Kevin's accident and would not be its cause. However, violation of a statute established to protect against driving the wrong way down a road and injuring others driving on the proper side of the road would be negligence *per se*. That very type of harm occurred, and it appears Kevin is liable.

Although difficult to do, a presumption of negligence can be rebutted by proof of excuse or justification. It is possible that Kevin diverted his car because of conditions beyond his control (such as an object in the road, an unforeseeable failure of his steering mechanism, a sudden heart attack, or an illegal action by another car squeezing by on his right side).

ARE OWNERS LIABLE FOR NEGLIGENCE OF OTHER DRIVERS?

Clearly an owner-driver is liable for injuries to others caused by his or her own negligent driving. Under the principle of **vicarious liability** (liability for acts of another), the owner may also be liable for harm caused when someone else is the driver, if one of the following conditions applies:

1. The driver is the employee or agent of the owner, and is acting within the scope of his or her employment. See the discussion of the doctrine of *Respondeat superior* in Chapter 13.

2. The owner is negligent in lending or giving the car to someone who is not qualified to drive or is known by the owner to be an unsafe driver. The owner is also negligent if he or she lends or gives an automobile to another in a condition (e.g., with faulty brakes) that makes it unsafe to drive.

3. In a number of states*, owners are responsible whenever a member of their immediate family or household drives and a third party is injured

---

*Arizona, Colorado, Connecticut, Georgia, Kentucky, Louisiana (spouse only), Nebraska, Nevada, New Jersey, New Mexico, North Carolina, North Dakota, Oregon, South Carolina, Tennessee, Washington, and West Virginia.

because of the negligence of the driver. This is called the **family purpose doctrine**.

4. In several states, parents or guardians who sign a minor's application for a driver's license become liable for damage caused by the minor's negligent operation of the vehicle. As discussed earlier, there are usually dollar limits to the amount of this liability.

5. Many different variations and combinations of state statutes impose liability when an owner permits another to use the vehicle (called *permissive use*). In several states, owners are liable when a person they allow to use the vehicle negligently injures a third party.[23] In a few states, owners are liable only for permissive use when they have furnished a car to a minor who negligently injures a third party.[24] As noted earlier, there often are limits on the extent of liability under these statutes.

If the driver is an employee of the owner and is acting within the scope of employment, the owner-employer is liable without limit under the doctrine of *Respondeat superior*. A driver, even though an employee, is always liable (without limit) for his or her own torts.

Walter Johnson was driving down Main Street on his way to deliver a package for Racehorse Delivery Service. Unfortunately, Johnson was distracted for a second and ran into the rear of Marisa Woode's new Saturn automobile. Luckily, Marisa was not hurt, but the car was damaged and repairs cost $3,000. Who is legally responsible for the harm to Marisa's car?

Walter is, of course, liable for his own negligence. Walter Johnson was also an employee of Racehorse and he injured another while driving the automobile on company business. As Johnson was within the scope of his employment, Racehorse Delivery Service is also liable under the doctrine of *Respondeat superior*. Marisa can sue both Johnson and Racehorse, but she can collect her actual damages only once.

Karl Mellon parked his car in the street and ran into the post office to mail a parcel. In his haste, he forgot to remove the ignition key. When he returned, the car was gone. The police later reported that his stolen car had been in a collision with a motorcycle, injuring its rider, Joanna Denton. Denton later sued Mellon. Is he liable?

No. Although leaving the key in an unattended car is negligent and, in some states, a violation of a statute, the owner has no duty to protect the public from unexpected and illegal activities of thieves. The theft and negligent use of stolen property is an intervening and supervening act. A contrary argument can be advanced that Karl's carelessness created a danger and a result that was predictable.[25] However, most states have rejected such an extension of liability to a careless automobile owner theft victim.

Luella Wilson, a 91-year-old Vermont grandmother, enjoyed her own home, friends, and family and had more than $500,000 in the bank. She lent her grandnephew, Willard Stuart, money to buy a car. After a night of drug and alcohol use, he was involved in a serious accident. A passenger in his car, Mark Vince, was paralyzed from the waist down and lost a leg. Stuart had no driver's license, no assets, and no automobile insurance. The victim sued Luella, alleging that she knew Willard did not have a license and used drugs and that she was therefore negligent in lending him the money to buy the car. Luella did not appear at the trial because she was ill. What was the verdict?

The jury held for the plaintiff against Luella Wilson in the amount of $950,000. This case of negligent lending attracted considerable attention and was appealed. The Vermont Supreme Court did not reverse the trial court verdict, but did order a new trial to determine whether the automobile dealership and the salesperson who sold Willard the car should share Luella's liability.[26] At the new trial, the parties reached an out-of-court settlement, with the plaintiff dismissing his claim against Luella.[27] The out-of-court settlement relieved Luella of her liability, but it did not change the rule of law in this case, which found liability for a person other than a driver in a case of negligent entrustment (loan of the car or in this case the means to get the car).

A common extension of liability to persons who neither own nor were driving the car involved in an accident occurs under a **dramshop statute**, a state law making it a crime for a tavern proprietor or employee to serve intoxicants to an obviously drunk patron or someone under the legal drinking age. Injured victims of accidents caused by these patrons have successfully sued the bars and restaurants when they can prove that a dramshop statute was violated.[28] A few cases have found liability against social hosts of parties where intoxicating beverages or drugs were served and shortly afterward the guests were involved in automobile accidents.[29] Wisdom and prudence dictate: If you drink, don't drive. Arranging for a designated driver, one who does not drink alcoholic beverages or take any mood-altering substances, avoids the problem. Furthermore, as a host or hostess, do not have "open bars" or serve drinks of alcoholic beverages to the point of intoxication of your guests.

ARE DRIVERS LIABLE FOR INJURIES TO GUESTS IN THEIR CARS?

Generally, a driver has a responsibility not only to persons outside the vehicle but also to passengers inside the vehicle. The duty is that of ordinary and usual care for the safety of others. Issues of comparative negligence and assumption of the risk must also be considered when appropriate. In years past a driver usually could not be held liable to guest passengers for injuries caused by the driver's ordinary negligence, because of special protective statutes called **guest statutes**. Today, only a minority of states have retained guest statutes.[30] Idaho's guest statute is representative of the content of such protections for motor vehicle drivers.

LIABILITY OF MOTOR OWNER TO GUEST

No person transported by the owner or operator of a motor vehicle as his guest without payment for such transportation shall have a cause for damages against such owner or operator or for injuries, death or loss, in case of accident, unless such accident shall have been intentional on the part of the said owner or operator or caused by his intoxication or gross negligence.

The provisions of this section shall not relieve a public carrier or any owner or operator of a motor vehicle while the same is being demonstrated to a prospective purchaser of responsibility for injuries sustained by a passenger being transported by such public carrier or by such owner or operator.[31]

Proponents of guest statutes argue that when the drivers are insured, there can be collusion in staged accidents to defraud insurance companies. Even in the absence of fraud, a negligent driver who is a relative (e.g., a parent) of the guest (e.g., a child) who receives dollar damages would indirectly profit from his or her own negligence. Guest statutes also prevent possible fraudulent claims by guests who may be the only witnesses to a single-car accident. Texas courts have upheld the Texas guest statute, holding that the legislature is justified in seeking to prevent possible fraudulent claims against insurers.[32]

As social views have changed, most states have abolished guest statutes. The rationale for change has been that the recovery will probably come from an insurance company, and if you buy insurance to compensate strangers who you might injure, you probably would want to have the same protection for relatives and friends who are your guests.

Even when a state has a guest statute, liability exists when the plaintiff can prove that death or injury resulted from intoxication or willful misconduct of the driver. Thus, in our earlier example, Luella Wilson's nephew Willard Stuart, who was high on drugs and alcohol, was not protected from the lawsuit by a guest statute. He was, however, judgment-proof, which led the injured plaintiff to seek other possible defendants who were not judgment-proof.

DRIVING UNDER THE INFLUENCE (DUI)

People who drive under the influence (DUI)* of mind-altering chemicals are a major social problem in the United States. Drunk driving is the major cause of accidents on the highways and is an ingredient in most fatal accidents. "Drunk drivers kill almost 25,000 people annually, more than are murdered each year."[33] In addition, DUI has been identified as the crime most often committed by otherwise law-abiding persons. "The vast majority of Americans occasionally drive after drinking. Alcoholics who have access to a car habitually drive after drinking."[34] "About 1.4 million arrests are made annually for driving under the influence of alcohol or narcotics (1 in every 123 licensed drivers)."[35]

Several organizations try to protect the rights of people who are victims of such criminal activity. These organizations include MADD (Mothers Against Drunk Driving) and SADD (Students Against Drunk Driving). They have had a significant effect on public attitudes and on the enactment of laws concerning driving under the influence. In the past decade, all 50 states have joined in making

The Fatality Analysis Reporting System (FARS) contains data on all vehicle crashes in the United States that occur on a public roadway and involve a fatality. This Web site provides instant access to FARS data via the Query Engine, Wizard, and Reports Library. http://alcoholism.tqn.com/msubdrive.htm

"Mothers Against Drunk Driving (MADD) is more than just a bunch of angry moms. We're real people, moms, dads, young people, and other individuals just trying to make a difference. We are determined to stop drunk driving and to support victims of this violent crime." http://alcoholism.tqn.com/msubdrive.htm

---

*Also referred to as Driving While Intoxicated (DWI).

21 the minimum age for purchasing alcohol legally. The penalties for DUI have increased with longer jail sentences, driver's license revocations, and bigger fines.

Several friends were at Lawrence Harberson's apartment celebrating the end of the school year. Beer was flowing freely. Harberson, a 260-pound star tackle on the college football team, had finished his first 12-ounce beer when he opened a second. Waving the beer can, he jumped into his car and rammed the pedal to the metal, burning tire rubber as he sped off to collect his girlfriend Marcie at the nearby airport. While en route, he was stopped by a highway patrol officer for exceeding the posted speed limit by 20 mph or more. Is he also guilty of driving under the influence of alcohol?

Probably not, although he could be required to demonstrate his sobriety. One beer is not likely to intoxicate or adversely influence a 260-pound person's body mechanisms (see Exhibit 10–3). However, he could be cited for carrying an open container of alcoholic beverage in his car.

When stopped under suspicion of intoxication, a driver is required to submit to a **field sobriety test**. It is a preliminary test at the scene, where the driver may be asked to walk a straight line, stand on one foot, or perform some other similar act. A person who appears intoxicated may be taken to a police station and asked for a sample of breath, blood, or urine to be analyzed for alcoholic or drug content.

Refusing to submit to a chemical test by exercising your constitutional right against self-incrimination may cause forfeiture of your driver's license. Every person who accepts a license to drive impliedly consents to sobriety tests upon police suspicion, with probable cause, of the driver's intoxication. The driver has a right to a proper warning of the possible effect of the law, and a right to a court or administrative hearing, before the license is revoked.

The percentage of drugs in the blood system necessary to classify a person as DUI has been lowered in most states in recent years. In all states but Massachusetts, South Carolina, and the District of Columbia, driving with a blood-alcohol concentration of 0.10 or above satisfies the crime. It need not be proven that the driver is intoxicated. Driving with a blood-alcohol content level at or above the stated percentage is a violation of law and therefore cannot be contested. Several states, including California and Florida, have established 0.08 as the *per se* level. The means of measurement varies, but almost all states provide for blood, breath, or urine tests or some combination of tests. In several states, the percentage standard is much lower for minors than for adults, and sometimes evidence of any consumption of alcoholic beverage leads to an automatic suspension of the driver's license.

Criminal penalties for driving under the influence can be severe. In a representative state, a jail sentence of from two days to six months is imposed if one is convicted two or more times for drunk driving within five years; a judge who fails to send the defendant to jail must write a formal opinion justifying such leniency. It is also common that a first conviction leads to an automatic driver's license suspension of 90 to 120 days. A fine of from $500 to $2,500 or more is also assessed. Under certain circumstances, the vehicle may be impounded or even forfeited. In addition, the defendant's automobile insurance premiums will rise.

Seventeen percent of randomly selected drivers in 1996 from 10 P.M. and 3 A.M. on Friday and Saturday nights had measurable alcohol and 2.8 percent were legally DUI. See an article about this by the Insurance Institute for Highway Safety and the national Highway Traffic Safety Administration.
http://www.hwysafety.org/press/press12.htm

1998 state law facts regarding DUI/DWI laws as of September 1998 can be found at
http://www.hwysafety.org/facts/dui.htm

We have discussed the judicial and administrative expenses and penalties in DUI cases. You can examine some of the nonjudicial costs of a DUI at
http://www.idir.net/~jay/nonjud.html

Exhibit 10–3: Blood-Alcohol Concentration Levels per Body Weight

0.08% DUI* CHARTS

DRINKING ALCOHOL AND DRIVING AT ANY AGE IS ILLEGAL

Prepared by DMV in cooperation with the CHP, Office of Traffic Safety, Department of Alcohol and Drug Programs and Department of Justice, State of California.

There is no safe way to drive after drinking. Even one drink can make you an unsafe driver. Drinking affects your **BLOOD ALCOHOL CONCENTRATION (BAC)**. It is illegal to drive with a **BAC** of .08% (.04% if you have a commercial driver license or .01% or more if under 21). Even a **BAC** below .08% does not mean that it is safe or legal to drive. The charts show the **BAC** zones for various numbers of drinks and time periods.

HOW TO USE THESE CHARTS: Find the chart that includes your weight. Look at the total number of drinks you have had and compare that to the time shown. You can quickly tell if you are at risk of being arrested.* If your **BAC** level is in the grey zone, your chances of having a collision are 5 times higher than if you had no drinks, and 25 times higher if your **BAC** level falls into the black zone.

REMEMBER: "One drink" is a 1¼-ounce shot of 80-proof liquor (even if it's mixed with non-alcoholic drinks), a 4-ounce glass of wine, or 10 ounces of 5.7% beer. If you have larger or stronger drinks; drink on an empty stomach; are tired, sick, or upset; or have taken medicines or drugs, you can be **UNSAFE WITH FEWER DRINKS**.

TECHNICAL NOTE: These charts are intended to be guides and are not legal evidence of the actual blood alcohol concentration. Although it is possible for anyone to exceed the designated limits, the charts have been constructed so that fewer than 5 persons in 100 will exceed these limits when drinking the stated amounts on an empty stomach. Actual values can vary by body type, sex, health status, and other factors.

*VC §23152, §23153, §23136, §23140 **DUI**/Driving under the influence of alcohol and/or other drugs.

BAC Zones:	90 to 109 lbs.	110 to 129 lbs.	130 to 149 lbs.	150 to 169 lbs.	170 to 189 lbs.	190 to 209 lbs.	210 lbs.& Up
TIME FROM 1st DRINK	TOTAL DRINKS 1 2 3 4 5 6 7 8	TOTAL DRINKS 1 2 3 4 5 6 7 8	TOTAL DRINKS 1 2 3 4 5 6 7 8	TOTAL DRINKS 1 2 3 4 5 6 7 8	TOTAL DRINKS 1 2 3 4 5 6 7 8	TOTAL DRINKS 1 2 3 4 5 6 7 8	TOTAL DRINKS 1 2 3 4 5 6 7 8
1 hr							
2 hrs							
3 hrs							
4 hrs							

SHADINGS IN THE CHARTS ABOVE MEAN: ☐ (.01%–.04%) May be DUI—DEFINITELY DUI IF UNDER 21 YRS. OLD

▨ (.05%–.07%) Likely DUI—DEFINITELY DUI IF UNDER 21 YRS. OLD   ■ (.08% Up) Definitely DUI

A study in 1988 of the effect of a single DUI on insurance costs found increases as high as $2,030 per year for three years in Baltimore, Maryland.[36] The costs are undoubtedly much higher today. A single DUI can lead to cancellation of insurance and an inability to rent an automobile when out of town or on vacation for up to three years after conviction. It is clear that the cost of DUI starts at about $5,000 the first year (not including court costs and attorney's fees) and continues for several years while your new insurance company surcharges coverage premiums.*

It should be noted that the legal tolerance of drinking while boating has lessened in many states in recent years. In 1998, Georgia's new tougher boating law provides for a loss of boating privileges, up to a $1,000 fine, and one year of jail upon conviction of the first offense.

MUST OWNERS MAINTAIN THEIR VEHICLES IN GOOD REPAIR?

Owners of motor vehicles are legally required to maintain them in safe operating condition. One appellate court stated this generally applicable duty in the following words:

> *Generally speaking, it is the duty of one driving a motor vehicle along a public highway to see that it is properly equipped so that it may be at all times controlled to the end that it be not a menace to the safety of others or of their property. The law requires that such a vehicle be equipped with brakes adequate to its quick stopping when necessary for the safety of its occupants or of others, and it is equally essential that it be maintained in such a condition as to mechanical efficiency and fuel supply that it may not become a menace to, or an obstruction of, other traffic by stopping on the road. But if the person in charge of such vehicle has done all that can be reasonably expected of a person of ordinary prudence to see that his vehicle is in proper condition, and an unforeseen failure of a part of his equipment occurs, it does not necessarily follow that he must be deemed guilty of negligence as a matter of law.[37]*

A driver is not liable for injuries suffered by strangers from an unforeseeable mechanical failure of his or her automobile. Furthermore, if the driver is injured, he or she might recover damages from the manufacturer (or an intermediary) on the theory of strict product liability. The driver must prove that the defendant placed the product (automobile or component part thereof) on the market, knowing that it was to be used without inspection for defects by the consumer. The driver additionally must show personal injury as a result of a defect in the design or manufacture of the article while it was being used properly. There can be no recovery, however, if the driver was aware that such defect made the article unsafe for its intended use.

---

*The California State Automobile Association estimated at least $5,000 for a first-time DUI. Included in the costs is the fine (typically between $390 to $1,700), attorney's fees, courts' assessment fees, raised insurance premiums, court-ordered educational programs, and vehicle and impoundment fees. *Via*, November/December 1998, 11. Coors Sacramento, California, Drive Sober Campaign estimated a similar figure in this ad: "Your first DUI: 1 hour in cuffs, 4 hours in jail, 3 hours getting your car back, 2 days at the DMV, 2 days community service, 15 weeks of DUI classes, 4 months without your license, 2 nights DUI victim impacts sessions, 7 years with 2 points on driving record, 3 years probation, plus $5,249 in fees, assessments, and fines." *Sacramento News and Review*, 17 December 1998.

When Alberta Ayers stopped for a cup of coffee at the Summit Cafe, she mentioned a "short pedal" on the hydraulic brakes of her heavy-duty truck. She had to "pump" the brake pedal to get a braking response. Nevertheless, after her coffee break she proceeded down the mountain road until the brakes did not hold and the rig went out of control, ultimately careening over the side of the road and landing 200 feet below. Was the manufacturer or seller of the truck or of the brakes liable?

No. Even if the brakes were defective in design or manufacture, Ayers knew of the condition and was negligent by returning to the highway, especially in the mountains without a checkup, adjustment, or repair.

Both federal and state governments assist owners by prescribing a variety of safety standards for motor vehicles.[38] Not only are manufacturers required to manufacture motor vehicles meeting minimum safety standards, but also in recent years many states (through court opinions and legislative statutes) have increased the responsibilities of drivers for their own safety.[39] The most common personal safety equipment is the mandatory use of safety seat belts. With respect to motorcycles, protective headgear must be worn while driving.

The driver of a rented vehicle is generally not responsible for the vehicle's condition, except for obvious and/or known dangers that create an unreasonable risk of harm to the driver or others. Examples of such dangers include missing headlights or brakes that obviously need to be adjusted or repaired. The operator of a leased vehicle, unlike a rented vehicle, is treated the same as an owner-driver.

ARE THERE SPECIAL LAWS FOR RENTED VEHICLES?

When you rent an automobile, you contract for the use rather than the ownership of personal property. The legal term for this relationship is a *bailment,* which, as explained earlier, is a temporary right of possession of the goods of another. In a sale or a gift, title is transferred; in a bailment, possession is transferred, but not title. The rental car company is a **bailor**, and the renter a **bailee**. Although bailment law has very well-defined rights and duties, the most important determinant of the relationship is the language of the rental agreement, which is the controlling written contract.

Laws relating to rental car bailments vary significantly among the states, but two rules are uniform. The first uniform rule is that the rental car company has a duty to provide a vehicle that is safe to use and in good driving condition. A bailee has rights both in contract and tort if harmed because of a breach of this duty. Second, the bailor has a right to expect the car to be returned in the same condition in which it was rented, minus ordinary wear and tear. The bailee is responsible for harm to the car even if it was not the bailee's fault. Rental companies suggest special collision insurance (called *collision damage waivers*) to cover this risk. As this insurance is very costly (rental companies make a sizeable profit with this add-on fee), many states have restricted rental car company practices promoting such special coverage.[40] If you have collision insurance on your own automobile, your policy typically will cover this risk (minus the deductible) on any rental car (however, check your specific policy to determine your specific coverage). Credit card companies often provide collision wavier coverage as an important fringe benefit for their customers. Of course, for the benefit to apply, the customer must use the credit card when renting the vehicle.

Joua Landini landed at Metropolitan airport and walked over to the Maxi Car Rental agency to pick up his reserved auto. After he provided his license and credit card to the rental company, the agent refused to rent him an automobile. She told Joua that the two speeding violations found when she did a computer search of his driving disqualified him from renting from Maxi. Joua insists that Maxi rent him a car, arguing that the search was an invasion of his privacy.

The rental company has a legitimate interest in public information, which lets it determine the level of risk it takes when renting to a particular customer. If the renter has certain types of recent traffic violations or a certain violation "point level," the rental company may refuse to rent or may charge a higher rental amount. This has become a common business practice of rental car companies, and neither court case nor legislation has yet successfully curbed this practice.

The driving record requirements at the world's largest automobile rental company can be found at http://www.hertz.com/policy/us/gen_license.html

Another type of bailment exists when you leave your car with valet parking, or even in a parking lot. Here you, the driver, are the bailor and the parking lot is the bailee. Self-service parking lots are generally not considered bailments because the parking lot owners do not take control or possession of the automobile. Even if a bailment exists, the bailee often will limit or disclaim liability by posting signs and including disclaimer language on the claim ticket.

ARE THERE SPECIAL LAWS FOR COMMON CARRIERS?

A **common carrier** of passengers agrees to transport, in exchange for money, anybody applying for passage, assuming there is available space and no legal justification for refusal.[41] Bus lines, taxicabs, railroads, airlines, and subway systems are all classified as common carriers. Common carriers are required to be licensed and are regulated by federal, and sometimes state, agencies. Regulations usually cover routes, safety measures, operating methods, rates, passenger contracts and treatment, and luggage handling. At the heart of the relationship are two legal concepts: (1) specific obligations or duties are owed to passengers created by a contract of transport and (2) general duties are also owed as a matter of public policy. These general duties are independent of private contract and arise from the carrier's position as a public utility.[42] These common carrier legal duties are very important for passenger safety and baggage care.

Mark Oglesby and Mark Finken, both seventh graders, were riding on the Milwaukee County bus. A group of about twenty youths stormed the bus, some entering through its windows. The hoodlums demanded money of Finken; when he refused, they beat him. Oglesby and Finken eventually were able to flee the scene. During the entire course of events, the bus driver, although watching in her rear-view mirror, made no attempt to intervene. Did the bus driver breach a duty owed Oglesby and Finken?

Yes. Common carriers are responsible for the safety of their passengers. Because common carriers are open to everyone, the public reasonably expects to be safe. Although the carriers are not insurers of the passengers' safety, their duty is described as either high, or the highest, duty of care.[43] This duty includes inspection of equipment, safe means of access and departure, use of protective restraints such as seat belts in airlines and possibly even in buses,[44] and protection from fellow passengers.[45] In the preceding case, the court stated, "It was reasonable to infer . . . that the assault would not have occurred had the driver ordered the youths off the bus for their rowdiness, warned them, or notified them she was summoning the police."[46]

A common carrier is also responsible for the safe transport and return of a passenger's baggage, as covered by that passenger's ticket or fare. If there is no extraordinary excuse (such as confiscation of the baggage by police), the carrier is responsible for loss or damage to the baggage, without proof of fault. Statutes regulating baggage transport typically provide that although liability may not be eliminated, it may be limited by contract to certain defined amounts. Such partial disclaimers are allowed as long as the passenger is given the right to have the monetary limit raised after paying an additional fee. As baggage transport contracts generally include a disclaimer, it behooves the passenger to protect valuable goods through a suitable declaration of higher value and payment of an additional fee.

A recurring complaint about airline travel is the "bumping" of passengers (leaving them behind) with confirmed reservations. Airlines do not guarantee their schedules and, following deregulation of the industry in the 1980s, many consumer protections for passengers have been left to carrier discretion. Department of Transportation regulations do require airline companies to ask passengers for volunteers to stay behind for compensation. However the regulations do not specify compensation, which is up to airline discretion. If sufficient volunteers are found, the problem is solved, if not, then there are several possibilities depending on when the bumped passengers will ultimately arrive at their destination. Although there are some mandated rules for bumping passengers, much of what the airline does will be its own choice.

A discussion of airline passenger rights can be found at
http://www.thetrip.com/strategies/flight/0018txt.html
and
http://flyana.com/index.html

What Is the Financial Responsibility Law?

Jill Searle and Bob Ranney were in an automobile collision that occurred when their speeding cars collided at the campus entrance on the way to morning classes at Nashville University. The collision created a terrible traffic jam, and several hundred students missed their first morning class. Many regarded the event as a festive occasion because no one was hurt and everyone had an excuse from class. Each car sustained at least $500 worth of damage. Searle and Ranney notified their respective insurance companies and relaxed with the thought that both had adequate coverage. Have they overlooked anything important?

Yes. Although proof of insurance is important and notifying their insurance companies is wise, they must also notify the state about the accident. Tennessee, like most states, has a **financial responsibility law**. Such laws require that within 15 days each driver involved in an automobile accident, regardless of fault, must provide proof of financial responsibility and also report to the state any accident that causes more than a modest amount of property damage (such as $500) or in which someone is injured (no matter how slightly) or killed. The financial responsibility requirement is usually met by purchase of a minimum amount of automobile insurance. Drivers who do not have automobile insurance usually must either pay a cash deposit or post a bond. The cash deposit or bond (a form of guarantee) is proof of financial responsibility.

Failure to report a serious accident (e.g., $500 damage, injury, or death) can lead to suspension or revocation of your driver's license. If you do not have insurance and cannot establish financial responsibility, your driver's license will be suspended in most states until proof is presented. The minimum financial responsibility requirements vary among the states. A common required amount is $25,000 for injury to or death of any one person in any one accident, $50,000 for injury to or death of more than one person, and $10,000 for property damage. Many states have compulsory insurance laws in addition to financial responsibility laws. All states have at least one or the other.[47] Insurance salespersons and brokers should know your state's minimum coverage requirements.

Financial responsibility requirements, as the name suggests, are designed to provide some assurance that persons who use the highways and negligently injure others will pay resulting claims. Damages awarded by a court may far exceed the statutory responsibility limits. Furthermore, since financial responsibility need not be demonstrated until after an accident has occurred, there is no guarantee that any particular driver is complying with the law. Indeed, socially irresponsible persons who violate the rights of others are the least likely to buy the needed insurance. Even states that require motor vehicle insurance are left with many liability issues unresolved. The minimum coverage required is typically low, unregistered (and uninsured) automobiles are still driven, and unlicensed (and uninsured) drivers still drive.

Negligently backing his car and house trailer from a parking spot across a mountain road, Malcolm Maclede caused a major accident in which three persons were seriously injured and two $27,000 automobiles were totally wrecked. Medical expenses alone exceeded $70,000 within a year, and one victim had to be confined to a bed, presumably for the rest of her life. All three victims were adults with families, and none could work for a year or longer. Maclede had the minimum insurance coverage required by the financial responsibility law. Is Malcolm guilty of a crime? Will he lose all his assets in civil litigation? Can he escape punishment through bankruptcy?

Maclede is not guilty of a crime because he was not criminally negligent. If he had been intoxicated, he would have faced manslaughter and possibly even murder charges (see Chapter 6 for examples). He will, no doubt, lose all of his assets not otherwise subject to preexisting creditors' claims, unless he is very wealthy. He can escape his civil liability through bankruptcy, but all his nonexempt assets could be seized. **Exempt assets** are assets that every debtor is permitted to keep, such as an inexpensive automobile, personal clothes and effects, tools of his or her trade, a television, and a residential homestead. The moral is that all drivers should carry adequate public liability coverage for bodily injury to others as a

Read about the Utah Motor Vehicle Financial Responsibility Law at http://www.ps.ex.state.ut.us/dl/dhb/chapter6.html

matter of prudent self-interest as well as of social justice and concern for other human beings.

PURCHASING AUTOMOBILE INSURANCE

Owners of a car absolutely, unequivocally, and without reservation need to protect themselves against losses that may arise from, for example, a collision, vandalism, or theft, and especially against the overwhelming losses that could arise from injury to oneself or others as a result of an auto accident. The typical family automobile insurance policy covers the named insured (and spouse, if any) and residents of the same household (including children, even when they are temporarily away from home, as when attending a distant school). The policy also covers other persons when they are using the vehicle with the permission of the named insured. Persons in the household other than the named insured cannot give permission to others to use the family car with continuing coverage by the policy. When an insured person drives another owner's car with permission, the driver's policy provides additional supplementary coverage if the owner's policy is insufficient to cover a valid claim or judgment.

A short discussion of various forms of automobile insurance coverage terms can be found at http://www.insurance.ca.gov/CSD/Auto.htm

WHAT TYPES OF AUTOMOBILE INSURANCE ARE AVAILABLE?

> When Tosh Takimota celebrated his 20th birthday, his parents gave him his first new car. "Remember," his father said, "you won't be driving one horse, you'll be driving 100 of them. That can be worse than a stampede. So before you use these keys, let's see our insurance agent and make sure you're adequately covered." What sort of insurance coverage does Tosh need?

Tosh needs all four basic types of automobile insurance—liability, medical-payments, uninsured-motorist, and physical-damage—to meet the hazards caused by motor vehicles and those who drive them.

Liability Insurance

A policy of **liability insurance** (also called personal-liability or *PL insurance*) will pay a specified amount of money for bodily injury and **property damage** (also called *PD insurance*) to other persons occurring as the result of the negligence of the insured or other drivers covered by the policy. If your state mandates that all drivers have insurance coverage, this is the coverage required. Personal-liability and property-damage coverage compensates others who are injured by the negligence of the insured. Personal-liability coverage pays claims against the insured for losses resulting from the injury or death of the victim(s). Property-damage coverage pays claims resulting from damage to the car or other property of the victim(s). PL and PD coverage can be purchased in most states with a single liability limit, such as $50,000. In other words, the insurance company provides $50,000 coverage for both personal and property losses suffered by injured victims. Some policies are written with "split limits," such as $10,000/$20,000/$5,000 (that is, in any one accident the company pays up to $10,000 for injury or death to any one person or $20,000 to all persons, and $5,000 for property damage).

Medical-Payments Insurance

Medical-payments insurance covers medical and funeral expenses incurred by the insured (and family members of the insured's household) as a result of an automobile accident. Usually this protection is extended to guests who are injured while occupying the insured's automobile. Payments are made without reference to fault. If the named insured or family members are injured by a motor vehicle while they are pedestrians, or if they are injured while occupying another motor vehicle, they also will be protected by this coverage.

If a person already has adequate health insurance, this additional coverage may be unnecessary. Of course, guests in the insured's car may not have health insurance, and for their sake this comparatively inexpensive coverage should be considered.

Stranded in downtown Atlanta without his wallet, which had been picked from his pocket, Dean Labordee desperately needed a ride to the airport for a return flight to Detroit. (His airline ticket was safely tucked in his breast pocket.) Frantically, he "hot-wired" the first idle car he came upon (an Oldsmobile owned by Thad Turner) and headed for the airport. Labordee had been drinking, and within a block he crashed into a telephone pole. Before it was all over, his medical payments totaled $18,789. Will Thad Turner's medical-payments policy (limit $20,000) have to cover Labordee's damage?

No. In order for Turner's medical-payments insurance to apply, he must have given the driver, Labordee, permission to use his vehicle. Labordee did not have Turner's permission; he had stolen Turner's car. Labordee's own medical-payments coverage is inapplicable, as is the rest of his automobile insurance policy, because, as a thief, he was using a vehicle without a reasonable belief of permission. However, if Labordee also carried ordinary health insurance, his medical expenses would be covered.

Uninsured-Motorist Insurance

There is a type of insurance that provides for injuries and damages resulting from accidents involving hit-and-run drivers and those without insurance.

Pedro Perez was at the wheel of his car, patiently waiting for a green light, when he was rear-ended with a horrendous crash. He was wearing a shoulder harness, but his neck and back were snapped in a violent whiplash. Although conscious, he was dazed and could not identify the hit-and-run driver or car that backed off, made a U-turn, and then sped away. What type of automobile insurance protects Perez in this situation?

Perez can recover his medical expenses (and in about one-half the states, his property damages within low limits) under **uninsured-motorist insurance**. For a relatively modest premium, this policy typically pays between $15,000 and $25,000 for bodily injury suffered by the insured as a result of being struck by a hit-and-run driver who escapes without being identified, or by an identified but uninsured or judgment-proof driver who is at fault. Some states require uninsured-motorist insurance to be included in all PL/PD policies.

Physical-Damage Coverage

Two types of insurance are available to pay for damages to your own automobile: collision and comprehensive. **Collision** pays for damage to the insured's motor vehicle caused by a collision, no matter who is at fault. If the other party was at fault, your automobile insurance company will have a right of **subrogation**. Subrogation is the right to succeed to or substitute for the rights of another. In insurance law, if the insurance company pays a claimant, it has the right to reimbursement from the wrongdoer.

    Comprehensive (also called *other-than-collision loss*) protects against any losses to the insured's vehicle except those caused by collision. Thus, comprehensive applies if the vehicle is stolen, vandalized, or otherwise damaged (as by fire, earthquake, flood, or sandstorm). The policy does not pay for loss caused by theft of personal effects (e.g., clothing, cameras, or luggage) left in the vehicle or for the theft of radio or stereo equipment, although these may be covered by special endorsement or addition to the policy.

WHO IS PROTECTED BY AUTOMOBILE INSURANCE?

    Sally and Ben McFarland have a teenage daughter, Karen. All drive the family car. Are all covered by the couple's automobile insurance policy?

Yes, if the insurance company is properly informed that everyone drives the family car. As all family members are likely to be significant drivers, the insurance company has a right to be told which members of the family drive in order to properly estimate its risk and charge the appropriate insurance premium (price paid for the policy). With respect to an owned automobile identified in a policy, the following persons are normally insured:

1. The named insured and spouse, if residing in the same household.

2. Declared residents of the same household. (This applies even if the person is temporarily away from the residence; for example, if Karen goes to school in another state.)

3. Other persons who use the automobile with the permission of the named insured. This coverage is provided to nonresident drivers who infrequently drive the insured vehicle.

4. Other persons who might be liable because of negligence of the insured. This could be the employer of the insured, if Sally or Ben McFarland got into an accident while on company business.

    Under most policies, if you sell your car and buy another, your automobile coverage continues for at least 30 days, or at most until the next policy anniversary date. Thus, you are fully protected in case you are in an accident during the short transition period. However, the company should be notified promptly so it can make the necessary changes to your policy, including an adjustment in the premium.

While on vacation in Glacier National Park, Nelson Salbeck borrowed a four-wheel drive vehicle from some friends and took off on a cross-country trip. Does his automobile insurance policy cover him while he drives the borrowed vehicle?

Yes. Salbeck and relatives who reside in his household are all covered when they drive nonowned passenger automobiles with the permission of the vehicle's owner. A **nonowned automobile** is defined as an automobile or trailer not owned by, or furnished for, the regular use of the named insured. Insurance carried by the owner of the vehicle provides the basic coverage. Salbeck's insurer would pay only amounts in excess of the owner's policy limits.

When Nelson Salbeck came home, he learned that his adult son, Jack, who still lived with his parents, had bought a new car with a manual gearshift and had insured it in his own name. Salbeck asked if he might try it out; Jack said yes, and Nelson took off. He had an accident in which the car was damaged, and both a pedestrian and Nelson were injured, all because of his negligence in shifting gears. Did Nelson's insurance cover him?

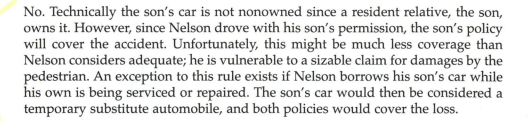

No. Technically the son's car is not nonowned since a resident relative, the son, owns it. However, since Nelson drove with his son's permission, the son's policy will cover the accident. Unfortunately, this might be much less coverage than Nelson considers adequate; he is vulnerable to a sizable claim for damages by the pedestrian. An exception to this rule exists if Nelson borrows his son's car while his own is being serviced or repaired. The son's car would then be considered a temporary substitute automobile, and both policies would cover the loss.

Aaron Dittmar bought a stand-alone trailer for camping trips and mounted a light trail motorcycle to the rear of the trailer. Are these vehicles covered by Dittmar's automobile insurance policy?

The trailer is covered, without an added premium, for PL and PD only if it is designed for use with a private passenger automobile and is not used for business or commercial purposes. Motorcycles, dune buggies, all-terrain vehicles (ATVs), mopeds, motor homes, and other similar vehicles are generally excluded from coverage unless specially added to the policy. Of course, individual policies may be written directly for a motorcycle or other vehicle.

A policy effective within the United States generally does not cover the insured in other countries unless specially endorsed in exchange for an extra premium. Most U.S. policies apply to travel while in Canada, but U.S. drivers need to carry proof of insurance coverage while driving there. Most U.S. insurance is not considered sufficient in Mexico. Before driving in Mexico, a driver should purchase a policy covering Mexican travel. Such policies are sold in both countries. It is extremely important that you review your automobile liability and property-damage coverage with your insurance agent before you leave to travel by car in foreign countries. Otherwise, you could be burdened with a non-covered judgment and might even be jailed pending trial because of lack of local insurance to cover possible damages.

WHAT IS NO-FAULT INSURANCE?

No-fault is a type of insurance requiring each driver to look to his or her own insurance carrier for reimbursement of losses after an accident. Injured victims cannot sue negligent drivers. Under no-fault, every driver is required to buy insurance. After an accident, each company pays the physical injury damages suffered by its insured up to some prescribed limit, regardless of fault. The label "no-fault" means that the insured will be paid even if he or she caused the accident. There are different versions of no-fault insurance, but in its purest conceptual form neither party may sue the other, nor may the insurance companies sue by right of subrogation after making payment. With pure no-fault, the insured may not recover any damages for pain and suffering, which is often the largest portion of jury verdicts. If there is a dispute as to the proper amount of damages to be paid, an administrator decides after a hearing. Each party collects from his or her own company for medical or funeral expenses and lost wages (usually for a limited time), both for themselves and for other occupants of the cars.

A fact sheet on no-fault auto insurance is located at http://www.citizen.org/ congress/civjus/nofault/ auto.html

No-fault insurance replaces the typical method of establishing responsibility for wrongs related to automobile accidents. It replaces the tort fault system and thus it is a system itself. The closest existing parallel is workers' compensation insurance, which replaced the fault system for most work-related injures. All the states that have adopted no-fault systems have implemented modified versions of the pure concept. For instance, in a modified plan if an accidental death, permanent injury, or disfigurement results, or if medical expenses exceed a specified minimum (such as $2,500 or $5,000, or 90 days of disability), it is called the "threshold for suit." When the "threshold" is met, the general prohibition against suits is waived. If it is then proved that the other party's negligence caused the accident, a larger sum may be recovered, including all special damages (for medical expenses, loss of wages, or destruction of property) and payment of general damages for pain, suffering, and disfigurement.

Massachusetts pioneered no-fault in 1971 and almost one-half of the states have followed with a variety of no-fault plans.* Some states have adopted plans and then abandoned or modified them.** Other states have considered the idea but rejected it. At the federal level, repeated unsuccessful efforts have been made to enact a comprehensive national plan,[48] excluding only those states that have acceptable equivalent plans. Individuals who are not satisfied with recovery schedules under no-fault can, of course, buy additional health or

---

*States with some type of no-fault plan as of 1998: Arkansas, Colorado, Delaware, Florida, Hawaii, Kansas, Kentucky, Maryland, Massachusetts, Michigan, Minnesota, New Jersey, New York, North Dakota, Oregon, Pennsylvania, South Carolina, Texas, Utah, Washington, and the District of Columbia.
**Connecticut, Georgia, New Jersey, Nevada, and Pennsylvania have repealed no-fault plans. The Illinois Supreme Court declared an Illinois plan unconstitutional.

medical-payments, accident, and disability insurance coverage for themselves. Most no-fault plans exclude property damage, so drivers should continue to buy such protection, both comprehensive and collision.

CAN AUTOMOBILE INSURANCE PREMIUMS BE MINIMIZED?

Tim and Jane Quinn are graduate students working at multiple jobs to support themselves and their infant child. Every dollar is important in the family budget. They wonder how they can economize on insurance for the car they are buying. They know that if either of them negligently injures or kills another person while driving, they would be hard-pressed to pay a judgment that could be for hundreds of thousands of dollars. Even if they could clear themselves of such a judgment by bankruptcy, they do not want to lose all of their savings, let alone hurt others and have no hope of making good the loss. Also, they do not want a discharge in bankruptcy on their credit records. What automobile insurance should they buy?

Comparison of state auto insurance laws can be found at http://www.citizen.org/congress/civjus/nofault/statelaws.htm

The Quinns have limited freedom of choice if they are buying their car on credit. A lender seller will insist that the buyers carry collision and comprehensive insurance until the vehicle is paid in full. Because of the Quinns fear of incurring a huge debt in damages, they decide to add personal-liability and property-damage coverage to their automobile insurance package. They find that they can substantially increase the amount from a basic 10/20/5 to 100/300/50 for perhaps only 40 percent higher premiums. This "bargain rate" for the larger amount of coverage is economical for insurance companies because most claims are for small amounts. Yet, it is also better for the policyholder, because the big risk is a financially devastating judgment.

In three to five years, when the car is paid for,* the Quinns can drop the expensive collision and comprehensive coverage, because even total destruction of the car would not be a catastrophic loss. At the least, they should then contract for the maximum **deductible**. Thus, they would pay, perhaps, the first $500 cost of any damage to the car, the deductible. The premiums would then be lower. Indeed, if a loss occurs, it might be wise to make no claim unless the damage far exceeds the deductible, because the company might raise the premium the year following the claim. After a series of small claims, some companies cancel policies at renewal time. In some states, statutes or administrative bodies limit insurance companies' right to raise premiums or cancel policies.

The Quinns can also save on automobile insurance now by driving carefully and avoiding moving violation citations, which lead to rate increases and cancellations. An insurance company may legally refuse to insure an applicant for any reason related to the hazard insured against: a bad driving record because of accidents that are the fault of the driver, moving traffic violations, employment in a line of work with an unfavorable loss experience (such as bartending, barbering,

---

*The Quinns might avoid this expensive coverage by buying a good used car for cash. The first year's depreciation in value is highest; money can be put into a savings account and in five or six years be enough to pay cash for a new car.

acting, or soldiering), physical or mental handicaps, or a reputation of being a *deadbeat* (slow-pay or no-pay debtor).

A person who cannot otherwise get insurance may qualify for a risk assignment policy (or assigned risk). Most insurance companies supply policies on a risk assignment basis as a condition of state law for handling other, less risky business. Under risk assignment plans, companies may be required to accept the unwanted business on a rotating basis in proportion to the volume of policies voluntarily sold in the state by each firm. The plans usually provide minimal coverage at very high premiums.

Companies often offer significant discounts to young men and women who have successfully completed approved driver education courses. Insurance company records show those who have received such training are less likely to be involved in accidents. Some companies give discounts to drivers who do not drink or smoke, who travel very little and do not commute to work, or who drive compact cars. Young drivers may qualify for discounts if they are superior students on the scholastic honor roll or maintain a "B" average. Insurance companies have evidence that such persons have fewer accidents, and so the rate discrimination is legal.

WHAT SHOULD YOU DO IF INVOLVED IN AN ACCIDENT?

The following suggestions are made to help protect your legal rights in the event that you have an accident while driving a car. More important, they may help to protect human lives, including your own.

1. If your car is not stopped by the accident, park it in a safe place, immediately ahead of the accident area and preferably off the highway. To hit-and-run is a serious criminal offense and morally wrong. If possible, post someone to warn oncoming vehicles, place warning flares, or do both. If you hit an unattended car or damage other property, leave your name, address, telephone number, and automobile license number on a note inside the car or under the windshield wiper.

2. Provide first-aid to anyone injured if you are qualified to do so. Do not move anyone unless absolutely necessary, lest you aggravate injuries.

3. Call, or have someone call, for an ambulance, if necessary. As soon as practical, see a doctor if you or others have been injured. This is important because some serious injuries are not immediately apparent.

4. Call, or have someone call, the highway patrol or local police when anyone is injured or killed, or if there is serious property damage. Get the name or number of the officer who investigates the accident. Although the officer's name will be on the police report, you will not receive this report for several days. Persons protecting your interests (e.g., your insurance company or your attorney) will want to begin their investigation of the accident immediately.

5. Even before the police arrive, write down (or have someone else write down) the vehicle license numbers, names, addresses, and phone numbers of all witnesses (they might leave the scene after a few minutes). Get the same information from the driver and occupants of the other vehicle. Also ask the other driver for the name of his or her insurance company.

6. Do not admit responsibility for the accident. Any such admission of fault would be later held against you in court. Right after an accident is not the time to make dramatic conclusions, especially since they may be wrong.

7. Notify your insurance company if the other party is injured or has suffered property damage, and/or if you intend to submit a claim for personal injuries and/or damages to your car.

8. As soon after the accident as possible, write down the full details of what happened immediately before, at the time of, and immediately after the accident. A map or sketch of the scene may help. Note the weather and road conditions, visibility (sun, moon, lights), time, speed estimates, and skid marks. If you can, get pictures of the cars and any skid marks.

9. If the accident was serious, have your family contact an attorney as soon as possible. If you do not have an attorney, find one. (Methods of attorney selection are discussed in Chapter 4.) The attorney may have a professional photographer take pictures of the scene, including skid marks, aided by your notes of the event.

10. Notify the appropriate government agency, using its preprinted forms, to comply with the state's financial responsibility law.

11. If an insurance claims adjuster for the other driver contacts you or your family, refer them to your attorney. Be careful not to admit fault to the adjuster, who openly or with concealed equipment may be recording any conversation. Do not make any settlement until you know the extent of your damages. You cannot know that information until after you have been released by your doctor and have received legal advice. If you are an innocent victim of another driver's negligence, you may be entitled to damages sufficient to cover (a) medical and hospital expenses, present and future; (b) damage to property (car, clothing); (c) loss of wages, actual and prospective; and (d) payment for pain, suffering, and disfigurement. When damages are high, you are well advised to hire an attorney. Even after the attorney's fee, you will probably receive a sum larger than any direct offer from an insurance claims adjuster.

12. You will probably want to have your damaged car repaired. The insurance company may require two or more written estimates from reliable repair shops. The insurance company will pay you on the basis of the lower estimate. If it seems that a defect in your vehicle caused the accident, consult your attorney before you repair the car. The attorney may arrange to have an expert examine the suspect parts to preserve them as evidence.

CASE

JAMISON V. THE PANTRY, INC.

Court of Appeals of South Carolina. 301 S.C. 443, 392 S.E.2d 474 (1990)

After attending a football game, Willis DeBruhl, a minor, drives to a convenience store and buys some beer. That is illegal in South Carolina. He apparently returns to the car and shares the beer with his buddy. Sometime later, DeBruhl is involved in a head-on collision with another vehicle, killing himself and the driver of the other vehicle and injuring passengers in that vehicle. An action was brought on behalf of the deceased driver and passengers against the convenience store. The trial court granted a directed verdict for the defendant on the grounds that the plaintiffs failed to prove that "any beer purchased at The Pantry was ever consumed prior to this accident [and] that any beer purchased from The Pantry was [a] proximate cause of the accident in question." The plaintiffs appealed.

GOOLSBY, Judge: These personal injury actions against The Pantry, Inc. arise out of an alleged unlawful sale of beer. The actions were consolidated for trial. The trial court directed a verdict in The Pantry's favor. The question on appeal concerns only the sufficiency of the evidence as to proximate cause. We reverse and remand.

The three complaints, among other things, allege that The Pantry sold beer to Willis Dean DeBruhl, a minor, that DeBruhl's consumption of the beer resulted in a head-on collision that injured Jamison and Kyle Ruff and fatally injured Opal Ruff, and that the sale of the beer by The Pantry was a proximate cause of the collision and of the injuries the collision brought about.

At trial, the trial judge granted The Pantry's motion for a directed verdict, finding simply that "as a matter of law there [is] insufficient evidence to submit the case to the jury." The grounds for The Pantry's motion were that Jamison and the Ruffs failed to prove that "any beer purchased at The Pantry was ever consumed prior to this accident [and] that any beer purchased from The Pantry was [a] proximate cause of the accident in question."

In determining the question of whether the trial judge properly granted The Pantry's motion for a directed verdict, we are required, as was the trial judge, to view the evidence and all reasonable inferences that can be drawn therefrom in the light most favorable to Jamison and the Ruffs and if there is even a "scintilla of evidence" tending to prove the allegations of the complaints, the motion should have been denied. Because a direction of a verdict is not favored, a case must be clear, certain, or indisputable to warrant a trial judge's granting of a motion seeking a directed verdict.

A review of the evidence and its reasonable inferences in the light most favorable to Jamison and the Ruffs follows.

On September 5, 1986, Mark Uggiano talked to DeBruhl, a nineteen-year-old, at a high school football game and arranged to meet him after the game at The Pantry. Thirty or forty minutes after leaving the game, Uggiano met DeBruhl and Richard Derodo in Dusty Bend at The Pantry, a convenience store. DeBruhl, who was not intoxicated at the time, bought a case of beer from The Pantry.*

*We infer from the following that DeBruhl was not intoxicated:

Q. (By Mr. Hardaway): Did you see Willis Dean DeBruhl on September the 5th, 1986?

A. (By Mr. Uggiano): Yes, sir.

Q. When did you first see him?

A. I saw him at the football game at Camden High.

Q. Did he appear to be drunk?

A. No, sir, he didn't.

Q. When you saw Willis Dean DeBruhl at The Pantry when he came there that night, describe what he looked like then.

A. Nothing out of the ordinary, same way.

Q. Was he drunk?

A. Not that I could tell.

And from the following:

Q. (By Mr. Pulliam): . . . In your opinion, as an eyewitness, was he drunk or intoxicated when he went into [The] Pantry?

A. (By Mr. Uggiano): As far as I know, no.

The beer, which The Pantry was licensed to sell, was put into a paper bag and DeBruhl carried it to his car. DeBruhl got into the car and handed the beer to Uggiano who sat on the back seat. The beer DeBruhl purchased was the only beer in the car.**

**We infer from the following that the beer bought by DeBruhl from The Pantry was the only beer in the car:

Q. (By Mr. Hardaway): Was there any particular reason for ya'll to meet at this particular Pantry?

A. (By Mr. Uggiano): To buy beer so that we could head out to sorority night.

Q. How much beer did he buy?

A. A case.

Q. How much beer did Willis Dean DeBruhl buy that night?

A. I only saw a case.

Q. (By Mr. Mathews): Now, when Dean went into The Pantry and he came back out, did he give you something in the back seat?

A. He gave me the beer.

Q. Did you see any other beer in the car at that time?

A. No, sir. I didn't.

Q. (By Mr. Hardaway): When . . . Willis Dean DeBruhl bought that beer and brought it back to the car, was there any other beer in the car?

A. Not that I could see.

Q. Were there any other coolers in the car?

A. Not that I know of.

At 10:45 P.M., a mile from The Pantry, DeBruhl's car collided head-on with another car. The collision killed both DeBruhl and the driver of the other car, Opal Ruff, and injured the passengers in her car, Jamison and Kyle Ruff. DeBruhl was the at-fault driver.

A highway patrolman found opened beer cans inside the car, along with unopened beer cans in a paper bag and inside an ice chest. DeBruhl's blood alcohol level was determined to be .135. This amount of alcohol is sufficient to bring a person under its influence to such an extent as to impair the person's faculties. (A person is under the influence of alcohol or drugs when the ingestion of alcohol or drugs results in the impairment of the person's faculties.)

We think the evidence just recited supports the inferences that DeBruhl purchased beer at The Pantry no later than about 9:58 p.m., or approximately 47 minutes before the accident at 10:45 P.M., that the beer sold DeBruhl by The Pantry was the only beer in the car, that DeBruhl consumed from the opened cans found in his car some of the beer purchased from The Pantry, and that his consumption of the beer caused him to be under the influence of alcohol and impaired his driving ability.***

***We determined the time this way: the game ended at approximately 9:30 P.M.; a quarter of high school football is 12 minutes; Uggiano left the game either at the end of the third quarter or at the start of the fourth; assuming it actually took only 12 minutes to play the 12-minute quarter, which is highly unlikely, Uggiano left the game at approximately 9:18 P.M.; and he met DeBruhl at The Pantry 30 or 40 minutes later, or at approximately 9:48 or 9:58 P.M. Had it taken longer than 12 minutes to play the fourth quarter, then Uggiano, obviously, would have left the game earlier than approximately 9:18 P.M. and would have met DeBruhl earlier than approximately 9:48 or 9:58 P.M. Viewing the evidence as suggesting that Uggiano left the game at approximately 9:18 P.M. and not earlier favors The Pantry and not Jamison and the Ruffs.

We also think the evidence just recited supports the inference that The Pantry's sale of beer to DeBruhl, a minor, in violation of Sections 61-9-40 and 61-9-410 of the South Carolina Code of Laws* was a proximate cause of the injuries suffered by Jamison and the Ruffs. It was reasonably foreseeable that a nineteen-year-old who was sold a case of beer by a convenience store in violation of statutes would consume a portion of the beer, would become intoxicated, would drive an automobile, would collide with another vehicle, and would injure or kill someone.

A jury issue existed, therefore, regarding whether The Pantry's sale of the beer to DeBruhl in violation of Sections 61-9-40 and 61-9-410 was a proximate cause of the injuries sustained by Jamison and the Ruffs.

REVERSED AND REMANDED
SANDERS, C.J., and SHAW, J., concur.

FOR CRITICAL ANALYSIS

1. Willis DeBruhl was the negligent driver, why is The Pantry the defendant?

2. The case was reversed and remanded in favor of the Plaintiffs—is the case over?

3. Assuming that DeBruhl has automobile insurance, what type of coverage applies to this type of claim? If his policy limits are less than damages proved, would his estate be personally liable? His parents?

4. Assume that when DeBruhl purchased the beer from The Pantry he used a fake identification that showed he was of legal age. Would it make any difference as to the case against The Pantry?

CHAPTER QUESTIONS AND PROBLEMS

1. Scott had not quite mastered the stick shift in his new four-wheel-drive truck. While parking in a shopping center lot, he shifted into forward when he wanted reverse. With a sickening crunch, his truck rammed into the side of a new limousine, causing $5,000 in damages. His own vehicle needed $2,000 in repairs. Scott purchased his car with a loan from Schools Credit Union. Since he had repaid only 25 percent of the loan, Schools Credit Union was listed as the legal owner of the truck. Who is liable for the damages to the limousine?

2. Darryl Galloway is 14 years old, but he has been driving autos, trucks, and all-terrain vehicles on his family's 3,000-acre cattle ranch for more than five years without a driver's license. Sometimes he drives on a neighbor's land and sometimes on nearby U.S. forest service land.

*Section 61-9-40 of the South Carolina Code of Laws (1976) (Rev.1990) provides in part as follows:

(A) It is unlawful for any person to sell beer . . . to a person under twenty years of age and effective September 14, 1986, under twenty-one years of age. Any person making such unlawful sale must be, upon conviction, fined not less than one hundred dollars nor more than two hundred dollars or imprisoned not less than thirty days nor more than sixty days, or both, in the discretion of the court. . . .

Section 61-9-410 provides in part as follows:

No holder of a permit authorizing the sale of beer . . . or any servant, agent, or employee of the permittee shall knowingly do any of the following acts upon the licensed premises covered by the holder's permit:

(1) sell beer or wine to a person under twenty years of age and effective September 14, 1986, under twenty-one years of age;. . . .

A violation of . . . the foregoing provision[ ] is a ground for the revocation or suspension of the holder's permit.

Is he or are his parents guilty of violating the state's vehicle code?

3. A driver was seated behind the steering wheel of her car, which was stopped in the fast lane of the highway. The car started drifting backwards, its transmission in neutral, while the driver was trying to start the car. Officers tried without success to find out what she was doing. A field sobriety test showed probable cause for a breath test, which she failed with a .13 reading. What criminal offenses might the driver face, if any? [*People v. Garcia*, 214 Cal App. 3d. Supp.1, 262 Cal.Rptr. 915 (Calif., 1989).]

4. As Alyse Brooks was easing from her tight parking space in the three-story "Park Yourself" garage, she creased the side of the neighboring vehicle, a 1975 Pinto, with her front bumper. She stopped, looked, and left, thinking it was an old car not even worth spending the $100 it would take for repairs. Has Brooks violated any law?

5. David was the proud purchaser of a new Yamaha motorcycle from Anderson Vehicle Sales with a six-month limited warranty. About two-and-a-half months and 3,115 miles after its purchase, a tapping noise in the engine caused David to bring the cycle in for repairs. The seller agreed that the repairs were under warranty, but through misdiagnosis, a wait for parts, and another wait for additional parts, the cycle was in the shop for two months. At that time, David informed Anderson Vehicle Sales that the limited warranty was inadequate and he was exercising his right to revoke under the UCC. Three-and-a-half months after repairs began, the cycle was as good as new. Could David revoke his acceptance and demand his purchase price returned? [*Kelynack v. Yamaha Motor Corporation*, 152 Mich. App. 505, 394 N.W.2d 17 (Mich., 1986).]

6. Following an extra-inning baseball game, won by the San Francisco Giants, thousands of fans were pouring onto the local highways, where visibility was poor due to fog. On the main highway, 37 vehicles smashed into one another in a massive chain collision. If it is established that Douglas Burham, driver of the second car in line, was at fault because he rear-ended the first car, is he liable for damages to all the other damaged vehicles?

7. Dunning borrowed Brady's car with his permission. Due to carelessness in making a U-turn, Dunning was involved in a collision. The driver of the other vehicle was faultless and neither his person nor his heavy-duty truck suffered damage. Brady's car needed $1,500 worth of bodywork. Both Dunning and Brady have collision insurance coverage, each providing for a $250 deductible. Which policy, if either, will pay for Brady's loss?

8. Joann liked Ford Grenadas so well that she purchased a used one three years newer than her previous Grenada. Within three days the car needed valve work, relocation of the radiator, and various other repairs. O'Neal Ford agreed to make these repairs under a limited guarantee that appeared in the contract of sale. Joann sent O'Neal Ford a letter revoking acceptance under rights provided by the UCC and requested a return of her payments. Can a buyer revoke acceptance of a used car under the UCC? Does the fact that she was given a limited warranty prohibit her claim of revocation? [*O'Neal Ford, Inc. v. Earley*, 13 Ark. App. 189, 681 S.W.2d 414 (Ark., 1985).]

9. You intend to drive your automobile into a foreign country for a four-month vacation. What legal issues regarding the car's use should you consider prior to your trip?

10. Parthworthy owned the Old Eagle Tavern, located with a beautiful view overlooking Deadman Canyon. One Saturday night the bartender, Tran Ong,

was serving Craig Hamada "Long Island Iced Teas" (an especially potent alcoholic drink) from 8 P.M. until 2 A.M. Tran knew that Craig would have to drive some 15 miles to get home. Craig left for home at 2 A.M., after "one more for the road," and had gone only two miles before crashing into an oncoming car driven by Shelia. Shelia was killed; the relaxed Craig was uninjured. Shelia's mother brought a wrongful death action against Craig Hamada, Tran Ong, and the Old Eagle Tavern. Discuss.

11. Quicken's Business Law Partner. You wish to buy your friend Sean's used 1995 Toyota 4-Runner. Will the Motor Vehicle Bill of Sale available in Business Law Partner Documents financial section meet your

needs for a contract? What is the importance of the VIN number? Will Sean need to state the odometer mileage on the contract? What is the effect of the "as is" clause? Do you want an arbitration clause? If so is it available or would you need to add it? Are there other provisions not included that you might wish to add?

12. Use Business Law Partner to get the latest information of your state's lemon laws. Go to the document section and look in consumer contracts. Follow the instruction to get the information.

13. Listen to Arthur Miller's description of types of property in the financial category of Business Law Partner.

NOTES

1. Judy Crichton, *America 1900: The Turning Point* (New York: Henry Holt & Company, 1998), 262.
2. Crichton, 262.
3. Crichton, 264.
4. California Civil Code § 657.
5. 15 U.S.C. 2301 et seq.
6. A "lemon" has been defined as "something or someone that proves to be unsatisfactory or undesirable: DUD, FAILURE . . ." *John v. John Deere Co.*, 306 N.W.2d 231 (South Dakota, 1981).
7. UCC §§ 2-601, 2-602, and 2-607.
8. UCC § 2-608(1)(b) and (2).
9. For examples of lemon laws see Arizona Rev. Stat. Ann. §§ 44-1261 to 1265; California Civil Code § 1793.2; Colorado Rev. Stat. §§ 42-12-101 to 107; Florida Stat. Ann. § 681.10-108; Illinois Rev. Stat. Ch. 121 1/2, § 1201-08, Indiana Code § 24-5-13-1 to 24; Kansas Stat. Ann. § 50-645; Michigan Comp. Laws Ann. § 257.1401; Minnesota Stat. Ann. § 325F.665; Ohio Rev. Code Ann. §§ 1345.71 to .77; Washington Revised Code §§ 19.118.010-070; N.Y. General Business Law § 198-a; and Wisconsin Stat. Ann. § 218.015.
10. *John L. Hughes v. Chrysler Motors Corp.*, 197 Wis.2d 973, 542 N.W.2d 148 (Wis., 1996).
11. *Hughes v. Chrysler*, at 986.
12. A short but useful discussion of automobile leasing versus buying exists in the April 1998 issue of *Consumer Reports* pp. 18–19. A comparison of leasing versus purchasing has been included in the April Annual Auto issue for several years.
13. *Potente v. Peugeot*, 62 Ohio Misc.2d 335, 598 N.E.2d 907 (1991).
14. The states that do not provide lemon laws protection for lease transactions are Alabama, Alaska, Colorado,

Michigan, Missouri, Nebraska, New Mexico, Pennsylvania, Ohio, Virginia, and West Virginia. *Consumer Reports*, July 1998, p. 11.
15. *The Wall Street Journal*, 29 April 1994. In one of these cases, the trial court awarded the plaintiffs $105 million after a young man died in a fiery crash. The verdict was later overturned on appeal. *General Motors Corp. v. Moseley*, 447 S.E. 2d 302 (1994). The case was settled (along with three others) in 1995 for an undisclosed sum. *National Law Journal*, 25 September 1945, A6. The trial is the subject of a Court Television program available to the professor from West Publishing for classroom use.
16. *Shimoda v. Bundy*, 142 P. 109 (California, 1914).
17. *Lee v. State*, 187 Kan. 566, 358 P.2d 765 (Kansas, 1961).
18. For example, see Calif. Vehicle Code § 17709, for 15/30/5 liability amounts.
19. See, for example, Calif. Civil Code § 1714.1.
20. *Lovett v. Hitchcock*, 192 Cal. App. 2d 806, 14 Cal. Rptr. 117 (1961).
21. North Carolina General Statute § 90-21.14.
22. North Carolina General Statute § 90-21.14.
23. Among those states are California, District of Columbia, Florida, Idaho, Iowa, Maryland (when present in the car), Massachusetts, Michigan, Minnesota, Mississippi (when present in the car), New York, Puerto Rico, Rhode Island, and Tennessee (when present in the car).
24. Delaware, Idaho, Kansas, Maine, Pennsylvania, and Utah.
25. See *Ney v. Yellow Cab Co.*, 2 Ill.2d 74, 117 N.E.2d 74 (Illinois, 1954) and *Hergenrether v. East*, 61 Cal.2d 440, 393 P.2d 164, 39 Cal.Rptr. 4 (1964).
26. *Vince v. Wilson*, 151 Vt. 425, 561 A.2d 103 (Vermont, 1989).
27. *Sacramento Bee*, 21 February 1990.
28. *Wanna v. Miller*, 136 N.W.2d 563 (North Dakota, 1965).

29. *Coulter v. Superior Court*, 21 Cal.3d 144, 577 P.2d 669, 145 Cal.Rptr. 534 (1978). This case, along with California's Dramshop liability, was later abrogated by statute. See California Business and Professional Code § 25602 and Civil Code § 1714(C).

30. Some representative states with some form of guest statute are Alabama, Idaho, Indiana, Ohio, and Texas.

31. Idaho Code Title 49-§2415

32. *Tisko v. Harrison*, 500 S.W.2d 565 (Texas, 1973).

33. D. Foley, *Stop DWI: Successful Community Responses to Drunk Driving*, (Lexington MA: Lexington Books, 1986), 1. The number of alcohol traffic fatalities dropped in 1986 but by 1996 were back to about 25,000 per year, according to the NHTSA Fatality Analysis Reporting System.

34. Foley, 1.

35. http://www.cdc.gov/ncipc/duip/drving.htm   Federal Bureau of Investigation, U.S. Department of Justice. *Uniform Crime Reports: Crime in the United States*, Washington DC, 1995 & 1996.

36. "What a DUI Costs," *Aide Magazine*, August 1988, 10.

37. *Rath v. Bankston*, 101 Cal.App. 274 281 P. 1081 (Calif., 1929).

38. National Traffic and Motor Vehicle Safety Act of 1966, Title 15 § 1381 et seq.

39. "The Seat Belt Defense," 35 *Am. Jur. Trials* 349.

40. California Business and Professional Code § 22325.

41. *Rathbun v. Ocean Accident & Guarantee Corporation*, 299 Ill. 562, 132 N.E. 754 (Illinois, 1921).

42. *McNeill v. Durham C. R. Co.*, 135 N.C. 682, 47 S.E. 765 (North Carolina, 1904).

43. *Kasanof v. Embry-Riddle Co.*, 157 Fla. 677, 26 So.2d 889 (Florida, 1946).

44. A California jury held a bus company negligent for failure to equip buses with safety belts. *Greyhound Lines v. Superior Court*, 3 Cal. App. 3d 356, 83 Cal.Rptr. 343 (1970).

45. *Lopez v. Southern California Rapid Transit Dist.*, 40 Cal.3d 780, 710 P.2d 907, 221 Cal.Rptr. 840 (1985).

46. *Finken by Gutknecht v. Milwaukee County*, 120 Wis.2d 69, 353 N.W.2d 827 (Wisconsin, 1984).

47. *Insurance Facts* (New York: Insurance Information Institute, 1987), 104.

48. Congress introduced a national no-fault bill in 1998. *The Times-Picayune*, 25 September 1998.

RENTERS AND LANDLORDS

*I*f you lived here you'd be home now.

**Advertising banner on apartment complex
close to downtown and visible from
commuter's freeway, San Francisco, CA**

Millions of adult Americans live in dwellings they do not own. This circumstance has continued throughout the twentieth century. Called **tenants**, these people rent their living quarters, mostly in cities and suburban areas.

Around the turn of the twentieth century, young people were migrating from rural America, from their farm homes with nearby churches and stores. Although there were tens of thousands of farmers who grew most of what they ate and traded for the rest—horseshoes, nails, sugar, salt—the call of the cities was compelling. Electrification was years away for most farms, while city lights symbolized a new promise. Furthermore, increasing crop production drove prices down while railroad freight rates rose, forcing many to migrate to cities such as New York, Kansas City, and Chicago. These rural migrants were joining the droves of European immigrants—500,000 in 1900 alone.

The big cities offered crowded rooming houses, apartments, high-density tenements, "flophouses," cellars, hotels, and even lesser accommodations to their immigrants and residents in slums.* Individual sleeping spaces might be rented in an apartment, with four men sleeping "broadside" on a sofa, their legs extending out onto chairs. Of course, there were luxurious apartment suites in the exclusive neighborhoods, but rural migrants could not even dream of living in such splendor. "To the people of soil, the cities, with their saloons, gambling halls, and masses of foreign people speaking strange tongues, seemed the source of much that was wrong with contemporary America, and these godless places were . . . luring away innocent country children with promises of easier money and a more stimulating way of life."[1] Unwelcome, rural migrants were "having difficulty dealing with their new image as backward rubes, hayseeds, or country

---

*As the result of buildings and railroad construction, one-half of the original forests in America had been clear-cut and destroyed by 1900. The writings of John Muir (1838–1914) gave rise to the idea of conservation. The Sierra Club and Audubon Societies were born and Congress responded with its first law to protect an endangered species—the buffalo.

bumpkins, butt of the jokes of smooth-talking, unscrupulous city folk who mocked them as allegedly bereft of intelligence, sophistication, or any sense of fun."[2] And they were forced to live in the most dreadful conditions imaginable. For example, around 1900, more than 2.5 million head of livestock would be butchered in Kansas City—with nothing wasted. "But the grime, the noise, and the stench from the stockyards intruded into every corner of the town," penetrating tenements everywhere. Even in the midst of such filth could be found "'squatters shacks' surrounded by refuse and smoky, evil-smelling fires."[3]

New York was the first city to appoint a Tenement Commission to solve the problems of renters who were jammed into squalid, disease-infested apartments with six or more people in windowless rooms, with peeling walls and leaking pipes. Many cities today have commissions responsible to administer laws, such as rent controls, that are designed to protect renters. The plight of the poor who rent was, and some believe still is, unfortunate. But as you will learn, renters today are protected by a plethora of legal rights that were unknown at the beginning of the twentieth century. Rent gouging at the turn of the century set the tone for future conflicts in perspective between landlords and their tenants. That issue continues today, but expressed as a landlord's right to a fair return on the investment. Regardless of how the issue is expressed, its solution, satisfactory to both sides, continues to elude society.

Why do people rent their living accommodations? Lack of funds to buy is usually the primary reason, although personal preference influences many. In some desirable areas home prices have escalated to the extent that fully employed families cannot afford to live close to downtown employment centers. These families must therefore either choose to rent in unglamorous, high-density apartment buildings or commute to suburban areas where home prices are lower. As a result, most choose to buy and commute rather than to rent and walk or take public transportation.

Traditionally it has been understood that the financial benefits of renting are bleak. The rent that tenants pay edges upward, reflecting continuing inflation (or, more precisely, the rising costs of new construction and increasing expenses of operation and maintenance). As the demand for apartments increases, new construction must occur or vacancies become impossible to find; rents respond accordingly by increasing further.

The cost of home ownership also is high, largely because of population increases and demographic shifts that occur as more people become parents and new buyers in the housing marketplace. Many young people in metropolitan areas who desire to own their homes cannot qualify as purchasers because of the prices and high down-payments required. These reluctant renters contribute to overall low vacancy rates, and thus to the economic pressure for higher rents. One result of demand for home ownership has been the conversion of apartment units into condominiums, thereby further reducing the number of apartments available for rent.

When housing shortages intensify, causing rents to escalate, a clamor for government remedial action is heard. Some local governments, especially in crowded metropolitan areas and university towns, respond with rent controls; others with laws restricting condominium conversions. Government-subsidized apartment building programs for poor families are demanded in populous areas. In response, some frightened communities curtail the rental housing supply by enacting growth-limitation laws, out of fear that any new growth will disturb existing lifestyles and may reduce property values in the city's core or vicinity. Subsidized high-density housing also requires expanded public services (e.g., police and fire protection and community services) financed, at least in part, by higher taxes. So the desire to avoid higher taxes fuels the resistance to uncontrolled growth, even though new development contributes to the revenues of local governments in many ways (e.g., property tax and sales tax revenues).

As we shall explain more fully in the following chapter about home owner-ship, the traditional economic benefits of home ownership may be in sharp de-cline in response to new characteristics of employment in the new millennium. Renters traditionally lament that each month they are "throwing their money away" while home owners are "buying an equity." Renters may take some solace in our observation that the efficacy of this classic theory is in doubt as the twenty-first century begins.

The overall inventory of available housing, and the laws that guarantee at least minimum health and safety standards to renters, have improved indescrib-ably since 1900. Suburban apartment buildings are characterized by many ameni-ties, such as recreational and laundry facilities. However, much substandard housing still exists, usually within our great cities, much of which is rented to the elderly and the poor.

From the foregoing it should be clear that laws affecting housing necessarily reflect some kind of social policy. Almost everyone agrees that the housing in-dustry, both rental and homeowner, must be regulated by law—the most notable of which is called NIMBY (not in my backyard).

Unfortunately, the relationship between tenants and the owners of rental properties, legally called **landlords**, often is characterized by misunderstanding, controversy, and even ill will. Many of the legal problems experienced by these parties may be anticipated simply from the nature of the relationship. Landlords desire to control rent and maintenance standards and to pick and choose selec-tively from among tenant applicants who, in turn, rely on civil rights and con-sumer laws for protection against discrimination. Tenants also benefit from the forces of competition when vacancy factors are high and landlords accordingly are anxious to rent.

Once in occupancy, tenants do not have any compelling economic incentive to maintain the rented premises. They have no proprietary interest in the prop-erty; all monetary benefit goes to the landlords. And landlords have an incentive to maintain their rental premises only if the expenditures are covered by rental re-ceipts. Rising maintenance costs, taxes, and utility charges lead to rent increases, which can be onerous for the poor and create hostility even in tenants who are well able to pay. No tenant appreciates a rent increase. Moreover, tenants often are considered, by some, to be in a lower social position because they rent rather than own. This erosion of self-esteem is heightened by the insecurity caused by the landlords' continuing ability to remove tenants under certain circumstances.

The law governing the landlord–tenant relationship evolved from concepts, now archaic, that related to an agrarian, feudal society in England. Those con-cepts are largely irrelevant to the relationship as it is, or as reformers think it should be, in our urbanized, egalitarian democracy. For example, in the eyes of the law, a **lease** of a dwelling historically was considered primarily a conveyance of a property interest, not a traditional contract with reciprocal rights and duties. Accordingly, the landlord owed no continuing duty of maintenance because the tenant had the right of exclusive possession of the "leasehold" or "property."

Thus, repairs had to be made by the tenant if they were to be made at all. The rule of *caveat emptor* (Latin: "let the buyer beware") clearly applied to tenants.

In modern times, though, legislatures and courts increasingly approach the landlord–tenant relationship in a more enlightened manner. For example, most states now consider a lease to be primarily a contract with reciprocal rights and duties. Thus, a landlord now may be required by law to repair and maintain the rented premises. In most states, legislatures have adopted comprehensive statutory schemes that have replaced or modified the historic common-law rules. The following laws now in effect in many states exemplify significant departures from the common law:

- The landlord must maintain the premises in *habitable* (reasonably livable) conditions, unless the tenant agrees otherwise. The tenant's agreement cannot be coerced.

- If the landlord fails to maintain the premises, the tenant, under specified conditions, may do so—spending (typically) up to one month's rent—which then may be deducted from the next installment of rent due.

- The landlord cannot evict a tenant in retaliation for exercising any tenant right; if the attempt is made, the landlord may be held liable for punitive damages up to a specified cap (of perhaps $1,000).

- Landlords must refund **security deposits** promptly (often within two weeks of vacancy). The deposits may be retained by the landlord only to repair or clean the premises, and then only by following procedures typically set forth by statute. Statutory damages may be imposed for a failure to comply with these laws. Nonrefundable security deposits are not legal in modern law.

- Charges by the landlord for cleaning or damage repair, if withheld from security deposits, must be itemized and explained. The landlord typically has the burden of proving, in court, the reasonableness of each levy contested by the former tenant.

- Landlords owe their tenants and perhaps their guests a continuing duty of safety under certain circumstances.

Cory, in Unit 5 of Shady Tree Apartments, had plugged a portable space heater, television, and hot plate for coffee into a long extension cord that was designed for low amperage use, such as a radio. It was plugged into the bedroom socket. Hours after Cory fell asleep with all three appliances on, the electric socket overheated and started a fire. There was extensive damage before the fire was extinguished, partly because the nearby fire extinguisher in the hallway was not operative. What liabilities have arisen?

Tenants, as well as landlords, are obligated by law to use reasonable care. In this example, Cory's negligence was primarily responsible for the fire damage. He is lucky that other tenants were not injured or even killed. The landlord, however, must share in the extent of the damages attributable to negligently maintaining the fire extinguisher.

Unfortunately, rental property reform has evolved slowly, which has led to various disruptive developments: organizations of militant tenant groups, legislatively imposed rent controls, and increasing reluctance of investors and lenders to become involved in the purchase or operation of rental properties in certain geographical areas, thus aggravating the shortages of needed housing (especially for low- and moderate-income tenants). Another trend has been the willingness of public interest attorneys to misuse procedural laws to further exacerbate the landlord–tenant relationship. Even with reform, the amounts of money in dispute are relatively small and many tenants simply move away without claiming or enforcing their rights.

Many apartments are constructed especially for low-income renters. These apartments are subsidized under programs authorized by the U.S. Housing Act. Administered by the Department of Housing and Urban Development (HUD), these programs seek to improve landlord–tenant relations in many ways, e.g., by eliminating onerous clauses from its leases and rental agreements. For example, *distraint clauses* (which authorize the landlord to seize the tenant's property for unpaid rent) and *exculpatory clauses* (which immunize the landlord from responsibility for all injuries or losses caused by negligence), discussed later, have been eliminated from standard HUD leases. Even so, tenants of public housing projects still must rely on state law to protect other basic legal rights as renters. Another disruptive trend has been the willingness of public interest attorneys to misuse procedural laws to further exacerbate the landlord–tenant relationship.*

Clearly there are opposing public policy issues, e.g., housing for everyone in our nation and respect for property rights of owners of rental properties. Legislatures and enlightened courts will no doubt continue the movement toward uniformity in landlord–tenant laws of the various states. Meanwhile, prospective tenants need to bargain carefully and effectively with landlords to minimize the risk of possible future costly conflict. It is important to understand that state laws protect you primarily after you become a tenant. It is the responsibility of prospective tenants to fend for themselves in negotiating rental terms and in obtaining the often specific and detailed protections that are provided by state statutes. Without any doubt, an "ounce of prevention" in making rental commitments is worth a "pound of cure" for both landlords and their renters.

THE CONFLICTING PERSPECTIVES OF RENTERS AND LANDLORDS

The landlord and tenant are involved in a business relationship. One must accept this fact in order to understand landlord–tenant law. The landlord's primary concern is that total rent received be sufficient to cover all cash outlays, including periodic major expenditures to replace carpets and appliances, to repair roofs, and to repaint building interiors and exteriors. As cash outlays rise with inflation, pressure grows to raise rents sufficiently to cover these outlays. The renters of

*The movie *Pacific Heights*, widely available in video rental stores, captures the essence of combative relationships between renters and landlords in an emotionally charged and entertaining fashion.

modern projects often enjoy rising incomes and are able to pay higher rents, with the result that the owners' project continues to appreciate in value. (Note that the preceding overview pertains primarily to those multifamily projects that rent to more affluent segments of society.)

Millions of other dwelling units are rented by low-income persons who cannot afford any increases in their rent, which already represents a formidable portion of their total income. Some multifamily dwellings languish in disrepair and gradually become uninhabitable. Mainstream thinking is that laws designed to force landlords to spend money for adequate maintenance and repair would actually hurt low-income tenants, who could not afford to pay necessary resulting increases in rent. They would be forced to move, possibly onto the streets, joining the ranks of the homeless. This conundrum has prompted the production of huge housing projects for low-income renters under government subsidies.

Typically, the owner, especially of a large apartment complex, prefers to avoid personal contact with tenants, and so hires an on-site manager to handle the day-to-day business of the apartment—collecting rent, paying bills, maintaining the building, or employing others to perform some, or all, of these tasks. The on-site manager, or *resident manager,* is the person with whom the residents must deal, at least initially, in solving whatever problems arise. Unfortunately, some resident managers try to do as little work as possible in exchange for the customary rent-free apartment and small salary. Thus, tenant complaints may fall upon "deaf ears" where the owner-landlord is a passive investor, secure in anonymity and absence from the premises.

Owners of larger complexes frequently hire property management firms that specialize in managing apartments. These organizations supervise the resident manager, the collection of rents and payment of bills, and maintenance and repairs. They often charge a percentage of the gross rent collected for their services, which tend to be more systematic and efficient than those found in owner-supervised projects.

The manager, whether an individual or a professional organization, is the owner's agent, and agency law governs the relationship (see Chapter 13). It extends to all activities connected with the conduct of the rental business, including the receipt of notices and complaints. It therefore is a wise policy for tenants to make complaints in writing to the resident manager, retaining a copy for themselves as well.

The nature of the rental business obviously places the landlord and tenant in conflicting financial positions. On the one hand, as owner of the property the landlord is in the superior position, having both business experience and the availability of professional help from attorneys and accountants. On the other hand, government regulation, modernization of applicable state laws, and enlightenment of the renting public has done much to equalize the strength of the parties. But to bargain effectively over the terms of a lease, a tenant should understand what terms are negotiable and what potential problems can be solved in advance. Unfortunately, the bargaining power is often so lopsided in favor of the landlord that the tenant has little choice but to "sign on the dotted line" or "keep on looking." This is so because most consumer protection laws become operative only after one becomes a tenant—the negotiating process is left to the prospect and landlord. Often the landlord presents a form lease full of disclaimers and frequently printed in difficult-to-understand legalese: a classic *adhesion contract* (discussed in Chapter 8). Many state laws protect tenants from unfair provisions within the leases they sign, on the basis of public policy. State laws are found in statutes and in the common-law decisions of courts.

> Kristin Benet moved into the Berkshire Arms apartment complex during registration week at the University of Washington. Vacancies at rental rates that Kristin could afford were scarce, and she was especially pleased to be able to walk to school because she did not own a car. Harry Hammer, the resident owner and manager, began "hitting" on Kristin the day she moved in. At first, Harry made remarks about her "fine body" and what a "sensational lover" he was, and how "she could have the time of her life with him." Week after week the harassment continued, becoming more graphic in its innuendos and more threatening to Kristin. Fearing the need to abandon her coveted apartment, Kristin visited the campus legal adviser, Sherlock, and asked what she could do, if anything. Sherlock advised her that apartments were not businesses and tenants are not employees, therefore the sexual harassment laws did not apply to protect her. Until she was "assaulted" or "battered" by Harry, there was nothing she could do. Was Sherlock right?

Don't "kill the messenger," but Sherlock may well be right. Sexual harassment against persons in their homes may be more oppressive than at their workplaces, but is far less protected. Being forced to abandon a desirable apartment or home is a considerable loss. But what statutory laws protect Kristin from Harry's obnoxious behavior? Federal laws apply to larger employers whose business presumptively affects interstate commerce. State employment laws protect *employees* of local (intrastate) businesses, and some extend specified protections to tenants. Under the common law, if the harassment became very obnoxious and offensive, Kristin could bring an action for the tort of intentional infliction of mental distress and seek punitive damages as well as compensation for her anguish.

On occasion, federal laws also protect tenants.

> Sidney Gotrocks owns the Laguna Apartments, an exclusive oceanfront complex. Sidney, appealing to upper-class retirees, charges high rents and restricts the behavior of his tenants with clauses in the lease agreements and in exhaustive written "rules." These rules are intended to assure privacy, to maintain the quiet and peaceful co-existence of the tenants, and to preserve the aesthetics of the structures. One of the restrictions prohibits the installation of any kind of antennae or satellite dish on the balconies or in the patios of apartments. Sidney also is the principal shareholder of the local cable TV corporation that services his apartments. Craig Stanley, a Silicon Valley technocrat, installed a satellite dish in his Laguna Apartments patio to assist him in his work. Sidney, after repeatedly demanding removal of the dish, instigated eviction proceedings. Can Sidney evict Craig?

No. Despite Craig's agreement not to install any antennae, his behavior is protected by rules of the Federal Communications Commission. The FCC, a federal administrative agency, has adopted a rule that prohibits a blanket prohibition of

http://

For information about
residential or vacation rentals,
senior housing, moving,
resources, and a wealth of
other relevant data, visit
http://www.rent.net

viewers to use competing technologies. Reasonable rules of how such a satellite dish may be used would be appropriate. Under the doctrine of supremacy, the rules of the FCC supersede all contrary state laws or private contracts, such as Sidney's lease.[4]

WHAT KINDS OF LEASES ARE AVAILABLE?

A lease transfers possession of a dwelling or apartment unit from the owner (called **lessor**) to the renter (called **lessee**) in exchange for **rent**. With a lease, the landlord transfers to the tenant the exclusive right to use and possess a designated space (apartment unit) for a period of time in exchange for a promise to pay rent periodically. The landlord is the **lessor**; the tenant is the **lessee**. A lease usually is, and always ought to be, in written form. Leases for more than one year (or three years, in some states) must be in writing and signed by the party to be obligated in order to be enforceable under state statutes of frauds. Ideally, both parties should sign. However, no law is violated if a landlord and tenant choose to abide by an oral lease, even though it may be unenforceable. If there is no complaint, there is no consequence. A lease contains the mutual promises of the parties. Because a lease involves both the transfer of a property interest (possession) and reciprocal agreements, it is both a conveyance of a property interest and a contract.

A resident's occupancy (or tenancy) commonly is called a lease if it continues for a fixed period of time (e.g., "I have a one-year lease"). On the other hand, if the tenancy is agreed to last indefinitely, usually renewing automatically from month to month, it commonly is called simply a **rental agreement**. (e.g., "I have a month-to-month rental agreement"). Technically, both tenancies are created by a lease and are called a *tenancy for years* and a *periodic tenancy*, respectively. Both types are discussed later in this chapter.

LEGAL REQUIREMENTS OF A LEASE

A lease document must (1) express the intention to establish the relationship of landlord–tenant; (2) state that exclusive possession transfers to the tenant at the beginning of the lease term; (3) provide for the landlord to retake possession of the property upon termination of the lease; (4) describe the leased premises, usually with its street address and unit number; and (5) provide for the length of the lease (its term), the amount of rent, and payment dates. Most lease documents are supplied by landlords who obtain them from trade associations or from purveyors of business forms. In addition to the minimum legal requirements of a lease, as noted previously, most lease forms contain many difficult-to-understand clauses regarding legal remedies for the landlord. Prospective tenants are well-advised to read lease forms completely and to insist on clarification of any words and phrases they do not understand. But realistically, most prospective tenants will gloss over most of this "fine print" and trust that they are adequately protected by law. Later in this chapter a checklist is provided for prospective tenants to help them in negotiating with landlords about the standardized or customized forms.

TENANCY FOR YEARS

The unique characteristic of a **tenancy for years** lease is that it is always for a stated period of time, usually one year.* The main advantage of such a lease to the lessee-tenant is that all terms, including the amount of rent and duration of occupancy, are fixed by the lease and cannot be changed by the lessor-landlord until the lease expires. However, the lease may authorize the landlord to change the detailed *operating rules* for the rental premises during the period of the lease. For example, the hours during which a swimming pool may be used may be changed during the leasehold. Nonetheless, the tenant can rely on a fixed, or predictable, rent for a stated period while enjoying occupancy of the dwelling.

The main disadvantage to tenants is the inability to move during the lease term without ensuring that the landlord will continue to collect the agreed-upon rent. Likewise, a main advantage to the lessor is that rental income is uninterrupted for the term of the lease; there will be no need to advertise the premises or to prepare them for another resident. This is a significant advantage, since new tenants rarely can be found to replace departing tenants precisely when vacancies occur. Consequently, even brief periods of vacancy, during which apartments are readied and replacement tenants are sought, contribute to a *vacancy factor*. When tenant turnover is high, vacancy factors are larger and the financial return to the owner is less.

A disadvantage to the owner is that the rent is locked for the duration of the lease and cannot be increased to reflect increases in operating expenses. However, some landlords include an adjustable rent feature in their leases that limit annual increases to some percentage, say 4 percent, as an alternative to an absolutely fixed amount of rent. Or, in very long-term leases, the rent may fluctuate with a standard cost-of-living index. This protects landlords from a decline in their net cash flow caused by increasing operating expenses. And tenants thus know they will, or may, face an increase in rent each year, but at least it is limited in amount.

PERIODIC TENANCY

A **periodic tenancy** is commonly called a *month-to-month tenancy* because most landlords prefer to do business on a monthly basis rather than, for example, a weekly basis. As with a tenancy for years, a month-to-month tenancy should be put in writing. Such a document is commonly called a *rental agreement* (although it really is a lease). The fact that it is in writing minimizes the possibility of future controversy caused by misunderstandings by either party.

A unique characteristic of a month-to-month tenancy is that it continues indefinitely for successive monthly periods until properly terminated, again in writing, by the lessor or the lessee.

The main advantage of a month-to-month tenancy to the resident is the freedom to vacate without further liability for rent by giving a relatively short notice (usually a minimum of 30 days). The main advantage to the landlord is the freedom to increase the rent or to evict a "problem" tenant by giving the same short notice. The tenant who is faced with an unacceptable rent increase may choose simply to move elsewhere.

---

*Technically, this variety of leasehold is called an *estate for years*, even though it terminates in a fixed period of time, which is often less than one year. Thus, a six-month lease creates an estate for years, also called a tenancy for years.

There are other methods of occupying a nonowned living unit, but they are very uncommon. Examples are a *tenancy at will* and a *holdover tenancy* (both with indefinite occupancy, terminable at landlord's or tenant's pleasure), as well as a **tenancy at sufferance** (unauthorized occupancy following termination of a previous tenancy). This latter is not really a tenancy as it is created by a tenant wrongfully retaining possession of property. Unlike a trespasser, however, the tenant at sufferance previously was lawfully in possession.

LAW AND PUBLIC POLICY IN THE LANDLORD–TENANT RELATIONSHIP

Under basic principles of contract law in former years, landlords were generally free to rent to whomever they pleased upon whatever terms they pleased. Of course, then and now, the marketplace dictates a cap on maximum rent, since it must be competitive if vacancies are to be minimized. But in addition to market forces, some metropolitan areas now have comprehensive **rent-control** or rent-stabilization laws that regulate increases of rent and criteria for eviction.*

Rent control repeatedly has been ruled constitutional despite the contention that it constitutes the compulsory "taking" of private property without "just compensation." The constitutionality of rent control depends upon the actual existence of a housing shortage with its concomitant ill effects. Under those circumstances, rent control is deemed to be a rational curative measure. Opponents of rent control contend it is a disguised tax on landlords, discriminating unfairly against them by taking their wealth to subsidize renters, a burden that should be imposed on the total society. Still others argue that rent controls result in the deterioration of rental units because artificially low rents are not sufficient to cover the increasing costs of maintenance and repairs. The buildings are not maintained and often are finally abandoned and permitted to become veritable urban wasteland.

Almost all rent-control laws exempt new construction from coverage to avoid the possibility of discouraging new residential developments. Landlords can recapture some of their losses from rent control by setting very high rents for new tenants when vacancies occur. For example, university towns such as Berkeley, California, are characterized by rental accommodations because streams of students come and go on a regular basis. Thus, strict rent control, called "vacancy control," under which landlords cannot raise the rents on newly vacated apartments to their market value, has been in effect in Berkeley for more than 20 years. This has angered landlords and triggered attempts to preempt the Berkeley city laws with a new state law permitting increases to market value of all vacancies. The landlords have been successful: effective in 1999 landlords throughout California can raise the rents on vacant units to whatever the "traffic will bear."[5]

---

*Restrictions on eviction are necessary to prevent landlords from avoiding rent restrictions by periodically evicting tenants for no reason, and then renting to new tenants at increased rates. Valid cause to evict in jurisdictions that regulate eviction would include such defaults as failure to pay rent or deliberate damage to the premises.

Under one alternative to rent control, government agencies make direct cash subsidies (e.g., through rent vouchers) to qualified low-income renters who can then pay market rental rates. This alternative tends to shift the burden of subsidized housing from landlords to taxpayers in general. Needless to say, landlords prefer voucher systems to rent control.

The landlord is generally free to include in the lease noise limitations, parking regulations, restrictions on wall hangings, restrictions on the number of guests and frequency of parties, and so on. Some landlords are strict in such matters, others lax. Renters generally are informed about restrictions when their tenancy begins, although the enforcement policy often is not spelled out. Nevertheless, the remedy available to the landlord for violation of such rules is the same as for nonpayment of rent: eviction, plus monetary damages when appropriate.

The power of the landlord to exclude prospective tenants is not without limitation. Although illegal for more than two decades, racial discrimination in housing still exists. This phenomenon is attributable to weak enforcement as well as to apparent regional preferences for segregated lifestyles by persons of different races. The Fair Housing Amendments Act of 1988,[6] has been hailed as the strongest modern legislation to combat housing discrimination. Its primary weapons include the possible award of generous damages (no limit is specified) as well as necessary reasonable attorney fees, coupled with an overall expanded role of the federal government for proven, illegal discrimination. New classes of persons now protected from exclusionary discrimination are children, the physically disabled, and the mentally impaired. AIDS sufferers also cannot be excluded from rental housing. Qualified senior citizen complexes may discriminate on the basis of age. Traditional protection from discrimination in housing is continued in the categories of sex (gender), race, color, religion, ancestry, or national origin. Other areas of historical discrimination that are ignored by the act are lack of wealth (minimum income restrictions), marital status (unmarried couples), family size (separate bedrooms for each child), and sexual preference (homosexual relationships). However, state civil rights or human rights laws now protect some of these categories.* California long has protected against discrimination on the basis of sex (gender), sexual orientation, race, color, religion, ancestry, national origin, blindness or other physical disability, and children.[7]

Certain possible terms of leases or rental agreements generally are declared to be against public policy and unenforceable by landlords. Nonrefundable security deposit clauses** and exculpatory clauses—explained later in this chapter—are examples.

Timothy Whalen, attorney at law and former state legislator, owns the Shannon Rose Apartments in Billings, Montana. Taylor, a 48-year-old janitor, was renting an apartment from Whalen. When Taylor was late for

---

*The New York Court of Appeals, noting that the term "family member" was not specifically defined in the applicable statute, held that it included a gay life-partner under the New York rent-control laws. The court did not create a constitutional right to same-sex marriage generally. *Braschi v. Stahl Assoc. Co.*, 74 N.Y.2d 201, 544 N.Y.S.2d 784, 543 N.E.2d (New York, 1989).

**Even where it is against public policy to have a nonrefundable cleaning *deposit*, it may be possible to have a nonrefundable cleaning *fee*. See, e.g., Washington statutes, Landlord and Tenant, 59.18.130.

the payment of rent, Whalen surreptitiously changed Taylor's locks, re-fused to accept the late rent when Taylor returned, and gave him a small part of his deposit. Taylor moved to the Esquire Motor Inn that night. Whalen personally moved into Taylor's apartment, and then sued him for damages and attorney fees. Taylor countered, asking for damages and possession, but was confronted with a clause in the rental agreement that said: *Acceptance of a refund of deposit shall constitute a full release of landlord from any claims of tenants whatsoever*. Is Taylor's claim for damages for wrongful eviction waived?

No. Such a waiver is against public policy. Under the Montana statutes, Taylor was entitled to three months' rent because attorney Whalen used the clause knowing it was illegal. Furthermore, Whalen was evicted from his own apartment and possession was awarded to Taylor.[8] How this interesting example ultimately worked out is not public information. Whalen was evicted, and presumably Taylor moved back in. Under these circumstances Whalen would, no doubt, be tempted to serve Taylor with a 30-day notice to vacate—a normal eviction procedure. However, attorney Whalen might then face an action by Taylor for retaliatory eviction, a variety of wrongful eviction that is discussed later.

Unfortunately, a tenant may unwittingly sign rental papers that include an unenforceable provision and ignorantly submit to its consequences. For example, an unsophisticated or illiterate tenant who agrees in a written contract that the security deposit is nonrefundable might make no effort to obtain a refund. The unscrupulous landlord who obtained the illegal waiver is not likely to volunteer a refund that the tenant doesn't request.

Prospective tenants always should read and obtain explanations for the lease and rules forms with which they are presented. For example, many states require the landlord to pay interest on the amount of security deposit that is refunded at the end of the lease term. However, a trusting tenant who does not understand this benefit may simply not receive it. Thus, an explanation should be asked at the beginning as to the landlord's policy in this regard and his or her answer should be noted.

LEGAL REMEDIES FOR LANDLORDS

DAMAGES AND EVICTION

If a tenant fails to pay rent (defaults) and leaves the premises (**abandonment**) the landlord may sue the tenant for accrued rent and damages. Damages may include the cost of repairs for physical damage to the premises, as well as the rent the landlord would have received if the tenant had completely performed the rental contract. In a month-to-month tenancy, for example, the landlord is typically entitled by state statute to one month's notice of the tenant's intention to terminate (not necessarily on the first day of the month) and is also entitled to receive rent for that full period. Reciprocally, the tenant has the same legal right to receive notice of the landlord's intention to raise the rent or to terminate the lease.

In a tenancy for years (a lease with fixed term), the landlord is entitled to rent payment for the entire unexpired portion of the lease term. However, the landlord would have to deduct from that amount any rent actually received from any successor tenant. In other words, the landlord is not entitled to obtain double rent for the premises: once from the tenant who abandoned and once again from a replacement tenant. As a practical matter, a tenant who simply "buys himself out of the lease" by paying rent for the full unexpired term would be unlikely to learn if his former landlord in fact collected double rent. Sometimes landlords do not sue for damages because their defaulting tenants "skip" leaving no forwarding address, or are without financial resources and are therefore "judgment-proof." Many rental agreements also include a provision allowing the landlord to recover reasonable attorney fees incurred in settling the matter after an abandonment.*

When the tenant remains in possession after default in the payment of rent, the situation becomes more complex. The tenant may have defaulted in the payment of rent because of some personal circumstance, and remained in possession simply because there was nowhere else to go. Or, the tenant may have defaulted in rent because of what the tenant believed was just cause, such as a continuing failure of the landlord to maintain habitability (e.g., to repair the heating system). Regardless of why the tenant-in-possession defaulted in the payment of rent, the landlord will typically seek to reclaim possession by evicting the tenant.

Under common-law rules, a landlord could forcibly **evict** (expel) tenants who were in default and then literally throw their possessions into the street. **Forcible eviction** is now prohibited in all states.

> Shariya was two months behind in the rent for her one-bedroom apartment near Brigham Young University. Her landlord, Sahun Hong, waited until she left for school and then, by prearrangement, opened her apartment with his master key and caused two workers to box all of her possessions. Five mover's boxes containing all of Shariya's belongings were carefully set on the ground outside her former apartment. Sahun changed the lock to the apartment. When Shariya returned after classes and discovered what had happened, she burst into tears. Sahun was nowhere to be found. Has Shariya been lawfully evicted for nonpayment of rent?

No. The self-help remedy of **peaceable eviction** is also prohibited in all states. Although the landlord is entitled to possession of the property ultimately, statutory remedies compel the landlord to follow court procedures. In this case, Shariya could sue her landlord for **wrongful eviction** and, in many states, could recover punitive damages even though she was behind in her rent. Note that Shariya's situation is different from those situations where tenants abandon their rental unit and leave their personal property behind.

> Emmit Smith rented a small apartment in Butte, Montana. He lost his job and was looking for work and missed his December 1st rent payment. Landlord Harry Hammer repeatedly demanded the overdue rent, threatening eviction. Emmit, finding no work, traveled to Chicago to visit his

---

*In many states, the inclusion of a clause giving a landlord the right to recover attorney fees in a lease dispute is interpreted, as a matter of law, to allow for the recovery of reasonable attorney fees by the prevailing party, landlord *or* tenant.

niece and to look for work over the Christmas holiday. When the rent was due again on January 1st, a bitter cold front had hit the area, dropping temperatures to 20 degrees below zero. Hammer, angry about the late rent, turned off the heat to Emmit's apartment and left a note on the table that said: "no rent—no heat." Emmit, returning on January 5th, abandoned the freezing apartment within days and took up residence in a downtown "homeless" shelter. Can Harry sue Emmit for the unpaid rent?

Yes. However, the apartment was not habitable from the date the heat was cut off. Thus, no rent would accrue for that period. Also, to Harry's chagrin, Emmit, like Shariya in the previous example, could sue for wrongful eviction. Landlords cannot indirectly evict a tenant by cutting off services, such as water, heat, electricity, and so forth. Unless a tenant voluntarily complies with a request or demand that the tenant vacate the premises, court remedies must be obtained. As a practical matter, it would be very unlikely that Harry would pursue litigation against the insolvent Emmit who, very likely, would be unaware and uninterested in his legal rights.

All states provide for statutory remedies that enable a landlord to resolve the problem of a defaulting tenant who remains in possession. These proceedings generally are called *summary proceedings,* although different terms for the process are used in different states. Other common titles are **unlawful detainer**, *dispossessory warrant* proceedings, and *forcible entry* proceedings.

Uniformly, the purpose of summary proceedings is to secure possession of the premises quickly, pending any subsequent and time-consuming litigation concerning collection of unpaid rent, forfeiture of deposits, or monetary damages. Because summary proceedings for eviction are so important, involving a person's shelter, most states

1. Require a notice to precede the litigation, giving the tenant a **grace period** to **cure** the default.

2. Make trial by jury available to decide disputed factual contentions, although this option imposes expenses upon the tenant and landlord and practically requires hiring attorneys.

3. Permit the tenant who acted in good faith to continue occupancy by paying all overdue rent and court costs even after loss of the case.

4. Give the proceedings priority of hearing time on court calendars, which are frequently crowded.

Eviction, when decreed by the court, is effected by the marshal, sheriff, or other designated officer who physically removes the tenants (if necessary) and places their personal belongings, if abandoned, in a municipal warehouse or other designated place. Personal property may be redeemed by the tenant upon payment of storage fees. Some states give landlords a *lien* (a formal, legal claim) on all of the tenant's property abandoned in the apartment. The practical effect is to guarantee the landlord that the value of the property ultimately will be applied to unpaid rent as well as to storage costs. However, the landlord must instigate court proceedings to cause the property to be sold.

Although the disposition of abandoned personal property may sound unreasonably harsh at first blush, the tenant has the opportunity and responsibility to make other arrangements. For example, only under exceptional circumstances are valuable goods left behind by an evicted tenant. Warehouses that store belongings must be paid for their services, and usually enjoy a statutory **possessory lien** to help assure payment of storage fees through sale of the goods, if necessary. Either way, the handling of such a tenant's property is unpleasant for all persons who are involved.

The typical defense to a summary proceeding for eviction is exemplified by the tenant who testifies: "Yes, I admit I did not pay the rent. But that was because the toilet does not work," or "there's a big leak in the roof." This response may or may not be a proper defense to the eviction proceedings, depending on who has the duty to repair and maintain under the contractual terms of the lease, or under applicable statutes. Unfortunately, most tenants are not adequately informed as to the laws of their state and do not know whether they can successfully resist eviction on the grounds that the premises are not habitable. The tenant facing summary eviction is in a difficult position. It is possible to simply appear in court at the designated time and testify as to the conditions that render the premises uninhabitable. But many lease forms provide for the recovery of attorney fees in addition to rent and court costs. In some metropolitan areas, public interest attorneys are available through nearby law schools or legal aid services, but they are restricted to low-income tenants. Hiring a private attorney is an expensive proposition, although specialists can be identified from advertisements and may be reasonably priced due to the volume of these routine cases they handle. Unfortunately, many tenants with proper defenses of non-habitability probably give up the fight and simply move on.

On the other hand, landlords can be made to suffer from "tenants from hell" who do not pay their rent on time or at all. Many public interest lawyers are experts in resisting evictions, both properly and improperly. It is unethical for an attorney to use legal procedures to stall an eviction for which there is known to be no legal justification, and court-ordered sanctions (monetary fines) can be imposed to punish such unethical behavior. But as a practical matter, it is almost impossible to determine if an attorney is employing judicial tactics for ethical or unethical reasons.

SECURITY DEPOSITS

Security deposits are lump-sum cash payments commonly demanded by landlords to protect them from various forms of loss that may result when a lessee-tenant defaults, or if unpaid rent is due when the lease ends. The legal right to the return of a security deposit depends on how it is characterized by the court interpreting the documents involved. It may be considered (1) an advance payment of rent, (2) a bonus for the landlord for renting to the tenant, (3) liquidated or agreed-upon damages that may later be owed to the landlord, or (4) security for the tenant's performance. Let's look at each of these interpretations.

First, the deposit may be designated as an advance payment of rent (called *prepaid rent*), usually for the first and last month of the occupancy. It serves to give the landlord security because the tenant has something to lose if the premises are abandoned. In such event, the rental unit is paid for while the landlord locates another tenant. But advance rent is rent; it cannot be retained by the landlord as compensation for damage or cleaning.

Another use of the security deposit is as a "bonus," or "key money" paid to a landlord when desirable rental quarters are hard to find. It is owned by the landlord and is not refundable under any circumstances.

A third use is as **liquidated damages**, an amount of money the parties agree will compensate the landlord for any property damages that may occur in the future, whether or not the actual amount for repairing the damage turns out to be more or less. Liquidated damage clauses are seldom found in leases because state laws limit their use, for example, to situations were actual damages would be very difficult to prove.

On the other hand, a security deposit is commonly used as a security fund held by the landlord to be applied against any actual losses incurred by the landlord from any default by the tenant. Any portion of the security deposit in excess of actual damages must be refunded to the tenant; if actual damages exceed the amount of deposit, the tenant remains liable for their payment.

The prospective tenant should insist that a clearly understandable provision in the lease explains the ultimate disposition of the security deposit. Although a true security deposit (as distinguished from prepaid rent) is the tenant's money until properly applied to damages, the landlord is not, in most jurisdictions, obligated to pay any interest on it to the tenant.

Disputes often arise in connection with the return of security deposits because of disagreement as to the condition of the premises at the beginning and at the end of the term. Also, there can be differences in opinion as to what constitutes ordinary wear and tear, which is generally defined as deterioration attributable to the passage of time and reasonable use by a tenant rather than abuse or wrongful conduct.

Harry, Sally, Kristina, and Jocelyn rented a home in the neighborhood of the university they were attending. The home was owned by an elderly widow who had moved to an apartment in a nearby city to be closer to her children following the death of her husband. The rent was mailed to her each month. After Harry and his roommates moved out at the end of their two-year lease, they wrote and asked for return of their $1,000 security deposit. A rental management company reported to the widow that paths were worn in the carpets, the paint around all light switches and door handles was scratched and stained, grease spatters on the walls around the kitchen stove and sink were permanent, there were permanent water stains on the drapes caused by outside sprinklers that had been showering the open windows, the toilet was "running" constantly and two faucets were dripping, the linoleum in the kitchen and bathrooms was curling at the edges and needed replacement, there was a hole in a window screen, and there was water damage to the subfloor around the shower in each bathroom. Can the widow use the security deposit to repair the items?

Probably not. All of the items would ordinarily and gradually occur in any house occupied by four college students. These kinds of deterioration are called **ordinary wear and tear** in the law. Over time, interior paint will fade, discolor, and even crack; carpets will wear down, especially in high-traffic areas; curtains will sag, lose their shape, and discolor from the sun's rays and from oxidation; sediment in water will accumulate around rubber washers and cause faucets to leak; caulking around showers and tubs will discolor, crack, and ultimately leak; wood surfaces around door handles and cupboard pulls will mar from fingers and fingernails, and so forth. Sprinkler damage is not the tenant's responsibility, nor is the window screen damage unless caused by one of the tenants. Tenants are not legally responsible for correcting these types of damage.

Examples of damage beyond ordinary wear and tear, which usually are indeed the tenant's responsibility, include cigarette burns on furniture, unremovable stains on carpets, chipped porcelain in sinks, burns on rugs and floors from fireplace embers, broken windows or damaged light fixtures, scratched and gouged walls, animal urine on carpeting or flooring, and graffiti on walls and ceiling.

Damages are treated differently than cleanliness. Dirt is not damage, nor is it ordinary wear and tear. A tenant is obligated to return the premise to the landlord in as clean a condition as at the beginning of the term. The landlord cannot legally retain security deposits to make the premises more clean, even if the deposit is labeled a "cleaning deposit" in the paperwork. Sometimes the distinction between cleanliness and damage is fuzzy, as when an oven has been used but left uncleaned over a long period of time, or when toilet bowl stains become permanent from lack of periodic cleaning.

Generally, the landlord and tenant are free to contract as they please. However, because of their unequal bargaining power, courts will not enforce certain terms that frequently appear in landlord–tenant agreements because they are "against public policy." For example, a security deposit that is agreed to be nonrefundable nonetheless must be refunded to the extent it is not applied to some proper purpose, such as the repair of damage to the apartment.

LEGAL REMEDIES FOR TENANTS

IMPLIED WARRANTY OF HABITABILITY

Under archaic principles of common law, a landlord had no continuing duty to maintain the rented premises; the tenant had the duty to maintain and repair. Under modern law, the landlord does have a continuing duty to provide and to maintain habitability and to make repairs unless otherwise provided in the lease agreement.[9] This duty, called the **implied warranty of habitability**, means that the landlord guarantees that there are no concealed defects in the facilities (i.e., those that are vital to the use of the premises for residential purposes) because of faulty original construction or deterioration from age or normal usage. This warranty applies to the condition of the premises at the time the rental arrangement is made.

> Becker fell against an untempered, frosted-glass shower door in the apartment he rented from IRM Corp. Becker broke and lacerated his arm. The landlord was not aware the doors were made of untempered glass, and therefore was not aware of any risk to tenants. Becker sued under a theory of strict product liability, arguing that the landlord should be held liable just like the manufacturer of any defective product. What was the result?

Becker won in a 1985 case in which the California Supreme Court agreed that landlords were strictly liable (without fault) for damages caused by products in the apartments they rented. Courts in other states balked and refused to apply this new interpretation of law. Later the California courts abandoned the rule, ruling that a tenant *cannot* reasonably expect that the landlord will have eliminated defects of which the landlord was unaware and which would not have been disclosed by a reasonable inspection. Thus, the implied warranty of habitability does not support an action for strict liability. In the *Becker* case, even if the landlord had inspected the apartment, the untempered type of glass would not have been apparent. The landlord therefore was not negligent, and Becker would lose if the case arose today.[10] Still, a landlord must exercise due care in the management of the rental property to avoid foreseeable injury to tenants and others.

The implied warranty of habitability gives a tenant a reasonable expectation that the landlord has inspected the rental dwelling and corrected any defects disclosed by that inspection that would render the dwelling uninhabitable. The tenant further can expect that the landlord will maintain the property in a habitable condition by repairing promptly any conditions of which the landlord has actual or constructive notice that arise during the tenancy. Some states, however, reject the implied warranty of habitability.

Robert Flain, visiting a friend who rented a home in Casper, Wyoming, fell down the rickety stairs leading to the basement and was seriously injured. There were no handrails on the dimly lit stairs. Flain sues the landlord for bodily injury from negligence. Can Flain win his case?

Not in Wyoming, which follows the old common-law rule under which a landlord owes no duty of care to tenants or their guests. Wyoming is a "Let the Tenant Beware" state, unlike the vast majority of states that have established an implied warranty of habitability.[11] Under the modern rule, a jury would have decided whether the condition of the staircase violated an implied warranty of habitability. Even in Wyoming, the landlord owes a duty of reasonable care in maintaining the premises *over which control is retained*, such as hallways and parking lots.

Under the more modern view, the landlord is responsible for necessary maintenance and repairs arising during the lease term (e.g., stopped-up toilet, broken air conditioner, burned-out water heater, leaky faucet). However, the parties are free to include a provision in their lease specifying that the tenant will make specified or all repairs. Unfortunately, in part due to their unequal bargaining power, the lessee-tenant frequently agrees to make specified repairs, thereby effectively canceling any implied warranty of habitability. Unless so specified, the landlord has an ongoing duty to make repairs. Repairs made necessary because of the negligence of the tenant are, of course, the responsibility of the tenant.

Generally, the warranty of habitability applies to major physical defects in the property that affect the tenant's quality of life (e.g., a serious leak in the roof). The landlord has a reasonable time to repair such major defects. A defect that is merely unattractive or annoying, such as a crack in a wall, probably will not violate the warranty. Unless the crack is a structural defect or affects the residence's heating capabilities, it generally is not serious enough to make the property uninhabitable. In deciding whether a defect violates the landlord's warranty, courts may consider the following:

1.   Did the tenant cause the defect, or is the tenant otherwise responsible for it?

2. How long has the defect existed?

3. What is the age of the building? A newer building is expected to have fewer problems.

4. What is the defect's impact—present and potential—on the tenant's health, safety, and activities, such as sleeping and eating?

5. Is the defect in violation of housing, building, or sanitation codes?

The landlord is responsible for maintaining common areas, such as halls, stairways, and elevators. This duty requires repair of defects of which the landlord has actual knowledge and those the landlord should know about.

Tenants have duties also. Lease agreements contain clauses requiring tenants to comply with the law and incorporate rules that purport to regulate conduct. The state has an obligation to provide for the health, safety, and welfare of the public, and thus has an interest in tenant life. State statutes* may require tenants to keep premises as clean and sanitary as conditions of premises permit (slum property less sanitary than a suburban garden apartment); to dispose of all rubbish and trash; to pay for any fumigation necessary for removal of any infestation caused by the tenant (e.g., cockroaches, fleas, lice); to properly use all plumbing, heating, and appliances; to not intentionally trash the premises (may be a crime); and to not engage in or permit drug-related activities in the premises. As a practical matter, police are not aware of any tenant violations until some commotion occurs, or until a landlord calls them to press criminal charges.** The police power also extends to homeowners, but in a slightly different way. For example, municipal ordinances ordinarily require trash to be disposed of, limit the kinds of animals owned (public health hazard), limit noise levels, and prohibit certain activities (practicing with firearms). But the renters in apartments may be more closely regulated because of the high-density and, hence, close proximity of families, the semipublic nature of the premises that can themselves invite mischief, as well as the property interest of landlords.

As already noted, courts and state legislatures consistently have been abandoning the old common-law rules and have been imposing certain duties upon landlords to maintain and repair their premises reasonably, unless otherwise agreed. In this way, the common law is continually expanding, meeting new and changing circumstances.

The **covenant of quiet enjoyment** is a duty implied by law and declared by courts to be an incident of the landlord–tenant relationship. The historical covenant merely provides that the tenant will not be put out of possession (i.e., evicted) by any act or failure of the landlord. Courts have extended this principle so that any substantial interference with the tenant's use of the premises is considered a violation of the implied covenant of quiet enjoyment.

Brenda and Julie, MBA students, were roommates at Shady Tree Apartments, which were managed by Mrs. Marta Johnson. Billy Baba, who lived next door, hosted loud and boisterous "Monday night

*See, e.g., Washington statutes, Landlord and Tenant, 59.18.130.
**Recall from Chapter 6 that the attempt to obtain a monetary advantage by threatening prosecution of a crime is a variety of the felony called *extortion*. There is a world of difference between calling the police and *threatening* to call the police unless monetary restitution is made.

football" parties; on Thursday nights, he threw wild and noisy "TGIF" parties. As many as 20 to 30 people routinely attended these parties, which lasted until long after midnight. After their repeated complaints to Marta Johnson that they couldn't sleep or study, Brenda and Julie suddenly broke their one-year lease and moved out. Seven months remained on their lease and their rent was $900 per month. Can Marta Johnson sue Brenda and Julie for the unpaid rent?

Not if Brenda and Julie provide documented strong evidence of the offensiveness of Billy Baba's parties. The law treats certain serious and wrongful conduct, or neglect by a landlord, as a **constructive eviction**, which is equivalent to an actual wrongful, physical eviction. Violation of the covenant of quiet enjoyment is one example of wrongful conduct or neglect. Julie and Brenda could sue their landlord Marta Johnson for tort damages (i.e., including mental distress and suffering) and moving costs on the theory of a wrongful eviction. Some courts would award them damages for any increase in rent they were required to pay for a similar apartment. In some states they could ask for punitive damages, although the failure to provide peace and quiet doesn't appear to be particularly egregious conduct. Note that Brenda and Julie would have no basis to sue Billy Baba for damages. Billy was committing no tort even if he was breaking the published rules of the apartment by hosting noisy parties.*

Less egregious conduct by a landlord also may be considered a constructive eviction, i.e., a violation of the covenant of quiet enjoyment. For example, in cases where a clogged sewer pipe caused foul odors, where there was lack of heat, and where the landlord permitted occupants of other parts of the buildings to carry on lewd activities, courts have found a violation of the implied covenant of quiet enjoyment. These examples do not mean that occasional noise is prohibited. But when persistent offensive and disturbing conduct reaches the level of a *constructive eviction*, the tenant becomes free to abandon the premises without further responsibility for rent and may sue the landlord for wrongful eviction. In most states, the premises must be vacated if the tenant chooses to sue for a constructive eviction.[12]

In addition to this developing private duty upon landlords to maintain rental premises, most cities and towns have housing ordinances designed to protect the health, safety, and welfare of renters and the public, and to prevent the deterioration of dwellings to substandard or slum conditions. These ordinances may impose alleged hardships upon landlords, but they are constitutional exercises of the police power. Typically, for example, these ordinances require that flush toilets, lavatory sinks, bathtubs and showers, kitchen stoves and refrigerators, heating systems, and similar essentials be maintained by the landlord in good operating order.

Failure to comply with housing codes or ordinances may subject a landlord to government sanctions. But the landlord's obligation is to the municipality and not to the tenant, who, accordingly, cannot bring an action to enforce such codes

---

*Some cities have adopted "noise" ordinances that make persistent noise-making (above a specified decibel level) an infraction punishable by fine. At some level of boisterousness, party-making may constitute the misdemeanor crime of disturbing the peace. Under the common law, persistent excessive noise may be declared a civil nuisance and enjoined by a court of equity.

and ordinances. The tenant is entitled to complain to the appropriate local official and wait for administrative enforcement of the housing code.

A **retaliatory eviction** (an eviction for revenge) occurs when a landlord evicts a tenant because the tenant insisted upon enforcement of some right, such as by complaining to a local official of a building code violation. Most states, by statute, specifically prohibit retaliatory evictions and provide remedies for occasions when they occur. Aggrieved tenants, however, must prove by a preponderance of the evidence that the eviction was motivated by revenge and not for valid reasons.*

Many housing codes impose reciprocal duties of cleanliness and housekeeping upon the tenant, but enforcement is rare, as the landlord usually is reluctant to register a complaint that will invite inspection of the premises by an official.

If the landlord fails to maintain the premises, what remedy is available to the tenant? Under such circumstances, and depending on the terms of the lease and the state statutes involved, one of the following situations exists:

- The landlord is breaching an implied warranty of habitability or an implied covenant of quiet enjoyment (whether the duty was created by court decision or by statute).

- The landlord is violating a term in the rental agreement or lease.

- The tenant has the duty to repair and there is no remedy against the landlord.

If the landlord persists in violating a duty to maintain or repair, the tenant is free to declare the lease terminated and abandon the premises. This breach of duty will be a good defense for the tenant in any action the landlord might later pursue seeking unpaid rent.

More likely, however, the tenant desires to remain in possession as originally agreed, and simply wants the landlord to fulfill the duty of maintaining, and if necessary repairing, the premises. Most states require the tenant to pay the rent and then sue for *redress*. Damages recoverable for breach of the covenant of quiet enjoyment or the implied warranty of habitability are measured by the difference between the rental value of the premises actually received and the rental value if the premises had been as "covenanted" or as "warranted." Thus, the costly testimony of expert witnesses as to their opinion of these values may be necessary. Such a suit brought in small claims court may also instigate a retaliatory eviction by the landlord and, thereby, escalate the legal proceedings beyond the willingness of the tenant to proceed. Unfortunately, there often is a practical side to legal remedies that often look better on paper than they turn out to be when applied in real life.

In most states, legislators have created new remedies for tenants. Some statutes permit the tenant to make necessary repairs and deduct their cost from the rent. The amount of the deduction from rent due usually is limited to a maximum of one month's rent. This remedy of "repair and deduct" is subject to various procedures and limitations. Some states have permitted **abatement**, temporary suspension of the duty of rent payment, as long as the premises remain uninhabitable.

---

*The obvious defense for an aggressive "landlord's attorney" to assert in a case for retaliatory eviction is that the tenant broke the lease or violated the rules and deserved eviction. This explains why some apartments have very strict rules that are enforced only when necessary to get rid of an undesirable tenant.

http://

To determine the statutory scheme enforced by your state, visit http://www.law.cornell.edu/topics/landlord_tenant.html

http://

For general information concerning housing for and protection of low-income tenants in subsidized housing, begin with the home page of HUD at http://www.hud.gov/

A tenant facing eviction because of a failure to pay rent may admit the charge, but may claim legal justification because of the landlord's failure to maintain the premises. Where an implied warranty of habitability or an expanded covenant of quiet enjoyment exists, the tenant's contention is "relevant" and may constitute a valid defense to the summary proceedings for eviction. Every prospective renter should inquire as to which party will have the duty to maintain and repair. Where feasible, the tenant should negotiate to impose that burden upon the landlord, and have it stated in the terms of the lease; otherwise, the tenant should give long and careful thought to the potential financial burdens of making periodic repairs before blithely assuming that responsibility.

As noted earlier, some real estate scholars believe that forcing landlords to repair and maintain will hurt low-income tenants who are unable to afford increases in rent levels. However, the U.S. Department of Housing and Urban Affairs (HUD) now is extensively involved in financing and maintaining low-rent housing.

LANDLORD NEGLIGENCE CAUSING BODILY INJURY

The laws of torts apply to landlords and tenants just as they do to everybody else. Thus, if a landlord punches a tenant in the nose, a battery has occurred. But unlike other common situations, such as strangers driving automobiles on a freeway, landlords are in a special position of trust and responsibility for the safety of their tenants. In legal terms, landlords owe a duty of reasonable care for the safety of their tenants. States may adopt statutes that declare a specified duty of a landlord. For example, in California apartment landlords have a duty to install and maintain deadbolt locks and must provide locking devices on windows and on all exterior doors that lead to common areas, such as lobbies.[13] The specific duties of landlords that are required by law become an issue when tenants are injured by the criminal activities of third persons. On the one hand, landlords are not police officers and have no general responsibility to protect the public or tenants from criminal acts—tenants are in more risk from one another than from third parties. However, landlords do have the duty to take all reasonably necessary management steps to protect tenants from unreasonable risks of criminal activity.

Alicia Gomez, a 12-year-old girl, was waiting for an elevator in the lobby of the 150-unit apartment building in New York City where she lived. She saw a man enter through the back door of the lobby, which was always ajar because it did not fit its frame correctly. The man entered the elevator with Alicia and several other people, but he did not push a button to select a floor. When Alicia exited the elevator, the man followed, forced her to the building's roof, and then raped her. Alicia sued the landlord for negligently failing to maintain the back door. The trial court dismissed her case on the basis that there was no evidence the assailant was an intruder. The assailant could have been another tenant, and thus the broken door would not be the proximate cause of the crime. The fact that no one recognized the assailant is not sufficient proof that he was an intruder—in a large apartment building nobody would recognize every tenant or tenant's guest. Alicia appealed. What was the result on appeal?

Alicia won on appeal. The court was persuaded that the man was an intruder because he made no attempt to conceal his identity although he knew there were other tenants about who might recognize a neighbor. The fact that the assailant did not push an elevator button also caused the court to view him as an intruder, although a tenant rapist who was following Alicia would not know which button to push until she got off the elevator. The court held that a jury could find the landlord liable to Alica for the negligent failure to maintain a properly locked rear door.[14] The entrance of a criminal through an unlocked door is reasonably foreseeable, at least in high-crime areas. If doors to the lobby of the building never were locked, and if that fact was made known to prospective tenants, there would be no liability for the crimes of third parties (unless locked doors were required by statute). But, by providing locked doors, the landlord was obligated to keep them operating in good repair.

Rebecca lived in a mid-rise apartment building with 25 units. One evening she opened her door into the common area hallway, only to be accosted by two unmasked men who, after pushing her back into her apartment, beat and robbed her. She sued her landlord for negligence in failing to maintain functioning locks on any of the three entrances—the front door, back door, or roof door. The landlord defended on the basis that there was no proof that the assailants were "intruders" and thus no evidence that the unlocked doors were the proximate cause of Rebecca's injuries. Who wins?

Rebecca wins. Because the assailants were unmasked, the court reasoned, they probably were not residents of the building. Rebecca does not need to prove absolutely that the assailants were strangers who gained access through the unlocked doors—only that it is more likely than not.[15] Thus, the liability of a landlord in New York City under these circumstances depends on whether or not an assailant is wearing a mask. The premise is that tenants, for whom there would be no liability, would wear masks, while strangers who entered through an unlocked door would not bother.

As noted above, landlords are not guarantors of the safety of tenants from criminal acts by third persons. But when criminal acts are foreseeable, a landlord can be held liable for failing to take steps to prevent a crime, such as by failing to install sufficient exterior lighting. Whether or not criminal acts were foreseeable is influenced by the existence of similar criminal acts on or near the premises.

Norman Bates owns Bates Garden Apartments, which are managed by Doak Walker. There are four buildings, a swimming pool, laundry room, and extensive landscaping. On the day that Carly asked for and received a rental application for Unit #15, the following circumstances existed:

- A pardoned sex offender and stalker was living in Unit #13.
- Over the preceding two years, no less than six master keys had become misplaced, stolen, or kept by former gardeners or maintenance workers.
- The few night lights above the parking area were out of order.

- The chlorine level in the pool had not been checked for three months and the sides were slimy to the touch.
- Norman had received an annual notification that the drinking water serving the area was below federal minimum guidelines.
- There was lead in the hot water piping and in the paint used in most apartment units.
- The entire apartment, built by Bates' father some 25 years earlier, had asbestos insulation.
- The apartment was located in an earthquake and flood zone, and renter's insurance therefore was more costly than otherwise.
- There were no safety locks on the sliding glass doors that led from bedrooms to patios.
- Last year there had been a murder in Unit #15 involving a teenage gang member.
- Homicide police had visited the previous month inquiring about the tenant who lived in Unit #17. They assured Bates that the tenant was not a suspect yet.
- Doak Walker once had been convicted of voluntary manslaughter but had fully served his three-year sentence. Norman Bates was unaware of this fact, and had no idea of the history of the gardener who carried a master key and hung out in the apartment workshop all day.
- The locks on Unit #15 had not been rekeyed during the residency of the preceding three tenants, the most recent of whom had been evicted for verbally harassing other tenants.

Which of the preceding circumstances does the law require landlords to reveal to prospective tenants?

This example is not as bizarre as it may first appear to be. The laws protecting prospective buyers of homes are more protective than the laws protecting prospective renters. As you will learn in Chapter 12, although the laws of the states are not uniform, taken together they require disclosure to the buyer of most of the preceding circumstances. These same states do not require such advance disclosures to renters.

Although Carly may not have been told of these strange circumstances before she rented, she is owed reasonable care by her landlord. To put it differently, suppose that Carly rented unit #15 and subsequently was gravely injured as the proximate result of action related to any of the listed circumstances. Could she sue and recover damages from Norman Bates for negligently failing to inform her? The general answer is yes, even though she was not informed of the circumstances at the outset. Let's consider some laws that apply differently to renters than to buyers:

1. Home sellers must inform buyers of convicted sex offenders who are neighbors, or minimally how the buyers can learn the residence of nearby offenders. Although the courts have not applied Megan's Law (discussed fully in Chapter 9) to renters yet, it is likely they will do so.

2. Home sellers in many states must inform buyers of earthquake and flood zones, of water quality, of the presence of lead or asbestos, and even

whether or not water heaters are strapped to walls. Although ignored now, can it be too far in the new millennium before courts will protect prospective tenants with comparable zealousness?

3. In Minnesota, owners of apartments are required by law to screen prospective managers, and cannot hire persons who have been convicted of, for example, stalking, rape, or murder.* Can we expect other states to follow suit in the near future? Of course, homeowners do not have managers, but many are subject to homeowner associations. Should they be screened?

4. As already noted, deadbolt locks often are required by law on apartments, as are smoke alarms, and locks on windows and doors to outside entrances to common areas. Homeowners must also install smoke alarms but are free to provide whatever other security devices they choose.

5. Home sellers in some states must inform buyers of any unnatural deaths that have occurred in the home (other than by AIDS), such as by murder or suicide. Renters need not be informed even though they are just as likely to be affected psychologically as buyers.

In considering whether or not the law ought to protect renters to the same degree as it protects buyers, ask yourself whether you feel, as a renter, entitled to be informed of the items listed in the Bates Garden Apartments example. Under law, the landlord makes an implied (unwritten) representation that the premises are fit for use as a dwelling. Are the Bates Garden Apartments fit? There is a pertinent distinction between the nature of disclosures to buyers on the one hand and to renters on the other. Buyers are concerned about matters that affect the value of the home they are about to purchase, while renters are not. Renters are more concerned with disclosures that pertain to their safety and enjoyment of the premises. Perhaps that distinction will influence the evolving laws concerning what information landlords must provide to prospective renters.

There are unique risks of harm, especially to females, from living in apartments that typically do not have "neighborhood crime watch" programs, are located in high-density locations that often provide housing for the more transient and less affluent members of society, and that may be more likely to house convicted sex offenders than residential neighborhoods.

Rosa, a very meticulous person, lived alone in a one-bedroom apartment near Sacramento State University, where she was a sophomore. The apartment manager, Willard, 23, had a long history of sex-related accusations while he was a juvenile. There were accusations of "peeping," "stalking," and "flashing." Willard had been accused, investigated, suspected, and warned but never convicted. One afternoon Rosa returned home from school and soon developed a sense of uneasiness—it was as if something in her apartment was not precisely the way it had been left. The next day Rosa left concealed threads and buttons balancing on dresser drawers—when she returned, her greatest fears were realized.

---

*The Kari Koskinen Manager Background Check Act was adopted in response to the murder of Kari Koskinen by her apartment manager, who, unbeknownst to her, was a convicted felon.

The buttons and threads had fallen. Someone had been in her dresser. What legal remedy does the terrified Rosa have?

None, as a practical matter. Rosa is unaware of the suspicious circumstances surrounding Willard, who may be innocent. Although Rosa has been injured mentally, an attorney would be very unlikely to sue the landlord on the basis of a general suspicion with the hope of finding evidence later. Unlike Carly in the preceding Norman Bates example, Rosa had no tangible evidence nor physical injury to support a claim of wrongdoing upon which a case could be filed. Testimony might show that Willard had been negligently hired, or that the master keys had been carelessly managed, or that the locks on Rosa's door had not been changed. But without additional evidence, a lawsuit would be unlikely.* Rosa probably would confront Willard, her apartment manager, with her suspicions. This dilemma points out the vulnerability of tenants, like Rosa, whose regular comings and goings are obvious to persons on the premises who possess master keys.

Recognizing the opportunity for abusive violations of tenant privacy, some states have enacted statutes addressing the problem. For example, Minnesota has adopted the Tenant's Right to Privacy Act, under which a $100 fine, payable to the tenant, is imposed for each illegal entry. Apartment managers are entitled to enter and inspect the premises, or to make repairs, but only after reasonable notice is given to the tenant. Thus, statutes restricting entries by landlords may do little to help in situations like Rosa's where an illegal entry is intended for illegal purposes. It would not be illegal or necessarily negligent for the apartment owner to hire someone with Willard's background as apartment manager. Minnesota also requires the screening of applicants for apartment manager jobs and makes it illegal to hire convicted felons. But even that law would not disqualify Willard.

Lai owned a vicious dog, a doberman, which she believed was necessary for her protection while she was in her apartment and outside while jogging. She paid additional rent each month for the privilege of keeping the dog. While the dog was exercising on the apartment lawn, it attacked and severely injured Albert East, a guest who was visiting his girlfriend who also lived in the complex. East sued the landlord for his injuries, primarily because Lai carried no personal liability insurance. What will the result be?

East probably will win if the landlord knew, or should have known, the dangerous propensity of the dog.** As soon as an animal's dangerous propensity is known, a prudent landlord should request the tenant to immediately remove the animal from the premises. If the tenant fails to act, his or her lease should be

---

*You may recall that attorneys can obtain information by using written interrogatories and depositions. But those devices are available only after civil litigation has been commenced. Attorneys ethically cannot use a lawsuit as a device to search for evidence to justify the filing of the case. If that were done for Rosa, and if Willard were innocent, and if the keys had been properly maintained, the attorney personally might be held accountable by a lawsuit for malicious prosecution—a serious intentional tort.

**Lai is, of course, liable for the damages caused by her dog. If the landlord were held responsible and paid the claim, he or she theoretically could seek indemnification from Lai. But the problem is a practical one—the tenant is judgment-proof.

terminated by the landlord to avoid injury to others as well as personal liability. While eviction proceedings are underway, the landlord should seek the assistance of local officials and, if reasonably necessary under the circumstances, warn other tenants and others likely to be endangered, such as postal employees. The landlord would be wise to include a provision in the lease agreement that if pets exhibit any dangerous tendencies, they must be removed within a few days or the tenant shall be evicted. Some landlords refuse to rent to tenants with animals. The landlord is not responsible for injuries caused by tenants' pets that previously have exhibited no dangerous propensities, or are not inherently dangerous.

An **exculpatory clause** is a provision in a lease or rental agreement under which the tenant agrees that the landlord shall not be liable for negligence. At common law, through the use of exculpatory clauses, landlords could effectively escape liability for personal injuries caused by their negligence in maintaining the premises or caused by physical defects in the premises. Liability could not be avoided for willful or wanton misconduct, for this would be against public policy. Legislatures in most states now prohibit broad exculpatory clauses, or severely limit their scope, and courts in the remaining states have modernized the common law by ruling that exculpatory clauses are often unenforceable, being against public policy.

ASSIGNING AND SUBLETTING

A lease may prohibit the future transfer of possession of the rented premises by the resident to a substitute tenant. Such a transfer is called an **assignment** or, more commonly, a **sublease.** (Technically, an assignment is the transfer of the full unexpired term of the lease, while a sublease is the transfer of less than the full term. The distinction is ignored for the purposes of this discussion.)

The lessor usually does not want another person, of unknown desirability as a tenant, to appear suddenly as a subtenant. On the other hand, a tenant who has permission to assign thereby has a practical escape route from the lease if it becomes necessary (e.g., when a change of employment occurs). A typical compromise is for the lessor to permit an assignment "subject to approval." If such a term is provided in the lease, the approval must not be unreasonably withheld by the lessor. Solid reasons to withhold approval of a prospective substitute tenant would be a poor credit record or a history of evictions from prior rental units. Following a proper assignment, the former tenant is released from liability for future rent, although this is not necessarily so. For example, a tenant may choose to sublease to a new, substitute tenant but at a slightly reduced rent. The landlord, presented with a request to approve this arrangement, would no doubt ask the original tenant to remain responsible on the original lease and to personally make up any discounted rent. The landlord is legally bound to be reasonable in approving proposed subleases but is not required to accept discounted rent or any other material alteration in the original lease.

Jill, Maria, and Crissy, juniors at Podunk University, had signed a lease on a three-bedroom condominium at the beginning of the school year. They agreed to share the $900 per month rent plus all utilities equally. Consider each of the following situations:

1. Crissy needed to drop out of school for a quarter, but intended to return for the last quarter.
2. Crissy flunked out of school and needed to return to her hometown.
3. Crissy developed personality conflicts with her roommates and wanted out of the lease so she could move into campus housing.

What are Crissy's options under each of the three scenarios?

Under the first alternative, Crissy could *sublease* to a substitute tenant who would agree to pay Crissy's share of the rent and utilities. The landlord could refuse to permit the sublease, but only for good reason, such as if the proposed sublessee had a history of damaging apartments and fighting with landlords about repairs. Crissy would remain responsible for her share of the rent, and could continue making payments personally while collecting from her sublessee. Or Crissy could permit her sublessee to make payments directly with Jill and Maria. If Crissy's subtenant agreed to pay only $250 rent each month, Crissy would be responsible to make up the $50 per month deficiency. This arrangement would at least minimize Crissy's loss. Crissy would return at the end of the sublease and resume her living arrangement with her roommates.

Under the second alternative, Crissy could *assign* her lease to a substitute tenant who could agree to pay Crissy's share of the rent and utilities until the end of the lease. Crissy would have no right to return and resume living in the premises following assignment of the entire unexpired term of her lease. The landlord could, but need not, release Crissy from the lease completely. Otherwise, the same consequences follow that pertain to the first alternative.

Under the third alternative, Crissy has the power to simply move out and abandon her lease. However, she cannot "abandon" or avoid her legal obligations to pay rent. If Jill and Maria paid the entire $900 each month, they would have the right to sue Crissy to recover rent (and utilities) they paid on her behalf. The landlord could evict Jill and Maria if they paid only $600 rent each month. Each individual tenant is fully responsible for the entire rent; if all the rent is not collected, the remedy of eviction is available to the landlord.

Under all three alternatives, Jill and Maria would have a very significant interest in the course of action Crissy selected. They would have to live with any substitute tenant and would undoubtedly be concerned about Crissy's willingness to continue her obligations to pay the rent. Proposed roommates are well advised to consider the impact of possible future changes in their circumstances.

HOW CAN A RENTER'S PROBLEMS BE MINIMIZED?

The bargaining power of renters may be slight in communities where vacancies are scarce. Lease and rental agreement forms are commonly supplied by the prospective landlord and favor the owner's legal position. And landlords tend to know more about the applicable laws and customs. How then may a prospective tenant minimize the risk of controversy, litigation, and victimization? Here are some suggestions:

1. *Correctly estimate the economics of the transaction.* In addition to the rent, the prospective tenant should determine, by inquiring, as precisely as possible all expenses that will be involved in the rental. Each utility service paid by the tenant (which may or may not include water, gas, electricity, sewage, heating oil, garbage and trash collection, and telephone) should be estimated. Increased commuting costs (in time and money) should be estimated. What penalty, if any, is levied for a tardy rent payment? Are rents increased each year, and if so, by how much? Ask when the last rent increase was made. Consider asking for a longer-term lease to protect against future increases in rent, provided you are reasonably sure you won't be under pressure to move because of a job change or family situation. It sounds simple, but many make the mistake of miscalculating their total housing cost. Don't bite off more than you can comfortably chew.

2. *Clarify the landlord's interpretation of the future disposition of all required security deposits.* Often the landlord's forms are not sufficiently clear as to how security deposits are to be used. Ascertain how any deductions, if applicable, are to be calculated; when deposits will be refunded; what the landlord means by ordinary wear and tear; and whether full refunds will be made if there is no damage and the premises are left as clean as when you moved in. Ask when the dwelling was last painted on the inside, who will be responsible for repainting, and when. Is interest paid on returned deposits? Make thorough notes while obtaining this information. On important items, later send the landlord a memo stating your understanding of the oral agreement, and keep a copy.

3. *Ask about security and prior criminal activity in the building and vicinity.* Everyone expects to be safe and secure in his or her "castle." Unfortunately, some areas are more vulnerable than others to burglaries or even felonious assaults and rapes. The inquiry may prompt the installation of deadbolt locks, window security pins, exterior lighting, or other apparatus designed to reduce the chance of such occurrences, if they have not been previously installed. Although it is true that landlords could lie about this unfavorable information, they are unlikely to do so. If proven, such a lie would subject the landlord to the risk of substantial punitive damages that may not be covered by liability insurance. Landlords are reluctant to accept such serious risks.

4. *Ask about master keys and authorized entry.* Many leases and rental agreements do not mention the circumstances under which the landlord may enter the rented premises in the absence of the tenant. Entry should be authorized for an emergency (e.g., a broken water pipe), but otherwise prior notice should be given to the tenant and an appointment made at a mutually convenient time, and for agreed-upon purposes. This discussion should lead to the question of who has a master key and when the locks were last changed. It is not a major task to adjust a lock to reject prior keys. The landlord's manager or agent customarily will have a master key for emergencies. But there is no good reason why the gardener's master key that fits the maintenance shop must also fit your entry door.

http://

To find available apartments or homes and to obtain directions, maps, and distances to your college or work, consult http://www.mapquest.com and http://www.movequest.com

5. *Ask who has the duty to make needed repairs within the dwelling.* The land-lord should regularly have assumed, or should now agree to assume, the responsibility for making all repairs required as a result of normal wear and tear. The tenant should be required to make only those repairs ne-cessitated by the tenant's negligence (e.g., carelessly allowing a spoon to lodge in a garbage disposal) or willfulness (e.g., throwing a beer bottle through a window).

6. *Prepare a thorough inventory of the rented premises and their contents* (see Exhibit 11–1). Before moving into the rented apartment or dwelling, in-spect the premises for both cleanliness and damage. List your findings room by room. Be accurate and do not exaggerate, a tactic that most likely would serve little purpose other than to anger the landlord. As soon as the inventory is prepared, deliver a signed copy to the landlord (or agent) and obtain a signed copy in return. Keep your copy with your valuable papers for future reference. If the landlord challenges the

Exhibit 11–1: Inventory of Rented Premises and Their Condition

Room	Damage	Cleanliness
Kitchen	Chip in counter near stove burners	Dust and debris behind refrigerator
		Linoleum clean but not waxed; several cuts and loose patches
		Encrusted stains in oven and on stove top
Living room	Electrical outlet cracked	Windows spotted and streaked with dirt
	Hole in ceiling from former hanging object	Stain on carpet near front entry, about 1 foot square
	Holes in wallboard from picture hangers	
	Carpet torn near entry into kitchen	

Landlord _____

Tenant _____

accuracy of the information, suggest a confirming joint inspection. Sometimes color snapshots are useful, especially if the premises are furnished.

7. *If extraordinary unanticipated expenses compel a tardy payment of rent, advise the landlord in advance.* Often, late charges will be waived in exchange for such prompt and courteous notice; indeed, the desired mutual respect in your landlord and tenant relationship may even be strengthened. A partial payment of rent on time is recommended.

8. *Upon departure at term's end, compare the premises to the inventory and ask for a joint inspection with the landlord.* The best times for discussing the condition of the premises (for cleanliness and for damage) are the day of arrival and the day of departure. Comparison of the premises to the previously prepared inventory helps to avoid misunderstandings and disputes. Usually, an agreement can be made on the spot as to the ultimate disposition of the security deposit.

The foregoing suggestions have been arranged in checklist form for quick review (see Exhibit 11–2).

In the event these suggestions do not avoid a serious misunderstanding with the landlord, the best recourse is ADR (alternative dispute resolution), if available. If not, take the matter to the appropriate court, usually a small claims court. In many states, no attorney is necessary to do this, and whatever assistance is required may be obtained from a designated clerk or administrative official. All documents should be available for the court, including your personal notes taken at the time the lease was negotiated and the inventory prepared upon taking occupancy. This procedure is relatively inexpensive and will usually result in a satisfactory solution for the well-prepared tenant who has a valid claim. The successful tenant, depending on the state, may recover attorney fees (if they were actually paid) and double or triple the amount of deposits wrongfully retained by the landlord. In some states, landlords successfully avoid small claims suits by concealing their identity and address, which makes the service of process practically impossible. Only the resident manager is known to the tenant. But a persistent tenant can obtain needed information from the local tax assessor's office or from the record of fictitious business names maintained by the clerk of each county, which lists the true names of owners. In other states, the apartment manager is the agent for accepting process (service of small claims court papers), and that solves the problem. You should ask for this information when initially renting the apartment.

The specific laws governing renters and landlords vary from state to state in considerable detail. We have included a representative sample of them to broaden your understanding and sharpen your analytical skills. However, we believe the information contained in Exhibit 11–2 is so valuable to you that we recommend you reproduce it for use in the future when renting accommodations.*

Exhibit 11–2:   Suggestions for Prospective Renters

BEFORE SIGNING A LEASE, FIND OUT:

Projected expenses (Stay within your budget!)

- What are the personal expenses connected with living in the rental unit?
- What cash is due upon moving in (e.g., prepaid rent, cleaning deposit, security deposit, telephone deposit)?
- What are the average utility rates? Are additional deposits required?

Deposits

- What is the disposition of all deposits at the end of the lease? Is a full refund possible?
- Is interest paid on deposits? Are deposits held in a separate account?
- Will your landlord or manager inspect the premises with you on the day of your departure at the end of the lease?

Condition of premises

- What is the condition of each room: ceiling, walls, drapes, carpet, and all doors?
- What date was the unit last painted, the drapes cleaned, and the carpets professionally shampooed? Who pays for these items if they are necessary at the end of the lease?
- What is the operating condition of each appliance? (Check them out.)
- How does your landlord define "ordinary wear and tear"? Who is expected to pay for it at the end of the lease?
- How clean does the landlord expect the unit to be at the end of the lease? (Tell him or her that you will prepare a room-by-room checklist for both of you.)
- Are all lightbulbs new? Who must replace them? Are any exterior lights wired into the tenant's system, with the cost of electricity added to the tenant's electrical bill?
- What are policies regarding alterations, hanging framed paintings, pictures, bookcases, decals, adhesive shelf paper, etc.?

Safety

- Under what circumstances will the landlord enter your apartment in your absence?
- Who has master keys? When were the locks last changed? Are there deadbolt locks in the entry doors?
- What security measures are in effect? Is there a roving security patrol?
- Are fire extinguishers provided in or near your prospective unit?
- How soon do police and firefighters respond to a call in that area?
- What lighting exists in and around the unit at night? Are the parking areas well lit at night? (You should visit the prospective unit in the middle of the night to see for yourself.)
- What security problems have there been in the past? Assults, burglaries, or thefts from cars?
- What is the policy about confidentiality of your rental application?
- Who are the neighboring tenants? Have there been any prior noise, safety, or other problems with them, or with traffic on fronting or nearby streets during rush hours?
- Are there safety pins or other devices for securing sliding glass doors?
- Are all windows equipped with screens? Are they in good condition?

Rights and responsibilities

- What are the rules of the rental property regarding television and stereo use, swimming, parking, guests, parties, laundry facilities, and the like?
- Under what circumstances may a tenant break the lease? What about a job change, flunking out of college, illness, marriage, divorce, or birth of a child?

Exhibit 11–2: Suggestions for Prospective Renters *(continued)*

- Does a tenant have the option to substitute another person as tenant? What are criteria for the landlord's approval of a sublease, if required?
- When is the rent due? What is the delinquent rent penalty? What excuses are acceptable for late payments of rent without incurring any penalty, such as a check lost in the mail, a bank error, or an illness?
- In student housing, or other joint housing arrangements, is each of several roommates fully responsible for rent? (All occupants should sign the lease.)
- Who is responsible for repairs (e.g., roof leaks, plumbing failure, sewer drain blockage, and garbage disposal and appliance breakdowns)? Has there been a history of such problems in your prospective unit?
- Who is to be telephoned if problems arise late at night, or on Sundays or holidays?
- What is the name and address of the owner (with the understanding that you will deal directly with the manager without disturbing the owner)?
- Who pays for utilities (electricity, gas, water, sewer, and refuse disposal)?
- What are the rules concerning pets?

In case of disputes
- Will any disputes be handled by ADR or by court action?
- Will tenant's attorney's fees be paid by the landlord if the tenant wins in a court preceding? And vice-versa?

UPON SIGNING A LEASE AND BEFORE MOVING IN, DO:

- Make and date written notes of your understanding of your conversations with the landlord. Carefully enumerate subjects that do not appear to be covered in your lease.
- Prepare a detailed list of any damages on the premises (e.g., chipped counters, stains, cuts or tears in the carpeting, cracks around door handles, tears or bends in screens, caulking cracks and stains in the bathroom, stains in the drapes, stains around heating and air conditioning vents, cracks in windows, and so forth). Be thorough, because when you leave, the landlord will assuredly be.
- Prepare an inventory of all furniture and items on the premises, noting the condition of each.
- Prepare a list on cleanliness of the unit, room by room. Pay special attention to the kitchen appliances and bathroom facilities.
- Deliver a signed copy of these lists (but not your notes) to the landlord. Invite verification by personal inspection. Obtain a signed copy for your records.
- Do not be lulled into complacency by the personality of the landlord. After all, landlords change periodically, and you may be dealing with a different face when checkout time comes.

BEFORE MOVING OUT, DO:

- Make the unit as clean as it was when you moved in, or hire a professional cleaner to do so.
- Compare the original damage list to the unit's present condition. Arrange for repairs, or bargain with the landlord for an agreed-on amount of deduction from deposit.
- Insist on a personal inspection of your unit by the landlord in your presence. Make notes of what is said. If possible, get the landlord to admit that the place is clean and the damage is as you indicate.
- Give your new mailing address to the landlord for your refund; ask when you can expect to receive it.

CASES

MARINA POINT, LTD. V. WOLFSON
California Supreme Court, 180 Cal.Rptr. 496 (1982)

BACKGROUND AND FACTS: A landlord refused to rent an apartment to any family with a minor child. The landlord contended that middle-aged persons, having worked long and hard, having raised their own children, and having paid both their taxes and their dues to society, deserve to spend their remaining years in a relatively quiet, peaceful, and tranquil environment of their own choice. This right is lost in the presence of children, who are rowdier, noisier, more mischievous, and more boisterous than adults.

The trial court agreed, holding that the exclusionary rental policy was reasonable and not arbitrary, and therefore not barred by a state statute that prohibited arbitrary discrimination in business establishments. On appeal, a majority of the California Supreme Court reversed the trial court and held the exclusion improper.

Justice Tobriner: . . . . the basic rights guaranteed by (the California civil rights statute) would be drastically undermined if, as the landlord contends, a business enterprise could exclude from its premises or services entire classes of the public simply because the owner of the enterprise had some reason to believe that the class, taken as a whole, might present greater problems than other groups. Under such an approach, for example, members of entire occupations or avocations, e.g., sailors or motorcyclists, might find themselves excluded as a class from some places of public accommodation simply because that, as a statistical matter, members of their occupation or avocation were more likely than others to be involved in a disturbance. . . . the exclusion of individuals . . . on the basis of class or group affiliation basically conflicts with the individual nature of the right afforded by the (civil rights statute) of access to such enterprises.

. . . the exclusionary practice at issue in this case is clearly distinguishable from the age-limited admission policies of retirement communities or housing complexes reserved for older citizens. Such facilities are designed for the elderly and in many instances have particular appurtenances and exceptional arrangements for their specified purposes.

Judgement reversed.

FOR CRITICAL ANALYSIS:

In the foregoing case, there was no issue concerning due process or equal protection under the U.S. Constitution because there is no "state action" in the apartment rental business. The rule of the Marina Point case has been extended to apply to nonprofit homeowners' associations that attempt to restrict condominium occupancy to adults. On the one hand, exclusion of children as a class is not permitted. On the other hand, however, housing accommodations exclusively for the elderly are permitted. What is the difference?

FRANCES V. PLAZA PACIFIC EQUITIES, INC.
Nevada Supreme Court, 847 P.2d 722 (Nev. 1993)

Michael, age 5, was playing with his two brothers at the apartment swimming pool where they lived. Catherine, a friend of Michael's mother, was babysitting while at the pool and several other adults were lounging about. When it was time to leave, Catherine noticed young Michael's still body lying at the bottom of the pool. The water was murky and it was difficult to see Michael, who later died from drowning.

Frances sued Sierra Woods Apartments, owner and manager, for the negligent wrongful death of her son. It later was learned that the day before the incident, the pool was closed because the chemical balance was improper and the water lacked clarity. Testimony at trial revealed that the pool water was cloudy or murky on the day following the tragic event. At that time, the Washoe County Health Department issued several citations to Plaza for conditions around the complex, including an abnormal disinfectant level, a lack of a proper grate over the pool drain, a cloudy pool, and the absence of a first-aid kit.

At trial the jury found that although Plaza was negligent, its negligence was not the "proximate cause of the death" and returned a verdict for defendant. Frances appealed on various grounds, including the issue of proximate cause.

PER CURIAM. The jury received numerous instructions at the end of trial, including instruction number 35 outlining proximate cause. Proximate cause has been defined as "any cause which in natural and continuous sequence, unbroken by any efficient intervening cause, produces the injury complained of and without which the result would not have occurred" . . . . In Nevada, issues of negligence and proximate cause are usually factual issues to be determined by the trier of fact. (citations). . . .

The jury was presented with substantial evidence of the deleterious condition of the pool as it existed at the time of Michael's drowning. Dr. Osinski testified at length of the negligent manner in which the pool was operated and maintained. . . .

As previously noted, the jury was given an instruction defining proximate cause. However, the jurors exhibited confusion over the concept and reached a verdict which manifestly ignored or misapplied the jury instruction.

This court has long adhered to the rule that where there is a conflict in the evidence, the verdict or decision will not be disturbed on appeal. (citation). However, we have recognized an exception where "there is plain error in the record or . . . a showing of manifest injustice." (citations). . . .This case readily evokes the exception because of the jury's obvious disregard of the proximate cause instruction with its resulting injustice. . . .

We are therefore constrained to grant a new trial.

FOR CRITICAL ANALYSIS:

1. The appellate court ruled that it is "obvious" that murky swimming pool water was a proximate cause of the death of the child Michael. The assumption is that if the water had been clear, someone would have seen and rescued Michael in time to save his life. Is murky water a more "obvious" cause than the proximate cause by a babysitter failing to watch the child?

2. This case does not involve a warranty of habitability, nor the common-law rule of "Let the Tenant Beware" because the pool is in a common area. Thus, the general law of negligence applies under which a landlord owes tenants a duty of reasonable care—a question of fact for a jury.

CHAPTER QUESTIONS AND PROBLEMS

1. Arlene, Sherry, and Marguerite, college students, are roommates in an apartment they leased for one year. Their rent is $600 a month. If for an important reason (e.g., an ill family member, failure from school, or marriage) the women need to break their lease six months before its termination, may they do so? What are the consequences of "breaking" their lease? If only Marguerite needs to leave, and Arlene and Sherry desire to remain, what are the probable consequences?

2. Several tenants, including Dorothy Detling, sued their landlord, C. E. Edelbrock, for damages, alleging that their leased premises were infested with rodents and roaches, were missing screens, and had exposed electrical wiring. They also alleged that the heating boiler was defective, that rubbish was strewn in passageways, and that the common area stairs were unstable. Does the landlord have a duty to prevent these kinds of conditions from occurring, or are such repairs and maintenance tasks the responsibility of the tenants? If you conclude that the landlord was at fault, must these tenants move out of the premises because they have been constructively evicted? [*Detling v. Edelbrock*, 671 S.W.2d 265 (Missouri, 1984).]

3. Lewis Crowell's father rented an apartment from the Dallas Housing Authority. The apartment contained a defective gas heater that leaked carbon monoxide gas. The lease, signed by the senior Crowell, contained an exculpatory clause stating that the landlord was not liable for negligence. Lewis's father died of carbon monoxide poisoning from the defective gas heater. Lewis sued for damages based upon the landlord's negligence. What was the result? [*Crowell v.

Housing Authority, 495 S.W.2d 887 (Texas, 1973).]

4. Assume that a landlord, who was angry because a tenant's rent was unpaid, entered the tenant's apartment with a master key, placed all of the tenant's possessions in a refuse-disposal container, and changed the locks on the door. What would be the tenant's legal remedy? Assume that a landlord's agent (i.e., an apartment manager) wrongfully entered and snooped through the tenant's personal belongings, but did not steal or damage anything. What would be the tenant's legal remedy?

5. Note that you have special permission to make a copy of Exhibit 11–2 without infringing on the publisher's legal copyright. Please make your personal copy now or at your earliest convenience. Even though you are probably settled in for the semester or school year, it is not too late to benefit from a careful, conscientious application of the questions in the exhibit to your own present living accommodations if you are currently a renter.

   Make the effort and take the time to ask and to answer every one of the questions that is applicable to you. (Ideally, of course, we wish you could have done this before you signed your lease or rental agreement.) After you have answered as many questions as you can (always in writing), talk to your landlord and, in a friendly manner, ask her or him to help you answer the remaining questions. (Blame us, the authors, for this assignment if any blame is forthcoming.)

6. Angela, bitten by her neighbor's monkey, sued her landlord for damages for negligence. The apartment lease forms did not allow the keeping of animals except small, caged birds. What should

the result be? Would your answer be different if the lease permitted all pets? [*Jendralski v. Black*, 222 Cal.Rptr. 396 (1986).]

7. What arguments can you make to support the notion that tenants should earn interest on the portion of their security deposits that are refunded? Can you think of any opposing arguments?

8. Before making an apartment available for rent, the landlord legally must take which of the following actions?
   a. Provide a freshly painted unit.
   b. Provide the unit with sterilized bathroom facilities.
   c. Rekey the entry locks to the unit.
   d. Deflea and deodorize the unit if a cat or dog had been kept in the premises.
   e. Provide a clean oven.
   f. Arrange for repair of all damages done by the previous tenant.
   g. Disclose to prospective tenants any security problems that have occurred in the complex.
   h. Provide the unit with a fire extinguisher.

9. If a landlord files a court action against a former improvident tenant for unpaid rent and for damages to the rental unit, and obtains a judgment for damages, how can the landlord "get blood out of a turnip"?

10. Notes jotted down on paper are not a contract and are not clauses in a written lease or rental agreement. Why then should prospective tenants who ask pertinent questions of a landlord who is offering rentals make written notation of the answers received?

NOTES

1. Traxel, *1898: The Birth of the American Century* (New York: Alfred A. Knopf, 1998), 21.
2. Traxel, 21.
3. Judy Crichton, *America 1900* (New York: Henry Holt Co. 1998), 22.
4. The first publicized application of the FCC rule occurred in 1988. Associated Press, Washington, 21 November 1998.
5. Charles Burress, *San Francisco Chronicle*, 2 January 1999.
6. Public Law No. 100-430, 102 Statutes 1619 (1988) amending 42 U.S.C. Sec. 3601-3619, signed by then President Ronald Reagan in September 1988, took effect in March 1989.
7. Unruh Civil Rights Act, California Civil Code, § 51 *et. seq.*
8. Based on *Whalen v. Taylor*, 925 P.2d 462 (Montana, 1996).
9. Uniform Residential Landlord and Tenant Act (URLTA).
10. Strict liability established by *Becker v. IRM Corp.*, 38 Cal.3d 454, 698 P.2d 116, 213 Cal.Rpt. 213 (California 1985) and disapproved by *Peterson v. Superior Court*, 10 Cal.4th 1185, 899 P.2d 905, 43 Cal.Rptr.2d 836 (1995).
11. Based on *Ortega v. Flain*, 902 P.2d 199 (Wyoming, 1995). In this case, the Wyoming Supreme Court unashamedly explains why it is unwilling to change its common law to comply with the modern trend.
12. See, e.g., *Yee v. Weiss*, 877 P.2d 510, 110 Nev. 657 (1994) and *Barton v. MTB Enterprises, Inc.*, 889 P.2d 476 (Utah App., 1995).
13. California Civil Code, § 1941.3.
14. Based on *Gomez v. N.Y. City Housing Authority*, 98 N.Y. Int. 0148 (1998).
15. Based on *Burgos v. Aqueduct Realty Corp.*, 98 N.Y. Int. 0148 (1998).

12

HOME OWNERSHIP

Mid pleasures and palaces though we may roam, Be it ever so humble, there's no place like home.

John Howard Payne

http://

For population, housing, and a wealth of similar statistical information begin at the U.S. Census Bureau home page at http://www.census.gov/

Most people want to own their own home. The desire is so prevalent it often is called "The American Dream." This dream has become a reality for 65 percent of the U.S. population, but remains beyond the reach of others. In most areas of the country, home prices have gone up sharply during the last years of the twentieth century to levels too high for many would-be buyers. But permanent federal and state programs designed to bring home ownership within the financial means of moderate- and low-income families promise to extend their success well into the new millennium. Of course, many renters could afford to purchase homes but choose to rent for personal reasons, such as freedom from the responsibilities of home ownership.

There are two traditional kinds of benefits of home ownership: amenity and economic. We begin by examining these characteristics separately.

CHARACTERISTICS OF HOME OWNERSHIP

AMENITIES

Amenities are conveniences that flow from living in a single-family residence, or home. The kinds of available amenities have changed dramatically over the course of the twentieth century. In 1900, the homes of average Americans did not contain indoor plumbing, cooking was done on oil- or wood-fueled stoves, and there was no electricity in the rural and farm areas. There were no refrigerators, no microwave ovens, no washing machines, no hot showers, no garages for cars and storage. There was no wall-to-wall carpeting, fiberglass insulation, or water-based paint. Of course, the affluent in their mansions were the first to receive the amenities of electricity, indoor plumbing, water closet toilets, and central heat. Upscale Victorian homes and mansions were well-equipped and beautiful—ordinary homes were merely functional. But for average Americans, home

544

ownership offered far more amenities, space, and privacy, not to mention a greater sense of satisfaction, than was enjoyed by dwellers of rented apartments and rooms.

Entering the new millennium, most American homes feature extensive creature comforts such as swimming pools and entertainment centers—amenities far beyond the imaginations of your grandparents in their day, but with which you are quite familiar. Homeowners today enjoy the option of selecting a neighborhood with compatible people, away from congestion, street noise, and commotion. Home buyers may make their choice based on the quality of schools or a host of other intangibles that contribute to an improved lifestyle. Home ownership usually provides a safer environment for children and adults alike.

Even renters enjoy far more amenities than before, with common-use swimming pools, tennis courts, workout facilities, laundry rooms, and game rooms with televisions and computers. Modern apartments are more spacious, better lit, and fully equipped with modern appliances and creature comforts such as central heat and air conditioning. Renters argue that they have an additional amenity—the absence of mowing, trimming, weeding, cleaning rain gutters, waiting and paying for roof and plumbing repairs, and painting. These renters-by-choice are proof that one person's delight is another person's agony.

ECONOMICS

Economic aspects of home ownership partly offset the benefits from amenities. Sometimes furnishing a house may involve credit purchases at high interest rates. Acquiring a home in a suburban area usually boosts the costs of commuting, including higher automobile insurance rates. For example, a no-car or one-car family renting an apartment in the inner city may need two cars if they move to a home in the suburbs. In crowded metropolitan areas, such as the New York and San Francisco Bay areas, many persons take public transportation or commute 50 miles or more, enduring gridlock on highways for the privilege of living in an affordable suburban house with a yard.

In addition to large outlays of money when the home is acquired and furnished, the monthly expenses may prove burdensome. Homeowner insurance premiums, utility bills, property taxes, and repair and maintenance expenses must be paid in addition to principal and interest on the mortgage loan. Most of these expenses are included in the rent of the apartment dweller, but in reduced amount because of the economics of scale of multiple units.

Along with the considerable monthly expenses of home ownership, there is compelling evidence that in the early years of the new millennium the traditional economic advantages of home ownership may be diminishing. If correct, this is a dynamic new aspect in home ownership. Traditional economic benefits of home ownership consist of (1) increasing value, called *appreciation*, (2) *equity buildup* as mortgage debt is paid off, and (3) *tax benefits* from deducting interest and property tax expenses. Appreciation and equity buildup are depicted in Exhibit 12–1.

Although the effect will be discussed in more detail later, notice that equity buildup from the systematic repayment of the mortgage debt occurs with significance only after about six to eight years. Furthermore, appreciation usually begins in earnest after five or so years, in part because transaction costs (sales commissions) consume about 6 percent of the home's value when it is purchased. Because of the slow start of both equity buildup and appreciation, the economic

Exhibit 12–1: The Economics of Home Ownership

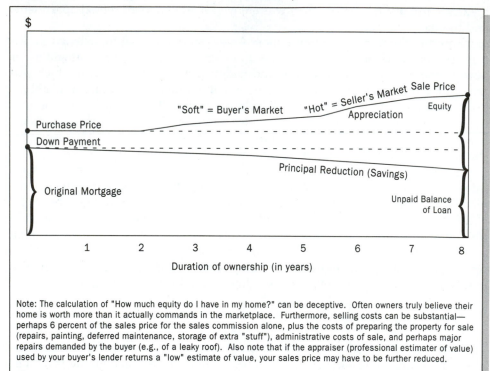

Note: The calculation of "How much equity do I have in my home?" can be deceptive. Often owners truly believe their home is worth more than it actually commands in the marketplace. Furthermore, selling costs can be substantial—perhaps 6 percent of the sales price for the sales commission alone, plus the costs of preparing the property for sale (repairs, painting, deferred maintenance, storage of extra "stuff"), administrative costs of sale, and perhaps major repairs demanded by the buyer (e.g., of a leaky roof). Also note that if the appraiser (professional estimator of value) used by your buyer's lender returns a "low" estimate of value, your sales price may have to be further reduced.

benefits of home ownership become attractive only after five or more years elapse from the date of purchase.

As the twenty-first century begins, changes in traditional employment also are occurring. For example, unlike your grandparents and parents, who may have held only one or two different jobs during their working years, it is likely that you will change jobs as frequently as every five to eight years. The transitory nature of the modern work force is the product of many new changes. For one example, consider that many jobs in technology change as its science changes. Also consider that companies downsize for modern efficiencies, sometimes taking employment across our country's borders in search of cheaper labor. Some companies expand by opening new plants and even administrative centers overseas for economies. In other words, the work force is becoming globalized, shifting and moving to meet necessary economies and the needs of opening markets. At the same time, we have become a service/technology/communications economy with frequent employee turnover and "outsourcing" (hiring contractors for specific tasks instead of employees). Furthermore, the two-income family is now well established, and one spouse's job change can force the other to change jobs as well.

None of the foregoing was occurring at the beginning of the twentieth century. On the contrary, America was a melting pot of labor with more jobs of all descriptions available for the new European immigrants who were flooding our borders every year. In some industries, children would follow in the footsteps of their fathers at the plant and begin their own lifetime jobs. Today, however, our nation is rapidly changing from a manufacturing economy often characterized by lifetime employment in huge plants. A major consequence of changing jobs every five to eight years on average is that the traditional economic benefits of home ownership—equity buildup and appreciation—will essentially cease to exist.

We will consider other examples of this unhappy phenomenon in later sections of this chapter dealing with property taxation, other new financial burdens, transaction costs, and the new, costly burdens placed upon sellers—all of which are helping to erode traditional twentieth century economic benefits of home ownership. Thus, for many, the benefit of home ownership will be primarily amenity, not economic, benefit. Those modern and mobile persons will consider the opportunity of *renting* single-family homes to obtain all of the amenities of home ownership.

HOW DO YOU FIND HOMES AVAILABLE FOR SALE?

Most homes are in subdivisions, a term that derives from the real estate business of dividing a tract of land into separate lots that are suitable for individual ownership of new homes. Served by common sewer trunk lines, water and electric delivery systems, and interior streets, the subdividing of land through economies of scale has made home ownership a financially realistic option for most Americans. Two general categories of homes that are located in subdivisions may be available: pre-owned or newly constructed.

NEW SUBDIVISION HOMES

New subdivision homes are houses built mostly by one company offering a limited variety of floor plans. They may be constructed before being offered to buyers, or be sold before construction by display of model homes to prospective buyers. Some companies catering to more affluent customers offer custom homes that are built according to floor plans selected by each buyer. New subdivisions are often called planned developments because they offer a common design and architectural scheme with common areas shared by all homeowners, such as large entry streets with beautiful medians and, sometimes, gates, interior parks, and common landscaping. These planned subdivisions typically are governed by a **homeowner's association (HOA)** composed of residents who volunteer or are elected by owners within the subdivision. Monthly fees are collected from owners within the subdivision and are used to maintain the common facilities. Rules also are designed and enforced to maintain property values in the subdivision. For example, the parking of RVs, boats, or disabled cars on interior streets often is prohibited. There are differing views of the role of HOAs, and they are discussed later in this chapter under "Help from CC&Rs."

One advantage to buying a new subdivision home is that the developer-seller probably will offer a financing package (prearranged loan terms) for qualified (in terms of creditworthiness) buyers, sometimes at very favorable interest rates. One disadvantage is that the character of the neighborhood is not established because many homes are new, practically new, or may not be constructed until after the purchase is made. Subdivisions do evolve by gradually reflecting the nature of the persons and families that buy and then maintain the houses.

For information about the management of planned developments and other residential developments with common areas, *from the perspective of the community association*, visit their national headquarters at http://www.caionline.org/

Developers of new subdivision homes usually advertise heavily in local newspapers. Prospects who visit a new subdivision are usually given written data and shown furnished model homes. Once the decision to buy is made, the developer-seller provides many services to the buyer, assisting with the necessary paperwork and otherwise making the purchase experience as simple and expeditious as possible.

PRE-OWNED SUBDIVISION HOMES

Homes in mature subdivisions may have been sold several times over the years. As noted earlier, with the average length of employment shortening to perhaps seven years on average, it follows that homes will be owned by families for fewer years than ever before in the twentieth century. Mature subdivisions offer well-defined benefits because their character has become stabilized. Subdivisions become neighborhoods with well-known characteristics that influence the prices charged by sellers. Most available homes that are for sale are pre-owned.

Prospective buyers of pre-owned subdivision homes typically rely upon the services of real estate sales companies who hire *sales agents* to assist buyers and sellers. Prospective buyers often telephone for appointments with real estate companies whose signs they have seen in front of homes that are for sale in the desired area. Sales agents then provide prospective buyers with a plethora of information about homes that are for sale in the area. Once a home is selected, the sales agent assists the buyer in consummating the purchase.

CUSTOM HOME

A person who wants to build a custom home must do the preliminary work of locating an available lot. Some custom home builders have plans and lots available in new subdivisions and will build a custom home, provided it meets certain standards consistent with other houses in the area. Otherwise, the services of an architect or building designer, as well as those of a building contractor—someone licensed by the state to supervise all aspects of home construction—and lending institution must be obtained. Persons desiring a custom home can obtain names of possible builders from advertisements in the Yellow Pages and local newspapers as well as by contacting local architects and savings and loan associations for recommendations. Many prospective buyers of custom homes tour desirable areas of the community and obtain leads as to architects and contractors from homes that are under construction or already built. The decision to hire a contractor to build a custom home should be carefully made, preferably after interviewing previous customers of each contractor under consideration.

You should understand that general contractors are supervisors who usually perform no personal construction services. Rather, they select and hire subcontractors to grade the lot, pour the concrete foundation, frame and plumb the structure, etc. Perhaps that is why they are called "general" contractors—they act as generals commanding the workers. The building contractor you hire may not know any of the subcontractors who will perform the actual construction services. Thus, quality can vary widely. Furthermore, all subcontractors have the right to put liens or claims, called **mechanic's liens**, on your property if the general contractor you hired fails to make all payments. Mechanic's liens protect claims of workers for their wages by giving them claims on the owner's property.

If unpaid, the owner of the property is liable to the workers even if the owner already has paid the general contractor for the work done. Because the law does not require the general contractor even to visit your home while it is being constructed (although most do), you may rightfully come to feel neglected and even abused. These few summary points should serve to etch in your mind the rule: ALWAYS obtain the assistance of an attorney who has considerable experience in construction law and litigation before hiring any building contractor.

OTHER AVAILABLE HOMES

Three other types of homes are available in both the new and pre-owned markets: the cooperative apartment, the condominium, and the manufactured (mobile) home.

Cooperative Apartments

For **cooperative apartments**, a corporation is formed to acquire land and erect a multifamily (apartment) building. Interested persons buy sufficient shares (of capital stock) in the corporation to obtain rights to proprietary leases that entitle them to live in one of the units and to use the *common areas* (such as stairs, elevators, swimming pools, parking spaces, and gardens). The corporation arranges for a single mortgage loan on the property and pays taxes and other costs, allocating proportional responsibility to the resident shareholders. Any owner of shares may sell the shares and assign the lease to someone else, who is then entitled to reside in the seller's unit. Shares offered for sale often are advertised for direct sale or submitted to sales agents in the area.

Condominium

The **condominium** is a more common variety of home ownership than the cooperative. Each owner of a "condo" receives a deed conveying title to a particular unit and arranges individual financing for its purchase. Only the areas used in common are owned in common, typically by a corporation whose stock is owned by the unit owners. In some condominiums, the common areas are owned as a *tenancy-in-common* (a form of co-ownership) among all the unit owners. The corporation hires professionals to maintain the building exteriors and common areas, and the owners share the related costs. Condominiums vary in type from townhouses with common walls, to the John Hancock skyscraper in Chicago, with commercial establishments on lower floors and residences on upper floors.

All condominiums are governed by a homeowner's association (HOA) with a set of corporation by-laws and rules. Prudent buyers should carefully read all applicable governing rules, making certain there are no surprises (e.g., no dogs allowed in common areas) that would make their purchase undesirable.* Pre-owned condominiums are advertised individually and also offered through multiple-listing services as with single family detached residences.

Condominiums are especially attractive to people who must (or prefer to) travel extensively because all exterior maintenance is performed by the HOA. Many condominiums offer as many or even more amenities than typical homes.

For a wealth of practical and current housing information begin at the home page of the National Association of Home Builders (NAHB) at http://www.nahb.com

http://

---

*State laws require the seller of a condominium to submit copies of specified documents, such as by-laws, rules, and restrictions, to the buyer before the sale is complete to reduce the risk of unpleasant surprises later.

For example, many offer common areas that include pools, jacuzzi tubs, workout facilities, dog runs, etc. Historically, condominiums have not appreciated as rapidly as single-family homes. But recall, those people who must move every five to eight years from single family-homes probably will not enjoy any significant appreciation either.

Manufactured Homes

Manufactured homes are constructed in a factory and delivered to a lot in a specially designed subdivision or park. Once called mobile homes, they are available at prices starting near $25,000 and sometimes exceeding $100,000. Once they are placed in a park, owners have no expectation of moving them. This expectation is so rooted that one state enacted a statute requiring owners of mobile home parks to pay toward their tenants' relocation costs if their park is closed. Regardless of its helpful intent, the statute was declared unconstitutional.[1] Rent must be paid to the owner of the mobile home park for use of the lot upon which the home is placed. Because the homes are compact and relatively modest, and include much built-in furniture, they have a special appeal for budget-minded couples, both young and old. Financing is typically available only for shorter terms than customary for mortgage financing of conventionally built homes. The term of the loan may be as short as seven years with larger down payments (as much as one-third of the purchase price) than for standard homes. Dealers of mobile homes typically advertise in both the Yellow Pages and in local newspapers.

Because of a history of poor construction, sometimes causing bodily injury, as well as hard sale tactics, the entire manufactured home industry is regulated by federal statutes.[2] Related types of homes not in wide acceptance but nonetheless sometimes available are prefabricated and kit homes. The idea is to produce part or most of the components inexpensively on an assembly line, then to ship the components to their final site for assembly. Difficulties include compliance with local building codes and zoning requirements.

For a wide selection of information, search the Web under "manufactured homes." Many manufacturers and sales companies from around the nation promote their products online and provide useful data.

http://

WHAT FACTORS INFLUENCE HOME SELECTION?

Within a price range permitted by the buyer's budget, the most important factor in selecting a particular house from those available is usually its location. Location influences commuting time to work and shopping areas, availability of police and fire protection, utility services, refuse and sewer disposal facilities, school districts and houses of worship, ambulance and medical care services, access to public transportation and highways, proximity to public and private recreational facilities, and whether the home is in the path of community decline or growth. Specific location can indicate whether the neighborhood is deteriorating; whether surrounding properties are of comparable value; whether local traffic, noise, or commotion is excessive; whether airplanes fly low patterns overhead; whether factories with fumes, smoke, and noise are nearby; whether television reception is poor in the area or cable is available; whether neighbors are likely to be compatible socially and economically; whether there are deed restrictions and zoning regulations that increase or decrease values; whether ground waters are clean; whether high-voltage overhead electrical cables are nearby; whether the building is in a flood plain or vulnerable to earthquakes, and so forth. Some of these issues are not as obvious in their implications as you may think. For example, on the one hand, it is well established that electric power lines create electromagnetic field radiation (called EMFR); on the other hand, the effects on humans living nearby are in dispute. Most studies have focused on neighborhood electric power lines, which probably should be avoided if possible. Even so, EMFR, to a lesser degree and only for intermittent periods, is also created by home appliances, such as electric razors, hair dryers, toasters, food mixers, vacuum cleaners, electric radios, electric garage openers and, of course, computers.[3]

Another significant criterion for evaluating a house is the configuration of the house itself. Does the lot drain well? Is it located on a corner? Where does the sun shine in the morning and afternoon? Is there sufficient privacy? How old is the house? Are bathrooms and kitchen up-to-date and functional? What is the condition of the electrical system, the plumbing, and the heating and cooling systems? When must the roof be redone? Is the house well insulated? Does the house contain asbestos, radon gas, or lead in its paint or plumbing systems? Are the rooms adequate for storage, furniture, and appliances? A myriad of other common-sense questions should be considered. If you lack the necessary expertise to ask and answer such questions, get assistance from someone who knows how to help you. **Home inspection services**—professionals who evaluate and report upon all important aspects of a house—are widely available to assist buyers in making good decisions and are available by referral from sales agents or through advertisements in the Yellow Pages. (The legal obligation of sellers to reveal certain characteristics of their homes to prospective buyers is discussed later.) Prospective home buyers should remember one axiom of business: "Money is made on the buy"; in other words, buy wisely, and even if you do not plan to move from the house in the foreseeable future, "well bought is half-sold."

For information about home inspection services, begin with the National Association of Home Inspectors (NAHI) home page at http://www.nahi.org/

FIXER-UPPERS

A special category of pre-owned home may be appealing to certain budget-minded buyers who are handy with tools. **Fixer-uppers** are properties where building and landscaping have been allowed to deteriorate to some considerable degree. These properties are often sold through foreclosure sales and at auctions by government agencies. Although the price for a fixer-upper may seem very attractive, prospective buyers must be very careful to ensure that no serious and prohibitively expensive structural defects exist that make even the most modest price unacceptable. If the home suffers only superficial or limited deterioration, obsolescence, and disrepair, it may be a bargain for buyers who have the skill and the will to do most of the cleaning, painting, repairing, and planting themselves.

HOW DO REAL ESTATE AGENTS SERVE BUYERS AND SELLERS?

The real estate business is composed of *brokers* and *sales agents*.

Real estate brokers must obtain a license from the state that authorizes them to hire sales agents. Brokers need not be but often are corporations that hire many agents to perform the necessary services to sellers and buyers. Brokers act as managers and rarely meet with buyers or sellers whose personal contact almost

There is information about various real estate issues at the Lectric Library. http://www.lectlaw.com/ref.html

always is with a sales agent. **Real estate sales agents** also are licensed by the state, and perform all of the day-to-day services and provide information as necessary to bring sellers and buyers of homes together and to make sales transactions happen. The success of home purchasers and sellers is affected by the services they receive from real estate sales agents, and their role cannot be ignored.

Sales agents do not receive salaries from the brokerage firms that employ them. Instead they typically receive a portion, say 50 percent or more, of the sales commissions they generate. Thus, if a sales agent produces a commission of $12,000 by handling a home sale with a price of $200,000 (a 6 percent commission), he or she will be paid $6,000 by the broker, who will retain the other one-half. Top sales agents command commission splits with their brokers of 60 to 80 percent.

SERVICE TO SELLERS

An owner desiring to sell usually hires a real estate brokerage company by negotiating with a sales agent. The owner understands that all future dealings will be directly with the sales agent—none with the broker. The employment of the agent, who is called the **listing agent,*** is accomplished by using a form of employment contract that usually is presented to the homeowner by the agent. The employment contract, or listing, serves to hire the real estate broker (acting through the sales agent) to hunt for a suitable buyer.

The effect of the standard employment contract, or listing, subject to many regional variables, is that the prospective seller and the real estate agent exchange promises as follows: Seller promises to pay a commission of a negotiable percentage (often 6 percent) of the actual sales price if an acceptable offer to purchase is made by a qualified buyer (regardless of who finds the buyer) within a prescribed time period (often three to six months). The real estate broker promises to use "diligence" in hunting for a buyer. It is difficult, if not impossible, to prove in court that an incompetent agent failed to "use due diligence" in hunting for a buyer. That is why few sellers who become disenchanted with their listing agents sue them in court.

Rupert and Kimberly East signed a standard *exclusive listing* with Acme Real Estate for the sale of their home on specified terms. Shortly thereafter, at a social gathering, they met a couple—the Auburns—who were interested in buying a house similar to the East's. The Auburns came by and decided to make an offer to purchase it in an amount that was satisfactory to the Easts. Rupert telephoned their agent to cancel the listing because they had found their own buyer. Their sales agent, Sam Saltsman, responded: "Fine, you may mail me a check for the 6 percent commission you owe." Do Mr. and Mrs. East owe a commission even though their sales agent did no work and did not find the buyer?

---

*The term "listing" is a word of art the original source of which has eluded your authors. Colloquial information suggests that it originally referred to a "list" of homes that were available for sale in an area—the composite list being called "multiple listing." As a verb, "listing" meant adding a new seller's home to the list. An agent who persuades a new seller to engage his or her services uses a "listing agreement" and then is referred to as the "listing agent" or simply the "lister." The price the new seller hopes to obtain is called the "listing price." All of these usages appear to be accurate except when used to describe the listing agreement, which as indicated in the text is actually a variety of *employment contract*—a more daunting phrase.

Yes. The commission is owed because the variety of employment contract known as an **exclusive listing** requires payment of a commission regardless of who finds the buyer. Sometimes owners find their own buyers, sometimes buyers simply appear on their own accord, sometimes other sales agents find buyers, and, of course, sometimes the hired agent finds a buyer. In each of these situations, the commission is owed to the exclusive listing agent. Rupert and Kimberly would not owe any commission if they had asked for and signed a different kind of employment contract—an "exclusive-agency." **Exclusive-agency listings**, under which owners who find their own buyers do not pay commissions, are widely available to new sellers who are smart enough to ask for them. Such a listing is preferable from the seller's standpoint because, through luck or accident, a buyer may be found or appear without any agent.

As noted, listing agents promise to use diligence in hunting for a suitable buyer. This is accomplished by submitting data about the new seller's home to a regional database called the **multiple listing service**.* All real estate brokers subscribe to this service and thereby gain access to specific data (e.g., address, square footage, number of baths and bedrooms, all amenities, etc.) about all homes in the region that are "on the market" for sale. Thus, the subscribing broker has available for the firm's sales agents all of the information necessary to present to prospective buyers. Putting a home "into multiple listing" alone probably satisfies the promise by the listing agent to use due diligence. As a result, some "listing agents" never perform additional services to find a suitable buyer—a practice that always angers sellers who wait expectantly for "action" on their listings.

Although the terms of the agreement between seller and the listing brokerage firm are completely negotiable, as a practical matter most sellers routinely accept the deal as proposed by the listing agent. Curiously, real estate agents customarily do not promise to spend any specified amount of money on advertising, but prudent sellers can negotiate for that useful provision.

At the time a new seller hires a sales agent, a "listing price" will be agreed upon and stated in the listing form. Some agents earn the initial goodwill of prospective sellers by suggesting a very high "listing price," creating the impression that the home is worth more than might be the case. When the broker finds a purchaser who is willing to buy at a price lower than the listing price, and the owner accepts the offer, payment of the commission cannot be refused on the grounds that the broker failed to find a buyer at the listed price. Acceptance of the lower price effectively amends the listing (or employment contract) to provide for a commission based on the actual sales price. Indeed, the only reason to include a listing price in the listing agreement is to provide a measure of damages the agent might obtain if the seller should fire the agent and withdraw the residence from the market during the listing period. Absent a listing price, the discharged agent would be entitled to damages equal to the reasonable value of the services rendered to the date of termination. With a listing price, the discharged agent is entitled to damages equal to a stated percentage, often 5 percent, of the listing price. Thus sellers would be better off with no listing price in the listing agreement.

To view online listings visit
http://www.listinglink.com

http://

---

*Various companies already are online purporting to act as multiple listing services in that information about homes for sale across the United States is made available. This phenomenon is in its infancy as this text is written (1999) and, although promising, has not yet become effective. If curious, simply use your Web browser and search under "real estate" to review state-of-the-art advertisements and promotions.

Recall that the listing agreement is a fully negotiable employment contract. Before hiring a real estate broker to sell your home, you are well advised to negotiate for some, if not all, of the following provisions:

- The right to pay no commission if you find your own buyer. Often a potential buyer may transfer to your workplace or surface through recommendations of your friends and acquaintances.

- A short listing period, perhaps as little as 30 days, with the understanding it will be extended in 30-day increments if the agent is satisfactorily "pushing" the property. Remember, once your agent is hired for an extended period, there is no legal right to end the listing. How can you be sure your agent will provide good service?

- A reduced commission, perhaps 5 or even 4 percent, if the property is readily saleable and market conditions are good. Always calculate what percentage of your *equity* a 6 (or other) percent commission of the *sales price* represents. You will be surprised, and probably shocked. Use this information in negotiating for a reduced commission percentage rate.

- Restrictions on when sales agents and their prospects will be permitted to enter the house, especially if you are still residing there. You can require the presence of your agent on each occasion your house is shown to others. (The sign in front of your house can read "shown by appointment.") Or you can accept a lock box arrangement whereby any agent can enter at any time.

- A specified advertising budget, to be paid by the agent. Your Sunday newspaper carries many real estate advertisements, because they are effective. Make sure an ad for your house is professionally made and will appear there. Line ads are not considered expensive, and you could make your negotiations with the agent in this regard very persuasive by offering to pay one-half the budget. If one agent refuses to advertise, consider listing with a competing agent, of which there always are many. The more unique your home, the more useful is tailor-made advertisements.

- Electronic advertisements, including interior and exterior photographs, are becoming more popular and more effective as their availability gains recognition and acceptance. From the seller's standpoint, they can't hurt and will be offered by some agents in the area, especially if demanded during the negotiating process.

In addition to negotiating the terms of the listing agreement, and at the same time, prospective sellers should fully discuss each of the following matters with prospective listing agents:

- Ask for a sample of text of different advertisements that will be published in identified newspaper(s). Also ask for samples of information sheets that are placed in dispensing boxes in front of houses next to their proper "For Sale" signs. Ask how the information sheets will be distributed, and make sure they will contain all the relevant information about nearby shopping, transportation systems, schools, churches, parks, police and fire stations, and so forth.

- Will there be an agent tour? What steps will the listing agent take to ensure that most of the other agents in the area will attend the agent tour?

- How and when will the house be shown to potential buyers by all other agents? You do not want to have agents arriving with prospective buyers at unexpected times during your daily routine.

- A list of all repairs thought necessary to put the house in condition for sale. Also, obtain advice with regard to what disclosures about the condition of the house you will need to make in contracting with a buyer. (More about sellers' disclosures later in this chapter.) It will take you two weeks to get the house ready for sale, then sign the listing in two weeks when it is ready.

- What is the absolutely lowest price you should consider accepting? This will be useful later when your agent begins bringing you offers to consider. Do not disclose to your agent the actual lowest price you would accept, or any other information that might suggest you have an urgent need to sell.

- What is the estimate of the net cash proceeds from escrow, assuming various sales prices? This will avoid any surprises from exaggerated expectations concerning how much cash you ultimately will receive.

- What is the highest reasonably possible selling price, and how was it derived? Have the agent provide a list of all sales of comparable homes in your area within the past 12 months, indicating which ones were handled by the subject brokerage firm. This information is easily obtained by sales agents. Agents tend to specialize by geographical area (their "farm"), and agents who work successfully in your area will probably get better results sooner than agents who customarily work other areas.

- Will the seller be permitted to hold any earnest money deposit received? If not, why not? If it is deposited in an escrow or trustee account, it will be difficult for the seller to obtain it if the sale is not consummated. And will any earnest money deposit be restricted to a certified check or money order? If not, why not? How will the earnest money deposit be divided if the prospective buyer defaults (backs out) before escrow closes?

- How much effort will the agent who signs the listing personally expend? Will your agent accompany potential buyers or simply send them by? Or will your agent rely on other agents to sell the property, while spending his or her time obtaining new listings? Will your agent "**qualify**" each and every prospect to make sure they are financially able to buy your home, or are simply curious "lookers"?

- Is an immediate termite inspection advisable? If major repairs are to be made, shouldn't you know that before signing a contract obligating you to sell? If not, why not? Similar concerns exist about the condition of the roof or about major structural problems.

- What are the current terms of financing available for a buyer of your home? Should you offer an assumption of the existing loan and carryback of some of the unpaid balance? If financing is not available for the potential buyers of your home, should you consider a lease-option and make a quick deal? What will you owe your agent if you make a lease-option during the listing period? If you handle a lease-option arrangement, is it excluded from the listing?

- Is it really necessary to conduct an open house? (Many agents conduct open houses primarily to obtain listings from other persons in the neighborhood who may be considering selling. This technique is especially attractive to a modestly successful agent who happens to land one upscale listing. It may produce other upscale listings and generate considerable profits.) Most prospects do not spend hours slowly driving around the city hoping to see "open house" signs on desirable homes. Rather, they seek counsel from sales agents who know what's available and who can show the house to the prospect.

- Precisely what does the broker intend to do, step by step, in diligently hunting for a buyer? Will your agent exchange referrals with other brokers nationwide? Are new employment centers opening that may provide clues about potential buyers moving into your area? Will a handsome flyer or prospectus about your house be prepared and widely distributed to all other agents in the community?

A candid discussion of these topics with the prospective agent will illuminate many areas of concern and forestall potential misunderstandings.

Finally, do not sign a proffered listing agreement before obtaining the names and current addresses/telephone numbers of two or more former sellers. Ask the references if they were satisfied with the negotiating process; if they felt pressured to drop their price; if they thought the agent was working hard for them all the time; if they were surprised by closing costs and repairs they had to make; and if they would hire the agent again. In addition to obtaining references from former employers, you might consider asking prospective agents for their resumés, indicating their education and work experiences. After all, you routinely will be asked as much when applying for employment positions.

The greatest benefits from hiring an agent to assist in the sale of your home is the experience of the agent (1) in directing you how to prepare your home for sale, (2) in knowing and explaining the market data in general and how it specifically affects the price of your home, and (3) in aggressively urging all other agents in the community to show your home to their prospects, and providing them with a professional brochure of its features.

There are risks in hiring a listing agent. Your property may be placed in multiple listings and be quietly forgotten, with your agent doing nothing more than hoping that some other agent somewhere will stumble upon it (out of the thousands that are multiple-listed). If your agent knows what your absolute lowest possible acceptable price is, that too often will be the top offer you will receive. If your agent knows that your job has changed and you are desperate to sell, that information may find its way to prospective buyers who then will "bottom fish" (offer below-market prices). If no prospects appear as the weeks and months drift by, you cannot fire your listing agent for inactivity. If your listing agent is not competent and experienced, you may face problems with disclosing or withholding material information, with obtaining a reasonable termite clearance, and with demands by prospective buyers for repairs, fixups, and other costly changes. Care in employing a listing agent should be no less than the obvious care required in employing any professional person who will be charged with important responsibilities on your behalf.

SERVICE TO BUYERS

Real estate sales agents are authorized by law to solicit for new "listings" from prospective sellers. This often is referred to as the "listing" function. These agents often send flyers to homeowners asking if they will be selling soon and recommending themselves as agents. Sales agents also are authorized to take prospective buyers to and show homes that are on the market but that were listed by other agents, even from competing brokerage companies. This often is referred to as the "selling" function. By tradition, the commission paid by the seller is split evenly between the brokers in charge of the listing and selling functions.

It is important to distinguish between these two functions, and to understand how the seller's commission is distributed. An example may clarify this distinction.

> Sam Seller employed Larry Lister of Cold Realty to hunt for a buyer for his home on Shady Tree Lane, and promised to pay a 6 percent commission if a ready, willing, and able purchaser was found who agreed to pay a $200,000 purchase price. Sallie Saleslady noticed Sam's home in the electronic multiple listing service while she was sitting at her desk in the Tigar Realty Co. Sallie thought this might be the right home for Betty Buyer, with whom she had been working, and arranged to show Sam's home to her. Betty Buyer loved the home and asked Sallie to prepare an offer to purchase and handle all the necessary details. As a result, Betty bought Sam's home and a commission of $12,000 was payable. Who gets the money?

In the listing agreement, Sam promised to pay the brokerage firm, Cold Realty, the $12,000 commission. But since the buyer was found by Tigar Realty Co., it received one-half, $6,000, directly from Cold Realty. Cold Realty splits 50–50 with its agents, and so paid Larry Lister $3,000, his share. Tigar Realty, however, had agreed to a 60–40 split with its leading producers, and so paid $3,600 to Sallie for her efforts in finding the buyer, and kept $2,400 for itself. Thus it is said that finding a listing is worth one-half of the commission while finding a buyer is worth the other one-half. Sallie was representing the buyer, Betty, against the best interests of Sam Seller who, nevertheless, ends up paying her fee. Thus it is said that the buyer ordinarily pays no commission.*

With the understanding of how both listing and selling agents are paid, we can consider what services are provided.

The *listing agent* provides specific information about the homes for sale to the multiple listing service; causes a For Sale sign to be displayed on the property;

---

*Although the buyer pays no cash to any agent in the transaction, the buyer is paying the sales price. If the sales price was "inflated" by $12,000 in this example, the economic "loss" of the commission would fall upon Betty the buyer. For those of you who enjoy financial analysis, note that most of the purchase price is financed over many years—thus, Betty's economic "loss" is spread over the same period of time. The word *loss* is in quotation marks because it is descriptive—there is no loss when a valuable service is received for a fair price paid.

prepares a flyer or brochure for distribution to other agents who farm (specialize in) the area; and organizes an agent's tour of the home featuring refreshments and a semi-party atmosphere. The home then is officially "on the market." Interested persons may respond to the sign in the front yard and telephone the listing agent. The listing agent then becomes a selling agent, like Sallie Saleslady, and shows the house. If that buyer makes a purchase, it is called a *double-ender* because the listing agent and the selling agent are one and the same person, who collects "both ends" of the commission, or $6,000 in our preceding example. The agent in a double-ender is a *dual agent* representing both the seller and the buyer. This fact must be disclosed to the parties because there is a serious conflict of interest and the temptation is great for the agent to, for example, recommend a speciously low purchase price to the seller. On the other hand, an interested buyer might telephone any brokerage company in town, and one of their salespersons will show the house, just as Sallie showed the house that had been listed by Larry.

In either of the preceding situations, the agent representing the buyer (called the *buyer's agent*) will prepare a written offer to purchase, called a **deposit receipt**. The buyer's agent will negotiate with the seller's (listing) agent by exchanging counteroffers. Once a real estate purchase agreement is signed by seller and buyer, the agents will play a less active roll. The agents will assist in arranging for a home inspection, a termite inspection, and any other service providers who may be needed. Sellers and buyers typically rely on their agents for a wide variety of suggestions and information, but should also read all documents and give the transaction the personal attention that its importance deserves.

Real estate brokerage companies, quick to seize an opportunity presented by the Internet, are beginning to offer concierge services to buyers and homeowners for no charge. Also called "home provider" services or "home-link," the concierge service provides homeowners with references to all kinds of service providers, for repairs, cleaning, gardening, child care/house sitting, or perhaps legal, accounting or any other service—all at discount prices. Home products also may be obtained through these services. Service providers pay real estate brokerage companies a fee, anywhere from $500 to $15,000 every three months to place an advertising "banner" on the company's Web site. Thus homeowners have a single source to find a provider for any service or product that is desired. Real estate companies expect to attract new listings, produce advertising income, and obtain referral fees from providers. Consumer advocates express concern that the quality of services and products referred to home owners may be lacking.[4]

HOW IS AN OFFER TO PURCHASE A HOME MADE?

An offer to purchase real property, such as a home, should be made in writing. Otherwise, under the statute of frauds, it is unenforceable should either party dispute its terms or even deny its existence. The offer must state essential terms, such as a description of the property, the purchase price, and payment terms. The offer is usually made on a form document called a **purchase agreement and deposit receipt**, or simply deposit receipt.* The deposit receipt is a standard form with

*The term "deposit receipt" is a misnomer because, once signed by the parties, it is a binding contract between seller and buyer. A purchase contract also serves the dual role of acting as a receipt for any refundable "good faith deposit" that may accompany it, hence, the derivation of its euphemistic phrase "deposit receipt."

many blanks to be completed by the buyer with the assistance of the real estate agent. The deposit receipt cannot be drafted by a real estate agent because that would constitute the illegal practice of law. But filling in blanks in a form contract is permitted.

The process of negotiating back and forth on behalf of the seller and buyer, thereby avoiding the intransigence that typically is created by eye-to-eye dealings, is the single most valuable service provided by agents. Some contend that preparation of the written purchase agreement is the primary service rendered for sellers and buyers, but attorneys could easily be hired to perform that service for considerably less than a real estate commission—and may even recommend that the contract be bypassed. The role of attorneys in sales transactions is discussed later in this chapter.

WHAT IS THE EFFECT OF AN ACCEPTED OFFER?

When a written purchase contract is prepared for and signed by the buyer, it becomes a formal *offer to purchase** and will be delivered to the seller's agent.

A good-faith deposit made by the buyer usually accompanies a purchase agreement. In theory, the deposit is to assure the seller that the buyer is not a mere "tire kicker" and intends to purchase the property. **Liquidated damages** are an amount of money agreed upon between contracting parties to fairly represent all losses of the innocent party if the contract is wrongfully broken. Such a provision is common and eliminates the necessity of litigation, since a solution already has been agreed upon. The earnest money serves as liquidated damages in the event of a broken contract. If the buyer wrongfully fails to complete the purchase, the deposit can be retained by the seller as liquidated damages for the breach of the contract of purchase. There is no legal requirement that a buyer include a deposit with the offer, but it is a customary sign of serious intent and ability to buy, and a seller would most likely refuse to accept an offer without one. Often the earnest money deposit will approximate 1 percent of the purchase price. But, there is one "fly in the ointment" for the seller who attempts to retain the earnest money deposit after a buyer defaults.

Sam Seller signed a contract to sell his home to Betty Buyer. A $1,500 earnest money deposit had accompanied the deposit receipt and was on deposit at the Acme Escrow and Title Company. Then Betty found a home she liked better and bought it. Sam never saw her again. A few days later Sam telephoned Acme and asked them to send the now-forfeited $1,500 deposit to him. To his dismay, ACME declined and referred him to the listing agent, Larry. Sam immediately called Larry asking about the money. What do you suppose Larry said?

In all likelihood, Larry said, "Like it says in the listing, I get one-half of the forfeited deposit money for my troubles in finding the buyer." Sam learned, by reference to the listing contract, that Larry was indeed entitled to one-half of the money for finding the "deadbeat" buyer. If Sam had bothered to read the listing form before signing it, he could have deleted that provision.

---

*An offer confers upon the seller a power to create a binding contract, simply by acceptance (signing the offer). Usually, the seller will make a responsive counteroffer, and after reciprocal negotiations a final contract will emerge.

Audra made a written, signed offer to purchase Sam Seller's home. Sam signed and returned the offer, thereby creating a binding contract. Subsequently, pending "close of escrow" (the usual moment when ownership passes to the buyer), Sam refused to complete the transaction. Audra believed that Sam did this because he found out that his house was worth a lot more money than his selling price. Audra contacted her attorney. What advice will she receive?

Audra's attorney will advise her that she has two legal remedies. In the first, she can proceed *in equity* and request the court to order Sam Seller to comply with the agreement. This remedy is called *specific performance* and is available when dollar damages would be inadequate. Money damages would be inadequate here because every parcel of land is considered by the courts as unique (no two parcels can be in the same place) and cannot be substituted for in the marketplace, as can, for example, an automobile. When Audra won such a lawsuit, the court would order Sam to convey ownership as promised. Audra, of course, would have to pay the price, as promised.

In the alternative remedy, Audra can sue *at law* and request the court to assess damages against Sam in an amount equal to her out-of-pocket expenses plus the benefit of her bargain, if any. (This "benefit of the bargain" could be the difference between the low purchase price of the home and its higher fair market value.) Audra's decision would depend primarily on how unique the property was to her as compared to the amount of monetary damages she could recover.

In addition, and as a separate matter, if Sam Seller had "listed" the property with a real estate brokerage firm, he would be obligated to pay the firm a commission, even though the sale was never completed. This is so because the broker had found in Audra a "ready, willing, and able buyer" who had signed a written offer to buy on terms originally specified by the seller. Listing agreements typically contain language protecting real estate agents from nonpayment by sellers who change their minds and withdraw their properties from the market either before or after signing sales contracts. If sellers want an "out" in their listing agreements, they must negotiate for them before they are signed.

WHAT ARE DISCLOSURE LAWS?

In the common law, the seller of a home is not required to disclose patent (visible) defects to a buyer, the theory being that the buyer should be alert enough to see and discover such defects. Latent (hidden) defects that were known to the seller need not be revealed; if asked, the seller cannot lie, but ordinary sales "puffing" is legal. In a general sense, the common law holds "let the buyer beware." Under this version of the common law, many cases evolved that distinguish between those lies by sellers for which there was liability, and those for which there was not.

C.J. Thomas and his wife Joan were home when their real estate sales agent brought a prospective buyer, Art Shab, for a viewing. During

For links on many environmental issues that relate to housing and development, visit http://www.envl-info.com

introductions, Art asked whether the neighbors ever made unusually loud noises or otherwise caused problems, and whether the house was insulated. C.J. answered that the neighbors "were quiet" and "yes, the building was well insulated." In truth, as C.J. knew, the neighbors were extremely boisterous, often screaming profanities at each other in the early hours, and their children were known to break neighborhood windows with BB guns, empty garbage cans over neighbors' fences, and race their motorcycles up and down the street. Likewise, as C.J. also knew, the house was not insulated. Art purchased the home and shortly thereafter learned the truth about the neighbors and the insulation. He contacted his attorney seeking to revoke the purchase, claiming fraud. Will Art Shab succeed?

Art will succeed if the seller (1) made a representation (2) of a material fact, (3) knowing the statement to be false, (4) which asserted fact was reasonably relied upon by the buyer, and (5) induced the buyer to consummate the purchase. Under the common law, the falsehood concerning the "quiet neighbors" is irrelevant because it is only a personal opinion. What is admirable to some is anathema to others. However, the presence or absence of insulation is a fact. If the absence of insulation would be obvious (patent) to an ordinary layman, Art would again be out of luck—a buyer cannot close his or her eyes to the obvious and then complain after the sale. But the presence or absence of insulation is usually not readily ascertainable. Therefore, Art may pursue either of two common-law remedies. He may seek to recover the cost to cure the defect (by installing insulation) as compensatory damages, and he could also seek, and might receive, an additional sum as exemplary or punitive damages because of the intentional deception or fraud by C.J.* Alternatively, Art may *rescind* the purchase, give up possession of the house to C.J., and receive reimbursement for his down payment and other monies expended in the purchase. This is the remedy authorized by the New York court in the *Stambovsky* case you will find at the end of this chapter.

Note that the remedies available to Art are based on the common-law tort called *misrepresentation* (also called *fraud and deceit*). Some states have modern disclosure statutes, discussed shortly, that change the common law under which C.J. would be responsible for both misrepresentations.

Following are examples of statements of personal opinion, often exaggerated. A seller may make them to a prospective buyer without fear of liability for damages or of a demand for rescission:

- "This house is really worth much more than I'm asking."
- "This is the finest home in the area."
- "This is the best-constructed home you will ever live in."
- "Will taxes go up in this neighborhood? Never!"
- "The value of this house will increase at least 5 percent per year."

Statements such as the following *may* justify a rescission or action for damages, if they are false:

---

*Some states, such as Washington, do not permit the award of punitive damages. Punitive damages were explained fully in Chapter 7.

- "A new roof was installed on this house two years ago."
- "During the rainy season, all excess surface water drains off almost immediately."
- "There are no termites, no dry rot."
- "The foundation was not damaged by the earthquake."
- "There is no asbestos in the house."

A more difficult question arises when a seller, knowing of some important latent defect, such as a fractured foundation, simply doesn't say anything to the prospective buyer. No lies are told, but important information is withheld. Under the common law and in some states, a seller has no general duty to speak. The rationale is that the buyer is free to investigate and to inquire; if asked, the seller's answers must be truthful. The problem is that most buyers are not qualified or prepared to ask all possibly relevant questions. For example, how many buyers would be likely to ask if there is radon gas emission within the premises or if the neighbors have threatened to sue about location of the new backyard fence, or if there is landfill on the property?

As the twenty-first century begins there is a new trend under which state laws require sellers to disclose increasing amounts of information, not limited to the traditional material questions of fact. The real estate industry largely favors this trend. Why would an industry favor laws that increase the disclosure burdens (and liabilities) of their customers-sellers? Licensed real estate agents carry information back and forth between negotiating buyers and sellers who almost never meet eye-to-eye. Salesmanship and negotiating success require that agents serve as buffers between and out of the presence of sellers and buyers, alternately conveying persuasive information back and forth. Thus, when buyers believe they have been lied to by the seller, *they normally sue the sales agents as well*, contending that the agent also knew, or should have known, of the false information. The National Association of Realtors™ (NAR) is a huge trade association that exists for the purpose of serving its members. In so doing it continually lobbies for new laws to protect its members from lawsuits, among other things. Thus, it favors laws that shift burdens of disclosure from sales agents to sellers by creating legal defenses for agents. This influence, and the push for consumer protection, have created a recent trend called "let the seller beware" which began in California. Under relatively new laws, all sellers of homes are required by statute to disclose a great deal of specific information about the property they offer for sale. In theory, the buyer is entitled to be informed of virtually anything that may influence the value or subjective desirability of the property about to be purchased. Thus informed, the real estate agent is off the hook and unlikely to be sued after a buyer discovers some bothersome defect. Sellers, however, can be and are sued if they fail to disclose all specified information or if their disclosures are inaccurate.

The trend of law requires the seller to disclose, in writing and as soon as practicable before close of escrow, information that is either known to, or *can be ascertained by*, the seller. For example, one category of disclosure requires preparation of a checklist of items on the premises, such as a range, dishwasher, washer/dryer hookup, burglar alarm, and so forth. Another category of disclosure requires notice to the buyer if any of the systems or appliances are not in good working order. Yet another category requires notice of any defects or malfunctions in the roof,

For wide-ranging information *from the perspective of real estate agents*, visit http://www.newREALTOR.com/

ceiling, floor, foundation, driveway, plumbing, sewer/septic system, etc. A final category calls for disclosure of general knowledge the seller has about any easements, absence of a building permit for any additions that have been made, a landfill under the house, settling or sliding incidents, flooding or drainage problems, zoning violations, and even neighborhood noise problems. Furthermore, both the seller's agent and any buyer's agent must inspect the property and report to the prospective buyer any problems they observe. Unlike the seller, if the agent does not observe a defect, he or she is not responsible to discover and disclose it.

If the seller is negligent or dishonest in making any disclosure that later comes to the buyer's attention, a suit for money damages is authorized by statute. The sale, however, cannot be rescinded (undone).[5]

Brent Lanfield and his wife Lorri, having lived frugally for several years while accumulating sufficient money for a down payment, purchased their first home from the Maxwell family. A month after escrow closed, while Lorri was mowing the lawn, a next-door neighbor dropped by, introduced himself, and asked, "Did you know that the Maxwell's grandson committed suicide in the upstairs bedroom of your new house?" Brent and Lorri were shocked by this discovery, and in the ensuing weeks became increasingly ill at ease because of it. They consulted Ms. Monica Smith, attorney at law, for advice. Should the law provide the Lanfields with a remedy against the Maxwells?

It is unfortunately true that occurrence of a human being's death in a house can have an adverse effect on its future resale value. In times past, for some people, a house wasn't a home unless and until both births and deaths had occurred within its walls. Today, rightly or wrongly, knowledge of a natural death from old age may affect potential buyers differently than death by suicide. Death on the premises from any cause may adversely affect the willingness of some people to purchase the property. Under common-law principles, the Maxwells probably had no duty to reveal the fact of their grandson's death because it was not a material defect in the real property as distinguished from the subjective attitudes of members in the buying public. For example, nondisclosure of a nearby tuberculosis clinic provides no common-law remedy for a buyer who is distressed by its presence and who would have offered less purchase money if the truth had been known. TB clinics do not distribute contagion and subjective thoughts to the contrary are irrelevant. However, in states where the common law has been modified by comprehensive disclosure statutes, sellers must disclose the occurrence of prior deaths from any cause (except AIDS), or face the likelihood of an action for damages measured by the impact of such fact upon the market value of the property.

Justin and Michelle Goodbright, with two daughters ages 8 and 10, were especially attracted to the excellent schools that were located near the Waterford subdivision. After searching for months, they finally found and purchased a "custom" home at 2204 Shady Tree Court for $345,000. Unbeknownst to them, Rodney Weasel, a former convict who was twice convicted of sexual offenses involving minor children, was living nearby at 2214 Shady Tree Court. Was the seller, or the seller's agent, required to inform the Goodbrights of this, to them shocking, bit of information?

Under Megan's Law, as discussed earlier in Chapter 6, police routinely notify residents in neighborhoods of the residency of sexual predators. Notification is passive in some communities (available by telephone) or active (delivered door-to-door) in others. A seller may or may not be aware of the nearby residence of a sexual predator. Furthermore, if such a disclosure is made to a prospective buyer like the Goodbrights, surely the sale will not occur. Should the financial ramifications of where a sex predator chooses to live fall upon the shoulders of his neighbors? Should an agent, who is in the business of knowing what is going on relative to market values in the area, be excused from responsibility to tell buyers while the seller is not?

Relative to Megan's Law, the National Association of Realtors lobbies for laws that straddle the fence by requiring disclosure to the buyer only of the police telephone number (or other source) to obtain the addresses of sexual predators. If prospective buyers ask the real estate sales agent who is showing the home, "Are there any sexual predators nearby?" the NAR position is to answer, "You can check by calling 555-6463 or by . . . ." After doing this, no further disclosure need be made.

Future homeowners and sellers should be alarmed that the value of all homes in the vicinity would drop substantially on the happenstance of a convict moving nearby. If the notoriety through posting of pictures and shunning, if not ridicule, drives convicts from subdivisions in the suburbs, the problem may be transferred to renters. That is, convicts may be effectively pushed into the large, highly populated and densely housed cities, as renters, where their anonymity is possible. Under that scenario, the attendant risks of harm will have been shifted from the children of homeowners in the suburbs to the children of renters in the cities.

Laws about home ownership and real estate can be found under the key word "real property" at the WWW Virtual Law Library, main index: http://www.law.indiana.edu/law/v-lib/lawindex.html or at http://www.law.cornell.edu/index.html

How Can a Buyer Finance Purchase of a Home?

Most buyers do not have the cash to pay the entire purchase price of a home. Even if they did, they may prefer to make a relatively low down payment and borrow the balance of the purchase price, because they can then invest the rest of their savings elsewhere. The assumption is that with climbing wages or salaries, it will become progressively easier to pay off the fixed amount of the loan as time goes by.

Buyers desiring to borrow money to purchase a home will be required to sign, and to be legally bound by, two very important documents: the promissory note and the mortgage.

The Promissory Note

A **promissory note** evidences the loan (see Exhibit 12–2). It is signed by the borrower, called the **maker**, and delivered to the lender, called the **payee**, when the

Exhibit 12–2: Example of Promissory Note for $100,000

PROMISSORY NOTE
SECURED BY DEED OF TRUST

$100,000   June 1, 200_

FOR VALUE RECEIVED, I PROMISE TO PAY TO _____
(the lender/payee) _____, OR ORDER, AT _____
(lender's address) _____ THE PRINCIPAL SUM OF $100,000, WITH
INTEREST FROM THIS DATE UNTIL PAID AT THE RATE OF _____ PERCENT A YEAR ON THE
BALANCE REMAINING FROM TIME TO TIME UNPAID. PRINCIPAL AND INTEREST SHALL BE DUE
AND PAYABLE IN MONTHLY INSTALLMENTS OF $_____, OR MORE,* COMMENCING
ON THE _____ DAY OF _____, 200_, AND CONTINUING THEREAFTER UNTIL THE PRINCIPAL
AND INTEREST ARE FULLY PAID.

UPON ANY DEFAULT IN THIS NOTE OR IN THE TERMS OF THE DEED OF TRUST SECURING THIS
LOAN, THE UNPAID PRINCIPAL AND ACCRUED INTEREST SHALL AT ONCE BECOME DUE AND
PAYABLE, WITHOUT NOTICE, AT THE OPTION OF THE HOLDER OF THIS NOTE.

MAKER AGREES TO PAY COURT COSTS AND REASONABLE ATTORNEY FEES INCURRED BY
PAYEE IN CONNECTION WITH THE ENFORCEMENT OF THIS NOTE.

IF ANY MONTHLY INSTALLMENT IS RECEIVED BY PAYEE MORE THAN 10 DAYS AFTER ITS
DUE DATE, LATE CHARGES OF _____ PERCENT OF SAID PAYMENT, BEING THE SUM OF
$_____ EACH PAYMENT, ALSO WILL BE DUE AND PAYABLE.

PRIVILEGE IS RESERVED TO MAKE ADDITIONAL PRINCIPAL PAYMENTS NOT TO EXCEED A
TOTAL OF $_____ IN ANY TWELVE-MONTH PERIOD DURING THE FIRST 36 MONTHS
OF THIS LOAN.

                                              _____
                                    /s/   Maker

---

*The phrase "or more" gives the borrower the option to make additional payments of principal. Technically, if the phrase is not included in the note, the loan is said to be "locked in," meaning that the borrower cannot make larger or additional monthly payments to retire the debt earlier. However, most states have declared that "locked in" home-purchase loans are against public policy, and unenforceable; therefore, lenders customarily add a provision, such as found at the bottom of this exemplar note, specifically authorizing additional principal payments in specified amounts.

sale is completed. As evidence of the debt, the note contains important information pertaining to the loan. The note is not a contract, rather it is evidence of the existent of a debt. The most important information it contains is:

- The names of the maker and the payee.
- The amount of the debt.
- The interest rate.
- The amount of the monthly payments (of principal and interest).
- The due date of payments.
- The delinquency date of payments after which a penalty is charged.
- The penalty for delinquent payments.
- The obligation of the debtor to pay creditor's collection and attorney fees, if applicable.

The Mortgage

The lender will not trust the borrower as the sole source for repayment of the loan. Too much money is involved. The lender will require the home to be put up as **collateral**, or security. If the borrower *defaults* (fails to make the proper monthly payments in repayment of the loan), the lender may take the home, sell it, and apply the proceeds of the sale to pay off the balance of the loan. This procedure is called **foreclosure**. The document that establishes the home as collateral is called a **mortgage**. The borrower or debtor is called the **mortgagor**; the lender or creditor is called the **mortgagee**.* Most home loans are paid on time, although the national rate of foreclosures fluctuates considerably from year to year.

When the home mortgage loan is completely paid off by the homeowner, the lender will return the mortgage to the borrower, who then may "burn the mortgage" or, perhaps, frame it. In the case of a deed of trust, the full repayment will be evidenced by a *deed of reconveyance*, or simply "recon" as it is called. In both situations, the lender also will return the original promissory note to the borrower, marked "paid in full."

What if a Home Owner Defaults on Monthly Loan Payments?

Upon default by the owner, the lender may simply do nothing for awhile, giving the homeowner extra time to pay, or may start foreclosure proceedings. Both deeds of trust and mortgages contain many formal promises of the homeowner, such as to pay property taxes as they come due, to keep casualty insurance in force, to maintain the property, and to comply with all applicable laws. The mortgage lenders require these promises because they may have to foreclose on the property in the future and want it to be in good condition at that time.

A breach of any of these promises or of the promise to make monthly payments is called a *default*, for which the lender's basic remedy is foreclosure. Lenders do not like foreclosure any more than borrowers do. As a practical matter, long before foreclosure will be commenced by an unpaid lender, many attempts will be made to help solve the debtor's financial problem.

If the remedy of foreclosure becomes necessary, most lenders will choose foreclosure by private sale, which is called **nonjudicial foreclosure**, under which no court proceedings are necessary. Mortgages (and deeds of trust) contain a provision, called the *power-of-sale clause*, that authorizes a private foreclosure sale without court supervision. The date and place where the foreclosure sale will occur must be advertised in a local newspaper, and a notice will be posted in the county courthouse. Before the sale, the homeowner may *reinstate* the loan by paying all delinquent monthly payments as well as late-payment charges and any costs and fees to date. This valuable **right of reinstatement** exists even though the borrower may have agreed within the terms of the promissory note that upon

---

*Not all states use the mortgage, or real mortgage as it is sometimes called. Other states use a "deed of trust" to accomplish the same result. The debtor is called the *trustor* and the lender the *beneficiary*. Even in these states, the deed of trust is usually called a mortgage. There are technical differences between mortgages and deeds of trust that need not concern home buyers and sellers. Both documents serve to empower lenders to foreclose upon a home as indicated above.

default the entire unpaid balance becomes immediately due and payable. Such a provision is called an **acceleration clause** (because the loan due date is accelerated to the present), but its impact is overridden by the right of reinstatement.

If the defaulting homeowner does not reinstate (or, alternatively, completely pay off) the loan, a **foreclosure sale** will occur after about four months from the date the borrower's default was formally recorded. At the sale, the trustee accepts the highest cash bid and conveys title to the successful buyer by deed. If no bidders offer cash in at least the amount of the unpaid balance of the mortgage loan, the lender will bid its debt, that is, cancel its loan in exchange for ownership of the property. Thus, the lender either obtains payment of its loan in full from some cash bidder, or cancels its loan and acquires ownership of the house.

Houses owned by institutional lenders that have been acquired through foreclosure are called **real estate owned (REOs)** and make attractive purchase opportunities for home buyers. Oftentimes institutional owners of REOs will provide buyers with attractive financing to complete the purchase, as well as keep the price at an attractive level. These REO owners are not in the business of owning homes, and thus will work with interested home buyers who may "take them off our hands."

Sometimes homes are sold, before foreclosure occurs, for less than the unpaid balance of their original mortgages in what are called **short sales**. A short sale is any sale during foreclosure where the asking price is less than the unpaid amount of the mortgage on the home. Short sales were frequent in the early 1990s when home prices fell, leaving many people saddled with homes worth less than the mortgages they owed. Many simply "walked away," leaving the banks with the choice of proceeding through foreclosure and then selling the homes as REOs, or simply accepting short sales during foreclosure to cut their losses.

Homeowners who are not making their monthly mortgage payments receive advance notice of the date and place of their foreclosure sale, and are entitled to remain in possession of the home until the sale takes place and a new owner of the property takes possession.

Proceeds of foreclosure sales go to the creditor to satisfy the homeowner's debt. Any excess (unlikely), of course, belongs to the homeowner whose home was sold. But if there was any significant potential excess (i.e., equity) at the time of the foreclosure sale, it is unlikely the loan would have been permitted to remain in default.

The creditor may be entitled to a **deficiency judgment**, a court judgment against the debtor in an amount equal to the difference between the unpaid mortgage balance and the fair market value of the property. This represents the amount of money lost by the creditor as a result of the foreclosure. But such a judgment can be obtained only through a court-ordered and supervised foreclosure called **judicial foreclosure**, and most lenders prefer nonjudicial foreclosures by private sale because they are quicker, less expensive, and don't require the services of an attorney. Furthermore, following judicial foreclosure, the debtor has one year within which to reclaim the property—called the one-year **right of redemption**—by fully reimbursing the person who made the winning bid at the judicial-foreclosure sale. So the only advantage to a judicial foreclosure is the possibility of a deficiency judgment, which could be uncollectible anyway (because the debtor lacks funds or assets).

Sometimes borrowers facing foreclosure offer a deed to the property to the lender to avoid the bad-credit implications of foreclosure. Such a deed is called a *deed in lieu of foreclosure.* Although these are more common in commercial property finances, they can offer advantages and disadvantages to other borrowers and lenders. From the homeowner's perspective, a deed in lieu of foreclosure can avoid the impact of a foreclosure upon his or her credit history. On the other hand, unless otherwise agreed, possession must be given immediately to the lender instead of several months later, following foreclosure sale. A deed in lieu of foreclosure also cancels any possibility of a deficiency judgment by the lender. From the lender's perspective, there is an advantage in that the delay and possible deterioration of the property while foreclosure is pending are avoided. If no deficiency judgment is possible or desirable, the deed in lieu of foreclosure should be satisfactory. However, the lender acquiring title by a deed in lieu of foreclosure takes the property subject to any junior liens, such as a mechanic's lien, an unpaid home-equity loan, or a carryback mortgage, that are on the property. Such liens would be wiped out if title were obtained by foreclosure sale. The decision to use a deed in lieu of foreclosure should be supported by professional advice.

State **homestead** laws do not apply to home buyers who fail to make payments required under purchase-money mortgages. Rather, these laws are designed to protect the family home from other, unsecured creditors.* State homestead laws vary in many details, including the scope of protection they afford homeowners.** The purpose of all homestead laws is to protect a family's ability to obtain a place of residence free from the threat of existing creditors.

TYPES OF FINANCING

There are three general sources of financing available for home buyers: new financing, assumption of existing financing, and seller's financing. We discuss these alternatives in order.

New Loans

Several different types of new, or original, loans are available to persons who desire to purchase a home. Most loans are made by savings and loan associations, banks, mortgage brokers, and mortgage bankers. **Mortgage brokers** prepare loan packages (applications and other documents) for borrowers, which they send to other lenders who actually advance the funds and make the loan. These brokers often work with a pool of many lenders and try to find the most attractive loan terms for borrowers. **Mortgage bankers**, on the other hand, make loans that they may later resell for cash, which is used again as working capital.

All lenders supply the information and forms necessary to apply for a mortgage loan. Usually loan application fees, and sometimes appraisal charges, must be paid even if the applicant fails to qualify for, or abandons, the *loan commitment.*

---

*State homestead laws currently in force should not be confused with a series of United States Homestead Acts beginning in 1862, which gave clear title to 162 acres of federal public land to any person who occupied and cultivated the land for five years. By the 1950s, the federal government had thus given away about 250,000,000 acres of land west of the Mississippi River.

**For example, in California a creditor can cause a forced sale of the debtor's family home, but the first net proceeds (above the purchase-money mortgage) up to $45,000 (for a married couple) go to the debtor and can be used to purchase a substitute home. Any excess goes to the creditor. See California Code of Civil Procedure, § 704 *et. seq.* In Florida, on the other hand, regardless of the value of the residence, no sale can be forced during the lifetime of the debtor. See Donna L. Seiden, "An Update on the Legal Chameleon: Florida's Homestead Exemption and Restrictions." 40 *University of Florida Law Review* 919 (1988). It is noted that O. J. Simpson moved from California to Florida and purchased an expensive home before the conclusion of the civil trial that assessed damages of $35 million against him for the wrongful deaths of Nicole Simpson and Ronald Goldman.

A loan commitment is a lender's written agreement to make a loan to the borrower upon specified terms and conditions. But lenders do not ordinarily make loan commitments until the buyer has signed a purchase agreement. Then the prospective lender can have the home appraised and make other lending evaluations. However, it is increasingly popular for prospective buyers to get either **pre-approved** or **pre-qualified** for financing. For pre-approval, lenders will require a credit check and often written verification of employment. Pre-qualification is an estimate of the borrowing power of the prospective buyer based upon hypothetical information. Neither is a legal commitment by the lender to make a loan. Only a written loan commitment is binding. However, pre-approval and pre-qualifying are useful because they tend to assure sellers that the buyer is financially able to purchase the home that is for sale.

Loan terms are said to be completely negotiable, but in reality lenders advertise the terms of loans they are willing to make and rarely depart from such limitations. Nevertheless, astute borrowers who take the time to comparison-shop for available financing often save many dollars. Many mortgage brokers and even lenders advertise online the up-to-the-hour terms of available loans and offer assistance in making applications. Lenders compete aggressively to make loans to home purchasers, who are well advised to shop and to fully discuss the opportunities with their sales agent.

Once loans are made (or "originated") in the primary market—that is, the market composed of savings and loan associations, banks, and others that issue new loans—they are sold to buyers in the secondary mortgage market, which is a market of agencies and buyers who are competing to purchase new loans. Selling home loans gives lenders the cash with which to make additional new loans to buyers in the primary mortgage market. The major buyers in the secondary mortgage market are government agencies known widely by their acronyms, **Fannie Mae (FNMA)**, **Freddie Mac (FHLMC)**, and **Ginnie Mae (GNMA)**.* Since these buyers purchase home mortgages, they can specify the terms of the loans that they will purchase, by interest rate, length for repayment, loan-to-value ratio, qualifications of borrower, etc. Nonconforming loans will not be purchased. Institutions then will make only those kinds of loans they can sell in the secondary market. These guidelines by mortgage buyers are regularly reviewed and updated to keep pace with changing market conditions and emerging social policies.

Buying loans is one way these three agencies—FNMA, FHLMC, and GNMA—fulfill their responsibility to stabilize the mortgage-money market. For example, when money is "tight" (difficult to borrow and with rising interest rates), these agencies purchase loans from lenders, thereby making more cash available to them for new loans. When money is "loose" (easy to borrow and with declining interest rates), these agencies will sell loans at attractive prices, thereby taking money out of effective circulation. Such transactions help prevent wide fluctuations in interest rates that would endanger the health of the economy.

---

*Federal National Mortgage Association, Federal Home Loan Corporation, and Government National Mortgage Association, respectively. These quasi-governmental agencies buy and sell mortgages to influence interest rates and to provide for the availability of funds for new mortgage lending. For example, if Fannie Mae announced that it would purchase mortgage loans made to recent college graduates for 100 percent of the purchase price of homes they bought, with interest at 7 percent, banks would immediately make such loans. Thus, public policy is influenced by the secondary mortgage market.

Well-informed real estate agents check the fluctuations in the mortgage markets every day, and especially keep abreast of trends, all to help home buyers and sellers make smart decisions.

Conventional Loans. A conventional loan is one in which the terms are not directly influenced by government regulations or subsidies. The bank that is not going to sell its mortgages can make the loan on any terms it desires. Such a lender is called a **portfolio lender** because the loan is retained in the lender's own portfolio of outstanding loans. Lenders usually require a larger down payment for these loans than for loans to be sold.

Most conventional loans are, however, sold in the secondary market, in which case the buyer must qualify for the guidelines of Fannie Mae or Freddie Mac. These guidelines declare that if the down payment is less than 20 percent, the buyer must purchase **private mortgage insurance (PMI)** to guarantee the loan purchaser against loss in case of default by the homeowner/borrower. The premium for PMI is collected monthly along with principal and interest payments. Thus, PMI achieves the same security for the ultimate holder of the home buyer's mortgage loan as does government insurance, as explained shortly. In effect, mortgage buyers invest in risk free mortgages—they are either paid by the homeowner or by an insurance company.

Redlining is a prohibited practice by a few lenders designed to avoid making loans to minority persons. The word is derived from a practice of drawing red circles around minority neighborhoods, especially any areas in which repayment histories have been poor. Excuses are used to justify making loans in those redlined areas.

Federal Housing Administration (FHA) Loan. In FHA loans, repayment is insured by the U.S. government, and so the lender (or current mortgage holder) is not likely to lose its money. In a sense, the U.S. Government "cosigns" the borrower's loan. Since the loan is insured, lenders are able to accept transactions where the down payment is as little as 3 percent of the purchase price. The FHA establishes limits on the amount of loans it will insure. These loan "ceilings" vary by metropolitan area, ranging in amount from $109,032 in low-cost housing areas to $197,621 in high-cost areas to substantially above $225,000 in very expensive areas. These ceilings on single-family loans change from time to time.

Prospective home buyers obtain FHA loans simply by requesting an appropriate loan application from any authorized FHA lender, such as most savings and loan associations, banks, and mortgage brokers. All real estate sales agents keep informed as to the FHA loan ceilings, which change from time to time.

Veteran's Administration (VA) Loan. In a VA loan, repayment to the lender is guaranteed by the U.S. government because the borrower is a qualified veteran. No down payment is required for these loans unless the price paid for the home exceeds its "reasonable value" as determined by the VA appraisal (a professional estimate of value). In such cases, the excess must be paid in cash by the veteran. The VA does not have loan ceilings, but lenders adhere to guidelines set by Ginnie Mae and Fannie Mae.

Selecting the Best New Financing. The principal sources of all of these loans are savings and loan associations, commercial banks, and mortgage brokers who represent insurance companies, pension funds, and a variety of other organizations. The terms of available loans, such as their interest rates, change from time to time,

For general information about or assistance relative to discrimination in housing or lending, visit the home page of the U.S. Department of Housing and Urban Development (HUD) at http://www.hud.gov/

For updates on the FHA loan ceiling in your area, and for other services provided by the FHA, visit http://www.hud.gov/local/stl/stlmoll.html or http://www.hud.gov/fha/fhahome.html

and differ somewhat between lenders. A prudent buyer will shop for a lender willing to offer the most advantageous package of terms. Real estate sales agents are familiar with aggressive (very competitive) lenders in the area and ought to be consulted, as well as one or more mortgage brokers. As indicated earlier, many lenders are online with up-to-date financing packages. Generally, borrowers seek the highest **loan ratio** (lowest down payment), longest loan repayment period, lowest interest rate, and lowest loan charges. The reasons why borrowers usually seek these terms are described in the following paragraphs.

Veterans may qualify for a VA loan or, in many states, for state assistance. In California, a direct loan is obtainable from a state agency. Although the interest rate for such loans fluctuates with the cost of money to the state, it is generally far below the conventional loan market rate. Oregon and Wisconsin offer their veterans a benefit in the form of a loan repayment guarantee, but not a direct loan. Veterans almost always will receive better deals under VA programs than from other lenders.

Some of the factors a borrower should consider in determining which loan is best are the repayment term (longer is usually better), interest rate (the lower the better), qualification requirements (the more relaxed the better), and amount of the loan (the larger the better). We have suggested what is "better" only as a general guide; obviously, what is better for you will depend on your particular situation.

Loans where the interest rate remains the same during the life of the loan are called **fixed-rate mortgages**. Types of loans where the interest rate may (will) fluctuate are called **variable-interest-rate mortgages (VIRMs)** or **adjustable-rate mortgages (ARMs)**. Borrowers should examine carefully what caps, or limits, are placed on periodic fluctuations. Caps may restrict how high the interest rate can ultimately go, how much it can increase at any one adjustment, and how often adjustments can be made. Prudent borrowers will make certain that they understand the parameters of any ARM they are considering. All real estate sales agents should be able to explain the pros and cons of an ARM given the prevailing interest rate at the time the information is requested.

Repayment Term. The longer the time span is during which the loan must be repaid, the lower the monthly payment. For example, the monthly payment to **amortize** (pay off) an 8 percent loan of $100,000 *over 15 years* is $955.70. In addition to principal and interest of $955.70, the borrower also must pay property taxes and casualty insurance (both discussed later). Lenders often require those payments on a monthly basis, which are then held in "impound accounts" until remitted to the appropriate insurance company and tax collector. Principal, interest, taxes, and insurance are often referred to by the acronym **PITI**. If PMI (private mortgage insurance), discussed earlier, is required by the lender, its premium is also tacked onto the monthly payment.

The same $100,000 loan repaid *over a 30-year period* at 8 percent interest requires a monthly payment of $733.80, which is $221.90 a month less than the 15-year loan. These "savings" in monthly payments are offset by the increased amount of total interest that must be paid because of the longer-term loan. For example, the purchaser of a $115,000 home who borrows $100,000 of the purchase price at 8 percent will pay $172,026 ($955.70 × 12 × 15) over 15 years, whereas the total cost would be $264,168 ($733.80 × 12 × 30) if the term of the $100,000 loan were 30 years. This $92,142 difference is interest paid because of the longer term.

The example given is intended only to demonstrate the change in monthly loan payments when the term of the loan is extended from 15 to 30 years.

There are distinct advantages in taking a loan with a longer term, particularly for the younger family:

1. The longer repayment term gives young buyers extra cash in early years while their family increases in size and cost of support.

2. The young buyer's income is probably rising, so postponed payments will be easier to make in the future.

3. Continuing inflation provides "cheaper" dollars in greater numbers, which will help pay off the loan later.

4. Buyers might otherwise need to rely on costlier installment credit (18 percent or more a year) to buy goods wanted now and services needed now if extra cash goes into larger payments on the home.

5. The tax deduction for interest paid on the mortgage remains available over the longer term. But note, it is more profitable to pay no interest than to obtain a tax deduction for interest that is paid.

A long-term loan can, of course, be paid off much earlier if the borrower chooses to make extra principal payments each month. Most loans permit an additional payment of principal each month without penalty. After 5 years of payments, there typically is no limit on the size of extra principal payments that may be made. The longer-term loan gives the borrower the choice, whereas a shorter-term loan requires the larger payment each month regardless of changing financial circumstances.

There are limits on the available term, typically 30 years for FHA and VA loans. Conventional lenders who sell their loans in the secondary mortgage market also are limited to 30-year terms; however, loans allowing up to 40 years for repayment are possible with portfolio lenders.

Interest Rate. The price of borrowing money is **interest**. The higher the interest rate, the higher the monthly payment (which includes both principal and interest). For example, a real estate loan of $100,000 over 30 years at 8 percent interest requires a monthly payment of $733.80. If the interest is reduced to 7 percent, the monthly payment decreases to $665.31, a savings of $68.49 each month. Thus, the total payments under the 8 percent loan would be $264,168 ($733.80 x 12 x 30) and only $239,512 ($665.31 x 12 x 30) for the 7 percent loan, a savings of $24,656. Exhibit 12–3 gives a more complete idea of monthly payments necessary to amortize (pay off) various loan amounts, to be repaid over 30 years,* with interest rates varying, for example, at 7 percent, 8 percent, and 9 percent (payments for property taxes and insurance are not included).

Although interest payments on home loans are tax-deductible, interest payments (or carrying charges) on consumer loans or credit purchases for cars, furniture, and so forth, are not—unless financed with a **home-equity loan**, a consumer loan secured by the equity in a home. This would explain the popularity of home-equity loans.

---

*As noted earlier in this chapter, most homeowners no longer live in one home for 30 years, making payments on the same mortgage until it is paid off. But homeowners who move ordinarily resume monthly mortgage payments on each successive home they purchase, and thus do make mortgage payments for 30 years or even longer. On average, in our highly mobile society, most new home buyers will move between five and eight years after purchasing a home.

Exhibit 12–3: Interest Rates and Amortization

30-Year, Fixed-Rate Loan

A Original Loan Amount	B Monthly Payment	C Total Paid Over 30-Year Life of Loan*
7% Interest		
$50,000	$332.66	$119,758
$75,000	$498.98	$179,633
$150,000	$997.97	$359,269
$200,000	$1,330.62	$479,023
8% Interest		
$50,000	$366.90	$132,084
$75,000	$550.35	$198,126
$150,000	$1,100.70	$396,252
$200,000	$1,467.60	$528,336
9% Interest		
$50,000	$402.30	$144,828
$75,000	$603.45	$217,242
$150,000	$1,206.90	$434,484
$200,000	$1,609.20	$579,312

For current mortgage information visit http://www.interest.com/

*The total paid over the life of the loan is the sum of all monthly payments of principal and interest. Not included are taxes and insurance. Interest can be calculated by subtracting the original loan amount from the total paid over the life of the loan (column C minus column A). Mortgage interest is tax-deductible, resulting in savings that are related to the taxpayer's marital status and annual earnings.

Increased pressures for realistic financing, with monthly payments within the average budget, as well as for stability within the mortgage markets, have resulted in new variations of loans. As noted, the adjustable-rate mortgage (ARM) provides for the periodic increase or decrease in interest rate depending on prevailing interest levels. Because lenders of ARMs are protected against being locked into a low rate should prevailing rates increase, they are willing to begin the loan at an interest rate lower than is available for fixed-rate mortgages. These "teaser" rates may last for only a year or two before automatically "triggering" up to the market rate. If market interest rates decrease, the borrower is protected against being locked into a higher rate.

Borrowers of fixed-rate mortgages found themselves locked into an unfavorable position in the last years of the twentieth century as interest rates plummeted. As a result, there has been a blizzard of refinancing in which these borrowers obtained much lower interest rate loans. A refinancing occurs when a homeowner replaces the existing mortgage with a new mortgage at a lower interest rate, and sometimes for a greater amount of money that produces cash for other purchases or needs or even for investment. In refinancing, many of these smart borrowers switched to fixed-rate loans, capitalizing on very attractive interest rates that cannot rise regardless of prevailing rates. Interest rates fluctuate upward and then downward over time, making the question "Should I apply for a fixed-rate or a variable-rate mortgage?" impossible to answer with scientific precision. Everyone desires a VIRM when interest rates are falling and a fixed-rate mortgage when interest rates are rising.

To avoid the possibility that the monthly payment may become unbearably high, the loan contract can call for maintenance of the same monthly payment even when the interest rate automatically increases in step with the relevant index, simply by extending the term of the loan. Other VIRMs may maintain the same monthly payment, even though the variable interest rate has increased, by adding the monthly difference owed but unpaid to the unpaid balance of the loan. This is called **negative amortization** because the unpaid principal balance of the loan is actually getting larger each month. If you don't pay what you owe this year, you end up owing more next year. Consequently, the owner's equity is decreasing each month, unless the amount of negative amortization is exceeded by gains in appreciation.

Another variation is the **graduated-payment mortgage**, where early payments are kept artificially low (through reduced interest rates), then increased later to artificially high levels (above-market interest rates). This arrangement is geared to young persons who are beginning their careers. Much of the interest is deferred to later years when income has risen and interest can be repaid without undue hardship.

Yet another variation is the rollover mortgage, where an existing mortgage loan is replaced entirely, every three to five years, as agreed, with a new loan at then-current interest rates. The borrower usually is not charged loan fees or processing costs for the new loan. Lenders can be and are very creative in tailoring new loans to the perceived needs and desires of new home buyers like you. Pressure on the housing supply, and financing availability, will no doubt prompt new government subsidy programs and private sector financing ingenuity. Whatever happens, the purchase of living accommodations will continue to be the most significant financial undertaking and legal contract transaction entered into by most adults.

Points and Annualized Percentage Rate (APR). Interest rates should not be confused with loan charges, called **points**, which are one-time charges made by a lender at the time the home loan is made (originated). These charges are computed much like any percentage commission. They have ranged from about 1 percent to 3 percent. Thus, two points on a $100,000 loan would mean a charge of $2,000. Points are said to be a payment designed to bring the effective, or true, profit of the loan in line with prevailing interest rates. They also serve to generate cash for the lender to pay a loan broker's commission. Often the seller pays the points to the lender in order to avoid losing the sale, because on FHA and VA loans the buyer-borrower cannot be charged more than one point, which is considered a **loan origination fee**. This limitation reduces buyers' closing costs (which are discussed in detail later); but sellers who can do so may boost their sales price to make up the difference, thus indirectly passing this added cost to their buyers.

To show borrowers more clearly what their borrowing costs are, points are computationally treated as additional annualized interest. Thus, an 8 percent loan (with no points charged) may have an 8.75 percent **annualized percentage rate (APR)** if points are charged. When shopping for loans, prospective borrowers should compare the APRs of loans, and not their stated interest rate. All lenders must provide to prospective borrowers the APRs of each of their available financing packages.

Amount of Loan. The greater the amount of money that can be borrowed to purchase a home, the lower the required down payment. Lenders will loan up to a specified percentage of the **appraised value** of the home—that is, the value assigned by a professional appraiser chosen by the lender. Conventional lenders might lend up to 90 percent of the appraised value and require the borrower to guarantee its repayment through the purchase of private mortgage insurance (PMI). Thus, to purchase a home appraised at and selling for $100,000, a loan of $90,000 can be made, requiring a $10,000 down payment.* Other portfolio lenders may require a larger down payment. FHA loan limits are adjusted from time to time by government regulation, but always are more liberal than conventional loan limits. For example, the FHA typically permits (will insure) loans with as little as a 5 percent down payment. Current FHA and market data may be obtained from any real estate sales agent or lending institution. Online mortgage services, mentioned earlier, also publish the terms of available financing.

To learn about appraisers, visit http://www.asc.gov

Loan Qualification Requirements. To obtain a loan to purchase a home a borrower must meet creditworthiness criteria set by the lender. For a conventional loan, for example, a lender may require that monthly payments of principal and interest not exceed 40 percent of the borrower's total monthly income. Spouses, or unrelated co-owners of a home, may pool their respective incomes and credit standings to qualify for a loan. For government-subsidized loans, such as FHA and VA loans, qualifications are set by administrative regulation. Furthermore, purchasers of mortgages in the secondary mortgage market dictate borrower-qualification requirements as a precondition to purchase of their loans. The process of evaluating a borrower's qualifications for a specified loan is called **loan underwriting**. All of these qualifying rules use ratios that compare the borrower's anticipated monthly housing expense and total monthly obligations to monthly gross income.

Mortgage borrowers must have good credit histories or their applications will be denied. Generally, loan applicants are categorized by *alphabet lenders* as either A, B, C, or D, depending on their credit histories. B and C borrowers have histories reflecting significant financial problems (missed payments), but they are not "deadbeats" (persons with disastrous credit histories). When even regional recessions occur, tens of thousands of homeowners may slip from category A to categories B and C. Unfortunately, these rating changes occur to victims of corporate downsizings, plant closings, regional economic slumps, and similar catastrophes that do not truly reflect upon their character as borrowers. B and C borrowers can qualify for mortgage loans, but will face higher than usual loan-to-value (LTV) requirements, meaning that larger down payments are required (e.g., 25 percent for B and 35 percent for C applicants). To assist these borrowers, many lenders typically permit a larger percentage of their income to be absorbed by monthly payments (up to 45 and even 50 percent is common, whereas category A borrowers cannot commit more than 38 percent of their income to PITI). This permits credit-impaired B and C borrowers to qualify if they are willing to commit both a larger down payment and a substantial portion of their income to home ownership.

Qualifying criteria often change, but current requirements are readily available free of charge from offices of real estate brokerage firms, mortgage brokers, banks and savings and loans, and online mortgage information providers.

*The actual cash requirements of the buyer will be somewhat higher than $10,000 because of closing costs, which are explained later.

Assumption of Existing Loan. The obligation of an existing mortgage may be transferred from the debtor (homeowner who desires to sell) to another person (a prospective buyer) who desires to become obligated to its monthly payments. This transfer of obligation is called an **assumption of mortgage**.

Equity is the market value of a property minus the unpaid balance of loans against it. Frequently, sellers of a home have only a small equity in their property. In such a situation, the purchasers may not need to borrow directly; rather, they may desire to assume the loan of the sellers, especially if its interest rate is attractive.

Laura Shields wanted to sell her home for $100,000. She still owed $88,000 against it as represented by a promissory note payable to the bank in monthly installments of $724, including interest at 9 percent. The note was secured by a deed of trust on the home. Mark Hendricks offered to buy the house by paying Laura $12,000 for her equity and by assuming her loan for the balance of the purchase price. Laura contacted her attorney, Colleen Strong, to find out what would happen if she accepted Mark's offer and if, at some future time, Mark failed to make his newly assumed monthly payment. What would attorney Strong advise her?

Laura's attorney would advise her that when Mark assumed the bank loan, he would become a debtor of the bank. The bank could either accept him as the sole debtor, and release Laura from the loan, or keep both Laura and Mark as debtors. In either case, if the bank is not paid each month on time, the trustee (or mortgagee) can cause the house to be sold at public auction with the proceeds going to the bank in satisfaction of the debt. This may not bother Laura since she already would have received $12,000 for her equity; however, her credit rating could be affected adversely if the bank foreclosed in the future since her name would remain on the defaulted note. In addition, if the loan were federally insured, such as an FHA loan, and the sales price at foreclosure was less than the unpaid balance due on the loan, Laura could be made to pay the bank any deficiency (unpaid balance) on the loan remaining after a foreclosure sale. For this reason, most sellers whose mortgage is being assumed by a buyer request a **release of liability** from the lender at the time of the sale. A release will be given by the lender only if the assuming purchaser has a satisfactory credit record, or if the loan balance is small compared to the value of the security (the house). Generally speaking, it is easier for a prospective buyer to qualify for assumption of an existing loan than to qualify for a new loan.

Some states have **anti-deficiency laws** that apply to conventional purchase-money loans, which are any loan the proceeds of which are used by the borrower to purchase a home. As their name implies, anti-deficiency laws prohibit the collection of any deficiency by the creditor following foreclosure sale. A deficiency would arise if the proceeds of the foreclosure sale were less than the amount then owed on the defaulted loan, plus certain costs. These debtor laws date back to the Great Depression of the 1930s, when many people lost their homes and substantial equities through foreclosures but ended up still owing money to their lenders. If a home is fully paid for, and then a mortgage is given for a loan, this statutory protection generally is not available. No doubt legislators believe such borrowers are not vulnerable seekers of shelter, but sophisticated borrowers for profit. For the same reason, **construction loans** for the purpose of building a house generally are not protected, nor are **refinance loans** that are taken out to replace an existing loan. Another type of unprotected loan is the currently popular home-equity loan, whereby a homeowner borrows for miscellaneous purposes, such as traveling, paying tuition, or buying expensive consumer goods. As noted earlier, interest within limits on home-equity loans is tax-deductible whereas interest on consumer debt is not, which helps explain their popularity. Note, though, that income tax laws change frequently; professional advice always should be obtained before making financial decisions based upon supposed tax consequences. As stated, these home-equity loans are subject to deficiency judgments if a foreclosure sale should fail to generate enough cash to pay them off in full.

Most mortgages cannot be assumed without the consent of the mortgagee (beneficiary) because they contain **due-on-sale clauses** that trigger payment of the entire unpaid balance upon any sale of the home. However, assumption is permitted by lenders if the buyer (who is assuming the existing mortgage) agrees to pay an assumption fee, and often an increased interest rate if the loan has a fixed rate. Financing the purchase of a home by assuming its existing mortgage is one alternative that sometimes is attractive, and sales agents often promote the possibility of a loan assumption as an additional selling point for their listings that have assumable mortgages. But at other times loan assumption is less appropriate than new financing.

Seller's Financing

Sometimes prospective buyers do not have sufficient funds for a substantial down payment, or are unable to qualify for a new loan under then-existing underwriting (borrower qualification) requirements. As an alternative to "hard" money loans from institutional lenders in which cash is borrowed for the purchase price, a "soft" money (paper) loan from the seller may be appropriate. Soft money here refers to simply paying the purchase price by giving the seller a promissory note for the amount owed. The seller takes on the role of a creditor; receives a note secured by deed of trust; and conveys title to the buyer. This kind of transaction gave rise to the sagacious wife's tale "buy with paper—sell for cash."

Carryback Mortgage Financing. Sellers of homes that are free and clear of any loans may themselves finance, or "carry," their buyers. In this situation, the buyer usually makes a small down payment and signs a promissory note in favor of the seller. The seller, like a bank, will not be content with the mere promise of the buyer to pay the unpaid balance but will want the home as collateral. The seller will then require the buyer to execute a carryback mortgage (or deed of trust).

If the buyer fails to make payments when due, the trustee (or mortgagee) will sell the property in a foreclosure auction and apply the cash proceeds to satisfying the defaulted debt. This would be a purchase-money mortgage (or deed of trust), and the seller could not obtain a deficiency judgment against the buyer-debtor if the proceeds of sale were inadequate to pay off the loan. The seller would simply absorb any such loss.

Creative Financing. Sometimes a seller will finance a portion of the sales price (say, 30 percent), accept cash (say, 10 percent), and transfer the existing mortgage loan (say, 60 percent) to the purchaser who assumes the existing mortgage. This is an example of a combination carryback mortgage and assumption transaction, often called **creative financing**. The carryback mortgage accepted by the seller as part of creative financing is a **second mortgage** (entitled to any proceeds at foreclosure sale only if the institutional first mortgage is paid in full). Second mortgages can be risky for the lender, who, in this instance, is the seller. One reason why buyers may suggest creative financing is because they are unable to qualify for new financing. Sellers should consider whether they want to accept credit risks that well-managed financial institutions will not accept. When creative financing is agreed to and an existing mortgage is assumed, institutional lenders normally will charge an assumption fee and increase the existing interest rate in the assumed loan. Their risk is less than the seller's because of their lower LTV ratio and first priority to foreclosure proceeds. Generally, assumption fees and interest rate hikes are not attractive to most buyers; on the other hand, it is easier to qualify to assume an existing loan than it is to qualify for a new loan. Creative financing is most popular when it is offered by sellers as a sales inducement in a sluggish real estate market.

Contract for Deed or Installment-Land Contract. As an alternative method of financing, the buyer and seller may enter into an **installment-land contract**, also called a **contract for deed**. Under this arrangement, the seller will not immediately convey title to the buyer, who simply moves in and begins making monthly payments. Rather, title is retained by the seller until the buyer has made monthly payments for many years. This method is used when a buyer cannot qualify for a loan and has no money for a down payment. In these circumstances, the buyer simply makes monthly payments to the seller for, say 20 years, at which time the seller conveys title to the buyer in exchange for payment of the balance of the purchase price.

From the buyer's standpoint, this generally is not a good way to buy a home, but when no other financing is available, it does solve the immediate problem. This type of transaction may be tempting to a budget-conscious buyer because closing costs can be eliminated, no legal assistance is necessary, the cost of title insurance (discussed later) may be avoided, and appraisal fees and lender's up-front fees (points) are avoided. Even the down payment may be small. However, some of these are false savings—the seller may inflate the price of the house as compensation for the other munificent terms offered to the buyer.

The buyer under a contract for deed who fails to make a monthly payment theoretically may be evicted, as would a defaulting tenant, and would have no asset to show for the payments made to date. Because the buyer did not receive title, there is no apparent need for the seller to foreclose and regain title. Simple eviction theoretically is a potent remedy for the unpaid seller.

However, if payments have been made regularly for a long time under an installment-land contract, a court of equity, in the vast majority of states, will require the seller to recognize that the buyer has acquired some reasonable amount of equity in the property. This remedy, however, requires a lawsuit by the buyer, who could be out of possession of the residence pending the litigation. Following litigation, there would be a foreclosure sale; any balance received in excess of the unpaid balance on the contract would go to the defaulting buyer.[6] As a practical matter, buyers under land contracts who have been in possession for only a short period probably will not profit from a lawsuit to establish an equity in the property, because most payments during early years go primarily to interest and do not reduce the principal amount of the loan very much.

Wareham Rossi owned a cabin that was situated on five acres in the mountains. His listing agent, Larry, advised him to sell under a land contract for a small down payment of $1,000, thereby eliminating appraisal fees, title insurance premium, points, and most other closing costs so the property would attract a wider number of possible buyers. A buyer made an offer to pay $150,000 (which was a good price) with $3,000 down payment, interest at 8 percent, and principal and interest payable at $1,100 per month for ten years, at which time the unpaid balance would be paid in full. Following Larry's advice, Wareham accepted the offer while unaware that the buyer, Hammer Studkin, was a leader of the Hell's Angels. Studkin and his buddies moved in and never made a monthly payment. Seven months later, and the day before Wareham's lawsuit for eviction was due to be heard in court, Studkin leased the premises to Irwin Goodheart for one year, for $10,000 rent, all paid in advance. Goodheart moved in; Hammer and his buddies moved out; and the judge ruled that eviction was not a proper remedy because Mr. Studkin was an "owner" and not a mere "tenant." Wareham consulted his new attorney Colleen Strong. What advice would Ms. Strong give Wareham?

This hypothetical situation illustrates many of the problems that can be encountered when using an installment-land contract. Hammer Studkin was buying the property and had the right to lease it to a third person, such as Mr. Goodheart. His transaction netted him seven months of occupancy and a net cash profit of $7,000 ($10,000 prepaid rent less $3,000 down payment). The original down payment was much too small, as Mr. Rossi discovered; his out-of-pocket losses were not nearly covered. It is doubtful that Mr. Rossi can evict Mr. Goodheart if he leased the premises in good faith. Colleen Strong probably would advise a lawsuit be filed against the real estate agent, Larry, for negligence in recommending acceptance of the deal. However, it is doubtful that Colleen would take the case on a contingency. She also would be unlikely to sue Hammer Studkin who, if he could be found and served with the lawsuit papers, would probably be judgment-proof. Ms. Strong might recommend a **quiet title action** (declaration as to who owns real property) to achieve clear title in Mr. Rossi's name, and possibly to force a negotiated settlement with Mr. Goodheart. But she would, no doubt, ask for a substantial retainer fee before commencing such a lawsuit.

What should Wareham Rossi have done? If he used the land contract method, he should have received a larger down payment, prohibited leasing of the premises, and posted the premises with a form declaring the "owner's nonresponsibility" for any third-party claims, as for repairs or for possession by a subtenant. Better yet, Mr. Rossi should have sold the premises in a more orthodox fashion. For example, if the premises had been leased with an option to buy, as discussed shortly, Rossi could have simply evicted any occupant in the ordinary manner of all evictions.

Generally speaking, both parties to a land contract should proceed very carefully and receive professional advice.

Lease with Option to Buy

A buyer who has inadequate funds for a down payment and who may have difficulty qualifying for a new loan may sometimes be able to purchase a home by leasing it with an **option to buy**. This gives the renter an absolute right to purchase the property at a future date at a fixed price upon established terms. The renter who would like to buy now hopes to be better able financially to complete the purchase a few years in the future. A typical lease would be for five years. A portion of each month's lease payment would be "credited" to and earmarked as down payment on the purchase price. This gradual buildup of equity helps reduce or even eliminate the need for a down payment when the option is exercised. Any appreciation in the value of the residence above the agreed-upon option price would further benefit the buyer. Meanwhile, lease payments are made, equity is growing, and opportunity exists for the buyer to enjoy his or her future home while saving for a down payment. The seller, on the other hand, receives the advantage of delaying income taxes by delaying the sale to some future year, and receives tax deductions permitted for rental property (depreciation, interest, taxes, maintenance if applicable, insurance, supplies, and so forth) while waiting. Because a future sale already is in the works, a real estate commission may be avoided. What is more, tenants with an option to buy probably will be excellent residents, making improvements and caring for the property as if it were their own.

Leases with options to buy can be a panacea for buyers and sellers alike. Lease-option forms are readily available from stationery stores and sellers of legal forms. But like most transactions involving a considerable sum of money, precautions should be taken by both parties. For example, if the seller should go into bankruptcy or foreclosure during the term of the lease, and consequently be unable to deliver title in the future, the tenant-buyer could lose his or her rent credit. Professional legal assistance is advisable before entering a lease-option purchase contract.

WHAT IS ESCROW?

To complete the purchase of a house, many things need to be done simultaneously. At the moment title passes, the buyer wants to be certain that title insurance and fire insurance (discussed later) are in effect; the seller wants to receive the amount of the sales price; the lender wants the promissory note and mortgage or deed of trust; the real estate broker wants the earned commission, and so forth. Because it would be impractical for all these persons to meet and hand some documents out with the left hand while simultaneously taking other documents in with the right, the practice of hiring a third-party intermediary (called the **escrow agent**, or simply **escrow**) developed.

Title companies, escrow departments of banks, escrow companies, and sometimes real estate brokers and attorneys may act as escrow agents. The escrow agent collects the required monies and documents from all the interested persons as necessary, and then, at the **close of escrow**, disburses and distributes them to the appropriate persons. Close of escrow is execution of the contract; title is conveyed to the buyer and cash is delivered to the seller, and so forth.

Each party interested in a real estate transaction signs **escrow instructions** that are prepared from standard forms by escrow agents, or by attorneys for the parties. The escrow instructions command the escrow agent as to what each person will put into escrow and what is expected out of it upon its close. For example, in simplified form, the seller may instruct the escrow officer as follows: "I hand you a duly executed grant deed that you are authorized and instructed to record and deliver to the buyer upon the receipt on my behalf of $150,000, the sales price." The escrow agent who complies with all of the instructions will not be liable for any losses suffered by any of the parties.

The escrow instructions must dovetail or the escrow cannot close. For example, if a mistake is made such that the instructions direct the escrow agent to accept $150,000 for the seller but for the buyer to pay only $145,000, there is a conflict and the escrow cannot close. Sometimes, errors are made and instructions of the buyer and seller conflict as to how some of the money should be disbursed by the escrow officer. Facing conflicting demands or instructions that do not dovetail, the escrow officer may file a court action called **interpleader**, deposit the contested funds with the clerk of the court, and withdraw completely, leaving the buyer and seller with the problem of settling their dispute in court. The rationale is that the escrow officer is a mere stakeholder who is obligated to follow instructions as received. When instructions conflict, the stakeholder should be allowed to withdraw.

The escrow officer is a disinterested stakeholder owing allegiance to neither seller nor buyer. Therefore you should not rely upon escrow agents for advice about the merits or consequences of any real estate transaction. In fact, escrow agents are reluctant to say anything to anybody that might be construed as advice. This "mere stakeholder" concept is so clearly defined in the law that even if an escrow officer knows that the buyer is about to be defrauded in a transaction pending in escrow, nothing can be said and no warning can be given. The theory underlying such law is that if escrow officers were permitted to offer advice or suggestions, it would lead to claims of negligent advice (malpractice), bias, and deal-wrecking by disappointed consumers. As a practical matter, sellers and buyers do sign many important papers (standard forms) in the presence of the escrow agent, who generally explains their meanings. These papers include written escrow instructions, deeds, and even promissory notes and mortgages provided by the buyer's lender. Do buyers and sellers rely upon escrow agents? Most do.

In some states, such as New York, attorneys commonly perform all services necessary to close escrow, that is, they serve as escrow officers. More commonly, banks, professional escrow companies, or title companies provide escrow services. Escrows charge fees for their services—it is up to the parties to negotiate how they will be allocated between buyer and seller. Usually the parties agree to allocate escrow costs "in accordance with the customs and practices" of the county.

CLOSING COSTS

Buyers and sellers negotiate how to share a variety of costs that are necessary to close escrow when homes are sold. This array of expenses commonly are called **closing costs**.

Michelle Chen was buying Henry Foster's home for $145,000. She had arranged financing of $130,000 from a savings and loan association and anticipated putting down $15,000 of her own cash to make the purchase price. Will she be required to pay more than $15,000 into escrow?

Yes. The seller will likely have prepaid real property taxes and fire insurance premiums, some amount of which will have to be reimbursed by the buyer. Thus, if seller has prepaid say $1,000 for the period that extends six months after the close of escrow, the buyer must reimburse that sum. The buyer is responsible for property taxes following the sale.

The same sort of allocation results with prepaid casualty (fire) insurance. Furthermore, the buyer will probably pay the cost of a boundary survey if needed, termite inspection, loan fees (points), and perhaps title, notary, and recording fees. All of these costs and more make up what are commonly called closing costs. Some participants call them garbage fees.

It is customarily the responsibility of the seller to pay any transfer taxes (taxes imposed upon the transfer of ownership of real property, based upon its sales price) and to pay for any corrective repairs determined to be necessary because of damage by termites or dry rot (wood damage from water penetration). Almost all details of the purchase of a home are appropriate matters for inclusion in the contract between seller and buyer, and are freely negotiable. Real estate sales agents should be capable of estimating closing costs for their clients.

THE LEGAL SIGNIFICANCE OF CLOSE OF ESCROW

The term *close of escrow* already has been defined as the final distribution of cash and documents to the seller and buyer. At the close of escrow, the deed to the buyer and mortgage to the lender are **recorded** in the official records of the county. Recording is a process by which a county official date and time stamps deeds and mortgages, then photographs and files them in the official records. These records are open to the public and are the original records relied upon by attorneys or title companies when a title search is made. Original documents are returned to the parties.

Prior to close of escrow, the buyer has promised to buy, the seller has promised to sell, the lender has promised to lend, the broker has earned a commission, and so forth. All of these contractual promises are executory, that is, still to be performed. Upon the close of escrow, the buyer has received title to and possession of the home and is its owner; the seller has sold, received the net purchase price, and no longer owns any interest in the property; the lender has made the loan, which the buyer has promised to repay; the broker has received the agreed-upon commission. Most of the promises have been executed or performed. Sometimes, in complicated transactions, the parties will be present with their attorneys at a final meeting called the closing. Many of the documents will be reviewed for the last time and then signed. Although the transaction is completed at close of escrow, the buyer, as borrower, must of course continue to make future payments on the loan as required by the note.

Although it is possible to agree that the seller will retain possession for a period subsequent to close of escrow, or that the buyer will move into the home before close of escrow, these terms are invitations to trouble. The best practice is to have a final walk-through just prior to close of escrow, and to have possession change immediately thereafter. The purpose of a walk-through is to ensure that the condition of the property is the same as it was when the agreement to purchase was made.

In brief, the sale is a *fait accompli* (French: "fact or deed accomplished," presumably irrevocably) when escrow closes. However, some rights and responsibilities linger beyond close of escrow. For example, buyers and sellers continue to have the right to sue each other for fraud or deceit up until the statute of limitations extinguishes their claims. But generally speaking, most buyers and sellers consider the transaction completed when escrow closes.

WHAT IS TITLE INSURANCE?

In some states, such as New York, attorneys perform title searches and render legal opinions regarding the quality of title to property. These opinions are called **abstracts of title**. In most states, however, title insurance companies guarantee property purchasers that they have accurately searched the public records. **Standard title insurance** is a policy of insurance whereby the owner of a home may ensure that there are no surprises lurking in the official records that pertain to his or her newly acquired property. The insurance covers a narrow range of losses, up to a specified face amount of the policy. Title insurance is unlike any other variety of insurance, such as life insurance, where the event of loss is unpredictable. Title insurance does not insure against unpredictable losses. Rather, it insures against losses that may occur from the failure to reveal to the owner any recorded documents—which should have been found absent negligence by the title insurance company.

At the time the title insurance policy is issued, the owner is given a list of recorded documents pertaining to the property, which might include earlier deeds, mortgages, and liens. As briefly noted earlier, recorded documents have been physically date-time stamped, photographed, filed in the public records, and indexed alphabetically by the surnames of the parties to the document. You can visit the recorder of your county and examine any recorded document. The process of recording permanently establishes the sequence in which the documents pertaining to a particular parcel of real property were recorded (date-time stamped). In general, claims that are first in time are first in right, so such formal recording in the official records obviously is important.

The accuracy of the list of recorded documents is guaranteed by the policy of title insurance. Losses arising from something in the public records that was somehow not found by the title insurance company (and therefore not placed on the list) are made good by the title insurance company. Losses therefore are unlikely. Visions of a senior attorney wearing a green visor while hunched over a desk under a dimly-lit light, diligently searching through piles of documents hunting for some defect in the title to real property, are dated to the beginning of the twentieth century. Technology, especially micro fiche and the computer, have revolutionized the process of title searching. Title companies in larger metropolitan areas are in the process of indexing all recorded documents in huge databases, making their existence remotely accessible at the touch of a button in every branch office.

In addition to the accuracy of a list of recorded documents, standard coverage title insurance covers a few losses that may arise from matters not readily ascertainable from the official records, such as forgery of a deed in the chain of title, lack of capacity of parties who are grantors (perhaps through mental incompetency), or lack of delivery of a deed to a former owner. Losses from forgery are unlikely because documents must be **notarized** (signed in the presence of an official who is called a notary public) before being recorded. Losses from lack of capacity of previous owners also are unlikely because court judgments declaring a person incompetent (lacking in capacity) are available in official records. Nor is lack of delivery of deed a likely defect since the law presumes delivery whenever a document, such as a deed, is recorded.

> Percy Fairchild bought a one-acre homesite in the country, on which he planned to build a home and enjoy a "gentleman's farm" with an extensive garden and a variety of animals. In connection with the purchase he acquired a standard policy of title insurance. Thereafter, he began leveling the land for a foundation for his home and outbuildings. He promptly was served with a lawsuit in which a neighbor to the rear, Georgette Simpson, was the plaintiff. Georgette alleged that she owned an easement (right to use) across the middle of Fairchild's lot because she had used it for 15 years for access to the county road. She requested the court to enjoin the construction to protect her easement. Percy asked his lawyer to cross-complain against the title insurance company for the apparent defect in his title. Will he win?

Percy will probably lose his case with Georgette and will certainly lose his cross-complaint against the title company. Among defects in title that are *not* covered by standard title insurance are unrecorded **easements**, i.e., legal rights to use the land of another, that are not recorded in the official records. Some easements are prepared by deeds and are recorded in the official records. But many easements do not appear in the public records. They are created by adjacent landowners who repeatedly use neighboring land for access over many years. These **prescriptive easements** are not evidenced by any documents, and therefore do not appear in the public records. In Georgette's case, the court would not bar Percy from any use of his land but could order him to make suitable some portion of his land for continued periodic access by Georgette. It is important to note that if a defect is disclosed by the title insurer in its policy, any losses from that defect are not covered by insurance. That is, the risk of loss is that the insurer (title company) will negligently overlook a recorded document, and thus fail to inform the insured (home owner) of its existence.

Other exclusions from coverage in standard title insurance policies are boundary discrepancies and errors about how many acres or square feet are contained within the parcel.

Many lenders require **extended coverage insurance** (also called an **American Land Title Association** insurance policy) against loss from any defect, including such unrecorded matters as the presence of tenants or adverse possessors who may assert a future claim of ownership in the property. An **adverse possessor** is anyone who physically occupies and pays taxes on someone else's property for a number of years, such as five, under some color or claim of ownership. Such interlopers can be awarded ownership rights by judicial proceeding even though they never paid a cent for the property. Extended insurance (ALTA) costs more than standard coverage because the title insurance company must make an on-site physical inspection in addition to the customary search of the official records. Presumably such an on-site inspection would reveal to the title insurer that someone is adversely possessing the property or encroaching its boundaries, causing that fact to be noted as an exception to coverage and thereby placing the risk of loss upon the buyer. As a practical matter in the buying and selling of homes, adverse possession would be extraordinarily unlikely and on-site inspections are not made.

Unfortunately for home buyers, the premium charged for title insurance is a function of the sales price of the insured property, not a function of the insurer's risk. That is, the premium is calculated as a scaled percentage of the purchase price of the home each time it sells, whether or not there is any increased risk of loss to the title insurance company. Therefore, the buyer of a new subdivision home faces a purchase price that already includes the accumulated costs of premiums for title insurance that were paid by the developer and again by the builder. The buyer must pay again for title insurance that already has been twice paid for, all on the same lot and all, perhaps, in the same year.[7] Should the buyer resell the home immediately, the next buyer would face another title insurance premium based on the new purchase price. This *layering* of premiums without commensurate risks of loss has prompted title insurers to offer discounts on homes that are repeatedly sold within a short time.

Title insurance premiums are a major part of closing costs in the sale of every home. Buyers and sellers are free to negotiate as to who will pay the title insurance premium, and are well-advised to do so. Any thoughts of avoiding the purchase of title insurance should be set aside because mortgage lenders require it as a condition to making their loans.

ROLE OF ATTORNEY IN HOME TRANSACTIONS

On the one hand it would be prudent to simply advise all prospective sellers and buyers of homes to consult with an attorney to draft or at least to review all documents involved. However, it is unrealistic to engage the services of an attorney for each step in the process, which occur at different times and places. For example, the employment contract (listing) is negotiated early on, usually in the prospective seller's home. Should an attorney assist in this important transaction? Perhaps months later an offer to purchase (deposit receipt) will be received. Should an attorney review this document, consult with the seller's agent, and participate by drafting counteroffers? Can an attorney be expected to drop all other business to review a routine, standard form purchase offer, most of which require acceptance within a couple of days? Should an attorney be taken to the title company once a deal is made, to help instruct the escrow? And a few days later, to review the proposed written escrow instructions? In a more perfect world all parties to important transactions would benefit from more perfect advice—but practicalities interfere. As a general proposition, most buyers and sellers of homes do not consult attorneys; rather, they rely upon the advice and recommendations of their real estate sales agents who, in turn, rely upon standard forms and customs and practices they have followed for years. And yes, many sellers and buyers end up unhappy or even outraged by how they feel mistreated following a home purchase. The more costly the transaction, the more likely the services of attorneys should be considered.

Dave and Kathy McDaniel were in the market for a home priced around $215,000. While deciding whether to buy a pre-owned or newly built home, they contacted their attorney, Ms. Colleen Strong, for advice about available financing. What would attorney Strong's advice likely be?

Their attorney would probably advise the McDaniels that financing is primarily an economic, not a legal, question. The most knowledgeable persons concerning the availability of home loans and their terms are found in real estate sales and loan brokerage firms. Additional useful information is obtainable from local banks, savings and loan institutions, and the Federal Housing Administration (FHA). Attorney Strong might properly suggest, however, that she review all significant documents before they are signed. Sales agents loathe the involvement of attorneys, who never seem to be available at critical times when the parties are ready to sign a document and who raise many questions, some of which may create buyers' or sellers' remorse. Agents often refer to attorneys as "deal killers." Nonetheless, Ms. Strong might review any purchase agreement.

The advice of attorneys always is essential in complex arrangements in which one party is in a position to take advantage of the other. The hiring of a general contractor to build a custom home is one important example that was emphasized earlier.

Because most questions that arise in buying homes are simple and repetitive, real estate agents develop considerable expertise and are usually qualified to assist buyers in the preparation of purchase agreements without the need for legal assistance. However, agents are primarily in the business of selling and are not qualified or authorized to render legal opinions to prospective buyers or sellers. A prudent buyer who asks questions and receives fuzzy, nonresponsive, or incomplete answers would be well-advised to obtain legal assistance before signing any contracts. Fees for contract review are likely to be modest because attorneys can perform such routine services in a short time—if that is their specialization.

One decision that more often than not should be carefully made, perhaps requiring the services of an attorney, concerns choice in legal form of title, which we consider next.

How May Title to Your Home Be Held?

Title may be held (1) by one person, which is termed **in severalty**, (2) by two or more persons (co-owners) as **tenants-in-common**, (3) by two or more persons (co-owners) as **joint tenants** *with right of survivorship*, or (4) by two or more persons (co-owners) as partnership property. About half the states permit a variation of joint tenancy between husband and wife called **tenancy by the entireties**. Some states (Arizona, California, Idaho, Louisiana, Nevada, New Mexico, Texas, and Washington) have community property and a few have marital property, both a variation of co-ownership by married couples.

When two or more persons decide to purchase a residence, a decision must be made as to the legal form of joint ownership to be used.

Mr. and Mrs. Robert Ramirez were buying their first home. Just before close of escrow, they were advised by their real estate agent to take title in joint tenancy. * Should they do so? What alternatives should they consider?

Owning a home in joint tenancy is a common form of ownership by married couples. Upon the death of one joint tenant, transfer of ownership to the survivor is expedient because the property need not go through probate (discussed in Chapter 14). Joint tenancy property cannot, however, be affected by a will, and may be vulnerable to death tax problems in large estates.

In some states, Mr. and Mrs. Ramirez would probably take title as *tenants by the entireties*, with essentially the same effect as if they were joint tenants. In any of the states where available, they might consider taking title as *community property*, so that each spouse's one-half share could be disposed of by will, if so desired. Community property ownership also offers income tax advantages to the surviving spouse when his or her highly appreciated house is sold following the other's death. One community property state, Washington, requires that married couples own their home as community property.

If two or more unrelated persons decide to pool their resources in order to improve their quality of life by purchasing a home, they would, no doubt, prefer to retain the right to individually will their undivided interests to their respective relatives or loved ones. They would accordingly select the tenancy-in-common form of home ownership.

Jinna Roberts and Kathy Jennings, unrelated, owned Sky High Ranch as joint tenants. Upon learning that their respective interests would go to the survivor of them regardless of their respective wills, they decided to change their ownership form. May they do so?

Yes. Jinna and Kathy can simply convey the property to themselves as tenants-in-common. Then both may will their respective equal shares to anyone they choose. For example, if Jinna should die without leaving a will, her undivided one-half interest would go to her closest surviving heirs. Such surviving heirs would, under law, become tenants-in-common with Kathy.

A **deed** is the document that transfers or conveys title (ownership) of real property from one person to another. A valid deed must contain the following:

1. The names of the seller (grantor) and the buyer (grantee).
2. Words evidencing an intent to transfer title (i.e., I hereby "grant," or "convey" to).
3. A legally sufficient description of the real property deeded.
4. The grantor's (and usually the spouse's) signature(s).

---

*This advice is dangerously close to constituting the unauthorized practice of law. A more prudent agent would provide his or her clients with published materials generally describing the alternatives available and add that they should obtain any further advice from an attorney. Even the publishers of "how-to" legal books, such as Nolo Press, have been challenged by lawyers for engaging in the practice of law. As a practical matter, agents often respond, "I cannot give you legal advice, but I can say that most of my clients choose joint tenancy."

Finally, to be valid, a deed must be delivered from the grantor to the grantee. Most deeds are recorded in the official records of the county in which the property is located, and must be recorded if title insurance is to be purchased. But unrecorded deeds are legally valid.

Typically, a **quitclaim deed** is used to change the manner in which title is held. It is a deed by which a person merely gives up any claim he or she may have to specified property. The transferor makes no promises or warranties to the transferee about the condition of the property or quality of title conveyed. A quitclaim deed seems strange to most people. After all, what value is a deed where the person transferring title to you does not promise ownership? Actually, quitclaim deeds are used often in situations where ownership rights are uncertain, and serve to clarify title in the official records. The quitclaim deed is appropriate when land is transferred by gift or to clear some possible "**cloud on title**"—some obstacle to clear title, such as an old abandoned leasehold that might otherwise be the basis for a later lawsuit.

In contrast to a quitclaim deed, a warranty deed is used for transfers of real property by sale. By its use, the grantor impliedly makes certain covenants or promises:

1. The grantor has full ownership of the exact interest being conveyed.
2. The property is free of liens or claims of third persons except as disclosed in the deed.
3. The title will not be challenged by third persons.
4. The grantor will execute any further documents that may be required to perfect the grantee's title.

In states where title insurance policies provide considerable assurance that there will be no surprises found in the official records, the simple **grant deed** is commonly used. By use of the word "grant," the grantor (seller) impliedly warrants that (1) he or she has not previously conveyed the property to someone else and (2) the estate (ownership) conveyed is free from prior encumbrances by the grantor, unless disclosed.

Married persons can change the form of ownership of property held as community property to tenancy-in-common or joint tenancy, or vice-versa, by deed. Under some circumstances, courts have held that even though held in joint tenancy, the husband and wife actually intended to and did hold the property as community property. The result of such a ruling is a tax advantage, in that surviving owners of community property pay considerably less income tax on any future sale than do surviving joint tenants.

See a copy of a quitclaim deed at http://www.4closure.com/forms13.html

SELLING YOUR HOME YOURSELF

Some homeowners desire to sell their home without using an agent in order to avoid paying the negotiable sales commission, which often is 6 percent of the sales price. If a home sells for $150,000 and there is a mortgage outstanding with unpaid balance of $130,000, the owner's equity is $20,000. A 6 percent commission equals $9,000 (.06 × $150,000), which equals 45 percent of the owner's equity ($9,000/$20,000). For this reason, some homeowners do not hire sales agents.

Sellers who do not utilize agents are referred to as *FSBO* ("for sale by owner") pronounced somewhat disrespectfully as "fizzbo."

Selling without an agent is not as easy as it might seem at first blush because of the lack of cooperation of real estate agents. They will take their prospective buyers to listed homes, which if purchased will produce a commission, and will avoid non-commission paying FSBOs. But selling without an agent is realistic under certain circumstances.

FSBO sellers cannot place their houses in the privately owned multiple listing service. But FSBO sellers can create a beautiful and informative brochure containing all of the amenities of the house and of the neighborhood. Or a Web site can be created complete with photographs and information about schools, shopping, transportation, etc. Most sellers can arrange for effective advertising simply by consulting with specialists at the local newspaper. If the property is on a street with significant traffic flows, even if only at certain hours, a suitable "for sale" sign might be posted.

Once a buyer is obtained, all the paperwork necessary (escrow instructions) can be accomplished by the title company or escrow company that is selected to close the escrow. Once the escrow instructions are prepared and signed, they constitute a legally binding contract.

Pending preparation of the escrow instructions and before they are signed, the parties should hire an attorney to prepare a purchase agreement, if they want one. Generally it is in the seller's interest not to have such a contract, because the seller without a contract can continue to receive offers that might be higher or more favorable. In short, the seller's property is not technically "off the market" until a contract is signed. Signed purchase agreements protect buyers and agents more than sellers.*

Problems face FSBOs in preparing their property for sale; in determining the highest price they might receive; in dealing face-to-face with buyers who expect to benefit from dickering about the price; in separating qualified buyers from "lookers"; and in retaining confidence in their ability to handle the sale in the face of many licensed agents who may contact them attempting to obtain a listing. But the problems can be solved and the benefits to the seller can be substantial, especially in a **seller's market** (i.e., where the demand for homes exceeds the available supply, and properties offered for sale are promptly sold).

A FSBO can pass along some of the commission savings to his or her buyer (e.g., through price reduction or inclusion of items of personal property), thereby making the deal especially attractive.

A more effective possibility for a seller who hopes to save on the costs of selling is to make an **open listing** under which one-half of a normal commission is offered to be paid to any agent who brings a buyer to whom the property is sold. An open listing can be created by making the statement on the sales brochure, on a Web page, on the sign in the front yard, or by any other form of communication. Because agents who bring buyers typically produce only one-half of the total commission (the other one-half, or 3 percent, going to the listing office), they will

*The effect of a real estate purchase agreement is that the seller's property is "off the market" and subsequent, more lucrative offers must be rejected. The deal may linger on for longer than anticipated, all the while "handcuffing" the seller. Meanwhile, all the buyer has at risk is an earnest money deposit, which sometimes is represented by an uncashed check. Even then the deposit is refundable under most circumstances. Thus, the seller has great risk from such a contract while the buyer has little or none.

respond to open listings for, typically, 3 percent. Thus, in the preceding example, the seller would pay a commission of $4,500 instead of $9,000.

HOW IS A HOME TAXED?

A home may be located within the boundaries of both a county and a city as well as within various municipal taxing districts, all of which may impose taxes on property to finance schools, colleges, flood control districts, mosquito abatement districts, air pollution control districts, parks, water systems, sewers, and so on. Generally these needs are expressed in a *combined budget*, which reflects the money local government must obtain from its residents in order to function for another fiscal year.

Taxation of real property, including homes, is the principal method by which local governments obtain needed funds. Theoretically, all properties are taxed in proportion to their current values, whether they are residential, commercial, industrial, or whatever. The county assessor appraises each property at its **market value** (called **full cash value**) and declares a uniform fraction of that amount to be its **assessed value**. Some states assess at full cash value. These values are approximations of fair market values because assessors cannot possibly keep all properties within a jurisdiction currently appraised on a year-to-year basis.

Whether a full cash value or fractional assessment (some arbitrary portion, or fraction, of full cash value) is used has no effect on the amount of property tax paid by the homeowner. These "assessed" values are listed on the assessment roll.

The applicable combined budget is then divided by the total assessed value of all taxable property in the county to arrive at the property tax rate—the percentage that must be applied to the assessed value of each parcel of taxable property in the county to determine how much its share of the entire budget should be.

In this way, property owners are taxed in proportion to the value of the property they own. A property worth 30 percent more than another property will be liable for 30 percent more in taxes, if both are within the same municipal taxing districts. Also, a home worth $75,000 will be liable for exactly the same amount of tax as a service station worth $75,000, if both are within the same districts.*

Owners who believe their taxes are unfairly high in comparison with similar properties may informally request a reappraisal by the tax assessor, or formally appeal to the specified appeals body (such as the local Board of Equalization). If unsuccessful here, they can appeal to a court, but courts generally do not overrule administrative agencies, especially on matters of taxation.

If government expenditures (initially proposed in budgets) *increase*, property taxes increase. If government expenditures are *constant*, total tax revenues are constant, regardless of whether assessed values increase or *decrease*. If government expenditures decrease, property taxes decrease, regardless of whether assessed values increase or decrease.

---

*Some states, following California's lead, have adopted property tax limitations that apply to older, but not recently sold properties. Therefore, a home that recently sold for $75,000 may be chargeable with more property tax than a home or service station also worth $75,000 but which has been owned a number of years. In effect, new homeowners thus subsidize owners who have owned their homes for some years. This result of higher taxes for newer homes of comparable values is another example of how the traditional economic benefits of home ownership are eroding as we begin the twenty-first century.

$$\frac{\text{Total expenditures, i.e.,}}{\text{the budget}} = \text{Tax rate} \times \frac{\text{Your assessed}}{\text{value}} = \frac{\text{Your}}{\text{tax*}}$$

Of course, any individual's property may be reappraised and if its assessed value goes up, its specific tax bill will rise. Conversely, a person whose property goes down in assessed value in relationship to other properties will pay a lower tax. Increases or decreases in assessed values or tax rates have nothing to do with increased total taxes, which can occur only when government expenditures increase. In other words, if all assessed values rise, but budgeted expenses remain constant, total taxes collected will remain constant. Rising and falling property taxes are a function of rising and falling county budgets.

Typically, all assessed values in a county are increased annually by some percentage to reflect estimated general inflationary pressures. A constant tax rate thus will produce an increase in the budget, producing, in turn, higher taxes for everyone's property.[8]

Not all real estate is subject to property taxes. Property owned by any type of governmental organization is exempt from taxation. Thus, when private property is acquired by local government, as for a public park or school, property tax collections are reduced. If total expenditures are to be maintained, or increased, the remaining private property must contribute more to taxes assessed and collected. Federal lands and the lands under highways and streets are all exempt from taxation. Rising property values automatically provide increases in funds for local governments when tax rates are constant; thus, inflation fuels local budgets. If the preceding statement is unclear to you, reconsider the preceding formula for how your property taxes are computed.

Property taxes typically are paid twice a year, in December and April, although they accrue daily. Some lenders require their borrowers to pay taxes monthly, along with their payments of principal and interest. These lenders then forward the collected property taxes to the local tax collector twice a year. The funds collected monthly are held in an **impound account** by the lender until disbursed to the tax collector. A small amount of interest is paid to the borrower by some lenders for these prepayments of taxes. The reason lenders prefer impounds is that it gives them an assurance that the homeowner has set aside enough money to pay the taxes when due. When negotiating for a home mortgage, borrowers can ask that they pay all property taxes and insurance bills directly, avoiding the impounding process. This gives the homeowner use of the cash until the periodic tax and insurance bills arrive.

WHAT IS FIRE INSURANCE?

A private home is the costliest single asset the typical adult is likely ever to acquire. The greatest hazard both buyer and lender face is the possibility that a fire

---

*Notice that so long as all property is assessed upon the same basis, whether that basis is full cash value, 25 percent of full cash value, or 10 percent of full cash value, the particular basis used in your community will not affect the amount of tax paid by any one homeowner.

may break out and damage or completely destroy the building and contents. To protect their respective interests, both lenders and buyers generally agree that the latter shall purchase appropriate casualty (fire) insurance. Casualty insurance on a home is generally provided in what is called a **homeowner's policy**. Essentially, the basic policy covers the dwelling, together with equipment and fixtures, such as heating and air conditioning equipment and the contents, including furniture, clothing, and other household goods. Coverage also exists for loss of use of the home following a casualty, and often medical benefits. Homeowner's policies also contain liability coverage protecting against, for example, injuries to guests. Many additional coverages are available for added premiums, such as damages from windstorm, from hail, from an explosion, or from earthquake or flood.

WHAT IS NEIGHBOR LAW?[9]

Disputes between neighbors frequently center around noise, encroachments of tree roots and limbs, boundary lines, and obstructions of views. Various laws, both statutory and common law, comprise **neighbor law**. Court decisions are infrequent largely because the picayune nature of many neighbor squabbles do not justify spending the substantial sums that are required to pursue formal litigation remedies. Neighbor disputes, however, are notable for their intensity and longevity. Lawyers and judges alike prefer to remain uninvolved, knowing that even after a court rules the neighbors will find something else to fight about. Most neighbor quarrels are resolved by local officials in small claims courts (fully discussed in Chapter 3), and many are resolved by simple resignation and tolerance of annoyances that are part of "life."

HELP FROM LOCAL OFFICIALS

Many common neighbor disputes have been anticipated and are regulated by local ordinance. Ordinances prohibit allowing city property to become blighted (a condition of disrepair), and they often prohibit the accumulation of weeds, debris, rubbish, etc. Anti-blight ordinances may apply to fences, sidewalks, windows, and driveways as well as structures. Graffiti may be considered a form of blight. Some local ordinances address possible public health problems, such as garbage, debris, and weeds or other rubbish that encourages the breeding of rats and insects or are conducive to fires. Offended neighbors can obtain assistance from city officials, who will compel repairs of unsightly messes or impose fines upon persons responsible. Local ordinances also prohibit unreasonably loud noises, sometimes applying to such activities as late-night basketball, blaring outdoor stereos, and even screaming and fighting neighbors. Police can be called to enforce such ordinances. What is reasonable sound is sometimes determined by measurement of decibels and their relationship to the time of day ("quiet times" may be included within the ordinance) and the type of applicable zoning. Some states have criminal statutes prohibiting noise that is so loud that it "disturbs the peace."

The traffic, crime, and fear engendered by continuous drug dealing in a house also may be prohibited by ordinances that provide neighbors with small claims court remedies against landlords and owners of such nuisances. Courts have imposed damages upon landlords of such crack houses and this ultimately leads to evictions to forestall future penalties.

Local ordinances also impose restrictions on irresponsible animal owners. Under the common law the owner of an animal, such as a dog, is absolutely liable for damages caused when it bites someone. Ordinances often make illegal continuous dog barking and howling and require leashes when dogs (and sometimes cats)[10] are off their owner's property. Offended neighbors can seek assistance from city officials to enforce pooper scooper ordinances if they are in effect, or can sue for trespass if they aren't. The number of dogs and cats per household also is often regulated. In at least one instance, the number of geese that can be kept (often as substitutes for watch dogs) also is regulated.[11]

Local zoning ordinances also regulate how property may be used. Zoning laws typically prohibit running a business at a residence if it attracts customers and creates traffic. Persons who perform "outsource" work at home do not violate residential ordinances unless repeated customer and car traffic is thereby generated. Even running garage sales every weekend is probably illegal in most residentially zoned communities. Ordinances also regulate the use and storage of motor vehicles. For example, recreational vehicles (RVs) sometimes must be shielded by fencing or vegetation. Cars cannot be stored in driveways in a state of disassembly and disrepair for indefinite times, under many ordinances. And most communities prohibit the continuous parking of cars on public streets.

HELP FROM CC&RS

Condominium projects and planned unit subdivisions are regulated by deed restrictions, called **covenants, conditions & restrictions (CC&Rs)**. These restrictions are binding upon the owners and occupants of homes within the subdivision. The purpose of the CC&Rs is to maintain property values within the community and to contribute to a safe, neat, and pleasing environment.* A wide range of neighbor disputes may be solved by application of the CC&Rs to the problem. For example, CC&Rs almost always cover noise problems, regulate the time of day when swimming pools may be used, when basketball may be played and whether its court may be lighted, and so on. Colors of fences as well as their style, height, material, and location are usually regulated, both by local ordinance and by applicable CC&Rs.

When a dispute arises, the CC&Rs include a mechanism, or procedure, by which complaints can be brought to the attention of the homeowner's association (HOA).

Earlier in this chapter a general comparison of the amenities between owning and renting a home was presented. Homeowner's associations and the rules they enforce are considered by many to equalize, or at least to resemble, the restrictive rules found in apartments. In other words, the owned home is less like a "castle" and more like a rented apartment.

---

*Nationwide, there are more than 150,000 developments governed by community associations, housing perhaps 32 million people, or one in eight Americans, according to the Community Associations Institute in Alexandria, Virginia. Subdividers create community associations in nearly all new developments to manage and levy fees for common facilities and obligations such as road and landscaping maintenance. Some provide for the collection of monthly fees from each lot owner specifically to fund roving patrols who assist the publicly funded police in maintaining security within their borders. To some homeowners, these associations are overbearing mini-governments without checks and balances. Typically, elections are conducted periodically and only homeowners can be elected to serve on an association's governing board. *The Wall Street Journal*, 21 September 1994.

Phyllis Hammond lived in Taromina, a 92-unit oceanfront co-operative in
Florida, when its HOA ended its ban on cats. Phyllis scurried out and
bought a 10-pound cat named Sam for $100. Weeks later the co-op board
of directors reinstated its prior ban on cats as pets, and ordered Phyllis to
get Sam out of her one-bedroom apartment. Legal battles ensued, and before long Phyllis, who was living on a modest pension and social security,
had spent $8,063, mostly in attorney fees; the co-op board had likewise
spent $11,000. The governing rules provided that in legal skirmishes, the
prevailing party was entitled to reimbursement of attorney fees from the
losing side. In disgust, Phyllis offered to get rid of Sam, sell her apartment, and end the dispute if each side would pay its own attorney fees.
The board refused, "on principle" according to its lawyer.[12] How can
Phyllis end the dispute?

Phyllis cannot end the dispute. All too often, attorney fees become the tail that
wags the dog (or cat in Phyllis' situation) in litigation. HOA rules typically provide that the prevailing party is entitled to recover their attorney fees, which may
greatly exceed the amount in controversy, as the Phyllis Hammond case demonstrates. Because of the frequency and ferocity of litigation between owners and
HOAs, California requires that such disputes be submitted to non-binding arbitration before litigation can be pursued. The theory is that arbitration may cool off
the parties sufficiently that some compromise will follow.

HELP FROM COURT

Many people develop zealously protective attitudes about their trees. As trees
grow, their limbs may extend across lot lines, offering both their fruit to the neighbor (sometimes welcome) as well as their dripping sap, falling leaves and limbs,
and bird droppings (seldom welcome). Furthermore, your neighbor's trees can be
counted on to clog up your rain gutters and downspouts (never welcome). Roots
can and do extend across lot lines, and sometimes even a tree's trunk will cross
the line. Any physical protrusion across a boundary line is called an **encroachment**. Problems arise when neighbors want to cut limbs off their neighbor's tree,
or cut the tree down entirely, especially if its roots are uprooting the fence, driveway, or even a nearby structure. Of equally provoking concern is loss of sunlight,
allergic reaction to drifting pollen, and, of course, loss of an ocean, valley, or
mountain view. The location of a tree's trunk determines its ownership. If
the trunk overlaps a lot line, it is jointly owned by both homeowners whether
they like the idea or not. If a wrongdoer (whether or not a neighbor) kills a
landowner's tree, the victim may recover compensatory damages (cost of replacement, or dimunition in value of the land, plus out-of-pocket costs) and punitive damages if applicable. Many states have adopted statutes prescribing
damages for crimes against trees, doubling or trebling compensatory damages
and sometimes permitting the recovery of attorney fees.[13] In some states
wrongful tree killing is a crime, a misdemeanor punishable by both fine and/or
imprisonment.[14]

In the common law there is a right of self-help. Under the doctrine of self-help,
a person has the right to personally secure or enforce some legal right so long as

no violent confrontation is involved.* But, in a modern application of the rule, neighbors can simply cut off any encroaching limbs or roots of trees. This conduct may offend the tree's owner, but it is permitted in all states under the common law. However, the trimming is generally at the neighbor's expense, and cannot result in killing the tree—if it does die, the neighbor can be sued for damages for loss of the tree. This is noteworthy because some trees can add a substantial amount to the value of a home. In most states, the neighbor has no other remedy than to trim the tree back to the boundary, unless real damage has been caused (for example, by partially falling onto the roof.)** When substantial injury has occurred, or is threatened, the encroaching tree qualifies as a **nuisance**. Any unreasonable interference with the use and enjoyment of real property is called a nuisance, and it may be enjoined by court (through its issuance of an injunction) and/or damages may be awarded. Tree owners clearly must keep their trees from becoming a nuisance, i.e., from encroaching *and* damaging their neighbors' property.

The owner of a fruit tree owns its fruit, even if the fruit is growing on a limb that is overhanging the boundary fence. This rule makes it clear that the public cannot legally pull off a road to pick fruit from orchard trees that overhang onto the public right of way. If the owner of a fruit tree desired to enter upon the neighbor's property to retrieve fruit, the issue of trespass would arise. It is unclear whether the law would uphold an owner's fundamental right to exclude persons from the property, or would create a limited right in the owner of a fruit tree to trespass on another's property to retrieve fruit.

Janice Turner was angry that her neighbor's Strawberry Blush cling peach tree was overhanging the fence. She said nothing to her neighbor, Scott Harlow, during the following months. In August the tree was laden with beautiful ripe fruit, much of which was clinging to the limbs overhanging Janice's property. Janice then smugly trimmed the limbs back to the fence line and, after the limbs were severed, picked the peaches, canning some and simply enjoying the others. Scott learned of the timely trimming and sued in small claims court for the value of the peaches Janice had taken. What arguments support each side, and what decision should the judge make?

Janice would argue that she exercised her common-law right of self-help by trimming the encroaching limbs back to the property line. Scott might counter that her real intention was to steal his fruit. He could argue that the limbs and fruit remained his property even after they were trimmed, and that Janice is guilty of the tort of conversion. (Conversion was explained in Chapter 7.) The law on this point is nonexistent; the judge would simply have to make a decision without the benefit of the doctrine of *stare decisis*. What decision would you make as judge?

Homeowners enjoy sunlight, free-flowing breezes, and sometimes good views. However, in the common law there is no right to light, air, or view, which

---

*The classic example of the mostly outdated rule of self-help is the right to trespass (go onto another person's property) to retrieve a stolen horse, so long as a violent confrontation can be avoided. It is usually preferable to summon and rely upon proper officials to execute the law.

**California, Louisiana, and Washington permit suits against owners of encroaching trees even if no serious damage has occurred, on the theory such trees are a private nuisance.

may be impaired from growing trees (or even buildings) on neighboring property. This harsh rule has been modified by local ordinances in some areas near the ocean or with other scenic view potential. These ordinances do not prohibit growing trees that may someday obstruct a neighbor's view. The court is authorized to balance the owner's rights with the desirability of a view for the neighbor, whether or not trimming to the extent of providing a filtered view, or even topping or windowing (cutting out a window to provide a partial view) would be a satisfactory solution. CC&Rs also may regulate the protection of views from growing trees.

Disputes in connection with fences, as noted above, may be resolved by resort to local officials, who will enforce ordinances regulating fences, or by resort to HOA officials, who will enforce applicable CC&Rs. Sometimes, however, a property owner will erect a spite fence, creating a dispute that will require going to court for relief. Any fence that is built to annoy or vex a neighbor, and that has no reasonable value to its owner, is called a **spite fence**. Many states have statutes defining spite fences as nuisances and authorizing lawsuits for their removal and recovery of damages.[15] Proof that a fence is intended to annoy or vex may be easier to produce than it seems. Often a spite fence is deliberately made to look like a monstrosity, to further annoy the neighbor. The existence of ongoing hostility between the neighbors is evidence of a malicious intent. If a fence does not contribute materially to needed privacy, or does not effectively fence anything inside, or does not effectively stop intruders, strong evidence exists that it is a spite fence. Made-up reasons, such as "needed to support my climbing roses" are not likely to be persuasive. Courts can order the removal of spite fences, award compensatory damages, and even punitive damages in outrageous cases.

Neighbor disputes can make life less enjoyable. Prospective home buyers are well-advised to extend their enquires beyond the four corners of the lots they are considering for purchase. Much about the neighborhood can be learned from asking nearby residents pertinent questions. Letter carriers also are available for questions, and often are experts in any ongoing neighborhood disputes. The location of trees, condition of fences, establishment of boundary lines through survey, as well as a late-night visit on Friday or Saturday can all contribute to making a well-informed purchase.

Sometimes families rent homes in subdivisions in which most homes are owned. This situation can exacerbate problems on occasion when renters are less concerned than owners with long-term neighbor relations. Some think that renters are less likely to maintain proper outside appearances of the home they rent, as by storing old vehicles or making repairs in front or by not picking up loose papers, etc. Owners of homes that are rented also often are accused of ignoring exterior appearances through marginal landscaping services, deteriorated paint and roof conditions, and permissiveness toward all **blight**. Blight in real estate refers to any condition that negatively affects property values in a neighborhood. Examples of blight include foil in or bars over windows; toys constantly left asunder; motorcycles on lawn areas; moss growing on roofs; cracked windows; makeshift visible repairs; exposed garbage cans; etc. Neighbors who are offended by nearby blight have little recourse in the law, no recourse in CC&Rs if none are applicable, and little assistance from government officials unless more serious violations of law also are taking place.

Sometimes the American Dream can become an American Nightmare—it pays to be a smart buyer.

CASES

STAMBOVSKY V. ACKLEY
169 A.D.2d 254, 572 N.Y.S.2d 672 (New York, 1991)

*Jeffrey Stambovsky, the plaintiff, was horrified to discover that the house he contracted to buy was widely believed to be possessed by ghosts. These ghosts had reportedly been seen by the defendant seller and member of her family on numerous occasions over the nine years prior to the sale of the house. The defendant had reported the presence of ghosts in both a national publication (*Readers' Digest*) and the local press. The plaintiff buyer, a resident of New York City, did not know about the "reputation" of the house in Nyack Village, where the house was located. Plaintiff brought this lawsuit to rescind the contract to buy the house and to have his down payment of $33,000 returned to him. The New York trial court dismissed the plaintiff's lawsuit before the trial, holding that the doctrine of caveat emptor applied to real estate transactions and Stambovsky was expected to investigate any facts important to him in a sale. Stambovsky appealed. On appeal, Stambovsky argued that the seller, Ackley, who knew about the ghosts, had a responsibility to tell him the house was haunted. The appellate court agreed and held the plaintiff had a right to pursue his lawsuit and have a trial.*

Justice Rubin delivered the opinion: The unusual facts of this case, as disclosed by the record, clearly warrant a grant of equitable relief to the buyer who, as a resident of New York City, cannot be expected to have any familiarity with the folklore of the Village of Nyack. Not being a "local," plaintiff could not readily learn that the home he had contracted to purchase is haunted. Whether the source of the spectral apparitions seen by defendant seller are parapsychic (paranormal psychological phenomena, e.g., telepathy or clairvoyance) or psychogenic (originating in the mind), having reported their presence in both a national publication (*Readers' Digest*) and the local press (in 1977 and 1982, respec-

tively), defendant is estopped to deny their existence and, as a matter of law, the house is haunted.

More to the point, however, no divination is required to conclude that it is defendant's promotional efforts in publicizing her close encounters with these spirits which fostered the home's reputation in the community. In 1989, the house was included in a five-home walking tour of Nyack and described in a November 27th newspaper article as "a riverfront Victorian (with ghost)." The impact of the reputation thus created goes to the very essence of the bargain between the parties, greatly impairing both the value of the property and its potential for resale. The extent of this impairment may be presumed for the purpose of reviewing the disposition of this motion to dismiss the cause of action for rescission . . . and represents merely an issue of fact for resolution at trial.

While I agree with supreme court that the real estate broker, as agent for the seller, is under no duty to disclose to a potential buyer the phantasmal reputation of the premises and that, in his pursuit of a legal remedy for fraudulent misrepresentation against the seller, plaintiff hasn't a ghost of a chance, I am nevertheless moved by the spirit of equity to allow the buyer to seek rescission of the contract of sale and recovery of his down payment.

New York law fails to recognize any remedy for damages incurred as a result of the seller's mere silence, applying instead the strict rule of caveat emptor. Therefore, the theoretical basis for granting relief, even under the extraordinary facts of this case, is elusive if not ephemeral. "Pity me not but lend thy serious hearing to what I shall unfold." [William Shakespeare, *Hamlet*, Act 1, Scene V (Ghost)]

From the perspective of a person in the position of plaintiff herein, a very practical problem arises with respect to the discovery of a paranormal phenomenon: "Who you gonna' call?" as the title song to the movie *Ghostbusters* asks. Applying the strict rule of caveat emptor to a contract involving a house possessed by poltergeists conjures up visions of a psychic or medium routinely accompanying the structural engineer and Terminix man on an inspection of every home subject to a contract of sale. It portends that the prudent attorney will establish an escrow account lest the subject of the transaction come back to haunt him and his client—or pray that his malpractice insurance coverage extends to supernatural disasters. In the interest of avoiding such untenable consequences, the notion that a haunting is a condition which can and should be ascertained upon reasonable inspection of the premises is a hobgoblin [a goblin or gremlin or elf that is mischievous but not malicious] which should be exercised from the body of legal precedent and laid quietly to rest.

It has been suggested by a leading authority that the ancient rule which holds that mere nondisclosure does not constitute actionable misrepresentation "finds proper application in cases where the fact undisclosed is patent, or the plaintiff has equal opportunities for obtaining information which he may be expected to utilize, or the defendant has no reason to think that he is acting under any misapprehension" [Prosser, Law of Torts, § 106 at 696 (4th ed., 1971)] However, with respect to transaction in real estate, New York adheres to the doctrine of caveat emptor and imposes no duty upon the vendor to disclose any information concerning the premises . . . unless there is a confidential or fiduciary relationship between the parties . . . or some conduct on the part of the seller which constitutes "active concealment. . . ."

Caveat emptor is not so all-encompassing a doctrine of common law as to render every act of nondisclosure immune from redress, whether legal or equitable. "In regard to the necessity of giving information which has not been asked, the rule differs somewhat at laws and in equity, and while the law courts would permit no recovery of damages against a vendor, because of mere concealment of facts under certain circumstances, yet if the vendee refused to complete the contract because of the concealment of a material fact on the part of the other, equity would refuse to compel him so to do, because equity only compels the specific performance of a contract which is fair and open, and in regard to which all material matters known to each have been communicated to the other." [*Rothmiller v. Stein*, and cases cited therein] Common law is not moribund. *Ex facto jus oritur* (law arises out of facts). Where fairness and common sense dictate that an exception should be created, the evolution of the law should not be stifled by rigid application of a legal maxim.

The doctrine of caveat emptor requires that a buyer act prudently to assess the fitness and value of his purchase and operates to bar the purchaser who fails to exercise due care from seeking the equitable remedy of rescission. . . . It should be apparent, however, that the most meticulous inspection and search would not reveal the presence of poltergeists at the premises or unearth the property's ghoulish reputation in the community. Therefore, there is no sound policy reason to deny plaintiff relief for failing to discover a state of affairs which the most prudent purchaser would not be expected to even contemplate. Where a condition which has been created by the seller materially impairs the value of the contract and is peculiarly within the knowledge of the seller or unlikely to be discovered by a prudent purchaser exercising due care with respect to the subject transaction, nondisclosure constitutes a basis for rescission as a matter of equity. Any other outcome places upon the buyer not merely the obligation to exercise care in his purchase but rather to be omniscient with respect to any fact which may affect the bargain. No practical purpose is served by imposing such a burden upon a purchaser. To the contrary, it encourages predatory business practice and offends the principle that equity will suffer no wrong to be without a remedy.

Defendant's contention that the contract of sale, particularly the merger, or "as is" clause, bars recovery of the buyer's deposit is unavailing. Even an express disclaimer will not be given effect where the facts are peculiarly within the knowledge of the party invoking it. . . . Moreover, a fair reading of the merger clause reveals that it expressly disclaims only representations made with respect to the physical condition of the premises and merely makes general reference to representations concerning "any other matter or things affecting or relating to the aforesaid premises." As broad as this language may be, a reasonable interpretation is that its effect is limited to tangible or physical matters and does not extend to paranormal phenomena. Finally, if the language of the contract is to be construed as broadly as defendant urges to encompass the presence of poltergeists in the house, it cannot be said that she has delivered the premises "vacant" in accordance with her obligation under the provisions of the contract rider.

Application of the remedy of rescission, within the bounds of the narrow exception to the doctrine of caveat emptor set forth herein, is entirely appropriate to relieve the unwitting purchaser from the consequences of a most unnatural bargain.

The court reinstated the cause of action for rescission of the contract of purchase.

All concurred except J. P. Milonas and J. Smith, who dissented in an opinion by Justice Smith: I would affirm the dismissal of the complaint. . . . The parties herein were represented by counsel and dealt at arm's length. . . . There is no allegation that defendants, by some specific act, other than the failure to speak, deceived the plaintiff. . . . Finally, if the doctrine of caveat emptor is to be discarded, it should be for a reason more substantive than a poltergeist. The existence of a poltergeist is no more binding upon the defendants than it is upon this court. Based upon the foregoing, the motion court properly dismissed the complaint.

FOR CRITICAL ANALYSIS

Early in his opinion, Justice Rubin made the following statement: ". . . . defendant (seller) is estopped to deny their (the ghosts) existence and, as a matter of law, the house is haunted."

1. Does this mean that all future buyers must be told the house is haunted because, as a matter of law, it is? Or does this rule apply only to the seller in this case?

2. Is this case precedent for the rule of law that whenever a person behaves as if a situation is true, that the law holds the person to that situation even if it's false? Can you think of limitations or qualifications that ought to limit such a rule of law?

3. New York follows the common law rule of "caveat emptor" (Let the buyer beware). Did the majority opinion discard the rule, as suggested by the dissenting Justices, or did it distinguish the rule in some way?

KAMP V. STEBENS
517 v. N.W. 2d 227 (Iowa App., 1994)

Richard Stebens received a building permit to build a 16-foot breezeway connecting his garage to his house. Wayne Wille, a planner for the city of Davenport, testified that once attached by the breezeway, Mr. Stebens's garage was a "dwelling structure with a maximum height limitation of 35 feet. As an unattached garage, or "accessory structure," Stebens's garage was restricted to a height of 15 feet. Stebens obtained the building permit and built the breezeway because his garage was 17 feet high, in clear violation of the height-limitation ordinance for "accessory structures."

Mr. Wayne Wille's testimony was given in an action brought by Kamp, Stebens's neighbor, to declare the structure a nuisance and require it be brought into compliance with the law. The trial court found that the garage, attached to the house or not, was an "accessory" building and subject to the height restriction of 15 feet. The court concluded the garage was, therefore, a nuisance, and ordered the structure reduced in height. Stebens appealed.

Senior Judge Critelli wrote the opinion: We adopt the language of the trial court when it stated: "Under the plain language of the various ordinance sections, garages are considered accessory buildings and accessory uses whether detached from or attached to the main building, also referred to as the principal use." In referring to the use of the "breezeway" process of converting the new garage to part of the existing house, the trial court used terms such as "circumvent," "ploy to frustrate," and we might add "subterfuge" as a descriptive term of such process. . . .

Stebens's property line, which adjoined Kamp's property, is at least 15 feet higher than Kamp's property, and Stebens was given a variance to construct this garage within 1 foot of the property line. It is one thing to allow a neighbor to construct a garage within 1 foot of a property line, particularly one so many feet above the neighbor's property and retaining wall, and another thing to treat that constructed garage as being part of an existing house which has a maximum . . . limitation of up to 35 feet in height. We agree with the trial court that it is highly unlikely that the board of adjustment would have permitted a structure of up to 35 feet in height within 1 foot of

the property line and retaining wall under these full circumstances and the existing topography. That is the result, or at least a possibility, if one considers that the garage becomes a part of the house by this connecting process. We affirm the trial court in its determination that Stebens has violated the city ordinance and he should be ordered to reconstruct the upper portion of his garage to bring it into compliance with the height limitation of the ordinance, to wit, 15 feet. Judgment affirmed.

FOR CRITICAL ANALYSIS

1. If the complaining neighbor waited until after the offensive garage was built before filing suit, why wasn't he or she "estopped" from complaining later, when correction of the problem would be so costly? Didn't the complaining neighbor behave as if the garage was legal during construction the same as the sellers in the *Ackley* case behaved as if there were ghosts?

2. Do you have any reason to believe that homeowners in your neighborhood have constructed improvements, such as a swimming pool, or a small flat for an elderly relative, or a large back porch without first obtaining a permit? Should all violations of building and permitting codes result in removal of the improvement? Or should an adjustment in property taxes be made as a sufficient penalty? Which improvements should be removed, as in the *Kamp* case, and which should be permitted to remain?

CHAPTER QUESTIONS AND PROBLEMS

1. What is the amount of the standard real estate commission charged by brokerage firms in your community? Assume you own a home in which your equity is $25,000, and that you are about to sell

for $125,000. If your agent's commission rate is 6 percent, what is the commission rate expressed as a percentage of your equity? How much difference in effort do you suspect a sales agent expends in listing a home in which the owner has a $50,000 equity? What conclusions can be drawn from your analysis? Would a prospective seller be wise to engage the services of a listing agent on an hourly basis? Why or why not?

2. What specific services are rendered to a homeowner by a licensed real estate agent who has "listed" the property?

3. What questions should you ask the seller, or the seller's agent, before buying a house for your personal residence?

4. In 1950 Michael and Albina Klos purchased a lot from the Molenda family, who continued to live right next door. Rather than survey the property, the buyers and sellers paced off the lot and placed stakes in the ground as boundary markers. After Mr. Molenda's death in 1983, his widow hired a surveyor to determine the exact property line. The property line turned out to be 30" closer to the Klos house. Mrs. Molenda immediately dug up 30" of the Klos's grass and erected a fence on the true property line. Should the court require dismantling of the fence and award ownership of the 30" strip to Michael and Albina? [*Klos v. Molenda*, 355 Pa.Super. 399, 513 A.2d 490 (Pennsylvania, 1986).]

5. If you were selling your home, and a prospective buyer offered a very attractive price, and suggested the use of a land contract with only $1,000 down payment, what factors would you take into consideration?

6. If you were applying for a loan at a savings and loan association for the purpose of buying a home, which three of the following factors would be the most important to you?
   a. A relatively low interest rate.
   b. A relatively long repayment term.
   c. The right to prepay principal payments without penalty.
   d. A relatively low "late payment" penalty.
   e. The right to have someone else assume your loan without any assumption fee and without any increase in the interest rate.
   f. The absence of the requirement that you pay the lender's attorney fees incurred by the lender because of your default in making monthly payments.
   g. The absence of an acceleration clause that made the entire unpaid balance of the loan all due upon any default in monthly payments.

7. As a prospective buyer of your first home, what disadvantages would there be in leasing with an option to buy?

8. Would you prefer to finance the purchase of your home with a fixed-rate mortgage or with a variable-rate mortgage that begins with an interest rate one full percentage point rate lower than the former? Why?

9. Would you prefer to own a single-family detached home or a condominium? What are your perceptions of the advantages and disadvantages of each?

10. What is the primary reason you hope to be a homeowner in the future? If you will buy and sell a home on five different occasions over your working career, would you still prefer to be a homeowner? Explain.

NOTES

1. *Guimont v. Clarke*, 121 Wash.2d 586, 854 P.2d 1 (Washington, 1993).
2. National Manufactured Housing Construction & Safety Standards Act of 1974, 42 U.S. C. 5402 *et. seq.*
3. *The National Law Journal*, 8 February 1993, p. 20.
4. Kenneth R. Harney, *Homeowners Concierge Service Is Latest Thing*, San Francisco Examiner, 31 January 1999.
5. California Civil Code, § 1102 *et. seq.*

6. *Skendzel v. Marshall*, 261 Ind. 226, 301 N.E.2d 641 (Indiana, 1973). A leading case on protecting buyers under install-ment-land contracts.

7. Todd Juchau, "Is 'Title Insurance' Insurance?" Thesis for Master's in Business Administration, California State University, Sacramento, 1994.

8. To see how one state handles property tax, visit the Georgia Property Tax Division Web site at http://www2.state.ga.us/Departments/DOR/ptd/

9. Nolo Press publishes books on self-help legal topics, in-cluding neighbor law. For information, visit their Web site at http://www.nolo.com.

10. Peoria, Illinois County Code, § 5-19.

11. Albany, California Municipal Ordinance, § 10-3.6.

12. *San Francisco Chronicle*, 3 May 1994.

13. See, e.g., California Civil Code, § 3346; Maine Revised Statutes Ann., Title 14, § 7552; Alabama Code, § 35-14-1.

14. Michigan Comp. Laws Ann., § 750.382, California Penal Code, Sec, 384(a).

15. See, e.g., California Civil Code, § 841.4; Maine Revised Statutes, Title 17, § 2801; Massachusetts Gen. Laws Ann., § 49.21; Mich. Comp. Laws Ann., § 561.02; New Hampshire Rev. Stat. Ann., § 476.1; Rhode Island Gen. Laws, § 34-10-20, and Wisconsin Stat. Ann., § 844.10.

13

EMPLOYEE AND EMPLOYER RIGHTS AND DUTIES

I'm a great believer in luck, and I find the harder I work the more I have of it.

Thomas Jefferson, 1743–1826

Our environment sustains us well but only as a result of considerable, continuing, tiring, and sometimes fatiguing personal labor. Most adults and many minors must devote a substantial portion of their waking hours to gainful employment. A small number of people in the workforce are self-employed; most are *employees*, working for others under contracts of hire. Those who coordinate the work may be self-employed owners of business firms. More often they are employees themselves, typically in the service of corporations, partnerships, or sole proprietorships.

A CHANGING WORK ENVIRONMENT

In George Washington's time, approximately 90 percent of all Americans could be classified as farmers. In 1997, our total population of 267,954,764 included a civilian labor force of 136.3 million workers. Of that number, only 2.7 percent worked in farming, forestry, and fishing. Thus, our agricultural revolution has enabled 1.5 percent of our entire population to produce more than enough food to feed the nation.[1] The industrial and agricultural revolutions of the last hundred or so years shifted most people into urban areas, where manufacturing and various service activities expanded. In more recent times, mechanization, automation, robotization, and siliconization has reduced the need for factory workers and miners.

At the beginning of the twentieth century, workers had to adjust to new types of machines, ones they did not understand. Instead of the steam engine, which mechanically inclined workers could observe and figure out, the internal combustion engine befuddled many. Even a greater challenge to understanding were electrical machines, which operated quite differently from the earliest machines; how and why these machines worked was past the understanding of most laborers. Most of us have long since reconciled everyday dependence on a world we don't quite understand. Pictures are transmitted to satellites and received in homes through cable or satellite receivers with hundreds of viewing options available. We can log on to the Internet and find out how to safely thaw the frozen turkey in time to save Thanksgiving dinner. We can record movies for our own use and make phone calls from almost anywhere in the world, including Mt. Everest.[2] In 1899, only the wildest ranting of a mad scientist or science fiction writer could have predicted the cooperative construction of a space station by several countries. Yet just when we have become somewhat comfortable with machines we don't understand, the pace of change again appears to be accelerating. Silicon-based technology and biomedical research are making groundbreaking advances almost weekly. The discussions presented to the common person make little sense. However, workers in both the early 1900s and 2000s face a future with rapid change and exciting new possibilities.

NEW WORK ALIGNMENT

Dramatic realignments in work have occurred in this century. In 1997, 29.1 percent of American workers were in managerial and professional occupations; 29.6 percent in technical, sales, and administrative support; 13.5 percent in service occupations; 25.1 percent in manufacturing, mining, transportation, and crafts; 2.7 percent in farming, forestry, and fishing; and 4.9 percent unemployed.[3] In the 1998–1999 Occupational Outlook Handbook, the jobs with the highest predicted growth rates all require a college degree and relate to the computer industry. They include database administrators, computer support specialists, computer scientists, computer engineers, and systems analysts. The next several areas of predicted employment growth are in the health industry and relate in part to a growing aged population.[4] College degrees were a rare commodity in 1900, but now they are necessary for most of the best employment opportunities.

The pace of change in science and technology has increased in recent decades, stimulated by discoveries and inventions best exemplified by the computer. Among the most evident effects of this accelerated pace of change in employer–employee relations has been corporate downsizing: emphasis on cutbacks in numbers of middle-level managers and lower-level line workers. This has been made possible by machines and technology that improve efficiency in all steps, from accounting through production, warehousing, and marketing. Concurrently the internationalization of much business has greatly expanded world trade and intensified competition. The Bureau of Labor Statistics tells us that more than 21 million persons did some work at home as part of their primary job; instead of agriculture, repair work, or production, however, nearly 9 out of 10 of these workers were in white-collar occupations. We enter the new century armed with knowledge from the recent past that many common jobs may soon disappear and new job titles may require tasks and functions that today are unknown.

EXPANDED ROLE OF WOMEN

During the past three decades, women have earned a greatly expanded role in the nation's civilian labor force. Census Bureau figures tell us that in 1960 there were 69.6 million persons in the labor force, and 33.4 percent were women. By 1992, the civilian labor force included 45.6 percent women.[5]

There had been temporary bulges in such employment when women helped win the production battles of World Wars One and Two, but more permanent shifts have followed, encouraged by changed attitudes, inflationary pressures on single-earner families, continued mechanization and simplification of household chores, a trend toward smaller families, and legal protection against traditional gender discrimination. Although the civil rights movement has been primarily an effort by African Americans to gain legal equality, women may be the primary beneficiaries of the resulting remedial legislation. A notable failure for women, however, was the unsuccessful campaign between 1972 and 1982 to add an Equal Rights Amendment to the Constitution. That measure provided that "Equality of rights under the law shall not be denied or abridged by the United States or by any state on account of sex." Ratification required approval by 38 states; only 35 approved it before the deadline. Fortunately, most essential employment rights are ensured by law. Today there are very few bona fide jobs that might justify exclusively hiring an employee of a particular sex (or color, or religion). Even the concept of equal pay for comparable work is gaining in acceptance. Regrettably, however, full equality of opportunity remains a sought-after goal. In a 1998 study, the Institute for Women's Policy Research estimated that if current wage patterns continue "the average 25-year-old woman who works full-time, year-round for 40 years will earn $523,000 less than the average 25-year-old man."*[6]

How Does the Law Affect Workers and the Workplace?

Legislation and court decisions affect or control a wide range of issues concerning employment.

1. *Who may work?* Labor of persons under age 18 is limited and strictly regulated under federal and state laws. Thus, persons aged 16 or 17 are barred from hazardous work, including driving motor vehicles, mining, logging, and wrecking. Persons aged 14 or 15 may work in office or sales jobs and in retail, food service, and gasoline service, but not during school hours. Under specified conditions, persons of any age may deliver newspapers; act in movies, theater, radio, or TV; and work on any farm owned or operated by their parents. Other regulations are prescribed by the secretary of labor.[7] Many laws are designed to prevent discrimination in hiring, training, promoting, and dismissing employees simply because of their race, color, gender, national origin, religion, disability, or advanced age (40 to 70).[8]

2. *What work may be done?* By statute, scores of occupations from commercial aviator to X-ray technician require a license obtainable only by persons who have prescribed education and experience and pass qualifying examinations. Many are required to continue formal education to keep their skills current.

Visit the 'Lectric Law Library's Lawcopedia™ on employment and labor law Web site at http://www.lectlaw.com/temp.html

---

*Of course, there are many assumptions underlying such an estimation, such as comparability of work requirements, regions, and weighting of averages.

3. *When may the work be done?* Generally, one day in each week must be set aside for rest and recreation. Traditionally, Sunday has been so designated. Legal provision of this day of rest has been upheld by the U.S. Supreme Court as a valid state exercise of the police power in the interest of public health and general welfare. (Reasonable exceptions to Sunday closing laws permit sale of commodities necessary for health and recreation. This does not violate the equal protection or due-process clauses of the Fourteenth Amendment.[9]) Annual vacations of one week or longer are not mandated by law but are generally provided as a fringe benefit. Most states, by statute or executive proclamation, observe some ten federal holidays that are legally designated by the president and Congress specifically for the District of Columbia and for federal employees. Many states add one or more local legal holidays of their own.

4. *Where may the work be done?* Extensive legislation and administrative regulations prescribe minimal acceptable environmental conditions in workplaces.[10] Some 25 states (including California, Florida, Illinois, Michigan, New York, and Pennsylvania) have **right-to-know laws**. These require disclosure to workers of information about any hazardous chemical substances they are likely to be exposed to on the job.

5. *How may the work be done?* The Occupational Safety and Health Administration (OSHA) has outlawed many tasks, such as those involving repetitive hand, arm, and wrist motions that cause crippling injuries from tendonitis. In 1990, members of the Newspaper Guild, a union of editorial employees, had suffered tendonitis injuries from repeated work at video display terminals. Under an agreement with Cal-OSHA, the newspaper involved (the *Fresno Bee*) agreed to spend $750,000 in corrective action for new furniture, adjustable chairs, support tables, and special training sessions.[11]

6. *How many consecutive hours of work may be required in certain occupations?* Regulations control the maximum number of hours that bus drivers and airline pilots can be on duty without time off for sleep.

7. *How much must be paid for labor?* At both the federal and state levels, minimum wage laws have been in effect since the great depression. They are coupled with regulations of the maximum hours of work that employers may demand without the payment of "time-and-a-half" for overtime.[12]

8. *Do workers have the legal right to unionize?* Federal and state laws guarantee most workers the right to organize into unions of their own choice, and require employers to bargain collectively with the representatives of such unions over wages, hours, and a broad spectrum of conditions of employment.[13]

The law's concern with the employment process is pervasive. It precedes hiring, applies during employment, continues through dismissal, and extends into retirement. An expensive, legally mandated public education system provides lifelong learning opportunities that facilitate useful employment. Without proper knowledge and skills, one is likely to be underemployed or unemployed throughout one's life. Legal involvement continues when jobs are lost because of an economic recession, and public funds pay unemployment compensation.[14] A permanent worker who is dismissed without just cause may sue for damages under developing tort law. (The tort of wrongful discharge is discussed more fully later in this chapter.)

LEGAL CLASSIFICATION OF EMPLOYEES

The world of work has been a prime concern of lawmakers over the centuries. Rules enforceable in court enable businesses to fulfill their needs of providing goods and services to many customers. They also govern the employer–employee relationship, of which there are three basic types: principal–agent, employer–ordinary employee, and contracting employer–independent contractor.

PRINCIPAL–AGENT RELATIONSHIP

Agency is described in technical language by the authoritative *Restatement of Agency* as "the fiduciary relation which results from the manifestation of consent by one person to another that the other shall act on his behalf and subject to his control, and consent by the other, so to act."[15] In less arcane terms, this means that the principal is a special type of employer who hires an **agent** to act for the **principal** in negotiating and transacting business with customers. The agent receives and accepts authority from the principal to carry out the principal's business as directed.

Agents may be authorized to make contracts with customers on behalf of their principals. When made, the contracts are treated as legally binding between the customer and the employer, although negotiated by the agent. If every business customer had to deal directly with the owner, business as we know it could not exist. Agency law enables a business owner (as principal) to employ any number of persons (as agents) to enter into contracts with third parties for the sale or purchase of goods and / or services on behalf of the principal. Because an agent can legally bind his or her employer (the principal) to contracts that are made, the law declares the agent to be a *fiduciary* and imposes a high obligation of trustworthiness upon the agent. A **fiduciary** relationship exists when the law requires one person to treat another with the most scrupulous good faith and honesty (e.g., an attorney toward a client, a trustee toward a beneficiary in a trust, and a partner toward another partner in a partnership have fiduciary relationships). Obviously, a key to the expansion and success of business is to find and retain competent, honest, and industrious agents. The following hypothetical example illustrates how an agent may perform legal acts that bind the principal.

The 'Lectric Law Library's summary of agency law is at http://www.lectlaw.com/d-a.html

Bruce is hired as the booking agent for a rock group, the Understanding Slugs. He negotiates and signs a contract for the group to appear in one evening performance at the Wisconsin State Fair in Milwaukee. Two months before the show date, Bruce informs the Milwaukee producer that the group cannot appear as scheduled because "they'll be tied up in a two-week appearance in Vegas—a big break we just can't walk away from." Are the Understanding Slugs liable to the Milwaukee producer for damages for breach of the earlier contract?

Yes, the group is liable. They are legally bound by the acts of their agent just as is the Milwaukee producer to the group. Following are highlights of the agency relationship:

- Agency is a relationship between two persons, the *principal*, or employer who wants to get something done, and the *agent*, or employee who is authorized by the principal to do the specified job as a representative of the principal.

- The relationship is always *consensual*. Both principal and agent must expressly or impliedly consent to the relationship. For example, as a favor Juanita agrees to act as Lou's agent to buy two tickets to the big game. Lou reimburses Juanita for the price paid, but gives her no more than a "thank you" for the service. (Had Juanita bought the tickets without Lou's consent, he would have no obligation to pay.) The relationship is also usually—although not always—*contractual*, meaning that generally both parties give and receive consideration (see Chapter 8). For example, under an employment contract, Craig serves as Molly's agent (sales representative) in the Chicago territory. Craig makes contracts on Molly's behalf and binds her to perform. She pays him a salary and/or commission for his services.

- The agent represents and acts on behalf of the principal in dealings with third parties. The resulting contract is legally binding on the principal, provided the agent acted within the scope of his or her authority as given by the principal. Usually the agent is not bound to the third party to perform the contract.

- However, an agent who acts beyond the scope of his or her authority is personally liable to the third party. If in doubt as to the nature and scope of the agent's authority, the third party should check directly with the principal, asking (1) Is he/she your agent and (2) What is your agent's authority (e.g., to sell, to buy) and on what terms?

The hospital workers were excited to find that former Major League Baseball pitcher Mickey Lolich was checking into St. Joseph's Medical Center. When the healthcare workers checked the identity of their patient, they found out it was not Lolich but someone named Leroy Fulton. Is Mickey Lolich liable for the health bills incurred by Leroy Fulton in his name?

If an agent exceeds his or her authority, the principal is ordinarily not liable. It is then also true that if a person attempts to pass him or herself off as someone else, that person is liable but the "real" person, in this case Lolich, is not. Apparently, Leroy was also bumming beers and giving autographs. Don't assume that someone is who he or she claims to be without carefully checking. Leroy was arrested on suspicion of forgery and theft.[16]

- The agent, in effect, walks in the shoes of the principal, even when out of the principal's presence. The principal has the continuing right to control the agent, but while alone, the agent may make a foolish contract and the principal must honor it as long as the agent's acts were authorized. Note that even if the agent violates explicit orders, the principal would be liable to affected innocent third parties (e.g., the agent sells goods below a minimum price set by the principal, or grants credit in violation of stated company policy). The principal is likewise responsible for the torts the agent committed while within the scope of authorized behavior under a doctrine called *Respondeat superior* (discussed shortly).

- An official notice (e.g., legal summons and complaint) given to a duly authorized agent is legally deemed to be a notice to the principal. Also, the agent is duty bound to perform as promised and to use reasonable care (which could be appropriate skilled care, as when the agent is a lawyer or real estate broker).

- Agency is a fiduciary relationship in which the agent must act in scrupulous good faith and honesty toward the principal, always placing the interests of the principal first. He or she must be loyal, never serving two adverse parties (e.g., the buyer and the seller in a transaction) at the same time, unless both are fully informed and consent. Of course, an agent may be employed by a group of associated principals. Also, an attorney at law may be employed by two or more persons to prepare a partnership agreement as long as all clients give their informed consent, and the attorney treats them with impartiality and balanced fairness. Any agent must account to the principal for all receipts and disbursements and must never keep a secret profit.*

EMPLOYER–ORDINARY EMPLOYEE

An **ordinary employee** is a person hired to perform services for another, the employer, and the employee's physical conduct is controlled by, or is subject to control by, the employer. As mentioned, the employment relationship is usually a contractual relationship. Employees who transact business with third parties have a dual status; they are both ordinary employees and agents.

> Donna owns a dress shop. She employs Myra, Roxanne, and Nita as salespeople and Kari as a janitor. Donna is the employer, and Myra, Roxanne, Nita, and Kari obviously work for Donna. Which of the employed parties are employees and which are agents? Are the terms mutually exclusive?

Myra, Roxanne, Nita, and Kari are all employees. All but Kari are agents. The classifications are not mutually exclusive and many employees are agents and vice-versa. The key to an employer–employee relationship is the extent of the employer's right to control the employee's acts. Ordinary employees usually do not have *independent* business discretion. The salespeople in the dress shop are told how to handle and display merchandise and how to record sales. When they actually sell the dresses, however, they act as agents as well as ordinary employees because they have been given the authority by Donna to sell goods to customers.

---

*The burden of the fiduciary obligation is upon the agent and operates to safeguard the principal. The principal, although not a fiduciary, is still expected to deal fairly. For example, a company (the principal) must account to the agent for all receipts and commissions owed and must never retain any as a secret profit.

These sales are contracts between the customers and Donna. Kari, the janitor, has no authority to sell dresses or make any contracts for Donna; thus, Kari is an ordinary employee but not an agent.

The employer is liable to third parties for injuries caused by the negligence of employees while they are acting within the scope of their employment under a common-law doctrine called **Respondeat superior.** This legal doctrine imposes vicarious—that is, indirect—liability on an employer for the wrongful acts of an agent or employee that occur while the agent or employee is on the job. The Latin term *Respondeat superior* means "let the master respond." Vicarious liability occurs even though the employer has not been careless. Because liability exists even without the fault of the employer, the doctrine is similar to the theory of strict liability in tort.

The discussion in this text refers to employer and employee, but the terms *principal* and *agent* and even *master* and *servant*, are also often used when discussing *Respondeat superior*. If the appropriate control over the actor by the employer exists, then so does liability, despite any inconsistency in the use of terms.

The doctrine of *Respondeat superior* has three supporting theories. The first concerns the issue of control. An employer has the right to control the acts of the agent or employee and is thus responsible for injuries arising out of such service. The second theory is economic in nature. Since the employer profits from the employee's or agent's service, he or she should also suffer the losses. The third reason is practical and is referred to as the *deep-pocket theory*. The employer is more likely to be able to pay for the losses than the employee and/or agent. In other words, the employer usually has more money; this is where the saying "the employer has the deep pockets" comes from.

It is important to note that there are limitations on the employer's or principal's vicarious liability. An employer is responsible only for the wrongful conduct of an employee/agent occurring in "the scope of the employment." Generally, the act must be of a kind the worker was employed to do. It must also have occurred within authorized time and space limits and must have been activated, at least in part, by a purpose to serve the employer.

The employer is responsible only for the torts of the employee while the employee is on the job—or, in legal terms, is "acting within the scope of employment." There are several questions used to determine if the employee's act occurred within the scope of employment. The answers to all these questions assist a court or jury in determining whether the employee was on the job for purposes of the doctrine of *Respondeat superior*.

1. *Did the employer authorize the act?* If the answer is yes, then the act is probably within the scope of employment.

2. *What was the time, place, and purpose of the act?* If it occurred on the worksite, then the employee was probably on the job. The employee is generally not acting within the scope of employment, while commuting to or from work.

3. *Was the act one commonly performed by employees for the employer?* If yes, the employee was acting within the scope of employment.

4. *To what extent was the employer's interest advanced by the act?* If the act would ordinarily benefit the employer, then the employee was acting within the scope of employment.

5. *To what extent were the private interests of the employee involved?* If the act was primarily to benefit the employee, then perhaps the employee was not on the job. For example, an employee takes a break during the day and goes downtown to shoot a game of pool. An accident occurs while driving to the pool hall. The employee is probably not within the scope of employment.

6. *Did the employer furnish the means or instrumentality (for example, a truck or a machine) by which the injury was inflicted?* If the employee is using the employer's truck, he or she is more likely to be considered within the scope of employment.

7. *Did the employer expect that the employee would do the act?* Had the employee done the act before? If the answer is yes to both questions, the employee is more likely to be within the scope of employment.

8. *Did the act involve the commission of a serious crime?* If the act is a serious intentional wrong, the employee is not usually considered to be within the scope of employment, unless the employer requested that the employee perform that wrongful act.

Walter Johnson was driving down Main Street on his way to deliver a package for Racehorse Delivery Service. Unfortunately, Walter was distracted for a second and ran into the rear of Felicia Fresno's new Saturn automobile. Luckily, Felicia was not hurt, but the car suffered $3,000 in damages. Who is legally responsible for the harm to Felicia's car?

Johnson is, of course, liable for his own negligence. Because Johnson was an employee of Racehorse and because he injured another while driving the automobile on company business, Johnson was within the scope of his employment, making Racehorse Delivery also liable. Although Felicia can sue both Johnson and Racehorse, she will collect her actual damages only once; she will not receive twice that amount.

Many state and federal employment laws apply to employer–employee relationships. These laws cover such issues as social security, withholding of income taxes, workers' compensation benefits, unemployment compensation, workplace safety laws, employment discrimination, unionization, and the like. These laws do not apply to employer–independent contractor relationships, discussed next.

CONTRACTING EMPLOYER–INDEPENDENT CONTRACTOR

Independent contractors are not ordinary employees; they are engaged to accomplish some task, such as to build a warehouse. The party who contracts for their service has little control over how the job specified in the service contract is performed. The *Restatement of Agency* 2d §2 defines an independent contractor as

> [A] person who contracts with another to do something for him but who is not controlled by the other nor subject to the other's right to control with respect to his physical conduct in the performance of the undertaking. He may or may not be an agent.

Read "Independent Contractor v. Employer: Is There Really a Choice?" at the 'Lectric Law Library's Web site at http://www.lectlaw.com/files/emp25

If someone is an independent contractor rather than an employee, then the doctrine of *Respondeat superior* does not apply, certain tax obligations of the employer do not arise, and obligations under various employment laws such as the Civil Rights Act of 1964 do not arise.* In determining whether someone is an employee or an independent contractor, the following questions are important:

1. *What control does the employer exercise over the details of the work?* Little or no control suggests the worker is an independent contractor.

2. *Does the employed person work in an occupation or business distinct from that of the employer?* A different business suggests an independent contractor.

3. *Is the work usually done under the employer's direction, or by an unsupervised specialist?* Little or no supervision suggests an independent contractor.

4. *Does the employer supply tools or equipment required at the place of work?* Not supplying tools or equipment suggests an independent contractor.

5. *How long is the period of employment?* The shorter the period, the more likely that the person is employed as an independent contractor.

6. *What is the method of payment—by time period or upon completion of the job?* Payment upon completion suggests an independent contractor.

7. *What degree of skill is required of the person employed?* A high degree of skill suggests an independent contractor.

Building contractors and their subcontractors are examples of independent contractors. A property owner does not control the specific way in which either of these professionals performs the work. Truck drivers who own their equipment and hire out on an *ad hoc* basis are independent contractors. However, truck drivers who drive company trucks are usually ordinary employees. Collection agents and real estate brokers are usually independent contractors.

The relationship between a contracting employer and an independent contractor also may or may not be an agency relationship. Attorneys are often independent contractors who advise their clients and who also act as agents when they negotiate contracts on behalf of their clients with third parties.

The fact that the contracting employer has little or no control over the way in which the independent contractor does his or her work emphasizes the responsibility of the independent contractor to perform that work competently, although not as fiduciaries.

Yellow page community directories list many such independent contractors, from accountants to locksmiths to word-processing specialists. Many operate sizable firms, and employ their own staffs of ordinary employees and agents. What is their appeal? Usually they are experts in their specialized fields, and they perform jobs (such as painting houses) that are required only occasionally by the

---

*Thus, when interviewing lawyers or real estate agents who are to be hired, a prospective client can ask questions that would not be permissible if directed to candidate employees. "Are you married?" "Have you been arrested?" "Are you a Democrat?" "Do you believe in equality of the sexes?" "Do you contribute to the ACLU (American Civil Liberties Union)?" would all be legal questions to ask. Furthermore, the hiring principal could discriminate for or against candidates based on the answers to those questions. Interestingly, candidates to be engaged as independent contractors rarely even submit resumés to their prospective principals.

persons who employ them. An employer who hires independent contractors is relieved of the burdens of hiring and maintaining such specialists in a permanent workforce. Eliminated also are troublesome and costly chores of recordkeeping, payment of wages and workers' compensation insurance premiums, and the provision of fringe benefits such as medical insurance. However, as noted below, the relationship can be misused. The nature of the relationship is ultimately determined by its legal characteristics, not how the parties designate it. In other words, simply because an employer calls someone performing services for him or her an independent contractor does not necessarily make it so. The relationship may instead really be an employer–ordinary employee relationship with its attendant consequences.

> In 1989 the General Accounting Office estimated that the U.S. government was losing between $1.6 billion and $8 billion annually because some employers failed to withhold taxes from paychecks of ordinary employees who were improperly classified as independent contractors. Construction companies were major offenders. Legally, when the employer controls the location, the hours, and the quality of work, the individuals are in fact ordinary employees, and the employer must withhold and transmit their income and social security taxes.[17]

In the early months of President Clinton's first term, another employee tax problem surfaced when it was determined that certain prospective presidential appointees had failed to pay social security taxes for their domestic help, presumably because of ignorance of the complex applicable law. Further investigation disclosed that the practice was widespread. It was estimated that three-quarters of all household employers had failed to pay applicable social security and Medicare taxes. The law passed in 1950 required such payments for domestic workers who earned more than $50 in a three-month period, or more than $200 in a year. In October 1994, Congress approved a new "nanny tax" law that permits affected employers to pay their household employees' social security taxes as part of their own annual 1040 income tax returns, rather than file separate quarterly reports as in the past. The tax is payable on any domestic helper's wages that exceed $1,100 a year, which is substantially more than the former threshold of $50 a quarter.[18]

Nanitax Newsletter by Home/Work Solutions, Inc., Setering, VA 20165. http://www.4nannytaxes.com/tips.htm

http://

ECONOMIC SAFETY NETS FOR EMPLOYEES

In every state, society intervenes when a worker is hurt on the job by providing for compensation under applicable workers' compensation laws (see Chapter 7). The worker who is permanently disabled, on or off the job, may qualify for social security disability payments, as may the worker's dependents. Upon reaching retirement age, the worker eventually qualifies for benefit payments, and dependent survivors of a deceased worker may qualify for survivors' benefits under social security.[19] If a private employer has voluntarily provided a private pension to supplement social security retirement payments, the worker is again protected by the federal **Employee Retirement Income Security Act (ERISA)**, which regulates such plans. Under ERISA, the Pensions Benefit Guaranty Corporation (PBGC) was created to ensure the financial soundness of about 100,000 plans for some 40 million workers and retirees in the private sector. Needed reserves come from insurance premiums paid by the participating private employers.[20]

In 1986, the LTV Corporation, a Dallas-based steel and aerospace company, filed for bankruptcy. It used a Chapter 11 proceeding (as discussed in Chapter 7) that permitted LTV to reorganize and continue operating with reduced debts. At that time, its private pension plan for its 100,000 workers had about $2.3 billion in liabilities for promised benefits. PBGC promptly declared these LTV pension plans terminated and assumed responsibility for paying the pensions. However, by 1987 LTV had negotiated a new pension plan with its unions, leaving the PBGC burdened with the heavy deficit of LTV's prior plans. The PBGC objected, saying the new plan required the use of the insurance fund to pay retirees the same pensions they would normally have received if the termination had never occurred. When the PBGC ordered LTV to resume responsibility for administering and financing the original plans, LTV refused. Lower federal courts upheld the refusal, saying the order was "arbitrary and capricious." The PBGC appealed to the U.S. Supreme Court. How did the Court rule?

The U.S. Supreme Court agreed with the PBGC. Justice Henry Blackmun, writing for the majority, stated that the law gives the PBGC "the power to restore terminated plans in any case in which the PBGC determines such action to be appropriate and consistent with its duties." The PBGC authority, he noted, "is not contrary to clear congressional intent and is based on a permissible construction" of the 1974 Employment Retirement Income Security Act.[21] (See Chapter 5 for a discussion of the potent powers of administrative agencies.) If the PBGC were barred from ordering financially able companies to restore their private employee pension plans, the resulting financial burden could climb into billions of dollars beyond its insurance reserves. In June 1994, then Labor Secretary Robert Reich disclosed that private corporate employers underfinance pension plans covering about 8 million workers and retirees. He told the Senate Finance Committee, "We're not there yet," when asked whether the problem is similar to the scandal-ridden multibillion-dollar bailout of the savings and loan industry. However, he urged the committee to provide strong reform "before the problem becomes another economic crisis."[22]

INDIVIDUAL PENSION PLANS

Because most private employers do not provide pension plans to supplement social security, the federal Internal Revenue Code allows qualified workers to individually set aside a certain percentage of earned income, tax-free until retirement, in **Individual Retirement Accounts (IRAs)**. Some employers contribute to their employees' IRA accounts under what are called **simplified employee pension plans (SEP plans)**. Under *401(k) plans*, companies with profit sharing or stock bonus plans may contribute cash to a trust account for their employees. Funds for retirement may also be set aside by means of appropriate salary reduction or by forgoing a salary increase. Self-employed persons may establish **Keogh retirement plans**, which serve the same purpose.[23] Such private arrangements prudently provide retirement funds in addition to the maximum social security payments, which are meant to lay a minimum "floor" rather than an ideal customized "ceiling" for retirement needs.

In 1998 Congress authorized a new IRA named after Senator William Roth of Delaware. The so-called **Roth IRA** provides for tax-free income, as opposed to the traditional IRA's tax-deferred income. To qualify for the Roth IRA, a taxpayer must have earned income at least equal to the amount set aside (currently $2,000 annually for Roth and other IRAs), and there are maximum incomes over which a taxpayer cannot participate in this program. Tax-free income means just that—the income is tax-free.

Technical and planning information on Roth IRAs for practitioners and consumers can be found at http://www.rothiras.com/

> Cory Finley invests $2,000 in a Roth IRA at the age of 20. He makes no further investment. Assuming he waits until age 65 to make any withdrawal and the single investment earns an 8 percent annual compounded return, what would his tax-free investment be worth?

The power of compounding is astounding. After 45 years, Cory's $2,000 investment in a tax-free IRA would be worth $63,840 if invested at 8 percent. In all likelihood, Cory would invest additional funds in the account and the amount available at age 65 would be much greater. For example, assume Cory invests $2,000 a year from age 20 to 65, receiving a consistent 8 percent return; in this case, the value of his account at retirement would be $834,852. If he waits until age 68 to retire, he will be a millionaire ($1,058,685) on this $2,000 a year investment alone.

Is There a Constitutional Right to Work?

Do you have a constitutional right to work for pay? The answer is no. The U.S. Constitution does not recognize any right to work for pay. In 1946, however, Congress enacted the **Employment Act**, which was a philosophical commitment to provide full employment by "all practical means" for persons who are able, willing, and seeking to work. Initially, these practical means included a federal job-finding program under the leadership of the U.S. Training and Employment Service; the gathering and interpreting of economic data; the advising of the president and Congress via the Council of Economic Advisers; and the strategic use of the fiscal weapons of federal taxing and spending, as well as the federal monetary weapons of controlling the supply of money and credit through actions of the Federal Reserve Board of Governors.*

We have never achieved 100 percent employment. The reasons are numerous. Federal Reserve measures are limited in their accuracy and effectiveness. Some jobs are seasonal, as in professional sports and farming. Also, every year

---

*Controls available to the Federal Reserve Board of Governors include (1) changing the discount rate (interest) charged to member banks when they exchange promissory notes for cash (a lower rate releases more money into the economy), (2) buying or selling U.S. government securities (buying them from member banks releases more money into the economy), and (3) increasing or decreasing the reserves that member banks must maintain (lowering the reserves releases more money into the economy).

thousands of high school and college graduates attempt to enter into, and must be absorbed by, the full-time job market. Additionally, the supply and demand for products and services are in a constant state of flux in our competitive business world, and countless variables affect the nation's economy. A theory currently gaining support among economists is that there is, in fact, a natural and unavoidable rate of unemployment.*

Laura Lanier was pleased and honored when she was discharged from the U.S. Army, but now she needed a job in the private sector and could not find one. She heard that her state had enacted a "right-to-work" law, and so she went to a state employment office, described her skills as a truck driver, and demanded a job. "It's my legal right," she said. Must she be employed?

No. *Right-to-work laws*, which have been enacted in 21 states,** in no way guarantee every able and willing person a job. The term was coined to gain voter support for legislation outlawing *union shops* (discussed later in this chapter). Many believe that such laws are actually designed to weaken unions rather than to protect jobs or an authentic right to work. In states with right-to-work laws, a worker is not obligated to join or to pay dues to a union in order to get or keep a job. Note, however, that even in states without such laws, most workers do not belong to unions. In the preceding situation, Laura, as a veteran, may legally be given preferential treatment in competition with non-veterans for federal civil service jobs. (Many states and local governments allow some such bonus.) Thus, 5 points may be added to a veteran's score on qualifying tests for federal jobs, and 10 points may be added if the applicant has a service-connected disability and was disabled while in uniform.

EQUAL PAY FOR EQUAL WORK

Disappointed in her quest for civilian employment after leaving the Army, Laura Lanier enrolled as a student in a private business school. Within a year, she was qualified as a computer operator. The inventory control department of a wholesale hardware supply house hired her to work as a computer operator. Her performance and output soon equaled that of several male computer operators who had been with the company for periods ranging from three to ten years. All of the men were paid more than Laura. Was this a violation of federal equal pay legislation?

The federal **Equal Pay Act of 1963** specifically prohibited wage discrimination on the basis of gender for equal work in jobs that require equal skill, effort, and

---

*This theory is advanced by Edmund Phelps in his book, *Structural Slumps: The Modern Equilibrium Theory of Unemployment Interest and Assets* (Cambridge, MA: Harvard University Press, 1994). Phelps refers to a rate below which unemployment cannot fall without causing the economy to "overheat" with higher prices. That, in turn, brings on adjustments or corrections in the economy. These then push unemployment back up again.
**Alabama, Arizona, Arkansas, Florida, Georgia, Idaho, Iowa, Kansas, Louisiana, Mississippi, Nebraska, Nevada, North Carolina, North Dakota, South Carolina, South Dakota, Tennessee, Texas, Utah, Virginia, and Wyoming.

responsibility and that are performed under similar working conditions. However, the law permits inequality in pay on the basis of (1) seniority, (2) merit, (3) quality or quantity of production, or (4) any factor other than sex (e.g., a shift differential, a higher rate maintained for an employee reassigned to a lower-rate job because of "exigencies of the employer's needs," a training program, or higher sales commissions because of higher profits on goods sold). The employer must, however, act in good faith without unlawful discrimination in assignment and evaluation of work. Thus, in Laura's case, there was no violation if the pay differentials were based on seniority.

Unfortunately for women—and for the country—employment practices over many decades have placed most women employees in positions of less responsibility and lower wages than those held by most men. This condition tends to be maintained by the practice of some women who accept less demanding part-time employment in order to work concurrently as homemakers and caregivers (of children or elderly relatives). In past decades, women also often left gainful employment after marrying. Years later, they may seek to reenter the job market as full-time employees but are at a further disadvantage because others have outpaced them in seniority and experience.

The Institute for Women's Policy Research (IWPR) is an independent, nonprofit, scientific research organization incorporated in the District of Columbia in 1987.
http://www.iwpr.org/

Continued advancement in the ongoing campaign to equalize employment opportunities for women (as well as for minority members of both sexes) will probably require additional years during which women (and minority members) qualify through formal education and experience for the better and the best jobs. It will also require continued enforcement of existing equal employment opportunity legislation. Major employers have been compelled by legal action to pay millions of dollars in retroactive wage adjustments for past discrimination. Publicity given to prominent cases alerts other employers to the importance of complying with the law. Any person who believes that he or she has been victimized may file a complaint with the federal Equal Employment Opportunity Commission at one of its regional offices. Although more burdensome for the employee, a private action may also be brought. The aggrieved individual may even rely on the federal Civil Rights Act of 1866, a post-Civil War law that forbids employment discrimination on account of race or color.[24]

It is a grim fact that women, who constitute the majority in our nation, as a class of workers earn less than men do. U.S. Census Bureau demographer Suzanne Bianchi has reported that since the 1950s, every generation of women entering the nation's labor force has been much better educated and more committed to continuous full-time gainful employment than the group of women existing in that labor force. As a result, the annual earnings of women employed full-time rose from 60 percent of earnings of comparable males to 72 percent.[25]

This trend continues, but a "glass ceiling" remains firmly in place for women in many offices, shops, and laboratories. In the Civil Rights Act of 1991, Congress established the Glass Ceiling Commission[26] to study the business practices of federal contractors that affect the promotion of women and minorities through the corporate hierarchy. This is done on a selective basis by the Office of Federal Contract Compliance Programs (OFCCP) through corporate management audits known as *glass ceiling audits.*[27] The commission concluded that "independent research has shown that companies that go the extra mile in hiring and promoting minorities and women are more profitable. A study of the Standard and Poors 500 by Covenant Investment Management found that businesses committed to promoting minority and women workers had an average annualized return on investment of 18.3 percent over a five-year period, compared with only 7.9 percent for those with the most shatter-proof glass ceilings."[28]

COMPARABLE WORTH IN THE FUTURE— THE OUTLOOK FOR WOMEN

For a variety of reasons, certain jobs tend to be held mostly by women—and most of these jobs pay less than most jobs held by men. When different pay scales are based on differences in work performed, there is no unlawful discrimination under present laws. However, under the theory of **comparable worth**, jobs that have equal social and economic value should be paid equally. Thus, it is said, the services of a registered nurse who helps to keep you alive are worth at least as much as those of a licensed electrician who helps to provide light and power in your hospital room. The problem is that it is extremely difficult to measure with precision and fairness all the elements and variables that should determine the dollar value of different jobs at different times in different places. Presumably, the economic forces of supply and demand should automatically decide the question. Realistically, this function of the free market is distorted by such factors as traditional attitudes, long-established seniority rights, union pressures, government licensing regulations, and willingness or ability to make a commitment to long-term, full-time, career-type employment.

The Canadian province of Ontario passed a law in 1987 designed to introduce comparable-worth standards to both government units and private companies with at least ten employees. It requires employers to define job classes by grouping positions with similar qualifications and duties that are recruited and paid in similar ways. Jobs are ranked in terms of skill, effort, responsibility, and working conditions. For each female-dominated class (60 percent or more), the employer must seek a comparably rated male class. If the women are paid less, they must get a raise.

The Institute for Women's Policy Research has created a composite index considering several women's issues including employment and earnings, political participation, and economic autonomy. It then ranked the various states on the criteria. The five best states in 1998 were District of Columbia (they know it's not a state), Connecticut, Maryland, New Hampshire, and Vermont. The five worst states were all southern states: Mississippi, Tennessee, Kentucky, Arkansas, and West Virginia.[29]

WHAT IS THE MINIMUM WAGE?

The Fair Labor Standards Act of 1938 (FLSA) set a minimum standard hourly wage for industrial workers engaged in interstate commerce, and set the maximum workweek at 40 hours. The wage rate has been periodically increased (it was 25 cents in 1950, for example); since September 1997, the rate has been $5.15 for all workers who are at least 20 years old. Persons under 20 may be hired for 90 days for no less than $4.25 an hour. The act is complex, with exemptions and exceptions specifically detailed in the law (i.e., employers of tipped employees [those customarily receiving $30 or more a month in tips] may consider those tips as part of the wages and may pay as low as $2.13 per hour). Among those employees exempt from minimum pay requirements, as well as overtime provisions

Find minimum wage information at the Department of Labor's Web site at http://www.dol.gov/dol/asp/public/programs/handbook/minwage.htm

of FLSA, are academic employees, farm workers on small farms, casual babysitters, and administrative employees.

LAWS AGAINST DISCRIMINATION

Employees in G. R. Coleman's machine shop in a small New England town reflected the social makeup of the community. All were white, Anglo-American, Protestant, male, and highly skilled. Coleman was proud of his business and its products, and he ascribed much of its success to the homogeneity of the workforce. He therefore refused to hire Samara Fuguady when she applied for work in the mechanical drafting department. A native of southern Egypt, she was a naturalized American citizen, had extremely dark skin, and was a practicing Muslim. Samara had ten years of experience and excellent references. "It's not that I'm prejudiced," Coleman said, "but your presence would be disruptive and no one would be happy—least of all you." Is Coleman within his legal rights in refusing to hire Samara?

No. The **Civil Rights Act of 1964 (Title VII)** makes it unlawful for an employer "to fail or refuse to hire or to discharge any individual, or otherwise to discriminate against any individual, with respect to compensation, terms, conditions, or privileges of employment because of such individual's race, color, religion, sex, or national origin."[30] A group of persons defined by one or more of these criteria (race, color, gender, nation origin, or religion) is referred to as a **protected class**. Coleman appears to be using color, national origin, and religion as a reason to not hire—a clear case of illegal discrimination.

Title VII covers all employers and labor unions affecting interstate commerce *with 15 or more workers,* and all employment agencies. It applies to all state and local governments. A special section of the law forbids discrimination in most federal government employment. Many states have passed legislation prohibiting discrimination among those employers *with less than 15 employees.*

Discrimination is prohibited whether it is intentional (called **disparate treatment**) or unintentional (called **disparate impact**). "'Disparate treatment' . . . is the most easily understood type of discrimination. The employer simply treats some people less favorably than others because of their race, color, religion, sex, or national origin. Proof of discriminatory motive is critical, although it can in some cases be inferred from the mere fact of differences of treatment."[31] "By contrast, disparate impact cases involve some facially neutral employment criterion which has an adverse impact upon a protected group. If the inquiry in a disparate treatment case focuses upon the existence of discriminatory intent, the inquiry in a disparate impact case is generally directed toward the business justification for the disputed employment test or practice."[32]

Under Title VII, as amended, discrimination in employment practices is permitted only if in conformance with a bona fide (1) seniority system, (2) merit system, (3) system that measures earnings by quantity or quality of production, or (4) system that is based on the results of a professionally developed ability test (or criteria) not designed or intended to discriminate on any of the barred bases,

The Department of Labor Small Business HANDBOOK with laws, regulations, and technical assistance services can be found at http://www.dol.gov/dol/asp/public/programs/handbook/contents.htm

provided that the test is *job-related*, meaning that persons who do well on the test do well on the job, and vice-versa.

To prevail in a case, a plaintiff needs to satisfy three steps: (1) "The plaintiff has the burden of proving by the preponderance of the evidence a prima facie case of discrimination. (2) If the plaintiff succeeds in proving the prima facie case, the burden shifts to the defendant 'to articulate some legitimate, nondiscriminatory reason for the employee's rejection.' (3) Should the defendant carry this burden, the plaintiff must then have an opportunity to prove by a preponderance of the evidence that the legitimate reasons offered by the defendant were not its true reasons, but were a pretext for discrimination. The defendant need not persuade the court that it was actually motivated by the proffered reasons, but it is sufficient if the defendant's evidence raises a genuine issue of fact as to whether it discriminated against the plaintiff. To accomplish this, the defendant must clearly set forth, through the introduction of admissible evidence, the reasons for the plaintiff's rejection."[33]

Remedies available to a successful plaintiff include reinstatement or hiring, a court order to eliminate discriminatory practices, or a restoration of lost wages and damages. Although punitive damages are available, there is a statutory cap on total damages based on the number of employees working for the employer ($300,000 maximum for an employer of 500 employees). A prevailing plaintiff in a Title VII action is ordinarily entitled to recover attorney's fees and costs.[34]

The Role of EEOC

Congress made important amendments to the Civil Rights Act of 1964 with the Equal Employment Opportunity Act of 1972. For the first time, the federal **Equal Employment Opportunity Commission (EEOC)** was given power to institute civil actions in court to eliminate violations of the law. Formerly, it had to rely on informal methods, such as conferences and conciliation, which an employer could ignore.* The individual victim often was unwilling or financially unable to take the grievance to court.

Title VII charges must be filed with EEOC within 180 days of the alleged discriminatory act. In states or localities where there is an antidiscrimination law and an agency authorized to grant or seek relief, a charge may be presented to that state or local agency instead of EEOC (the time requirements may differ). Strict time frames govern filing charges of employment discrimination, failure to file undermines the ability of EEOC to act on an aggrieved person's behalf and may terminate a injured victim's right to a private lawsuit. Filing a complaint with the EEOC or appropriate state equivalent and complying with EEOC rules is required before filing a private lawsuit.

Race and Color Discrimination

A company's standards, policies, or practices for selecting or promoting employees are illegal if they discriminate on the basis of race or color. Discrimination in

---

*The authors of this text are proponents of Alternative Dispute Resolution, such as mediation and conciliation, but acknowledge that non-adversary alternatives are more effective to solve the conflict when a lawsuit is a viable option for the plaintiff if ADR does not work. This is particularly true in situations with significant power imbalances.

employment conditions and benefits are also illegal. For example, an employer cannot grant higher Christmas bonuses to whites than to blacks.

> Julie Deffenbaugh, a white manager of the jewelry department at Wal-Mart in Arlington, Texas, began dating Truce Williams, a black sales associate in another department. The store manager saw them together after work, obviously as a couple. The store manager told Deffenbaugh that she "would never move up with the company being associated with a black man and that Wal-Mart frowned upon fraternization with[in] the company." Deffenbaugh responded that her personal business was not the company's concern, "because it did not affect [her] job performance." Later her supervisor fired her, purportedly for shopping while on company time. Prior to the discovery of the interracial relationship, Deffenbaugh's employment record was spotless. Deffenbaugh sued Wal-Mart, claiming that she was discharged because she was dating a black male. Wal-Mart claimed that Deffenbaugh was not a member of a protected class because she was white and could not sue on the basis of Title VII. What was the result?

Deffenbaugh's jury verdict of $19,000 in compensatory damages was upheld, and a punitive damage award of $75,000 was allowed. Title VII prohibits discrimination in employment premised on an interracial relationship. "A reasonable juror could find that Deffenbaugh was discriminated against because of her race (white), if that discrimination was premised on the fact that she, a white person, had a relationship with a black person."[35] A more complicated case and one more representative of the type of discrimination that African Americans have been subjected to is the case of *Roberts v. Texaco*. In 1996 this case, which involved the revelation of audiotapes featuring Texaco executives discussing the hiding of evidence and speaking of blacks in a disparaging way, made headlines nationwide. The case was settled for $176.1 million.[36]

In the leading case of *Griggs v. Duke Power Co.*, the U.S. Supreme Court has unanimously held that it is a violation of the Civil Rights Act of 1964 for an employer to require a high school diploma and a passing score on a general intelligence test for employment or promotion when neither can be demonstrably related to job performance.[37] This tends to open the door to some minority and nonminority members who lack the benefit of high school education but are willing and capable workers. Moreover, the Court held that employment and personnel management practices, procedures, or tests neutral on their face and even neutral in terms of intent cannot be maintained if they operate to "freeze" the status quo of prior discriminatory employment practices. Thus, disparate hiring of relatively few women or minorities is illegal unless truly *necessitated* by lawful business purposes or requirements. In the case of *Ward's Cove Packing Co., Inc. v. Atonio*,[38] the Supreme Court held that it does not matter whether or not an employer intends to discriminate in its hiring practices. If the requirements for employment are unrelated to job performance yet operate to exclude minority groups, the requirements violate Title VII. Accordingly, the plaintiff, that is, the would-be employee, needs merely to prove that the employer's policy has a disparate impact on women or minorities of qualified people in the particular workforce (*not* in the much wider labor market). To overcome these facts, the employer

Garland's Digest on Employment Discrimination Law can be found at http://www.garlands-digest.com/sample/recentcases.html

http://

must prove that the practice is required by *business necessity* and is essential for the job, a heavy burden of proof.[39] But the employer is not compelled to hire and promote to meet specified quotas.

NATIONAL-ORIGIN DISCRIMINATION

It is unlawful under Title VII to discriminate against any employee or applicant on the basis of national origin. National origin includes birthplace, ancestry, culture, and linguistic characteristics common to a specific ethnic group. Title VII is joined by the Immigration Reform and Control Act of 1986 (IRCA),[40] which prohibits discrimination based on citizenship. The IRCA covers employers of four or more employees and proscribes discrimination against any person (other than an unauthorized alien) in hiring, discharge, or recruiting or referring for a fee because of national origin or citizenship status.*

Kufi, a Ghanaian-born black man, was employed in the laundry at Rivercity Resort Hotel. He made several unsuccessful attempts to transfer to the accounting department. Kufi had completed high school in Ghana and studied business at several universities in the United Kingdom. After emigrating to the U.S., he also took classes at two community colleges and completed 30 units at California State University in pursuit of a bachelor's degree in finance. Rivercity told Kufi that his accent was a barrier to all positions in the accounting department. Kufi filed a discrimination claim. Is an accent sufficient reason to deny Kufi the transfer?

In order to succeed with a defense based on accent and English usage, Rivercity must show that Kufi's accent or manner of speaking would have a detrimental effect on job performance (clear enunciation was a requisite job requirement and Kufi did not meet that requirement). A legitimate nondiscriminatory reason to not hire the applicant must be shown. In the case upon which this hypothetical is based, the court found that the plaintiff "speaks fluent, understandable English. His speech was clear and understandable during a whole day on the witness stand during which he underwent probing cross-examination." The hotel lost the case.[41]

Whereas discrimination against a person on the basis of national origin is illegal, it is also illegal to hire an alien who is not authorized to work in the U.S. All employers (agricultural and nonagricultural) are prohibited from knowingly employing aliens not legally entitled to work in the U.S. The definition of "knowingly hiring" has been greatly expanded in recent years. The applicable law now states: "Knowing is defined as including not only actual knowledge, but also constructive knowledge—knowledge which may fairly be inferred through notice of

---

*While the IRCA prohibits discrimination on the basis of citizenship, it also requires verification of legal status of all workers. Employers are required to check workers' documents to confirm the identity and work eligibility of all persons hired. The U.S. Immigration and Naturalization Service (INS) requires employers to (1) hire only those persons authorized to work in the United States, (2) ask all new employees to show documents that establish both identity and work authorization, and (3) complete the INS Employment Eligibility Verification Form I-9 for every new employee— U.S. citizens and noncitizens alike.

certain facts and certain circumstances which would lead a person, through the exercise of reasonable care, to know about certain conditions."

RELIGIOUS DISCRIMINATION

Title VII prohibits employers from discriminating on the basis of an employee's religious beliefs. Prohibited discrimination may be overt and blatant or a more subtle failure to reasonably accommodate an employee's religious beliefs. The plaintiff must establish four elements of a *prima facie* case of discrimination: "(1) he is a member of or practices a particular religion; (2) he is qualified to perform the job at issue; (3) he has suffered some adverse employment action; and (4) someone outside the protected class of which he is a member was treated differently."[42] Plaintiff must show that he possessed a bona fide religious belief that was not reasonably accommodated.

Officer Rodriguez, a patrol officer in the Chicago Police Department (CPD), was among those assigned to guard an abortion clinic during various demonstrations. A lifelong Roman Catholic, Officer Rodriguez believed clinic activities to be wrongful, and he requested that he not be assigned to guard the clinic. Rodriguez was offered a transfer to a district without an abortion clinic, but he refused. Thereupon, CPD refused to exempt Rodriguez from the duty, claiming department policy prohibited an officer from refusing any assignment. Must the employer agree not to assign Officer Rodriguez to such duty as an accommodation to his religion?

The court held for the Chicago Police Department. "Because the CPD provided Officer Rodriguez with the option of transferring to a district without an abortion clinic and such a transfer would have eliminated the conflict between his job responsibilities and his religious beliefs, we conclude that the City has satisfied its duty of reasonable accommodation under Title VII."[43]

GENDER DISCRIMINATION

The Equal Employment Opportunity Act of 1972 (EEOA), amending the Civil Rights Act of 1964, dramatically changed employment law relating to women. Before 1972, state law often prohibited the employment of women in certain jobs. For example, many state statutes barred women from working at night, working as a bartender, or working more than a certain number of hours per day or week. The EEOA struck down most of these limiting laws. Employers are forbidden to classify jobs as male or female and they cannot have separate male and female seniority lists.

Some 115 female flight attendants brought a class action suit against Pan American World Airways, Inc., in 1984. The women had been suspended, denied promotion, or fired for being overweight. The airline had used different tables of heights and weights, classifying men under the heading of "large frames" and women under "medium frames." The resulting difference between the two sexes was 11 pounds for a person 5'7" tall. Did the corporation's standards discriminate illegally against women?

Yes. The federal district court in San Francisco found the weight standards discriminatory against the female employees, while reserving the issue of damages for later determination. Pan American began an appeal, but dropped it in 1989. Without admitting bias, it agreed to pay the attendants $2.35 million. It also adopted a more flexible weight policy with a new "large frame" category for women. Under it, a 5'7" woman of medium frame should weigh 139 pounds; for a 5'7" woman with a large frame, the acceptable weight could be as much as 150 pounds. Moreover, the attendant could add up to three pounds upon reaching the age of 35, and again at ages 45 and 55.[44]

A defense to sex discrimination case is the existence of a Bona Fide Occupational Qualification (BFOQ). A BFOQ is a job requirement that, although discriminatory, is essential to the job in question.

Four male Adult Corrections Officers (ACOs) at the Women's Community Correctional Center (WCCC) on the Island of Oahu filed a Title VII sexual discrimination claim after the WCCC assigned only female Correction Officers to 6 of 41 available watch posts. The WCCC claimed that gender was a BFOQ because the protested watch sites were shower and toilet areas and the purpose of the restriction was to protect female inmates and to prevent allegations of sexual misconduct. Is gender a BFOQ in this case?

The court said yes. "Each designated female-only post is residential and requires the ACO on duty to observe the inmates in the showers and toilet areas for the prison's own security or provides unsupervised access to the inmates. The state's legitimate penological interests outweigh whatever interests the male ACOs may have in standing the watches of their choice. Viewing the evidence in the light most favorable to the plaintiffs, the defendants have met their burden of demonstrating that their policy is reasonably necessary to the operation of the WCCC. The defendants have established these six female-only posts are a reasonable response to the concerns about inmate privacy and allegations of abuse by male ACOs."[45]

The following case illustrates how the well-intended protection of one group can hurt another.

Johnson Controls, Inc., of Milwaukee, produces batteries. The manufacturing process exposes workers to levels of airborne lead considered harmful to a fetus and may cause birth defects. In 1982, Johnson instituted a program banning women from all jobs in the division where the airborne lead level was 25 micrograms per cubic meter or higher, unless they presented a doctor's certificate of sterility. It also barred women from jobs where the lead level was below 25 micrograms if the jobs could lead to promotion to more dangerous areas. Female employees working in the lead division were transferred to other divisions without loss of pay or seniority. The United Auto Workers union claimed that this was illegal sex discrimination and filed a complaint with the Equal Employment Opportunity Commission on behalf of seven involuntarily transferred women (and one man who had been denied transfer to a lower lead-level division because women got priority in transfers). A federal civil rights suit followed, and the district judge awarded summary judgment to Johnson without trial, although a 1982 amendment to Title VII (the Pregnancy Discrimination Act) declared that "women affected by pregnancy or childbirth . . . shall be treated the same for all employment related purposes . . . as other persons not so affected but similar in their ability or inability to work." The UAW appealed. How did the appellate court rule?

The Court of Appeals, in a 7–4 ruling, upheld the trial court. The appellate court declared that "the physical differences between the human sexes creates a distinction between men and women that accords with our previous recognition that Title VII permits distinctions based upon the real sex-based differences between men and women, especially those related to childbirth." If generally applied, the ruling could have barred as many as 20 million women from employment in workplaces where similar toxic chemical exposure exists. Proponents argued that the obvious discrimination is a business necessity: to provide a safe work environment and to avoid potential liability for lawsuits. Being male, they said, is a Bona Fide Occupational Qualification (BFOQ) reasonably required for normal operation of that particular business and a valid exception to Title VII.[46] In the UAW's final appeal, the U.S. Supreme Court reversed the appellate court, and in its opinion stated, "The PDA's (Pregnancy Discrimination Act) amendment to Title VII contains a BFOQ standard of its own: unless pregnant employees differ from others in their ability or inability to work, they must be treated the same as other employees. . . . Title VII and the PDA simply do not allow a woman's dismissal because of her failure to submit to sterilization."[47]

Sexual Harassment

Sexual harassment in the workplace is a form of illegal gender discrimination. Sexual harassment occurs when job opportunities, promotions, and the like are given on the basis of sexual favors. Harassment also occurs when an employee is subjected to a work environment where the employee must put up with sexual comments, jokes, or physical contact that is sexually offensive.

The EEOC has defined two types of sexual harassment in its guidelines:

1. *Quid pro quo*. "Unwelcome sexual advances, requests for sexual favors, and other verbal or physical conduct of a sexual nature constitute 'quid pro quo' sexual harassment when (1) submission to such conduct is made either explicitly or implicitly a term or condition of an individual's employment, or (2) submission to or rejection of such conduct by an individual is used as the basis for employment decisions affecting such individual."

2. **Hostile Environment.** Conduct in a hostile environment "has the purpose or effect of unreasonably interfering with an individual's work performance or creating an intimidating, hostile, or offensive working environment." The EEOC considers several factors to determine whether a hostile environment exists: "(1) whether the conduct was verbal or physical or both; (2) how frequently it was repeated; (3) whether the conduct was hostile or patently offensive; (4) whether the alleged

The law firm of Morgan, Lewis and Bockius, with offices in several states and countries, provides a newsletter with brief well-written discussions of current trends in employment law. http://www.mlb.com/

harasser was a coworker or supervisor; (5) whether others joined in perpetrating the harassment; and (6) whether the harassment was directed at more than one individual. No one factor controls. An assessment is made based upon the totality of the circumstances."[48]

Rena Weeks began work as Martin Greenstein's secretary on July 23, 1991. Greenstein was a partner at Baker & McKenzie, the world's largest law firm. "On August 8, the Thursday of her third week at the firm, Weeks had lunch with several persons, including Greenstein, at a local restaurant. As they left the restaurant, Greenstein gave her some M & M candies, which she put into the breast pocket of her blouse. A short time later, as they walked to Greenstein's car, Greenstein pulled Weeks back, put his arm over her shoulder, put his hand in her breast pocket and dropped more candies into the pocket. He then put his knee in her lower back, pulled her shoulders back, and said, 'Let's see which breast is bigger.'"[49] Is this behavior sexual harassment causing liability for Greenstein and his employer, Baker & McKenzie?

A San Francisco jury said yes, awarding Weeks $50,000 in compensatory damages. They said yes to this jury instruction, "Has plaintiff Rena Weeks proved by clear and convincing evidence that defendant Baker & McKenzie (a) had advance knowledge of the unfitness of defendant Martin R. Greenstein and with a conscious disregard of the rights or safety of others continued to employ him, or (b) ratified the conduct of Mr. Greenstein which is found to be oppression or malice?"[50] The jury awarded Wells $7.1 million in total punitive damages.* The trial court judge reduced the punitive damage award to $3.5 million, an amount later upheld on appeal. In upholding the punitive damage award against Baker & McKenzie, the court stated, "In all events, there is substantial evidence that at the time Weeks was hired, Baker & McKenzie and its relevant managing agents were well aware that Greenstein was likely to create a hostile work environment for women, and that Baker & McKenzie consistently failed to take measures reasonably designed to protect women from Greenstein's abuse. The failure to place reports of Greenstein's misconduct in his own personnel file so as to warn future supervisors of that conduct in and of itself demonstrates a conscious disregard for the rights and safety of other employees. No formal action was taken by the firm to prevent Greenstein from creating a hostile work environment."[51]

As laudable a goal as nondiscriminatory treatment is, difficulty among people of good will can still arise. An employee wrongfully accused of discriminatory treatment may be discharged without a full and accurate investigation to protect the employer from sexual harassment claims.[52] Except in limited circumstances, the wrongfully accused employee has no legal recourse.**

---

*A discerning reader might note that the damage total in this case exceeds the maximum provided under Title VII of the Civil Rights Act. The case could have been a Title VII case, but it instead was pled under the California Civil Rights Law, which lacks the federal damage limitation. The Fair Employment and Housing Act (FEHA) Gov. Code, § 129000 et seq.

**Employees protected by a just cause provision of a labor contract are among those with some protection. In union contracts issues of employee discipline including discharge usually provide for a grievance mechanism which culminates in a neutral arbitration. In the typical labor contact, an arbitrator ultimately decides if the employee was a harasser and if discharge is consistent with fair treatment under the contract.

The risk and complexity of civil rights lawsuits often lead defendants to settle cases out of court. In 1992, the State Farm Insurance Company settled a class action sex-discrimination lawsuit for $157 million to be paid to 814 women plaintiffs. The federal district court had already ruled (in 1985) that State Farm had engaged in discriminatory practices. In 1988, the court approved an agreement between State Farm and aggrieved employees whereby the company agreed that for the next ten years at least 50 percent of all sales agents hired would be women, to help remedy past violations. This affirmative action remedy was based on evidence of discriminatory practices that had occurred between 1970 and 1974, a period during which State Farm had hired 586 agents in California, but only one was a woman. Many women had applied for positions, but had been rejected. One of the witnesses, Muriel Kraszewski, who worked for the company as an insurance agent's assistant, testified that when she applied for a job as a sales agent, she was told that a college degree was a prerequisite. Yet at that time State Farm was hiring male sales agents who did not have college degrees. Later she was told that State Farm would not hire women for work as agents. At the time this settlement was the largest in the history of civil rights litigation for any type of discrimination. Divided by the number of plaintiffs, however, the average award shrank to $19,287.

AGE DISCRIMINATION

Harry Rockwell lost his job with the Majestic Admiral Products Corporation when he was 45 years old. A friend told him about a similar job that had just become available in the Crescent Moon Company because of the death of the incumbent. When Rockwell applied, the personnel manager said, "You are eminently qualified for the assignment, except that you're too old. We're looking for a bright young college graduate with maybe five years of experience. We want him or her to grow with the company." Does Rockwell have any legal recourse?

Yes. Three years after the Civil Rights Act became law, Congress passed the **Age Discrimination in Employment Act of 1967 (ADEA)**, which prohibits "arbitrary age discrimination in employment" of persons between 40 and 70 years of age. It makes it unlawful for an employer in interstate commerce to fail or refuse to hire, to discharge any individual, or otherwise to discriminate against persons with respect to compensation, term, conditions, or privileges of employment, because of age. This law also applies to employment agencies and unions. It permits discrimination when age is a Bona Fide Occupational Qualification, and it recognizes the propriety of disciplining or even discharging a person for good cause.

A 54-year-old plant manager who earned $15.75 an hour was temporarily laid off when the company plant was closed for the winter. When spring came, the manager was replaced by a 43-year-old worker who earned $8.05 per hour. The older manager, who had worked for the company for 27 years, was not given a chance to accept a lower wage rate. Was the action of the company permissible under the ADEA?

No. The court, which referred to the firm's dismissal of the manager as "industrial capital punishment," held that the manager's termination in these circumstances violated the ADEA.[53]

The ADEA applies to "a person (including a corporation) engaged in an industry affecting commerce who has 20 or more employees for each working day in each of 20 or more calendar weeks in the current or preceding calendar year."[54] If the older manager had refused the pay reduction, the result would have been different.

An "'employee' means an individual employed by any employer except that the term 'employee' shall not include any person elected to public office in any State or political subdivision of any State by the qualified voters thereof, or any person chosen by such officer to be on such officer's personal staff, or an appointee on the policymaking level or an immediate adviser with respect to the exercise of the constitutional or legal powers of the office."[55]

In Missouri, four judges were appointed to preside over state courts under the Missouri Non-Partisan Court Plan. They had been retained in office through elections, but became subject to mandatory retirement at the age of 70 under a provision of the Missouri State Constitution. Must they retire?

Yes. The U.S. Supreme Court held that the judges qualified as appointees on the policymaking level because performance of their duties required "discretion concerning issues of public importance." Moreover, the Court said that if the Congress had wanted the ADEA to apply to state judges, it could have plainly said so.[56] The ADEA is joined by the Workers Benefit Protection Act,[57] making it illegal for a business to use a worker's past-40 age as the basis for discriminatory treatment in awarding employee benefits.

Almost all states have enacted their own laws barring employment discrimination on the basis of race, sex, religion, national origin, and advanced age. Most states call for equal pay for equal work and also follow the federal model of protecting the employment rights of handicapped persons. Also, the developing tort law of wrongful dismissal (discussed later in the chapter) may protect permanent employees against arbitrary discharge without good cause.

WHAT IS MEANT BY "AFFIRMATIVE ACTION" IN EMPLOYMENT PRACTICES?

Because of many years of discrimination in employment against women and minorities, government administrators have made special efforts to provide them with more opportunities for gainful employment. By threatening to terminate lucrative supply and research contracts, federal government departments have pressured companies to adopt **affirmative action programs**. Essentially, these require positive efforts to hire and promote minorities and women, in percentages roughly equal to their representation in the neighboring communities (sometimes referred to as the "potential applicant pool"). This has sometimes caused **reverse discrimination** against qualified nonminority male employees and applicants. The presumption, however, is that such persons are better able to fend for themselves in the job market; they can look for and find suitable employment where there are no federal contracts that might require affirmative corrective action. It should be noted that Title VII neither requires nor denies affirmative action as a remedy for discriminatory practices.

> The Acme Electronics Company, a Texas-based corporation, sold most of its output to the U.S. government. It had operated for the past ten years in a city near the Mexican border, where many citizens of Mexican ancestry resided. After a preliminary screening of applicants for an important job in its computer center, Adam Ramirez (a Mexican American of Latino and Native American ancestry) and Richard Ellis (an Anglo American) were the final contenders. Both were university graduates and appeared to be qualified or qualifiable with a minimal amount of training. Ellis, however, had five extra years of experience. He was highly recommended by his previous employer. Most of Acme's employees were white males. Whom should Acme hire?

To protect its federal supply contracts, Acme should hire Ramirez. Some legal experts question the constitutionality of affirmative action. Efficiency experts insist that employment and promotion should be based on merit. Opponents of affirmative action say that the Civil Rights Act of 1964 calls for neutrality, with no discrimination for or against anyone. Proponents argue that with neutrality, corrective action might take a generation or longer, and that is too long.

The Supreme Court has not been as helpful as many critics would like on the issues of affirmative action, perpetuating a contentious political debate over its efficacy and legality. In 1979, the Supreme Court did give its stamp of approval to a private, voluntary arrangement negotiated by the Kaiser Aluminum and Chemical Co. with the United Steelworkers Union. This program set up a skilled craft-training program with half the slots arbitrarily reserved for blacks and half for whites. At the time, although there was a 30 percent black population in the geographical area of the plant, fewer than 2 percent of the skilled craftworkers were black. Brian Weber, a white, was passed over for skilled craft training and challenged the company and union plan as discriminatory. He lost.[58] The Court's approval of this private, voluntary affirmative action plan to correct manifest racial imbalance automatically legitimized some 175,000 similar plans already in existence at that time, and others that have been added since then. Moreover, one effect was to shield such employers from charges that the plans impliedly admitted prior bias for which they could be sued. Eight years after the *Weber* case, the U.S. Supreme Court upheld a local government agency's voluntary affirmative action program.

> Among seven finalists seeking promotion to road dispatcher, Diane Joyce had a lower score than Paul Johnson on qualifying tests and interviews. However, since not even one of the 238 job positions of the pertinent job classification was held by a woman, the employer (Transportation Agency of Santa Clara County, California) voluntarily adopted an affirmative action program and promoted Ms. Joyce to the position. Johnson claimed this violated his rights under Title VII, and the trial court agreed. The Court of Appeals reversed, and Johnson appealed to the U.S. Supreme Court. How did it rule?[59]

The judgment of the Court of Appeals was affirmed. The Court opined that the employer had acted reasonably in considering the sex of Ms. Joyce because of "'a manifest imbalance' that reflected under representation of women in 'traditionally segregated job categories.'" She was one of seven applicants, all classified as "qualified and eligible," and the agency director was authorized to promote any one of the seven. Johnson remains an employee who may seek other promotions in the future.

In 1996, California voters passed a constitutional amendment by initiative, Proposition 209. The key provision of the initiative is "The state shall not discriminate against, or grant preferential treatment to, any individual or group on the basis of race, sex, color, ethnicity, or national origin in the operation of public employment, public education, or public contracting." Court challenges to the initiative have been unsuccessful.[60] The effect of the initiative has been the curtailment of affirmative action programs of the nature in the preceding case.

> Cheryl Hopwood, a white Texas resident, applied for admission to the University of Texas School of Law, one of the nation's leading law schools. She was denied admission although her application credentials were impressive, including a 3.8 undergraduate grade-point average and a 160 score on the Law School Admissions Test (83rd percentile). She sued, claiming she was "subjected to unconstitutional racial discrimination by the law school's evaluation of [her] admissions applications."[61] The University of Texas School of Law admissions process separated the files of black and Mexican American applicants and enrollment decisions were made separately, accepting GPA and test scores lower than Ms. Hopwood's. Was Ms. Hopwood successful in her lawsuit?

Whether she was successful depends on what you mean by success. The Federal Court of Appeals held that the "University of Texas School of Law may not use race as a factor in deciding which applicants to admit in order to achieve a diverse student body, to combat the perceived effects of a hostile environment at the law school, to alleviate the law school's poor reputation in the minority community, or to eliminate any present effects of past discrimination by actors other than the law school."[62] Ms. Hopwood, however, was not admitted to the school and she received only $1 in damages.[63] The Supreme Court declined to hear an appeal of the *Hopwood* case,[64] and the extent to which employers, particularly public employers, may use affirmative action is in some doubt.

AMERICANS WITH DISABILITIES ACT (ADA)

In July 1990, President Bush signed another landmark civil rights law, one that may, in time, prove to be the most significant legislation enacted during his term in office. The **Americans with Disabilities Act of 1990 (ADA)** has been hailed as a declaration of independence for some 43 million disabled Americans. The ADA applies to both the public and private sectors and goes well beyond prior existing protective legislation at the state and federal levels. The ADA applies to practices in employment, public and private accommodations, transportation, and telecommunications facilities. Business firms and other establishments must improve access for the disabled if "readily achievable" without "undue hardship." This hardship could involve the nature and cost of the accommodation in comparison to the overall size of the firm and its financial resources.

Employers with 15 or more employees are legally forbidden to discriminate in employment of disabled people who are capable of performing the essential functions of the job. Note that the act does not require employment of anyone who is unqualified for the job, nor does it require preferential treatment for the disabled.

Among the key issues in the law is the definition of a disability deserving of legal protection and the definition of reasonable accommodation. "An individual with a disability under the ADA is a person who has a physical or mental impairment that substantially limits one or more major life activities, has a record of such an impairment, or is regarded as having such an impairment. Major life activities are activities that an average person can perform with little or no difficulty such as walking, breathing, seeing, hearing, speaking, learning, and working."[65]

Rock Island County Metro Link has a federally required reduced fare program that makes transportation services available at a reduced rate for persons with disabilities. The application form for this program states, "Applicants do not qualify if their sole disability is . . . AIDS. . . ." Mr. Hamlyn has AIDS, which has caused him to have significant difficulty walking more than one block and boarding or alighting from a standard bus. Is Rock Island's exclusion from the reduced fare program illegal under the ADA?

Yes. AIDS is considered a disability under the ADA. In the court's opinion, "it is undisputed that the AIDS infection renders Mr. Hamlyn physically "unable . . . to utilize mass transportation facilities and services as effectively as persons who are not so affected." This exclusion is discriminatory under the ADA. Title II of the ADA provides that "no qualified individual with a disability shall, by reason of such disability, be excluded from participation in or be denied the benefits of the services, programs, or activities of a public entity, or be subject to discrimination by such entity."[66]

A "reasonable accommodation may include, but is not limited to, making existing facilities used by employees readily accessible to and usable by persons with disabilities; job restructuring; modification of work schedules; providing additional unpaid leave; reassignment to a vacant position; acquiring or modifying equipment or devices; adjusting or modifying examinations, training materials, or policies; and providing qualified readers or interpreters. Reasonable accommodation may be necessary to apply for a job, to perform job functions, or to enjoy the benefits and privileges of employment that are enjoyed by people without disabilities. An employer is not required to lower production standards to make an accommodation. An employer generally is not obligated to provide personal use items such as eyeglasses or hearing aids."[67]

Salley began working at Circuit City as a video sales counselor. Within two years, she became a store manager. Circuit City had a drug policy, providing that managers "will work to ensure that employees are free from the effects of alcohol and illegal substances, whether consumed on or off Company property." Within a year of becoming a store manager,

Salley told a superior of his significant drug activity and addiction, but told him that it was a thing of the past. Salley was assured that no action would be taken against him. Unfortunately, he suffered a relapse into drug and alcohol addiction. Circuit City discovered his drug use and other apparent violations of company drug policy, including missing work time because of drug use and alleged drug involvement with a subordinate, whose drug use he failed to report. Circuit City fired Salley two days after he signed a statement admitting his misconduct. Was Salley's firing in violation of the ADA?

No.[68] While an employer is required to reasonably accommodate a person with a disability (drug addiction is a protected disability) they are not required to tolerate disobedience and violation of company rules. "[F]or purposes of [the ADA], the term 'qualified individual with a disability' shall not include any employee or applicant who is currently engaging in the illegal use of drugs, when the covered entity acts on the basis of such use." The court upheld Salley's dismissal stating "an employer may hold an alcoholic or drug-dependent employee" to the same qualification standards for employment or job performance and behavior that such entity holds other employees, even if any unsatisfactory performance or behavior is related to the drug use or alcoholism of such employee. "[No] reasonable jury could conclude that Salley was discharged for his disability rather than his drug use and concomitant violations of Circuit City's drug policy."[69]

Casual inspection of office and factory buildings, as well as of stores, theaters, and various other facilities open to the public, confirms the fact that great improvement has been made in accessibility for disabled persons. Not as successful have been efforts to open doors to their gainful employment. According to a 1994 survey by Lou Harris & Associates, two out of three disabled persons are not working, a ratio unchanged since 1986. Yet 79 percent of those who are unemployed would rather have a job. Moreover, they are half as likely as persons who are without significant disabilities to attend sports events, live music performances, and movies. Obviously, availability of transportation remains a major obstacle.[70]

An employer is not expected to make accommodations that will impose an undue hardship on the operation of the employer's business. Undue hardship has been defined to mean "an action that requires significant difficulty or expense when considered in relation to factors such as a business' size, financial resources, and the nature and structure of its operation."[71]

As with other protected classes, certain questions and tests are prohibited. Among prohibited questions are those asking about the existence, nature, or severity of a disability. Job-related questions are allowed, such as: Can you keyboard or work with the newest Rivercity Software? Passing a medical examination may be a qualification for a job as long as it is required of all applicants for the same job and is somehow job- and business-related.

Your textbook authors need to be aware of the hazards of "Repetitive Strain Injury" in the preparation of this text. Read about the problem at http://www.engr.unl.edu/ee/eeshop/rsi.html

WHAT ARE BASIC DUTIES OF EMPLOYEES?

Two weeks after being employed as a deckhand on Plato Pamasi's 180-foot yacht, *The Invincible*, Jake Morgan refused to obey an order of the

Chief Mate Ben Blight to swing over the side on a rope ladder and scrape and repaint a rusted section of the hull. Morgan argued that nothing had been said about such dirty and potentially dangerous duties when he was hired. Moreover, he said, "I'm too tired. Why don't you do it?" May he be fired without recourse?

Yes. Scraping and painting are customary duties of deckhands. This was reasonably implied, if not explicitly expressed, in their employment agreement. The agreement could have been expressed in words (spoken or written) or implied from conduct of the parties, or from customs of people in that occupation. Also, being too tired during working hours is no excuse for refusal to do a job. An employee is duty bound to obey reasonable orders and to comply with reasonable rules. However, one cannot be required to do anything that is illegal, immoral, or contrary to public policy, nor can one be compelled to do work not covered by the employment contract. Thus, if Morgan had been hired as a steward or engine room mechanic, he could properly refuse to do the scraping and painting of the hull.

The Supreme Court has decided, however, that a worker may refuse to do a job that appears to be unreasonably dangerous. The specific task in question involved walking on angle-iron frames of a wire mesh screen suspended about 20 feet above the shop floor, to remove objects that had dropped onto the screen from overhead conveyor belts. Only ten days before, a coworker had fallen to his death while doing similar work. The U.S. Labor Department supported the worker's position, claiming authority under OSHA (the Occupational Safety and Health Act), which seeks to guarantee a hazard-free working environment for employees.[72]

An employee is neither a slave nor an indentured servant bound to remain for a prescribed time. One has the *power* to quit at any time—simply leave the job. But there is no legal *right* to quit when to do so breaches a contract in which one has promised to work for a specified period of time. For this reason, an employee who quits without good cause before the contract ends may be liable for damages. However, employers seldom sue their rank-and-file employees. A lawsuit would be costly, other employees would resent it, and any sizable judgment obtained would probably be uncollectible. The implied or expressed duration of the contract is usually short, perhaps a month or a year. But, of course, it may be extended by formal or informal renewals into permanent employment, which could last until retirement.

Many employment contracts are entered into informally, for an indefinite or open-ended period of time, with no detailed agreement as to the rights and duties of the parties. Traditionally, such employment is **at will,** with both parties free to terminate the relationship at any time without liability (other than payment by the employer for services rendered to date, or sometimes to the end of the pay period). Indeed, employees under such contracts continue to have the right to quit at will without liability. However, in a number of states the employer may be held liable for the tort of **wrongful discharge** of a permanent employee, or for illegal discrimination against any employee. Discharge is legal if it is for good cause (e.g., insubordination or intoxication of the worker on the job, or lack of business, or bankruptcy for the employer). To the chagrin of many employers who wish to avoid such liability, a worker who started in a contract of employment *at will* may gradually become a permanent employee with the simple passage of time. As a result, many employers now explicitly state that employment is at will and may be terminated at any time by either party without liability. They take this precaution in oral and in written contracts as well as in employee handbooks.

Nevertheless, courts and legislators throughout the country continue to grapple with the difficult issue of wrongful discharge. At stake is the propriety and viability of extending to many workers something comparable to the security now enjoyed by tenured faculty in the employ of colleges and universities. At the same time the law is attempting to provide security to employees, however, the nature of employment, especially in the technology and communications fields, may be gradually normalizing a twenty-first century concept that many specific jobs and even careers are expected to change every five to seven years as science and services evolve. Certainly the employer and the employee can explicitly agree on the duration of the intended employment, but in the past the vast majority of employment contracts have probably failed to address this matter, or they have confused or contradicted it as the actual employment continued over many years.

Three rules appear to be emerging in courts that have been confronted with the issue:

1. As a matter of public policy, the employer is guilty of a tort and vulnerable to a claim for substantial damages if the employee is demoted, transferred, or fired as a "whistleblower" for disclosing company fraud or for refusing to follow company orders to commit perjury or other illegal acts.

2. The employer may also be liable in tort when an employee is fired in violation of the covenant (promise) implied in every contract to perform all promises in good faith (i.e., with honesty) and fair dealing.

3. The employer is liable for a breach of contract if the employee is fired in violation of a contractual agreement of continued employment. More often this would be the case when the court finds an *implied* contractual agreement not to fire unless there is good cause to discharge. The implied agreement may be evidenced by favorable job evaluations over a long period of time, especially when accompanied by promotions and salary boosts.

In a 1998 case, a California employer sued for wrongful discharge was ultimately held legally blameless for firing a manager accused of sexual harassment. The manager claimed that he was not guilty of the accusations made against him by two female coworkers, which led to his termination. The jury in the trial court agreed that the manager had not harassed the women and awarded him $1.8 million. Nevertheless, the jury award was overturned and the company was found blameless because it had acted on a reasonable, good faith belief that the allegations were true.[73]

An employee who has been wrongfully discharged often faces insurmountable obstacles to meaningful relief. In the words of Lewis Maitby, director of the ACLU (American Civil Liberties Union) National Task Force on Civil Liberties in the Workplace, "The average employee who has been wrongfully terminated has as much chance of getting a jury trial as sprouting wings and flying to the moon."[74] Mr. Maitby was indulging in hyperbole, provoked no doubt by his observations of the barriers that do exist. He and others have accordingly supported acceptance of the Model Employment Termination Act (META), which was approved in 1991 by the 300 state-appointed uniform law commissioners. It was originally proposed for adoption as uniform legislation (like the Uniform Commercial Code), but was finally approved as a model act that permits individual states to adopt alternative provisions.

The META is designed to give American workers protection against arbitrary dismissal under the generally prevailing practice of employing workers at will, with no assurance of job security. Relief under the META is limited to reinstatement with full or partial back pay. If reinstatement is not feasible, limited severance pay is to be provided. As with workers' compensation, jury trials are discouraged, tort actions (with possible compensatory and punitive damages) are not allowed, and arbitration is provided. The act is limited to private employers of five or more employees who have worked more than part-time for the same employer for at least one year. Workers may still be fired for a good cause (e.g., theft, substance abuse, and "inadequate performance," as well as for economic reasons based on "honest business judgment"). Thus far, there has been little support for the act within state legislatures.

A highly valued employee who quits during the specified term of a written contract to take a better-paying job elsewhere cannot be compelled to return to his or her job. But a court of equity might grant the first employer an **injunction** barring the employee from working for anyone else during the contract term. To defy the court order would mean citation for contempt and a possible fine, as well as a judgment for damages. The second employer might also be guilty of the tort of interference with a contract or an economically advantageous situation—some authors call this a *contort*—a contract tainted by a tort. The tort is known as **interference with an economically advantageous relationship** and is defined as the knowing and wrongful interference with the performance of an existing valid contract.

Generally, there must be a contract in existence between two parties, and the defendant must induce one of the parties to breach the contract. Thus, a computer software manufacturer might wrongfully induce a talented software designer to breach a fixed-term employment contract with the plaintiff and join the defendant's staff at a higher salary. This must be distinguished from the common case where an employee has the right to quit *at will*, and does so in order to join another company. Legitimate advertising and other forms of solicitation, such as the promise of higher income and greater responsibilities, may encourage this move. Employees, acting collectively, may legally interfere with the commercial expectations of their employers by a lawful strike. Note also that employers may compete with one another, vigorously but fairly, for business in the open market. This is true even when the practice drives some competitors into bankruptcy as customers flock to the aggressive firm that offers a better deal (in quantity, price, service, delivery, credit, etc.).

A legal drama in 1984–1988 between Texaco and Pennzoil over which suitor would buy Getty Oil provided the factual basis, and the tort of intentional interference with contractual relations the legal weapon, for the largest civil award in world history. In the Texaco–Pennzoil case, the tort was committed when Texaco prevented the performance or full execution of the terms of a binding "agreement in principle" between Pennzoil and Getty. Although there was no formal written contract between Pennzoil and Getty, they had been engaged in a serious business relationship with a reasonable expectation of successful completion.*

The **Family and Medical Leave Act of 1993 (FMLA)** requires employers with 50 or more employees to grant employees leave for certain family purposes related to child care and family health. All public agencies (state and local government) and local education agencies (schools) are covered without need of meeting the 50-employee test. The act allows an employee to use up to 12 weeks leave in any 12-month period but does not require that the leave be paid, although the employer must continue any provided health benefits. The employer may require the employee to use paid benefits as part of leave (e.g., the employee has three weeks of vacation available). Among the reasons deemed proper for family leave are birth or adoption of a child; placement of a foster child in an employee's care; care of a seriously ill spouse, parent, or child; or a serious health condition that renders the employee unable to perform any essential functions of the job. After any leave is taken, the employee must be restored to the same or similar position in the company.

ACME Company provides in its employee handbook that the Family and Medical Leave Act applies to the company's employees. An employee seeking leave is denied same and the company claims as a defense to a family leave claim that it employs fewer than 50 employees. Is this a good defense?

Yes. Federal statutes apply to companies according to the jurisdictional requirements of the statute. As the act applies only to employers with 50 or more employees, FMLA does not apply to ACME Company. "The agreement between the parties that ACME would comply with the requirements of the FMLA does not bring the parties within the Act itself, because to do so would effectively enable them to contract around the Court's lack of subject matter jurisdiction. Although such an agreement may have enhanced the terms of the contractual relationship between the parties, it does not provide the federal courts with jurisdiction to hear cases under the Act."[75]

Every employee is duty bound to use reasonable skill in performing assigned work, to perform it conscientiously (i.e., to do "an honest day's work for an honest day's wages"), and to do nothing contrary to the interests of the employer. For

---

*In 1984, a jury in Houston, Texas, awarded the Pennzoil Company $7.53 billion in compensatory damages and $3 billion in punitive damages, an unprecedented total judgment of $10.53 billion. Three years later, the Texas intermediate Court of Appeals affirmed the judgment but reduced the punitive damages to $1 billion. In April 1987, Texaco filed for bankruptcy in a Chapter 11 proceeding (which allows temporary freedom from creditor claims while the company formulates a strategy to pay its debts), delaying payment of the judgment and permitting continued operations while avoiding forced liquidation (i.e., selling all of its assets and paying all debts to the extent possible). After the Texas Supreme Court affirmed the judgment that November, Texaco planned to appeal to the U.S. Supreme Court. However, on Christmas Day, Pennzoil agreed to accept Texaco's "final settlement offer" of $3 billion—still a colossal penalty (20 percent of Texaco's total net worth, and three times the net worth of Pennzoil). In 1994, the drama continued on another stage. Pennzoil has paid $800 million in taxes and had used the $2.2 billion balance to buy Chevron Corporation stock, claiming that the stock constituted "replacement property similar to property lost to Texaco." The IRS disagreed and demanded an additional $906 million. In October 1994, the parties reached a compromise, and Pennzoil paid another $265 million in taxes and $189 million in interest. *The Wall Street Journal*, 17 October 1994, A4. The case is the subject of a best selling book, James Shannon, *Texaco and the $10 Billion Jury* (New York: Prentice Hall, 1988).

example, one may not sabotage equipment, steal supplies, or sell company secrets to competitors.

> Ed Block was a stationary engineer in charge of a battery of boilers at the Metropole Chemical Works. Safety valves would prevent a major explosion, but the equipment could be seriously damaged even if the fail-safe devices worked perfectly. All controls had to be closely monitored and regulated. One day Block's wife left him after a prolonged argument over their son, who had been arrested on a narcotics possession charge. Perhaps understandably, but not excusably, Block had consumed a large bottle of bourbon before he went to work on the swing shift. Within an hour, he was sound asleep at the control panel. The boilers soon overheated and shut down automatically. Repairs would cost at least $5,000, to say nothing of the cost of disrupted production and spoiled goods in process, worth perhaps another $50,000. Is Block liable for the loss?

Yes. Theoretically, an employee may be charged with the cost of the employer's products he or she spoils or the value of equipment damaged either intentionally or through negligence. Practically, most employers seldom go beyond dismissing the errant employee. They absorb such spoilage costs as part of the price of doing business, and pass them along to consumers in higher prices for finished products. Insurance sometimes helps cover the costs.

WHAT ARE BASIC RIGHTS AND COMMON BENEFITS OF EMPLOYEES?

Every employee is entitled to compensation for services as agreed on with the employer. If no figure is specified, the prevailing or customary wage applies, or whatever would be reasonable under the circumstances. Sometimes, as in many sales jobs, pay in the form of commissions is related to particular performance, such as a specified percentage of all sales made. A common variation is a contract that calls for payment of a minimum base salary or "draw," to be offset by commissions earned. The employee retains any excess commissions. State laws commonly require payment every two weeks, or sometimes weekly.

In any event, the employee does not receive all of the earnings. Legally, the employer must withhold federal income taxes (and, in some states, state income taxes) and social security taxes and pay them directly to the appropriate government agencies. By agreement with the employee, deductions are also common for such purposes as buying insurance, government savings bonds, or company stock; paying off company credit union loans; paying union dues (called the check off); or putting money into savings accounts.

If wages are not paid, an employee has the right to sue for money owed. Special legislation in most states and under federal bankruptcy laws gives the employee a preference or priority over the employer's other creditors.

> Darleen Gorski was employed as a sales engineer by the Apogee Corporation at a salary of $2,000 a month plus a commission of 5 percent

of all net sales made in excess of a minimum specified at the beginning of each year. The company supplied her with a car and agreed to pay all expenses of its operation and maintenance. (Apogee had so many agents on the road that it set aside the equivalent of premiums on automobile insurance and was thus self-insured.) At the end of the first month, Gorski submitted an itemized bill of $409 for gas and oil and $1,175 to cover the cost of replacing wheels and tires and a tape deck that had been stolen. Were the items claimed by Gorski collectible as part of her compensation?

No. Although Gorski was entitled to both sums, technically the $409 was *reimbursement* for expenses properly incurred, and the $1,175 was indemnification for a loss suffered. Neither is *compensation* for services rendered; neither is it inculpable in taxable income.

WORKING CONDITIONS

The most-cited OSHA violations are at http://www.insure-it.com/oshatop20.htm

Every employee is entitled to reasonably safe working conditions. The federal **Occupational Safety and Health Act of 1970** broadly requires the employer in interstate commerce to furnish employment and a place of employment that are free from recognized hazards that cause or are likely to cause death or serious physical harm. The enforcement arm of the act is the Occupational Safety and Health Administration (OSHA). OSHA represents that between 1970 and 1996 the workplace death rate has been cut in half; still, about 17 Americans die every day on the job.[76]

The law extends to such diverse items as equipment, protective clothing, vapor and noise levels, and in-plant health facilities. The law requires that companies log injuries and correct unsafe conditions as well as notify employees of their rights to bring notice of unsafe conditions to the attention of OSHA. It provides for inspections, investigations, issuance of citations, judicial review, and penalties for violations. All states have a variety of similar local regulations governing production in intrastate commerce.

Carlos Gutierrez preferred to be a low-profile employee. However, in a previous job he had been a safety inspector and his new employer, Rivercity Cleaners, appeared to be in clear violation of several OSHA safety standards. After his supervisor refused to act, he notified the appropriate state OSHA. They inspected Rivercity and found violations of protective equipment requirements, violations of portable fire extinguisher requirements, and violations related to electrical components and equipment and walking-working surfaces. Rivercity fired Carlos for disloyalty. Does Carlos have any remedy?

Yes he does. Retaliation against workers who exercise their right to report unsafe working conditions under the Occupational Safety and Health Act is prohibited. Workers must contact an OSHA office almost immediately after learning of the alleged discriminatory action in order to protect their rights. OSHA will investigate the complaint and upon finding merit will order reinstatement or other remedies. The Department of Labor reached settlements with various employers involving

41 workers in New York and New Jersey, who reported workplace hazards and were discharged or otherwise penalized as a result. "Under the terms of settlement agreements reached between employers and the U.S. Labor Department's Occupational Safety and Health Administration (OSHA), the 41 workers received a total of $211,231 in back wages. Other remedies included reinstatement, restoration of vacations and 401K benefits, informal negotiated settlements between the complainants and their employers, and the requirement that employers display posters on the rights of employees."[77]

FRINGE BENEFITS

An employee has no constitutional right to fringe benefits, but legislation, competition, and union pressure have made them an integral part of most employment contracts. Such benefits are provided in addition to the regular wage or salary. Social security, no doubt the most important fringe benefit, is mandated by the Social Security Act of 1935. Financed by taxes paid by both employers and employees, the massive social security program provides benefits to more than 40 million persons, a growing number that includes retirees (who generally start receiving pensions at the age of 65), dependent survivors of insured persons, and qualified disabled workers and disabled dependents. It also encompasses the Medicare program of health benefits for qualified retirees, their dependents, qualified disabled persons under 65, and qualified workers and their dependents of any age who need dialysis treatment or a kidney transplant.

Since the Social Security Act was enacted in 1935, people are living longer and are having fewer children, and Congress has repeatedly increased benefits, extending them to additional groups and requiring increased payments to compensate for increases in the cost of living. As a result, to keep the program economically viable well beyond the year 2000, changes have been made and more will surely be made—in social security taxes levied, in benefits paid, and in income taxes on benefits received by wealthier recipients. The large numbers of comparatively young immigrants entering the United States (legally and illegally) and joining the domestic workforce should help to keep the social security tax revenues higher than disbursements.* There is no real justification for fears that the program will collapse in bankruptcy before today's children become tomorrow's retirees.

Many private and public employers supplement social security retirement benefits with their own pension, stock-purchase, and profit-sharing plans. Some provide a *simplified employee pension* (SEP) plan, whereby they contribute to the employee's individual retirement account (IRA). Vacations and holidays with pay, and medical and dental insurance are very valuable fringe benefits for most employed persons. Some employers also offer a variety of less significant benefits. These include life insurance; legal-aid plans; sick leave; prenatal, child, and

---

*In May 1994, the Urban Institute of Washington, D.C., a respected nonpartisan research organization, released the results of a study on immigration. Ironically, in a nation composed almost completely of immigrants and their descendants, many call for much tighter control and restraint of legal and illegal immigration. However, the Urban Institute reported that legal and illegal immigrants together pay between $25 billion and $30 billion more in taxes each year than they receive in public services. Although there are an estimated 2.7 to 3.7 million illegal immigrants in the United States, the study found that they have no negative effect on wages or the job markets (partly because they often do menial labor and seasonal fruit and vegetable harvesting that citizens refuse to do). M. Sandalow, *San Francisco Chronicle*, 25 May 1994.

elder care; maternity and paternity leave; adoption assistance; social, recreational, physical fitness, and continuing education programs; and employer-assisted housing. The dollar value of fringe benefits often equals as much as 20 to 30 percent of the monetary wages paid. The appeal of fringe benefits is enhanced by the fact that most are tax-free to the employees and tax-deductible as business expenses to the employers.

EMPLOYEE STOCK OWNERSHIP PLANS (ESOPs)

A relatively new fringe benefit could significantly affect the traditional dichotomy that many persons perceive between the interests of capital and labor—the **Employee Stock Ownership Plan (ESOP)**. The basic concept of employees acquiring stock in the company that employs them is not new. For example, for decades Sears, Roebuck & Co. has encouraged and helped its employees to buy Sears stock. It is a promising way of sharing the wealth, building employee loyalty, and stimulating productivity—much needed as international competition intensifies. The concept gained new prominence under a provision of the federal Tax Reduction Act of 1975, which gives special tax benefits to participating employers. A subsidy is given to the company's ESOP, a trust that buys company stock. The company invests the money received for the stock in new plants and equipment, and after seven years the stock can be distributed to the employees. Under a variation, the ESOP borrows money to buy company stock. The company guarantees the loan and agrees to pay it off. As the loan is paid off, shares are allocated to employees in proportion to their pay. Workers who quit or retire may take their allocation of shares, to hold or sell them.

Unions have been wary of the idea because it could divide worker loyalty, employers have been indifferent, some sociologists and economists see a contradiction in the idea of a worker's capitalism, and employees themselves generally prefer immediate benefits and fear the risks of stock ownership with its fluctuating value and returns. In any event, ESOPs have increased in popularity as a management technique to ward off unfriendly takeovers by corporate raiders and as an alternative to boosts in wages and fringe benefits. ESOPs are technical undertakings and employees may logically believe equity ownership will translate into company control. That assumption would be incorrect as the voting interest on the ESOP shares is retained by the prior equity owners and the other non-ESOP shareholders. For example, in a family-held corporation engaging in an ESOP plan, the stock held by the family will continue to control the company.

The National Center for Employee Ownership estimated that 10,000 ESOP plans were in effect in 1989, with some 10 million worker-owners participating, and the numbers have grown since then. United Airlines (UAL), the nation's largest air carrier, with 76,000 workers and some 550 airliners, became the largest ESOP company in July 1994.* United thus becomes number one in the list of the

---

*UAL Corporation shareholders approved transfer of a 55 percent ownership share to employees represented by unions of the pilots and the machinists. In exchange for the stake, worth some $4.8 billion, the pilots, machinists, and nonunion employees agreed to wage reductions for five to six years, and to work-rule changes and reductions in fringe benefits, to help the airline survive and thrive in this extremely competitive field. (The company had not earned a profit for four years.) As part of the deal, the employees selected the new chairman and chief executive officer (Gerald Greenwald) and will have three seats on the 12-member board of directors. A report by union president Ken Thiede stated that halfway through the distribution period there had not been a single employee layoff and the stock value had increased 260 percent.

ten largest companies offering ESOP: United Airlines, Procter & Gamble, Atlantic Richfield, Allied Signal, Phillips Petroleum, Lockheed, Ashland Oil, Textron, Colgate Palmolive, and FMC.[78]

EMPLOYER DUTY TO "WARN"

Rivercity Industries, a manufacturer of ceramic kitchenware, had an unprofitable 1998–1999. Efforts to return to profitability or find a buyer for the company were unsuccessful. On June 26, 1999, the bank that had been lending funds to the company informed management that they would no longer do so. The company decided to go out of business and close its three plants; termination notices were sent to workers on June 29, effective the next day. Several employees sued, alleging that the company had failed to provide the required 60-day notice of the plant closing required by federal law. What was the result?

Following a long-established practice in Western European countries, the federal **WARN Act (Worker Adjustment and Retraining Notification Act)** took effect early in 1989.[79] Generally, it requires managers of fairly large business enterprises* to give employees at least 60-day advance notice before either a *plant closing*** or a *mass layoff*.*** Certain exceptions are permitted. For example, if the closing or layoff is due to business circumstances that were not reasonably foreseeable, the notice must be given only as soon as the closing or layoff becomes reasonably foreseeable. In the case of Rivercity Industries, the plant closing falls within two exceptions requiring the 60-day notice: the "unforeseeable business circumstance" when the bank withdrew support and the "faltering company" exception (the company's inability to sustain its economic viability). The WARN Act requires that a company's notice provide the affected employees with a clear and detailed explanation of the reasons why full notice was not provided.[80]

PRIVACY RIGHTS

New technology can alter old habits and customs within a short time. For example, the introduction of computers into our lives has aided business but at the expense of legal and ethical tradeoffs. Many find the tradeoffs disturbing, particularly in relation to privacy rights.

Computers make it possible to accumulate, store, and retrieve vast amounts of information. Virtually all institutions with which we deal—insurance

---

*Covered by the act is any business enterprise that employs at any single site at least 100 full-time employees, or 100 or more employees (full-time or part-time) who, in the aggregate, work at least 4,000 hours a week.

**Plant closing means the permanent or temporary shutdown of a single site of employment, or one or more operating units within a single site, if it will result in an employment loss at that site during any 30-day period for 50 or more full-time employees. A full-time employee is one who works an average of 20 or more hours a week and has worked at least 6 months in the preceding 12-month period. An employment loss includes termination, a layoff for more than 6 months, or a loss of at least half of the employees' working hours for 6 consecutive months.

***A mass layoff is a reduction in the workforce that, during any 30-day period, causes one-third of the employees or 50 employees (whichever is less) to be terminated, laid off for more than 6 months, or to lose at least half of their working hours for 6 consecutive months. If at least 300 employees are affected by the mass layoff, notice is required regardless of the percentage of the employees who are affected.

companies, mail-order houses, banks, and credit card companies—gather information about us. They store that information in their computer files. Government agencies, such as the U.S. Census Bureau, the Social Security Administration, and the Internal Revenue Service, also collect and store data.

These businesses and agencies collect information on income, expenses, marital status, and other personal history and habits. When we apply for a driver's license, a credit card, or even telephone service, information about us is gathered and stored. Frequently, this personal information finds its way to potential or present employers. Seldom—if ever—do most persons give permission for, or even know about, the use of this information.

In recent years, the right to privacy has become a significant employment issue. As in many other areas of social life, the law attempts to balance competing interests to arrive at fair policies. Employers are interested in minimizing employee theft, loss of trade secrets, and misuse of company property while maximizing productivity; employees are interested in being treated with respect and dignity while remaining free of intrusion into their private lives. Employers today must be careful not to violate their employees' rights to privacy and personal security. Areas of concern include drug testing, the use of lie-detector tests, and electronic monitoring. Employees must realize that they should have modest expectations of privacy at the workplace. Personal e-mail, items kept in their desks, phone conversations, and the like may be subject to company monitoring and retrieval.

A new privacy issue is facing one class of employees: those who have previously been convicted of a serious felony but have served their time and returned to society as good citizens. As discussed earlier in Chapter 9, cities in all the states now make available to the public the names, addresses, crime committed, and date of release of all persons once convicted of serious sexual offenses and, in some cases, homicide. If the public dissemination of such information is disruptive in the former convict's place of employment, is it a proper basis for discharge? The answer is undoubtedly yes, because convicts are not within any protected class of persons. However, unanswered is the question: If these sometimes wholly reformed persons are driven from the neighborhoods and from employment by public disclosure of their records, will the interests of society be served? Or is further criminality assured? If public disclosure will be disruptive in the workplace, can an employer ask job candidates if they wear the "Scarlet Letter" and discriminate on that basis?

Drug Testing in the Workplace

Drug and alcohol abuse has been estimated to cost industry between $50 and $100 billion in absenteeism, impaired performance, and accidents each year. Naturally, employers are concerned about a decline in job performance and other harm resulting from drug abuse. Some employers therefore test employees to uncover drug use. But the tests are not always reliable. Even when tests are accurate, a question exists as to whether they violate employees' right to privacy.

If the employer is a government agency, testing is subject to the requirements of the U.S. Constitution. Employees have a Fourth Amendment right to be "secure in their persons . . . against unreasonable searches and seizures." So the administration of drug tests is constitutional only if there is a reasonable basis for suspecting the employee's use of drugs—or if drug use in a particular government job could threaten public safety.

The Department of Transportation required employees working on oil and gas pipelines to submit to random drug testing. All employees were subject to the rule whether they were suspected of drug use or not. Does the Department of Transportation's drug-testing rule violate employees' constitutional rights?

No. The government's interest in promoting public safety was held to outweigh employees' privacy interests.[81] To date, appellate court decisions conflict on whether and when drug testing violates employees' privacy rights.

Constitutional limitations do not usually restrict private employers. However, some state constitutions and statutes do restrict and regulate private drug testing. Also some collective-bargaining agreements regulate drug testing, specifying when and how it is or is not permitted. It is often required for participants in important competitive sporting events, such as track and field meets and certain Olympic events.

Donna refused to take her employer's drug test. Her employer maintained a drug-free workplace, requiring all employees to be subject to a random drug-testing program. Donna, a mechanical engineer and 15-year employee, was asked to report immediately for a urinalysis drug test. She refused and told her supervisor she had no intention of being tested and did not believe in the program. After additional unsuccessful attempts to get Donna to comply, the company fired her. Donna sought unemployment insurance and was denied because she lost her job because of "willful misconduct." Donna claims that the drug-testing policy is a humiliating invasion of her privacy and was adopted without the consent of the employees. Did the company have the right to require Donna to take the drug test, and can unemployment benefits be denied her?

Donna's reasons for declining the test are unknown, but the cost is clear. In the case upon which this scenario is based, the company's drug-testing program was upheld and the denial of unemployment compensation was deemed proper. "The avoidance of injury, as well as concern for vicarious liability that can accrue to the employer, are legitimate interests of the employer that must be accorded substantial weight. Appellant's objection that Duquesne Light adopted the testing program without having obtained the employees' consent is groundless. The creation of rules and requirements that govern the workplace is the prerogative of the employer. We conclude that the testing program of [the employer] was narrowly tailored to meet the employer's needs and that it did not unduly intrude on appellant's privacy interests. Hence, it was reasonable. Appellant's failure to cooperate with the program was without good cause. Willful misconduct was properly found, and the denial of unemployment benefits was, therefore, proper."[82]

Lie-Detector Tests

At one time, many employers required job applicants and employees to take lie-detector tests (called *polygraphs*) to determine if the individual was honestly answering questions asked by the employer. Many employees considered these

Find the Employee Polygraph Protection Act by using the U.S. House of Representatives Office of the Law Revision Counsel searchable U.S. Code http://uscode.house.gov/usc.htm

http://

tests to be an invasion of their right to privacy and their privilege against self-incrimination. Other critics believe lie-detector tests create a dangerous fantasy that the truth can be ascertained because most experts seriously doubt the tests' accuracy.

In 1988 Congress passed the Employee Polygraph Protection Act, which severely restricted the use of polygraphs. This act prohibits certain employers from (1) requiring, suggesting, requesting, or causing employees or job applicants to take lie-detector tests; (2) using, accepting, referring to, or asking about the results of lie-detector tests taken by employees or applicants; and (3) taking or threatening negative employment-related action against employees or applicants based on results of lie-detector tests or because they refused to take the tests.

Some employers are exempted from these prohibitions, notably federal, state, and local government employers, certain security service firms, and companies manufacturing and distributing controlled substances. Other employers may use polygraph tests when investigating losses attributable to theft, including suspected embezzlement, and theft of trade secrets. In all cases where lie-detector tests are still permitted, however, stringent procedural requirements are imposed on employers. Employees may always refuse to submit to polygraph testing, but this may make them vulnerable to dismissal for good cause.

Monitoring Job Performance

Another workplace privacy issue involves the monitoring of employees' performance by employers. Today, some employers electronically monitor employees' use of computer terminals or company telephones. Some employers use video cameras to evaluate employees' performance.

Current federal law recognizes the right of employers to listen in on telephone conversations to monitor employees' performance, but state laws vary. An employer may often avoid state laws by simply informing employees subject to monitoring that the company may be listening. In areas such as this, there is very little case law, and an employer may wish to consider carefully whether the need to monitor employees' performance outweighs the employees' right to privacy, as well as the possible negative effect on general employee morale and productivity. If the company's monitoring is formally challenged, a court will balance the purposes of the search against its effect on the employee's privacy. The existence of other available methods for accomplishing the employer's goals will be considered as alternatives.

Fred Ardmeyer's employer had assured all employees that their e-mail communications would not be accessed and used by the employer against its employees for disciplinary reasons. Fred sent several work-related e-mails to his supervisor. The messages also included threats to "kill the backstabbing bastards" and referred to a planned holiday party as the "Jim Jones Koolaid affair." Fred was fired. Fred sued, claiming his termination violated "public policy which precludes an employer from terminating an employee in violation of the employee's right to privacy as embodied in Pennsylvania common law." Was Fred's lawsuit successful?

In the case on which this hypothetical is based the court found for the employer, stating, "we do not find a reasonable expectation of privacy in e-mail communications voluntarily made by an employee to his supervisor over the company e-mail system notwithstanding any assurances that such communications would not be intercepted by management. Once plaintiff communicated the alleged unprofessional comments to a second person (his supervisor) over an e-mail system, which was apparently utilized by the entire company, any reasonable expectation of privacy was lost. Significantly, the defendant did not require plaintiff, as in the case of a urinalysis or personal property search, to disclose any personal information about himself. Rather, plaintiff voluntarily communicated the alleged unprofessional comments over the company e-mail system. We find no privacy interests in such communications."[83]

RIGHTS REGARDING UNIONS

Have workers always had the right to join with coworkers in unions? The answer is no. The history of relations between labor and capital is long and stormy. More precisely, in many cases, it is a record of relations between union leaders selected by workers and professional managers hired by the investors who are the owners of capital. In 1806 a group of Philadelphia boot and shoemakers (called *cordwainers*) who joined together were found guilty of common-law criminal conspiracy and were fined.[84] In another classic case about 35 years later, *Commonwealth v. Hunt*, the Supreme Court of Massachusetts rejected the idea that a combination of workers was criminal simply because of their concerted action. The proper test, the court said, was the purpose of the combination; if intended "to induce all those engaged in the same occupation to become members," it was lawful. "Such an association might be used to afford each other assistance in time of poverty, sickness, or distress; or to raise their intellectual, moral, and social condition, or to make improvement in their art; or for other proper purposes."[85]

Nevertheless, **unions** continued to be harassed by court action instituted by employers who resisted any erosion of their decision-making power. For example, the federal Sherman Anti-Trust Act of 1890 was enacted to protect trade and commerce against unlawful restraints and monopolies of business firms, but was also applied by courts to unions. Injunctions were often used to restrain concerted labor activity such as **picketing** (patrolling outside a business location to encourage workers to join the union, to gain recognition from the employer, or to gain sympathy and support from third parties during a strike). But the pendulum eventually did swing in the opposite direction to favor labor and union organization. For example, in 1940 the Supreme Court recognized peaceful picketing as a form of free speech protected by the First Amendment. In 1988, the Court upheld a local law that banned picketing in front of any particular or private home, but marching through a residential neighborhood or in front of an entire block of homes is not prohibited.[86]

STATUTES GOVERNING LABOR–MANAGEMENT RELATIONS

During the Great Depression (1929–1939), many new socioeconomic laws were enacted as part of the New Deal of President Franklin D. Roosevelt. In the labor field, two important laws survived challenges to their constitutionality: the Anti-Injunction Act and the National Labor Relations Act.

The **Anti-Injunction Act of 1932** (popularly known as the Norris-La Guardia Act, after its prime movers) restricts the issuance of injunctions by the federal

The Web site of the Institute of Labor Relations at Cornell is at http://www.workindex.com Web links on labor relations are at http://law.house.gov/100.htm

courts against unions peacefully striking in labor disputes.[87] Together with the Clayton Act of 1914, it effectively exempts unions from prosecution as monopolistic trusts or conspiracies in restraint of trade. Norris-La Guardia also outlaws **yellow dog contracts**, under which an employee—as a condition of employment—agrees never to join a union.

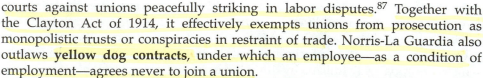

The **National Labor Relations Act of 1935 (Wagner Act)** recognizes the right of employees to form, join, or assist unions and to bargain collectively with employers through representatives of their own choosing.[88] **Collective bargaining** is the right given to a union to bargain with the employer over the terms of employment, including wages, hours, job security, and benefits covering all members of the worker group. Once a union is recognized as the bargaining agent of a group of workers, the union has the exclusive authority to bargain for all members of the group. Accordingly, an employee is no longer free to bargain individually with the company. The recognized union not only has the right to bargain for all members of the group, it has the duty. It cannot refuse to represent a worker in the group even if he or she is not a member of the union. The Wagner Act listed and outlawed five **unfair labor practices** of employers, including, most notably, interfering with employees in their right to form unions and firing an employee for filing charges under the act.

- Interference, restraint, or coercion with the organization or practice of union activities
- Wrongful domination of unions
- Encouragement or discouragement of unions by discriminating against union members
- Refusal to bargain with the union
- Discrimination against any employee seeking protection under the act

Antonio Mondalli and Jack Smith were the two youngest and toughest workers at the Iceberg Cold Storage and Ice Company. When their request for a wage boost to match community levels was denied, they started to persuade other workers in the plant to join them in forming a local union, or to affiliate with the Teamsters Union. When Artemus Finley, owner-manager of Iceberg, heard of the talk, he promptly fired Mondalli and Smith. Do they have any recourse under the law?

Yes. They can file a complaint with the nearest office of the National Labor Relations Board. For intrastate businesses, in some states they could apply to a comparable state board. In either case, the board could order their reinstatement with back pay.

The Pendulum Swings Back

Some critics claimed that in applying the Wagner Act, the National Labor Relations Board favored the revitalized unions unfairly. And so the pendulum eventually swung back with two new laws that restrained unions (but did not deprive them of their basic rights). The **Labor-Management Relations Act of 1947 (Taft-Hartley Act)**[89] amended the Wagner Act and added a list of unfair labor practices of unions, including, most notably, coercion of employees in their right to join or to refuse to join a union. It outlawed the **closed shop**, which mandated that one must belong to the union before getting a job, and it banned **secondary boycotts**, in which pressure is brought by striking workers against neutral third parties who supply or buy from the affected employer. For example, workers on strike at a furniture factory may not legally picket the independent retail stores that sell the furniture.

In an **open shop**, a union may be recognized as the sole bargaining agent for all employees in the particular group or bargaining unit, but any person may be hired and retained without joining the union.

What About Farm Workers?

Farm workers are not covered by the Taft-Hartley Act or by other federal labor laws. Therefore, the late Cesar Chavez and his striking United Farm Workers Union were able to utilize the secondary boycott by picketing stores that handle grapes and lettuce from nonunionized farms. This apparent advantage to farm workers is more than offset by the fact that employers are not legally obliged to recognize farm workers unions or to bargain collectively with them. However, California has pioneered with a state law granting to farm workers the rights to organize and bargain collectively. Significantly, in 1988 the U.S. Supreme Court partially revived the secondary boycott weapon for all unions. It permitted a union to pass out handbills urging shoppers and others at a shopping center not to patronize any of some 85 stores, even though the stores were not involved in the dispute. The dispute arose when E. J. De Bartolo Corporation hired Wilson to build a store in the mall. Wilson, in turn, hired the H.J. High Construction Company to work on the project. High had provoked the union's ire because it allegedly was paying substandard wages. The Court held that Congress had not intended "to proscribe peaceful handbilling, unaccompanied by picketing, urging a consumer boycott of a neutral employer."[90]

Legal Injunctions

The Taft-Hartley Act reintroduced the injunction against strikes, but made it available only at the request of the National Labor Relations Board or of the president of the United States in cases of disputes that endanger the national health and welfare. After an 80-day **cooling-off period** in such cases, during which time the issues are investigated and reported on by a public board, the strike may resume—to be ended possibly by government seizure and operation under an act of Congress. This extreme option is very seldom utilized. Courts may also issue injunctions against illegal strikes or lockouts and illegal activity in connection with either, such as mass picketing or violence in a strike or lockout.

> Loren Hilton was a rugged individualist, and as a matter of principle he opposed joining any mutual help organization. He was also a highly skilled toolmaker. Some time after Advanced Avionics Corporation hired him, the company signed an agreement with the toolmakers union that called for a union shop. Must Hilton now join the union if he wants to keep his job?

Yes. In a **union shop** an employee must join the union within 30 days after being hired. It is legal under the Taft-Hartley Act although, as noted before, some states have enacted "right-to-work" laws that outlaw this limited approach to union security and stability. Employers who accept the union shop reason that if they have to deal with a union, it may as well include all workers in the bargaining unit. There is likely to be less internal discord; the union leaders feel more secure and are less likely to make outrageous demands or promises to justify their existence. Also, since the union provides benefits, the members understandably believe all workers should share the costs; thus, those who do not join the union are regarded contemptuously as freeloaders.

A variation of the union shop is the **agency shop**, in which all employees in the bargaining unit (nonmembers as well as members) support the union by paying union dues as a condition of employment. Nonmembers must accept the union as their agent to conduct negotiations with the employer and to conclude employment contracts on behalf of all the employees within the bargaining unit. Many public-employee labor unions have agency-shop agreements that apply to nonmembers. The union cannot use any of such agency-shop dues for activities not directly related to collective bargaining.

The **Labor-Management Reporting and Disclosure Act of 1959 (Landrum-Griffin Act)** is sometimes called the bill of rights of union members, because it guarantees their right to participate in union affairs, protects their freedom to speak up in union meetings, and requires that they be kept informed about the union's financial condition.[91]

Raul Keroupian had joined the union at his plant shortly before the day of the meeting at which officers were to be selected. When nominations were made from the floor, someone moved to elect the entire incumbent slate by acclamation. Keroupian swallowed nervously, then stood up and said, "I don't think we can do that; it would be illegal." There were hoots and catcalls from the back of the room. Was he correct?

Yes. Among other things, the Landrum-Griffin Act prescribes that every local labor organization must elect its officers at least once every three years by secret ballot among the members in good standing.

DO MOST WORKERS BELONG TO UNIONS?

In 1997, only 14.1 percent of our nation's total force of employed wage and salary workers were union members. "Union membership has fallen steadily from 20.1 percent in 1983."*[92] Comparatively few professional workers, government employees (other than public school teachers), and white-collar workers belong to unions. Largest union membership is in the transportation and public utilities industries, followed by manufacturing and mining. Moreover, many union members are employed in open shops where union membership is not required as a

*It is ironic that while unions were in decline in this country during the 1980s (see Lipsci, *Unions in Transition—Entering the Second Century*, [San Francisco: Institute for Contemporary Studies, 1986]), the Solidarity union movement came into being in Poland. The union's leader, Lech Walesa, won the Nobel Peace Prize in 1983 and spoke before a joint session of Congress in 1989. The example of the Poles became a historical model for other nations that had been behind the Iron Curtain. They, too, asserted a significant measure of independence with more democratic rule.

condition of getting or keeping a job, or in firms where no union is recognized as the representative of all employees.

> Although a union had been selected by a majority of the workers in his department, Virgil Redman refused to join. There was no union-shop agreement, and he insisted on making his own "deal with the boss." "After all," he said, "I've been doing it that way for more than 30 years. We're both satisfied. I don't intend to stop now." May Redman make his own contract with his employer governing his compensation and other terms of employment?

No. When a union is designated as the bargaining representative for workers in a given unit, *collective bargaining* requires the union to represent all workers in that unit, including nonmembers. This is true even when only a bare majority of eligible workers participated in the representation election, and consequently only a minority of the total eligible workers voted for the union. The same phenomenon can be found in political elections and campus elections when there is a light turnout.

Thus simple numerical totals of union membership are misleading; they may reflect lethargy rather than ardent support. On the other hand, they may underestimate the true scope of union influence. Unions are very strong in certain key industries: steel, aerospace, automobiles, coal mining, transportation, printing, and construction. A major strike in any one of these could have serious repercussions throughout the economy. Moreover, the wages and conditions set forth in union contracts tend to become models for other labor contracts. And unions may exert pressure on legislatures through lobbying efforts made possible by their unity and access to large sums of money from the dues of many members.

Do Most Workers Engage in Strikes?

Most workers are not unionized, and unions normally call strikes, so that means that most workers do not engage in strikes. A **strike** is a concerted refusal by employees to perform the services for which they were hired. Strikers do not quit permanently; they consider themselves employees and plan to return to their old jobs when the strike ends. By then, they hope that their employer will have acceded to all or some of their demands. The strike is the ultimate weapon of unions, just as the ultimate weapon of employers is the **lockout**—a shutdown of operations in response to union activity or demands. Neither is used casually or frequently, although the strike is much more common.

The number of major work stoppages in 1997 was a record low, according to the U.S. Department of Labor's Bureau of Labor Statistics. There were 29 major work stoppages during 1997, idling 339,000 workers and resulting in about 4.5 million days of idleness (about 1 out of every 10,000 available workdays).[93] The percentage of days lost in 1997 was .01 percent compared to .3 percent in 1947 when the data was first collected. The peak percentage of work stoppage was 1959 with .43 percent.

Such statistics do not reflect the full impact of a labor strike or lockout, however. They do not show the indirect or secondary effect on other companies that are forced to cut back or even shut down because markets or sources of needed supplies are cut off. Nor do they reflect the inconvenience and added cost or deprivation imposed on the disputants as well as on innocent third parties. A strike of a major automobile manufacturer that buys component parts from thousands of suppliers and ships autos to hundreds of dealers quickly sends shock waves throughout the nation's economy. Layoffs in the main plant are followed by cutbacks in satellite shops and dealerships. The 1998–1999 lockout of the National Basketball Association led to the loss of much of the entire season of basketball, affecting not only the players and owners but concessionaires, T-shirt salespersons, parking lot attendants, and even scalpers.

Society accepts these costs, even as it accepts the costs of competition that sometimes forces business firms to close at great loss to investors and other dependent parties. *Compulsory arbitration* of labor disputes might eliminate strikes, but most people reject the idea of having a third party (or panel) make decisions on the issues, which will then be binding as a matter of law. Some disputants are not eager even to utilize a government or private *conciliation and mediation service*, in which a neutral party uses reason, advice, and persuasion to bring labor and management together in a voluntary settlement.

Once labor and management agree on the terms of an employment contract, it is common practice to include a clause requiring arbitration of disputes that may arise over the interpretation and operation of the detailed provisions of the contract. For example, workers may claim that their duties qualify them for a higher-paying wage classification or they may charge a supervisor with unfair discrimination against them when assigned dangerous or unpleasant tasks.

WHAT KINDS OF STRIKES ARE THERE?

Pat McGillicuddy was unhappy with the wages, hours, work schedule, plant rules, heating and lighting of the workroom, fringe benefits (there were none), and supervision at his place of employment. One day, after weeks of grumbling and complaining to his coworkers, he got up from his workbench, put on his coat and hat, and shouted so that all in the large room could hear, "I strike!" Then he walked out the door and started to picket in front of the building. Was he on strike?

Because there was no union ordering the strike nor combined action by a group of workers, Pat McGillicuddy was not on strike. It is an individual's protest, and his employer can take the action to mean that he has quit and can be replaced.

When there is a union and it orders all members to walk out in an **economic strike** (over wages, hours, or conditions of employment), the employer may legally hire **strikebreakers** as permanent replacements. After the strike is over, however, if the jobs again become available, the employer must rehire the strikers, provided they have not taken substantially equivalent permanent jobs elsewhere. On the other hand, when the strike is an **unfair labor practice strike** prompted by one or more unfair labor practices of the employer, the striking workers retain full rights to their jobs and must be restored to them when the strike ends. Moreover, the offending employer must pay back wages to the strikers.

A number of cases in recent years have involved illegal strikes by government employees such as firefighters, police, and teachers. Feelings have been intense and court orders to return to work have been defied. In the case of an illegal strike of air traffic controllers in 1981, then-President Ronald Reagan ordered dismissal of some 11,000 strikers and their temporary replacement by U.S. Air Force controllers. Permanent civilian replacements were hired and trained, and few of the striking controllers were rehired. This action was permitted under the Taft-Hartley Act because the walkout was an economic strike (a strike over wages, hours, or conditions of employment) rather than an unfair labor practice strike.

More than a decade later, union leaders and members continue to protest this rule as one that tilts the scales unfairly to favor employers in an economic struggle over terms of employment. Congress has declined to consider a major revision of the national labor laws, but Congress may eventually change the controversial rule.

The Snug Fit Shoe Corporation had a three-year contract with its production workers under a collective-bargaining agreement. The union vote approving the contract had been very close, and initial dissatisfaction had gradually turned into outspoken protest. After 16 months, the workers defied their leaders and announced through a spokesperson: "We're on strike. To prevent strikebreakers from taking our jobs, we're going to stay right here in the plant." A sit-down strike had begun. Friends and relatives brought the strikers' sleeping bags and food for a long stay. Was the strike legal?

No. **Sit-down strikes**, in which workers retain possession of the employer's property, are illegal.[94] Moreover, this was a **wildcat strike**, one that is in violation of the contract and of the union's own rules. As such, it constituted an unfair labor practice on the part of the workers, and the employer could hire permanent replacements for the strikers, who could be evicted by the police and be subject to punishment. Sometimes workers of one employer walk out when workers of another employer go on strike or are locked out. This is a **sympathy strike** and obviously is more serious than the common union labor practice of refusing to cross a picket line. It is a variation of an economic strike and the employer may treat it as such.

ARBITRATION OF EMPLOYMENT DISPUTES

Collective-bargaining agreements often provide for arbitration of disputes arising during the term of the labor agreement. For example, a common provision in a labor contract restricts management discretion in employee discipline and termination. The provision will provide that no discharge or discipline can occur except upon a showing of "just cause" (a limitation upon the common-law "at will" doctrine) and in a provided fashion. If the subject union member is displeased with discipline, he or she can grieve under agreed processes, which ultimately lead to a hearing by a neutral arbitrator.

The Manager of Safety & Security at a convalescence hospital became aware that "S," a PBX Operator with some receptionist responsibilities, was wearing nose jewelry, namely a small silver hoop in her left nostril. She informed "S" not to wear this at work other than on breaks and lunch periods. An accommodation was later reached allowing "S" to wear a Band-Aid over the small hoop while working. "S" believed that the Band-Aid over her nose hoop violated provisions of the collective bargaining agreement, and she filed a grievance. The case went to arbitration. How did the arbitrator rule?

Most disputes involving discipline over unusual hairstyles, body piercing, and clothing choices are resolved in the employer's favor. The employer's right to set dress standards is allowable management discretion unless it is a subterfuge for prohibited discrimination. In this case, the arbitrator noted that the company had "Dress Guidelines" prohibiting extremes in jewelry. The arbitrator gave great "deference to management's interpretation and application of its dress and grooming standards. [The company] did not violate the Agreement when it prohibited the Grievant from wearing a ring or hoop through her nose while on duty as a PBX Operator. Therefore, the grievance shall be denied."[95]

Whereas arbitration in union–labor contracts is common, is it common in nonunion employment situations? Until recently, the answer was no.

The American Arbitration Association has an excellent Web site for information about employer/employee arbitration labor and otherwise at http://www.adr.org/

Interstate/Johnson Lane Corporation (Interstate) hired Robert Gilmer as a manager of Financial Services in May 1981. Gilmer was required by his employer to register as a securities representative with the New York Stock Exchange (NYSE). His registration application provided for arbitration of any controversy arising out of a registered representative's employment or termination of employment. Interstate terminated Gilmer's employment at age 62. Thereafter, he filed a charge with the Equal Employment Opportunity Commission (EEOC) and brought suit in the District Court, alleging that he had been discharged in violation of the Age Discrimination in Employment Act of 1967 (ADEA). Interstate moved to compel arbitration. Was Gilmer forced to arbitrate his ADEA claim?

He was. Gilmer argued that U.S. Supreme Court precedent provided that employees were free to file civil rights suits without regard to agreements to arbitrate such claims and that Congress intended to protect ADEA claimants from a waiver of the judicial forum. The Court held otherwise, stating that earlier cases were restricted to collective-bargaining employment contracts. "An important concern therefore was the tension between collective representation and individual statutory rights, a concern not applicable to the present case. Finally, those cases were not decided under the FAA [Federal Arbitration Act], which reflects a 'liberal federal policy favoring arbitration agreements.' Therefore, those cases provide no basis for refusing to enforce Gilmer's agreement to arbitrate his ADEA claim." The U.S. Supreme Court required Gilmer to submit all his claims (including ADEA) to compulsory binding arbitration.[96]

The *Gilmer* case technically did not deal with an employment contract, although it appears no one except perhaps the U.S. Supreme Court believed that. Gilmer's arbitration agreement was in a securities exchange registration form, not an employment contract. Because of this, the Court failed to address the specific language of the FAA, which states it does not apply to contracts of employment of "seamen, railroad employees, or any other class of workers engaged in foreign or interstate commerce."

Despite the language of the FAA most, but not all, courts since *Gilmer* have upheld agreements to arbitrate employment disputes.[97] Further consideration by the U.S. Supreme Court appears needed as binding arbitration as a condition of employment is still a contentious issue giving rise to much litigation. Among the concerns voiced by opponents to employment arbitration are that arbitrators are drawn from a non-neutral source, arbitration rules are biased toward employers, limitations on discovery, no appeal, and additional cost to the employee.

In response to a threatened boycott by The National Employment Lawyers Association, a special task force composed of individuals representing management, labor, employment, civil rights organizations, private administrative agencies, government, and the American Arbitration Association drafted "The Due Process Protocol for Mediation and Arbitration of Statutory Disputes Arising Out of the Employment Relationship." The Due Process Protocol has been endorsed by the American Arbitration Association, the American Bar Association Labor and Employment Section, the American Civil Liberties Union, the Federal Mediation and Conciliation Service, the National Academy of Arbitrators, and the National Society of Professionals in Dispute Resolution.[98] The Due Process Protocol "recognizes the dilemma inherent in the timing of an agreement to mediate and/or arbitrate statutory disputes" but does not take a position on whether an employer can require a pre-dispute, binding arbitration program as a condition of employment.[99]

CASES

PRICE WATERHOUSE V. HOPKINS
490 U.S. 228, 109 S.Ct. 1775 (1989)

Ann B. Hopkins worked for five years as a minor manager in the Washington, D.C., office of Price Waterhouse, a major accounting firm, when she was proposed as a candidate for partnership. Of the 662 partners in the firm at that time, 7 were women. Of the 32 partners who submitted comments, 13 supported her bid, 3 recommended it be placed on hold, and 8 recommended that she be denied partnership (the remaining 8 said they had no informed opinion about her). The firm's Admission Committee and its Policy Board placed her candidacy "on hold." She brought a sex-discrimination charge against the firm under Title VII of the Civil Rights *Act of 1964. The District Court ruled in her favor, and the Circuit Court of Appeals affirmed in part, reversed in part, and remanded the case to the District Court. The case came to the U.S. Supreme Court on certiorari. In a 6–3 vote, the Supreme Court approved the findings of the District Court but remanded the case for determination under the proper standard of evidence (i.e., by a preponderance of the evidence).*

On remand, the District Court again held Price Waterhouse liable and ordered the firm to accept her as a partner, retroactive to 1982, and to pay her $371,000 in back salary and interest.

When Price Waterhouse again appealed, the District of Columbia Circuit Court of Appeals again affirmed.

Justice Brennan wrote the opinion: The partners in Hopkins' office praised her character as well as her accomplishments, describing her in their joint statement as "an outstanding professional" who had a "deft touch," a "strong character, independence and integrity. . . ." Evaluations such as these led [trial] Judge Gesell to conclude that Hopkins "had no difficulty dealing with clients and her clients appear to have been very pleased with her work" and that she "was generally viewed as a highly competent project leader who worked long hours, pushed vigorously to meet deadlines and demanded much from the multidisciplinary staffs with which she worked. . . ." On too many occasions, however, Hopkins' aggressiveness apparently spilled over into abrasiveness. . . . Both "[s]upporters and opponents of her candidacy," stressed Judge Gesell, "indicated that she was sometimes overly aggressive, unduly harsh, difficult to work with and impatient with staff."

There were clear signs, though, that some of the partners reacted negatively to Hopkins' personality because she was a woman. One partner described her as "macho;" another suggested that she "overcompensated for being a woman;" a third advised her to take "a course at charm school." Several partners criticized her use of profanity; in response, one partner suggested that those partners objected to her swearing only "because it's a lady using foul language." Another supporter explained that Hopkins "ha[d] matured from a tough-talking somewhat masculine hard-nosed [manager] to an authoritative, formidable, but much more appealing lady [partner] candidate." But it was the man who, as Judge Gesell found, bore responsibility for explaining to Hopkins the reasons for the Policy Board's decision to place her candidacy on hold who delivered the coup de grace: in order to improve her chances for partnership, Thomas Beyer

advised, Hopkins should "walk more femininely, talk more femininely, dress more femininely, wear make-up, have her hair styled, and wear jewelry. . . ."

The Court of Appeals affirmed the district court's ultimate conclusion, but departed from its analysis in one particular: it held that even if a plaintiff proves that discrimination played a role in an employment decision, the defendant will not be found liable if it proves, by clear and convincing evidence, that it would have made the same decision in the absence of discrimination. . . . Under this approach, an employer is not deemed to have violated Title VII if it proves that it would have made the same decision in the absence of an impermissible motive, whereas under the district court's approach the employer's proof in that respect only avoids equitable relief. We decide today that the Court of Appeals had the better approach, but that both courts erred in requiring the employer to make its proof by clear and convincing evidence. . . .

We have, in short, been here before. Each time, we have concluded that the plaintiff who shows that an impermissible motive played a motivating part in an adverse employment decision has thereby placed upon the defendant the burden to show that it would have made the same decision in the absence of the unlawful motive. Our decision today treads this well-worn path. . . .

In saying that gender played a motivating part in an employment decision, we mean that, if we asked the employer at the moment of the decision what its reasons were and if we received a truthful response, one of those reasons would be that the applicant or employee was a woman. In the specific context of sex stereotyping, an employer who acts on the basis of a belief that a woman cannot be aggressive, or that she must not be, has acted on the basis of gender. . . .

The very premise of a mixed-motives case is that a legitimate reason was present, and indeed, in this case, Price Waterhouse already has made this showing by convincing Judge Gesell that Hopkins' interpersonal problems were a legitimate concern. The employer instead must show that its legitimate reason, standing alone, would have induced it to make the same decision. . . .

The courts below held that an employer who has allowed a discriminatory impulse to play a motivating part in an employment decision must prove by clear and convincing evidence that it would have made the same decision in the absence of discrimination. We are persuaded that the better rule is that the employer must make this showing by a preponderance of the evidence. . . .

Although Price Waterhouse does not concretely tell us how its proof was preponderant even if it was not clear and convincing, this general claim is implicit in its request for the less stringent standard. Since the lower courts required Price Waterhouse to make its proof by clear and convincing evidence, they did not determine whether Price Waterhouse had proved by *a preponderance of the evidence* that it would have placed Hopkins' candidacy on hold even if it had not permitted sex-linked evaluations to play a part in the decision-making process. Thus, we shall remand this case so that that determination can be made. . . .

In finding that some of the partners' comments reflected sex stereotyping, the district court relied in part on Dr. Fiske's expert testimony. . . .

Indeed, we are tempted to say that Dr. Fiske's expert testimony was merely icing on Hopkins' cake. It takes no special training to discern sex stereotyping in a description of an aggressive female employee as requiring "a course at charm school." Nor, turning to Thomas Beyer's memorable advice to Hopkins, does it require expertise in psychology to know that, if an employee's flawed "interpersonal skills" can be corrected by a soft-hued suit or a new shade of lipstick, perhaps it is the employee's sex and not her interpersonal skills that has drawn the criticism. . . .

We hold that when a plaintiff in a Title VII case proves that her gender played a motivating part in an employment decision, the defendant may avoid a finding of liability only by proving by a preponderance of the evidence that it would have made the same decision even if it had not taken the plaintiff's gender into account. Because the courts below erred by deciding that the defendant must make this proof by clear and convincing evidence, we reverse the Court of Appeals' judgment against Price Waterhouse on liability and remand the case to that court for further proceedings. It is so ordered.

For Critical Analysis

1. Is this case about sexual harassment or gender discrimination? What is the difference?

2. Does this case suggest to you that if your reason for a particular decision is nondiscriminatory that liability could still occur if your explanation suggested discrimination is involved?

3. Preponderance of the evidence and clear and convincing evidence are both discussed as burdens of proof. Which standard does the court ultimately require and for what and why? Does this decision favor the employer or the employee?

4. Do we know the ultimate result of this controversy from this opinion? Explain.

RAYMOND J. GONZALES V. SOUTHWEST SECURITY AND PROTECTION AGENCY, INC.

Court of Appeals of New Mexico, 100 N.M. 54, 665 P.2d 810 (1983)

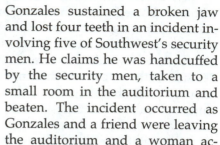

Raymond Gonzales, assaulted by security guards at a wrestling match, brought this action against the city, the sponsor of the wrestling match, the security company, and the individual security guards for damages resulting from false imprisonment, battery, and negligent hiring, training, supervising, and retaining of certain personnel. The District Court entered judgment in favor of the plaintiff against the security company and certain guards. The security company appealed, claiming that the doctrine of Respondeat superior *did not apply when employee torts were intentional and that Southwest Security was not independently negligent. The Court of Appeals held that (1) as the guards' conduct was naturally incident to the company's business, the company was properly held liable for intentional torts committed by the guards, and (2) substantial evidence supported findings that the company was negligent in equipping, training, supervising, and retaining the guards, and that its negligence caused the patron's injuries.*

Judge Lopez wrote the opinion of the court:
Plaintiff sued for damages resulting from false imprisonment, battery and negligent hiring, training, supervision and retention of certain personnel. A bench trial was had and plaintiff was awarded $15,000.00. Defendant appeals. We affirm.

Plaintiff, Raymond Gonzales (Gonzales), sued the City of Albuquerque (City), Fundamentals, Inc. (Fundamentals), Southwest Security and Protection Agency (Southwest) and five security guard employees of Southwest. The suit arose out of an episode where Gonzales received injuries while attending a wrestling match sponsored by Fundamentals. The match was held in the civic auditorium owned by the city, which it rented to Fundamentals. Southwest was hired by Fundamentals to provide security services for the event.

Gonzales sustained a broken jaw and lost four teeth in an incident involving five of Southwest's security men. He claims he was handcuffed by the security men, taken to a small room in the auditorium and beaten. The incident occurred as Gonzales and a friend were leaving the auditorium and a woman accosted him for having thrown beer during the matches. Security guards intervened and told Gonzales and his friend to leave. Once outside the auditorium the woman again accosted Gonzales's friend, setting off a substantial disturbance. When the security guards arrived Gonzales was a bystander. Nevertheless, the guards threw Gonzales to the ground, handcuffed him and took him to a small room where he was beaten. Throughout the incident Gonzales apparently was calm and did not provoke the guards.

Default judgment was entered against Southwest employees Mike and Alex Sedillo and David Chavez. At trial the City, Fundamentals and Southwest employee Ysidro Victor Vigil were found to be free of fault. Judgment in favor of Gonzalez was entered against Southwest and its employee Denny Sanchez. Southwest appeals.

On appeal Southwest contends (1) that it should not be held responsible for the intentional torts of its employees; and (2) that substantial evidence does not support the trial court finding it negligent.

Point 1: An Employer's Liability for the Intentional Torts of Its Employees. An employer is liable for the intentional torts of its employees if the torts are committed in the course and scope of employment. Whether an employee's conduct is within the course and scope of employment is a question of fact. In the case at bar, the question is whether the security guards' imprisonment and battering of Gonzales was within the course and scope of their employment. In resolution of this question we note that local decisions exist regarding an employee's intentional torts; however, none address the activity of private security personnel.

The definition of "the course and scope of employment" is variable. [The court has] adopted the following test of whether conduct was within the course of employment: ". . . an act is within the 'course of employment' if (1) it be something fairly and naturally incident to the business, and if (2) it be done while the servant was engaged upon the master's business and be done, although mistakenly or illadvisedly, with a view to further the master's interests, or from some impulse of emotion which naturally grew out of or was incident to the attempt to perform the master's business, and did not arise wholly from some external, independent, and personal motive on the part of the servant to do the act upon his own account."

In addition to the test delineated above, the instant case requires additional considerations because of the nature of Southwest's and the security guards' work. The Restatement of Agency addresses the use of force as follows: A master is subject to liability for the intended tortious harm by a servant to the person or things of another by an act done in connection with the servant's employment, although the act was unauthorized, if the act was not unexpectable in view of the duties of the servant. Restatement (Second) of Agency § 249 (1958). Comment c to § 245 adds the following: c. Nature of employment. Whether or not an employment involves or is likely to lead to the use of force against the person of another is a question to be decided upon the facts of the individual case. To create liability for a battery by a servant upon a third person, the employment must be one which is likely to bring the servant into conflict with others. The making of contracts, or the compromise, settlement, or collection of accounts, does not ordinarily have this tendency. On the other hand, the employment of servants to guard or to recapture property, to take possession of land, or to deal with chattels which are in the possession of another, is likely to lead to altercations, and the master may become liable, in spite of instructions that no force shall be exerted against the person of the possessor.

In this case Southwest provided the security personnel with uniforms, handcuffs, guns, nightsticks and the authority to keep peace. Evidence at trial showed that Gonzales's injuries were inflicted, at least in part, by a guard's use of a nightstick. Moreover, Gonzales was handcuffed during the beating. We therefore have a situation where not only did Southwest's employees beat a person, but the beating was facilitated by instrumentalities provided by Southwest.

According to the foregoing facts and authority, we conclude that the trial court properly determined that the guards' conduct was naturally incident to Southwest's business. The trial court also properly determined that the guards' conduct substantially arose out of an attempt to perform Southwest's business. Finally, from our review of the record, we hold that substantial evidence supports the trial court's finding that Southwest was liable for its employees' intentional torts.

Point 2. Whether Substantial Evidence Supports Finding Southwest Negligent. Southwest contends the trial court's finding of negligence is not supported by substantial evidence. [In the New Mexico Supreme Court decision in *F & T Co. v. Woods* (1979)], the court held that defendant could not be liable for negligently hiring or retaining an employee because there was no showing that defendant's omissions proximately caused plaintiff's injuries. The principle [sic] reason proximate causation was lacking was because defendant's employee was acting outside the scope of employment, without defendant's authority and without instrumentalities provided by defendant, when plaintiff was harmed. In the case at bar, however, we have held that the guards were acting within the scope of their employment, and were using instrumentalities provided by Southwest, when Gonzales's injuries occurred. We therefore begin with a vast factual disparity between *F & T Co. v. Woods* and the case at bar.

The specific error alleged by Southwest is that the guards' intentional torts were neither foreseeable nor the cause of Gonzales' harm. While the terms "foreseeability" and "proximate causation" evade precise definition, the meaning of these terms is well known in the law. The existence of causation is ordinarily a question of fact. In the case at bar the court concluded that Southwest negligently equipped, trained, supervised and retained the guards, and that Southwest's negligence was the cause of Gonzales's harm. These conclusions were based on the following findings:

12. Southwest Security did not adequately investigate the background and the character of the individual Defendants herein prior to hiring them as security guards.

13. Southwest Security did not adequately supervise their security guards in general and in particular on the evening of August 19, 1979.

14. Southwest Security failed to adequately train the security guards in the use of weapons such as clubs and handcuffs which were provided to Mike Z. Sedillo, Alex Sedillo, Denny Sanchez and David Chavez.

15. Southwest Security failed to adequately instruct its employees in the proper method of restraining and arresting individuals.

16. There was at least one other prior beating of an individual by employees of Southwest Security and in particular Mike Z. Sedillo which occurred [sic] at a wrestling match and Southwest Security was or should have been aware of such incident(s) and failed to take appropri-

ate action to avoid further incident(s) of this nature.

17. The negligence of Southwest Security as specified above proximately caused the damages which resulted to Raymond J. Gonzales.

The findings quoted above are supported by evidence in the record. Testimony at trial revealed that Southwest's guards previously had mistreated people, that supervisors or owners of Southwest knew or should have known of such treatment, and that Southwest knew violence was pervasive at similar events held in the auditorium. From these facts we conclude that substantial evidence supports the trial court's findings that Southwest was negligent and that its negligence caused Gonzales's injuries.

The judgement of the trial court is affirmed. Appellate costs are to be paid by Southwest.

FOR CRITICAL ANALYSIS

1. Employers are not usually liable for an employee's intentional torts. What about this fact situation persuaded the court to hold the employer liable?

2. Did the court hold Southwest liable under the doctrine of *Respondeat superior* and also hold them negligent? If these are different theories, explain the difference.

3. Could Southwest sue the security guards for any payments they are required to make to Mr. Gonzales? Explain your answer.

4. What precautions can a company such as Southwest Security and Protection Agency employ to avoid or reduce liability in the future?

CHAPTER QUESTIONS AND PROBLEMS

1. Problems abound in the area of employment. The following questions indicate some of the more difficult and challenging ones. What are your suggestions for answers and solutions?

   a. Do minimum-wage laws discourage employment of young persons, especially the unskilled, and thus encourage idleness and crime? Should the minimum-wage laws be eliminated or modified for minors and young adults?

   b. Subtle illegal discrimination because of sex, color, religion, age, and national origin still exists in many places. How can it be further reduced or eliminated? How can victims of discrimination facilitate that elimination?

   c. Should the federal government be the employer of last resort for those who cannot find jobs in the private sector? What meaningful work could such persons do?

   d. Are current workers' compensation benefits for job-related injuries and deaths reasonable? What do they encompass in your state?

   e. Should workers be encouraged to buy shares of stock in the corporations that employ them, under ESOPs or other plans?

   f. Should all states enact "right-to-work" laws?

   g. Should labor strikes and management lockouts be forbidden, and labor–management disputes be settled by compulsory arbitration?

   h. Are unions obsolescent or obsolete? If not, why, when, where, and how should union membership be encouraged? Should employers be required to rehire all strikers (after the strike is ended), even in an economic strike?

   i. Should "comparable-worth" laws be enacted at the federal and state levels? Would women be the only beneficiaries of such legislation?

   j. Since people live longer now than when the Social Security Act was enacted in 1935, should the normal retirement age be advanced from 65 to 70?

   k. Should racial and other special-interest or minority quotas and affirmative action policies for employment and educational (e.g., college admission) opportunities be legally forbidden?

2. Generally, an employer has the right to fire an employee at will, even as the employee has the right to quit at will. These rights can be negated by both parties by means of an *express written and signed agreement*, as, for example, when a college football coach is hired "for three years." An employer's power to fire may also be limited if there is an *implied agreement* not to discharge without cause. How could such an implied agreement be created?

3. A probationary police officer in the Globe, Arizona, police department was fired. The officer sued the city for wrongful discharge, claiming he was terminated because he had discovered that a man who had been arrested, convicted, and who was serving time for vagrancy was doing so under a law that had been repealed. The officer told a court official of the situation, pointing out that the detention was illegal. The judicial official informed the police chief. The chief fired the officer, saying, "he did not appreciate 'big city cops' coming to Globe to tell him how to run his department." A probationary civil service employee may generally be dismissed at will; a "just cause" need not be stated or proved. Was this firing nevertheless a wrongful discharge? [*Wagner v. City of Globe*, 150 Ariz. 82, 722 P.2d 250 (Arizona, 1986).]

4. Consider the following ethical issues:
   a. Is it legal for an employer to require an employee to lie when dealing with customers in order to make a sale?
   b. Should an auto mechanic be required by his employer to replace parts prematurely in order to boost the income of the shop?

5. Could employees who are professional types, such as attorneys at law, doctors of medicine, dentists, and college professors, form and join labor unions? If so, what would be some pros and cons of unionization by such professionals?

6. Salvatore Monte was the president of Kenrich Petrochemicals, Inc., a family-owned business. Helen Chizmar had been Kenrich's office manager for 24 years. Office managers are considered management and are not eligible for union membership. Among the clerical staff Helen supervised were her sister, daughter, and daughter-in-law. In May 1987, Helen's three relatives and other clerical staff members designated the Oil, Chemical and Atomic Workers International Union as their union. Helen was not involved. Monte found out that the office was unionizing. Angry at the news, he told Helen that someone else could do her job for "$20,000 less" and fired her. Later, he told another employee that one of his reasons for firing Helen was that he "was not going to put up with any union (expletive)." A few days later, he told the clerical workers that if they voted for the union they would have to "start from scratch. No benefits, no salary, no vacations." Still later, during negotiations with the union, Monte said that he planned to "get rid of the whole family." Helen's family complained to the National Labor Relations Board that the firing of Helen was an unfair labor practice. The NLRB agreed and ordered that Helen be reinstated with back pay. Kenrich appealed. Can the NLRB order

the reinstatement of a supervisor (manager) who, although not a member of the union, was fired in retaliation for participation by her relatives in a union organization campaign? [*Kenrich Petrochemicals, Inc. v. National Labor Relations Board*, 907 F.2d 400 (3rd cir., 1990).]

7. After a strike was legally called, Phil Thornbush joined coworkers on "picket duty" at their place of work, an intrastate business. There was no violence, and only two picketers at a given time marched in front of the plant, day and night. Thornbush and his partner were arrested and convicted under a state statute that made loitering and picketing a misdemeanor. They appealed, claiming the state violated their federal constitutional right to free speech. Should the convictions be reversed?

8. In Question 7, after the arrest almost all of the striking employees, as well as scores of sympathizers, gathered at the plant entrance. A strikebreaker's car was overturned and burned; rocks were thrown into plant windows. Police were called and order was restored, but the plant manager feared a recurrence in the future. What defensive legal steps might she take?

9. The technicians at television station KTVE went out on strike in a dispute over the terms of a proposed contract. The strike dragged on for weeks. Ordinary picketing seemed to be ineffective, so some of the strikers prepared and distributed 5,000 handbills, which in sharp language disparaged the quality of KTVE programs. The employer fired those responsible for the printing and distribution. As an employer, was KTVE guilty of an unfair labor practice?

10. April, an agent employed by Prototype, Inc., was driving her own car and rushing to an important luncheon meeting scheduled with a prospective customer. She saw the amber light in the signal ahead, but to stop and wait would delay

her at least four minutes, and she was already late. So she pushed the accelerator down, even though the light had changed to red, and raced ahead at 50 mph through the intersection—*almost.* Before she got across, her car collided with Lamare's truck, which had legally entered on the far right side. Lamare was injured and the truck was demolished.

a. Is April's employer, the principal Prototype, liable?

b. Would the employer be liable if April were an ordinary employee?

c. Would the employer be liable if April were an independent contractor?

d. Would your answer be different in a, b, and c above if April were violating not only the speed limit, but also Prototype's explicit orders not to go faster than 35 mph in town?

e. Is April personally liable to Lamare?

f. Is April personally liable to Prototype?

NOTES

1. *1997 World Fact Book,* Central Intelligence Agency, http://www.odci.gov/cia/publications/factbook/country-frame.html.

2. Jon Krakauer, *Into Thin Air,* (New York: Villard, 1987).

3. *1997 World Fact Book.*

4. Bureau of Labor Statistics, Department of Labor, *Occupational Outlook Handbook,* 1996–2006 (1998), http://stats.bls.gov/news.release/ooh.table1.htm.

5. U.S. Bureau of the Census, *Statistical Abstract of the United States, 1993* (Washington, D.C.: U.S. Government Printing Office, 1994), table 623.

6. "Working Women: Equal Pay—About the Data," AFL-CIO Web page, http://www.aflcio.org/women/.

7. Fair Labor Standards Act of 1938, 29 U.S.C. § 201 *et seq.* (AKA Wages and Hours Act). Similar legislation in many states governs intrastate commerce.

8. Civil Rights Act of 1964 (notably Title VII) as amended, 42 U.S.C. § 2000e *et seq.* There is similar legislation in most states governing intrastate commerce.

9. *McGowan v. Maryland,* 366 U.S. 420, 81 S.Ct. 1101 (1961) and *Braunffeld v. Brown,* 366 U.S. 599, 81 S.Ct. 1144 (1961).

10. Occupational Safety and Health Act of 1970, 29 U.S.C. § 651 *et seq.*

11. "Bee Writers Suffer from Repetitive Motions," *San Francisco Chronicle;* and "Bee Agrees to End Writers' Pains with New Equipment," *San Francisco Chronicle,* 23 June 1990.

12. Fair Labor Standards Act of 1938, 29 U.S.C. § 201 *et seq.*

13. National Labor Relations Act of 1935, 29 U.S.C. § 151 *et seq.* (Wagner Act); and National Labor Management Relations Act of 1947, 29 U.S.C. § 141 *et seq.* (Taft-Hartley Act).

14. Social Security Act of 1935, 42 U.S.C. § 301 *et seq.*

15. Restatement of the Law of Agency 2d, § 1.

16. *Sacramento Bee,* 18 September 1998.

17. P.L. Posner, Associate Director, General Accounting Office, quoted in *Insight,* 12 June 1989, 24.

18. See IRS Publication 926, "Household Employer's Tax Guide."

19. Social Security Act of 1935.

20. Employment Retirement Income Security Act (ERISA), 29 U.S.C. § 1001 *et seq.*

21. *Pension Benefit Guaranty Corporation v. The LTV Corporation,* 496 U.S. 633, 110 S.Ct. 2668 (1990).

22. "Some Private Pension Plans at Risk: Reform Needed Now," *San Francisco Chronicle,* 16 June 1994.

23. J.K. Lasser, *Your Income Tax, 1993,* (New York: Prentice Hall, 1992).

24. Civil Rights Act of 1866, 42 U.S.C. § 1981 *et seq.*

25. A. Otten, "People Patterns," *The Wall Street Journal.*

26. 42 U.S.C. § 2000.

27. A.G. Greever and P. E. Hargroves, U.S. Inspectors Look for Glass Ceilings, *The Wall Street Journal,* 30 May 1994.

28. From the Chairperson's Introduction in "A Solid Investment: Making Full Use of the Nation's Human Capital—Recommendations of the Federal Glass Ceiling Commission" Washington, D.C., November 1995.

29. *The Status of Women in the States,* 2nd ed. 1998–99, http://www.iwpr.org/STATES98.HTM.

30. Civil Rights Act of 1964, 42 U.S.C. § 703(a)(l).

31. *International Brotherhood of Teamsters v. United States,* 431 U.S. 324, 97 S.Ct. 1843, (1977).

32. *United States v. Meyers,* 906 F.Supp. 1494 (Wyoming, 1995).

33. *Texas Department of Community Affairs v. Burdine,* 450 U.S. 248, 101 S.Ct. 1089 (1981) and *McDonnell Douglas Corp. v. Green,* 411 U.S. 792, 93 S.Ct. 1817 (1973).

34. 42 U.S.C.A. S 2000e-5(k). In the case of *Parton v. GTE North, Inc.,* 971 F2d 150 (8th cir., 1992), an award of attorneys' fees under Title VII was upheld, even though the plaintiff was awarded only $1 in nominal damages for her claim of hostile environment sexual harassment.

35. *Deffenbaugh-Williams v. Wal-Mart, Inc.,* 156 F.3d 581 (5th cir., 1998).

36. "Portrait of a Company Behaving Badly," *Time,* 16 March 1998, and *The Wall Street Journal,* 15 July 1997. For a different perspective see *The Wall Street Journal,* 12 August 1997.

37. *Griggs v. Duke Power Co.,* 401 U.S. 424, 91 S.Ct. 849 (1971).

38. *Ward's Cove Packing Company, Inc. v. Atonio,* 490 U.S. 642, 109 S. Ct. 2115 (1989).

39. *Watkins v. Scott Paper Co.,* 530 F.2d 1159, 5th cert. denied, 429 U.S. 861, 97 S.C. 163 (1976).

40. 29 U.S.C. § 1802.

41. *Odima v. Westin Tucson Hotel,* 53 F.3d 1484 (9th cir., 1995).

42. *Mann v. Frank,* 7 F.3d 1365, 1370 (8th cir., 1993)

43. *Rodriguez v. Chicago,* 156 F.3d 771 (7th cir., 1998)

44. *Independent Union of Flight Attendants v. Pan American World Airways, Inc.,* Case #84-4600, Federal District Court, San Francisco, Nov. 27, 1989. This is a decision in a federal trial court where generally no opinions are written or published.

45. *Robino v. Iranon,* 145 F.3d 1109 (9th cir., 1998).

46. *International Union, United Automobile, Aerospace and Agricultural Implement Workers of America, UAW, et al., v. Johnson Controls, Inc.*, 886 F.2d 871 (7th cir., 1989).

47. *United AutoWorkers v. Johnson Controls, Inc.*, 499 U.S. 187, 111 S.Ct. 1196 (1991).

48. EEOC Guidelines for Sexual Harassment.

49. *Weeks v. Baker & McKenzie*, 63 Cal.App.4th 1128, 74 Cal.Rptr.2d 510 (1998).

50. *Weeks v. Baker & McKenzie.*

51. *Weeks v. Baker & McKenzie* at 1160. Additional information can be found by reading the following articles. *National Law Journal*, 12 September 1999, A4 (col. 1); *National Law Journal*, 14 November 1994, A4 (col. 1); *National Law Journal*, 18 May 1998, A5 (col. 1); and *National Law Journal*, 14 September 1998, A4 (col. 2).

52. *Cotran v. Rollins Hudig Hall Int'l Inc.*, 17 Cal.4th 93 (1998).

53. *Metz v. Transit Mix, Inc.*, 828 F.2d 1202 (7th cir., 1987).

54. Age Discrimination in Employment Act of 1967, an Amendment of Title VII of the Civil Rights Act of 1964, 29 U.S.C. § 630 (b).

55. 29 U.S.C. § 630(f).

56. *Gregory v. Ashcroft*, 501 U.S. 492, 111 S.Ct. 2395 (1991).

57. 29 U.S.C. §623.

58. *United Steelworkers of America v. Weber*, 444 U.S. 889, 99 S.Ct. 2721 (1979).

59. *Johnson v. Transportation Agency, Santa Clara County, California*, 480 U.S. 616, 107 S.Ct. 1442 (1987).

60. *The Coalition for Economic Equity v. Wilson*, 122 F.3d 692 (9th cir., 1977), Cert. Denied 118 S.Ct. 397 (1997).

61. *Hopwood v. Texas* 78 F.3d 932 (5th cir., 1996).

62. *Hopwood v. Texas.*

63. *National Law Journal*, 20 April 1998, A8, (col. 3).

64. *National Law Journal*, 15 July 1996, A10, (col. 2).

65. The U.S. Equal Employment Opportunity Commission definition, http://www.eeoc.gov.

66. *Hamlyn v. Rock Island County Metro Mass Transit Dist.*, 986 F.Supp. 1126 (C.D. Ill., 1997).

67. *Hamlyn v. Rock Island County Metro Mass Transit Dist.*

68. 42 U.S.C. § 12114(a) and (b).

69. 42 U.S.C. § 12114(c). *Salley v. Circuit City Stores, Inc.*, 160 F.3d 977 (3rd cir., 1998).

70. *The Wall Street Journal*, 7 June 1994.

71. http://www.eeoc.gov.

72. *Whirlpool Corporation v. Marshall, Secretary of Labor*, 445 U.S. 1, 100 S.Ct, 883 (1980).

73. Michael Higgins, "Choosing Sides," *ABA Journal*, March 1998, 36. *Cotran v. Rollins Hudig Hall Int'l*, 1998 WL 1336 (California 1998).

74. *The National Law Journal*, 14 October 1991, 1.

75. *Douglas v. E.G. Baldwin & Associates*, 150 F.3d 604 (6th cir. 4 August 1998).

76. OSHA Vital Facts 1997, Occupational Safety and Health Association.

77. OSHA Region 2 News Release: NY 225, 8 December 1998.

78. "United—Nation's Largest Airline Now Largest ESOP" *The Wall Street Journal*, 13 July 1994, and "United Airlines First Among Big Corporations in Employee Ownership," *San Francisco Chronicle*, 13 July 1994.

79. Worker Adjustment and Retraining Notification Act of 1988, 29 U.S.C. §§ 2101-2109.

80. Based on the case *Alarcon v. Keller Industries, Inc.*, 27 F.3d 386 (9th cir., 1994).

81. *Electrical Workers Local 1245 v. Skinner*, 913 F.2d 1454 (9th cir., 1990).

82. *Rebel v. Unemployment Compensation Board of Review*, 1998 WL 890250 (Pennsylvania, 1988).

83. *Smyth v. The Pillsbury Co.*, 914 F.Supp. 97 (E.D.Pennsylvania 1996).

84. *Commonwealth v. Pullis* (Philadelphia Cordwainers Case). Philadelphia Mayor's Court, 3 Commons and Gilmore (1806).

85. *Commonwealth v. Hunt*, 45 Mass. (4 Met.) 111, 38 Am. Dec. 316 (1842).

86. *Thornhill v. Alabama*, 310 U.S. 88, 60 S. Ct. 736 (1940) and *Frisby v. Schultz*, 487 U.S. 474, 108 S.Ct. 2495 (1988).

87. Anti-Injunction Act of 1932, 29 U.S.C. § 101 *et seq.*

88. National Labor Relations Act of 1935.

89. National Labor-Management Relations Act of 1947.

90. California Agricultural Labor Relations Act of 1975, Labor Code, § 1140 *et seq.; E.J. De Bartolo Corp. v. Florida Gulf Coast Building and Construction Trade Council & NLRB*, 485 U.S. 568, 108 S.Ct. 1392 (1988).

91. Labor-Management Reporting and Disclosure Act of 1959, 29 U.S.C. § 401 *et seq.*

92. U.S. Department of Labor Bureau of Labor Statistics, Press Release, 30 January 1998.

93. USDL 98-57 Press Release, 12 February 1998, http://stats.bls.gov.

94. *NLRB v. Fansteel Metallurgical Corporation*, 306 U.S. 240, 59 S.Ct. 490 (1939).

95. 103 Lab. Arb. (BNA) 988 (1994).

96. *Robert D. Gilmer v. Interstate/Johnson Lane Corporation*, 500 U.S. 20, 111 S.Ct. 1647 (1991).

97. Examples of cases denying arbitration include *Prudential Ins. Co. of America v. Lai* 42 F.3d 1299 (9th cir., 1994), *Renteria v. Prudential Ins. Co. of America* 113 F.3d 1104 (9th cir., 1997), and *Loftis v. Brown & Williamson FEP* 1754 (M.D. 73 N.C., 1997). Examples of cases upholding arbitration include *Cole v. Burns Intl. Security Serv.*, 105 F.3d 1465, (D.C. cir., 1997), *Brookwood v. Bank of America*, 45 Cal.App.4th 1667, 53 Cal.Rptr.2d 515 (1996), and *Piper Funds v. Piper Cap. Mgmt.*, 71 F.3d 298 (8th cir., 1995).

98. http://www.adr.org/.

99. http://www.adr.org/ Statement by the American Arbitration Association.

WILLS, TRUSTS, AND PROBATE

*I*n youth my wings were strong and tireless,
   But I did not know the mountains.
   In age I knew the mountains,
But my weary wings could not follow my vision—
Genius is wisdom and youth.

Headstone of Alexander Throckmorton
Edgar Lee Masters, 1864-1950
from **Spoon River Anthology**

To most of us the subject of death is unpleasant, so we avoid discussing it. We are, of course, willing to acknowledge that death happens. But it happens "to others, not to me! At least not yet!"

The inevitability of one's death should be calmly recognized as a reason for appropriate planning starting at least by midlife. By law, upon death, title to assets of the **decedent** (a more technical and less personal way of saying that a person has recently died) must go to someone, generally through the procedures of a probate court. It is true that "You can't take it with you!" But with prudent planning, and using such legal instruments as a will and perhaps a trust, you can arrange to have your property distributed consistent with your wishes. Moreover, your foresight can guarantee that your **heirs** (those who are legally entitled to your estate if you leave no will), as well as other intended beneficiaries or "objects of your bounty" will receive more, and that the government death-tax collectors will receive less. The topic is important.

We have tried in each chapter of this text to look back at the late nineteenth and early twentieth centuries and forward to the twenty-first century. One hundred years ago, only the rich needed to do estate planning (wills and trusts), but today its importance has increased for the rich and middle class alike. At the beginning of the twenty-first century, taxes are a significant potential burden on the passing of wealth to heirs, and many Americans have estates substantial enough to desire protection from high federal tax rates. In 1900, there was no federal income tax or federal estate and gift tax. Many of the legal methods used in estate planning discussed in this chapter existed in the late nineteenth century, but many did not. There were no living wills, medical directives, A and B trusts for tax planning, or "Avoid Probate" seminars and self-help books. And to advocate legally assisted suicide would itself have been suicidal. Property that might be transferred in the year 2001 will include such items as a computer, automobile, airplane, Microsoft common stock, high-definition television set, vacation-share condominium, and cryo-freeze container complete with instructions. These gifts will not be found if you search the probate records of 1901 wills. Instead, you will find horses, wagons, guns, family bibles, books, tools, and (if lucky) the family farm. An attorney in 1901 needed to ask clients the names of all of their children born of any marriage or born outside of marriage (the last part asked with great delicacy). An attorney of 2001 must now ask clients about frozen eggs and sperm when trying to establish potential heirs and estate claims. What will the attorneys of the year 2101 need to ask?

WHAT IS ESTATE PLANNING?

Two Web sites with lists to Estate Planning Sites on the Internet are http://hometown.aol.com/ dmk58/eplinks.html and http://www.ca-probate. com/links.htm

Estate planning is an ongoing analysis of what a person owns or expects to own (assets), and what he or she owes to others (liabilities). It involves short-range tactics and long-range strategies to maximize benefits for the individual and the estate (and dependents) while still alive, and for the heirs and other beneficiaries who will own the estate after the individual's death. As personal income and expenses change, and as needs and wants also change over the years, the estate plans must change as well, or they can cause more harm than good. For example, estate plans typically must be adjusted following a divorce, the birth of a child, receipt of a substantial inheritance, or changes in the number and circumstances of intended beneficiaries. An estate plan may involve continuing education, investing, saving for major purchases, borrowing for such things as a residence, and providing for retirement.

Estate plans usually include the following four major objectives:

1. *To provide for the financial needs of the planner while alive.* If married, the financial needs of the spouse and other dependents are an important concern.

2. *To reflect the desires of the planner.* That is, the plan should provide appropriately for beneficiaries who are thought to be deserving, and possibly charities, while excluding potential beneficiaries who are deemed undeserving or not in need.

3. *To minimize or legitimately avoid taxes.* Taxes include (a) income taxes payable both during life, and also after the planner's death, and (b) estate and inheritance taxes (**death taxes**) payable after the planner's death.

4. *To minimize or avoid the delays, costs, and publicity of probate.* **Probate** is the process of proving the validity of a will in court, coupled with the ability to monitor the administration of the decedent's estate.

Even for persons of modest wealth and income, the importance and value of proper estate planning cannot be overstated. All aspects of such planning have legal consequences, but our focus is on the transfer of property to others before or after death, and on trusts and wills as they relate to probate.

WHAT TAX BURDENS CAN THE
ESTATE PLANNER REDUCE OR AVOID?

The federal government imposes an **estate tax** on the total net assets of a person at death. Thus, it is a levy on the *giving of property* to others after death. A few state governments also impose estate taxes on property transferred at death.* More states impose an **inheritance tax**** upon the *receiving of property* from the estate of a decedent. The individual who inherits the property pays state inheritance tax. Inheritance and estate taxes together are called death taxes, as mentioned earlier.

Inheritance tax rates vary from state to state. The inheritance tax rate increases or decreases depending on the amount received and the relationship of the recipient to the decedent (spouses and close relatives pay less than friends). Many states, including California, Colorado, Florida, Illinois, Minnesota, Texas, and Washington, impose no death taxes.***

Federal estate taxes provide for a **unified estate and gift tax**[1] (see Exhibit 14–1). By imposing a federal tax on gifts, federal law prevents a person from avoiding payment of death taxes by making large gifts, especially "deathbed gifts," of their assets. This tax system requires the taxpayer to keep track of larger gifts and combine the total value of these lifetime gifts with the value of property transferred at death. Taxes are based on the total value of these gifts, after deduction of a *unified credit* (exemption). The unified credit effectively allows a transfer totaling $675,000 in property value before the individual's estate is taxed (in years 2000 and 2001). Once $675,000 is transferred by gift or will, the estate tax is imposed. The amount of the exemption is scheduled to increase to $1,000,000 in 2006. (See Exhibit 14–2 for the tax exemption increases between 1999 and 2006.)[2]

Most gifts are totally free of tax. An individual may make annual tax-free gifts of up to $10,000**** to each of any number of *donees* (recipients of gifts). Such gifts are called *exemptions*. (A husband and wife together may give $20,000 each year.) If a gift is $10,000 or less, the gift has no federal tax consequences, and no tax return need be filed. Use of the tax-free exclusion allows a considerable amount of money or property to be given tax-free over time.

Answers to frequently asked questions on estate and gift taxes are available at the Nolo Press Web site at http://www.nolo.com/chunkEP/ep70-74.html

http://

Over a period of 15 years, Clint and Mary Hamilton gave each of their three children the maximum tax-free gift each year ($10,000 each, or $20,000 together) without using any of either spouse's unified credit: three children times $20,000 per year tax-free gift times 15 years equals $900,000 of tax-free gifts. Moreover, they can continue such tax-free giving as long as they live.

---

*States that assess estate taxes are Massachusetts, Mississippi, New York, and Ohio.

**States assessing inheritance taxes are Connecticut, Delaware, Indiana, Iowa, Kansas, Kentucky, Louisiana, Maryland, Michigan, Montana, Nebraska, New Hampshire, New Jersey, North Carolina, Oklahoma, Pennsylvania, South Dakota, and Tennessee.

***Even the states that have no death taxes generally impose a death tax on estates that are subject to federal estate tax. The tax imposed takes advantage of a credit allowed for state death taxes under the federal law. The net effect on a person's estate, however, is nil, as the amount paid the state is deducted from the amount that would have otherwise been paid the federal government.

****Beginning in 1999, the amount of the tax-free gift is indexed for inflation. The computational method is complicated—so much for tax simplification.

Exhibit 14–1: Unified Federal Estate Tax Rate Schedule

Column A Net Taxable Estate Over	Column B Net Taxable Estate Not Over	Column C Tax on Amount in Column A	Column D Rate of Tax on Excess Over Amount In Column A (Percent)
0	$ 10,000	0	18%
$ 10,000	20,000	$ 1,800	20
20,000	40,000	3,800	22
40,000	60,000	8,200	24
60,000	80,000	13,000	26
80,000	100,000	18,200	28
100,000	150,000	23,800	30
150,000	250,000	38,800	32
250,000	500,000	70,800	34
500,000	750,000	155,800	37
750,000	1,000,000	248,300	39
1,000,000	1,250,000	345,800	41
1,250,000	1,500,000	448,300	43
1,500,000	2,000,000	555,800	45
2,000,000	2,500,000	780,800	49
2,500,000	3,000,000	1,025,800	53
3,000,000	infinity	1,290,800	55

Most modest estates are distributed free of federal tax. Large estates are heavily taxed, although appropriate estate planning can reduce and even eliminate this burden. The effective tax after deduction of the unified credit begins at 37 percent of the gift and increases to a maximum of 55 percent. Wealthy persons avoid taxes (both income and estate) by making exempt gifts, by utilizing trusts, and by making thoughtful wills. Wills and trusts are also used to direct property to pre-ferred persons, called *beneficiaries*. The most common type of tax-reduction trusts are marital trusts and generation-skipping trusts, both of which are described later in this chapter.

Some popular methods of transferring valuable property to avoid estate and gift taxes and income taxes after death were made less attractive by the Tax

Exhibit 14–2: Unified Federal Estate Tax Credit Exemption

Year	Exemption Amount
1999	$650,000
2000 and 2001	$675,000
2002 and 2003	$700,000
2004	$850,000
2005	$950,000
2006 and after	$1,000,000

Reform Act of 1986. Tax laws typically affect behavior. The government often encourages certain conduct through enactment of particular tax laws (e.g., home ownership is encouraged because of the deductibility from taxable income of property taxes on the home, and also of the interest paid on real estate loans incurred to buy the home). Tax laws also stimulate the creative energies of tax advisors, who seek ways to reduce tax burdens for their clients. Not all such tax-avoidance behaviors are desired by those who draft tax laws. The result is that every few years tax laws are amended to encourage some social policies and to discourage others.* It is an oft-repeated ritual of Congress.

MATTERS CONCERNING WILLS

WHAT IS A WILL?

A man who dies without a will has lawyers for his heirs.

Anonymous

A **will** is the proper written legal expression of a person's wishes for the distribution of his or her property after death. A person who dies with a will dies **testate**; without a will, **intestate**. Upon death without a will, state statutes control the distribution of property. Generally statutes prefer descendants to ascendants. In other words, children or grandchildren, instead of parents or grandparents, will inherit from the deceased. If there are any lineals (grandparents, parent, child, grandchild, etc.) then collaterals (aunts, uncles, siblings, or cousins) will not inherit. If a person dies without any heirs whatsoever (not even distant cousins), the decedent's assets escheat (transfer) to the state (usually the state of the decedent's permanent residence) to benefit the public in general.

A person who dies leaving a will is called a **testator**. The court responsible for administering any legal problems surrounding a will is usually called a *probate court* and sometimes a *surrogate* or *chancery court*. A gift of real estate by will is a **devise**, and a gift of personal property by will is a **bequest**, or **legacy**. When someone dies, a *personal representative* settles affairs of the estates. An **executor** is a personal representative named in a will. An **administrator** is the personal representative appointed by the court for someone who dies without a will. An administrator may also be appointed if a person fails to name an executor in a will, or names an executor who lacks the capacity to serve, or writes a will that the court refuses to admit to probate (because, for example, it was not properly witnessed). A will that is "admitted to probate" has been accepted by the court as the valid last will of the decedent.

A will is a conditional document. Although valid when properly created, it has no immediate legal effect. It becomes operative at the testator's death. Hence,

---

*One such loophole (a legal method to avoid taxes that was not planned by legislators) was the transfer of property to children through an irrevocable but temporary trust, called a Clifford Trust. The transfer was irrevocable for at least ten years, during which time the income belonged to the child and was the child's taxable income (at a much lower rate). After ten years, the property would return to the donor. The Tax Reform Act of 1986 closed this loophole by taxing income from a Clifford Trust to a child under 14 at the same rate as the donor would be taxed.

the will "speaks upon the author's death." Therefore, if the testator destroys it, or writes a more recent will, the older will is automatically nullified. This conditional feature makes a will a unique document, adding importance to proving its validity (a process called *authentication*) after the death of the testator.

To be valid, wills normally must strictly follow state statutory requirements regarding both the right and the process of making a will. A will can serve other purposes besides the distribution of property; it can recommend appointment of a guardian for minor children or incapacitated adults, and it can nominate a personal representative to settle the legal affairs of the deceased. Indeed, a well-drafted will provides many important advantages:

1. *Property is distributed as the testator wishes.* Gifts may be made to charities, to distant relatives, to friends, or to employees. Some beneficiaries may receive more, some less. Unique assets, such as family heirlooms, go to specified donees (beneficiaries).

2. *The possibility of a disaster that kills both husband and wife, and possibly one or more children, can be anticipated and accommodated.* Although unlikely, this is a real danger that is increased by modern means of transportation. A properly drafted will can eliminate multiple costly, tax-burdened probates that may be required when couples or adult family members die in close succession over a period of days or weeks from injuries sustained in a common calamity.

3. *Death taxes may be avoided or reduced.* This is accomplished by taking the **marital deduction** (tax deduction allowed a surviving spouse that is not available to single persons) or by utilizing appropriate trusts. Also, the will may direct the executor to pay inheritance taxes, as well as estate taxes from the *residuary property* (property not specifically identified and given to a beneficiary) of the estate. Therefore, assuming assets are sufficient, gifts to named beneficiaries will not be reduced by death taxes.

4. *Confusion is minimized when specific property owned by the testator is identified, and beneficiaries are correctly designated.* The will also minimizes the possibility of lawsuits among contending claimants—for example, a claim that "He gave it to me before he died."

5. *The testator may nominate appropriate guardian(s) for minor children and their estates.* The will may name both a guardian of the person (handles personal decisions in lieu of parent) and a guardian of the estate (handles the child's assets). Nominations by a testator are generally honored, but the welfare of the child (or children) is the primary concern of the court. If a natural parent survives, this problem does not arise. If there is no nomination, the court makes the appointment independently.

6. *A personal representative (usually called an executor) may be designated in the will to handle the estate.* Otherwise, or if the nominated executor refuses to serve, the probate court will name an administrator. A statutory commission, or fee, is ultimately payable to the personal representative from the assets in the estate,* although it is very common for the

---

*It is important to note the statutory fees to both personal representatives and their attorneys who assist them during probate proceedings are maximums, not prescribed fees. That is, beneficiaries can encourage competitive bids from probate attorneys as an additional way to maximize the estate. Personal representatives often waive fees because such fees are taxable income. If they otherwise inherit the property, there may be a lesser tax or no tax.

personal representative to waive the fee if he or she is also the principal beneficiary under the will.

If a will does not waive it, a **fidelity bond** is required. A fidelity bond insures against losses caused by the dishonest performance of duties by a personal representative (or by a guardian of the children, if any is named and accepts the task). While this provides added protection, it is an expense to the estate. However, it often is prudent to require the posting of a fidelity bond for estates that consist of large amounts of cash. The judgment of trustworthy persons can be affected through control of large sums of cash, as opposed to other "less liquid" types of assets such as real property, automobiles, jewelry, or investments. Such a bond may be unnecessary altogether when the estate consists of no liquid assets or the executor is also the sole primary beneficiary. Generally, a person not trustworthy enough to be appointed without a bond should not be appointed.

More detail about this chapter's topics can be found in "CRASH COURSE in WILLS & TRUSTS," by Michael T. Palermo, Attorney at Law; Certified Financial Planner. http://www.mtpalermo.com/

7. *The will can give funeral instructions*, although this can and should also be done in a letter of "last instructions" (described next), separate from the will and immediately available to a close relative or friend upon death.

Accompaniments to Wills

Ideally, a personal or family balance sheet, listing assets and liabilities, should accompany a will and be updated periodically. A **letter of last instructions**, as mentioned above, should also be prepared. This letter is not binding on the executor, but it is helpful in disclosing the location of assets and liabilities. It can indicate how the testator would like details requiring immediate attention to be handled such as a donation of body organs under the Uniform Anatomical Gift Act. Note that letters of last instructions, or even explanations for survivors, can be prepared by the testator in many ways: in writing, in an audio recording, or even in a video recording. These instructions are not legally binding, but can be useful in explaining why, for example, someone was disinherited.

Types of Gifts

Gifts by will can be specific, general, or residuary. A *specific* devise or bequest describes particular property—for example, a bequest of an inscribed gold watch or a specified collection of rare books. A *general* bequest usually specifies a sum of money but does not single out any particular item of property. Sometimes a will provides that any assets remaining after specific gifts are made, and after debts are paid, are to be distributed through a **residuary clause**. Such a clause is useful because the testator can never be exactly sure what property will remain following payment of debts and taxes. Sample gift clauses in a will follow.*

1. *A specific bequest.* I give my grandfather's gold ring with the initials GSH to my son, Scott Bradshaw of Mountain Oaks, Colorado.

2. *A general bequest.* I give the sum of Ten Thousand Dollars ($10,000) from my account number ZXY1117865 in First Hoosier Bank to the American Cancer Society, 1244 Normal, Decatur, Indiana.

---

*These gifts are examples assuming the testator owns and has the right to give away this property through the will. For example, in a community property state, a spouse has the right to will only his or her share of community property and all of his or her separate property.

3. *A specific devise.* I give my real property situated in Shorewood County, Milwaukee, Wisconsin, and commonly known as 1278 University Lane, to my sister, Carolyn A. Hamilton.

4. *A residuary gift.* I give the residue of my estate, both real and personal property, to my wife, Patricia A. Jenkins-Bradshaw.

HOW DOES ONE CREATE A VALID WILL?

A will must comply with statutory formalities that are designed to ensure that the testator understood his or her actions at the time the will was made. These formalities are intended to help prevent fraud. If not precisely followed, the will is void. The decedent's property is then distributed according to state laws of intestacy.

Three types of wills are generally recognized as valid: formal (or witnessed) typed or printed wills; informal (or holographic), handwritten wills; and, in a very limited situation almost never applicable, oral wills.*

What Is a Formal or Witnessed Will?

The **formal will** is usually drafted by a lawyer and is generally prepared on a computer, word processor, or typewriter. It must be signed at the end (subscribed) by the testator. The subscription must be made in the presence of witnesses, or in their presence the testator must acknowledge that the will was previously made by him or her or under his or her direction. Most states require the following to create a valid formal will.

1. *The testator must have testamentary capacity.* The testator must be of legal age and sound mind *at the time the will is made.* The legal age for executing a will varies, but in most states 18 is the minimum age. Thus, a will of a 21-year-old decedent, written when she was 16, is invalid, i.e., without legal effect.

    The concept of "being of sound mind" refers to the testator's ability to formulate and understand his or her plan to distribute property, coupled with intent that the will put into effect the distribution plan. Although the testator must be competent when executing the will, illiteracy or physical or mental infirmity caused by old age (such as senility) do not necessarily prevent the making of a valid will. Where there is physical or mental infirmity, it is advisable to have a medical doctor as one witness who can testify that the condition did not affect the soundness of the testator's mind at the execution of the will.

Michael Taylor signed a new will three days before he died of AIDS. The new will left most of his $3.5 million estate to a charitable trust for the decorative arts. The next largest gift was to his companion, who was to

---

*An oral will, also called a nuncupative will, is valid only when the testator is in fear of imminent death (e.g., an accident victim with fatal injuries). Under a typical statute, two persons must hear the orally expressed intentions. Most states limit the property that a testator may dispose of in this manner to personal property of no more than a small designated sum (usually $1,000). Because of these limitations and special requirements, nuncupative wills are seldom used. Nuncupative wills are recognized in Georgia, Indiana, Kansas, Louisiana, Mississippi, Missouri, Nevada, New Hampshire, North Carolina, Ohio, Tennessee, Texas, Vermont, and Washington.

receive property worth about $400,000. His 87-year-old mother challenged the will. What is the result?

A San Francisco superior court jury held that Michael, in a weakened condition in the final days of his illness, was subjected to undue influence by his companion. He lacked the freedom of will necessary to express his true intent, and the will was declared void.[3]

2. *The will must be in writing.* The writing itself can be informal as long as it complies with statutory requirements. A will can be handwritten in crayon or ink. It can be written on a sheet or scrap of paper, on a paper bag, or on a piece of cloth. A will also can refer to a memorandum that, although not a will, contains information necessary to carry out the will.

Fran's will directed that a sum of money be divided among a group of charities named in a memorandum that Fran gave to Meehum *the same day the will was signed*. Can the charities obtain their bequest?

The list of charities is legally included or "incorporated by reference" into the will, but only if it existed and was sufficiently described when the will was signed. This practice is not desirable and should be avoided because of the opportunities it presents for error or even fraud.

3. *A will must be signed by the testator.* It is a fundamental requirement in almost all jurisdictions that the testator's signature appear at the end of the will. Each jurisdiction dictates what is a legally sufficient signature. Initials, an "X" or other mark, and words like "Mom" have all been held valid when shown that the testator intended them to be a signature.

4. *A formal will must be witnessed.* A will must be witnessed by at least two witnesses or it is invalid.* The number of witnesses, their qualifications, and how a will should be witnessed are set out in state statutes. Most states require that a witness be disinterested—that is, not a beneficiary under the will. There are no age requirements for witnesses, but they must be mentally competent.

   The purpose of statutes that require witnesses is to verify that the testator actually executed (signed) the will and had the required intent and capacity at that time. A witness does not have to read the contents of the will. Typically, the testator and witnesses must all sign in the sight or the presence of one another. The act of witnessing the signing of a will and thereafter signing the will to that effect is called **attestation**.

5. *Sometimes a will must be published.* A will is **published** by an oral declaration by the maker to the witnesses that the document they are about to sign is his or her "last will and testament."

   Will formalities are strictly enforced by probate courts and provide added assurance of validity. After all, the testator is dead when the will

See the actual wills of famous people on this Court TV Web site at http://www.courttv.com/legaldocs/newsmakers/wills/ See even more wills at http://www.ca-probate.com/wills.htm

---

*Vermont requires three witnesses.

"speaks," and not able to challenge fraudulent claims. If witnesses are also dead at that time and cannot supply appropriate affidavits (sworn statements in writing), their handwriting on the will may be authenticated by other means. This complication is usually avoided through the use of witnesses who are younger than the testator.

One variation of a formal will is a **statutory will**, a standardized form will authorized by the legislature, with blanks to be completed by the testator. Statutory wills were devised to provide for the simple and usual circumstances of persons who may otherwise die intestate. States authorizing such wills commonly provide that no changes to the pre-printed form are permitted.*

Wills can be complicated or simple. The will in Exhibit 14–3 is the actual complete will of the retired Chief Justice of the United States Warren E. Burger, now deceased. Because of the size of his estate, the lack of planning and appropriate assignment of executor powers his heirs undoubtedly lost substantial amounts of

Exhibit 14–3: The Last Will and Testament of Warren E. Burger

---

LAST WILL AND TESTAMENT OF WARREN E. BURGER

I hereby make and declare the following to be my last will and testament.

1. My executors will first pay all claims against my estate;

2. The remainder of my estate will be distributed as follows: one-third to my daughter, Margaret Elizabeth Burger Rose and two-thirds to my son, Wade A. Burger;

3. I designate and appoint as executors of this will, Wade A. Burger and J. Michael Luttig.

IN WITNESS WHEREOF, I have hereunto set my hand to this my Last Will and Testament this 9th day of June, 1994.

/s/Warren E. Burger

We hereby certify that in our presence on the date written above WARREN E. BURGER signed the foregoing instrument and declared it to be his Last Will and Testament and that at this request in his presence and in the presence of each other we have signed our names below as witnesses.

/s/Nathaniel E. Brady residing at 120 F St., NW, Washington, DC

/s/Alice M. Khu residing at 3041 Meeting St., Falls Church, VA

---

*The National Conference of Commissioners of Uniform State Laws approved a Uniform Statutory Will Act providing a simple will statute that could be adopted by interested states. Four states adopted the statutory will including California (Probate Code §6200 et seq.), Michigan (Comp. Laws Ann. §700.123c), Maine, (Rev. Stat. Ann. Tit. 18-A, § 2-514), and Wisconsin (Stat. §853.50 et seq.). No state has adopted a statutory will since the mid-1980s and it appears the National Conference no longer is actively promoting this Uniform Act.

money to taxes and administrative costs. The irony of his lack of careful planning is real and instructive.

What Is a Holographic Will?

An exception to the formal witnessed will exists in many states. A **holographic will** is a type of self-prepared will written, signed, and dated with a complete date, all entirely in the handwriting of the testator. About half the states* recognize this type of will, although the exact requirements often vary slightly. If the will is appropriately witnessed and other formalities are observed, the document is considered a formal will even though handwritten by the testator.

> Dave Decker, married to Dora May Decker and father of one child (female) named Dora June Decker, decided to make a will entirely in his own handwriting. He was sure a person could validly make such a will. He carefully wrote on a blank sheet of paper, "I give all I own to Dora." He signed and dated the paper. As an afterthought, he took the document to his office and asked his friend, Arthur Bamish, to sign and date his paper as a witness for him. Is the document a valid will?

No, the will is not valid in this particular case. In many states, a person may prepare a valid holographic will without witnesses, in one's own handwriting, signed and dated by oneself. Even if Dave's state is one of these, though his will is nevertheless invalid. Why? Dave had a wife and daughter, both named Dora. When he dies, the probate court cannot be sure to whom he intended to leave his property. Consequently, his will is void because of the uncertainty as to the identity of the beneficiary. Such ambiguity invalidates a will.**

Dave Decker also failed to meet an additional requirement in some states that he declare to the witnesses when he signed the will, that it is a will, and specifically ask them to serve as witnesses. Dave did not tell his witness, Arthur Bamish, that the document was his will, nor did he sign, or acknowledge his signature, in Bamish's presence. (Recall that witnesses must sign in the presence of the testator. Some states also require that witnesses sign in the presence of each other.)

In most states that permit holographic wills, requirements must be followed precisely. A major objection to the holographic will is the absence of witnesses. Probate courts are concerned, among other things, with the possibility of forgery and undue influence. As holographic wills are usually not witnessed, there is little protection against forgery or undue influence. Probate judges have ruled many attempted holographic wills invalid because they were partially typed (thus not entirely in the handwriting of the testator) or not dated.

A few states, such as Colorado and California, have liberalized the requirements for a holographic will, allowing typed or printed provisions ". . . if the

---

*Alaska, Arizona, California, Colorado, Idaho, Kentucky, Louisiana, Maine, Michigan, Mississippi, Montana, Nebraska, Nevada, New Jersey, North Carolina, North Dakota, Oklahoma, South Dakota, Tennessee, Texas, Utah, Virginia, West Virginia, and Wyoming.

**Once a will is invalidated, state laws substitute a statutory will for the testator, more formally called statutes of succession. Under a state statutory will or law of succession, either the wife will inherit all the property, or both the wife and daughter will share in Decker's estate in a specified proportion depending on the nature of the state's property law and the statutory will.

signature and the material provisions are in the handwriting of the testator."[4] Even where holographic wills are legally acceptable, the wisdom of preparing one is questionable. Many people fail to express their intentions clearly. They also may fail to take advantage of readily available techniques to minimize estate taxes and other costs (such as appropriate executor powers and waiver of bond). A person who insists on proceeding without professional legal assistance would be well-advised to study one of the self-help books containing standard forms and provisions.

> *[An] individual, trying to avoid leaving anything to her daughter (a drug addict), carefully specified each piece of property in her will and which heir was to receive it. However, after writing her will, she received a large inheritance from her father. Because the inheritance was not listed in her will, under the intestacy laws of the state of Texas, the inheritance passed to her daughter — clearly not her intent. These are. . . . horror stories I have come across that could have been prevented if the people involved had consulted an attorney rather than written their wills.*

Daniel Palmer, Attorney at Law, Texas[5]

Shortly after Christine McCarthy and Stephen Kapcar married in 1972, Kapcar named Christine as beneficiary of an Atena Life Insurance Co. group life insurance policy. Within a year of the marriage, Kapcar was diagnosed with multiple sclerosis. He developed severe tremors, underwent brain surgery to alleviate the tremors, and became legally blind in 1974. Within a few years they separated and in 1978 Kapcar divorced Christine. Neither the divorce decree nor a property settlement mentioned the Aetna policy. Stephen Kapcar died in 1984 a quadriplegic, having spent the last seven years of his life—unemployed—living with his father. According to the terms of a holographic will written in 1977, Kapcar stated that "I will all my personal belongings, stock certificates, bank accounts, insurance benefits, and any other earthly belongings to my father. This will voids my previous will bequeathing my belongings to Christine B. Kapcar." Kapcar never changed the named beneficiary (Christine) on the Aetna policy. Christine claimed the proceeds of the insurance policy. Did the holographic will transfer the interest in the life insurance policy to Kapcar's father?

The admonition that people should seek legal counsel to prepare wills is not made simply to line lawyers' pockets with gold. Any competent attorney would have asked questions about Kapcar's assets, including life insurance policies, and Kapcar would have been directed to change the beneficiary according to his wishes. The predictable result in this case was that the self-prepared will was insufficient to change the beneficiary in the life insurance policy, and the divorced wife prevailed over the faithful father. "To hold that a change in beneficiary may be made by testamentary disposition alone would open up a serious question as to payment of life insurance policies. It is in the public interest that an insurance company may pay a loss to the beneficiary designated in the policy as promptly after the death of the insured as may reasonably be done. If there is uncertainty as to the beneficiary upon the death of the insured, in all cases where the right to change the beneficiary had been reserved there would always be a question as to whom the proceeds of the insurance should be paid. If paid to the beneficiary, a will might later be probated designating a different disposition of the fund, and it would be a risk that few companies would be willing to take."[6]

HOW DO YOU REVOKE A WILL?

The maker of a will may revoke it at any time during the maker's lifetime. Revocation can be partial or complete, and it should follow certain specified formalities. A testator can revoke a will by a physical act such as intentionally burning, tearing, canceling, obliterating, or destroying it. Having someone else destroy the will at the maker's direction and in the maker's presence also revokes the will. The intention to destroy the will is essential.

Another writing, called a *codicil*, may also revoke a will. A codicil is a written instrument, separate from the will, that amends or revokes provisions in the will. A codicil makes it unnecessary to redraft the entire will if its maker wants to change only part of it. A codicil can also be used to revoke an entire will. In either case, the codicil must be created with the same formalities required for the will, and it must refer to the will.

A *second* or *new will* can be executed to revoke the first. The second will must use specific language such as, "This will hereby revokes all prior wills." If the first will is not revoked, then some courts will admit both wills into probate. The second will is treated as a codicil. It is good idea to keep copies of prior wills—but they should be clearly marked and preferably initialed and dated to indicate that they are revoked and superseded by the will executed on (name the date).

CAN A PROBATE COURT DISTRIBUTE PROPERTY CONTRARY TO THE TERMS OF A WILL?

In most states, a failure to provide for a spouse or child can partially revoke a will, in which case a probate court can compel distribution of an estate contrary to the stated terms of a will. A **pretermitted heir** is a child either unintentionally left out of a will or one born after the will is made. Most states have pretermitted heir statutes that give to a pretermitted child a statutory share of the testator's property. This statutory shares overrides the will, unless the child received some gift in the will, or his or her exclusion was deliberate, expressly and clearly made. If a child (or grandchild, if the child has died and there is a surviving grandchild) is not mentioned in the will, and no provision was made for the child outside the will, the law assumes that the omission was an inadvertent mistake. A parent testator may ignore and exclude a child in his or her will, but must do so expressly. Likewise, in some states spouses sometimes can be omitted from receiving the decedent's property only if the will specifies that such omission of the spouse is purposeful.

Sometimes a testator identifies a specific gift of property in a will, but then disposes of it before the will "speaks." For example, the testator wills his savings account at the Texarkana Bank of Austin to Johnny Raye, but when the testator dies, no such account exists at the Texarkana Bank of Austin. Even if an account can be found at another bank in Austin the gift will fail. The executor is power-less to substitute other property to Johnny Raye. Instead, the property will be dis-tributed as otherwise specified in the will (e.g., in a residual disposition clause). This is called **ademption**: disposing of something given to a donee in a will. Thus, the provision in the will is inoperative and impossible to carry out. The person for whom the gift was originally intended does not receive it, even though the will was not revoked.

Fuller claimed that although he was found guilty of first-degree murder, technically he did not kill his grandmother because his girlfriend did. Can a beneficiary speed up a gift in a will by accelerating the testator's death, or as Sam Spade would say it, "can you do the person in and still inherit"?

Because a will is a document subject to change at the whim of the testator, it has been the subject of much intrigue in fiction, and in life (or in death—pardon the pun). A potential heir can be written out of a will anytime the testator wishes. States have passed laws to protect individuals from impatient and evil beneficia-ries. For example, anyone convicted of a crime that caused the death of a testator cannot receive benefits under the will. Fuller's claim was based on the court nar-rowly construing a so-called "slayer statute."* "We conclude that the term 'kills' as used in [the statute] refers to a person who causes the death of another by bringing about that effect."[7]

Probate court is the place of proving the validity of a will. It is also where wills are challenged or contested. The usual grounds for challenging a will are:

1. The testator lacked capacity.
2. The testator was subject to undue influence.
3. The will was not properly executed.
4. Someone defrauded the testator into executing this particular will.

To discourage will contests, will drafters often include a *no-contest* or *incon-testability clause* in the will. Such a clause might read:

> *If any beneficiary under this Will in any manner, directly or indirectly, contests or attacks the Will or any of its provisions, any share of interest in my estate given that contesting beneficiary under the Will is revoked and shall be disposed of as if that contesting beneficiary had died before me.*

Such a clause discourages beneficiaries from asserting frivolous will-contest lawsuits. However, when an entire will is ruled invalid, the incontestability clause as well as all other provisions are rendered void. The estate therefore would be distributed by intestate succession, or in some cases, by the terms of a prior will.

---

*The Colorado law applied to Fuller provides an example of a slayer statute, §15-11-803, C.R.S. (1987 Repl.Vol. 6B). (1) A . . . devisee who kills the decedent and, as a result thereof, is convicted of . . . the crime of murder in the first or second degree or manslaughter, as said crimes are defined in Sections 18-3-102 to 18-3- 104, C.R.S., is not en-titled to any benefits under the will or under this article, and the estate of the decedent passes as if the killer had predeceased the decedent. Property appointed by the will of the decedent to or for the benefit of the killer passes as if the killer had predeceased the decedent.

WHAT IF THE TESTATOR IS THE VICTIM OF UNDUE INFLUENCE?

Valid wills express the maker's intention to transfer and distribute his or her property after death. If it can be shown that the will was the result of improper pressure brought by another person, the will is void because it does not truly express the maker's intention.

Undue influence is sometimes inferred by the court if the testator ignores his or her blood relatives, who are normally the "natural objects of his bounty," and instead names a nonrelative as a beneficiary. The likelihood of undue influence is greater if the beneficiary is a person who was in constant close physical contact with the deceased and therefore able to influence the making of the will. When a nurse or friend who cares for the deceased during a comparatively short span of time before the death benefits to the exclusion of close family members, questions of undue influence inevitably arise. Even a spouse may be suspected of undue influence if children from a former marriage are excluded.

> Use the searchable index at the Fleming and Curti, Professional Law Corporation Elder Law Issues Web site. Put undue influence in the searchable index and read the examples.
> http://desert.net/elder/issues.html

J. Seward Johnson died in 1983 from prostrate cancer, leaving his entire estate to his wife of 12 years, Barbara Piasecka Johnson. Mrs. Johnson had worked as a chambermaid and cook at the Johnson mansion before their marriage in 1971. Mr. Johnson's six children, by a prior marriage, contested the will, claiming that their father had been the victim of undue influence by his wife and had been "terrorized" into signing the will just before his death. The estate valuation exceeded $500 million. Did the children succeed in their will contest?

After a four-month legal battle in New York's Surrogate Court, the parties reached an out-of-court settlement. Mrs. Johnson received $350 million, and the remainder was divided between the children and a charitable oceanographic research foundation that had been founded by the testator in 1971.[8]

Will-signing ceremonies are sometimes videotaped to show that the ritual prescribed by law was correctly followed. Such tapes also provide evidence as to the demeanor (behavior and possibly competence) of the testator. Such videotapes have been used effectively to defend challenges to the validity of wills.[9]

WHAT HAPPENS TO THE ESTATE OF A PERSON WHO DIES WITHOUT LEAVING A WILL?

Each state regulates how property shall be distributed when a resident of the state dies without leaving a will. Such laws attempt to carry out the presumed intent and wishes of the decedent. These statutes are called **intestacy laws** and, as briefly noted earlier in the chapter, provide for the distribution of property to designated heirs.

The rules of descent vary from state to state. The law always provides that the debts of the decedent must first be paid with assets of the estate. Then there is usually a special statutory provision for the rights of the surviving spouse and children. A surviving spouse generally receives one-half of the estate, if there is also a surviving child who gets the other half. The surviving spouse gets one-third if there are two or more children, the children share in equal portions the remaining two-thirds. When no children or grandchildren survive the decedent, the surviving spouse gets the entire estate.

Allen dies intestate (without a will) and is survived by his wife, Della, and his children, Duane and Tara. Allen's property passes according to intestacy laws. After Allen's outstanding debts are paid, Della will ordinarily receive one-third to one-half interest in the property; Duane and Tara will receive equal shares of the remainder.

State distribution laws specify the order in which heirs of an intestate have claims against the estate. When there is no surviving spouse or child, then the grandchildren, brothers and sisters, and, in some states, parents of the decedent follow in that sequence to receive the entire estate.

Because state laws differ so widely, few generalizations can be made about the laws of descent and distribution. It is necessary to refer to the exact terms of the applicable statutes to answer questions about intestate distribution in any given state. Exhibit 14–4 shows a typical pattern of intestate distribution of property (in this case, in Indiana).

MATTERS CONCERNING PROBATE

Is it the eccentric nature of the customers or the probate system itself that generates so much attention? I think it is a little bit of both.

Probate Judge Pat Gregory, Harris County, Texas[10]

WHAT IS PROBATE?

Probate is a court proceeding where wills are proved to be valid or invalid and estates of decedents are administered and ultimately properly distributed. Probate serves several useful purposes. It provides an opportunity for unsecured creditors of the decedent to submit claims for payment from the estate. If they fail to submit a claim, they risk having their debts canceled, with no future claims against the beneficiaries who get the estate assets.* Death taxes are also normally paid as part of the probate process. If the court finds a valid will, the net assets (after all debts and liabilities of the decedent are paid) are distributed to named beneficiaries. If there is no valid will, the probate court will accomplish similar tasks by complying with the state's law of intestate succession. Probate laws vary from state to state. A Uniform Probate Code has been adopted by 18 states. Note that applicable death taxes are payable whether or not there is a probate proceeding.

---

*Secured debts (for example, a note secured by a testator's real property) remain secured. In other words, the beneficiary who receives the property receives it subject to the security interest held by the creditor.

Exhibit 14–4:   Intestate Distribution of Property under Indiana Law

Deceased	Survived by	Spouse	Parent(s)	Child(ren)	Siblings (Brothers & Sisters)	Grandparents
HUSBAND or WIFE	Spouse only	All Property				
	Spouse and one or more Children	1/2[a]		1/2[b]		
	Spouse Child(ren) Parent(s)	1/2		1/2[b]		
	Spouse and Parent(s) only	3/4	1/4			
	Child(ren) and Parent(s) only			All Property		
WIDOW, WIDOWER, or SINGLE or DIVORCED	Child(ren)			All Property		
	Child(ren) and Parent(s)			All Property		
	Parent(s) only		All Property			
	Parent(s) and Siblings[c]		1/2		1/2[b,c]	
	Siblings				All Property[b]	
	Grand-parents only					All Property
	No Spouse, Parent issue, Siblings or Grand-parents[d]					
	No Relatives[e]					

[a]Limitations exist for a childless spouse when children by a prior marriage survive the decedent.
[b]Descendants of a deceased take the deceased person's share.
[c]Assumes both parents are living and there are two or more siblings. Each parent takes as a sibling but receives at least 1/4 interest. For example, one parent and one sibling each would receive 1/2 share. If there are one parent and six siblings, the parent would get 1/4 and the six siblings would divide 3/4 share.
[d]All property to aunts and uncles. If an aunt or uncle is deceased but leaves a surviving child, the child or children receive the aunt or uncle's share.
[e]All property goes (escheats) to the state.

SOURCE: Indiana code, § 29–1–2–1.

CAN PROBATE BE AVOIDED?

Probate has important disadvantages. It takes time, generally a minimum of six months, often one to two years, sometimes longer. During this time, title to property is uncertain, as it is not yet transferred to the beneficiaries pending proof of the will and payment of the debts of the estate. The trauma of a loved one's death may be aggravated by the inability to use assets that the survivor badly needs.

Appropriate planning and a well-chosen executor advised by a competent lawyer should minimize or eliminate problems caused by probate delay. In addition, the facts about the estate and its disposition become a matter of public record. If the probate is of the estate of a prominent person, famous or infamous, information about the estate and beneficiaries is often publicized in the media.

Probate fees are payable to the personal representative (executor or administrator) and to the attorney who handles the estate. Sometimes the executor is a principal or sole beneficiary and will waive probate fees (which are taxable as earned income for income tax purposes) to increase the inheritance (which may be tax-free depending on size, or may be taxable at death tax rates that are lower than the executor's income tax bracket).

In California, the following percentages of the probated estate's gross value are the maximum fees that may generally be received by both the executor and the attorney:[11]

4 percent of the first	$15,000	$600
3 percent of the next	$85,000	$2,550
2 percent of the next	$900,000	$18,000
1 percent of the next	$9,000,000	$90,000
.5 percent of the next	$15,000,000	$75,000

A reasonable amount to be determined by the court of any amount over $25,000,000.

In some states, statutory maximum fees are higher than California; in other states, they are lower. The amount of the lawyer's fee is negotiable and an executor may reach an agreement in which the attorney agrees to accept a fee less than the statutory amount. However, the statutory fee is typically the amount paid. Costs of appraisal, tax returns, and property management are extra. If unusual or extraordinary services are provided, such as defense against a claim that the will is invalid, a court will usually allow a higher fee. If a state does not provide a statutory fee, the usual practice is for the attorney to bill by the hour.

Many states have laws that allow distribution of assets without probate proceedings. Less formal methods of transferring title are used for estates with small property values. In some states, for example, merely filling out standard forms can pass savings and checking accounts, title to cars, and certain other property. And summary proceedings are often available when there is only one heir, notably a spouse. A vast majority of states provide for a Transfer on Death (TOD) of securities free of probate under the Uniform Transfer-On-Death Security Registration Act. The securities need to be held in an account, which provides for this type of transfer, and the specific details must be carefully planned.[12] Some very populous states do not have TOD laws including California and New York.

A majority of states provide for **family settlement agreements**—private agreements among the beneficiaries. Once a will is admitted to probate, the family members can agree to settle among themselves the distribution of the decedent's assets. However, a court order is still needed to protect the estate from possible future claims of creditors and to clear title to estate assets.

The use of summary procedures in estate administration saves time and money. The expenses of a personal representative's commission, attorneys' fees, and appraisers' fees can thus be eliminated or at least minimized.

Some persons with larger estates (not eligible for summary procedures) nonetheless try to avoid probate and its related costs. With proper estate planning, the size of the probate estate may be substantially reduced. The following are types of property transfers that bypass probate:

1. Undivided interests in property owned by the decedent in joint tenancy (or tenancy by the entireties) goes to the survivor(s) without probate under the right of survivorship (see Chapter 12).

2. In community property states, only one-half of the community property will go through probate, since the surviving spouse already owns the other half.

3. Life insurance proceeds are paid directly to beneficiaries, unless the estate is named as the beneficiary (e.g., to provide cash for payment of death taxes, thus avoiding forced liquidation of other assets, such as equity in a business).

4. Certain U.S. government bonds are paid directly to the person listed on the front of the bond as POD ("paid on death").

5. Property previously transferred to an *inter vivos trust* (discussed later in the chapter) is not probated.

Not all of these methods are suitable for every estate, but they are alternatives to probate administration.

What Are the Duties of an Executor?

One day Robert Yu received the sad news of the death of his wealthy uncle, Wilbur Yu. A few days later he received some good news and some bad news. The good news: he was named a beneficiary in his uncle's will and was to receive a gift of 1,000 shares of International Business Machines common stock. The bad news (or so he regarded it): he was named executor of his uncle's will. Should he accept the appointment?

Probably yes. If he declines, the court will appoint a substitute administrator. If he accepts the nomination, an attorney he selects to handle the estate in probate court will do the legal work and will guide him in the proper performance of his duties. Both will be entitled to payment authorized by statute, plus compensation for extraordinary time or expenditures (e.g., defending or pursuing litigation on behalf of their estate, or negotiating sales of real property). This compensation is usually adequate and even generous, at least for larger estates. Compensation is usually limited by statute based on the gross value of the estate (total value of assets without regard to liabilities). Executor and attorney fees are often the same for a complicated estate consisting of various business and assorted assets, as they are for an estate consisting of one bank account, if the values of each estate are the same. This anomaly flows from the misunderstanding of most executors that attorney fees provided by statute are maximums generally allowed. In fact, a lower fee can be paid if agreed to between the executor and the attorney.

The duties of an executor are important and generally include the following. Note that many of these services are provided by the lawyer employed by the executor to assist with administration of the estate.

1. Complying with decedent's special instructions for funeral and burial.

2. Locating and notifying witnesses to the will.

3. Notifying heirs (i.e., persons who would get the estate if there were no will) and beneficiaries named in the will, preferably meeting with them, if convenient.

4. Arranging for bond, if necessary, to cover faithful performance of his or her duties as executor.

5. Notifying the post office to send the decedent's mail to the executor and discontinuing telephone and other services as appropriate.

6. Opening a bank account for the estate.

7. Assisting the attorney in identifying creditors and arranging for payment of debts.

8. Identifying, inventorying, and safeguarding all probate assets. Safeguarding may require getting or maintaining adequate fire, property, and liability insurance. Safeguarding may also involve excluding relatives of the deceased from plundering estate assets.

9. Reviewing nonprobate assets (joint tenancy and trusts) for appropriate action to ensure legal transfer.

10. Offering the will for probate in court and being formally appointed by the court as executor. This appointment is referred to as *receiving letters testamentary*.

11. Reviewing and taking appropriate action regarding the decedent's financial records: leases, mortgages, notes, life insurance policies, pensions, social security, stocks, bonds, saving accounts, checking accounts, etc.

12. Collecting any dividends, interest, and/or rent and paying any rent, interest, insurance premiums, or other obligations.

13. Having assets appraised when advisable or required.

14. If decedent had a business, acting to continue proper operation if feasible and appropriate, or to sell and liquidate if necessary.

15. Publishing statutorily required notice to creditors and reviewing and paying claims.

16. Keeping detailed records of receipts (income) and disbursements (expenses and debt payments).

17. Determining cash requirements for taxes (income and estate) probate expenses, valid claims, and cash bequests, and deciding which assets are to be used or liquidated for these needs.

18. With the aid of an accountant, filing income tax returns (final return of decedent, tax returns for the estate while administration continues) and death taxes (inheritance and/or estate) and making necessary payments.

19. Preparing a final estate accounting to submit to the court (listing assets, receipts, disbursements, sales with gains and losses, and reconciliation of beginning and ending balances).

20. Transferring title to real and personal property to beneficiaries (and sometimes trustees) in accordance with the probate court decree of distribution under the will, obtaining receipts for them.

21. Obtaining formal court approval of the settlement of the estate and final discharge as the executor.

WHAT IS THE UNIFORM PROBATE CODE?

A Uniform Probate Code (UPC) has been adopted in whole or in substantial part by 18 states, including Arizona, Colorado, Florida, and Michigan. Under the UPC, a person must be 18 or older and of sound mind to make a will. The will must be in writing and signed by the testator (or in the testator's name by someone else in the testator's presence, by his or her direction). Two competent witnesses must witness the will. They need not be present when the testator signs, but must be present later when the testator acknowledges the signature on the will. The code permits holographic wills.[13] A major goal of the creators of any uniform code is that it be adopted by most states in order to provide uniform law throughout the country. Because of the mobility of our society, compelling arguments exist for uniformity in probate law, yet the goal of general acceptance of the UPC remains elusive.

You can access a typical state's version of the Uniform Probate Code (in this case, South Dakota's) at the Uniform Code Web site, maintained by Cornell Law School at http://www.law.cornell.edu/uniform/probate.html

WHAT ARE LIVING WILLS AND OTHER ADVANCED DIRECTIVES?

The population of the United States is aging primarily because people are living longer thanks to some remarkable advances in pharmacology and in medical practice, as well as diet. Increases in the number of aged persons influences social, political, and economic policy and related law. There is a growing acceptance of a document called a **living will**, which allows an individual to instruct his or her family, and medical personnel, about the medical procedures to follow—or more particularly, to abstain from—under specified circumstances.

Twenty-five-year-old Nancy Cruzan lapsed into a permanent coma after an automobile accident. Five years after the accident, Nancy's parents sought a court order to remove a feeding tube from Nancy who had been existing in a "vegetative state" since the accident. Without medical assistance, Nancy would die. Were Nancy's parents able to get the order from the court?

National attention focused on the "right to die" issue in 1987 after the lawsuit brought by Nancy Cruzan's parents. After several years of court battles, a Missouri circuit court granted her parent's wishes and the feeding tubes were removed. Twelve days after the court order, Nancy died. Among the reasons for the long court battle was the absence of any written evidence as to what Nancy Cruzan's desires might be. A living will would have provided the written evidence that Nancy Cruzan's parents lacked.

All states now have passed statutes providing for **advance medical directives (AMD)**, instructions to others about the care they wish, or do not wish, to receive if they become terminally ill or incapacitated. **Incapacity** is the lack of legal capacity to make important decisions. It can result from a serious illness, an accident causing a coma, or even old age if coupled with Alzheimer's disease. The most common AMD is the aforementioned living wills.

The term *living will* is misleading because a living will has nothing to do with the transfer of property after death. A less confusing term used in many states is **directive to physicians**. A related directive is the durable power of attorney for healthcare, discussed later. Whatever the name, it is a document directed to physicians to consider the ill or injured person's wishes regarding the use of life-support systems. All 50 states now provide for living wills, but requirements vary. (A living will should not be confused with a living trust, which is discussed later in the chapter.)

Some living will statutes require that the living will be created after a patient has learned of a terminal illness but not before. This type of living will obviously would not have assisted Nancy Cruzan's parents, because her condition occurred without notice or time to plan. Also, Nancy was not just permanently ill; she was brain dead in a permanent coma.

Living wills must be witnessed by two or more disinterested (meaning free from any selfish motive or interest) persons, and prepared using a specific format or form.[14] If a form is legally invalid in execution, it may still be used in court to show the desires of the ill person if he or she is unable to testify.

A **durable power of attorney for healthcare** is a more flexible document than the living will. It authorizes another person to make healthcare decisions for a person who is incapacitated. It is one type of power of attorney. A **power of attorney** is a common legal document allowing the creator, a principal, to empower another (agent) to act on his or her behalf, usually in regard to financial and property decisions. These documents can authorize another to perform any act that the principal could otherwise do. They also can be limited in scope to authorize specified and limited acts, such as selling specific shares of stock. Note that the person nominated is known as the *attorney-in-fact*, and he or she need not be and usually is not an attorney at law. (The term *attorney* literally means "representative.") An ordinary power of attorney ends with the *incapacity* or death of the person giving the power; it automatically terminates at that point. The powers granted by a durable power of attorney, however, do not end with the incapacitation of its creator.

A durable power of attorney can be created in some states to authorize financial decisions, as well as health care decisions, but here we are discussing the *durable power of attorney for healthcare*, a phrase describing a durable power of attorney that limits the attorney-in-fact to healthcare decisions. Such durable powers of attorney are often created to be "springing" documents, written so as to provide power to the designated representative only upon the occurrence of a healthcare crisis. In other words, the power is given to the attorney-in-fact only upon the occurrence of certain specified events or conditions.

In any form, a durable power of attorney gives the attorney-in-fact, usually a close relative or friend, the power to make healthcare decisions for a person who becomes incapacitated through serious illness, accident, or any other means. The decisions authorized include life-and-death decisions such as whether to order the withdrawal of life-support systems for the incapacitated party. The durable power is not necessarily restricted to life-and-death health decisions, however. For example, if a person who is incapacitated needs elective surgery, the durable power of attorney may allow the designated person to approve of the surgery.

A durable power of attorney for healthcare typically requires the signature of at least one disinterested witness, and must contain exact, approved statutory language. Often the signature of the creator of the power must be attested and certified by a notary public.*

As with a living will a durable power of attorney can be revoked by the principal creator at any time before incapacity. Note that the durable power of attorney differs from the living will in two important ways: (1) it can be created at any time—one need not be terminally ill—and (2) it delegates very extensive and critical decision-making powers to another person. Therefore, that person should be selected carefully. While these documents are well-advised and useful, they should be created with great care and thoughtful consideration.

Mabel Bradshaw was elderly and concerned about being able to handle her affairs in the future. She wished to grant a power of attorney to her daughter Ann, who could then manage her property and make decisions about her medical care if she, Mabel, became incapacitated. Would you advise Mabel to create a power of attorney or a durable power of attorney?

Mabel's wishes suggest that a durable power of attorney is more appropriate. This will permit Ann to handle Mabel's healthcare decisions and also authorize Ann to make decisions about Mabel's property and investments should Mabel become unable to do so.

A petition to remove the life-support system for George Vogel was accompanied by this affidavit of Dr. Jonathan Sumner: "George Vogel suffered a major stroke that has left him in a vegetative state. He can move, but has no awareness; he further has no intellectual function. He is being kept alive solely by the use of a gastric tube through his nose in which material, in the consistency of eggnog, is fed into his body. George Vogel is not aware of his surroundings, nor is there any possibility that he will ever be in any other state other than the vegetative state that he presently suffers." Testimony was also offered by his sister-in-law that Vogel, prior to his recent illness, had said "he did not wish to be kept alive by having tubes inserted into his body and that he would not wish to be kept alive solely by artificial means." A non-physician guardian appointed by the court opposed the petition, stating that Mr. Vogel was neither brain dead ("his brain stem is operative") nor terminally ill. Mr. Vogel had not prepared any advanced directive and he was not otherwise terminally ill. What was the order of the court?

The court denied the petition, stating, "A distinction must be drawn between those who are unable to care for themselves due to infirmities of illness, age or

---

*As law in this area is relatively new, it varies a great deal from state to state. Specific state statutes must be consulted before creating either a living will or durable power of attorney. Considerable thought need also be given to the selection of the attorney-in-fact. He or she should be someone you trust implicitly and who knows and is willing to abide by your wishes in trying times. In both the living will and either type of durable power of attorney, the instructions can be as detailed for the attorney-in-fact as one might wish, including exactly what to do in a variety of circumstances.

other physical disabilities and those who are brain-dead or terminally ill, without hope of recovery and are being kept alive solely by use of artificial means made available by the techniques of modern medicine and technology. [I]t is a function of humanity to care for those who are unable to care for themselves by reason of illness, age or infirmities."[15] Clearly the legal response to Mr. Vogel's condition would have been different had he prepared an appropriate advance directive.

In 1991 the federal government passed the Patient Self-Determination Act, which requires that, before being admitted to certain healthcare facilities participating in Medicare or Medicaid (including hospitals), patients must be informed of the right to execute advance directives and have an opportunity to inform the healthcare facility of their wishes regarding heroic measures to sustain life.[16]

Laws dealing with these sensitive matters are still in an early stage of development.* States are establishing, and liberalizing, their statutes involving living wills and durable powers of attorney to allow persons greater flexibility. Requirements for the creation and use of the document will undoubtedly continue to vary until a greater consensus emerges as to the proper way to deal with issues of natural death.[17]

DOES A TERMINALLY ILL PERSON HAVE THE LEGAL RIGHT TO COMMIT SUICIDE?

The issue of whether **suicide** (the taking of one's own life) is morally correct is one of many issues upon which Americans lack consensus. Most religious codes of conduct, and certainly legal rules generally label it a wrongful act. Currently no state in the United States explicitly condones suicide; and only one state, Oregon,[18] has legalized assisted suicide. **Euthanasia**, also called mercy killing, is the affirmative act of bringing about the immediate death of another, allegedly in a painless way; it is generally administered by one who thinks that the dying person wishes to die because of a terminal or extremely painful disease. The advanced directives discussed earlier provide that only extraordinary and heroic measures to resuscitate can be refused or continued. Euthanasia involves an aggressive act of putting the patient to death without his or her prior authorization, an act most likely to be treated as some form of criminal homicide.

> Washington law provides that "[a] person is guilty of promoting a suicide attempt when he knowingly causes or aids another person to attempt suicide." Such promotion is a felony punishable by up to five years' imprisonment and up to a $10,000 fine. Four Washington physicians who treat terminally ill patients, along with three gravely ill plaintiffs (since deceased) sued the Washington State Attorney General, claiming that

http://

Read the text of the Oregon Death With Dignity Act at http://www.finalexit.org/ORdwdAct.html

---

*Together, living will statutes and durable powers of attorney are often part of a "Natural Death Act" or "Rights of Terminally Ill" statute. Some states provide that family members or close friends can make medical decisions for incompetent patients who have not provided advance directives. Also, approximately 20 states provide for non-hospital do-not-resuscitate orders. The typical DNR order is written on an official form provided by the state department of health. Upon presentation to a paramedic, emergency room technician, or any other health professional, all resuscitation efforts must be stopped.

Washington law has kept the physicians from assisting these patients in ending their lives. This legal barrier violated "a liberty interest protected by the Fourteenth Amendment which extends to a personal choice by a mentally competent, terminally ill adult to commit physician assisted suicide." Was the claim successful?

The U.S. Supreme Court considered this important issue in 1987 and rejected the plaintiffs' arguments.[19] The Court acknowledged the blurring of the issue given that Washington had in 1979 passed a Natural Death Act allowing the "withholding or withdrawal of life sustaining treatment" at a patient's direction and providing that such an act "shall not, for any purpose, constitute a suicide."[20] In rejecting the physicians' arguments, the Court recognized that "for over 700 years, the Anglo American common law tradition has punished or otherwise disapproved of both suicide and assisting suicide."[21] "The history of the law's treatment of assisted suicide in this country has been and continues to be one of the rejection of nearly all efforts to permit it." "[We] conclude that the asserted 'right' to assistance in committing suicide is not a fundamental liberty interest protected by the Due Process Clause. Throughout the Nation, Americans are engaged in an earnest and profound debate about the morality, legality, and practicality of physician-assisted suicide. Our holding permits this debate to continue, as it should in a democratic society."[22] The Court noted that since the enactment Oregon's "Death With Dignity Act," which legalized physician-assisted suicide, several other states had considered similar proposals, though none had been enacted.[23]

If you pay any attention to current events, you have heard of Dr. Jack Kevorkian, a retired pathologist and advocate for physician-assisted suicide. He has admittedly assisted in the suicide of several terminally ill patients. At least one source has credited Dr. Kevorkian with assisting in the death of over 130 persons.[24] He has been charged with various homicide offenses in his home state of Michigan, with the charges eventually being dropped or, in three instances resulting in an acquittal by jury (indubitable examples of juror abrogation, as discussed in Chapter 3). In November 1998, the prestigious CBS television program *60 Minutes* used videotape provided by Dr. Kevorkian showing his participation in the death of a terminally ill ALS patient.[25] Millions of Americans were able to witness physician-assisted suicide in prime time. This portrayed act led to a second-degree murder conviction in March of 1999 and a sentence of 10 to 15 years in prison.

Read the chronology of events surrounding the passage and implementation of the Oregon Death With Dignity Act at http://www.oregondwd.org/chron.htm

---

MATTERS CONCERNING TRUSTS

Put not your trust in money, but put your money in trust.

Oliver Wendell Holmes, Jr., 1841–1935
(Associate Justice of the United States Supreme Court, 1902–1932)

WHAT ARE TRUSTS?

Marisa Fabor and her husband, Brandon, are worried. They fear that when their children, Kathy and Tom, inherit the family farm, they will sell it and squander the proceeds within a short time; the children "simply do not know the value of a dollar." What can Marisa and Brandon do to keep their children from squandering their inheritance?

One solution is the creation of a **trust**. This is done by transferring legal title to property from the owner (called a **settlor** or sometimes called the *trustor* or *donor*) to another (called a **trustee**) to hold for the benefit of, and someday distribute to, the specified **beneficiary**. A trust becomes a separate legal entity, governed by its trustee. Thus, the trustee is anyone who holds property for the benefit of another, called the *trust beneficiary*. In the preceding situation, Marisa and Brandon would be the settlors, Kathy and Tom would be the beneficiaries. The person or business firm selected by Marisa and Brandon to manage the trust would be the trustee. They could select themselves as co-trustees and name others as successor trustees upon their deaths.

How property is to be distributed is determined by the settlor and stated in the trust document. The trustee receives possession and legal title to the property for the duration of the trust, until it is distributed to the beneficiaries. Pending distribution, the beneficiary owns the *equitable title* to the property, which is a beneficial interest but without the right to possess or transfer the property. A trust can be created for any legal purpose consistent with public policy. Its essential elements are as follows:

Read about trusts at this Cornell Law School Web site at http://www.law.cornell.edu/topics/estates_trusts.html

1. The settlor must be competent to create a trust.

2. The settlor must intend to create a trust.

3. The trust must be created for a proper purpose.

4. Money or property sufficiently identified to allow title to pass must be transferred to the trust.

5. A beneficiary must be designated.

6. Although a writing is not absolutely required to create a trust, it is expected.

7. The trust instrument should name a trustee with appropriate capacity.

If Marisa and Brandon transfer their farm to the First Bank of Minnesota, in trust, for the benefit of their children, the couple will have created a trust. This arrangement is illustrated in Exhibit 14–5.

A frequent use for trusts is to provide funds for a child's education. These trusts are created both in wills and as *inter vivos* trusts. The amount of assets or cash necessary to accomplish the purpose of this trust obviously changes over time. If Yale is your child's goal (or the parent's), note that the estimated cost of attending Yale for one academic year in 1998–1999 was $33,200. Tuition and fees cost was $23,780. If you could find a working time machine and travel back to 1900, you would find Yale's tuition a more reasonable $155 per year; room rent, $200; board, $200; books, $35 to $45; and subscriptions, society dues, etc., $100; clothing and incidentals, $150—making a total of $850.[26]

WHO MAY BE A TRUSTEE AND WHAT DOES A TRUST COST?

Any settlor who creates a trust may serve as his or her own trustee. However, unless the trust is a living trust, the settlor usually chooses a competent and

Exhibit 14–5:   Trust Arrangement

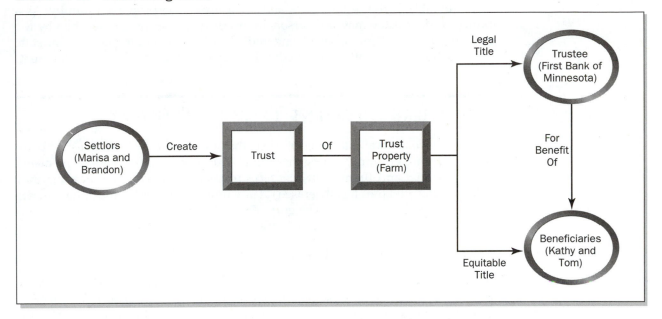

trustworthy relative or friend or a commercial trust company with its staff of experts. In addition, many financial corporations, such as banks, offer their services as commercial trustees. Anyone nominated as a trustee is free to decline to serve. If a successor or alternate is not named in the trust document, the court will usually name a trustee.

If compensation is not mentioned in the trust document, the trustee has a right to be paid for his or her services. The fees are determined consistent with state law or as allowed by the probate court. The settlor can provide in the trust document how, or even whether, the trustee is to be paid for services. If the court sets the fee, it will determine what is reasonable in view of the size of the estate, time required to administer it, services performed, and results achieved.

In trusts created during the settlor's life, like Marisa and Brandon's, the fees are negotiated. Common percentages are three-fourths of one percent of the fair market value of real estate and obligations secured by real estate, and three-fifths of one percent of the fair market value of other assets in the trust estate. The percentage may be less for a very large trust (e.g., one with assets in excess of $1 million). Corporate trustees frequently charge one-tenth of one percent as an "acceptance fee" when the trust takes effect, and a one percent "distribution fee" for all amounts they distribute. Trustees, like attorneys and personal representatives in probate proceedings, are also entitled to extra compensation for special services and expenses, as for defending the trust in a lawsuit.

WHAT ARE THE DUTIES OF A TRUSTEE?

The trustee is a fiduciary to the beneficiary of the trust; that is, the trustee owes to the beneficiary a duty of highest care, honesty, and loyalty. The legal responsibilities of trustees are the same in both *inter vivos* and testamentary trusts, discussed shortly.

A trustee is duty bound to manage the assets of the trust properly. The trustee is accountable to the beneficiaries and must invest the property carefully. As a fiduciary, the trustee may not personally profit from the trust, other than by the payment provided for services rendered.* Trustee duties are specified in state statutes, but they are often modified or further explained by the trust document.

ARE THERE DIFFERENT TYPES OF TRUSTS?

There are two general categories of trusts that are commonly used in estate planning. *Inter vivos* (Latin: "among the living") trusts are those created before death, such as Marisa and Brandon's. *Inter vivos* trusts may be *revocable*, meaning they can be terminated (i.e., legally erased) at any time, or *irrevocable*, meaning they are permanent. A second general category of trust is the **testamentary trust**, which is created by will and which becomes effective upon the death of the testator.

IRREVOCABLE *INTER VIVOS* TRUSTS

If the trust is an **irrevocable *inter vivos* trust**, it cannot be revoked, nor can the property be returned to the settlor. Income from the trust is taxable to whoever receives it. Thus, shifting it in trust to someone in a lower tax bracket can reduce the amount of tax paid on one's income property. An irrevocable trust can also keep property out of a settlor's estate at death and avoid the cost and delay of probate.[27] A marital life estate trust (to be discussed later) may also limit payment of death taxes.

In the trust example, Marisa and Brandon Fabor (settlors) can name themselves as trustees, or they could name another person or a bank or trust company to perform the task.** The Fabors could create a trust with provisions that become operative upon the death of the surviving spouse, including the following:***

- The children shall receive a limited amount of income from the trust as spending money, but most of their needs shall be paid for directly by the trustee (to shield such funds from possible creditors of the children).
- The children cannot give away or sell their rights in the trust.
- Creditors of the children cannot reach the trust principal.
- The trustee may spend part of the principal of the trust, if necessary, for the welfare of the children (using discretionary power to "invade the corpus" or use the "body" of the principal amount, in addition to interest or profit earned on the principal).
- The trustee shall transfer 25 percent of the trust to each child when he or she attains age 30 and the balance at age 40. (The ages used here are arbitrary. The parents, reflecting their opinion of when their children will have matured and could safely be given the assets, could select any age.

*Payment for duties performed as a trustee is obviously not considered a conflict of interest. Also, if the trustee is a beneficiary of the trust, receiving benefits from the trust consistent with the trust terms does not violate the duty of the trustee.
**Professional trustees charge fees for their services, and their use may not be appropriate except in very substantial trusts.
***These provisions create a type of spendthrift trust that is discussed on page 697.

Also, the trustee could be given the power to decide the time for appropriate distributions within some constraint.) Alternatively, the parents could direct that the principal remains intact and go to the then-living grandchildren. This would eliminate a possible levy of estate taxes on the trust assets when their own children—the initial beneficiaries—die.

A major disadvantage of the irrevocable trust is that it cannot be changed to meet new circumstances. A will can be changed frequently to reflect new thoughts about how assets ought to be distributed upon death (of course, after death a will is irrevocable). And that distribution could be made under the terms of a testamentary trust included in their wills.

REVOCABLE *INTER VIVOS* TRUSTS

The Fabors may be reluctant to make the trust irrevocable, because they might need the money for themselves before they die. Therefore, they might create a **revocable *inter vivos* trust**. Here they can change the terms, beneficiaries, or completely terminate the trust at any time, regaining full control over the principal. All trust income would be taxable to them as owners, however, and the value of the trust principal would be taxed as part of the estate of the spouse who is last to die. Death taxes would not be affected one way or the other by this trust. On the other hand, the trust assets will not be probated if the trust exists, is funded, and is not revoked prior to their deaths.

WHAT IS A LIVING TRUST?

The **living trust** is a popular term for a type of *inter vivos* trust designed to avoid probate. A person may desire to avoid probate because of its costs, and also to maintain privacy in the settlement of family affairs. The living trust is often less expensive than probate, and it is private. However, a living trust will not by itself reduce death taxes.

With the living trust, the settlor transfers all of her or his property into a revocable living trust. To illustrate, assume that the trust is created jointly by husband and wife; the settlors can be joint trustees, or one alone may serve as the trustee. During their lives, they each may be the beneficiary of the trust. At the death of the first settlor, certain benefits of the trust shift to one or more other person(s), and the surviving settlor becomes the sole trustee, perhaps with the power to name a co-trustee.

Read about Living Trusts at the American Association of Retired Persons Web site at http://www.aarp.org/getans/consumer/wills.html

http://

Don and Pat Lee have a gross estate of $900,000 and a net estate (after payment of debts) of $800,000. They wish to avoid probate expenses for whichever of them is the surviving spouse. Ultimately, they wish to minimize shrinkage of estate assets for their only child, Kelly. They decide to create a living trust. Will it accomplish their goals?

Yes. They create a living trust, transferring all or most of their property into the trust. For example, if they own real property, their ownership interest is conveyed by deed to the trust. Thereafter, the trust is legal owner of the real property. Other property, stocks, bonds, and pension contracts are also transferred to them as trustees of the trust.

The Lees name themselves co-trustees with the surviving spouse also named as the successor trustee, anticipating the inevitability of death. (They might name additional successor trustees as well.) They also name the beneficiary (or beneficiaries) who will receive distributions from the trust after the death of the settlors. At the death of the first spouse, the property remains in the trust and the trust becomes irrevocable as to the decedent's property. At the death of the second spouse, the property is distributed to the named beneficiary (or beneficiaries) in compliance with the terms of the trust.

Thus, the costs directly attributable to probate are not incurred. Deciding the cost savings, however, can be tricky and misleading. In California, for example, fees for an executor and an attorney to probate an estate with a gross value of $450,000 would be $20,300. (See the earlier discussion about probate fees.) However, the fee savings are probably overstated. It is common and usual when the executor is the heir for executor fees to be waived, and if all or most of the property is community, and the spouse is the heir, he or she may elect an alternate procedure to probate, which eliminates most of the fees. When the property is probated at the time of Pat's death (assuming that her gross estate now totals $900,000), the probate fees would be $38,300. (An assumption is made that Pat has lived within her income and the estate is larger because Pat received Don's property.) It should be noted that the executor might waive his or her $19,150 executor fee, so again the probate costs are probably overstated. If the property has been placed in the living trust, there are no probate fees at either death. Alternatively, there are only minimal fees to transfer the property to the surviving beneficiary (or beneficiaries). The total probate fee savings, in California, thus could be as much as $58,600 ($20,300 + 38,300), but are more likely to be to be around $20,000. Although this example assumes a marital living trust, a living trust would also reduce probate fees for the estate of a single person.

There are costs involved when creating the trust, when transferring title to the property into the trust, when managing the trust, and when making its final distributions. Attorney and Certified Public Accountant (CPA) fees may be incurred at every stage. In addition, probate fees are a deductible expense on the decedent's final income tax filing, and so the amount of savings by using the trust is somewhat overstated. Other reductions in probate fees can be made through waving executor's fees (which is common) and negotiating attorney fees below the statutory maximum. What the living trust does require is advance planning about fees that may be triggered upon death.

As a special caution, living trusts are marketed in ways that can lead to abuse. For example, the living trust is often sold in hotel seminars as a magic, painless way to save money for one's heirs. Sellers often overcharge for a form trust, failing to spend sufficient time with the client determining whether a living trust makes sense for that individual's estate plan, appropriately transfer property into the trust, provide for monitoring of the trust, and arrange for how the settlors will have their future questions about the trust answered. While a living trust may be a good idea for many, it is not automatically a good idea for everyone. Unless you are a sophisticated investor and estate planner, you should obtain competent professional advice about your particular situation.

The simple living trust discussed here makes the most sense for unconditional gifts to family members. The trustee is expected to be the settlor. (In a marital living trust, both spouses are joint trustees, with the surviving spouse being the successor trustee). The trustee's duties are expected to be simple; the most important and complex of these is the distribution of the property. But the trust must be kept current, with title to property kept in the name of the trust. That can be an annoying burden to some persons. Valuations that are a normal part of probate and are certain to occur are often forgotten in private trust administration. Failure to appraise trust property and to obtain stepped-up valuations for assets can lead to significantly higher income taxes for heirs when inherited assets are ultimately sold.

The following situations are among those that suggest extreme caution in the creation of a living trust and necessitate the advice of an attorney.

1. *A minor child is among the beneficiaries.* Special attention must be taken for the care of the minor child, and property should remain subject to the trust at least until the minor reaches majority.

2. *Long-term care of the settlors is contemplated* (e.g., a senior center or nursing home). This situation contemplates planning for the best and most appropriate use of your assets to allow for maximum healthcare while preserving property for your heirs.

3. *Long-term care of a beneficiary is contemplated* (e.g., a developmentally disabled child or a spouse who is mentally incapacitated). This situation contemplates a more complex trust and significant long-term responsibilities.

4. *Conditional gifts to beneficiaries are contemplated* (e.g., in the Lee case, property to Kelly if she graduates from college). Conditional gifts create increased responsibilities for the trustee. If the trustee has discretionary powers, conflict between the beneficiary and the trustee is possible.

5. *The value of the estate is significant, and estate taxes are to be paid* (e.g., a significant amount might be $800,000). Note that the estate tax exemption continues to increase through the year 2006. Depending on whether the estate is liquid (i.e., cash, stocks, and bonds) or not (i.e., real property, most partnership interests, or a sole proprietorship business), determining and accumulating the money to pay the death taxes may complicate the duties of the trustee.

6. *You have or expect to have a substantial number of unsecured debts.* One of the advantages of probate is the provision for an orderly method of paying debtors of the decedent—a living trust does not extinguish the debts of the settlor. Creditors expect to be paid, and without probate the process may be awkward. Secured property (e.g., real property with a mortgage or an automobile with a secured interest) will be transferred subject to its indebtedness. Unsecured creditors have a claim against all property of the decedent. If the amount of debt is small, there will be little difficulty; if debts are significant, then careful plans should be made to pay them. Creditor claims complicate the trustee's duties and can cloud the title to property for intended beneficiaries for some time.

7. *You are in business and your personal trust assets are used from time to time as security for business loans.* Private lenders will inspect your trust documents and may well require changes be made to the trust terms. If you later require additional financing, a second lender may also desire changes to the trust documents, which require approval of the first lender if it is willing. In any case, it gets complicated and the settlor loses

control of the terms of the trust. This caution applies also to nonbusiness situations where you intend that trust property act as security for a loan.

None of these situations makes a living trust inappropriate. Indeed, the same or similar problems arise when there is no trust. However, if they or other complications are likely, then how the estate planner wishes these complications to be addressed should be considered in deciding whether a trust is appropriate and, if so, how it should be drafted.

TESTAMENTARY TRUSTS

A trust created in a will is called a *testamentary trust*. Although it is created when the will is made, the trust does not take effect until the settlor's death. If the will setting up a testamentary trust is invalid, then the trust will also be invalid. The property that was supposed to be in the trust will then pass according to intestacy laws, not according to the terms of the trust. Since the property is part of the decedent's estate, a testamentary trust does not avoid estate taxes or probate fees, nor provide the privacy of *inter vivos* trusts.

MARITAL LIFE ESTATE TRUSTS

Don and Pat may wish to reduce federal death taxes on their estate. The living trust discussed earlier does not accomplish that goal. A **marital life estate trust**, also called an *A and B trust*, can, however, significantly reduce death taxes to the ultimate benefit of the beneficiaries if it is created before the first spouse dies. In this trust, once the first spouse dies, the surviving spouse receives a life interest in the property and someone else (the designated beneficiary) has a **remainder interest** (the interest remaining after the life interest). An owner of a life interest can use the property for life, but cannot convey it away by contract or will. At the death of the owner of the life interest, the owner of the remainder interest (usually a child or children) automatically becomes the sole owner of the property. This trust, whether created *inter vivos* or by will, does restrict the freedom of the surviving spouse to use the property as he or she might wish. The person(s) owning the remainder interest is (are) therefore protected from diversion and unjustified dispersion of the trust property.

How does the A and B trust work? Assume Don dies first in 1999 and all property is to go to Pat. In an estate without a trust, there would be no death tax because federal law allows an unlimited amount of property to be transferred to a spouse without tax, by means of the marital deduction. In an estate with a trust, Don's $400,000 share of the net community property is transferred first to Pat, and then to Kelly, in the following fashion: Pat receives a right to the income from the $400,000 for the rest of her life, and may be authorized to invade (consume) the principal if necessary to maintain her health and continued well-being. Kelly has a right to the principal upon Pat's death. There are no federal death taxes because the interest to Pat is exempt as a marital transfer, and the value of the interest to Kelly is less than the 1999 $650,000 estate tax exemption. Thus, at the death of the first spouse there are no federal estate tax savings. Depending on the state however, there may be state death taxes.

Upon the death of the second spouse—Pat in our example—the tax treatment between the two situations is quite different. If no A and B trust exists, Pat's entire net estate, valued at $800,000, would go to Kelly. As the starting tax rate after the $650,000 exemption is 37 percent on the first $100,000 and 39 percent on the next $50,000, the amount of the tax would be $56,500.

Net estate		$800,000
Exempt estate		650,000
Amount to be taxed		$150,000
Rate of tax	37% of 100,000	$37,000
Rate of tax	39% of 50,000	$19,500
Total federal estate tax		$56,500

If a marital life estate trust had been created, only the $400,000 solely owned by Pat is transferred at her death because the value of Don's estate had already been transferred to Kelly. Remember that Kelly already had a right as remainder owner to the first $400,000 inheritance from Don, when Pat, the life beneficiary, died. Pat's death did not create the interest in the trust, it perfected it. As the $400,000 inherited from Pat is less than the amount allowed to pass tax-free, there is no tax. The net tax savings to Kelly is $56,500 if the A and B trust is created. If Don and Pat created this type of trust as an *inter vivos* trust, they could protect the estate from both probate fees and federal death taxes. The larger the estate, the larger the potential savings. Exhibit 14–6 portrays the amount of an estate that can pass free from estate tax with and without an A & B trust.

There are, of course, additional costs of creating and maintaining the trusts and a loss of deductions on the decedent's final tax return. Actual predicted savings for an individual should be determined in consultation with tax and estate planning advisors. The general admonition is to seek competent legal and tax advice for any kind of trust, which has significant, sometimes undesirable consequences to the settlors. Fortunately, such trusts are usually revocable by either settlor before either dies. Thus, the trust can be revoked or amended if circumstances or wishes change before either one of them dies.

THE RULE AGAINST PERPETUITIES

As noted at the beginning of this chapter, there is an old saying that "you can't take it with you." The law cannot get around that truism, but instruments such as trusts and wills do the next best thing: they legitimately avoid probate fees and death taxes. Moreover, they allow a person to control who is to receive the property upon her or his death, and to instruct and/or restrict how that property may

See the tip from Ernst & Young's Personal Financial Planning Guide, Second Edition on Marital Trusts at http://www.wiley.co.uk/products/subject/finance/ey/pfg-tips/tip044.html Read some estate planning strategies from the J. Lion Financial Group at http://jlionfinancial.com

Exhibit 14–6: The Value of Property That Can Pass Free from Estate Tax without and with an A & B Trust

Year	No Trust	With an A & B Trust	Estimated Tax Savings With A & B Trust
1999	$650,000	$1,300,000	$259,000
2000 and 2001	$675,000	$1,350,000	$260,750
2002 and 2003	$700,000	$1,400,000	$283,000
2004	$850,000	$1,700,000	$358,500
2005	$950,000	$1,900,000	$415,500
2006 and after	$1,000,000	$2,000,000	$445,000

be used. However, the **rule against perpetuities** limits this control as it applies to trusts and other legal instruments that restrict the use and free transferability of property in the future. Under this rule, title in property must vest (i.e., some beneficiary must get full and unrestricted possession and ownership of the property) no later than a life or lives in being, plus 21 years.

The details of this rule are very complicated and beyond the scope of this text. But the purpose of the rule is simple and understandable. The rule against perpetuities is meant to prevent a trust from accumulating and compounding income for perhaps ten generations, by which time a small sum may have grown to a prodigious amount. It also keeps assets under the control of living persons rather than straitjacketed by donors long since dead. The rule does not generally apply to charitable gifts. A gift of real property to a church, so long as no alcohol is served on the property, would not violate the rule. Such a restriction can last for hundreds of years, whereupon a violation (i.e., liquor is served on the land) could lead to a reversion of the property to the donor's heirs (who may well be hard to find and who will be surprised to learn of their interest).

TAXATION OF GENERATION-SKIPPING TRUSTS

There are special rules to tax certain large generation-skipping transfers of wealth. Trusts are usually used for such transfers. For example, in a **generation-skipping trust**, a father (first generation) creates a trust under which his daughter (second generation) receives the income while she lives. When she dies, the principal goes to her child, a son (third generation). There is a death tax when the father dies, but no second tax when the daughter dies. The daughter's generation has been skipped as to estate tax liability because the daughter never received or controlled the principal. (Of course, when her child dies, any property from the trust still in his possession would be part of his estate for tax purposes.) This technique of tax avoidance is effective only for a trust that, on the death of the second generation member (the daughter in our example), has a value of less than $1 million. Any value in excess of $1 million is routinely taxed.[28]

ARE THERE OTHER USES OF TRUSTS?

H. Pauline Amesbury dearly loves her husband, who is 15 years her senior and in his 80s. She is terminally ill and afraid that when she dies first, as is likely, he will be unable to manage the family estate alone. He might be talked into foolish investments, or worse, into remarriage to someone interested only in his money. What can Pauline do to protect her husband against such developments?

She can create an *inter vivos* or testamentary trust, specifying that he shall receive the income during his lifetime and that the trustee may use the principal, if necessary, for his welfare. When he dies, the property will not appear in his estate, where it would boost his estate tax. Instead, it will be distributed as prescribed in Pauline's trust, perhaps to go to their children, or even held for their grandchildren. The effect is the same as in the marital life estate trust, even if only one spouse creates the trust, as long as the settlor spouse is the first to die.

The trust instrument could name charities or other beneficiaries selected by H. Pauline Amesbury herself, or designated by Mr. Amesbury if he is given a

power of appointment—a designation in a will or trust giving him the power to decide who gets the money or property or to designate how the money or property will be used. This useful estate-planning tool allows the trust to postpone deciding which child or children or other beneficiaries receive what gifts. In these ways, a trust can frustrate would-be fortune hunters who prey on wealthy and unsophisticated beneficiaries.

Sometimes trusts make sense when the beneficiary is ill, mentally retarded, or very old. Settlors may even create a trust naming themselves as the beneficiaries and a bank or trust company as the trustees, to spare themselves the burden of managing their estate. One may also create a trust and name it as beneficiary of insurance policies on one's life. This arrangement is often preferable to allowing the insurance proceeds to go as a lump sum to a beneficiary unequipped to handle such a sum.

A **discretionary sprinkling and accumulation trust** may be appropriate when flexibility is vital to meet the changing needs of family-member beneficiaries. The trustee is authorized to decide who among the designated beneficiaries is to receive periodic payments of income, or principal, or both. Beneficiaries who need more can be given more; those who need less get less. To help the trustee distribute the trust funds, the trust specifies guidelines, which might include maintaining a stated standard of living or comfort and general welfare for beneficiaries and allowing special payment for educational or medical fees. Income not paid is accumulated and ultimately distributed as part of the principal.

A trust designed for the benefit of a segment of the public or of the public in general is a **charitable trust**. It differs from a private trust in that the identities of the beneficiaries are uncertain. Usually, to be deemed a charitable trust, a trust must be created for charitable, educational, religious, or scientific purposes.

A trust created to provide for the maintenance of a beneficiary by preventing his or her improvidence with the bestowed funds is a **spendthrift trust**. Essentially, the beneficiary receives or is permitted to draw only a certain portion of the total amount of which he or she is the beneficial owner. Most states permit spendthrift trust provisions that prohibit creditors from taking possession of the assets of the trust before they are distributed to the beneficiaries.

A special type of trust created when one person deposits money in a bank in his or her own name as a trustee for another is a **Totten trust**. This trust is tentative in that it is revocable at will until the depositor dies or completes the gift in his or her lifetime by some unequivocal act or declaration (for example, delivery of the funds to the intended beneficiary). If the depositor should die before the beneficiary dies and if the depositor has not revoked the trust expressly or impliedly, a presumption arises that an absolute trust has been created for the benefit of the beneficiary. At the death of the depositor, the beneficiary obtains property rights to the balance on hand.

Is Joint Tenancy an Effective Way to Avoid Probate?

Joint tenancy (or the similar tenancy by the entireties between spouses in some states) is a form of ownership for two or more persons to hold real and personal property (see Chapter 12). One of the most important aspects of joint tenancy is its *survivorship feature*.

Al and Beth own a house in joint tenancy. If Beth dies, Al automatically becomes the sole owner of the house immediately and without probate. Full title passes to Al even if Beth left a will that attempted to give her interest in the house to her mother, Sue. Surviving joint tenants automatically receive the interests of a deceased joint-tenancy owner. As Al's interest is perfected at the moment of Beth's death, there is no interest left to convey by will.

Depending on the circumstances and desires of the co-owners, this survivorship feature is either a reason to own property in joint tenancy or a reason not to own property in this manner. Because the ownership transfers automatically at the death of a joint tenant to the remaining tenant(s), joint-tenancy property is not subject to probate. Indeed, it is an effective way to avoid probate. However, like most living trusts, a transfer by joint tenancy will not reduce death taxes because the transfer itself may be subject to such taxes because of its value. Other disadvantages to holding title to property in joint tenancy include:

1. Either joint tenant can secretly terminate the tenancy while alive by conveying his or her interest to another person. The owner of the conveyed interest will not be a joint tenant but a tenant in common with the other joint owner(s).

2. Creditors may terminate the tenancy by claims against the interest of one of the tenants. Such a claim may require sale of the asset to satisfy the claim. Such actions can tie up and cloud title to the property, even though the creditor's claim is generally good only against the debtor's interest in the property.

3. The establishment of joint tenancy in property other than a bank account might be considered a gift. To the extent that its value exceeds $10,000 in a given year, the gift is a federal taxable event.

4. Following the death of a joint tenant, there may be adverse capital gains treatment for the surviving tenant when the property is subsequently sold. Explanation of such complex tax consequences is beyond the scope of this text. The moral is as follows: If you are dealing with significant financial interests, seek legal and tax advice as to the most appropriate manner of joint ownership for you and your co-owners.

WHAT ARE CONSERVATORSHIPS AND GUARDIANSHIPS?

Peter White, age 78, is a millionaire who sometimes acts in a way his family considers eccentric. His son Ed has been particularly disturbed since Peter bought a large sailboat and announced his intention to sail to the South Pacific with an all-female crew. Ed contacted an attorney to inquire how he might stop his father from squandering the family fortune. Can Ed tie up his father's money?

Not unless there is more to the story. Peter appears to be capable of handling his own affairs, including his personal needs and financial resources. However, if he were physically or mentally unable to handle his affairs (including the sailboat!), his son could petition the court to declare a **conservatorship**. A responsible person would be named the *conservator*, to manage the assets and personal affairs of the *conservatee*. The conservator will make periodic reports to the court showing the business and personal transactions that have occurred. Although the conservatee is without authority to handle his or her own affairs, he or she ordinarily can still make, or modify, a last will. A conservatorship cannot and will not be declared simply to stop an eccentric person from overspending and thereby dissipating his or her estate.

An alternative procedure, called a **guardianship**, is available for those who, for any reasons, are unable to care for themselves or their estates. Usually a guardianship is created to provide for a minor whose parents are dead, but an adult who is infirm may be judicially declared incompetent and placed in a guardianship. The person subject to a guardianship is called a *ward*. The person in charge of the ward's personal and financial affairs is called the *guardian*.

Under a typical guardianship statute, in order to declare one a ward, proof must show that the person is substantially unable to provide for his or her own personal needs (food, clothing, shelter, medical care)—in other words, to manage his or her finances. Isolated incidents of negligence or improvidence will not suffice as evidence of substantial inability. The alleged incompetent has the right to appear at the court hearing and to oppose the petition with the aid of counsel. A proposed conservatee has similar rights, and either party may call for a jury trial if provided by state law. If the petition is granted, the court monitors the activities of the person in charge, requiring periodic reports. Both guardianships and conservatorships are usually costly to the estate of the protected party.

The California Advocates for Nursing Home Reform (CANHR) Web site is not directly related to our text discussion, but this important Web site for people with loved ones in nursing home care can be found at http://www.canhr.org/

A new area of practice is elder law, well represented at the Elder Law Section of the New York State Bar Association Web site at http://www.nysba.org/ sections/elder/elderlinks.html

PRINCIPAL ELEMENTS OF ESTATE PLANNING

Although you probably have little personal need for an estate plan at this early stage of your life, the following guidelines may be valuable in the future, and perhaps now for members of your family. Also see Exhibit 14–7 for a useful checklist.

1. Prepare a personal or family balance sheet to show assets and liabilities. Keep accurate records of dates along with evidence of the acquisition costs of assets, including real property and its improvements (with receipts, for future tax purposes). Prepare a budget to monitor your earnings, spending, saving, and investing on a monthly and annual basis.

2. Consider life insurance if appropriate for the needs of beneficiaries. (Be sure you understand the difference between term and ordinary life policies.) Select a suitable settlement option for each policy.

3. Consider creation of trusts (*inter vivos* or testamentary, or both). Consider using a living trust to avoid probate and death taxes.

4. You (and your spouse, if married) should prepare a will specifying the recipients of all your possessions. Prepare a will even if you use a trust

Exhibit 14–7:   Trust Arrangement

WHERE TO FIND MY IMPORTANT PAPERS

Name _____ Social Security Number _____

My valuable papers are stored in these locations (address plus where to look):
A. Residence _____
B. Safe-deposit box(es) _____
C. Other _____

Item	A	B	C		Item	A	B	C
My will (original)	___	___	___		Retirement papers	___	___	___
Powers of appointment	___	___	___		Deferred compensation; IRA papers	___	___	___
Spouse's will (original)	___	___	___		Titles and deeds	___	___	___
Location and combination of safe	___	___	___		Notes (mortgages)	___	___	___
Trust agreements					List of stored & loaned items			
As settlor	___	___	___		(item, bailee, and address)	___	___	___
As beneficiary	___	___	___		Motor vehicle ownership records	___	___	___
Life insurance policy(ies)	___	___	___		Birth certificates (mine, spouse's			
Health insurance policy(ies)	___	___	___		and children's)	___	___	___
Homeowner's insurance policy	___	___	___		Military enlistment and			
Motor vehicle and other insurance					discharge papers	___	___	___
policy(ies) (including boats)	___	___	___		Marriage certificate(s)	___	___	___
Employment contract(s)	___	___	___		Divorce/separation records	___	___	___
Partnership agreement(s)	___	___	___		Contracts	___	___	___
List of checking, savings accounts	___	___	___		Important receipts*	___	___	___
List of credit cards with numbers	___	___	___		Important warranties	___	___	___
Brokerage account records	___	___	___		Other	___	___	___
Stock certificates	___	___	___			___	___	___
Bonds	___	___	___					
Notes receivable	___	___	___					
Notes payable	___	___	___					

*Including receipts for capital improvements to residence.

IMPORTANT NAMES, ADDRESSES AND PHONE NUMBERS
Beneficiaries under my will (list)

_____

_____

_____

_____

Attorney _____
Accountant _____
Insurance agent _____
Stock broker _____
Medical doctor _____
Date prepared _____
People to whom copies have been given _____
1. _____
2. _____
3. _____
4. _____

to avoid probate. Let your heirs celebrate if there is insufficient property to require probate because you effectively and economically transferred your estate by other means.

5. Write a letter of or record your final instructions. Leave a version of Exhibit 14–7 explaining where important records and assets are located.

6. Consider donating your body organs at death and prepare appropriate documents. Make your intentions known to others (e.g., on a card in your wallet, as such information should be immediately accessible).

7. Consider execution of a living will and/or a durable power of attorney to permit implementation of your wishes if you become terminally ill or incapacitated.

8. Consider the transfer of certain assets into joint tenancy so that they will pass to the surviving joint tenant, avoiding probate. If married and living in a community property state, consider holding your jointly owned property as community property.

9. Make tax-free *inter vivos* gifts to reduce the size of your estate and thus reduce the level of income taxes and death taxes that will have to be paid upon your death. A salutary side effect is to help the donees when they need the money most and not years later when unpredictable destiny forces a distribution by death.

10. Review pension plans to determine how much retirement income you can expect from these sources, including social security.

11. Consider investments in annuities to supplement a fixed income expected from pensions. Annuities can be created from the lump-sum proceeds of cash surrender values of life insurance policies.

12. Keep in mind the possible assistance obtainable from workers' compensation insurance and social security in case of accidental injury or death on the job, and from unemployment insurance, in case of forced idleness.

13. If one of your major assets is a stock in a closely held corporation, prepare and execute a buy-sell agreement coupled with qualified plans for deferred compensation through profit sharing or company pension plans.

14. If one of your major assets is an interest in a partnership, prepare and execute a suitable buy-sell agreement and arrange for life insurance or some other means of providing cash to fund the purchase.

15. If one of your major assets is a sole proprietorship, provide a funded plan that will provide for the continuation of the company or a liquidation under favorable circumstances.

16. Review and update your plan anytime there is a change in your personal status, or at least every few years. An outdated plan may be worse than no plan.

CASES

ESTATE OF DOROTHY SOUTHWORTH v. NORTH SHORE ANIMAL LEAGUE

Court of Appeal, Second District, Division 6, California, 51 Cal.App.4th 564, 59 Cal.Rptr.2d 272 (1996)

Dorothy Southworth requested information from the North Shore Animal League (NSAL) about its lifetime pet care program. NSAL sent Dorothy the information, included a request that Dorothy return an enclosed pet care registration card, and told Dorothy to contact her attorney about including a bequest to NSAL in her estate. Dorothy did not return the registration card to NSAL; however, after additional correspondence she did return a donor card to NSAL. In a blank space following the printed words, "I am not taking action now, but my intention is," Dorothy wrote, "my entire estate is to be left to North Shore Animal League" and she signed and dated the donor card. On January 14, 1994, Dorothy Southworth died without a will. NSAL asked that the donor card be admitted to probate as a holographic will and the trial court ruled in its favor, stating that the card "substantially complies with all the Probate Code requirements for a holographic will." The intestate heirs, suppressing their natural love for animals, appealed.

GILBERT, Associate Justice

Facts

Decedent never married and had no children. On March 4, 1986, in response to decedent's request for information, NSAL sent a letter to her describing its lifetime pet care program and explaining how to register for it. NSAL asked that she return its enclosed pet care registration card, contact her attorney to include her bequest to NSAL in her estate and send a copy of the bequest to NSAL. NSAL informed her that "[e]ven if you don't currently have a will, we'll accept your Registration on good faith and maintain an Active file on your pet while you're arranging the Bequest." Decedent never returned the registration card to NSAL.

NSAL sent a donor card to the decedent. It stated: "Your newest gift to the North Shore Animal League will help get more homeless dogs and cats out of cages and into new homes." The donor card thanked her "for your interest in making a bequest to the League." It explained that she could change her life insurance policy or provide for animals in her will by calling her attorney. It sought gifts and legacies and asked her to complete and return the donor card.

On April 19, 1989, she returned the donor card to NSAL. [There had been other occasional contact in the intervening 3 years.] The card provided three options: a. naming NSAL as a beneficiary of a life insurance policy, b. changing one's will to leave securities or cash to NSAL, or c. not taking immediate action, but stating her intentions.

On the card, the decedent circled printed option (c) which states: "I am not taking action now, but my intention is [in the blank space provided she wrote] My entire estate is to be left to North Shore Animal League."

The donor card also included a printed statement which reads, "The total amount that the animal shelter will someday receive is [she wrote in the blank space] $500,000." The card then stated, "I would like the money used for:

"Food and shelter for the animals
"Adoption Fund to advertise for new owners
"Spaying and Neutering Program
"Unrestricted use[.]"

Decedent placed an "x" next to the food and spaying options listed. She signed and dated the donor card.

On May 10, 1989, NSAL sent a thank you letter to decedent for "letting us know that you will remember the North Shore Animal League in your will." The letter requested that decedent "have your attorney send us a copy of your will[.]"

The Neptune Society [where she had arranged for her cremation] asked for additional information to complete the death certificate, pursuant to amendments to the Probate Code. Decedent returned Neptune's supplemental form and stated that there are "[n]o living relatives" and to "[p]lease notify North Shore Animal League." She included NSAL's address, telephone numbers and the name of the executive director of NSAL. She signed the supplemental form and dated it October 20, 1989.

On September 2, 1992, NSAL sent a letter to decedent acknowledging that in March 1989 she wrote NSAL to state that she intended to take action leading to its becoming one of the beneficiaries of her estate. NSAL requested a meeting with decedent, thanking her for her "kind thoughts and generous support." She never responded to this request.

Jeanette Southworth, Jack Southworth, Michael Hulse and Arthur Hulse assigned part of their alleged interests in the estate to [Francis V.] See. Jeanette and Jack are the surviving half-siblings of decedent. Michael and Arthur Hulse are the children of another half-sister of decedent who predeceased her.

The See contestants argued that the donor card should be denied admission into probate as a holographic will because not all of its material provisions are in the handwriting of the decedent and there is no showing of testamentary intent at the time she signed the card. NSAL argued that the donor card reflected decedent's testamentary intent and satisfied the statutory requirements for a holographic will.

The trial court concluded that decedent's handwritten statement on the donor card that "[m]y entire estate is to be left to North Shore Animal League" substantially complies with all the Probate Code requirements for a holographic will. The court viewed the preprinted parts of the donor card and the $500,000 sum written in to be immaterial. The court interpreted the preprinted words stating that "I

am not taking action now, but my intention is . . ." to mean that she did not want to immediately transfer her funds to NSAL, but intended to bequeath them upon her death. The trial court admitted the donor card to probate as the last will of the decedent. Jeanette and Jack Southworth, and Francis V. See, appeal from the judgment.

Discussion

The facts are stipulated. "Where, as here, there is no conflict in the evidence, the validity of the holographic instrument must be determined entirely by reference to the applicable statutes and principles of law." Interpretation of statutes is a question of law and our fundamental task is to ascertain the intent of the Legislature.

Former Civil Code section 1277 stated that "[a] [h]olographic will is one that is entirely written, dated and signed by the hand of the testator himself. It is subject to no other form, . . . and need not be witnessed." (Emphasis added.) Section 1277 was strictly construed.

In 1931, the Legislature reenacted former Civil Code section 1277 as section 53 of the Probate Code and added a third sentence . . . "No address, date or other matter written, printed or stamped upon the document, which is not incorporated in the provisions which are in the handwriting of the decedent, shall be considered as any part of the will."

In Estate of Black, the decedent wrote out her will on three identical, commercially-printed one-page will forms. In the blanks provided, she wrote her signature and place of domicile, and on the third page she inserted the name and gender of her executor, the date of the instrument and the city and state where she executed it. She either struck out or ignored other printed language regarding residuary gifts, the appointment of an executor, attesting witnesses and a testimonium clause.

"Using virtually all of the remaining space on each of the three pages, testatrix expressed in her own handwriting a detailed testamentary disposition of her estate, including specific devises and legacies to individuals and a charitable institution and a bequest of her residuary estate."

The trial court denied probate because the testatrix incorporated some of the printed language, even though it concerned perfunctory procedural matters in the form will. Our Supreme Court reversed because "none of the incorporated material is either material to the substance of the will or essential to its validity as a testamentary disposition. . . ." (Estate of Black, 181 Cal.Rptr. 222.)

The Black court explained that "[t]he policy of the law is toward a construction favoring validity, in determining whether a will has been executed in conformity with statutory requirements." Moreover, we affirmed ([in the] Estate of Baker) "the tendency of both the courts and the Legislature . . . toward greater liberality in accepting a writing as an holographic will. . . ." "Substantial compliance with the statute, and not absolute precision is all that is required. . . ." Courts are to use common sense in evaluating whether a document constitutes a holographic will.

The Black court recognized that "[i]f testators are to be encouraged by a statute like ours to draw their own wills, the courts should not adopt, upon purely technical reasoning, a construction which would result in invalidating such wills in half the cases." That sensible admonition is no less appropriate today. The law recognizes that such wills are generally made by people without legal training. The primary purpose of the statutory holographic will provisions is to prevent fraud. Because counterfeiting another's handwriting "is exceedingly difficult," these statutes require the material provisions of holographic wills to be in the testator's handwriting.

Whether a document should be admitted to probate as a holographic will depends on proof of its authorship and authenticity, and whether the words establish that it was intended to be the author's last will and testament at the time she wrote it.

Our high court explained that four questions are pertinent in evaluating whether a document should be invalidated as a holographic will due to printed language in the document: "Was the particular provision relevant to the substance of the will? Was it essential to the will's validity? Did the testator intend to incorporate the provision? Would invalidation of the holograph defeat the testator's intent?"

Accordingly, in 1983, the year after our Supreme Court decided Black, our Legislature replaced Probate Code section 53 with Probate Code section 6111. Section 6111 provides, in pertinent part, that "(a) A will . . . is valid as a holographic will, whether or not witnessed, if the signature and the material provisions are in the handwriting of the testator." In 1990, the Legislature added subdivision (c) which provides that "Any statement of testamentary intent contained in a holographic will may be set forth either in the testator's own handwriting or as part of a commercially printed form will."

There is no question that the handwriting on the document at issue is that of Dorothy Southworth, and that she signed and dated it. Unlike Black, however, the document is not a commercially-printed will form. It is a donor card for a charity. It was not drafted to serve as a will. The card provides the option of informing NSAL that the donor has or intends to instruct one's attorney to change his or her will.

Furthermore, the printed language Southworth incorporated from the donor card does not evince her present testamentary intent. Instead of striking the material printed words which state "I am not taking action now, but my intention is," she chose to incorporate those words with her handwritten statement, "My entire estate is to be left to North Shore Animal League." The material printed language together with her handwriting evince a future intent; not present testamentary intent.

Although other extrinsic evidence, such as her letter to NSAL of September 4, 1987, and the supplemental Neptune form she signed on October 20, 1989, shows that Southworth desired to leave her estate to

NSAL, neither the donor card at issue nor the handwriting on it substantially complies with probate code requirements for holographic wills. Although courts may consider statements made before and after a holographic will is made and the surrounding circumstances, evidence of present testamentary intent provided by the instrument at issue is paramount.

Here, Southworth incorporated printed language stating that she was not taking any action when she executed it. It does not establish her testamentary intent at the time she executed it. It only states her intention to make a will in the future.

The judgment is reversed. The parties are to bear their own costs.

FOR CRITICAL ANALYSIS

1. What were the appellate courts reasons in holding there was no valid holographic will? Do you agree with the court? Explain.

2. What could NSAL have done, if anything, to increase its chances of inheriting from Ms. Southworth?

3. Identify the heirs who are claiming Ms. Southworth's estate and their relation to Ms. Southworth. Why had Ms. Southworth told the Neptune Society she had no "living relatives"?

4. Are the rules for holographic wills too technical? Explain your answer.

McCONNELL v. BEVERLY ENTERPRISES-CONNECTICUT, INC.

Supreme Court of Connecticut, 209 Conn. 692, 553 A.2d 596 (1989)

The husband and children of a comatose, terminally ill patient brought an action seeking to terminate life-support services being provided to Carol M. McConnell by a private nursing home, Danbury Pavilion Healthcare. Carol McConnell was the 57-year-old wife of the plaintiff John E. McConnell and the mother of the three other co-plaintiffs. By profession, she was a registered nurse. Her last nursing positions were as head nurse and manager of the emergency room at Danbury Hospital. On January 18, 1985, Mrs. McConnell sustained a severe head injury as the result of an automobile accident. She had not regained consciousness, despite excellent medical care. She was in an irreversible persistent vegetative state with no prospect of improvement. In the opinion of her attending physician, her condition was terminal. Her life was sustained by means of a gastrostomy tube through which she received nutrition and hydration. The Superior Court entered judgment for patient's husband and children, and the state attorney general and the patient's guardian ad litem took appeal.

Chief Justice Peters wrote the opinion: This case concerns the right of a family, on behalf of a patient who is presently in a terminal coma, to implement the patient's clearly expressed wish for the removal of a gastrostomy tube that is artificially providing nutrition and hydration for the patient.

[T]he Removal of Life Support Systems Act in which the legislature, cognizant of a common law right of self-determination and of a constitutional right to privacy, sought to provide a statutory mechanism to implement these important rights. We must decide what role this act plays in the present litigation. The trial court held that the plaintiffs were entitled to relief without regard to the act, which the court construed to be nonexclusive. The defendants, by contrast, maintain that the act governs and precludes the relief sought by the plaintiffs. There is, however, a middle ground, a construction of the act that is consistent with the plaintiffs' affirmative claims for relief.

Although the United States Constitution does not expressly provide a right to privacy, the United States Supreme Court has recognized a right to privacy in the penumbra of the Bill of Rights, specifically in the protection of the First, Third, Fourth and Fifth amendments. "[T]he Court has recognized that a right of personal privacy, or a guarantee of certain areas or zones of privacy, does exist under the Constitution." Justice Brandeis has referred to this right as "the right to be let alone—the most comprehensive of rights and the right most valued by civilized men." Although the court has recently construed this right to privacy narrowly; it has held that personal rights that are "implicit in the concept of ordered liberty"; or "deeply rooted in this Nation's history and tradition" are included in this guarantee of personal privacy. The court has found that contraception, procreation, marriage, and education implicate privacy rights.

The right to refuse medical treatment has been specifically recognized as a subject of constitutional protection. "This court has also long held that '[e]very human being of adult years and sound mind has a right to determine what shall be done with his own body. . . .'" Court after court has recognized the existence of a right, in principle and in properly guarded circumstances, to the removal of medical treatments that artificially prolong life.

Many of the cases upholding a right of self-determination for terminally ill individuals have urged legislatures to enact guidelines for appropriate private decision-making in these heart-rending dilemmas. When the legislature has attempted to respond to this urgent request for statutory assistance, we have an obligation to pursue the applicability of statutory criteria before resorting to an exploration of residual common law rights, if any such rights indeed remain. We must therefore decide whether a reasonable construction of our act ever permits the removal of a gastrostomy tube.

Careful examination of our act discloses that the legislature approached the appropriate treatment for very sick patients by establishing three guiding principles. First, if a patient, in the eyes of his or her attending physician, is not in a terminal condition, "beneficial medical treatment and nutrition and hydration must be provided." Second, if a patient, to the contrary, is deemed by his or her physician to be in a terminal condition, life sustaining technology may be removed, in the exercise of the physician's best medical judgment, when that judgment has received the informed consent of the patient's next of kin or guardian and when it coincides with the expressed wishes of the patient. Third, even the removal of life sustaining technology must be done in a manner consistent with providing "comfort care and pain alleviation" for the patient. Under the act, the patient's attending physician must deem "the patient to be in a terminal condition." For the purposes of the act, "'[t]erminal condition' means the final stage of an incurable or irreversible medical condition which, in the opinion of the attending physician, will result in death." Dr. Robert Ruxin serves as Mrs. McConnell's attending physician and he testified that he deemed her to be in a terminal condition. While there was testimony to the contrary on this issue, the act places the responsibility for reaching the conclusion with the attending physician, contemplating a decision to discontinue treatment reached after consultation between the attending physician and the family or next of kin, unimpeded by courts, other medical experts or ethicists.

Ruxin reached his conclusion after numerous examinations of Mrs. McConnell. He deemed her to be in an incurable, irreversible, persistent vegetative state, a condition that ultimately will lead to her death. The trial court found Ruxin's testimony credible and we have discovered nothing in the trial transcripts to warrant disturbing this finding.

The Statute requires that the attending physician obtain the informed consent of the patient's next of kin prior to removing a life support system. The fact that the rest of the McConnell family (husband John, daughters Kathleen and Amy, and son James), all over the age of majority, have brought this action indicates that they consent to the removal of the gastrostomy tube. Furthermore, the testimony of all four demonstrates positively that they reached their decision out of love and concern for their mother and wife and respect for her wishes. There is not a hint in the trial court testimony of any ulterior motive on the part of any of the plaintiffs.

Finally, pursuant to the act, the attending physician must consider "the patient's wishes as expressed by the patient directly, through his next of kin or legal guardian. . . ." The trial court found clear and convincing evidence that Mrs. McConnell had expressed "forcefully and without wavering" that artificial means should not be employed to prolong her life. We conclude that the trial court did not err in this finding.

That Mrs. McConnell desired that her family not prolong her life should she ever suffer an injury that left her in a vegetative state could not have been clearer. She worked as a registered nurse in an emergency room, and therefore often saw the tragedy that befell those who suffered severe head injuries. The court heard testimony from a co-worker, Marie Kornhaas, that Mrs. McConnell did not believe in the use of respirators, feeding tubes or other life-sustaining systems, and that if she were ever placed on such a system, she hoped that Kornhaas would do what she could to stop it.

The trial court heard testimony from all of Mrs. McConnell's immediate family that she was extremely concerned about head injuries, warning her children often about the dangers of motorcycles and small cars. Her husband described her as having "a phobia about head injury." She had also been adamant that her own mother, when dying of cancer, not be placed on any life support system. Finally, each member of her immediate family testified absolutely, without hesitation, that Mrs. McConnell did not believe in life support systems, including gastrostomy tubes, for herself, that she would want the tube removed from her and that they sought to carry out her wishes. We therefore conclude that the record sustains those findings of fact by the trial court that are required by the act to be shown as a condition for the withdrawal of life support systems.

III

In his brief, the Attorney General raises the specter of suicide, claiming that the state has a compelling interest in preventing it and that to allow Mrs. McConnell to carry out her wish to discontinue food and nutrition would be to allow her to commit suicide. We are not persuaded that a suicide would occur in this case.

It is well-established that the state may not base a criminal prosecution on the exercise of a constitutional right. Because we hold that the legislature in enacting the Removal of Life Support Systems Act sought to establish a workable mechanism by which individuals may implement their common law and constitutional rights, it follows that by exercising these rights, the individual cannot become criminally liable.

Furthermore, we agree with the majority of jurisdictions that have addressed this issue in holding that the removal of a gastrostomy tube is not the "death producing agent," set in motion with the intent of causing her own death. In exercising her right of self-determination, Mrs. McConnell merely seeks to be free of extraordinary mechanical devices and to allow nature to take its course. Thus, death will be by natural causes underlying the disease, not by self-inflicted injury.

There is no error.

In this opinion CALLAHAN, GLASS and COVELLO, J.J., concur.

FOR CRITICAL ANALYSIS

1. Why did the State Attorney General oppose the family's wishes? Was it appropriate that they do so?

2. What does this sentence mean, "The trial court held that the plaintiffs were entitled to relief without regard to the act, which the court construed to be nonexclusive"?

3. Do you agree with the doctor's diagnosis that the Mrs. McConnell was in a "terminal condition"? Remember this diagnosis was made before removal

of the gastrostomy tube—after removal it is clear she would be. How would Mrs. McConnell's situation be anymore terminal than anyone else, including you?

4. Assume a person makes a conscious decision to stop taking nutrition and hydration (eating and drinking). Is that

suicide? Is it illegal? At some time the person would become unconscious before death, would it be wrongful to provide hydration and nutrition by a feeding tube against the person's wishes? If it were administered could the person demand removal upon regaining consciousness?

CHAPTER QUESTIONS AND PROBLEMS

1. Joe Mariano never made a will. Now he is flat on his back in a hospital bed after being injured in a crash of his private plane. Both his arms are in casts and he has extensive internal injuries. But his mind is alert and he can talk. Realizing that the prognosis is bad, he calls for his lawyer. Can they prepare a formal, witnessed will, even though Mariano cannot write his name?

2. When Pauline Puffington died, she left her entire estate of $3 million to a trust for the care of her 12 dogs and 14 cats. After the pet's deaths, the principal was to be paid to a designated society for the prevention of cruelty to animals. Relatives challenged the will, proving not only that she was eccentric and senile when she made it, but also that she was insane when she died. Can the will be enforced?

3. Mary Dorsett was convinced that making a will was tantamount to writing one's own death warrant. Even after she married and had given birth to the twins, she did nothing to ensure the economical transfer of her estate to her family after her death. She was a hardworking dentist and had acquired an estate of $250,000 by age 30. Then she suddenly died of a heart attack. Under the state's law of intestacy, her husband received one-third of her separate

property and the twins, age 5, shared the balance equally. What expenses and burdens might she have avoided for her widower?

4. Richard Kalfus murdered his wife, Domenica. He pled guilty and was sentenced to prison. Her husband and two infant children survived Domenica. She left no will. Under New Jersey's law of intestate succession, a husband is entitled to a one-third share of personal property if children also survive the deceased parent. The statute made no reference to the effect of wrongful acts by an heir. Is Richard entitled to his intestate share of Domenica's estate? [*Estate of Kalfus v. Kalfus*, 81 N.J. Super. 435, 195 A.2d 903 (N.J., 1963).]

5. Harry Gordon died at the age of 83. The sole beneficiary in his will was a charitable organization. The attorney who drafted Mr. Gordon's will was the regional vice president of the organization and his practice was located in the same building as the charity. All witnesses to the will were officers of the corporation, as were the executors. The original of the will was kept in the charity's offices. The will was executed seven years before Mr. Gordon's death. Would there be a presumption of undue influence? Was undue influence present? [*Herman v. Kogan*, 487 So.2d 48 (Fla., 1986).]

6. The will of Warren E. Burger, Chief Justice of United States from 1969 until 1986, is included as Exhibit 14–3 in this chapter. He prepared the will himself. Is it a holographic will? What improvements to his will could you advise?

7. Discuss some of the situations in which a directive to physician would apply. A durable power of attorney? What ethical dilemmas do these instruments create?

8. What is the difference between a revocable and an irrevocable trust? Identify a circumstance where each would be appropriate.

9. First Virginia Bank of Tidewater was the trustee of testamentary marital trust. In the course of the bank's service as trustee, it invested $40,000 in real estate investment trusts (REIT). The investment became worthless. The beneficiaries of the trust brought suit, complaining that the bank had violated the Virginia statutory "prudent man rule," which guided trustees in careful investment of trust assets. The bank defended, alleging the settlor had granted the bank broad discretion, obviating the "prudent man rule." Language in the will authorized real estate investments and to hold or sell investments ". . .without liability on the part of any fiduciary for depreciation in the value. . . ." Can a settlor supersede a statutory standard for a trustee? Did the testator settlor do so in this case? [*Hoffman v. First Virginia Bank of Tidewater*, 220 Va. 834, 263 S.E. 402 (Va., 1980).]

10. J. T. Payne executed a valid will on June 29, 1934. On April 24, 1956, a will with singed edges was offered to the probate court. Three of his children challenged the will, contending the deceased had revoked it. A witness at the trial testified that in July of 1934, J. T. Payne said, "I am going to get rid of this damn will right now," and he threw it on live coals in the fireplace. Payne's wife rescued the document and, with it still smoking on one end, put it into her apron. No language of the will offered in probate was obliterated or obscured. Can this be considered a valid will? [*Payne v. Payne*, 3213 Ga. 613, 100 S.E.2d 450 (Ga., 1957).]

11. Sung Fong had two strong obsessions during a long, eventful life: to become a millionaire and to "go it alone." He never married and now, at age 90, has a net worth of more than $10 million, almost all in stocks and bonds. He has no enemies, explaining with a chuckle that he's outlived them all. He has no true friends and no known relatives. With his health failing rapidly, he's added a third goal: to pay no death tax to the government. "Not one cent," he repeats. Can you tell him how to accomplish this last strange goal?

12. Quicken's Business Law Partner. Answer each of the following questions. Check your answer with the answer Arthur Miller gives on Quicken's Business Law Partner.
    a. Why should I prepare a will?
    b. What happens if I die without a will?
    c. Does a will cover all my property?
    d. How do I change my will after it's been signed?
    e. What is probate? How can I avoid it?
    f. What does it mean when a will is contested?
    g. What does it mean to be an executor?

Notes

1. Internal Revenue Code, §26 U.S.C. 2001.
2. Internal Revenue Code, §26 U.S.C. 2010.
3. *San Francisco Chronicle*, 17 March 1989.
4. Colorado Statutes §§ 15-11-503 and Calif. Probate Code § 6111.
5. Dear Abby, *San Francisco Chronicle*, 19 June 1989.

6. *Stone v. Stephens*, 155 Ohio St. 595, 99 NE2d 766 (1951) and *McCarthy, f/n/a Christine Kapcar v. Aetna Life Insurance Co. v. Kapcar*, 1998 WL 802773 (N.Y.).

7. *Estate of Walker v. Russell Eastern Star Home of Colorado, Inc.*, 847 P.2d 162 (Colorado 1992).

8. *The Guide to American Law*, Supplement 1991 (St. Paul, Minn: West Publishing, 1991), 405.

9. T. Zickefoose, "Videotaped Wills: Ready for Primetime," 9 Probate Law Journal 139 (1989).

10. "Probate Texas Style," *The National Law Journal*, 22 May 1989.

11. Calif. Probate Code § 10800.

12. Alaska is one of about 40 states with a TOD statute. Two important sections are provided as an illustration. AS 13.33.307. Ownership On Death of Owner. On death of a sole owner or the last to die of all multiple owners, ownership of securities registered in beneficiary form passes to the beneficiary or beneficiaries who survive all owners. On proof of death of all owners and compliance with any applicable requirements of the registering entity, a security registered in beneficiary form may be reregistered in the name of the beneficiary or beneficiaries who survived the death of all owners. Until division of the security after the death of all owners, multiple beneficiaries surviving the death of all owners hold their interests as tenants in common. If no beneficiary survives the death of all owners, the security belongs to the estate of the deceased sole owner or the estate of the last to die of all multiple owners.

    AS 13.33.309. Nontestamentary Transfer On Death. (a) A transfer on death resulting from a registration in beneficiary form is effective by reason of the contract regarding the registration between the owner and the registering entity and AS 13.33.301-13.33.310 and is not testamentary. (b) AS 13.33.301-13.33.310 do not limit the rights of creditors of security owners against beneficiaries and other transferees under other laws of this state.

13. AS 13.33.309., §§ 2-502 and 2-505.

14. Forms and individual state requirements are available from Choice In Dying, 200 Varick Street, New York, NY, 10014-4810.

15. *Vogel v. Forman*, 134 Misc.2d 395, 512 N.Y.S.2d 622 (1986).

16. PL 101-508, 42 U.S.C. §1395cc(a)(1).

17. Forms and individual state requirements are available from Choice In Dying, 200 Varick Street, New York, NY, 10014.

18. Oregon voters passed the Oregon Death With Dignity Act on November 4, 1994. Ore. Rev. Stat. §§127.800 *et seq.* http://detroitsuburbs.miningco.com/library/weekly/aa020298.htm. See the case of *Lee v. Oregon*, for a discussion of early litigation to stop operative use of the act, 107 F.3d 1382 (9th cir., 1997).

19. *Washington et al. v. Glucksberg et al.* 521 U.S. 702, 117 S.Ct. 2258 (1997). Also see *Vacco, Attorney General of New York et al. v. Quill et al.*, 521 U.S. 793 S.Ct. 2293, 117 S.Ct. 2293 (1997).

20. Wash. Rev. Code §70.122.070(1).

21. *Washington et al. v. Glucksberg et al.*

22. *Washington et al. v. Glucksberg et al.*

23. Alaska H. B. 371 (1996); Ariz. S. B. 1007 (1996); Cal. A. B. 1080, A. B. 1310 (1995); Colo. H. B. 1185 (1996); Colo. H. B. 1308 (1995); Conn. H. B. 6298 (1995); Ill. H. B. 691, S. B. 948 (1997); Iowa Code Ann. §§707A.2, 707A.3 (Supp. 1997); Me. H. P. 663 (1997); Me. H. P. 552 (1995); Md. H. B. 474 (1996); Md. H. B. 933 (1995); Mass. H. B. 3173 (1995); Mich. H. B. 6205 (1996); Mich. S. B. 556 (1996); Mich. H. B. 4134 (1995); Miss. H. B. 1023 (1996); N. H. H. B. 339 (1995); N. M. S. B. 446 (1995); N. Y. S. B. 5024 (1995); N. Y. A. B. 6333 (1995); Neb. L. B. 406 (1997); Neb. L. B. 1259 (1996); R. I. Gen. Laws §§ 11-60-1, 11-60-3 (Supp. 1996); Vt. H. B. 109 (1997); Vt. H. B. 335 (1995); Wash. S. B. 5596 (1995); Wis. A. B. 174, S. B. 90 (1995); Senate of Canada, Of Life and Death, Report of the Special Senate Committee on Euthanasia and Assisted Suicide A-156 (June 1995) (describing unsuccessful proposals, between 1991-1994, to legalize assisted suicide). Also, on April 30, 1997, President Clinton signed the Federal Assisted Suicide Funding Restriction Act of 1997, which prohibits the use of federal funds in support of physician assisted suicide. Pub. L. 105-12, 111 Stat. 23 (codified at 42 U.S.C. § 14401 *et seq*).

24. "Assisted-Suicide Pioneer," ABC News Internet Ventures.

25. Jon Shure, "TV news getting worse? Now that's a no-brainer," *New Jersey Lawyer*, 30 November 1998.

26. Judy Crichton, *America 1900: The Turning Point* (New York: Henry Holt and Company, 1998), 64.

27. Internal Revenue Code, 26 U.S.C. § 671-677.

28. Internal Revenue Code, 26 U.S.C. §§ 2631 and 2601 *et seq.*

Appendix A

DECLARATION OF INDEPENDENCE

In Congress, July 4, 1776

A Declaration by the Representatives of the United States of America, in General Congress assembled

When in the Course of human Events, it becomes necessary for one People to dissolve the Political Bands which have connected them with another, and to assume among the Powers of the Earth, the separate and equal Station to which the Laws of Nature and of Nature's God entitle them, a decent Respect to the Opinions of Mankind requires that they should declare the causes which impel them to the Separation.

We hold these Truths to be self-evident, that all Men are created equal, that they are endowed by their Creator with certain unalienable Rights, that among these are Life, Liberty, and the Pursuit of Happiness—That to secure these Rights, Governments are instituted among Men, deriving their just Powers from the Consent of the Governed, that whenever any Form of Government becomes destructive of these Ends, it is the Right of the People to alter or to abolish it, and to institute new Government, laying its Foundation on such Principles, and organizing its Powers in such Form, as to them shall seem most likely to effect their Safety and Happiness. Prudence, indeed, will dictate that Governments long established should not be changed for light and transient Causes; and accordingly all Experience hath shewn, that Mankind are more disposed to suffer, while Evils are sufferable, than to right themselves by abolishing the Forms to which they are accustomed. But when a long Train of Abuses and Usurpations, pursuing invariably the same Object, evinces a Design to reduce them under absolute Despotism, it is their Right, it is their Duty, to throw off such Government, and to provide new Guards for their future Security. Such has been the patient Sufferance of these Colonies; and such is now the Necessity which constrains them to alter their former Systems of Government. The History of the present King of Great-Britain is a History of repeated Injuries and Usurpations, all having in direct Object the Establishment of an absolute Tyranny over these States. To prove this, let Facts be submitted to a candid World.

He has refused his Assent to Laws, the most wholesome and necessary for the public Good.

He has forbidden his Governors to pass Laws of immediate and pressing Importance, unless suspended in their Operation till his Assent should be obtained; and when so suspended, he has utterly neglected to attend to them.

He has refused to pass other Laws for the Accommodation of large Districts of People, unless those People would relinquish the Right of Representation in the Legislature, a Right inestimable to them, and formidable to Tyrants only.

He has called together Legislative Bodies at Places unusual, uncomfortable, and distant from the Depository of their public Records, for the sole Purpose of fatiguing them into Compliance with his Measures.

He has dissolved Representative Houses repeatedly, for opposing with manly Firmness his Invasions on the Rights of the People.

He has refused for a long Time, after such Dissolutions, to cause others to be elected; whereby the Legislative Powers, incapable of Annihilation, have returned to the People at large for their exercise; the State remaining in the mean time exposed to all the Dangers of Invasion from without, and Convulsions within.

He has endeavoured to prevent the Population of these States; for that Purpose obstructing the Laws for Naturalization of Foreigners; refusing to pass others to encourage their Migration hither, and raising the Conditions of new Appropriations of Lands.

He has obstructed the Administration of Justice, by refusing his Assent to Laws for establishing Judiciary Powers.

He has made Judges dependent on his Will alone, for the Tenure of their offices, and the Amount and Payments of their Salaries.

He has erected a Multitude of new Offices, and sent hither Swarms of Officers to harrass our People, and eat out their Substance.

He has kept among us, in Times of Peace, Standing Armies, without the consent of our Legislatures.

He has affected to render the Military independent of and superior to the Civil Power.

He has combined with others to subject us to a Jurisdiction foreign to our Constitution, and unacknowledged by our Laws; giving his Assent to their Acts of pretended Legislation:

For quartering large Bodies of Armed Troops among us:

For protecting them, by a mock Trial, from Punishment for any Murders which they should commit on the Inhabitants of these States:

For cutting off our Trade with all Parts of the World:

For imposing Taxes on us without our Consent:

For depriving us, in many Cases, of the Benefits of Trial by Jury:

For transporting us beyond Seas to be tried for pretended Offences:

For abolishing the free System of English Laws in a neighbouring Province, establishing therein an arbitrary Government, and enlarging its Boundaries, so as to render it at once an Example and fit Instrument for introducing the same absolute Rule into these Colonies:

For taking away our Charters, abolishing our most valuable Laws, and altering fundamentally the Forms of our Governments:

For suspending our own Legislatures, and declaring themselves invested with Power to legislate for us in all Cases whatsoever.

He has abdicated Government here, by declaring us out of his Protection and waging War against us.

He has plundered our Seas, ravaged our Coasts, burnt our Towns, and destroyed the Lives of our People.

He is, at this Time, transporting large Armies of foreign Mercenaries to compleat the Works of Death, Desolation, and Tyranny, already begun with circumstances of Cruelty and Perfidy, scarcely paralleled in the most barbarous Ages, and totally unworthy the Head of a civilized Nation.

He has constrained our fellow Citizens taken Captive on the high Seas to bear Arms against their Country, to become the Executioners of their Friends and Brethren, or to fall themselves by their Hands.

He has excited domestic Insurrections amongst us, and had endeavoured to bring on the Inhabitants of our Frontiers, the merciless Indian Savages, whose known Rule of Warfare, is an undistinguished Destruction, of all Ages, Sexes and Conditions.

In every stage of these Oppressions we have Petitioned for Redress in the most humble Terms: Our repeated Petitions have been answered only by repeated Injury. A Prince, whose Character is thus marked by every act which may define a Tyrant, is unfit to be the Ruler of a free People.

Nor have we been wanting in Attentions to our British Brethren. We have warned them from Time to Time of Attempts by their Legislature to extend an unwarrantable Jurisdiction over us. We have reminded them of the Circumstances of our Emigration and Settlement here. We have appealed to their native Justice and Magnanimity, and we have conjured them by the Ties of our common Kindred to disavow these Usurpations, which would inevitably interrupt our Connections and Correspondence. They too have been deaf to the Voice of Justice and of Consanguinity. We must, therefore, acquiesce in the Necessity, which denounces our Separation, and hold them, as we hold the rest of Mankind, Enemies in War, in Peace, Friends.

We, therefore, the Representatives of the UNITED STATES OF AMERICA, in General Congress Assembled, appealing to the Supreme Judge of the World for the Rectitude of our Intentions, do, in the Name, and by Authority of the good People of these Colonies, solemnly Publish and Declare, That these United Colonies are, and of Right ought to be, Free and Independent States; that they are absolved from all Allegiance to the British Crown, and that all political Connection between them and the State of Great-Britain, is and ought to be totally dissolved; and that as Free and Independent States they have full Power to levy War, conclude Peace, contract Alliances, establish Commerce, and to do all other Acts and Things which Independent States may of right do. And for the support of this Declaration, with a firm Reliance on the Protection of Divine Providence, we mutually pledge to each other our Lives, our Fortunes, and our sacred Honor.

Appendix B

CONSTITUTION OF THE UNITED STATES OF AMERICA*

We the People of the United States, in Order to form a more perfect Union, establish Justice, insure domestic Tranquility, provide for the common defence, promote the general Welfare, and secure the Blessings of Liberty to ourselves and our Posterity, do ordain and establish this Constitution for the United States of America.

ARTICLE I

Section 1. All legislative Powers herein granted shall be vested in a Congress of the United States, which shall consist of a Senate and House of Representatives.

Section 2. The House of Representatives shall be composed of Members chosen every second Year by the People of the several States, and the Electors in each State shall have the Qualifications requisite for Electors of the most numerous Branch of the State Legislature.

No Person shall be a Representative who shall not have attained to the Age of twenty five Years, and been seven Years a Citizen of the United States, and who shall not, when elected, be an Inhabitant of that State in which he shall be chosen.

Representatives and direct (Taxes)[1] shall be apportioned among the several States which may be included within this Union, according to their respective Numbers (which shall be determined by adding to the whole Number of free Persons, including those bound to Service for a Term of Years, and excluding Indians not taxed, three fifths of all other Persons).[2] The actual Enumeration shall be made within three Years after the first Meeting of the Congress of the United States, and within every subsequent Term of ten Years, in such Manner as they shall by Law direct. The Number of Representatives shall not exceed one for every thirty Thousand, but each State shall have at Least one Representative; and until such enumeration shall be made, the State of New Hampshire shall be entitled to chuse three, Massachusetts eight, Rhode Island and Providence Plantations one, Connecticut five, New York six, New Jersey four, Pennsylvania eight, Delaware one, Maryland six, Virginia ten, North Carolina five, South Carolina five, and Georgia three.

When vacancies happen in the Representation from any State, the Executive Authority thereof shall issue Writs of Election to fill such Vacancies.

The House of Representatives shall chuse their Speaker and other Officers; and shall have the sole Power of Impeachment.

---

* The spelling, capitalization, and punctuation of the original have been retained here. Parentheses indicate passages that have been altered by amendments to the Constitution.
1. Modified by the Sixteenth Amendment.
2. Modified by the Fourteenth Amendment.

Section 3. The Senate of the United States shall be composed of two Senators from each State (chosen by the Legislature thereof),[3] for six Years; and each Senator shall have one Vote.

Immediately after they shall be assembled in Consequence of the first Election, they shall be divided as equally as may be into three Classes. The Seats of the Senators of the first Class shall be vacated at the Expiration of the second Year, of the second Class at the Expiration of the fourth Year, and of the third Class at the Expiration of the sixth Year, so that one third may be chosen every second Year (and if Vacancies happen by Resignation, or otherwise, during the Recess of the Legislature of any State, the Executive thereof may make temporary Appointments until the next Meeting of the Legislature, which shall then fill such Vacancies).[4]

No Person shall be a Senator who shall not have attained to the Age of thirty Years, and been nine Years a Citizen of the United States, and who shall not, when elected, be an Inhabitant of that State for which he shall be chosen.

The Vice President of the United States shall be President of the Senate, but shall have no Vote, unless they be equally divided.

The Senate shall chuse their other Officers, and also a President pro tempore, in the Absence of the Vice President, or when he shall exercise the Office of President of the United States.

The Senate shall have the sole Power to try all Impeachments. When sitting for that Purpose, they shall be on Oath or Affirmation. When the President of the United States is tried, the Chief Justice shall preside: And no Person shall be convicted without the Concurrence of two thirds of the Members present.

Judgment in Cases of Impeachment shall not extend further than to removal from Office, and disqualification to hold and enjoy any Office of honor, Trust or Profit under the United States; but the Party convicted shall nevertheless be liable and subject to Indictment, Trial, Judgment and Punishment, according to Law.

Section 4. The Times, Places and Manner of holding Elections for Senators and Representatives, shall be prescribed in each State by the Legislature thereof; but the Congress may at any time by Law make or alter such Regulations, except as to the Places of chusing Senators.

(The Congress shall assemble at least once in every Year, and such Meeting shall be on the first Monday in December, unless they shall by Law appoint a different Day.)[5]

Section 5. Each House shall be the Judge of the Elections, Returns and Qualifications of its own Members, and a Majority of each shall constitute a Quorum to do Business; but a smaller Number may adjourn from day to day, and may be authorized to compel the Attendance of absent Members, in such Manner, and under such Penalties as each House may provide.

Each House may determine the Rules of its Proceedings, punish its Members for disorderly Behaviour, and, with the Concurrence of two thirds, expel a Member.

Each House shall keep a Journal of its Proceedings, and from time to time publish the same, excepting such Parts as may in their Judgment require Secrecy; and the Yeas and Nays of the Members of either House on any question shall, at the Desire of one fifth of those Present, be entered on the Journal.

Neither House, during the Session of Congress, shall, without the Consent of the other, adjourn for more than three days, nor to any other Place than that in which the two Houses shall be sitting.

Section 6. The Senators and Representatives shall receive a Compensation for their Services, to be ascertained by Law, and paid out of the Treasury of the United States. They shall in all Cases, except Treason, Felony and Breach of the Peace, be privileged from Arrest during their Attendance at the Session of their respective Houses, and in going to and returning from the same; and for any Speech or Debate in either House, they shall not be questioned in any other Place.

No Senator or Representative shall, during the Time for which he was elected, be appointed to any civil Office under the Authority of the United States, which shall have been created, or the Emoluments whereof shall have been encreased during such time; and no Person holding any Office under the United States, shall be a Member of either House during his Continuance in Office.

Section 7. All Bills for raising Revenue shall originate in the House of Representatives; but the Senate may propose or concur with Amendments as on other Bills.

Every Bill which shall have passed the House of Representatives and the Senate, shall, before it becomes a Law, be presented to the President of the United States; If he approve he shall sign it, but if not he shall return it, with his Objections to the House in which it shall have originated, who shall

---

3. Repealed by the Seventeenth Amendment.
4. Modified by the Seventeenth Amendment.
5. Changed by the Twentieth Amendment.

enter the Objections at large on their Journal, and proceed to reconsider it. If after such Reconsideration two thirds of that House shall agree to pass the Bill, it shall be sent, together with the Objections, to the other House, by which it shall likewise be reconsidered, and if approved by two thirds of that House, it shall become a Law. But in all such Cases the Votes of both Houses shall be determined by yeas and Nays, and the Names of the Persons voting for and against the Bill shall be entered on the Journal of each House respectively. If any Bill shall not be returned by the President within ten Days (Sundays excepted) after it shall have been presented to him, the Same shall be a Law, in like Manner as if he had signed it, unless the Congress by their Adjournment prevent its Return, in which Case it shall not be a Law.

Every Order, Resolution, or Vote to Which the Concurrence of the Senate and House of Representatives may be necessary (except on a question of Adjournment) shall be presented to the President of the United States; and before the Same shall take Effect, shall be approved by him, or being disapproved by him, shall be repassed by two thirds of the Senate and House of Representatives, according to the Rules and Limitations prescribed in the Case of a Bill.

Section 8. The Congress shall have Power To lay and collect Taxes, Duties, Imposts and Excises, to pay the Debts and provide for the common Defence and general Welfare of the United States; but all Duties, Imposts and Excises shall be uniform throughout the United States;

To borrow money on the credit of the United States;

To regulate Commerce with foreign Nations, and among the several States, and with the Indian Tribes;

To establish a uniform Rule of Naturalization, and uniform Laws on the subject of Bankruptcies throughout the United States;

To coin Money, regulate the Value thereof, and of foreign Coin, and fix the Standard of Weights and Measures;

To provide for the Punishment of counterfeiting the Securities and current Coin of the United States.

To establish Post Offices and Post Roads;

To promote the Progress of Science and useful Arts, by securing for limited Times to Authors and Inventors the exclusive Right to their respective Writings and Discoveries;

To constitute Tribunals inferior to the supreme Court;

To define and punish Piracies and Felonies committed on the high Seas, and Offences against the Law of Nations;

To declare War, grant Letters of Marque and Reprisal, and make Rules concerning Captures on Land and Water;

To raise and support Armies, but no Appropriation of Money to that Use shall be for a longer Term than two Years;

To provide and maintain a Navy;

To make Rules for Government and Regulation of the land and naval Forces;

To provide for calling forth the Militia to execute the Laws of the Union, suppress Insurrections and repel Invasions;

To provide for organizing, arming, and disciplining the Militia, and for governing such Part of them as may be employed in the Service of the United States, reserving to the States respectively, the Appointment of the Officers, and the Authority of training the Militia according to the discipline prescribed by Congress;

To exercise exclusive Legislation in all Cases whatsoever, over such District (not exceeding ten Miles square) as may, by Cession of Particular States, and the Acceptance of Congress, become the Seat of the Government of the United States, and to exercise like Authority over all Places purchased by the Consent of the Legislature of the State in which the Same shall be, for the Erection of Forts, Magazines, Arsenals, dock-Yards, and other needful Buildings;—And

To make all Laws which shall be necessary and proper for carrying into Execution the foregoing Powers, and all other Powers vested by this Constitution in the Government of the United States, or in any Department or Officer thereof.

Section 9. The Migration or Importation of Such Persons as any of the States now existing shall think proper to admit, shall not be prohibited by the Congress prior to the Year one thousand eight hundred and eight, but a Tax or duty may be imposed on such Importation, not exceeding ten dollars for each Person.

The Privilege of the Writ of Habeas Corpus shall not be suspended, unless when in Cases of Rebellion or Invasion the public Safety may require it.

No Bill of Attainder or ex post facto Law shall be passed.

(No Capitation, or other direct, Tax shall be laid, unless in Proportion to the Census or Enumeration herein before directed to be taken.)[6]

No Tax or Duty shall be laid on Articles exported from any State.

6. Modified by the Sixteenth Amendment.

No Preference shall be given by any Regulation of Commerce or Revenue to the Ports of one State over those of another; nor shall Vessels bound to, or from, one State, be obliged to enter, clear, or pay Duties in another.

No Money shall be drawn from the Treasury, but in Consequence of Appropriations made by Law; and a regular Statement and Account of the Receipts and Expenditures of all public Money shall be published from time to time.

No Title of Nobility shall be granted by the United States; And no Person holding any Office of Profit or Trust under them, shall, without the Consent of the Congress accept of any present, Emolument, Office, or Title, of any kind whatever, from any King, Prince, or foreign State.

Section 10. No state shall enter into any Treaty, Alliance, or Confederation; grant Letters of Marque and Reprisal; coin Money; emit Bills of Credit; make any Thing but gold and silver Coin a Tender in Payment of Debts; pass any Bill of Attainder, ex post facto Law, or Law impairing the Obligation of Contracts, or grant any Title of Nobility.

No State shall, without the Consent of the Congress, lay any Imposts or Duties on Imports or Exports, except what may be absolutely necessary for executing its inspection Laws; and the net Produce of all Duties and Imposts, laid by any State on Imports or Exports, shall be for the Use of the Treasury of the United States; and all such Laws shall be subject to the Revision and Controul of the Congress.

No State shall, without the Consent of Congress, lay any Duty of Tonnage, keep Troops, or Ships of War in time of Peace, enter into any Agreement or Compact with another State, or with a foreign Power, or engage in War, unless actually invaded, or in such imminent Danger as will not admit of delay.

ARTICLE II

Section 1. The executive Power shall be vested in a President of the United States of America. He shall hold his Office during the Term of four Years, and, together with the Vice President, chosen for the Same Term, be elected, as follows:

Each State shall appoint, in such Manner as the Legislature thereof may direct, a Number of Electors, equal to the whole Number of Senators and Representatives to which the State may be entitled in the Congress; but no Senator or Representative, or Person holding an Office of Trust or Profit under the United States, shall be appointed an Elector.

(The Electors shall meet in their respective States and vote by Ballot for two Persons of whom one at least shall not be an Inhabitant of the same State with themselves. And they shall make a List of all the Persons voted for, and of the Number of Votes for each; which List they shall sign and certify, and transmit sealed to the Seat of the Government of the United States, directed to the President of the Senate. The President of the Senate shall, in the Presence of the Senate and House of Representatives, open all the Certificates, and the Votes shall then be counted. The Person having the greatest Number of Votes shall be the President, if such Number be a Majority of the whole Number of Electors appointed; and if there be more than one who have such Majority, and have an equal Number of Votes, then the House of Representatives shall immediately chuse by Ballot one of them for President; and if no Person have a Majority, then from the five highest on the List the said House shall in like Manner chuse the President. But in chusing the President, the Votes shall be taken by States, the Representation from each State having one Vote; A quorum for this Purpose shall consist of a Member or Members from two thirds of the States, and a Majority of all the States shall be necessary to a Choice. In every Case, after the Choice of the President, the Person having the greater Number of Votes of the Electors shall be the Vice President. But if there should remain two or more who have equal Votes, the Senate shall chuse from them by Ballot the Vice President.)[7]

The Congress may determine the Time of chusing the Electors, and the Day on which they shall give their Votes; which Day shall be the same throughout the United States.

No person except a natural born Citizen, or a Citizen of the United States, at the time of the Adoption of this Constitution, shall be eligible to the Office of President; neither shall any Person be eligible to that Office who shall not have attained to the Age of thirty five Years, and been fourteen Years a Resident within the United States.

(In Case of the Removal of the President from Office, or of his Death, Resignation, or Inability to discharge the Powers and Duties of the said Office, the Same shall devolve on the Vice President, and the Congress may by Law provide for the Case of

---

7. Changed by the Twelfth Amendment.

Removal, Death, Resignation or Inability, both of the President and Vice President, declaring what Officer shall then act as President, and such Officer shall act accordingly, until the Disability be removed, or a President shall be elected.)[8]

The President shall, at stated Times, receive for his Services, a Compensation, which shall neither be increased nor diminished during the Period for which he shall have been elected, and he shall not receive within that Period any other Emolument from the United States, or any of them.

Before he enter on the Execution of his Office, he shall take the following Oath or Affirmation: "I do solemnly swear (or affirm) that I will faithfully execute the Office of President of the United States, and will to the best of my Ability, preserve, protect and defend the Constitution of the United States."

Section 2. The President shall be Commander in Chief of the Army and Navy of the United States, and of the Militia of the several States, when called into the actual Service of the United States; he may require the Opinion, in writing, of the principal Officer in each of the Executive Departments, upon any Subject relating to the Duties of their respective Offices, and he shall have Power to grant Reprieves and Pardons for Offences against the United States, except in Cases of Impeachment.

He shall have Power, by and with the Advice and Consent of the Senate, to make Treaties, provided two thirds of the Senators present concur; and he shall nominate, and by and with the Advice and Consent of the Senate, shall appoint Ambassadors, other public Ministers and Consuls, Judges of the Supreme Court, and all other Officers of the United States, whose Appointments are not herein otherwise provided for, and which shall be established by Law; but the Congress may by Law vest the Appointment of such inferior Officers, as they think proper, in the President alone, in the Courts of Law, or in the Heads of Departments.

The President shall have Power to fill up all Vacancies that may happen during the Recess of the Senate, by granting Commissions which shall expire at the End of their next Session.

Section 3. He shall from time to time give to the Congress Information of the State of the Union, and recommend to their Consideration such Measures as he shall judge necessary and expedient; he may, on extraordinary Occasions, convene both Houses, or either of them, and in Case of Disagreement between them, with Respect to the Time of Adjournment, he may adjourn them to such Time as he shall think proper; he shall receive Ambassadors and other public Ministers; he shall take Care that the Laws be faithfully executed, and shall Commission all the Officers of the United States.

Section 4. The President, Vice President and all civil Officers of the United States, shall be removed from Office on Impeachment for, and Conviction of, Treason, Bribery, or other high Crimes and Misdemeanors.

ARTICLE III

Section 1. The judicial Power of the United States, shall be vested in one supreme Court, and in such inferior Courts as the Congress may from time to time ordain and establish. The Judges, both of the supreme and inferior Courts, shall hold their Offices during good Behaviour, and shall, at stated Times, receive for their Services, a Compensation, which shall not be diminished during their Continuance in Office.

Section 2. The judicial Power shall extend to all Cases, in Law and Equity, arising under this Constitution, the Laws of the United States, and Treaties made, or which shall be made, under their Authority;—to all Cases affecting Ambassadors, other public Ministers and Consuls;—to all Cases of admiralty and maritime Jurisdiction;—to Controversies to which the United States shall be a Party;—to Controversies between two or more States; (—between a State and Citizens of another State;—)[9] between Citizens of different States,—between Citizens of the same State claiming Lands under the Grants of different States, (and between a State, or the Citizens thereof, and foreign States, Citizens or Subjects.)[10]

In all Cases affecting Ambassadors, other public Ministers and Consuls, and those in which a State shall be a Party, the supreme Court shall have original Jurisdiction. In all the other Cases before mentioned, the supreme Court shall have appellate Jurisdiction, both as to Law and Fact, with such Exceptions, and under such Regulations as the Congress shall make.

The Trial of all Crimes, except in Cases of Impeachment, shall be by Jury; and such Trial shall be held in the State where the said Crimes shall

---

8. Repealed by the Seventeenth Amendment.
9. Modified by the Seventeenth Amendment.
10. Changed by the Twentieth Amendment.

have been committed; but when not committed within any State, the Trial shall be at such Place or Places as the Congress may by Law have directed.

Section 3. Treason against the United States, shall consist only in levying War against them, or in adhering to their Enemies, giving them Aid and Comfort. No Person shall be convicted of Treason unless on the Testimony of two Witnesses to the same overt Act, or on Confession in open Court.

The Congress shall have Power to declare the Punishment of Treason, but no Attainder of Treason shall work Corruption of Blood, or Forfeiture except during the Life of the Person attainted.

ARTICLE IV

Section 1. Full Faith and Credit shall be given in each State to the public Acts, Records, and judicial Proceedings of every other State. And the Congress may by general Laws prescribe the Manner in which such Acts, Records and Proceedings shall be proved, and the Effect thereof.

Section 2. The Citizens of each State shall be entitled to all Privileges and Immunities of Citizens in the several States.

A Person charged in any State with Treason, Felony, or other Crime, who shall flee from Justice, and be found in another State, shall on Demand of the executive Authority of the State from which he fled, be delivered up, to be removed to the State having Jurisdiction of the Crime.

(No Person held to Service or Labour in one State, under the Laws thereof, escaping into another, shall, in Consequence of any Law or Regulation therein, be discharged from such Service or Labour, but shall be delivered up on Claim of the Party to whom such Service or Labour may be due.)[11]

Section 3. New States may be admitted by the Congress into this Union; but no new State shall be formed or erected within the Jurisdiction of any other State; nor any State be formed by the Junction of two or more States, or Parts of States, without the Consent of the Legislatures of the States concerned as well as of the Congress.

The Congress shall have Power to dispose of and make all needful Rules and Regulations respecting the Territory or other Property belonging to the United States; and nothing in this Constitution shall be so construed as to Prejudice any Claims of the United States, or of any particular State.

Section 4. The United States shall guarantee to every State in this Union a Republican Form of Government, and shall protect each of them against Invasion, and on Application of the Legislature, or of the Executive (when the Legislature cannot be convened) against domestic Violence.

ARTICLE V

The Congress, whenever two thirds of both Houses shall deem it necessary, shall propose Amendments to this Constitution, or, on the Application of the Legislatures of two thirds of the several States, shall call a Convention for proposing Amendments, which, in either Case, shall be valid to all Intents and Purposes, as Part of this Constitution, when ratified by the Legislatures of three fourths of the several States, or by Conventions in three fourths thereof, as the one or the other Mode of Ratification may be proposed by the Congress; Provided that no Amendment which may be made prior to the Year One thousand eight hundred and eight shall in any Manner affect the first and fourth Clauses in the Ninth Section of the first Article; and that no State, without its Consent, shall be deprived of its equal Suffrage in the Senate.

ARTICLE VI

All Debts contracted and Engagements entered into, before the Adoption of this Constitution, shall be as valid against the United States under this Constitution, as under the Confederation.

This Constitution, and the Laws of the United States which shall be made in Pursuance thereof; and all Treaties made, or which shall be made, under the Authority of the United States, shall be the supreme Law of the Land; and the Judges in every State shall be bound thereby, any Thing in the Constitution or Laws of any State to the Contrary notwithstanding.

The Senators and Representatives before mentioned, and the Members of the several State Legislatures, and all executive and judicial Officers, both of the United States and of the several States, shall be bound by Oath or Affirmation, to support

---

11. Repealed by the Thirteenth Amendment.

this Constitution: but no religious Test shall ever be required as a Qualification to any Office or public Trust under the United States.

ARTICLE VII

The Ratification of the Conventions of nine States, shall be sufficient for the Establishment of this Constitution between the States so ratifying the Same.

Done in Convention by the Unanimous Consent of the States present the Seventeenth Day of September in the Year of our Lord one thousand seven hundred and Eighty seven and of the Independence of the United States of America the Twelfth. In witness whereof we have hereunto subscribed our Names,

Go. WASHINGTON
Presid't. and deputy from Virginia

Attest
William Jackson
Secretary

Delaware
Geo Read
Gunning Bedford jun
John Dickinson
Richard Basset
Jaco. Broom

Massachusetts
Nathaniel Gorham
Rufus King

Connecticut
Wm. Saml. Johnson
Roger Sherman

New York
Alexander Hamilton

New Jersey
Wh. Livingston
David Brearley.
Wm. Paterson.
Jona Dayton

Virginia
John Blair
James Madison Jr.

North Carolina
Wm. Blount
Richd. Dobbs Spaight.
Hu. Williamson

South Carolina
J. Rutledge
Charles Cotesworth
  Pinckney
Charles Pinckney
Pierce Butler.

Georgia
William Few
Abr. Baldwin

New Hampshire
John Langdon
Nicholas Gilman

Pennsylvania
B. Franklin
Thomas Mifflin
Robt. Morris
Geo. Clymer
Thos. FitzSimons

Jared Ingersoll
James Wilson.
Gouv. Morris

Maryland
James McHenry
Dan of St. Thos. Jenifer
Danl Carroll

Amendment I[12]

Congress shall make no law respecting an establishment of religion, or prohibiting the free exercise thereof; or abridging the freedom of speech, or of the press; or the right of the people peaceably to assemble, and to petition the Government for a redress of grievances.

Amendment II

A well regulated Militia, being necessary to the security of a free State, the right of the people to keep and bear Arms, shall not be infringed.

Amendment III

No Soldier shall, in time of peace be quartered in any house, without the consent of the Owner, nor in time of war, but in a manner to be prescribed by law.

Amendment IV

The right of the people to be secure in their persons, houses, papers, and effects, against unreasonable searches and seizures, shall not be violated, and no Warrants shall issue, but upon probable cause, supported by Oath or affirmation, and particularly describing the place to be searched, and the persons or things to be seized.

Amendment V

No person shall be held to answer for a capital, or otherwise infamous crime, unless on a presentment or indictment of a Grand Jury, except in cases arising in the land or naval forces, or in the Militia, when in actual service in time of War or public danger; nor shall any person be subject for the same offence to be twice put in jeopardy of life or limb; nor shall be compelled in any criminal case to be a witness against himself, nor be deprived of life, liberty, or property, without due process of law; nor shall private property be taken for public use, without just compensation.

---

12. The first ten amendments were passed by Congress on September 15, 1789, and were ratified on December 15, 1791. Collectively they are referred to as the *Bill of Rights*.

Amendment VI

In all criminal prosecutions, the accused shall enjoy the right to a speedy and public trial, by an impartial jury of the State and district wherein the crime shall have been committed, which district shall have been previously ascertained by law, and to be informed of the nature and cause of the accusation; to be confronted with the witnesses against him; to have compulsory process for obtaining witnesses in his favor, and to have the Assistance of Counsel for his defence.

Amendment VII

In Suits at common law, where the value in controversy shall exceed twenty dollars, the right of trial by jury shall be preserved, and no fact tried by jury, shall be otherwise re-examined in any Court of the United States, than according to the rules of the common law.

Amendment VIII

Excessive bail shall not be required, nor excessive fines imposed, nor cruel and unusual punishments inflicted.

Amendment IX

The enumeration in the Constitution, of certain rights, shall not be construed to deny or disparage others retained by the people.

Amendment X

The powers not delegated to the United States by the Constitution, nor prohibited by it to the States, are reserved to the States respectively, or to the people.

Amendment XI (Ratified on February 7, 1795)

The Judicial power of the United States shall not be construed to extend to any suit in law or equity, commenced or prosecuted against one of the United States by Citizens of another State, or by Citizens or Subjects of any Foreign State.

Amendment XII (Ratified on June 15, 1804)

The Electors shall meet in their respective states, and vote by ballot for President and Vice-President, one of whom, at least, shall not be an inhabitant of the same state with themselves; they shall name in their ballots the person voted for as President, and in distinct ballots the person voted for as Vice-President, and they shall make distinct lists of all persons voted for as President, and of all persons voted for as Vice-President, and of the number of votes for each, which lists they shall sign and certify, and transmit sealed to the seat of the government of the United States, directed to the President of the Senate;—The President of the Senate shall, in the presence of the Senate and House of Representatives, open all the certificates and the votes shall then be counted;—The person having the greatest number of votes for President, shall be the President, if such number be a majority of the whole number of Electors appointed; and if no person have such majority, then from the persons having the highest numbers not exceeding three on the list of those voted for as President, the House of Representatives shall choose immediately, by ballot, the President. But in choosing the President, the votes shall be taken by states, the representation from each state having one vote; a quorum for this purpose shall consist of a member or members from two-thirds of the states, and a majority of all the states shall be necessary to a choice. (And if the House of Representatives shall not choose a President whenever the right of choice shall devolve upon them, before the fourth day of March next following, then the Vice-President shall act as President, as in the case of the death or other constitutional disability of the President.)[13] The person having the greatest number of votes as Vice-President, shall be the Vice-President, if such number be a majority of the whole number of Electors appointed, and if no person have a majority, then from the two highest numbers on the list, the Senate shall choose the Vice-President; a quorum for the purpose shall consist of two-thirds of the whole number of Senators, and a majority of the whole number shall be necessary to a choice. But no person constitutionally ineligible to the office of President shall be eligible to that of Vice-President of the United States.

Amendment XIII (Ratified on December 6, 1865)

Section 1. Neither slavery nor involuntary servitude, except as a punishment for crime whereof the party shall have been duly convicted, shall exist within the United States, or any place subject to their jurisdiction.

Section 2. Congress shall have power to enforce this article by appropriate legislation.

13. Changed by the Twentieth Amendment.

Amendment XIV (Ratified on July 9, 1868)

Section 1. All persons born or naturalized in the United States, and subject to the jurisdiction thereof, are citizens of the United States and of the State wherein they reside. No State shall make or enforce any law which shall abridge the privileges or immunities of citizens of the United States; nor shall any State deprive any person of life, liberty, or property, without due process of law; nor deny to any person within its jurisdiction the equal protection of the laws.

Section 2. Representatives shall be apportioned among the several States according to their respective numbers, counting the whole number of persons in each State, excluding Indians not taxed. But when the right to vote at any election for the choice of electors for President and Vice President of the United States, Representatives in Congress, the Executive and Judicial offices of a State, or the members of the Legislature thereof, is denied to any of the male inhabitants of such State, being (twenty-one)[14] years of age, and citizens of the United States, or in any way abridged, except for participation in rebellion, or other crime, the basis of representation therein shall be reduced in the proportion which the number of such male citizens shall bear to the whole number of male citizens (twenty-one)[15] years of age in such State.

Section 3. No person shall be a Senator or Representative in Congress, or elector of President and Vice President, or hold any office, civil or military, under the United States, or under any State, who having previously taken an oath, as a member of Congress, or as an officer of the United States, or as a member of any State legislature, or as an executive or judicial officer of any State, to support the Constitution of the United States, shall have engaged in insurrection or rebellion against the same, or given aid or comfort to the enemies thereof. But Congress may by a vote of two-thirds of each House, remove such disability.

Section 4. The validity of the public debt of the United States, authorized by law, including debts incurred for payment of pensions and bounties for services in suppressing insurrection or rebellion, shall not be questioned. But neither the United States nor any State shall assume or pay any debt or obligation incurred in aid of insurrection or rebellion against the United States, or any claim for the loss or emancipation of any slave, but all such debts, obligations and claims shall be held illegal and void.

Section 5. The Congress shall have power to enforce, by appropriate legislation, the provisions of this article.

Amendment XV (Ratified on February 3, 1870)

Section 1. The right of citizens of the United States to vote shall not be denied or abridged by the United States or by any State on account of race, color, or previous condition of servitude.

Section 2. The Congress shall have power to enforce this article by appropriate legislation.

Amendment XVI (Ratified on February 3, 1913)

The Congress shall have power to lay and collect taxes on incomes, from whatever source derived, without apportionment among the several States, and without regard to any census or enumeration.

Amendment XVII (Ratified on April 8, 1913)

The Senate of the United States shall be composed of two Senators from each State, elected by the people thereof, for six years; and each Senator shall have one vote. The electors in each State shall have the qualifications requisite for electors of the most numerous branch of the State legislatures.

When vacancies happen in the representation of any State in the Senate, the executive authority of such State shall issue writs of election to fill such vacancies: Provided, That the legislature of any State may empower the executive thereof to make temporary appointments until the people fill the vacancies by election as the legislature may direct.

This amendment shall not be so construed as to affect the election or term of any Senator chosen before it becomes valid as part of the Constitution.

Amendment XVIII (Ratified on January 16, 1919)

Section 1. After one year from the ratification of this article the manufacture, sale, or transportation of intoxicating liquors within, the importation thereof into, or the exportation thereof from the United States and all territory subject to the

---

14. Changed by the Twenty-sixth Amendment.
15. Ibid.

jurisdiction thereof for beverage purposes is hereby prohibited.

Section 2. The Congress and the several States shall have concurrent power to enforce this article by appropriate legislation.

Section 3. This article shall be inoperative unless it shall have been ratified as an amendment to the Constitution by the legislatures of the several States, as provided in the Constitution, within seven years from the date of the submission hereof to the States by the Congress.[16]

Amendment XIX (Ratified on August 18, 1920)

The right of citizens of the United States to vote shall not be denied or abridged by the United States or by any State on account of sex.

Congress shall have power to enforce this article by appropriate legislation.

Amendment XX (Ratified on January 23, 1933)

Section 1. The terms of the President and Vice President shall end at noon on the 20th day of January, and the terms of Senators and Representatives at noon on the 3d day of January, of the years in which such terms would have ended if this article had not been ratified, and the terms of their successors shall then begin.

Section 2. The Congress shall assemble at least once in every year, and such meeting shall begin at noon on the 3d day of January, unless they shall by law appoint a different day.

Section 3. If, at the time fixed for the beginning of the term of the President, the President elect shall have died, the Vice President elect shall become President. If the President shall not have been chosen before the time fixed for the beginning of his term, or if the President elect shall have failed to qualify, then the Vice President elect shall act as President until a President shall have qualified; and the Congress may by law provide for the case wherein neither a President elect nor a Vice President elect shall have qualified, declaring who shall then act as President, or the manner in which one who is to act shall be selected, and such person shall act accordingly until a President, or Vice President shall have qualified.

Section 4. The Congress may by law provide for the case of the death of any of the persons from whom the House of Representatives may choose a President whenever the right of choice shall have devolved upon them, and for the case of the death of any of the persons from whom the Senate may choose a Vice President whenever the right of choice shall have devolved upon them.

Section 5. Sections 1 and 2 shall take effect on the 15th day of October following the ratification of this article.

Section 6. This article shall be inoperative unless it shall have been ratified as an amendment to the Constitution by the legislatures of three-fourths of the several States within seven years from the date of its submission.

Amendment XXI (Ratified on December 5, 1933)

Section 1. The eighteenth article of amendment to the Constitution of the United States is hereby repealed.

Section 2. The transportation or importation into any State, Territory, or possession of the United States for delivery or use therein of intoxicating liquors, in violation of the laws thereof, is hereby prohibited.

Section 3. This article shall be inoperative unless it shall have been ratified as an amendment to the Constitution by conventions in the several States, as provided in the Constitution, within seven years from the date of the submission hereof to the States by the Congress.

Amendment XXII (Ratified on February 27, 1951)

Section 1. No person shall be elected to the office of the President more than twice, and no person who has held the office of President, or acted as President, for more than two years of a term to which some other person was elected President shall be elected to the office of President more than once. But this Article shall not apply to any person holding the office of President when this Article was proposed by the Congress, and shall not prevent any person who may be holding the office of President, or acting as President, during the term

---

16. The Eighteenth Amendment was repealed by the Twenty-first Amendment.

within which this Article becomes operative from holding the office of President or acting as President during the remainder of such term.

Section 2. This article shall be inoperative unless it shall have been ratified as an amendment to the Constitution by the legislatures of three-fourths of the several States within seven years from the date of its submission to the States by the Congress.

Amendment XXIII (Ratified on March 29, 1961)

Section 1. The District constituting the seat of Government of the United States shall appoint in such manner as the Congress may direct:

A number of electors of President and Vice President equal to the whole number of Senators and Representatives in Congress to which the District would be entitled if it were a State, but in no event more than the least populous State; they shall be in addition to those appointed by the states, but they shall be considered, for the purposes of the election of President and Vice President, to be electors appointed by a State; and they shall meet in the District and perform such duties as provided by the twelfth article of amendments.

Section 2. The Congress shall have power to enforce this article by appropriate legislation.

Amendment XXIV (Ratified on January 23, 1964)

Section 1. The right of citizens of the United States to vote in any primary or other election for President or Vice President, for electors for President or Vice President, or for Senator or Representative in Congress, shall not be denied or abridged by the United States or any State by reason of failure to pay any poll tax or other tax.

Section 2. The Congress shall have power to enforce this article by appropriate legislation.

Amendment XXV (Ratified on February 10, 1967)

Section 1. In case of the removal of the President from office or of his death or resignation, the Vice President shall become President.

Section 2. Whenever there is a vacancy in the office of the Vice President, the President shall nominate a Vice President who shall take office upon confirmation by a majority vote of both Houses of Congress.

Section 3. Whenever the President transmits to the President pro tempore of the Senate and the Speaker of the House of Representatives his written declaration that he is unable to discharge the powers and duties of his office, and until he transmits to them a written declaration to the contrary, such powers and duties shall be discharged by the Vice President as Acting President.

Section 4. Whenever the Vice President and a majority of either the principal officers of the executive departments or of such other body as Congress may by law provide, transmit to the President pro tempore of the Senate and the Speaker of the House of Representatives their written declaration that the President is unable to discharge the powers and duties of his office, the Vice President shall immediately assume the powers and duties of the office as Acting President.

Thereafter, when the President transmits to the President pro tempore of the Senate and the Speaker of the House of Representatives his written declaration that no inability exists, he shall resume the powers and duties of his office unless the Vice President and a majority of either the principal officers of the executive department or of such other body as Congress may by law provide, transmit within four days to the President pro tempore of the Senate and the Speaker of the House of Representatives their written declaration and the President is unable to discharge the powers and duties of his office. Thereupon Congress shall decide the issue, assembling within forty-eight hours for that purpose if not in session. If the Congress, within twenty-one days after receipt of the latter written declaration, or, if Congress is not in session, within twenty-one days after Congress is required to assemble, determines by two-thirds vote of both Houses that the President is unable to discharge the powers and duties of his office, the Vice President shall continue to discharge the same as Acting President; otherwise, the President shall resume the powers and duties of his office.

Amendment XXVI (Ratified on July 1, 1971)

Section 1. The right of citizens of the United States, who are eighteen years of age or older, to vote shall not be denied or abridged by the United States or by any State on account of age.

Section 2. The Congress shall have power to enforce this article by appropriate legislation.

Amendment XXVII (Ratified on May 7, 1992)

No law, varying the compensation for the services of the Senators and Representatives, shall take effect, until an election of Representatives shall have intervened.

Appendix C
LEGAL RESEARCH

Understanding the Law, Third Edition, presents legal rules that help to solve a variety of problems that people commonly confront in their personal and business relations. When a legal problem or question arises, the law or laws appling to that particular situation in that particular jurisdiction must be determined. In our discussion of general rules of law, a rule presented may or may not apply in your particular state. Sometimes the rules of different states on a given matter may differ fundamentally. If differences do exist, the decisive rule is the one that applies in the particular state involved.

Both lawyers and students of law conduct legal research to find the legal rule(s) that apply to specific problems, as well as those that form the body of a larger area of law. Legal research over the years has been conducted as library research, but today much research is conducted through computer terminals accessing proprietary databases or legal research sites on the Internet.

Legal research is the search for authority to determine what the applicable law is, or to support your legal arguments; it is the search for primary law. **Primary law** consists of established rules from constitutions, statutes, administrative agency regulations and rules, treaties, and judicial decisions. Primary law is law stated without interpretation by commentators. It is law issued directly from an authoritative source, such as Congress or an appellate court. In important legal matters, one cites existing primary law in support of contentions made; if primary law of the appropriate jurisdiction is not available, one may present primary law from other jurisdictions or discussions of applicable law from secondary sources.

Law from other than primary sources is gathered from **secondary materials**, which include encyclopedias and other books that present some writer's opinion of what the law is or should be. This textbook is a secondary source. Secondary materials also assist a researcher in finding primary law and in understanding broad areas of the law.

Here we discuss how to begin legal research, sources for primary law, database legal research, some types of secondary materials, and Internet research.

WHERE TO BEGIN

There are many ways to begin legal research. Among the benefits of a formal legal education is knowledge about how and where to look for answers to legal questions. For example, a person may want to know if the cost of repairing a flood-damaged home is a deductible expense for income tax purposes. This is a legal question. The inquirer is interested in applicable federal statutes and regulations, and in administrative interpretations and court enforcement of those laws. Once the answer is obtained for federal income taxes, a similar inquiry may be necessary if state income taxes are also payable. State law may or may not treat the expense in the same way.

Experience and knowledge assist one in classifying legal problems and suggesting where the applicable law to resolve the problem is likely to be found. The more knowledgeable one is about the problem being researched, the more specific the initial inquiry is likely to be. Conversely, the less knowledgeable one is, the more general the initial search.

While there are several good methods to begin a search for the answer to a legal problem, the index/descriptive word approach suggested by the West Publishing Company is among the most helpful. Most legal materials, with the exception of court cases, are indexed by topics. Identifying appropriate index topics can quickly take the researcher to a discussion of the law that is of interest. The key to the index approach is the identification of multiple index possibilities. Note that legal materials are generally indexed according to the historical descriptions of legal issues, which are not always obvious. For example, a problem involving a child under the age of 18 might lead you to think logically of such terms as "child," "minor," or "youth." However, the term *legal description of a minor* historically was *infant*, and that is often how the information you now seek is indexed. The more index possibilities you identify at the beginning of your search, the more likely you are to find the information you seek. Indexing the key words, phrases, and issues can be aided by following this time-tested method from *West's Research Techniques*.

When analyzing your fact situation for the purpose of searching for cases or statutes in point (i.e., that apply), it is helpful to ask yourself, "What words describe the parties concerned; the places or things involved; the basis of the action or issue; the possible defense or defenses; and the relief sought?"

Parties: Persons of a particular class, occupation, or relation; e.g., children, collectors, heirs, or any person who is either directly or indirectly necessary to a proper determination of the action.

Places and Things: Objects that necessarily must exist before any cause of action or dispute can arise; objects perceptible through the senses; e.g., automobiles, sidewalks, derricks, or garages are words describing the places or things that must exist before a cause of action alleging negligent use or defective condition can arise regarding them.

Basis of Action or Issue: Some wrong suffered by reason of another's neglect of duty; e.g., loss (of goods); some affirmative wrong—boycott, ejection, assault; some legal obligation ignored—stop, look, and listen; or the violation of some statutory or constitutional provision—eight-hour law, the Civil Rights Act, or restriction of free speech.

Defense: Some reason in law or fact why the plaintiff should not recover; e.g., failure of consideration, act of God, assumption of risk, infancy.

Relief Sought: Legal remedy sought; e.g., restraining order, restitution, damages, annulment.

THE SEARCH FOR PRIMARY LAW

Primary law consists of court opinions, constitutions, statutes, and administrative regulations.

State Court Decisions

For most state trial court cases, the judges do not write opinions, and decisions are not published. New York and a few other states do publish selected opinions of their trial courts, but decisions of the state trial courts generally are filed in the office of the clerk of the court, where they are available for public inspection. These decisions include findings of fact and conclusion of law but do not have the authority or "*stare decisis* effect" of appellate court decisions and related opinions.

Written decisions of the appellate courts are published and distributed. They generally include opinions that give reasons for the judgments. The reported appellate decisions are published in volumes called *Reports*, which are numbered consecutively. State appellate court decisions are found in the state reports of that particular state. More and more states are now making appellate court opinions available on the Internet. At this time, however, most older cases still are available only in books and on private databases.

Additionally, state court opinions appear in regional units of the *National Reporter System*, published by West Publishing Company. Most lawyers and libraries have the West reporters because they report cases more quickly and are distributed more widely than the state-published reports. In fact, many states (e.g., Texas) have eliminated their own official reports in favor of West's *National Reporter System*. The *National Reporter System* divides the states into the following geographical areas: Atlantic (A. or A.2d), South Eastern (S.E. or S.E.2d), South Western (S.W. or S.W.2d), North Western (N.W. or N.W.2d), North Eastern (N.E. or N.E.2d), Southern (So. or So.2d), and Pacific (P. or P.2d).

After appellate decisions have been published, they are normally referred to (cited) by the name of the case; the volume, name, and page of the state's official reporter (if different from West's *National*

Reporter System); the volume, unit, and page number of the *National Reporter*; and the volume, name, and page number of any other selected reporter. (Citing a reporter by volume number, name, and page number, in that order, is common to all citations.) This information is included in what is called the **citation**. When more than one reporter is cited for the same case, each reference is called a *parallel citation*. For example, consider the following case: *People v. Segal*, 54 N.Y. 2d 58, 429 N.E.2d 107 (New York, 1981). We see that the opinion in this case may be found in volume 54 of the official *New York Reporter*, Second Series, on page 58. The parallel citation is to Volume 429 of the *North Eastern Reporter*, Second Series, and page 107. In reprinting appellate opinions in this text, in addition to the citation, we give the state of the court hearing the case and the year of the court's decision (New York, 1981).

A few states—including those with intermediate appellate courts, such as California, Illinois, and New York—have more than one reporter for opinions given their courts.

Federal Court Decisions

Federal trial court decisions are published unofficially in West's *Federal Supplement* (F.Supp.), and decisions of the circuit courts of appeal are reported unofficially in West's *Federal Reporter* (F. or F.2d). Cases concerning federal bankruptcy law are published unofficially in West's *Bankruptcy Reporter* (Bankr.). Decisions of the United States Supreme Court are reported in West's *Supreme Court Reporter* (S.Ct.), and the *United States Reports* (U.S.).

The *United States Reports* is the official edition of all decisions of the United States Supreme Court for which there are written opinions. Published by the federal government, the series includes reports of Supreme Court cases dating from the term of August 1791, although originally many of the decisions were not reported in the early volumes.

West's *Supreme Court Reporter* is an unofficial edition dating from the Court's term in October 1882. Preceding each of its case reports is a summary of the case with *headnotes* (brief editorial statements of the law involved in the case, numbered to correspond to numbers in the report). The headnotes are also given classification numbers that serve to cross-reference each headnote to other headnotes on similar points throughout the *National Reporter System* and other West publications. This facilitates research of all relevant cases on a given point. This is important because, as may be evident from the doctrine of *stare decisis*, a lawyer's goal in undertaking legal research is to find an authority that is similar "on all fours": where the facts are very close and the same questions of law are involved.

Case Titles

In the title of a case, such as *Ardmeyer v. Rau*, the *v.* or *vs.* stands for versus, which means "against." In the trial court, Ardmeyer was the plaintiff—the person who filed the suit. Rau was the defendant. If the case is appealed, however, the appellate court will sometimes place the name of the party appealing the decision first, so that the case may be called *Rau v. Ardmeyer*. Since some appellate courts retain the trial court order of names, it is often impossible to distinguish the plaintiff from the defendant by the title of a reported appellate court decision. The student must carefully read the facts of each case in order to identify the legal status of each party. Otherwise, the discussion by the appellate court is difficult to understand.

Terminology

The following terms and phrases are frequently encountered in court opinions and legal publications. Because it is important to understand what these terms and phrases mean, we define and discuss them here.

Decisions and Opinions. Most decisions reached by reviewing, or appellate, courts are explained in writing. A *decision* contains the opinion (the court's reasons for its decision), the rules of law that apply, and the judgment (outcome). There are four possible types of written *opinions* for any particular case decided by an appellate court. When all justices agree on an opinion, it is written for the entire court and is called a **unanimous opinion**. When there is not a unanimous opinion, a **majority opinion** is written, outlining the views of the majority of the justices deciding the case. Often, a justice who feels strongly about making or emphasizing a point that was not made or emphasized in the unanimous or majority opinion will write a **concurring opinion**. That means that the judge or justice agrees (concurs) with the judgment given in the unanimous or majority opinion, but for different reasons. In other than unanimous opinions, a judge or justice who does not agree (i.e., dissents) with the majority reasoning or holding often writes a **dissenting opinion**. The dissenting opinion is important because it may form the basis of the arguments used years later in overruling the precedent of the majority opinion.

Judges and Justices. The terms *judge* and *justice* are usually synonymous and represent two designations given to judges in various courts. All members of the U.S. Supreme Court, for example, are referred to as justices. And justice is the formal title usually given to judges of appellate courts, although this is not always so. Thus, in New York, a justice is a trial judge of the trial court (which is called the Supreme Court), whereas a member of the Court of Appeals (the state's highest court) is called a judge. The term *justice* is commonly abbreviated to J., and *justices* to JJ. A Supreme Court case might refer to Justice Kennedy as Kennedy, J.; or to Chief Justice Rehnquist as Rehnquist, C. J.

Appellants and Appellees. The **appellant** is the party who appeals a case to another court or jurisdiction from the court or jurisdiction in which the case was originally brought. Sometimes, an appellant who appeals from a judgment is referred to as the **petitioner**. The **appellee** is the party against whom the appeal is taken. Sometimes, an appellee is referred to as the **respondent**.

Updating Case Law Research

Case law is printed chronologically, by its decision date. One can never know by reading the case itself whether it has been subsequently reheard by the same court, reversed by a later higher court, or even whether the doctrines declared in the opinion have been rendered moot for later disputants by an act of the legislature. Yet that information is critical for one relying upon the holding of a court opinion. Imagine a lawyer's embarrassment (and perhaps malpractice) when citing an apparently leading dispositive case, when he or she is told by the opposing counsel that "the case was overruled two months ago."

Although other sources exist, *Sheppard's Citations* or *Citators* provide the primary protection against such errors as an overruled case. These publications track and then report when and where reported cases are cited. Assume you are interested in the case of *Boyson v. Thorn* cited in 98 Cal. 578. You can find the case citation in *Sheppard's Citators*, where accompanying the citation is a list of every published case in the U.S. that has cited *Boyson* since it was issued. *Sheppard's* also provides coding notes indicating among other things, whether the case has been overruled, criticized, or followed. The primary limitation of *Sheppard's* is the delay between the publication of updated *Citators* and brand-new cases. For example, if a case were overruled last week, *Sheppard's Citators* will not show that—except on a database service where the information is often available within hours of the issuance of a new case through a computer search. (Fortunately, most leading cases are not overruled.)

Constitutional Law

The federal government and the states have separate constitutions that define the general organization, powers, and limits of governments. The U.S. Constitution is the supreme law of the land. A law in violation of the Constitution, no matter what its source, will be declared unconstitutional and will not be enforced. Similarly, unless it conflicts with the U.S. Constitution, every state constitution is supreme within the borders of that state. The U.S. Constitution defines the powers and limitations of the federal government. All powers not granted to the federal government are retained by the states or by the people.

Constitutions are published and available for research in the same publications that provide the text of federal and state **codes** (systematic collections of law, rules, or regulations).

Statutory Law

Statutes enacted by the U.S. Congress and the various state legislative bodies are another source of law, generally called **statutory law**. Statutory law also includes the ordinances passed by cities and counties. Today, legislative bodies and regulatory agencies exercise an ever-increasing role in lawmaking. Much of the work of modern courts is interpreting what the rulemakers meant when a statute was enacted and applying it to a particular set of facts. When Congress passes laws, and the president signs them, they are collected in a publication titled *United States Statutes at Large*. When state legislatures pass laws, and state governors sign them, they are collected in similar state publications. These publications arrange laws chronologically by date of enactment. Most frequently, however, laws are cited in their codified form—that is, the form in which they appear in the federal and state codes.

In these codes, laws are compiled by subject. For example, the *United States Code* (U.S.C.) arranges all existing federal laws of a public and permanent nature by 50 subjects. Each of the subjects into which U.S.C. arranges the laws has a title and a title number. For example, laws relating to commerce and trade are collected in Title 15, which is titled "Commerce and Trade." (Titles may be divided into chapters and subchapters. Within Title 15, for instance, Chapter 1 includes laws concerning monopolies.) Within each subdivision, statutes are assigned numbers, which are referred to as section numbers. A U.S.C. citation includes titles and section numbers. Thus, a reference to "15 U.S.C. Section 1" means that the statute can be found in Section 1 of Title 15. ("Section" may also be designated by the symbol §.)

Sometimes, a citation includes the abbreviation "*et seq.*—(e.g., 15 U.S.C. Section 1 *et seq.*) *Et seq.* (Latin: *et sequens*) means "and the following." This is a reference to sections that concern the same subject as the numbered section and follow it in sequence.

State codes follow the U.S.C. pattern of law arranged by subject. They may be called Codes, Revisions, Compilations, Consolidations, General Statutes, or Statutes, depending on the preference of the specific state. In some codes, subjects are designated by number. In others, they are designated by name. For example, "13 Pennsylvania Consolidated Statutes Section 1101" means the statute can be found in Section 1101 of Title 13 of the Pennsylvania code. "California Commercial Code Section 1101" means the statute can be found in Section 1101 under the commercial heading of the California code. Abbreviations may be used. For example, "13 Pennsylvania Consolidated Statutes Section 1101" may be abbreviated "13 Pa. C.S. § 1101," and "California Commercial Code Section 1101" may be abbreviated "Cal. Com. Code § 1101."

Commercial publications of these laws and regulations are available and are often more helpful than the official publications. For example, West Publishing Company publishes the *United States Code Annotated* (U.S.C.A.). U.S.C.A. contains the complete text of laws included in U.S.C., as well as notes of short summaries of court decisions that interpret and apply specific sections of the statutes, plus the text of presidential proclamations and executive orders. U.S.C.A. also includes research aids, such as cross-references to related statutes, historical notes, and library references. A citation to U.S.C.A. is similar to a citation to U.S.C. (e.g., 15 U.S.C.A. Section 1.)

Commercial publishers provide comparable publications for state statutes. For example, in California two private compilations of California statutory law exists, West's *Annotated Codes* and Deering's *Codes Annotated*. Each provides helpful features similar to those found in U.S.C.A.

Updating Statutory Law Research

There are two major benefits to placing statutes into organized codes. It is easier to index the law and thus to help those researchers who wish to find a specific provision of the law when they do not know the appropriate legal citation. The second benefit is provided by *pocket-parts*. Once a code is published, it is almost immediately out of date. When the legislature passes a new statute or amends an existing one, the code must be changed. Publishing a new set of books each year so as to be temporarily current is wasteful and expensive beyond reason. Pocket-parts meet the need of accuracy and efficiency. Several times during the course of the year, the publisher issues to purchasers of its book supplements that update the main text. These supplements are commonly placed in a pouch or pocket in the back inside cover of the book. They are indexed to correspond to the sections in the main body of the work.

To find an appropriate statute in the main text and then fail to check and examine any pocket-part is a critical error in legal research. In annotated codes or constitutions, these pocket-parts also provide summaries of new recent cases that have interpreted statutes listed in the main text.

Administrative Law

Rules and regulations adopted by federal administrative agencies are compiled in the *Code of Federal Regulations* (C.F.R.). Like U.S.C., C.F.R. is divided into 50 titles. Rules within each title are assigned section numbers. A full citation to C.F.R. includes title and section numbers. For example, a reference to "17 C.F.R. Section 230.504" means the rule can be found in Section 230.504 of Title 17.

State administrative offices generally also have their regulations listed in a state administrative code.

Updating Administrative Law Research

The procedure for updating administrative law research is as follows: Check each book to see if it provides pocket-parts; if so, consult them. If the publication does not provide pocket-parts, check the publication date; the older it is, the less confidence you can have in any source you have identified therein. State administrative regulations are sometimes available in loose-leaf form. If so, check the date on the page consulted and check the beginning of the volume to see when the last loose-leaf additions were made available to the library.

COMPUTER-ASSISTED LEGAL RESEARCH

Internet

Throughout this textbook we have made references to Internet sites that give you additional, background, or follow-up information about the topics we are discussing. If you went to the referenced site, you engaged in legal research. If you wish to research your own topic, using an Internet search engine will be helpful. You can use your favorite search engine to find the information you seek or you can try some of our favorites. Use the Index/Descriptive word approach discussed on page 725.

- Internet Legal Resource Guide: http://www.ilrg.com/

- 'Lectric Library: http://www.lectlaw.com/ref.html

- Findlaw: http://www.findlaw.com/

- Hieros Gamos: http://www.hg.org/hghm.html

- Law.com: http://www.laws.com/

- The World Wide Web Virtual Law Library: http://www.law.indiana.edu/law/v-lib/lawindex.html

- The U.S. House of Representatives Internet Law Library: http://law.house.gov

- Cornell Law School Legal Information Institute: http://www.law.cornell.edu/index.html

- LawCrawler: http://lawcrawler.findlaw.com/

- The Meta-Index for U.S. Legal Research: http://gsulaw.gsu.edu/metaindex/

- Yahoo: http://www.yahoo.com/law/

Database

Computers have made possible the streamlining of the legal research techniques used by businesses, lawyers, and members of the judiciary. Today a number of databases—collections of information useful to anyone doing legal research—can be accessed through several high-speed data-delivery systems. The two most common systems are WEST-LAW and LEXIS-NEXIS. WESTLAW is a computer-assisted legal research service of West Publishing Company. LEXIS-NEXIS is a similar service of Reed Elsevier, Inc. Each system has database-access software that allows the researcher to interact with the delivery system. These providers also allow for Internet access through code entry sites.

A computer user needs to satisfy four conditions to gain access to vast banks of legal research materials. First, he or she must have appropriate computer hardware, such as an IBM-compatible computer or an Apple computer. Second, the computer must be equipped with a modem to transmit data over existing transmission lines. Third, the user must have system database-access software to make it possible for the researcher to interact with the delivery system. Fourth, she or he needs a license or agreement with a data provider for access to the databank.

In WESTLAW, user interaction with the data-delivery system can be initiated from a computer terminal or a personal computer running a special WESTLAW access program literally anywhere in the world. The WESTLAW user sends a query, or message, to the computer. A user can ask about a specific case, statute, or administrative regulation. Cases can be retrieved by either case

citation or case name. A person can check to see if cases have been cited as precedent in later cases or whether a case has been overruled. The user can use descriptive or key words to search material by topic. The query is then processed and documents are identified that satisfy the search request. The information is transmitted back to the user, where it is seen on a video display terminal (VDT). The documents displayed on the VDT can be stored on the user's hard or floppy drives, saved at site, or printed.

There are numerous benefits to using the database systems.

1. Users need not duplicate large libraries available on the database systems:

2. Data systems allow researchers to speed up the research effort.

3. The database may identify source material that manual research might overlook.

4. Updating and checking for accuracy is tedious and boring. This effort can be automated and time spent on the effort reduced.

5. Data services provide the means to identify time spent on each project, allowing for ease in billing to a particular client.

6. Staying at your desk with computer and proper software minimizes time spent in traffic and parking problems.

Much of the research for this textbook was completed using both WESTLAW and LEXIS-NEXIS and a home computer. These systems are still expensive for most private users, although they have become more reasonable in recent years. Also, many university libraries provide access privileges for currently enrolled students to one or more of these databases.

In short, WESTLAW, LEXIS-NEXIS, and similar computerized data-search systems allow access to virtually all cases, statutes, and federal regulations. Access is almost immediate and requires a minimum of physical effort. Often the latest cases can be found through a database before they are available at a local law school or law office library.

CD-ROM

Most hard copy legal publications are now available on CD-ROM. An amazing amount of information can be coded on this easy-to-retrieve format. Index searches using correct combinations of terms can be conducted in nanoseconds to retrieve on-point (relevant) information. Unlike database services, CD-ROM (like hardback publications) do require updating for changes in law occurring after the publication of the CD. Frequently updating CD disks, manually updating using database services, or hard copy sources can overcome some problems inherent in the use of this format. CD-ROM materials can be purchased or leased. In either option, most users pay a flat fee for the materials, and a usage fee similar to the one charged when accessing either LEXIS-NEXIS or WESTLAW.

SECONDARY SOURCES OF LEGAL INFORMATION

There are numerous legal publications that meet different needs of lawyers, judges, and others interested in the law. Some provide general discussions of the law; others provide excellent methods to find the appropriate and important primary law sources. The following are major secondary sources of law.

Dictionaries
Dictionaries provide definitions of terms and pronunciation guides. The leading authoritative legal dictionaries are *Ballentine's Law Dictionary* and *Black's Law Dictionary*. West Publishing Company also publishes an elaborate dictionary called *Words and Phrases*. The definitions are taken from actual court opinions and feature pocket-parts to keep the publication current.

Legal Encyclopedias
Encyclopedias report the whole of the law without commentary or analysis. Some encyclopedias are national in scope (*American Jurisprudence* and *Corpus Juris Secundum*); others are statewide (*California Jurisprudence*). These books are very useful starting points when you want a general overview of almost any important legal topic. They also often provide useful citations to important cases and statutes. When using an encyclopedia, be sure to check applicable pocket-parts or supplemental books.

Topical Publications
Publishers offer topical publication in areas of legal practice where great detail and current status may be critical. Taxation, employment law, and securities regulation exemplify areas where topical publications are available. The publications are often loose-leaf, to facilitate insertion of current supplements. Again, when using topical publications check for pocket-parts or supplemental books.

Restatements of the Law
A *Restatement* is a product of extensive consultation and research by scholars, judges, and practitioners on specific areas of law, such as torts, contracts, and agency. Each *Restatement* includes a synthesis of state black letter law (i.e., principles accepted by appellate courts and/or included in statutes), commentaries, and examples of the application of listed rules of law to specific problems. Although a *Restatement* has no binding force of law, courts often cite *Restatement* provisions because of their clarity and precision in stating the law. Such citation gives the quoted *Restatement* rule the force of law in that particular jurisdiction. Here again, when using *Restatements*, check for pocket-parts and or supplemental volumes.

Treatises and Texts
Treatises are books, limited in topical content, that cover either one area of law or a group of closely related areas of law. Treatises are usually more comprehensive than encyclopedias in their discussion of a given topic. They often contain critical commentary in addition to the expository text treatment. Other tests that serve this purpose are also available.

Digests
Digests are elaborate indexes to court decisions. They provide a short synopsis of parts of the court opinions (usually the headnotes) and are arranged and indexed by topic and subtopic. Digests exist for federal court opinions (*Federal Digest* and *Supreme Court Digest*), for all state opinions (*American Digest System*), and for some populous states. Check the pocket-parts.

Annotated Reports
Annotated reports are publications of selected cases accompanied by a thorough discussion, summary, and synthesis of other reported cases on the same or similar topic. They provide a very valuable source for finding citations of similar cases. Annotated reports are updated but by different means depending on the policy of the publisher. Consult the source on how to find updated information.

Annotated Codes
Annotated codes are private publications that generally contain the entire applicable federal or state code and constitution, along with summary capsule annotations to cases that have construed or interpreted the statutes. Also included are references to

legislative history and cross-references to related statutes. Check for pocket-parts.

Law Journals

Law journals are periodicals that contain scholarly articles on the law written by professors, judges, practitioners, and sometimes law students. Leading law schools usually publish them, although professional associations such as the American Bar Association also sponsor such learned journals.

Self-Help Books

A growing number of books are published by commercial publishers and professional organizations advising laypersons how to perform legal tasks. The quality of these books varies widely, but Nolo Press in Berkeley, California, has earned a reputation for providing high-quality self-help books at reasonable prices. Great care should be exercised in using self-help books. Pay particular attention to their publication dates.

Practice Books

Some books are published to assist lawyers in procedural requirements for performing certain legal tasks. They are often provided by continuing education organizations and give very specific directions on how to perform certain legal tasks in areas such as criminal procedure, family law, and wills and trusts. The books are usually too complicated for use by laypersons.

SOURCES TO ASSIST YOU IN YOUR LEGAL RESEARCH

The following excellent books present more detailed information on legal research:

- Morris Cohen and Kent Olson, *Cohen's Legal Research in a Nutshell*, 4th ed., (St. Paul, MN: West/Wadsworth, 1996).

- Steven Elias and Susan Levinkind, *Legal Research Online and in the Library*, (Berkeley CA: Nolo Press, 1998).

- Stephen Elias and Susan Levinkind, *Legal Research: How to Find & Understand the Law*, 6th ed., (Berkeley CA: Nolo Press, 1998).

- Marjorie Rombauer, *Legal Problem Solving, Analysis, Research and Writing*, 5th ed., (St. Paul, MN: West Publishing Co., 1991).

- William Statsky, *Legal Research and Writing: Some Starting Points*, 3rd ed., (Cincinnati, OH: Intl Thomson Pub Education Group, 1998).

- *West's Law Finder, A Legal Research Manual* (St. Paul, MN: West Publishing Co., 1991).

Glossary

A and B trust A husband-and-wife trust wherein after the first spouse dies, the surviving spouse receives a life interest in the trust property, and someone else (the designated beneficiary) has a remainder interest. An A and B trust is also called a *marital life estate trust*.

abandonment When a tenant leaves rented premises with no intent to return or honor legal obligations under the lease.

abatement Temporary suspension of a tenant's duty to pay rent because the rented premises have become uninhabitable.

abortion, illegal Termination of a human pregnancy in a manner that violates the law of the state in which it occurs (for example, during the minority of the female without prior notification to one or more of her parents or, in the alternative, without the consent of a judge).

abortion, legal Termination of a human pregnancy in conformity with the law of the state in which it occurs (for example, by a licensed physician during the first trimester, i.e., three months from conception).

absolute liability A theory of liability in which the victim need not prove negligence or wrongful intent.

absolute privilege A total right under the law to do or not do some act.

absolute privilege to defame Total protection from liability for defamation. Legislators enjoy it for statements made during official sessions, and judges and others enjoy it during judicial proceedings. See also "conditional or qualified privilege to defame."

abstract of title A chronological history of recorded documents that affect the title to a parcel of real property.

acceleration clause A clause in a note that declares the unpaid balance of the loan to be immediately due and payable upon the happening of any of a number of specified events called "events of default." Typical events that will accelerate a mortgage loan are sale of the home, default in monthly payments, or failure to maintain casualty insurance. See also "right of reinstatement."

acceptance Affirmative response to the terms of an offer, creating a contract. See also "offer."

accessories after the fact Persons who harbor, conceal, or otherwise voluntarily and intentionally aid a known perpetrator of a crime to escape arrest or punishment. They are guilty of criminal conduct, but not of the perpetrator's crime.

accessories before the fact Persons who encourage or assist a perpetrator of a crime—for example, by planning, advising, or standing guard during its commission. They are as guilty as the perpetrator (principal), but in some states to a lesser degree and with lesser punishment.

accessory A person who, though not present at the scene of a crime, aided and abetted the principal in its commission. In some states, an accessory is any person who, though not present at the scene

732

of the crime, aided the perpetrator in escaping apprehension—all other participants in the crime are principals.

accident A sudden, unexpected, unintended happening that causes injury and/or death and/or loss of property. Depending on the circumstances, legal fault may or may not exist.

accomplice A person who, in cooperation with the principal offender, is associated in a crime before, during, or after its commission. An accomplice is also called an *aider and abettor*. See "aid and abet."

accord and satisfaction A party agrees (by accord) to accept some substitute for the promised performance of a contract, which is then provided (the satisfaction).

accusation Formal commencement of a criminal case by a specified public official such as a district attorney or by a grand jury.

accusatory pleading A document specifying the crime committed and accusing the defendant of its commission.

acquitted Found not guilty of a crime by judgment of the court following a jury verdict, or by a judge's decision if there is no jury.

actual cause (or causation) An element of negligence meaning that the negligent person's carelessness is the reason for the loss by the victim; in other words, when injury to person or property results from the tortfeasor's action or failure to act.

ademption Without revocation, the elimination of a specific gift of property listed in a will because it no longer exists (e.g., a diamond ring is lost, stolen, or destroyed), or it is transferred in life to the named beneficiary or to someone else.

adhesion contract A contract drafted by a dominant party and then presented to the other party—the adhering party—on a "take it or leave it" basis.

adjudicate To hear and decide a dispute in a judicial action or court proceeding.

adjustable-rate mortgage See "variable-interest-rate mortgage (VIRM)."

administrative agencies Collectively, sub-branches of the executive branch of federal, state, and local governments. Administrative agencies may possess legislative, executive, and judicial powers in specialized technical areas where appropriate regulation requires action by experts.

administrative hearing An oral proceeding before an administrative agency to hear and decide some factual question related to agency action.

administrative law The body of law concerned with the power of administrative agencies. Administrative law consists of rules, regulations, orders, and adjudications. Also the composite body of substantive law created by the various administrative agencies in the performance of their assigned tasks.

administrative law judge A government employee appointed to hear and decide matters in administrative agency hearings.

Administrative Procedure Act (APA) of 1946 Law that mandates procedures for federal administrative agencies.

administrative process The administration of law by nonjudicial government agencies.

administrator A person appointed by a court to supervise disposition of the estate of a decedent who dies without leaving a valid will (i.e., intestate).

ADR See "alternative dispute resolution (ADR)."

adultery Sexual intercourse by a married person with someone other than the offender's spouse.

advance directive A general term describing the instructions prepared in advance of a life-threatening condition as to what care should be given or not given in the event of incapacitation (*incapacitation* being the lack of legal capacity to make important decisions). The most common advance directives are called *living wills, directives to physicians, durable powers of attorney, and durable powers of attorney for health-care decisions.*

adversary system The jurisprudential system in which the parties to a legal dispute are opponents. Their attorneys advocate a great variety of theories of benefit to the cause of their clients both before and during the trial, and on any appeal. This system is thought by many to be the best method of eliciting the truth and producing a just result. The judge acts as an independent magistrate rather than prosecutor, as found in many foreign countries which have an inquisitorial system.

adverse possession The creation of ownership of real property through its possession for a prescribed number of years without the consent of its owner.

affidavit A signed written statement of facts, confirmed by oath or affirmation of the signer, before a person authorized to administer such oath (e.g., a notary public).

affirmative action Policies and practices designed to assure employment of women and of minorities until their percentages in the work force approximate their percentages in the community.

affirmative action employment programs Programs that require preference in hiring be given to some statutorily protected group.

affirmed The confirmation of a lower court's judgment or order because the prior decision is deemed to be correct and free from prejudicial error.

Age Discrimination in Employment Act of 1967 Federal law that added "advanced age" (over age 40) to attributes listed in the Civil Rights Act of 1964 that may not be used negatively in employment decisions.

agency Relationship in which, by mutual consent, an employee (the agent) is authorized to represent and bind an employer (the principal) in business dealings with third parties. An agent is a fiduciary of the principal.

agency shop A company or department in which all employees in the bargaining unit must pay union dues (or some comparable fee) irrespective of whether they are union members.

agent A person employed by a principal to deal with third parties and to make contracts binding the principal to the third parties. An agent is a fiduciary of the principal.

aid and abet To help or assist another in committing a crime or tort.

alimony Maintenance payment by one spouse to the other spouse following dissolution of their marriage. Alimony may be rehabilitative (terminates at a specified time) or permanent (indefinite in duration). Alimony is also called *maintenance*.

allegations of fact Plaintiff's statement of alleged facts, contained in the complaint that serves to commence a civil action.

alternative dispute resolution (ADR) A term that describes various methods of resolving disputes through means other than the judicial process.

American Arbitration Association (AAA) Private nonprofit organization organized to provide education, training, and administrative assistance to parties who use nonjudicial methods—that is, alternative dispute resolution (ADR)—for resolving disputes.

American Land Title Association insurance policy A standardized form of extended title insurance coverage that is more comprehensive than the customary policy.

Americans with Disabilities Act (ADA) of 1990 Federal law that bars discrimination in the employment of capable handicapped persons by both private and public employers, and that requires reasonable accommodations for their special needs.

amicus curiae [Latin for "friend of the court"] One—not a party to a lawsuit—who submits a brief containing arguments in favor of the position of the plaintiff or the defendant. An *amicus curiae* usually appears only at the appellate level when a case has generated broad public interest.

amnesty Action by a legislature or chief executive to abolish and legally forget a specified offense, generally of a political nature such as alleged treason or desertion by a large group. Contrasted to a *pardon*, which remits or abates punishment imposed on an individual, generally for a felony.

amortization Repayment of a note secured by mortgage through agreed upon monthly payments of principal and interest over the life of the loan. A mortgage loan amortizes very slowly during the early years of its term because most of each monthly payment represents interest on the borrowed money. As the unpaid balance decreases, however, an increasing percentage of each monthly payment is used to reduce the principal (because less interest is due on the declining principal), and amortization of the debt thus accelerates.

annualized percentage rate (APR) The rate of interest a borrower is paying to a mortgage lender when points and lender's fees are considered as interest rather than mere expenses of the transaction. Thus, the contract rate of interest (stated in the note) is always less than the APR, which computationally spreads several one-time charges, such as points, over the life of the loan and recomputes that stated interest rate. This consumer protection device also informs consumers of the true annual costs of loans or credit transactions (e.g., 1.5 percent a month is realistically 18 percent a year).

annulment A court decree canceling a marriage because of some defect that existed when the marriage was entered. An annulment states that no valid marriage ever existed, whereas a divorce or dissolution terminates a valid marriage.

answer A document containing a defendant's allegations of fact. It is filed by the defendant, with the clerk of the court, after receiving a summons and complaint. A copy is given to the plaintiff (or the plaintiff's lawyer).

antenuptial agreement A contract whereby two persons who are contemplating marriage specify certain future mutual rights and obligations as marriage partners. For example, persons entering marriage might specify how they will divide listed assets if a divorce occurs. These binding contracts are also called *premarital agreements* or *prenuptial agreements*.

anti-deficiency law A state law protecting a homeowner from payment of any deficiency (or unpaid balance) if a mortgage foreclosure sale fails to produce sufficient money to satisfy the underlying debt in full. It applies only to a purchase-money mortgage incurred to buy the home.

Anti-Injunction Act of 1932 (Norris-LaGuardia Act) Federal law that restricts the issuance of injunctions in labor disputes, outlaws yellow dog contracts, and exempts unions from legal attack as monopolies.

appeal Formal request to a higher court to review any action of a lower court.

appellant The party who appeals to a higher court for review of lower court rulings.

appellate court Court that reviews decisions of prior courts for substantive and procedural correctness. The court has authority to affirm, modify, or reverse rulings of the lower court. Also known as an *appeals court*.

appellee The party, on appeal, who defends the earlier court determination. Also called the *respondent*.

appraisal Professional expert's opinion or estimate of the value of real or personal property.

appraised value Opinion of a professional appraiser of the fair market value of property, usually stated in a formal writing.

APR See "annualized percentage rate (APR)."

arbitrary and capricious Action taken impulsively or in bad faith and without good or valid reason.

arbitration Alternative to litigation whereby conflicting parties select a neutral third party (or parties) to hear and decide their dispute. Arbitration can be binding or nonbinding. See also "court-annexed arbitration."

arbitrator A private person selected by parties in conflict to hear and decide their dispute. Arbitrators are usually selected because of their expertise in the subject area of the dispute.

armed robbery Robbery committed with the use of a lethal weapon, such as a gun or a knife.

arraignment The formal charging in a court of law of a person accused of a crime. In this criminal court proceeding, following arrest, the charge is read to the accused. He or she is advised of constitutional rights and must enter a plea (e.g., guilty, not guilty, nolo contendere, not guilty by reason of insanity).

arrest To take a person into custody in order to charge him or her with commission of a crime. An arrest may be made with or without a warrant, depending on the circumstances.

arson The intentional and malicious burning of a building or other property for unlawful purposes.

articles of incorporation Document that, minimally, states the name, address (for service of legal process), purpose(s), and capital structure of a proposed profit-seeking corporation. When dated and signed by the incorporator(s), it is filed in the proper state office, at which moment the corporation comes into existence.

as is A phrase indicating that property is sold without warranty as to quality or condition.

assault, civil The tort of creating apprehension in the mind of the victim that he or she is about to be touched in a harmful or offensive way. There is no requirement that the actor have the present ability to inflict actual harm.

assault, criminal The crime of unlawful attempt, coupled with present ability, to commit a battery. There is no touching required in an assault.

assessed value The value assigned to real property by a local official called an *assessor* for the purpose of levying a property tax. In some states, the assessed value is a designated fraction (e.g., one-fourth) of the appraised or full cash value.

asset Anything of value that is owned. An asset is distinguished from a *liability*, which is indebtedness.

assigned risk A high-risk applicant seeking automobile liability insurance who is rejected by an insurance company and is then directed, by random rotating choice, to a designated insurer from a pool that includes all insurers in the state. Minimal coverage must be provided, although higher premiums are usually charged.

assignment (a) The transfer of some or all rights under a contract to another person. (b) The transfer by a tenant of his or her leasehold interest for its unexpired time. See also "sublease."

assumption fee A one-time charge made by the lender of an existing mortgage loan for accepting a new debtor (usually a buyer who has agreed to take over, or *assume*, the unpaid balance of the seller's existing loan). The fee, which is agreed upon in the note, often is six months' interest—a substantial amount.

assumption of loan An agreement by one person (usually a buyer) to *assume* (i.e., take upon himself or herself) all the obligations of an existing loan of another person (usually the seller). In periods of rising interest rates, it is sometimes desirable for a buyer to assume an existing loan on a home to be purchased rather than to obtain new financing at a higher interest rate.

assumption of risk When a plaintiff with knowledge of the facts of a dangerous condition voluntarily exposes himself or herself to the particular risk of injury.

attempt Intention of the accused to commit a crime and a substantial step toward its commission. This is a crime in itself. However, evil thought and even simple preparation are not enough to constitute an attempt—a substantial step toward the crime must be taken. If the crime is completed, the attempt "merges" into the crime.

attestation The act of witnessing the signing of a document and thereafter signing, as evidence that you have witnessed it.

attorney at law A person licensed to practice law, and usually called a *lawyer, attorney, counsel,* or *counselor*. In England such a person is called a *solicitor*; or a *barrister* if engaged in conducting trials.

attorney-client privilege The right of a client to keep communications with his or her attorney confidential and free from disclosure.

attractive-nuisance doctrine The doctrine under which minors who trespass may collect damages if attracted onto the defendant's premises where they are injured by a man-made instrumentality that has special appeal to children (such as a railroad turntable or an unfenced swimming pool).

at will A term used, for example, to indicate that an employment contract may be terminated at any time by either the employee or the employer without any liability (beyond payment for services rendered up to the time of departure or discharge).

auction sale   Public sale in which an auctioneer solicits offers, or bids; normally the goods are sold to the highest bidder.

automated teller machine (ATM)   Machine that allows bank customers to transact certain business without the direct help of bank employees. ATMs receive deposits, dispense funds from checking and savings accounts, make credit card advances, and receive payments.

automobile insurance   Insurance against hazards flowing directly from the ownership and operation of motor vehicles.

automobile medical payments coverage   Automobile insurance that pays the medical expenses of the insured and of other occupants of the insured's vehicle who are injured in an accident, regardless of who caused the accident.

award   The final decision of an arbitrator or other nonjudicial officer in the resolution of a dispute.

bad faith   The deliberate failure to fulfill some duty or contractual obligation owed to another (e.g., a purposeful failure by an insurance company to pay a lawful claim).

bail   Security posted with the court to assure that the accused, if released before trial, will voluntarily return for further criminal proceedings.

bail bond   A document signed by both the accused and a bail bondsman, binding the bail bondsman to pay a specified sum of money to the state if the accused fails to appear in court as directed.

bailee   One who rightfully receives temporary possession of personal property from another, the bailor, in a bailment.

bailment   A delivery of personal property to another by which that person has the right to temporary possession. Often, though not always, bailment is created by contract.

bailor   One who transfers temporary possession of personal property to another, the bailee.

balloon payment   The unpaid balance of a mortgage loan due in one payment at the end of an agreed upon period of time. A loan might require interest-only payments for three years and then a balloon payment of the entire amount of principal originally borrowed.

bankruptcy   Proceedings under federal law whereby all assets of a debtor (excluding certain exempt property) are distributed to his or her creditors. The debtor is then "discharged," or excused from the legal obligation to pay most of the debts. See also "Chapter 7 bankruptcy," "Chapter 11 reorganization," and "Chapter 13 adjustment of debts."

bar association   A professional organization of attorneys who are licensed to practice law.

bar examination   Test given to otherwise qualified lawyer candidates (generally law school graduates), the purpose of which is to assure possession of minimum standards of knowledge of the law before engaging in its practice.

bargaining unit   The department of a company, or other group of employees, that is deemed appropriate (by the National Labor Relations Board) for collective-bargaining purposes, based on common or related skills and duties.

battery   Any harmful or offensive touching of another human being without excuse or consent. Usually (but not necessarily) battery involves violent infliction of injury.

beneficiary   (a) The person designated by the insured to receive the proceeds of an insurance policy. (b) The person (also called a donee) designated by the settlor (or testator or donor) to receive the benefit of property in a trust. (c) A third party who receives the benefit of a contract between two other persons. (d) The creditor under a deed of trust.

benefit of the bargain   The respective consideration that each party in a contractual agreement is entitled to receive.

bequest   A gift of personal property by will. See "devise."

Better Business Bureau   A voluntary private agency, sponsored by the Chamber of Commerce, whose purpose is to encourage ethical business practice and to inform consumers of fraudulent sales schemes.

beyond a reasonable doubt   A term applied in a criminal trial to a quantum evidence that fully satisfies and entirely convinces the jury that the defendant is guilty as charged.

bias   A preconceived belief about some person or fact that makes it difficult to be neutral, dispassionate, or fair in evaluating that person's rights and duties, guilt or innocence.

bigamy   The crime of willfully and knowingly contracting a second marriage while still lawfully married to another spouse.

bilateral contract   Agreement in which both parties exchange binding promises.

bilateral mistake   See "mutual mistake."

bill of attainder   Act of the legislature inflicting capital punishment upon a named person or member of a specific group without trial and conviction. Such a law is forbidden by the U.S. Constitution.

Bill of Rights   The first ten amendments to the U.S. Constitution.

blue-collar crime   Crimes committed by persons of comparatively lower social status and economic wealth, often involving violence (such as robbery and battery), in contrast to white-collar crimes such as income tax evasion and fraudulent sales practices.

blue laws Statutes that regulate or prohibit commercial activities and amusements on Sundays.

blue sky laws Statutes that regulate the sale of corporate securities. They seek to prevent fraudulent promotion and sale of highly speculative or worthless stock and other securities.

board of directors A group of usually three or more persons elected by the stockholders to set basic company policies and to appoint the top executives who actively manage a business corporation. The board also declares dividends, to distribute profits to stockholders.

bodily injury and property damage insurance Automobile insurance that protects against the risk of liability for injuring or killing another or damaging her/his property as a result of negligence.

bond (a) A written obligation to pay a sum of money upon the happening of a specified event. (b) A written promise by a borrower to pay a lender a fixed sum of interest for a prescribed time, and to repay the principal of a loan on a stated date. (If payable within a year, it may be referred to as a *promissory note*.)

booking Administrative practice that occurs when an arrested person is brought to a police station following arrest but before incarceration in jail. Booking typically includes recording of name, address, and alleged crime, as well as fingerprinting, photographing, and blood testing for alcohol.

breach of contract Failure without legal excuse to perform a promise made in a legally binding agreement.

breach of legal duty Failure to act as an ordinary prudent person is required by law to act, under the given circumstances.

briefs Written arguments addressed to the appellate court by counsel for appellant and by counsel for appellee, including points of law and what they claim to be authoritative case support for their respective positions.

broker, real estate A person licensed by the state to engage in the business of negotiating the buying and selling of real property, and to employ licensed real estate sales agents to assist in this business.

burden of proof The duty to produce evidence as a trial progresses. In a civil case, alleged facts must be proved by a preponderance of the evidence. In a criminal case, the required measure of proof is that alleged guilt must be proved beyond a reasonable doubt and to a moral certainty.

burglary The crime of unlawfully entering premises, structures, and vehicles with intent to commit larceny (theft) or any other felony.

business invitee A person who is expressly or impliedly invited onto the premises by the occupier of land for business purposes designed to produce a profit.

busing Compulsory movement of children by bus to particular public schools to achieve a higher level of racial integration. Less controversial purposes include safety of the children and economy in the utilization of facilities.

but-for test A test to determine causation in negligence by asking, "But for" the defendant's negligence, would the accident have occurred?

buy-and-sell agreement A contract under which business partners (or stockholders in a closely held corporation) reciprocally agree to sell and buy their interests in the firm to the remaining member(s) upon the death or disability of any one of the owners.

bylaws Private rules for the internal government of a business corporation. Normally adopted by the board of directors of the corporation.

cancellation (of contract) Termination of a contract by a buyer with return of the parties to their original status, because of a breach of contract by the seller. The buyer may still sue for damages suffered. The reciprocal is also true if the buyer breaches the contract.

cap The maximum interest rate that a variable-interest-rate mortgage can reach. There is an "overall" cap that is the highest amount the variable rate may become during the entire life of the loan. A "periodic" cap is the maximum amount the interest rate may increase in any one jump. Usually interest rates may "trigger" every six months, or every year, and rise or fall in sync with index levels, unless capped or limited at some lesser level by prior agreement.

capital (a) Money and credit used to start and continue a business. (b) Total assets of a business. (c) Owner's equity in a corporation, consisting of common (and sometimes preferred) stock and retained earnings.

capital crime A crime for which the death penalty may be imposed in states where authorized and at the federal level.

capital gain The profit realized from the sale or exchange of a capital asset (i.e., generally a thing of value owned). In other words, the *gain* is the difference between (a) what was originally paid for the property (to buy or build) minus accumulated depreciation (in the case of investment property), plus accumulated costs of major improvements, and (b) its net sales price.

capital punishment Death penalty for a crime.

case A controversy brought before a court for decision. There are two broad categories of cases: see "case at law" and "case in equity."

case at law A case in which the relief sought is monetary damages, and in which a jury may be used to decide questions of fact.

case citation A reference that identifies a legal case and indicates where it may be found in a reporter system that publishes opinions of appellate cases. For example: *Commonwealth of Mass. v. Geagan*, 339 Mass. 487, 159 N.E.2d 870 (1959).

case-in-chief The case presented by each party in a trial. It includes calling witnesses and introducing into evidence documents, photographs, or whatever else is relevant to the issues in a trial.

case in equity A case in which the plaintiff seeks specific performance, an injunction, an accounting, dissolution of marriage, or other nonmonetary relief because the remedy at law is inadequate or unavailable. The judge, alone, decides questions of facts as well as those of law.

case law All reported judicial decisions; the law that comes from judges' opinions in lawsuits.

causation The act or means by which a specified effect is produced. See also "actual causation" and "proximate causation."

cause of action An existing right to seek and to receive judicial relief, assuming the factual allegations of the plaintiff are true.

caveat emptor [Latin for "let the buyer beware"] A phrase meaning that before purchase a buyer should investigate and then rely on his or her own judgment regarding obvious or readily discoverable shortcomings of the goods or services.

caveat venditor [Latin for "let the seller beware"] A phrase meaning that a seller should exercise appropriate care to assure that goods sold (or services rendered) are of fair value and suitable for human use, or be subjected to possible legal sanctions.

CC&Rs See "covenants, conditions, and restrictions (CC&Rs)."

cease and desist A command from an administrative agency that the subject party refrain from specified activities.

certificate of incorporation See "charter."

certificate of ownership A legal document issued by a state government showing who owns a vehicle (i.e., has legal and/or equitable title to it).

certificate of registration A legal document issued by a state government permitting operation of a motor vehicle on the highways of the state.

certiorari [Latin for "to be informed of"] A writ or order by which the U.S. Supreme Court exercises its discretionary power to decide which lower court cases it will hear.

challenge (of juror) Any prospective trial juror may be challenged *for cause* if his or her bias or prejudice is indicated. Statutes also provide that prospective trial jurors may be challenged *peremptorily* for any reason other than their race or gender. The decision to exclude a juror for cause is made by the judge; the decision to exclude a juror peremptorily is made by a party acting through his or her attorney. Peremptory challenges are limited in number.

champerty An illegal agreement with a party to a suit for a portion of any recovery in exchange for paying the litigant's lawsuit expenses.

Chapter 7 bankruptcy Voluntary or involuntary proceeding (also called *straight bankruptcy*) whereby a debtor surrenders all property, excluding certain exempt property, to the court for liquidation. Proceeds are distributed to creditors and most debts are discharged.

Chapter 11 reorganization Voluntary or involuntary proceeding whereby the debtor remains in possession and control of the business. The creditors and the debtor agree on a plan that permits the business to continue after creditors accept a portion of their claims as payment in full. Owners also accept less for their equity in the business.

Chapter 13 adjustment of debts Bankruptcy court-approved plan whereby an individual or a small business is shielded against involuntary bankruptcy while unsecured creditors receive at least as much as they would in Chapter 7 liquidation bankruptcy. Payments are normally made over a period up to three years, but no longer than five years.

charitable trust A trust designed for the benefit of a segment of the public or of the public in general.

charter (of corporation) A permit issued by the government to do business as a corporation. In some states, a *certificate of incorporation* and *articles of incorporation* serve the same purpose.

chattel See "property."

check-off An agreement between an employer and a union whereby the employer deducts union dues from employees' pay and forwards the funds directly to the union.

citation (a) An abbreviation that refers to the written decision of a published appellate court case, usually including its name, volume and page numbers, and year of publication. (b) Accusation that an infraction has occurred, as in traffic citation.

citizen's arrest The taking into custody by a private citizen of a person who allegedly committed a felony in the citizen's presence, or of a person who allegedly committed a misdemeanor that constitutes a breach of the peace then in progress.

civil action or civil dispute A lawsuit commenced for the purpose of resolving a civil conflict. Distinguished from a criminal action.

civil law (a) The branch of law dealing with civil rights and civil duties and their enforcement. (b) The total system of law embracing civil and criminal matters, used in the ancient Roman Empire and copied on the continent of Europe in modern times. In ancient times the law was defined by experts and imposed from above by the emperor. Roman civil law is contrasted to English *common law*.

civil rights See "rights, civil."

Civil Rights Act of 1964 Federal law (specifically Title VII) that makes it unlawful for employers of 15 or more persons, engaged in interstate commerce, to discriminate with respect to employment against any individual because of such person's race, color, religion, sex, or national origin.

class action When all members of a group of persons who have suffered the same or similar injury join together in a single lawsuit against the alleged wrongdoer. The group must be so numerous that it is impracticable to bring all members before the court individually. Therefore, they are collectively represented by only one or a few members. However, all members must have a definable common interest in the disputed situations of law and fact, and all are bound to the court's decision.

clemency A formal act of kindness, mercy, and leniency by a governor or the president in commuting (i.e., reducing) a criminal penalty or granting a pardon.

client One who employs an attorney to provide legal advice or other assistance.

close corporation A corporation whose stock is owned by one person or very few persons. Also known as a *closely held corporation* or *a family corporation*.

closed shop A place of employment where workers must join a union before they can be hired. Made illegal by the Taft-Hartley Act.

closely held corporation A corporation in which the common stock is owned by only one or a small number of shareholders. Also known as a *close corporation* or a *closed corporation*.

close of escrow The time when all required monies and documents from all interested persons are distributed by the escrow agent to the appropriate persons in connection with the sale/purchase of real property.

closing costs Charges for various services that arise in connection with the purchase and sale of a home. The charges are paid upon close of escrow by the buyer and seller in accordance with the terms of their agreement and escrow instructions. Examples of closing costs are termite-inspection charges, loan fees, title insurance premiums, notary public fees, and transfer taxes.

cloud on title Any dormant or actively pursued claim to the possession of or title to real property that is unresolved or contested. An unresolved claim may be evidenced by a written document, whether recorded or not, or by some physical characteristic, such as a ditch.

codes A compilation of statutes that are grouped together by subject matter, i.e., a vehicle code.

codicil A document prepared to change but not revoke an existing will.

cohabitation Living together as husband and wife. It is *notorious cohabitation* if done without complying with the legal formalities of marriage.

cohabitation agreement An agreement between notoriously cohabiting persons concerning financial or property matters.

collateral Money or other property made available as security by a debtor to a creditor, through physical possession or legal right, to guarantee repayment of a loan.

collaterals Relatives who are brother, sister, uncle, aunt, cousins and so forth. See also "lineals."

collective bargaining The process of negotiation by representative(s) of the employees' union and representative(s) of an employer for an employment contract that provides terms and conditions of employment.

collision insurance Automobile insurance that protects against the risk of loss from damages to one's own automobile in a collision regardless of who is at fault.

commerce The exchange of goods or commodities for payment in cash, credit, services, or other goods, often between parties separated from each other in time and space, and usually accomplished by means of legal contracts.

commerce clause A part of the U.S. Constitution which provides Congress with the power to pass laws to provide for trade with foreign countries and among states.

commercial impracticability When performance as agreed is rendered impracticable by occurrence of a contingency, the nonoccurrence of which was a basic assumption of the parties when they made the contract.

commercial property Property used in trade or commerce, contrasted to *residential*.

commercial speech Oral, written, and other forms of communication used in advertising and in other business activities. It is protected to some extent by the First Amendment.

commingling The mixing together of community property and separate property to the extent that the properties cannot be traced back to their original status. Commingled property becomes totally community property.

commission, real estate The compensation a home seller agrees to pay the listing sales agent if a ready, willing, and able buyer is found. The commission rate is negotiable and is calculated as a percentage of the sales price of the home, not the seller's equity in the home.

common area Any area available for use by all the residents of a multifamily residential development, such as sidewalks, swimming pools, landscaping, parking spaces, hallways, and recreation rooms.

common carrier A carrier that transports for payment all persons who apply for passage, assuming space is available and there is no legal excuse for refusal.

common law The total system of law that originated in medieval England and was adopted by the United States at the time of the American Revolution. Expressed originally in opinions and judgments of the courts, it is judge-made law that reflects the customs and usages of the people. Contrasted to Roman *civil law*, it is found throughout the English-speaking world. Common law is also called *unwritten law*.

common-law marriage The bond formed when a man and a woman live together in the manner of a husband and a wife for the number of years prescribed by state laws, though without observing the legal formalities of marriage. This is a legal form of marriage in some states.

common stock Shares representing ownership in a business corporation. They have no contractual rate or amount of dividend payment but are usually coupled with the right to vote for directors.

community property All property acquired (in a community-property state) by the husband or the wife during marriage other than by gift or inheritance, and other than as profits or income from separate property. See also "separate property."

commutation Reduction, by a state governor or by the U.S. president, of punishment for a crime—for example, changing a death sentence to life imprisonment.

company union A union formed, sponsored, or financed by the employer of its members, and thus subject to possible domination or control by that employer. The National Labor Relations Act of 1935 banned such unions.

comparable-worth theory The theory that the same wage or salary should be paid for jobs that have equal societal and economic value based on such factors as required preparation, skill, effort, responsibility, and working conditions.

comparative negligence Negligence of the plaintiff that does not bar recovery of damages but may reduce the amount of recovery proportionally.

compensatory damages Amount awarded by a court to make good or replace the actual loss suffered by a plaintiff. In the case of a breach of contract, this amount is equivalent to the actual dollar loss suffered because the defendant did not perform as promised. See also "general damages" and "special damages."

competent parties Parties who are legally qualified (i.e., have the *capacity*) to make a binding contractual agreement.

complaint, civil A document filed by the plaintiff with the court and served on the defendant to inform her or him of the facts constituting an alleged cause of action.

complaint, criminal (a) A written statement filed by complainant containing facts that indicate a crime has been committed and that the accused committed it. (b) An accusation of a misdemeanor.

composition of creditors A plan whereby all or most of the creditors of a defaulting debtor mutually agree to accept less than the full amount due each. In some plans, the time for payment is extended.

comprehensive insurance Automobile insurance that protects against losses from having one's car stolen or damaged other than by collision (e.g., by falling trees, sandstorm).

compulsory arbitration See "arbitration."

compulsory process (a) The right guaranteed by the Sixth Amendment to every person accused of a crime to require witnesses to appear in his or her favor, by court order. (b) Official action to force a person to appear as a witness in court, administrative hearing, or before a legislature.

conciliation and mediation of labor disputes Process by which a neutral third party attempts to negotiate a voluntary settlement of a labor dispute.

concurrent jurisdiction Power of more than one court to hear a case.

concurring opinion A written opinion wherein a judge agrees (concurs) with the result reached by another judge, but does so for different reasons than those stated by the other judge.

conditional (or qualified) privilege to defame Protection from liability for defamation extended, for example, to employers who, in good faith and without negligence, critically discuss employee qualifications with third parties. See "absolute privilege to defame."

condominium A residential or business building in which individuals own, and receive title to, separate units or apartments. Each owner is responsible for financing his or her own purchase. Common areas (such as the land, entry hall, and elevators) are owned in common and managed collectively by all owners of the individual units through a community association.

conflict of interest In a situation where one party is obligated to represent another, a real, perceived, or potential situation exists where the interests of the representing party and represented party are pposed. Conflict of interest can occur in attorney–client situations or where a member of the board of directors of a corporation is representing a corporation in such a way as to receive personal benefit.

consanguinity The blood relationship of persons who are descended from a common ancestor.

consequential damages Amount awarded by a court to make good or replace indirect but foreseeable economic loss resulting from a party's breach of contract (e.g., the value of an expected crop that was not produced because of seed that did not conform to agreed-upon specifications).

conservatorship A legal relationship created by a court to allow a person, the *conservator*, to manage the assets and personal affairs of another, the *conservatee*, who is not competent to manage his or her affairs.

consideration The price or inducement (for example, reciprocal promises) to enter a contract.

consortium The reciprocal legal right of companionship, cooperation, aid, affection, and sexual relations of each spouse from and to the other.

conspiracy An agreement by two or more persons to commit a crime. In most states, one or more of the conspirators must commit an overt act in furtherance of the criminal plan.

constitution A written document defining fundamental legal principles for governance of the people within the country or state. It may include grants of power and limitations of power.

constitutionalism The principles of constitutional government; adherence to them, including, notably, restrictions and limitations on government power.

construction loan A short-term real estate loan, secured by mortgage, intended to finance building costs. Upon completion, the loan is paid, when long-term financing is obtained.

constructive eviction Indirect eviction of a tenant by means of the landlord's failure to correct an intolerable interference or defects in the premises, which effectively drives the tenant out. For example, a landlord's failure to prevent neighboring tenants from making outrageous noises throughout the night can constitute constructive eviction.

Consumer Credit Protection Act Federal law requiring full disclosure to borrowers or consumers of the cost of credit as an annual percentage rate (APR) and in total dollars. This act is also known as the Truth in Lending Act.

Consumer Product Safety Commission Independent federal agency charged with implementing the Consumer Product Safety Act of 1972 by setting safety standards for most potentially dangerous consumer products.

contempt of court Willful defiance of the authority of a court, affront to its dignity, or willful disobedience of its lawful orders.

contingent fee A fixed percentage of the monetary recovery obtained by a lawyer for a client. It is agreed on in advance and accepted in full payment for services rendered. If the representation produces no recovery, no fee is due under the contingent-fee agreement.

continuation agreement Contract between partners to permit continuation of a partnership business after dissolution, thus avoiding the *winding-up period* and forestalling termination. See also "winding-up period."

contract A legally enforceable agreement to do or not to do a specified thing.

contract for deed An installment sales contract whereby the buyer, although in possession of the premises, promises to make monthly payments for years before title is conveyed from the seller by deed.

contributing to the delinquency of a minor Any conduct by an adult that encourages or assists a person under the age of 18 in any unlawful activity.

contributory negligence The negligence of a plaintiff that helped to cause a tort. In many states such a plaintiff is barred or restricted from claiming damages if injured.

conventional loan A home-purchase mortgage the repayment of which is not guaranteed by an agency of the federal government. The lender relies exclusively upon the value of the collateral and the creditworthiness of the borrower in making the loan.

conversion Unauthorized taking of the personal property of another and wrongfully exercising rights of ownership. Conversion is an intentional tort.

convicted Found guilty of a crime by a judgment of the court following a jury verdict or the judge's decision. See also "acquitted."

cooling-off period Three-day period during which a person who borrows money on the security of a second mortgage on the borrower's home may rescind. Most states also permit a three-day cancellation period for door-to-door sales and for home-improvement contracts.

cooperative apartment An apartment owned by a corporation formed to acquire land and erect the building. Interested persons buy shares in the corporation to obtain the right to live in one of the units.

corporation A legal entity with rights of a human person, created by compliance with applicable law for some designated purpose. A corporation may or may not seek profits. It is generally characterized by unlimited life, transferable shares, limited liability for owners, and centralized management.

corpus **(of a trust)** [Latin for "body"] The principal or capital sum, as distinguished from income, of the trust estate.

corpus delicti [Latin for "body of a crime"] The two essential elements of every crime: evidence that (a) harm has occurred, (b) most probably because of a criminal act. Such evidence may be provided by a corpse with gunshot wounds or by a burned building with lingering gas fumes, for example.

corrective advertising Advertisements required by order of the Federal Trade Commission to inform the public of errors or misstatements in earlier advertisements by the same company.

court (a) A government body that administers justice by applying laws to civil controversies and criminal offenses. Under the control of the judge(s), it also includes attorneys, clerks, and others to conduct and facilitate its proceedings. (b) The place where trials are held. (c) Sometimes the term is used as a synonym for *judge(s)*.

court-annexed arbitration A type of nonbinding arbitration required by some courts before the parties may proceed to trial.

court costs Fees charged by the court to cover some of the administrative costs of processing the paperwork (e.g., filing a complaint) connected with litigation.

covenant A formal promise or binding agreement.

covenant not to compete A promise not to engage in a competing business or profession. Such covenants are generally illegal unless part of an otherwise enforceable contract for the sale of a business or for employment. In such case, they are legal only if they are drafted to be reasonable regarding time, scope, and geographic area, and are necessary to protect the interests of the contracting parties.

covenant of good faith and fair dealing Agreement implied under the Uniform Commercial Code that contracting merchants shall always act with honesty and observe standards of fair dealing in the trade.

covenant of quiet enjoyment See "implied covenant of quiet enjoyment."

covenants, conditions, and restrictions (CC&Rs) A written set of limitations, in deeds or other recorded documents, on the future use of real property. For example, for residential use, they may require minimum-sized homes, with specified fencing, and so forth. Enforcement is often delegated to a homeowners' association (HOA). See also "deed restrictions."

creative financing Any financing for the purchase of a home in which the seller accepts a note secured by mortgage for all or part of the purchase price. Creative financing is also called *seller's financing*.

credit Legal right given by one person (the creditor) to another (the debtor) to incur a debt, coupled with a promise to pay it later, usually with interest.

credit card A small card, usually made of plastic, identifying the holder by signature (and sometimes by photograph), issued by banks, stores, and other agencies to permit the holder to obtain goods, services, or money on credit up to a specified limit.

Credit Card Act of 1970 Federal law that regulates issuance and enforcement of credit cards.

crime An offense against the public resulting from violation of a criminal statute.

criminal action, case, or dispute A trial before a jury (if demanded by either party) in which the government (state or federal) prosecutes a person charged with a crime.

criminal facilitation The crime of assisting the commission of a crime by another person.

criminal intent The requisite guilty state of mind [Latin *mens rea*, for "guilty mind"] to hold a person responsible for a particular crime.

criminal law The branch of law dealing with crimes and their punishment.

criminal negligence Conduct that is without criminal intent and yet is so careless, or occurs in such reckless disregard of another's safety, that criminal penalties are prescribed by statute.

cruel and unusual punishment Criminal punishment in which the duration of sentence in jail is totally disproportionate to the offense, or the prisoner is subjected to inhuman torture or merciless abuse, or the method of the punishment is unacceptable to society, or the punishment is arbitrary. Cruel and unusual punishment is prohibited by the Eighth Amendment to the U.S. Constitution.

cure a default To bring current any past-due payments of rent or of monthly payments on a home-purchase mortgage, or to correct any other default, such as removing a dog from rented premises where they are prohibited.

custom-built home A home built according to specifications (e.g., floor plan, building materials, interior design) selected by its buyer. Custom-built homes are usually constructed on subdivision lots or sometimes on rural acreage.

damages Money awarded by a court to a plaintiff for injury or economic loss caused by the defendant. There are various types, including compensatory, consequential, general, incidental, liquidated, nominal or token, punitive or exemplary, special, and treble. See each of these entries.

dangerous instrumentality A gun or other object that may cause harm when given to a child without instruction as to its proper use.

dangerous propensity A child's harmful habit that may result in injury to others, such as throwing rocks at automobiles.

death taxes Taxes imposed on the estate of the decedent (that is, an *estate* tax on the privilege of giving) and on the gifts received by the donee(s) (that is, an *inheritance* tax on the privilege of receiving).

decedent A deceased person.

deceit Fraudulent misrepresentation made knowingly to mislead another person who is thereby misled and injured. Deceit is also called *fraud*.

decisional law The written decisions of appellate courts, also referred to as the common law and case law.

declaratory judgment A judicial action where a court states the rights and duties of parties without specifically ordering that anything be done. Declaratory judgment is also called *declaratory relief*.

decree of dissolution A court judgment ending a marriage.

deductible clause A provision in an insurance policy whereby the insured bears modest losses up to a prescribed sum (e.g., $50, $100, or a little more) in exchange for reduced premiums. Typically there is no deduction from full coverage when the loss is substantial.

deed Any document used to transfer any ownership interest in real property. Many types of deeds are used in a variety of property transfers. For example, *grant deeds* and *warranty deeds* are commonly used in the sale of homes; they include certain guarantees by the transferor that are implied by law. A *trustee's deed* transfers ownership to the purchaser of property at a foreclosure sale. See also "deed of reconveyance," "deed of trust," and "quitclaim deed."

deed of reconveyance A deed used by a trustee to return title to real property to the trustor (borrower) when he or she pays off a loan that was secured by a trust deed. See also "deed."

deed of trust A deed used by a borrower (called *trustor*) to transfer the legal title to real property to a disinterested stakeholder (the *trustee*) to hold as security or collateral for the benefit of the lender (the *beneficiary*). When the loan is paid in full, the legal title is reconveyed to the trustor. Also called a *trust deed*. See also "deed of reconveyance."

deed restrictions A clause included within a deed that restricts the future use of the real property that is being conveyed. For example, property can be conveyed subject to the restriction that it be used only for residential purposes. Covenants, conditions, and restrictions (CC&Rs) may be included within a deed, incorporated by reference into a deed, or contained in a separate document that, like a deed, is recorded and legally restricts the future use of the property.

de facto [Latin for "in fact" or "actually"] A situation that exists in fact whether or not it is lawful (e.g., the term *de facto segregation* is often used to refer to a separation of races caused by social selection, living patterns, and economic conditions). See also "*de jure*."

defamation False statement, either oral (called *slander*) or written (called *libel*), that tends to injure the reputation of the victim. It may be civil (a tort) as well as criminal (a crime).

default Failure of a party to do what is legally required (e.g., failing to keep a contractual promise, or failing to file an answer to a complaint).

default judgment Court-awarded judgment based on the defendant's failure to answer the summons and complaint or to appear at the trial to contest the claim of the plaintiff.

defective (or voidable) marriage A marriage that may be legally nullified by the innocent party through court action, thereby restoring both parties to the legal status of persons who have never been married to each other.

defendant (a) In a civil trial, the person from whom money damages or other relief is sought by the plaintiff. (b) In a criminal trial, the accused.

defense Some reason in law or fact why the plaintiff should not recover in a civil action (e.g., failure of consideration, act of God, assumption of risk) or why the defendant is not guilty as charged in a criminal action.

deficiency judgment Judgment against a debtor for the unpaid balance still due after repossession and resale of goods that were sold on credit, or after judicial foreclosure of a real estate mortgage.

de jure [Latin for "by law" or "lawfully"] Of right; done in compliance with law; legitimate; lawful, whether or not such is true in actual fact (e.g., the term *de jure segregation* is often used to refer to officially sanctioned racial discrimination). See also "*de facto*."

delegation Transfer of some or all contractual duties to another person.

deliberate The review, discussion, and weighing of evidence presented at a trial by a jury.

democracy [Greek for "rule by the people"] System of government in which power is vested in the people and exercised by them directly, or indirectly as through a system of representation involving free elections.

demurrer A motion filed by a defendant in response to a summons and complaint when allegations of the complaint, even if true, are insufficient to state a cause of action. In federal courts, and in many states, the same result is achieved by a motion to dismiss.

de novo **review** An entirely new hearing (including witnesses and other evidence) as contrasted to an appeal (limited to a review of the law as applied).

deposition Questioning of a witness or adverse party to an action, under oath, by the opposing attorney before the trial. Depositions are conducted in the presence of a court reporter and the person's own counsel. They are the principal type of discovery procedure.

deposit receipt Idiom for a legally binding contract to purchase and sell a specific parcel of real property. See also "purchase contract and deposit receipt."

depreciated value The value of property after deduction of a percentage of its original value because of aging and/or use.

depreciation (a) In tax law, a tax deduction allowed by law for taxpayers who own certain kinds of assets. Such a tax deduction permits a taxpayer to pay a smaller income tax than otherwise would be due; for example, apartment house owners are entitled to large income tax deductions for depreciation. (b) In other than tax law, a decline in value, or the opposite of appreciation in value.

detention The brief stopping of a suspicious person by a police officer for the limited purpose of determining if a crime has been or is being committed in the proximity of the detainee.

devise A gift of real property by will. See "bequest."

dictum **(pl.** *dicta***)** [Latin for "remark(s)"] Any part of a court opinion that is unnecessary to the resolution of dispute before the court. Such digression by a judge is not binding on later courts.

diminished capacity Reduced ability to exercise one's freedom of will or to choose between right and wrong. Possibly delusion induced by drugs, diminished capacity may negate the presence of specific criminal intent required for first-degree murder.

directive to physicians A signed document communicating the signer's wishes regarding the use of life-support systems in the treatment of a terminal illness.

director (of corporation) One of a group of persons (called a *board*) legally charged with the determination of major policies for management of a business corporation, appointment of top executives, and the declaration of dividends.

disability insurance A form of insurance that provides replacement income for a person who is unable to work because of a disability (illness or injury).

disbarment Revocation of an attorney's license to practice law. A disbarred attorney may seek reinstatement at a future date.

discharge of contract Completion of contractual obligation(s).

disclaimer (a) A written or oral statement stating that a warranty does not exist. (b) Refusal of an insurer to accept certain types of liability. (c) Rejection of an estate or right offered to a person. (d) Renunciation of a claim or power. (e) Negation or limitation of a warranty in the sale of goods.

discovery procedures Methods used under court order during the period between commencement of a lawsuit and the date of trial to learn facts about the dispute. See also "deposition," "motion to produce," "request for admission of facts," and "written interrogatories."

discretionary sprinkling and accumulation trust A trust where the trustee is authorized to decide who among the designated beneficiaries is to receive periodic payments of income or principal, and when.

disparate-impact A facially neutral employment criterion, which has an adverse discriminatory impact upon a protected group.

disparate-treatment Less favorable treatment than others because of race, color, religion, gender, age, or national origin.

disputants Opposing parties in conflict.

dissenting opinion A written opinion by a judge or judges who vote(s) contrary to and in disagreement with the majority opinion and holding of the court.

dissolution Termination of marriage relationship by court judgment. Dissolution is called *divorce* in some states.

diversity of citizenship A basis of jurisdiction in federal courts. It requires that plaintiff and defendant be involved in an actual controversy, be citizens of different states, and that a minimum of $75,000 be sought in damages.

divided interest Interest in property such as a parcel of land, held by a person either separately or in severalty—for example, by the owner of a condominium.

dividend (a) Profit of a corporation distributed proportionally to stockholders by order of the board of directors. (b) Refund of overpaid premiums by an insurance company.

divorce Termination of a marriage relationship by court judgment. Divorce is called *dissolution* in some states.

divorce from bed and board A modification of the spousal relationship in which the parties are forbidden to cohabit but do not dissolve the marriage. Support may be paid, and property is divided as in a divorce. See also "separate maintenance."

doctrine of supremacy The constitutional doctrine that applies whenever the United States and a state or local government enact laws on the same subject which conflict. Under this constitutional doctrine, the federal law prevails.

domestic law The laws of the United States, as distinguished from the laws relating to foreign nations. Sometimes also refers to the law of domestic relations, i.e., family law.

domestic torts Torts based on negligent or intentional conduct by one spouse causing bodily injury or property damage to the other.

donee The person to whom a gift is made in life or by will.

donor A person who makes a gift in life or by will.

double jeopardy A second criminal prosecution against a person for the same single offense, after the person has been found innocent of the crime in the prior trial.

double taxation of corporate income After corporate net income has already been taxed, it is taxed again as personal income if it is distributed to the shareholders as dividends.

dower and curtesy Dower is the common-law right of a married woman to a life estate in the property of her husband upon his death. Curtesy is the comparable right of a husband to property of his wife upon her death. Dower and curtesy have no application in community-property jurisdictions and have been abolished or modified in most other states.

down payment The purchase price of a home less the net amount of funds that can be borrowed equals the amount of cash the buyer will have to deposit into escrow to complete the purchase—i.e., the down payment. Broadly, the amount paid for real or personal property in cash in addition to the debt incurred for the balance due.

dramshop statute A state law making it a crime for a tavern proprietor or employee to serve intoxicants to an obviously inebriated customer.

driving under the influence (DUI) Violating the law by driving while one's judgment and ability to react are impaired by alcohol or other mind-altering drugs.

due-on-sale clause A clause found in most promissory notes secured by home-purchase mortgages that accelerates the due date of the loan to the date the home is sold. A due-on-sale clause is one variety of *acceleration clause*, the purpose of which is to *call* an existing loan (legally demand its payment in full) because of some act of the borrower, such as selling the collateral, e.g., the home.

due process of law The requirement that legal proceedings (including arrest, civil and criminal trials, and punishment) comply with the U.S. Constitution and other applicable substantive and procedural laws.

durable power of attorney A document authorizing another person to make health-care (and sometimes other) decisions for a person even after he/she has become incapacitated. See also "power of attorney."

duress Any threat of, or actual, physical harm that deprives a person of the freedom of will to choose and decide.

duty, legal The obligation enforceable in court to recognize and respect the person, property, and rights of others. Legal duty is the reciprocal of *legal right*.

easement The right to use the real property of another for a limited purpose (e.g., access to a beach or public road).

economic strike A strike in which workers seek a change in wages, hours, and/or conditions of employment. See also "unfair labor practice strike."

Electronic Fund Transfer Act Federal law that authorizes financial institutions to transfer funds through accounts without the use of paper instruments (e.g., checks or drafts).

emancipation Parental consent to a minor to handle her or his own financial affairs. It normally also ends parental duties of supported care.

embezzlement The crime of stealing property that, before the theft, was lawfully in the possession of the thief (e.g., when a cashier steals money from the company cash register).

eminent domain The constitutional power of the government to take private property for public use upon payment of just compensation.

employee A person who agrees by contract to perform work as directed and controlled by an employer in exchange for compensation (usually consisting of wages or salary and fringe benefits).

Employee Stock Ownership Plans (ESOPs) Plans encouraged by federal income tax benefits whereby employees become owners of stock in the corporation that employs them.

Employment Act of 1946 Federal law committing the federal government to encourage employment for all persons able to, willing to, and seeking to work.

employment at will Typical employment contract under which both the employee and the employer may end the relationship at any time without liability (other than payment for services already rendered, generally).

Employment Retirement Income Security Act (ERISA) Federal legislation regulating private pension plans that supplement social security.

enabling statute A statute that authorizes an administrative agency to perform specified actions. The statute that creates the agency typically empowers it to act.

enact To establish a law by proper vote of members of the legislative branch of government and (normally) with executive approval (i.e., by signature of the president or responsible governor).

encroachment Construction (e.g., building or fence) or vegetation (e.g., tree limb or ground cover) that physically intrudes upon or overlaps the real property of another. An encroachment can be a *nuisance*, enjoinable by court judgment.

endorsements, policy Clauses that supplement standard policies of insurance. May be printed forms added to policies.

entrapment A defense to criminal charges if the crime was induced by police encouragement, but not if police merely provided an opportunity for the accused to commit the criminal act.

entrepreneur One who organizes, owns, and manages a business.

environmental impact statement (EIS) A report required by law before any major federal action that might affect the environment can be taken. The report analyzes the effects of the proposed development or action on the surrounding natural and fabricated environment in accordance with the National Policy Act of 1969.

environmental law Federal, state, and local statutory and administrative laws designed to protect the environment.

Equal Credit Opportunity Act of 1974 Federal law that forbids discrimination in the extension of credit because of sex, marital status, race, or other specified qualities of the applicant.

Equal Employment Opportunity Act (EEOA) of 1972 Federal law that created the Equal Employment Opportunity Commission.

Equal Employment Opportunity Commission (EEOC) Federal agency created by the Equal Employment Opportunity Act of 1972 that authorized the federal government to use its resources to enforce the Civil Rights Act of 1964 for private persons.

Equal Pay Act (1963) Federal law that mandates the same wage or salary for women and men for equal work done in jobs performed under similar conditions. Different wages are permitted when justified by such factors as seniority, quality and quantity of output, and any basis (such as night shift) other than gender.

equal-pay laws Statutes that prohibit discrimination in wages for equal work because of the gender of the employee. The federal Equal Pay Act of 1963 was the first law of this type.

equal-protection clause The clause in the Fourteenth Amendment to the U.S. Constitution declaring that "no state shall . . . deny to any person within its jurisdiction the equal protection of the laws." The thrust of the mandate is to prohibit unreasonable discrimination. This clause is the basis for much civil rights litigation by minorities and women.

equitable distribution The division and distribution by the court of marital property to the spouses upon divorce or dissolution—not applicable in community-property states, where each spouse owns one-half of all community property.

equitable maxims General rules applied by courts to cases in equity (e.g., "Those who seek equity, must do equity" and "Equity aids the vigilant and not those who sleep on their rights").

equitable owner An owner who has possession and use of the property although someone else may retain the legal title.

equitable title Title possessed by the beneficial owner of goods who has possession and use, as in installment (on-credit) sales where the seller retains the legal title as security until paid in full.

equity The net interest of a homeowner in the property, representing the excess of the value of the property over loans or other legal claims outstanding against it.

equity, action in A civil trial held without a jury when relief sought by the plaintiff is equitable in nature, such as an injunction, or a divorce or dissolution of a marriage.

escrow [from Old French for "roll of writings"] An arrangement common in real estate transactions whereby the buyer and seller (and/or the borrower and lender) designate a neutral third party as an agent to carry out instructions for gathering and distributing documents and funds as necessary.

escrow agent A person paid to perform all the administrative tasks necessary to close a real estate escrow. Escrow agents are similar to stakeholders, but are not fiduciaries. They merely carry out instructions received from buyers and sellers, who cannot rely upon escrow agents for information about their real estate transactions.

estate The totality of interest(s) that a person has in property.

estate planning The process of arranging a person's property and estate, taking into account the laws of wills, taxes, insurance, property, and trusts so as to gain maximum benefit of all laws while carrying out the person's wishes for use of the property during his or her lifetime and disposition of the property upon his or her death.

estate tax A tax imposed by the federal government and some states on the privilege of giving property to another person after death of the donor.

ethics Norms of just and morally correct conduct.

euthanasia The act of allowing one to die by withholding extraordinary medical measures, or putting to death by painless means a person suffering from an incurable disease or condition of an extremely painful nature. Euthanasia is also called *mercy killing*.

evict The act of expelling a tenant from rented premises.

eviction, legal The legal process by which landlords expel tenants who are in breach of their lease contracts. Because eviction is considered a draconian remedy, legal proceedings to evict require prior notice to the tenant, who must be given opportunity to be heard in court.

eviction, wrongful Any unlawful conduct by the landlord designed to evict a tenant for any reason. An example is changing locks on doors.

evidence Everything presented by disputing parties and witnesses that the "finder of fact" is entitled to consider in arriving at a determination of the facts.

exclusionary rule The court-made rule that precludes the use in criminal court proceedings of any evidence improperly obtained by the prosecution.

exclusive-agency listing Employment contract between an owner of real property and a licensed agent in which the owner may find a buyer and sell the property without liability for payment of commission, but must pay the listing agent if that agent—or any other licensed agent—finds the buyer.

exclusive listing Employment contract in which the owner of real property agrees to pay a licensed agent a certain commission regardless of who finds the buyer to whom the property is sold. Also called an *exclusive right to sell*.

exculpatory clause Provision in a contractual agreement (e.g., a lease) by which a party agrees not to hold the other party responsible for his or her negligence.

executed contract A contract that has been fully performed by both parties.

executive branch The government officials responsible for execution or effectuation of constitutional mandates and statutes enacted by the legislative branch. See "judicial branch" and "legislative branch."

executive clemency A formal act of kindness, mercy, and leniency by a governor, or by the president, in commuting a criminal penalty or granting a pardon.

executive order (or directive) A lawful order by the president of the United States, the governor of a state, or the head of a local government given without the concurrence of the legislative branch. An example is the 1990 executive order of President George H. Bush calling certain units of the U.S. military reserve to active duty in the Middle East for the Persian Gulf War.

executive privilege The right of the president of the United States to refuse to disclose information because of national security considerations, provided that there is no overriding reason for disclosure as determined by judicial review.

executor A person named by a testator to dispose of her or his estate after death as directed in the will and in compliance with law.

executory contract A valid contract in which something remains to be done by either or both parties.

exemplary damages See "punitive damages."

exempt assets Property that a debtor can protect against seizure resulting from execution of judgment by a judgment creditor or a trustee in a bankruptcy distribution.

ex parte [Latin for "for/with one party"] Term usually used in conjunction with some legal action occurring after only one side of the dispute has been heard.

expert witness Anyone qualified by knowledge and skill, experience, training or education to offer a credible and useful opinion upon some material issue in a trial.

ex post facto **law** [Latin for "after the fact"] A statute that retroactively makes previously lawful conduct a crime. Such a statute is unconstitutional.

express contract An agreement stated in words, spoken or written.

express powers The powers specifically delegated to the U.S. government by the Constitution.

express warranty A warranty given by a seller to a buyer orally or in writing.

extended coverage title insurance Coverage for title defects as described within the American Land and Title Insurance form of insurance contract.

extortion The crime of obtaining money or other property by wrongful use of actual or threatened force or violence to the victim or the victim's family. The threat may be to accuse the victim of a crime or to expose any secret tending to subject the victim to hatred, contempt, or ridicule.

fair comment A privilege that legitimates certain statements on matters of public concern that might otherwise be considered defamatory. See "privileged communication."

Fair Credit Billing Act of 1974 A federal law that permits users of credit cards to challenge correctness of charges, without penalty.

Fair Credit Reporting Act of 1970 A federal law that enables consumers to check and correct credit information about themselves in the files of credit-reporting companies.

Fair Debt Collection Practices Act of 1977 A federal law that outlaws certain unreasonably harsh collection practices previously used by professional debt collectors.

Fair Labor Standards Act of 1938 (FLSA) A New Deal statute that mandated worker protections, including the maximum 8-hour workday, 40-hour workweek, and protection of child labor.

false arrest Taking custody of another, without proper legal authority, to be held or restrained in order to answer a civil claim or criminal charge. Because this action restrains the person's liberty, it is also *false imprisonment*.

false imprisonment The wrongful restraint of the personal liberty of another.

Family and Medical Leave Act of 1993 (FMLS) A federal law requiring employers with 50 or more employees to grant employees leave for certain family purposes related to child care and family health.

family-purpose doctrine A law in some states that holds the owner of a motor vehicle vicariously responsible whenever a member of his or her immediate family or household drives and a third party is injured because of the negligence of the driver.

family-settlement agreement A law of probate in some states allowing family members to agree to settle among themselves the distribution of a decedent's assets.

Fannie Mae The slang expression for the Federal National Mortgage Association, a corporation created by the National Housing Act to establish a secondary mortgage market by purchasing existing home-purchase mortgages. The cash paid for existing mortgages thus becomes available to lenders for new mortgage loans.

featherbedding Causing or attempting to cause an employer to pay for services by employees that are not actually performed or are not to be performed, such as requiring unneeded extra workers (e.g., brakemen on modern trains).

federal Refers to the U.S. government and its activities. The United States is a federation of 50 sovereign states.

Federal Housing Administration (FHA) A federal agency in the U.S. Department of Housing and Urban Development (HUD). The FHA insures (guarantees) the repayment of home-purchase mortgages and provides housing subsidies, thus making financing available to home buyers, and to owners and developers of housing projects.

Federal Insurance Contribution Act (FICA) A federal law authorizing a tax to finance social security benefits (unemployment, disability, retirement, and survivors' benefits payments). FICA deductions are automatically made by employers from employees' paychecks.

federalism A government consisting of a union of states under an umbrella of federal government.

federal law Includes the U.S. Constitution, statutes enacted by Congress, international treaties, Presidential orders, rules promulgated by federal agencies, and decisions of federal courts.

Federal Register The official publication of the federal government for promulgating all agency rules and regulations.

Federal Reporter Volumes containing decisions and opinions of U.S. courts of appeals.

Federal Savings and Loan Insurance Corporation (FSLIC) The federal agency charged with assuring the collectibility of deposits and savings accounts (up to $100,000 per covered account) in savings and loan associations (S&Ls). The failure of hundreds of these associations led Congress to create and fund the Resolution Trust Corporation in 1990, an agency responsible for liquidating and selling off insolvent S&Ls.

Federal Trade Commission (FTC) A federal agency charged with regulating business to prevent unfair competition and to protect consumers against false advertising and other unfair trade practices.

fee (or fee simple) Complete ownership of real property. A fee simple is distinguished, for example, from a life estate, which is ownership limited in its duration.

felon Person convicted of a felony.

felony A serious crime (such as murder) that is punishable by death or imprisonment for more than one year.

felony-murder rule A rule in some states mandating that all participants in a dangerous felony are guilty of murder in the first degree if a killing occurs during its commission (e.g., the driver of a getaway car in a bank robbery where one of the robbers was killed by a guard).

fictitious name A name other than the true name(s) [i.e., the forename(s) and family surname(s)] used to identify a sole proprietorship or partnership. State statutes generally require filing with the county clerk the true name(s) along with the assumed name(s) to inform the public of the facts.

fidelity bond A bond insuring against losses caused by a fraudulent performance of duties by a personal representative (for example, an executor or guardian).

fiduciary relationship A relationship between two persons wherein one has an obligation to perform services with scrupulous good faith and honesty (e.g., an attorney toward a client, a trustee toward a beneficiary in a trust, and a partner toward another partner in a partnership have a fiduciary relationship).

field sobriety test A simple test used to determine the reactions of a motor vehicle driver who is suspected of driving under the influence of alcohol or another drug. The test is administered at the scene of the arrest.

financial-responsibility law A statute requiring that after an automobile accident of specified severity, any driver not covered by insurance must post specified cash or equivalent bond (e.g., $35,000 in California) or lose his or her driver's license and vehicle registration until released from the potential liability for damages.

financial statement A written summary of the financial condition or operating results of a business (most commonly the balance sheet and income statement).

financing package A presentation of prearranged loan terms that are available for qualified (in terms of creditworthiness) borrowers who desire to purchase a home.

firm offer A written offer signed by a merchant that remains open for a specified time, up to three months. It is binding even though the offeree does not pay for the right (i.e., the option to buy the goods at the stated price).

first degree A measurement in law of the degree of culpability (blameworthiness) of the perpetrator of a crime. A perpetrator of first-degree murder, for example, is guilty of the highest culpability known in the law.

first-degree murder Premeditated murder perpetrated with malice aforethought; e.g., by an explosive device or poison, or while lying in wait, or during commission of a specified dangerous felony such as robbery, rape, or arson.

fixed-rate mortgage A traditional home-purchase mortgage in which the interest rate and the monthly payment do not fluctuate during the life of the loan.

fixer-upper A house that needs extensive work and repair, usually of a cosmetic nature, before it can be sold at a higher price. When major structural repairs are necessary, the substantial costs may not be covered or recouped through the rise in its fair market value.

for cause See "challenge of a juror."

forcible eviction An illegal eviction technique by which a landlord confronts a tenant, forcibly removes all personal items, and changes locks on the unit.

foreclosure Process by which secured real property is confiscated at the direction of the unpaid creditor and sold to the highest bidder. Cash proceeds go to retire or reduce the unpaid debt. There are two kinds of foreclosure. Judicial foreclosure is accomplished through court proceedings much as other litigation. Nonjudicial foreclosure, the more commonly occurring, is accomplished without resort to courts or lawyers. It takes place through a private sale conducted by a trustee under the direction of the unpaid creditor.

foreclosure, judicial The forced sale, following a court proceeding, of an owner's real property to raise money to satisfy the creditor's claim for the unpaid balance of the loan that is in default.

foreclosure, nonjudicial The involuntary sale, without court proceedings, of an owner's real property to raise money to satisfy the unpaid balance of the loan that is in default.

foreclosure sale Sale of a debtor's real property to raise cash with which to reduce or retire the unpaid debt. A foreclosure sale may be of two varieties, by a court official following judicial foreclosure or by a trustee following nonjudicial foreclosure.

foreseeability The ability of a reasonably prudent person to anticipate in advance that injury to person and/or property is likely to result from a specified act or failure to act. Foreseeability is an essential element of the tort of negligence.

formal contract Agreement that must use prescribed language.

formal will A typewritten or computer-printed will executed in compliance with law and signed or acknowledged by the testator in the presence of witnesses who also sign the document.

form prescribed by law Any written expression or particular language that may be required for a valid, fully enforceable contract (e.g., a promissory note).

franchise (a) The right obtained by a person or group through contract with a manufacturer or distributor to sell a branded item in a given location. (b) The right granted by government to conduct certain activities (such as the sale of gas or electricity throughout a county) as monopolies. (c) The right to vote for candidates for public office.

franchisee A person or group who obtains a franchise from a manufacturer or distributor-franchisor.

franchisor A manufacturer or distributor who grants a franchise to a franchisee.

fraud A knowingly false representation of a material fact, made through words or conduct, with intent to deceive a victim, who is induced to contract in reliance on the lie, and who is thereby injured. Fraud is also called *deceit*.

Freddie Mac The slang expression for the Federal Home Loan Mortgage Corporation, a corporation that participates in the secondary mortgage market by buying and selling conventional, FHA, and VA (Veteran's Administration) mortgages.

Freedom of Information Act (FOIA) A federal law requiring the federal government to disclose most public "records" to "any person" on request.

fringe benefits Direct and indirect compensation, other than in money wages, to employees by an employer for services rendered. Examples include health and life insurance, vacations, and stock purchase plans.

full cash value The appraised value of real property determined for the purpose of calculating the annual property tax.

future interest Any possessory or ownership interest in real property that will *vest* (become perfected) at some future date. For example, the owners of the remainder interest following a life estate have future interests in the property that will vest upon the death of the life tenant.

garnishment A legal proceeding in which a plaintiff-creditor gets a court order compelling a third party (such as the employer of the defendant-debtor) to pay monies earned by the defendant to the plaintiff. Garnishment is also called *attachment*.

general damages Amount awarded by a court to pay the plaintiff for nonmonetary losses (e.g., pain and suffering) that resulted from an injury, without reference to any special circumstances of the plaintiff. General damages are a type of compensatory damages.

general jurisdiction Authorization of a court to hear and decide virtually any type of case occurring within the political boundaries of the geographical area in which it is located.

general partner A partner who manages the firm, shares equally with other general partners in its profits and losses (unless otherwise agreed), and is liable to third parties without limit for partnership debts.

general partnership A partnership in which all members are general partners. See also "limited partnership."

generation-skipping trust A trust created whereby the settlors of the first generation (parents) arrange for their child(ren) (the second generation) to receive the income while they are alive, but not the principal, which is reserved for the grandchild(ren) (the third generation) after the death of the second generation.

genuine assent When consent of both parties to be bound by a contract is freely given and is not negated by fraud, duress, undue influence, and/or certain mistakes.

gerrymandering The intentional drawing of a political district by a political party that is in power so as to give itself, or a racial minority, a majority of voters in as many districts as possible while concentrating the voting power of the other party into as few districts as possible. With this technique, an incumbent party may control a legislature even though it generates only the same number of votes as the other party. In some cases, the result would be the same even if the incumbent party generates fewer votes for its candidates.

gift tax A tax imposed on donors at the federal and state levels on the value of certain gifts made by living persons, with the exception of gifts to charities.

Ginnie Mae The slang expression for the Government National Mortgage Association, a federal corporation that purchases mortgages in the secondary mortgage market.

good faith A general obligation imposed by the Uniform Commercial Code on both sellers and buyers to practice honesty in business conduct and contracts.

goods Tangible, movable personal property.

Good Samaritan Reference to a Biblical story where a person (a Samaritan) came to the aid of a stranger in desperate need. Refers to statutes today that protect volunteers from liability for ordinary negligence while aiding persons in need.

goodwill, business Intangible asset of a business that is developed through supplier confidence and customer satisfaction with sales and service, stimulating future sales and profits.

Government-in-the-Sunshine Act A federal law requiring that most meetings of federal agencies be open for public observation and that advance notice be given of agency meetings, listing the expected topics of discussion.

grace period A period of time during which a tardy payment on a debt, a home-purchase mortgage or rent will be accepted without penalty. The grace period is the time between the due date of a payment and the delinquent date, following which a penalty may be assessed.

graduated-payment mortgage A home-purchase mortgage and promissory note that features artificially low monthly payments for the initial few years as an inducement for borrowers whose incomes and creditworthiness are expected to improve in the future.

grandfather clause Any provision in a statute that exempts a specified class of persons from some change or new requirement in the law.

grand jury An appointed body of citizens formed both to investigate the operations of government and to issue indictments against persons suspected of criminal conduct. Indictments are one

procedure to instigate either state or federal criminal proceedings.

grand theft Theft of personal property of substantial value, as declared by statute. Because of the substantial value of the stolen property, grand theft is a felony. However, sometimes theft of a specific type of property is grand theft regardless of its value, as, for example, theft of a horse or hunting dog.

grant deed A document that conveys the ownership of real property, and impliedly warrants that the grantor has not previously conveyed the property to another and that the property is free from undisclosed encumbrances.

guardian A person appointed by the court (in a guardianship proceeding) to supervise and take care of the person and/or the estate of another.

guardian ad litem [Latin for `for the suit"] A guardian appointed by the court to prosecute or defend any action for a minor as party.

guardianship A court-established arrangement whereby an adult guardian is appointed to take care of the person and/or the estate of a minor.

guest A person who rides for free in another person's vehicle.

guest statute Law that pertains to guests of a driver of a motor vehicle. In some states a guest cannot sue the driver if injured, unless the driver is guilty of intoxication, willful misconduct, or gross negligence that causes the accident and resulting injury or death. In other states a guest may sue the driver for ordinary negligence.

habeas corpus [Latin for "you have the body"] A legal writ or court order to release a prisoner from allegedly unlawful confinement so that he or she can appear before a court for proper remedial action. The petitioner seeks release.

habitability, implied warranty of See "implied warranty of habitability."

hate crime Any crime the motivation for which was persecution of a victim because of race, religion, sexual orientation, or political beliefs. Hate crimes usually result in enhancement of the penalty otherwise imposed. In some instances, hate crimes are treated as separate offenses with specified penalties.

hate speech Words spoken, written, or symbolized (e.g., by placing burning crosses on private lawns) that express irrational and false ideas that insult and demean certain persons or classes or persons. Such speech, often illegal, may encourage violent attacks on innocent people.

hearsay evidence Evidence not based on personal observation or knowledge of the witness, but consisting of repetition of what someone else has said. Hearsay is generally not admissible to prove a fact, but exceptions exist.

hedonic damages Monetary damages for the future loss of the pleasures of life suffered by a deceased or severely injured victim.

heirs Persons designated by law to receive the estate of a decedent who leaves no will (i.e., dies intestate).

holder of mortgage The present owner of a mortgage loan, to whom monthly payments are made by the homeowner. Mortgage loans are often transferred from one holder to another investor.

holographic will An unwitnessed will. States that allow such a will usually require it to be written in longhand by the testator, signed, and dated.

home equity loan A loan for any purpose, (e.g., to pay off credit card balances that carry higher interest rates, or to pay for college tuition, a new car, a vacation, or home improvements) that is collateralized by a mortgage on the borrower's home. Although the mortgage securing a home equity loan typically incurs higher interest than a home-purchase mortgage, its interest is deductible from federal and state income taxes, which helps explain its popularity.

home inspection services Professional businesses that inspect residential properties to discover any defects that might influence the decision of a prospective buyer either to buy or to offer a lower price. They can also alert prospective sellers to needed repairs.

homeowners' association (HOA) Association of people who own homes, condominiums, or cooperatives in a given area, formed for the purpose of improving or maintaining the quality of that area. HOAs are often formed by the developers/builders of planned unit developments to manage and maintain the property in which all owners have a common, undivided interest. Such associations commonly supervise the property deed CC&Rs.

homeowner's policy of insurance Insurance that typically covers losses of the homeowner's property from specified casualties, such as fire and water damage, as well as the possible liability of the owner for specified damages he or she may cause to another person through negligent behavior (other than with a motor vehicle or boat). A casualty-loss homeowner's policy (e.g., coverage of fire losses) does not necessarily include liability protection for the homeowner, however.

homestead exemption An exemption for the homeowner from the valid claims of creditors who otherwise could take substantially all of the debtor's assets in satisfaction of debts. The exemption protects a specified amount of the equity in the homeowner's residence from levy and execution by a creditor.

homicide The killing of a human being by another human being.

hostile environment Conduct by others in the workplace that has the purpose or effect of unrea-sonably interfering with an individual's work performance or creating an intimidating, hostile, or offensive working environment.

hung jury A jury that cannot reach a verdict because of inability or unwillingness of a sufficient number of jurors to agree on disputed facts.

immaterial evidence Evidence that is not important or essential to the proof of facts in dispute. Counsel may successfully object to its introduction by the opponent.

immunity from prosecution The granting by a court of freedom from liability for a specified crime. A person who has been granted this immunity possesses no privilege against self-incrimination and may be compelled to testify about the event in question.

impeach (a) To discredit, dispute, disparage, or contradict a witness's testimony. (b) Proceeding against a political figure for a crime or misfeasance before the proper political forum.

implied covenant of quiet enjoyment (a) An implied obligation of a landlord to maintain reasonably comfortable living conditions for the tenant in the rented premises, without disturbance by hostile claimants. (b) An implied promise by the seller of real property that he or she will defend against claims or lawsuits by others who may challenge the buyer's title to the property.

implied-in-fact contract Contractual agreement manifested by conduct or body language (e.g., purchase of items from vendors in noisy stadiums during sporting events).

implied-in-law contract Not a true contract, but an obligation imposed on one party to prevent unjust enrichment of another. Also called "quasi-contract."

implied powers The authority of Congress to make such laws as are "necessary and proper" for effective performance of duties under its powers that are expressly granted.

implied warranty A warranty implied by actions or law whether or not it is specifically mentioned in a contract. See also "warranty."

implied warranty of habitability (a) An implied guarantee in a lease that there are no concealed defects in the rented premises existing at the beginning of the lease term. (b) An implied obligation upon a landlord to maintain leased premises in a condition fit for use and enjoyment by the tennant through the term of the lease.

impossibility When it is impossible through no fault of the obligor to perform an obligation as promised in a contract.

impound account An account held by a mortgage lender in which to accumulate sufficient funds to pay all annual property taxes and property and liability insurance premiums. The funds are taken from the borrower's monthly mortgage payment and accumulated until the periodic taxes and insurance premiums are due.

incapacity   Lack of legal capacity to make important decisions. Minority is an example of incapacity to make contracts.

incest   Sexual intercourse between relatives who are *lineals* (grandparents, parents, children, etc.) or *collaterals* (brothers/sisters, aunts/uncles, etc.) of those degrees of closeness in which marriage is prohibited by state law.

incidental damages   Amount awarded by a court after a breach of a sales contract to cover reasonable expenses incurred by a party (e.g., to inspect, transport, and care for goods rightfully rejected by a buyer).

incompetent evidence   Evidence that the court will not permit counsel to present during trial because of some defect in the qualification of the witness or in the nature of the evidence.

indemnification   Payment by one person (e.g., an employer) to another person (e.g., an employee) to make up for a loss suffered by the latter in performance of the job.

independent contractor   A person who is hired to do a specific job, and who retains control over how that job is done.

independent regulatory agency   An administrative body empowered to regulate some policy area led by officials who cannot be dismissed by the president of the United States except for good cause.

indeterminate sentence law   A statute that provides for a range (such as one to five years) rather than a specific period of incarceration for a crime, the exact time to be determined by a designated authority after confinement begins.

indict   The act by a grand jury of declaring, after an evidentiary hearing, that there is probable cause that a named person has committed a specific crime and should stand trial to determine his or her guilt or innocence. The official declaration of a grand jury is an *indictment*.

indictment   An accusation of felony filed by a grand jury. See also "information."

Individual Retirement Account (IRA)   Federally authorized private pension plans supplementing social security whereby qualified employees contribute a certain percentage of their income, tax-free, to their retirement accounts until retirement. The money is then normally distributed in installments beginning by April 1 following the year the employee reaches the age 70½, when it is subject to the personal income tax.

information   An accusation of a criminal offense. Unlike an indictment by a grand jury, it is issued following a preliminary hearing before a judge who decides if the defendant should be required to stand trial or be released.

informed consent   Agreement of a patient to undergo surgical procedures or administration of experimental drugs after full disclosure of the risk involved and available alternatives.

infraction   Any minor crime (e.g., parking violation) that is not punishable by incarceration, but only by fine. Accordingly, trial by jury is not required or permitted.

inheritance tax   A tax imposed by most states on the privilege of receiving property from a decedent.

initiative   An electoral process for making new statutes or changing the constitution by filing appropriate formal petitions to be voted upon by legislature (and governor) or by the total electorate. The initiative is not available in all states.

injunction   An order of a court of equity forbidding an action that is considered injurious to the plaintiff. Injunctions are used when dollar damages are unavailable or would be an inadequate remedy (e.g., to restrain the scope of picketing when violence is threatened in a strike).

in loco parentis   [Latin for "in the place of a parent"] Term meaning that a person other than a parent is charged with a parent's rights, duties, and responsibilities.

in personam **jurisdiction**   The power of a court over a person, usually obtained by personal service of a summons on the defendant while he or she is within the boundaries of the state in which the suit is commenced.

in propria persona   [Latin for "in one's own proper person"] Term meaning the person represents herself or himself in a legal action without the appearance of an attorney.

inquisitorial system   A legal system used in some countries that allows the judge to investigate, question witnesses, and seek out evidence during a trial.

in rem **jurisdiction**   The power of a court to declare rights against the world rather than solely against the named defendant(s). If the legal question involves ownership of real property located in Alaska, for example, the court with authority to hear the case would be the appropriate trial court in Alaska.

insanity, legal   Mental disease or defect that causes the accused to lack substantial and sufficient capacity either to appreciate the criminality (wrongfulness) of his or her conduct or to conform his or her conduct to the requirements of the law. Definitions of insanity vary among the states.

in severalty   Form of ownership under which a sole person owns an interest in real property. The term is confusing because it appears to be related to the word *several*. Actually, it relates to the word *separate*.

installment land contract   A method of selling real property in which the seller retains title during the years that the buyer in possession is making monthly payments. Equitable title passes to the buyer after all or most payments have been made. This contract is also called a *contract for deed*.

insurable interest A sufficient interest in property to where its loss or destruction would cause an economic loss to the owner or possessor. Required to enforce an insurance policy.

intangible property Property recognized by law even though it has no physical existence. Warranty rights under a contract to buy an automobile and ownership of shares in a corporation are examples of intangible personal property. The legal right of the telephone company to bury and maintain telephone lines across your property is an intangible real property interest, called an *easement*.

intentional infliction of mental distress Outrageous conduct that causes mental, if not immediate physical, suffering by the victim.

intentional tort Where the tortfeasor deliberately performs a wrongful act that injures an innocent victim.

interest The price, usually expressed as an annualized rate (percentage), for use of a sum of money (principal) obtained from a lender.

interference with an economically advantageous relationship When a tortfeasor knowingly and wrongfully interferes with the promised performance of another person's contract. The term may also refer to violations of antitrust laws and to other unfair competitive practices.

international law The branch of law governing relations between and among sovereign nations.

interpleader A legal proceeding to resolve conflicting claims (e.g., to funds in an escrow account).

interrogatories A form of discovery used by attorneys, consisting of written questions directed to a party or witness who is expected to reply with written answers under oath.

inter-spousal immunity The traditional ban on lawsuits between spouses to avoid possible resulting disruption of family harmony. The modern trend is to allow such lawsuits.

interstate commerce Commercial trading or transportation between or among two or more states. The U.S. Constitution (Article I) delegates to Congress power to regulate such commerce.

intervening cause A cause of an accident or other injury that legally excuses the wrongdoer who originally sets a series of events in motion.

intervenor A neutral third party who assists parties in resolving their private conflicts (e.g., *conciliator* or *mediator*) or acts as a decision maker in such conflicts (e.g., *arbitrator*).

inter vivos [Latin for "between the living"] A term applied to a gift or trust. An *inter vivos gift* is made from one living person to another. This is a way to transfer title to personal property. An *inter vivos*

trust is created during the life of the trustor to take effect during her or his lifetime. Such a trust contrasts with *a testamentary trust*, which takes effect upon the death of the trustor or testator.

intestate (or intestacy) The status of a person who has died without leaving a valid will.

intestate law Statutory prescription for distribution, among heirs, of the estate of a decedent who has died leaving no will.

intrastate commerce Commercial trading or transportation within any one state. Under the Tenth Amendment of the U.S. Constitution, the power to regulate intrastate commerce is reserved to the respective concerned states.

invidious discrimination Discrimination by a government or private business against a person based on ethnicity, religion, or national origin, for which there is a legal remedy.

invitee One who enters another's land with the permission (implied or express) of the owner or occupier, for a matter of business benefiting the owner or occupier.

involuntary manslaughter The unintentional killing of another person because of gross negligence, or as a result of dangerous and unlawful conduct (e.g., killing a pedestrian while speeding).

irrelevant evidence Evidence that does not relate to or have a bearing upon a question of fact in dispute during a trial. The objection of "Irrelevant" may be made to a question during a trial.

irresistible impulse The motivation whereby an accused, because of a diseased mind, could not avoid committing a criminal act even if he or she knew it was wrong. An acceptable test of legal insanity in a few states.

irrevocable trust A trust that cannot be terminated or revoked by the trustor who created it.

issue arbitration Only part of a dispute is submitted to arbitration and thereafter decided by the arbitrator.

joint and several liability Responsibility both together and individually. Joint and several liability applies in contracts (as when two or more persons sign a promissory note as makers) and in torts (as when two or more wrongdoers cause the injury together). Of course, the plaintiff is entitled to only one full recovery of his or her total damages.

joint custody Responsibility shared by both parents, following a divorce, annulment, or separation, to guide and support their child(ren).

joint tenancy A method of co-ownership of property by two or more persons. Upon the death of any co-owner, his or her percentage interest goes to the surviving joint tenant(s) regardless of the decedent's last will. This right of survivorship is the basic incident of joint-tenancy ownership.

joint tortfeasors Two or more persons who together commit a tort.

judge The official who presides over a trial court. See also "court."

judgment The final determination or decision of the court as to the rights and duties of the parties in a lawsuit.

judgment creditor A person who has won a judgment but has not been fully paid.

judgment debtor A person against whom a judgment for payment of money has been entered but who has not yet made or completed that payment.

judgment non obstante veredicto **(or** *n.o.v.***)** [Latin for "notwithstanding the verdict"] A decision by a judge that overrules the verdict of the jury.

judgment-proof Financial condition of a person who lacks the assets to pay any judgment rendered against him or her.

judicial activist A judge or court that is readily willing to announce or apply new rules of law through interpretation without regard to precedents or legal trends.

judicial branch Judges who are the government officials responsible for determining the constitutionality of legislative and executive actions and adjudicating rights and duties of persons involved in disputes. They interpret and apply the laws. See also "executive branch" and "legislative branch."

judicial foreclosure See "foreclosure."

judicial process The administration of law by the courts.

judicial review Power of the U.S. Supreme Court to declare unconstitutional an act of Congress, a presidential order, or a state law.

jurisdiction The power of a court to decide a controversy and to award appropriate relief. Jurisdiction may also refer to the geographic area in which the court has authority and the types of cases it has power to hear.

jury A group of men and women selected according to pre-established procedures to ensure lack of bias, who are sworn under oath to inquire of certain matters of fact, and declare the truth based on evidence presented to them. A jury is also referred to as a trier of fact.

jury, trial A group, usually consisting of 12 adults, but sometimes a smaller number, who are selected and sworn to review evidence in civil and criminal trials, and to return a verdict consistent with their view of the evidence. Also *petit* [French for "small"] *jury*.

jury deliberation A thoughtful and thorough discussion by a jury of the facts of a case in light of the applicable law before determining their verdict.

jury instructions Rules of law and charges provided by the judge to the jury for guidance in reaching a verdict. The instructions include essential facts that must be proved by the prevailing party; they also state the law applicable to the cause of action.

jury nullification The power of a jury in a criminal trial to disregard the law and unanimously find the defendant innocent, although there is ample evidence to support a verdict of guilty. Although a judge can set aside a guilty verdict in a criminal case, the judge cannot reverse a finding of innocent. A judge can order a mistrial upon a showing of jury misconduct, but refusing to find an accused guilty is not juror misconduct. "The jury has the power to bring in a verdict in the teeth of both law and facts."

justices Judges in appellate courts.

juvenile court A court with special jurisdiction of a parental nature over delinquent, dependent, and neglected children.

Keogh Retirement Plan Federally authorized private pension plans whereby self-employed persons may contribute a percentage of their earnings, tax-free, to a trust account until retirement.

kidnapping The crime of unlawful seizure and movement of a victim from one place to another against his or her will.

Labor Management Relations Act See "National Labor Management Relations Act of 1947."

Labor-Management Reporting and Disclosure Act of 1959 (Landrum-Griffin Act) Federal law that mandates open, democratic internal government of unions.

Labor Relations Act See "National Labor Relations Act of 1935."

laches, doctrine of A doctrine that bars *stale* (old) lawsuits in civil cases in courts of equity. The doctrine of laches may be applied by the court to bar a claim when the petitioner has unreasonably delayed his or her pursuit of the claim, and this delay has prejudiced or harmed the case of the respondent. The doctrine of laches may bar a claim that is otherwise timely under the *statute of limitations*.

land contract An agreement by an owner of real property to sell to a buyer who takes possession immediately but does not obtain legal title until all or most payments have been made to the seller. See also "installment land contract."

landlord The owner of residential property who leases it to a tenant, or renter, in exchange for rent.

landlord's lien A statutory lien in favor of an unpaid landlord that provides a mechanism for storage of the tenant's belongings and ultimate sale of them to pay unpaid rent (plus storage costs).

larceny The crime of stealing property from another who is not then present. Larceny is also called *theft*.

larceny by trick Theft accomplished by deceit or subterfuge wherein the victim turns over property, especially money, to the perpetrator.

last will See "will."

law General principles and detailed rules of human conduct that are enforceable in civil and criminal courts and by administrative agencies.

lawyer See "attorney at law."

lease A contract, usually written, by which the relationship of landlord and tenant is created. Leases are also called *rental agreements*.

leasehold The legal interest a tenant has in residential property leased from the landlord. A leasehold is usually created by a written contract called a *lease*.

legacy A disposition of personal property by will. Also called a "bequest."

legal assistants Persons qualified through education, training, and/or work experience to be employed or retained by a lawyer, law office, government agency, or other entity in a capacity or function that involves the performance, under the ultimate direction and supervision of an attorney, of specifically delegated substantive legal work. This work, for the most part, requires sufficient knowledge of legal concepts that, absent such assistants, the attorney would perform the task. Legal assistants are also called "paralegals."

legal owner An owner who has legal title, for example, as security for repayment of a loan or payment of the purchase price of real property or personal property, such as an automobile. Legal title is transferred to the equitable owner when the debt is paid in full.

legal separation A court order permitting spouses to live apart with necessary related orders for child custody and child support, support of the wife (or husband), and division of property (as in dissolution), but the marriage endures.

legal service plans Insurance plans designed to make legal services available to members of unions or other organizations, such as business firms.

Legal Services Corporation (LSC) A federally funded corporation that distributes federal tax dollars to state programs that provide legal assistance in noncriminal proceedings to persons financially unable to afford such services.

legislative branch The government officials who are responsible for enacting statutory laws. See also "executive branch" and "judicial branch."

legislative veto A legislative device whereby Congress may include within a statute a means for Congressional review of the executive branch's implementation of the law.

legitimate Status of a person who is the issue of his or her natural, married parents. The child of an unmarried mother is *illegitimate*.

legitimation Irrevocable acknowledgment by a natural father that, although not married to the mother of a child, he is the male parent.

lemon Something, usually a product such as an automobile, that proves to be unsatisfactory because of serious defects that remain after repeated attempts to correct them.

lemon laws State statutes designed to assist the buyer of seriously defective goods to obtain a replacement or full refund.

lessee A party to a lease who pays rent to the landlord in exchange for the possession and use of real property, such as a person who rents an apartment.

lessor A party to a lease who receives rent from a tenant in exchange for the possession and use of real property by the tenant. The lessor is more commonly called the *landlord*.

letter of last instructions A document prepared by a person instructing his or her personal representative (executor or administrator) as to the nature and location of assets and liabilities and suggesting appropriate action to be taken after death. Such letters are useful but not legally binding.

liability Any legal obligation or debt (e.g., money owed).

libel The customary written or printed form of defamation. It may also be committed by defamatory pictures, statues, or signs—all of which are more durable than spoken defamatory words (slander).

license Permission, often formal, to do something specific (e.g., to drive or to enter property).

licensee Person who holds a license. Includes person who enters another's land with permission (implied or express) of the owner or possessor, for the visitor's convenience.

licensor Organization or person who grants a license to another.

lien A formal, legal claim to a possessory or ownership interest in the real property of another.

life estate An ownership interest in property characterized by the right to its possession for the duration of the owner's life. At the death of the owner (called the *life tenant*) possession may (a) revert to the person (called the *grantor*) who created the life estate, (b) go to a designated person (called the *remainderman*), or (c) go to a successor life tenant. Upon death of a life tenant, the value of the life estate is extinguished, and therefore no death taxes are payable. A life estate may be created by deed or will, and it may be created so as to continue until the death of someone other than the life tenant.

limited jurisdiction Limitation on a court as to the types of cases it can hear and decide.

limited liability company (LLC) A variation of the S-type corporation but with no limit on the number of owners (or members) or on the nature of the financial structure. The liability of the owners is limited to the amount of their investment in the company, and they are not subject to double taxation of their profits, as are owners of stock in conventional corporations.

limited liability of stockholders   Refers to the fact that regardless of the number of shares owned, a stockholder is normally not liable for the debts of the corporation beyond the extent of his or her investment. This limited liability is considered a primary advantage of corporate ownership.

limited liability partnership (LLP)   A variation of the general partnership in which if the firm (of lawyers, for example) is sued by a client for malpractice, only the lawyer(s) actually guilty of the tortious conduct is (are) liable without limit. Of course, firm assets and firm professional liability insurance would first be exhausted.

limited partner   Partner whose liability for partnership debts extends only to his or her capital investment. Substantial limitations exist as to the extent such partners may participate in management of the partnership.

limited partnership   A partnership form authorized by state statute in which at least one member is a general partner who manages the firm and has unlimited liability for its debts, but the liability of the other partner(s) is limited to the amount of their capital investment(s). See also "general partnership."

lineals   Relatives who are in a direct line of descent, as parents, children, grandchildren. See also "collaterals."

line item veto   Selective veto, by the executive, of a specific proposed expenditure as it appears on a separate line in a fiscal budget, without vetoing the entire budget or legislative bill.

liquidated damages   Amount of damages that contracting parties have previously agreed would be fair payment in case of breach. This amount will be unacceptable by a court if it is so large as to constitute a penalty.

list   As a verb, the act by a prospective seller of hiring a real estate agent to hunt for a buyer for his or her real property. For example, "I am going to list my house with ABC Realty." The document that establishes the employment relationship is called a *listing*. See "listing agreement."

listing agreement   An employment contract between the owner of real property and a licensed agent authorizing the latter to hunt for a buyer of the property on specified terms. Preprinted types of listing agreement forms include exclusive, exclusive-agency, net, and open listings. See each of these entries.

litigation   Any pending lawsuit.

litigious   Excessively inclined to resolve disputes and claims through lawsuits rather than by negotiation or other methods.

living trust   A popular term for a revocable *inter vivos trust* whose primary purpose is to avoid probate. See "inter vivos."

living will   A document, usually authorized by state statute, that directs any attending physician to comply with the wishes of the drafter regarding the use of life-support systems in the treatment of a terminal illness. Also called a *directive to physicians*.

loan-origination fee   A lump-sum fee paid by a mortgage borrower to the lender, who in turn pays all or a portion of it to the mortgage broker who introduced the borrower to the lender. Often the fee is called *points* when it is charged to the borrower and a *loan-origination fee* when paid by the lender to the mortgage broker.

loan ratio   The ratio of a prospective loan amount to the appraised value of a home. For example, a buyer who needed to borrow $100,000 to buy a home with an appraised value of $125,000 would ask the lender to accept a loan ratio of 80 percent ($100,000/125,000=80%). Also called the *loan-to-value ratio*.

loan shark   A person who charges usurious (exorbitantly as well as illegally high) interest for the loan of money and commonly threatens or uses violence to compel payment.

loan underwriting   The process of evaluating the acceptability of a prospective borrower's loan application. Underwriters adhere to rules, policies, and company practices to determine whether or not a specific loan ought to be made or denied.

lobbying   Efforts by individuals and representatives of special-interest groups to persuade legislators (and sometimes administrators) to enact, amend, or rescind specified laws.

lockout   A shutdown of operations by an employer in response to union demands or to achieve other changes in an employment contract.

long-arm statute   A state law authorizing a court to hear cases brought against nonresidents under specified circumstances. It requires certain minimal contacts with the defendant, such as involvement in an automobile accident while driving in the state, or conducting business within the state that claims to have jurisdiction.

magistrates   (a) State judges of the justice court or other lower courts with jurisdiction over relatively minor offenses and small claims (b) U.S. officials who perform specified judicial services in the prosecution of federal crimes.

Magnuson-Moss Warranty Act of 1975   Federal law that protects ultimate consumers of personal, family, and household goods by defining effects of full and limited warranties.

maintenance   (a) Financial support or promotion of litigation in which one has no legitimate interest. See also "champerty." (b) Term used interchangeably with *alimony*.

majority opinion A written opinion by a judge outlining the views of the majority of the judges of the court deciding the case.

maker The creator of a promissory note.

malice Evil intent; a desire to inflict injury or suffering; a cold-blooded state of mind.

malice aforethought The highest degree of criminal culpability, characterized by a cold and malignant heart and a mental predetermination to do the wrongful act without legal justification or excuse.

malicious prosecution A sham lawsuit brought for the purpose of vexing, harassing, or forcing the payment of money from the defendant.

malpractice Violation of a duty of due care by a professional person.

manslaughter The unlawful killing of another person without malice aforethought. Usually classified as *voluntary* or *involuntary*, depending on the degree of culpability involved. *Vehicular manslaughter* is a special category for negligent killing by automobile.

marital deduction A tax deduction allowing a surviving spouse to receive an estate from the deceased spouse free of federal estate tax.

marital fault The legal basis necessary in some states to obtain a divorce, such as repeated infidelity. In those states where marital fault is not a prerequisite for divorce, it is irrelevant.

marital life estate trust Reciprocal trust executed by a husband and wife with the other spouse as a life beneficiary. These trusts are also called *A and B trusts*.

marital property Property acquired during marriage.

market value The price property would bring if offered for sale in a fair market (not at auction or in a forced sale) by a willing and fully informed (but not compelled) seller, after ample time to find a willing and fully informed (but not compelled) buyer. The price is such as would be fixed by negotiation and mutual agreement. Market value is distinguished from market price, which is what the property might actually be sold for at a given time.

material alteration Any deliberate, *unilateral* (by one of the parties), important change that is made in a written contract, without legal excuse.

mayhem The crime of unlawfully depriving the victim of some member of his or her body; disfiguring, disabling, or rendering the member useless or otherwise permanently disfiguring the body.

mechanic's lien A legal claim of a contractor or worker who helped construct, improve, or repair a building (or repair a product, such as a car). It may be asserted against the property itself for any sum unpaid. A similar claim is given by law to suppliers of materials for construction projects.

med-arb An alternative dispute resolution (ADR) process that combines mediation and arbitration.

The intervenor is appointed to mediate the dispute. If the mediation is unsuccessful, the intervenor is authorized to resolve the dispute by arbitration with a binding award.

mediation The use of a neutral third party to assist parties in voluntarily resolving their dispute(s).

medical-payments insurance Coverage available in conjunction with automobile insurance—for example, to pay medical, surgical, dental, and funeral expenses suffered by the insured or any member of the insured's household who is injured while occupying or being struck by an automobile. Coverage may be extended to other persons occupying the owned automobile.

mens rea [Latin for "guilty mind"] The intent necessary to be convicted of most criminal acts.

merchant A businessperson who regularly deals in goods of the kind involved in a sales contract.

meretricious A relationship between cohabiting, but unmarried, persons that includes sexual relations. Usage of the term is decreasing.

mini-trial A nonbinding version of alternative dispute resolution (ADR) where the disputing parties, usually sizable business organizations, participate in an informal trial-like proceeding. Each side agrees to the procedural rules, including an exchange of information and selection of a neutral advisor. The presentation is made before officials of the parties who possess authority to settle disputes.

minor A person below the age of legal competence. For most purposes, in most states, minority ends at age 18. For some purposes, such as the purchase and consumption of alcoholic beverages, it may end later, up to the age of 21.

***Miranda* warnings** Warnings directed to a suspect by police before a *custodial* (while in custody) interrogation may occur. The warnings include disclosure of the right to remain silent, of the fact that anything said can and will be used against the person in court, and of the accused's right to have a lawyer present during the questioning.

misdemeanor A crime punishable by fine or by incarceration in a county jail up to a year, or by both.

misrepresentation A false statement made intentionally, knowing it is not true. A negligent misrepresentation is a false statement made carelessly. See also "deceit" and "fraud."

mistrial A trial that has failed to conclude properly because of some defect or because of the inability of the proper number of jurors to concur in a verdict. For example, inflammatory remarks by an attorney to a jury may result in a mistrial before the jury returns a verdict. A new trial is usually scheduled to follow a mistrial.

mobile home A compact movable home, available for a relatively low price, and generally securely set down in a "mobile home park" and not removed thereafter.

Model Business Corporations Act A model act concerning the corporation form of business, first drafted in 1933. Although not adopted in full by any state, it has significantly influenced the corporation codes of most states.

money Coins and paper currency authorized by the federal government as a medium of exchange and as legal tender for payment of debts.

moot question A question (a) open to argument and not settled by court decision, (b) purely hypothetical or academic, or (c) no longer important.

mortgage (or real mortgage) The contract in which the buyer of real property typically gives a lender a lien or claim against the real property which serves as collateral for a loan of money, often borrowed to pay part of the purchase price. As borrower, the buyer signs a related contract—a promissory note—for the amount of the loan. Foreclosure and forced sale of the real property may follow if payments are not made as promised. In some states the same results are achieved with a *deed of trust*.

mortgage banker A business that makes real estate loans with its own capital, as well as with institutional funds, and then sells the loans in the secondary mortgage market.

mortgage broker A person licensed to engage in the business of bringing together borrowers and lenders of mortgage funds. Mortgage brokers typically are paid a commission based upon the volume of loans they originate.

mortgagee The lender of funds secured by a mortgage. In states where deeds of trust are used instead of mortgages, the lender of funds (creditor) is called the *beneficiary*.

mortgagor The borrower of funds secured by a mortgage. In states where deeds of trust are used instead of mortgages, the borrower (debtor) is called the *trustor*.

Mosaic Code The Ten Commandments, or Decalogue, delivered to Moses on Mount Sinai. Some ethicists believe the commandments include a succinct statement of the *natural law*.

motion A formal request by counsel addressed to a court or other tribunal for a particular decision or act (e.g., motion for directed verdict).

motion for change of venue Request to a judge by counsel to transfer the trial to a different geographic location within the jurisdiction of the court.

motion for directed verdict Request to a judge by counsel to enter a particular verdict instead of allowing the jury to do so because there are insufficient facts to allow any other verdict.

motion for summary judgment Request to a judge by counsel to award judgment because there are no significant questions of fact in the lawsuit.

motion *in limine* An application to a court requesting that the court make a pretrial decision,

usually about excluding evidence expected to be introduced by the party opposing the motion

motion to dismiss See "demurrer."

motion to produce Request to a judge by counsel to compel the opposing party to provide specified evidence to the court. This is a type of discovery procedure.

motive A reason for doing, or not doing, an act. Motive is not synonymous with criminal intent. Intent is essential for proof of crime; motive is not. However, a good motive is no excuse for criminal conduct.

moving party The party making a request of a court.

multiple-listing service An organization of real estate brokers who exchange information about listings of property they have obtained. All member brokers (and their sales agents) may seek buyers for any of the multiple-listed properties. Any agent who finds a ready, willing, and able buyer of a listed property shares the commission earned with the agent who obtained the original listing agreement with the seller.

murder The unlawful killing of a human being with malice aforethought. Usually classified as first-degree (or capital murder) or second-degree (or noncapital murder), depending on the degree of culpability involved. In some states murder includes the unlawful killing of a fetus.

mutual assent A proper exchange of an offer and its acceptance by the parties forming a contract.

mutual mistake Where both parties to a contract labor under the same error about an important fact in their agreement. Also called a *bilateral mistake*.

National Labor Management Relations Act of 1947 (Taft-Hartley Act) A federal law that lists unfair labor practices of unions. It outlaws the closed shop and the secondary boycott.

National Labor Relations Act of 1935 (Wagner Act) A federal law that recognizes the right of workers to organize into unions of their own choice, and the duty of employers to bargain collectively with the unions over wages, hours, and conditions of employment. It provides a list of unfair labor practices by management.

natural law The higher law believed by some ethicists to be above and beyond man's power to change.

natural rights Inalienable rights of every human being that exist by virtue of natural law, notably to life, liberty, and property.

necessaries Goods and services ordinarily required by and appropriate to an incompetent person's station in life, yet not available and/or not provided by parent or guardian.

negative amortization A monthly increase in the unpaid principal balance of a mortgage loan resulting when the borrower does not make the required monthly interest payments in full. Unpaid monthly interest is converted (called *capitalized*) into unpaid principal, causing the unpaid principal balance to increase each month. When a cap prevents the monthly payment of an adjustable-rate mortgage from rising to the amount required by the index rate of interest, the borrowers pay only the capped amount each month. But the amount of interest accruing each month continues, resulting in negative amortization.

negative injunction An order of a court of equity forbidding specified action (e.g., continued sale of goods manufactured in violation of a patent owned by the plaintiff).

negligence Failure to act as a reasonable, careful person would act under the same or similar circumstances, thereby causing injury that was foreseeable.

negligence per se [Latin for "of itself"] (a) The unexcused violation of a statute or ordinance which is automatically deemed to be negligent conduct without argument or proof as to the particular surrounding circumstances. (b) Certain conduct that is deemed negligent because of its obvious breach of duty (e.g., driving a vehicle on a residential street at 90 mph is negligence per se).

negotiation Communication between disputing parties for the purposes of persuasion and settlement without litigation. Negotiation is bargaining.

neighborhood dispute center Private or public organizations that provide trained mediators to assist parties in resolving consumer and neighbor disputes.

neighbor law The body of laws and rules found in state statutes; in county and city ordinances; in covenants, conditions, and restrictions (CC&Rs); and in court decisions that govern the legal issues that arise between residential neighbors.

net listing Employment contract in which the owner of real property agrees that, as compensation for finding a ready, willing, and able buyer, the licensed agent will retain all sums received by the seller that are in excess of a specified net amount.

net worth The difference between total assets and total liabilities of a person or organization. (If liabilities exceed assets, the negative difference is called a *deficit*. In a corporation, a deficit is the excess of liabilities and capital stock over assets.)

neutral An unbiased third party who assists others in the resolution of their disputes. Includes arbitrators, mediators, and ombudspersons.

neutral expert fact-finding A nonbinding alternative dispute resolution (ADR) process in which an appointed third-party expert investigates and/or hears facts on selected issues and makes advisory findings of fact.

no-fault divorce A divorce granted by a court without either party having to prove fault in the other party. The rapidly disappearing traditional type of divorce used to be granted only to an innocent spouse, on proof that the other spouse was guilty of some misconduct, such as infidelity, mental cruelty, or desertion.

no-fault insurance A type of automobile insurance, mandatory for all motorists in some states, that provides benefits to the insured, regardless of fault of parties to the accident.

nolo contendere, **plea of** [Latin for "I will not contest it"] Equivalent to a plea of guilty, but it cannot be regarded as admission of guilt in any subsequent civil trial against the defendant.

nominal (or token) damages Insignificant amount (such as $1) awarded by a court when the defendant has violated the rights of the plaintiff but no monetary loss has been suffered or can be proved.

nonbinding arbitration A form of arbitration in which the arbitrator's finding is not binding on the parties.

noncapital crime A homicide for which the death penalty may not be imposed even if such penalty is authorized for other crimes by the state in which the crime is committed.

nonjudicial foreclosure See "foreclosure."

non-owned automobile An automobile or trailer not owned by, or furnished for, the regular use of the named insured.

nonsupport Failure to contribute money, in accordance with one's ability, to the maintenance of a parent or child as required by law.

notarized Signed in the presence of a person licensed by the state to perform identification services as a notary public. Most real estate documents, such as deeds, deeds of trust, mortgages, and written easements, must be notarized before they can be recorded in the official records of the county in which the property is located.

note A written contract which is the best evidence of the existence of a debt. A note contains all of the essential terms of the loan, including the dollar amount, interest rate, signature of the borrower, due date, and other important matters. Also called *promissory note*.

notice of default Notice used to inform the public (including the debtor) of an impending private foreclosure sale under a real estate mortgage and to commence the statutory time period that must elapse before a sale can take place.

novation A three-party agreement in which a creditor accepts a new party who agrees to assume the debt and to release the prior debtor.

nuisance Any unreasonable and continuous interference with the use and enjoyment of real property. For example, an overhanging tree that threatens the safety of a neighbor is a nuisance. Intangibles, such as sound, also can be a nuisance if unreasonable and continuous.

nullification of marriage A court judgment terminating a defective or voidable marriage (for example, one involving a person below the age of legal consent).

nuncupative will An oral will.

objective theory of contracts A theory that the words and conduct of an offeror mean whatever a reasonable person in the offeree's position would think they mean, as opposed to what the offeror may have actually meant.

obscene Material or conduct is obscene if, considered as a whole, its predominant appeal is to prurient interest, i.e., a morbid interest in nudity, sex, or excretion. Community standards, as distinguished from national standards, are used by the jury in applying this definition to material or conduct alleged to be obscene.

Occupational Safety and Health Administration (OSHA) A federal agency charged with defining and enforcing minimum standards of health and safety in the workplace. Assisted in some states by state OSHA officials.

offer A promise by one person (the offeror) to do or to give consideration (something of value) in exchange for sought-for consideration through acceptance by another person (the offeree). See also "acceptance."

offeree In contracts, the party to whom an offer is made by the offeror.

offeror In contracts, the party who makes an offer.

officers (of corporation) Persons selected by directors and given delegated authority to manage the day-to-day business affairs of a corporation. Officers typically include a president, vice-president(s), secretary, and treasurer.

ombudsperson A proactive neutral party who investigates and determines facts and suggests resolutions to disputes.

opening statements Summaries by counsel of plaintiff and of defendant indicating what they expect to prove in the ensuing trial.

open listing Employment contract in which the owner of real property agrees to pay a commission only to the agent who produces a ready, willing, and able buyer. Thus, an owner may sign several open listings, each with a different agent and pay only one commission. The owner may also sell the property without the aid of any agents and pay no commission.

open shop A company or department where union membership is not required to get or keep a job.

option The right to purchase property at an established price at any time within a specified period. The optionee (potential buyer) pays option money to the owner in exchange for this right.

option contract An agreement concerning the right to buy or sell something to another at a certain price within a certain time. It often refers to rights to buy or sell real or personal property.

order of examination A judicially authorized inquiry as to the assets of a judgment debtor.

ordinance A written law enacted by a city or county. An example is a zoning ordinance that governs the use of land.

ordinary care The standard of care that would have been exercised by an ordinary, reasonably prudent person under the same or similar circumstances.

ordinary wear and tear Deterioration in a residential rental property that is attributable to the passage of time (e.g., fading of draperies), and not to abuse by the tenant.

outrageous conduct Intentional conduct that does not involve assault or battery yet inflicts extreme emotional trauma on the victim.

owner A person who has legal and/or equitable title to property, with related rights and duties, or benefits and burdens. See also "equitable owner" and "legal owner."

paralegal A person qualified to perform a wide range of legal tasks under the guidance of an attorney. See also "legal assistant."

pardon Release of a convicted criminal from all punishment for his or her crime through an act of the governor of the state or president of the United States.

parole Release from a prison on specified conditions involving good behavior. If these conditions are violated, the prisoner is returned to prison to complete the original sentence.

parol-evidence rule The rule that when contracting parties have put their complete agreement into writing, no prior or contemporaneous oral or written terms may be unilaterally added later to change the written contract, absent proof of fraud, mistake, or illegality.

participating preferred stock Shares of preferred stock, the owners of which are entitled to receive additional dividends (beyond the regular agreement amount) when payments are made to common stockholders of the corporation.

parties Persons of a particular class, occupation, or relation (e.g., children, creditors, heirs), or any persons who are either directly or indirectly necessary to a proper determination of the legal action before a court.

partnership An association of two or more persons to carry on, as co-owners, a business for a profit. Also known as a "general partnership."

paternity action A lawsuit to determine whether or not the defendant is the natural father of a child.

payee Person in whose favor a check, draft, or promissory note is drawn.

peaceful eviction An improper eviction technique by which a landlord surreptitiously enters the absent tenant's apartment, removes the tenant's belongings, and changes locks to the unit. It is peaceable in the sense that no eye-to-eye, person-to-person confrontation takes place, as in a forcible eviction.

Pension Benefit Guaranty Corporation (PBGC) Created under the Employee Retirement Income Security Act to assure financial soundness of specified private pension plans.

peremptory challenge See "challenge (of juror)."

performance That which each party to a contract promises to do.

periodic tenancy A leasehold interest that continues indefinitely for successive periods (usually monthly) until properly terminated by either the lessor (landlord) or lessee (tenant).

perjury Lying about material facts when testifying under oath.

personal-liability insurance Contract that protects the insured from civil liability that may arise from his or her action in causing injury or death to another person.

personal property All property that is not *real property*, i.e., property other than land and things permanently attached to it.

petition A written request to a court asking it to take a particular action.

petitioner (a) In many courts, term used interchangeably with the term *plaintiff* to mean the moving party in a lawsuit. (b) Moving party in an action in equity. (c) Used synonymously with the term *appellee*. (d) Moving party in an arbitration case.

petty larceny Theft of personal property of a value less than that specified by statute. If the value exceeds the statutory minimum, often $500, the crime becomes grand larceny.

petty theft Theft of a thing of little value, as specified by statute. Because of the small value, the crime is a misdemeanor.

picketing Patrolling by strikers or sympathizers, generally at the entrances to a business plant, during a labor dispute. Pickets usually carry placards urging workers to join the strikers and urging suppliers and customers to refuse to deal with the employer.

pilferage Stealing of small goods from storage, usually by employees of the owner or of the warehouse operator.

pimping The crime of enticing a female to engage in prostitution. Also called *pandering* and *procuring*.

PITI An acronym for *principal, interest, taxes*, and *insurance*, which represent the four basic repetitive expenses of buying real property with borrowed funds. Lenders qualify prospective borrowers upon their ability to make the monthly payment of PITI.

plaintiff In trial, the person trying to recover money damages or other relief from a defendant.

planned unit development (PUD) A subdivision that is designed and built functionally integrated, featuring common areas (such as private roadways, parks, and landscaping), uniformity of aesthetically attractive building design, and ongoing regulation by a homeowners' association (HOA).

plea Response of the accused to criminal charges. In most states it may be (a) guilty, (b) not guilty, (c) nolo contendere, or (d) not guilty by reason of insanity.

plea bargain A binding agreement in which an accused agrees to plead guilty (or nolo contendere) if the court agrees to a specified punishment in advance. Plea bargains avoid the time, expense, and outcome uncertainty of a trial.

pleadings The complaint of the plaintiff and answer of the defendant in a lawsuit.

PMI See "private mortgage insurance (PMI)."

points A one-time charge made by a lender when a home loan is originated. One point is 1 percent of the loan.

police power The inherent power of the government to make laws and impose reasonable regulations for the health, safety, morals, or general welfare of the public, even when this limits individual freedom.

polygraph (tests) "Lie detector" tests using an electromechanical device for recording dramatic changes in body functions during interrogation.

portfolio lender A lender of home-purchase funds that does not expect to sell its mortgages in the secondary mortgage market. Because such lenders keep their loans within their own portfolio of loans, they can be more flexible (liberal) in the terms of the loans they offer prospective home buyers.

positive law Law enacted by governmental authority, such as legislatures, courts, and administrative agencies, as distinguished from natural law.

possession The custody and control of property coupled with the right to use it.

possessory lien A lien that empowers a creditor to retain possession of the collateral until the debt is paid or until it is sold to the highest bidder in accordance with law. Typically a mechanic has a possessory lien on the automobile that is repaired. On the other hand, an attorney does not have a possessory lien on the client's files.

power of appointment Authority given to a person (the donee) under a trust or will to designate or appoint the person(s) who shall receive specified assets after a specified event (such as death of the donee or death of the testator).

power of attorney A document authorizing another person to act as one's agent. A general power of attorney authorizes the agent (called the *attorney-in-fact*) to do all acts not prohibited by law for another (called the *principal*). A special power of attorney authorizes the attorney-in-fact to do a limited and specified class of acts for the principal.

power of sale A clause found in a mortgage or deed of trust that, upon a default in monthly payments, authorizes the creditor (mortgagee or beneficiary) to cause the collateral for the loan (i.e., the debtor's home) to be sold to the highest bidder at a private sale. Without a power-of-sale clause, foreclosing creditors would be required to file a court action for foreclosure, a time-consuming and costly process, before the collateral could be sold.

precedent A court decision on a question of law that gives authority or direction on a similar question of law in a later case with similar facts. See also "stare decisis."

preemption Assertion by the federal government of authority to regulate a field (such as certain labor relations). States cannot enforce conflicting laws in such fields. (The same principle applies between state and local governments.) Preemption is also called *supremacy*.

preferred stock Shares that represent ownership in a business corporation and whose holders are entitled to dividends of a fixed amount before any payment is made to shareholders of common stock.

Pregnancy Discrimination Act (1978) Federal law that requires employers to treat women affected by pregnancy or related medical conditions just as they would treat other temporarily disabled employees (e.g., regarding accrual of seniority status, and return to work). This act is an amendment to the Civil Rights Act of 1964.

preliminary hearing An examination in open court by a judge to determine whether sufficient evidence exists to hold the accused for trial. Preliminary hearings are not used when a grand jury issues an indictment.

prenuptial Occurring prior to the commencement of marital status. Prenuptial agreements are made before marriage but concern property matters during marriage. These binding agreements are also called *antenuptial agreements* and *premarital agreements*.

preponderance of evidence Standard of determining civil liability, that the weight of the evidence offered to prove a matter is more probable than not.

prescriptive easements Easements, usually of access, over the land of another person, created by a continuous, open (visible) use without the consent of the landowner for a long period of time, usually five years or more in most states.

pretermitted heir A child who was not specifically provided for in life and was not mentioned in his or her parent's will. Statutes typically declare that such child, or the issue of a deceased child, shares in the estate as though the testator had died intestate.

pretermmited heir statute A statute giving rights of inheritance to a testator's children (or grandchildren) when they are not named in the will and not provided for by settlement in life.

pretrial proceeding (Conference or Hearing) In the months before a civil trial is scheduled to begin, several pretrial proceedings may occur. One type is a settlement conference attended by the attorneys, parties, and judge to determine if the case can be amicably settled without a trial. Another type is a conference attended by the attorneys and the judge to formalize the issues to be determined at trial and to decide whether to have a jury, among other matters.

prima facie [Latin for "on first appearance"] Term describing a fact presumed to be true unless disproved by some contrary evidence. With reference to a legal case, such fact will prevail unless and until contradicted and overcome by other evidence.

primary law Law stated without interpretation by commentators. Primary law consists of established rules from constitutions, statutes, administrative agency regulations and rules, treaties, and judicial decisions.

principal The person who empowers an agent to enter contract(s) on her or his behalf.

prior restraint (a) Legal measures to prevent anticipated illegal conduct before it takes place, such as the banning of a parade expected to cause a riot. (b) Constitutional—First Amemdment—prohibition of restraints on a publication before it is actually published. Exceptions to the rule include certain obscene publications, certain publications that invade personal privacy, and publications that create clear and present danger to the public.

privacy, invasion of right of Violation of the fundamental right of every person who has done no wrong to be simply left alone.

private judging The use of a legally trained arbitrator who follows formal judicial procedures in hearing a case outside a court. The final award is entered as a judgment in many states, with the right of judicial appeal allowed.

private law That body of law regulating the rights and duties that exist between private persons (including private corporations). Contract law is an example of private law.

private mortgage insurance (PMI) Insurance to protect a lender in the event that a borrower defaults in the repayment of a mortgage loan. Premiums for PMI are paid monthly by the borrower along with the monthly mortgage payment.

privilege A legal right to do or refrain from doing something enjoyed by only some persons or classes (e.g., immunity of judges from liability for defamation for statements made during judicial proceedings).

privilege against self-incrimination The right of any person, including one accused of a crime, to remain silent when what might be said could indicate guilt. The Fifth Amendment to the U.S.

Constitution provides that "No person . . . shall be compelled in any criminal case to be a witness against himself. . . ."

privileged communication A right and duty one has to withhold communications from legal proceedings because of some special relationship (e.g., attorney-client, physician-patient, husband-wife, priest-penitent).

privity of contract Applies to a direct contractual relationship between parties, as exists, for example, with a consumer-buyer dealing with the retail-seller but not with the wholesaler or manufacturer of the goods (who are farther away in the chain of distribution).

probate The process of proving the validity of a will in court, coupled with the related matter of administering the decedent's estate. Involves payment of debts to creditors and distribution of remaining assets to heirs and/or named beneficiaries.

probation Release of a convicted criminal before sentence begins on condition of good behavior and under supervision of a probation officer. If this condition is violated, incarceration begins.

pro bono publico [Latin for "for the public good"] When an attorney provides legal services free of charge to poor but worthy clients or causes.

procedural law General principles and detailed rules that define the methods of administering substantive law.

process Legal documents or writs (orders issued from a court) used to compel a defendant in a lawsuit to answer a complaint and appear in court.

process server A person who serves (delivers) a copy of the summons and complaint, or other legal document, upon a party or witness at the request of the opposing party to civil litigation.

product liability A general area of law holding manufacturers and sellers of goods liable to buyers, users, and perhaps bystanders for harm caused when goods are defective.

professional ethics Written rules of prohibited conduct that are adopted by and binding upon members of a professional group.

profit The excess of revenues or receipts of a business over costs or expenses. The profit is also called *net income*.

promisee The person to whom a contractual promise has been made. See also "offeree."

promisor The person who makes a contractual promise. See also "offeror."

promissory note, negotiable A written promise to pay to a named person or to the bearer of the note a certain sum of money in the future. The note may contain the terms of the loan, such as the due date, repayment schedule, interest rate, and so forth. To be a negotiable promissory note, it must comply with Article III of the Uniform Commercial Code.

property Anything that may be owned. Classified broadly as *real* and *personal* property. See "personal property" and "real property."

property-damage insurance Contract that protects the insured with coverage for liability arising from his or her damaging the property of another.

property-tax rate The factor that, when multiplied by the assessed value of a parcel of taxable real property, produces the amount of annual property tax the owner must pay. The factor is computed annually by local government officials who divide the county budget by the assessed value of all taxable real property in the county [e.g., assuming this factor to be 1.25 percent (.0125), the annual tax on a home assessed at $150,000 would be $1,875 (since .0125 x 150,000 = 1,875)].

pro se [Latin for "for himself or herself"] See "in propria persona."

prosecutor An attorney employed by the government to pursue legal proceedings against persons accused of crime. The prosecutor represents the state, or the people, in criminal trials.

prospectus A formal report published prior to the issuance of securities by a corporation, containing basic important facts about the company and its operations.

protected class A classification of persons defined by one or more of these criteria: race, color, gender, national origin, age, or religion.

provocative-act rule The rule that all participants in a dangerous felony are guilty of murder in the first degree if a lawful killing occurs in response to some threatening act by one of the felons. An example is a killing of an innocent bystander by a police officer who fires in response to gun-waving by one of the fleeing felons.

proximate cause (or causation) An action that, in natural and continuous sequence, unbroken by an intervening force or cause, produces the injury, and without which the effect or result would not have occurred.

proxy A written power of attorney signed by a shareholder authorizing another person to vote on her or his behalf at a meeting of the stockholders of the corporation.

publication of defamatory material Communicating defamatory material about a person(s) to one or more other persons.

public defender A lawyer provided by the community for a person who is accused of a serious crime (felony) and cannot afford to hire counsel.

public-interest law firm A nonprofit law firm that offers assistance in areas such as employment, minority rights, civil rights, political rights, family law, and environmental law.

public law That body of law directly concerned with public rights and obligations, such as constitutional, administrative, criminal, and international law.

public policy A fundamental guideline under which courts condemn or validate actions depending on whether the conduct is deemed to be contrary to or supportive of the commonweal or good of society.

published A legal rule of wills in some states requiring a declaration by the maker of the will to the witnesses that the document they are about to sign is indeed his or her will.

puffing Seller's talk; claims about the quality of goods, usually exaggerated; not considered fraud.

punitive (or exemplary) damages Amount awarded by a court, to the victim of an intentional tort, in addition to compensatory damages; designed to punish the tortfeasor and serve as an example to others.

purchase contract and deposit receipt A contract by which a seller agrees to sell, and the buyer agrees to buy, a specified parcel of real property at a specified price and upon specified terms.

purchase-money mortgage A loan the proceeds of which are used to purchase a home. The lender retains a nonpossessory equitable interest in the home as security for repayment of the loan.

quasi [Latin for "as if"] A term used in conjunction with other words to mean having a legal status only by operation or construction of law. For example, "quasi-contract" means an agreement that resembles a contract and may be enforced as one even when some essential element of a contract is missing. Designed to prevent unjust enrichment of one of the parties.

questions of fact Circumstances or matters surrounding and involved in a case that is being tried by a court. These questions refer to events that allegedly took place in the past and are now in dispute. The jury decides if the information provided is true.

questions of law Principles and rules of human conduct determined by the judge to be applicable in a case being tried by a court. For example, the definition of murder is a question of law within the province of the judge and not the jury.

quid pro quo [Latin: "this for that"] Expression often is used in sexual harassment situations when sexual favors or demands are a term or condition of an individual's employment, or the basis for employment decisions affecting such individual. Also used as a synonym for consideration.

quiet enjoyment The sense of ownership, such as freedom from interference by others (who claim a superior legal right to occupy the premises) that a tenant is entitled to receive as an implied incident of a lease.

quiet title action Action "against the world" initiated by a person who claims ownership of a particular parcel of real property. The action forces any person in the world who has a claim to ownership or possession of the property either to step forward and assert the claim or to lose it forever.

quitclaim deed A deed to real property in which the transferor conveys whatever ownership interest he or she may possess, which may be none. The transferor makes no warranties and therefore cannot be held liable if the title transferred proves to be faulty. A quitclaim deed is commonly used to correct errors in recorded titles. See also "deed."

racial quota Required hiring of specific numbers of minorities and/or women to rectify past discrimination. Affirmative action programs are legal but the U.S. Supreme Court has rejected quotas.

Racketeer Influenced and Corrupt Organization Act (RICO) of 1970 A federal law passed to control attempts by organized crime to invest money gained from illegal racketeering in legitimate business activities. The scope of this law is broad and creates both civil and criminal remedies for activities defined as racketeering, which include 26 types of federal crimes and 9 state felonies.

rape, forcible An unlawful act of sexual intercourse, against the will of the victim. Consent obtained by trick or threat or through the use of intoxicants or narcotics is not considered true consent.

rape-shield statute A statute that protects victims from courtroom questioning about prior sexual experiences with persons other than the defendant.

real estate agent A person licensed by the state to negotiate the buying and selling of real property while employed and supervised by a licensed real estate broker.

real estate owned (REO) Institutional lenders, such as banks and savings and loan associations, sometimes receive title to properties secured by loans that are in default, following foreclosure sales. Typically these lenders then offer the reclaimed properties, called REOs, for sale.

real property Land and things permanently attached to it. Includes air space above, surface water, and subsurface waters, gases, and minerals.

reasonable accommodation Expression in some employment statutes requiring an employer to make modifications in workplace or job requirements to accommodate an employee.

reasonable person A hypothetical person used in the law as a standard for reasonable conduct. For example, failure to act as a reasonable person under given circumstances is usually deemed to be negligence. This may result in liability to others for injuries caused thereby.

recall A democratic process for removing public officials from their elective positions by a vote of the people taken after filing of a petition signed by the required number of qualified voters.

receiving stolen property The crime of knowingly receiving stolen property. Proof of knowledge may be inferred from the circumstances.

recidivist A criminal who is a repeat offender. Violation of statutes against recidivism may increase a lesser penalty to life imprisonment.

recognizance A written promise by the accused that if released without posting bail, he or she will return voluntarily for further criminal proceedings. See also "bail."

referendum A democratic process whereby a state legislature submits (refers) proposed laws, or existing laws, to the electorate for approval or rejection.

refinance loan A loan, secured by mortgage, the proceeds of which are used primarily to pay off, or retire, an existing mortgage loan. Refinancing occurs when interest rates drop, encouraging homeowners to pay off existing high-interest-rate loans with new lower-interest-rate loans.

registered buyer-owner The buyer of a car on credit, who, as the equitable owner, gets possession and use of the vehicle while making payments. The seller (or lender) remains the legal owner until the car is paid for in full. See also "owner."

regulations Rules promulgated by an administrative agency under authority given to the agency by the enabling statute.

Regulatory Flexibility Act Federal law requiring federal agencies to consider the effects of their regulatory actions on small businesses and other small entities and to minimize any undue disproportionate burden.

regulatory offense A violation of a rule promulgated by an administrative agency.

rehabilitative alimony Financial support paid by one former spouse to the other for a definite period of time during which the recipient is expected to prepare for financial independence (e.g., by vocational education)

reinstatement of mortgage A procedure in which, upon payment to a foreclosing creditor of all delinquent sums and related fees within a prescribed period of time, the original loan terms are reinstated as if no default had occurred. The right of reinstatement belongs to the debtor or her or his assigns. See also "right of reinstatement."

relevant evidence Evidence that is related to the facts in dispute. See also "irrelevant evidence."

remainderman The person designated to receive complete ownership of property upon termination of a life estate. For example, when a man, in his will, leaves real property to his widow for her life, and then to their children, the children are called remaindermen. See also "life estate."

remainder trust A trust that distributes (gives) the remaining property interest to an identified beneficiary (or beneficiaries) after the termination of a life estate.

remanded The status of a case sent back to a lower court from which it had been appealed, with binding instructions as to its disposal or further required proceedings.

remedies Relief provided by courts to redress wrongs and to enforce rights. Examples are monetary damages, orders for specific performance, injunctions, and other appropriate relief.

rent Money paid by a renter to the landlord in exchange for the possession and use of rental property. Rent may also take the form of personal services, or the transfer of any asset in lieu of money.

rental agreement A contract, usually written, between a landlord and tenant. Technically it is a lease. See also "lease."

rental unit One unit in a multi-unit residential structure that is available to be rented. Urban apartments that are owned by their occupants are technically condominiums.

rent control Government regulation of how much rent a landlord may charge for the possession and use of rental premises. Rent controls have not been imposed on commercial properties.

renter (a) One who receives payment in exchange for the use of one's property by another. (b) One who pays rent for the use of another's property; a tenant.

REO See "real estate owned (REO)."

replevin Legal action to recover possession of goods (personal property) wrongfully taken or retained by a defendant.

reporter A set of books that contain the written opinions of justices of specified appellate courts. These volumes contain the decisional or unwritten law. Volumes in the reporters and the cases they contain are arranged in chronological order and accessible by case name or subject matter index.

reprieve Postponement, or stay of execution (i.e., of enforcement) of the judgment, after conviction for a crime.

republic A system of government with the supreme power in the people, who exercise it by representatives chosen through the votes of qualified voters (i.e., qualified by age, citizenship, and registration).

request for admission of facts A request submitted to counsel by the opposing attorney before trial for the acknowledgment of facts that are not in dispute and yet are relevant and material. This is a type of discovery procedure.

rescission An equitable remedy that annuls a contract and returns the parties to the relationship they had before the contract was made.

residual powers Any power not expressly delegated to the United States by the U.S. Constitution nor prohibited by it to the states, and hence reserved to the states, or to the people.

residuary clause Any part of the will which disposes of property not expressly disposed of by other provisions of the will.

res ipsa loquitur [Latin for "the thing speaks for itself "] A doctrine under which negligence is inferred when the instrumentality causing the injury was under control of the defendant and an injury occurred that normally would not occur in the absence of negligence by the defendant. This doctrine is frequently relied on by victims of medical malpractice. To avoid liability the defendant must prove he or she was not negligent.

Resolution Trust Corporation (RTC) A corporation created by Congress to salvage savings and loan companies and thrift institutions from insolvencies that resulted from imprudent lending practices during the 1980s. The RTC takes full control of such insolvent institutions and auctions their real estate holdings to raise money with which to reimburse depositors.

respondeat superior [Latin for "let the master answer"] A legal doctrine holding employers liable for injuries caused third persons by their employees who were negligent while acting in the course and within the scope of their employment.

respondent (a) The person against whom an appeal is taken. See also "appellee." (b) The person against whom a *motion* is filed. (c) Party who is notified to respond and proceed to arbitration.

Restatement of the Law A series of authoritative volumes on major areas of law (e.g., contracts, agency, and torts) written by scholars of the nonprofit American Law Institute.

restitution Return of what has been received or stolen, as when a contract is rescinded or when a thief repays stolen money or returns other stolen property.

retainer fee (a) A sum of money paid to an attorney for a promise to remain available to the client for consultation when needed and requested. (b) Fees paid in advance that are held in a trust account to be drawn down (taken) by the attorney as work progresses.

retaliatory eviction An eviction carried out by a landlord primarily for revenge, or retaliation, against a particular tenant who has in some way angered the landlord.

reverse discrimination Label given to the results of affirmative action programs by opponents who claim that such programs discriminate against male and white workers.

reversionary interest (a) Something of value (such as the right to borrow against the policy) that a life insurance policyholder may retain when giving the policy to another person. (b) The future interest in real property retained by the grantor of a life estate.

revocable trust A trust that may be terminated or revoked by the trustor who created it.

right of redemption Right of a debtor to recover, within one year, the property sold at a judicial foreclosure sale. The debtor must reimburse the purchaser of the foreclosure sale and must retire any unpaid amount owing the original unpaid creditor who initiated the sale. A right of redemption is in the nature of a real property interest and is freely saleable.

right of reinstatement The right of a defaulting debtor to reinstate the loan by payment of all money due for prior months including late charges, even though the note and mortgage declare that the *entire* unpaid balance is immediately due in full upon any default.

right of retraction A defense against libel favoring certain publications, such as newspapers. Even if a paper defames someone, prompt publication of a retraction, or admission of error, may be a complete or partial defense against a claim for damages.

rights, civil Rights that a person has as a human being and by virtue of U.S. citizenship. These rights are found in constitutions and state and federal civil rights laws. They include the rights to equal protection of the law and to due process of law.

rights, fundamental Basic rights that a person has under the U.S. Constitution, such as the rights of freedom of speech, press, religion, and assembly.

rights, legal Rights to recognition and protection of one's person, property, and other interests, enforceable in court. Legal rights may include civil, natural, and political rights. They are the reciprocal of legal duties.

rights, natural Rights that a person has by virtue of being human, such as the right to life, liberty, and the pursuit of happiness.

rights, political Rights that citizens share in government, including the right to vote and to hold public office.

right-to-know law Statute that requires informing workers of the hazards from chemicals that they are likely to be exposed to on the job.

right-to-work laws Statutes enacted in about 20 states that provide that a person cannot be required to join a union as a condition of receiving or retaining a job. Most of them also ban any obligation to pay dues to a union.

robbery The crime of stealing property from another person in his or her immediate presence through the use of force or fear.

Roman civil law See "civil law."

Roth IRA A form of Individual Retirement Account authorized by federal law that allows a taxpayer to shelter all earnings in the account from federal income taxes.

rule against perpetuities A rule that requires remainder interests in property to *vest* (i.e., to take effect) no later than a life or any number of identified lives in being, plus 21 years.

sale A contract in which title (ownership) of property passes from seller to buyer. Possession usually transfers at the time of sale.

same-sex marriage The bond formed when persons of the same sex live together as spouses though without the legal formalities. Same-sex marriages are not legal in the U.S., but are legal in some countries (e.g., Denmark, Norway, and Sweden).

satisfaction of judgment Proof that a debt created by a judgment of the court has been paid by the defendant.

S corporation A closely held corporation that is treated as a partnership for federal tax purposes. Income is regarded as taxable personal income to the stockholders, whether distributed or retained in the business. One effect is avoidance of the customary double taxation of corporate net income.

search and seizure A phrase that describes any search of one's person or property and the process of taking evidence into custody by an officer of the law. Evidence obtained by police in an unreasonable search and seizure (e.g., without a proper warrant) is tainted with illegality and may not be used against the accused under the so-called *exclusionary rule.*

secondary boycott Occurs when striking workers picket or use other pressure against a neutral third party who supplies or buys from the struck employer.

secondary materials Law from other than *primary sources* (e.g., encyclopedias, dictionaries, treatises and texts, and other books that present some writer's opinion of what the law is or should be).

secondary mortgage market A financial market in which existing mortgages are bought and sold. The market is composed of investors, private institutions (such as pension funds and insurance companies), and government agencies, who purchase mortgages, thereby making funds available for new mortgages.

second degree A measurement in law of the degree of culpability of the perpetrator of a crime—less than first degree.

second mortgage A loan secured by a mortgage that is originated subsequent to an existing mortgage. In real estate, "first in time is first in right." Upon default and sale of property to satisfy indebtedness, a first mortgagee must be paid in full (or the creditor-mortgagee may accept the collateralized home, free and clear of all debt) before the holder of the second mortgage is entitled to receive anything.

secured loan Money borrowed in exchange for a pledge by the borrower of specific assets that may be forfeited if repayment is not made as promised.

secured transaction Any transaction, regardless of form, that is intended to create a security interest in personal property.

security Collateral for loan, available to the creditor if the debtor should default. In home-purchase loans, the home is the security for repayment of the mortgage debt.

security deposit A lump sum of cash paid by a tenant to his or her new landlord as security that the tenant will pay rent as agreed and will not damage the rented premises.

seduction The criminal act of enticing a person to engage in sexual intercourse by means of a false promise (as of marriage), but without physical force.

segregation Isolation or separate treatment, usually unequal, on the sole basis of race, color, creed, or national origin.

self-defense The legal right to use whatever force appears to be reasonably necessary to protect oneself (or specified others) from great and imminent bodily injury by an assailant.

self-help A common-law rule that, under certain circumstances, a person can legally take action to resolve a problem without resort to a court or the legal system (e.g., to trespass for the purpose of recovering stolen property, or to tear down an encroaching fence). Generally, self-help is no longer a lawful remedy; an aggrieved person must resort to peaceful judicial alternatives.

self-incrimination See "privilege against self-incrimination."

separate maintenance A partial termination of marriage in which the spouses live apart while support if paid. Property normally is not divided. See also "divorce from bed and board" and "legal separation."

separate property Property, real or personal, either brought into a marriage at the outset or acquired during marriage by gift or inheritance, together with the profits therefrom. To retain this status, it must be treated as such, in formal records, for example. See also "community property."

separation The status of spouses who are by judicial decree living apart, i.e., no longer cohabiting.

separation agreement A contract between spouses who are contemplating a divorce. See also "antenuptial agreement."

separation of powers The Constitutional doctrine dividing and confining certain powers of the U.S. government into the legislative, the executive, and the judicial branches.

SEPs See "simplified employee pension plans (SEPs)."

Service Core of Retired Executives (SCORE) A sizeable group of experienced retired business executives who provide expert counselling and training to new small-business entrepreneurs without charge, under the auspices of the federal Small Business Administration.

settlor A person who establishes a trust. A settlor is also called a *trustor*.

severalty Separate or individual ownership of property by one person or ownership as separate property by a married person.

sex perversion Criminal violation of state laws prohibiting sodomy, oral copulation, and/or lewd or lascivious acts with a child.

sexual harassment A form of illegal gender discrimination wherein (1) job opportunities, promotions, and the like are given on the basis of sexual favors or (2) the employee is subjected to a work environment where the employee must put up with sexual comments, jokes, or physical contact that is sexually offensive.

shareholder See "stockholder."

shares See "stock."

shoplifting Surreptitiously stealing merchandise from displays in a retail store.

short sale (a) The sale of property (such as a home) for less than the unpaid balance of a loan in which the property serves as security. (b) The sale of securities, commodities, or foreign currency that is not actually owned by the seller who hopes to "cover" (i.e., buy back at a lower price) contracts for the goods previously sold—and thus earn a profit.

simple contracts All oral and written contracts that are not classified as formal contracts which require a specified form to be enforceable (e.g., contracts under seal).

simplified employee pension plans (SEPs) Private employee pension plans authorized by federal law whereby employers contribute to their employees' individual retirement accounts.

sitdown strike Illegal strike in which strikers remain in their places of employment but refuse to work.

Small Business Administration (SBA) Federal administrative agency that provides information, advice, and financial assistance to business managers and qualified small-business firms.

small claims court A court with jurisdiction to decide civil controversies of a relatively minor or insignificant nature as far as society in general is concerned.

sobriety checkpoint A method used by police authorities of stopping automobiles at random locations and inspecting the drivers to determine whether they are guilty of DUI (driving under the influence of alcohol or drugs).

social contract (a) An agreement setting forth rights, duties, and obligations of government officials and the people governed (e.g., a constitution). (b) In political philosophy, a theory that human beings associate together for mutual protection and well-being, and the government rests on and depends on their consent.

sole proprietorship A business owned and typically operated by one person, who receives all profits and is liable for all losses.

solicitation The crime of assisting or encouraging another person to commit a crime.

sovereign immunity Traditional legal rule that "the king can do no wrong," hence, government is not liable for the torts of its agents and employees. The modern trend is away from recognition of such immunity.

special damages Amount awarded by a court to pay for monetary out-of-pocket losses resulting from the specific or special circumstances of the plaintiff (e.g., for medical expenses, loss of wages, and destruction of property). Special damages are a type of compensatory damages.

specific performance Remedy available in a court of equity for a buyer to get possession and title to real property and to goods that are unique, when the seller refuses to deliver under a valid sales contract. Dollar damages that are the customary remedy are deemed inadequate.

specious lawsuit (a) Any lawsuit brought against the authors of this text. (b) A lawsuit which on its face may appear to have validity but is in fact totally without merit.

spendthrift trust A trust created to provide for the maintenance of an improvident beneficiary by limiting his or her control of the corpus (the principal of the trust) and by barring access by creditors. Only a small portion is given to the beneficiary at any one time, and major expenses may be paid directly by the trustee.

spite fence A fence erected primarily to vex, annoy, or "spite" a neighbor. Such fences usually block the targeted neighbor's view, or access, or are constructed so shabbily as to detract from the value of the neighbor's property.

spousal immunity A doctrine of the common law that tort actions between spouses are prohibited because of a public policy to protect the harmony of the marital relationship from adversarial and disruptive legal proceedings.

standard of care The legal duty to behave as a hypothetical reasonably prudent person would behave under the same or similar circumstances.

standard title insurance Customary title insurance coverage that does not include the special coverage included within the more expensive American Land Title Association policy, which includes physical inspection of the premises as well as a review of the official records in a title search.

standing to sue doctrine   A person's right or capacity to bring a lawsuit because he or she has a legally protectible interest at stake in the litigation.

stare decisis   [Latin for "to stand by decided cases"] The common-law doctrine that binds an inferior (subordinate) court to follow and apply decisions and interpretations of higher courts when similar cases arise. Also called the *doctrine of precedents*.

state law   Includes state constitutions, statutes enacted by state legislatures, rules promulgated by state agencies, and the decisions of state courts.

statute of frauds   A state statute requiring certain types of contracts to be evidenced by a writing and to be signed by the party to be charged, or by her or his authorized agent.

statute of limitations   A statute that bars civil or criminal proceedings unless brought within a specified period of time after the act occurred. Note that there is no statute of limitations for murder. See also "statute of repose."

statute of repose   A type of statute of limitations that specifies an absolute time from the date of sale during which the cause of action must be brought to collect damages for defects in the product.

statutes   Laws enacted by Congress and by state legislatures.

statutory rape   Sexual intercourse between a male, usually 18 or older, and a consenting female, usually 17 or younger. State statutes vary the penalties depending on the age of the victim. Also called *unlawful intercourse*.

statutory will   A form will authorized by state law with blanks to be completed by the testator.

stock   Certificate of ownership of a share or interest in a business corporation. May be common or preferred, with further subdivisions depending on related rights.

stock dividend   A distribution declared by directors of a corporation in the form of shares of the corporation's stock rather than cash. An appropriate accounting transfer is made from "earned surplus" to "capital." The dividend is not taxable to the recipient unless a share received is sold and a profit is realized.

stockholder   A person who owns one or more shares of the capital stock of a profit-seeking corporation. The stockholder's liability for losses is normally limited to the amount of the capital investment made through purchase and retention of the stock.

stock split   Occurs when directors of a corporation divide each share of stock into a larger number of shares. There is no accounting transfer from "earned surplus" to "capital" as in a stock divi-

dend. However, if the stock has par value or stated value, such values are accordingly changed. There is no tax due from the stockholder unless a share is sold and a profit is realized.

strict constructionist   A judge or court that is reluctant to create new rules by departing from clear precedent, leaving the creation of new laws primarily to the legislative branch of government.

strict liability   A legal theory applicable when a defective or hazardous product is sold and the user-victim is injured. The victim need not prove negligence, wrongful intent, breach of warranty, or privity of contract.

strike, labor   A concerted refusal by employees to perform the services for which they were hired, generally in order to gain recognition of a union, or improvements in wages, hours, or conditions of employment.

strike, sympathy   A strike called by workers in a company or department where there is no labor dispute in order to support striking workers employed elsewhere.

strike-breakers   Persons hired to take the place of workers who are out on strike. If it is an economic strike, the strike-breakers may be retained as permanent replacements.

subdivision home   Any home built in a tract of land that previously has been subdivided into lots. Most subdivision homes are designed and built by one builder to conform to a variety of three or four floor plans.

subject-matter jurisdiction   The power of a court to hear and decide cases of the general class to which the subject in question belongs, e.g., probate matters or domestic relations.

sublease   The transfer by a tenant of less than the full, unexpired term of the lease to a subtenant.

subornation of perjury   Crime of persuading another person to commit perjury.

subpoena   An order directing a person to appear at a certain time and place for the purpose of giving testimony as a witness.

subpoena duces tecum   [Latin for "under penalty bring with you"] A judicial order to bring specified documents or physical evidence to court.

subrogation   The substitution of a third party for the creditor in a claim against a debtor. For example, an insurance company may pay the claim of its insured against the defendant, and then sue the defendant in the name of the insured for damages resulting from an auto accident.

subsequent illegality   When terms of a contract, legal at inception, cannot be performed legally.

substantial performance   When a party to a contract honestly performs most essentials of the contract, but there is some minor omission or deviation which can be corrected, or compensated for in a reduction of the price.

substantive law General principles and detailed rules that define legal rights and duties. Substantive law is contrasted to *procedural law*.

suffrage The right to vote in political elections.

summary jury trial A nonbinding alternative dispute resolution (ADR) process in which parties present their cases to a private mock jury, which then gives the parties an advisory verdict.

summation The review of the evidence presented to the court by each lawyer in oral argument at the close of the trial, before the jury retires and before the judge renders a decision.

summons A document issued by a clerk of the court at the request of the plaintiff when a complaint is filed. After service on the defendant, judgment will be taken if the complaint is not answered within the statutory time (e.g., 15 or 30 days). A summons is prepared by the plaintiff's attorney. See also "complaint."

surrogate mother A female who is artificially inseminated, carries the fetus to term, and who then relinquishes her parental rights to the biological father. Surrogacy services are performed pursuant to a contract in return for money.

sustain Agreement by the judge with an argument by an attorney. For example, if an attorney objects to the introduction of certain evidence and the judge agrees to the objection, the judge sustains the objection.

symbolic speech Communication of ideas by conduct and/or use of material objects, without the use of words. The expression may be deemed a form of speech protected by the First Amendment (e.g., use of black arm bands to protest the war in Vietnam).

tangible property Property that has physical existence and can be touched. An automobile is tangible personal property; a house is tangible real property.

tax deductibility Legal right to exclude an expense or expenditure from gross income, thereby reducing taxable income and its concomitant tax.

tax evasion The intentional and illegal violation of federal and state tax laws. In contrast, tax avoidance is legitimate and an ongoing concern of accountants and tax lawyers under pressure from their clients.

tenancy at sufferance A tenant remaining in possession of real property without permission of the landlord after the expiration of a lawful term.

tenancy at will A lawful possession of a tenancy without a definite duration. Tenancy at will can be terminated by either the landlord or the tenant at any time. (Statutes may require a short advance notice by landlords.)

tenancy by the entirety A form of co-ownership of property between husband and wife in some states. As with joint-tenancy ownership, the spouses have a right of survivorship. See also "joint tenancy."

tenancy for years A leasehold interest that expires at a specified time. It need not actually be for years in duration.

tenancy in common A form of co-ownership of property by two or more persons. Upon the death of any co-owner, his or her percentage interest passes by intestate succession or by last will. Unlike joint tenancy, there is no right of survivorship by co-owners.

tenant A party to a lease who pays rent to the landlord in exchange for the possession and use of real property (e.g., a person who rents an apartment).

testamentary trust Trust created by a valid will.

testate The legal status of a person who dies leaving a valid will.

testator (a) Person who makes a valid will. (b) Person who dies leaving a valid will.

theft The crime of stealing property from another who is not then present. Depending on the nature or value of the property stolen, it is either petty theft (*misdemeanor*) or grand theft (*felony*).

third-party beneficiary One who is not a party to a contract, yet benefits from it. May be (a) a donee beneficiary, a third party who receives the benefit as a gift; or (b) a creditor beneficiary named because of an existing enforceable claim against one of the parties; or (c) an incidental beneficiary who may benefit from the contract but has no legally enforceable rights under it.

title Full and complete ownership of property. It may be separated into *legal title* (ownership) and *equitable title* (possession). For example, the purchaser of a home may agree to make payments for years before receiving full ownership from the seller. While waiting for legal title from the seller, the buyer is enjoying possession (equitable ownership) of the home. See also "equitable title" and "legal title."

title insurance A variety of insurance designed to insure against loss suffered by a homeowner or mortgage lender if title to the property is not as described by the insurer. Unlike most insurance, the premium is paid in total at the beginning of the period to be covered, it is measured in amount by the value of the property rather than by the risk of its loss, and it extends for as long as the insured continues to own the property, be it a week or 50 years or more.

Title VII Literally refers to number 7, but its usual use is to refer to one of the operative parts of the Civil Rights Act of 1964.

TOD (Transfer on Death) A method authorized by state statute allowing for the transfer of registered securities to a named beneficiary free of probate under the Uniform Transfer-on-Death Security Registration Act.

token damages See "nominal (or token) damages."

tort A private wrong committed by one person (the tortfeasor) that injures another (the victim) in person and/or property, and for which society allows the legal remedy of monetary damages.

tortfeasor A wrongdoer who commits a private injury to another person by breaching a duty recognized by law.

Totten trust A trust for bank depositors whereby they deposit money in a bank in the settlor's own name as a trustee for another person. It is revocable at will until the depositor dies or completes the gift in his or her lifetime by some unequivocal act or declaration.

treble damages Amount of compensatory damages as determined by a jury or judge, multiplied by 3, in order to punish the wrongdoers and serve as an example to others. Treble damages are available, for example, by statute for victims of certain violations of federal antitrust laws.

trespass Wrongful interference with the real or personal property of another. Trespass commonly refers to entry onto another's rural land without authority or permission (implied or express).

trespass to chattel A brief, temporary, unauthorized interference with the personal-property rights of another.

trial Formal procedure before a court conducted to resolve disputed questions of fact and of law.

trial courts Tribunals that conduct trials, as distinguished from courts that conduct appeals of cases decided by trial courts.

trial *de novo* A new trial that takes place as if the first trial had not occurred.

trier of fact See Jury.

trust A legal relationship in which one party (called trustor, settlor, or donor) transfers legal title in property to a second party (trustee) for the benefit of a third party (beneficiary, or donee).

trustee A person who holds property in a trust for the benefit of another, the beneficiary.

trustee's deed A deed from a trustee, under a deed of trust provided to the successful bidder at a nonjudicial foreclosure sale.

trustee's sale Auction-type sale conducted by a trustee under the direction of the unpaid creditor (called the beneficiary) of a mortgage (or deed of trust).

trustor The person who creates a trust. The trustor is also called a *settlor* or donor.

Truth in Lending Act See "Consumer Credit Protection Act."

unanimous opinion A written opinion of the court wherein all judges agree on the holding and the stated reasons for it.

unconscionable contract A contract in which one party is treated unfairly, oppressively, and with bad faith. The court may refuse to enforce the contract, or may modify it to eliminate the part that is unconscionable.

undue influence Wrongful persuasion, often by a fiduciary or other trusted individual, which deprives the victim of freedom of will in making a contract.

unenforceable contract A contract that was initially valid but can no longer be enforced, e.g., because of the running out of a statute of limitations.

unfair labor practice Certain practices of employers, and also certain practices of unions, that are prohibited by federal or state law.

unfair labor practice strike A strike in which the workers are protesting an unfair labor practice of their employer. See "economic strike."

unified estate and gift tax A federal tax levied on the transfer of property through an estate at the time of death or on a taxable transfer by gift. The estate or the donor is responsible for payment of the tax. A unified credit is available to be applied against the transfer tax.

Uniform Commercial Code (UCC) One of several uniform laws drafted by the National Conference of Commissioners of Uniform State Laws. It covers a wide range of commercial activity and has been generally adopted by all states.

Uniform Residential Landlord and Tenant Act (URLTA) A uniform law modernizing common-law rules that govern the landlord-tenant relationship. In general, the act adopts contract principles and imposes implied duties upon landlords.

unilateral contract A contract in which the promisor seeks performance of a requested act. Upon performance of the act, the contract is formed and the promisor is obligated to fulfill his or her promise.

unilateral mistake A situation in which one of the parties to a contract labors under some error about an important fact in the agreement.

uninsured motorist insurance Automobile insurance that protects against the risk of loss from bodily injury (and in some states, from property damage) suffered by an insured driver because of the negligence of either an uninsured driver or a hit-and-run driver.

union Association of workers formed to bargain collectively with employers over wages, hours, and conditions of employment.

union shop A place of employment where newly hired workers must join the union within 30 days of being hired.

unlawful detainer A statutory remedy for a landlord to evict a renter who has defaulted in the payment of rent or who has broken the terms of the lease in some other manner. It is a summary judicial proceeding (i.e., not a full-blown trial on all issues before a jury). In some states it is called a *dispossessory-warrant proceeding* or a *forcible-entry proceeding*.

unwritten law Laws that are enforced by courts and are included in their written opinions (cases) but not in statutes or ordinances. Also called "common law."

usury Interest charged for the use of borrowed money that exceeds the maximum rate allowed by state law. Institutional lenders are commonly exempt from usury laws.

valid Legally enforceable (for example, a proper contract).

valid contract An agreement that complies with all requisites of the law for enforceability.

variable-interest-rate mortgage (VIRM) A home-purchase mortgage and promissory note in which the interest rate may fluctuate, up or down, in sync with a published index. This type of mortgage is also called an *adjustable-rate mortgage*.

vehicular manslaughter The wrongful killing of another person by a perpetrator driving a vehicle in a reckless and dangerous manner (e.g., in some cases while under the influence of alcohol or other drug). Some states have created, by statute, this special category of vehicular manslaughter to embrace all wrongful conduct involving the operation of automobiles resulting in homicide. Other states govern homicides by automobiles under their all-encompassing manslaughter statutes.

venue [French for "to come"] The local place, within the geographical boundaries of a larger jurisdiction, where a case is generally most appropriately tried.

venue, change of Transfer of a case for trial to another county or judicial district within the same jurisdiction, usually because of local prejudice against the defendant.

verdict The expressed decision of the jury on questions of fact submitted to it for determination, based on evidence presented during trial.

Veteran's Administration (VA) loan A home-purchase mortgage loan made to any eligible veteran by the federal Veteran's Administration. The VA was established in 1944 by the Serviceman's Readjustment Act to assist veterans in becoming homeowners.

vicarious liability The responsibility of one person for the wrongful acts of another. For example, the owner of a vehicle is vicariously liable for the damages caused by the negligence of the driver.

vicarious-murder rule A rule holding that an aider and abettor of a murder may also be guilty of the crime even though another person was the actual killer.

victim The person who is the object of a crime or tort.

victimless crime Any crime that allegedly hurts only the wrongdoer, if anyone (e.g., unusual sexual practices by consenting adults in private, prostitution, public drunkenness, use of marijuana and other hard drugs, usury, and illegal gambling). Reformers contend that such acts should be decriminalized, although participants frequently suffer painful consequences such as disease and loss of money, and society is often burdened with resulting costs of medical care, family decline, and welfare support.

violation The act of disobeying or breaking a law or rule. Violation is also the act of doing harm to another person's rights, and of seducing or ravishing.

voluntary manslaughter The wrongful and intentional killing of another person during the heat of passion, or under the influence of alcohol or drugs, or while engaged in some reckless and dangerous activity (such as driving while under the influence of a drug).

void Without legal force or binding effect.

voidable contract An agreement that may be legally enforced or may be rejected by a party. For example, a contract between a minor and an adult is voidable or valid at the option of the minor.

void agreement A misnomer, because such attempted contract is a nullity. One or more essential element of a valid contract is missing in the attempt to make a contract.

voir dire [Old French for "to speak the truth"] Process of questioning prospective jurors to ascertain whether they have any bias that would make difficult or unlikely their impartiality in determining questions of fact during a trial.

voluntary arbitration See "arbitration."

voluntary rescission When both parties voluntarily agree to return to the status quo as it existed before a contract was made. See also "rescission."

wage-earner receivership A plan under which a court-appointed trustee collects all nonexempt wages of the debtor and distributes them pro rata to the creditors, who meanwhile may not garnish wages or repossess goods of the debtor.

waive To give up a right, such as the Constitutional right to a trial by jury.

ward A person, usually a child, subject to a guardianship.

warrant A written authorization of a judge or magistrate to arrest or search a specific person and/or place.

warranty Assurance given by the seller of goods concerning the title to, or the quality or performance of, the product sold. A warranty may be express (oral or written) or *implied* by law even if not mentioned by the seller.

warranty against encumbrances An implied warranty that goods will be delivered free of liens and encumbrances that are not otherwise noted.

warranty against infringement An implied warranty by a merchant-seller that goods are free of any rightful claim, such as a patent.

warranty deed A type of deed with several warranties implied by law to protect the buyer.

warranty of fitness for particular purpose A warranty that arises when the buyer, having stated the intended use of the goods, relies on the seller's selection of goods.

warranty of merchantability An implied warranty in a sale by a merchant that the goods are of fair, average quality and fit for the ordinary purpose(s) for which such goods are used.

warranty of title An implied warranty to a buyer that the seller has and is transferring good title.

waste Conduct that is destructive to real property and that is perpetrated by an owner/debtor, life tenant, or renter who is in possession. The conduct is wrongful because it damages or reduces the value of property for others who have a beneficial interest in it. The wronged party can sue the party in tort, for damages for waste. Damage by a trespasser, although wrongful, is considered not waste but trespass.

white-collar crime Illegal acts committed usually without violence by persons of comparatively high social status and economic wealth. Examples are embezzlement, fraudulent sale of securities, and tax evasion. White-collar crime is contrasted to blue-collar crime, such as robbery and battery.

wildcat strike An unlawful strike of union members that takes place without the approval of the union leaders.

will Legal expression (usually in writing, signed and witnessed) of a person's directions as to how property owned is to be disposed of after death. A will is also called the *last will and testament*.

winding-up period After dissolution of a partnership, the time during which outstanding debts are paid, assets are sold, and partners' investments are returned if possible. The partnership is then legally terminated. The term may also be applied to the winding-up process of liquidating a corporation.

Worker Adjustment and Retraining Notification Act (WARN) of 1989 A federal law that requires business managers to give employees 60 days advance notice of a plant closing or mass layoff.

workers' compensation Medical treatment, rehabilitation benefits, and disability payments for workers injured on the job. It is paid for by employer-financed insurance.

work furlough A rehabilitative program for prisoners under which they may participate in part-time gainful employment even while they are serving time in a prison or jail.

writ of *certiorari* A procedural document whereby an appellate court exercises its discretionary power to accept jurisdiction of a pending case.

writ of execution Order of the court directing the sheriff to confiscate property of the defendant. The property is then sold to satisfy the award of dollar damages given to the plaintiff at a trial.

writ of *habeas corpus* [Latin: "you have the body"] A judicial command to bring a prisoner to court for further legal proceedings.

written interrogatories See "interrogatories."

written law The statutes and ordinances of federal, state, and local governments, and the published rules of administrative agencies.

wrongful-death statute A law allowing the heirs of a deceased person to sue whoever caused the decedent's death, and to collect any court-awarded damages.

wrongful discharge The wrongful dismissal of a permanent employee (i.e., discharge without good cause). Wrongful discharge is a tort.

yellow dog contract An employment contract in which a worker agrees not to join a union. This type of contract was outlawed by the Anti-Injunction Act of 1932.

Index

NOTE: Footnote material is denoted by an "f" following the page number.